Unit Conversions (Equivalents)

Length

1 in. = 2.54 cm (defined)
1 cm = 0.3937 in.
1 ft = 30.48 cm
1 m = 39.37 in. = 3.281 ft
1 mi = 5280 ft = 1.609 km
1 km = 0.6214 mi
1 nautical mile (U.S.) = 1.151 mi = 6076 ft = 1.852 km
1 fermi = 1 femtometer (fm) = 10^{-15} m
1 angstrom (Å) = 10^{-10} m = 0.1 nm
1 light-year (ly) = 9.461×10^{15} m
1 parsec = 3.26 ly = 3.09×10^{16} m

Volume

1 liter (L) = 1000 mL = 1000 cm^3 = 1.0×10^{-3} m^3 = 1.057 qt (U.S.) = 61.02 in.^{3}
1 gal (U.S.) = 4 qt (U.S.) = 231 in.^{3} = 3.785 L = 0.8327 gal (British)
1 quart (U.S.) = 2 pints (U.S.) = 946 mL
1 pint (British) = 1.20 pints (U.S.) = 568 mL
1 m^3 = 35.31 ft^3

Speed

1 mi/h = 1.4667 ft/s = 1.6093 km/h = 0.4470 m/s
1 km/h = 0.2778 m/s = 0.6214 mi/h
1 ft/s = 0.3048 m/s (exact) = 0.6818 mi/h = 1.0973 km/h
1 m/s = 3.281 ft/s = 3.600 km/h = 2.237 mi/h
1 knot = 1.151 mi/h = 0.5144 m/s

Angle

1 radian (rad) = 57.30° = 57°18′
1° = 0.01745 rad
1 rev/min (rpm) = 0.1047 rad/s

Time

1 day = 8.640×10^4 s
1 year = 3.156×10^7 s

Mass

1 atomic mass unit (u) = 1.6605×10^{-27} kg
1 kg = 0.06852 slug
[1 kg has a weight of 2.20 lb where $g = 9.80$ m/s^2.]

Force

1 lb = 4.44822 N
1 N = 10^5 dyne = 0.2248 lb

Energy and Work

1 J = 10^7 ergs = 0.7376 ft·lb
1 ft·lb = 1.356 J = 1.29×10^{-3} Btu = 3.24×10^{-4} kcal
1 kcal = 4.19×10^3 J = 3.97 Btu
1 eV = 1.6022×10^{-19} J
1 kWh = 3.600×10^6 J = 860 kcal
1 Btu = 1.055×10^3 J

Power

1 W = 1 J/s = 0.7376 ft·lb/s = 3.41 Btu/h
1 hp = 550 ft·lb/s = 746 W

Pressure

1 atm = 1.01325 bar = 1.01325×10^5 N/m^2 = 14.7 lb/in.^{2} = 760 torr
1 lb/in.^{2} = 6.895×10^3 N/m^2
1 Pa = 1 N/m^2 = 1.450×10^{-4} lb/in.^{2}

SI Derived Units and Their Abbreviations

Quantity	Unit	Abbreviation	In Terms of Base Units†
Force	newton	N	kg·m/s^2
Energy and work	joule	J	kg·m^2/s^2
Power	watt	W	kg·m^2/s^3
Pressure	pascal	Pa	kg/(m·s^2)
Frequency	hertz	Hz	s^{-1}
Electric charge	coulomb	C	A·s
Electric potential	volt	V	kg·m^2/(A·s^3)
Electric resistance	ohm	Ω	kg·m^2/(A^2·s^3)
Capacitance	farad	F	A^2·s^4/(kg·m^2)
Magnetic field	tesla	T	kg/(A·s^2)
Magnetic flux	weber	Wb	kg·m^2/(A·s^2)
Inductance	henry	H	kg·m^2/(s^2·A^2)

† kg = kilogram (mass), m = meter (length), s = second (time), A = ampere (electric current).

Metric (SI) Multipliers

Prefix	Abbreviation	Value
yotta	Y	10^{24}
zeta	Z	10^{21}
exa	E	10^{18}
peta	P	10^{15}
tera	T	10^{12}
giga	G	10^9
mega	M	10^6
kilo	k	10^3
hecto	h	10^2
deka	da	10^1
deci	d	10^{-1}
centi	c	10^{-2}
milli	m	10^{-3}
micro	μ	10^{-6}
nano	n	10^{-9}
pico	p	10^{-12}
femto	f	10^{-15}
atto	a	10^{-18}
zepto	z	10^{-21}
yocto	y	10^{-24}

Douglas C. Giancoli

Physics
Physics 3 C

Custom Edition for University of California, Irvine

Taken from:
Physics for Scientists and Engineers with Modern Physics, Fourth Edition
by Douglas C. Giancoli

Cover Art: Courtesy of Photodisc/Getty Images

Taken from:

Physics for Scientists and Engineers with Modern Physics, Fourth Edition
by Douglas C. Giancoli
Copyright © 2009, 2000, 1989, 1984 by Douglas C. Giancoli, Inc.
Published by Prentice Hall
Upper Saddle River, New Jersey 07458

Pearson Learning Solutions, 501 Boylston Street, Suite 900, Boston, MA 02116
A Pearson Education Company
www.pearsoned.com

Printed in the United States of America

6 7 8 9 10 V0UD 19 18 17 16 15

000200010270758333

SS

ISBN 10: 1-256-36375-8
ISBN 13: 978-1-256-36375-0

MasteringPhysics® Instructions for Physics 2, Physics 3 and Physics 7 students.

MasteringPhysics® will be used for online homework and tutorial for Physics 2, Physics 3 and Physics 7.

- All Physics 2, Physics 3 and Physics 7 students are **required to have a student access code** for MasteringPhysics®.
- Once you **purchase** a MasteringPhysics® student access code, it is **valid for 2 years** and may be used every quarter (including summer) during that time.
- Each student access code may only be used **for one course per quarter**.

What You Need:

- ◆ **A valid email address:** it is recommended that you use your uci.edu email address. Your MasteringPhysics® access code is linked to the email address you enter.
- ◆ **Student access code:** included in the Student Access Kit that is packaged with your new textbook.
- ◆ **The ZIP code for UCI: 92697**
- ◆ **Your 8-digit UCI student ID number**
- ◆ **A Course ID:** ▬▬▬▬▬▬▬▬▬ (Instructor provides this)

Register

- Go to http://www.masteringphysics.com
- Under "Students" Click **Register.**
- To register using the Student Access Code inside the MasteringPhysics® Student Access Kit, select **Yes, I have an access code**. Click **Continue.**
- **License Agreement and Privacy Policy:** Click **I Accept** to indicate that you have read and agree to the license agreement and privacy policy.
- Select the appropriate option under "Do you have a Pearson Education account?" and supply the requested information. Upon completion, the **Confirmation & Summary** page confirms your registration. This information will also be emailed to you for your records. You can either click **Log In Now** or return to www.masteringphysics.com later.

Log In

- Go to http://www.masteringphysics.com
- Click **Login to MasteringPhysics.**
- Enter your Login Name and Password and click **Log In.**

Enroll in Your Instructor's Course and/or Access the Self-Study Area

Upon first login, you'll be prompted to do one or more of the following:

- **Join your MasteringPhysics course** by entering the **MasteringPhysics Course ID** provided by your instructor.
- **Enter your 8-digit UCI student ID number when prompted.** If you don't use your correct student ID to enroll, you won't get credit for the homework you do. So check this carefully.

Click **Save** and **OK**.

Note: When assignments are created, you may access them in the Assignments Due Soon area, or by clicking the "Assignments" tab. Otherwise, click on Study Area to access self-study material.

Keyboard shortcuts for entering mathematical expressions

When you finish adding values in any of the math templates:
Press the right or left arrow keys to move outside of the specially formatted area and to exit template insertion mode.

To move between the top and bottom parts of a fraction: Use the up and down arrow keys.

For this Math Format Template	Type this...	For this Greek Letter/ Symbol	Type this...	For this Greek Letter/ Symbol	Type this...	For Special Functions, type...
2.56	. (Period)	α	\alpha	τ	\tau	acos
y_1	_ (Underscore)	β	\beta	ϕ	\phi	acot
x^2	^	γ	\gamma	χ	\chi	acsc
$\sin(\theta)$	(and)	δ	\delta	ψ	\psi	asec
$[2\pi r]$	[and]	ϵ	\epsilon	ω	\omega	asin
$K + U$	+	η	\eta	$\hbar$	\hbar	atan
$x_f - x_i$	− (Hyphen)	θ	\theta	Δ	\Delta	cos
$7 \cdot 10^{-8}$	*	κ	\kappa	Σ	\Sigma	cot
$\frac{1}{2}mv^2$	/	λ	\lambda	Φ	\Phi	csc
$\sqrt{2gh}$	\sqrt	μ	\mu	Ψ	\Psi	e
$\sqrt[n]{x}$	\nrt	ν	\nu	Ω	\Omega	ln
$|\vec{a}|$	|	π	\pi	$\mathcal{E}$	\EMF	log
$\vec{V}$	\vec	ρ	\rho			sec
$\hat{j}$	\hat	σ	\sigma			sin
						tan

Contents

Volume 1

14 OSCILLATIONS 369

15 WAVE MOTION 395

16 SOUND 424

Volume 2

31 MAXWELL'S EQUATIONS AND ELECTROMAGNETIC WAVES 812

subtends a ~~~~~~~~~ ~~~~~. As shown in Fig. 33–33a, the object is placed at the focal poin~ **magnifying gla~** ~~~~ converging lens produces a virtual image, which ~ comparison of part (a) o~ ~~ f the eye is to focus on it. If the eye is relaxed, ~iewed at the near point wit~ ~f when you "focus" on the object ~ ~bject subtends at the eye is much la~ part (b), in which **magnification** or **magnifying power**, *M* eye, re~ ~~~~~~~~gular angle subtended by an object when usin~ ~~ ~~ ratio of the unaided eye, with the object at the nea~ ~~e subtended using the normal eye): ~ ~~ the eye (*N* = 25 cm for a

$$M = \frac{\theta'}{\theta},$$ (33–5)

where θ and θ' are shown in Fig. 33–33. ~write *M* in terms of the focal length by noting that $\theta = h/N$ (Fig. 33– ~ $\theta' = h/d_o$ (Fig. 33–33a), where *h* is the height of the object and we ass~ ~gles are small so θ and θ' equal ~heir sines and tangents. If the eye is ~ ~r least eye strain), the image will ~ at infinity and the object will b~ at the focal point; see Fig. 33–34. $d_o = f$ and $\theta' = h/f$. Th~

APPLICATIONS (SELECTED)

Preface

I was motivated from the beginning to write a textbook different from others that present physics as a sequence of facts, like a Sears catalog: "here are the facts and you better learn them." Instead of that approach in which topics are begun formally and dogmatically, I have sought to begin each topic with concrete observations and experiences students can relate to: start with specifics and only then go to the great generalizations and the more formal aspects of a topic, showing *why* we believe what we believe. This approach reflects how science is actually practiced.

Why a Fourth Edition?

Two recent trends in physics texbooks are disturbing: (1) their revision cycles have become short—they are being revised every 3 or 4 years; (2) the books are getting larger, some over 1500 pages. I don't see how either trend can be of benefit to students. My response: (1) It has been 8 years since the previous edition of this book. (2) This book makes use of physics education research, although it avoids the detail a Professor may need to say in class but in a book shuts down the reader. And this book still remains among the shortest.

This new edition introduces some important new pedagogic tools. It contains new physics (such as in cosmology) and many new appealing applications (list on previous page). Pages and page breaks have been carefully formatted to make the physics easier to follow: no turning a page in the middle of a derivation or Example. Great efforts were made to make the book attractive so students will want to *read* it.

Some of the new features are listed below.

What's New

Chapter-Opening Questions: Each Chapter begins with a multiple-choice question, whose responses include common misconceptions. Students are asked to answer before starting the Chapter, to get them involved in the material and to get any preconceived notions out on the table. The issues reappear later in the Chapter, usually as Exercises, after the material has been covered. The Chapter-Opening Questions also show students the power and usefulness of Physics.

APPROACH paragraph in worked-out numerical Examples: A short introductory paragraph before the Solution, outlining an approach and the steps we can take to get started. Brief NOTES after the Solution may remark on the Solution, may give an alternate approach, or mention an application.

Step-by-Step Examples: After many Problem Solving Strategies (more than 20 in the book), the next Example is done step-by-step following precisely the steps just seen.

Exercises within the text, after an Example or derivation, give students a chance to see if they have understood enough to answer a simple question or do a simple calculation. Many are multiple choice.

Greater clarity: No topic, no paragraph in this book was overlooked in the search to improve the clarity and conciseness of the presentation. Phrases and sentences that may slow down the principal argument have been eliminated: keep to the essentials at first, give the elaborations later.

$\vec{F}, \vec{v}, \vec{B}$ *Vector notation, arrows*: The symbols for vector quantities in the text and Figures now have a tiny arrow over them, so they are similar to what we write by hand.

Cosmological Revolution: With generous help from top experts in the field, readers have the latest results.

Page layout: more than in the previous edition, serious attention has been paid to how each page is formatted. Examples and all important derivations and arguments are on facing pages. Students then don't have to turn back and forth. Throughout, readers see, on two facing pages, an important slice of physics.

New Applications: LCDs, digital cameras and electronic sensors (CCD, CMOS), electric hazards, GFCIs, photocopiers, inkjet and laser printers, metal detectors, underwater vision, curve balls, airplane wings, DNA, how we actually *see* images. (Turn back a page to see a longer list.)

Examples modified: more math steps are spelled out, and many new Examples added. About 10% of all Examples are Estimation Examples.

This Book is Shorter than other complete full-service books at this level. Shorter explanations are easier to understand and more likely to be read.

Content and Organizational Changes

- **Rotational Motion**: Chapters 10 and 11 have been reorganized. All of angular momentum is now in Chapter 11.
- **First law of thermodynamics**, in Chapter 19, has been rewritten and extended. The full form is given: $\Delta K + \Delta U + \Delta E_{int} = Q - W$, where internal energy is E_{int}, and U is potential energy; the form $Q - W$ is kept so that $dW = P\,dV$.
- Kinematics and Dynamics of Circular Motion are now treated together in Chapter 5.
- Work and Energy, Chapters 7 and 8, have been carefully revised.
- Work done by friction is discussed now with energy conservation (energy terms due to friction).
- Chapters on Inductance and AC Circuits have been combined into one: Chapter 30.
- Graphical Analysis and Numerical Integration is a new optional Section 2–9. Problems requiring a computer or graphing calculator are found at the end of most Chapters.
- Length of an object is a script ℓ rather than normal l, which looks like 1 or I (moment of inertia, current), as in $F = I\ell B$. Capital L is for angular momentum, latent heat, inductance, dimensions of length $[L]$.
- Newton's law of gravitation remains in Chapter 6. Why? Because the $1/r^2$ law is too important to relegate to a late chapter that might not be covered at all late in the semester; furthermore, it is one of the basic forces in nature. In Chapter 8 we can treat real gravitational potential energy and have a fine instance of using $U = -\int \vec{F} \cdot d\vec{\ell}$.
- New Appendices include the differential form of Maxwell's equations and more on dimensional analysis.
- Problem Solving Strategies are found on pages 30, 58, 64, 96, 102, 125, 166, 198, 229, 261, 314, 504, 551, 571, 600, 685, 716, 740, 763, 849, 871, and 913.

Organization

Some instructors may find that this book contains more material than can be covered in their courses. The text offers great flexibility. Sections marked with a star * are considered optional. These contain slightly more advanced physics material, or material not usually covered in typical courses and/or interesting applications; they contain no material needed in later Chapters (except perhaps in later optional Sections). For a brief course, all optional material could be dropped as well as major parts of Chapters 1, 13, 16, 26, 30, and 35, and selected parts of Chapters 9, 12, 19, 20, 33, and the modern physics Chapters. Topics not covered in class can be a valuable resource for later study by students. Indeed, this text can serve as a useful reference for years because of its wide range of coverage.

Versions of this Book

Complete version: 44 Chapters including 9 Chapters of modern physics.

Classic version: 37 Chapters including one each on relativity and quantum theory.

3 Volume version: Available separately or packaged together (Vols. 1 & 2 or all 3 Volumes):

Volume 1: Chapters 1–20 on mechanics, including fluids, oscillations, waves, plus heat and thermodynamics.

Volume 2: Chapters 21–35 on electricity and magnetism, plus light and optics.

Volume 3: Chapters 36–44 on modern physics: relativity, quantum theory, atomic physics, condensed matter, nuclear physics, elementary particles, cosmology and astrophysics.

Thanks

Many physics professors provided input or direct feedback on every aspect of this textbook. They are listed below, and I owe each a debt of gratitude.

Mario Affatigato, Coe College
Lorraine Allen, United States Coast Guard Academy
Zaven Altounian, McGill University
Bruce Barnett, Johns Hopkins University
Michael Barnett, Lawrence Berkeley Lab
Anand Batra, Howard University
Cornelius Bennhold, George Washington University
Bruce Birkett, University of California Berkeley
Dr. Robert Boivin, Auburn University
Subir Bose, University of Central Florida
David Branning, Trinity College
Meade Brooks, Collin County Community College
Bruce Bunker, University of Notre Dame
Grant Bunker, Illinois Institute of Technology
Wayne Carr, Stevens Institute of Technology
Charles Chiu, University of Texas Austin
Robert Coakley, University of Southern Maine
David Curott, University of North Alabama
Biman Das, SUNY Potsdam
Bob Davis, Taylor University
Kaushik De, University of Texas Arlington
Michael Dennin, University of California Irvine
Kathy Dimiduk, University of New Mexico
John DiNardo, Drexel University
Scott Dudley, United States Air Force Academy
John Essick, Reed College
Cassandra Fesen, Dartmouth College
Alex Filippenko, University of California Berkeley
Richard Firestone, Lawrence Berkeley Lab
Mike Fortner, Northern Illinois University
Tom Furtak, Colorado School of Mines
Edward Gibson, California State University Sacramento
John Hardy, Texas A&M
J. Erik Hendrickson, University of Wisconsin Eau Claire
Laurent Hodges, Iowa State University
David Hogg, New York University
Mark Hollabaugh, Normandale Community College
Andy Hollerman, University of Louisiana at Lafayette
William Holzapfel, University of California Berkeley
Bob Jacobsen, University of California Berkeley
Teruki Kamon, Texas A&M
Daryao Khatri, University of the District of Columbia
Jay Kunze, Idaho State University

Jim LaBelle, Dartmouth College
M.A.K. Lodhi, Texas Tech
Bruce Mason, University of Oklahoma
Dan Mazilu, Virginia Tech
Linda McDonald, North Park College
Bill McNairy, Duke University
Raj Mohanty, Boston University
Giuseppe Molesini, Istituto Nazionale di Ottica Florence
Lisa K. Morris, Washington State University
Blaine Norum, University of Virginia
Alexandria Oakes, Eastern Michigan University
Michael Ottinger, Missouri Western State University
Lyman Page, Princeton and WMAP
Bruce Partridge, Haverford College
R. Daryl Pedigo, University of Washington
Robert Pelcovitz, Brown University
Vahe Peroomian, UCLA
James Rabchuk, Western Illinois University
Michele Rallis, Ohio State University
Paul Richards, University of California Berkeley
Peter Riley, University of Texas Austin
Larry Rowan, University of North Carolina Chapel Hill
Cindy Schwarz, Vassar College
Peter Sheldon, Randolph-Macon Woman's College
Natalia A. Sidorovskaia, University of Louisiana at Lafayette
James Siegrist, UC Berkeley, Director Physics Division LBNL
George Smoot, University of California Berkeley
Mark Sprague, East Carolina University
Michael Strauss, University of Oklahoma
Laszlo Takac, University of Maryland Baltimore Co.
Franklin D. Trumpy, Des Moines Area Community College
Ray Turner, Clemson University
Som Tyagi, Drexel University
John Vasut, Baylor University
Robert Webb, Texas A&M
Robert Weidman, Michigan Technological University
Edward A. Whittaker, Stevens Institute of Technology
John Wolbeck, Orange County Community College
Stanley George Wojcicki, Stanford University
Edward Wright, UCLA
Todd Young, Wayne State College
William Younger, College of the Albemarle
Hsiao-Ling Zhou, Georgia State University

I owe special thanks to Prof. Bob Davis for much valuable input, and especially for working out all the Problems and producing the Solutions Manual for all Problems, as well as for providing the answers to odd-numbered Problems at the end of this book. Many thanks also to J. Erik Hendrickson who collaborated with Bob Davis on the solutions, and to the team they managed (Profs. Anand Batra, Meade Brooks, David Currott, Blaine Norum, Michael Ottinger, Larry Rowan, Ray Turner, John Vasut, William Younger). I am grateful to Profs. John Essick, Bruce Barnett, Robert Coakley, Biman Das, Michael Dennin, Kathy Dimiduk, John DiNardo, Scott Dudley, David Hogg, Cindy Schwarz, Ray Turner, and Som Tyagi, who inspired many of the Examples, Questions, Problems, and significant clarifications.

Crucial for rooting out errors, as well as providing excellent suggestions, were Profs. Kathy Dimiduk, Ray Turner, and Lorraine Allen. A huge thank you to them and to Prof. Giuseppe Molesini for his suggestions and his exceptional photographs for optics.

For Chapters 43 and 44 on Particle Physics and Cosmology and Astrophysics, I was fortunate to receive generous input from some of the top experts in the field, to whom I owe a debt of gratitude: George Smoot, Paul Richards, Alex Filippenko, James Siegrist, and William Holzapfel (UC Berkeley), Lyman Page (Princeton and WMAP), Edward Wright (UCLA and WMAP), and Michael Strauss (University of Oklahoma).

I especially wish to thank Profs. Howard Shugart, Chair Frances Hellman, and many others at the University of California, Berkeley, Physics Department for helpful discussions, and for hospitality. Thanks also to Prof. Tito Arecchi and others at the Istituto Nazionale di Ottica, Florence, Italy.

Finally, I am grateful to the many people at Prentice Hall with whom I worked on this project, especially Paul Corey, Karen Karlin, Christian Botting, John Christiana, and Sean Hogan.

The final responsibility for all errors lies with me. I welcome comments, corrections, and suggestions as soon as possible to benefit students for the next reprint.

D.C.G.

email: Paul.Corey@Pearson.com

Post: Paul Corey
　　　One Lake Street
　　　Upper Saddle River, NJ 07458

About the Author

Douglas C. Giancoli obtained his BA in physics (summa cum laude) from the University of California, Berkeley, his MS in physics at the Massachusetts Institute of Technology, and his PhD in elementary particle physics at the University of California, Berkeley. He spent 2 years as a post-doctoral fellow at UC Berkeley's Virus lab developing skills in molecular biology and biophysics. His mentors include Nobel winners Emilio Segrè and Donald Glaser.

He has taught a wide range of undergraduate courses, traditional as well as innovative ones, and continues to update his texbooks meticulously, seeking ways to better provide an understanding of physics for students.

Doug's favorite spare-time activity is the outdoors, especially climbing peaks (here on a dolomite summit, Italy). He says climbing peaks is like learning physics: it takes effort and the rewards are great.

Online Supplements (partial list)

MasteringPhysics™ (www.masteringphysics.com) is a sophisticated online tutoring and homework system developed specially for courses using calculus-based physics. Originally developed by David Pritchard and collaborators at MIT, MasteringPhysics provides **students** with individualized online tutoring by responding to their wrong answers and providing hints for solving multi-step problems when they get stuck. It gives them immediate and up-to-date assessment of their progress, and shows where they need to practice more. MasteringPhysics provides **instructors** with a fast and effective way to assign tried-and-tested online homework assignments that comprise a range of problem types. The powerful post-assignment diagnostics allow instructors to assess the progress of their class as a whole as well as individual students, and quickly identify areas of difficulty.

WebAssign (www.webassign.com)

CAPA and LON-CAPA (www.lon-capa.org)

Student Supplements (partial list)

Student Study Guide & Selected Solutions Manual (Volume I: 0-13-227324-1, Volumes II & III: 0-13-227325-X) by Frank Wolfs

Student Pocket Companion (0-13-227326-8) by Biman Das

Tutorials in Introductory Physics (0-13-097069-7) by Lillian C. McDermott, Peter S. Schaffer, and the Physics Education Group at the University of Washington

Physlet® Physics (0-13-101969-4) by Wolfgang Christian and Mario Belloni

Ranking Task Exercises in Physics, Student Edition (0-13-144851-X) by Thomas L. O'Kuma, David P. Maloney, and Curtis J. Hieggelke

E&M TIPERs: Electricity & Magnetism Tasks Inspired by Physics Education Research (0-13-185499-2) by Curtis J. Hieggelke, David P. Maloney, Stephen E. Kanim, and Thomas L. O'Kuma

Mathematics for Physics with Calculus (0-13-191336-0) by Biman Das

To Students

HOW TO STUDY

1. Read the Chapter. Learn new vocabulary and notation. Try to respond to questions and exercises as they occur.
2. Attend all class meetings. Listen. Take notes, especially about aspects you do not remember seeing in the book. Ask questions (everyone else wants to, but maybe you will have the courage). You will get more out of class if you read the Chapter first.
3. Read the Chapter again, paying attention to details. Follow derivations and worked-out Examples. Absorb their logic. Answer Exercises and as many of the end of Chapter Questions as you can.
4. Solve 10 to 20 end of Chapter Problems (or more), especially those assigned. In doing Problems you find out what you learned and what you didn't. Discuss them with other students. Problem solving is one of the great learning tools. Don't just look for a formula—it won't cut it.

NOTES ON THE FORMAT AND PROBLEM SOLVING

1. Sections marked with a star (*) are considered **optional**. They can be omitted without interrupting the main flow of topics. No later material depends on them except possibly later starred Sections. They may be fun to read, though.
2. The customary **conventions** are used: symbols for quantities (such as m for mass) are italicized, whereas units (such as m for meter) are not italicized. Symbols for vectors are shown in boldface with a small arrow above: $\vec{\mathbf{F}}$.
3. Few equations are valid in all situations. Where practical, the **limitations** of important equations are stated in square brackets next to the equation. The equations that represent the great laws of physics are displayed with a tan background, as are a few other indispensable equations.
4. At the end of each Chapter is a set of **Problems** which are ranked as Level I, II, or III, according to estimated difficulty. Level I Problems are easiest, Level II are standard Problems, and Level III are "challenge problems." These ranked Problems are arranged by Section, but Problems for a given Section may depend on earlier material too. There follows a group of General Problems, which are not arranged by Section nor ranked as to difficulty. Problems that relate to optional Sections are starred (*). Most Chapters have 1 or 2 Computer/Numerical Problems at the end, requiring a computer or graphing calculator. Answers to odd-numbered Problems are given at the end of the book.
5. Being able to solve **Problems** is a crucial part of learning physics, and provides a powerful means for understanding the concepts and principles. This book contains many aids to problem solving: (a) worked-out **Examples** and their solutions in the text, which should be studied as an integral part of the text; (b) some of the worked-out Examples are **Estimation Examples**, which show how rough or approximate results can be obtained even if the given data are sparse (see Section 1–6); (c) special **Problem Solving Strategies** placed throughout the text to suggest a step-by-step approach to problem solving for a particular topic—but remember that the basics remain the same; most of these "Strategies" are followed by an Example that is solved by explicitly following the suggested steps; (d) special problem-solving Sections; (e) "Problem Solving" marginal notes which refer to hints within the text for solving Problems; (f) **Exercises** within the text that you should work out immediately, and then check your response against the answer given at the bottom of the last page of that Chapter; (g) the Problems themselves at the end of each Chapter (point 4 above).
6. **Conceptual Examples** pose a question which hopefully starts you to think and come up with a response. Give yourself a little time to come up with your own response before reading the Response given.
7. **Math** review, plus some additional topics, are found in Appendices. Useful data, conversion factors, and math formulas are found inside the front and back covers.

USE OF COLOR

Vectors

A general vector

    resultant vector (sum) is slightly thicker

    components of any vector are dashed

Displacement ($\vec{\mathbf{D}}, \vec{\mathbf{r}}$)

Velocity ($\vec{\mathbf{v}}$)

Acceleration ($\vec{\mathbf{a}}$)

Force ($\vec{\mathbf{F}}$)

    Force on second or

    third object in same figure

Momentum ($\vec{\mathbf{p}}$ or $m\vec{\mathbf{v}}$)

Angular momentum ($\vec{\mathbf{L}}$)

Angular velocity ($\vec{\boldsymbol{\omega}}$)

Torque ($\vec{\boldsymbol{\tau}}$)

Electric field ($\vec{\mathbf{E}}$)

Magnetic field ($\vec{\mathbf{B}}$)

Electricity and magnetism

Electric field lines

Equipotential lines

Magnetic field lines

Electric charge (+)   ⊕   or   ● +

Electric charge (−)   ⊖   or   ● −

Electric circuit symbols

Wire, with switch S

Resistor

Capacitor

Inductor

Battery

Ground

Optics

Light rays

Object

Real image (dashed)

Virtual image (dashed and paler)

Other

Energy level (atom, etc.)

Measurement lines   ⊢—1.0 m—⊣

Path of a moving object

Direction of motion or current

An object attached to a coil spring can exhibit oscillatory motion. Many kinds of oscillatory motion are sinusoidal in time, or nearly so, and are referred to as being simple harmonic motion. Real systems generally have at least some friction, causing the motion to be damped. The automobile spring shown here has a shock absorber (yellow) that purposefully dampens the oscillation to make for a smooth ride. When an external sinusoidal force is exerted on a system able to oscillate, resonance occurs if the driving force is at or near the natural frequency of oscillation.

14

Oscillations

CHAPTER-OPENING QUESTION—Guess now!

A simple pendulum consists of a mass m (the "bob") hanging on the end of a thin string of length ℓ and negligible mass. The bob is pulled sideways so the string makes a 5.0° angle to the vertical; when released, it oscillates back and forth at a frequency f. If the pendulum was raised to a 10.0° angle instead, its frequency would be

(a) twice as great.
(b) half as great.
(c) the same, or very close to it.
(d) not quite twice as great.
(e) a bit more than half as great.

10.0° ℓ

m

CONTENTS

Many objects vibrate or oscillate—an object on the end of a spring, a tuning fork, the balance wheel of an old watch, a pendulum, a plastic ruler held firmly over the edge of a table and gently struck, the strings of a guitar or piano. Spiders detect prey by the vibrations of their webs; cars oscillate up and down when they hit a bump; buildings and bridges vibrate when heavy trucks pass or the wind is fierce. Indeed, because most solids are elastic (see Chapter 12), they vibrate (at least briefly) when given an impulse. Electrical oscillations are necessary in radio and television sets. At the atomic level, atoms vibrate within a molecule, and the atoms of a solid vibrate about their relatively fixed positions. Because it is so common in everyday life and occurs in so many areas of physics, oscillatory motion is of great importance. Mechanical oscillations are fully described on the basis of Newtonian mechanics.

14-1 Oscillations of a Spring

FIGURE 14–1 A mass oscillating at the end of a uniform spring.

FIGURE 14–2 Force on, and velocity of, a mass at different positions of its oscillation cycle on a frictionless surface.

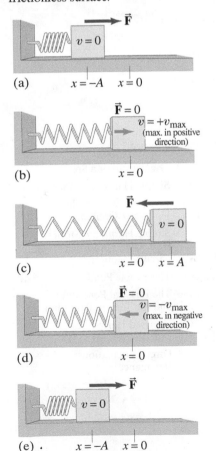

When an object **vibrates** or **oscillates** back and forth, over the same path, each oscillation taking the same amount of time, the motion is **periodic**. The simplest form of periodic motion is represented by an object oscillating on the end of a uniform coil spring. Because many other types of oscillatory motion closely resemble this system, we will look at it in detail. We assume that the mass of the spring can be ignored, and that the spring is mounted horizontally, as shown in Fig. 14–1a, so that the object of mass m slides without friction on the horizontal surface. Any spring has a natural length at which it exerts no force on the mass m. The position of the mass at this point is called the **equilibrium position**. If the mass is moved either to the left, which compresses the spring, or to the right, which stretches it, the spring exerts a force on the mass that acts in the direction of returning the mass to the equilibrium position; hence it is called a *restoring force*. We consider the common situation where we can assume the restoring force F is directly proportional to the displacement x the spring has been stretched (Fig. 14–1b) or compressed (Fig. 14–1c) from the equilibrium position:

$$F = -kx. \qquad \text{[force exerted by spring]} \quad \textbf{(14–1)}$$

Note that the equilibrium position has been chosen at $x = 0$ and the minus sign in Eq. 14–1 indicates that the restoring force is always in the direction opposite to the displacement x. For example, if we choose the positive direction to the right in Fig. 14–1, x is positive when the spring is stretched (Fig. 14–1b), but the direction of the restoring force is to the left (negative direction). If the spring is compressed, x is negative (to the left) but the force F acts toward the right (Fig. 14–1c).

Equation 14–1 is often referred to as Hooke's law (Sections 7–3, 8–2 and 12–4), and is accurate only if the spring is not compressed to where the coils are close to touching, or stretched beyond the elastic region (see Fig. 12–15). Hooke's law works not only for springs but for other oscillating solids as well; it thus has wide applicability, even though it is valid only over a certain range of F and x values.

The proportionality constant k in Eq. 14–1 is called the *spring constant* for that particular spring, or its *spring stiffness constant*. To stretch the spring a distance x, one has to exert an (external) force on the free end of the spring with a magnitude at least equal to

$$F_{\text{ext}} = +kx. \qquad \text{[external force on spring]}$$

The greater the value of k, the greater the force needed to stretch a spring a given distance. That is, the stiffer the spring, the greater the spring constant k.

Note that the force F in Eq. 14–1 is *not* a constant, but varies with position. Therefore the acceleration of the mass m is not constant, so we *cannot* use the equations for constant acceleration developed in Chapter 2.

Let us examine what happens when our uniform spring is initially compressed a distance $x = -A$, as shown in Fig. 14–2a, and then released on the frictionless surface. The spring exerts a force on the mass that pushes it toward the equilibrium position. But because the mass has inertia, it passes the equilibrium position with considerable speed. Indeed, as the mass reaches the equilibrium position, the force on it decreases to zero, but its speed at this point is a maximum, v_{max} (Fig. 14–2b). As the mass moves farther to the right, the force on it acts to slow it down, and it stops for an instant at $x = A$ (Fig. 14–2c). It then begins moving back in the opposite direction, accelerating until it passes the equilibrium point (Fig. 14–2d), and then slows down until it reaches zero speed at the original starting point, $x = -A$ (Fig. 14–2e). It then repeats the motion, moving back and forth symmetrically between $x = A$ and $x = -A$.

EXERCISE A An object is oscillating back and forth. Which of the following statements are true at some time during the course of the motion? (*a*) The object can have zero velocity and, simultaneously, nonzero acceleration. (*b*) The object can have zero velocity and, simultaneously, zero acceleration. (*c*) The object can have zero acceleration and, simultaneously, nonzero velocity. (*d*) The object can have nonzero velocity and nonzero acceleration simultaneously.

EXERCISE B A mass is oscillating on a frictionless surface at the end of a horizontal spring. Where, if anywhere, is the acceleration of the mass zero (see Fig. 14–2)? (*a*) At $x = -A$; (*b*) at $x = 0$; (*c*) at $x = +A$; (*d*) at both $x = -A$ and $x = +A$; (*e*) nowhere.

To discuss oscillatory motion, we need to define a few terms. The distance x of the mass from the equilibrium point at any moment is called the **displacement**. The maximum displacement—the greatest distance from the equilibrium point—is called the **amplitude**, A. One **cycle** refers to the complete to-and-fro motion from some initial point back to that same point—say, from $x = -A$ to $x = A$ and back to $x = -A$. The **period**, T, is defined as the time required to complete one cycle. Finally, the **frequency**, f, is the number of complete cycles per second. Frequency is generally specified in hertz (Hz), where $1\,\text{Hz} = 1$ cycle per second (s^{-1}). It is easy to see, from their definitions, that frequency and period are inversely related, as we saw earlier (Eqs. 5–2 and 10–8):

$$f = \frac{1}{T} \quad \text{and} \quad T = \frac{1}{f}; \qquad\qquad \textbf{(14–2)}$$

for example, if the frequency is 5 cycles per second, then each cycle takes $\frac{1}{5}\,\text{s}$.

The oscillation of a spring hung vertically is essentially the same as that of a horizontal spring. Because of gravity, the length of a vertical spring with a mass m on the end will be longer at equilibrium than when that same spring is horizontal, as shown in Fig. 14–3. The spring is in equilibrium when $\Sigma F = 0 = mg - kx_0$, so the spring stretches an extra amount $x_0 = mg/k$ to be in equilibrium. If x is measured from this new equilibrium position, Eq. 14–1 can be used directly with the same value of k.

⚠ CAUTION

For vertical spring, measure displacement (x or y) from the vertical equilibrium position

| **EXERCISE C** If an oscillating mass has a frequency of 1.25 Hz, it makes 100 oscillations in (a) 12.5 s, (b) 125 s, (c) 80 s, (d) 8.0 s.

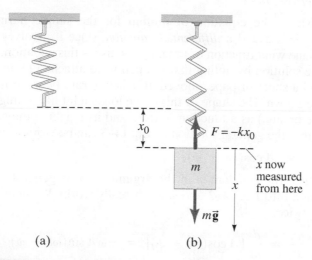

FIGURE 14–3
(a) Free spring, hung vertically.
(b) Mass m attached to spring in new equilibrium position, which occurs when $\Sigma F = 0 = mg - kx_0$.

EXAMPLE 14–1 **Car springs.** When a family of four with a total mass of 200 kg step into their 1200-kg car, the car's springs compress 3.0 cm. (a) What is the spring constant of the car's springs (Fig. 14–4), assuming they act as a single spring? (b) How far will the car lower if loaded with 300 kg rather than 200 kg?

APPROACH We use Hooke's law: the weight of the people, mg, causes a 3.0-cm displacement.

SOLUTION (a) The added force of $(200\,\text{kg})(9.8\,\text{m/s}^2) = 1960\,\text{N}$ causes the springs to compress $3.0 \times 10^{-2}\,\text{m}$. Therefore (Eq. 14–1), the spring constant is

$$k = \frac{F}{x} = \frac{1960\,\text{N}}{3.0 \times 10^{-2}\,\text{m}} = 6.5 \times 10^4\,\text{N/m}.$$

(b) If the car is loaded with 300 kg, Hooke's law gives

$$x = \frac{F}{k} = \frac{(300\,\text{kg})(9.8\,\text{m/s}^2)}{(6.5 \times 10^4\,\text{N/m})} = 4.5 \times 10^{-2}\,\text{m},$$

or 4.5 cm.

NOTE In (b), we could have obtained x without solving for k: since x is proportional to F, if 200 kg compresses the spring 3.0 cm, then 1.5 times the force will compress the spring 1.5 times as much, or 4.5 cm.

FIGURE 14–4 Photo of a car's spring. (Also visible is the shock absorber, in blue—see Section 14–7.)

14–2 Simple Harmonic Motion

Any oscillating system for which the net restoring force is directly proportional to the negative of the displacement (as in Eq. 14–1, $F = -kx$) is said to exhibit **simple harmonic motion** (SHM). Such a system is often called a **simple harmonic oscillator** (SHO). We saw in Chapter 12 (Section 12–4) that most solid materials stretch or compress according to Eq. 14–1 as long as the displacement is not too great. Because of this, many natural oscillations are simple harmonic or close to it.

EXERCISE D Which of the following represents a simple harmonic oscillator: (a) $F = -0.5x^2$, (b) $F = -2.3y$, (c) $F = 8.6x$, (d) $F = -4\theta$?

Let us now determine the position x as a function of time for a mass attached to the end of a simple spring with spring constant k. To do so, we make use of Newton's second law, $F = ma$. Since the acceleration $a = d^2x/dt^2$, we have

$$ma = \Sigma F$$

$$m\frac{d^2x}{dt^2} = -kx,$$

where m is the mass[†] which is oscillating. We rearrange this to obtain

$$\frac{d^2x}{dt^2} + \frac{k}{m}x = 0, \qquad\qquad \text{[SHM]} \quad \textbf{(14–3)}$$

which is known as the **equation of motion** for the simple harmonic oscillator. Mathematically it is called a *differential equation*, since it involves derivatives. We want to determine what function of time, $x(t)$, satisfies this equation. We might guess the form of the solution by noting that if a pen were attached to an oscillating mass (Fig. 14–5) and a sheet of paper moved at a steady rate beneath it, the pen would trace the curve shown. The shape of this curve looks a lot like it might be **sinusoidal** (such as cosine or sine) as a function of time, and its height is the amplitude A. Let us then guess that the general solution to Eq. 14–3 can be written in a form such as

$$x = A\cos(\omega t + \phi), \qquad\qquad \textbf{(14–4)}$$

where we include the constant ϕ in the argument to be general.[‡] Let us now put this trial solution into Eq. 14–3 and see if it really works. We need to differentiate the $x = x(t)$ twice:

$$\frac{dx}{dt} = \frac{d}{dt}[A\cos(\omega t + \phi)] = -\omega A\sin(\omega t + \phi)$$

$$\frac{d^2x}{dt^2} = -\omega^2 A\cos(\omega t + \phi).$$

We now put the latter into Eq. 14–3, along with Eq. 14–4 for x:

$$\frac{d^2x}{dt^2} + \frac{k}{m}x = 0$$

$$-\omega^2 A\cos(\omega t + \phi) + \frac{k}{m}A\cos(\omega t + \phi) = 0$$

or

$$\left(\frac{k}{m} - \omega^2\right)A\cos(\omega t + \phi) = 0.$$

Our solution, Eq. 14–4, does indeed satisfy the equation of motion (Eq. 14–3) for

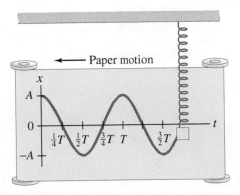

FIGURE 14–5 Sinusoidal nature of SHM as a function of time. In this case, $x = A\cos(2\pi t/T)$.

[†]In the case of a mass, m', on the end of a spring, the spring itself also oscillates and at least a part of its mass must be included. It can be shown—see the Problems—that approximately one-third the mass of the spring, m_s, must be included, so then $m = m' + \frac{1}{3}m_s$ in our equation. Often m_s is small enough to be ignored.

[‡]Another possible way to write the solution is the combination $x = a\cos\omega t + b\sin\omega t$, where a and b are constants. This is equivalent to Eq. 14–4 as can be seen using the trigonometric identity $\cos(A \pm B) = \cos A\cos B \mp \sin A\sin B$.

any time t, but only if $(k/m - \omega^2) = 0$. Hence

$$\omega^2 = \frac{k}{m}. \qquad \textbf{(14–5)}$$

Equation 14–4 is the general solution to Eq. 14–3, and it contains two arbitrary constants A and ϕ, which we should expect because the second derivative in Eq. 14–3 implies that two integrations are needed, each yielding a constant. They are "arbitrary" only in a calculus sense, in that they can be anything and still satisfy the differential equation, Eq. 14–3. In real physical situations, however, A and ϕ are determined by the **initial conditions**. Suppose, for example, that the mass is started at its maximum displacement and is released from rest. This is, in fact, what is shown in Fig. 14–5, and for this case $x = A \cos \omega t$. Let us confirm it: we are given $v = 0$ at $t = 0$, where

$$v = \frac{dx}{dt} = \frac{d}{dt}[A \cos(\omega t + \phi)] = -\omega A \sin(\omega t + \phi) = 0. \qquad [\text{at } t = 0]$$

For v to be zero at $t = 0$, then $\sin(\omega t + \phi) = \sin(0 + \phi)$ is zero if $\phi = 0$ (ϕ could also be $\pi, 2\pi$, etc.), and when $\phi = 0$, then

$$x = A \cos \omega t,$$

as we expected. We see immediately that A is the amplitude of the motion, and it is determined initially by how far you pulled the mass m from equilibrium before releasing it.

Consider another interesting case: at $t = 0$, the mass m is at $x = 0$ and is struck, giving it an initial velocity toward increasing values of x. Then at $t = 0$, $x = 0$, so we can write $x = A \cos(\omega t + \phi) = A \cos \phi = 0$, which can happen only if $\phi = \pm \pi/2$ (or $\pm 90°$). Whether $\phi = +\pi/2$ or $-\pi/2$ depends on $v = dx/dt = -\omega A \sin(\omega t + \phi) = -\omega A \sin \phi$ at $t = 0$, which we are given as positive ($v > 0$ at $t = 0$); hence $\phi = -\pi/2$ because $\sin(-90°) = -1$. Thus our solution for this case is

$$x = A \cos\left(\omega t - \frac{\pi}{2}\right)$$

$$= A \sin \omega t,$$

where we used $\cos(\theta - \pi/2) = \sin \theta$. The solution in this case is a pure sine wave, Fig. 14–6, where A is still the amplitude.

Many other situations are possible, such as that shown in Fig. 14–7. The constant ϕ is called the **phase angle**, and it tells us how long after (or before) $t = 0$ the peak at $x = A$ is reached. Notice that the value of ϕ does not affect the shape of the $x(t)$ curve, but only affects the displacement at some arbitrary time, $t = 0$. Simple harmonic motion is thus always *sinusoidal*. Indeed, simple harmonic motion is *defined* as motion that is purely sinusoidal.

Since our oscillating mass repeats its motion after a time equal to its period T, it must be at the same position and moving in the same direction at $t = T$ as it was at $t = 0$. Since a sine or cosine function repeats itself after every 2π radians, then from Eq. 14–4, we must have

$$\omega T = 2\pi.$$

Hence

$$\omega = \frac{2\pi}{T} = 2\pi f,$$

where f is the frequency of the motion. Strictly speaking, we call ω the **angular frequency** (units are rad/s) to distinguish it from the frequency f (units are $\text{s}^{-1} = \text{Hz}$); sometimes the word "angular" is dropped, so the symbol ω or f needs to be specified. Because $\omega = 2\pi f = 2\pi/T$, we can write Eq. 14–4 as

$$x = A \cos\left(\frac{2\pi t}{T} + \phi\right) \qquad \textbf{(14–6a)}$$

or

$$x = A \cos(2\pi f t + \phi). \qquad \textbf{(14–6b)}$$

FIGURE 14–6 Special case of SHM where the mass m starts, at $t = 0$, at the equilibrium position $x = 0$ and has initial velocity toward positive values of x ($v > 0$ at $t = 0$).

FIGURE 14–7 A plot of $x = A \cos(\omega t + \phi)$ when $\phi < 0$.

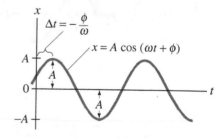

Because $\omega = 2\pi f = \sqrt{k/m}$ (Eq. 14–5), then

$$f = \frac{1}{2\pi}\sqrt{\frac{k}{m}}, \tag{14–7a}$$

$$T = 2\pi\sqrt{\frac{m}{k}}. \tag{14–7b}$$

Note that the *frequency and period do not depend on the amplitude*. Changing the amplitude of a simple harmonic oscillator does not affect its frequency. Equation 14–7a tells us that the greater the mass, the lower the frequency; and the stiffer the spring, the higher the frequency. This makes sense since a greater mass means more inertia and therefore a slower response (or acceleration); and larger k means greater force and therefore quicker response. The frequency f (Eq. 14–7a) at which a SHO oscillates naturally is called its **natural frequency** (to distinguish it from a frequency at which it might be forced to oscillate by an outside force, as discussed in Section 14–8).

The simple harmonic oscillator is important in physics because whenever we have a net restoring force proportional to the displacement $(F = -kx)$, which is at least a good approximation for a variety of systems, then the motion is simple harmonic—that is, sinusoidal.

EXAMPLE 14–2 **Car springs again.** Determine the period and frequency of the car in Example 14–1a after hitting a bump. Assume the shock absorbers are poor, so the car really oscillates up and down.

APPROACH We put $m = 1400$ kg and $k = 6.5 \times 10^4$ N/m from Example 14–1a into Eqs. 14–7.

SOLUTION From Eq. 14–7b,

$$T = 2\pi\sqrt{\frac{m}{k}} = 2\pi\sqrt{\frac{1400\text{ kg}}{6.5 \times 10^4\text{ N/m}}} = 0.92\text{ s},$$

or slightly less than a second. The frequency $f = 1/T = 1.09$ Hz.

EXERCISE E By how much should the mass on the end of a spring be changed to halve the frequency of its oscillations? (*a*) No change; (*b*) doubled; (*c*) quadrupled; (*d*) halved; (*e*) quartered.

EXERCISE F The position of a SHO is given by $x = (0.80\text{ m})\cos(3.14t - 0.25)$. The frequency is (*a*) 3.14 Hz, (*b*) 1.0 Hz, (*c*) 0.50 Hz, (*d*) 9.88 Hz, (*e*) 19.8 Hz.

Let us continue our analysis of a simple harmonic oscillator. The velocity and acceleration of the oscillating mass can be obtained by differentiation of Eq. 14–4, $x = A\cos(\omega t + \phi)$:

$$v = \frac{dx}{dt} = -\omega A\sin(\omega t + \phi) \tag{14–8a}$$

$$a = \frac{d^2x}{dt^2} = \frac{dv}{dt} = -\omega^2 A\cos(\omega t + \phi). \tag{14–8b}$$

The velocity and acceleration of a SHO also vary sinusoidally. In Fig. 14–8 we plot the displacement, velocity, and acceleration of a SHO as a function of time for the case when $\phi = 0$. As can be seen, the speed reaches its maximum

$$v_{\text{max}} = \omega A = \sqrt{\frac{k}{m}}\,A \tag{14–9a}$$

when the oscillating object is passing through its equilibrium point, $x = 0$. And the speed is zero at points of maximum displacement, $x = \pm A$. This is in accord with our discussion of Fig. 14–2. Similarly, the acceleration has its maximum value

$$a_{\text{max}} = \omega^2 A = \frac{k}{m}\,A \tag{14–9b}$$

which occurs where $x = \pm A$; and a is zero at $x = 0$, as we expect, since $ma = F = -kx$.

FIGURE 14–8 Displacement, x, velocity, dx/dt, and acceleration, d^2x/dt^2, of a simple harmonic oscillator when $\phi = 0$.

(a)

(b)

(c)

For the general case when $\phi \neq 0$, we can relate the constants A and ϕ to the initial values of x, v, and a by setting $t = 0$ in Eqs. 14–4, 14–8, and 14–9:

$$x_0 = x(0) = A \cos \phi$$

$$v_0 = v(0) = -\omega A \sin \phi = -v_{max} \sin \phi$$

$$a_0 = a(0) = -\omega^2 A \cos \phi = -a_{max} \cos \phi.$$

EXAMPLE 14–3 | ESTIMATE | A vibrating floor. A large motor in a factory causes the floor to vibrate at a frequency of 10 Hz. The amplitude of the floor's motion near the motor is about 3.0 mm. Estimate the maximum acceleration of the floor near the motor.

APPROACH Assuming the motion of the floor is roughly SHM we can make an estimate for the maximum acceleration using Eq. 14–9b.

SOLUTION Given $\omega = 2\pi f = (2\pi)(10 \text{ s}^{-1}) = 62.8 \text{ rad/s}$, then Eq. 14–9b gives

$$a_{max} = \omega^2 A = (62.8 \text{ rad/s})^2 (0.0030 \text{ m}) = 12 \text{ m/s}^2.$$

NOTE The maximum acceleration is a little over g, so when the floor accelerates down, objects sitting on the floor will actually lose contact momentarily, which will cause noise and serious wear.

PHYSICS APPLIED
Unwanted floor vibrations

EXAMPLE 14–4 | Loudspeaker. The cone of a loudspeaker (Fig. 14–9) oscillates in SHM at a frequency of 262 Hz ("middle C"). The amplitude at the center of the cone is $A = 1.5 \times 10^{-4} \text{ m}$, and at $t = 0$, $x = A$. (a) What equation describes the motion of the center of the cone? (b) What are the velocity and acceleration as a function of time? (c) What is the position of the cone at $t = 1.00 \text{ ms} (= 1.00 \times 10^{-3} \text{ s})$?

APPROACH The motion begins $(t = 0)$ with the cone at its maximum displacement $(x = A$ at $t = 0)$. So we use the cosine function, $x = A \cos \omega t$, with $\phi = 0$.

SOLUTION (a) The amplitude $A = 1.5 \times 10^{-4} \text{ m}$ and

$$\omega = 2\pi f = (6.28 \text{ rad})(262 \text{ s}^{-1}) = 1650 \text{ rad/s}.$$

The motion is described as

$$x = A \cos \omega t = (1.5 \times 10^{-4} \text{ m}) \cos(1650 t),$$

where t is in seconds.

(b) The maximum velocity, from Eq. 14–9a, is

$$v_{max} = \omega A = (1650 \text{ rad/s})(1.5 \times 10^{-4} \text{ m}) = 0.25 \text{ m/s},$$

so

$$v = -(0.25 \text{ m/s}) \sin(1650 t).$$

From Eq. 14–9b the maximum acceleration is $a_{max} = \omega^2 A = (1650 \text{ rad/s})^2 (1.5 \times 10^{-4} \text{ m}) = 410 \text{ m/s}^2$, which is more than 40 g's. Then

$$a = -(410 \text{ m/s}^2) \cos(1650 t).$$

(c) At $t = 1.00 \times 10^{-3} \text{ s}$,

$$x = A \cos \omega t = (1.5 \times 10^{-4} \text{ m}) \cos[(1650 \text{ rad/s})(1.00 \times 10^{-3} \text{ s})]$$

$$= (1.5 \times 10^{-4} \text{ m}) \cos(1.65 \text{ rad}) = -1.2 \times 10^{-5} \text{ m}.$$

NOTE Be sure your calculator is set in RAD mode, not DEG mode, for these $\cos \omega t$ calculations.

FIGURE 14–9 Example 14–4. A loudspeaker cone.

⚠ **CAUTION**
Always be sure your calculator is in the correct mode for angles

EXAMPLE 14-5 **Spring calculations.** A spring stretches 0.150 m when a 0.300-kg mass is gently attached to it as in Fig. 14–3b. The spring is then set up horizontally with the 0.300-kg mass resting on a frictionless table as in Fig. 14–2. The mass is pushed so that the spring is compressed 0.100 m from the equilibrium point, and released from rest. Determine: (a) the spring stiffness constant k and angular frequency ω; (b) the amplitude of the horizontal oscillation A; (c) the magnitude of the maximum velocity v_{max}; (d) the magnitude of the maximum acceleration a_{max} of the mass; (e) the period T and frequency f; (f) the displacement x as a function of time; and (g) the velocity at $t = 0.150$ s.

APPROACH When the 0.300-kg mass hangs at rest from the spring as in Fig. 14–3b, we apply Newton's second law for the vertical forces: $\Sigma F = 0 = mg - kx_0$, so $k = mg/x_0$. For the horizontal oscillations, the amplitude is given, and the other quantities can be found from Eqs. 14–4, 14–5, 14–7, and 14–9. We choose x positive to the right.

SOLUTION (a) The spring stretches 0.150 m due to the 0.300-kg load, so

$$k = \frac{F}{x_0} = \frac{mg}{x_0} = \frac{(0.300 \text{ kg})(9.80 \text{ m/s}^2)}{0.150 \text{ m}} = 19.6 \text{ N/m}.$$

From Eq. 14–5,

$$\omega = \sqrt{\frac{k}{m}} = \sqrt{\frac{19.6 \text{ N/m}}{0.300 \text{ kg}}} = 8.08 \text{ s}^{-1}.$$

(b) The spring is now horizontal (on a table). It is compressed 0.100 m from equilibrium and is given no initial speed, so $A = 0.100$ m.

(c) From Eq. 14–9a, the maximum velocity has magnitude

$$v_{max} = \omega A = (8.08 \text{ s}^{-1})(0.100 \text{ m}) = 0.808 \text{ m/s}.$$

(d) Since $F = ma$, the maximum acceleration occurs where the force is greatest—that is, when $x = \pm A = \pm 0.100$ m. Thus its magnitude is

$$a_{max} = \frac{F}{m} = \frac{kA}{m} = \frac{(19.6 \text{ N/m})(0.100 \text{ m})}{0.300 \text{ kg}} = 6.53 \text{ m/s}^2.$$

[This result could also have been obtained directly from Eq. 14–9b, but it is often useful to go back to basics as we did here.]

(e) Equations 14–7b and 14–2 give

$$T = 2\pi \sqrt{\frac{m}{k}} = 2\pi \sqrt{\frac{0.300 \text{ kg}}{19.6 \text{ N/m}}} = 0.777 \text{ s}$$

$$f = \frac{1}{T} = 1.29 \text{ Hz}.$$

(f) The motion begins at a point of maximum compression. If we take x positive to the right in Fig. 14–2, then at $t = 0, x = -A = -0.100$ m. So we need a sinusoidal curve that has its maximum negative value at $t = 0$; this is just a negative cosine:

$$x = -A \cos \omega t.$$

To write this in the form of Eq. 14–4 (no minus sign), recall that $\cos \theta = -\cos(\theta - \pi)$. Then, putting in numbers, and recalling $-\cos \theta = \cos(\pi - \theta) = \cos(\theta - \pi)$, we have

$$x = -(0.100 \text{ m}) \cos 8.08t$$
$$= (0.100 \text{ m}) \cos(8.08t - \pi),$$

where t is in seconds and x is in meters. Note that the phase angle (Eq. 14–4) is $\phi = -\pi$ or $-180°$.

(g) The velocity at any time t is dx/dt (see also part c):

$$v = \frac{dx}{dt} = \omega A \sin \omega t = (0.808 \text{ m/s}) \sin 8.08t.$$

At $t = 0.150$ s, $v = (0.808 \text{ m/s}) \sin(1.21 \text{ rad}) = 0.756 \text{ m/s}$, and is to the right (+).

EXAMPLE 14–6 **Spring is started with a push.** Suppose the spring of Example 14–5 is compressed 0.100 m from equilibrium $(x_0 = -0.100\text{ m})$ but is given a shove to create a velocity in the $+x$ direction of $v_0 = 0.400\text{ m/s}$. Determine (a) the phase angle ϕ, (b) the amplitude A, and (c) the displacement x as a function of time, $x(t)$.

APPROACH We use Eq. 14–8a, at $t = 0$, to write $v_0 = -\omega A \sin\phi$, and Eq. 14–4 to write $x_0 = A \cos\phi$. Combining these, we can obtain ϕ. We obtain A by using Eq. 14–4 again at $t = 0$. From Example 14–5, $\omega = 8.08\text{ s}^{-1}$.

SOLUTION (a) We combine Eqs. 14–8a and 14–4 at $t = 0$ and solve for the tangent:

$$\tan\phi = \frac{\sin\phi}{\cos\phi} = \frac{(v_0/-\omega A)}{(x_0/A)} = -\frac{v_0}{\omega x_0} = -\frac{0.400\text{ m/s}}{(8.08\text{ s}^{-1})(-0.100\text{ m})} = 0.495.$$

A calculator gives the angle as $26.3°$, but we note from this equation that both the sine and cosine are negative, so our angle is in the third quadrant. Hence

$$\phi = 26.3° + 180° = 206.3° = 3.60\text{ rad}.$$

(b) Again using Eq. 14–4 at $t = 0$, as given in the Approach above,

$$A = \frac{x_0}{\cos\phi} = \frac{(-0.100\text{ m})}{\cos(3.60\text{ rad})} = 0.112\text{ m}.$$

(c) $x = A\cos(\omega t + \phi) = (0.112\text{ m})\cos(8.08t + 3.60)$.

14–3 Energy in the Simple Harmonic Oscillator

When forces are not constant, as is the case here with simple harmonic motion, it is often convenient and useful to use the energy approach, as we saw in Chapters 7 and 8.

For a simple harmonic oscillator, such as a mass m oscillating on the end of a massless spring, the restoring force is given by

$$F = -kx.$$

The potential energy function, as we saw in Chapter 8, is given by

$$U = -\int F\,dx = \tfrac{1}{2}kx^2,$$

where we set the constant of integration equal to zero so $U = 0$ at $x = 0$ (the equilibrium position).

The total mechanical energy is the sum of the kinetic and potential energies,

$$E = \tfrac{1}{2}mv^2 + \tfrac{1}{2}kx^2,$$

where v is the velocity of the mass m when it is a distance x from the equilibrium position. SHM can occur only if there is no friction, so the total mechanical energy E remains constant. As the mass oscillates back and forth, the energy continuously changes from potential energy to kinetic energy, and back again (Fig. 14–10). At the extreme points, $x = A$ and $x = -A$, all the energy is stored in the spring as potential energy (and is the same whether the spring is compressed or stretched to the full amplitude). At these extreme points, the mass stops for an instant as it changes direction, so $v = 0$ and:

$$E = \tfrac{1}{2}m(0)^2 + \tfrac{1}{2}kA^2 = \tfrac{1}{2}kA^2. \qquad (14\text{–}10\text{a})$$

Thus, the *total mechanical energy of a simple harmonic oscillator is proportional to the square of the amplitude.* At the equilibrium point, $x = 0$, all the energy is kinetic:

$$E = \tfrac{1}{2}mv^2 + \tfrac{1}{2}k(0)^2 = \tfrac{1}{2}mv_{\text{max}}^2, \qquad (14\text{–}10\text{b})$$

where v_{max} is the maximum velocity during the motion. At intermediate points the energy is part kinetic and part potential, and because energy is conserved

$$E = \tfrac{1}{2}mv^2 + \tfrac{1}{2}kx^2. \qquad (14\text{–}10\text{c})$$

We can confirm Eqs. 14–10a and b explicitly by inserting Eqs. 14–4 and 14–8a into this last relation:

$$E = \tfrac{1}{2}m\omega^2 A^2 \sin^2(\omega t + \phi) + \tfrac{1}{2}kA^2 \cos^2(\omega t + \phi).$$

Substituting with $\omega^2 = k/m$, or $kA^2 = m\omega^2 A^2 = mv_{\text{max}}^2$, and recalling the important trigonometric identity $\sin^2(\omega t + \phi) + \cos^2(\omega t + \phi) = 1$, we obtain Eqs. 14–10a and b:

$$E = \tfrac{1}{2}kA^2 = \tfrac{1}{2}mv_{\text{max}}^2.$$

[Note that we can check for consistency by solving this equation for v_{max}, and we do get Eq. 14–9a.]

(a)

(b)

(c)

(d)

FIGURE 14–10 Energy changes from potential energy to kinetic energy and back again as the spring oscillates. Energy bar graphs (on the right) are described in Section 8–4.

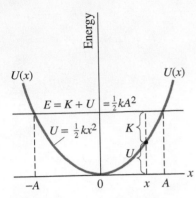

FIGURE 14–11 Graph of potential energy, $U = \frac{1}{2}kx^2$. $K + U = E = $ constant for any point x where $-A \leq x \leq A$. Values of K and U are indicated for an arbitrary position x.

We can now obtain an equation for the velocity v as a function of x by solving for v in Eq. 14–10c:

$$v = \pm\sqrt{\frac{k}{m}(A^2 - x^2)} \qquad \text{(14–11a)}$$

or, since $v_{max} = A\sqrt{k/m}$,

$$v = \pm v_{max}\sqrt{1 - \frac{x^2}{A^2}}. \qquad \text{(14–11b)}$$

Again we see that v is a maximum at $x = 0$, and is zero at $x = \pm A$.

The potential energy, $U = \frac{1}{2}kx^2$, is plotted in Fig. 14–11 (see also Section 8–9). The upper horizontal line represents a particular value of the total energy $E = \frac{1}{2}kA^2$. The distance between the E line and the U curve represents the kinetic energy, K, and the motion is restricted to x values between $-A$ and $+A$. These results are, of course, consistent with our full solution of the previous Section.

Energy conservation is a convenient way to obtain v, for example, if x is given (or vice versa), without having to deal with time t.

EXAMPLE 14–7 Energy calculations. For the simple harmonic oscillation of Example 14–5, determine (a) the total energy, (b) the kinetic and potential energies as a function of time, (c) the velocity when the mass is 0.050 m from equilibrium, (d) the kinetic and potential energies at half amplitude ($x = \pm A/2$).

APPROACH We use conservation of energy for a spring–mass system, Eqs. 14–10 and 14–11.

SOLUTION (a) From Example 14–5, $k = 19.6\,\text{N/m}$ and $A = 0.100\,\text{m}$, so the total energy E from Eq. 14–10a is

$$E = \tfrac{1}{2}kA^2 = \tfrac{1}{2}(19.6\,\text{N/m})(0.100\,\text{m})^2 = 9.80 \times 10^{-2}\,\text{J}.$$

(b) We have, from parts (f) and (g) of Example 14–5, $x = -(0.100\,\text{m})\cos 8.08t$ and $v = (0.808\,\text{m/s})\sin 8.08t$, so

$$U = \tfrac{1}{2}kx^2 = \tfrac{1}{2}(19.6\,\text{N/m})(0.100\,\text{m})^2\cos^2 8.08t = (9.80 \times 10^{-2}\,\text{J})\cos^2 8.08t$$

$$K = \tfrac{1}{2}mv^2 = \tfrac{1}{2}(0.300\,\text{kg})(0.808\,\text{m/s})^2\sin^2 8.08t = (9.80 \times 10^{-2}\,\text{J})\sin^2 8.08t.$$

(c) We use Eq. 14–11b and find

$$v = v_{max}\sqrt{1 - x^2/A^2} = (0.808\,\text{m/s})\sqrt{1 - (\tfrac{1}{2})^2} = 0.70\,\text{m/s}.$$

(d) At $x = A/2 = 0.050\,\text{m}$, we have

$$U = \tfrac{1}{2}kx^2 = \tfrac{1}{2}(19.6\,\text{N/m})(0.050\,\text{m})^2 = 2.5 \times 10^{-2}\,\text{J}$$

$$K = E - U = 7.3 \times 10^{-2}\,\text{J}.$$

CONCEPTUAL EXAMPLE 14–8 Doubling the amplitude. Suppose the spring in Fig. 14–10 is stretched twice as far (to $x = 2A$). What happens to (a) the energy of the system, (b) the maximum velocity of the oscillating mass, (c) the maximum acceleration of the mass?

RESPONSE (a) From Eq. 14–10a, the total energy is proportional to the square of the amplitude A, so stretching it twice as far quadruples the energy ($2^2 = 4$). You may protest, "I did work stretching the spring from $x = 0$ to $x = A$. Don't I do the same work stretching it from A to $2A$?" No. The force you exert is proportional to the displacement x, so for the second displacement, from $x = A$ to $2A$, you do more work than for the first displacement ($x = 0$ to A). (b) From Eq. 14–10b, we can see that when the energy is quadrupled, the maximum velocity must be doubled. [$v_{max} \propto \sqrt{E} \propto A$.] (c) Since the force is twice as great when we stretch the spring twice as far, the acceleration is also twice as great: $a \propto F \propto x$.

EXERCISE G Suppose the spring in Fig. 14–10 is compressed to $x = -A$, but is given a push to the right so that the initial speed of the mass m is v_0. What effect does this push have on (a) the energy of the system, (b) the maximum velocity, (c) the maximum acceleration?

14–4 Simple Harmonic Motion Related to Uniform Circular Motion

Simple harmonic motion has a simple relationship to a particle rotating in a circle with uniform speed. Consider a mass m rotating in a circle of radius A with speed v_M on top of a table as shown in Fig. 14–12. As viewed from above, the motion is a circle. But a person who looks at the motion from the edge of the table sees an oscillatory motion back and forth, and this corresponds precisely to SHM as we shall now see. What the person sees, and what we are interested in, is the projection of the circular motion onto the x axis, Fig. 14–12. To see that this motion is analogous to SHM, let us calculate the x component of the velocity v_M which is labeled v in Fig. 14–12. The two right triangles indicated in Fig. 14–12 are similar, so

$$\frac{v}{v_M} = \frac{\sqrt{A^2 - x^2}}{A}$$

or

$$v = v_M \sqrt{1 - \frac{x^2}{A^2}}.$$

This is exactly the equation for the speed of a mass oscillating with SHM, Eq. 14–11b, where $v_M = v_{max}$. Furthermore, we can see from Fig. 14–12 that if the angular displacement at $t = 0$ is ϕ, then after a time t the particle will have rotated through an angle $\theta = \omega t$, and so

$$x = A \cos(\theta + \phi) = A \cos(\omega t + \phi).$$

But what is ω here? The linear velocity v_M of our particle undergoing rotational motion is related to ω by $v_M = \omega A$, where A is the radius of the circle (see Eq. 10–4, $v = R\omega$). To make one revolution requires a time T, so we also have $v_M = 2\pi A/T$ where $2\pi A$ is the circle's circumference. Hence

$$\omega = \frac{v_M}{A} = \frac{2\pi A/T}{A} = 2\pi/T = 2\pi f$$

where T is the time required for one rotation and f is the frequency. This corresponds precisely to the back-and-forth motion of a simple harmonic oscillator. Thus, the projection on the x axis of a particle rotating in a circle has the same motion as a mass undergoing SHM. Indeed, we can say that the projection of circular motion onto a straight line is simple harmonic motion.

The projection of uniform circular motion onto the y axis is also simple harmonic. Thus uniform circular motion can be thought of as two simple harmonic motions operating at right angles.

(a)

(b)

FIGURE 14–12 Analysis of simple harmonic motion as a side view (b) of circular motion (a).

14–5 The Simple Pendulum

A **simple pendulum** consists of a small object (the pendulum bob) suspended from the end of a lightweight cord, Fig. 14–13. We assume that the cord does not stretch and that its mass can be ignored relative to that of the bob. The motion of a simple pendulum moving back and forth with negligible friction resembles simple harmonic motion: the pendulum oscillates along the arc of a circle with equal amplitude on either side of its equilibrium point and as it passes through the equilibrium point (where it would hang vertically) it has its maximum speed. But is it really undergoing SHM? That is, is the restoring force proportional to its displacement? Let us find out.

FIGURE 14–13 Strobe-light photo of an oscillating pendulum photographed at equal time intervals.

FIGURE 14–14 Simple pendulum.

FIGURE 14–15 The swinging motion of this lamp, hanging by a very long cord from the ceiling of the cathedral at Pisa, is said to have been observed by Galileo and to have inspired him to the conclusion that the period of a pendulum does not depend on amplitude.

🚶 PHYSICS APPLIED
Pendulum clock

The displacement of the pendulum along the arc is given by $x = \ell\theta$, where θ is the angle (in radians) that the cord makes with the vertical and ℓ is the length of the cord (Fig. 14–14). If the restoring force is proportional to x or to θ, the motion will be simple harmonic. The restoring force is the net force on the bob, equal to the component of the weight, mg, tangent to the arc:

$$F = -mg \sin\theta,$$

where g is the acceleration of gravity. The minus sign here, as in Eq. 14–1, means that the force is in the direction opposite to the angular displacement θ. Since F is proportional to the sine of θ and not to θ itself, the motion is _not_ SHM. However, if θ is small, then $\sin\theta$ is very nearly equal to θ when the latter is specified in radians. This can be seen by looking at the series expansion[†] of $\sin\theta$ (or by looking at the trigonometry Table in Appendix A), or simply by noting in Fig. 14–14 that the arc length x ($= \ell\theta$) is nearly the same length as the chord ($= \ell \sin\theta$) indicated by the straight dashed line, _if_ θ _is small_. For angles less than 15°, the difference between θ (in radians) and $\sin\theta$ is less than 1%. Thus, to a very good approximation for small angles,

$$F = -mg \sin\theta \approx -mg\theta.$$

Substituting $x = \ell\theta$ or $\theta = x/\ell$, we have

$$F \approx -\frac{mg}{\ell} x.$$

Thus, for small displacements, the motion is essentially simple harmonic, since this equation fits Hooke's law, $F = -kx$. The effective force constant is $k = mg/\ell$. Thus we can write

$$\theta = \theta_{max} \cos(\omega t + \phi)$$

where θ_{max} is the maximum angular displacement and $\omega = 2\pi f = 2\pi/T$. To obtain ω we use Eq. 14–5, where for k we substitute mg/ℓ: that is,[‡] $\omega = \sqrt{k/m} = \sqrt{(mg/\ell)/m}$, or

$$\omega = \sqrt{\frac{g}{\ell}}. \qquad\qquad [\theta \text{ small}] \quad \textbf{(14–12a)}$$

Then the frequency f is

$$f = \frac{\omega}{2\pi} = \frac{1}{2\pi}\sqrt{\frac{g}{\ell}}, \qquad\qquad [\theta \text{ small}] \quad \textbf{(14–12b)}$$

and the period T is

$$T = \frac{1}{f} = 2\pi\sqrt{\frac{\ell}{g}}. \qquad\qquad [\theta \text{ small}] \quad \textbf{(14–12c)}$$

The mass m of the pendulum bob does not appear in these formulas for T and f. Thus we have the surprising result that the period and frequency of a simple pendulum do not depend on the mass of the pendulum bob. You may have noticed this if you pushed a small child and then a large one on the same swing.

We also see from Eq. 14–12c that the period of a pendulum does not depend on the amplitude (like any SHM, Section 14–2), as long as the amplitude θ is small. Galileo is said to have first noted this fact while watching a swinging lamp in the cathedral at Pisa (Fig. 14–15). This discovery led to the invention of the pendulum clock, the first really precise timepiece, which became the standard for centuries.

Because a pendulum does not undergo _precisely_ SHM, the period does depend slightly on the amplitude, the more so for large amplitudes. The accuracy of a pendulum clock would be affected, after many swings, by the decrease in amplitude due to friction. But the mainspring in a pendulum clock (or the falling weight in a grandfather clock) supplies energy to compensate for the friction and to maintain the amplitude constant, so that the timing remains precise.

[†]$\sin\theta = \theta - \dfrac{\theta^3}{3!} + \dfrac{\theta^5}{5!} - \dfrac{\theta^7}{7!} + \cdots$.

[‡]Be careful not to think that $\omega = d\theta/dt$ as in rotational motion. Here θ is the angle of the pendulum at any instant (Fig. 14–14), but we use ω now to represent _not_ the rate this angle θ changes, but rather a constant related to the period, $\omega = 2\pi f = \sqrt{g/\ell}$.

EXERCISE H If a simple pendulum is taken from sea level to the top of a high mountain and started at the same angle of 5°, it would oscillate at the top of the mountain (a) slightly slower, (b) slightly faster, (c) at exactly the same frequency, (d) not at all—it would stop, (e) none of these.

EXERCISE I Return to the Chapter-Opening Question, p. 369, and answer it again now. Try to explain why you may have answered differently the first time.

EXAMPLE 14-9 **Measuring g.** A geologist uses a simple pendulum that has a length of 37.10 cm and a frequency of 0.8190 Hz at a particular location on the Earth. What is the acceleration of gravity at this location?

APPROACH We can use the length ℓ and frequency f of the pendulum in Eq. 14-12b, which contains our unknown, g.

SOLUTION We solve Eq. 14–12b for g and obtain
$$g = (2\pi f)^2 \ell = (6.283 \times 0.8190 \, s^{-1})^2 (0.3710 \, m) = 9.824 \, m/s^2.$$

EXERCISE J (a) Estimate the length of a simple pendulum that makes one swing back and forth per second. (b) What would be the period of a 1.0-m-long pendulum?

*14–6 The Physical Pendulum and the Torsion Pendulum

Physical Pendulum

The term physical pendulum refers to any real extended object which oscillates back and forth, in contrast to the rather idealized simple pendulum where all the mass is assumed concentrated in the tiny pendulum bob. An example of a physical pendulum is a baseball bat suspended from the point O, as shown in Fig. 14–16. The force of gravity acts at the center of gravity (CG) of the object located a distance h from the pivot point O. The physical pendulum is best analyzed using the equations of rotational motion. The torque on a physical pendulum, calculated about point O, is

$$\tau = -mgh \sin\theta.$$

Newton's second law for rotational motion, Eq. 10–14, states that

$$\Sigma\tau = I\alpha = I\frac{d^2\theta}{dt^2},$$

where I is the moment of inertia of the object about the pivot point and $\alpha = d^2\theta/dt^2$ is the angular acceleration. Thus we have

$$I\frac{d^2\theta}{dt^2} = -mgh \sin\theta$$

or

$$\frac{d^2\theta}{dt^2} + \frac{mgh}{I}\sin\theta = 0,$$

where I is calculated about an axis through point O. For small angular amplitude, $\sin\theta \approx \theta$, so we have

$$\frac{d^2\theta}{dt^2} + \left(\frac{mgh}{I}\right)\theta = 0. \qquad \text{[small angular displacement]} \quad \textbf{(14–13)}$$

This is just the equation for SHM, Eq. 14–3, except that θ replaces x and mgh/I replaces k/m. Thus, for small angular displacements, a physical pendulum undergoes SHM, given by

$$\theta = \theta_{max}\cos(\omega t + \phi),$$

where θ_{max} is the maximum angular displacement and $\omega = 2\pi/T$. The period, T, is (see Eq. 14–7b, replacing m/k with I/mgh):

$$T = 2\pi\sqrt{\frac{I}{mgh}}. \qquad \text{[small angular displacement]} \quad \textbf{(14–14)}$$

$$d_\perp(= h \sin\theta)$$

FIGURE 14–16 A physical pendulum suspended from point O.

FIGURE 14–17 Example 14–10.

EXAMPLE 14–10 **Moment of inertia measurement.** An easy way to measure the moment of inertia of an object about any axis is to measure the period of oscillation about that axis. (a) Suppose a nonuniform 1.0-kg stick can be balanced at a point 42 cm from one end. If it is pivoted about that end (Fig. 14–17), it oscillates with a period of 1.6 s. What is its moment of inertia about this end? (b) What is its moment of inertia about an axis perpendicular to the stick through its center of mass?

APPROACH We put the given values into Eq. 14–14 and solve for I. For (b) we use the parallel-axis theorem (Section 10–7).

SOLUTION (a) Given $T = 1.6$ s, and $h = 0.42$ m, Eq. 14–14 gives

$$I = mghT^2/4\pi^2 = 0.27 \text{ kg·m}^2.$$

(b) We use the parallel-axis theorem, Eq. 10–17. The CM is where the stick balanced, 42 cm from the end, so

$$I_{CM} = I - mh^2 = 0.27 \text{ kg·m}^2 - (1.0 \text{ kg})(0.42 \text{ m})^2 = 0.09 \text{ kg·m}^2.$$

NOTE Since an object does not oscillate about its CM, we cannot measure I_{CM} directly, but the parallel-axis theorem provides a convenient method to determine I_{CM}.

Torsion Pendulum

Another type of oscillatory motion is a **torsion pendulum**, in which a disc (Fig. 14–18) or a bar (as in Cavendish's apparatus, Fig. 6–3) is suspended from a wire. The twisting (torsion) of the wire serves as the elastic force. The motion here will be SHM since the restoring torque is very closely proportional to the negative of the angular displacement,

$$\tau = -K\theta,$$

where K is a constant that depends on the wire stiffness. Then

$$\omega = \sqrt{K/I}.$$

There is no small angle restriction here, as there is for the physical pendulum (where gravity acts), as long as the wire responds linearly in accordance with Hooke's law.

FIGURE 14–18 A torsion pendulum. The disc oscillates in SHM between θ_{max} and $-\theta_{max}$.

14–7 Damped Harmonic Motion

The amplitude of any real oscillating spring or swinging pendulum slowly decreases in time until the oscillations stop altogether. Figure 14–19 shows a typical graph of the displacement as a function of time. This is called **damped harmonic motion**. The damping[†] is generally due to the resistance of air and to internal friction within the oscillating system. The energy that is dissipated to thermal energy is reflected in a decreased amplitude of oscillation.

Since natural oscillating systems are damped in general, why do we even talk about (undamped) simple harmonic motion? The answer is that SHM is much easier to deal with mathematically. And if the damping is not large, the oscillations can be thought of as simple harmonic motion on which the damping is superposed, as represented by the dashed curves in Fig. 14–19. Although damping does alter the frequency of vibration, the effect is usually small if the damping is small. Let us look at this in more detail.

The damping force depends on the speed of the oscillating object, and opposes the motion. In some simple cases the damping force can be approximated as being directly proportional to the speed:

$$F_{damping} = -bv,$$

where b is a constant.[‡] For a mass oscillating on the end of a spring, the restoring force of the spring is $F = -kx$; so Newton's second law ($ma = \Sigma F$) becomes

$$ma = -kx - bv.$$

We bring all terms to the left side of the equation and substitute $v = dx/dt$ and

FIGURE 14–19 Damped harmonic motion. The solid red curve represents a cosine times a decreasing exponential (the dashed curves).

[†]To "damp" means to diminish, restrain, or extinguish, as to "dampen one's spirits."
[‡]Such velocity-dependent forces were discussed in Section 5–6.

$a = d^2x/dt^2$ to obtain

$$m\frac{d^2x}{dt^2} + b\frac{dx}{dt} + kx = 0, \qquad (14\text{--}15)$$

which is the equation of motion. To solve this equation, we guess at a solution and then check to see if it works. If the damping constant b is small, x as a function of t is as plotted in Fig. 14–19, which looks like a cosine function times a factor (represented by the dashed lines) that decreases in time. A simple function that does this is the exponential, $e^{-\gamma t}$, and the solution that satisfies Eq. 14–15 is

$$x = Ae^{-\gamma t}\cos\omega't, \qquad (14\text{--}16)$$

where A, γ, and ω' are assumed to be constants, and $x = A$ at $t = 0$. We have called the angular frequency ω' (and not ω) because it is not the same as the ω for SHM without damping $(\omega = \sqrt{k/m})$.

If we substitute Eq. 14–16 into Eq. 14–15 (we do this in the optional subsection below), we find that Eq. 14–16 is indeed a solution if γ and ω' have the values

$$\gamma = \frac{b}{2m} \qquad (14\text{--}17)$$

$$\omega' = \sqrt{\frac{k}{m} - \frac{b^2}{4m^2}}. \qquad (14\text{--}18)$$

Thus x as a function of time t for a (lightly) damped harmonic oscillator is

$$x = Ae^{(-b/2m)t}\cos\omega't. \qquad (14\text{--}19)$$

Of course a phase constant, ϕ, can be added to the argument of the cosine in Eq. 14–19. As it stands with $\phi = 0$, it is clear that the constant A in Eq. 14–19 is simply the initial displacement, $x = A$ at $t = 0$. The frequency f' is

$$f' = \frac{\omega'}{2\pi} = \frac{1}{2\pi}\sqrt{\frac{k}{m} - \frac{b^2}{4m^2}}. \qquad (14\text{--}20)$$

The frequency is lower, and the period longer, than for undamped SHM. (In many practical cases of light damping, however, ω' differs only slightly from $\omega = \sqrt{k/m}$.) This makes sense since we expect damping to slow down the motion. Equation 14–20 reduces to Eq. 14–7a, as it should, when there is no damping $(b = 0)$. The constant $\gamma = b/2m$ is a measure of how quickly the oscillations decrease toward zero (Fig. 14–19). The time $t_L = 2m/b$ is the time taken for the oscillations to drop to $1/e$ of the original amplitude; t_L is called the "mean lifetime" of the oscillations. Note that the larger b is, the more quickly the oscillations die away.

The solution, Eq. 14–19, is not valid if b is so large that

$$b^2 > 4mk$$

since then ω' (Eq. 14–18) would become imaginary. In this case the system does not oscillate at all but returns directly to its equilibrium position, as we now discuss.

Three common cases of *heavily damped* systems are shown in Fig. 14–20. Curve C represents the situation when the damping is so large $(b^2 \gg 4mk)$ that it takes a long time to reach equilibrium; the system is **overdamped**. Curve A represents an **underdamped** situation in which the system makes several swings before coming to rest $(b^2 < 4mk)$ and corresponds to a more heavily damped version of Eq. 14–19. Curve B represents **critical damping**: $b^2 = 4mk$; in this case equilibrium is reached in the shortest time. These terms all derive from the use of practical damped systems such as door-closing mechanisms and **shock absorbers** in a car (Fig. 14–21), which are usually designed to give critical damping. But as they wear out, underdamping occurs: a door slams and a car bounces up and down several times whenever it hits a bump.

In many systems, the oscillatory motion is what counts, as in clocks and watches, and damping needs to be minimized. In other systems, oscillations are the problem, such as a car's springs, so a proper amount of damping (i.e., critical) is desired. Well-designed damping is needed for all kinds of applications. Large buildings, especially in California, are now built (or retrofitted) with huge dampers to reduce earthquake damage.

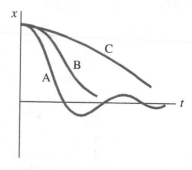

FIGURE 14–20 Underdamped (A), critically damped (B), and overdamped (C) motion.

FIGURE 14–21 Automobile spring and shock absorber provide damping so that a car won't bounce up and down endlessly.

Attached to car frame

Piston

Viscous fluid

Attached to car axle

FIGURE 14–22 Example 14–11.

EXAMPLE 14–11 **Simple pendulum with damping.** A simple pendulum has a length of 1.0 m (Fig. 14–22). It is set swinging with small-amplitude oscillations. After 5.0 minutes, the amplitude is only 50% of what it was initially. (a) What is the value of γ for the motion? (b) By what factor does the frequency, f', differ from f, the undamped frequency?

APPROACH We assume the damping force is proportional to angular speed, $d\theta/dt$. The equation of motion for damped harmonic motion is

$$x = Ae^{-\gamma t}\cos\omega' t, \quad \text{where} \quad \gamma = \frac{b}{2m} \quad \text{and} \quad \omega' = \sqrt{\frac{k}{m} - \frac{b^2}{4m^2}},$$

for motion of a mass on the end of a spring. For the simple pendulum without damping, we saw in Section 14–5 that

$$F = -mg\theta$$

for small θ. Since $F = ma$, where a can be written in terms of the angular acceleration $\alpha = d^2\theta/dt^2$ as $a = \ell\alpha = \ell d^2\theta/dt^2$, then $F = m\ell d^2\theta/dt^2$, and

$$\ell\frac{d^2\theta}{dt^2} + g\theta = 0.$$

Introducing a damping term, $b(d\theta/dt)$, we have

$$\ell\frac{d^2\theta}{dt^2} + b\frac{d\theta}{dt} + g\theta = 0,$$

which is the same as Eq. 14–15 with θ replacing x, and ℓ and g replacing m and k.

SOLUTION (a) We compare Eq. 14–15 with our equation just above and see that our equation $x = Ae^{-\gamma t}\cos\omega' t$ becomes an equation for θ with

$$\gamma = \frac{b}{2\ell} \quad \text{and} \quad \omega' = \sqrt{\frac{g}{\ell} - \frac{b^2}{4\ell^2}}.$$

At $t = 0$, we rewrite Eq. 14–16 with θ replacing x as

$$\theta_0 = Ae^{-\gamma \cdot 0}\cos\omega' \cdot 0 = A.$$

Then at $t = 5.0\,\text{min} = 300\,\text{s}$, the amplitude given by Eq. 14–16 has fallen to $0.50\,A$, so

$$0.50A = Ae^{-\gamma(300\,\text{s})}.$$

We solve this for γ and obtain $\gamma = \ln 2.0/(300\,\text{s}) = 2.3 \times 10^{-3}\,\text{s}^{-1}$.

(b) We have $\ell = 1.0\,\text{m}$, so $b = 2\gamma\ell = 2(2.3 \times 10^{-3}\,\text{s}^{-1})(1.0\,\text{m}) = 4.6 \times 10^{-3}\,\text{m/s}$. Thus $(b^2/4\ell^2)$ is very much less than $g/\ell\,(= 9.8\,\text{s}^{-2})$, and the angular frequency of the motion remains almost the same as that of the undamped motion. Specifically (see Eq. 14–20),

$$f' = \frac{1}{2\pi}\sqrt{\frac{g}{\ell}}\left[1 - \frac{\ell}{g}\left(\frac{b^2}{4\ell^2}\right)\right]^{\frac{1}{2}} \approx \frac{1}{2\pi}\sqrt{\frac{g}{\ell}}\left[1 - \frac{1}{2}\frac{\ell}{g}\left(\frac{b^2}{4\ell^2}\right)\right]$$

where we used the binomial expansion. Then, with $f = (1/2\pi)\sqrt{g/\ell}$ (Eq. 14–12b),

$$\frac{f - f'}{f} \approx \frac{1}{2}\frac{\ell}{g}\left(\frac{b^2}{4\ell^2}\right) = 2.7 \times 10^{-7}.$$

So f' differs from f by less than one part in a million.

*Showing $x = Ae^{-\gamma t}\cos\omega' t$ is a Solution

We start with Eq. 14–16, to see if it is a solution to Eq. 14–15. First we take the first and second derivatives

$$\frac{dx}{dt} = -\gamma Ae^{-\gamma t}\cos\omega' t - \omega' Ae^{-\gamma t}\sin\omega' t$$

$$\frac{d^2x}{dt^2} = \gamma^2 Ae^{-\gamma t}\cos\omega' t + \gamma A\omega' e^{-\gamma t}\sin\omega' t + \omega'\gamma Ae^{-\gamma t}\sin\omega' t - \omega'^2 Ae^{-\gamma t}\cos\omega' t.$$

We next substitute these relations back into Eq. 14–15 and reorganize to obtain

$$Ae^{-\gamma t}\left[(m\gamma^2 - m\omega'^2 - b\gamma + k)\cos \omega't + (2\omega'\gamma m - b\omega')\sin \omega't\right] = 0. \quad \textbf{(i)}$$

The left side of this equation must equal zero for all times t, but this can only be so for certain values of γ and ω'. To determine γ and ω', we choose two values of t that will make their evaluation easy. At $t = 0$, $\sin \omega't = 0$, so the above relation reduces to $A(m\gamma^2 - m\omega'^2 - b\gamma + k) = 0$, which means[†] that

$$m\gamma^2 - m\omega'^2 - b\gamma + k = 0. \quad \textbf{(ii)}$$

Then at $t = \pi/2\omega'$, $\cos \omega't = 0$ so Eq. (i) can be valid only if

$$2\gamma m - b = 0. \quad \textbf{(iii)}$$

From Eq. (iii) we have

$$\gamma = \frac{b}{2m}$$

and from Eq. (ii)

$$\omega' = \sqrt{\gamma^2 - \frac{b\gamma}{m} + \frac{k}{m}} = \sqrt{\frac{k}{m} - \frac{b^2}{4m^2}}.$$

Thus we see that Eq. 14–16 is a solution to the equation of motion for the damped harmonic oscillator as long as γ and ω' have these specific values, as already given in Eqs. 14–17 and 14–18.

14–8 Forced Oscillations; Resonance

When an oscillating system is set into motion, it oscillates at its natural frequency (Eqs. 14–7a and 14–12b). However, a system may have an external force applied to it that has its own particular frequency and then we have a **forced oscillation**.

For example, we might pull the mass on the spring of Fig. 14–1 back and forth at a frequency f. The mass then oscillates at the frequency f of the external force, even if this frequency is different from the **natural frequency** of the spring, which we will now denote by f_0 where (see Eqs. 14–5 and 14–7a)

$$\omega_0 = 2\pi f_0 = \sqrt{\frac{k}{m}}.$$

In a forced oscillation the amplitude of oscillation, and hence the energy transferred to the oscillating system, is found to depend on the difference between f and f_0 as well as on the amount of damping, reaching a maximum when the frequency of the external force equals the natural frequency of the system—that is, when $f = f_0$. The amplitude is plotted in Fig. 14–23 as a function of the external frequency f. Curve A represents light damping and curve B heavy damping. The amplitude can become large when the driving frequency f is near the natural frequency, $f \approx f_0$, as long as the damping is not too large. When the damping is small, the increase in amplitude near $f = f_0$ is very large (and often dramatic). This effect is known as **resonance**. The natural frequency f_0 of a system is called its **resonant frequency**.

A simple illustration of resonance is pushing a child on a swing. A swing, like any pendulum, has a natural frequency of oscillation that depends on its length ℓ. If you push on the swing at a random frequency, the swing bounces around and reaches no great amplitude. But if you push with a frequency equal to the natural frequency of the swing, the amplitude increases greatly. At resonance, relatively little effort is required to obtain a large amplitude.

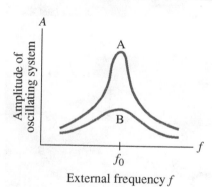

FIGURE 14–23 Resonance for lightly damped (A) and heavily damped (B) systems. (See Fig. 14–26 for a more detailed graph.)

[†]It would also be satisfied by $A = 0$, but this gives the trivial and uninteresting solution $x = 0$ for all t—that is, no oscillation.

FIGURE 14–24 This goblet breaks as it vibrates in resonance to a trumpet call.

FIGURE 14–25 (a) Large-amplitude oscillations of the Tacoma Narrows Bridge, due to gusty winds, led to its collapse (1940). (b) Collapse of a freeway in California, due to the 1989 earthquake.

(a)

(b)

The great tenor Enrico Caruso was said to be able to shatter a crystal goblet by singing a note of just the right frequency at full voice. This is an example of resonance, for the sound waves emitted by the voice act as a forced oscillation on the glass. At resonance, the resulting oscillation of the goblet may be large enough in amplitude that the glass exceeds its elastic limit and breaks (Fig. 14–24).

Since material objects are, in general, elastic, resonance is an important phenomenon in a variety of situations. It is particularly important in structural engineering, although the effects are not always foreseen. For example, it has been reported that a railway bridge collapsed because a nick in one of the wheels of a crossing train set up a resonant oscillation in the bridge. Indeed, marching soldiers break step when crossing a bridge to avoid the possibility that their normal rhythmic march might match a resonant frequency of the bridge. The famous collapse of the Tacoma Narrows Bridge (Fig. 14–25a) in 1940 occurred as a result of strong gusting winds driving the span into large-amplitude oscillatory motion. The Oakland freeway collapse in the 1989 California earthquake (Fig. 14–25b) involved resonant oscillation of a section built on mudfill that readily transmitted that frequency.

We will meet important examples of resonance later. We will also see that vibrating objects often have not one, but many resonant frequencies.

*Equation of Motion and Its Solution

We now look at the equation of motion for a forced oscillation and its solution. Suppose the external force is sinusoidal and can be represented by

$$F_{ext} = F_0 \cos \omega t,$$

where $\omega = 2\pi f$ is the angular frequency applied externally to the oscillator. Then the equation of motion (with damping) is

$$ma = -kx - bv + F_0 \cos \omega t.$$

This can be written as

$$m\frac{d^2x}{dt^2} + b\frac{dx}{dt} + kx = F_0 \cos \omega t. \tag{14–21}$$

The external force, on the right of the equation, is the only term that does not involve x or one of its derivatives. Problem 68 asks you to show that

$$x = A_0 \sin(\omega t + \phi_0) \tag{14–22}$$

is a solution to Eq. 14–21, by direct substitution, where

$$A_0 = \frac{F_0}{m\sqrt{(\omega^2 - \omega_0^2)^2 + b^2\omega^2/m^2}} \tag{14–23}$$

and

$$\phi_0 = \tan^{-1}\frac{\omega_0^2 - \omega^2}{\omega(b/m)}. \tag{14–24}$$

Actually, the general solution to Eq. 14–21 is Eq. 14–22 plus another term of the form of Eq. 14–19 for the natural damped motion of the oscillator; this second term approaches zero in time, so in many cases we need to be concerned only with Eq. 14–22.

The amplitude of forced harmonic motion, A_0, depends strongly on the difference between the applied and the natural frequency. A plot of A_0 (Eq. 14–23) as a function of the applied frequency, ω, is shown in Fig. 14–26 (a more detailed version of Fig. 14–23) for three specific values of the damping constant b. Curve A $(b = \frac{1}{6}m\omega_0)$ represents light damping, curve B $(b = \frac{1}{2}m\omega_0)$ fairly heavy damping, and curve C $(b = \sqrt{2}m\omega_0)$ overdamped motion. The amplitude can become large when the driving frequency is near the natural frequency, $\omega \approx \omega_0$, as long as the damping is not too large. When the damping is small, the increase in amplitude near $\omega = \omega_0$ is very large and, as we saw, is known as *resonance*.

The natural oscillating frequency $f_0 (= \omega_0/2\pi)$ of a system is its *resonant frequency*.[†] If $b = 0$, resonance occurs at $\omega = \omega_0$ and the resonant peak (of A_0) becomes infinite; in such a case, energy is being continuously transferred into the system and none is dissipated. For real systems, b is never precisely zero, and the resonant peak is finite. The peak does not occur precisely at $\omega = \omega_0$ (because of the term $b^2\omega^2/m^2$ in the denominator of Eq. 14–23), although it is quite close to ω_0 unless the damping is very large. If the damping is large, there is little or no peak (curve C in Fig. 14–26).

*Q value

The height and narrowness of a resonant peak is often specified by its **quality factor** or **Q value**, defined as

$$Q = \frac{m\omega_0}{b}.$$ (14–25)

In Fig. 14–26, curve A has $Q = 6$, curve B has $Q = 2$, and curve C has $Q = 1/\sqrt{2}$. The smaller the damping constant b, the larger the Q value becomes, and the higher the resonance peak. The Q value is also a measure of the width of the peak. To see why, let ω_1 and ω_2 be the frequencies where the square of the amplitude A_0 has half its maximum value (we use the square because the power transferred to the system is proportional to A_0^2); then $\Delta\omega = \omega_1 - \omega_2$, which is called the *width* of the resonance peak, is related to Q by

$$\frac{\Delta\omega}{\omega_0} = \frac{1}{Q}.$$ (14–26)

This relation is accurate only for weak damping. The larger the Q value, the narrower will be the resonance peak relative to its height. Thus a large Q value, representing a system of high quality, has a high, narrow resonance peak.

[†]Sometimes the resonant frequency is defined as the actual value of ω at which the amplitude has its maximum value, and this depends somewhat on the damping constant. Except for very heavy damping, this value is quite close to ω_0.

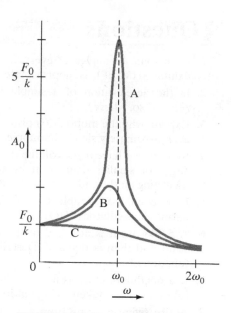

FIGURE 14–26 Amplitude of a forced harmonic oscillator as a function of ω. Curves A, B, and C correspond to light, heavy, and overdamped systems, respectively ($Q = m\omega_0/b = 6, 2, 0.71$).

Summary

An oscillating object undergoes **simple harmonic motion** (SHM) if the restoring force is proportional to the displacement,

$$F = -kx.$$ (14–1)

The maximum displacement from equilibrium is called the **amplitude**.

The **period**, T, is the time required for one complete cycle (back and forth), and the **frequency**, f, is the number of cycles per second; they are related by

$$f = \frac{1}{T}.$$ (14–2)

The period of oscillation for a mass m on the end of an ideal massless spring is given by

$$T = 2\pi\sqrt{\frac{m}{k}}.$$ (14–7b)

SHM is **sinusoidal**, which means that the displacement as a function of time follows a sine or cosine curve. The general solution can be written

$$x = A\cos(\omega t + \phi)$$ (14–4)

where A is the amplitude, ϕ is the **phase angle**, and

$$\omega = 2\pi f = \sqrt{\frac{k}{m}}.$$ (14–5)

The values of A and ϕ depend on the **initial conditions** (x and v at $t = 0$).

During SHM, the total energy $E = \frac{1}{2}mv^2 + \frac{1}{2}kx^2$ is continually changing from potential to kinetic and back again.

A **simple pendulum** of length ℓ approximates SHM if its amplitude is small and friction can be ignored. For small amplitudes, its period is given by

$$T = 2\pi\sqrt{\frac{\ell}{g}},$$ (14–12c)

where g is the acceleration of gravity.

When friction is present (for all real springs and pendulums), the motion is said to be **damped**. The maximum displacement decreases in time, and the mechanical energy is eventually all transformed to thermal energy. If the friction is very large, so no oscillations occur, the system is said to be **overdamped**. If the friction is small enough that oscillations occur, the system is **underdamped**, and the displacement is given by

$$x = Ae^{-\gamma t}\cos\omega't,$$ (14–16)

where γ and ω' are constants. For a **critically damped** system, no oscillations occur and equilibrium is reached in the shortest time.

If an oscillating force is applied to a system capable of vibrating, the amplitude of vibration can be very large if the frequency of the applied force is near the **natural** (or **resonant**) **frequency** of the oscillator; this is called **resonance**.

Questions

1. Give some examples of everyday vibrating objects. Which exhibit SHM, at least approximately?

2. Is the acceleration of a simple harmonic oscillator ever zero? If so, where?

3. Explain why the motion of a piston in an automobile engine is approximately simple harmonic.

4. Real springs have mass. Will the true period and frequency be larger or smaller than given by the equations for a mass oscillating on the end of an idealized massless spring? Explain.

5. How could you double the maximum speed of a simple harmonic oscillator (SHO)?

6. A 5.0-kg trout is attached to the hook of a vertical spring scale, and then is released. Describe the scale reading as a function of time.

7. If a pendulum clock is accurate at sea level, will it gain or lose time when taken to high altitude? Why?

8. A tire swing hanging from a branch reaches nearly to the ground (Fig. 14–27). How could you estimate the height of the branch using only a stopwatch?

FIGURE 14–27 Question 8.

9. For a simple harmonic oscillator, when (if ever) are the displacement and velocity vectors in the same direction? When are the displacement and acceleration vectors in the same direction?

10. A 100-g mass hangs from a long cord forming a pendulum. The mass is pulled a short distance to one side and released from rest. The time to swing over and back is carefully measured to be 2.0 s. If the 100-g mass is replaced by a 200-g mass, which is then pulled over the same distance and released from rest, the time will be (a) 1.0 s, (b) 1.41 s, (c) 2.0 s, (d) 2.82 s, (e) 4.0 s.

11. Two equal masses are attached to separate identical springs next to one another. One mass is pulled so its spring stretches 20 cm and the other is pulled so its spring stretches only 10 cm. The masses are released simultaneously. Which mass reaches the equilibrium point first?

12. Does a car bounce on its springs faster when it is empty or when it is fully loaded?

13. What is the approximate period of your walking step?

14. What happens to the period of a playground swing if you rise up from sitting to a standing position?

*15. A thin uniform rod of mass m is suspended from one end and oscillates with a frequency f. If a small sphere of mass $2m$ is attached to the other end, does the frequency increase or decrease? Explain.

16. A tuning fork of natural frequency 264 Hz sits on a table at the front of a room. At the back of the room, two tuning forks, one of natural frequency 260 Hz and one of 420 Hz are initially silent, but when the tuning fork at the front of the room is set into vibration, the 260-Hz fork spontaneously begins to vibrate but the 420-Hz fork does not. Explain.

17. Why can you make water slosh back and forth in a pan only if you shake the pan at a certain frequency?

18. Give several everyday examples of resonance.

19. Is a rattle in a car ever a resonance phenomenon? Explain.

20. Over the years, buildings have been able to be built out of lighter and lighter materials. How has this affected the natural oscillation frequencies of buildings and the problems of resonance due to passing trucks, airplanes, or by wind and other natural sources of vibration?

Problems

14–1 and 14–2 Simple Harmonic Motion

1. (I) If a particle undergoes SHM with amplitude 0.18 m, what is the total distance it travels in one period?

2. (I) An elastic cord is 65 cm long when a weight of 75 N hangs from it but is 85 cm long when a weight of 180 N hangs from it. What is the "spring" constant k of this elastic cord?

3. (I) The springs of a 1500-kg car compress 5.0 mm when its 68-kg driver gets into the driver's seat. If the car goes over a bump, what will be the frequency of oscillations? Ignore damping.

4. (I) (a) What is the equation describing the motion of a mass on the end of a spring which is stretched 8.8 cm from equilibrium and then released from rest, and whose period is 0.66 s? (b) What will be its displacement after 1.8 s?

5. (II) Estimate the stiffness of the spring in a child's pogo stick if the child has a mass of 35 kg and bounces once every 2.0 seconds.

6. (II) A fisherman's scale stretches 3.6 cm when a 2.4-kg fish hangs from it. (a) What is the spring stiffness constant and (b) what will be the amplitude and frequency of oscillation if the fish is pulled down 2.5 cm more and released so that it oscillates up and down?

7. (II) Tall buildings are designed to sway in the wind. In a 100-km/h wind, for example, the top of the 110-story Sears Tower oscillates horizontally with an amplitude of 15 cm. The building oscillates at its natural frequency, which has a period of 7.0 s. Assuming SHM, find the maximum horizontal velocity and acceleration experienced by a Sears employee as she sits working at her desk located on the top floor. Compare the maximum acceleration (as a percentage) with the acceleration due to gravity.

8. (II) Construct a Table indicating the position x of the mass in Fig. 14–2 at times $t = 0, \frac{1}{4}T, \frac{1}{2}T, \frac{3}{4}T, T,$ and $\frac{5}{4}T$, where T is the period of oscillation. On a graph of x vs. t, plot these six points. Now connect these points with a smooth curve. Based on these simple considerations, does your curve resemble that of a cosine or sine wave?

9. (II) A small fly of mass 0.25 g is caught in a spider's web. The web oscillates predominately with a frequency of 4.0 Hz. (a) What is the value of the effective spring stiffness constant k for the web? (b) At what frequency would you expect the web to oscillate if an insect of mass 0.50 g were trapped?

10. (II) A mass m at the end of a spring oscillates with a frequency of 0.83 Hz. When an additional 680-g mass is added to m, the frequency is 0.60 Hz. What is the value of m?

11. (II) A uniform meter stick of mass M is pivoted on a hinge at one end and held horizontal by a spring with spring constant k attached at the other end (Fig. 14–28). If the stick oscillates up and down slightly, what is its frequency? [Hint: Write a torque equation about the hinge.]

FIGURE 14–28
Problem 11.

12. (II) A balsa wood block of mass 55 g floats on a lake, bobbing up and down at a frequency of 3.0 Hz. (a) What is the value of the effective spring constant of the water? (b) A partially filled water bottle of mass 0.25 kg and almost the same size and shape of the balsa block is tossed into the water. At what frequency would you expect the bottle to bob up and down? Assume SHM.

13. (II) Figure 14–29 shows two examples of SHM, labeled A and B. For each, what is (a) the amplitude, (b) the frequency, and (c) the period? (d) Write the equations for both A and B in the form of a sine or cosine.

FIGURE 14–29   Problem 13.

14. (II) Determine the phase constant ϕ in Eq. 14–4 if, at $t = 0$, the oscillating mass is at (a) $x = -A$, (b) $x = 0$, (c) $x = A$, (d) $x = \frac{1}{2}A$, (e) $x = -\frac{1}{2}A$, (f) $x = A/\sqrt{2}$.

15. (II) A vertical spring with spring stiffness constant 305 N/m oscillates with an amplitude of 28.0 cm when 0.260 kg hangs from it. The mass passes through the equilibrium point $(y = 0)$ with positive velocity at $t = 0$. (a) What equation describes this motion as a function of time? (b) At what times will the spring be longest and shortest?

16. (II) The graph of displacement vs. time for a small mass m at the end of a spring is shown in Fig. 14–30. At $t = 0$, $x = 0.43$ cm. (a) If $m = 9.5$ g, find the spring constant, k. (b) Write the equation for displacement x as a function of time.

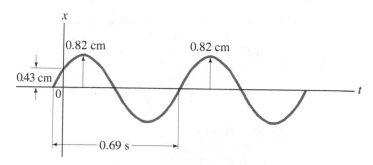

FIGURE 14–30   Problem 16.

17. (II) The position of a SHO as a function of time is given by $x = 3.8\cos(5\pi t/4 + \pi/6)$ where t is in seconds and x in meters. Find (a) the period and frequency, (b) the position and velocity at $t = 0$, and (c) the velocity and acceleration at $t = 2.0$ s.

18. (II) A tuning fork oscillates at a frequency of 441 Hz and the tip of each prong moves 1.5 mm to either side of center. Calculate (a) the maximum speed and (b) the maximum acceleration of the tip of a prong.

19. (II) An object of unknown mass m is hung from a vertical spring of unknown spring constant k, and the object is observed to be at rest when the spring has extended by 14 cm. The object is then given a slight push and executes SHM. Determine the period T of this oscillation.

20. (II) A 1.25-kg mass stretches a vertical spring 0.215 m. If the spring is stretched an additional 0.130 m and released, how long does it take to reach the (new) equilibrium position again?

21. (II) Consider two objects, A and B, both undergoing SHM, but with different frequencies, as described by the equations $x_A = (2.0 \text{ m})\sin(2.0t)$ and $x_B = (5.0 \text{ m})\sin(3.0t)$, where t is in seconds. After $t = 0$, find the next three times t at which both objects simultaneously pass through the origin.

22. (II) A 1.60-kg object oscillates from a vertically hanging light spring once every 0.55 s. (a) Write down the equation giving its position y (+ upward) as a function of time t, assuming it started by being compressed 16 cm from the equilibrium position (where $y = 0$), and released. (b) How long will it take to get to the equilibrium position for the first time? (c) What will be its maximum speed? (d) What will be its maximum acceleration, and where will it first be attained?

23. (II) A bungee jumper with mass 65.0 kg jumps from a high bridge. After reaching his lowest point, he oscillates up and down, hitting a low point eight more times in 43.0 s. He finally comes to rest 25.0 m below the level of the bridge. Estimate the spring stiffness constant and the unstretched length of the bungee cord assuming SHM.

24. (II) A block of mass m is supported by two identical parallel vertical springs, each with spring stiffness constant k (Fig. 14–31). What will be the frequency of vertical oscillation?

FIGURE 14–31
Problem 24.

25. (III) A mass m is connected to two springs, with spring constants k_1 and k_2, in two different ways as shown in Fig. 14–32a and b. Show that the period for the configuration shown in part (a) is given by

$$T = 2\pi \sqrt{m\left(\frac{1}{k_1} + \frac{1}{k_2}\right)}$$

and for that in part (b) is given by

$$T = 2\pi \sqrt{\frac{m}{k_1 + k_2}}.$$

Ignore friction.

(a)

FIGURE 14–32
Problem 25.

(b)

26. (III) A mass m is at rest on the end of a spring of spring constant k. At $t = 0$ it is given an impulse J by a hammer. Write the formula for the subsequent motion in terms of m, k, J, and t.

14–3 Energy in SHM

27. (I) A 1.15-kg mass oscillates according to the equation $x = 0.650 \cos 7.40t$ where x is in meters and t in seconds. Determine (a) the amplitude, (b) the frequency, (c) the total energy, and (d) the kinetic energy and potential energy when $x = 0.260$ m.

28. (I) (a) At what displacement of a SHO is the energy half kinetic and half potential? (b) What fraction of the total energy of a SHO is kinetic and what fraction potential when the displacement is one third the amplitude?

29. (II) Draw a graph like Fig. 14–11 for a horizontal spring whose spring constant is 95 N/m and which has a mass of 55 g on the end of it. Assume the spring was started with an initial amplitude of 2.0 cm. Neglect the mass of the spring and any friction with the horizontal surface. Use your graph to estimate (a) the potential energy, (b) the kinetic energy, and (c) the speed of the mass, for $x = 1.5$ cm.

30. (II) A 0.35-kg mass at the end of a spring oscillates 2.5 times per second with an amplitude of 0.15 m. Determine (a) the velocity when it passes the equilibrium point, (b) the velocity when it is 0.10 m from equilibrium, (c) the total energy of the system, and (d) the equation describing the motion of the mass, assuming that at $t = 0$, x was a maximum.

31. (II) It takes a force of 95.0 N to compress the spring of a toy popgun 0.175 m to "load" a 0.160-kg ball. With what speed will the ball leave the gun if fired horizontally?

32. (II) A 0.0125-kg bullet strikes a 0.240-kg block attached to a fixed horizontal spring whose spring constant is 2.25×10^3 N/m and sets it into oscillation with an amplitude of 12.4 cm. What was the initial speed of the bullet if the two objects move together after impact?

33. (II) If one oscillation has 5.0 times the energy of a second one of equal frequency and mass, what is the ratio of their amplitudes?

34. (II) A mass of 240 g oscillates on a horizontal frictionless surface at a frequency of 3.0 Hz and with amplitude of 4.5 cm. (a) What is the effective spring constant for this motion? (b) How much energy is involved in this motion?

35. (II) A mass resting on a horizontal, frictionless surface is attached to one end of a spring; the other end is fixed to a wall. It takes 3.6 J of work to compress the spring by 0.13 m. If the spring is compressed, and the mass is released from rest, it experiences a maximum acceleration of 15 m/s². Find the value of (a) the spring constant and (b) the mass.

36. (II) An object with mass 2.7 kg is executing simple harmonic motion, attached to a spring with spring constant $k = 280$ N/m. When the object is 0.020 m from its equilibrium position, it is moving with a speed of 0.55 m/s. (a) Calculate the amplitude of the motion. (b) Calculate the maximum speed attained by the object.

37. (II) Agent Arlene devised the following method of measuring the muzzle velocity of a rifle (Fig. 14–33). She fires a bullet into a 4.648-kg wooden block resting on a smooth surface, and attached to a spring of spring constant $k = 142.7$ N/m. The bullet, whose mass is 7.870 g, remains embedded in the wooden block. She measures the maximum distance that the block compresses the spring to be 9.460 cm. What is the speed v of the bullet?

FIGURE 14–33   Problem 37.

38. (II) Obtain the displacement x as a function of time for the simple harmonic oscillator using the conservation of energy, Eqs. 14–10. [Hint: Integrate Eq. 14–11a with $v = dx/dt$.]

39. (II) At $t = 0$, a 785-g mass at rest on the end of a horizontal spring ($k = 184$ N/m) is struck by a hammer which gives it an initial speed of 2.26 m/s. Determine (a) the period and frequency of the motion, (b) the amplitude, (c) the maximum acceleration, (d) the position as a function of time, (e) the total energy, and (f) the kinetic energy when $x = 0.40A$ where A is the amplitude.

40. (II) A pinball machine uses a spring launcher that is compressed 6.0 cm to launch a ball up a 15° ramp. Assume that the pinball is a solid uniform sphere of radius $r = 1.0$ cm and mass $m = 25$ g. If it is rolling without slipping at a speed of 3.0 m/s when it leaves the launcher, what is the spring constant of the spring launcher?

14–5 Simple Pendulum

41. (I) A pendulum has a period of 1.35 s on Earth. What is its period on Mars, where the acceleration of gravity is about 0.37 that on Earth?

42. (I) A pendulum makes 32 oscillations in exactly 50 s. What is its (a) period and (b) frequency?

43. (II) A simple pendulum is 0.30 m long. At $t = 0$ it is released from rest starting at an angle of 13°. Ignoring friction, what will be the angular position of the pendulum at (a) $t = 0.35$ s, (b) $t = 3.45$ s, and (c) $t = 6.00$ s?

44. (II) What is the period of a simple pendulum 53 cm long (a) on the Earth, and (b) when it is in a freely falling elevator?

45. (II) A simple pendulum oscillates with an amplitude of 10.0°. What fraction of the time does it spend between $+5.0°$ and $−5.0°$? Assume SHM.

46. (II) Your grandfather clock's pendulum has a length of 0.9930 m. If the clock loses 26 s per day, how should you adjust the length of the pendulum?

47. (II) Derive a formula for the maximum speed v_{max} of a simple pendulum bob in terms of g, the length ℓ, and the maximum angle of swing θ_{max}.

*14–6 Physical Pendulum and Torsion Pendulum

*48. (II) A pendulum consists of a tiny bob of mass M and a uniform cord of mass m and length ℓ. (a) Determine a formula for the period using the small angle approximation. (b) What would be the fractional error if you use the formula for a simple pendulum, Eq. 14–12c?

*49. (II) The balance wheel of a watch is a thin ring of radius 0.95 cm and oscillates with a frequency of 3.10 Hz. If a torque of 1.1×10^{-5} m·N causes the wheel to rotate 45°, calculate the mass of the balance wheel.

*50. (II) The human leg can be compared to a physical pendulum, with a "natural" swinging period at which walking is easiest. Consider the leg as two rods joined rigidly together at the knee; the axis for the leg is the hip joint. The length of each rod is about the same, 55 cm. The upper rod has a mass of 7.0 kg and the lower rod has a mass of 4.0 kg. (a) Calculate the natural swinging period of the system. (b) Check your answer by standing on a chair and measuring the time for one or more complete back-and-forth swings. The effect of a shorter leg is a shorter swinging period, enabling a faster "natural" stride.

*51. (II) (a) Determine the equation of motion (for θ as a function of time) for a torsion pendulum, Fig. 14–18, and show that the motion is simple harmonic. (b) Show that the period T is $T = 2\pi\sqrt{I/K}$. [The balance wheel of a mechanical watch is an example of a torsion pendulum in which the restoring torque is applied by a coil spring.]

*52. (II) A student wants to use a meter stick as a pendulum. She plans to drill a small hole through the meter stick and suspend it from a smooth pin attached to the wall (Fig. 14–34). Where in the meter stick should she drill the hole to obtain the shortest possible period? How short an oscillation period can she obtain with a meter stick in this way?

FIGURE 14–34
Problem 52.

*53. (II) A meter stick is hung at its center from a thin wire (Fig. 14–35a). It is twisted and oscillates with a period of 5.0 s. The meter stick is sawed off to a length of 70.0 cm. This piece is again balanced at its center and set in oscillation (Fig. 14–35b). With what period does it oscillate?

(a)

(b)

FIGURE 14–35 Problem 53.

*54. (II) An aluminum disk, 12.5 cm in diameter and 375 g in mass, is mounted on a vertical shaft with very low friction (Fig. 14–36). One end of a flat coil spring is attached to the disk, the other end to the base of the apparatus. The disk is set into rotational oscillation and the frequency is 0.331 Hz. What is the torsional spring constant $K (\tau = -K\theta)$?

Aluminum disk   Coil spring

Air bearing

FIGURE 14–36 Problem 54.

*55. (II) A plywood disk of radius 20.0 cm and mass 2.20 kg has a small hole drilled through it, 2.00 cm from its edge (Fig. 14–37). The disk is hung from the wall by means of a metal pin through the hole, and is used as a pendulum. What is the period of this pendulum for small oscillations?

FIGURE 14–37
Problem 55.

14-7 Damping

56. (II) A 0.835-kg block oscillates on the end of a spring whose spring constant is $k = 41.0\,\text{N/m}$. The mass moves in a fluid which offers a resistive force $F = -bv$, where $b = 0.662\,\text{N·s/m}$. (a) What is the period of the motion? (b) What is the fractional decrease in amplitude per cycle? (c) Write the displacement as a function of time if at $t = 0$, $x = 0$, and at $t = 1.00\,\text{s}$, $x = 0.120\,\text{m}$.

57. (II) Estimate how the damping constant changes when a car's shock absorbers get old and the car bounces three times after going over a speed bump.

58. (II) A physical pendulum consists of an 85-cm-long, 240-g-mass, uniform wooden rod hung from a nail near one end (Fig. 14–38). The motion is damped because of friction in the pivot; the damping force is approximately proportional to $d\theta/dt$. The rod is set in oscillation by displacing it 15° from its equilibrium position and releasing it. After 8.0 s, the amplitude of the oscillation has been reduced to 5.5°. If the angular displacement can be written as $\theta = Ae^{-\gamma t}\cos\omega' t$, find (a) γ, (b) the approximate period of the motion, and (c) how long it takes for the amplitude to be reduced to $\frac{1}{2}$ of its original value.

FIGURE 14–38
Problem 58.

85 cm

$\theta_0 = 15°$

59. (II) A damped harmonic oscillator loses 6.0% of its mechanical energy per cycle. (a) By what percentage does its frequency differ from the natural frequency $f_0 = (1/2\pi)\sqrt{k/m}$? (b) After how many periods will the amplitude have decreased to $1/e$ of its original value?

60. (II) A vertical spring of spring constant 115 N/m supports a mass of 75 g. The mass oscillates in a tube of liquid. If the mass is initially given an amplitude of 5.0 cm, the mass is observed to have an amplitude of 2.0 cm after 3.5 s. Estimate the damping constant b. Neglect buoyant forces.

61. (III) (a) Show that the total mechanical energy, $E = \frac{1}{2}mv^2 + \frac{1}{2}kx^2$, as a function of time for a lightly damped harmonic oscillator is

$$E = \tfrac{1}{2}kA^2 e^{-(b/m)t} = E_0 e^{-(b/m)t},$$

where E_0 is the total mechanical energy at $t = 0$. (Assume $\omega' \gg b/2m$.) (b) Show that the fractional energy lost per period is

$$\frac{\Delta E}{E} = \frac{2\pi b}{m\omega_0} = \frac{2\pi}{Q},$$

where $\omega_0 = \sqrt{k/m}$ and $Q = m\omega_0/b$ is called the **quality factor** or **Q value** of the system. A larger Q value means the system can undergo oscillations for a longer time.

62. (III) A glider on an air track is connected by springs to either end of the track (Fig. 14–39). Both springs have the same spring constant, k, and the glider has mass M. (a) Determine the frequency of the oscillation, assuming no damping, if $k = 125\,\text{N/m}$ and $M = 215\,\text{g}$. (b) It is observed that after 55 oscillations, the amplitude of the oscillation has dropped to one-half of its initial value. Estimate the value of γ, using Eq. 14–16. (c) How long does it take the amplitude to decrease to one-quarter of its initial value?

FIGURE 14–39
Problem 62.

14-8 Forced Oscillations; Resonance

63. (II) (a) For a forced oscillation at resonance ($\omega = \omega_0$), what is the value of the phase angle ϕ_0 in Eq. 14–22? (b) What, then, is the displacement at a time when the driving force F_{ext} is a maximum, and at a time when $F_{\text{ext}} = 0$? (c) What is the phase difference (in degrees) between the driving force and the displacement in this case?

64. (II) Differentiate Eq. 14–23 to show that the resonant amplitude peaks at

$$\omega = \sqrt{\omega_0^2 - \frac{b^2}{2m^2}}.$$

65. (II) An 1150 kg automobile has springs with $k = 16{,}000\,\text{N/m}$. One of the tires is not properly balanced; it has a little extra mass on one side compared to the other, causing the car to shake at certain speeds. If the tire radius is 42 cm, at what speed will the wheel shake most?

*66. (II) Construct an accurate resonance curve, from $\omega = 0$ to $\omega = 2\omega_0$, for $Q = 6.0$.

*67. (II) The amplitude of a driven harmonic oscillator reaches a value of $23.7F_0/k$ at a resonant frequency of 382 Hz. What is the Q value of this system?

68. (III) By direct substitution, show that Eq. 14–22, with Eqs. 14–23 and 14–24, is a solution of the equation of motion (Eq. 14–21) for the forced oscillator. [*Hint*: To find $\sin\phi_0$ and $\cos\phi_0$ from $\tan\phi_0$, draw a right triangle.]

*69. (III) Consider a simple pendulum (point mass bob) 0.50 m long with a Q of 350. (a) How long does it take for the amplitude (assumed small) to decrease by two-thirds? (b) If the amplitude is 2.0 cm and the bob has mass 0.27 kg, what is the initial energy loss rate of the pendulum in watts? (c) If we are to stimulate resonance with a sinusoidal driving force, how close must the driving frequency be to the natural frequency of the pendulum (give $\Delta f = f - f_0$)?

General Problems

70. A 62-kg person jumps from a window to a fire net 20.0 m below, which stretches the net 1.1 m. Assume that the net behaves like a simple spring. (a) Calculate how much it would stretch if the same person were lying in it. (b) How much would it stretch if the person jumped from 38 m?

71. An energy-absorbing car bumper has a spring constant of 430 kN/m. Find the maximum compression of the bumper if the car, with mass 1300 kg, collides with a wall at a speed of 2.0 m/s (approximately 5 mi/h).

72. The length of a simple pendulum is 0.63 m, the pendulum bob has a mass of 295 g, and it is released at an angle of 15° to the vertical. (a) With what frequency does it oscillate? (b) What is the pendulum bob's speed when it passes through the lowest point of the swing? Assume SHM. (c) What is the total energy stored in this oscillation assuming no losses?

73. A simple pendulum oscillates with frequency f. What is its frequency if the entire pendulum accelerates at $0.50\,g$ (a) upward, and (b) downward?

74. A 0.650-kg mass oscillates according to the equation $x = 0.25 \sin(5.50t)$ where x is in meters and t is in seconds. Determine (a) the amplitude, (b) the frequency, (c) the period, (d) the total energy, and (e) the kinetic energy and potential energy when x is 15 cm.

75. (a) A crane has hoisted a 1350-kg car at the junkyard. The crane's steel cable is 20.0 m long and has a diameter of 6.4 mm. If the car starts bouncing at the end of the cable, what is the period of the bouncing? [Hint: Refer to Table 12–1.] (b) What amplitude of bouncing will likely cause the cable to snap? (See Table 12–2, and assume Hooke's law holds all the way up to the breaking point.)

76. An oxygen atom at a particular site within a DNA molecule can be made to execute simple harmonic motion when illuminated by infrared light. The oxygen atom is bound with a spring-like chemical bond to a phosphorus atom, which is rigidly attached to the DNA backbone. The oscillation of the oxygen atom occurs with frequency $f = 3.7 \times 10^{13}$ Hz. If the oxygen atom at this site is chemically replaced with a sulfur atom, the spring constant of the bond is unchanged (sulfur is just below oxygen in the Periodic Table). Predict the frequency for a DNA molecule after the sulfur substitution.

77. A "seconds" pendulum has a period of exactly 2.000 s. That is, each one-way swing takes 1.000 s. What is the length of a seconds pendulum in Austin, Texas, where $g = 9.793$ m/s²? If the pendulum is moved to Paris, where $g = 9.809$ m/s², by how many millimeters must we lengthen the pendulum? What is the length of a seconds pendulum on the Moon, where $g = 1.62$ m/s²?

78. A 320-kg wooden raft floats on a lake. When a 75-kg man stands on the raft, it sinks 3.5 cm deeper into the water. When he steps off, the raft oscillates for a while. (a) What is the frequency of oscillation? (b) What is the total energy of oscillation (ignoring damping)?

79. At what displacement from equilibrium is the speed of a SHO half the maximum value?

80. A diving board oscillates with simple harmonic motion of frequency 2.5 cycles per second. What is the maximum amplitude with which the end of the board can oscillate in order that a pebble placed there (Fig. 14–40) does not lose contact with the board during the oscillation?

FIGURE 14–40
Problem 80.

81. A rectangular block of wood floats in a calm lake. Show that, if friction is ignored, when the block is pushed gently down into the water and then released, it will then oscillate with SHM. Also, determine an equation for the force constant.

82. A 950-kg car strikes a huge spring at a speed of 25 m/s (Fig. 14–41), compressing the spring 5.0 m. (a) What is the spring stiffness constant of the spring? (b) How long is the car in contact with the spring before it bounces off in the opposite direction?

950 kg

FIGURE 14–41
Problem 82.

83. A 1.60-kg table is supported on four springs. A 0.80-kg chunk of modeling clay is held above the table and dropped so that it hits the table with a speed of 1.65 m/s (Fig. 14–42). The clay makes an inelastic collision with the table, and the table and clay oscillate up and down. After a long time the table comes to rest 6.0 cm below its original position. (a) What is the effective spring constant of all four springs taken together? (b) With what maximum amplitude does the platform oscillate?

FIGURE 14–42
Problem 83.

84. In some diatomic molecules, the force each atom exerts on the other can be approximated by $F = -C/r^2 + D/r^3$, where r is the atomic separation and C and D are positive constants. (a) Graph F vs. r from $r = 0.8D/C$ to $r = 4D/C$. (b) Show that equilibrium occurs at $r = r_0 = D/C$. (c) Let $\Delta r = r - r_0$ be a small displacement from equilibrium, where $\Delta r \ll r_0$. Show that for such small displacements, the motion is approximately simple harmonic, and (d) determine the force constant. (e) What is the period of such motion? [Hint: Assume one atom is kept at rest.]

85. A mass attached to the end of a spring is stretched a distance x_0 from equilibrium and released. At what distance from equilibrium will it have (a) velocity equal to half its maximum velocity, and (b) acceleration equal to half its maximum acceleration?

86. Carbon dioxide is a linear molecule. The carbon–oxygen bonds in this molecule act very much like springs. Figure 14–43 shows one possible way the oxygen atoms in this molecule can oscillate: the oxygen atoms oscillate symmetrically in and out, while the central carbon atom remains at rest. Hence each oxygen atom acts like a simple harmonic oscillator with a mass equal to the mass of an oxygen atom. It is observed that this oscillation occurs with a frequency of $f = 2.83 \times 10^{13}$ Hz. What is the spring constant of the C—O bond?

FIGURE 14–43
Problem 86, the
CO_2 molecule.

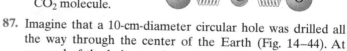

87. Imagine that a 10-cm-diameter circular hole was drilled all the way through the center of the Earth (Fig. 14–44). At one end of the hole, you drop an apple into the hole. Show that, if you assume that the Earth has a constant density, the subsequent motion of the apple is simple harmonic. How long will the apple take to return? Assume that we can ignore all frictional effects. [Hint: See Appendix D.]

FIGURE 14–44
Problem 87.

88. A thin, straight, uniform rod of length $\ell = 1.00\,\text{m}$ and mass $m = 215\,\text{g}$ hangs from a pivot at one end. (a) What is its period for small-amplitude oscillations? (b) What is the length of a simple pendulum that will have the same period?

89. A mass m is gently placed on the end of a freely hanging spring. The mass then falls 32.0 cm before it stops and begins to rise. What is the frequency of the oscillation?

90. A child of mass m sits on top of a rectangular slab of mass $M = 35\,\text{kg}$, which in turn rests on the frictionless horizontal floor at a pizza shop. The slab is attached to a horizontal spring with spring constant $k = 430\,\text{N/m}$ (the other end is attached to an immovable wall, Fig. 14–45). The coefficient of static friction between the child and the top of the slab is $\mu = 0.40$. The shop owner's intention is that, when displaced from the equilibrium position and released, the slab and child (with no slippage between the two) execute SHM with amplitude $A = 0.50\,\text{m}$. Should there be a weight restriction for this ride? If so, what is it?

FIGURE 14–45
Problem 90.

91. Estimate the effective spring constant of a trampoline.

92. In Section 14–5, the oscillation of a simple pendulum (Fig. 14–46) is viewed as linear motion along the arc length x and analyzed via $F = ma$. Alternatively, the pendulum's movement can be regarded as rotational motion about its point of support and analyzed using $\tau = I\alpha$. Carry out this alternative analysis and show that

$$\theta(t) = \theta_{\text{max}} \cos\left(\sqrt{\frac{g}{\ell}}\, t + \phi\right),$$

where $\theta(t)$ is the angular displacement of the pendulum from the vertical at time t, as long as its maximum value is less than about 15°.

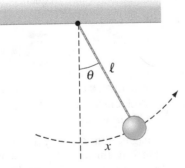

FIGURE 14–46
Problem 92.

*93. (II) A mass m on a frictionless surface is attached to a spring with spring constant k as shown in Fig. 14–47. This mass–spring system is then observed to execute simple harmonic motion with a period T. The mass m is changed several times and the associated period T is measured in each case, generating the following data Table:

Mass m (kg)	Period T (s)
0.5	0.445
1.0	0.520
2.0	0.630
3.0	0.723
4.5	0.844

(a) Starting with Eq. 14–7b, show why a graph of T^2 vs. m is expected to yield a straight line. How can k be determined from the straight line's slope? What is the line's y-intercept expected to be? (b) Using the data in the Table, plot T^2 vs. m and show that this graph yields a straight line. Determine the slope and (nonzero) y-intercept. (c) Show that a nonzero y-intercept can be expected in our plot theoretically if, rather than simply using m for the mass in Eq. 14–7b, we use $m + m_0$, where m_0 is a constant. That is, repeat part (a) using $m + m_0$ for the mass in Eq. 14–7b. Then use the result of this analysis to determine k and m_0 from your graph's slope and y-intercept. (d) Offer a physical interpretation for m_0, a mass that appears to be oscillating in addition to the attached mass m.

FIGURE 14–47   Problem 93.

*94. (III) *Damping proportional to v^2.* Suppose the oscillator of Example 14–5 is damped by a force proportional to the square of the velocity, $F_{\text{damping}} = -cv^2$, where $c = 0.275\,\text{kg/m}$ is a constant. Numerically integrate[†] the differential equation from $t = 0$ to $t = 2.00\,\text{s}$ to an accuracy of 2%, and plot your results.

[†]See Section 2–9.

Answers to Exercises

A: (a), (c), (d).

B: (b).

C: (c).

D: (b), (d).

E: (c).

F: (c).

G: All are larger.

H: (a).

I: (c).

J: (a) 25 cm; (b) 2.0 s.

Waves—such as these water waves—spread outward from a source. The source in this case is a small spot of water oscillating up and down briefly where a rock was thrown in (left photo). Other kinds of waves include waves on a cord or string, which also are produced by a vibration. Waves move away from their source, but we also study waves that seem to stand still ("standing waves"). Waves reflect, and they can interfere with each other when they pass through any point at the same time.

Wave Motion

CHAPTER-OPENING QUESTION—Guess now!

You drop a rock into a pond, and water waves spread out in circles.

(a) The waves carry water outward, away from where the rock hit. That moving water carries energy outward.

(b) The waves only make the water move up and down. No energy is carried outward from where the rock hit.

(c) The waves only make the water move up and down, but the waves do carry energy outward, away from where the rock hit.

W hen you throw a stone into a lake or pool of water, circular waves form and move outward, as shown in the photos above. Waves will also travel along a cord that is stretched out flat on a table if you vibrate one end back and forth as shown in Fig. 15–1. Water waves and waves on a cord are two common examples of **mechanical waves**, which propagate as oscillations of matter. We will discuss other kinds of waves in later Chapters, including electromagnetic waves and light.

FIGURE 15–1 Wave traveling on a cord. The wave travels to the right along the cord. Particles of the cord oscillate back and forth on the tabletop.

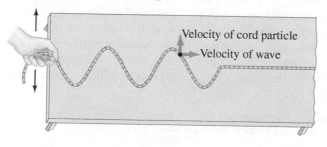

Velocity of cord particle
Velocity of wave

CONTENTS

If you have ever watched ocean waves moving toward shore before they break, you may have wondered if the waves were carrying water from far out at sea onto the beach. They don't.† Water waves move with a recognizable velocity. But each particle (or molecule) of the water itself merely oscillates about an equilibrium point. This is clearly demonstrated by observing leaves on a pond as waves move by. The leaves (or a cork) are not carried forward by the waves, but simply oscillate about an equilibrium point because this is the motion of the water itself.

CONCEPTUAL EXAMPLE 15–1 | **Wave vs. particle velocity.** Is the velocity of a wave moving along a cord the same as the velocity of a particle of the cord? See Fig. 15–1.

RESPONSE No. The two velocities are different, both in magnitude and direction. The wave on the cord of Fig. 15–1 moves to the right along the tabletop, but each piece of the cord only vibrates to and fro. (The cord clearly does not travel in the direction that the wave on it does.)

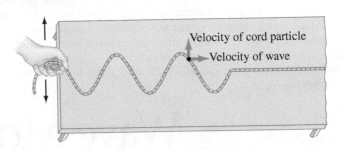

Velocity of cord particle
Velocity of wave

FIGURE 15–1 (repeated)
Wave traveling on a cord. The wave travels to the right along the cord. Particles of the cord oscillate back and forth on the tabletop.

Waves can move over large distances, but the medium (the water or the cord) itself has only a limited movement, oscillating about an equilibrium point as in simple harmonic motion. Thus, although a wave is not matter, the wave pattern can travel in matter. A wave consists of oscillations that move without carrying matter with them.

Waves carry energy from one place to another. Energy is given to a water wave, for example, by a rock thrown into the water, or by wind far out at sea. The energy is transported by waves to the shore. The oscillating hand in Fig. 15–1 transfers energy to the cord, and that energy is transported down the cord and can be transferred to an object at the other end. All forms of traveling waves transport energy.

EXERCISE A Return to the Chapter-Opening Question, page 395, and answer it again now. Try to explain why you may have answered differently the first time.

15–1 Characteristics of Wave Motion

Let us look a little more closely at how a wave is formed and how it comes to "travel." We first look at a single wave bump, or **pulse**. A single pulse can be formed on a cord by a quick up-and-down motion of the hand, Fig. 15–2. The hand pulls up on one end of the cord. Because the end section is attached to adjacent sections, these also feel an upward force and they too begin to move upward. As each succeeding section of cord moves upward, the wave crest moves outward along the cord. Meanwhile, the end section of cord has been returned to its original position by the hand. As each succeeding section of cord reaches its peak position, it too is pulled back down again by tension from the adjacent section of cord. Thus the source of a traveling wave pulse is a disturbance, and cohesive forces between adjacent sections of cord cause the pulse to travel. Waves in other media are created

FIGURE 15–2 Motion of a wave pulse to the right. Arrows indicate velocity of cord particles.

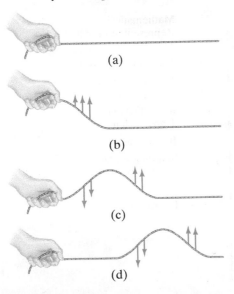

(a)

(b)

(c)

(d)

†Do not be confused by the "breaking" of ocean waves, which occurs when a wave interacts with the ground in shallow water and hence is no longer a simple wave.

and propagate outward in a similar fashion. A dramatic example of a wave pulse is a tsunami or tidal wave that is created by an earthquake in the Earth's crust under the ocean. The bang you hear when a door slams is a sound wave pulse.

A **continuous** or **periodic wave**, such as that shown in Fig. 15–1, has as its source a disturbance that is continuous and oscillating; that is, the source is a *vibration* or *oscillation*. In Fig. 15–1, a hand oscillates one end of the cord. Water waves may be produced by any vibrating object at the surface, such as your hand; or the water itself is made to vibrate when wind blows across it or a rock is thrown into it. A vibrating tuning fork or drum membrane gives rise to sound waves in air. And we will see later that oscillating electric charges give rise to light waves. Indeed, almost any vibrating object sends out waves.

The source of any wave, then, is a vibration. And it is a *vibration* that propagates outward and thus constitutes the wave. If the source vibrates sinusoidally in SHM, then the wave itself—if the medium is perfectly elastic—will have a sinusoidal shape both in space and in time. (1) In space: if you take a picture of the wave in space at a given instant of time, the wave will have the shape of a sine or cosine as a function of position. (2) In time: if you look at the motion of the medium at one place over a long period of time—for example, if you look between two closely spaced posts of a pier or out of a ship's porthole as water waves pass by—the up-and-down motion of that small segment of water will be simple harmonic motion. The water moves up and down sinusoidally in time.

Some of the important quantities used to describe a periodic sinusoidal wave are shown in Fig. 15–3. The high points on a wave are called *crests*; the low points, *troughs*. The **amplitude**, A, is the maximum height of a crest, or depth of a trough, relative to the normal (or equilibrium) level. The total swing from a crest to a trough is twice the amplitude. The distance between two successive crests is called the **wavelength**, λ (the Greek letter lambda). The wavelength is also equal to the distance between *any* two successive identical points on the wave. The **frequency**, f, is the number of crests—or complete cycles—that pass a given point per unit time. The **period**, T, equals $1/f$ and is the time elapsed between two successive crests passing by the same point in space.

FIGURE 15–3 Characteristics of a single-frequency continuous wave moving through space.

The **wave velocity**, v, is the velocity at which wave crests (or any other part of the waveform) move forward. The wave velocity must be distinguished from the velocity of a particle of the medium itself as we saw in Example 15–1.

A wave crest travels a distance of one wavelength, λ, in a time equal to one period, T. Thus the wave velocity is $v = \lambda/T$. Then, since $1/T = f$,

$$v = \lambda f. \tag{15–1}$$

For example, suppose a wave has a wavelength of 5 m and a frequency of 3 Hz. Since three crests pass a given point per second, and the crests are 5 m apart, the first crest (or any other part of the wave) must travel a distance of 15 m during the 1 s. So the wave velocity is 15 m/s.

EXERCISE B You notice a water wave pass by the end of a pier with about 0.5 s between crests. Therefore (*a*) the frequency is 0.5 Hz; (*b*) the velocity is 0.5 m/s; (*c*) the wavelength is 0.5 m; (*d*) the period is 0.5 s.

15–2 Types of Waves: Transverse and Longitudinal

When a wave travels down a cord—say, from left to right as in Fig. 15–1—the particles of the cord vibrate up and down in a direction transverse (that is, perpendicular) to the motion of the wave itself. Such a wave is called a **transverse wave** (Fig. 15–4a). There exists another type of wave known as a **longitudinal wave**. In a longitudinal wave, the vibration of the particles of the medium is *along* the direction of the wave's motion. Longitudinal waves are readily formed on a stretched spring or Slinky by alternately compressing and expanding one end. This is shown in Fig. 15–4b, and can be compared to the transverse wave in Fig. 15–4a.

(a)

FIGURE 15–4   (a) Transverse wave; (b) longitudinal wave.

(b)

A series of compressions and expansions propagate along the spring. The *compressions* are those areas where the coils are momentarily close together. *Expansions* (sometimes called *rarefactions*) are regions where the coils are momentarily far apart. Compressions and expansions correspond to the crests and troughs of a transverse wave.

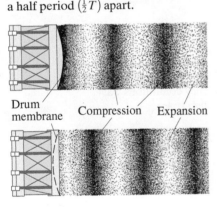

FIGURE 15–5   Production of a sound wave, which is longitudinal, shown at two moments in time about a half period $(\frac{1}{2}T)$ apart.

An important example of a longitudinal wave is a sound wave in air. A vibrating drumhead, for instance, alternately compresses and rarefies the air in contact with it, producing a longitudinal wave that travels outward in the air, as shown in Fig. 15–5.

As in the case of transverse waves, each section of the medium in which a longitudinal wave passes oscillates over a very small distance, whereas the wave itself can travel large distances. Wavelength, frequency, and wave velocity all have meaning for a longitudinal wave. The wavelength is the distance between successive compressions (or between successive expansions), and frequency is the number of compressions that pass a given point per second. The wave velocity is the velocity with which each compression appears to move; it is equal to the product of wavelength and frequency, $v = \lambda f$ (Eq. 15–1).

A longitudinal wave can be represented graphically by plotting the density of air molecules (or coils of a Slinky) versus position at a given instant, as shown in Fig. 15–6. Such a graphical representation makes it easy to illustrate what is happening. Note that the graph looks much like a transverse wave.

(a)

FIGURE 15–6   (a) A longitudinal wave with (b) its graphical representation at a particular instant in time.

(b)

Velocity of Transverse Waves

The velocity of a wave depends on the properties of the medium in which it travels. The velocity of a transverse wave on a stretched string or cord, for example, depends on the tension in the cord, F_T, and on the mass per unit length of the cord, μ (the Greek letter mu, where here $\mu = m/\ell$). For waves of small amplitude, the relationship is

$$v = \sqrt{\frac{F_T}{\mu}}. \qquad \begin{bmatrix} \text{transverse} \\ \text{wave on a cord} \end{bmatrix} \quad \textbf{(15–2)}$$

Before giving a derivation of this formula, it is worth noting that at least qualitatively it makes sense on the basis of Newtonian mechanics. That is, we do expect the tension to be in the numerator and the mass per unit length in the denominator. Why? Because when the tension is greater, we expect the velocity to be greater since each segment of cord is in tighter contact with its neighbor. And, the greater the mass per unit length, the more inertia the cord has and the more slowly the wave would be expected to propagate.

EXERCISE C A wave starts at the left end of a long cord (see Fig. 15–1) when someone shakes the cord back and forth at the rate of 2.0 Hz. The wave is observed to move to the right at 4.0 m/s. If the frequency is increased from 2.0 to 3.0 Hz, the new speed of the wave is (a) 1.0 m/s, (b) 2.0 m/s, (c) 4.0 m/s, (d) 8.0 m/s, (e) 16.0 m/s.

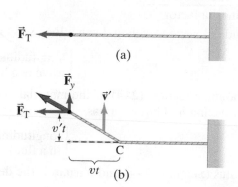

FIGURE 15–7 Diagram of simple wave pulse on a cord for derivation of Eq. 15–2. The vector shown in (b) as the resultant of $\vec{F}_T + \vec{F}_y$ has to be directed along the cord because the cord is flexible. (Diagram is not to scale: we assume $v' \ll v$; the upward angle of the cord is exaggerated for visibility.)

We can make a simple derivation of Eq. 15–2 using a simple model of a cord under a tension F_T as shown in Fig. 15–7a. The cord is pulled upward at a speed v' by the force F_y. As shown in Fig. 15–7b all points of the cord to the left of point C move upward at the speed v', and those to the right are still at rest. The speed of propagation, v, of this wave pulse is the speed of point C, the leading edge of the pulse. Point C moves to the right a distance vt in a time t, whereas the end of the cord moves upward a distance $v't$. By similar triangles we have the approximate relation

$$\frac{F_T}{F_y} = \frac{vt}{v't} = \frac{v}{v'},$$

which is accurate for small displacements ($v't \ll vt$) so that F_T does not change appreciably. As we saw in Chapter 9, the impulse given to an object is equal to its change in momentum. During the time t the total upward impulse is $F_y t = (v'/v)F_T t$. The change in momentum of the cord, Δp, is the mass of cord moving upward times its velocity. Since the upward moving segment of cord has mass equal to the mass per unit length μ times its length vt we have

$$F_y t = \Delta p$$

$$\frac{v'}{v} F_T t = (\mu vt)v'.$$

Solving for v we find $v = \sqrt{F_T/\mu}$ which is Eq. 15–2. Although it was derived for a special case, it is valid for any wave shape since other shapes can be considered to be made up of many tiny such lengths. But it is valid only for small displacements (as was our derivation). Experiment is in accord with this result derived from Newtonian mechanics.

EXAMPLE 15–2 **Pulse on a wire.** An 80.0-m-long, 2.10-mm-diameter copper wire is stretched between two poles. A bird lands at the center point of the wire, sending a small wave pulse out in both directions. The pulses reflect at the ends and arrive back at the bird's location 0.750 seconds after it landed. Determine the tension in the wire.

APPROACH From Eq. 15–2, the tension is given by $F_T = \mu v^2$. The speed v is distance divided by the time. The mass per unit length μ is calculated from the density of copper and the dimensions of the wire.

SOLUTION Each wave pulse travels 40.0 m to the pole and back again $(= 80.0\,\text{m})$ in $0.750\,\text{s}$. Thus their speed is $v = (80.0\,\text{m})/(0.750\,\text{s}) = 107\,\text{m/s}$. We take (Table 13–1) the density of copper as $8.90 \times 10^3\,\text{kg/m}^3$. The volume of copper in the wire is the cross-sectional area (πr^2) times the length ℓ, and the mass of the wire is the volume times the density: $m = \rho(\pi r^2)\ell$ for a wire of radius r and length ℓ. Then $\mu = m/\ell$ is

$$\mu = \rho\pi r^2 \ell/\ell = \rho\pi r^2 = (8.90 \times 10^3\,\text{kg/m}^3)\pi(1.05 \times 10^{-3}\,\text{m})^2 = 0.0308\,\text{kg/m}.$$

Thus, the tension is $F_T = \mu v^2 = (0.0308\,\text{kg/m})(107\,\text{m/s})^2 = 353\,\text{N}.$

Velocity of Longitudinal Waves

The velocity of a longitudinal wave has a form similar to that for a transverse wave on a cord (Eq. 15–2); that is,

$$v = \sqrt{\frac{\text{elastic force factor}}{\text{inertia factor}}}.$$

In particular, for a longitudinal wave traveling down a long solid rod,

$$v = \sqrt{\frac{E}{\rho}}, \qquad \left[\begin{array}{l}\text{longitudinal} \\ \text{wave in a long rod}\end{array}\right] \quad \textbf{(15–3)}$$

where E is the elastic modulus (Section 12–4) of the material and ρ is its density. For a longitudinal wave traveling in a liquid or gas,

$$v = \sqrt{\frac{B}{\rho}}, \qquad \left[\begin{array}{l}\text{longitudinal wave} \\ \text{in a fluid}\end{array}\right] \quad \textbf{(15–4)}$$

where B is the bulk modulus (Section 12–4) and ρ again is the density.

PHYSICS APPLIED
Space perception
by animals, using sound waves

EXAMPLE 15–3 **Echolocation.** Echolocation is a form of sensory perception used by animals such as bats, toothed whales, and dolphins. The animal emits a pulse of sound (a longitudinal wave) which, after reflection from objects, returns and is detected by the animal. Echolocation waves can have frequencies of about 100,000 Hz. (*a*) Estimate the wavelength of a sea animal's echolocation wave. (*b*) If an obstacle is 100 m from the animal, how long after the animal emits a wave is its reflection detected?

APPROACH We first compute the speed of longitudinal (sound) waves in sea water, using Eq. 15–4 and Tables 12–1 and 13–1. The wavelength is $\lambda = v/f$.

SOLUTION (*a*) The speed of longitudinal waves in sea water, which is slightly more dense than pure water, is

$$v = \sqrt{\frac{B}{\rho}} = \sqrt{\frac{2.0 \times 10^9\,\text{N/m}^2}{1.025 \times 10^3\,\text{kg/m}^3}} = 1.4 \times 10^3\,\text{m/s}.$$

Then, using Eq. 15–1, we find

$$\lambda = \frac{v}{f} = \frac{(1.4 \times 10^3\,\text{m/s})}{(1.0 \times 10^5\,\text{Hz})} = 14\,\text{mm}.$$

(*b*) The time required for the round-trip between the animal and the object is

$$t = \frac{\text{distance}}{\text{speed}} = \frac{2(100\,\text{m})}{1.4 \times 10^3\,\text{m/s}} = 0.14\,\text{s}.$$

NOTE We shall see later that waves can be used to "resolve" (or detect) objects only if the wavelength is comparable to or smaller than the object. Thus, a dolphin can resolve objects on the order of a centimeter or larger in size.

*Deriving Velocity of Wave in a Fluid

We now derive Eq. 15–4. Consider a wave pulse traveling in a fluid in a long tube, so that the wave motion is one dimensional. The tube is fitted with a piston at the end and is filled with a fluid which, at $t = 0$, is of uniform density ρ and at uniform pressure P_0, Fig. 15–8a. At this moment the piston is abruptly made to start moving to the right with speed v', compressing the fluid in front of it. In the (short) time t the piston moves a distance $v't$. The compressed fluid itself also moves with speed v', but the leading edge of the compressed region moves to the right at the characteristic speed v of compression waves in that fluid; we assume the wave speed v is much larger than the piston speed v'. The leading edge of the compression (which at $t = 0$ was at the piston face) thus moves a distance vt in time t as shown in Fig. 15–8b. Let the pressure in the compression be $P_0 + \Delta P$, which is ΔP higher than in the uncompressed fluid. To move the piston to the right requires an external force $(P_0 + \Delta P)S$ acting to the right, where S is the cross-sectional area of the tube. (S for "surface area"; we save A for amplitude.) The *net* force on the compressed region of the fluid is

$$F_{net} = (P_0 + \Delta P)S - P_0 S = S\,\Delta P$$

since the uncompressed fluid exerts a force $P_0 S$ to the left at the leading edge. Hence the impulse given to the compressed fluid, which equals its change in momentum, is

$$F_{net}\,t = \Delta m v'$$
$$S\,\Delta P\,t = (\rho S v t)v',$$

where $(\rho S v t)$ represents the mass of fluid which is given the speed v' (the compressed fluid of area S moves a distance vt, Fig. 15–8, so the volume moved is Svt). Hence we have

$$\Delta P = \rho v v'.$$

From the definition of the bulk modulus, B (Eq. 12–7):

$$B = -\frac{\Delta P}{\Delta V/V_0} = -\frac{\rho v v'}{\Delta V/V_0},$$

where $\Delta V/V_0$ is the fractional change in volume due to compression. The original volume of the compressed fluid is $V_0 = Svt$ (see Fig. 15–8), and it has been compressed by an amount $\Delta V = -Sv't$ (Fig. 15–8b). Thus

$$B = -\frac{\rho v v'}{\Delta V/V_0} = -\rho v v'\left(\frac{Svt}{-Sv't}\right) = \rho v^2,$$

and so

$$v = \sqrt{\frac{B}{\rho}},$$

which is what we set out to show, Eq. 15–4.

The derivation of Eq. 15–3 follows similar lines, but takes into account the expansion of the sides of a rod when the end of the rod is compressed.

Other Waves

Both transverse and longitudinal waves are produced when an **earthquake** occurs. The transverse waves that travel through the body of the Earth are called S waves (S for shear), and the longitudinal waves are called P waves (P for pressure) or *compression* waves. Both longitudinal and transverse waves can travel through a solid since the atoms or molecules can vibrate about their relatively fixed positions in any direction. But only longitudinal waves can propagate through a fluid, because any transverse motion would not experience any restoring force since a fluid is readily deformable. This fact was used by geophysicists to infer that a portion of the Earth's core must be liquid: after an earthquake, longitudinal waves are detected diametrically across the Earth, but not transverse waves.

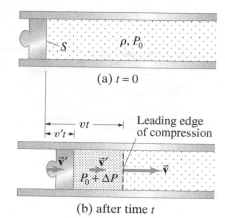

(a) $t = 0$

(b) after time t

FIGURE 15–8 Determining the speed of a one-dimensional longitudinal wave in a fluid contained in a long narrow tube.

PHYSICS APPLIED
Earthquake waves

FIGURE 15–9 A water wave is an example of a *surface wave*, which is a combination of transverse and longitudinal wave motions.

FIGURE 15–10 How a wave breaks. The green arrows represent the local velocity of water molecules.

Besides these two types of waves that can pass through the body of the Earth (or other substance), there can also be *surface waves* that travel along the boundary between two materials. A wave on water is actually a surface wave that moves on the boundary between water and air. The motion of each particle of water at the surface is circular or elliptical (Fig. 15–9), so it is a combination of transverse and longitudinal motions. Below the surface, there is also transverse plus longitudinal wave motion, as shown. At the bottom, the motion is only longitudinal. (When a wave approaches shore, the water drags at the bottom and is slowed down, while the crests move ahead at higher speed (Fig. 15–10) and "spill" over the top.)

Surface waves are also set up on the Earth when an earthquake occurs. The waves that travel along the surface are mainly responsible for the damage caused by earthquakes.

Waves which travel along a line in one dimension, such as transverse waves on a stretched string, or longitudinal waves in a rod or fluid-filled tube, are *linear* or *one-dimensional waves*. Surface waves, such as the water waves pictured at the start of this Chapter, are *two-dimensional waves*. Finally, waves that move out from a source in all directions, such as sound from a loudspeaker or earthquake waves through the Earth, are *three-dimensional waves*.

15–3 Energy Transported by Waves

Waves transport energy from one place to another. As waves travel through a medium, the energy is transferred as vibrational energy from particle to particle of the medium. For a sinusoidal wave of frequency f, the particles move in simple harmonic motion (Chapter 14) as a wave passes, and each particle has energy $E = \frac{1}{2}kA^2$ where A is the maximum displacement (amplitude) of its motion, either transversely or longitudinally (Eq. 14–10a). Using Eq. 14–7a we can write $k = 4\pi^2 mf^2$, where m is the mass of a particle (or small volume) of the medium. Then in terms of the frequency f and amplitude A,

$$E = \tfrac{1}{2}kA^2 = 2\pi^2 mf^2 A^2.$$

FIGURE 15–11 Calculating the energy carried by a wave moving with velocity v.

For three-dimensional waves traveling in an elastic medium, the mass $m = \rho V$, where ρ is the density of the medium and V is the volume of a small slice of the medium. The volume $V = S\ell$ where S is the cross-sectional area through which the wave travels (Fig. 15–11), and we can write ℓ as the distance the wave travels in a time t as $\ell = vt$, where v is the speed of the wave. Thus $m = \rho V = \rho S\ell = \rho Svt$ and

$$E = 2\pi^2 \rho Svtf^2 A^2. \tag{15–5}$$

From this equation we have the important result that *the energy transported by a wave is proportional to the square of the amplitude, and to the square of the frequency.* The average *rate* of energy transferred is the average power P:

$$\overline{P} = \frac{E}{t} = 2\pi^2 \rho Svf^2 A^2. \tag{15–6}$$

Finally, the **intensity**, I, of a wave is defined as the average power transferred across unit area perpendicular to the direction of energy flow:

$$I = \frac{\overline{P}}{S} = 2\pi^2 v\rho f^2 A^2. \tag{15–7}$$

If a wave flows out from the source in all directions, it is a three-dimensional wave. Examples are sound traveling in the open air, earthquake waves, and light waves.

If the medium is isotropic (same in all directions), the wave from a point source is a *spherical wave* (Fig. 15–12). As the wave moves outward, the energy it carries is spread over a larger and larger area since the surface area of a sphere of radius r is $4\pi r^2$. Thus the intensity of a wave is

$$I = \frac{\overline{P}}{S} = \frac{\overline{P}}{4\pi r^2}.$$

If the power output $\overline{P}$ is constant, then the intensity decreases as the inverse square of the distance from the source:

$$I \propto \frac{1}{r^2}. \qquad\qquad \text{[spherical wave]} \quad \textbf{(15–8a)}$$

If we consider two points at distances r_1 and r_2 from the source, as in Fig. 15–12, then $I_1 = \overline{P}/4\pi r_1^2$ and $I_2 = \overline{P}/4\pi r_2^2$, so

$$\frac{I_2}{I_1} = \frac{\overline{P}/4\pi r_2^2}{\overline{P}/4\pi r_1^2} = \frac{r_1^2}{r_2^2}. \qquad\qquad \textbf{(15–8b)}$$

Thus, for example, when the distance doubles $(r_2/r_1 = 2)$, then the intensity is reduced to $\frac{1}{4}$ of its earlier value: $I_2/I_1 = \left(\frac{1}{2}\right)^2 = \frac{1}{4}$.

The amplitude of a wave also decreases with distance. Since the intensity is proportional to the square of the amplitude (Eq. 15–7), $I \propto A^2$, the amplitude A must decrease as $1/r$, so that I can be proportional to $1/r^2$ (Eq. 15–8a). Hence

$$A \propto \frac{1}{r}.$$

To see this directly from Eq. 15–6, consider again two different distances from the source, r_1 and r_2. For constant power output, $S_1 A_1^2 = S_2 A_2^2$ where A_1 and A_2 are the amplitudes of the wave at r_1 and r_2, respectively. Since $S_1 = 4\pi r_1^2$ and $S_2 = 4\pi r_2^2$, we have $(A_1^2 r_1^2) = (A_2^2 r_2^2)$, or

$$\frac{A_2}{A_1} = \frac{r_1}{r_2}.$$

When the wave is twice as far from the source, the amplitude is half as large, and so on (ignoring damping due to friction).

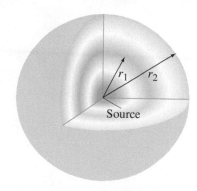

FIGURE 15–12 Wave traveling outward from a point source has spherical shape. Two different crests (or compressions) are shown, of radius r_1 and r_2.

EXAMPLE 15–4 **Earthquake intensity.** The intensity of an earthquake P wave traveling through the Earth and detected 100 km from the source is 1.0×10^6 W/m². What is the intensity of that wave if detected 400 km from the source?

APPROACH We assume the wave is spherical, so the intensity decreases as the square of the distance from the source.

SOLUTION At 400 km the distance is 4 times greater than at 100 km, so the intensity will be $\left(\frac{1}{4}\right)^2 = \frac{1}{16}$ of its value at 100 km, or $(1.0 \times 10^6$ W/m²$)/16 = 6.3 \times 10^4$ W/m².

NOTE Using Eq. 15–8b directly gives

$$I_2 = I_1 r_1^2/r_2^2 = (1.0 \times 10^6 \text{ W/m}^2)(100 \text{ km})^2/(400 \text{ km})^2 = 6.3 \times 10^4 \text{ W/m}^2.$$

The situation is different for a one-dimensional wave, such as a transverse wave on a string or a longitudinal wave pulse traveling down a thin uniform metal rod. The area remains constant, so the amplitude A also remains constant (ignoring friction). Thus the amplitude and the intensity do not decrease with distance.

In practice, frictional damping is generally present, and some of the energy is transformed into thermal energy. Thus the amplitude and intensity of a one-dimensional wave decrease with distance from the source. For a three-dimensional wave, the decrease will be greater than that discussed above, although the effect may often be small.

15–4 Mathematical Representation of a Traveling Wave

Let us now consider a one-dimensional wave traveling along the x axis. It could be, for example, a transverse wave on a cord or a longitudinal wave traveling in a rod or in a fluid-filled tube. Let us assume the wave shape is sinusoidal and has a particular wavelength λ and frequency f. At $t = 0$, suppose the wave shape is given by

$$D(x) = A \sin \frac{2\pi}{\lambda} x, \qquad (15\text{–}9)$$

FIGURE 15–13 A traveling wave. In time t, the wave moves a distance vt.

as shown by the solid curve in Fig. 15–13: $D(x)$ is the **displacement**[†] of the wave (be it a longitudinal or transverse wave) at position x, and A is the **amplitude** (maximum displacement) of the wave. This relation gives a shape that repeats itself every wavelength, which is needed so that the displacement is the same at $x = 0$, $x = \lambda$, $x = 2\lambda$, and so on (since $\sin 4\pi = \sin 2\pi = \sin 0$).

Now suppose the wave is moving to the right with velocity v. Then, after a time t, each part of the wave (indeed, the whole wave "shape") has moved to the right a distance vt; see the dashed curve in Fig. 15–13. Consider any point on the wave at $t = 0$: say, a crest which is at some position x. After a time t, that crest will have traveled a distance vt so its new position is a distance vt greater than its old position. To describe this same point on the wave shape, the argument of the sine function must be the same, so we replace x in Eq. 15–9 by $(x - vt)$:

1-D wave moving in positive x direction

$$D(x, t) = A \sin\left[\frac{2\pi}{\lambda}(x - vt)\right]. \qquad (15\text{–}10\text{a})$$

Said another way, if you are riding on a crest, the argument of the sine function, $(2\pi/\lambda)(x - vt)$, remains the same ($= \pi/2, 5\pi/2$, and so on); as t increases, x must increase at the same rate so that $(x - vt)$ remains constant.

Equation 15–10a is the mathematical representation of a sinusoidal wave traveling along the x axis to the right (increasing x). It gives the displacement $D(x, t)$ of the wave at any chosen point x at any time t. The function $D(x, t)$ describes a curve that represents the actual shape of the wave in space at time t. Since $v = \lambda f$ (Eq. 15–1) we can write Eq. 15–10a in other ways that are often convenient:

1-D wave

moving in

positive x

direction

$$D(x, t) = A \sin\left(\frac{2\pi x}{\lambda} - \frac{2\pi t}{T}\right), \qquad (15\text{–}10\text{b})$$

where $T = 1/f = \lambda/v$ is the period; and

$$D(x, t) = A \sin(kx - \omega t), \qquad (15\text{–}10\text{c})$$

where $\omega = 2\pi f = 2\pi/T$ is the angular frequency and

$$k = \frac{2\pi}{\lambda} \qquad (15\text{–}11)$$

⚠ **CAUTION**

Don't confuse wave number k with spring constant k

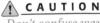

is called the **wave number**. (Do not confuse the wave number k with the spring constant k; they are very different quantities.) All three forms, Eqs. 15–10a, b, and c, are equivalent; Eq. 15–10c is the simplest to write and is perhaps the most common. The quantity $(kx - \omega t)$, and its equivalent in the other two equations, is called the **phase** of the wave. The velocity v of the wave is often called the **phase velocity**, since it describes the velocity of the phase (or shape) of the wave and it can be written in terms of ω and k:

$$v = \lambda f = \left(\frac{2\pi}{k}\right)\left(\frac{\omega}{2\pi}\right) = \frac{\omega}{k}. \qquad (15\text{–}12)$$

[†]Some books use $y(x)$ in place of $D(x)$. To avoid confusion, we reserve y (and z) for the coordinate positions of waves in two or three dimensions. Our $D(x)$ can stand for pressure (in longitudinal waves), position displacement (transverse mechanical waves), or—as we will see later—electric or magnetic fields (for electromagnetic waves).

For a wave traveling along the x axis to the left (decreasing values of x), we start again with Eq. 15–9 and note that the velocity is now $-v$. A particular point on the wave changes position by $-vt$ in a time t, so x in Eq. 15–9 must be replaced by $(x + vt)$. Thus, for a wave traveling to the left with velocity v,

$$D(x,t) = A \sin\left[\frac{2\pi}{\lambda}(x + vt)\right] \qquad \textbf{(15–13a)}$$

$$= A \sin\left(\frac{2\pi x}{\lambda} + \frac{2\pi t}{T}\right) \qquad \textbf{(15–13b)}$$

$$= A \sin(kx + \omega t). \qquad \textbf{(15–13c)}$$

1-D wave moving in negative x direction

In other words, we simply replace v in Eqs. 15–10 by $-v$.

Let us look at Eq. 15–13c (or, just as well, at Eq. 15–10c). At $t = 0$ we have

$$D(x,0) = A \sin kx,$$

which is what we started with, a sinusoidal wave shape. If we look at the wave shape in space at a particular later time t_1, then we have

$$D(x, t_1) = A \sin(kx + \omega t_1).$$

That is, if we took a picture of the wave at $t = t_1$, we would see a sine wave with a phase constant ωt_1. Thus, for fixed $t = t_1$, the wave has a sinusoidal shape in space. On the other hand, if we consider a fixed point in space, say $x = 0$, we can see how the wave varies in time:

$$D(0, t) = A \sin \omega t$$

where we used Eq. 15–13c. This is just the equation for simple harmonic motion (Section 14–2). For any other fixed value of x, say $x = x_1$, $D = A \sin(\omega t + k x_1)$ which differs only by a phase constant $k x_1$. Thus, at any fixed point in space, the displacement undergoes the oscillations of simple harmonic motion in time. Equations 15–10 and 15–13 combine both these aspects to give us the representation for a **traveling sinusoidal wave** (also called a **harmonic wave**).

The argument of the sine in Eqs. 15–10 and 15–13 can in general contain a phase angle ϕ, which for Eq. 15–10c is

$$D(x,t) = A \sin(kx - \omega t + \phi),$$

to adjust for the position of the wave at $t = 0$, $x = 0$, just as in Section 14–2 (see Fig. 14–7). If the displacement is zero at $t = 0$, $x = 0$, as in Fig. 14–6 (or Fig. 15–13), then $\phi = 0$.

Now let us consider a general wave (or wave pulse) of any shape. If frictional losses are small, experiment shows that the wave maintains its shape as it travels. Thus we can make the same arguments as we did right after Eq. 15–9. Suppose our wave has some shape at $t = 0$, given by

$$D(x,0) = D(x)$$

where $D(x)$ is the displacement of the wave at x and is not necessarily sinusoidal. At some later time, if the wave is traveling to the right along the x axis, the wave will have the same shape but all parts will have moved a distance vt where v is the phase velocity of the wave. Hence we must replace x by $x - vt$ to obtain the amplitude at time t:

$$D(x,t) = D(x - vt). \qquad \textbf{(15–14)}$$

Similarly, if the wave moves to the left, we must replace x by $x + vt$, so

$$D(x,t) = D(x + vt). \qquad \textbf{(15–15)}$$

Thus, any wave traveling along the x axis must have the form of Eq. 15–14 or 15–15.

EXERCISE D A wave is given by $D(x,t) = (5.0 \, \text{mm}) \sin(2.0x - 20.0t)$ where x is in meters and t is in seconds. What is the speed of the wave? (a) 10 m/s, (b) 0.10 m/s, (c) 40 m/s, (d) 0.005 m/s, (e) 2.5×10^{-4} m/s.

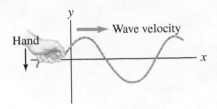

FIGURE 15–14 Example 15–5. The wave at $t = 0$ (the hand is falling). Not to scale.

EXAMPLE 15–5 **A traveling wave.** The left-hand end of a long horizontal stretched cord oscillates transversely in SHM with frequency $f = 250\,\text{Hz}$ and amplitude 2.6 cm. The cord is under a tension of 140 N and has a linear density $\mu = 0.12\,\text{kg/m}$. At $t = 0$, the end of the cord has an upward displacement of 1.6 cm and is falling (Fig. 15–14). Determine (a) the wavelength of waves produced and (b) the equation for the traveling wave.

APPROACH We first find the phase velocity of the transverse wave from Eq. 15–2; then $\lambda = v/f$. In (b), we need to find the phase ϕ using the initial conditions.

SOLUTION (a) The wave velocity is

$$v = \sqrt{\frac{F_T}{\mu}} = \sqrt{\frac{140\,\text{N}}{0.12\,\text{kg/m}}} = 34\,\text{m/s}.$$

Then

$$\lambda = \frac{v}{f} = \frac{34\,\text{m/s}}{250\,\text{Hz}} = 0.14\,\text{m} \qquad \text{or} \qquad 14\,\text{cm}.$$

(b) Let $x = 0$ at the left-hand end of the cord. The phase of the wave at $t = 0$ is not zero in general as was assumed in Eqs. 15–9, 10, and 13. The general form for a wave traveling to the right is

$$D(x, t) = A \sin(kx - \omega t + \phi),$$

where ϕ is the phase angle. In our case, the amplitude $A = 2.6\,\text{cm}$; and at $t = 0$, $x = 0$, we are given $D = 1.6\,\text{cm}$. Thus

$$1.6 = 2.6 \sin \phi,$$

so $\phi = \sin^{-1}(1.6/2.6) = 38° = 0.66\,\text{rad}$. We also have $\omega = 2\pi f = 1570\,\text{s}^{-1}$ and $k = 2\pi/\lambda = 2\pi/0.14\,\text{m} = 45\,\text{m}^{-1}$. Hence

$$D = (0.026\,\text{m}) \sin\left[(45\,\text{m}^{-1})x - (1570\,\text{s})t + 0.66\right]$$

which we can write more simply as

$$D = 0.026 \sin(45x - 1570t + 0.66),$$

and we specify clearly that D and x are in meters and t in seconds.

*15–5 The Wave Equation

Many types of waves satisfy an important general equation that is the equivalent of Newton's second law of motion for particles. This "equation of motion for a wave" is called the **wave equation**, and we derive it now for waves traveling on a stretched horizontal string.

We assume the amplitude of the wave is small compared to the wavelength so that each point on the string can be assumed to move only vertically and the tension in the string, F_T, does not vary during a vibration. We apply Newton's second law, $\Sigma F = ma$, to the vertical motion of a tiny section of the string as shown in Fig. 15–15. The amplitude of the wave is small, so the angles θ_1 and θ_2 that the string makes with the horizontal are small. The length of this section is then approximately Δx, and its mass is $\mu\,\Delta x$, where μ is the mass per unit length of the string. The net vertical force on this section of string is $F_T \sin \theta_2 - F_T \sin \theta_1$. So Newton's second law applied to the vertical (y) direction gives

$$\Sigma F_y = ma_y$$

$$F_T \sin \theta_2 - F_T \sin \theta_1 = (\mu\,\Delta x) \frac{\partial^2 D}{\partial t^2}. \qquad \textbf{(i)}$$

FIGURE 15–15 Deriving the wave equation from Newton's second law: a segment of string under tension F_T.

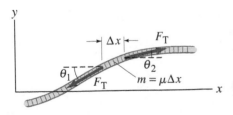

We have written the acceleration as $a_y = \partial^2 D/\partial t^2$ since the motion is only vertical, and we use the partial derivative notation because the displacement D is a function of both x and t.

Because the angles θ_1 and θ_2 are assumed small, $\sin\theta \approx \tan\theta$ and $\tan\theta$ is equal to the slope s of the string at each point:

$$\sin\theta \approx \tan\theta = \frac{\partial D}{\partial x} = s.$$

Thus our equation (i) at the bottom of the previous page becomes

$$F_T(s_2 - s_1) = \mu\,\Delta x\,\frac{\partial^2 D}{\partial t^2}$$

or

$$F_T\frac{\Delta s}{\Delta x} = \mu\frac{\partial^2 D}{\partial t^2}, \qquad \textbf{(ii)}$$

where $\Delta s = s_2 - s_1$ is the difference in the slope between the two ends of our tiny section. Now we take the limit of $\Delta x \to 0$, so that

$$F_T\lim_{\Delta x \to 0}\frac{\Delta s}{\Delta x} = F_T\frac{\partial s}{\partial x}$$

$$= F_T\frac{\partial}{\partial x}\left(\frac{\partial D}{\partial x}\right) = F_T\frac{\partial^2 D}{\partial x^2}$$

since the slope $s = \partial D/\partial x$, as we wrote above. Substituting this into the equation labeled (ii) above gives

$$F_T\frac{\partial^2 D}{\partial x^2} = \mu\frac{\partial^2 D}{\partial t^2}$$

or

$$\frac{\partial^2 D}{\partial x^2} = \frac{\mu}{F_T}\frac{\partial^2 D}{\partial t^2}.$$

We saw earlier in this Chapter (Eq. 15–2) that the velocity of waves on a string is given by $v = \sqrt{F_T/\mu}$, so we can write this last equation as

$$\frac{\partial^2 D}{\partial x^2} = \frac{1}{v^2}\frac{\partial^2 D}{\partial t^2}. \qquad \textbf{(15–16)}$$

This is the **one-dimensional wave equation**, and it can describe not only small amplitude waves on a stretched string, but also small amplitude longitudinal waves (such as sound waves) in gases, liquids, and elastic solids, in which case D can refer to the pressure variations. In this case, the wave equation is a direct consequence of Newton's second law applied to a continuous elastic medium. The wave equation also describes electromagnetic waves for which D refers to the electric or magnetic field, as we shall see in Chapter 31. Equation 15–16 applies to waves traveling in one dimension only. For waves spreading out in three dimensions, the wave equation is the same, with the addition of $\partial^2 D/\partial y^2$ and $\partial^2 D/\partial z^2$ to the left side of Eq. 15–16.

The wave equation is a *linear* equation: the displacement D appears singly in each term. There are no terms that contain D^2, or $D(\partial D/\partial x)$, or the like in which D appears more than once. Thus, if $D_1(x, t)$ and $D_2(x, t)$ are two different solutions of the wave equation, then the linear combination

$$D_3(x, t) = aD_1(x, t) + bD_2(x, t),$$

where a and b are constants, is also a solution. This is readily seen by direct substitution into the wave equation. This is the essence of the *superposition principle*, which we discuss in the next Section. Basically it says that if two waves pass through the same region of space at the same time, the actual displacement is the sum of the separate displacements. For waves on a string, or for sound waves, this is valid only for small-amplitude waves. If the amplitude is not small enough, the equations for wave propagation may become nonlinear and the principle of superposition would not hold and more complicated effects may occur.

EXAMPLE 15–6 **Wave equation solution.** Verify that the sinusoidal wave of Eq. 15–10c, $D(x, t) = A \sin(kx - \omega t)$, satisfies the wave equation.

APPROACH We substitute Eq. 15–10c into the wave equation, Eq. 15–16.

SOLUTION We take the derivative of Eq. 15–10c twice with respect to t:

$$\frac{\partial D}{\partial t} = -\omega A \cos(kx - \omega t)$$

$$\frac{\partial^2 D}{\partial t^2} = -\omega^2 A \sin(kx - \omega t).$$

With respect to x, the derivatives are

$$\frac{\partial D}{\partial x} = k A \cos(kx - \omega t)$$

$$\frac{\partial^2 D}{\partial x^2} = -k^2 A \sin(kx - \omega t).$$

If we now divide the second derivatives we get

$$\frac{\partial^2 D/\partial t^2}{\partial^2 D/\partial x^2} = \frac{-\omega^2 A \sin(kx - \omega t)}{-k^2 A \sin(kx - \omega t)} = \frac{\omega^2}{k^2}.$$

From Eq. 15–12 we have $\omega^2/k^2 = v^2$, so we see that Eq. 15–10 does satisfy the wave equation (Eq. 15–16).

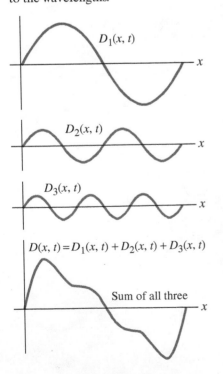

FIGURE 15–16 The superposition principle for one-dimensional waves. The composite wave formed from three sinusoidal waves of different amplitudes and frequencies $(f_0, 2f_0, 3f_0)$ is shown at the bottom at a certain instant in time. The displacement of the composite wave at each point in space, at any time, is the algebraic sum of the displacements of the component waves. Amplitudes are shown exaggerated; for the superposition principle to hold, they must be small compared to the wavelengths.

15–6 The Principle of Superposition

When two or more waves pass through the same region of space at the same time, it is found that for many waves *the actual displacement is the vector* (or *algebraic*) *sum of the separate displacements.* This is called the **principle of superposition**. It is valid for mechanical waves as long as the displacements are not too large and there is a linear relationship between the displacement and the restoring force of the oscillating medium.[†] If the amplitude of a mechanical wave, for example, is so large that it goes beyond the elastic region of the medium, and Hooke's law is no longer operative, the superposition principle is no longer accurate.[‡] For the most part, we will consider systems for which the superposition principle can be assumed to hold.

One result of the superposition principle is that if two waves pass through the same region of space, they continue to move independently of one another. You may have noticed, for example, that the ripples on the surface of water (two-dimensional waves) that form from two rocks striking the water at different places will pass through each other.

Figure 15–16 shows an example of the superposition principle. In this case there are three waves present on a stretched string, each of different amplitude and frequency. At any time, such as at the instant shown, the actual displacement at any position x is the algebraic sum of the displacements of the three waves at that position. The actual wave is not a simple sinusoidal wave and is called a *composite* (or *complex*) *wave.* (Amplitudes are exaggerated in Fig. 15–16.)

It can be shown that any complex wave can be considered as being composed of many simple sinusoidal waves of different amplitudes, wavelengths, and frequencies. This is known as *Fourier's theorem.* A complex periodic wave of period T can be represented as a sum of pure sinusoidal terms whose frequencies are integral multiples of $f = 1/T$. If the wave is not periodic, the sum becomes an integral (called a *Fourier integral*). Although we will not go into the details here, we see the importance of considering sinusoidal waves (and simple harmonic motion): because any other wave shape can be considered a sum of such pure sinusoidal waves.

[†]For electromagnetic waves in vacuum, Chapter 31, the superposition principle always holds.

[‡]Intermodulation distortion in high-fidelity equipment is an example of the superposition principle not holding when two frequencies do not combine linearly in the electronics.

CONCEPTUAL EXAMPLE 15–7 | **Making a square wave.** At $t = 0$, three waves are given by $D_1 = A \cos kx$, $D_2 = -\frac{1}{3} A \cos 3kx$, and $D_3 = \frac{1}{5} A \cos 5kx$, where $A = 1.0$ m and $k = 10$ m^{-1}. Plot the sum of the three waves from $x = -0.4$ m to $+0.4$ m. (These three waves are the first three Fourier components of a "square wave.")

RESPONSE The first wave, D_1, has amplitude of 1.0 m and wavelength $\lambda = 2\pi/k = (2\pi/10)$ m $= 0.628$ m. The second wave, D_2, has amplitude of 0.33 m and wavelength $\lambda = 2\pi/3k = (2\pi/30)$ m $= 0.209$ m. The third wave, D_3, has amplitude of 0.20 m and wavelength $\lambda = 2\pi/5k = (2\pi/50)$ m $= 0.126$ m. Each wave is plotted in Fig. 15–17a. The sum of the three waves is shown in Fig. 15–17b. The sum begins to resemble a "square wave," shown in blue in Fig. 15–17b.

When the restoring force is not precisely proportional to the displacement for mechanical waves in some continuous medium, the speed of sinusoidal waves depends on the frequency. The variation of speed with frequency is called **dispersion**. The different sinusoidal waves that compose a complex wave will travel with slightly different speeds in such a case. Consequently, a complex wave will change shape as it travels if the medium is "dispersive." A pure sine wave will not change shape under these conditions, however, except by the influence of friction or dissipative forces. If there is no dispersion (or friction), even a complex linear wave does not change shape.

15–7 Reflection and Transmission

When a wave strikes an obstacle, or comes to the end of the medium in which it is traveling, at least a part of the wave is reflected. You have probably seen water waves reflect off a rock or the side of a swimming pool. And you may have heard a shout reflected from a distant cliff—which we call an "echo."

A wave pulse traveling down a cord is reflected as shown in Fig. 15–18. The reflected pulse returns inverted as in Fig. 15–18a if the end of the cord is fixed; it returns right side up if the end is free as in Fig. 15–18b. When the end is fixed to a support, as in Fig. 15–18a, the pulse reaching that fixed end exerts a force (upward) on the support. The support exerts an equal but opposite force downward on the cord (Newton's third law). This downward force on the cord is what "generates" the inverted reflected pulse.

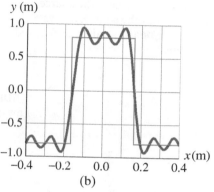

FIGURE 15–17 Example 15–7. Making a square wave.

FIGURE 15–18 Reflection of a wave pulse on a cord lying on a table. (a) The end of the cord is fixed to a peg. (b) The end of the cord is free to move.

(a)   (b)

FIGURE 15–19 When a wave pulse traveling to the right along a thin cord (a) reaches a discontinuity where the cord becomes thicker and heavier, then part is reflected and part is transmitted (b).

Consider next a pulse that travels down a cord which consists of a light section and a heavy section, as shown in Fig. 15–19. When the wave pulse reaches the boundary between the two sections, part of the pulse is reflected and part is transmitted, as shown. The heavier the second section of the cord, the less the energy that is transmitted. (When the second section is a wall or rigid support, very little is transmitted and most is reflected, as in Fig. 15–18a.) For a periodic wave, the frequency of the transmitted wave does not change across the boundary since the boundary point oscillates at that frequency. Thus if the transmitted wave has a lower speed, its wavelength is also less $(\lambda = v/f)$.

FIGURE 15–20 Rays, signifying the direction of motion, are always perpendicular to the wave fronts (wave crests). (a) Circular or spherical waves near the source. (b) Far from the source, the wave fronts are nearly straight or flat, and are called plane waves.

For a two- or three-dimensional wave, such as a water wave, we are concerned with **wave fronts**, by which we mean all the points along the wave forming the wave crest (what we usually refer to simply as a "wave" at the seashore). A line drawn in the direction of motion, perpendicular to the wave front, is called a **ray**, as shown in Fig. 15–20. Wave fronts far from the source have lost almost all their curvature (Fig. 15–20b) and are nearly straight, as ocean waves often are; they are then called **plane waves**.

For reflection of a two- or three-dimensional plane wave, as shown in Fig. 15–21, the angle that the incoming or *incident wave* makes with the reflecting surface is equal to the angle made by the reflected wave. This is the **law of reflection**:

the angle of reflection equals the angle of incidence.

The "angle of incidence" is defined as the angle (θ_i) the incident ray makes with the perpendicular to the reflecting surface (or the wave front makes with a tangent to the surface), and the "angle of reflection" is the corresponding angle (θ_r) for the reflected wave.

FIGURE 15–21
Law of reflection: $\theta_r = \theta_i$.

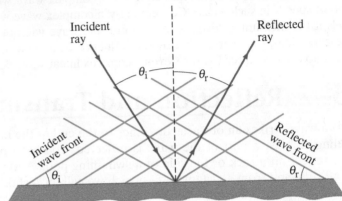

15–8 Interference

Interference refers to what happens when two waves pass through the same region of space at the same time. Consider, for example, the two wave pulses on a cord traveling toward each other as shown in Fig. 15–22. In Fig. 15–22a the two pulses have the same amplitude, but one is a crest and the other a trough; in Fig. 15–22b they are both crests. In both cases, the waves meet and pass right by each other. However, in the region where they overlap, the resultant displacement is the *algebraic sum of their separate displacements* (a crest is considered positive and a trough negative). This is another example of the principle of superposition. In Fig. 15–22a, the two waves have opposite displacements at the instant they pass one another, and they add to zero. The result is called **destructive interference**. In Fig. 15–22b, at the instant the two pulses overlap, they produce a resultant displacement that is greater than the displacement of either separate pulse, and the result is **constructive interference**.

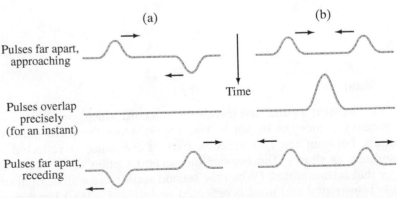

FIGURE 15–22 Two wave pulses pass each other. Where they overlap, interference occurs: (a) destructive, and (b) constructive.

[You may wonder where the energy is at the moment of destructive interference in Fig. 15–22a; the cord may be straight at this instant, but the central parts of it are still moving up or down.]

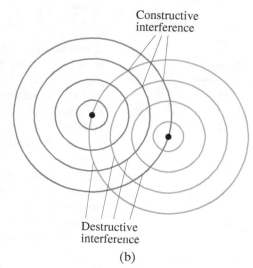

(a)

(b)

FIGURE 15–23 (a) Interference of water waves. (b) Constructive interference occurs where one wave's maximum (a crest) meets the other's maximum. Destructive interference ("flat water") occurs where one wave's maximum (a crest) meets the other's miminum (a trough).

When two rocks are thrown into a pond simultaneously, the two sets of circular waves interfere with one another as shown in Fig. 15–23a. In some areas of overlap, crests of one wave repeatedly meet crests of the other (and troughs meet troughs), Fig. 15–23b. Constructive interference is occurring at these points, and the water continuously oscillates up and down with greater amplitude than either wave separately. In other areas, destructive interference occurs where the water does not move up and down at all over time. This is where crests of one wave meet troughs of the other, and vice versa. Figure 15–24a shows the displacement of two identical waves graphically as a function of time, as well as their sum, for the case of constructive interference. For constructive interference (Fig. 15–24a), the two waves are **in phase**. At points where destructive interference occurs (Fig. 15–24b) crests of one wave repeatedly meet troughs of the other wave and the two waves are **out of phase** by one-half wavelength or 180°. The crests of one wave occur a half wavelength behind the crests of the other wave. The relative phase of the two water waves in Fig. 15–23 in most areas is intermediate between these two extremes, resulting in *partially* destructive interference, as illustrated in Fig. 15–24c. If the amplitudes of two interfering waves are not equal, fully destructive interference (as in Fig. 15–24b) does not occur.

FIGURE 15–24 Graphs showing two identical waves, and their sum, as a function of time at three locations. In (a) the two waves interfere constructively, in (b) destructively, and in (c) partially destructively.

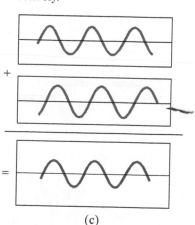

(a)

(b)

(c)

15–9 Standing Waves; Resonance

FIGURE 15–25 Standing waves corresponding to three resonant frequencies.

If you shake one end of a cord and the other end is kept fixed, a continuous wave will travel down to the fixed end and be reflected back, inverted, as we saw in Fig. 15–18a. As you continue to vibrate the cord, waves will travel in both directions, and the wave traveling along the cord, away from your hand, will interfere with the reflected wave coming back. Usually there will be quite a jumble. But if you vibrate the cord at just the right frequency, the two traveling waves will interfere in such a way that a large-amplitude **standing wave** will be produced, Fig. 15–25. It is called a "standing wave" because it does not appear to be traveling. The cord simply appears to have segments that oscillate up and down in a fixed pattern. The points of destructive interference, where the cord remains still at all times, are called **nodes**. Points of constructive interference, where the cord oscillates with maximum amplitude, are called **antinodes**. The nodes and antinodes remain in fixed positions for a particular frequency.

Standing waves can occur at more than one frequency. The lowest frequency of vibration that produces a standing wave gives rise to the pattern shown in Fig. 15–25a. The standing waves shown in Figs. 15–25b and 15–25c are produced at precisely twice and three times the lowest frequency, respectively, assuming the tension in the cord is the same. The cord can also vibrate with four loops (four antinodes) at four times the lowest frequency, and so on.

The frequencies at which standing waves are produced are the **natural frequencies** or **resonant frequencies** of the cord, and the different standing wave patterns shown in Fig. 15–25 are different "resonant modes of vibration." A standing wave on a cord is the result of the interference of two waves traveling in opposite directions. A standing wave can also be considered a vibrating object at resonance. Standing waves represent the same phenomenon as the resonance of a vibrating spring or pendulum, which we discussed in Chapter 14. However, a spring or pendulum has only one resonant frequency, whereas the cord has an infinite number of resonant frequencies, each of which is a whole-number multiple of the lowest resonant frequency.

Consider a string stretched between two supports that is plucked like a guitar or violin string, Fig. 15–26a. Waves of a great variety of frequencies will travel in both directions along the string, will be reflected at the ends, and will travel back in the opposite direction. Most of these waves interfere with each other and quickly die out. However, those waves that correspond to the resonant frequencies of the string will persist. The ends of the string, since they are fixed, will be nodes. There may be other nodes as well. Some of the possible resonant modes of vibration (standing waves) are shown in Fig. 15–26b. Generally, the motion will be a combination of these different resonant modes, but only those frequencies that correspond to a resonant frequency will be present.

FIGURE 15–26   (a) A string is plucked. (b) Only standing waves corresponding to resonant frequencies persist for long.

(a)

(b)

$\ell = \frac{1}{2}\lambda_1$

Fundamental or first harmonic, f_1

$\ell = \lambda_2$

First overtone or second harmonic, $f_2 = 2f_1$

$\ell = \frac{3}{2}\lambda_3$

Second overtone or third harmonic, $f_3 = 3f_1$

To determine the resonant frequencies, we first note that the wavelengths of the standing waves bear a simple relationship to the length ℓ of the string. The lowest frequency, called the **fundamental frequency**, corresponds to one antinode (or loop). And as can be seen in Fig. 15–26b, the whole length corresponds to one-half wavelength. Thus $\ell = \frac{1}{2}\lambda_1$, where λ_1 stands for the wavelength of the fundamental frequency. The other natural frequencies are called **overtones**; for a vibrating string they are whole-number (integral) multiples of the fundamental, and then are also called **harmonics**, with the fundamental being referred to as the **first harmonic**.[†] The next mode of vibration after the fundamental has two loops and is called the **second harmonic** (or first overtone), Fig. 15–26b. The length of the string ℓ at the second harmonic corresponds to one complete wavelength: $\ell = \lambda_2$. For the third and fourth harmonics, $\ell = \frac{3}{2}\lambda_3$, and $\ell = 2\lambda_4$, respectively, and so on. In general, we can write

$$\ell = \frac{n\lambda_n}{2}, \qquad \text{where } n = 1, 2, 3, \cdots.$$

The integer n labels the number of the harmonic: $n = 1$ for the fundamental, $n = 2$ for the second harmonic, and so on. We solve for λ_n and find

$$\lambda_n = \frac{2\ell}{n}, \qquad n = 1, 2, 3, \cdots. \qquad \begin{bmatrix} \text{string fixed} \\ \text{at both ends} \end{bmatrix} \quad \textbf{(15–17a)}$$

To find the frequency f of each vibration we use Eq. 15–1, $f = v/\lambda$, and we see that

$$f_n = \frac{v}{\lambda_n} = n\frac{v}{2\ell} = nf_1, \qquad n = 1, 2, 3, \cdots, \qquad \textbf{(15–17b)}$$

where $f_1 = v/\lambda_1 = v/2\ell$ is the fundamental frequency. We see that each resonant frequency is an integer multiple of the fundamental frequency.

Because a standing wave is equivalent to two traveling waves moving in opposite directions, the concept of wave velocity still makes sense and is given by Eq. 15–2 in terms of the tension F_T in the string and its mass per unit length $(\mu = m/\ell)$. That is, $v = \sqrt{F_T/\mu}$ for waves traveling in both directions.

EXAMPLE 15–8 **Piano string.** A piano string is 1.10 m long and has a mass of 9.00 g. (a) How much tension must the string be under if it is to vibrate at a fundamental frequency of 131 Hz? (b) What are the frequencies of the first four harmonics?

APPROACH To determine the tension, we need to find the wave speed using Eq. 15–1 $(v = \lambda f)$, and then use Eq. 15–2, solving it for F_T.

SOLUTION (a) The wavelength of the fundamental is $\lambda = 2\ell = 2.20$ m (Eq. 15–17a with $n = 1$). The speed of the wave on the string is $v = \lambda f = (2.20 \text{ m})(131 \text{ s}^{-1}) = 288$ m/s. Then we have (Eq. 15–2)

$$F_T = \mu v^2 = \frac{m}{\ell}v^2 = \left(\frac{9.00 \times 10^{-3} \text{ kg}}{1.10 \text{ m}}\right)(288 \text{ m/s})^2 = 679 \text{ N}.$$

(b) The frequencies of the second, third, and fourth harmonics are two, three, and four times the fundamental frequency: 262, 393, and 524 Hz, respectively.

NOTE The speed of the wave on the string is *not* the same as the speed of the sound wave that the piano string produces in the air (as we shall see in Chapter 16).

A standing wave does appear to be standing in place (and a traveling wave appears to move). The term "standing" wave is also meaningful from the point of view of energy. Since the string is at rest at the nodes, no energy flows past these points. Hence the energy is not transmitted down the string but "stands" in place in the string.

Standing waves are produced not only on strings, but on any object that is struck, such as a drum membrane or an object made of metal or wood. The resonant frequencies depend on the dimensions of the object, just as for a string they depend on its length. Large objects have lower resonant frequencies than small objects. All musical instruments, from stringed instruments to wind instruments (in which a column of air vibrates as a standing wave) to drums and other percussion instruments, depend on standing waves to produce their particular musical sounds, as we shall see in Chapter 16.

[†]The term "harmonic" comes from music, because such integral multiples of frequencies "harmonize."

Mathematical Representation of a Standing Wave

As we saw, a standing wave can be considered to consist of two traveling waves that move in opposite directions. These can be written (see Eqs. 15–10c and 15–13c)

$$D_1(x, t) = A \sin(kx - \omega t) \quad \text{and} \quad D_2(x, t) = A \sin(kx + \omega t)$$

since, assuming no damping, the amplitudes are equal as are the frequencies and wavelengths. The sum of these two traveling waves produces a standing wave which can be written mathematically as

$$D = D_1 + D_2 = A[\sin(kx - \omega t) + \sin(kx + \omega t)].$$

From the trigonometric identity $\sin \theta_1 + \sin \theta_2 = 2 \sin\frac{1}{2}(\theta_1 + \theta_2)\cos\frac{1}{2}(\theta_1 - \theta_2)$, we can rewrite this as

$$D = 2A \sin kx \cos \omega t. \tag{15–18}$$

If we let $x = 0$ at the left-hand end of the string, then the right-hand end is at $x = \ell$ where ℓ is the length of the string. Since the string is fixed at its two ends (Fig. 15–26), $D(x, t)$ must be zero at $x = 0$ and at $x = \ell$. Equation 15–18 already satisfies the first condition ($D = 0$ at $x = 0$) and satisfies the second condition if $\sin k\ell = 0$ which means

$$k\ell = \pi, 2\pi, 3\pi, \cdots, n\pi, \cdots$$

where $n =$ an integer. Since $k = 2\pi/\lambda$, then $\lambda = 2\ell/n$, which is just Eq. 15–17a.

Equation 15–18, with the condition $\lambda = 2\ell/n$, is the mathematical representation of a standing wave. We see that a particle at any position x vibrates in simple harmonic motion (because of the factor $\cos \omega t$). All particles of the string vibrate with the same frequency $f = \omega/2\pi$, but the amplitude depends on x and equals $2A \sin kx$. (Compare this to a traveling wave for which all particles vibrate with the same amplitude.) The amplitude has a maximum, equal to $2A$, when $kx = \pi/2, 3\pi/2, 5\pi/2$, and so on—that is, at

$$x = \frac{\lambda}{4}, \frac{3\lambda}{4}, \frac{5\lambda}{4}, \cdots.$$

These are, of course, the positions of the antinodes (see Fig. 15–26).

EXAMPLE 15–9 **Wave forms.** Two waves traveling in opposite directions on a string fixed at $x = 0$ are described by the functions

$$D_1 = (0.20\,\text{m}) \sin(2.0x - 4.0t) \quad \text{and} \quad D_2 = (0.20\,\text{m}) \sin(2.0x + 4.0t)$$

(where x is in m, t is in s), and they produce a standing wave pattern. Determine (a) the function for the standing wave, (b) the maximum amplitude at $x = 0.45\,\text{m}$, (c) where the other end is fixed ($x > 0$), (d) the maximum amplitude, and where it occurs.

APPROACH We use the principle of superposition to add the two waves. The given waves have the form we used to obtain Eq. 15–18, which we thus can use.

SOLUTION (a) The two waves are of the form $D = A \sin(kx \pm \omega t)$, so

$$k = 2.0\,\text{m}^{-1} \quad \text{and} \quad \omega = 4.0\,\text{s}^{-1}.$$

These combine to form a standing wave of the form of Eq. 15–18:

$$D = 2A \sin kx \cos \omega t = (0.40\,\text{m}) \sin(2.0x) \cos(4.0t),$$

where x is in meters and t in seconds.

(b) At $x = 0.45\,\text{m}$,

$$D = (0.40\,\text{m}) \sin(0.90) \cos(4.0t) = (0.31\,\text{m}) \cos(4.0t).$$

The maximum amplitude at this point is $D = 0.31\,\text{m}$ and occurs when $\cos(4.0t) = 1$.

(c) These waves make a standing wave pattern, so both ends of the string must be nodes. Nodes occur every half wavelength, which for our string is

$$\frac{\lambda}{2} = \frac{1}{2}\frac{2\pi}{k} = \frac{\pi}{2.0}\,\text{m} = 1.57\,\text{m}.$$

If the string includes only one loop, its length is $\ell = 1.57\,\text{m}$. But without more information, it could be twice as long, $\ell = 3.14\,\text{m}$, or any integral number times 1.57 m, and still provide a standing wave pattern, Fig. 15–27.

FIGURE 15–27 Example 15–9: possible lengths for the string.

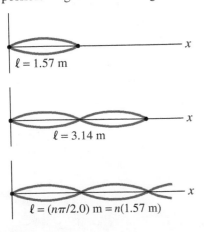

$\ell = 1.57\,\text{m}$

$\ell = 3.14\,\text{m}$

$\ell = (n\pi/2.0)\,\text{m} = n(1.57\,\text{m})$

(d) The nodes occur at $x = 0$, $x = 1.57\,\text{m}$, and, if the string is longer than $\ell = 1.57\,\text{m}$, at $x = 3.14\,\text{m}$, $4.71\,\text{m}$, and so on. The maximum amplitude (antinode) is 0.40 m [from part (b) above] and occurs midway between the nodes. For $\ell = 1.57\,\text{m}$, there is only one antinode, at $x = 0.79\,\text{m}$.

*15–10 Refraction†

When any wave strikes a boundary, some of the energy is reflected and some is transmitted or absorbed. When a two- or three-dimensional wave traveling in one medium crosses a boundary into a medium where its speed is different, the transmitted wave may move in a different direction than the incident wave, as shown in Fig. 15–28. This phenomenon is known as **refraction**. One example is a water wave; the velocity decreases in shallow water and the waves refract, as shown in Fig. 15–29 below. [When the wave velocity changes gradually, as in Fig. 15–29, without a sharp boundary, the waves change direction (refract) gradually.]

In Fig. 15–28, the velocity of the wave in medium 2 is less than in medium 1. In this case, the wave front bends so that it travels more nearly parallel to the boundary. That is, the *angle of refraction*, θ_r, is less than the *angle of incidence*, θ_i. To see why this is so, and to help us get a quantitative relation between θ_r and θ_i, let us think of each wave front as a row of soldiers. The soldiers are marching from firm ground (medium 1) into mud (medium 2) and hence are slowed down after the boundary. The soldiers that reach the mud first are slowed down first, and the row bends as shown in Fig. 15–30a. Let us consider the wave front (or row of soldiers) labeled A in Fig. 15–30b. In the same time t that A_1 moves a distance $\ell_1 = v_1 t$, we see that A_2 moves a distance $\ell_2 = v_2 t$. The two right triangles in Fig. 15–30b, shaded yellow and green, have the side labeled a in common. Thus

$$\sin \theta_1 = \frac{\ell_1}{a} = \frac{v_1 t}{a}$$

since a is the hypotenuse, and

$$\sin \theta_2 = \frac{\ell_2}{a} = \frac{v_2 t}{a}.$$

Dividing these two equations, we obtain the **law of refraction**:

$$\frac{\sin \theta_2}{\sin \theta_1} = \frac{v_2}{v_1}. \tag{15–19}$$

Since θ_1 is the angle of incidence (θ_i), and θ_2 is the angle of refraction (θ_r), Eq. 15–19 gives the quantitative relation between the two. If the wave were going in the opposite direction, the geometry would not change; only θ_1 and θ_2 would change roles: θ_1 would be the angle of refraction and θ_2 the angle of incidence. Clearly then, if the wave travels into a medium where it can move faster, it will bend the opposite way, $\theta_r > \theta_i$. We see from Eq. 15–19 that if the velocity increases, the angle increases, and vice versa.

Earthquake waves refract within the Earth as they travel through rock layers of different densities (and therefore the velocity is different) just as water waves do. Light waves refract as well, and when we discuss light, we shall find Eq. 15–19 very useful.

†This Section and the next are covered in more detail in Chapters 32 to 35 on optics.

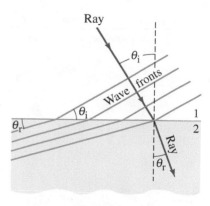

FIGURE 15–28 Refraction of waves passing a boundary.

FIGURE 15–29 Water waves refract gradually as they approach the shore, as their velocity decreases. There is no distinct boundary, as in Fig. 15–28, because the wave velocity changes gradually.

(a)

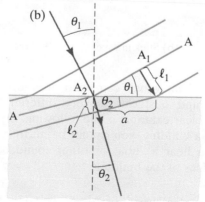

(b)

FIGURE 15–30 (a) Soldier analogy to derive (b) law of refraction for waves.

EXAMPLE 15–10 **Refraction of an earthquake wave.** An earthquake P wave passes across a boundary in rock where its velocity increases from 6.5 km/s to 8.0 km/s. If it strikes this boundary at 30°, what is the angle of refraction?

APPROACH We apply the law of refraction, Eq. 15–19, $\sin\theta_2/\sin\theta_1 = v_2/v_1$.

SOLUTION Since $\sin 30° = 0.50$, Eq. 15–19 yields

$$\sin\theta_2 = \frac{(8.0\,\text{m/s})}{(6.5\,\text{m/s})}(0.50) = 0.62.$$

So $\theta_2 = \sin^{-1}(0.62) = 38°$.

NOTE Be careful with angles of incidence and refraction. As we discussed in Section 15–7 (Fig. 15–21), these angles are between the wave front and the boundary line, or—equivalently—between the ray (direction of wave motion) and the line perpendicular to the boundary. Inspect Fig. 15–30b carefully.

*15–11 Diffraction

Waves spread as they travel. When they encounter an obstacle, they bend around it somewhat and pass into the region behind it, as shown in Fig. 15–31 for water waves. This phenomenon is called **diffraction**.

The amount of diffraction depends on the wavelength of the wave and on the size of the obstacle, as shown in Fig. 15–32. If the wavelength is much larger than the object, as with the grass blades of Fig. 15–32a, the wave bends around them almost as if they are not there. For larger objects, parts (b) and (c), there is more of a "shadow" region behind the obstacle where we might not expect the waves to penetrate—but they do, at least a little. Then notice in part (d), where the obstacle is the same as in part (c) but the wavelength is longer, that there is more diffraction into the shadow region. As a rule of thumb, *only if the wavelength is smaller than the size of the object will there be a significant shadow region*. This rule applies to *reflection* from an obstacle as well. Very little of a wave is reflected unless the wavelength is smaller than the size of the obstacle.

A rough guide to the amount of diffraction is

$$\theta(\text{radians}) \approx \frac{\lambda}{\ell},$$

where θ is roughly the angular spread of waves after they have passed through an opening of width ℓ or around an obstacle of width ℓ.

FIGURE 15–31 Wave diffraction. The waves are coming from the upper left. Note how the waves, as they pass the obstacle, bend around it, into the "shadow region" behind the obstacle.

FIGURE 15–32 Water waves passing objects of various sizes. Note that the longer the wavelength compared to the size of the object, the more diffraction there is into the "shadow region."

(a) Water waves passing blades of grass

(b) Stick in water

(c) Short-wavelength waves passing log

(d) Long-wavelength waves passing log

That waves can bend around obstacles, and thus can carry energy to areas behind obstacles, is very different from energy carried by material particles. A clear example is the following: if you are standing around a corner on one side of a building, you cannot be hit by a baseball thrown from the other side, but you can hear a shout or other sound because the sound waves diffract around the edges of the building.

Summary

Vibrating objects act as sources of **waves** that travel outward from the source. Waves on water and on a string are examples. The wave may be a **pulse** (a single crest) or it may be continuous (many crests and troughs).

The **wavelength** of a continuous wave is the distance between two successive crests (or any two identical points on the wave shape).

The **frequency** is the number of full wavelengths (or crests) that pass a given point per unit time.

The **wave velocity** (how fast a crest moves) is equal to the product of wavelength and frequency,

$$v = \lambda f. \qquad (15\text{--}1)$$

The **amplitude** of a wave is the maximum height of a crest, or depth of a trough, relative to the normal (or equilibrium) level.

In a **transverse wave**, the oscillations are perpendicular to the direction in which the wave travels. An example is a wave on a string.

In a **longitudinal wave**, the oscillations are along (parallel to) the line of travel; sound is an example.

The velocity of both longitudinal and transverse waves in matter is proportional to the square root of an elastic force factor divided by an inertia factor (or density).

Waves carry energy from place to place without matter being carried. The **intensity** of a wave (energy transported across unit area per unit time) is proportional to the square of the amplitude of the wave.

For a wave traveling outward in three dimensions from a point source, the intensity (ignoring damping) decreases with the square of the distance from the source,

$$I \propto \frac{1}{r^2}. \qquad (15\text{--}8a)$$

The amplitude decreases linearly with distance from the source.

A one-dimensional transverse wave traveling in a medium to the right along the x axis (x increasing) can be represented by a formula for the displacement of the medium from equilibrium at any point x as a function of time as

$$D(x, t) = A \sin\left[\left(\frac{2\pi}{\lambda}\right)(x - vt)\right] \qquad (15\text{--}10a)$$

$$= A \sin(kx - \omega t) \qquad (15\text{--}10c)$$

where

$$k = \frac{2\pi}{\lambda} \qquad (15\text{--}11)$$

and

$$\omega = 2\pi f.$$

If a wave is traveling toward decreasing values of x,

$$D(x, t) = A \sin(kx + \omega t). \qquad (15\text{--}13c)$$

[*Waves can be described by the **wave equation**, which in one dimension is $\partial^2 D / \partial x^2 = (1/v^2)\, \partial^2 D / \partial t^2$, Eq. 15–16.]

When two or more waves pass through the same region of space at the same time, the displacement at any given point will be the vector sum of the displacements of the separate waves. This is the **principle of superposition**. It is valid for mechanical waves if the amplitudes are small enough that the restoring force of the medium is proportional to displacement.

Waves reflect off objects in their path. When the **wave front** of a two- or three-dimensional wave strikes an object, the *angle of reflection* equals the *angle of incidence*, which is the **law of reflection**. When a wave strikes a boundary between two materials in which it can travel, part of the wave is reflected and part is transmitted.

When two waves pass through the same region of space at the same time, they **interfere**. From the superposition principle, the resultant displacement at any point and time is the sum of their separate displacements. This can result in **constructive interference**, **destructive interference**, or something in between depending on the amplitudes and relative phases of the waves.

Waves traveling on a cord of fixed length interfere with waves that have reflected off the end and are traveling back in the opposite direction. At certain frequencies, **standing waves** can be produced in which the waves seem to be standing still rather than traveling. The cord (or other medium) is vibrating as a whole. This is a resonance phenomenon, and the frequencies at which standing waves occur are called **resonant frequencies**. The points of destructive interference (no vibration) are called **nodes**. Points of constructive interference (maximum amplitude of vibration) are called **antinodes**. On a cord of length ℓ fixed at both ends, the wavelengths of standing waves are given by

$$\lambda_n = 2\ell/n \qquad (15\text{--}17a)$$

where n is an integer.

[*Waves change direction, or **refract**, when traveling from one medium into a second medium where their speed is different. Waves spread, or **diffract**, as they travel and encounter obstacles. A rough guide to the amount of diffraction is $\theta \approx \lambda/\ell$, where λ is the wavelength and ℓ the width of an opening or obstacle. There is a significant "shadow region" only if the wavelength λ is smaller than the size of the obstacle.]

Questions

1. Is the frequency of a simple periodic wave equal to the frequency of its source? Why or why not?

2. Explain the difference between the speed of a transverse wave traveling down a cord and the speed of a tiny piece of the cord.

3. You are finding it a challenge to climb from one boat up onto a higher boat in heavy waves. If the climb varies from 2.5 m to 4.3 m, what is the amplitude of the wave? Assume the centers of the two boats are a half wavelength apart.

4. What kind of waves do you think will travel down a horizontal metal rod if you strike its end (*a*) vertically from above and (*b*) horizontally parallel to its length?

5. Since the density of air decreases with an increase in temperature, but the bulk modulus B is nearly independent of temperature, how would you expect the speed of sound waves in air to vary with temperature?

6. Describe how you could estimate the speed of water waves across the surface of a pond.

7. The speed of sound in most solids is somewhat greater than in air, yet the density of solids is much greater (10^3 to 10^4 times). Explain.

8. Give two reasons why circular water waves decrease in amplitude as they travel away from the source.

9. Two linear waves have the same amplitude and speed, and otherwise are identical, except one has half the wavelength of the other. Which transmits more energy? By what factor?

10. Will any function of $(x - vt)$—see Eq. 15–14—represent a wave motion? Why or why not? If not, give an example.

11. When a sinusoidal wave crosses the boundary between two sections of cord as in Fig. 15–19, the frequency does not change (although the wavelength and velocity do change). Explain why.

12. If a sinusoidal wave on a two-section cord (Fig. 15–19) is inverted upon reflection, does the transmitted wave have a longer or shorter wavelength?

13. Is energy always conserved when two waves interfere? Explain.

14. If a string is vibrating as a standing wave in three segments, are there any places you could touch it with a knife blade without disturbing the motion?

15. When a standing wave exists on a string, the vibrations of incident and reflected waves cancel at the nodes. Does this mean that energy was destroyed? Explain.

16. Can the amplitude of the standing waves in Fig. 15–25 be greater than the amplitude of the vibrations that cause them (up and down motion of the hand)?

17. When a cord is vibrated as in Fig. 15–25 by hand or by a mechanical oscillator, the "nodes" are not quite true nodes (at rest). Explain. [*Hint*: Consider damping and energy flow from hand or oscillator.]

*18. AM radio signals can usually be heard behind a hill, but FM often cannot. That is, AM signals bend more than FM. Explain. (Radio signals, as we shall see, are carried by electromagnetic waves whose wavelength for AM is typically 200 to 600 m and for FM about 3 m.)

*19. If we knew that energy was being transmitted from one place to another, how might we determine whether the energy was being carried by particles (material objects) or by waves?

Problems

15–1 and 15–2 Characteristics of Waves

1. (I) A fisherman notices that wave crests pass the bow of his anchored boat every 3.0 s. He measures the distance between two crests to be 8.0 m. How fast are the waves traveling?

2. (I) A sound wave in air has a frequency of 262 Hz and travels with a speed of 343 m/s. How far apart are the wave crests (compressions)?

3. (I) Calculate the speed of longitudinal waves in (a) water, (b) granite, and (c) steel.

4. (I) AM radio signals have frequencies between 550 kHz and 1600 kHz (kilohertz) and travel with a speed of 3.0×10^8 m/s. What are the wavelengths of these signals? On FM the frequencies range from 88 MHz to 108 MHz (megahertz) and travel at the same speed. What are their wavelengths?

5. (I) Determine the wavelength of a 5800-Hz sound wave traveling along an iron rod.

6. (II) A cord of mass 0.65 kg is stretched between two supports 8.0 m apart. If the tension in the cord is 140 N, how long will it take a pulse to travel from one support to the other?

7. (II) A 0.40-kg cord is stretched between two supports, 7.8 m apart. When one support is struck by a hammer, a transverse wave travels down the cord and reaches the other support in 0.85 s. What is the tension in the cord?

8. (II) A sailor strikes the side of his ship just below the surface of the sea. He hears the echo of the wave reflected from the ocean floor directly below 2.8 s later. How deep is the ocean at this point?

9. (II) A ski gondola is connected to the top of a hill by a steel cable of length 660 m and diameter 1.5 cm. As the gondola comes to the end of its run, it bumps into the terminal and sends a wave pulse along the cable. It is observed that it took 17 s for the pulse to return. (a) What is the speed of the pulse? (b) What is the tension in the cable?

10. (II) P and S waves from an earthquake travel at different speeds, and this difference helps locate the earthquake "epicenter" (where the disturbance took place). (a) Assuming typical speeds of 8.5 km/s and 5.5 km/s for P and S waves, respectively, how far away did the earthquake occur if a particular seismic station detects the arrival of these two types of waves 1.7 min apart? (b) Is one seismic station sufficient to determine the position of the epicenter? Explain.

11. (II) The wave on a string shown in Fig. 15–33 is moving to the right with a speed of 1.10 m/s. (a) Draw the shape of the string 1.00 s later and indicate which parts of the string are moving up and which down at that instant. (b) Estimate the vertical speed of point A on the string at the instant shown in the Figure.

FIGURE 15–33 Problem 11.

12. (II) A 5.0 kg ball hangs from a steel wire 1.00 mm in diameter and 5.00 m long. What would be the speed of a wave in the steel wire?

13. (II) Two children are sending signals along a cord of total mass 0.50 kg tied between tin cans with a tension of 35 N. It takes the vibrations in the string 0.50 s to go from one child to the other. How far apart are the children?

*14. (II) **Dimensional analysis.** Waves on the surface of the ocean do not depend significantly on the properties of water such as density or surface tension. The primary "return force" for water piled up in the wave crests is due to the gravitational attraction of the Earth. Thus the speed v (m/s) of ocean waves depends on the acceleration due to gravity g. It is reasonable to expect that v might also depend on water depth h and the wave's wavelength λ. Assume the wave speed is given by the functional form $v = C g^\alpha h^\beta \lambda^\gamma$, where α, β, γ, and C are numbers without dimension. (a) In deep water, the water deep below does not affect the motion of waves at the surface. Thus v should be independent of depth h (i.e., $\beta = 0$). Using only dimensional analysis (Section 1–7), determine the formula for the speed of surface waves in deep water. (b) In shallow water, the speed of surface waves is found experimentally to be independent of the wavelength (i.e., $\gamma = 0$). Using only dimensional analysis, determine the formula for the speed of waves in shallow water.

15-3 Energy Transported by Waves

15. (I) Two earthquake waves of the same frequency travel through the same portion of the Earth, but one is carrying 3.0 times the energy. What is the ratio of the amplitudes of the two waves?

16. (II) What is the ratio of (a) the intensities, and (b) the amplitudes, of an earthquake P wave passing through the Earth and detected at two points 15 km and 45 km from the source?

17. (II) Show that if damping is ignored, the amplitude A of circular water waves decreases as the square root of the distance r from the source: $A \propto 1/\sqrt{r}$.

18. (II) The intensity of an earthquake wave passing through the Earth is measured to be $3.0 \times 10^6 \, \text{J/m}^2 \cdot \text{s}$ at a distance of 48 km from the source. (a) What was its intensity when it passed a point only 1.0 km from the source? (b) At what rate did energy pass through an area of $2.0 \, \text{m}^2$ at 1.0 km?

19. (II) A small steel wire of diameter 1.0 mm is connected to an oscillator and is under a tension of 7.5 N. The frequency of the oscillator is 60.0 Hz and it is observed that the amplitude of the wave on the steel wire is 0.50 cm. (a) What is the power output of the oscillator, assuming that the wave is not reflected back? (b) If the power output stays constant but the frequency is doubled, what is the amplitude of the wave?

20. (II) Show that the intensity of a wave is equal to the energy density (energy per unit volume) in the wave times the wave speed.

21. (II) (a) Show that the average rate with which energy is transported along a cord by a mechanical wave of frequency f and amplitude A is
$$\overline{P} = 2\pi^2 \mu v f^2 A^2,$$
where v is the speed of the wave and μ is the mass per unit length of the cord. (b) If the cord is under a tension $F_T = 135 \, \text{N}$ and has mass per unit length 0.10 kg/m, what power is required to transmit 120-Hz transverse waves of amplitude 2.0 cm?

15-4 Mathematical Representation of Traveling Wave

22. (I) A transverse wave on a wire is given by $D(x, t) = 0.015 \sin(25x - 1200t)$ where D and x are in meters and t is in seconds. (a) Write an expression for a wave with the same amplitude, wavelength, and frequency but traveling in the opposite direction. (b) What is the speed of either wave?

23. (I) Suppose at $t = 0$, a wave shape is represented by $D = A \sin(2\pi x/\lambda + \phi)$; that is, it differs from Eq. 15–9 by a constant phase factor ϕ. What then will be the equation for a wave traveling to the left along the x axis as a function of x and t?

24. (II) A transverse traveling wave on a cord is represented by $D = 0.22 \sin(5.6x + 34t)$ where D and x are in meters and t is in seconds. For this wave determine (a) the wavelength, (b) frequency, (c) velocity (magnitude and direction), (d) amplitude, and (e) maximum and minimum speeds of particles of the cord.

25. (II) Consider the point $x = 1.00$ m on the cord of Example 15–5. Determine (a) the maximum velocity of this point, and (b) its maximum acceleration. (c) What is its velocity and acceleration at $t = 2.50$ s?

26. (II) A transverse wave on a cord is given by $D(x, t) = 0.12 \sin(3.0x - 15.0t)$, where D and x are in m and t is in s. At $t = 0.20$ s, what are the displacement and velocity of the point on the cord where $x = 0.60$ m?

27. (II) A transverse wave pulse travels to the right along a string with a speed $v = 2.0$ m/s. At $t = 0$ the shape of the pulse is given by the function
$$D = 0.45 \cos(2.6x + 1.2),$$
where D and x are in meters. (a) Plot D vs. x at $t = 0$. (b) Determine a formula for the wave pulse at any time t assuming there are no frictional losses. (c) Plot $D(x, t)$ vs. x at $t = 1.0$ s. (d) Repeat parts (b) and (c) assuming the pulse is traveling to the left. Plot all 3 graphs on the same axes for easy comparison.

28. (II) A 524-Hz longitudinal wave in air has a speed of 345 m/s. (a) What is the wavelength? (b) How much time is required for the phase to change by 90° at a given point in space? (c) At a particular instant, what is the phase difference (in degrees) between two points 4.4 cm apart?

29. (II) Write the equation for the wave in Problem 28 traveling to the right, if its amplitude is 0.020 cm, and $D = -0.020$ cm, at $t = 0$ and $x = 0$.

30. (II) A sinusoidal wave traveling on a string in the negative x direction has amplitude 1.00 cm, wavelength 3.00 cm, and frequency 245 Hz. At $t = 0$, the particle of string at $x = 0$ is displaced a distance $D = 0.80$ cm above the origin and is moving upward. (a) Sketch the shape of the wave at $t = 0$ and (b) determine the function of x and t that describes the wave.

*15-5 The Wave Equation

*31. (II) Determine if the function $D = A \sin kx \cos \omega t$ is a solution of the wave equation.

*32. (II) Show by direct substitution that the following functions satisfy the wave equation: (a) $D(x, t) = A \ln(x + vt)$; (b) $D(x, t) = (x - vt)^4$.

*33. (II) Show that the wave forms of Eqs. 15–13 and 15–15 satisfy the wave equation, Eq. 15–16.

*34. (II) Let two linear waves be represented by $D_1 = f_1(x, t)$ and $D_2 = f_2(x, t)$. If both these waves satisfy the wave equation (Eq. 15–16), show that any combination $D = C_1 D_1 + C_2 D_2$ does as well, where C_1 and C_2 are constants.

*35. (II) Does the function $D(x, t) = e^{-(kx-\omega t)^2}$ satisfy the wave equation? Why or why not?

*36. (II) In deriving Eq. 15–2, $v = \sqrt{F_T/\mu}$, for the speed of a transverse wave on a string, it was assumed that the wave's amplitude A is much less than its wavelength λ. Assuming a sinusoidal wave shape $D = A \sin(kx - \omega t)$, show via the partial derivative $v' = \partial D/\partial t$ that the assumption $A \ll \lambda$ implies that the maximum transverse speed v'_{max} of the string itself is much less than the wave velocity. If $A = \lambda/100$ determine the ratio v'_{max}/v.

15-7 Reflection and Transmission

37. (II) A cord has two sections with linear densities of 0.10 kg/m and 0.20 kg/m, Fig. 15–34. An incident wave, given by $D = (0.050 \, \text{m}) \sin(7.5x - 12.0t)$, where x is in meters and t in seconds, travels along the lighter cord. (a) What is the wavelength on the lighter section of the cord? (b) What is the tension in the cord? (c) What is the wavelength when the wave travels on the heavier section?

$\mu_1 = 0.10 \, \text{kg/m}$ $\mu_2 = 0.20 \, \text{kg/m}$

FIGURE 15-34
Problem 37. $D = (0.050 \, \text{m}) \sin(7.5 x - 12.0 t)$

38. (II) Consider a sine wave traveling down the stretched two-part cord of Fig. 15–19. Determine a formula (a) for the ratio of the speeds of the wave in the two sections, v_H/v_L, and (b) for the ratio of the wavelengths in the two sections. (The frequency is the same in both sections. Why?) (c) Is the wavelength larger in the heavier cord or the lighter?

39. (II) Seismic reflection prospecting is commonly used to map deeply buried formations containing oil. In this technique, a seismic wave generated on the Earth's surface (for example, by an explosion or falling weight) reflects from the subsurface formation and is detected upon its return to ground level. By placing ground-level detectors at a variety of locations relative to the source, and observing the variation in the source-to-detector travel times, the depth of the subsurface formation can be determined. (a) Assume a ground-level detector is placed a distance x away from a seismic-wave source and that a horizontal boundary between overlying rock and a subsurface formation exists at depth D (Fig. 15–35a). Determine an expression for the time t taken by the reflected wave to travel from source to detector, assuming the seismic wave propagates at constant speed v. (b) Suppose several detectors are placed along a line at different distances x from the source as in Fig. 15–35b. Then, when a seismic wave is generated, the different travel times t for each detector are measured. Starting with your result from part (a), explain how a graph of t^2 vs. x^2 can be used to determine D.

FIGURE 15–35
Problem 39.

40. (III) A cord stretched to a tension F_T consists of two sections (as in Fig. 15–19) whose linear densities are μ_1 and μ_2. Take $x = 0$ to be the point (a knot) where they are joined, with μ_1 referring to that section of cord to the left and μ_2 that to the right. A sinusoidal wave, $D = A \sin[k_1(x - v_1 t)]$, starts at the left end of the cord. When it reaches the knot, part of it is reflected and part is transmitted. Let the equation of the reflected wave be $D_R = A_R \sin[k_1(x + v_1 t)]$ and that for the transmitted wave be $D_T = A_T \sin[k_2(x - v_2 t)]$. Since the frequency must be the same in both sections, we have $\omega_1 = \omega_2$ or $k_1 v_1 = k_2 v_2$. (a) Because the cord is continuous, a point an infinitesimal distance to the left of the knot has the same displacement at any moment (due to incident plus reflected waves) as a point just to the right of the knot (due to the transmitted wave). Thus show that $A = A_T + A_R$. (b) Assuming that the slope $(\partial D/\partial x)$ of the cord just to the left of the knot is the same as the slope just to the right of the knot, show that the amplitude of the reflected wave is given by

$$A_R = \left(\frac{v_1 - v_2}{v_1 + v_2}\right)A = \left(\frac{k_2 - k_1}{k_2 + k_1}\right)A.$$

(c) What is A_T in terms of A?

15–8 Interference

41. (I) The two pulses shown in Fig. 15–36 are moving toward each other. (a) Sketch the shape of the string at the moment they directly overlap. (b) Sketch the shape of the string a few moments later. (c) In Fig. 15–22a, at the moment the pulses pass each other, the string is straight. What has happened to the energy at this moment?

FIGURE 15–36
Problem 41.

42. (II) Suppose two linear waves of equal amplitude and frequency have a phase difference ϕ as they travel in the same medium. They can be represented by

$$D_1 = A \sin(kx - \omega t)$$
$$D_2 = A \sin(kx - \omega t + \phi).$$

(a) Use the trigonometric identity $\sin \theta_1 + \sin \theta_2 = 2 \sin\frac{1}{2}(\theta_1 + \theta_2) \cos\frac{1}{2}(\theta_1 - \theta_2)$ to show that the resultant wave is given by

$$D = \left(2A \cos\frac{\phi}{2}\right) \sin\left(kx - \omega t + \frac{\phi}{2}\right).$$

(b) What is the amplitude of this resultant wave? Is the wave purely sinusoidal, or not? (c) Show that constructive interference occurs if $\phi = 0, 2\pi, 4\pi$, and so on, and destructive interference occurs if $\phi = \pi, 3\pi, 5\pi$, etc. (d) Describe the resultant wave, by equation and in words, if $\phi = \pi/2$.

15–9 Standing Waves; Resonance

43. (I) A violin string vibrates at 441 Hz when unfingered. At what frequency will it vibrate if it is fingered one-third of the way down from the end? (That is, only two-thirds of the string vibrates as a standing wave.)

44. (I) If a violin string vibrates at 294 Hz as its fundamental frequency, what are the frequencies of the first four harmonics?

45. (I) In an earthquake, it is noted that a footbridge oscillated up and down in a one-loop (fundamental standing wave) pattern once every 1.5 s. What other possible resonant periods of motion are there for this bridge? What frequencies do they correspond to?

46. (I) A particular string resonates in four loops at a frequency of 280 Hz. Name at least three other frequencies at which it will resonate.

47. (II) A cord of length 1.0 m has two equal-length sections with linear densities of 0.50 kg/m and 1.00 kg/m. The tension in the entire cord is constant. The ends of the cord are oscillated so that a standing wave is set up in the cord with a single node where the two sections meet. What is the ratio of the oscillatory frequencies?

48. (II) The velocity of waves on a string is 96 m/s. If the frequency of standing waves is 445 Hz, how far apart are the two adjacent nodes?

49. (II) If two successive harmonics of a vibrating string are 240 Hz and 320 Hz, what is the frequency of the fundamental?

50. (II) A guitar string is 90.0 cm long and has a mass of 3.16 g. From the bridge to the support post $(= \ell)$ is 60.0 cm and the string is under a tension of 520 N. What are the frequencies of the fundamental and first two overtones?

51. (II) Show that the frequency of standing waves on a cord of length ℓ and linear density μ, which is stretched to a tension F_T, is given by

$$f = \frac{n}{2\ell}\sqrt{\frac{F_T}{\mu}}$$

where n is an integer.

52. (II) One end of a horizontal string of linear density 6.6×10^{-4} kg/m is attached to a small-amplitude mechanical 120-Hz oscillator. The string passes over a pulley, a distance $\ell = 1.50$ m away, and weights are hung from this end, Fig. 15–37. What mass m must be hung from this end of the string to produce (a) one loop, (b) two loops, and (c) five loops of a standing wave? Assume the string at the oscillator is a node, which is nearly true.

FIGURE 15–37
Problems 52 and 53.

53. (II) In Problem 52, Fig. 15–37, the length of the string may be adjusted by moving the pulley. If the hanging mass m is fixed at 0.070 kg, how many different standing wave patterns may be achieved by varying ℓ between 10 cm and 1.5 m?

54. (II) The displacement of a standing wave on a string is given by $D = 2.4 \sin(0.60x) \cos(42t)$, where x and D are in centimeters and t is in seconds. (a) What is the distance (cm) between nodes? (b) Give the amplitude, frequency, and speed of each of the component waves. (c) Find the speed of a particle of the string at $x = 3.20$ cm when $t = 2.5$ s.

55. (II) The displacement of a transverse wave traveling on a string is represented by $D_1 = 4.2 \sin(0.84x - 47t + 2.1)$, where D_1 and x are in cm and t in s. (a) Find an equation that represents a wave which, when traveling in the opposite direction, will produce a standing wave when added to this one. (b) What is the equation describing the standing wave?

56. (II) When you slosh the water back and forth in a tub at just the right frequency, the water alternately rises and falls at each end, remaining relatively calm at the center. Suppose the frequency to produce such a standing wave in a 45-cm-wide tub is 0.85 Hz. What is the speed of the water wave?

57. (II) A particular violin string plays at a frequency of 294 Hz. If the tension is increased 15%, what will the new frequency be?

58. (II) Two traveling waves are described by the functions

$$D_1 = A \sin(kx - \omega t)$$
$$D_2 = A \sin(kx + \omega t),$$

where $A = 0.15$ m, $k = 3.5$ m^{-1}, and $\omega = 1.8$ s^{-1}. (a) Plot these two waves, from $x = 0$ to a point $x(> 0)$ that includes one full wavelength. Choose $t = 1.0$ s. (b) Plot the sum of the two waves and identify the nodes and antinodes in the plot, and compare to the analytic (mathematical) representation.

59. (II) Plot the two waves given in Problem 58 and their sum, as a function of time from $t = 0$ to $t = T$ (one period). Choose (a) $x = 0$ and (b) $x = \lambda/4$. Interpret your results.

60. (II) A standing wave on a 1.64-m-long horizontal string displays three loops when the string vibrates at 120 Hz. The maximum swing of the string (top to bottom) at the center of each loop is 8.00 cm. (a) What is the function describing the standing wave? (b) What are the functions describing the two equal-amplitude waves traveling in opposite directions that make up the standing wave?

61. (II) On an electric guitar, a "pickup" under each string transforms the string's vibrations directly into an electrical signal. If a pickup is placed 16.25 cm from one of the fixed ends of a 65.00-cm-long string, which of the harmonics from $n = 1$ to $n = 12$ will not be "picked up" by this pickup?

62. (II) A 65-cm guitar string is fixed at both ends. In the frequency range between 1.0 and 2.0 kHz, the string is found to resonate only at frequencies 1.2, 1.5, and 1.8 kHz. What is the speed of traveling waves on this string?

63. (II) Two oppositely directed traveling waves given by $D_1 = (5.0 \text{ mm}) \cos[(2.0 \text{ m}^{-1})x - (3.0 \text{ rad/s})t]$ and $D_2 = (5.0 \text{ mm}) \cos[(2.0 \text{ m}^{-1})x + (3.0 \text{ rad/s})t]$ form a standing wave. Determine the position of nodes along the x axis.

64. (II) A wire is composed of aluminum with length $\ell_1 = 0.600$ m and mass per unit length $\mu_1 = 2.70$ g/m joined to a steel section with length $\ell_2 = 0.882$ m and mass per unit length $\mu_2 = 7.80$ g/m. This composite wire is fixed at both ends and held at a uniform tension of 135 N. Find the lowest frequency standing wave that can exist on this wire, assuming there is a node at the joint between aluminum and steel. How many nodes (including the two at the ends) does this standing wave possess?

*15–10 Refraction

*65. (I) An earthquake P wave traveling 8.0 km/s strikes a boundary within the Earth between two kinds of material. If it approaches the boundary at an incident angle of 52° and the angle of refraction is 31°, what is the speed in the second medium?

*66. (I) Water waves approach an underwater "shelf" where the velocity changes from 2.8 m/s to 2.5 m/s. If the incident wave crests make a 35° angle with the shelf, what will be the angle of refraction?

*67. (II) A sound wave is traveling in warm air (25°C) when it hits a layer of cold (−15°C) denser air. If the sound wave hits the cold air interface at an angle of 33°, what is the angle of refraction? The speed of sound as a function of temperature can be approximated by $v = (331 + 0.60\,T)$ m/s, where T is in °C.

*68. (II) Any type of wave that reaches a boundary beyond which its speed is increased, there is a maximum incident angle if there is to be a transmitted refracted wave. This maximum incident angle θ_{iM} corresponds to an angle of refraction equal to 90°. If $\theta_i > \theta_{iM}$, all the wave is reflected at the boundary and none is refracted, because this would correspond to $\sin \theta_r > 1$ (where θ_r is the angle of refraction), which is impossible. This phenomenon is referred to as *total internal reflection*. (a) Find a formula for θ_{iM} using the law of refraction, Eq. 15–19. (b) How far from the bank should a trout fisherman stand (Fig. 15–38) so trout won't be frightened by his voice (1.8 m above the ground)? The speed of sound is about 343 m/s in air and 1440 m/s in water.

FIGURE 15–38
Problem 68b.

*69. (II) A longitudinal earthquake wave strikes a boundary between two types of rock at a 38° angle. As the wave crosses the boundary, the specific gravity of the rock changes from 3.6 to 2.8. Assuming that the elastic modulus is the same for both types of rock, determine the angle of refraction.

*15–11 Diffraction

*70. (II) A satellite dish is about 0.5 m in diameter. According to the user's manual, the dish has to be pointed in the direction of the satellite, but an error of about 2° to either side is allowed without loss of reception. Estimate the wavelength of the electromagnetic waves (speed = 3×10^8 m/s) received by the dish.

General Problems

71. A sinusoidal traveling wave has frequency 880 Hz and phase velocity 440 m/s. (a) At a given time, find the distance between any two locations that correspond to a difference in phase of $\pi/6$ rad. (b) At a fixed location, by how much does the phase change during a time interval of 1.0×10^{-4} s?

72. When you walk with a cup of coffee (diameter 8 cm) at just the right pace of about one step per second, the coffee sloshes higher and higher in your cup until eventually it starts to spill over the top, Fig 15–39. Estimate the speed of the waves in the coffee.

FIGURE 15–39 Problem 72.

73. Two solid rods have the same bulk modulus but one is 2.5 times as dense as the other. In which rod will the speed of longitudinal waves be greater, and by what factor?

74. Two waves traveling along a stretched string have the same frequency, but one transports 2.5 times the power of the other. What is the ratio of the amplitudes of the two waves?

75. A bug on the surface of a pond is observed to move up and down a total vertical distance of 0.10 m, lowest to highest point, as a wave passes. (a) What is the amplitude of the wave? (b) If the amplitude increases to 0.15 m, by what factor does the bug's maximum kinetic energy change?

76. A guitar string is supposed to vibrate at 247 Hz, but is measured to actually vibrate at 255 Hz. By what percentage should the tension in the string be changed to get the frequency to the correct value?

77. An earthquake-produced surface wave can be approximated by a sinusoidal transverse wave. Assuming a frequency of 0.60 Hz (typical of earthquakes, which actually include a mixture of frequencies), what amplitude is needed so that objects begin to leave contact with the ground? [Hint: Set the acceleration $a > g$.]

78. A uniform cord of length ℓ and mass m is hung vertically from a support. (a) Show that the speed of transverse waves in this cord is $\sqrt{gh}$, where h is the height above the lower end. (b) How long does it take for a pulse to travel upward from one end to the other?

79. A transverse wave pulse travels to the right along a string with a speed $v = 2.4$ m/s. At $t = 0$ the shape of the pulse is given by the function

$$D = \frac{4.0 \text{ m}^3}{x^2 + 2.0 \text{ m}^2},$$

where D and x are in meters. (a) Plot D vs. x at $t = 0$ from $x = -10$ m to $x = +10$ m. (b) Determine a formula for the wave pulse at any time t assuming there are no frictional losses. (c) Plot $D(x,t)$ vs. x at $t = 1.00$ s. (d) Repeat parts (b) and (c) assuming the pulse is traveling to the left.

80. (a) Show that if the tension in a stretched string is changed by a small amount ΔF_T, the frequency of the fundamental is changed by an amount $\Delta f = \frac{1}{2}(\Delta F_T/F_T)f$. (b) By what percent must the tension in a piano string be increased or decreased to raise the frequency from 436 Hz to 442 Hz? (c) Does the formula in part (a) apply to the overtones as well?

81. Two strings on a musical instrument are tuned to play at 392 Hz (G) and 494 Hz (B). (a) What are the frequencies of the first two overtones for each string? (b) If the two strings have the same length and are under the same tension, what must be the ratio of their masses (m_G/m_B)? (c) If the strings, instead, have the same mass per unit length and are under the same tension, what is the ratio of their lengths (ℓ_G/ℓ_B)? (d) If their masses and lengths are the same, what must be the ratio of the tensions in the two strings?

82. The ripples in a certain groove 10.8 cm from the center of a 33-rpm phonograph record have a wavelength of 1.55 mm. What will be the frequency of the sound emitted?

83. A 10.0-m-long wire of mass 152 g is stretched under a tension of 255 N. A pulse is generated at one end, and 20.0 ms later a second pulse is generated at the opposite end. Where will the two pulses first meet?

84. A wave with a frequency of 220 Hz and a wavelength of 10.0 cm is traveling along a cord. The maximum speed of particles on the cord is the same as the wave speed. What is the amplitude of the wave?

85. A string can have a "free" end if that end is attached to a ring that can slide without friction on a vertical pole (Fig. 15–40). Determine the wavelengths of the resonant vibrations of such a string with one end fixed and the other free.

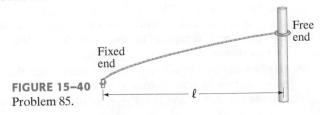

FIGURE 15–40
Problem 85.

86. A highway overpass was observed to resonate as one full loop ($\frac{1}{2}\lambda$) when a small earthquake shook the ground vertically at 3.0 Hz. The highway department put a support at the center of the overpass, anchoring it to the ground as shown in Fig. 15–41. What resonant frequency would you now expect for the overpass? It is noted that earthquakes rarely do significant shaking above 5 or 6 Hz. Did the modifications do any good? Explain.

Before modification

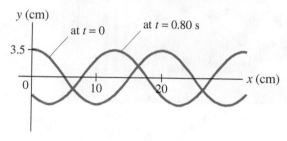

Added support

After modification

FIGURE 15–41 Problem 86.

87. Figure 15–42 shows the wave shape at two instants of time for a sinusoidal wave traveling to the right. What is the mathematical representation of this wave?

y (cm)

at t = 0   at t = 0.80 s

3.5

0   10   20   x (cm)

FIGURE 15–42 Problem 87.

88. Estimate the average power of a water wave when it hits the chest of an adult standing in the water at the seashore. Assume that the amplitude of the wave is 0.50 m, the wavelength is 2.5 m, and the period is 4.0 s.

89. A tsunami of wavelength 215 km and velocity 550 km/h travels across the Pacific Ocean. As it approaches Hawaii, people observe an unusual decrease of sea level in the harbors. Approximately how much time do they have to run to safety? (In the absence of knowledge and warning, people have died during tsunamis, some of them attracted to the shore to see stranded fishes and boats.)

90. Two wave pulses are traveling in opposite directions with the same speed of 7.0 cm/s as shown in Fig. 15–43. At $t = 0$, the leading edges of the two pulses are 15 cm apart. Sketch the wave pulses at $t = 1.0, 2.0$ and 3.0 s.

Distance (cm)

FIGURE 15–43 Problem 90.

91. For a spherical wave traveling uniformly away from a point source, show that the displacement can be represented by

$$D = \left(\frac{A}{r}\right) \sin(kr - \omega t),$$

where r is the radial distance from the source and A is a constant.

92. What frequency of sound would have a wavelength the same size as a 1.0-m-wide window? (The speed of sound is 344 m/s at 20°C.) What frequencies would diffract through the window?

*Numerical/Computer

*93. (II) Consider a wave generated by the periodic vibration of a source and given by the expression $D(x,t) = A\sin^2 k(x - ct)$, where x represents position (in meters), t represents time (in seconds), and c is a positive constant. We choose $A = 5.0$ m, $k = 1.0$ m^{-1}, and $c = 0.50$ m/s. Use a spreadsheet to make a graph with three curves of $D(x,t)$ from $x = -5.0$ m to $+5.0$ m in steps of 0.050 m at times $t = 0.0$, 1.0, and 2.0 s. Determine the speed, direction of motion, period, and wavelength of the wave.

*94. (II) The displacement of a bell-shaped wave pulse is described by a relation that involves the exponential function:

$$D(x,t) = Ae^{-\alpha(x-vt)^2}$$

where the constants $A = 10.0$ m, $\alpha = 2.0$ m^{-2}, and $v = 3.0$ m/s. (a) Over the range -10.0 m $\le x \le +10.0$ m, use a graphing calculator or computer program to plot $D(x,t)$ at each of the three times $t = 0$, $t = 1.0$, and $t = 2.0$ s. Do these three plots demonstrate the wave-pulse shape shifting along the x axis by the expected amount over the span of each 1.0-s interval? (b) Repeat part (a) but assume $D(x,t) = Ae^{-\alpha(x+vt)^2}$.

Answers to Exercises

A: (c).

B: (d).

C: (c).

D: (a).

"If music be the food of physics, play on."
[See Shakespeare, *Twelfth Night*, line 1.]

Stringed instruments depend on transverse standing waves on strings to produce their harmonious sounds. The sound of wind instruments originates in longitudinal standing waves of an air column. Percussion instruments create more complicated standing waves.

Besides examining sources of sound, we also study the decibel scale of sound level, sound wave interference and beats, the Doppler effect, shock waves and sonic booms, and ultrasound imaging.

C H A P T E R

16

Sound

CONTENTS

CHAPTER-OPENING QUESTION—Guess now!

A pianist plays the note "middle C." The sound is made by the vibration of the piano string and is propagated outward as a vibration of the air (which can reach your ear). Comparing the vibration on the string to the vibration in the air, which of the following is true?

(a) The vibration on the string and the vibration in the air have the same wavelength.
(b) They have the same frequency.
(c) They have the same speed.
(d) Neither wavelength, frequency, nor speed are the same in the air as on the string.

Sound is associated with our sense of hearing and, therefore, with the physiology of our ears and the psychology of our brain, which interprets the sensations that reach our ears. The term *sound* also refers to the physical sensation that stimulates our ears: namely, longitudinal waves.

We can distinguish three aspects of any sound. First, there must be a *source* for a sound; as with any mechanical wave, the source of a sound wave is a vibrating object. Second, the energy is transferred from the source in the form of longitudinal sound *waves*. And third, the sound is *detected* by an ear or by a microphone. We start this Chapter by looking at some aspects of sound waves themselves.

16–1 Characteristics of Sound

We saw in Chapter 15, Fig. 15–5, how a vibrating drumhead produces a sound wave in air. Indeed, we usually think of sound waves traveling in the air, for normally it is the vibrations of the air that force our eardrums to vibrate. But sound waves can also travel in other materials.

Two stones struck together under water can be heard by a swimmer beneath the surface, for the vibrations are carried to the ear by the water. When you put your ear flat against the ground, you can hear an approaching train or truck. In this case the ground does not actually touch your eardrum, but the longitudinal wave transmitted by the ground is called a sound wave just the same, for its vibrations cause the outer ear and the air within it to vibrate. Sound cannot travel in the absence of matter. For example, a bell ringing inside an evacuated jar cannot be heard, nor does sound travel through the empty reaches of outer space.

The **speed of sound** is different in different materials. In air at 0°C and 1 atm, sound travels at a speed of 331 m/s. We saw in Eq. 15–4 $\left(v = \sqrt{B/\rho}\right)$ that the speed depends on the elastic modulus, B, and the density, ρ, of the material. Thus for helium, whose density is much less than that of air but whose elastic modulus is not greatly different, the speed is about three times as great as in air. In liquids and solids, which are much less compressible and therefore have much greater elastic moduli, the speed is larger still. The speed of sound in various materials is given in Table 16–1. The values depend somewhat on temperature, but this is significant mainly for gases. For example, in air at normal (ambient) temperatures, the speed increases approximately 0.60 m/s for each Celsius degree increase in temperature:

$$v \approx (331 + 0.60\,T)\ \text{m/s}, \qquad \text{[speed of sound in air]}$$

where T is the temperature in °C. Unless stated otherwise, we will assume in this Chapter that $T = 20$°C, so that[†] $v = \left[331 + (0.60)(20)\right]$ m/s = 343 m/s.

TABLE 16–1 Speed of Sound in Various Materials (20°C and 1 atm)

Material	Speed (m/s)
Air	343
Air (0°C)	331
Helium	1005
Hydrogen	1300
Water	1440
Sea water	1560
Iron and steel	≈ 5000
Glass	≈ 4500
Aluminum	≈ 5100
Hardwood	≈ 4000
Concrete	≈ 3000

CONCEPTUAL EXAMPLE 16–1 **Distance from a lightning strike.** A rule of thumb that tells how close lightning has struck is, "one mile for every five seconds before the thunder is heard." Explain why this works, noting that the speed of light is so high (3×10^8 m/s, almost a million times faster than sound) that the time for light to travel to us is negligible compared to the time for the sound.

RESPONSE The speed of sound in air is about 340 m/s, so to travel 1 km = 1000 m takes about 3 seconds. One mile is about 1.6 kilometers, so the time for the thunder to travel a mile is about $(1.6)(3) \approx 5$ seconds.

PHYSICS APPLIED

How far away is the lightning?

| **EXERCISE A** What would be the rule used in Example 16–1 in terms of kilometers?

Two aspects of any sound are immediately evident to a human listener: "loudness" and "pitch." Each refers to a sensation in the consciousness of the listener. But to each of these subjective sensations there corresponds a physically measurable quantity. **Loudness** is related to the intensity (energy per unit time crossing unit area) in the sound wave, and we shall discuss it in Section 16–3.

The **pitch** of a sound refers to whether it is high, like the sound of a piccolo or violin, or low, like the sound of a bass drum or string bass. The physical quantity that determines pitch is the frequency, as was first noted by Galileo. The lower the frequency, the lower the pitch; the higher the frequency, the higher the pitch.[‡] The best human ears can respond to frequencies from about 20 Hz to almost 20,000 Hz. (Recall that 1 Hz is 1 cycle per second.) This frequency range is called the **audible range**. These limits vary somewhat from one individual to another. One general trend is that as people age, they are less able to hear high frequencies, so the high-frequency limit may be 10,000 Hz or less.

[†]We treat the 20°C ("room temperature") as accurate to 2 significant figures.

[‡]Although pitch is determined mainly by frequency, it also depends to a slight extent on loudness. For example, a very loud sound may seem slightly lower in pitch than a quiet sound of the same frequency.

CAUTION

*Do not confuse
ultrasonic (high frequency)
with supersonic (high speed)*

PHYSICS APPLIED

Autofocusing camera

FIGURE 16–1 Example 16–2.
Autofocusing camera emits an
ultrasonic pulse. Solid lines
represent the wave front of the
outgoing wave pulse moving to the
right; dashed lines represent the
wave front of the pulse reflected off
the person's face, returning to the
camera. The time information allows
the camera mechanism to adjust the
lens to focus at the proper distance.

Sound waves whose frequencies are outside the audible range may reach the ear, but we are not generally aware of them. Frequencies above 20,000 Hz are called **ultrasonic** (do not confuse with *supersonic*, which is used for an object moving with a speed faster than the speed of sound). Many animals can hear ultrasonic frequencies; dogs, for example, can hear sounds as high as 50,000 Hz, and bats can detect frequencies as high as 100,000 Hz. Ultrasonic waves have many useful applications in medicine and other fields, which we discuss later in this Chapter.

EXAMPLE 16–2 **Autofocusing with sound waves.** Older autofocusing cameras determine the distance by emitting a pulse of very high frequency (ultrasonic) sound that travels to the object being photographed, and include a sensor that detects the returning reflected sound, as shown in Fig. 16–1. To get an idea of the time sensitivity of the detector, calculate the travel time of the pulse for an object (*a*) 1.0 m away, and (*b*) 20 m away.

APPROACH If we assume the temperature is about 20°C, then the speed of sound is 343 m/s. Using this speed v and the total distance d back and forth in each case, we can obtain the time ($v = d/t$).

SOLUTION (*a*) The pulse travels 1.0 m to the object and 1.0 m back, for a total of 2.0 m. We solve for t in $v = d/t$:

$$t = \frac{d}{v} = \frac{2.0 \text{ m}}{343 \text{ m/s}} = 0.0058 \text{ s} = 5.8 \text{ ms}.$$

(*b*) The total distance now is $2 \times 20 \text{ m} = 40 \text{ m}$, so

$$t = \frac{40 \text{ m}}{343 \text{ m/s}} = 0.12 \text{ s} = 120 \text{ ms}.$$

NOTE Newer autofocus cameras use infrared light ($v = 3 \times 10^8 \text{ m/s}$) instead of ultrasound, and/or a digital sensor array that detects light intensity differences between adjacent receptors as the lens is automatically moved back and forth, choosing the lens position that provides maximum intensity differences (sharpest focus).

Sound waves whose frequencies are below the audible range (that is, less than 20 Hz) are called **infrasonic**. Sources of infrasonic waves include earthquakes, thunder, volcanoes, and waves produced by vibrating heavy machinery. This last source can be particularly troublesome to workers, for infrasonic waves—even though inaudible—can cause damage to the human body. These low-frequency waves act in a resonant fashion, causing motion and irritation of the body's organs.

FIGURE 16–2 Longitudinal sound
wave traveling to the right, and its
graphical representation in terms of
pressure.

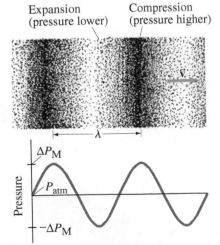

Expansion
(pressure lower)

Compression
(pressure higher)

16–2 Mathematical Representation of Longitudinal Waves

In Section 15–4, we saw that a one-dimensional sinusoidal wave traveling along the x axis can be represented by the relation (Eq. 15–10c)

$$D = A\sin(kx - \omega t), \tag{16–1}$$

where D is the displacement of the wave at position x and time t, and A is its *amplitude* (maximum value). The wave number k is related to the wavelength λ by $k = 2\pi/\lambda$, and $\omega = 2\pi f$ where f is the frequency. For a transverse wave—such as a wave on a string—the displacement D is perpendicular to the direction of wave propagation along the x axis. But for a longitudinal wave the displacement D is *along the direction of wave propagation*. That is, D is parallel to x and represents the displacement of a tiny volume element of the medium from its equilibrium position.

Longitudinal (sound) waves can also be considered from the point of view of variations in pressure rather than displacement. Indeed, longitudinal waves are often called **pressure waves**. The pressure variation is usually easier to measure than the displacement (see Example 16–7). As can be seen in Fig. 16–2, in a wave "compression" (where molecules are closest together), the pressure is higher than normal, whereas in an expansion (or rarefaction) the pressure is less than normal.

Figure 16–3 shows a graphical representation of a sound wave in air in terms of (a) displacement and (b) pressure. Note that the displacement wave is a quarter wavelength, or 90° ($\pi/2$ rad), out of phase with the pressure wave: where the pressure is a maximum or minimum, the displacement from equilibrium is zero; and where the pressure variation is zero, the displacement is a maximum or minimum.

Pressure Wave Derivation

Let us now derive the mathematical representation of the pressure variation in a traveling longitudinal wave. From the definition of the bulk modulus, B (Eq. 12–7),

$$\Delta P = -B(\Delta V/V),$$

where ΔP represents the pressure difference from the normal pressure P_0 (no wave present) and $\Delta V/V$ is the fractional change in volume of the medium due to the pressure change ΔP. The negative sign reflects the fact that the volume decreases ($\Delta V < 0$) if the pressure is increased. Consider now a layer of fluid through which the longitudinal wave is passing (Fig. 16–4). If this layer has thickness Δx and area S, then its volume is $V = S \Delta x$. As a result of pressure variation in the wave, the volume will change by an amount $\Delta V = S \Delta D$, where ΔD is the change in thickness of this layer as it compresses or expands. (Remember that D represents the displacement of the medium.) Thus we have

$$\Delta P = -B \frac{S \Delta D}{S \Delta x}.$$

To be precise, we take the limit of $\Delta x \to 0$, so we obtain

$$\Delta P = -B \frac{\partial D}{\partial x}, \tag{16–2}$$

where we use the partial derivative notation since D is a function of both x and t. If the displacement D is sinusoidal as given by Eq. 16–1, then we have from Eq. 16–2 that

$$\Delta P = -(BAk) \cos(kx - \omega t). \tag{16–3}$$

(Here A is the displacement amplitude, not area which is S.) Thus the pressure varies sinusoidally as well, but is out of phase from the displacement by 90° or a quarter wavelength, as in Fig. 16–3. The quantity BAk is called the **pressure amplitude**, ΔP_M. It represents the maximum and minimum amounts by which the pressure varies from the normal ambient pressure. We can thus write

$$\Delta P = -\Delta P_M \cos(kx - \omega t), \tag{16–4}$$

where, using $v = \sqrt{B/\rho}$ (Eq. 15–4), and $k = \omega/v = 2\pi f/v$ (Eq. 15–12), then

$$\begin{aligned} \Delta P_M &= BAk \\ &= \rho v^2 Ak \\ &= 2\pi \rho v Af. \end{aligned} \tag{16–5}$$

16–3 Intensity of Sound: Decibels

Loudness is a sensation in the consciousness of a human being and is related to a physically measurable quantity, the **intensity** of the wave. Intensity is defined as the energy transported by a wave per unit time across a unit area perpendicular to the energy flow. As we saw in Chapter 15, intensity is proportional to the square of the wave amplitude. Intensity has units of power per unit area, or watts/meter^2 (W/m^2).

The human ear can detect sounds with an intensity as low as 10^{-12} W/m^2 and as high as 1 W/m^2 (and even higher, although above this it is painful). This is an incredibly wide range of intensity, spanning a factor of 10^{12} from lowest to highest. Presumably because of this wide range, what we perceive as loudness is not directly proportional to the intensity. To produce a sound that sounds about twice as loud requires a sound wave that has about 10 times the intensity. This is roughly valid at any sound level for frequencies near the middle of the audible range. For example, a sound wave of intensity 10^{-2} W/m^2 sounds to an average human being like it is about twice as loud as one whose intensity is 10^{-3} W/m^2, and four times as loud as 10^{-4} W/m^2.

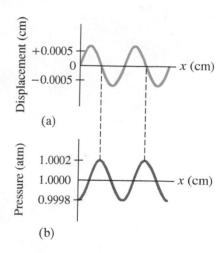

FIGURE 16–3 Representation of a sound wave in space at a given instant in terms of (a) displacement, and (b) pressure.

FIGURE 16–4 Longitudinal wave in a fluid moves to the right. A thin layer of fluid, in a thin cylinder of area S and thickness Δx, changes in volume as a result of pressure variation as the wave passes. At the moment shown, the pressure will increase as the wave moves to the right, so the thickness of our layer will decrease, by an amount ΔD.

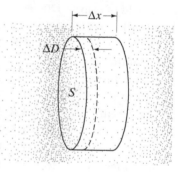

PHYSICS APPLIED
Wide range of human hearing

Sound Level

Because of this relationship between the subjective sensation of loudness and the physically measurable quantity "intensity," sound intensity levels are usually specified on a logarithmic scale. The unit on this scale is a **bel**, after the inventor Alexander Graham Bell, or much more commonly, the **decibel** (dB), which is $\frac{1}{10}$ bel (10 dB = 1 bel). The **sound level**, β, of any sound is defined in terms of its intensity, I, as

$$\beta \text{ (in dB)} = 10 \log \frac{I}{I_0}, \qquad \qquad \text{(16–6)}$$

where I_0 is the intensity of a chosen reference level, and the logarithm is to the base 10. I_0 is usually taken as the minimum intensity audible to a good ear—the "threshold of hearing," which is $I_0 = 1.0 \times 10^{-12} \text{ W/m}^2$. Thus, for example, the sound level of a sound whose intensity $I = 1.0 \times 10^{-10} \text{ W/m}^2$ will be

$$\beta = 10 \log \left(\frac{1.0 \times 10^{-10} \text{ W/m}^2}{1.0 \times 10^{-12} \text{ W/m}^2} \right) = 10 \log 100 = 20 \text{ dB},$$

since log 100 is equal to 2.0. (Appendix A has a brief review of logarithms.) Notice that the sound level at the threshold of hearing is 0 dB. That is, $\beta = 10 \log 10^{-12}/10^{-12} = 10 \log 1 = 0$ since $\log 1 = 0$. Notice too that an increase in intensity by a factor of 10 corresponds to a sound level increase of 10 dB. An increase in intensity by a factor of 100 corresponds to a sound level increase of 20 dB. Thus a 50-dB sound is 100 times more intense than a 30-dB sound, and so on.

Intensities and sound levels for a number of common sounds are listed in Table 16–2.

⚠️ **CAUTION**

0 dB does not mean zero intensity

TABLE 16–2
Intensity of Various Sounds

Source of the Sound	Sound Level (dB)	Intensity (W/m²)
Jet plane at 30 m	140	100
Threshold of pain	120	1
Loud rock concert	120	1
Siren at 30 m	100	1×10^{-2}
Truck traffic	90	1×10^{-3}
Busy street traffic	80	1×10^{-4}
Noisy restaurant	70	1×10^{-5}
Talk, at 50 cm	65	3×10^{-6}
Quiet radio	40	1×10^{-8}
Whisper	30	1×10^{-9}
Rustle of leaves	10	1×10^{-11}
Threshold of hearing	0	1×10^{-12}

EXAMPLE 16–3 **Sound intensity on the street.** At a busy street corner, the sound level is 75 dB. What is the intensity of sound there?

APPROACH We have to solve Eq. 16–6 for intensity I, remembering that $I_0 = 1.0 \times 10^{-12} \text{ W/m}^2$.

SOLUTION From Eq. 16–6

$$\log \frac{I}{I_0} = \frac{\beta}{10},$$

so

$$\frac{I}{I_0} = 10^{\beta/10}.$$

With $\beta = 75$, then

$$I = I_0 10^{\beta/10} = (1.0 \times 10^{-12} \text{ W/m}^2)(10^{7.5}) = 3.2 \times 10^{-5} \text{ W/m}^2.$$

NOTE Recall that $x = \log y$ is the same as $y = 10^x$ (Appendix A).

🚶 **PHYSICS APPLIED**

Loudspeaker response ($\pm 3 \, dB$)

EXAMPLE 16–4 **Loudspeaker response.** A high-quality loudspeaker is advertised to reproduce, at full volume, frequencies from 30 Hz to 18,000 Hz with uniform sound level ± 3 dB. That is, over this frequency range, the sound level output does not vary by more than 3 dB for a given input level. By what factor does the intensity change for the maximum change of 3 dB in output sound level?

APPROACH Let us call the average intensity I_1 and the average sound level β_1. Then the maximum intensity, I_2, corresponds to a level $\beta_2 = \beta_1 + 3$ dB. We then use the relation between intensity and sound level, Eq. 16–6.

SOLUTION Equation 16–6 gives

$$\beta_2 - \beta_1 = 10 \log \frac{I_2}{I_0} - 10 \log \frac{I_1}{I_0}$$

$$3 \text{ dB} = 10 \left(\log \frac{I_2}{I_0} - \log \frac{I_1}{I_0} \right)$$

$$= 10 \log \frac{I_2}{I_1}$$

because $(\log a - \log b) = \log a/b$ (see Appendix A). This last equation gives

$$\log \frac{I_2}{I_1} = 0.30,$$

or

$$\frac{I_2}{I_1} = 10^{0.30} = 2.0.$$

So $\pm 3 \text{ dB}$ corresponds to a doubling or halving of the intensity.

It is worth noting that a sound-level difference of 3 dB (which corresponds to a doubled intensity, as we just saw) corresponds to only a very small change in the subjective sensation of apparent loudness. Indeed, the average human can distinguish a difference in sound level of only about 1 or 2 dB.

EXERCISE B If an increase of 3 dB means "twice as intense," what does an increase of 6 dB mean?

CONCEPTUAL EXAMPLE 16–5 **Trumpet players.** A trumpeter plays at a sound level of 75 dB. Three equally loud trumpet players join in. What is the new sound level?

RESPONSE The intensity of four trumpets is four times the intensity of one trumpet $(= I_1)$ or $4I_1$. The sound level of the four trumpets would be

$$\beta = 10 \log \frac{4I_1}{I_0} = 10 \log 4 + 10 \log \frac{I_1}{I_0}$$

$$= 6.0 \text{ dB} + 75 \text{ dB} = 81 \text{ dB}.$$

EXERCISE C From Table 16–2, we see that ordinary conversation corresponds to a sound level of about 65 dB. If two people are talking at once, the sound level is (a) 65 dB, (b) 68 dB, (c) 75 dB, (d) 130 dB, (e) 62 dB.

Normally, the loudness or intensity of a sound decreases as you get farther from the source of the sound. In interior rooms, this effect is altered because of reflections from the walls. However, if a source is in the open so that sound can radiate out freely in all directions, the intensity decreases as the inverse square of the distance,

$$I \propto \frac{1}{r^2},$$

as we saw in Section 15–3. Over large distances, the intensity decreases faster than $1/r^2$ because some of the energy is transferred into irregular motion of air molecules. This loss happens more for higher frequencies, so any sound of mixed frequencies will be less "bright" at a distance.

FIGURE 16–5 Example 16–6. Airport worker with sound-intensity-reducing ear covers (headphones).

EXAMPLE 16–6 **Airplane roar.** The sound level measured 30 m from a jet plane is 140 dB. What is the sound level at 300 m? (Ignore reflections from the ground.)

APPROACH Given the sound level, we can determine the intensity at 30 m using Eq. 16–6. Because intensity decreases as the square of the distance, ignoring reflections, we can find I at 300 m and again apply Eq. 16–6 to obtain the sound level.

SOLUTION The intensity I at 30 m is

$$140\,\text{dB} = 10\log\left(\frac{I}{10^{-12}\,\text{W/m}^2}\right)$$

or

$$14 = \log\left(\frac{I}{10^{-12}\,\text{W/m}^2}\right).$$

We raise both sides of this equation to the power 10 (recall $10^{\log x} = x$) and have

$$10^{14} = \frac{I}{10^{-12}\,\text{W/m}^2},$$

so $I = (10^{14})(10^{-12}\,\text{W/m}^2) = 10^2\,\text{W/m}^2$. At 300 m, 10 times as far, the intensity will be $\left(\frac{1}{10}\right)^2 = 1/100$ as much, or $1\,\text{W/m}^2$. Hence, the sound level is

$$\beta = 10\log\left(\frac{1\,\text{W/m}^2}{10^{-12}\,\text{W/m}^2}\right) = 120\,\text{dB}.$$

Even at 300 m, the sound is at the threshold of pain. This is why workers at airports wear ear covers to protect their ears from damage (Fig. 16–5).

NOTE Here is a simpler approach that avoids Eq. 16–6. Because the intensity decreases as the square of the distance, at 10 times the distance the intensity decreases by $\left(\frac{1}{10}\right)^2 = \frac{1}{100}$. We can use the result that 10 dB corresponds to an intensity change by a factor of 10 (see text just before Example 16–3). Then an intensity change by a factor of 100 corresponds to a sound-level change of $(2)(10\,\text{dB}) = 20\,\text{dB}$. This confirms our result above: $140\,\text{dB} - 20\,\text{dB} = 120\,\text{dB}$.

Intensity Related to Amplitude

The intensity I of a wave is proportional to the square of the wave amplitude, as we saw in Chapter 15. We can therefore relate the amplitude quantitatively to the intensity I or level β, as the following Example shows.

EXAMPLE 16–7 **How tiny the displacement is.** (a) Calculate the displacement of air molecules for a sound having a frequency of 1000 Hz at the threshold of hearing. (b) Determine the maximum pressure variation in such a sound wave.

APPROACH In Section 15–3 we found a relation between intensity I and displacement amplitude A of a wave, Eq. 15–7. The amplitude of oscillation of air molecules is what we want to solve for, given the intensity. The pressure is found from Eq. 16–5.

SOLUTION (a) At the threshold of hearing, $I = 1.0 \times 10^{-12}\,\text{W/m}^2$ (Table 16–2). We solve for the amplitude A in Eq. 15–7:

$$A = \frac{1}{\pi f}\sqrt{\frac{I}{2\rho v}}$$

$$= \frac{1}{(3.14)(1.0 \times 10^3\,\text{s}^{-1})}\sqrt{\frac{1.0 \times 10^{-12}\,\text{W/m}^2}{(2)(1.29\,\text{kg/m}^3)(343\,\text{m/s})}}$$

$$= 1.1 \times 10^{-11}\,\text{m},$$

where we have taken the density of air to be $1.29\,\text{kg/m}^3$ and the speed of sound in air (assumed 20°C) as 343 m/s.

NOTE We see how incredibly sensitive the human ear is: it can detect displacements of air molecules which are actually less than the diameter of atoms (about $10^{-10}\,\text{m}$).

(b) Now we are dealing with sound as a pressure wave (Section 16–2). From Eq. 16–5,

$$\Delta P_M = 2\pi \rho v A f$$
$$= 2\pi(1.29\,\text{kg/m}^3)(343\,\text{m/s})(1.1 \times 10^{-11}\,\text{m})(1.0 \times 10^3\,\text{s}^{-1}) = 3.1 \times 10^{-5}\,\text{Pa}$$

or 3.1×10^{-10} atm. Again we see that the human ear is incredibly sensitive.

By combining Eqs. 15–7 and 16–5, we can write the intensity in terms of the pressure amplitude, ΔP_M:

$$I = 2\pi^2 v \rho f^2 A^2 = 2\pi^2 v \rho f^2 \left(\frac{\Delta P_M}{2\pi \rho v f} \right)^2$$

$$I = \frac{(\Delta P_M)^2}{2 v \rho}. \tag{16–7}$$

The intensity, when given in terms of pressure amplitude, thus does not depend on frequency.

The Ear's Response

The ear is not equally sensitive to all frequencies. To hear the same loudness for sounds of different frequencies requires different intensities. Studies averaged over large numbers of people have produced the curves shown in Fig. 16–6. On this graph, each curve represents sounds that seemed to be equally loud. The number labeling each curve represents the **loudness level** (the units are called *phons*), which is numerically equal to the sound level in dB at 1000 Hz. For example, the curve labeled 40 represents sounds that are heard by an average person to have the same loudness as a 1000-Hz sound with a sound level of 40 dB. From this 40-phon curve, we see that a 100-Hz tone must be at a level of about 62 dB to be perceived as loud as a 1000-Hz tone of only 40 dB.

The lowest curve in Fig. 16–6 (labeled 0) represents the sound level, as a function of frequency, for the *threshold of hearing*, the softest sound that is just audible by a very good ear. Note that the ear is most sensitive to sounds of frequency between 2000 and 4000 Hz, which are common in speech and music. Note too that whereas a 1000-Hz sound is audible at a level of 0 dB, a 100-Hz sound must be nearly 40 dB to be heard. The top curve in Fig. 16–6, labeled 120 phons, represents the *threshold of pain*. Sounds above this level can actually be felt and cause pain.

Figure 16–6 shows that at lower sound levels, our ears are less sensitive to the high and low frequencies relative to middle frequencies. The "loudness" control on some stereo systems is intended to compensate for this low-volume insensitivity. As the volume is turned down, the loudness control boosts the high and low frequencies relative to the middle frequencies so that the sound will have a more "normal-sounding" frequency balance. Many listeners, however, find the sound more pleasing or natural without the loudness control.

FIGURE 16–6 Sensitivity of the human ear as a function of frequency (see text). Note that the frequency scale is "logarithmic" in order to cover a wide range of frequencies.

16–4 Sources of Sound: Vibrating Strings and Air Columns

The source of any sound is a vibrating object. Almost any object can vibrate and hence be a source of sound. We now discuss some simple sources of sound, particularly musical instruments. In musical instruments, the source is set into vibration by striking, plucking, bowing, or blowing. Standing waves are produced and the source vibrates at its natural resonant frequencies. The vibrating source is in contact with the air (or other medium) and pushes on it to produce sound waves that travel outward. The frequencies of the waves are the same as those of the source, but the speed and wavelengths can be different. A drum has a stretched membrane that vibrates. Xylophones and marimbas have metal or wood bars that can be set into vibration. Bells, cymbals, and gongs also make use of a vibrating metal. Many instruments make use of vibrating strings, such as the violin, guitar, and piano, or make use of vibrating columns of air, such as the flute, trumpet, and pipe organ. We have already seen that the pitch of a pure sound is determined by the frequency. Typical frequencies for musical notes on the "equally tempered chromatic scale" are given in Table 16–3 for the octave beginning with middle C. Note that one octave corresponds to a doubling of frequency. For example, middle C has frequency of 262 Hz whereas C′ (C above middle C) has twice that frequency, 524 Hz. [Middle C is the C or "do" note at the middle of a piano keyboard.]

TABLE 16–3 Equally Tempered Chromatic Scale[†]

Note	Frequency (Hz)
C	262
C♯ or D♭	277
D	294
D♯ or E♭	311
E	330
F	349
F♯ or G♭	370
G	392
G♯ or A♭	415
A	440
A♯ or B♭	466
B	494
C′	524

[†]Only one octave is included.

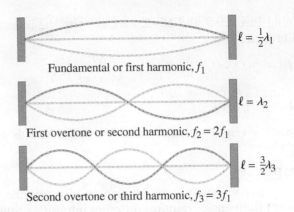

$\ell = \frac{1}{2}\lambda_1$

Fundamental or first harmonic, f_1

$\ell = \lambda_2$

First overtone or second harmonic, $f_2 = 2f_1$

$\ell = \frac{3}{2}\lambda_3$

Second overtone or third harmonic, $f_3 = 3f_1$

FIGURE 16–7 Standing waves on a string—only the lowest three frequencies are shown.

Stringed Instruments

(a)

(b)

FIGURE 16–8 The wavelength of (a) an unfingered string is longer than that of (b) a fingered string. Hence, the frequency of the fingered string is higher. Only one string is shown on this guitar, and only the simplest standing wave, the fundamental, is shown.

We saw in Chapter 15, Fig. 15–26b, how standing waves are established on a string, and we show this again here in Fig. 16–7. Such standing waves are the basis for all stringed instruments. The pitch is normally determined by the lowest resonant frequency, the **fundamental**, which corresponds to nodes occurring only at the ends. The string vibrating up and down as a whole corresponds to a half wavelength as shown at the top of Fig. 16–7; so the wavelength of the fundamental on the string is equal to twice the length of the string. Therefore, the fundamental frequency is $f_1 = v/\lambda = v/2\ell$, where v is the velocity of the wave on the string (*not* in the air). The possible frequencies for standing waves on a stretched string are whole-number multiples of the fundamental frequency:

$$f_n = nf_1 = n\frac{v}{2\ell}, \qquad n = 1, 2, 3, \cdots$$

where $n = 1$ refers to the fundamental and $n = 2, 3, \cdots$ are the overtones. All of the standing waves, $n = 1, 2, 3, \cdots$, are called harmonics,[†] as we saw in Section 15–9.

When a finger is placed on the string of a guitar or violin, the effective length of the string is shortened. So its fundamental frequency, and pitch, is higher since the wavelength of the fundamental is shorter (Fig. 16–8). The strings on a guitar or violin are all the same length. They sound at a different pitch because the strings have different mass per unit length, μ, which affects the velocity on the string, Eq. 15–2,

$$v = \sqrt{F_T/\mu}. \qquad \text{[stretched string]}$$

Thus the velocity on a heavier string is lower and the frequency will be lower for the same wavelength. The tension F_T may also be different. Adjusting the tension is the means for tuning the pitch of each string. In pianos and harps the strings are of different lengths. For the lower notes the strings are not only longer, but heavier as well, and the reason is illustrated in the following Example.

EXAMPLE 16–8 **Piano strings.** The highest key on a piano corresponds to a frequency about 150 times that of the lowest key. If the string for the highest note is 5.0 cm long, how long would the string for the lowest note have to be if it had the same mass per unit length and was under the same tension?

APPROACH Since $v = \sqrt{F_T/\mu}$, the velocity would be the same on each string. So the frequency is inversely proportional to the length ℓ of the string ($f = v/\lambda = v/2\ell$).

SOLUTION We can write, for the fundamental frequencies of each string, the ratio

$$\frac{\ell_L}{\ell_H} = \frac{f_H}{f_L},$$

where the subscripts L and H refer to the lowest and highest notes, respectively. Thus $\ell_L = \ell_H(f_H/f_L) = (5.0\,\text{cm})(150) = 750\,\text{cm},$ or 7.5 m. This would be ridiculously long (≈ 25 ft) for a piano.

NOTE The longer strings of lower frequency are made heavier, of higher mass per unit length, so even on grand pianos the strings are less than 3 m long.

[†]When the resonant frequencies above the fundamental (that is, the overtones) are integral multiples of the fundamental, as here, they are called harmonics. But if the overtones are not integral multiples of the fundamental, as is the case for a vibrating drumhead, for example, they are not harmonics.

EXERCISE D Two strings have the same length and tension, but one is more massive than the other. Which plays the higher note?

⚠ CAUTION

*Speed of standing wave on string
≠ speed of sound wave in air*

EXAMPLE 16–9 **Frequencies and wavelengths in the violin.** A 0.32-m-long violin string is tuned to play A above middle C at 440 Hz. (*a*) What is the wavelength of the fundamental string vibration, and (*b*) what are the frequency and wavelength of the sound wave produced? (*c*) Why is there a difference?

APPROACH The wavelength of the fundamental string vibration equals twice the length of the string (Fig. 16–7). As the string vibrates, it pushes on the air, which is thus forced to oscillate at the same frequency as the string.

SOLUTION (*a*) From Fig. 16–7 the wavelength of the fundamental is

$$\lambda = 2\ell = 2(0.32 \text{ m}) = 0.64 \text{ m} = 64 \text{ cm}.$$

This is the wavelength of the standing wave on the string.

(*b*) The sound wave that travels outward in the air (to reach our ears) has the same frequency, 440 Hz. Its wavelength is

$$\lambda = \frac{v}{f} = \frac{343 \text{ m/s}}{440 \text{ Hz}} = 0.78 \text{ m} = 78 \text{ cm},$$

where v is the speed of sound in air (assumed at 20°C), Section 16–1.

(*c*) The wavelength of the sound wave is different from that of the standing wave on the string because the speed of sound in air (343 m/s at 20°C) is different from the speed of the wave on the string ($= f\lambda = 440 \text{ Hz} \times 0.64 \text{ m} = 280 \text{ m/s}$) which depends on the tension in the string and its mass per unit length.

NOTE The frequencies on the string and in the air are the same: the string and air are in contact, and the string "forces" the air to vibrate at the same frequency. But the wavelengths are different because the wave speed on the string is different than that in air.

Stringed instruments would not be very loud if they relied on their vibrating strings to produce the sound waves since the strings are too thin to compress and expand much air. Stringed instruments therefore make use of a kind of mechanical amplifier known as a *sounding board* (piano) or *sounding box* (guitar, violin), which acts to amplify the sound by putting a greater surface area in contact with the air (Fig. 16–9). When the strings are set into vibration, the sounding board or box is set into vibration as well. Since it has much greater area in contact with the air, it can produce a more intense sound wave. On an electric guitar, the sounding box is not so important since the vibrations of the strings are amplified electronically.

Wind Instruments

Instruments such as woodwinds, the brasses, and the pipe organ produce sound from the vibrations of standing waves in a column of air within a tube (Fig. 16–10). Standing waves can occur in the air of any cavity, but the frequencies present are complicated for any but very simple shapes such as the uniform, narrow tube of a flute or an organ pipe. In some instruments, a vibrating reed or the vibrating lip of the player helps to set up vibrations of the air column. In others, a stream of air is directed against one edge of the opening or mouthpiece, leading to turbulence which sets up the vibrations. Because of the disturbance, whatever its source, the air within the tube vibrates with a variety of frequencies, but only frequencies that correspond to standing waves will persist.

For a string fixed at both ends, Fig. 16–7, we saw that the standing waves have nodes (no movement) at the two ends, and one or more antinodes (large amplitude of vibration) in between. A node separates successive antinodes. The lowest-frequency standing wave, the *fundamental*, corresponds to a single antinode. The higher-frequency standing waves are called **overtones** or **harmonics**, as we saw in Section 15–9. Specifically, the first harmonic is the fundamental, the second harmonic (= first overtone) has twice the frequency of the fundamental, and so on.

(a)

(b)

FIGURE 16–9 (a) Piano, showing sounding board to which the strings are attached; (b) sounding box (guitar).

FIGURE 16–10 Wind instruments: flute (left) and clarinet.

(a) Displacement of air

First harmonic = fundamental
$$\ell = \tfrac{1}{2}\lambda_1$$
$$f_1 = \frac{v}{2\ell}$$
←[motion of air molecules]

Second harmonic
$$\ell = \lambda_2$$
$$f_2 = \frac{v}{\ell} = 2f_1$$

Overtones

Third harmonic
$$\ell = \tfrac{3}{2}\lambda_3$$
$$f_3 = \frac{3v}{2\ell} = 3f_1$$

(b) Pressure variation in the air

FIGURE 16–11 Graphs of the three simplest modes of vibration (standing waves) for a uniform tube open at both ends ("open tube"). These simplest modes of vibration are graphed in (a), on the left, in terms of the motion of the air (displacement), and in (b), on the right, in terms of air pressure. Each graph shows the wave format at two times, A and B, a half period apart. The actual motion of molecules for one case, the fundamental, is shown just below the tube at top left.

PHYSICS APPLIED
Wind instruments

The situation is similar for a column of air in a tube of uniform diameter, but we must remember that it is now air itself that is vibrating. We can describe the waves either in terms of the flow of the air—that is, in terms of the *displacement* of air—or in terms of the *pressure* in the air (see Figs. 16–2 and 16–3). In terms of displacement, the air at the closed end of a tube is a displacement node since the air is not free to move there, whereas near the open end of a tube there will be an antinode because the air can move freely in and out. The air within the tube vibrates in the form of longitudinal standing waves. The possible modes of vibration for a tube open at both ends (called an **open tube**) are shown graphically in Fig. 16–11. They are shown for a tube that is open at one end but closed at the other (called a **closed tube**) in Fig. 16–12. [A tube closed at *both* ends, having no connection to the outside air, would be useless as an instrument.] The graphs in part (a) of each Figure (left-hand sides) represent the displacement amplitude of the vibrating air in the tube. Note that these are graphs, and that the air molecules themselves oscillate *horizontally*, parallel to the tube length, as shown by the small arrows in the top diagram of Fig. 16–11a (on the left). The exact position of the antinode near the open end of a tube depends on the diameter of the tube, but if the diameter is small compared to the length, which is the usual case, the antinode occurs very close to the end as shown. We assume this is the case in what follows. (The position of the antinode may also depend slightly on the wavelength and other factors.)

Let us look in detail at the open tube, in Fig. 16–11a, which might be an organ pipe or a flute. An open tube has displacement antinodes at both ends since the air is free to move at open ends. There must be at least one node within an open tube if there is to be a standing wave at all. A single node corresponds to the *fundamental frequency* of the tube. Since the distance between two successive nodes, or between two successive antinodes, is $\tfrac{1}{2}\lambda$, there is one-half of a wavelength within the length of the tube for the simplest case of the fundamental (top diagram in Fig. 16–11a): $\ell = \tfrac{1}{2}\lambda$, or $\lambda = 2\ell$. So the fundamental frequency is $f_1 = v/\lambda = v/2\ell$, where v is the velocity of sound in air (the air in the tube). The standing wave with two nodes is the *first overtone* or *second harmonic* and has half the wavelength ($\ell = \lambda$) and twice the frequency of the fundamental. Indeed, in a uniform tube open at both ends, the frequency of each overtone is an integral multiple of the fundamental frequency, as shown in Fig. 16–11a. This is just what is found for a string.

For a closed tube, shown in Fig. 16–12a, which could be an organ pipe, there is always a displacement node at the closed end (because the air is not free to move) and an antinode at the open end (where the air can move freely). Since the distance between a node and the nearest antinode is $\tfrac{1}{4}\lambda$, we see that the fundamental in a closed tube corresponds to only one-fourth of a wavelength within the length of the tube: $\ell = \lambda/4$, and $\lambda = 4\ell$. The fundamental frequency is thus $f_1 = v/4\ell$, or half that for an open pipe of the same length. There is another

TUBE CLOSED AT ONE END

(a) Displacement of air

First harmonic = fundamental
$\ell = \frac{1}{4}\lambda_1$
$f_1 = \frac{v}{4\ell}$

Third harmonic
$\ell = \frac{3}{4}\lambda_3$
$f_3 = \frac{3v}{4\ell} = 3f_1$

Fifth harmonic
$\ell = \frac{5}{4}\lambda_5$
$f_5 = \frac{5v}{4\ell} = 5f_1$

Overtones

(b) Pressure variation in the air

FIGURE 16–12 Modes of vibration (standing waves) for a tube closed at one end ("closed tube"). See caption for Fig. 16–11.

difference, for as we can see from Fig. 16–12a, only the odd harmonics are present in a closed tube: the overtones have frequencies equal to 3, 5, 7, ... times the fundamental frequency. There is no way for waves with 2, 4, 6, ... times the fundamental frequency to have a node at one end and an antinode at the other, and thus they cannot exist as standing waves in a closed tube.

Another way to analyze the vibrations in a uniform tube is to consider a description in terms of the *pressure* in the air, shown in part (b) of Figs. 16–11 and 16–12 (right-hand sides). Where the air in a wave is compressed, the pressure is higher, whereas in a wave expansion (or rarefaction), the pressure is less than normal. The open end of a tube is open to the atmosphere. Hence the pressure variation at an open end must be a *node*: the pressure does not alternate, but remains at the outside atmospheric pressure. If a tube has a closed end, the pressure at that closed end can readily alternate to be above or below atmospheric pressure. Hence there is a pressure *antinode* at a closed end of a tube. There can be pressure nodes and antinodes within the tube. Some of the possible vibrational modes in terms of pressure for an open tube are shown in Fig. 16–11b, and for a closed tube are shown in Fig. 16–12b.

EXAMPLE 16–10 **Organ pipes.** What will be the fundamental frequency and first three overtones for a 26-cm-long organ pipe at 20°C if it is (a) open and (b) closed?

APPROACH All our calculations can be based on Figs. 16–11a and 16–12a.

SOLUTION (a) For the open pipe, Fig. 16–11a, the fundamental frequency is

$$f_1 = \frac{v}{2\ell} = \frac{343 \text{ m/s}}{2(0.26 \text{ m})} = 660 \text{ Hz}.$$

The speed v is the speed of sound in air (the air vibrating in the pipe). The overtones include all harmonics: 1320 Hz, 1980 Hz, 2640 Hz, and so on.

(b) For a closed pipe, Fig. 16–12a, the fundamental frequency is

$$f_1 = \frac{v}{4\ell} = \frac{343 \text{ m/s}}{4(0.26 \text{ m})} = 330 \text{ Hz}.$$

Only odd harmonics are present: the first three overtones are 990 Hz, 1650 Hz, and 2310 Hz.

NOTE The closed pipe plays 330 Hz, which, from Table 16–3, is E above middle C, whereas the open pipe of the same length plays 660 Hz, an octave higher.

Pipe organs use both open and closed pipes, with lengths from a few centimeters to 5 m or more. A flute acts as an open tube, for it is open not only where you blow into it, but also at the opposite end. The different notes on a flute are obtained by shortening the length of the vibrating air column, by uncovering holes along the tube (so a displacement antinode can occur at the hole). The shorter the length of the vibrating air column, the higher the fundamental frequency.

Flute. A flute is designed to play middle C (262 Hz) as the fundamental frequency when all the holes are covered. Approximately how long should the distance be from the mouthpiece to the far end of the flute? (This is only approximate since the antinode does not occur precisely at the mouthpiece.) Assume the temperature is 20°C.

APPROACH When all holes are covered, the length of the vibrating air column is the full length. The speed of sound in air at 20°C is 343 m/s. Because a flute is open at both ends, we use Fig. 16–11: the fundamental frequency f_1 is related to the length ℓ of the vibrating air column by $f = v/2\ell$.

SOLUTION Solving for ℓ, we find

$$\ell = \frac{v}{2f} = \frac{343 \text{ m/s}}{2(262 \text{ s}^{-1})} = 0.655 \text{ m} \approx 0.66 \text{ m}.$$

EXERCISE E To see why players of wind instruments "warm up" their instruments (so they will be in tune), determine the fundamental frequency of the flute of Example 16–11 when all holes are covered and the temperature is 10°C instead of 20°C.

EXERCISE F Return to the Chapter-Opening Question, page 424, and answer it again now. Try to explain why you may have answered differently the first time.

*16–5 Quality of Sound, and Noise; Superposition

Whenever we hear a sound, particularly a musical sound, we are aware of its loudness, its pitch, and also of a third aspect called its *timbre* or "quality." For example, when a piano and then a flute play a note of the same loudness and pitch (say, middle C), there is a clear difference in the overall sound. We would never mistake a piano for a flute. This is what is meant by the timbre or *quality* of a sound. For musical instruments, the term *tone color* is also used.

Just as loudness and pitch can be related to physically measurable quantities, so too can quality. The quality of a sound depends on the presence of overtones—their number and their relative amplitudes. Generally, when a note is played on a musical instrument, the fundamental as well as overtones are present simultaneously. Figure 16–13 illustrates how the *principle of superposition* (Section 15–6) applies to three wave forms, in this case the fundamental and first two overtones (with particular amplitudes): they add together at each point to give a composite **waveform** (by which we mean the displacement as a function of position at a given time). Normally, more than two overtones are present. [Any complex wave can be analyzed into a superposition of sinusoidal waves of appropriate amplitudes, wavelengths, and frequencies—see Section 15–6. Such an analysis is called a *Fourier analysis*.]

The relative amplitudes of the overtones for a given note are different for different musical instruments, which is what gives each instrument its characteristic quality or timbre. A bar graph showing the relative amplitudes of the harmonics for a given note produced by an instrument is called a *sound spectrum*. Several typical examples for different musical instruments are shown in Fig. 16–14. The fundamental usually has the greatest amplitude, and its frequency is what is heard as the pitch.

The manner in which an instrument is played strongly influences the sound quality. Plucking a violin string, for example, makes a very different sound than pulling a bow across it. The sound spectrum at the very start (or end) of a note (as when a hammer strikes a piano string) can be very different from the subsequent sustained tone. This too affects the subjective tone quality of an instrument.

An ordinary sound, like that made by striking two stones together, is a noise that has a certain quality, but a clear pitch is not discernible. Such a noise is a mixture of many frequencies which bear little relation to one another. A sound spectrum made of that noise would not show discrete lines like those of Fig. 16–14. Instead it would show a continuous, or nearly continuous, spectrum of frequencies. Such a sound we call "noise" in comparison with the more harmonious sounds which contain frequencies that are simple multiples of the fundamental.

FIGURE 16–13 The displacements of the fundamental and first two overtones are added at each point to get the "sum," or composite waveform.

FIGURE 16–14 Sound spectra for different instruments. The spectra change when the instruments play different notes. The clarinet is a bit complicated: it acts like a closed tube at lower frequencies, having only odd harmonics, but at higher frequencies all harmonics occur as for an open tube.

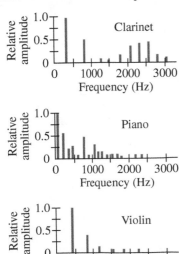

16–6 Interference of Sound Waves; Beats

Interference in Space

We saw in Section 15–8 that when two waves simultaneously pass through the same region of space, they interfere with one another. Interference also occurs with sound waves.

Consider two large loudspeakers, A and B, a distance d apart on the stage of an auditorium as shown in Fig. 16–15. Let us assume the two speakers are emitting sound waves of the same single frequency and that they are in phase: that is, when one speaker is forming a compression, so is the other. (We ignore reflections from walls, floor, etc.) The curved lines in the diagram represent the crests of sound waves from each speaker at one instant in time. We must remember that for a sound wave, a crest is a compression in the air whereas a trough—which falls between two crests—is a rarefaction. A human ear or detector at a point such as C, which is the same distance from each speaker, will experience a loud sound because the interference will be constructive—two crests reach it at one moment, two troughs reach it a moment later. On the other hand, at a point such as D in the diagram, little if any sound will be heard because destructive interference occurs—compressions of one wave meet rarefactions of the other and vice versa (see Fig. 15–24 and the related discussion on water waves in Section 15–8).

An analysis of this situation is perhaps clearer if we graphically represent the waveforms as in Fig. 16–16. In Fig. 16–16a, it can be seen that at point C, constructive interference occurs since both waves simultaneously have crests or simultaneously have troughs when they arrive at C. In Fig. 16–16b we see that, to reach point D, the wave from speaker B must travel a greater distance than the wave from A. Thus the wave from B lags behind that from A. In this diagram, point E is chosen so that the distance ED is equal to AD. Thus we see that if the distance BE is equal to precisely one-half the wavelength of the sound, the two waves will be exactly out of phase when they reach D, and destructive interference occurs. This then is the criterion for determining at what points destructive interference occurs: destructive interference occurs at any point whose distance from one speaker is one-half wavelength greater than its distance from the other speaker. Notice that if this extra distance (BE in Fig. 16–16b) is equal to a whole wavelength (or 2, 3, … wavelengths), then the two waves will be in phase and *constructive interference* occurs. If the distance BE equals $\frac{1}{2}, 1\frac{1}{2}, 2\frac{1}{2}, \ldots$ wavelengths, *destructive interference* occurs.

It is important to realize that a person at point D in Fig. 16–15 or 16–16 hears nothing at all (or nearly so), yet sound is coming from both speakers. Indeed, if one of the speakers is turned off, the sound from the other speaker will be clearly heard.

If a loudspeaker emits a whole range of frequencies, only specific wavelengths will destructively interfere completely at a given point.

EXAMPLE 16–12 **Loudspeakers' interference.** Two loudspeakers are 1.00 m apart. A person stands 4.00 m from one speaker. How far must this person be from the second speaker to detect destructive interference when the speakers emit an 1150-Hz sound? Assume the temperature is 20°C.

APPROACH To sense destructive interference, the person must be one-half wavelength closer to or farther from one speaker than from the other—that is, at a distance $= 4.00\,\text{m} \pm \lambda/2$. We can determine λ since we know f and v.

SOLUTION The speed of sound at 20°C is 343 m/s, so the wavelength of this sound is (Eq. 15–1)

$$\lambda = \frac{v}{f} = \frac{343\,\text{m/s}}{1150\,\text{Hz}} = 0.30\,\text{m}.$$

For destructive interference to occur, the person must be one-half wavelength farther from one loudspeaker than from the other, or 0.15 m. Thus the person must be 3.85 m or 4.15 m from the second speaker.

NOTE If the speakers are less than 0.15 m apart, there will be no point that is 0.15 m farther from one speaker than the other, and there will be no point where destructive interference could occur.

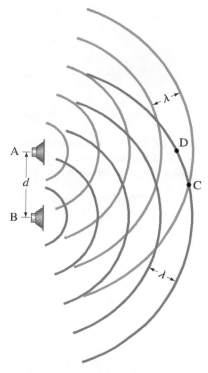

FIGURE 16–15 Sound waves from two loudspeakers interfere.

FIGURE 16–16 Sound waves of a single frequency from loudspeakers A and B (see Fig. 16–15) constructively interfere at C and destructively interfere at D. [Shown here are graphical representations, not the actual longitudinal sound waves.]

(a)

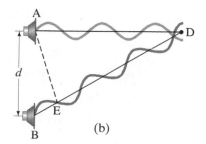

(b)

FIGURE 16–17 Beats occur as a result of the superposition of two sound waves of slightly different frequency.

Beats—Interference in Time

We have been discussing interference of sound waves that takes place in space. An interesting and important example of interference that occurs in time is the phenomenon known as **beats**: If two sources of sound—say, two tuning forks—are close in frequency but not exactly the same, sound waves from the two sources interfere with each other. The sound level at a given position alternately rises and falls in time, because the two waves are sometimes in phase and sometimes out of phase due to their different wavelengths. The regularly spaced intensity changes are called beats.

To see how beats arise, consider two equal-amplitude sound waves of frequency $f_A = 50\,\text{Hz}$ and $f_B = 60\,\text{Hz}$, respectively. In 1.00 s, the first source makes 50 vibrations whereas the second makes 60. We now examine the waves at one point in space equidistant from the two sources. The waveforms for each wave as a function of time, at a fixed position, are shown on the top graph of Fig. 16–17; the red line represents the 50-Hz wave, and the blue line represents the 60-Hz wave. The lower graph in Fig. 16–17 shows the sum of the two waves as a function of time. At time $t = 0$ the two waves are shown to be in phase and interfere constructively. Because the two waves vibrate at different rates, at time $t = 0.05\,\text{s}$ they are completely out of phase and interfere destructively. At $t = 0.10\,\text{s}$, they are again in phase and the resultant amplitude again is large. Thus the resultant amplitude is large every 0.10 s and drops drastically in between. This rising and falling of the intensity is what is heard as beats.[†] In this case the beats are 0.10 s apart. That is, the **beat frequency** is ten per second, or 10 Hz. This result, that the beat frequency equals the difference in frequency of the two waves, is valid in general, as we now show.

Let the two waves, of frequencies f_1 and f_2, be represented at a fixed point in space by

$$D_1 = A \sin 2\pi f_1 t$$

and

$$D_2 = A \sin 2\pi f_2 t.$$

The resultant displacement, by the principle of superposition, is

$$D = D_1 + D_2 = A(\sin 2\pi f_1 t + \sin 2\pi f_2 t).$$

Using the trigonometric identity $\sin\theta_1 + \sin\theta_2 = 2\sin\frac{1}{2}(\theta_1 + \theta_2)\cos\frac{1}{2}(\theta_1 - \theta_2)$, we have

$$D = \left[2A\cos 2\pi\left(\frac{f_1 - f_2}{2}\right)t\right]\sin 2\pi\left(\frac{f_1 + f_2}{2}\right)t. \qquad (16\text{–}8)$$

We can interpret Eq. 16–8 as follows. The superposition of the two waves results in a wave that vibrates at the average frequency of the two components, $(f_1 + f_2)/2$. This vibration has an amplitude given by the expression in brackets, and this amplitude varies in time, from zero to a maximum of $2A$ (the sum of the separate amplitudes), with a frequency of $(f_1 - f_2)/2$. A beat occurs whenever $\cos 2\pi[(f_1 - f_2)/2]t$ equals $+1$ or -1 (see Fig. 16–17); that is, two beats occur per cycle, so the beat frequency is twice $(f_1 - f_2)/2$ which is just $f_1 - f_2$, the difference in frequency of the component waves.

[†]Beats will be heard even if the amplitudes are not equal, as long as the difference in amplitude is not great.

The phenomenon of beats can occur with any kind of wave and is a very sensitive method for comparing frequencies. For example, to tune a piano, a piano tuner listens for beats produced between his standard tuning fork and that of a particular string on the piano, and knows it is in tune when the beats disappear. The members of an orchestra tune up by listening for beats between their instruments and that of a standard tone (usually A above middle C at 440 Hz) produced by a piano or an oboe. A beat frequency is perceived as an intensity modulation (a wavering between loud and soft) for beat frequencies below 20 Hz or so, and as a separate low tone for higher beat frequencies (audible if the tones are strong enough).

PHYSICS APPLIED
Tuning a piano

EXAMPLE 16–13 **Beats.** A tuning fork produces a steady 400-Hz tone. When this tuning fork is struck and held near a vibrating guitar string, twenty beats are counted in five seconds. What are the possible frequencies produced by the guitar string?

APPROACH For beats to occur, the string must vibrate at a frequency different from 400 Hz by whatever the beat frequency is.

SOLUTION The beat frequency is

$$f_{beat} = 20 \text{ vibrations}/5\text{ s} = 4\text{ Hz}.$$

This is the difference of the frequencies of the two waves. Because one wave is known to be 400 Hz, the other must be either 404 Hz or 396 Hz.

16–7 Doppler Effect

You may have noticed that you hear the pitch of the siren on a speeding fire truck drop abruptly as it passes you. Or you may have noticed the change in pitch of a blaring horn on a fast-moving car as it passes by you. The pitch of the engine noise of a racecar changes as the car passes an observer. When a source of sound is moving toward an observer, the pitch the observer hears is higher than when the source is at rest; and when the source is traveling away from the observer, the pitch is lower. This phenomenon is known as the **Doppler effect**[†] and occurs for all types of waves. Let us now see why it occurs, and calculate the difference between the perceived and source frequencies when there is relative motion between source and observer.

Consider the siren of a fire truck at rest, which is emitting sound of a particular frequency in all directions as shown in Fig. 16–18a. The sound waves are moving at the speed of sound in air, v_{snd}, which is independent of the velocity of the source or observer. If our source, the fire truck, is moving, the siren emits sound at the same frequency as it does at rest. But the sound wavefronts it emits forward, in front of it, are closer together than when the fire truck is at rest, as shown in Fig. 16–18b. This is because the fire truck, as it moves, is "chasing" the previously emitted wavefronts, and emits each crest closer to the previous one. Thus an observer on the sidewalk in front of the truck will detect more wave crests passing per second, so the frequency heard is higher. The wavefronts emitted behind the truck, on the other hand, are farther apart than when the truck is at rest because the truck is speeding away from them. Hence, fewer wave crests per second pass by an observer behind the moving truck (Fig. 16–18b) and the perceived pitch is lower.

(a) At rest

(b) Fire truck moving

FIGURE 16–18 (a) Both observers on the sidewalk hear the same frequency from a fire truck at rest. (b) Doppler effect: observer toward whom the fire truck moves hears a higher-frequency sound, and observer behind the fire truck hears a lower-frequency sound.

[†]After J. C. Doppler (1803–1853).

(a) Source fixed

(b) Source moving

FIGURE 16–19 Determination of the frequency shift in the Doppler effect (see text). The red dot is the source.

We can calculate the frequency shift perceived by making use of Fig. 16–19, and we assume the air (or other medium) is at rest in our reference frame. (The stationary observer is off to the right.) In Fig. 16–19a, the source of the sound is shown as a red dot, and is at rest. Two successive wave crests are shown, the second of which has just been emitted and so is still near the source. The distance between these crests is λ, the wavelength. If the frequency of the source is f, then the time between emissions of wave crests is

$$T = \frac{1}{f} = \frac{\lambda}{v_{\text{snd}}}.$$

In Fig. 16–19b, the source is moving with a velocity v_{source} toward the observer. In a time T (as just defined), the first wave crest has moved a distance $d = v_{\text{snd}} T = \lambda$, where v_{snd} is the velocity of the sound wave in air (which is the same whether the source is moving or not). In this same time, the source has moved a distance $d_{\text{source}} = v_{\text{source}} T$. Then the distance between successive wave crests, which is the wavelength λ' the observer will perceive, is

$$\begin{aligned} \lambda' &= d - d_{\text{source}} \\ &= \lambda - v_{\text{source}} T \\ &= \lambda - v_{\text{source}} \frac{\lambda}{v_{\text{snd}}} \\ &= \lambda \left(1 - \frac{v_{\text{source}}}{v_{\text{snd}}} \right). \end{aligned}$$

We subtract λ from both sides of this equation and find that the shift in wavelength, $\Delta\lambda$, is

$$\Delta\lambda = \lambda' - \lambda = -\lambda \frac{v_{\text{source}}}{v_{\text{snd}}}.$$

So the shift in wavelength is directly proportional to the source speed v_{source}. The frequency f' that will be perceived by our stationary observer on the ground is given by

$$f' = \frac{v_{\text{snd}}}{\lambda'} = \frac{v_{\text{snd}}}{\lambda \left(1 - \dfrac{v_{\text{source}}}{v_{\text{snd}}} \right)}.$$

Since $v_{\text{snd}}/\lambda = f$, then

$$f' = \frac{f}{\left(1 - \dfrac{v_{\text{source}}}{v_{\text{snd}}} \right)}. \qquad \begin{bmatrix} \text{source moving toward} \\ \text{stationary observer} \end{bmatrix} \quad \textbf{(16–9a)}$$

Because the denominator is less than 1, the observed frequency f' is greater than the source frequency f. That is, $f' > f$. For example, if a source emits a sound of frequency 400 Hz when at rest, then when the source moves toward a fixed observer with a speed of 30 m/s, the observer hears a frequency (at 20°C) of

$$f' = \frac{400\,\text{Hz}}{1 - \dfrac{30\,\text{m/s}}{343\,\text{m/s}}} = 438\,\text{Hz}.$$

Now consider a source moving *away* from the stationary observer at a speed v_{source}. Using the same arguments as above, the wavelength λ' perceived by our observer will have the minus sign on d_{source} (second equation on this page) changed to plus:

$$\begin{aligned} \lambda' &= d + d_{\text{source}} \\ &= \lambda \left(1 + \frac{v_{\text{source}}}{v_{\text{snd}}} \right). \end{aligned}$$

The difference between the observed and emitted wavelengths will be $\Delta\lambda = \lambda' - \lambda = +\lambda(v_{\text{source}}/v_{\text{snd}})$. The observed frequency of the wave, $f' = v_{\text{snd}}/\lambda'$, will be

$$f' = \frac{f}{\left(1 + \dfrac{v_{\text{source}}}{v_{\text{snd}}} \right)}. \qquad \begin{bmatrix} \text{source moving away from} \\ \text{stationary observer} \end{bmatrix} \quad \textbf{(16–9b)}$$

If a source emitting at 400 Hz is moving away from a fixed observer at 30 m/s, the observer hears a frequency $f' = (400\,\text{Hz})/[1 + (30\,\text{m/s})/(343\,\text{m/s})] = 368\,\text{Hz}$.

The Doppler effect also occurs when the source is at rest and the observer is in motion. If the observer is traveling *toward* the source, the pitch heard is higher than that of the emitted source frequency. If the observer is traveling *away* from the source, the pitch heard is lower. Quantitatively the change in frequency is different than for the case of a moving source. With a fixed source and a moving observer, the distance between wave crests, the wavelength λ, is not changed. But the velocity of the crests with respect to the observer *is* changed. If the observer is moving toward the source, Fig. 16–20, the speed v' of the waves relative to the observer is a simple addition of velocities: $v' = v_{snd} + v_{obs}$, where v_{snd} is the velocity of sound in air (we assume the air is still) and v_{obs} is the velocity of the observer. Hence, the frequency heard is

$$f' = \frac{v'}{\lambda} = \frac{v_{snd} + v_{obs}}{\lambda}.$$

Because $\lambda = v_{snd}/f$, then

$$f' = \frac{(v_{snd} + v_{obs})f}{v_{snd}},$$

or

$$f' = \left(1 + \frac{v_{obs}}{v_{snd}}\right)f. \qquad \begin{bmatrix} \text{observer moving toward} \\ \text{stationary source} \end{bmatrix} \quad \textbf{(16–10a)}$$

If the observer is moving away from the source, the relative velocity is $v' = v_{snd} - v_{obs}$, so

$$f' = \left(1 - \frac{v_{obs}}{v_{snd}}\right)f. \qquad \begin{bmatrix} \text{observer moving away} \\ \text{from stationary source} \end{bmatrix} \quad \textbf{(16–10b)}$$

EXAMPLE 16–14 **A moving siren.** The siren of a police car at rest emits at a predominant frequency of 1600 Hz. What frequency will you hear if you are at rest and the police car moves at 25.0 m/s (*a*) toward you, and (*b*) away from you?

APPROACH The observer is fixed, and the source moves, so we use Eqs. 16–9. The frequency you (the observer) hear is the emitted frequency f divided by the factor $(1 \pm v_{source}/v_{snd})$ where v_{source} is the speed of the police car. Use the minus sign when the car moves toward you (giving a higher frequency); use the plus sign when the car moves away from you (lower frequency).

SOLUTION (*a*) The car is moving toward you, so (Eq. 16–9a)

$$f' = \frac{f}{\left(1 - \dfrac{v_{source}}{v_{snd}}\right)} = \frac{1600\ \text{Hz}}{\left(1 - \dfrac{25.0\ \text{m/s}}{343\ \text{m/s}}\right)} = 1726\ \text{Hz} \approx 1730\ \text{Hz}.$$

(*b*) The car is moving away from you, so (Eq. 16–9b)

$$f' = \frac{f}{\left(1 + \dfrac{v_{source}}{v_{snd}}\right)} = \frac{1600\ \text{Hz}}{\left(1 + \dfrac{25.0\ \text{m/s}}{343\ \text{m/s}}\right)} = 1491\ \text{Hz} \approx 1490\ \text{Hz}.$$

EXERCISE G Suppose the police car of Example 16–14 is at rest and emits at 1600 Hz. What frequency would you hear if you were moving at 25.0 m/s (*a*) toward it, and (*b*) away from it?

When a sound wave is reflected from a moving obstacle, the frequency of the reflected wave will, because of the Doppler effect, be different from that of the incident wave. This is illustrated in the following Example.

EXAMPLE 16–15 **Two Doppler shifts.** A 5000-Hz sound wave is emitted by a stationary source. This sound wave reflects from an object moving 3.50 m/s toward the source (Fig. 16–21). What is the frequency of the wave reflected by the moving object as detected by a detector at rest near the source?

APPROACH There are actually two Doppler shifts in this situation. First, the moving object acts like an observer moving toward the source with speed $v_{obs} = 3.50$ m/s (Fig. 16–21a) and so "detects" a sound wave of frequency (Eq. 16–10a) $f' = f[1 + (v_{obs}/v_{snd})]$. Second, reflection of the wave from the moving object is equivalent to the object reemitting the wave, acting effectively as a moving source with speed $v_{source} = 3.50$ m/s (Fig. 16–21b). The final frequency detected, f'', is given by $f'' = f'/[1 - v_{source}/v_{snd}]$, Eq. 16–9a.

SOLUTION The frequency f' that is "detected" by the moving object is (Eq. 16–10a):

$$f' = \left(1 + \frac{v_{obs}}{v_{snd}}\right)f = \left(1 + \frac{3.50 \text{ m/s}}{343 \text{ m/s}}\right)(5000 \text{ Hz}) = 5051 \text{ Hz}.$$

The moving object now "emits" (reflects) a sound of frequency (Eq. 16–9a)

$$f'' = \frac{f'}{\left(1 - \dfrac{v_{source}}{v_{snd}}\right)} = \frac{5051 \text{ Hz}}{\left(1 - \dfrac{3.50 \text{ m/s}}{343 \text{ m/s}}\right)} = 5103 \text{ Hz}.$$

Thus the frequency shifts by 103 Hz.

NOTE Bats use this technique to be aware of their surroundings. This is also the principle behind Doppler radar as speed-measuring devices for vehicles and other objects.

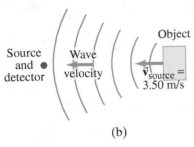

FIGURE 16–21 Example 16–15.

The incident wave and the reflected wave in Example 16–15, when mixed together (say, electronically), interfere with one another and beats are produced. The beat frequency is equal to the difference in the two frequencies, 103 Hz. This Doppler technique is used in a variety of medical applications, usually with ultrasonic waves in the megahertz frequency range. For example, ultrasonic waves reflected from red blood cells can be used to determine the velocity of blood flow. Similarly, the technique can be used to detect the movement of the chest of a young fetus and to monitor its heartbeat.

For convenience, we can write Eqs. 16–9 and 16–10 as a single equation that covers all cases of both source and observer in motion:

$$f' = f\left(\frac{v_{snd} \pm v_{obs}}{v_{snd} \mp v_{source}}\right). \qquad \begin{bmatrix} \text{source and} \\ \text{observer moving} \end{bmatrix} \quad \textbf{(16–11)}$$

PHYSICS APPLIED
Doppler blood-flow meter and other medical uses

PROBLEM SOLVING
Getting the signs right

To get the signs right, recall from your own experience that the frequency is higher when observer and source approach each other, and lower when they move apart. Thus the upper signs in numerator and denominator apply if source and/or observer move toward each other; the lower signs apply if they are moving apart.

EXERCISE H How fast would a source have to approach an observer for the observed frequency to be one octave above (twice) the produced frequency? (a) $\frac{1}{2}v_{snd}$, (b) v_{snd}, (c) $2v_{snd}$, (d) $4v_{snd}$.

Doppler Effect for Light

The Doppler effect occurs for other types of waves as well. Light and other types of electromagnetic waves (such as radar) exhibit the Doppler effect: although the formulas for the frequency shift are not identical to Eqs. 16–9 and 16–10, as discussed in Chapter 44, the effect is similar. One important application is for weather forecasting using radar. The time delay between the emission of radar pulses and their reception after being reflected off raindrops gives the position of precipitation. Measuring the Doppler shift in frequency (as in Example 16–15) tells how fast the storm is moving and in which direction.

Another important application is to astronomy, where the velocities of distant galaxies can be determined from the Doppler shift. Light from distant galaxies is shifted toward lower frequencies, indicating that the galaxies are moving away from us. This is called the **redshift** since red has the lowest frequency of visible light. The greater the frequency shift, the greater the velocity of recession. It is found that the farther the galaxies are from us, the faster they move away. This observation is the basis for the idea that the universe is expanding, and is one basis for the idea that the universe began as a great explosion, affectionately called the "Big Bang" (Chapter 44).

⊗ PHYSICS APPLIED

Doppler effect for EM waves and weather forecasting

⊗ PHYSICS APPLIED

Redshift in cosmology

*16–8 Shock Waves and the Sonic Boom

An object such as an airplane traveling faster than the speed of sound is said to have a **supersonic speed**. Such a speed is often given as a **Mach**[†] number, which is defined as the ratio of the speed of the object to the speed of sound in the surrounding medium. For example, a plane traveling 600 m/s high in the atmosphere, where the speed of sound is only 300 m/s, has a speed of Mach 2.

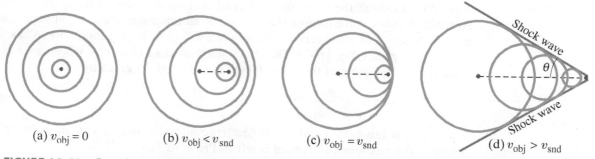

(a) $v_{obj} = 0$ (b) $v_{obj} < v_{snd}$ (c) $v_{obj} = v_{snd}$ (d) $v_{obj} > v_{snd}$

FIGURE 16–22 Sound waves emitted by an object (a) at rest or (b, c, and d) moving. (b) If the object's velocity is less than the velocity of sound, the Doppler effect occurs; (d) if its velocity is greater than the velocity of sound, a shock wave is produced.

When a source of sound moves at subsonic speeds (less than the speed of sound), the pitch of the sound is altered as we have seen (the Doppler effect); see also Fig. 16–22a and b. But if a source of sound moves faster than the speed of sound, a more dramatic effect known as a **shock wave** occurs. In this case, the source is actually "outrunning" the waves it produces. As shown in Fig. 16–22c, when the source is traveling *at* the speed of sound, the wave fronts it emits in the forward direction "pile up" directly in front of it. When the object moves faster, at a supersonic speed, the wave fronts pile up on one another along the sides, as shown in Fig. 16–22d. The different wave crests overlap one another and form a single very large crest which is the shock wave. Behind this very large crest there is usually a very large trough. A shock wave is essentially the result of constructive interference of a large number of wave fronts. A shock wave in air is analogous to the bow wave of a boat traveling faster than the speed of the water waves it produces, Fig. 16–23.

FIGURE 16–23 Bow waves produced by a boat.

[†]After the Austrian physicist Ernst Mach (1838–1916).

FIGURE 16–24 (a) The (double) sonic boom has already been heard by person A on the left. The front shock wave is just being heard by person B in the center. And it will shortly be heard by person C on the right. (b) Special photo of supersonic aircraft showing shock waves produced in the air. (Several closely spaced shock waves are produced by different parts of the aircraft.)

When an airplane travels at supersonic speeds, the noise it makes and its disturbance of the air form into a shock wave containing a tremendous amount of sound energy. When the shock wave passes a listener, it is heard as a loud *sonic boom*. A sonic boom lasts only a fraction of a second, but the energy it contains is often sufficient to break windows and cause other damage. Actually, a sonic boom is made up of two or more booms since major shock waves can form at the front and the rear of the aircraft, as well as at the wings, etc. (Fig. 16–24). Bow waves of a boat are also multiple, as can be seen in Fig. 16–23.

PHYSICS APPLIED
Sonic boom

When an aircraft approaches the speed of sound, it encounters a barrier of sound waves in front of it (see Fig. 16–22c). To exceed the speed of sound, the aircraft needs extra thrust to pass through this "sound barrier." This is called "breaking the sound barrier." Once a supersonic speed is attained, this barrier no longer impedes the motion. It is sometimes erroneously thought that a sonic boom is produced only at the moment an aircraft is breaking through the sound barrier. Actually, a shock wave follows the aircraft at all times it is traveling at supersonic speeds. A series of observers on the ground will each hear a loud "boom" as the shock wave passes, Fig. 16–24. The shock wave consists of a cone whose apex is at the aircraft. The angle of this cone, θ (see Fig. 16–22d), is given by

$$\sin \theta = \frac{v_{\text{snd}}}{v_{\text{obj}}}, \qquad (16\text{–}12)$$

where v_{obj} is the velocity of the object (the aircraft) and v_{snd} is the velocity of sound in the medium. (The proof is left as Problem 75.)

*16–9 Applications: Sonar, Ultrasound, and Medical Imaging

*Sonar

PHYSICS APPLIED
Sonar: depth finding, Earth soundings

The reflection of sound is used in many applications to determine distance. The **sonar**[†] or pulse-echo technique is used to locate underwater objects. A transmitter sends out a sound pulse through the water, and a detector receives its reflection, or echo, a short time later. This time interval is carefully measured, and from it the distance to the reflecting object can be determined since the speed of sound in water is known. The depth of the sea and the location of reefs, sunken ships, submarines, or schools of fish can be determined in this way. The interior structure of the Earth is studied in a similar way by detecting reflections of waves traveling through the Earth whose source was a deliberate explosion (called "soundings"). An analysis of waves reflected from various structures and boundaries within the Earth reveals characteristic patterns that are also useful in the exploration for oil and minerals.

[†]Sonar stands for "*so*und *na*vigation *r*anging."

Sonar generally makes use of **ultrasonic** frequencies: that is, waves whose frequencies are above 20 kHz, beyond the range of human detection. For sonar, the frequencies are typically in the range 20 kHz to 100 kHz. One reason for using ultrasound waves, other than the fact that they are inaudible, is that for shorter wavelengths there is less diffraction (Section 15–11) so the beam spreads less and smaller objects can be detected.

*Ultrasound Medical Imaging

The diagnostic use of ultrasound in medicine, in the form of images (sometimes called *sonograms*), is an important and interesting application of physical principles. A **pulse-echo technique** is used, much like sonar, except that the frequencies used are in the range of 1 to 10 MHz $(1 \text{ MHz} = 10^6 \text{ Hz})$. A high-frequency sound pulse is directed into the body, and its reflections from boundaries or interfaces between organs and other structures and lesions in the body are then detected. Tumors and other abnormal growths, or pockets of fluid, can be distinguished; the action of heart valves and the development of a fetus can be examined; and information about various organs of the body, such as the brain, heart, liver, and kidneys, can be obtained. Although ultrasound does not replace X-rays, for certain kinds of diagnosis it is more helpful. Some kinds of tissue or fluid are not detected in X-ray photographs, but ultrasound waves are reflected from their boundaries. "Real-time" ultrasound images are like a movie of a section of the interior of the body.

PHYSICS APPLIED
Ultrasound medical imaging

The pulse-echo technique for medical imaging works as follows. A brief pulse of ultrasound is emitted by a transducer that transforms an electrical pulse into a sound-wave pulse. Part of the pulse is reflected as echoes at each interface in the body, and most of the pulse (usually) continues on, Fig. 16–25a. The detection of reflected pulses by the same transducer can then be displayed on the screen of a display terminal or monitor. The time elapsed from when the pulse is emitted to when each reflection (echo) is received is proportional to the distance to the reflecting surface. For example, if the distance from transducer to the vertebra is 25 cm, the pulse travels a round-trip distance of $2 \times 25 \text{ cm} = 0.50 \text{ m}$. The speed of sound in human tissue is about 1540 m/s (close to that of sea water), so the time taken is

$$t = \frac{d}{v} = \frac{(0.50 \text{ m})}{(1540 \text{ m/s})} = 320 \ \mu\text{s}.$$

The *strength* of a reflected pulse depends mainly on the difference in density of the two materials on either side of the interface and can be displayed as a pulse or as a dot (Figs. 16–25b and c). Each echo dot (Fig. 16–25c) can be represented as a point whose position is given by the time delay and whose brightness depends on the strength of the echo.

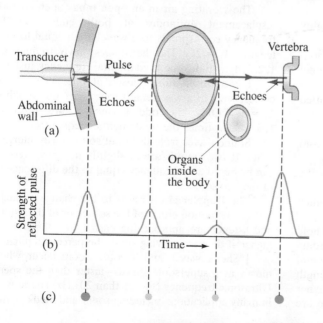

FIGURE 16–25 (a) Ultrasound pulse passes through the abdomen, reflecting from surfaces in its path. (b) Reflected pulses plotted as a function of time when received by transducer. The vertical dashed lines point out which reflected pulse goes with which surface. (c) Dot display for the same echoes: brightness of each dot is related to signal strength.

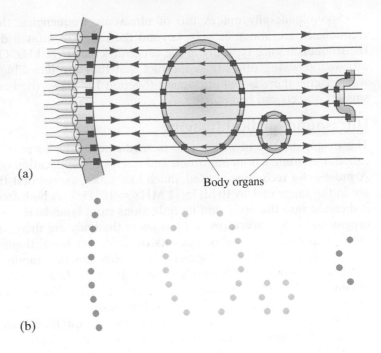

FIGURE 16-26 (a) Ten traces are made across the abdomen by moving the transducer, or by using an array of transducers. (b) The echoes are plotted as dots to produce the image. More closely spaced traces would give a more detailed image.

(a)

Body organs

(b)

FIGURE 16-27 Ultrasound image of a human fetus within the uterus.

A two-dimensional image can then be formed out of these dots from a series of scans. The transducer is moved, or an array of transducers is used, each of which sends out a pulse at each position and receives echoes as shown in Fig. 16–26a. Each trace can be plotted, spaced appropriately one below the other, to form an image on a monitor screen as shown in Fig. 16–26b. Only 10 lines are shown in Fig. 16–26, so the image is crude. More lines give a more precise image.[†] An ultrasound image is shown in Fig. 16–27.

[†]*Radar* used for aircraft involves a similar pulse-echo technique except that it uses electromagnetic (EM) waves, which, like light, travel with a speed of 3×10^8 m/s.

Summary

Sound travels as a longitudinal wave in air and other materials. In air, the speed of sound increases with temperature; at 20°C, it is about 343 m/s.

The **pitch** of a sound is determined by the frequency; the higher the frequency, the higher the pitch.

The **audible range** of frequencies for humans is roughly 20 Hz to 20,000 Hz (1 Hz = 1 cycle per second).

The **loudness** or **intensity** of a sound is related to the amplitude squared of the wave. Because the human ear can detect sound intensities from 10^{-12} W/m² to over 1 W/m², sound levels are specified on a logarithmic scale. The **sound level** β, specified in decibels, is defined in terms of intensity I as

$$\beta(\text{in dB}) = 10 \log\left(\frac{I}{I_0}\right), \qquad (16\text{--}6)$$

where the reference intensity I_0 is usually taken to be 10^{-12} W/m².

Musical instruments are simple sources of sound in which *standing waves* are produced.

The strings of a stringed instrument may vibrate as a whole with nodes only at the ends; the frequency at which this standing wave occurs is called the **fundamental**. The fundamental frequency corresponds to a wavelength equal to twice the length of the string, $\lambda_1 = 2\ell$. The string can also vibrate at higher frequencies, called **overtones** or **harmonics**, in which there are

one or more additional nodes. The frequency of each harmonic is a whole-number multiple of the fundamental.

In wind instruments, standing waves are set up in the column of air within the tube.

The vibrating air in an **open tube** (open at both ends) has displacement antinodes at both ends. The fundamental frequency corresponds to a wavelength equal to twice the tube length: $\lambda_1 = 2\ell$. The harmonics have frequencies that are 1, 2, 3, 4, … times the fundamental frequency, just as for strings.

For a **closed tube** (closed at one end), the fundamental corresponds to a wavelength four times the length of the tube: $\lambda_1 = 4\ell$. Only the odd harmonics are present, equal to 1, 3, 5, 7, … times the fundamental frequency.

Sound waves from different sources can interfere with each other. If two sounds are at slightly different frequencies, **beats** can be heard at a frequency equal to the difference in frequency of the two sources.

The **Doppler effect** refers to the change in pitch of a sound due to the motion either of the source or of the listener. If source and listener are approaching each other, the perceived pitch is higher; if they are moving apart, the perceived pitch is lower.

[*Shock waves and a sonic boom occur when an object moves at a supersonic speed—faster than the speed of sound. Ultrasonic-frequency (higher than 20 kHz) sound waves are used in many applications, including sonar and medical imaging.]

Questions

1. What is the evidence that sound travels as a wave?

2. What is the evidence that sound is a form of energy?

3. Children sometimes play with a homemade "telephone" by attaching a string to the bottoms of two paper cups. When the string is stretched and a child speaks into one cup, the sound can be heard at the other cup (Fig. 16–28). Explain clearly how the sound wave travels from one cup to the other.

FIGURE 16–28 Question 3.

4. When a sound wave passes from air into water, do you expect the frequency or wavelength to change?

5. What evidence can you give that the speed of sound in air does not depend significantly on frequency?

6. The voice of a person who has inhaled helium sounds very high-pitched. Why?

7. What is the main reason the speed of sound in hydrogen is greater than the speed of sound in air?

8. Two tuning forks oscillate with the same amplitude, but one has twice the frequency. Which (if either) produces the more intense sound?

9. How will the air temperature in a room affect the pitch of organ pipes?

10. Explain how a tube might be used as a filter to reduce the amplitude of sounds in various frequency ranges. (An example is a car muffler.)

11. Why are the frets on a guitar (Fig. 16–29) spaced closer together as you move up the fingerboard toward the bridge?

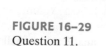

FIGURE 16–29
Question 11.

12. A noisy truck approaches you from behind a building. Initially you hear it but cannot see it. When it emerges and you do see it, its sound is suddenly "brighter"—you hear more of the high-frequency noise. Explain. [*Hint*: See Section 15–11 on diffraction.]

13. Standing waves can be said to be due to "interference in space," whereas beats can be said to be due to "interference in time." Explain.

14. In Fig. 16–15, if the frequency of the speakers is lowered, would the points D and C (where destructive and constructive interference occur) move farther apart or closer together?

15. Traditional methods of protecting the hearing of people who work in areas with very high noise levels have consisted mainly of efforts to block or reduce noise levels. With a relatively new technology, headphones are worn that do not block the ambient noise. Instead, a device is used which detects the noise, inverts it electronically, then feeds it to the headphones *in addition to* the ambient noise. How could adding *more* noise reduce the sound levels reaching the ears?

16. Consider the two waves shown in Fig. 16–30. Each wave can be thought of as a superposition of two sound waves with slightly different frequencies, as in Fig. 16–17. In which of the waves, (a) or (b), are the two component frequencies farther apart? Explain.

(a)

(b)

FIGURE 16–30 Question 16.

17. Is there a Doppler shift if the source and observer move in the same direction, with the same velocity? Explain.

18. If a wind is blowing, will this alter the frequency of the sound heard by a person at rest with respect to the source? Is the wavelength or velocity changed?

19. Figure 16–31 shows various positions of a child on a swing moving toward a person on the ground who is blowing a whistle. At which position, A through E, will the child hear the highest frequency for the sound of the whistle? Explain your reasoning.

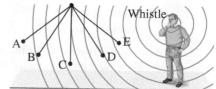

FIGURE 16–31
Question 19.

20. Approximately how many octaves are there in the human audible range?

21. At a race track, you can estimate the speed of cars just by listening to the difference in pitch of the engine noise between approaching and receding cars. Suppose the sound of a certain car drops by a full octave (frequency halved) as it goes by on the straightaway. How fast is it going?

Problems

[Unless stated otherwise, assume $T = 20°C$ and $v_{sound} = 343$ m/s in air.]

16–1 Characteristics of Sound

1. (I) A hiker determines the length of a lake by listening for the echo of her shout reflected by a cliff at the far end of the lake. She hears the echo 2.0 s after shouting. Estimate the length of the lake.

2. (I) A sailor strikes the side of his ship just below the waterline. He hears the echo of the sound reflected from the ocean floor directly below 2.5 s later. How deep is the ocean at this point? Assume the speed of sound in sea water is 1560 m/s (Table 16–1) and does not vary significantly with depth.

3. (I) (a) Calculate the wavelengths in air at 20°C for sounds in the maximum range of human hearing, 20 Hz to 20,000 Hz. (b) What is the wavelength of a 15-MHz ultrasonic wave?

4. (I) On a warm summer day (27°C), it takes 4.70 s for an echo to return from a cliff across a lake. On a winter day, it takes 5.20 s. What is the temperature on the winter day?

5. (II) A *motion sensor* can accurately measure the distance d to an object repeatedly via the sonar technique used in Example 16–2. A short ultrasonic pulse is emitted and reflects from any objects it encounters, creating echo pulses upon their arrival back at the sensor. The sensor measures the time interval t between the emission of the original pulse and the arrival of the first echo. (a) The smallest time interval t that can be measured with high precision is 1.0 ms. What is the smallest distance (at 20°C) that can be measured with the motion sensor? (b) If the motion sensor makes 15 distance measurements every second (that is, it emits 15 sound pulses per second at evenly spaced time intervals), the measurement of t must be completed within the time interval between the emissions of successive pulses. What is the largest distance (at 20°C) that can be measured with the motion sensor? (c) Assume that during a lab period the room's temperature increases from 20°C to 23°C. What percent error will this introduce into the motion sensor's distance measurements?

6. (II) An ocean fishing boat is drifting just above a school of tuna on a foggy day. Without warning, an engine backfire occurs on another boat 1.35 km away (Fig. 16–32). How much time elapses before the backfire is heard (a) by the fish, and (b) by the fishermen?

FIGURE 16–32
Problem 6.

7. (II) A stone is dropped from the top of a cliff. The splash it makes when striking the water below is heard 3.0 s later. How high is the cliff?

8. (II) A person, with his ear to the ground, sees a huge stone strike the concrete pavement. A moment later two sounds are heard from the impact: one travels in the air and the other in the concrete, and they are 0.75 s apart. How far away did the impact occur? See Table 16–1.

9. (II) Calculate the percent error made over one mile of distance by the "5-second rule" for estimating the distance from a lightning strike if the temperature is (a) 30°C, and (b) 10°C.

16–2 Mathematical Representation of Waves

10. (I) The pressure amplitude of a sound wave in air $(\rho = 1.29$ kg/m$^3)$ at 0°C is 3.0×10^{-3} Pa. What is the displacement amplitude if the frequency is (a) 150 Hz and (b) 15 kHz?

11. (I) What must be the pressure amplitude in a sound wave in air (0°C) if the air molecules undergo a maximum displacement equal to the diameter of an oxygen molecule, about 3.0×10^{-10} m? Assume a sound-wave frequency of (a) 55 Hz and (b) 5.5 kHz.

12. (II) Write an expression that describes the pressure variation as a function of x and t for the waves described in Problem 11.

13. (II) The pressure variation in a sound wave is given by
$$\Delta P = 0.0035 \sin(0.38\pi x - 1350\pi t),$$
where ΔP is in pascals, x in meters, and t in seconds. Determine (a) the wavelength, (b) the frequency, (c) the speed, and (d) the displacement amplitude of the wave. Assume the density of the medium to be $\rho = 2.3 \times 10^3$ kg/m^3.

16–3 Intensity of Sound; Decibels

14. (I) What is the intensity of a sound at the pain level of 120 dB? Compare it to that of a whisper at 20 dB.

15. (I) What is the sound level of a sound whose intensity is 2.0×10^{-6} W/m^2?

16. (I) What are the lowest and highest frequencies that an ear can detect when the sound level is 40 dB? (See Fig. 16–6.)

17. (II) Your auditory system can accommodate a huge range of sound levels. What is the ratio of highest to lowest intensity at (a) 100 Hz, (b) 5000 Hz? (See Fig. 16–6.)

18. (II) You are trying to decide between two new stereo amplifiers. One is rated at 100 W per channel and the other is rated at 150 W per channel. In terms of dB, how much louder will the more powerful amplifier be when both are producing sound at their maximum levels?

19. (II) At a painfully loud concert, a 120-dB sound wave travels away from a loudspeaker at 343 m/s. How much sound wave energy is contained in each 1.0-cm^3 volume of air in the region near this loudspeaker?

20. (II) If two firecrackers produce a sound level of 95 dB when fired simultaneously at a certain place, what will be the sound level if only one is exploded?

21. (II) A person standing a certain distance from an airplane with four equally noisy jet engines is experiencing a sound level of 130 dB. What sound level would this person experience if the captain shut down all but one engine?

22. (II) A cassette player is said to have a signal-to-noise ratio of 62 dB, whereas for a CD player it is 98 dB. What is the ratio of intensities of the signal and the background noise for each device?

23. (II) (a) Estimate the power output of sound from a person speaking in normal conversation. Use Table 16–2. Assume the sound spreads roughly uniformly over a sphere centered on the mouth. (b) How many people would it take to produce a total sound output of 75 W of ordinary conversation? [*Hint*: Add intensities, not dBs.]

24. (II) A 50-dB sound wave strikes an eardrum whose area is 5.0×10^{-5} m^2. (a) How much energy is received by the eardrum per second? (b) At this rate, how long would it take your eardrum to receive a total energy of 1.0 J?

25. (II) Expensive amplifier A is rated at 250 W, while the more modest amplifier B is rated at 45 W. (a) Estimate the sound level in decibels you would expect at a point 3.5 m from a loudspeaker connected in turn to each amp. (b) Will the expensive amp sound twice as loud as the cheaper one?

26. (II) At a rock concert, a dB meter registered 130 dB when placed 2.2 m in front of a loudspeaker on the stage. (a) What was the power output of the speaker, assuming uniform spherical spreading of the sound and neglecting absorption in the air? (b) How far away would the sound level be a somewhat reasonable 85 dB?

27. (II) A fireworks shell explodes 100 m above the ground, creating a colorful display of sparks. How much greater is the sound level of the explosion for a person standing at a point directly below the explosion than for a person a horizontal distance of 200 m away (Fig. 16–33)?

FIGURE 16–33
Problem 27.

28. (II) If the amplitude of a sound wave is made 2.5 times greater, (a) by what factor will the intensity increase? (b) By how many dB will the sound level increase?

29. (II) Two sound waves have equal displacement amplitudes, but one has 2.6 times the frequency of the other. (a) Which has the greater pressure amplitude and by what factor is it greater? (b) What is the ratio of their intensities?

30. (II) What would be the sound level (in dB) of a sound wave in air that corresponds to a displacement amplitude of vibrating air molecules of 0.13 mm at 380 Hz?

31. (II) (a) Calculate the maximum displacement of air molecules when a 330-Hz sound wave passes whose intensity is at the threshold of pain (120 dB). (b) What is the pressure amplitude in this wave?

32. (II) A jet plane emits 5.0×10^5 J of sound energy per second. (a) What is the sound level 25 m away? Air absorbs sound at a rate of about 7.0 dB/km; calculate what the sound level will be (b) 1.00 km and (c) 7.50 km away from this jet plane, taking into account air absorption.

16–4 Sources of Sound: Strings and Air Columns

33. (I) What would you estimate for the length of a bass clarinet, assuming that it is modeled as a closed tube and that the lowest note that it can play is a D♭ whose frequency is 69.3 Hz?

34. (I) The A string on a violin has a fundamental frequency of 440 Hz. The length of the vibrating portion is 32 cm, and it has a mass of 0.35 g. Under what tension must the string be placed?

35. (I) An organ pipe is 124 cm long. Determine the fundamental and first three audible overtones if the pipe is (a) closed at one end, and (b) open at both ends.

36. (I) (a) What resonant frequency would you expect from blowing across the top of an empty soda bottle that is 21 cm deep, if you assumed it was a closed tube? (b) How would that change if it was one-third full of soda?

37. (I) If you were to build a pipe organ with open-tube pipes spanning the range of human hearing (20 Hz to 20 kHz), what would be the range of the lengths of pipes required?

38. (II) Estimate the frequency of the "sound of the ocean" when you put your ear very near a 20-cm-diameter seashell (Fig. 16–34).

FIGURE 16–34
Problem 38.

39. (II) An unfingered guitar string is 0.73 m long and is tuned to play E above middle C (330 Hz). (a) How far from the end of this string must a fret (and your finger) be placed to play A above middle C (440 Hz)? (b) What is the wavelength on the string of this 440-Hz wave? (c) What are the frequency and wavelength of the sound wave produced in air at 25°C by this fingered string?

40. (II) (a) Determine the length of an open organ pipe that emits middle C (262 Hz) when the temperature is 15°C. (b) What are the wavelength and frequency of the fundamental standing wave in the tube? (c) What are λ and f in the traveling sound wave produced in the outside air?

41. (II) An organ is in tune at 22.0°C. By what percent will the frequency be off at 5.0°C?

42. (II) How far from the mouthpiece of the flute in Example 16–11 should the hole be that must be uncovered to play F above middle C at 349 Hz?

43. (II) A bugle is simply a tube of fixed length that behaves as if it is open at both ends. A bugler, by adjusting his lips correctly and blowing with proper air pressure, can cause a harmonic (usually other than the fundamental) of the air column within the tube to sound loudly. Standard military tunes like *Taps* and *Reveille* require only four musical notes: G4 (392 Hz), C5 (523 Hz), E5 (659 Hz), and G5 (784 Hz). (a) For a certain length ℓ, a bugle will have a sequence of four consecutive harmonics whose frequencies very nearly equal those associated with the notes G4, C5, E5, and G5. Determine this ℓ. (b) Which harmonic is each of the (approximate) notes G4, C5, E5, and G5 for the bugle?

44. (II) A particular organ pipe can resonate at 264 Hz, 440 Hz, and 616 Hz, but not at any other frequencies in between. (a) Show why this is an open or a closed pipe. (b) What is the fundamental frequency of this pipe?

45. (II) When a player's finger presses a guitar string down onto a fret, the length of the vibrating portion of the string is shortened, thereby increasing the string's fundamental frequency (see Fig. 16–35). The string's tension and mass per unit length remain unchanged. If the unfingered length of the string is ℓ = 65.0 cm, determine the positions x of the first six frets, if each fret raises the pitch of the fundamental by one musical note in comparison to the neighboring fret. On the equally tempered chromatic scale, the ratio of frequencies of neighboring notes is $2^{1/12}$.

FIGURE 16–35
Problem 45.

46. (II) A uniform narrow tube 1.80 m long is open at both ends. It resonates at two successive harmonics of frequencies 275 Hz and 330 Hz. What is (a) the fundamental frequency, and (b) the speed of sound in the gas in the tube?

47. (II) A pipe in air at 23.0°C is to be designed to produce two successive harmonics at 240 Hz and 280 Hz. How long must the pipe be, and is it open or closed?

48. (II) How many overtones are present within the audible range for a 2.48-m-long organ pipe at 20°C (a) if it is open, and (b) if it is closed?

49. (II) Determine the fundamental and first overtone frequencies for an 8.0-m-long hallway with all doors closed. Model the hallway as a tube closed at both ends.

50. (II) In a *quartz oscillator*, used as a stable clock in electronic devices, a transverse (shear) standing sound wave is excited across the thickness d of a quartz disk and its frequency f is detected electronically. The parallel faces of the disk are unsupported and so behave as "free ends" when the sound wave reflects from them (see Fig. 16–36). If the oscillator is designed to operate with the first harmonic, determine the required disk thickness if $f = 12.0$ MHz. The density and shear modulus of quartz are $\rho = 2650$ kg/m^3 and $G = 2.95 \times 10^{10}$ N/m^2.

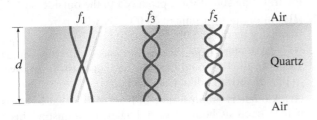

FIGURE 16–36 Problem 50.

51. (III) The human ear canal is approximately 2.5 cm long. It is open to the outside and is closed at the other end by the eardrum. Estimate the frequencies (in the audible range) of the standing waves in the ear canal. What is the relationship of your answer to the information in the graph of Fig. 16–6?

*16–5 Quality of Sound, Superposition

*52. (II) Approximately what are the intensities of the first two overtones of a violin compared to the fundamental? How many decibels softer than the fundamental are the first and second overtones? (See Fig. 16–14.)

16–6 Interference; Beats

53. (I) A piano tuner hears one beat every 2.0 s when trying to adjust two strings, one of which is sounding 370 Hz. How far off in frequency is the other string?

54. (I) What is the beat frequency if middle C (262 Hz) and C$^\sharp$ (277 Hz) are played together? What if each is played two octaves lower (each frequency reduced by a factor of 4)?

55. (II) A guitar string produces 4 beats/s when sounded with a 350-Hz tuning fork and 9 beats/s when sounded with a 355-Hz tuning fork. What is the vibrational frequency of the string? Explain your reasoning.

56. (II) The two sources of sound in Fig. 16–15 face each other and emit sounds of equal amplitude and equal frequency (294 Hz) but 180° out of phase. For what minimum separation of the two speakers will there be some point at which (a) complete constructive interference occurs and (b) complete destructive interference occurs. (Assume $T = 20$°C.)

57. (II) How many beats will be heard if two identical flutes, each 0.66 m long, try to play middle C (262 Hz), but one is at 5.0°C and the other at 28°C?

58. (II) Two loudspeakers are placed 3.00 m apart, as shown in Fig. 16–37. They emit 494-Hz sounds, in phase. A microphone is placed 3.20 m distant from a point midway between the two speakers, where an intensity maximum is recorded. (a) How far must the microphone be moved to the right to find the first intensity minimum? (b) Suppose the speakers are reconnected so that the 494-Hz sounds they emit are exactly out of phase. At what positions are the intensity maximum and minimum now?

FIGURE 16–37
Problem 58.

59. (II) Two piano strings are supposed to be vibrating at 220 Hz, but a piano tuner hears three beats every 2.0 s when they are played together. (a) If one is vibrating at 220.0 Hz, what must be the frequency of the other (is there only one answer)? (b) By how much (in percent) must the tension be increased or decreased to bring them in tune?

60. (II) A source emits sound of wavelengths 2.64 m and 2.72 m in air. (a) How many beats per second will be heard? (Assume $T = 20$°C.) (b) How far apart in space are the regions of maximum intensity?

16–7 Doppler Effect

61. (I) The predominant frequency of a certain fire truck's siren is 1350 Hz when at rest. What frequency do you detect if you move with a speed of 30.0 m/s (a) toward the fire truck, and (b) away from it?

62. (I) A bat at rest sends out ultrasonic sound waves at 50.0 kHz and receives them returned from an object moving directly away from it at 30.0 m/s. What is the received sound frequency?

63. (II) (a) Compare the shift in frequency if a 2300-Hz source is moving toward you at 18 m/s, versus you moving toward it at 18 m/s. Are the two frequencies exactly the same? Are they close? (b) Repeat the calculation for 160 m/s and then again (c) for 320 m/s. What can you conclude about the asymmetry of the Doppler formulas? (d) Show that at low speeds (relative to the speed of sound), the two formulas—source approaching and detector approaching—yield the same result.

64. (II) Two automobiles are equipped with the same single-frequency horn. When one is at rest and the other is moving toward the first at 15 m/s, the driver at rest hears a beat frequency of 4.5 Hz. What is the frequency the horns emit? Assume $T = 20$°C.

65. (II) A police car sounding a siren with a frequency of 1280 Hz is traveling at 120.0 km/h. (a) What frequencies does an observer standing next to the road hear as the car approaches and as it recedes? (b) What frequencies are heard in a car traveling at 90.0 km/h in the opposite direction before and after passing the police car? (c) The police car passes a car traveling in the same direction at 80.0 km/h. What two frequencies are heard in this car?

66. (II) A bat flies toward a wall at a speed of 7.0 m/s. As it flies, the bat emits an ultrasonic sound wave with frequency 30.0 kHz. What frequency does the bat hear in the reflected wave?

67. (II) In one of the original Doppler experiments, a tuba was played on a moving flat train car at a frequency of 75 Hz, and a second identical tuba played the same tone while at rest in the railway station. What beat frequency was heard in the station if the train car approached the station at a speed of 12.0 m/s?

68. (II) If a speaker mounted on an automobile broadcasts a song, with what speed (km/h) does the automobile have to move toward a stationary listener so that the listener hears the song with each musical note shifted up by one note in comparison to the song heard by the automobile's driver? On the equally tempered chromatic scale, the ratio of frequencies of neighboring notes is $2^{1/12}$.

69. (II) A wave on the surface of the ocean with wavelength 44 m is traveling east at a speed of 18 m/s relative to the ocean floor. If, on this stretch of ocean surface, a powerboat is moving at 15 m/s (relative to the ocean floor), how often does the boat encounter a wave crest, if the boat is traveling (a) west, and (b) east?

70. (III) A factory whistle emits sound of frequency 720 Hz. When the wind velocity is 15.0 m/s from the north, what frequency will observers hear who are located, at rest, (a) due north, (b) due south, (c) due east, and (d) due west, of the whistle? What frequency is heard by a cyclist heading (e) north or (f) west, toward the whistle at 12.0 m/s? Assume $T = 20°C$.

71. (III) The Doppler effect using ultrasonic waves of frequency 2.25×10^6 Hz is used to monitor the heartbeat of a fetus. A (maximum) beat frequency of 260 Hz is observed. Assuming that the speed of sound in tissue is 1.54×10^3 m/s, calculate the maximum velocity of the surface of the beating heart.

*16–8 Shock Waves; Sonic Boom

*72. (II) An airplane travels at Mach 2.0 where the speed of sound is 310 m/s. (a) What is the angle the shock wave makes with the direction of the airplane's motion? (b) If the plane is flying at a height of 6500 m, how long after it is directly overhead will a person on the ground hear the shock wave?

*73. (II) A space probe enters the thin atmosphere of a planet where the speed of sound is only about 45 m/s. (a) What is the probe's Mach number if its initial speed is 15,000 km/h? (b) What is the angle of the shock wave relative to the direction of motion?

*74. (II) A meteorite traveling 8800 m/s strikes the ocean. Determine the shock wave angle it produces (a) in the air just before entering the ocean, and (b) in the water just after entering. Assume $T = 20°C$.

*75. (II) Show that the angle θ a sonic boom makes with the path of a supersonic object is given by Eq. 16–12.

*76. (II) You look directly overhead and see a plane exactly 1.25 km above the ground flying faster than the speed of sound. By the time you hear the sonic boom, the plane has traveled a horizontal distance of 2.0 km. See Fig. 16–38. Determine (a) the angle of the shock cone, θ, and (b) the speed of the plane (the Mach number). Assume the speed of sound is 330 m/s.

FIGURE 16–38
Problem 76.

*77. (II) A supersonic jet traveling at Mach 2.2 at an altitude of 9500 m passes directly over an observer on the ground. Where will the plane be relative to the observer when the latter hears the sonic boom? (See Fig. 16–39.)

FIGURE 16–39 Problem 77.

General Problems

78. A fish finder uses a sonar device that sends 20,000-Hz sound pulses downward from the bottom of the boat, and then detects echoes. If the maximum depth for which it is designed to work is 75 m, what is the minimum time between pulses (in fresh water)?

79. A science museum has a display called a sewer pipe symphony. It consists of many plastic pipes of various lengths, which are open on both ends. (a) If the pipes have lengths of 3.0 m, 2.5 m, 2.0 m, 1.5 m and 1.0 m, what frequencies will be heard by a visitor's ear placed near the ends of the pipes? (b) Why does this display work better on a noisy day than on a quiet day?

80. A single mosquito 5.0 m from a person makes a sound close to the threshold of human hearing (0 dB). What will be the sound level of 100 such mosquitoes?

81. What is the resultant sound level when an 82-dB sound and an 89-dB sound are heard simultaneously?

82. The sound level 9.00 m from a loudspeaker, placed in the open, is 115 dB. What is the acoustic power output (W) of the speaker, assuming it radiates equally in all directions?

83. A stereo amplifier is rated at 175 W output at 1000 Hz. The power output drops by 12 dB at 15 kHz. What is the power output in watts at 15 kHz?

84. Workers around jet aircraft typically wear protective devices over their ears. Assume that the sound level of a jet airplane engine, at a distance of 30 m, is 130 dB, and that the average human ear has an effective radius of 2.0 cm. What would be the power intercepted by an unprotected ear at a distance of 30 m from a jet airplane engine?

85. In audio and communications systems, the *gain*, β, in decibels is defined as

$$\beta = 10 \log\left(\frac{P_{out}}{P_{in}}\right),$$

where P_{in} is the power input to the system and P_{out} is the power output. A particular stereo amplifier puts out 125 W of power for an input of 1.0 mW. What is its gain in dB?

86. For large concerts, loudspeakers are sometimes used to amplify a singer's sound. The human brain interprets sounds that arrive within 50 ms of the original sound as if they came from the same source. Thus if the sound from a loudspeaker reaches a listener first, it would sound as if the loudspeaker is the source of the sound. Conversely, if the singer is heard first and the loudspeaker adds to the sound within 50 ms, the sound would seem to come from the singer, who would now seem to be singing louder. The second situation is desired. Because the signal to the loudspeaker travels at the speed of light $(3 \times 10^8 \, \text{m/s})$, which is much faster than the speed of sound, a delay is added to the signal sent to the loudspeaker. How much delay must be added if the loudspeaker is 3.0 m behind the singer and we want its sound to arrive 30 ms after the singer's?

87. Manufacturers typically offer a particular guitar string in a choice of diameters so that players can tune their instruments with a preferred string tension. For example, a nylon high-E string is available in a low- and high-tension model with diameter 0.699 mm and 0.724 mm, respectively. Assuming the density ρ of nylon is the same for each model, compare (as a ratio) the tension in a tuned high- and low-tension string.

88. The high-E string on a guitar is fixed at both ends with length $\ell = 65.0 \, \text{cm}$ and fundamental frequency $f_1 = 329.6 \, \text{Hz}$. On an acoustic guitar, this string typically has a diameter of 0.33 mm and is commonly made of brass $(7760 \, \text{kg/m}^3)$, while on an electric guitar it has a diameter of 0.25 mm and is made of nickel-coated steel $(7990 \, \text{kg/m}^3)$. Compare (as a ratio) the high-E string tension on an acoustic versus an electric guitar.

89. The A string of a violin is 32 cm long between fixed points with a fundamental frequency of 440 Hz and a mass per unit length of $7.2 \times 10^{-4} \, \text{kg/m}$. (a) What are the wave speed and tension in the string? (b) What is the length of the tube of a simple wind instrument (say, an organ pipe) closed at one end whose fundamental is also 440 Hz if the speed of sound is 343 m/s in air? (c) What is the frequency of the first overtone of each instrument?

90. A tuning fork is set into vibration above a vertical open tube filled with water (Fig. 16–40). The water level is allowed to drop slowly. As it does so, the air in the tube above the water level is heard to resonate with the tuning fork when the distance from the tube opening to the water level is 0.125 m and again at 0.395 m. What is the frequency of the tuning fork?

FIGURE 16–40
Problem 90.

0.125 m
0.395 m

91. Two identical tubes, each closed at one end, have a fundamental frequency of 349 Hz at 25.0°C. The air temperature is increased to 30.0°C in one tube. If the two pipes are sounded together now, what beat frequency results?

92. Each string on a violin is tuned to a frequency $1\frac{1}{2}$ times that of its neighbor. The four equal-length strings are to be placed under the same tension; what must be the mass per unit length of each string relative to that of the lowest string?

93. The diameter D of a tube does affect the node at the open end of a tube. The end correction can be roughly approximated as adding $D/3$ to the effective length of the tube. For a closed tube of length 0.60 m and diameter 3.0 cm, what are the first four harmonics, taking the end correction into consideration?

94. A person hears a pure tone in the 500 to 1000-Hz range coming from two sources. The sound is loudest at points equidistant from the two sources. To determine exactly what the frequency is, the person moves about and finds that the sound level is minimal at a point 0.28 m farther from one source than the other. What is the frequency of the sound?

95. The frequency of a steam train whistle as it approaches you is 552 Hz. After it passes you, its frequency is measured as 486 Hz. How fast was the train moving (assume constant velocity)?

96. Two trains emit 516-Hz whistles. One train is stationary. The conductor on the stationary train hears a 3.5-Hz beat frequency when the other train approaches. What is the speed of the moving train?

97. Two loudspeakers are at opposite ends of a railroad car as it moves past a stationary observer at 10.0 m/s, as shown in Fig. 16–41. If the speakers have identical sound frequencies of 348 Hz, what is the beat frequency heard by the observer when (a) he listens from the position A, in front of the car, (b) he is between the speakers, at B, and (c) he hears the speakers after they have passed him, at C?

$v = 10.0 \, \text{m/s}$

C   B   A

FIGURE 16–41 Problem 97.

98. Two open organ pipes, sounding together, produce a beat frequency of 8.0 Hz. The shorter one is 2.40 m long. How long is the other?

99. A bat flies toward a moth at speed 7.5 m/s while the moth is flying toward the bat at speed 5.0 m/s. The bat emits a sound wave of 51.35 kHz. What is the frequency of the wave detected by the bat after that wave reflects off the moth?

100. If the velocity of blood flow in the aorta is normally about 0.32 m/s, what beat frequency would you expect if 3.80-MHz ultrasound waves were directed along the flow and reflected from the red blood cells? Assume that the waves travel with a speed of $1.54 \times 10^3 \, \text{m/s}$.

101. A bat emits a series of high-frequency sound pulses as it approaches a moth. The pulses are approximately 70.0 ms apart, and each is about 3.0 ms long. How far away can the moth be detected by the bat so that the echo from one pulse returns before the next pulse is emitted?

102. (a) Use the binomial expansion to show that Eqs. 16–9a and 16–10a become essentially the same for small relative velocity between source and observer. (b) What percent error would result if Eq. 16–10a were used instead of Eq. 16–9a for a relative velocity of 18.0 m/s?

103. Two loudspeakers face each other at opposite ends of a long corridor. They are connected to the same source which produces a pure tone of 282 Hz. A person walks from one speaker toward the other at a speed of 1.4 m/s. What "beat" frequency does the person hear?

104. A *Doppler flow meter* is used to measure the speed of blood flow. Transmitting and receiving elements are placed on the skin, as shown in Fig. 16–42. Typical sound-wave frequencies of about 5.0 MHz are used, which have a reasonable chance of being reflected from red blood cells. By measuring the frequency of the reflected waves, which are Doppler-shifted because the red blood cells are moving, the speed of the blood flow can be deduced. "Normal" blood flow speed is about 0.1 m/s. Suppose that an artery is partly constricted, so that the speed of the blood flow is increased, and the flow meter measures a Doppler shift of 780 Hz. What is the speed of blood flow in the constricted region? The effective angle between the sound waves (both transmitted and reflected) and the direction of blood flow is 45°. Assume the velocity of sound in tissue is 1540 m/s.

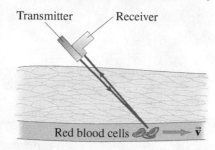

FIGURE 16–42
Problem 104.

105. The wake of a speedboat is 15° in a lake where the speed of the water wave is 2.2 km/h. What is the speed of the boat?

106. A source of sound waves (wavelength λ) is a distance ℓ from a detector. Sound reaches the detector directly, and also by reflecting off an obstacle, as shown in Fig. 16–43. The obstacle is equidistant from source and detector. When the obstacle is a distance d to the right of the line of sight between source and detector, as shown, the two waves arrive in phase. How much farther to the right must the obstacle be moved if the two waves are to be out of phase by $\frac{1}{2}$ wavelength, so destructive interference occurs? (Assume $\lambda \ll \ell, d$.)

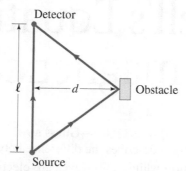

FIGURE 16–43
Problem 106.

107. A dramatic demonstration, called "singing rods," involves a long, slender aluminum rod held in the hand near the rod's midpoint. The rod is stroked with the other hand. With a little practice, the rod can be made to "sing," or emit a clear, loud, ringing sound. For a 75-cm-long rod, (a) what is the fundamental frequency of the sound? (b) What is its wavelength in the rod, and (c) what is the wavelength of the sound in air at 20°C?

108. Assuming that the maximum displacement of the air molecules in a sound wave is about the same as that of the speaker cone that produces the sound (Fig. 16–44), estimate by how much a loudspeaker cone moves for a fairly loud (105 dB) sound of (a) 8.0 kHz, and (b) 35 Hz.

FIGURE 16–44
Problem 108.

Rarefaction Compression

Motion of speaker cone
(exaggerated)

*### Numerical/Computer

*109. (III) The manner in which a string is plucked determines the mixture of harmonic amplitudes in the resulting wave. Consider a string exactly $\frac{1}{2}$-m long that is fixed at both its ends located at $x = 0.0$ and $x = \frac{1}{2}$ m. The first five harmonics of this string have wavelengths $\lambda_1 = 1.0$ m, $\lambda_2 = \frac{1}{2}$ m, $\lambda_3 = \frac{1}{3}$ m, $\lambda_4 = \frac{1}{4}$ m, and $\lambda_5 = \frac{1}{5}$ m. According to Fourier's theorem, any shape of this string can be formed by a sum of its harmonics, with each harmonic having its own unique amplitude A. We limit the sum to the first five harmonics in the expression

$$D(x) = A_1 \sin\left(\frac{2\pi}{\lambda_1} x\right) + A_2 \sin\left(\frac{2\pi}{\lambda_2} x\right)$$
$$+ A_3 \sin\left(\frac{2\pi}{\lambda_3} x\right) + A_4 \sin\left(\frac{2\pi}{\lambda_4} x\right) + A_5 \sin\left(\frac{2\pi}{\lambda_5} x\right),$$

and D is the displacement of the string at a time $t = 0$. Imagine plucking this string at its midpoint (Fig. 16–45a) or at a point two-thirds from the left end (Fig. 16–45b). Using a graphing calculator or computer program, show that the above expression can fairly accurately represent the shape in: (a) Fig. 16–45a, if
$A_1 = 1.00$,
$A_2 = 0.00$,
$A_3 = -0.11$,
$A_4 = 0.00$, and
$A_5 = 0.040$; and in
(b) Fig. 16–45b, if
$A_1 = 0.87$,
$A_2 = -0.22$,
$A_3 = 0.00$,
$A_4 = 0.054$, and
$A_5 = -0.035$.

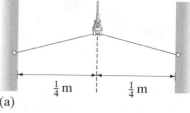

(a)

$\frac{1}{4}$ m $\quad$ $\frac{1}{4}$ m

$\frac{1}{3}$ m $\quad$ $\frac{1}{6}$ m

FIGURE 16–45
Problem 109. $\quad$ (b)

Answers to Exercises

A: 1 km for every 3 s before the thunder is heard.

B: 4 times as intense.

C: (b).

D: The less-massive one.

E: 257 Hz.

F: (b).

G: (a) 1717 Hz, (b) 1483 Hz.

H: (a).

Wireless technology is all around us: in this photo we see a Bluetooth earpiece for wireless telephone communication and a wi-fi computer. The wi-fi antenna is just visible at the lower left. All these devices work by electromagnetic waves traveling through space, based on the great work of Maxwell which we investigate in this Chapter. Modern wireless devices are applications of Marconi's development of long distance transmission of information a century ago.

We will see in this Chapter that Maxwell predicted the existence of EM waves from his famous equations. Maxwell's equations themselves are a magnificent summary of electromagnetism. We will also examine how EM waves carry energy and momentum.

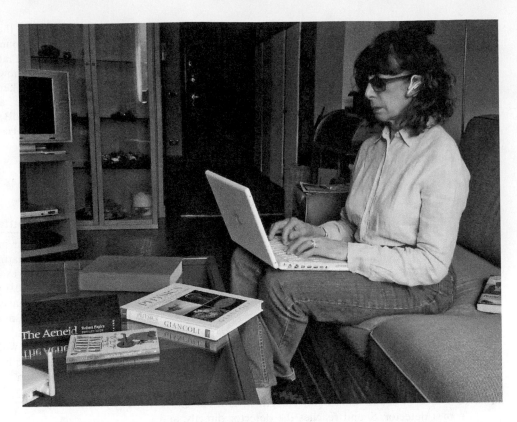

C H A P T E R
31

Maxwell's Equations and Electromagnetic Waves

CONTENTS

CHAPTER-OPENING QUESTION—Guess now!

Which of the following best describes the difference between radio waves and X-rays?

(a) X-rays are radiation while radio waves are electromagnetic waves.

(b) Both can be thought of as electromagnetic waves. They differ only in wavelength and frequency.

(c) X-rays are pure energy. Radio waves are made of fields, not energy.

(d) Radio waves come from electric currents in an antenna. X-rays are not related to electric charge.

(e) The fact that X-rays can expose film, and radio waves cannot, means they are fundamentally different.

The culmination of electromagnetic theory in the nineteenth century was the prediction, and the experimental verification, that waves of electromagnetic fields could travel through space. This achievement opened a whole new world of communication: first the wireless telegraph, then radio and television, and more recently cell phones, remote-control devices, wi-fi, and Bluetooth. Most important was the spectacular prediction that visible light is an electromagnetic wave.

The theoretical prediction of electromagnetic waves was the work of the Scottish physicist James Clerk Maxwell (1831–1879; Fig. 31–1), who unified, in one magnificent theory, all the phenomena of electricity and magnetism.

The development of electromagnetic theory in the early part of the nineteenth century by Oersted, Ampère, and others was not actually done in terms of electric and magnetic fields. The idea of the field was introduced somewhat later by Faraday, and was not generally used until Maxwell showed that all electric and magnetic phenomena could be described using only four equations involving electric and magnetic fields. These equations, known as **Maxwell's equations**, are the basic equations for all electromagnetism. They are fundamental in the same sense that Newton's three laws of motion and the law of universal gravitation are for mechanics. In a sense, they are even more fundamental, since they are consistent with the theory of relativity (Chapter 36), whereas Newton's laws are not. Because all of electromagnetism is contained in this set of four equations, Maxwell's equations are considered one of the great triumphs of human intellect.

Before we discuss Maxwell's equations and electromagnetic waves, we first need to discuss a major new prediction of Maxwell's, and, in addition, Gauss's law for magnetism.

FIGURE 31–1 James Clerk Maxwell (1831–1879).

31–1 Changing Electric Fields Produce Magnetic Fields; Ampère's Law and Displacement Current

Ampère's Law

That a magnetic field is produced by an electric current was discovered by Oersted, and the mathematic relation is given by Ampère's law (Eq. 28–3):

$$\oint \vec{\mathbf{B}} \cdot d\vec{\boldsymbol{\ell}} = \mu_0 I_{\text{encl}}.$$

Is it possible that magnetic fields could be produced in another way as well? For if a changing magnetic field produces an electric field, as discussed in Section 29–7, then perhaps the reverse might be true as well: that *a changing electric field will produce a magnetic field*. If this were true, it would signify a beautiful *symmetry* in nature.

To back up this idea that a changing electric field might produce a magnetic field, we use an indirect argument that goes something like this. According to Ampère's law, we divide any chosen closed path into short segments $d\vec{\boldsymbol{\ell}}$, take the dot product of each $d\vec{\boldsymbol{\ell}}$ with the magnetic field $\vec{\mathbf{B}}$ at that segment, and sum (integrate) all these products over the chosen closed path. That sum will equal μ_0 times the total current I that passes through a surface bounded by the path of the line integral. When we applied Ampère's law to the field around a straight wire (Section 28–4), we imagined the current as passing through the circular area enclosed by our circular loop, and that area is the flat surface 1 shown in Fig. 31–2. However, we could just as well use the sackshaped surface 2 in Fig. 31–2 as the surface for Ampère's law, since the same current I passes through it.

Now consider the closed circular path for the situation of Fig. 31–3, where a capacitor is being discharged. Ampère's law works for surface 1 (current I passes through surface 1), but it does not work for surface 2, since no current passes through surface 2. There is a magnetic field around the wire, so the left side of Ampère's law ($\int \vec{\mathbf{B}} \cdot d\vec{\boldsymbol{\ell}}$) is not zero; yet no current flows through surface 2, so the right side of Ampère's law *is* zero. We seem to have a contradiction of Ampère's law.

There is a magnetic field present in Fig. 31–3, however, only if charge is flowing to or away from the capacitor plates. The changing charge on the plates means that the electric field between the plates is changing in time. Maxwell resolved the problem of no current through surface 2 in Fig. 31–3 by proposing that there needs to be an extra term on the right in Ampère's law involving the changing electric field.

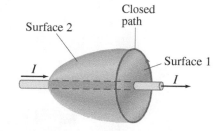

FIGURE 31–2 Ampère's law applied to two different surfaces bounded by the same closed path.

FIGURE 31–3 A capacitor discharging. A conduction current passes through surface 1, but no conduction current passes through surface 2. An extra term is needed in Ampère's law.

FIGURE 31–3 (repeated) See text.

Let us see what this term should be by determining it for the changing electric field between the capacitor plates in Fig. 31–3. The charge Q on a capacitor of capacitance C is $Q = CV$ where V is the potential difference between the plates (Eq. 24–1). Also recall that $V = Ed$ (Eq. 23–4) where d is the (small) separation of the plates and E is the (uniform) electric field strength between them, if we ignore any fringing of the field. Also, for a parallel-plate capacitor, $C = \epsilon_0 A/d$, where A is the area of each plate (Eq. 24–2). We combine these to obtain:

$$Q = CV = \left(\epsilon_0 \frac{A}{d} \right)(Ed) = \epsilon_0 AE.$$

If the charge on each plate changes at a rate dQ/dt, the electric field changes at a proportional rate. That is, by differentiating this expression for Q, we have:

$$\frac{dQ}{dt} = \epsilon_0 A \frac{dE}{dt}.$$

Now dQ/dt is also the current I flowing into or out of the capacitor:

$$I = \frac{dQ}{dt} = \epsilon_0 A \frac{dE}{dt} = \epsilon_0 \frac{d\Phi_E}{dt}$$

where $\Phi_E = EA$ is the **electric flux** through the closed path (surface 2 in Fig. 31–3). In order to make Ampère's law work for surface 2 in Fig. 31–3, as well as for surface 1 (where current I flows), we therefore write:

Ampère's law (general form)

$$\oint \vec{B} \cdot d\vec{\ell} = \mu_0 I_{\text{encl}} + \mu_0 \epsilon_0 \frac{d\Phi_E}{dt}. \tag{31–1}$$

This equation represents the general form of **Ampère's law**,[†] and embodies Maxwell's idea that a magnetic field can be caused not only by an ordinary electric current, but also by a changing electric field or changing electric flux. Although we arrived at it for a special case, Eq. 31–1 has proved valid in general. The last term on the right in Eq. 31–1 is usually very small, and not easy to measure experimentally.

EXAMPLE 31–1 Charging capacitor. A 30-pF air-gap capacitor has circular plates of area $A = 100 \text{ cm}^2$. It is charged by a 70-V battery through a 2.0-Ω resistor. At the instant the battery is connected, the electric field between the plates is changing most rapidly. At this instant, calculate (a) the current into the plates, and (b) the rate of change of electric field between the plates. (c) Determine the magnetic field induced between the plates. Assume $\vec{E}$ is uniform between the plates at any instant and is zero at all points beyond the edges of the plates.

APPROACH In Section 26–5 we discussed RC circuits and saw that the charge on a capacitor being charged, as a function of time, is

$$Q = CV_0(1 - e^{-t/RC}),$$

where V_0 is the voltage of the battery. To find the current at $t = 0$, we differentiate this and substitute the values $V_0 = 70 \text{ V}$, $C = 30 \text{ pF}$, $R = 2.0 \, \Omega$.

SOLUTION (a) We take the derivative of Q and evaluate it at $t = 0$:

$$\left. \frac{dQ}{dt} \right|_{t=0} = \left. \frac{CV_0}{RC} e^{-t/RC} \right|_{t=0} = \frac{V_0}{R} = \frac{70 \text{ V}}{2.0 \, \Omega} = 35 \text{ A}.$$

This is the rate at which charge accumulates on the capacitor and equals the current flowing in the circuit at $t = 0$.

(b) The electric field between two closely spaced conductors is given by (Eq. 21–8)

$$E = \frac{\sigma}{\epsilon_0} = \frac{Q/A}{\epsilon_0}$$

as we saw in Chapter 21 (see Example 21–13).

[†]Actually, there is a third term on the right for the case when a magnetic field is produced by magnetized materials. This can be accounted for by changing μ_0 to μ, but we will mainly be interested in cases where no magnetic material is present. In the presence of a dielectric, ϵ_0 is replaced by $\epsilon = K\epsilon_0$ (see Section 24–5).

Hence

$$\frac{dE}{dt} = \frac{dQ/dt}{\epsilon_0 A} = \frac{35\,\text{A}}{(8.85 \times 10^{-12}\,\text{C}^2/\text{N}\cdot\text{m}^2)(1.0 \times 10^{-2}\,\text{m}^2)} = 4.0 \times 10^{14}\,\text{V/m}\cdot\text{s}.$$

(c) Although we will not prove it, we might expect the lines of $\vec{\mathbf{B}}$, because of *symmetry*, to be circles, and to be perpendicular to $\vec{\mathbf{E}}$, as shown in Fig. 31–4; this is the same symmetry we saw for the inverse situation of a changing magnetic field producing an electric field (Section 29–7, see Fig. 29–27). To determine the magnitude of B between the plates we apply Ampère's law, Eq. 31–1, with the current $I_{\text{encl}} = 0$:

$$\oint \vec{\mathbf{B}}\cdot d\vec{\boldsymbol{\ell}} = \mu_0\epsilon_0 \frac{d\Phi_E}{dt}.$$

We choose our path to be a circle of radius r, centered at the center of the plate, and thus following a magnetic field line such as the one shown in Fig. 31–4. For $r \le r_0$ (the radius of plate) the flux through a circle of radius r is $E(\pi r^2)$ since E is assumed uniform between the plates at any moment. So from Ampère's law we have

$$B(2\pi r) = \mu_0\epsilon_0 \frac{d}{dt}(\pi r^2 E)$$

$$= \mu_0\epsilon_0 \pi r^2 \frac{dE}{dt}.$$

Hence

$$B = \frac{\mu_0\epsilon_0}{2} r \frac{dE}{dt}. \qquad\qquad [r \le r_0]$$

We assume $\vec{\mathbf{E}} = 0$ for $r > r_0$, so for points beyond the edge of the plates all the flux is contained within the plates (area $= \pi r_0^2$) and $\Phi_E = E\pi r_0^2$. Thus Ampère's law gives

$$B(2\pi r) = \mu_0\epsilon_0 \frac{d}{dt}(\pi r_0^2 E)$$

$$= \mu_0\epsilon_0 \pi r_0^2 \frac{dE}{dt}$$

or

$$B = \frac{\mu_0\epsilon_0 r_0^2}{2r} \frac{dE}{dt}. \qquad\qquad [r \ge r_0]$$

B has its maximum value at $r = r_0$ which, from either relation above (using $r_0 = \sqrt{A/\pi} = 5.6$ cm), is

$$B_{\text{max}} = \frac{\mu_0\epsilon_0 r_0}{2} \frac{dE}{dt}$$

$$= \tfrac{1}{2}(4\pi \times 10^{-7}\,\text{T}\cdot\text{m/A})(8.85 \times 10^{-12}\,\text{C}^2/\text{N}\cdot\text{m}^2)(5.6 \times 10^{-2}\,\text{m})(4.0 \times 10^{14}\,\text{V/m}\cdot\text{s})$$

$$= 1.2 \times 10^{-4}\,\text{T}.$$

This is a very small field and lasts only briefly (the time constant $RC = 6.0 \times 10^{-11}$ s) and so would be very difficult to measure.

Let us write the magnetic field B outside the capacitor plates of Example 31–1 in terms of the current I that leaves the plates. The electric field between the plates is $E = \sigma/\epsilon_0 = Q/(\epsilon_0 A)$, as we saw in part b, so $dE/dt = I/(\epsilon_0 A)$. Hence B for $r > r_0$ is,

$$B = \frac{\mu_0\epsilon_0 r_0^2}{2r} \frac{dE}{dt} = \frac{\mu_0\epsilon_0 r_0^2}{2r} \frac{I}{\epsilon_0 \pi r_0^2} = \frac{\mu_0 I}{2\pi r}.$$

This is the same formula for the field that surrounds a wire (Eq. 28–1). Thus the B field outside the capacitor is the same as that outside the wire. In other words, the magnetic field produced by the changing electric field between the plates is the same as that produced by the current in the wire.

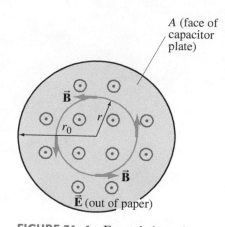

FIGURE 31–4 Frontal view of a circular plate of a parallel-plate capacitor. $\vec{\mathbf{E}}$ between plates points out toward viewer; lines of $\vec{\mathbf{B}}$ are circles. (Example 31–1.)

Displacement Current

Maxwell interpreted the second term on the right in Eq. 31–1 as being *equivalent* to an electric current. He called it a **displacement current**, I_D. An ordinary current I is then called a **conduction current**. Ampère's law can then be written

$$\oint \vec{B} \cdot d\vec{\ell} = \mu_0 (I + I_D)_{encl} \tag{31–2}$$

where

Displacement current

$$I_D = \epsilon_0 \frac{d\Phi_E}{dt}. \tag{31–3}$$

The term "displacement current" was based on an old discarded theory. Don't let it confuse you: I_D does not represent a flow of electric charge[†], nor is there a displacement.

31–2 Gauss's Law for Magnetism

We are almost in a position to state Maxwell's equations, but first we need to discuss the magnetic equivalent of Gauss's law. As we saw in Chapter 29, for a magnetic field $\vec{B}$ the *magnetic flux* Φ_B through a surface is defined as

$$\Phi_B = \int \vec{B} \cdot d\vec{A}$$

where the integral is over the area of either an open or a closed surface. The magnetic flux through a closed surface—that is, a surface which completely encloses a volume—is written

$$\Phi_B = \oint \vec{B} \cdot d\vec{A}.$$

In the electric case, we saw in Section 22–2 that the electric flux Φ_E through a closed surface is equal to the total net charge Q enclosed by the surface, divided by ϵ_0 (Eq. 22–4):

$$\oint \vec{E} \cdot d\vec{A} = \frac{Q}{\epsilon_0}.$$

This relation is Gauss's law for electricity.

We can write a similar relation for the magnetic flux. We have seen, however, that in spite of intense searches, no isolated magnetic poles (monopoles)—the magnetic equivalent of single electric charges—have ever been observed. Hence, **Gauss's law for magnetism** is

$$\oint \vec{B} \cdot d\vec{A} = 0. \tag{31–4}$$

FIGURE 31–5 Magnetic field lines for a bar magnet.

In terms of magnetic field lines, this relation tells us that as many lines enter the enclosed volume as leave it. If, indeed, magnetic monopoles do not exist, then there are no "sources" or "sinks" for magnetic field lines to start or stop on, corresponding to electric field lines starting on positive charges and ending on negative charges. Magnetic field lines must then be continuous. Even for a bar magnet, a magnetic field $\vec{B}$ exists inside as well as outside the magnetic material, and the lines of $\vec{B}$ are closed loops as shown in Fig. 31–5.

[†]The interpretation of the changing electric field as a current does fit in well with our discussion in Chapter 30 where we saw that an alternating current can be said to pass through a capacitor (although charge doesn't). It also means that Kirchhoff's junction rule will be valid even at a capacitor plate: conduction current flows into the plate, but no conduction current flows out of the plate—instead a "displacement current" flows out of one plate (toward the other plate).

31–3 Maxwell's Equations

With the extension of Ampère's law given by Eq. 31–1, plus Gauss's law for magnetism (Eq. 31–4), we are now ready to state all four of Maxwell's equations. We have seen them all before in the past ten Chapters. In the absence of dielectric or magnetic materials, **Maxwell's equations** are:

$$\oint \vec{E} \cdot d\vec{A} = \frac{Q}{\epsilon_0} \qquad (31\text{--}5a)$$

$$\oint \vec{B} \cdot d\vec{A} = 0 \qquad (31\text{--}5b)$$

$$\oint \vec{E} \cdot d\vec{\ell} = -\frac{d\Phi_B}{dt} \qquad (31\text{--}5c)$$

$$\oint \vec{B} \cdot d\vec{\ell} = \mu_0 I + \mu_0 \epsilon_0 \frac{d\Phi_E}{dt}. \qquad (31\text{--}5d)$$

MAXWELL'S EQUATIONS

The first two of Maxwell's equations are the same as Gauss's law for electricity (Chapter 22, Eq. 22–4) and Gauss's law for magnetism (Section 31–2, Eq. 31–4). The third is Faraday's law (Chapter 29, Eq. 29–8) and the fourth is Ampère's law as modified by Maxwell (Eq. 31–1). (We dropped the subscripts on Q_{encl} and I_{encl} for simplicity.)

They can be summarized in words: (1) a generalized form of Coulomb's law relating electric field to its sources, electric charges; (2) the same for the magnetic field, except that if there are no magnetic monopoles, magnetic field lines are continuous—they do not begin or end (as electric field lines do on charges); (3) an electric field is produced by a changing magnetic field; (4) a magnetic field is produced by an electric current or by a changing electric field.

Maxwell's equations are the basic equations for all electromagnetism, and are as fundamental as Newton's three laws of motion and the law of universal gravitation. Maxwell's equations can also be written in differential form; see Appendix E.

In earlier Chapters, we have seen that we can treat electric and magnetic fields separately if they do not vary in time. But we cannot treat them independently if they do change in time. For a changing magnetic field produces an electric field; and a changing electric field produces a magnetic field. An important outcome of these relations is the production of electromagnetic waves.

31–4 Production of Electromagnetic Waves

A magnetic field will be produced in empty space if there is a changing electric field. A changing magnetic field produces an electric field that is itself changing. This changing electric field will, in turn, produce a magnetic field, which will be changing, and so it too will produce a changing electric field; and so on. Maxwell found that the net result of these interacting changing fields was a *wave* of electric and magnetic fields that can propagate (travel) through space! We now examine, in a simplified way, how such **electromagnetic waves** can be produced.

Consider two conducting rods that will serve as an "antenna" (Fig. 31–6a). Suppose these two rods are connected by a switch to the opposite terminals of a battery. When the switch is closed, the upper rod quickly becomes positively charged and the lower one negatively charged. Electric field lines are formed as indicated by the lines in Fig. 31–6b. While the charges are flowing, a current exists whose direction is indicated by the black arrows. A magnetic field is therefore produced near the antenna. The magnetic field lines encircle the rod-like antenna and therefore, in Fig. 31–6, $\vec{B}$ points into the page ($\otimes$) on the right and out of the page ($\odot$) on the left. How far out do these electric and magnetic fields extend? In the static case, the fields extend outward indefinitely far. However, when the switch in Fig. 31–6 is closed, the fields quickly appear nearby, but it takes time for them to reach distant points. Both electric and magnetic fields store energy, and this energy cannot be transferred to distant points at infinite speed.

FIGURE 31–6 Fields produced by charge flowing into conductors. It takes time for the $\vec{E}$ and $\vec{B}$ fields to travel outward to distant points. The fields are shown to the right of the antenna, but they move out in all directions, symmetrically about the (vertical) antenna.

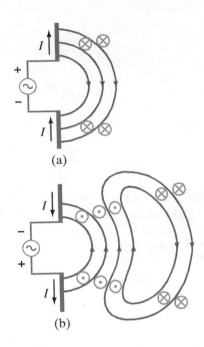

(a)

(b)

FIGURE 31–7 Sequence showing electric and magnetic fields that spread outward from oscillating charges on two conductors (the antenna) connected to an ac source (see the text).

FIGURE 31–8 (a) The radiation fields (far from the antenna) produced by a sinusoidal signal on the antenna. The red closed loops represent electric field lines. The magnetic field lines, perpendicular to the page and represented by blue $\otimes$ and $\odot$, also form closed loops. (b) Very far from the antenna the wave fronts (field lines) are essentially flat over a fairly large area, and are referred to as *plane waves*.

Now we look at the situation of Fig. 31–7 where our antenna is connected to an ac generator. In Fig. 31–7a, the connection has just been completed. Charge starts building up and fields form just as in Fig. 31–6. The + and − signs in Fig. 31–7a indicate the net charge on each rod at a given instant. The black arrows indicate the direction of the current. The electric field is represented by the red lines in the plane of the page; and the magnetic field, according to the right-hand rule, is into ($\otimes$) or out of ($\odot$) the page, in blue. In Fig. 31–7b, the voltage of the ac generator has reversed in direction; the current is reversed and the new magnetic field is in the opposite direction. Because the new fields have changed direction, the old lines fold back to connect up to some of the new lines and form closed loops as shown.[†] The old fields, however, don't suddenly disappear; they are on their way to distant points. Indeed, because a changing magnetic field produces an electric field, and a changing electric field produces a magnetic field, this combination of changing electric and magnetic fields moving outward is self-supporting, no longer depending on the antenna charges.

The fields not far from the antenna, referred to as the *near field*, become quite complicated, but we are not so interested in them. We are instead mainly interested in the fields far from the antenna (they are generally what we detect), which we refer to as the **radiation field**, or *far field*. The electric field lines form loops, as shown in Fig. 31–8, and continue moving outward. The magnetic field lines also form closed loops, but are not shown since they are perpendicular to the page. Although the lines are shown only on the right of the source, fields also travel in other directions. The field strengths are greatest in directions perpendicular to the oscillating charges; and they drop to zero along the direction of oscillation—above and below the antenna in Fig. 31–8.

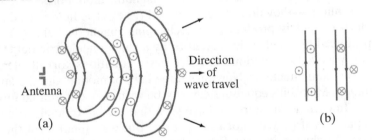

Antenna   Direction → of wave travel

(a)   **(b)**

The magnitudes of both $\vec{E}$ and $\vec{B}$ in the radiation field are found to decrease with distance as $1/r$. (Compare this to the static electric field given by Coulomb's law where $\vec{E}$ decreases as $1/r^2$.) The energy carried by the electromagnetic wave is proportional (as for any wave, Chapter 15) to the square of the amplitude, E^2 or B^2, as will be discussed further in Section 31–8, so the intensity of the wave decreases as $1/r^2$.

Several things about the radiation field can be noted from Fig. 31–8. First, *the electric and magnetic fields at any point are perpendicular to each other, and to the direction of wave travel.* Second, we can see that the fields alternate in direction ($\vec{B}$ is into the page at some points and out of the page at others; $\vec{E}$ points up at some points and down at others). Thus, the field strengths vary from a maximum in one direction, to zero, to a maximum in the other direction. The electric and magnetic fields are "in phase": that is, they each are zero at the same points and reach their maxima at the same points in space. Finally, very far from the antenna (Fig. 31–8b) the field lines are quite flat over a reasonably large area, and the waves are referred to as **plane waves**.

If the source voltage varies sinusoidally, then the electric and magnetic field strengths in the radiation field will also vary sinusoidally. The sinusoidal character of the waves is diagrammed in Fig. 31–9, which shows the field directions and magnitudes plotted as a function of position. Notice that $\vec{B}$ and $\vec{E}$ are perpendicular to each other and to the direction of travel (= the direction of the wave velocity $\vec{v}$). The direction of $\vec{v}$ can be had from a right-hand rule using $\vec{E} \times \vec{B}$: fingers along $\vec{E}$, then along $\vec{B}$, gives $\vec{v}$ along thumb.

[†]We are considering waves traveling through empty space. There are no charges for lines of $\vec{E}$ to start or stop on, so they form closed loops. Magnetic field lines always form closed loops.

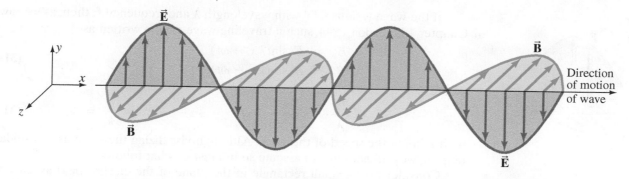

We call these waves electromagnetic (EM) waves. They are *transverse* waves because the amplitude is perpendicular to the direction of wave travel. However, EM waves are always waves of *fields*, not of matter (like waves on water or a rope). Because they are fields, EM waves can propagate in empty space.

As we have seen, EM waves are produced by electric charges that are oscillating, and hence are undergoing acceleration. In fact, we can say in general that

accelerating electric charges give rise to electromagnetic waves.

Electromagnetic waves can be produced in other ways as well, requiring description at the atomic and nuclear levels, as we will discuss later.

EXERCISE A At a particular instant in time, a wave has its electric field pointing north and its magnetic field pointing up. In which direction is the wave traveling? (*a*) South, (*b*) west, (*c*) east, (*d*) down, (*e*) not enough information.

FIGURE 31–9 Electric and magnetic field strengths in an electromagnetic wave. $\vec{\mathbf{E}}$ and $\vec{\mathbf{B}}$ are at right angles to each other. The entire pattern moves in a direction perpendicular to both $\vec{\mathbf{E}}$ and $\vec{\mathbf{B}}$.

31–5 Electromagnetic Waves, and Their Speed, Derived from Maxwell's Equations

Let us now examine how the existence of EM waves follows from Maxwell's equations. We will see that Maxwell's prediction of the existence of EM waves was startling. Equally startling was the speed at which they were predicted to travel.

We begin by considering a region of free space, where there are *no charges or conduction currents*—that is, far from the source so that the wave fronts (the field lines in Fig. 31–8) are essentially flat over a reasonable area. We call them **plane waves**, as we saw, because at any instant $\vec{\mathbf{E}}$ and $\vec{\mathbf{B}}$ are uniform over a reasonably large plane perpendicular to the direction of propagation. We choose a coordinate system, so that the wave is traveling in the x direction with velocity $\vec{\mathbf{v}} = v\hat{\mathbf{i}}$, with $\vec{\mathbf{E}}$ parallel to the y axis and $\vec{\mathbf{B}}$ parallel to the z axis, as in Fig. 31–9.

Maxwell's equations, with $Q = I = 0$, become

$$\oint \vec{\mathbf{E}} \cdot d\vec{\mathbf{A}} = 0 \tag{31–6a}$$

$$\oint \vec{\mathbf{B}} \cdot d\vec{\mathbf{A}} = 0 \tag{31–6b}$$

$$\oint \vec{\mathbf{E}} \cdot d\vec{\boldsymbol{\ell}} = -\frac{d\Phi_B}{dt} \tag{31–6c}$$

$$\oint \vec{\mathbf{B}} \cdot d\vec{\boldsymbol{\ell}} = \mu_0 \epsilon_0 \frac{d\Phi_E}{dt}. \tag{31–6d}$$

Notice the beautiful *symmetry* of these equations. The term on the right in the last equation, conceived by Maxwell, is essential for this symmetry. It is also essential if electromagnetic waves are to be produced, as we will now see.

FIGURE 31–10 Applying Faraday's law to the rectangle $(\Delta y)(dx)$.

If the wave is sinusoidal with wavelength λ and frequency f, then, as we saw in Chapter 15, Section 15–4, such a traveling wave can be written as

$$E = E_y = E_0 \sin(kx - \omega t)$$
$$B = B_z = B_0 \sin(kx - \omega t)$$

(31–7)

where

$$k = \frac{2\pi}{\lambda}, \qquad \omega = 2\pi f, \qquad \text{and} \qquad f\lambda = \frac{\omega}{k} = v,$$

(31–8)

with v being the speed of the wave. Although visualizing the wave as sinusoidal is helpful, we will not have to assume so in most of what follows.

Consider now a small rectangle in the plane of the electric field as shown in Fig. 31–10. This rectangle has a finite height Δy, and a very thin width which we take to be the infinitesimal distance dx. First we show that $\vec{E}$, $\vec{B}$, and $\vec{v}$ are in the orientation shown by applying Lenz's law to this rectangular loop. The changing magnetic flux through this loop is related to the electric field around the loop by Faraday's law (Maxwell's third equation, Eq. 31–6c). For the case shown, B through the loop is decreasing in time (the wave is moving to the right). So the electric field must be in a direction to oppose this change, meaning E must be greater on the right side of the loop than on the left, as shown (so it could produce a counterclockwise current whose magnetic field would act to oppose the change in Φ_B—but of course there is no current). This brief argument shows that the orientation of $\vec{E}$, $\vec{B}$, and $\vec{v}$ are in the correct relation as shown. That is, $\vec{v}$ is in the direction of $\vec{E} \times \vec{B}$. Now let us apply Faraday's law, which is Maxwell's third equation (Eq. 31–6c),

$$\oint \vec{E} \cdot d\vec{\ell} = -\frac{d\Phi_B}{dt}$$

to the rectangle of height Δy and width dx shown in Fig. 31–10. First we consider $\oint \vec{E} \cdot d\vec{\ell}$. Along the short top and bottom sections of length dx, $\vec{E}$ is perpendicular to $d\vec{\ell}$, so $\vec{E} \cdot d\vec{\ell} = 0$. Along the vertical sides, we let E be the electric field along the left side, and on the right side where it will be slightly larger, it is $E + dE$. Thus, if we take our loop counterclockwise,

$$\oint \vec{E} \cdot d\vec{\ell} = (E + dE)\,\Delta y - E\,\Delta y = dE\,\Delta y.$$

For the right side of Faraday's law, the magnetic flux through the loop changes as

$$\frac{d\Phi_B}{dt} = \frac{dB}{dt}\,dx\,\Delta y,$$

since the area of the loop, $(dx)(\Delta y)$, is not changing. Thus, Faraday's law gives us

$$dE\,\Delta y = -\frac{dB}{dt}\,dx\,\Delta y$$

or

$$\frac{dE}{dx} = -\frac{dB}{dt}.$$

Actually, both E and B are functions of position x and time t. We should therefore use partial derivatives:

$$\frac{\partial E}{\partial x} = -\frac{\partial B}{\partial t}$$

(31–9)

where $\partial E/\partial x$ means the derivative of E with respect to x while t is held fixed, and $\partial B/\partial t$ is the derivative of B with respect to t while x is kept fixed.

We can obtain another important relation between E and B in addition to Eq. 31–9. To do so, we consider now a small rectangle in the plane of $\vec{B}$, whose length and width are Δz and dx as shown in Fig. 31–11. To this rectangular loop we apply Maxwell's fourth equation (the extension of Ampère's law), Eq. 31–6d:

$$\oint \vec{B} \cdot d\vec{\ell} = \mu_0 \epsilon_0 \frac{d\Phi_E}{dt}$$

where we have taken $I = 0$ since we assume the absence of conduction currents.

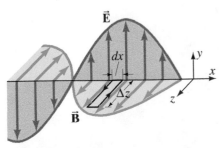

FIGURE 31–11 Applying Maxwell's fourth equation to the rectangle $(\Delta z)(dx)$.

Along the short sides (dx), $\vec{B} \cdot d\vec{\ell}$ is zero since $\vec{B}$ is perpendicular to $d\vec{\ell}$. Along the longer sides (Δz), we let B be the magnetic field along the left side of length Δz, and $B + dB$ be the field along the right side. We again integrate counterclockwise, so

$$\oint \vec{B} \cdot d\vec{\ell} = B \, \Delta z - (B + dB) \, \Delta z = -dB \, \Delta z.$$

The right side of Maxwell's fourth equation is

$$\mu_0 \epsilon_0 \frac{d\Phi_E}{dt} = \mu_0 \epsilon_0 \frac{dE}{dt} \, dx \, \Delta z.$$

Equating the two expressions, we obtain

$$-dB \, \Delta z = \mu_0 \epsilon_0 \frac{dE}{dt} \, dx \, \Delta z$$

or

$$\frac{\partial B}{\partial x} = -\mu_0 \epsilon_0 \frac{\partial E}{\partial t} \qquad (31\text{–}10)$$

where we have replaced dB/dx and dE/dt by the proper partial derivatives as before.

We can use Eqs. 31–9 and 31–10 to obtain a relation between the magnitudes of $\vec{E}$ and $\vec{B}$, and the speed v. Let E and B be given by Eqs. 31–7 as a function of x and t. When we apply Eq. 31–9, taking the derivatives of E and B as given by Eqs. 31–7, we obtain

$$kE_0 \cos(kx - \omega t) = \omega B_0 \cos(kx - \omega t)$$

or

$$\frac{E_0}{B_0} = \frac{\omega}{k} = v,$$

since $v = \omega/k$ (see Eq. 31–8 or 15–12). Since E and B are in phase, we see that E and B are related by

$$\frac{E}{B} = v \qquad (31\text{–}11)$$

at any point in space, where v is the velocity of the wave.

Now we apply Eq. 31–10 to the sinusoidal fields (Eqs. 31–7) and we obtain

$$kB_0 \cos(kx - \omega t) = \mu_0 \epsilon_0 \omega E_0 \cos(kx - \omega t)$$

or

$$\frac{B_0}{E_0} = \frac{\mu_0 \epsilon_0 \omega}{k} = \mu_0 \epsilon_0 v.$$

We just saw that $B_0/E_0 = 1/v$, so

$$\mu_0 \epsilon_0 v = \frac{1}{v}.$$

Solving for v we find

$$v = c = \frac{1}{\sqrt{\epsilon_0 \mu_0}}, \qquad (31\text{–}12)$$

where c is the special symbol for the speed of electromagnetic waves in free space. We see that c is a constant, independent of the wavelength or frequency. If we put in values for ϵ_0 and μ_0 we find

$$c = \frac{1}{\sqrt{\epsilon_0 \mu_0}} = \frac{1}{\sqrt{(8.85 \times 10^{-12} \, \text{C}^2/\text{N} \cdot \text{m}^2)(4\pi \times 10^{-7} \, \text{T} \cdot \text{m/A})}}$$

$$= 3.00 \times 10^8 \, \text{m/s}.$$

This is a remarkable result. For this is precisely equal to the measured speed of light!

EXAMPLE 31–2 **Determining $\vec{E}$ and $\vec{B}$ in EM waves.** Assume a 60.0-Hz EM wave is a sinusoidal wave propagating in the z direction with $\vec{E}$ pointing in the x direction, and $E_0 = 2.00 \text{ V/m}$. Write vector expressions for $\vec{E}$ and $\vec{B}$ as functions of position and time.

APPROACH We find λ from $\lambda f = v = c$. Then we use Fig. 31–9 and Eqs. 31–7 and 31–8 for the mathematical form of traveling electric and magnetic fields of an EM wave.

SOLUTION The wavelength is

$$\lambda = \frac{c}{f} = \frac{3.00 \times 10^8 \text{ m/s}}{60.0 \text{ s}^{-1}} = 5.00 \times 10^6 \text{ m}.$$

From Eq. 31–8 we have

$$k = \frac{2\pi}{\lambda} = \frac{2\pi}{5.00 \times 10^6 \text{ m}} = 1.26 \times 10^{-6} \text{ m}^{-1}$$

$$\omega = 2\pi f = 2\pi(60.0 \text{ Hz}) = 377 \text{ rad/s}.$$

From Eq. 31–11 with $v = c$, we find that

$$B_0 = \frac{E_0}{c} = \frac{2.00 \text{ V/m}}{3.00 \times 10^8 \text{ m/s}} = 6.67 \times 10^{-9} \text{ T}.$$

The direction of propagation is that of $\vec{E} \times \vec{B}$, as in Fig. 31–9. With $\vec{E}$ pointing in the x direction, and the wave propagating in the z direction, $\vec{B}$ must point in the y direction. Using Eqs. 31–7 we find:

$$\vec{E} = \hat{i}(2.00 \text{ V/m}) \sin\left[(1.26 \times 10^{-6} \text{ m}^{-1})z - (377 \text{ rad/s})t\right]$$

$$\vec{B} = \hat{j}(6.67 \times 10^{-9} \text{ T}) \sin\left[(1.26 \times 10^{-6} \text{ m}^{-1})z - (377 \text{ rad/s})t\right]$$

*Derivation of Speed of Light (General)

We can derive the speed of EM waves without having to assume sinusoidal waves by combining Eqs. 31–9 and 31–10 as follows. We take the derivative, with respect to t of Eq. 31–10

$$\frac{\partial^2 B}{\partial t \, \partial x} = -\mu_0 \epsilon_0 \frac{\partial^2 E}{\partial t^2}.$$

We next take the derivative of Eq. 31–9 with respect to x:

$$\frac{\partial^2 E}{\partial x^2} = -\frac{\partial^2 B}{\partial t \, \partial x}.$$

Since $\partial^2 B / \partial t \, \partial x$ appears in both relations, we obtain

$$\frac{\partial^2 E}{\partial t^2} = \frac{1}{\mu_0 \epsilon_0} \frac{\partial^2 E}{\partial x^2}. \tag{31–13a}$$

By taking other derivatives of Eqs. 31–9 and 31–10 we obtain the same relation for B:

$$\frac{\partial^2 B}{\partial t^2} = \frac{1}{\mu_0 \epsilon_0} \frac{\partial^2 B}{\partial x^2}. \tag{31–13b}$$

Both of Eqs. 31–13 have the form of the **wave equation** for a plane wave traveling in the x direction, as discussed in Section 15–5 (Eq. 15–16):

$$\frac{\partial^2 D}{\partial t^2} = v^2 \frac{\partial^2 D}{\partial x^2},$$

where D stands for any type of displacement. We see that the velocity v for Eqs. 31–13 is given by

$$v^2 = \frac{1}{\mu_0 \epsilon_0}$$

in agreement with Eq. 31–12. Thus we see that a natural outcome of Maxwell's equations is that E and B obey the wave equation for waves traveling with speed $v = 1/\sqrt{\mu_0 \epsilon_0}$. It was on this basis that Maxwell predicted the existence of electromagnetic waves and predicted their speed.

31–6 Light as an Electromagnetic Wave and the Electromagnetic Spectrum

The calculations in Section 31–5 gave the result that Maxwell himself determined: that the speed of EM waves in empty space is given by

$$c = \frac{E}{B} = \frac{1}{\sqrt{\epsilon_0 \mu_0}} = 3.00 \times 10^8 \, \text{m/s},$$

the same as the measured speed of light in vacuum.

Light had been shown some 60 years previously to behave like a wave (we'll discuss this in Chapter 34). But nobody knew what kind of wave it was. What is it that is oscillating in a light wave? Maxwell, on the basis of the calculated speed of EM waves, argued that light must be an electromagnetic wave. This idea soon came to be generally accepted by scientists, but not fully until after EM waves were experimentally detected. EM waves were first generated and detected experimentally by Heinrich Hertz (1857–1894) in 1887, eight years after Maxwell's death. Hertz used a spark-gap apparatus in which charge was made to rush back and forth for a short time, generating waves whose frequency was about 10^9 Hz. He detected them some distance away using a loop of wire in which an emf was produced when a changing magnetic field passed through. These waves were later shown to travel at the speed of light, 3.00×10^8 m/s, and to exhibit all the characteristics of light such as reflection, refraction, and interference. The only difference was that they were not visible. Hertz's experiment was a strong confirmation of Maxwell's theory.

The wavelengths of visible light were measured in the first decade of the nineteenth century, long before anyone imagined that light was an electromagnetic wave. The wavelengths were found to lie between 4.0×10^{-7} m and 7.5×10^{-7} m, or 400 nm to 750 nm $(1 \, \text{nm} = 10^9 \, \text{m})$. The frequencies of visible light can be found using Eq. 15–1 or 31–8, which we rewrite here:

$$c = \lambda f, \tag{31–14}$$

where f and λ are the frequency and wavelength, respectively, of the wave. Here, c is the speed of light, 3.00×10^8 m/s; it gets the special symbol c because of its universality for all EM waves in free space. Equation 31–14 tells us that the frequencies of visible light are between 4.0×10^{14} Hz and 7.5×10^{14} Hz. (Recall that $1 \, \text{Hz} = 1$ cycle per second $= 1 \, \text{s}^{-1}$.)

But visible light is only one kind of EM wave. As we have seen, Hertz produced EM waves of much lower frequency, about 10^9 Hz. These are now called **radio waves**, because frequencies in this range are used to transmit radio and TV signals. Electromagnetic waves, or EM radiation as we sometimes call it, have been produced or detected over a wide range of frequencies. They are usually categorized as shown in Fig. 31–12, which is known as the **electromagnetic spectrum**.

FIGURE 31–12
Electromagnetic spectrum.

Radio waves and microwaves can be produced in the laboratory using electronic equipment (Fig. 31–7). Higher-frequency waves are very difficult to produce electronically. These and other types of EM waves are produced in natural processes, as emission from atoms, molecules, and nuclei (more on this later). EM waves can be produced by the acceleration of electrons or other charged particles, such as electrons in the antenna of Fig. 31–7. Another example is X-rays, which are produced (Chapter 35) when fast-moving electrons are rapidly decelerated upon striking a metal target. Even the visible light emitted by an ordinary incandescent light is due to electrons undergoing acceleration within the hot filament.

We will meet various types of EM waves later. However, it is worth mentioning here that infrared (IR) radiation (EM waves whose frequency is just less than that of visible light) is mainly responsible for the heating effect of the Sun. The Sun emits not only visible light but substantial amounts of IR and UV (ultraviolet) as well. The molecules of our skin tend to "resonate" at infrared frequencies, so it is these that are preferentially absorbed and thus warm us up. We humans experience EM waves differently, depending on their wavelengths: Our eyes detect wavelengths between about 4×10^{-7} m and 7.5×10^{-7} m (visible light), whereas our skin detects longer wavelengths (IR). Many EM wavelengths we don't detect directly at all.

EXERCISE B Return to the Chapter-Opening Question, page 812, and answer it again now. Try to explain why you may have answered differently the first time.

⚠ CAUTION

Sound and EM waves are different

Light and other electromagnetic waves travel at a speed of 3×10^8 m/s. Compare this to sound, which travels (see Chapter 16) at a speed of about 300 m/s in air, a million times slower; or to typical freeway speeds of a car, 30 m/s (100 km/h, or 60 mi/h), 10 million times slower than light. EM waves differ from sound waves in another big way: sound waves travel in a medium such as air, and involve motion of air molecules; EM waves do not involve any material—only fields, and they can travel in empty space.

EXAMPLE 31–3 Wavelengths of EM waves. Calculate the wavelength (*a*) of a 60-Hz EM wave, (*b*) of a 93.3-MHz FM radio wave, and (*c*) of a beam of visible red light from a laser at frequency 4.74×10^{14} Hz.

APPROACH All of these waves are electromagnetic waves, so their speed is $c = 3.00 \times 10^8$ m/s. We solve for λ in Eq. 31–14: $\lambda = c/f$.

SOLUTION (*a*) $\lambda = \dfrac{c}{f} = \dfrac{3.00 \times 10^8 \text{ m/s}}{60 \text{ s}^{-1}} = 5.0 \times 10^6$ m,

or 5000 km. 60 Hz is the frequency of ac current in the United States, and, as we see here, one wavelength stretches all the way across the continental USA.

(*b*) $\lambda = \dfrac{3.00 \times 10^8 \text{ m/s}}{93.3 \times 10^6 \text{ s}^{-1}} = 3.22$ m.

The length of an FM antenna is about half this ($\frac{1}{2}\lambda$), or $1\frac{1}{2}$ m.

(*c*) $\lambda = \dfrac{3.00 \times 10^8 \text{ m/s}}{4.74 \times 10^{14} \text{ s}^{-1}} = 6.33 \times 10^{-7}$ m ($= 633$ nm).

EXERCISE C What are the frequencies of (*a*) an 80-m-wavelength radio wave, and (*b*) an X-ray of wavelength 5.5×10^{-11} m?

EXAMPLE 31–4 ESTIMATE Cell phone antenna. The antenna of a cell phone is often $\frac{1}{4}$ wavelength long. A particular cell phone has an 8.5-cm-long straight rod for its antenna. Estimate the operating frequency of this phone.

APPROACH The basic equation relating wave speed, wavelength, and frequency is $c = \lambda f$; the wavelength λ equals four times the antenna's length.

SOLUTION The antenna is $\frac{1}{4}\lambda$ long, so $\lambda = 4(8.5 \text{ cm}) = 34$ cm $= 0.34$ m. Then $f = c/\lambda = (3.0 \times 10^8 \text{ m/s})/(0.34 \text{ m}) = 8.8 \times 10^8$ Hz $= 880$ MHz.

NOTE Radio antennas are not always straight conductors. The conductor may be a round loop to save space. See Fig. 31–21b.

EXERCISE D How long should a $\frac{1}{4}\lambda$ antenna be for an aircraft radio operating at 165 MHz?

Electromagnetic waves can travel along transmission lines as well as in empty space. When a source of emf is connected to a transmission line—be it two parallel wires or a coaxial cable (Fig. 31–13)—the electric field within the wire is not set up immediately at all points along the wires. This is based on the same argument we used in Section 31–4 with reference to Fig. 31–7. Indeed, it can be shown that if the wires are separated by empty space or air, the electrical signal travels along the wires at the speed $c = 3.0 \times 10^8$ m/s. For example, when you flip a light switch, the light actually goes on a tiny fraction of a second later. If the wires are in a medium whose electric permittivity is ϵ and magnetic permeability is μ (Sections 24–5 and 28–9, respectively), the speed is not given by Eq. 31–12, but by

$$v = \frac{1}{\sqrt{\epsilon \mu}}.$$

FIGURE 31–13 Coaxial cable.

EXAMPLE 31–5 ESTIMATE Phone call time lag. You make a telephone call from New York to a friend in London. Estimate how long it will take the electrical signal generated by your voice to reach London, assuming the signal is (a) carried on a telephone cable under the Atlantic Ocean, and (b) sent via satellite 36,000 km above the ocean. Would this cause a noticeable delay in either case?

APPROACH The signal is carried on a telephone wire or in the air via satellite. In either case it is an electromagnetic wave. Electronics as well as the wire or cable slow things down, but as a rough estimate we take the speed to be $c = 3.0 \times 10^8$ m/s.

SOLUTION The distance from New York to London is about 5000 km.
(a) The time delay via the cable is $t = d/c \approx (5 \times 10^6 \text{ m})/(3.0 \times 10^8 \text{ m/s}) = 0.017$ s.
(b) Via satellite the time would be longer because communications satellites, which are usually geosynchronous (Example 6–6), move at a height of 36,000 km. The signal would have to go up to the satellite and back down, or about 72,000 km. The actual distance the signal would travel would be a little more than this as the signal would go up and down on a diagonal. Thus $t = d/c \approx 7.2 \times 10^7 \text{ m}/(3 \times 10^8 \text{ m/s}) = 0.24$ s.

NOTE When the signal travels via the underwater cable, there is only a hint of a delay and conversations are fairly normal. When the signal is sent via satellite, the delay *is* noticeable. The length of time between the end of when you speak and your friend receives it and replies, and then you hear the reply, is about a half second beyond the normal time in a conversation. This is enough to be noticeable, and you have to adjust for it so you don't start talking again while your friend's reply is on the way back to you.

EXERCISE E If you are on the phone via satellite to someone only 100 km away, would you hear the same effect?

EXERCISE F If your voice traveled as a sound wave, how long would it take to go from New York to London?

31–7 Measuring the Speed of Light

Galileo attempted to measure the speed of light by trying to measure the time required for light to travel a known distance between two hilltops. He stationed an assistant on one hilltop and himself on another, and ordered the assistant to lift the cover from a lamp the instant he saw a flash from Galileo's lamp. Galileo measured the time between the flash of his lamp and when he received the light from his assistant's lamp. The time was so short that Galileo concluded it merely represented human reaction time, and that the speed of light must be extremely high.

The first successful determination that the speed of light is finite was made by the Danish astronomer Ole Roemer (1644–1710). Roemer had noted that the carefully measured orbital period of Io, a moon of Jupiter with an average period of 42.5 h, varied slightly, depending on the relative position of Earth and Jupiter. He attributed this variation in the apparent period to the change in distance between the Earth and Jupiter during one of Io's periods, and the time it took light to travel the extra distance. Roemer concluded that the speed of light—though great—is finite.

Eight-sided rotating mirror

Observer

Stationary mirror

(Mt. Baldy)

Light source

(Mt. Wilson)

|←————35 km————→|

FIGURE 31–14 Michelson's speed-of-light apparatus (not to scale).

Since then a number of techniques have been used to measure the speed of light. Among the most important were those carried out by the American Albert A. Michelson (1852–1931). Michelson used the rotating mirror apparatus diagrammed in Fig. 31–14 for a series of high-precision experiments carried out from 1880 to the 1920s. Light from a source would hit one face of a rotating eight-sided mirror. The reflected light traveled to a stationary mirror a large distance away and back again as shown. If the rotating mirror was turning at just the right rate, the returning beam of light would reflect from one of the eight mirrors into a small telescope through which the observer looked. If the speed of rotation was only slightly different, the beam would be deflected to one side and would not be seen by the observer. From the required speed of the rotating mirror and the known distance to the stationary mirror, the speed of light could be calculated. In the 1920s, Michelson set up the rotating mirror on the top of Mt. Wilson in southern California and the stationary mirror on Mt. Baldy (Mt. San Antonio) 35 km away. He later measured the speed of light in vacuum using a long evacuated tube.

Today the speed of light, c, in vacuum is taken as

$$c = 2.99792458 \times 10^8 \text{ m/s},$$

and is defined to be this value. This means that the standard for length, the meter, is no longer defined separately. Instead, as we noted in Section 1–4, the meter is now formally defined as the distance light travels in vacuum in 1/299,792,458 of a second. We usually round off c to

$$c = 3.00 \times 10^8 \text{ m/s}$$

when extremely precise results are not required. In air, the speed is only slightly less.

31–8 Energy in EM Waves; the Poynting Vector

Electromagnetic waves carry energy from one region of space to another. This energy is associated with the moving electric and magnetic fields. In Section 24–4, we saw that the energy density u_E (J/m³) stored in an electric field E is $u_E = \frac{1}{2}\epsilon_0 E^2$ (Eq. 24–6). The energy density stored in a magnetic field B, as we discussed in Section 30–3, is given by $u_B = \frac{1}{2}B^2/\mu_0$ (Eq. 30–7). Thus, the total energy stored per unit volume in a region of space where there is an electromagnetic wave is

$$u = u_E + u_B = \frac{1}{2}\epsilon_0 E^2 + \frac{1}{2}\frac{B^2}{\mu_0}. \qquad (31\text{–}15)$$

In this equation, E and B represent the electric and magnetic field strengths of the wave at any instant in a small region of space. We can write Eq. 31–15 in terms of the E field alone, using Eqs. 31–11 $(B = E/c)$ and 31–12 $(c = 1/\sqrt{\epsilon_0\mu_0})$ to obtain

$$u = \frac{1}{2}\epsilon_0 E^2 + \frac{1}{2}\frac{\epsilon_0\mu_0 E^2}{\mu_0} = \epsilon_0 E^2. \qquad (31\text{–}16\text{a})$$

Note here that the energy density associated with the B field equals that due to the E field, and each contributes half to the total energy. We can also write the energy density in terms of the B field only:

$$u = \epsilon_0 E^2 = \epsilon_0 c^2 B^2 = \frac{B^2}{\mu_0}, \qquad (31\text{–}16\text{b})$$

or in one term containing both E and B,

$$u = \epsilon_0 E^2 = \epsilon_0 EcB = \frac{\epsilon_0 EB}{\sqrt{\epsilon_0\mu_0}} = \sqrt{\frac{\epsilon_0}{\mu_0}} EB. \qquad (31\text{–}16\text{c})$$

Equations 31–16 give the energy density in any region of space at any instant.

Now let us determine the energy the wave transports per unit time per unit area. This is given by a vector $\vec{S}$, which is called the **Poynting vector.**[†] The units of $\vec{S}$ are W/m². The direction of $\vec{S}$ is the direction in which the energy is transported, which is the direction in which the wave is moving.

[†]After J. H. Poynting (1852–1914).

Let us imagine the wave is passing through an area A perpendicular to the x axis as shown in Fig. 31–15. In a short time dt, the wave moves to the right a distance $dx = c\,dt$ where c is the wave speed. The energy that passes through A in the time dt is the energy that occupies the volume $dV = A\,dx = Ac\,dt$. The energy density u is $u = \epsilon_0 E^2$ where E is the electric field in this volume at the given instant. So the total energy dU contained in this volume dV is the energy density u times the volume: $dU = u\,dV = (\epsilon_0 E^2)(Ac\,dt)$. Therefore the energy crossing the area A per time dt is

$$S = \frac{1}{A}\frac{dU}{dt} = \epsilon_0 c E^2. \tag{31–17}$$

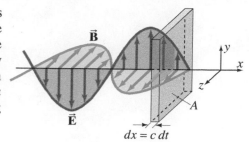

FIGURE 31–15 Electromagnetic wave carrying energy through area A.

Since $E = cB$ and $c = 1/\sqrt{\epsilon_0 \mu_0}$, this can also be written:

$$S = \epsilon_0 c E^2 = \frac{cB^2}{\mu_0} = \frac{EB}{\mu_0}.$$

The direction of $\vec{S}$ is along $\vec{v}$, perpendicular to $\vec{E}$ and $\vec{B}$, so the Poynting vector $\vec{S}$ can be written

$$\vec{S} = \frac{1}{\mu_0}(\vec{E} \times \vec{B}). \tag{31–18}$$

Equation 31–17 or 31–18 gives the energy transported per unit area per unit time at any *instant*. We often want to know the *average* over an extended period of time since the frequencies are usually so high we don't detect the rapid time variation. If E and B are sinusoidal, then $\overline{E^2} = E_0^2/2$, just as for electric currents and voltages (Section 25–7), where E_0 is the *maximum* value of E. Thus we can write for the magnitude of the Poynting vector, on the average,

$$\overline{S} = \frac{1}{2}\epsilon_0 c E_0^2 = \frac{1}{2}\frac{c}{\mu_0} B_0^2 = \frac{E_0 B_0}{2\mu_0}, \tag{31–19a}$$

where B_0 is the maximum value of B. This time averaged value of $\vec{S}$ is the **intensity**, defined as the average power transferred across unit area (Section 15–3). We can also write for the average value of S:

$$\overline{S} = \frac{E_{\text{rms}} B_{\text{rms}}}{\mu_0} \tag{31–19b}$$

where E_{rms} and B_{rms} are the rms values $\left(E_{\text{rms}} = \sqrt{\overline{E^2}}, B_{\text{rms}} = \sqrt{\overline{B^2}}\right)$.

EXAMPLE 31–6 *E* **and** *B* **from the Sun.** Radiation from the Sun reaches the Earth (above the atmosphere) at a rate of about $1350\,\text{J/s}\cdot\text{m}^2\,(= 1350\,\text{W/m}^2)$. Assume that this is a single EM wave, and calculate the maximum values of E and B.

APPROACH We solve Eq. 31–19a $\left(\overline{S} = \frac{1}{2}\epsilon_0 c E_0^2\right)$ for E_0 in terms of $\overline{S}$ using $\overline{S} = 1350\,\text{J/s}\cdot\text{m}^2$.

SOLUTION $\quad E_0 = \sqrt{\dfrac{2\overline{S}}{\epsilon_0 c}} = \sqrt{\dfrac{2(1350\,\text{J/s}\cdot\text{m}^2)}{(8.85 \times 10^{-12}\,\text{C}^2/\text{N}\cdot\text{m}^2)(3.00 \times 10^8\,\text{m/s})}}$

$\qquad\qquad = 1.01 \times 10^3\,\text{V/m}.$

From Eq. 31–11, $B = E/c$, so

$$B_0 = \frac{E_0}{c} = \frac{1.01 \times 10^3\,\text{V/m}}{3.00 \times 10^8\,\text{m/s}} = 3.37 \times 10^{-6}\,\text{T}.$$

NOTE Although B has a small numerical value compared to E (because of the way the different units for E and B are defined), B contributes the same energy to the wave as E does, as we saw earlier (Eqs. 31–15 and 16).

31–9 Radiation Pressure

If electromagnetic waves carry energy, then we might expect them to also carry linear momentum. When an electromagnetic wave encounters the surface of an object, a force will be exerted on the surface as a result of the momentum transfer ($F = dp/dt$), just as when a moving object strikes a surface. The force per unit area exerted by the waves is called **radiation pressure**, and its existence was predicted by Maxwell. He showed that if a beam of EM radiation (light, for example) is completely absorbed by an object, then the momentum transferred is

$$\Delta p = \frac{\Delta U}{c} \qquad \left[\begin{array}{c}\text{radiation}\\\text{fully}\\\text{absorbed}\end{array}\right] \quad \textbf{(31–20a)}$$

where ΔU is the energy absorbed by the object in a time Δt, and c is the speed of light.[†] If instead, the radiation is fully reflected (suppose the object is a mirror), then the momentum transferred is twice as great, just as when a ball bounces elastically off a surface:

$$\Delta p = \frac{2 \Delta U}{c}. \qquad \left[\begin{array}{c}\text{radiation}\\\text{fully}\\\text{reflected}\end{array}\right] \quad \textbf{(31–20b)}$$

If a surface absorbs some of the energy, and reflects some of it, then $\Delta p = a\,\Delta U/c$, where a is a factor between 1 and 2.

Using Newton's second law we can calculate the force and the pressure exerted by radiation on the object. The force F is given by

$$F = \frac{dp}{dt}.$$

The average rate that energy is delivered to the object is related to the Poynting vector by

$$\frac{dU}{dt} = \bar{S}A,$$

where A is the cross-sectional area of the object which intercepts the radiation. The radiation pressure P (assuming full absorption) is given by (see Eq. 31–20a)

$$P = \frac{F}{A} = \frac{1}{A}\frac{dp}{dt} = \frac{1}{Ac}\frac{dU}{dt} = \frac{\bar{S}}{c}. \qquad \left[\begin{array}{c}\text{fully}\\\text{absorbed}\end{array}\right] \quad \textbf{(31–21a)}$$

If the light is fully reflected, the pressure is twice as great (Eq. 31–20b):

$$P = \frac{2\bar{S}}{c}. \qquad \left[\begin{array}{c}\text{fully}\\\text{reflected}\end{array}\right] \quad \textbf{(31–21b)}$$

EXAMPLE 31–7 **ESTIMATE** **Solar pressure.** Radiation from the Sun that reaches the Earth's surface (after passing through the atmosphere) transports energy at a rate of about $1000\,\text{W/m}^2$. Estimate the pressure and force exerted by the Sun on your outstretched hand.

APPROACH The radiation is partially reflected and partially absorbed, so let us estimate simply $P = \bar{S}/c$.

SOLUTION $P \approx \dfrac{\bar{S}}{c} = \dfrac{1000\,\text{W/m}^2}{3 \times 10^8\,\text{m/s}} \approx 3 \times 10^{-6}\,\text{N/m}^2.$

An estimate of the area of your outstretched hand might be about 10 cm by 20 cm, so $A = 0.02\,\text{m}^2$. Then the force is

$$F = PA \approx (3 \times 10^{-6}\,\text{N/m}^2)(0.02\,\text{m}^2) \approx 6 \times 10^{-8}\,\text{N}.$$

NOTE These numbers are tiny. The force of gravity on your hand, for comparison, is maybe a half pound, or with $m = 0.2\,\text{kg}$, $mg \approx (0.2\,\text{kg})(9.8\,\text{m/s}^2) \approx 2\,\text{N}$. The radiation pressure on your hand is imperceptible compared to gravity.

[†]Very roughly, if we think of light as particles (and we do—see Chapter 37), the force that would be needed to bring such a particle moving at speed c to "rest" (i.e. absorption) is $F = \Delta p/\Delta t$. But F is also related to energy by Eq. 8–7, $F = \Delta U/\Delta x$, so $\Delta p = F\,\Delta t = \Delta U/(\Delta x/\Delta t) = \Delta U/c$ where we identify $(\Delta x/\Delta t)$ with the speed of light c.

EXAMPLE 31–8 **ESTIMATE** **A solar sail.** Proposals have been made to use the radiation pressure from the Sun to help propel spacecraft around the solar system. (a) About how much force would be applied on a 1 km × 1 km highly reflective sail, and (b) by how much would this increase the speed of a 5000-kg spacecraft in one year? (c) If the spacecraft started from rest, about how far would it travel in a year?

APPROACH Pressure P is force per unit area, so $F = PA$. We use the estimate of Example 31–7, doubling it for a reflecting surface $P = 2\overline{S}/c$. We find the acceleration from Newton's second law, and assume it is constant, and then find the speed from $v = v_0 + at$. The distance traveled is given by $x = \frac{1}{2}at^2$.

SOLUTION (a) Doubling the result of Example 31–7, the solar pressure is $2\overline{S}/c = 6 \times 10^{-6}\,\text{N/m}^2$. Then the force is $F \approx PA = (6 \times 10^{-6}\,\text{N/m}^2)(10^6\,\text{m}^2) \approx 6\,\text{N}$. (b) The acceleration is $a \approx F/m \approx (6\,\text{N})/(5000\,\text{kg}) \approx 1.2 \times 10^{-3}\,\text{m/s}^2$. The speed increase is $v - v_0 = at = (1.2 \times 10^{-3}\,\text{m/s}^2)(365\,\text{days})(24\,\text{hr/day})(3600\,\text{s/hr}) \approx 4 \times 10^4\,\text{m/s}$ ($\approx 150{,}000\,\text{km/h}!$). (c) Starting from rest, this acceleration would result in a distance of about $\frac{1}{2}at^2 \approx 6 \times 10^{11}\,\text{m}$ in a year, about four times the Sun-Earth distance. The starting point should be far from the Earth so the Earth's gravitational force is small compared to 6 N.

NOTE A large sail providing a small force over a long time can result in a lot of motion.

Although you cannot directly feel the effects of radiation pressure, the phenomenon is quite dramatic when applied to atoms irradiated by a finely focused laser beam. An atom has a mass on the order of 10^{-27} kg, and a laser beam can deliver energy at a rate of $1000\,\text{W/m}^2$. This is the same intensity used in Example 31–7, but here a radiation pressure of $10^{-6}\,\text{N/m}^2$ would be very significant on a molecule whose mass might be 10^{-23} to 10^{-26} kg. It is possible to move atoms and molecules around by steering them with a laser beam, in a device called "optical tweezers." Optical tweezers have some remarkable applications. They are of great interest to biologists, especially since optical tweezers can manipulate live microorganisms, and components within a cell, without damaging them. Optical tweezers have been used to measure the elastic properties of DNA by pulling each end of the molecule with such a laser "tweezers."

PHYSICS APPLIED
Optical tweezers

31–10 Radio and Television; Wireless Communication

PHYSICS APPLIED
Wireless transmission

Electromagnetic waves offer the possibility of transmitting information over long distances. Among the first to realize this and put it into practice was Guglielmo Marconi (1874–1937) who, in the 1890s, invented and developed wireless communication. With it, messages could be sent at the speed of light without the use of wires. The first signals were merely long and short pulses that could be translated into words by a code, such as the "dots" and "dashes" of the Morse code: they were digital wireless, believe it or not. In 1895 Marconi sent wireless signals a kilometer or two in Italy. By 1901 he had sent test signals 3000 km across the ocean from Newfoundland, Canada, to Cornwall, England. In 1903 he sent the first practical commercial messages from Cape Cod, Massachusetts, to England: the London *Times* printed news items sent from its New York correspondent. 1903 was also the year of the first powered airplane flight by the Wright brothers. The hallmarks of the modern age—wireless communication and flight—date from the same year. Our modern world of wireless communication, including radio, television, cordless phones, cell phones, Bluetooth, wi-fi, and satellite communication, are simply modern applications of Marconi's pioneering work.

The next decade saw the development of vacuum tubes. Out of this early work radio and television were born. We now discuss briefly (1) how radio and TV signals are transmitted, and (2) how they are received at home.

FIGURE 31–16 Block diagram of a radio transmitter.

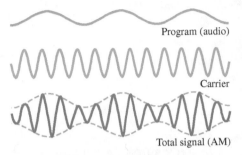

FIGURE 31–17 In amplitude modulation (AM), the amplitude of the carrier signal is made to vary in proportion to the audio signal's amplitude.

  PHYSICS APPLIED
AM and FM

FIGURE 31–18 In frequency modulation (FM), the frequency of the carrier signal is made to change in proportion to the audio signal's amplitude. This method is used by FM radio and television.

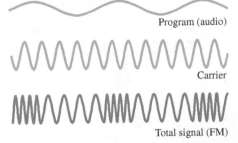

PHYSICS APPLIED
Radio and TV receivers

The process by which a radio station transmits information (words and music) is outlined in Fig. 31–16. The audio (sound) information is changed into an electrical signal of the same frequencies by, say, a microphone or magnetic read/write head. This electrical signal is called an audiofrequency (AF) signal, since the frequencies are in the audio range (20 to 20,000 Hz). The signal is amplified electronically and is then mixed with a radio-frequency (RF) signal called its **carrier frequency**, which represents that station. AM radio stations have carrier frequencies from about 530 kHz to 1700 kHz. For example, "710 on your dial" means a station whose carrier frequency is 710 kHz. FM radio stations have much higher carrier frequencies, between 88 MHz and 108 MHz. The carrier frequencies for broadcast TV stations in the United States lie between 54 MHz and 72 MHz, between 76 MHz and 88 MHz, between 174 MHz and 216 MHz, and between 470 MHz and 698 MHz.

The mixing of the audio and carrier frequencies is done in two ways. In **amplitude modulation** (AM), the amplitude of the high-frequency carrier wave is made to vary in proportion to the amplitude of the audio signal, as shown in Fig. 31–17. It is called "amplitude modulation" because the *amplitude* of the carrier is altered ("modulate" means to change or alter). In **frequency modulation** (FM), the *frequency* of the carrier wave is made to change in proportion to the audio signal's amplitude, as shown in Fig. 31–18. The mixed signal is amplified further and sent to the transmitting antenna, where the complex mixture of frequencies is sent out in the form of EM waves. In digital communication, the signal is put into a digital form (Section 29–8) which modulates the carrier.

A television transmitter works in a similar way, using FM for audio and AM for video; both audio and video signals (see Section 23–9) are mixed with carrier frequencies.

Now let us look at the other end of the process, the reception of radio and TV programs at home. A simple radio receiver is diagrammed in Fig. 31–19. The EM waves sent out by all stations are received by the antenna. The signals the antenna detects and sends to the receiver are very small and contain frequencies from many different stations. The receiver selects out a particular RF frequency (actually a narrow range of frequencies) corresponding to a particular station using a resonant *LC* circuit (Sections 30–6 and 30–9).

FIGURE 31–19 Block diagram of a simple radio receiver.

A simple way of tuning a station is shown in Fig. 31–20. A particular station is "tuned in" by adjusting C and/or L so that the resonant frequency of the circuit equals that of the station's carrier frequency. The signal, containing both audio and carrier frequencies, next goes to the *demodulator*, or *detector* (Fig. 31–19), where "demodulation" takes place—that is, the RF carrier frequency is separated from the audio signal. The audio signal is amplified and sent to a loudspeaker or headphones.

Modern receivers have more stages than those shown. Various means are used to increase the sensitivity and selectivity (ability to detect weak signals and distinguish them from other stations), and to minimize distortion of the original signal.[†]

A television receiver does similar things to both the audio and the video signals. The audio signal goes finally to the loudspeaker, and the video signal to the monitor, such as a *cathode ray tube* (CRT) or LCD screen (Sections 23–9 and 35–12).

One kind of antenna consists of one or more conducting rods; the electric field in the EM waves exerts a force on the electrons in the conductor, causing them to move back and forth at the frequencies of the waves (Fig. 31–21a). A second type of antenna consists of a tubular coil of wire which detects the magnetic field of the wave: the changing B field induces an emf in the coil (Fig. 31–21b).

FIGURE 31–20 Simple tuning stage of a radio.

FIGURE 31–21 Antennas. (a) Electric field of EM wave produces a current in an antenna consisting of straight wire or rods. (b) Changing magnetic field induces an emf and current in a loop antenna.

A satellite dish (Fig. 31–22) consists of a parabolic reflector that focuses the EM waves onto a "horn," similar to a concave mirror telescope (Fig. 33–38).

FIGURE 31–22 A satellite dish.

EXAMPLE 31–9 Tuning a station. Calculate the transmitting wavelength of an FM radio station that transmits at 100 MHz.

APPROACH Radio is transmitted as an EM wave, so the speed is $c = 3.0 \times 10^8$ m/s. The wavelength is found from Eq. 31–14, $\lambda = c/f$.

SOLUTION The carrier frequency is $f = 100$ MHz $= 1.0 \times 10^8$ s^{-1}, so

$$\lambda = \frac{c}{f} = \frac{(3.0 \times 10^8 \text{ m/s})}{(1.0 \times 10^8 \text{ s}^{-1})} = 3.0 \text{ m}.$$

NOTE The wavelengths of other FM signals (88 MHz to 108 MHz) are close to the 3.0-m wavelength of this station. FM antennas are typically 1.5 m long, or about a half wavelength. This length is chosen so that the antenna reacts in a resonant fashion and thus is more sensitive to FM frequencies. AM radio antennas would have to be very long to be either $\frac{1}{2}\lambda$ or $\frac{1}{4}\lambda$.

[†]For *FM stereo broadcasting*, two signals are carried by the carrier wave. One signal contains frequencies up to about 15 kHz, which includes most audio frequencies. The other signal includes the same range of frequencies, but 19 kHz is added to it. A stereo receiver subtracts this 19,000-Hz signal and distributes the two signals to the left and right channels. The first signal consists of the sum of left and right channels (L + R), so mono radios detect all the sound. The second signal is the difference between left and right (L − R). Hence the receiver must add and subtract the two signals to get pure left and right signals for each channel.

Other EM Wave Communications

The various regions of the radio-wave spectrum are assigned by governmental agencies for various purposes. Besides those mentioned above, there are "bands" assigned for use by ships, airplanes, police, military, amateurs, satellites and space, and radar. Cell phones, for example, are complete radio transmitters and receivers. In the U.S., CDMA cell phones function on two different bands: 800 MHz and 1900 MHz (= 1.9 GHz). Europe, Asia, and much of the rest of the world use a different system: the international standard called GSM (Global System for Mobile Communication), on 900-MHz and 1800-MHz bands. The U.S. now also has the GSM option (at 850 MHz and 1.9 GHz), as does much of the rest of the Americas. A 700-MHz band is now being made available for cell phones (it used to carry TV broadcast channels 52–69, now no longer used). Radio-controlled toys (cars, sailboats, robotic animals, etc.) can use various frequencies from 27 MHz to 75 MHz. Automobile remote (keyless) entry may operate around 300 MHz or 400 MHz.

Cable TV channels are carried as electromagnetic waves along a coaxial cable (see Fig. 31–13) rather than being broadcast and received through the "air." The channels are in the same part of the EM spectrum, hundreds of MHz, but some are at frequencies not available for TV broadcast. Digital satellite TV and radio are carried in the microwave portion of the spectrum (12 to 14 GHz and 2.3 GHz, respectively).

Summary

James Clerk Maxwell synthesized an elegant theory in which all electric and magnetic phenomena could be described using four equations, now called **Maxwell's equations**. They are based on earlier ideas, but Maxwell added one more—that a changing electric field produces a magnetic field. Maxwell's equations are

$$\oint \vec{E} \cdot d\vec{A} = \frac{Q}{\epsilon_0} \tag{31–5a}$$

$$\oint \vec{B} \cdot d\vec{A} = 0 \tag{31–5b}$$

$$\oint \vec{E} \cdot d\vec{\ell} = -\frac{d\Phi_B}{dt} \tag{31–5c}$$

$$\oint \vec{B} \cdot d\vec{\ell} = \mu_0 I + \mu_0 \epsilon_0 \frac{d\Phi_E}{dt}. \tag{31–5d}$$

The first two are Gauss's laws for electricity and for magnetism; the other two are Faraday's law and Ampère's law (as extended by Maxwell), respectively.

Maxwell's theory predicted that transverse **electromagnetic (EM) waves** would be produced by accelerating electric charges, and these waves would propagate through space at the speed of light c, given by

$$c = \frac{1}{\sqrt{\epsilon_0 \mu_0}} = 3.00 \times 10^8 \, \text{m/s}. \tag{31–12}$$

The wavelength λ and frequency f of EM waves are related to their speed c by

$$c = \lambda f, \tag{31–14}$$

just as for other waves.

The oscillating electric and magnetic fields in an EM wave are perpendicular to each other and to the direction of propagation. EM waves are waves of fields, not matter, and can propagate in empty space.

After EM waves were experimentally detected in the late 1800s, the idea that light is an EM wave (although of much higher frequency than those detected directly) became generally accepted. The **electromagnetic spectrum** includes EM waves of a wide variety of wavelengths, from microwaves and radio waves to visible light to X-rays and gamma rays, all of which travel through space at a speed $c = 3.00 \times 10^8 \, \text{m/s}$.

The energy carried by EM waves can be described by the **Poynting vector**

$$\vec{S} = \frac{1}{\mu_0} \vec{E} \times \vec{B} \tag{31–18}$$

which gives the rate energy is carried across unit area per unit time when the electric and magnetic fields in an EM wave in free space are $\vec{E}$ and $\vec{B}$.

EM waves carry momentum and exert a **radiation pressure** proportional to the intensity S of the wave.

Questions

1. An electric field $\vec{E}$ points away from you, and its magnitude is increasing. Will the induced magnetic field be clockwise or counterclockwise? What if $\vec{E}$ points toward you and is decreasing?

2. What is the direction of the displacement current in Fig. 31–3? (*Note*: The capacitor is discharging.)

3. Why is it that the magnetic field of a displacement current in a capacitor is so much harder to detect than the magnetic field of a conduction current?

4. Are there any good reasons for calling the term $\mu_0 \epsilon_0 \, d\Phi_E/dt$ in Eq. 31–1 as being due to a "current"? Explain.

5. The electric field in an EM wave traveling north oscillates in an east–west plane. Describe the direction of the magnetic field vector in this wave.

6. Is sound an electromagnetic wave? If not, what kind of wave is it?

7. Can EM waves travel through a perfect vacuum? Can sound waves?

8. When you flip a light switch, does the overhead light go on immediately? Explain.

9. Are the wavelengths of radio and television signals longer or shorter than those detectable by the human eye?

10. What does the wavelength calculated in Example 31–2 tell you about the phase of a 60-Hz ac current that starts at a power plant as compared to its phase at a house 200 km away?

11. When you connect two loudspeakers to the output of a stereo amplifier, should you be sure the lead wires are equal in length so that there will not be a time lag between speakers? Explain.

12. In the electromagnetic spectrum, what type of EM wave would have a wavelength of 10^3 km; 1 km; 1 m; 1 cm; 1 mm; 1 μm?

13. Can radio waves have the same frequencies as sound waves (20 Hz–20,000 Hz)?

14. Discuss how cordless telephones make use of EM waves. What about cellular telephones?

15. Can two radio or TV stations broadcast on the same carrier frequency? Explain.

16. If a radio transmitter has a vertical antenna, should a receiver's antenna (rod type) be vertical or horizontal to obtain best reception?

17. The carrier frequencies of FM broadcasts are much higher than for AM broadcasts. On the basis of what you learned about diffraction in Chapter 15, explain why AM signals can be detected more readily than FM signals behind low hills or buildings.

18. A lost person may signal by flashing a flashlight on and off using Morse code. This is actually a modulated EM wave. Is it AM or FM? What is the frequency of the carrier, approximately?

Problems

31–1 $\vec{B}$ Produced by Changing $\vec{E}$

1. (I) Determine the rate at which the electric field changes between the round plates of a capacitor, 6.0 cm in diameter, if the plates are spaced 1.1 mm apart and the voltage across them is changing at a rate of 120 V/s.

2. (I) Calculate the displacement current I_D between the square plates, 5.8 cm on a side, of a capacitor if the electric field is changing at a rate of 2.0×10^6 V/m·s.

3. (II) At a given instant, a 2.8-A current flows in the wires connected to a parallel-plate capacitor. What is the rate at which the electric field is changing between the plates if the square plates are 1.60 cm on a side?

4. (II) A 1500-nF capacitor with circular parallel plates 2.0 cm in diameter is accumulating charge at the rate of 38.0 mC/s at some instant in time. What will be the induced magnetic field strength 10.0 cm radially outward from the center of the plates? What will be the value of the field strength after the capacitor is fully charged?

5. (II) Show that the displacement current through a parallel-plate capacitor can be written $I_D = C\, dV/dt$, where V is the voltage across the capacitor at any instant.

6. (II) Suppose an air-gap capacitor has circular plates of radius $R = 2.5$ cm and separation $d = 1.6$ mm. A 76.0-Hz emf, $\mathscr{E} = \mathscr{E}_0 \cos \omega t$, is applied to the capacitor. The maximum displacement current is 35 μA. Determine (a) the maximum conduction current I, (b) the value of $\mathscr{E}_0$, (c) the maximum value of $d\Phi_E/dt$ between the plates. Neglect fringing.

7. (III) Suppose that a circular parallel-plate capacitor has radius $R_0 = 3.0$ cm and plate separation $d = 5.0$ mm. A sinusoidal potential difference $V = V_0 \sin(2\pi f t)$ is applied across the plates, where $V_0 = 150$ V and $f = 60$ Hz. (a) In the region between the plates, show that the magnitude of the induced magnetic field is given by $B = B_0(R) \cos(2\pi f t)$, where R is the radial distance from the capacitor's central axis. (b) Determine the expression for the amplitude $B_0(R)$ of this time-dependent (sinusoidal) field when $R \le R_0$, and when $R > R_0$. (c) Plot $B_0(R)$ in tesla for the range $0 \le R \le 10$ cm.

31–5 EM Waves

8. (I) If the electric field in an EM wave has a peak magnitude of 0.57×10^{-4} V/m, what is the peak magnitude of the magnetic field strength?

9. (I) If the magnetic field in a traveling EM wave has a peak magnitude of 12.5 nT, what is the peak magnitude of the electric field?

10. (I) In an EM wave traveling west, the B field oscillates vertically and has a frequency of 80.0 kHz and an rms strength of 7.75×10^{-9} T. Determine the frequency and rms strength of the electric field. What is its direction?

11. (II) The electric field of a plane EM wave is given by $E_x = E_0 \cos(kz + \omega t)$, $E_y = E_z = 0$. Determine (a) the direction of propagation and (b) the magnitude and direction of $\vec{B}$.

12. (III) Consider two possible candidates $E(x, t)$ as solutions of the wave equation for an EM wave's electric field. Let A and α be constants. Show that (a) $E(x, t) = Ae^{-\alpha(x-vt)^2}$ satisfies the wave equation, and that (b) $E(x, t) = Ae^{-(\alpha x^2 - vt)}$ does not satisfy the wave equation.

31–6 Electromagnetic Spectrum

13. (I) What is the frequency of a microwave whose wavelength is 1.50 cm?

14. (I) (a) What is the wavelength of a 25.75×10^9 Hz radar signal? (b) What is the frequency of an X-ray with wavelength 0.12 nm?

15. (I) How long does it take light to reach us from the Sun, 1.50×10^8 km away?

16. (I) An EM wave has frequency 8.56×10^{14} Hz. What is its wavelength, and how would we classify it?

17. (I) Electromagnetic waves and sound waves can have the same frequency. (a) What is the wavelength of a 1.00-kHz electromagnetic wave? (b) What is the wavelength of a 1.00-kHz sound wave? (The speed of sound in air is 341 m/s.) (c) Can you hear a 1.00-kHz electromagnetic wave?

18. (II) Pulsed lasers used for science and medicine produce very brief bursts of electromagnetic energy. If the laser light wavelength is 1062 nm (Neodymium–YAG laser), and the pulse lasts for 38 picoseconds, how many wavelengths are found within the laser pulse? How brief would the pulse need to be to fit only one wavelength?

19. (II) How long would it take a message sent as radio waves from Earth to reach Mars (a) when nearest Earth, (b) when farthest from Earth?

20. (II) An electromagnetic wave has an electric field given by
$$\vec{E} = \hat{i}(225 \text{ V/m}) \sin[(0.077 \text{ m}^{-1})z - (2.3 \times 10^7 \text{ rad/s})t].$$
(a) What are the wavelength and frequency of the wave? (b) Write down an expression for the magnetic field.

31–7 Speed of Light

21. (II) What is the minimum angular speed at which Michelson's eight-sided mirror would have had to rotate to reflect light into an observer's eye by succeeding mirror faces (1/8 of a revolution, Fig. 31–14)?

31–8 EM Wave Energy; Poynting Vector

22. (I) The $\vec{\mathbf{E}}$ field in an EM wave has a peak of 26.5 mV/m. What is the average rate at which this wave carries energy across unit area per unit time?

23. (II) The magnetic field in a traveling EM wave has an rms strength of 22.5 nT. How long does it take to deliver 335 J of energy to 1.00 cm^2 of a wall that it hits perpendicularly?

24. (II) How much energy is transported across a 1.00 cm^2 area per hour by an EM wave whose E field has an rms strength of 32.8 mV/m?

25. (II) A spherically spreading EM wave comes from a 1500-W source. At a distance of 5.0 m, what is the intensity, and what is the rms value of the electric field?

26. (II) If the amplitude of the B field of an EM wave is 2.5×10^{-7} T, (a) what is the amplitude of the E field? (b) What is the average power per unit area of the EM wave?

27. (II) What is the energy contained in a 1.00-m^3 volume near the Earth's surface due to radiant energy from the Sun? See Example 31–6.

28. (II) A 15.8-mW laser puts out a narrow beam 2.00 mm in diameter. What are the rms values of E and B in the beam?

29. (II) Estimate the average power output of the Sun, given that about 1350 W/m^2 reaches the upper atmosphere of the Earth.

30. (II) A high-energy pulsed laser emits a 1.0-ns-long pulse of average power 1.8×10^{11} W. The beam is 2.2×10^{-3} m in radius. Determine (a) the energy delivered in each pulse, and (b) the rms value of the electric field.

31. (II) How practical is solar power for various devices? Assume that on a sunny day, sunlight has an intensity of 1000 W/m^2 at the surface of Earth and that, when illuminated by that sunlight, a solar-cell panel can convert 10% of the sunlight's energy into electric power. For each device given below, calculate the area A of solar panel needed to power it. (a) A calculator consumes 50 mW. Find A in cm^2. Is A small enough so that the solar panel can be mounted directly on the calculator that it is powering? (b) A hair dryer consumes 1500 W. Find A in m^2. Assuming no other electronic devices are operating within a house at the same time, is A small enough so that the hair dryer can be powered by a solar panel mounted on the house's roof? (c) A car requires 20 hp for highway driving at constant velocity (this car would perform poorly in situations requiring acceleration). Find A in m^2. Is A small enough so that this solar panel can be mounted directly on the car and power it in "real time"?

32. (III) (a) Show that the Poynting vector $\vec{\mathbf{S}}$ points radially inward toward the center of a circular parallel-plate capacitor when it is being charged as in Example 31–1. (b) Integrate $\vec{\mathbf{S}}$ over the cylindrical boundary of the capacitor gap to show that the rate at which energy enters the capacitor is equal to the rate at which electrostatic energy is being stored in the electric field of the capacitor (Section 24–4). Ignore fringing of $\vec{\mathbf{E}}$.

33. (III) The Arecibo radio telescope in Puerto Rico can detect a radio wave with an intensity as low as 1×10^{-23} W/m^2. As a "best-case" scenario for communication with extraterrestrials, consider the following: suppose an advanced civilization located at point A, a distance x away from Earth, is somehow able to harness the entire power output of a Sun-like star, converting that power completely into a radio-wave signal which is transmitted uniformly in all directions from A. (a) In order for Arecibo to detect this radio signal, what is the maximum value for x in light-years (1 ly $\approx 10^{16}$ m)? (b) How does this maximum value compare with the 100,000-ly size of our Milky Way galaxy? The intensity of sunlight at Earth's orbital distance from the Sun is 1350 W/m^2.

31–9 Radiation Pressure

34. (II) Estimate the radiation pressure due to a 75-W bulb at a distance of 8.0 cm from the center of the bulb. Estimate the force exerted on your fingertip if you place it at this point.

35. (II) Laser light can be focused (at best) to a spot with a radius r equal to its wavelength λ. Suppose that a 1.0-W beam of green laser light $(\lambda = 5 \times 10^{-7}$ m$)$ is used to form such a spot and that a cylindrical particle of about that size (let the radius and height equal r) is illuminated by the laser as shown in Fig. 31–23. Estimate the acceleration of the particle, if its density equals that of water and it absorbs the radiation. [This order-of-magnitude calculation convinced researchers of the feasibility of "optical tweezers," p. 829.]

FIGURE 31–23
Problem 35.

$\lambda = 5 \times 10^{-7}$ m

36. (II) The powerful laser used in a laser light show provides a 3-mm diameter beam of green light with a power of 3 W. When a space-walking astronaut is outside the Space Shuttle, her colleague inside the Shuttle playfully aims such a laser beam at the astronaut's space suit. The masses of the suited astronaut and the Space Shuttle are 120 kg and 103,000 kg, respectively. (a) Assuming the suit is perfectly reflecting, determine the "radiation-pressure" force exerted on the astronaut by the laser beam. (b) Assuming the astronaut is separated from the Shuttle's center of mass by 20 m, model the Shuttle as a sphere in order to estimate the gravitation force it exerts on the astronaut. (c) Which of the two forces is larger, and by what factor?

37. (II) What size should the solar panel on a satellite orbiting Jupiter be if it is to collect the same amount of radiation from the Sun as a 1.0-m^2 solar panel on a satellite orbiting Earth?

38. (I) What is the range of wavelengths for (*a*) FM radio (88 MHz to 108 MHz) and (*b*) AM radio (535 kHz to 1700 kHz)?

39. (I) Estimate the wavelength for 1.9-GHz cell phone reception.

40. (I) The variable capacitor in the tuner of an AM radio has a capacitance of 2200 pF when the radio is tuned to a station at 550 kHz. What must the capacitance be for a station near the other end of the dial, 1610 kHz?

41. (II) A certain FM radio tuning circuit has a fixed capacitor $C = 620$ pF. Tuning is done by a variable inductance. What range of values must the inductance have to tune stations from 88 MHz to 108 MHz?

42. (II) A satellite beams microwave radiation with a power of 12 kW toward the Earth's surface, 550 km away. When the beam strikes Earth, its circular diameter is about 1500 m. Find the rms electric field strength of the beam at the surface of the Earth.

General Problems

43. A 1.60-m-long FM antenna is oriented parallel to the electric field of an EM wave. How large must the electric field be to produce a 1.00-mV (rms) voltage between the ends of the antenna? What is the rate of energy transport per square meter?

44. Who will hear the voice of a singer first: a person in the balcony 50.0 m away from the stage (see Fig. 31–24), or a person 1500 km away at home whose ear is next to the radio listening to a live broadcast? Roughly how much sooner? Assume the microphone is a few centimeters from the singer and the temperature is 20°C.

FIGURE 31–24 Problem 44.

45. Light is emitted from an ordinary lightbulb filament in wave-train bursts about 10^{-8} s in duration. What is the length in space of such wave trains?

46. Radio-controlled clocks throughout the United States receive a radio signal from a transmitter in Fort Collins, Colorado, that accurately (within a microsecond) marks the beginning of each minute. A slight delay, however, is introduced because this signal must travel from the transmitter to the clocks. Assuming Fort Collins is no more than 3000 km from any point in the U.S., what is the longest travel-time delay?

47. A radio voice signal from the *Apollo* crew on the Moon (Fig. 31–25) was beamed to a listening crowd from a radio speaker. If you were standing 25 m from the loudspeaker, what was the total time lag between when you heard the sound and when the sound entered a microphone on the Moon and traveled to Earth?

FIGURE 31–25
Problem 47.

48. Cosmic microwave background radiation fills all space with an average energy density of 4×10^{-14} J/m³. (*a*) Find the rms value of the electric field associated with this radiation. (*b*) How far from a 7.5-kW radio transmitter emitting uniformly in all directions would you find a comparable value?

49. What are E_0 and B_0 2.00 m from a 75-W light source? Assume the bulb emits radiation of a single frequency uniformly in all directions.

50. Estimate the rms electric field in the sunlight that hits Mars, knowing that the Earth receives about 1350 W/m² and that Mars is 1.52 times farther from the Sun (on average) than is the Earth.

51. At a given instant in time, a traveling EM wave is noted to have its maximum magnetic field pointing west and its maximum electric field pointing south. In which direction is the wave traveling? If the rate of energy flow is 560 W/m², what are the maximum values for the two fields?

52. How large an emf (rms) will be generated in an antenna that consists of a circular coil 2.2 cm in diameter having 320 turns of wire, when an EM wave of frequency 810 kHz transporting energy at an average rate of 1.0×10^{-4} W/m² passes through it? [*Hint:* you can use Eq. 29–4 for a generator, since it could be applied to an observer moving with the coil so that the magnetic field is oscillating with the frequency $f = \omega/2\pi$.]

53. The average intensity of a particular TV station's signal is 1.0×10^{-13} W/m² when it arrives at a 33-cm-diameter satellite TV antenna. (*a*) Calculate the total energy received by the antenna during 6.0 hours of viewing this station's programs. (*b*) What are the amplitudes of the E and B fields of the EM wave?

54. A radio station is allowed to broadcast at an average power not to exceed 25 kW. If an electric field amplitude of 0.020 V/m is considered to be acceptable for receiving the radio transmission, estimate how many kilometers away you might be able to hear this station.

55. A point source emits light energy uniformly in all directions at an average rate P_0 with a single frequency f. Show that the peak electric field in the wave is given by

$$E_0 = \sqrt{\frac{\mu_0 c P_0}{2\pi r^2}}.$$

56. Suppose a 35-kW radio station emits EM waves uniformly in all directions. (*a*) How much energy per second crosses a 1.0-m² area 1.0 km from the transmitting antenna? (*b*) What is the rms magnitude of the $\vec{E}$ field at this point, assuming the station is operating at full power? What is the rms voltage induced in a 1.0-m-long vertical car antenna (*c*) 1.0 km away, (*d*) 50 km away?

57. What is the maximum power level of a radio station so as to avoid electrical breakdown of air at a distance of 0.50 m from the transmitting antenna? Assume the antenna is a point source. Air breaks down in an electric field of about 3×10^6 V/m.

58. In free space ("vacuum"), where the net charge and current flow is zero, the speed of an EM wave is given by $v = 1/\sqrt{\epsilon_0 \mu_0}$. If, instead, an EM wave travels in a nonconducting ("dielectric") material with dielectric constant K, then $v = 1/\sqrt{K \epsilon_0 \mu_0}$. For frequencies corresponding to the visible spectrum (near 5×10^{14} Hz), the dielectric constant of water is 1.77. Predict the speed of light in water and compare this value (as a percentage) with the speed of light in a vacuum.

59. The metal walls of a microwave oven form a cavity of dimensions 37 cm $\times$ 37 cm $\times$ 20 cm. When 2.45-GHz microwaves are continuously introduced into this cavity, reflection of incident waves from the walls set up standing waves with nodes at the walls. Along the 37-cm dimension of the oven, how many nodes exist (excluding the nodes at the wall) and what is the distance between adjacent nodes? [Because no heating occurs at these nodes, most microwaves rotate food while operating.]

60. Imagine that a steady current I flows in a straight cylindrical wire of radius R_0 and resistivity ρ. (a) If the current is then changed at a rate dI/dt, show that a displacement current I_D exists in the wire of magnitude $\epsilon_0 \rho (dI/dt)$. (b) If the current in a copper wire is changed at the rate of 1.0 A/ms, determine the magnitude of I_D. (c) Determine the magnitude of the magnetic field B_D (T) created by I_D at the surface of a copper wire with $R_0 = 1.0$ mm. Compare (as a ratio) B_D with the field created at the surface of the wire by a steady current of 1.0 A.

61. The electric field of an EM wave pulse traveling along the x axis in free space is given by $E_y = E_0 \exp[-\alpha^2 x^2 - \beta^2 t^2 + 2\alpha\beta xt]$, where E_0, α, and β are positive constants. (a) Is the pulse moving in the $+x$ or $-x$ direction? (b) Express β in terms of α and c (speed of light in free space). (c) Determine the expression for the magnetic field of this EM wave.

62. Suppose that a right-moving EM wave overlaps with a left-moving EM wave so that, in a certain region of space, the total electric field in the y direction and magnetic field in the z direction are given by $E_y = E_0 \sin(kx - \omega t) + E_0 \sin(kx + \omega t)$ and $B_z = B_0 \sin(kx - \omega t) - B_0 \sin(kx + \omega t)$. (a) Find the mathematical expression that represents the standing electric and magnetic waves in the y and z directions, respectively. (b) Determine the Poynting vector and find the x locations at which it is zero at all times.

63. The electric and magnetic fields of a certain EM wave in free space are given by $\vec{E} = E_0 \sin(kx - \omega t)\hat{j} + E_0 \cos(kx - \omega t)\hat{k}$ and $\vec{B} = B_0 \cos(kx - \omega t)\hat{j} - B_0 \sin(kx - \omega t)\hat{k}$. (a) Show that $\vec{E}$ and $\vec{B}$ are perpendicular to each other at all times. (b) For this wave, $\vec{E}$ and $\vec{B}$ are in a plane parallel to the yz plane. Show that the wave moves in a direction perpendicular to both $\vec{E}$ and $\vec{B}$. (c) At any arbitrary choice of position x and time t, show that the magnitudes of $\vec{E}$ and $\vec{B}$ always equal E_0 and B_0, respectively. (d) At $x = 0$, draw the orientation of $\vec{E}$ and $\vec{B}$ in the yz plane at $t = 0$. Then qualitatively describe the motion of these vectors in the yz plane as time increases. [Note: The EM wave in this Problem is "circularly polarized."]

Answers to Exercises

A: (c).

B: (b).

C: (a) 3.8×10^6 Hz; (b) 5.5×10^{18} Hz.

D: 45 cm.

E: Yes; the signal still travels 72,000 km.

F: Over 4 hours.

Reflection from still water, as from a glass mirror, can be analyzed using the ray model of light.

Is this picture right side up? How can you tell? What are the clues? Notice the people and position of the Sun. Ray diagrams, which we will learn to draw in this Chapter, can provide the answer. See Example 32–3.

In this first Chapter on light and optics, we use the ray model of light to understand the formation of images by mirrors, both plane and curved (spherical). We also begin our study of refraction—how light rays bend when they go from one medium to another—which prepares us for our study in the next Chapter of lenses, which are the crucial part of so many optical instruments.

32

Light: Reflection and Refraction

CHAPTER-OPENING QUESTION—Guess now!

A 2.0-m-tall person is standing 2.0 m from a flat vertical mirror staring at her image. What minimum height must the mirror have if the person is to see her entire body, from the top of her head to her feet?

(a) 0.50 m.
(b) 1.0 m.
(c) 1.5 m.
(d) 2.0 m.
(e) 2.5 m.

The sense of sight is extremely important to us, for it provides us with a large part of our information about the world. How do we see? What is the something called *light* that enters our eyes and causes the sensation of sight? How does light behave so that we can see everything that we do? We saw in Chapter 31 that light can be considered a form of electromagnetic radiation. We now examine the subject of light in detail in the next four Chapters.

We see an object in one of two ways: (1) the object may be a *source* of light, such as a lightbulb, a flame, or a star, in which case we see the light emitted directly from the source; or, more commonly, (2) we see an object by light *reflected* from it. In the latter case, the light may have originated from the Sun, artificial lights, or a campfire. An understanding of how objects *emit* light was not achieved until the 1920s, and will be discussed in Chapter 37. How light is *reflected* from objects was understood earlier, and will be discussed here, in Section 32–2.

CONTENTS

32–1 The Ray Model of Light

A great deal of evidence suggests that *light travels in straight lines* under a wide variety of circumstances. For example, a source of light like the Sun casts distinct shadows, and the light from a laser pointer appears to be a straight line. In fact, we infer the positions of objects in our environment by assuming that light moves from the object to our eyes in straight-line paths. Our orientation to the physical world is based on this assumption.

This reasonable assumption is the basis of the **ray model** of light. This model assumes that light travels in straight-line paths called **light rays**. Actually, a ray is an idealization; it is meant to represent an extremely narrow beam of light. When we see an object, according to the ray model, light reaches our eyes from each point on the object. Although light rays leave each point in many different directions, normally only a small bundle of these rays can enter an observer's eye, as shown in Fig. 32–1. If the person's head moves to one side, a different bundle of rays will enter the eye from each point.

We saw in Chapter 31 that light can be considered as an electromagnetic wave. Although the ray model of light does not deal with this aspect of light (we discuss the wave nature of light in Chapters 34 and 35), the ray model has been very successful in describing many aspects of light such as reflection, refraction, and the formation of images by mirrors and lenses.[†] Because these explanations involve straight-line rays at various angles, this subject is referred to as **geometric optics**.

FIGURE 32–1 Light rays come from each single point on an object. A small bundle of rays leaving one point is shown entering a person's eye.

32–2 Reflection; Image Formation by a Plane Mirror

When light strikes the surface of an object, some of the light is reflected. The rest can be absorbed by the object (and transformed to thermal energy) or, if the object is transparent like glass or water, part can be transmitted through. For a very smooth shiny object such as a silvered mirror, over 95% of the light may be reflected.

When a narrow beam of light strikes a flat surface (Fig. 32–2), we define the **angle of incidence**, θ_i, to be the angle an incident ray makes with the normal (perpendicular) to the surface, and the **angle of reflection**, θ_r, to be the angle the reflected ray makes with the normal. It is found that the *incident and reflected rays lie in the same plane with the normal to the surface*, and that

the angle of reflection equals the angle of incidence, $\theta_r = \theta_i$.

This is the **law of reflection**, and it is depicted in Fig. 32–2. It was known to the ancient Greeks, and you can confirm it yourself by shining a narrow flashlight beam or a laser pointer at a mirror in a darkened room.

FIGURE 32–2 Law of reflection: (a) Shows a 3-D view of an incident ray being reflected at the top of a flat surface; (b) shows a side or "end-on" view, which we will usually use because of its clarity.

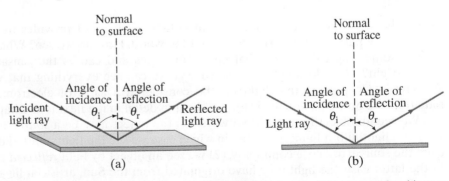

[†]In ignoring the wave properties of light we must be careful that when the light rays pass by objects or through apertures, these must be large compared to the wavelength of the light (so the wave phenomena of interference and diffraction, as discussed in Chapter 15, can be ignored), and we ignore what happens to the light at the edges of objects until we get to Chapters 34 and 35.

When light is incident upon a rough surface, even microscopically rough such as this page, it is reflected in many directions, as shown in Fig. 32–3. This is called **diffuse reflection**. The law of reflection still holds, however, at each small section of the surface. Because of diffuse reflection in all directions, an ordinary object can be seen at many different angles by the light reflected from it. When you move your head to the side, different reflected rays reach your eye from each point on the object (such as this page), Fig. 32–4a. Let us compare diffuse reflection to reflection from a mirror, which is known as **specular reflection**. ("Speculum" is Latin for mirror.) When a narrow beam of light shines on a mirror, the light will not reach your eye unless your eye is positioned at just the right place where the law of reflection is satisfied, as shown in Fig. 32–4b. This is what gives rise to the special image-forming properties of mirrors.

FIGURE 32–3 Diffuse reflection from a rough surface.

(a)

(b)

FIGURE 32–4 A narrow beam of light shines on (a) white paper, and (b) a mirror. In part (a), you can see with your eye the white light reflected at various positions because of diffuse reflection. But in part (b), you see the reflected light only when your eye is placed correctly $(\theta_r = \theta_i)$; mirror reflection is also known as specular reflection. (Galileo, using similar arguments, showed that the Moon must have a rough surface rather than a highly polished surface like a mirror, as some people thought.)

EXAMPLE 32–1 **Reflection from flat mirrors.** Two flat mirrors are perpendicular to each other. An incoming beam of light makes an angle of 15° with the first mirror as shown in Fig. 32–5a. What angle will the outgoing beam make with the second mirror?

APPROACH We sketch the path of the beam as it reflects off the two mirrors, and draw the two normals to the mirrors for the two reflections. We use geometry and the law of reflection to find the various angles.

FIGURE 32–5 Example 32–1.

(a)

(b)

SOLUTION In Fig. 32–5b, $\theta_1 + 15° = 90°$, so $\theta_1 = 75°$; by the law of reflection $\theta_2 = \theta_1 = 75°$ too. The two normals to the two mirrors are perpendicular to each other, so $\theta_2 + \theta_3 + 90° = 180°$ as for any triangle. Thus $\theta_3 = 180° - 90° - 75° = 15°$. By the law of reflection, $\theta_4 = \theta_3 = 15°$, so $\theta_5 = 75°$ is the angle the reflected ray makes with the second mirror surface.

NOTE The outgoing ray is parallel to the incoming ray. Red reflectors on bicycles and cars use this principle.

When you look straight into a mirror, you see what appears to be yourself as well as various objects around and behind you, Fig. 32–6. Your face and the other objects look as if they are in front of you, beyond the mirror. But what you see in the mirror is an **image** of the objects, including yourself, that are in front of the mirror.

FIGURE 32–6 When you look in a mirror, you see an image of yourself and objects around you. You don't see yourself as others see you, because left and right appear reversed in the image.

A "plane" mirror is one with a smooth flat reflecting surface. Figure 32–7 shows how an image is formed by a plane mirror according to the ray model. We are viewing the mirror, on edge, in the diagram of Fig. 32–7, and the rays are shown reflecting from the front surface. (Good mirrors are generally made by putting a highly reflective metallic coating on one surface of a very flat piece of glass.) Rays from two different points on an object (the bottle on the left in Fig. 32–7) are shown: two rays are shown leaving from a point on the top of the bottle, and two more from a point on the bottom. Rays leave each point on the object going in many directions, but only those that enclose the bundle of rays that enter the eye from each of the two points are shown. Each set of diverging rays that reflect from the mirror and enter the eye *appear* to come from a single point (called the image point) behind the mirror, as shown by the dashed lines. That is, our eyes and brain interpret any rays that enter an eye as having traveled straight-line paths. The point from which each bundle of rays seems to come is one point on the image. For each point on the object, there is a corresponding image point.

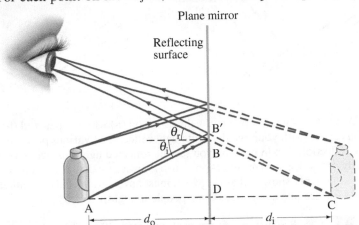

FIGURE 32–7 Formation of a virtual image by a plane mirror.

Let us concentrate on the two rays that leave point A on the object in Fig. 32–7, and strike the mirror at points B and B'. We use geometry for the rays at B. The angles ADB and CDB are right angles; and because of the law of reflection, $\theta_i = \theta_r$ at point B. Therefore, angles ABD and CBD are also equal. The two triangles ABD and CBD are thus congruent, and the length AD = CD. That is, the image appears as far behind the mirror as the object is in front. The **image distance**, d_i (perpendicular distance from mirror to image, Fig. 32–7), equals the **object distance**, d_o (perpendicular distance from object to mirror). From the geometry, we can also see that the height of the image is the same as that of the object.

The light rays do not actually pass through the image location itself in Fig. 32–7. (Note where the red lines are dashed to show they are our projections, not rays.) The image would not appear on paper or film placed at the location of the image. Therefore, it is called a **virtual image**. This is to distinguish it from a **real image** in which the light does pass through the image and which therefore could appear on film or in an electronic sensor, and even on a white sheet of paper or screen placed at the position of the image. Our eyes can see both real and virtual images, as long as the diverging rays enter our pupils. We will see that curved mirrors and lenses can form real images, as well as virtual. A movie projector lens, for example, produces a real image that is visible on the screen.

PHYSICS APPLIED
How tall a mirror do you need to see a reflection of your entire self?

EXAMPLE 32–2 How tall must a full-length mirror be? A woman 1.60 m tall stands in front of a vertical plane mirror. What is the minimum height of the mirror, and how close must its lower edge be to the floor, if she is to be able to see her whole body? Assume her eyes are 10 cm below the top of her head.

APPROACH For her to see her whole body, light rays from the top of her head and from the bottom of her foot must reflect from the mirror and enter her eye: see Fig. 32–8. We don't show two rays diverging from each point as we did in Fig. 32–7, where we wanted to find where the image is. Now that we know the image is the same distance behind a plane mirror as the object is in front, we only need to show one ray leaving point G (top of head) and one ray leaving point A (her toe), and then use simple geometry.

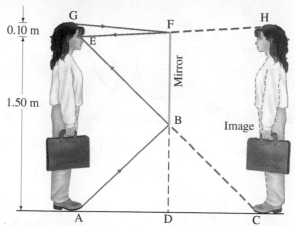

FIGURE 32–8 Seeing oneself in a mirror. Example 32–2.

0.10 m

1.50 m

G
F
E
H
Mirror
B
Image
A
D
C

SOLUTION First consider the ray that leaves her foot at A, reflects at B, and enters the eye at E. The mirror needs to extend no lower than B. The angle of reflection equals the angle of incidence, so the height BD is half of the height AE. Because AE = 1.60 m − 0.10 m = 1.50 m, then BD = 0.75 m. Similarly, if the woman is to see the top of her head, the top edge of the mirror only needs to reach point F, which is 5 cm below the top of her head (half of GE = 10 cm). Thus, DF = 1.55 m, and the mirror needs to have a vertical height of only (1.55 m − 0.75 m) = 0.80 m. The mirror's bottom edge must be 0.75 m above the floor.

NOTE We see that a mirror, if positioned well, need be only half as tall as a person for that person to see all of himself or herself.

EXERCISE A Does the result of Example 32–2 depend on your distance from the mirror? (Try it.)

EXERCISE B Return to the Chapter-Opening Question, page 837, and answer it again now. Try to explain why you may have answered differently the first time.

EXERCISE C Suppose you are standing about 3 m in front of a mirror in a hair salon. You can see yourself from your head to your waist, where the end of the mirror cuts off the rest of your image. If you walk closer to the mirror (*a*) you will not be able to see any more of your image; (*b*) you will be able to see more of your image, below your waist; (*c*) you will see less of your image, with the cutoff rising to be above your waist.

CONCEPTUAL EXAMPLE 32–3 | **Is the photo upside down?** Close examination of the photograph on the first page of this Chapter reveals that in the top portion, the image of the Sun is seen clearly, whereas in the lower portion, the image of the Sun is partially blocked by the tree branches. Show why the reflection is not the same as the real scene by drawing a sketch of this situation, showing the Sun, the camera, the branch, and two rays going from the Sun to the camera (one direct and one reflected). Is the photograph right side up?

RESPONSE We need to draw two diagrams, one assuming the photo on p. 837 is right side up, and another assuming it is upside down. Figure 32–9 is drawn assuming the photo is upside down. In this case, the Sun blocked by the tree would be the direct view, and the full view of the Sun the reflection: the ray which reflects off the water and into the camera travels at an angle below the branch, whereas the ray that travels directly to the camera passes through the branches. This works. Try to draw a diagram assuming the photo is right side up (thus assuming that the image of the Sun in the reflection is higher above the horizon than it is as viewed directly). It won't work. The photo on p. 837 is upside down.

Also, what about the people in the photo? Try to draw a diagram showing why they don't appear in the reflection. [*Hint*: Assume they are not sitting on the edge of poolside, but back from the edge a bit.] Then try to draw a diagram of the reverse (i.e., assume the photo is right side up so the people are visible only in the reflection). Reflected images are not perfect replicas when different planes (distances) are involved.

Branches
Direct ray
Camera or eye
Sun
Reflected ray
Water

FIGURE 32–9 Example 32–3.

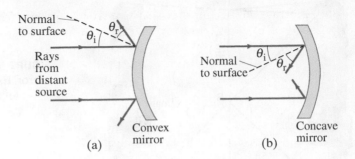

FIGURE 32–10 Mirrors with convex and concave spherical surfaces. Note that $\theta_r = \theta_i$ for each ray.

Normal to surface

θ_i θ_r

Rays from distant source

Convex mirror

(a)

Normal to surface

θ_i θ_r

Concave mirror

(b)

32–3 Formation of Images by Spherical Mirrors

Reflecting surfaces do not have to be flat. The most common *curved* mirrors are *spherical*, which means they form a section of a sphere. A spherical mirror is called **convex** if the reflection takes place on the outer surface of the spherical shape so that the center of the mirror surface bulges out toward the viewer (Fig. 32–10a). A mirror is called **concave** if the reflecting surface is on the inner surface of the sphere so that the mirror surface sinks away from the viewer (like a "cave"), Fig. 32–10b. Concave mirrors are used as shaving or cosmetic mirrors (Fig. 32–11a) because they magnify, and convex mirrors are sometimes used on cars and trucks (rearview mirrors) and in shops (to watch for thieves), because they take in a wide field of view (Fig. 32–11b).

FIGURE 32–11 (a) A concave cosmetic mirror gives a magnified image. (b) A convex mirror in a store reduces image size and so includes a wide field of view.

(a)   (b)

Focal Point and Focal Length

To see how spherical mirrors form images, we first consider an object that is very far from a concave mirror. For a distant object, as shown in Fig. 32–12, the rays from each point on the object that strike the mirror will be nearly parallel. *For an object infinitely far away* (the Sun and stars approach this), *the rays would be precisely parallel.*

Mirror

These rays strike the mirror, and they are essentially parallel.

FIGURE 32–12 If the object's distance is large compared to the size of the mirror (or lens), the rays are nearly parallel. They are parallel for an object at infinity (∞).

Now consider such parallel rays falling on a concave mirror as in Fig. 32–13. The law of reflection holds for each of these rays at the point each strikes the mirror. As can be seen, they are not all brought to a single point. In order to form a sharp image, the rays must come to a point. Thus a spherical mirror will not make as sharp an image as a plane mirror will. However, as we show below, if the mirror is small compared to its radius of curvature, so that a reflected ray makes only a *small angle* with the incident ray (2θ in Fig. 32–14), then the rays will cross each other at very nearly a single point, or **focus**. In the case shown in Fig. 32–14, the incoming rays are parallel to the **principal axis**, which is defined as the straight line perpendicular to the curved surface at its center (line CA in Fig. 32–14). The point F, where incident parallel rays come to a focus after reflection, is called the **focal point** of the mirror. The distance between F and the center of the mirror, length FA, is called the **focal length**, f, of the mirror. The focal point is also the *image point for an object infinitely far away* along the principal axis. The image of the Sun, for example, would be at F.

FIGURE 32–13 Parallel rays striking a concave spherical mirror do not intersect (or focus) at precisely a single point. (This "defect" is referred to as "spherical aberration.")

FIGURE 32–14 Rays parallel to the principal axis of a concave spherical mirror come to a focus at F, the focal point, as long as the mirror is small in width as compared to its radius of curvature, r, so that the rays are "paraxial"— that is, make only small angles with the horizontal axis.

Now we will show, for a mirror whose reflecting surface is small compared to its radius of curvature, that the rays very nearly meet at a common point, F, and we will also calculate the focal length f. In this approximation, we consider only rays that make a small angle with the principal axis; such rays are called **paraxial rays**, and their angles are exaggerated in Fig. 32–14 to make the labels clear. First we consider a ray that strikes the mirror at B in Fig. 32–14. The point C is the center of curvature of the mirror (the center of the sphere of which the mirror is a part). So the dashed line CB is equal to r, the radius of curvature, and CB is normal to the mirror's surface at B. The incoming ray that hits the mirror at B makes an angle θ with this normal, and hence the reflected ray, BF, also makes an angle θ with the normal (law of reflection). Note that angle BCF is also θ as shown. The triangle CBF is isosceles because two of its angles are equal. Thus we have length CF = BF. We assume the mirror surface is small compared to the mirror's radius of curvature, so the angles are small, and the length FB is nearly equal to length FA. In this approximation, FA = FC. But FA = f, the focal length, and CA = 2 × FA = r. Thus the focal length is half the radius of curvature:

$$f = \frac{r}{2}.$$ [spherical mirror] **(32–1)**

We assumed only that the angle θ was small, so this result applies for all other incident paraxial rays. Thus all paraxial rays pass through the same point F, the focal point.

Since it is only approximately true that the rays come to a perfect focus at F, the more curved the mirror, the worse the approximation (Fig. 32–13) and the more blurred the image. This "defect" of spherical mirrors is called **spherical aberration**; we will discuss it more with regard to lenses in Chapter 33. A **parabolic reflector**, on the other hand, will reflect the rays to a perfect focus. However, because parabolic shapes are much harder to make and thus much more expensive, spherical mirrors are used for most purposes. (Many astronomical telescopes use parabolic reflectors.) We consider here only spherical mirrors and we will assume that they are small compared to their radius of curvature so that the image is sharp and Eq. 32–1 holds.

Image Formation—Ray Diagrams

We saw that for an object at infinity, the image is located at the focal point of a concave spherical mirror, where $f = r/2$. But where does the image lie for an object not at infinity? First consider the object shown as an arrow in Fig. 32–15a, which is placed between F and C at point O (O for object). Let us determine where the image will be for a given point O′ at the top of the object.

(a) Ray 1 goes out from O′ parallel to the axis and reflects through F.

(b) Ray 2 goes through F and then reflects back parallel to the axis.

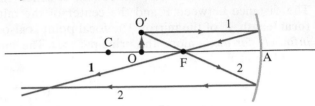

FIGURE 32–15 Rays leave point O′ on the object (an arrow). Shown are the three most useful rays for determining where the image I′ is formed. [Note that our mirror is not small compared to f, so our diagram will not give the precise position of the image.]

(c) Ray 3 is chosen perpendicular to mirror, and so must reflect back on itself and go through C (center of curvature).

Diverging rays heading toward eye

To do this we can draw several rays and make sure these reflect from the mirror such that the angle of reflection equals the angle of incidence. Many rays could be drawn leaving any point on an object, but determining the image position is simplified if we deal with three particularly simple rays. These are the rays labeled 1, 2, and 3 in Fig. 32–15 and we draw them leaving object point O′ as follows:

Ray 1 is drawn parallel to the axis; therefore after reflection it must pass along a line through F (Fig. 32–15a).

Ray 2 leaves O′ and is made to pass through F (Fig. 32–15b); therefore it must reflect so it is parallel to the axis.

Ray 3 passes through C, the center of curvature (Fig. 32–15c); it is along a radius of the spherical surface and is perpendicular to the mirror, so it is reflected back on itself.

RAY DIAGRAM

Finding the image position for a curved mirror

PROBLEM SOLVING

Image point is where reflected rays intersect

All three rays leave a single point O′ on the object. After reflection from a (small) mirror, the point at which these rays cross is the image point I′. All other rays from the same object point will also pass through this image point. To find the image point for any object point, only these three types of rays need to be drawn. Only two of these rays are needed, but the third serves as a check.

We have shown the image point in Fig. 32–15 only for a single point on the object. Other points on the object are imaged nearby, so a complete image of the object is formed, as shown by the dashed arrow in Fig. 32–15c. Because the light actually passes through the image itself, this is a **real image** that will appear on a piece of paper or film placed there. This can be compared to the virtual image formed by a plane mirror (the light does not actually pass through that image, Fig. 32–7).

The image in Fig. 32–15 can be seen by the eye when the eye is placed to the left of the image, so that some of the rays diverging from each point on the image (as point I′) can enter the eye as shown in Fig. 32–15c. (See also Figs. 32–1 and 32–7.)

Mirror Equation and Magnification

Image points can be determined, roughly, by drawing the three rays as just described, Fig. 32–15. But it is difficult to draw small angles for the "paraxial" rays as we assumed. For more accurate results, we now derive an equation that gives the image distance if the object distance and radius of curvature of the mirror are known. To do this, we refer to Fig. 32–16. The **object distance**, d_o, is the distance of the object (point O) from the center of the mirror. The **image distance**, d_i, is the distance of the image (point I) from the center of the mirror. The height of the object OO′ is called h_o and the height of the image, I′I, is h_i.

FIGURE 32–16 Diagram for deriving the mirror equation. For the derivation, we assume the mirror size is small compared to its radius of curvature.

Two rays leaving O′ are shown: O′FBI′ (same as ray 2 in Fig. 32–15) and O′AI′, which is a fourth type of ray that reflects at the center of the mirror and can also be used to find an image point. The ray O′AI′ obeys the law of reflection, so the two right triangles O′AO and I′AI are similar. Therefore, we have

$$\frac{h_o}{h_i} = \frac{d_o}{d_i}.$$

For the other ray shown, O′FBI′, the triangles O′FO and AFB are also similar because the angles are equal and we use the approximation AB = h_i (mirror small compared to its radius). Furthermore FA = f, the focal length of the mirror, so

$$\frac{h_o}{h_i} = \frac{\text{OF}}{\text{FA}} = \frac{d_o - f}{f}.$$

The left sides of the two preceding expressions are the same, so we can equate the right sides:

$$\frac{d_o}{d_i} = \frac{d_o - f}{f}.$$

We now divide both sides by d_o and rearrange to obtain

$$\frac{1}{d_o} + \frac{1}{d_i} = \frac{1}{f}. \tag{32–2}$$

Mirror equation

This is the equation we were seeking. It is called the **mirror equation** and relates the object and image distances to the focal length f (where $f = r/2$).

The **lateral magnification**, m, of a mirror is defined as the height of the image divided by the height of the object. From our first set of similar triangles above, or the first equation on this page, we can write:

$$m = \frac{h_i}{h_o} = -\frac{d_i}{d_o}. \tag{32–3}$$

The minus sign in Eq. 32–4 is inserted as a convention. Indeed, we must be careful about the signs of all quantities in Eqs. 32–2 and 32–3. Sign conventions are chosen so as to give the correct locations and orientations of images, as predicted by ray diagrams.

FIGURE 32–16 (Repeated from previous page.)

The sign conventions we use are: the image height h_i is positive if the image is upright, and negative if inverted, relative to the object (assuming h_o is taken as positive); d_i or d_o is positive if image or object is in front of the mirror (as in Fig. 32–16); if either image or object is behind the mirror, the corresponding distance is negative (an example can be seen in Fig. 32–18, Example 32–6). Thus the magnification (Eq. 32–3) is positive for an upright image and negative for an inverted image (upside down). We summarize sign conventions more fully in the Problem Solving Strategy following our discussion of convex mirrors later in this Section.

Concave Mirror Examples

EXAMPLE 32–4 **Image in a concave mirror.** A 1.50-cm-high diamond ring is placed 20.0 cm from a concave mirror with radius of curvature 30.0 cm. Determine (*a*) the position of the image, and (*b*) its size.

APPROACH We determine the focal length from the radius of curvature (Eq. 32–1), $f = r/2 = 15.0$ cm. The ray diagram is basically like that shown in Fig. 32–16 (repeated here on this page), since the object is between F and C. The position and size of the image are found from Eqs. 32–2 and 32–3.

SOLUTION Referring to Fig. 32–16, we have CA $= r = 30.0$ cm, FA $= f = 15.0$ cm, and OA $= d_o = 20.0$ cm.

(*a*) From Eq. 32–2,

$$\frac{1}{d_i} = \frac{1}{f} - \frac{1}{d}$$

$$= \frac{1}{15.0 \text{ cm}} - \frac{1}{20.0 \text{ cm}} = 0.0167 \text{ cm}^{-1}.$$

So $d_i = 1/(0.0167 \text{ cm}^{-1}) = 60.0$ cm. Because d_i is positive, the image is 60.0 cm in front of the mirror, on the same side as the object.

(*b*) From Eq. 32–3, the magnification is

$$m = -\frac{d_i}{d_o}$$

$$= -\frac{60.0 \text{ cm}}{20.0 \text{ cm}} = -3.00.$$

The image is 3.0 times larger than the object, and its height is

$$h_i = mh_o = (-3.00)(1.5 \text{ cm}) = -4.5 \text{ cm}.$$

The minus sign reminds us that the image is inverted, as in Fig. 32–16.

NOTE When an object is further from a concave mirror than the focal point, we can see from Fig. 32–15 or 32–16 that the image is always inverted and real.

CONCEPTUAL EXAMPLE 32–5 **Reversible rays.** If the object in Example 32–4 is placed instead where the image is (see Fig. 32–16), where will the new image be?

RESPONSE The mirror equation is *symmetric* in d_o and d_i. Thus the new image will be where the old object was. Indeed, in Fig. 32–16 we need only reverse the direction of the rays to get our new situation.

EXAMPLE 32–6 **Object closer to concave mirror.** A 1.00-cm-high object is placed 10.0 cm from a concave mirror whose radius of curvature is 30.0 cm. (*a*) Draw a ray diagram to locate (approximately) the position of the image. (*b*) Determine the position of the image and the magnification analytically.

APPROACH We draw the ray diagram using the rays as in Fig. 32–15, page 844. An analytic solution uses Eqs. 32–1, 32–2, and 32–3.

SOLUTION (*a*) Since $f = r/2 = 15.0$ cm, the object is between the mirror and the focal point. We draw the three rays as described earlier (Fig. 32–15); they are shown leaving the tip of the object in Fig. 32–17. Ray 1 leaves the tip of our object heading toward the mirror parallel to the axis, and reflects through F. Ray 2 cannot head toward F because it would not strike the mirror; so ray 2 must point as if it started at F (dashed line) and heads to the mirror, and then is reflected parallel to the principal axis. Ray 3 is perpendicular to the mirror, as before. The rays reflected from the mirror diverge and so never meet at a point. They appear, however, to be coming from a point behind the mirror. This point locates the image of the tip of the arrow. The image is thus behind the mirror and is *virtual*. (Why?)

(*b*) We use Eq. 32–2 to find d_i when $d_o = 10.0$ cm:

$$\frac{1}{d_i} = \frac{1}{f} - \frac{1}{d_o} = \frac{1}{15.0\text{ cm}} - \frac{1}{10.0\text{ cm}} = \frac{2 - 3}{30.0\text{ cm}} = -\frac{1}{30.0\text{ cm}}.$$

Therefore, $d_i = -30.0$ cm. The minus sign means the image is behind the mirror, which our diagram also told us. The magnification is $m = -d_i/d_o = -(-30.0\text{ cm})/(10.0\text{ cm}) = +3.00$. So the image is 3.00 times larger than the object. The plus sign indicates that the image is upright (same as object), which is consistent with the ray diagram, Fig. 32–17.

NOTE The image distance cannot be obtained accurately by measuring on Fig. 32–17, because our diagram violates the paraxial ray assumption (we draw rays at steeper angles to make them clearly visible).

NOTE When the object is located inside the focal point of a concave mirror ($d_o < f$), the image is always upright and vertical. And if the object O in Fig. 32–17 is you, you see yourself clearly, because the reflected rays at point O are diverging. Your image is upright and enlarged.

FIGURE 32–17 Object placed within the focal point F. The image is *behind* the mirror and is *virtual*, Example 32–6. [Note that the vertical scale (height of object = 1.0 cm) is different from the horizontal (OA = 10.0 cm) for ease of drawing, and reduces the precision of the drawing.]

It is useful to compare Figs. 32–15 and 32–17. We can see that if the object is within the focal point $(d_o < f)$, as in Fig. 32–17, the image is virtual, upright, and magnified. This is how a shaving or cosmetic mirror is used—you must place your head closer to the mirror than the focal point if you are to see yourself right-side up (see the photograph of Fig. 32–11a). If the object is *beyond* the focal point, as in Fig. 32–15, the image is real and inverted (upside down—and hard to use!). Whether the magnification has magnitude greater or less than 1.0 in the latter case depends on the position of the object relative to the center of curvature, point C. Practice making ray diagrams with various object distances.

The mirror equation also holds for a plane mirror: the focal length is $f = r/2 = \infty$, and Eq. 32–2 gives $d_i = -d_o$.

Seeing the Image

For a person's eye to see a sharp image, the eye must be at a place where it intercepts diverging rays from points on the image, as is the case for the eye's position in Figs. 32–15 and 32–16. Our eyes are made to see normal objects, which always means the rays are diverging toward the eye as shown in Fig. 32–1. (Or, for very distant objects like stars, the rays become essentially parallel, as in Fig. 32–12.) If you placed your eye between points O and I in Fig. 32–16, for example, *converging* rays from the object OO′ would enter your eye and the lens of your eye could not bring them to a focus; you would see a blurry image. [We will discuss the eye more in Chapter 33.]

FIGURE 32–18 You can see a clear inverted image of your face when you are beyond C $(d_o > 2f)$, because the rays that arrive at your eye are diverging. Standard rays 2 and 3 are shown leaving point O on your nose. Ray 2 (and other nearby rays) enters your eye. Notice that rays are diverging as they move to the left of image point I.

If *you* are the object OO′ in Fig. 32–16, situated between F and C, and are trying to see yourself in the mirror, you would see a blur; but the person whose eye is shown in Fig. 32–16 can see you clearly. You can see yourself clearly, but upside down, if you are to the left of C in Fig. 32–16, where $d_o > 2f$. Why? Because then the rays reflected from the image will be *diverging* at your position as demonstrated in Fig. 32–18, and your eye can then focus them. You can also see yourself clearly, and right-side up, if you are closer to the mirror than its focal point $(d_o < f)$, as we saw in Example 32–6, Fig. 32–17.

Convex Mirrors

The analysis used for concave mirrors can be applied to **convex** mirrors. Even the mirror equation (Eq. 32–2) holds for a convex mirror, although the quantities involved must be carefully defined. Figure 32–19a shows parallel rays falling on a convex mirror. Again spherical aberration is significant (Fig. 32–13), unless we assume the mirror's size is very small compared to its radius of curvature. The reflected rays diverge, but seem to come from point F behind the mirror. This is the **focal point**, and its distance from the center of the mirror (point A) is the **focal length**, f. It is easy to show that again $f = r/2$. We see that an object at infinity produces a virtual image in a convex mirror. Indeed, no matter where the object is

FIGURE 32–19 Convex mirror: (a) the focal point is at F, behind the mirror; (b) the image I of the object at O is virtual, upright, and smaller than the object. [Not to scale for Example 32–7.]

(a)

(b)

placed on the reflecting side of a convex mirror, the image will be virtual and upright, as indicated in Fig. 32–19b. To find the image we draw rays 1 and 3 according to the rules used before on the concave mirror, as shown in Fig. 32–19b. Note that although rays 1 and 3 don't actually pass through points F and C, the line along which each is drawn does (shown dashed).

The mirror equation, Eq. 32–2, holds for convex mirrors but the focal length f must be considered negative, as must the radius of curvature. The proof is left as a Problem. It is also left as a Problem to show that Eq. 32–3 for the magnification is also valid.

Spherical Mirrors

1. Always **draw a ray diagram** even though you are going to make an analytic calculation—the diagram serves as a check, even if not precise. From one point on the object, draw at least two, preferably three, of the easy-to-draw rays using the rules described in Fig. 32–15. The image point is where the reflected rays intersect or appear to intersect.

2. Apply the **mirror equation**, Eq. 32–2, and the **magnification equation**, Eq. 32–3. It is crucially important to follow the sign conventions—see the next point.

3. **Sign Conventions**
   (a) When the object, image, or focal point is on the reflecting side of the mirror (on the left in our drawings), the corresponding distance is positive. If any of these points is behind the mirror (on the right) the corresponding distance is negative.[†]
   (b) The image height h_i is positive if the image is upright, and negative if inverted, relative to the object (h_o is always taken as positive).

4. **Check** that the analytical solution is consistent with the ray diagram.

[†]Object distances are positive for material objects, but can be negative in systems with more than one mirror or lens—see Section 33–3.

EXAMPLE 32–7 **Convex rearview mirror.** An external rearview car mirror is convex with a radius of curvature of 16.0 m (Fig. 32–20). Determine the location of the image and its magnification for an object 10.0 m from the mirror.

APPROACH We follow the steps of the Problem Solving Strategy explicitly.
SOLUTION

1. **Draw a ray diagram.** The ray diagram will be like Fig. 32–19b, but the large object distance ($d_o = 10.0$ m) makes a precise drawing difficult. We have a convex mirror, so r is negative by convention.

2. **Mirror and magnification equations.** The center of curvature of a convex mirror is behind the mirror, as is its focal point, so we set $r = -16.0$ m so that the focal length is $f = r/2 = -8.0$ m. The object is in front of the mirror, $d_o = 10.0$ m. Solving the mirror equation, Eq. 32–2, for $1/d_i$ gives

$$\frac{1}{d_i} = \frac{1}{f} - \frac{1}{d_o} = \frac{1}{-8.0 \text{ m}} - \frac{1}{10.0 \text{ m}} = \frac{-10.0 - 8.0}{80.0 \text{ m}} = -\frac{18}{80.0 \text{ m}}.$$

Thus $d_i = -80.0 \text{ m}/18 = -4.4$ m. Equation 32–3 gives the magnification

$$m = -\frac{d_i}{d_o} = -\frac{(-4.4 \text{ m})}{(10.0 \text{ m})} = +0.44.$$

3. **Sign conventions.** The image distance is negative, -4.4 m, so the image is *behind* the mirror. The magnification is $m = +0.44$, so the image is *upright* (same orientation as object) and less than half as tall as the object.

4. **Check.** Our results are consistent with Fig. 32–19b.

Convex rearview mirrors on vehicles sometimes come with a warning that objects are closer than they appear in the mirror. The fact that d_i may be smaller than d_o (as in Example 32–7) seems to contradict this observation. The real reason the object seems farther away is that its image in the convex mirror is *smaller* than it would be in a plane mirror, and we judge distance of ordinary objects such as other cars mostly by their size.

PHYSICS APPLIED
Convex rearview mirror

FIGURE 32–20 Example 32–7.

TABLE 32–1 Indices of
Refraction†

Material	$n = \dfrac{c}{v}$
Vacuum	1.0000
Air (at STP)	1.0003
Water	1.33
Ethyl alcohol	1.36
Glass	
Fused quartz	1.46
Crown glass	1.52
Light flint	1.58
Lucite or Plexiglas	1.51
Sodium chloride	1.53
Diamond	2.42

†$\lambda = 589$ nm.

32–4 Index of Refraction

We saw in Chapter 31 that the speed of light in vacuum is

$$c = 2.99792458 \times 10^8 \,\text{m/s},$$

which is usually rounded off to

$$3.00 \times 10^8 \,\text{m/s}$$

when extremely precise results are not required.

In air, the speed is only slightly less. In other transparent materials such as glass and water, the speed is always less than that in vacuum. For example, in water light travels at about $\frac{3}{4}c$. The ratio of the speed of light in vacuum to the speed v in a given material is called the **index of refraction**, n, of that material:

$$n = \frac{c}{v}. \tag{32–4}$$

The index of refraction is never less than 1, and values for various materials are given in Table 32–1. For example, since $n = 2.42$ for diamond, the speed of light in diamond is

$$v = \frac{c}{n} = \frac{(3.00 \times 10^8 \,\text{m/s})}{2.42} = 1.24 \times 10^8 \,\text{m/s}.$$

As we shall see later, n varies somewhat with the wavelength of the light—except in vacuum—so a particular wavelength is specified in Table 32–1, that of yellow light with wavelength $\lambda = 589$ nm.

That light travels more slowly in matter than in vacuum can be explained at the atomic level as being due to the absorption and reemission of light by atoms and molecules of the material.

32–5 Refraction: Snell's Law

When light passes from one transparent medium into another with a different index of refraction, part of the incident light is reflected at the boundary. The remainder passes into the new medium. If a ray of light is incident at an angle to the surface (other than perpendicular), the ray changes direction as it enters the new medium. This change in direction, or bending, is called **refraction**.

Figure 32–21a shows a ray passing from air into water. Angle θ_1 is the angle the incident ray makes with the normal (perpendicular) to the surface and is called the **angle of incidence**. Angle θ_2 is the **angle of refraction**, the angle the refracted ray makes with the normal to the surface. Notice that the ray bends toward the normal when entering the water. This is always the case when the ray enters a medium where the speed of light is *less* (and the index of refraction greater, Eq. 32–4). If light travels from one medium into a second where its speed is *greater*, the ray bends away from the normal; this is shown in Fig. 32–21b for a ray traveling from water to air.

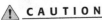

⚠ **CAUTION**

Angles θ_1 and θ_2 are measured from the perpendicular, not from surface

FIGURE 32–21 Refraction.
(a) Light refracted when passing from air (n_1) into water (n_2): $n_2 > n_1$.
(b) Light refracted when passing from water (n_1) into air (n_2): $n_1 > n_2$.

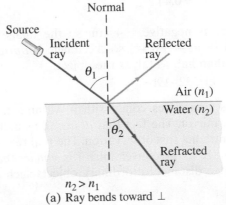

$n_2 > n_1$
(a) Ray bends toward $\perp$

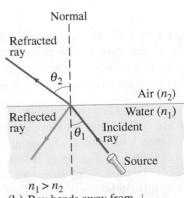

$n_1 > n_2$
(b) Ray bends away from $\perp$

FIGURE 32–22 Ray diagram showing why a person's legs look shorter when standing in waist-deep water: the path of light traveling from the bather's foot to the observer's eye bends at the water's surface, and our brain interprets the light as having traveled in a straight line, from higher up (dashed line).

Foot appears to be here

FIGURE 32–23 A straw in water looks bent even when it isn't.

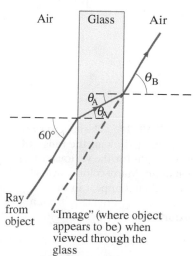

SNELL'S LAW
(LAW OF REFRACTION)

Refraction is responsible for a number of common optical illusions. For example, a person standing in waist-deep water appears to have shortened legs. As shown in Fig. 32–22, the rays leaving the person's foot are bent at the surface. The observer's brain assumes the rays to have traveled a straight-line path (dashed red line), and so the feet appear to be higher than they really are. Similarly, when you put a straw in water, it appears to be bent (Fig. 32–23).

Snell's Law

The angle of refraction depends on the speed of light in the two media and on the incident angle. An analytical relation between θ_1 and θ_2 in Fig. 32–21 was arrived at experimentally about 1621 by Willebrord Snell (1591–1626). It is known as **Snell's law** and is written:

$$n_1 \sin \theta_1 = n_2 \sin \theta_2. \tag{32–5}$$

θ_1 is the angle of incidence and θ_2 is the angle of refraction; n_1 and n_2 are the respective indices of refraction in the materials. See Fig. 32–21. The incident and refracted rays lie in the same plane, which also includes the perpendicular to the surface. Snell's law is the **law of refraction**. (Snell's law was derived in Section 15–10 where Eq. 15–19 is just a combination of Eqs. 32–5 and 32–4. We also derive it in Chapter 34 using the wave theory of light.)

It is clear from Snell's law that if $n_2 > n_1$, then $\theta_2 < \theta_1$. That is, if light enters a medium where n is greater (and its speed is less), then the ray is bent toward the normal. And if $n_2 < n_1$, then $\theta_2 > \theta_1$, so the ray bends away from the normal. This is what we saw in Fig. 32–21.

EXERCISE D Light passes from a medium with $n = 1.3$ into a medium with $n = 1.5$. Is the light bent toward or away from the perpendicular to the interface?

EXAMPLE 32–8 **Refraction through flat glass.** Light traveling in air strikes a flat piece of uniformly thick glass at an incident angle of 60°, as shown in Fig. 32–24. If the index of refraction of the glass is 1.50, (a) what is the angle of refraction θ_A in the glass; (b) what is the angle θ_B at which the ray emerges from the glass?

APPROACH We apply Snell's law at the first surface, where the light enters the glass, and again at the second surface where it leaves the glass and enters the air.

SOLUTION (a) The incident ray is in air, so $n_1 = 1.00$ and $n_2 = 1.50$. Applying Snell's law where the light enters the glass $(\theta_1 = 60°)$ gives

$$\sin \theta_A = \frac{1.00}{1.50} \sin 60° = 0.5774,$$

so $\theta_A = 35.3°$.

(b) Since the faces of the glass are parallel, the incident angle at the second surface is just θ_A (simple geometry), so $\sin \theta_A = 0.5774$. At this second interface, $n_1 = 1.50$ and $n_2 = 1.00$. Thus the ray re-enters the air at an angle $\theta_B (= \theta_2)$ given by

$$\sin \theta_B = \frac{1.50}{1.00} \sin \theta_A = 0.866,$$

and $\theta_B = 60°$. The direction of a light ray is thus unchanged by passing through a flat piece of glass of uniform thickness.

NOTE This result is valid for any angle of incidence. The ray is displaced slightly to one side, however. You can observe this by looking through a piece of glass (near its edge) at some object and then moving your head to the side slightly so that you see the object directly. It "jumps."

FIGURE 32–24 Light passing through a piece of glass (Example 32–8).

Air   Glass   Air

θ_B

θ_A

θ_A

60°

Ray from object

"Image" (where object appears to be) when viewed through the glass

FIGURE 32–25 Example 32–9.

EXAMPLE 32–9 **Apparent depth of a pool.** A swimmer has dropped her goggles to the bottom of a pool at the shallow end, marked as 1.0 m deep. But the goggles don't look that deep. Why? How deep do the goggles appear to be when you look straight down into the water?

APPROACH We draw a ray diagram showing two rays going upward from a point on the goggles at a small angle, and being refracted at the water's (flat) surface, Fig. 32–25. The two rays traveling upward from the goggles are refracted *away* from the normal as they exit the water, and so appear to be diverging from a point above the goggles (dashed lines), which is why the water seems less deep than it actually is.

SOLUTION To calculate the apparent depth d' (Fig. 32–25), given a real depth $d = 1.0$ m, we use Snell's law with $n_1 = 1.33$ for water and $n_2 = 1.0$ for air:

$$\sin \theta_2 = n_1 \sin \theta_1.$$

We are considering only small angles, so $\sin \theta \approx \tan \theta \approx \theta$, with θ in radians. So Snell's law becomes

$$\theta_2 \approx n_1 \theta_1.$$

From Fig. 32–25, we see that

$$\theta_2 \approx \tan \theta_2 = \frac{x}{d'} \quad \text{and} \quad \theta_1 \approx \tan \theta_1 = \frac{x}{d}.$$

Putting these into Snell's law, $\theta_2 \approx n_1 \theta_1$, we get

$$\frac{x}{d'} \approx n_1 \frac{x}{d}$$

or

$$d' \approx \frac{d}{n_1} = \frac{1.0 \text{ m}}{1.33} = 0.75 \text{ m}.$$

The pool seems only three-fourths as deep as it actually is.

32–6 Visible Spectrum and Dispersion

An obvious property of visible light is its color. Color is related to the wavelengths or frequencies of the light. (How this was discovered will be discussed in Chapter 34.) Visible light—that to which our eyes are sensitive—has wavelengths in air in the range of about 400 nm to 750 nm.[†] This is known as the **visible spectrum**, and within it lie the different colors from violet to red, as shown in Fig. 32–26. Light with wavelength shorter than 400 nm (= violet) is called **ultraviolet** (UV), and light with wavelength greater than 750 nm (= red) is called **infrared** (IR).[‡] Although human eyes are not sensitive to UV or IR, some types of photographic film and digital cameras do respond to them.

A prism can separate white light into a rainbow of colors, as shown in Fig. 32–27. This happens because the index of refraction of a material depends on the wavelength, as shown for several materials in Fig. 32–28. White light is a

FIGURE 32–26 The spectrum of visible light, showing the range of wavelengths for the various colors as seen in air. Many colors, such as brown, do not appear in the spectrum; they are made from a mixture of wavelengths.

[†]Sometimes the angstrom (Å) unit is used when referring to light: $1 \text{ Å} = 1 \times 10^{-10}$ m. Then visible light falls in the wavelength range of 4000 Å to 7500 Å.

[‡]The complete electromagnetic spectrum is illustrated in Fig. 31–12.

FIGURE 32–28 Index of refraction as a function of wavelength for various transparent solids.

FIGURE 32–27 White light passing through a prism is broken down into its constituent colors.

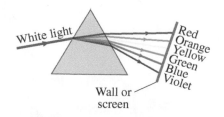

FIGURE 32–29 White light dispersed by a prism into the visible spectrum.

mixture of all visible wavelengths, and when incident on a prism, as in Fig. 32–29, the different wavelengths are bent to varying degrees. Because the index of refraction is greater for the shorter wavelengths, violet light is bent the most and red the least, as indicated. This spreading of white light into the full spectrum is called **dispersion**.

Rainbows are a spectacular example of dispersion—by drops of water. You can see rainbows when you look at falling water droplets with the Sun behind you. Figure 32–30 shows how red and violet rays are bent by spherical water droplets and are reflected off the back surface of the droplet. Red is bent the least and so reaches the observer's eyes from droplets higher in the sky, as shown in the diagram. Thus the top of the rainbow is red.

FIGURE 32–30 (a) Ray diagram explaining how a rainbow (b) is formed.

(a)

(b)

The visible spectrum, Fig. 32–26, does not show all the colors seen in nature. For example, there is no brown in Fig. 32–26. Many of the colors we see are a mixture of wavelengths. For practical purposes, most natural colors can be reproduced using three primary colors. They are red, green, and blue for direct source viewing such as TV and computer monitors. For inks used in printing, the primary colors are cyan (the color of the margin notes in this book), yellow, and magenta (the color we use for light rays in diagrams).

For any wave, its velocity v is related to its wavelength λ and frequency f by $v = f\lambda$ (Eq. 15–1 or 31–14). When a wave travels from one material into another, the frequency of the wave does not change across the boundary since a point (an atom) at the boundary oscillates at that frequency. Thus if light goes from air into a material with index of refraction n, the wavelength becomes (recall Eq. 32–4):

$$\lambda_n = \frac{v}{f} = \frac{c}{nf} = \frac{\lambda}{n} \tag{32–6}$$

where λ is the wavelength in vacuum or air and λ_n is the wavelength in the material with index of refraction n.

We said that color depends on wavelength. For example, for an object emitting 650 nm light in air, we see red. But this is true only in air. If we observe this same object when under water, it still looks red. But the wavelength in water λ_n is (Eq. 32–6) 650 nm/1.33 = 489 nm. Light with wavelength 489 nm would appear blue in air. Can you explain why the light appears red rather than blue when observed under water?

RESPONSE It must be that it is not the wavelength that the eye responds to, but rather the frequency. For example, the frequency of 650 nm red light in air is $f = c/\lambda = (3.0 \times 10^8 \text{ m/s})/(650 \times 10^{-9} \text{ m}) = 4.6 \times 10^{14} \text{ Hz}$, and does not change when the light travels from one medium to another. Only λ changes.

NOTE If we classified colors by frequency, the color assignments would be valid for any material. We typically specify colors by *wavelength* in air (even if less general) not just because we usually see objects in air, but because wavelength is what is commonly measured (it is easier to measure than frequency).

32–7 Total Internal Reflection; Fiber Optics

When light passes from one material into a second material where the index of refraction is less (say, from water into air), the light bends away from the normal, as for rays I and J in Fig. 32–31. At a particular incident angle, the angle of refraction will be 90°, and the refracted ray would skim the surface (ray K) in this

FIGURE 32–31 Since $n_2 < n_1$, light rays are totally internally reflected if the incident angle $\theta_1 > \theta_C$, as for ray L. If $\theta_1 < \theta_C$, as for rays I and J, only a part of the light is reflected, and the rest is refracted.

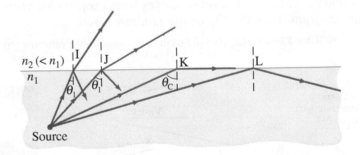

case. The incident angle at which this occurs is called the **critical angle**, θ_C. From Snell's law, θ_C is given by

$$\sin \theta_C = \frac{n_2}{n_1} \sin 90° = \frac{n_2}{n_1}. \tag{32–7}$$

For any incident angle less than θ_C, there will be a refracted ray, although part of the light will also be reflected at the boundary. However, for incident angles greater than θ_C, Snell's law would tell us that $\sin \theta_2$ is greater than 1.00. Yet the sine of an angle can never be greater than 1.00. In this case there is no refracted ray at all, and *all of the light is reflected*, as for ray L in Fig. 32–31. This effect is called **total internal reflection**. Total internal reflection can occur only when light strikes a boundary where the medium beyond has a lower index of refraction.

⚠ **CAUTION**

Total internal reflection (occurs only if refractive index is smaller beyond boundary)

EXERCISE E Fill a sink with water. Place a waterproof watch just below the surface with the watch's flat crystal parallel to the water surface. From above you can still see the watch reading. As you move your head to one side far enough what do you see, and why?

CONCEPTUAL EXAMPLE 32-11 | **View up from under water.** Describe what a person would see who looked up at the world from beneath the perfectly smooth surface of a lake or swimming pool.

RESPONSE For an air–water interface, the critical angle is given by

$$\sin \theta_C = \frac{1.00}{1.33} = 0.750.$$

Therefore, $\theta_C = 49°$. Thus the person would see the outside world compressed into a circle whose edge makes a 49° angle with the vertical. Beyond this angle, the person would see reflections from the sides and bottom of the lake or pool (Fig. 32–32).

(a)

(b)

FIGURE 32–32 (a) Light rays, and (b) view looking upward from beneath the water (the surface of the water must be very smooth). Example 32–11.

Diamonds achieve their brilliance from a combination of dispersion and total internal reflection. Because diamonds have a very high index of refraction of about 2.4, the critical angle for total internal reflection is only 25°. The light dispersed into a spectrum inside the diamond therefore strikes many of the internal surfaces of the diamond before it strikes one at less than 25° and emerges.

After many such reflections, the light has traveled far enough that the colors have become sufficiently separated to be seen individually and brilliantly by the eye after leaving the diamond.

Many optical instruments, such as binoculars, use total internal reflection within a prism to reflect light. The advantage is that very nearly 100% of the light is reflected, whereas even the best mirrors reflect somewhat less than 100%. Thus the image is brighter, especially after several reflections. For glass with $n = 1.50, \theta_C = 41.8°$. Therefore, 45° prisms will reflect all the light internally, if oriented as shown in the binoculars of Fig. 32–33.

FIGURE 32–33 Total internal reflection of light by prisms in binoculars.

EXERCISE F If 45.0° plastic lenses are used in binoculars, what minimum index of refraction must the plastic have?

Fiber Optics

Total internal reflection is the principle behind **fiber optics**. Glass and plastic fibers as thin as a few micrometers in diameter are common. A bundle of such tiny fibers is called a **light pipe** or cable, and light[†] can be transmitted along it with almost no loss because of total internal reflection. Figure 32–34 shows how light traveling down a thin fiber makes only glancing collisions with the walls so that total internal reflection occurs. Even if the light pipe is bent into a complicated shape, the critical angle still won't be exceeded, so light is transmitted practically undiminished to the other end. Very small losses do occur, mainly by reflection at the ends and absorption within the fiber.

Important applications of fiber-optic cables are in communications and medicine. They are used in place of wire to carry telephone calls, video signals, and computer data. The signal is a modulated light beam (a light beam whose intensity can be varied) and data is transmitted at a much higher rate and with less loss and less interference than an electrical signal in a copper wire. Fibers have been developed that can support over one hundred separate wavelengths, each modulated to carry up to 10 gigabits (10^{10} bits) of information per second. That amounts to a terabit (10^{12} bits) per second for the full one hundred wavelengths.

FIGURE 32–34 Light reflected totally at the interior surface of a glass or transparent plastic fiber.

Ⓧ **PHYSICS APPLIED**
Fiber optics in communications

[†]Fiber optic devices can use not only visible light but also infrared light, ultraviolet light, and microwaves.

(a)

(b)

FIGURE 32–35 (a) How a fiber-optic image is made. (b) Example of a fiber-optic device inserted through the mouth to view the gastro-intestinal tract, with image on screen.

The sophisticated use of fiber optics to transmit a clear picture is particularly useful in medicine, Fig. 32–35. For example, a patient's lungs can be examined by inserting a light pipe known as a bronchoscope through the mouth and down the bronchial tube. Light is sent down an outer set of fibers to illuminate the lungs. The reflected light returns up a central core set of fibers. Light directly in front of each fiber travels up that fiber. At the opposite end, a viewer sees a series of bright and dark spots, much like a TV screen—that is, a picture of what lies at the opposite end. Lenses are used at each end. The image may be viewed directly or on a monitor screen or film. The fibers must be optically insulated from one another, usually by a thin coating of material with index of refraction less than that of the fiber. The more fibers there are, and the smaller they are, the more detailed the picture. Such instruments, including bronchoscopes, colonoscopes (for viewing the colon), and endoscopes (stomach or other organs), are extremely useful for examining hard-to-reach places.

*32–8 Refraction at a Spherical Surface

We now examine the refraction of rays at the spherical surface of a transparent material. Such a surface could be one face of a lens or the cornea of the eye. To be general, let us consider an object which is located in a medium whose index of refraction is n_1, and rays from each point on the object can enter a medium whose index of refraction is n_2. The radius of curvature of the spherical boundary is R, and its center of curvature is at point C, Fig. 32–36. We now show that all rays leaving a point O on the object will be focused at a single point I, the image point, if we consider only paraxial rays: rays that make a small angle with the axis.

FIGURE 32–36 Rays from a point O on an object will be focused at a single image point I by a spherical boundary between two transparent materials $(n_2 > n_1)$, as long as the rays make small angles with the axis.

To do so, we consider a single ray that leaves point O as shown in Fig. 32–37. From Snell's law, Eq. 32–5, we have

$$n_1 \sin \theta_1 = n_2 \sin \theta_2.$$

We are assuming that angles θ_1, θ_2, α, β, and γ are small, so $\sin \theta \approx \theta$ (in radians), and Snell's law becomes, approximately,

$$n_1 \theta_1 = n_2 \theta_2.$$

Also, $\beta + \phi = 180°$ and $\theta_2 + \gamma + \phi = 180°$, so

$$\beta = \gamma + \theta_2.$$

Similarly for triangle OPC,

$$\theta_1 = \alpha + \beta.$$

FIGURE 32–37 Diagram for showing that all paraxial rays from O focus at the same point I $(n_2 > n_1)$.

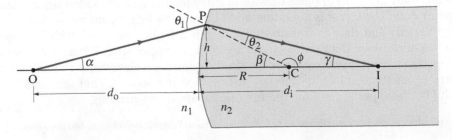

These three relations can be combined to yield

$$n_1\alpha + n_2\gamma = (n_2 - n_1)\beta.$$

Since we are considering only the case of small angles, we can write, approximately,

$$\alpha = \frac{h}{d_o}, \quad \beta = \frac{h}{R}, \quad \gamma = \frac{h}{d_i},$$

where d_o and d_i are the object and image distances and h is the height as shown in Fig. 32–37. We substitute these into the previous equation, divide through by h, and obtain

$$\frac{n_1}{d_o} + \frac{n_2}{d_i} = \frac{n_2 - n_1}{R}. \qquad (32\text{–}8)$$

For a given object distance d_o, this equation tells us d_i, the image distance, does not depend on the angle of a ray. Hence all paraxial rays meet at the same point I. This is true only for rays that make small angles with the axis and with each other, and is equivalent to assuming that the width of the refracting spherical surface is small compared to its radius of curvature. If this assumption is not true, the rays will not converge to a point; there will be spherical aberration, just as for a mirror (see Fig. 32–13), and the image will be blurry. (Spherical aberration will be discussed further in Section 33–10.)

We derived Eq. 32–8 using Fig. 32–37 for which the spherical surface is convex (as viewed by the incoming ray). It is also valid for a concave surface—as can be seen using Fig. 32–38—if we use the following conventions:

1. If the surface is convex (so the center of curvature C is on the side of the surface opposite to that from which the light comes), R is positive; if the surface is concave (C on the same side from which the light comes) R is negative.

2. The image distance, d_i, follows the same convention: positive if on the opposite side from where the light comes, negative if on the same side.

3. The object distance is positive if on the same side from which the light comes (this is the normal case, although when several surfaces bend the light it may not be so), otherwise it is negative.

For the case shown in Fig. 32–38 with a concave surface, both R and d_i are negative when used in Eq. 32–8. Note, in this case, that the image is virtual.

FIGURE 32–38 Rays from O refracted by a concave surface form a virtual image $(n_2 > n_1)$. Per our conventions, $R < 0$, $d_i < 0$, $d_o > 0$.

EXAMPLE 32–12 **Apparent depth II.** A person looks vertically down into a 1.0-m-deep pool. How deep does the water appear to be?

APPROACH Example 32–9 solved this problem using Snell's law. Here we use Eq. 32–8.

SOLUTION A ray diagram is shown in Fig. 32–39. Point O represents a point on the pool's bottom. The rays diverge and appear to come from point I, the image. We have $d_o = 1.0$ m and, for a flat surface, $R = \infty$. Then Eq. 32–8 becomes

$$\frac{1.33}{1.0\,\text{m}} + \frac{1.00}{d_i} = \frac{(1.00 - 1.33)}{\infty} = 0.$$

Hence $d_i = -(1.0\,\text{m})/(1.33) = -0.75$ m. So the pool appears to be only three-fourths as deep as it actually is, the same result we found in Example 32–9. The minus sign tells us the image point I is on the same side of the surface as O, and the image is virtual. At angles other than vertical, this conclusion must be modified.

FIGURE 32–39 Example 32–12.

Air: $n_2 = 1.00$

Water: $n_1 = 1.33$

EXAMPLE 32–13 **A spherical "lens."** A point source of light is placed at a distance of 25.0 cm from the center of a glass sphere $(n = 1.5)$ of radius 10.0 cm, Fig. 32–40. Find the image of the source.

APPROACH As shown in Fig. 32–40, there are two refractions, and we treat them successively, one at a time. The light rays from the source first refract from the convex glass surface facing the source. We analyze this first refraction, treating it as in Fig. 32–36, ignoring the back side of the sphere.

SOLUTION Using Eq. 32–8 (assuming paraxial rays) with $n_1 = 1.0$, $n_2 = 1.5$, $R = 10.0$ cm, and $d_o = 25.0$ cm − 10.0 cm = 15.0 cm, we solve for the image distance as formed at surface 1, d_{i1}:

$$\frac{1}{d_{i1}} = \frac{1}{n_2}\left(\frac{(n_2 - n_1)}{R} - \frac{n_1}{d_o}\right) = \frac{1}{1.5}\left(\frac{1.5 - 1.0}{10.0 \text{ cm}} - \frac{1.0}{15.0 \text{ cm}}\right) = -\frac{1}{90.0 \text{ cm}}.$$

Thus, the image of the first refraction is located 90.0 cm *to the left* of the front surface. This image (I_1) now serves as the object for the refraction occurring at the back surface (surface 2) of the sphere. This surface is concave so $R = -10.0$ cm, and we consider a ray close to the axis. Then the object distance is $d_{o2} = 90.0$ cm + 2(10.0 cm) = 110.0 cm, and Eq. 32–8 yields, with $n_1 = 1.5$, $n_2 = 1.0$,

$$\frac{1}{d_{i2}} = \frac{1}{1.0}\left(\frac{1.0 - 1.5}{-10.0 \text{ cm}} - \frac{1.5}{110.0 \text{ cm}}\right) = \frac{4.0}{110.0 \text{ cm}}$$

so $d_{i2} = 28$ cm. Thus, the final image is located a distance 28 cm from the back side of the sphere.

FIGURE 32–40 Example 32–13.

Summary

Light appears to travel along straight-line paths, called **rays**, at a speed v that depends on the **index of refraction**, n, of the material; that is

$$v = \frac{c}{n}, \tag{32–4}$$

where c is the speed of light in vacuum.

When light reflects from a flat surface, *the angle of reflection equals the angle of incidence*. This **law of reflection** explains why mirrors can form **images**.

In a **plane mirror**, the image is virtual, upright, the same size as the object, and is as far behind the mirror as the object is in front.

A **spherical mirror** can be concave or convex. A **concave** spherical mirror focuses parallel rays of light (light from a very distant object) to a point called the **focal point**. The distance of this point from the mirror is the **focal length** f of the mirror and

$$f = \frac{r}{2} \tag{32–1}$$

where r is the radius of curvature of the mirror.

Parallel rays falling on a **convex mirror** reflect from the mirror as if they diverged from a common point behind the mirror. The distance of this point from the mirror is the focal length and is considered negative for a convex mirror.

For a given object, the position and size of the image formed by a mirror can be found by ray tracing. Algebraically, the relation between image and object distances, d_i and d_o, and the focal length f, is given by the **mirror equation**:

$$\frac{1}{d_o} + \frac{1}{d_i} = \frac{1}{f}. \tag{32–2}$$

The ratio of image height to object height, which equals the magnification m of a mirror, is

$$m = \frac{h_i}{h_o} = -\frac{d_i}{d_o}. \tag{32–3}$$

If the rays that converge to form an image actually pass through the image, so the image would appear on film or a screen placed there, the image is said to be a **real image**. If the rays do not actually pass through the image, the image is a **virtual image**.

When light passes from one transparent medium into another, the rays bend or refract. The **law of refraction** (**Snell's law**) states that

$$n_1 \sin\theta_1 = n_2 \sin\theta_2, \tag{32–5}$$

where n_1 and θ_1 are the index of refraction and angle with the normal to the surface for the incident ray, and n_2 and θ_2 are for the refracted ray.

When light of wavelength λ enters a medium with index of refraction n, the wavelength is reduced to

$$\lambda_n = \frac{\lambda}{n}. \tag{32–6}$$

The frequency does not change.

The frequency or wavelength of light determines its color. The **visible spectrum** in air extends from about 400 nm (violet) to about 750 nm (red).

Glass prisms break white light down into its constituent colors because the index of refraction varies with wavelength, a phenomenon known as **dispersion**.

When light rays reach the boundary of a material where the index of refraction decreases, the rays will be **totally internally reflected** if the incident angle, θ_1, is such that Snell's law would predict $\sin \theta_2 > 1$. This occurs if θ_1 exceeds the critical angle θ_C given by

$$\sin \theta_C = \frac{n_2}{n_1}. \qquad (32\text{–}7)$$

Questions

1. What would be the appearance of the Moon if it had (a) a rough surface; (b) a polished mirrorlike surface?

2. Archimedes is said to have burned the whole Roman fleet in the harbor of Syracuse by focusing the rays of the Sun with a huge spherical mirror. Is this[†] reasonable?

3. What is the focal length of a plane mirror? What is the magnification of a plane mirror?

4. An object is placed along the principal axis of a spherical mirror. The magnification of the object is −3.0. Is the image real or virtual, inverted or upright? Is the mirror concave or convex? On which side of the mirror is the image located?

5. Using the rules for the three rays discussed with reference to Fig. 32–15, draw ray 2 for Fig. 32–19b.

6. Does the mirror equation, Eq. 32–2, hold for a plane mirror? Explain.

7. If a concave mirror produces a real image, is the image necessarily inverted?

8. How might you determine the speed of light in a solid, rectangular, transparent object?

9. When you look at the Moon's reflection from a ripply sea, it appears elongated (Fig. 32–41). Explain.

FIGURE 32–41
Question 9.

10. How can a spherical mirror have a negative object distance?

11. What is the angle of refraction when a light ray is incident perpendicular to the boundary between two transparent materials?

12. When you look down into a swimming pool or a lake, are you likely to overestimate or underestimate its depth? Explain. How does the apparent depth vary with the viewing angle? (Use ray diagrams.)

13. Draw a ray diagram to show why a stick or straw looks bent when part of it is under water (Fig. 32–23).

†Students at MIT did a feasibility study. See www.mit.edu.

14. When a wide beam of parallel light enters water at an angle, the beam broadens. Explain.

15. You look into an aquarium and view a fish inside. One ray of light from the fish as it emerges from the tank is shown in Fig. 32–42. The apparent position of the fish is also shown. In the drawing, indicate the approximate position of the actual fish. Briefly justify your answer.

FIGURE 32–42
Question 15.

16. How can you "see" a round drop of water on a table even though the water is transparent and colorless?

17. A ray of light is refracted through three different materials (Fig. 32–43). Rank the materials according to their index of refraction, least to greatest.

FIGURE 32–43
Question 17.

18. Can a light ray traveling in air be totally reflected when it strikes a smooth water surface if the incident angle is chosen correctly? Explain.

19. When you look up at an object in air from beneath the surface in a swimming pool, does the object appear to be the same size as when you see it directly in air? Explain.

20. What type of mirror is shown in Fig. 32–44?

FIGURE 32–44
Question 20.

21. Light rays from stars (including our Sun) always bend toward the vertical direction as they pass through the Earth's atmosphere. (a) Why does this make sense? (b) What can you conclude about the apparent positions of stars as viewed from Earth?

Problems

32-2 Reflection; Plane Mirrors

1. (I) When you look at yourself in a 60-cm-tall plane mirror, you see the same amount of your body whether you are close to the mirror or far away. (Try it and see.) Use ray diagrams to show why this should be true.

2. (I) Suppose that you want to take a photograph of yourself as you look at your image in a mirror 2.8 m away. For what distance should the camera lens be focused?

3. (II) Two plane mirrors meet at a 135° angle, Fig. 32–45. If light rays strike one mirror at 38° as shown, at what angle ϕ do they leave the second mirror?

FIGURE 32–45
Problem 3.

4. (II) A person whose eyes are 1.64 m above the floor stands 2.30 m in front of a vertical plane mirror whose bottom edge is 38 cm above the floor, Fig. 32–46. What is the horizontal distance x to the base of the wall supporting the mirror of the nearest point on the floor that can be seen reflected in the mirror?

FIGURE 32–46
Problem 4.

5. (II) Show that if two plane mirrors meet at an angle ϕ, a single ray reflected successively from both mirrors is deflected through an angle of 2ϕ independent of the incident angle. Assume $\phi < 90°$ and that only two reflections, one from each mirror, take place.

6. (II) Suppose you are 88 cm from a plane mirror. What area of the mirror is used to reflect the rays entering one eye from a point on the tip of your nose if your pupil diameter is 4.5 mm?

7. (II) Stand up two plane mirrors so they form a 90.0° angle as in Fig. 32–47. When you look into this double mirror, you see yourself as others see you, instead of reversed as in a single mirror. Make a ray diagram to show how this occurs.

FIGURE 32–47
Problems 7 and 8.

8. (III) Suppose a third mirror is placed beneath the two shown in Fig. 32–47, so that all three are perpendicular to each other. (a) Show that for such a "corner reflector," any incident ray will return in its original direction after three reflections. (b) What happens if it makes only two reflections?

32-3 Spherical Mirrors

9. (I) A solar cooker, really a concave mirror pointed at the Sun, focuses the Sun's rays 18.8 cm in front of the mirror. What is the radius of the spherical surface from which the mirror was made?

10. (I) How far from a concave mirror (radius 24.0 cm) must an object be placed if its image is to be at infinity?

11. (I) When walking toward a concave mirror you notice that the image flips at a distance of 0.50 m. What is the radius of curvature of the mirror?

12. (II) A small candle is 35 cm from a concave mirror having a radius of curvature of 24 cm. (a) What is the focal length of the mirror? (b) Where will the image of the candle be located? (c) Will the image be upright or inverted?

13. (II) You look at yourself in a shiny 9.2-cm-diameter Christmas tree ball. If your face is 25.0 cm away from the ball's front surface, where is your image? Is it real or virtual? Is it upright or inverted?

14. (II) A mirror at an amusement park shows an upright image of any person who stands 1.7 m in front of it. If the image is three times the person's height, what is the radius of curvature of the mirror? (See Fig. 32–44.)

15. (II) A dentist wants a small mirror that, when 2.00 cm from a tooth, will produce a 4.0× upright image. What kind of mirror must be used and what must its radius of curvature be?

16. (II) Some rearview mirrors produce images of cars to your rear that are smaller than they would be if the mirror were flat. Are the mirrors concave or convex? What is a mirror's radius of curvature if cars 18.0 m away appear 0.33 their normal size?

17. (II) You are standing 3.0 m from a convex security mirror in a store. You estimate the height of your image to be half of your actual height. Estimate the radius of curvature of the mirror.

18. (II) An object 3.0 mm high is placed 18 cm from a convex mirror of radius of curvature 18 cm. (a) Show by ray tracing that the image is virtual, and estimate the image distance. (b) Show that the (negative) image distance can be computed from Eq. 32–2 using a focal length of −9.0 cm. (c) Compute the image size, using Eq. 32–3.

19. (II) The image of a distant tree is virtual and very small when viewed in a curved mirror. The image appears to be 16.0 cm behind the mirror. What kind of mirror is it, and what is its radius of curvature?

20. (II) Use two techniques, (a) a ray diagram, and (b) the mirror equation, to show that the magnitude of the magnification of a concave mirror is less than 1 if the object is beyond the center of curvature C ($d_o > r$), and is greater than 1 if the object is within C ($d_o < r$).

21. (II) Show, using a ray diagram, that the magnification m of a convex mirror is $m = -d_i/d_o$, just as for a concave mirror. [Hint: Consider a ray from the top of the object that reflects at the center of the mirror.]

22. (II) Use ray diagrams to show that the mirror equation, Eq. 32–2, is valid for a convex mirror as long as f is considered negative.

23. (II) The magnification of a convex mirror is +0.55× for objects 3.2 m from the mirror. What is the focal length of this mirror?

24. (II) (a) Where should an object be placed in front of a concave mirror so that it produces an image at the same location as the object? (b) Is the image real or virtual? (c) Is the image inverted or upright? (d) What is the magnification of the image?

25. (II) A 4.5-cm tall object is placed 26 cm in front of a spherical mirror. It is desired to produce a virtual image that is upright and 3.5 cm tall. (a) What type of mirror should be used? (b) Where is the image located? (c) What is the focal length of the mirror? (d) What is the radius of curvature of the mirror?

26. (II) A shaving or makeup mirror is designed to magnify your face by a factor of 1.35 when your face is placed 20.0 cm in front of it. (a) What type of mirror is it? (b) Describe the type of image that it makes of your face. (c) Calculate the required radius of curvature for the mirror.

27. (II) A concave mirror has focal length f. When an object is placed a distance $d_o > f$ from this mirror, a real image with magnification m is formed. (a) Show that $m = f/(f - d_o)$. (b) Sketch m vs. d_o over the range $f < d_o < +\infty$ where $f = 0.45$ m. (c) For what value of d_o will the real image have the same (lateral) size as the object? (d) To obtain a real image that is much larger than the object, in what general region should the object be placed relative to the mirror?

28. (II) Let the focal length of a convex mirror be written as $f = -|f|$. Show that the magnification m of an object a distance d_o from this mirror is given by $m = |f|/(d_o + |f|)$. Based on this relation, explain why your nose looks bigger than the rest of your face when looking into a convex mirror.

29. (II) A spherical mirror of focal length f produces an image of an object with magnification m. (a) Show that the object is a distance $d_o = f\left(1 - \dfrac{1}{m}\right)$ from the reflecting side of the mirror. (b) Use the relation in part (a) to show that, no matter where an object is placed in front of a convex mirror, its image will have a magnification in the range $0 \le m \le +1$.

30. (III) An object is placed a distance r in front of a wall, where r exactly equals the radius of curvature of a certain concave mirror. At what distance from the wall should this mirror be placed so that a real image of the object is formed on the wall? What is the magnification of the image?

31. (III) A short thin object (like a short length of wire) of length ℓ is placed along the axis of a spherical mirror (perpendicular to the glass surface). Show that its image has length $\ell' = m^2\ell$ so the *longitudinal magnification* is equal to $-m^2$ where m is the normal "lateral" magnification, Eq. 32–3. Why the minus sign? [*Hint:* Find the image positions for both ends of the wire, and assume ℓ is very small.]

32–4 Index of Refraction

32. (I) The speed of light in ice is 2.29×10^8 m/s. What is the index of refraction of ice?

33. (I) What is the speed of light in (a) ethyl alcohol, (b) lucite, (c) crown glass?

34. (I) Our nearest star (other than the Sun) is 4.2 light years away. That is, it takes 4.2 years for the light to reach Earth. How far away is it in meters?

35. (I) How long does it take light to reach us from the Sun, 1.50×10^8 km away?

36. (II) The speed of light in a certain substance is 88% of its value in water. What is the index of refraction of that substance?

37. (II) Light is emitted from an ordinary lightbulb filament in wave-train bursts of about 10^{-8} s in duration. What is the length in space of such wave trains?

32–5 Snell's Law

38. (I) A diver shines a flashlight upward from beneath the water at a 38.5° angle to the vertical. At what angle does the light leave the water?

39. (I) A flashlight beam strikes the surface of a pane of glass ($n = 1.56$) at a 63° angle to the normal. What is the angle of refraction?

40. (I) Rays of the Sun are seen to make a 33.0° angle to the vertical beneath the water. At what angle above the horizon is the Sun?

41. (I) A light beam coming from an underwater spotlight exits the water at an angle of 56.0°. At what angle of incidence did it hit the air–water interface from below the surface?

42. (II) A beam of light in air strikes a slab of glass ($n = 1.56$) and is partially reflected and partially refracted. Determine the angle of incidence if the angle of reflection is twice the angle of refraction.

43. (II) A light beam strikes a 2.0-cm-thick piece of plastic with a refractive index of 1.62 at a 45° angle. The plastic is on top of a 3.0-cm-thick piece of glass for which $n = 1.47$. What is the distance D in Fig. 32–48?

FIGURE 32–48
Problem 43.

44. (II) An aquarium filled with water has flat glass sides whose index of refraction is 1.56. A beam of light from outside the aquarium strikes the glass at a 43.5° angle to the perpendicular (Fig. 32–49). What is the angle of this light ray when it enters (a) the glass, and then (b) the water? (c) What would be the refracted angle if the ray entered the water directly?

FIGURE 32–49
Problem 44.

45. (II) In searching the bottom of a pool at night, a watchman shines a narrow beam of light from his flashlight, 1.3 m above the water level, onto the surface of the water at a point 2.5 m from his foot at the edge of the pool (Fig. 32–50). Where does the spot of light hit the bottom of the pool, measured from the bottom of the wall beneath his foot, if the pool is 2.1 m deep?

FIGURE 32–50
Problem 45.

46. (II) The block of glass ($n = 1.5$) shown in cross section in Fig. 32–51 is surrounded by air. A ray of light enters the block at its left-hand face with incident angle θ_1 and reemerges into the air from the right-hand face directed parallel to the block's base. Determine θ_1.

FIGURE 32–51
Problem 46.

47. (II) A laser beam of diameter $d_1 = 3.0\,\text{mm}$ in air has an incident angle $\theta_1 = 25°$ at a flat air–glass surface. If the index of refraction of the glass is $n = 1.5$, determine the diameter d_2 of the beam after it enters the glass.

48. (II) Light is incident on an equilateral glass prism at a 45.0° angle to one face, Fig. 32–52. Calculate the angle at which light emerges from the opposite face. Assume that $n = 1.54$.

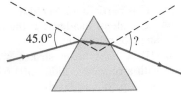

FIGURE 32–52
Problems 48 and 65.

49. (II) A triangular prism made of crown glass ($n = 1.52$) with base angles of 30.0° is surrounded by air. If parallel rays are incident normally on its base as shown in Fig. 32–53, what is the angle ϕ between the two emerging rays?

FIGURE 32–53
Problem 49.

50. (II) Show in general that for a light beam incident on a uniform layer of transparent material, as in Fig. 32–24, the direction of the emerging beam is parallel to the incident beam, independent of the incident angle θ. Assume the air on the two sides of the transparent material is the same.

51. (III) A light ray is incident on a flat piece of glass with index of refraction n as in Fig. 32–24. Show that if the incident angle θ is small, the emerging ray is displaced a distance $d = t\theta(n - 1)/n$, where t is the thickness of the glass, θ is in radians, and d is the perpendicular distance between the incident ray and the (dashed) line of the emerging ray (Fig. 32–24).

32–6 Visible Spectrum; Dispersion

52. (I) By what percent is the speed of blue light (450 nm) less than the speed of red light (680 nm), in silicate flint glass (see Fig. 32–28)?

53. (I) A light beam strikes a piece of glass at a 60.00° incident angle. The beam contains two wavelengths, 450.0 nm and 700.0 nm, for which the index of refraction of the glass is 1.4831 and 1.4754, respectively. What is the angle between the two refracted beams?

54. (II) A parallel beam of light containing two wavelengths, $\lambda_1 = 465\,\text{nm}$ and $\lambda_2 = 652\,\text{nm}$, enters the silicate flint glass of an equilateral prism as shown in Fig. 32–54. At what angle does each beam leave the prism (give angle with normal to the face)? See Fig. 32–28.

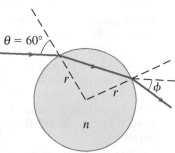

FIGURE 32–54
Problem 54.

55. (III) A ray of light with wavelength λ is incident from air at precisely 60° ($= \theta$) on a spherical water drop of radius r and index of refraction n (which depends on λ). When the ray reemerges into the air from the far side of the drop, it has been deflected an angle ϕ from its original direction as shown in Fig. 32–55. By how much does the value of ϕ for violet light ($n = 1.341$) differ from the value for red light ($n = 1.330$)?

FIGURE 32–55
Problem 55.

56. (III) For visible light, the index of refraction n of glass is roughly 1.5, although this value varies by about 1% across the visible range. Consider a ray of white light incident from air at angle θ_1 onto a flat piece of glass. (a) Show that, upon entering the glass, the visible colors contained in this incident ray will be dispersed over a range $\Delta\theta_2$ of refracted angles given approximately by

$$\Delta\theta_2 \approx \frac{\sin\theta_1}{\sqrt{n^2 - \sin^2\theta_1}}\frac{\Delta n}{n}.$$

[*Hint*: For x in radians, $(d/dx)(\sin^{-1} x) = 1/\sqrt{1 - x^2}$.] (b) If $\theta_1 = 0°$, what is $\Delta\theta_2$ in degrees? (c) If $\theta_1 = 90°$, what is $\Delta\theta_2$ in degrees?

32–7 Total Internal Reflection

57. (I) What is the critical angle for the interface between water and diamond? To be internally reflected, the light must start in which material?

58. (I) The critical angle for a certain liquid–air surface is 49.6°. What is the index of refraction of the liquid?

59. (II) A beam of light is emitted in a pool of water from a depth of 72.0 cm. Where must it strike the air–water interface, relative to the spot directly above it, in order that the light does *not* exit the water?

60. (II) A ray of light, after entering a light fiber, reflects at an angle of 14.5° with the long axis of the fiber, as in Fig. 32–56. Calculate the distance along the axis of the fiber that the light ray travels between successive reflections off the sides of the fiber. Assume that the fiber has an index of refraction of 1.55 and is $1.40 \times 10^{-4}\,\text{m}$ in diameter.

FIGURE 32–56 Problem 60.

61. (II) A beam of light is emitted 8.0 cm beneath the surface of a liquid and strikes the surface 7.6 cm from the point directly above the source. If total internal reflection occurs, what can you say about the index of refraction of the liquid?

62. (II) Figure 32–57 shows a liquid-detecting prism device that might be used inside a washing machine or other liquid-containing appliance. If no liquid covers the prism's hypotenuse, total internal reflection of the beam from the light source produces a large signal in the light sensor. If liquid covers the hypotenuse, some light escapes from the prism into the liquid and the light sensor's signal decreases. Thus a large signal from the light sensor indicates the absence of liquid in the reservoir. If this device is designed to detect the presence of water, determine the allowable range for the prism's index of refraction n. Will the device work properly if the prism is constructed from (inexpensive) lucite? For lucite, $n = 1.5$.

FIGURE 32–57 Problem 62.

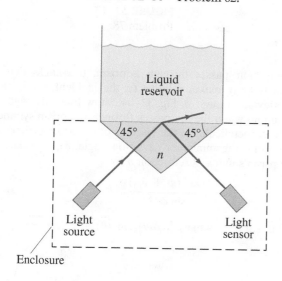

63. (II) Two rays A and B travel down a cylindrical optical fiber of diameter $d = 75.0\,\mu m$, length $\ell = 1.0\,km$, and index of refraction $n_1 = 1.465$. Ray A travels a straight path down the fiber's axis, whereas ray B propagates down the fiber by repeated reflections at the critical angle each time it impinges on the fiber's boundary. Determine the extra time Δt it takes for ray B to travel down the entire fiber in comparison with ray A (Fig. 32–58), assuming (a) the fiber is surrounded by air, (b) the fiber is surrounded by a cylindrical glass "cladding" with index of refraction $n_2 = 1.460$.

FIGURE 32–58 Problem 63.

64. (II) (a) What is the minimum index of refraction for a glass or plastic prism to be used in binoculars (Fig. 32–33) so that total internal reflection occurs at 45°? (b) Will binoculars work if their prisms (assume $n = 1.58$) are immersed in water? (c) What minimum n is needed if the prisms are immersed in water?

65. (III) Suppose a ray strikes the left face of the prism in Fig. 32–52 at 45.0° as shown, but is totally internally reflected at the opposite side. If the apex angle (at the top) is $\theta = 60.0°$, what can you say about the index of refraction of the prism?

66. (III) A beam of light enters the end of an optic fiber as shown in Fig. 32–59. (a) Show that we can guarantee total internal reflection at the side surface of the material (at point A), if the index of refraction is greater than about 1.42. In other words, regardless of the angle α, the light beam reflects back into the material at point A, assuming air outside.

FIGURE 32–59 Problem 66.

*32–8 Refraction at Spherical Surface

*67. (II) A 13.0-cm-thick plane piece of glass ($n = 1.58$) lies on the surface of a 12.0-cm-deep pool of water. How far below the top of the glass does the bottom of the pool seem, as viewed from directly above?

*68. (II) A fish is swimming in water inside a thin spherical glass bowl of uniform thickness. Assuming the radius of curvature of the bowl is 28.0 cm, locate the image of the fish if the fish is located: (a) at the center of the bowl; (b) 20.0 cm from the side of the bowl between the observer and the center of the bowl. Assume the fish is small.

*69. (III) In Section 32–8, we derived Eq. 32–8 for a convex spherical surface with $n_2 > n_1$. Using the same conventions and using diagrams similar to Fig. 32–37, show that Eq. 32–8 is valid also for (a) a convex spherical surface with $n_2 < n_1$, (b) a concave spherical surface with $n_2 > n_1$, and (c) a concave spherical surface with $n_2 < n_1$.

*70. (III) A coin lies at the bottom of a 0.75-m-deep pool. If a viewer sees it at a 45° angle, where is the image of the coin, relative to the coin? [*Hint:* The image is found by tracing back to the intersection of two rays.]

General Problems

71. Two identical concave mirrors are set facing each other 1.0 m apart. A small lightbulb is placed halfway between the mirrors. A small piece of paper placed just to the left of the bulb prevents light from the bulb from directly shining on the left mirror, but light reflected from the right mirror still reaches the left mirror. A good image of the bulb appears on the left side of the piece of paper. What is the focal length of the mirrors?

72. A slab of thickness D, whose two faces are parallel, has index of refraction n. A ray of light incident from air onto one face of the slab at incident angle θ_1 splits into two rays A and B. Ray A reflects directly back into the air, while B travels a total distance ℓ within the slab before reemerging from the slab's face a distance d from its point of entry (Fig. 32–60). (a) Derive expressions for ℓ and d in terms of D, n, and θ_1. (b) For normal incidence (i.e., $\theta_1 = 0°$) show that your expressions yield the expected values for ℓ and d.

FIGURE 32–60
Problem 72.

73. Two plane mirrors are facing each other 2.2 m apart as in Fig. 32–61. You stand 1.5 m away from one of these mirrors and look into it. You will see multiple images of yourself. (a) How far away from you are the first three images of yourself in the mirror in front of you? (b) Are these first three images facing toward you or away from you?

FIGURE 32–61
Problem 73.

74. We wish to determine the depth of a swimming pool filled with water by measuring the width $(x = 5.50\text{ m})$ and then noting that the bottom edge of the pool is just visible at an angle of $13.0°$ above the horizontal as shown in Fig. 32–62. Calculate the depth of the pool.

FIGURE 32–62
Problem 74.

75. A 1.80-m-tall person stands 3.80 m from a convex mirror and notices that he looks precisely half as tall as he does in a plane mirror placed at the same distance. What is the radius of curvature of the convex mirror? (Assume that $\sin\theta \approx \theta$.) [Hint: The viewing *angle* is half.]

76. The critical angle of a certain piece of plastic in air is $\theta_C = 39.3°$. What is the critical angle of the same plastic if it is immersed in water?

77. Each student in a physics lab is assigned to find the location where a bright object may be placed in order that a concave mirror, with radius of curvature $r = 46$ cm, will produce an image three times the size of the object. Two students complete the assignment at different times using identical equipment, but when they compare notes later, they discover that their answers for the object distance are not the same. Explain why they do not necessarily need to repeat the lab, and justify your response with a calculation.

78. A kaleidoscope makes symmetric patterns with two plane mirrors having a 60° angle between them as shown in Fig. 32–63. Draw the location of the images (some of them images of images) of the object placed between the mirrors.

FIGURE 32–63
Problem 78.

79. When light passes through a prism, the angle that the refracted ray makes relative to the incident ray is called the deviation angle δ, Fig. 32–64. Show that this angle is a minimum when the ray passes through the prism symmetrically, perpendicular to the bisector of the apex angle ϕ, and show that the minimum deviation angle, δ_m, is related to the prism's index of refraction n by

$$n = \frac{\sin\frac{1}{2}(\phi + \delta_m)}{\sin\phi/2}.$$

[Hint: For θ in radians, $(d/d\theta)(\sin^{-1}\theta) = 1/\sqrt{1 - \theta^2}$.]

FIGURE 32–64
Problems 79 and 80.

80. If the apex angle of a prism is $\phi = 72°$ (see Fig. 32–64), what is the minimum incident angle for a ray if it is to emerge from the opposite side (i.e., not be totally internally reflected), given $n = 1.58$?

81. **Fermat's principle** states that "light travels between two points along the path that requires the least time, as compared to other nearby paths." From Fermat's principle derive (a) the law of reflection $(\theta_i = \theta_r)$ and (b) the law of refraction (Snell's law). [Hint: Choose two appropriate points so that a ray between them can undergo reflection or refraction. Draw a rough path for a ray between these points, and write down an expression of the time required for light to travel the arbitrary path chosen. Then take the derivative to find the minimum.]

*82. Suppose Fig. 32–36 shows a cylindrical rod whose end has a radius of curvature $R = 2.0$ cm, and the rod is immersed in water with index of refraction of 1.33. The rod has index of refraction 1.53. Find the location and height of the image of an object 2.0 mm high located 23 cm away from the rod.

83. An optical fiber is a long transparent cylinder of diameter d and index of refraction n. If this fiber is bent sharply, some light hitting the side of the cylinder may escape rather than reflect back into the fiber (Fig. 32–65). What is the smallest radius r at a short bent section for which total internal reflection will be assured for light initially travelling parallel to the axis of the fiber?

FIGURE 32–65
Problem 83.

84. An object is placed 15 cm from a certain mirror. The image is half the height of the object, inverted, and real. How far is the image from the mirror, and what is the radius of curvature of the mirror?

85. The end faces of a cylindrical glass rod $(n = 1.51)$ are perpendicular to the sides. Show that a light ray entering an end face at any angle will be totally internally reflected inside the rod when it strikes the sides. Assume the rod is in air. What if it were in water?

86. The paint used on highway signs often contains small transparent spheres which provide nighttime illumination of the sign's lettering by retro-reflecting vehicle headlight beams. Consider a light ray from air incident on one such sphere of radius r and index of refraction n. Let θ be its incident angle, and let the ray follow the path shown in Fig. 32–66, so that the ray exits the sphere in the direction exactly antiparallel to its incoming direction. Considering only rays for which $\sin\theta$ can be approximated as θ, determine the required value for n.

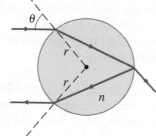

FIGURE 32–66
Problem 86.

*Numerical/Computer

*87. (II) The index of refraction, n, of crown flint glass at different wavelengths (λ) of light are given in the Table below.

λ (nm)	1060	546.1	365.0	312.5
n	1.50586	1.51978	1.54251	1.5600

Make a graph of n versus λ. The variation in index of refraction with wavelength is given by the Cauchy equation $n = A + B/\lambda^2$. Make another graph of n versus $1/\lambda^2$ and determine the constants A and B for the glass by fitting the data with a straight line.

*88. (III) Consider a ray of sunlight incident from air on a spherical raindrop of radius r and index of refraction n. Defining θ to be its incident angle, the ray then follows the path shown in Fig. 32–67, exiting the drop at a "scattering angle" ϕ compared with its original incoming direction. (a) Show that $\phi = 180° + 2\theta - 4\sin^{-1}(\sin\theta/n)$. (b) The parallel rays of sunlight illuminate a raindrop with rays of all possible incident angles from 0° to 90°. Plot ϕ vs. θ in the range $0° \le \theta \le 90°$, in 0.5° steps, assuming $n = 1.33$ as is appropriate for water at visible-light wavelengths. (c) From your plot, you should find that a fairly large fraction of the incident angles have nearly the same scattering angle. Approximately what fraction of the possible incident angles is within roughly 1° of $\phi = 139°$? [This subset of incident rays is what creates the rainbow. Wavelength-dependent variations in n cause the rainbow to form at slightly different ϕ for the various visible colors.]

FIGURE 32–67
Problem 88.

Answers to Exercises

A: No.

B: (b).

C: (a).

D: Toward.

E: The face becomes shiny: total internal reflection.

F: 1.414.

Of the many optical devices we discuss in this Chapter, the magnifying glass is the simplest. Here it is magnifying part of page 886 of this Chapter, which describes how the magnifying glass works according to the ray model. In this Chapter we examine thin lenses in detail, seeing how to determine image position as a function of object position and the focal length of the lens, based on the ray model of light. We then examine optical devices including film and digital cameras, the human eye, eyeglasses, telescopes, and microscopes.

subtends a ... As shown in Fig. 33–33a, the object is placed at the focal point ... magnifying glass ... converging lens produces a virtual image, which ... the eye is to focus on it. If the eye is relaxed, comparison of part (a) of ... case the object is exactly at the focal point. viewed at the near point with ... when you "focus" on the object ... object subtends at the eye is much la... part (b), in which ... eye, rev... **magnification** or **magnifying power**, M ... angular angle subtended by an object when using ... the ratio of the unaided eye, with the object at the near ... subtended using the normal eye): ... the eye ($N = 25$ cm for a

$$M = \frac{\theta'}{\theta},$$

(33–5)

where θ and θ' are shown in Fig. 33–33. $\theta' = h/d_o$ (Fig. 33–33a), where length by noting that $\theta = h/N$ (Fig. 33–... angles are small so θ and θ' equal h is the height of the object and we ass... at least eye strain), the image will ... heir sines and tangents. If the eye is ... at the focal point; see Fig. 33–34. ... at infinity and the object will b... $d_o = f$ and $\theta' = h/f$. Th...

CHAPTER 33

C H A P T E R

Lenses and Optical Instruments

CHAPTER-OPENING QUESTION—Guess now!

A converging lens, like the type used in a magnifying glass,

(a) always produces a magnified image (image taller than the object).
(b) can also produce an image smaller than the object.
(c) always produces an upright image.
(d) can also produce an inverted image (upside down).
(e) None of these statements are true.

The laws of reflection and refraction, particularly the latter, are the basis for explaining the operation of many optical instruments. In this Chapter we discuss and analyze simple lenses using the model of ray optics discussed in the previous Chapter. We then analyze a number of optical instruments, from the magnifying glass and the human eye to telescopes and microscopes. The importance of lenses is that they form images of objects, as shown in Fig. 33–1.

FIGURE 33–1 Converging lens (in holder) forms an image (large "F" on screen at right) of a bright object (illuminated "F" at the left).

Double convex Planoconvex Convex meniscus
(a) Converging lenses

Double concave Planoconcave Concave meniscus
(b) Diverging lenses

(c)

(d)

FIGURE 33–2 (a) Converging lenses and (b) diverging lenses, shown in cross section. Converging lenses are thicker in the center whereas diverging lenses are thinner in the center. (c) Photo of a converging lens (on the left) and a diverging lens (right). (d) Converging lenses (above), and diverging lenses (below), lying flat, and raised off the paper to form images.

33–1 Thin Lenses; Ray Tracing

The most important simple optical device is no doubt the thin lens. The development of optical devices using lenses dates to the sixteenth and seventeenth centuries, although the earliest record of eyeglasses dates from the late thirteenth century. Today we find lenses in eyeglasses, cameras, magnifying glasses, telescopes, binoculars, microscopes, and medical instruments. A thin lens is usually circular, and its two faces are portions of a sphere. (Cylindrical faces are also possible, but we will concentrate on spherical.) The two faces can be concave, convex, or plane. Several types are shown in Fig. 33–2 a and b in cross section.

Consider parallel rays striking the double convex lens shown in cross section in Fig. 33–3a. We assume the lens is made of material such as glass or transparent plastic, with index of refraction greater than that of the air outside. The **axis** of a lens is a straight line passing through the center of the lens and perpendicular to its two surfaces (Fig. 33–3). From Snell's law, we can see that each ray in Fig. 33–3a is bent toward the axis when the ray enters the lens and again when it leaves the lens at the back surface. (Note the dashed lines indicating the normals to each surface for the top ray.) If rays parallel to the axis fall on a thin lens, they will be focused to a point called the **focal point**, F. This will not be precisely true for a lens with spherical surfaces. But it will be very nearly true—that is, parallel rays will be focused to a tiny region that is nearly a point—if the diameter of the lens is small compared to the radii of curvature of the two lens surfaces. This criterion is satisfied by a **thin lens**, one that is very thin compared to its diameter, and we consider only thin lenses here.

The rays from a point on a distant object are essentially parallel—see Fig. 32–12. Therefore we can say that *the focal point is the image point for an object at infinity on the lens axis*. Thus, the focal point of a lens can be found by locating the point where the Sun's rays (or those of some other distant object) are brought to a sharp image, Fig. 33–4. The distance of the focal point from the center of the lens is called the **focal length**, f. A lens can be turned around so that light can pass through it from the opposite side. The focal length is *the same* on both sides, as we shall see later, even if the curvatures of the two lens surfaces are different. If parallel rays fall on a lens at an angle, as in Fig. 33–3b, they focus at a point F_a. The plane containing all focus points, such as F and F_a in Fig. 33–3b, is called the **focal plane** of the lens.

(a)

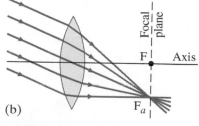

(b)

FIGURE 33–3 Parallel rays are brought to a focus by a converging thin lens.

FIGURE 33–4 Image of the Sun burning wood.

Any lens (in air) that is thicker in the center than at the edges will make parallel rays converge to a point, and is called a **converging lens** (see Fig. 33–2a). Lenses that are thinner in the center than at the edges (Fig. 33–2b) are called **diverging lenses** because they make parallel light diverge, as shown in Fig. 33–5. The focal point, F, of a diverging lens is defined as that point from which refracted rays, originating from parallel incident rays, seem to emerge as shown in Fig. 33–5. And the distance from F to the lens is called the **focal length**, f, just as for a converging lens.

FIGURE 33–5 Diverging lens.

Optometrists and ophthalmologists, instead of using the focal length, use the reciprocal of the focal length to specify the strength of eyeglass (or contact) lenses. This is called the **power**, P, of a lens:

$$P = \frac{1}{f}. \qquad\qquad (33-1)$$

The unit for lens power is the **diopter** (D), which is an inverse meter: $1\,\text{D} = 1\,\text{m}^{-1}$. For example, a 20-cm-focal-length lens has a power $P = 1/(0.20\,\text{m}) = 5.0\,\text{D}$. We will mainly use the focal length, but we will refer again to the power of a lens when we discuss eyeglass lenses in Section 33–6.

The most important parameter of a lens is its focal length f. For a converging lens, f is easily measured by finding the image point for the Sun or other distant objects. Once f is known, the image position can be calculated for any object. To find the image point by drawing rays would be difficult if we had to determine the refractive angles at the front surface of the lens and again at the back surface where the ray exits. We can save ourselves a lot of effort by making use of certain facts we already know, such as that a ray parallel to the axis of the lens passes (after refraction) through the focal point. To determine an image point, we can consider only the three rays indicated in Fig. 33–6, which uses an arrow (on the left) as the object, and a converging lens forming an image (dashed arrow) to the right. These rays, emanating from a single point on the object, are drawn as if the lens were infinitely thin, and we show only a single sharp bend at the center line of the lens instead of the refractions at each surface. These three rays are drawn as follows:

RAY DIAGRAM
Finding the image position formed by a thin lens

Ray 1 is drawn parallel to the axis, Fig. 33–6a; therefore it is refracted by the lens so that it passes along a line through the focal point F behind the lens. (See also Fig. 33–3a.)

Ray 2 is drawn on a line passing through the other focal point F′ (front side of lens in Fig. 33–6) and emerges from the lens parallel to the axis, Fig. 33–6b.

Ray 3 is directed toward the very center of the lens, where the two surfaces are essentially parallel to each other, Fig. 33–6c; this ray therefore emerges from the lens at the same angle as it entered; the ray would be displaced slightly to one side, as we saw in Example 32–8, but since we assume the lens is thin, we draw ray 3 straight through as shown.

The point where these three rays cross is the image point for that object point. Actually, any two of these rays will suffice to locate the image point, but drawing the third ray can serve as a check.

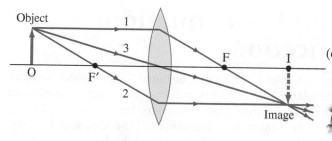

Center line

(a) Ray 1 leaves one point on object going parallel to the axis, then refracts through focal point behind the lens.

(b) Ray 2 passes through F′ in front of the lens; therefore it is parallel to the axis behind the lens.

(c) Ray 3 passes straight through the center of the lens (assumed very thin).

FIGURE 33–6 Finding the image by ray tracing for a converging lens. Rays are shown leaving one point on the object (an arrow). Shown are the three most useful rays, leaving the tip of the object, for determining where the image of that point is formed.

Using these three rays for one object point, we can find the image point for that point of the object (the top of the arrow in Fig. 33–6). The image points for all other points on the object can be found similarly to determine the complete image of the object. Because the rays actually pass through the image for the case shown in Fig. 33–6, it is a **real image** (see page 840). The image could be detected by film or electronic sensor, or actually seen on a white surface or screen placed at the position of the image (Fig. 33–7a).

FIGURE 33–7 (a) A converging lens can form a real image (here of a distant building, upside down) on a screen. (b) That same real image is also directly visible to the eye. [Figure 33–2d shows images (graph paper) seen by the eye made by both diverging and converging lenses.]

CONCEPTUAL EXAMPLE 33–1 **Half-blocked lens.** What happens to the image of an object if the top half of a lens is covered by a piece of cardboard?

RESPONSE Let us look at the rays in Fig. 33–6. If the top half (or any half of the lens) is blocked, you might think that half the image is blocked. But in Fig. 33–6c, we see how the rays used to create the "top" of the image pass through both the top and the bottom of the lens. Only three of many rays are shown—many more rays pass through the lens, and they can form the image. You don't lose the image, but covering part of the lens cuts down on the total light received and reduces the brightness of the image.

NOTE If the lens is partially blocked by your thumb, you may notice an out of focus image of part of that thumb.

(a)

Seeing the Image

The image can also be seen directly by the eye when the eye is placed behind the image, as shown in Fig. 33–6c, so that some of the rays diverging from each point on the image can enter the eye. We can see a sharp image only for rays *diverging* from each point on the image, because we see normal objects when diverging rays from each point enter the eye as was shown in Fig. 32–1. Your eye cannot focus rays converging on it; if your eye was positioned between points F and I in Fig. 33–6c, it would not see a clear image. (More about our eyes in Section 33–6.) Figure 33–7 shows an image seen (a) on a screen and (b) directly by the eye (and a camera) placed behind the image. The eye can see both real and virtual images (see next page) as long as the eye is positioned so rays diverging from the image enter it.

(b)

Diverging Lens

By drawing the same three rays emerging from a single object point, we can determine the image position formed by a diverging lens, as shown in Fig. 33–8. Note that ray 1 is drawn parallel to the axis, but does not pass through the focal point F' behind the lens. Instead it seems to come from the focal point F in front of the lens (dashed line). Ray 2 is directed toward F' and is refracted parallel to the lens axis by the lens. Ray 3 passes directly through the center of the lens. The three refracted rays seem to emerge from a point on the left of the lens. This is the image point, I. Because the rays do not pass through the image, it is a **virtual image**. Note that the eye does not distinguish between real and virtual images—both are visible.

FIGURE 33–8 Finding the image by ray tracing for a diverging lens.

33–2 The Thin Lens Equation; Magnification

We now derive an equation that relates the image distance to the object distance and the focal length of a thin lens. This equation will make the determination of image position quicker and more accurate than doing ray tracing. Let d_o be the object distance, the distance of the object from the center of the lens, and d_i be the image distance, the distance of the image from the center of the lens.

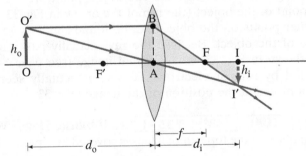

FIGURE 33–9 Deriving the lens equation for a converging lens.

Let h_o and h_i refer to the heights of the object and image. Consider the two rays shown in Fig. 33–9 for a converging lens, assumed to be very thin. The right triangles FI'I and FBA (highlighted in yellow) are similar because angle AFB equals angle IFI'; so

$$\frac{h_i}{h_o} = \frac{d_i - f}{f},$$

since length AB = h_o. Triangles OAO' and IAI' are similar as well. Therefore,

$$\frac{h_i}{h_o} = \frac{d_i}{d_o}.$$

We equate the right sides of these two equations (the left sides are the same), and divide by d_i to obtain

$$\frac{1}{f} - \frac{1}{d_i} = \frac{1}{d_o}$$

or

$$\frac{1}{d_o} + \frac{1}{d_i} = \frac{1}{f}. \tag{33–2}$$

THIN LENS EQUATION

This is called the **thin lens equation**. It relates the image distance d_i to the object distance d_o and the focal length f. It is the most useful equation in geometric optics.

(Interestingly, it is exactly the same as the mirror equation, Eq. 32–2). If the object is at infinity, then $1/d_o = 0$, so $d_i = f$. Thus the focal length is the image distance for an object at infinity, as mentioned earlier.

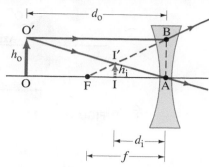

We can derive the lens equation for a diverging lens using Fig. 33–10. Triangles IAI′ and OAO′ are similar; and triangles IFI′ and AFB are similar. Thus (noting that length AB = h_o)

$$\frac{h_i}{h_o} = \frac{d_i}{d_o} \quad \text{and} \quad \frac{h_i}{h_o} = \frac{f - d_i}{f}.$$

When we equate the right sides of these two equations and simplify, we obtain

$$\frac{1}{d_o} - \frac{1}{d_i} = -\frac{1}{f}.$$

FIGURE 33–10 Deriving the lens equation for a diverging lens.

This equation becomes the same as Eq. 33–2 if we make f and d_i negative. That is, we take f to be *negative for a diverging lens*, and d_i negative when the image is on the same side of the lens as the light comes from. Thus Eq. 33–2 will be valid for both converging and diverging lenses, and for *all* situations, if we use the following **sign conventions**:

⚠ **CAUTION**

Focal length is negative for diverging lens

PROBLEM SOLVING

SIGN CONVENTIONS for lenses

1. The focal length is positive for converging lenses and negative for diverging lenses.

2. The object distance is positive if the object is on the side of the lens from which the light is coming (this is usually the case, although when lenses are used in combination, it might not be so); otherwise, it is negative.

3. The image distance is positive if the image is on the opposite side of the lens from where the light is coming; if it is on the same side, d_i is negative. Equivalently, the image distance is positive for a real image and negative for a virtual image.

4. The height of the image, h_i, is positive if the image is upright, and negative if the image is inverted relative to the object. (h_o is always taken as upright and positive.)

The **lateral magnification**, m, of a lens is defined as the ratio of the image height to object height, $m = h_i/h_o$. From Figs. 33–9 and 33–10 and the conventions just stated (for which we'll need a minus sign below), we have

$$m = \frac{h_i}{h_o} = -\frac{d_i}{d_o}. \tag{33–3}$$

For an upright image the magnification is positive ($h_i > 0$ and $d_i < 0$), and for an inverted image the magnification is negative ($h_i < 0$ and $d_i > 0$).

From sign convention 1, it follows that the power (Eq. 33–1) of a converging lens, in diopters, is positive, whereas the power of a diverging lens is negative. A converging lens is sometimes referred to as a **positive lens**, and a diverging lens as a **negative lens**.

Thin Lenses

1. Draw a **ray diagram**, as precise as possible, but even a rough one can serve as confirmation of analytic results. Choose one point on the object and draw at least two, or preferably three, of the easy-to-draw rays described in Figs. 33–6 and 33–8. The image point is where the rays intersect.

2. For analytic solutions, solve for unknowns in the **thin lens equation** (Eq. 33–2) and the **magnification equation** (Eq. 33–3). The thin lens equation involves reciprocals—don't forget to take the reciprocal.

3. Follow the **sign conventions** listed just above.

4. Check that your analytic answers are **consistent** with your ray diagram.

FIGURE 33–11 Example 33–2. (Not to scale.)

EXAMPLE 33–2 **Image formed by converging lens.** What is (a) the position, and (b) the size, of the image of a 7.6-cm-high leaf placed 1.00 m from a +50.0-mm-focal-length camera lens?

APPROACH We follow the steps of the Problem Solving Strategy explicitly.

SOLUTION

1. **Ray diagram.** Figure 33–11 is an approximate ray diagram, showing only rays 1 and 3 for a single point on the leaf. We see that the image ought to be a little behind the focal point F, to the right of the lens.

2. **Thin lens and magnification equations.** (a) We find the image position analytically using the thin lens equation, Eq. 33–2. The camera lens is converging, with $f = +5.00$ cm, and $d_o = 100$ cm, and so the thin lens equation gives

$$\frac{1}{d_i} = \frac{1}{f} - \frac{1}{d_o} = \frac{1}{5.00 \text{ cm}} - \frac{1}{100 \text{ cm}}$$

$$= \frac{20.0 - 1.0}{100 \text{ cm}} = \frac{19.0}{100 \text{ cm}}.$$

Then, taking the reciprocal,

$$d_i = \frac{100 \text{ cm}}{19.0} = 5.26 \text{ cm},$$

or 52.6 mm behind the lens.

(b) The magnification is

$$m = -\frac{d_i}{d_o} = -\frac{5.26 \text{ cm}}{100 \text{ cm}} = -0.0526,$$

so

$$h_i = mh_o = (-0.0526)(7.6 \text{ cm}) = -0.40 \text{ cm}.$$

The image is 4.0 mm high.

3. **Sign conventions.** The image distance d_i came out positive, so the image is behind the lens. The image height is $h_i = -0.40$ cm; the minus sign means the image is inverted.

4. **Consistency.** The analytic results of steps (2) and (3) are consistent with the ray diagram, Fig. 33–11: the image is behind the lens and inverted.

NOTE Part (a) tells us that the image is 2.6 mm farther from the lens than the image for an object at infinity, which would equal the focal length, 50.0 mm. Indeed, when focusing a camera lens, the closer the object is to the camera, the farther the lens must be from the sensor or film.

EXERCISE A If the leaf (object) of Example 33–2 is moved farther from the lens, does the image move closer to or farther from the lens? (Don't calculate!)

EXAMPLE 33–3 **Object close to converging lens.** An object is placed 10 cm from a 15-cm-focal-length converging lens. Determine the image position and size (a) analytically, and (b) using a ray diagram.

APPROACH We first use Eqs. 33–2 and 33–3 to obtain an analytic solution, and then confirm with a ray diagram using the special rays 1, 2, and 3 for a single object point.

SOLUTION (a) Given $f = 15$ cm and $d_o = 10$ cm, then

$$\frac{1}{d_i} = \frac{1}{15 \text{ cm}} - \frac{1}{10 \text{ cm}} = -\frac{1}{30 \text{ cm}},$$

and $d_i = -30$ cm. (Remember to take the reciprocal!) Because d_i is negative, the image must be virtual and on the same side of the lens as the object. The magnification

$$m = -\frac{d_i}{d_o} = -\frac{-30 \text{ cm}}{10 \text{ cm}} = 3.0.$$

⚠ **CAUTION**
Don't forget to take the reciprocal

The image is three times as large as the object and is upright. This lens is being used as a simple magnifying glass, which we discuss in more detail in Section 33–7. (b) The ray diagram is shown in Fig. 33–12 and confirms the result in part (a). We choose point O′ on the top of the object and draw ray 1, which is easy. But ray 2 may take some thought: if we draw it heading toward F′, it is going the wrong way—so we have to draw it as if coming from F′ (and so dashed), striking the lens, and then going out parallel to the lens axis. We project it back parallel, with a dashed line, as we must do also for ray 1, in order to find where they cross. Ray 3 is drawn through the lens center, and it crosses the other two rays at the image point, I′.

NOTE From Fig. 33–12 we can see that, whenever an object is placed between a converging lens and its focal point, the image is virtual.

FIGURE 33–12 An object placed within the focal point of a converging lens produces a virtual image. Example 33–3.

EXAMPLE 33–4 **Diverging lens.** Where must a small insect be placed if a 25-cm-focal-length diverging lens is to form a virtual image 20 cm from the lens, on the same side as the object?

APPROACH The ray diagram is basically that of Fig. 33–10 because our lens here is diverging and our image is in front of the lens within the focal distance. (It would be a valuable exercise to draw the ray diagram to scale, precisely, now.) The insect's distance, d_o, can be calculated using the thin lens equation.

SOLUTION The lens is diverging, so f is negative: $f = -25$ cm. The image distance must be negative too because the image is in front of the lens (sign conventions), so $d_i = -20$ cm. Equation 33–2 gives

$$\frac{1}{d_o} = \frac{1}{f} - \frac{1}{d_i} = -\frac{1}{25 \text{ cm}} + \frac{1}{20 \text{ cm}} = \frac{-4 + 5}{100 \text{ cm}} = \frac{1}{100 \text{ cm}}.$$

So the object must be 100 cm in front of the lens.

FIGURE 33–13 Exercise C.

(a)

(b)

EXERCISE B Return to the Chapter-Opening Question, page 866, and answer it again now. Try to explain why you may have answered differently the first time.

EXERCISE C Figure 33–13 shows a converging lens held above three equal-sized letters A. In (a) the lens is 5 cm from the paper, and in (b) the lens is 15 cm from the paper. Estimate the focal length of the lens. What is the image position for each case?

33–3 Combinations of Lenses

Optical instruments typically use lenses in combination. When light passes through more than one lens, we find the image formed by the first lens as if it were alone. This image becomes the *object* for the second lens, and we find the image then formed by this second lens, which is the final image if there are only two lenses. The total magnification will be the product of the separate magnifications of each lens, as we shall see. Even if the second lens intercepts the light from the first lens before it forms an image, this technique still works.

EXAMPLE 33–5 **A two-lens system.** Two converging lenses, A and B, with focal lengths $f_A = 20.0$ cm and $f_B = 25.0$ cm, are placed 80.0 cm apart, as shown in Fig. 33–14a. An object is placed 60.0 cm in front of the first lens as shown in Fig. 33–14b. Determine (a) the position, and (b) the magnification, of the final image formed by the combination of the two lenses.

APPROACH Starting at the tip of our object O, we draw rays 1, 2, and 3 for the first lens, A, and also a ray 4 which, after passing through lens A, acts as "ray 3" (through the center) for the second lens, B. Ray 2 for lens A exits parallel, and so is ray 1 for lens B. To determine the position of the image I_A formed by lens A, we use Eq. 33–2 with $f_A = 20.0$ cm and $d_{oA} = 60.0$ cm. The distance of I_A (lens A's image) from lens B is the object distance d_{oB} for lens B. The final image is found using the thin lens equation, this time with all distances relative to lens B. For (b) the magnifications are found from Eq. 33–3 for each lens in turn.

SOLUTION (a) The object is a distance $d_{oA} = +60.0$ cm from the first lens, A, and this lens forms an image whose position can be calculated using the thin lens equation:

$$\frac{1}{d_{iA}} = \frac{1}{f_A} - \frac{1}{d_{oA}} = \frac{1}{20.0 \text{ cm}} - \frac{1}{60.0 \text{ cm}} = \frac{3-1}{60.0 \text{ cm}} = \frac{1}{30.0 \text{ cm}}.$$

⚠ **CAUTION**

*Object distance for second lens is **not** equal to the image distance for first lens*

So the first image I_A is at $d_{iA} = 30.0$ cm behind the first lens. This image becomes the object for the second lens, B. It is a distance $d_{oB} = 80.0 \text{ cm} - 30.0 \text{ cm} = 50.0$ cm in front of lens B, as shown in Fig. 33–14b. The image formed by lens B, again using the thin lens equation, is at a distance d_{iB} from the lens B:

$$\frac{1}{d_{iB}} = \frac{1}{f_B} - \frac{1}{d_{oB}} = \frac{1}{25.0 \text{ cm}} - \frac{1}{50.0 \text{ cm}} = \frac{2-1}{50.0 \text{ cm}} = \frac{1}{50.0 \text{ cm}}.$$

Hence $d_{iB} = 50.0$ cm behind lens B. This is the final image—see Fig. 33–14b.

FIGURE 33–14 Two lenses, A and B, used in combination, Example 33–5. The small numbers refer to the easily drawn rays.

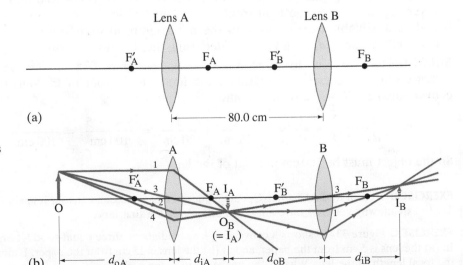

(b) Lens A has a magnification (Eq. 33–3)

$$m_A = -\frac{d_{iA}}{d_{oA}} = -\frac{30.0 \text{ cm}}{60.0 \text{ cm}} = -0.500.$$

Thus, the first image is inverted and is half as high as the object (again Eq. 33–3):

$$h_{iA} = m_A h_{oA} = -0.500 h_{oA}.$$

Lens B takes this image as object and changes its height by a factor

$$m_B = -\frac{d_{iB}}{d_{oB}} = -\frac{50.0 \text{ cm}}{50.0 \text{ cm}} = -1.000.$$

The second lens reinverts the image (the minus sign) but doesn't change its size. The final image height is (remember h_{oB} is the same as h_{iA})

$$h_{iB} = m_B h_{oB} = m_B h_{iA} = m_B m_A h_{oA} = (m_{\text{total}}) h_{oA}.$$

The total magnification is the product of m_A and m_B, which here equals $m_{\text{total}} = m_A m_B = (-1.000)(-0.500) = +0.500,$ or half the original height, and the final image is upright.

EXAMPLE 33–6 **Measuring f for a diverging lens.** To measure the focal length of a diverging lens, a converging lens is placed in contact with it, as shown in Fig. 33–15. The Sun's rays are focused by this combination at a point 28.5 cm, behind the lenses as shown. If the converging lens has a focal length f_C of 16.0 cm, what is the focal length f_D of the diverging lens? Assume both lenses are thin and the space between them is negligible.

APPROACH The image distance for the first lens equals its focal length (16.0 cm) since the object distance is infinity (∞). The position of this image, even though it is never actually formed, acts as the object for the second (diverging) lens. We apply the thin lens equation to the diverging lens to find its focal length, given that the final image is at $d_i = 28.5 \text{ cm}$.

SOLUTION If the diverging lens was absent, the converging lens would form the image at its focal point—that is, at a distance $f_C = 16.0 \text{ cm}$ behind it (dashed lines in Fig. 33–15). When the diverging lens is placed next to the converging lens, we treat the image formed by the first lens as the *object* for the second lens. Since this object lies to the right of the diverging lens, this is a situation where d_o is negative (see the sign conventions, page 871). Thus, for the diverging lens, the object is virtual and $d_o = -16.0 \text{ cm}$. The diverging lens forms the image of this virtual object at a distance $d_i = 28.5 \text{ cm}$ away (given). Thus,

$$\frac{1}{f_D} = \frac{1}{d_o} + \frac{1}{d_i} = \frac{1}{-16.0 \text{ cm}} + \frac{1}{28.5 \text{ cm}} = -0.0274 \text{ cm}^{-1}.$$

We take the reciprocal to find $f_D = -1/(0.0274 \text{ cm}^{-1}) = -36.5 \text{ cm}$.

NOTE If this technique is to work, the converging lens must be "stronger" than the diverging lens—that is, it must have a focal length whose magnitude is less than that of the diverging lens. (Rays from the Sun are focused 28.5 cm behind the combination, so the focal length of the total combination is $f_T = 28.5 \text{ cm}$.)

Image point made by first lens (object point for second lens)

Image made by second lens (final image)

FIGURE 33–15 Determining the focal length of a diverging lens. Example 33–6.

f_C

$f_T = 28.5 \text{ cm}$

*33–4 Lensmaker's Equation

In this Section, we will show that parallel rays are brought to a focus at a single point for a thin lens. At the same time, we will also derive an equation that relates the focal length of a lens to the radii of curvature of its two surfaces and its index of refraction, which is known as the lensmaker's equation.

In Fig. 33–16, a ray parallel to the axis of a lens is refracted at the front surface of the lens at point A_1 and is refracted at the back surface at point A_2. This ray then passes through point F, which we call the focal point for this ray. Point A_1 is a height h_1 above the axis, and point A_2 is height h_2 above the axis. C_1 and C_2 are the centers of curvature of the two lens surfaces; so the length $C_1 A_1 = R_1$, the radius of curvature of the front surface, and $C_2 A_2 = R_2$ is the radius of the second surface. We consider a double convex lens and by convention choose the radii of both lens surfaces as positive. The thickness of the lens has been grossly exaggerated so that the various angles would be clear. But we will assume that the lens is actually very thin and that angles between the rays and the axis are small. In this approximation, the sines and tangents of all the angles will be equal to the angles themselves in radians. For example, $\sin\theta_1 \approx \tan\theta_1 \approx \theta_1$ (radians).

FIGURE 33–16 Diagram of a ray passing through a lens for derivation of the lensmaker's equation.

To this approximation, then, Snell's law tells us that

$$\theta_1 = n\theta_2$$
$$\theta_4 = n\theta_3$$

where n is the index of refraction of the glass, and we assume that the lens is surrounded by air $(n = 1)$. Notice also in Fig. 33–16 that

$$\theta_1 \approx \sin\theta_1 = \frac{h_1}{R_1}$$

$$\alpha \approx \frac{h_2}{R_2}$$

$$\beta \approx \frac{h_2}{f}.$$

The last follows because the distance from F to the lens (assumed very thin) is f. From the diagram, the angle γ is

$$\gamma = \theta_1 - \theta_2.$$

A careful examination of Fig. 33–16 shows also that

$$\alpha = \theta_3 - \gamma.$$

This can be seen by drawing a horizontal line to the left from point A_2, which divides the angle θ_3 into two parts. The upper part equals γ and the lower part equals α. (The opposite angles between an oblique line and two parallel lines are equal.) Thus, $\theta_3 = \gamma + \alpha$. Furthermore, by drawing a horizontal line to the right from point A_2, we divide θ_4 into two parts. The upper part is α and the lower is β.

Thus

$$\theta_4 = \alpha + \beta.$$

We now combine all these equations:

$$\alpha = \theta_3 - \gamma = \frac{\theta_4}{n} - (\theta_1 - \theta_2) = \frac{\alpha}{n} + \frac{\beta}{n} - \theta_1 + \theta_2,$$

or

$$\frac{h_2}{R_2} = \frac{h_2}{nR_2} + \frac{h_2}{nf} - \frac{h_1}{R_1} + \frac{h_1}{nR_1}.$$

Because the lens is thin, $h_1 \approx h_2$ and all h's can be canceled from all the numerators. We then multiply through by n and rearrange to find that

$$\frac{1}{f} = (n - 1)\left(\frac{1}{R_1} + \frac{1}{R_2}\right). \tag{33-4}$$

This is called the **lensmaker's equation**. It relates the focal length of a thin lens to the radii of curvature of its two surfaces and its index of refraction. Notice that f for a thin lens does not depend on h_1 or h_2. Thus the position of the point F does not depend on where the ray strikes the lens. Hence, all rays parallel to the axis of a thin lens will pass through the same point F, which we wished to prove.

In our derivation, both surfaces are convex and R_1 and R_2 are considered positive.[†] Equation 33–4 also works for lenses with one or both surfaces concave; but for a concave surface, the radius must be considered *negative*.

Notice in Eq. 33–4 that the equation is *symmetrical* in R_1 and R_2. Thus, if a lens is turned around so that light impinges on the other surface, the focal length is the same even if the two lens surfaces are different.

> **EXAMPLE 33–7** **Calculating f for a converging lens.** A convex meniscus lens (Figs. 33–2a and 33–17) is made from glass with $n = 1.50$. The radius of curvature of the convex surface is 22.4 cm and that of the concave surface is 46.2 cm. (a) What is the focal length? (b) Where will the image be for an object 2.00 m away?
>
> **APPROACH** We use Eq. 33–4, noting that R_2 is negative because it refers to the concave surface.
>
> **SOLUTION** (a) $R_1 = 22.4$ cm and $R_2 = -46.2$ cm. Then
>
> $$\frac{1}{f} = (1.50 - 1.00)\left(\frac{1}{22.4 \text{ cm}} - \frac{1}{46.2 \text{ cm}}\right)$$
> $$= 0.0115 \text{ cm}^{-1}.$$
>
> So
>
> $$f = \frac{1}{0.0115 \text{ cm}^{-1}} = 87.0 \text{ cm}$$
>
> and the lens is converging. Notice that if we turn the lens around so that $R_1 = -46.2$ cm and $R_2 = +22.4$ cm, we get the same result.
> (b) From the lens equation, with $f = 0.870$ m and $d_o = 2.00$ m, we have
>
> $$\frac{1}{d_i} = \frac{1}{f} - \frac{1}{d_o} = \frac{1}{0.870 \text{ m}} - \frac{1}{2.00 \text{ m}}$$
> $$= 0.649 \text{ m}^{-1},$$
>
> so $d_i = 1/0.649 \text{ m}^{-1} = 1.54$ m.

FIGURE 33–17 Example 33–7.

EXERCISE D A Lucite planoconcave lens (see Fig. 33–2b) has one flat surface and the other has $R = -18.4$ cm. What is the focal length? Is the lens converging or diverging?

[†]Some books use a different convention—for example, R_1 and R_2 are considered positive if their centers of curvature are to the right of the lens, in which case a minus sign appears in their equivalent of Eq. 33–4.

33–5 Cameras: Film and Digital

The basic elements of a **camera** are a lens, a light-tight box, a shutter to let light pass through the lens only briefly, and in a digital camera an electronic sensor or in a traditional camera a piece of film (Fig. 33–18). When the shutter is opened for a brief "exposure," light from external objects in the field of view is focused by the lens as an image on the film or sensor. Film contains light-sensitive chemicals that change when light strikes them. In the development process, chemical reactions cause the changed areas to turn opaque, so the image is recorded on the film.[†]

You can see the image yourself if you remove the back of a conventional camera and view through a piece of tissue paper (on which an image can form) placed where the film should be with the shutter open.

Digital Cameras, Electronic Sensors (CCD, CMOS)

In a **digital camera**, the film is replaced by a semiconductor sensor. Two types are in common use: **CCD** (*charge-coupled device*) and **CMOS** (*complementary metal oxide semiconductor*). A CCD sensor is made up of millions of tiny **pixels** ("picture elements")—see Figs. 35–42 and 33–19. A 6-MP (6-megapixel) sensor[‡] would contain about 2000 pixels vertically by 3000 pixels horizontally over an area of perhaps $4 \times 6\,mm$ or even $24 \times 36\,mm$. Light reaching any pixel liberates electrons from the semiconductor. The more intense the light, the more charge accumulates during the brief exposure time. Conducting electrodes carry each pixel's charge (serially in time, row by row—hence the name "charge-coupled") to a central processor that stores the relative brightness of pixels, and allows reformation of the image later onto a computer screen or printer. A CCD is fully reusable. Once the pixel charges are transferred to memory, a new picture can be taken.

A CMOS sensor also uses a silicon semiconductor, and incorporates some electronics within each pixel, allowing parallel readout.

Color is achieved by red, green, and blue filters over alternating pixels as shown in Fig. 33–19, similar to a color CRT or LCD screen. The sensor type shown in Fig. 33–19 contains twice as many green pixels as red or blue (because green is claimed to have a stronger influence on the sensation of sharpness). The computer-analyzed color at each pixel is that pixel's intensity averaged with the intensities of the nearest-neighbor colors.

To reduce the amount of memory for each picture, compression programs average over pixels, but with a consequent loss of sharpness, or "resolution."

*Digital Artifacts

Digital cameras can produce image artifacts (artificial effects in the image not present in the original) resulting from the imaging process. One example using the "mosaic" of pixels (Fig. 33–19) is described in Fig. 33–20. An alternative technology uses a semitransparent silicon semiconductor layer system wherein different wavelengths of light penetrate silicon to different depths: each pixel is a sandwich of partly transparent layers, one for each color. The top layer can absorb blue light, allowing green and red light to pass through. The second layer absorbs green and the bottom layer detects the red. All three colors are detected by each pixel, resulting in better color resolution and fewer artifacts.

[†]This is called a *negative*, because the black areas correspond to bright objects and vice versa. The same process occurs during printing to produce a black-and-white "positive" picture from the negative. Color film has three emulsion layers (or dyes) corresponding to the three primary colors.

[‡]Each different color of pixel in a CCD is counted as a separate pixel. In contrast, in an LCD screen (Section 35–12), a group of three subpixels is counted as one pixel, a more conservative count.

⊕ PHYSICS APPLIED
The camera

FIGURE 33–18 A simple camera.

⊕ PHYSICS APPLIED
Digital cameras

FIGURE 33–19 Portion of a typical CCD sensor. A square group of four pixels $^{RG}_{GB}$ is sometimes called a "color pixel."

FIGURE 33–20 Suppose we take a picture that includes a thin black line (our object) on a white background. The *image* of this black line has a colored halo (red above, blue below) due to the mosaic arrangement of color filter pixels, as shown by the colors transmitted. Computer averaging can minimize color problems such as this (the green at top and bottom of image can be averaged with nearby pixels to give white or nearly so) but the image is consequently "softened" or blurred. The layered color pixel described in the text would avoid this artifact.

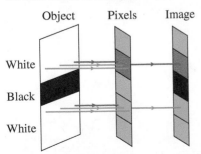

Camera Adjustments

There are three main adjustments on good-quality cameras: shutter speed, f-stop, and focusing. Although most cameras today make these adjustments automatically, it is valuable to understand these adjustments to use a camera effectively. For special or top-quality work, a manual camera is indispensable (Fig. 33–21).

Exposure time or shutter speed This refers to how quickly the digital sensor can make an accurate reading, or how long the shutter of a camera is open and the film or sensor exposed. It could vary from a second or more ("time exposures"), to $\frac{1}{1000}$s or less. To avoid blurring from camera movement, exposure times shorter than $\frac{1}{100}$s are normally needed. If the object is moving, even shorter exposure times are needed to "stop" the action. If the exposure (or sampling) time is not fast enough, the image will be blurred by camera shake no matter how many pixels a digital camera claims. Blurring in low light conditions is more of a problem with cell-phone cameras whose sensors are not usually the most sophisticated. Digital still cameras or cell phones that take short videos must have a fast enough "sampling" time and fast "clearing" (of the charge) time so as to take pictures at least 15 frames per second, and preferably 30 fps.

FIGURE 33–21 On this camera, the f-stops and the focusing ring are on the camera lens. Shutter speeds are selected on the small wheel on top of the camera body.

f-stop The amount of light reaching the film must be carefully controlled to avoid **underexposure** (too little light so the picture is dark and only the brightest objects show up) or **overexposure** (too much light, so that all bright objects look the same, with a consequent lack of contrast and a "washed-out" appearance). Most cameras these days make f-stop and shutter speed adjustments automatically. A high quality camera controls the exposure with a "stop" or iris diaphragm, whose opening is of variable diameter, placed behind the lens (Fig. 33–18). The size of the opening is controlled (automatically or manually) to compensate for bright or dark lighting conditions, the sensitivity of the sensor or film,[†] and for different shutter speeds. The size of the opening is specified by the **f-number** or **f-stop**, defined as

$$f\text{-stop} = \frac{f}{D},$$

where f is the focal length of the lens and D is the diameter of the lens opening (Fig. 33–18). For example, when a 50-mm-focal-length lens has an opening $D = 25\,\text{mm}$, we say it is set at $f/2$. When this lens is set at $f/8$, the opening is only $6\frac{1}{4}\,\text{mm}$ $\left(50/6\frac{1}{4} = 8\right)$. For faster shutter speeds, or low light conditions, a wider lens opening must be used to get a proper exposure, which corresponds to a smaller f-stop number. The smaller the f-stop number, the larger the opening and the more light passes through the lens to the sensor or film. The smallest f-number of a lens (largest opening) is referred to as the *speed* of the lens. The best lenses may have a speed of $f/2.0$, or even faster. The advantage of a fast lens is that it allows pictures to be taken under poor lighting conditions. Good quality lenses consist of several elements to reduce the defects present in simple thin lenses (Section 33–10). Standard f-stops are

1.0, 1.4, 2.0, 2.8, 4.0, 5.6, 8, 11, 16, 22, and 32

(Fig. 33–21). Each of these stops corresponds to a diameter reduction by a factor of about $\sqrt{2} \approx 1.4$. Because the amount of light reaching the film is proportional to the *area* of the opening, and therefore proportional to the diameter squared, each standard f-stop corresponds to a factor of 2 in light intensity reaching the film.

Focusing Focusing is the operation of placing the lens at the correct position relative to the sensor or film for the sharpest image. The image distance is smallest for objects at infinity (the symbol ∞ is used for infinity) and is equal to the focal length. For closer objects, the image distance is greater than the focal length, as can be seen from the lens equation, $1/f = 1/d_\text{o} + 1/d_\text{i}$ (Eq. 33–2). To focus on nearby objects, the lens must therefore be moved away from the sensor or film, and this is usually done on a manual camera by turning a ring on the lens.

[†]Different films have different sensitivities to light, referred to as the "film speed" and specified as an "ISO (or ASA) number." A "faster" film is more sensitive and needs less light to produce a good image. Faster films are grainier so offer less sharpness (resolution) when enlarged. Digital cameras may have a "gain" or "ISO" adjustment for sensitivity. Adjusting a CCD to be "faster" for low light conditions results in "noise," the digital equivalent of graininess.

FIGURE 33–22 Photos taken with a camera lens (a) focused on a nearby object with distant object blurry, and (b) focused on a more distant object with nearby object blurry.

(a)   (b)

If the lens is focused on a nearby object, a sharp image of it will be formed, but the image of distant objects may be blurry (Fig. 33–22). The rays from a point on the distant object will be out of focus—they will form a circle on the sensor or film as shown (exaggerated) in Fig. 33–23. The distant object will thus produce an image consisting of overlapping circles and will be blurred. These circles are called **circles of confusion**. To include near and distant objects in the same photo, you (or the camera) can try setting the lens focus at an intermediate position. For a given distance setting, there is a range of distances over which the circles of confusion will be small enough that the images will be reasonably sharp. This is called the **depth of field**. The depth of field varies with the lens opening. If the lens opening is smaller, only rays through the central part of the lens are accepted, and these form smaller circles of confusion for a given object distance. Hence, at smaller lens openings, a greater range of object distances will fit within the circle of confusion criterion, so the depth of field is greater.[†] For a sensor or film width of 36 mm (including 35-mm film cameras), the depth of field is usually based on a maximum circle of confusion diameter of 0.003 mm.

FIGURE 33–23 When the lens is positioned to focus on a nearby object, points on a distant object produce circles and are therefore blurred. (The effect is shown greatly exaggerated.)

Rays from nearby object (in focus)

Rays from distant object

"Circle of confusion" for distant object (greatly exaggerated)

EXAMPLE 33–8 **Camera focus.** How far must a 50.0-mm-focal-length camera lens be moved from its infinity setting to sharply focus an object 3.00 m away?

APPROACH For an object at infinity, the image is at the focal point, by definition. For an object distance of 3.00 m, we use the thin lens equation, Eq. 33–2, to find the image distance (distance of lens to film or sensor).

SOLUTION When focused at infinity, the lens is 50.0 mm from the film. When focused at $d_o = 3.00$ m, the image distance is given by the lens equation,

$$\frac{1}{d_i} = \frac{1}{f} - \frac{1}{d_o} = \frac{1}{50.0 \text{ mm}} - \frac{1}{3000 \text{ mm}} = \frac{3000 - 50}{(3000)(50.0) \text{ mm}} = \frac{2950}{150,000 \text{ mm}}.$$

We solve for d_i and find $d_i = 50.8$ mm, so the lens needs to move 0.8 mm away from the film or digital sensor.

[†]Smaller lens openings, however, result in reduced resolution due to diffraction (discussed in Chapter 35). Best resolution is typically found around $f/8$.

CONCEPTUAL EXAMPLE 33–9 **Shutter speed.** To improve the depth of field, you "stop down" your camera lens by two f-stops from $f/4$ to $f/8$. What should you do to the shutter speed to maintain the same exposure?

RESPONSE The amount of light admitted by the lens is proportional to the area of the lens opening. Reducing the lens opening by two f-stops reduces the diameter by a factor of 2, and the area by a factor of 4. To maintain the same exposure, the shutter must be open four times as long. If the shutter speed had been $\frac{1}{500}$ s, you would have to increase the exposure time to $\frac{1}{125}$ s.

*Picture Sharpness

The sharpness of a picture depends not only on accurate focusing and short exposure times, but also on the graininess of the film, or the number of pixels for a digital camera. Fine-grained films are "slower," meaning they require longer exposures for a given light level. Digital cameras have averaging (or "compression") programs, such as JPEG, which reduce memory size by averaging over pixels where little contrast is detected. Hence it is unusual to use all pixels available. They also average over pixels in low light conditions, resulting in a less sharp photo.

The quality of the lens strongly affects the image quality, and we discuss lens resolution and diffraction effects in Sections 33–10 and 35–4. The sharpness, or *resolution*, of a lens is often given as so many lines per millimeter, measured by photographing a standard set of parallel lines on fine-grain film or high quality sensor, or as so many dots per inch (dpi). The minimum spacing of distinguishable lines or dots gives the resolution; 50 lines/mm is reasonable, 100 lines/mm is quite good ($= 100$ dots/mm ≈ 2500 dpi on the sensor).

EXAMPLE 33–10 **Pixels and resolution.** A 6-MP (6-megapixel) digital camera offers a maximum resolution of 2000 × 3000 pixels on a 16-mm × 24-mm CCD sensor. How sharp should the lens be to make use of this resolution?

APPROACH We find the number of pixels per millimeter and require the lens to be at least that good.

SOLUTION We can either take the image height (2000 pixels in 16 mm) or the width (3000 pixels in 24 mm):

$$\frac{3000 \text{ pixels}}{24 \text{ mm}} = 125 \text{ pixels/mm}.$$

We would want the lens to be able to resolve at least 125 lines or dots per mm as well, which would be a very good lens. If the lens is not this good, fewer pixels and less memory could be used.

NOTE Increasing lens resolution is a tougher problem today than is squeezing more pixels on a CCD or CMOS. The sensor for high MP cameras must also be physically larger for greater light sensitivity (low light conditions).

EXAMPLE 33–11 **Blown-up photograph.** An enlarged photograph looks sharp at normal viewing distances if the dots or lines are resolved to about 10 dots/mm. Would an 8 × 10-inch enlargement of a photo taken by the camera in Example 33–10 seem sharp? To what maximum size could you enlarge this 2000 × 3000-pixel image?

APPROACH We assume the image is 2000 × 3000 pixels on a 16 × 24-mm CCD as in Example 33–10, or 125 pixels/mm. We make an enlarged photo 8 × 10 in. = 20 cm × 25 cm.

SOLUTION The short side of the CCD is 16 mm = 1.6 cm long, and that side of the photograph is 8 inches or 20 cm. Thus the size is increased by a factor of 20 cm/1.6 cm = 12.5× (or 25 cm/2.4 cm ≈ 10×). To fill the 8 × 10-in. paper, we assume the enlargement is 12.5×. The pixels are thus enlarged 12.5×; so the pixel count of 125/mm on the CCD becomes 10 per mm on the print. Hence an 8 × 10-inch print is just about the maximum possible for a sharp photograph with 6 megapixels. If you feel 7 dots per mm is good enough, you can enlarge to maybe 11 × 14 inches.

*Telephotos and Wide-angles

Camera lenses are categorized into normal, telephoto, and wide angle, according to focal length and film size. A **normal lens** covers the sensor or film with a field of view that corresponds approximately to that of normal vision. A normal lens for 35-mm film has a focal length in the vicinity of 50 mm. The best digital cameras aim for a sensor of the same size[†] (24 mm × 36mm). (If the sensor is smaller, digital cameras sometimes specify focal lengths to correspond with classic 35-mm cameras.) **Telephoto lenses** act like telescopes to magnify images. They have longer focal lengths than a normal lens: as we saw in Section 33–2 (Eq. 33–3), the height of the image for a given object distance is proportional to the image distance, and the image distance will be greater for a lens with longer focal length. For distant objects, the image height is very nearly proportional to the focal length. Thus a 200-mm telephoto lens for use with a 35-mm camera gives a 4× magnification over the normal 50-mm lens. A **wide-angle lens** has a shorter focal length than normal: a wider field of view is included, and objects appear smaller. A **zoom lens** is one whose focal length can be changed so that you seem to zoom up to, or away from, the subject as you change the focal length.

Digital cameras may have an **optical zoom** meaning the lens can change focal length and maintain resolution. But an "electronic" or **digital zoom** just enlarges the dots (pixels) with loss of sharpness.

Different types of viewing systems are used in cameras. In some cameras, you view through a small window just above the lens as in Fig. 33–18. In a **single-lens reflex** camera (SLR), you actually view through the lens with the use of prisms and mirrors (Fig. 33–24). A mirror hangs at a 45° angle behind the lens and flips up out of the way just before the shutter opens. SLRs have the advantage that you can see almost exactly what you will get. Digital cameras use an LCD display, and it too can show what you will get on the photo if it is carefully designed.

FIGURE 33–24 Single-lens reflex (SLR) camera, showing how the image is viewed through the lens with the help of a movable mirror and prism.

PHYSICS APPLIED
The eye

FIGURE 33–25 Diagram of a human eye.

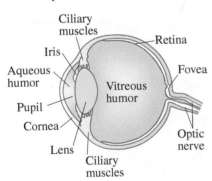

33–6 The Human Eye; Corrective Lenses

The human eye resembles a camera in its basic structure (Fig. 33–25), but is far more sophisticated. The interior of the eye is filled with a transparent gel-like substance called the *vitreous humor* with index of refraction $n = 1.337$. Light enters this enclosed volume through the cornea and lens. Between the cornea and lens is a watery fluid, the aqueous humor (*aqua* is "water" in Latin) with $n = 1.336$. A diaphragm, called the **iris** (the colored part of your eye), adjusts automatically to control the amount of light entering the eye, similar to a camera. The hole in the iris through which light passes (the **pupil**) is black because no light is reflected from it (it's a hole), and very little light is reflected back out from the interior of the eye. The **retina**, which plays the role of the film or sensor in a camera, is on the curved rear surface of the eye. The retina consists of a complex array of nerves and receptors known as *rods* and *cones* which act to change light energy into electrical signals that travel along the nerves. The reconstruction of the image from all these tiny receptors is done mainly in the brain, although some analysis may also be done in the complex interconnected nerve network at the retina itself. At the center of the retina is a small area called the **fovea**, about 0.25 mm in diameter, where the cones are very closely packed and the sharpest image and best color discrimination are found.

Unlike a camera, the eye contains no shutter. The equivalent operation is carried out by the nervous system, which analyzes the signals to form images at the rate of about 30 per second. This can be compared to motion picture or television cameras, which operate by taking a series of still pictures at a rate of 24 (movies) or 30 (U.S. television) per second; their rapid projection on the screen gives the appearance of motion.

[†]A "35-mm camera" uses film that is physically 35 mm wide; that 35 mm is not to be confused with a focal length. 35-mm film has sprocket holes, so only 24 mm of its height is used for the photo; the width is usually 36 mm for stills. Thus one frame is 24 mm × 36 mm. Movie frames are 18 mm × 24 mm.

The lens of the eye ($n = 1.386$ to 1.406) does little of the bending of the light rays. Most of the refraction is done at the front surface of the **cornea** ($n = 1.376$) at its interface with air ($n = 1.0$). The lens acts as a fine adjustment for focusing at different distances. This is accomplished by the ciliary muscles (Fig. 33–25), which change the curvature of the lens so that its focal length is changed. To focus on a distant object, the ciliary muscles of the eye are relaxed and the lens is thin, as shown in Fig. 33–26a, and parallel rays focus at the focal point (on the retina). To focus on a nearby object, the muscles contract, causing the center of the lens to thicken, Fig. 33–26b, thus shortening the focal length so that images of nearby objects can be focused on the retina, behind the new focal point. This focusing adjustment is called **accommodation**.

The closest distance at which the eye can focus clearly is called the **near point** of the eye. For young adults it is typically 25 cm, although younger children can often focus on objects as close as 10 cm. As people grow older, the ability to accommodate is reduced and the near point increases. A given person's **far point** is the farthest distance at which an object can be seen clearly. For some purposes it is useful to speak of a **normal eye** (a sort of average over the population), defined as an eye having a near point of 25 cm and a far point of infinity. To check your own near point, place this book close to your eye and slowly move it away until the type is sharp.

The "normal" eye is sort of an ideal. Many people have eyes that do not accommodate within the "normal" range of 25 cm to infinity, or have some other defect. Two common defects are nearsightedness and farsightedness. Both can be corrected to a large extent with lenses—either eyeglasses or contact lenses.

In **nearsightedness**, or *myopia*, the eye can focus only on nearby objects. The far point is not infinity but some shorter distance, so distant objects are not seen clearly. It is usually caused by an eyeball that is too long, although sometimes it is the curvature of the cornea that is too great. In either case, images of distant objects are focused in front of the retina. A diverging lens, because it causes parallel rays to diverge, allows the rays to be focused at the retina (Fig. 33–27a) and thus corrects this defect.

In **farsightedness**, or *hyperopia*, the eye cannot focus on nearby objects. Although distant objects are usually seen clearly, the near point is somewhat greater than the "normal" 25 cm, which makes reading difficult. This defect is caused by an eyeball that is too short or (less often) by a cornea that is not sufficiently curved. It is corrected by a converging lens, Fig. 33–27b. Similar to hyperopia is *presbyopia*, which refers to the lessening ability of the eye to accommodate as a person ages, and the near point moves out. Converging lenses also compensate for this.

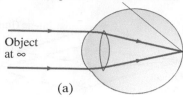

Focal point of lens and cornea

Object at ∞

(a)

Focal point of lens and cornea

Object

(b)

FIGURE 33–26 Accommodation by a normal eye: (a) lens relaxed, focused at infinity; (b) lens thickened, focused on a nearby object.

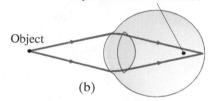

⊛ **PHYSICS APPLIED**
Corrective lenses

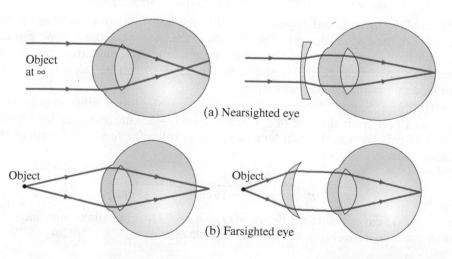

Object at ∞

(a) Nearsighted eye

Object

(b) Farsighted eye

FIGURE 33–27 Correcting eye defects with lenses: (a) a nearsighted eye, which cannot focus clearly on distant objects, can be corrected by use of a diverging lens; (b) a farsighted eye, which cannot focus clearly on nearby objects, can be corrected by use of a converging lens.

FIGURE 33–28 A cylindrical lens forms a line image of a point object because it is converging in one plane only.

Image (line)

Object (point)

Astigmatism is usually caused by an out-of-round cornea or lens so that point objects are focused as short lines, which blurs the image. It is as if the cornea were spherical with a cylindrical section superimposed. As shown in Fig. 33–28, a cylindrical lens focuses a point into a line parallel to its axis. An astigmatic eye may focus rays in one plane, such as the vertical plane, at a shorter distance than it does for rays in a horizontal plane. Astigmatism is corrected with the use of a compensating cylindrical lens. Lenses for eyes that are nearsighted or farsighted as well as astigmatic are ground with superimposed spherical and cylindrical surfaces, so that the radius of curvature of the correcting lens is different in different planes.

EXAMPLE 33–12 **Farsighted eye.** Sue is farsighted with a near point of 100 cm. Reading glasses must have what lens power so that she can read a newspaper at a distance of 25 cm? Assume the lens is very close to the eye.

APPROACH When the object is placed 25 cm from the lens, we want the image to be 100 cm away on the *same* side of the lens (so the eye can focus it), and so the image is virtual, as shown in Fig. 33–29, and $d_i = -100$ cm will be negative. We use the thin lens equation (Eq. 33–2) to determine the needed focal length. Optometrists' prescriptions specify the power $(P = 1/f$, Eq. 33–1) given in diopters $(1 \, \text{D} = 1 \, \text{m}^{-1})$.

SOLUTION Given that $d_o = 25$ cm and $d_i = -100$ cm, the thin lens equation gives

$$\frac{1}{f} = \frac{1}{d_o} + \frac{1}{d_i} = \frac{1}{25 \, \text{cm}} + \frac{1}{-100 \, \text{cm}} = \frac{4 - 1}{100 \, \text{cm}} = \frac{1}{33 \, \text{cm}}.$$

So $f = 33$ cm $= 0.33$ m. The power P of the lens is $P = 1/f = +3.0$ D. The plus sign indicates that it is a converging lens.

NOTE We chose the image position to be where the eye can actually focus. The lens needs to put the image there, given the desired placement of the object (newspaper).

FIGURE 33–29 Lens of reading glasses (Example 33–12).

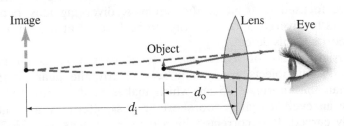

Image

Object

Lens

Eye

d_o

d_i

FIGURE 33–30 Example 33–13.

Object at ∞

I

17 cm (Far point)

2 cm

(a)

O

I

12 cm (Near point)

(b)

EXAMPLE 33–13 **Nearsighted eye.** A nearsighted eye has near and far points of 12 cm and 17 cm, respectively. (a) What lens power is needed for this person to see distant objects clearly, and (b) what then will be the near point? Assume that the lens is 2.0 cm from the eye (typical for eyeglasses).

APPROACH For a distant object $(d_o = \infty)$, the lens must put the image at the far point of the eye as shown in Fig. 33–30a, 17 cm in front of the eye. We can use the thin lens equation to find the focal length of the lens, and from this its lens power. The new near point (as shown in Fig. 33–30b) can be calculated for the lens by again using the thin lens equation.

SOLUTION (a) For an object at infinity $(d_o = \infty)$, the image must be in front of the lens 17 cm from the eye or $(17 \, \text{cm} - 2 \, \text{cm}) = 15$ cm from the lens; hence $d_i = -15$ cm. We use the thin lens equation to solve for the focal length of the needed lens:

$$\frac{1}{f} = \frac{1}{d_o} + \frac{1}{d_i} = \frac{1}{\infty} + \frac{1}{-15 \, \text{cm}} = -\frac{1}{15 \, \text{cm}}.$$

So $f = -15$ cm $= -0.15$ m or $P = 1/f = -6.7$ D. The minus sign indicates that it must be a diverging lens for the myopic eye.

(b) The near point when glasses are worn is where an object is placed (d_o) so that the lens forms an image at the "near point of the naked eye," namely 12 cm from the eye. That image point is $(12\,\text{cm} - 2\,\text{cm}) = 10\,\text{cm}$ in front of the lens, so $d_i = -0.10\,\text{m}$ and the thin lens equation gives

$$\frac{1}{d_o} = \frac{1}{f} - \frac{1}{d_i} = -\frac{1}{0.15\,\text{m}} + \frac{1}{0.10\,\text{m}} = \frac{-2 + 3}{0.30\,\text{m}} = \frac{1}{0.30\,\text{m}}.$$

So $d_o = 30\,\text{cm}$, which means the near point when the person is wearing glasses is 30 cm in front of the lens, or 32 cm from the eye.

Suppose contact lenses are used to correct the eye in Example 33–13. Since contacts are placed directly on the cornea, we would not subtract out the 2.0 cm for the image distances. That is, for distant objects $d_i = f = -17\,\text{cm}$, so $P = 1/f = -5.9\,\text{D}$. The new near point would be 41 cm. Thus we see that a contact lens and an eyeglass lens will require slightly different powers, or focal lengths, for the same eye because of their different placements relative to the eye. We also see that glasses in this case give a better near point than contacts.

PHYSICS APPLIED
Contact lenses

EXERCISE E What power contact lens is needed for an eye to see distant objects if its far point is 25 cm?

When your eyes are under water, distant underwater objects look blurry because at the water–cornea interface, the difference in indices of refraction is very small: $n = 1.33$ for water, 1.376 for the cornea. Hence light rays are bent very little and are focused far behind the retina, Fig. 33–31a. If you wear goggles or a face mask, you restore an air–cornea interface ($n = 1.0$ and 1.376, respectively) and the rays can be focused, Fig. 33–31b.

PHYSICS APPLIED
Underwater vision

(a)

(b)

FIGURE 33–31 (a) Under water, we see a blurry image because light rays are bent much less than in air. (b) If we wear goggles, we again have an air–cornea interface and can see clearly.

33–7 Magnifying Glass

Much of the remainder of this Chapter will deal with optical devices that are used to produce magnified images of objects. We first discuss the **simple magnifier**, or **magnifying glass**, which is simply a converging lens (see Chapter-Opening Photo).

How large an object appears, and how much detail we can see on it, depends on the size of the image it makes on the retina. This, in turn, depends on the angle subtended by the object at the eye. For example, a penny held 30 cm from the eye looks twice as tall as one held 60 cm away because the angle it subtends is twice as great (Fig. 33–32). When we want to examine detail on an object, we bring it up close to our eyes so that it subtends a greater angle. However, our eyes can accommodate only up to a point (the near point), and we will assume a standard distance of $N = 25\,\text{cm}$ as the near point in what follows.

FIGURE 33–32 When the same object is viewed at a shorter distance, the image on the retina is greater, so the object appears larger and more detail can be seen. The angle θ that the object subtends in (a) is greater than in (b). *Note*: This is not a normal ray diagram because we are showing only one ray from each point.

(a)

(b)

FIGURE 33–33 Leaf viewed (a) through a magnifying glass, and (b) with the unaided eye. The eye is focused at its near point in both cases.

A magnifying glass allows us to place the object closer to our eye so that it subtends a greater angle. As shown in Fig. 33–33a, the object is placed at the focal point or just within it. Then the converging lens produces a virtual image, which must be at least 25 cm from the eye if the eye is to focus on it. If the eye is relaxed, the image will be at infinity, and in this case the object is exactly at the focal point. (You make this slight adjustment yourself when you "focus" on the object by moving the magnifying glass.)

A comparison of part (a) of Fig. 33–33 with part (b), in which the same object is viewed at the near point with the unaided eye, reveals that the angle the object subtends at the eye is much larger when the magnifier is used. The **angular magnification** or **magnifying power**, M, of the lens is defined as the ratio of the angle subtended by an object when using the lens, to the angle subtended using the unaided eye, with the object at the near point N of the eye ($N = 25$ cm for a normal eye):

$$M = \frac{\theta'}{\theta}, \tag{33–5}$$

where θ and θ' are shown in Fig. 33–33. We can write M in terms of the focal length by noting that $\theta = h/N$ (Fig. 33–33b) and $\theta' = h/d_o$ (Fig. 33–33a), where h is the height of the object and we assume the angles are small so θ and θ' equal their sines and tangents. If the eye is relaxed (for least eye strain), the image will be at infinity and the object will be precisely at the focal point; see Fig. 33–34. Then $d_o = f$ and $\theta' = h/f$, whereas $\theta = h/N$ as before (Fig. 33–33b). Thus

$$M = \frac{\theta'}{\theta} = \frac{h/f}{h/N} = \frac{N}{f}. \quad \left[\begin{array}{c}\text{eye focused at } \infty; \\ N = 25 \text{ cm for normal eye}\end{array}\right] \tag{33–6a}$$

We see that the shorter the focal length of the lens, the greater the magnification.[†]

The magnification of a given lens can be increased a bit by moving the lens and adjusting your eye so it focuses on the image at the eye's near point. In this case, $d_i = -N$ (see Fig. 33–33a) if your eye is very near the magnifier.

[†]Simple single-lens magnifiers are limited to about 2 or 3× because of blurring due to spherical aberration (Section 33–10).

FIGURE 33–34 With the eye relaxed, the object is placed at the focal point, and the image is at infinity. Compare to Fig. 33–33a where the image is at the eye's near point.

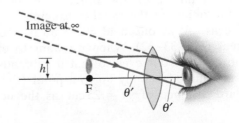

Then the object distance d_o is given by

$$\frac{1}{d_o} = \frac{1}{f} - \frac{1}{d_i} = \frac{1}{f} + \frac{1}{N}.$$

We see from this equation that $d_o = fN/(f + N) < f$, as shown in Fig. 33–33a, since $N/(f + N)$ must be less than 1. With $\theta' = h/d_o$ the magnification is

$$M = \frac{\theta'}{\theta} = \frac{h/d_o}{h/N} = \frac{N}{d_o} = N\left(\frac{1}{f} + \frac{1}{N}\right)$$

or

$$M = \frac{N}{f} + 1. \qquad \left[\begin{array}{l}\text{eye focused at near point, } N; \\ N = 25\,\text{cm for normal eye}\end{array}\right] \quad \textbf{(33–6b)}$$

We see that the magnification is slightly greater when the eye is focused at its near point, as compared to when it is relaxed.

EXAMPLE 33–14 **ESTIMATE** **A jeweler's "loupe."** An 8-cm-focal-length converging lens is used as a "jeweler's loupe," which is a magnifying glass. Estimate (a) the magnification when the eye is relaxed, and (b) the magnification if the eye is focused at its near point $N = 25\,\text{cm}$.

APPROACH The magnification when the eye is relaxed is given by Eq. 33–6a. When the eye is focused at its near point, we use Eq. 33–6b and we assume the lens is near the eye.

SOLUTION (a) With the relaxed eye focused at infinity,

$$M = \frac{N}{f} = \frac{25\,\text{cm}}{8\,\text{cm}} \approx 3\times.$$

(b) The magnification when the eye is focused at its near point $(N = 25\,\text{cm})$, and the lens is near the eye, is

$$M = 1 + \frac{N}{f} = 1 + \frac{25}{8} \approx 4\times.$$

33–8 Telescopes

A telescope is used to magnify objects that are very far away. In most cases, the object can be considered to be at infinity.

Galileo, although he did not invent it,[†] developed the telescope into a usable and important instrument. He was the first to examine the heavens with the telescope (Fig. 33–35), and he made world-shaking discoveries, including the moons of Jupiter, the phases of Venus, sunspots, the structure of the Moon's surface, and that the Milky Way is made up of a huge number of individual stars.

[†]Galileo built his first telescope in 1609 after having heard of such an instrument existing in Holland. The first telescopes magnified only three to four times, but Galileo soon made a 30-power instrument. The first Dutch telescope seems to date from about 1604, but there is a reference suggesting it may have been copied from an Italian telescope built as early as 1590. Kepler (see Chapter 6) gave a ray description (in 1611) of the Keplerian telescope, which is named for him because he first described it, although he did not build it.

FIGURE 33–35 (a) Objective lens (mounted now in an ivory frame) from the telescope with which Galileo made his world-shaking discoveries, including the moons of Jupiter. (b) Later telescopes made by Galileo.

(a)

(b)

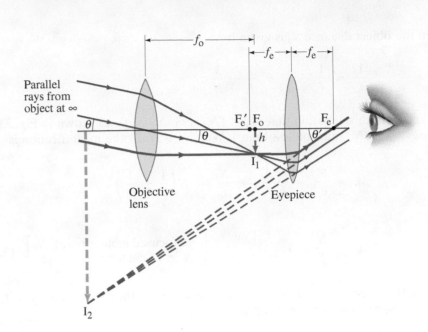

FIGURE 33–36 Astronomical telescope (refracting). Parallel light from one point on a distant object $(d_o = \infty)$ is brought to a focus by the objective lens in its focal plane. This image (I_1) is magnified by the eyepiece to form the final image I_2. Only two of the rays shown entering the objective are standard rays (2 and 3) as described in Fig. 33–6.

FIGURE 33–37 This large refracting telescope was built in 1897 and is housed at Yerkes Observatory in Wisconsin. The objective lens is 102 cm (40 inches) in diameter, and the telescope tube is about 19 m long. Example 33–15.

Several types of **astronomical telescope** exist. The common **refracting** type, sometimes called **Keplerian**, contains two converging lenses located at opposite ends of a long tube, as illustrated in Fig. 33–36. The lens closest to the object is called the **objective lens** (focal length f_o) and forms a real image I_1 of the distant object in the plane of its focal point F_o (or near it if the object is not at infinity). The second lens, called the **eyepiece** (focal length f_e), acts as a magnifier. That is, the eyepiece magnifies the image I_1 formed by the objective lens to produce a second, greatly magnified image, I_2, which is virtual and inverted. If the viewing eye is relaxed, the eyepiece is adjusted so the image I_2 is at infinity. Then the real image I_1 is at the focal point F_e' of the eyepiece, and the distance between the lenses is $f_o + f_e$ for an object at infinity.

To find the total angular magnification of this telescope, we note that the angle an object subtends as viewed by the unaided eye is just the angle θ subtended at the telescope objective. From Fig. 33–36 we can see that $\theta \approx h/f_o$, where h is the height of the image I_1 and we assume θ is small so that $\tan\theta \approx \theta$. Note, too, that the thickest of the three rays drawn in Fig. 33–36 is parallel to the axis before it strikes the eyepiece and therefore is refracted through the eyepiece focal point F_e on the far side. Thus, $\theta' \approx h/f_e$ and the **total magnifying power** (that is, angular magnification, which is what is always quoted) of this telescope is

$$ M = \frac{\theta'}{\theta} = \frac{(h/f_e)}{(h/f_o)} = -\frac{f_o}{f_e}, \qquad\qquad \text{[telescope]} \quad \textbf{(33–7)} $$

where we have inserted a minus sign to indicate that the image is inverted. To achieve a large magnification, the objective lens should have a long focal length and the eyepiece a short focal length.

EXAMPLE 33–15 **Telescope magnification.** The largest optical refracting telescope in the world is located at the Yerkes Observatory in Wisconsin, Fig. 33–37. It is referred to as a "40-inch" telescope, meaning that the diameter of the objective is 40 in., or 102 cm. The objective lens has a focal length of 19 m, and the eyepiece has a focal length of 10 cm. (a) Calculate the total magnifying power of this telescope. (b) Estimate the length of the telescope.

APPROACH Equation 33–7 gives the magnification. The length of the telescope is the distance between the two lenses.

SOLUTION (a) From Eq. 33–7 we find

$$ M = -\frac{f_o}{f_e} = -\frac{19\,\text{m}}{0.10\,\text{m}} = -190\times. $$

(b) For a relaxed eye, the image I_1 is at the focal point of both the eyepiece and the objective lenses. The distance between the two lenses is thus $f_o + f_e \approx 19\,\text{m}$, which is essentially the length of the telescope.

EXERCISE F A 40× telescope has a 1.2-cm focal length eyepiece. What is the focal length of the objective lens?

For an astronomical telescope to produce bright images of faint stars, the objective lens must be large to allow in as much light as possible. Indeed, the diameter of the objective lens (and hence its "light-gathering power") is an important parameter for an astronomical telescope, which is why the largest ones are specified by giving the objective diameter (such as the 10-meter Keck telescope in Hawaii). The construction and grinding of large lenses is very difficult. Therefore, the largest telescopes are **reflecting telescopes** which use a curved mirror as the objective, Fig. 33–38. A mirror has only one surface to be ground and can be supported along its entire surface[†] (a large lens, supported at its edges, would sag under its own weight). Often, the eyepiece lens or mirror (see Fig. 33–38) is removed so that the real image formed by the objective mirror can be recorded directly on film or on an electronic sensor (CCD or CMOS, Section 33–5).

(a) (b) (c) (d)

FIGURE 33–38 A concave mirror can be used as the objective of an astronomical telescope. Arrangement (a) is called the Newtonian focus, and (b) the Cassegrainian focus. Other arrangements are also possible. (c) The 200-inch (mirror diameter) Hale telescope on Palomar Mountain in California. (d) The 10-meter Keck telescope on Mauna Kea, Hawaii. The Keck combines thirty-six 1.8-meter six-sided mirrors into the equivalent of a very large single reflector, 10 m in diameter.

A **terrestrial telescope**, for viewing objects on Earth, must provide an upright image—seeing normal objects upside down would be difficult (much less important for viewing stars). Two designs are shown in Fig. 33–39. The **Galilean** type, which Galileo used for his great astronomical discoveries, has a diverging lens as eyepiece which intercepts the converging rays from the objective lens before they reach a focus, and acts to form a virtual upright image, Fig. 33–39a. This design is still used in opera glasses. The tube is reasonably short, but the field of view is small. The second type, shown in Fig. 33–39b, is often called a **spyglass** and makes use of a third convex lens that acts to make the image upright as shown. A spyglass must be quite long. The most practical design today is the **prism binocular** which was shown in Fig. 32–33. The objective and eyepiece are converging lenses. The prisms reflect the rays by total internal reflection and shorten the physical size of the device, and they also act to produce an upright image. One prism reinverts the image in the vertical plane, the other in the horizontal plane.

[†]Another advantage of mirrors is that they exhibit no chromatic aberration because the light doesn't pass through them; and they can be ground in a parabolic shape to correct for spherical aberration (Section 33–10). The reflecting telescope was first proposed by Newton.

FIGURE 33–39 Terrestrial telescopes that produce an upright image: (a) Galilean; (b) spyglass, or erector type.

(a) (b)

*33-9 Compound Microscope

Microscopes

The compound **microscope**, like the telescope, has both objective and eyepiece (or ocular) lenses, Fig. 33–40. The design is different from that for a telescope because a microscope is used to view objects that are very close, so the object distance is very small. The object is placed just beyond the objective's focal point as shown in Fig. 33–40a. The image I_1 formed by the objective lens is real, quite far from the objective lens, and much enlarged. The eyepiece is positioned so that this image is near the eyepiece focal point F_e. The image I_1 is magnified by the eyepiece into a very large virtual image, I_2, which is seen by the eye and is inverted. Modern microscopes use a third "tube" lens behind the objective, but we will analyze the simpler arrangement shown in Fig. 33–40a.

(a)

(b)

FIGURE 33–40 Compound microscope: (a) ray diagram, (b) photograph (illumination comes from the lower right, then up through the slide holding the object).

The overall magnification of a microscope is the product of the magnifications produced by the two lenses. The image I_1 formed by the objective lens is a factor m_o greater than the object itself. From Fig. 33–40a and Eq. 33–3 for the lateral magnification of a simple lens, we have

$$m_o = \frac{h_i}{h_o} = \frac{d_i}{d_o} = \frac{\ell - f_e}{d_o}, \tag{33–8}$$

where d_o and d_i are the object and image distances for the objective lens, ℓ is the distance between the lenses (equal to the length of the barrel), and we ignored the minus sign in Eq. 33–3 which only tells us that the image is inverted. We set $d_i = \ell - f_e$, which is true only if the eye is relaxed, so that the image I_1 is at the eyepiece focal point F_e. The eyepiece acts like a simple magnifier. If we assume that the eye is relaxed, the eyepiece angular magnification M_e is (from Eq. 33–6a)

$$M_e = \frac{N}{f_e}, \tag{33–9}$$

where the near point $N = 25 \text{ cm}$ for the normal eye. Since the eyepiece enlarges the image formed by the objective, the overall angular magnification M is the product of the lateral magnification of the objective lens, m_o, times the angular magnification, M_e, of the eyepiece lens (Eqs. 33–8 and 33–9):

$$M = M_e m_o = \left(\frac{N}{f_e}\right)\left(\frac{\ell - f_e}{d_o}\right) \qquad \text{[microscope]} \quad \textbf{(33–10a)}$$

$$\approx \frac{N\ell}{f_e f_o}. \qquad [f_o \text{ and } f_e \ll \ell] \quad \textbf{(33–10b)}$$

The approximation, Eq. 33–10b, is accurate when f_e and f_o are small compared to ℓ, so $\ell - f_e \approx \ell$, and the object is near F_o so $d_o \approx f_o$ (Fig. 33–40a). This is a good

890 CHAPTER 33 Lenses and Optical Instruments

approximation for large magnifications, which are obtained when f_o and f_e are very small (they are in the denominator of Eq. 33–10b). To make lenses of very short focal length, compound lenses involving several elements must be used to avoid serious aberrations, as discussed in the next Section.

EXAMPLE 33–16 **Microscope.** A compound microscope consists of a $10\times$ eyepiece and a $50\times$ objective 17.0 cm apart. Determine (a) the overall magnification, (b) the focal length of each lens, and (c) the position of the object when the final image is in focus with the eye relaxed. Assume a normal eye, so $N = 25$ cm.

APPROACH The overall magnification is the product of the eyepiece magnification and the objective magnification. The focal length of the eyepiece is found from Eq. 33–6a or 33–9 for the magnification of a simple magnifier. For the objective lens, it is easier to next find d_o (part c) using Eq. 33–8 before we find f_o.

SOLUTION (a) The overall magnification is $(10\times)(50\times) = 500\times$.
(b) The eyepiece focal length is (Eq. 33–9) $f_e = N/M_e = 25\,\text{cm}/10 = 2.5\,\text{cm}$. Next we solve Eq. 33–8 for d_o, and find

$$d_o = \frac{\ell - f_e}{m_o} = \frac{(17.0\,\text{cm} - 2.5\,\text{cm})}{50} = 0.29\,\text{cm}.$$

Then, from the thin lens equation for the objective with $d_i = \ell - f_e = 14.5$ cm (see Fig. 33–40a),

$$\frac{1}{f_o} = \frac{1}{d_o} + \frac{1}{d_i} = \frac{1}{0.29\,\text{cm}} + \frac{1}{14.5\,\text{cm}} = 3.52\,\text{cm}^{-1};$$

so $f_o = 1/(3.52\,\text{cm}^{-1}) = 0.28$ cm.
(c) We just calculated $d_o = 0.29$ cm, which is very close to f_o.

*33–10 Aberrations of Lenses and Mirrors

Earlier in this Chapter we developed a theory of image formation by a thin lens. We found, for example, that all rays from each point on an object are brought to a single point as the image point. This result, and others, were based on approximations for a thin lens, mainly that all rays make small angles with the axis and that we can use $\sin\theta \approx \theta$. Because of these approximations, we expect deviations from the simple theory, which are referred to as **lens aberrations**. There are several types of aberration; we will briefly discuss each of them separately, but all may be present at one time.

Consider an object at any point (even at infinity) on the axis of a lens with spherical surfaces. Rays from this point that pass through the outer regions of the lens are brought to a focus at a different point from those that pass through the center of the lens. This is called **spherical aberration**, and is shown exaggerated in Fig. 33–41. Consequently, the image seen on a screen or film will not be a point but a tiny circular patch of light. If the sensor or film is placed at the point C, as indicated, the circle will have its smallest diameter, which is referred to as the **circle of least confusion**. Spherical aberration is present whenever spherical surfaces are used. It can be reduced by using nonspherical (= aspherical) lens surfaces, but grinding such lenses is difficult and expensive. Spherical aberration can be reduced by the use of several lenses in combination, and by using primarily the central part of lenses.

PHYSICS APPLIED
Lens aberrations

FIGURE 33–41 Spherical aberration (exaggerated). Circle of least confusion is at C.

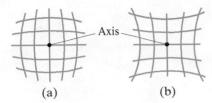

FIGURE 33–42 Distortion: lenses may image a square grid of perpendicular lines to produce (a) barrel distortion or (b) pincushion distortion. These distortions can be seen in the photograph of Fig. 33–2d.

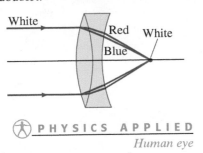

FIGURE 33–43 Chromatic aberration. Different colors are focused at different points.

FIGURE 33–44 Achromatic doublet.

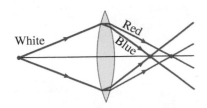

PHYSICS APPLIED

Human eye

For object points off the lens axis, additional aberrations occur. Rays passing through the different parts of the lens cause spreading of the image that is noncircular. There are two effects: **coma** (because the image of a point is comet-shaped rather than a circle) and **off-axis astigmatism.**† Furthermore, the image points for objects off the axis but at the same distance from the lens do not fall on a flat plane but on a curved surface—that is, the focal plane is not flat. (We expect this because the points on a flat plane, such as the film in a camera, are not equidistant from the lens.) This aberration is known as **curvature of field** and is a problem in cameras and other devices where the film is placed in a flat plane. In the eye, however, the retina is curved, which compensates for this effect.

Another aberration, **distortion**, is a result of variation of magnification at different distances from the lens axis. Thus a straight-line object some distance from the axis may form a curved image. A square grid of lines may be distorted to produce "barrel distortion," or "pincushion distortion," Fig. 33–42. The former is common in extreme wide-angle lenses.

All the above aberrations occur for monochromatic light and hence are referred to as *monochromatic aberrations*. Normal light is not monochromatic, and there will also be **chromatic aberration**. This aberration arises because of dispersion—the variation of index of refraction of transparent materials with wavelength (Section 32–6). For example, blue light is bent more than red light by glass. So if white light is incident on a lens, the different colors are focused at different points, Fig. 33–43, and have slightly different magnifications resulting in colored fringes in the image. Chromatic aberration can be eliminated for any two colors (and reduced greatly for all others) by the use of two lenses made of different materials with different indices of refraction and dispersion. Normally one lens is converging and the other diverging, and they are often cemented together (Fig. 33–44). Such a lens combination is called an **achromatic doublet** (or "color-corrected" lens).

To reduce aberrations, high-quality lenses are **compound lenses** consisting of many simple lenses, referred to as **elements**. A typical high-quality camera lens may contain six to eight (or more) elements. For simplicity we will usually indicate lenses in diagrams as if they were simple lenses.

The human eye is also subject to aberrations, but they are minimal. Spherical aberration, for example, is minimized because (1) the cornea is less curved at the edges than at the center, and (2) the lens is less dense at the edges than at the center. Both effects cause rays at the outer edges to be bent less strongly, and thus help to reduce spherical aberration. Chromatic aberration is partially compensated for because the lens absorbs the shorter wavelengths appreciably and the retina is less sensitive to the blue and violet wavelengths. This is just the region of the spectrum where dispersion—and thus chromatic aberration—is greatest (Fig. 32–28).

Spherical mirrors (Section 32–3) also suffer aberrations including spherical aberration (see Fig. 32–13). Mirrors can be ground in a parabolic shape to correct for aberrations, but they are much harder to make and therefore very expensive. Spherical mirrors do not, however, exhibit chromatic aberration because the light does not pass through them (no refraction, no dispersion).

---

† Although the effect is the same as for astigmatism in the eye (Section 33–6), the cause is different. Off-axis astigmatism is no problem in the eye because objects are clearly seen only at the fovea, on the lens axis.

Summary

A lens uses refraction to produce a real or virtual image. Parallel rays of light are focused to a point, called the **focal point**, by a **converging** lens. The distance of the focal point from the lens is called the **focal length** f of the lens.

After parallel rays pass through a **diverging** lens, they appear to diverge from a point, its focal point; and the corresponding focal length is considered negative.

The **power** P of a lens, which is

$$P = \frac{1}{f} \tag{33–1}$$

is given in diopters, which are units of inverse meters (m^{-1}).

For a given object, the position and size of the image formed by a lens can be found approximately by ray tracing.

Algebraically, the relation between image and object distances, d_i and d_o, and the focal length f, is given by the **thin lens equation**:

$$\frac{1}{d_o} + \frac{1}{d_i} = \frac{1}{f}. \qquad (33\text{–}2)$$

The ratio of image height to object height, which equals the **lateral magnification** m, is

$$m = \frac{h_i}{h_o} = -\frac{d_i}{d_o}. \qquad (33\text{–}3)$$

When using the various equations of geometric optics, it is important to remember the **sign conventions** for all quantities involved: carefully review them (page 871) when doing Problems.

When two (or more) thin lenses are used in combination to produce an image, the thin lens equation can be used for each lens in sequence. The image produced by the first lens acts as the object for the second lens.

[*The **lensmaker's equation** relates the radii of curvature of the lens surfaces and the len's index of refraction to the focal length of the lens.]

A **camera** lens forms an image on film, or on an electronic sensor (CCD or CMOS) in a digital camera, by allowing light in through a shutter. The image is focused by moving the lens relative to the film, and the **f-stop** (or lens opening) must be adjusted for the brightness of the scene and the chosen shutter speed. The f-stop is defined as the ratio of the focal length to the diameter of the lens opening.

The human **eye** also adjusts for the available light—by opening and closing the iris. It focuses not by moving the lens, but by adjusting the shape of the lens to vary its focal length. The image is formed on the retina, which contains an array of receptors known as rods and cones.

Diverging eyeglass or contact lenses are used to correct the defect of a nearsighted eye, which cannot focus well on distant objects. Converging lenses are used to correct for defects in which the eye cannot focus on close objects.

A **simple magnifier** is a converging lens that forms a virtual image of an object placed at (or within) the focal point. The **angular magnification**, when viewed by a relaxed normal eye, is

$$M = \frac{N}{f}, \qquad (33\text{–}6a)$$

where f is the focal length of the lens and N is the near point of the eye (25 cm for a "normal" eye).

An **astronomical telescope** consists of an **objective** lens or mirror, and an **eyepiece** that magnifies the real image formed by the objective. The **magnification** is equal to the ratio of the objective and eyepiece focal lengths, and the image is inverted:

$$M = -\frac{f_o}{f_e}. \qquad (33\text{–}7)$$

[*A compound **microscope** also uses objective and eyepiece lenses, and the final image is inverted. The total magnification is the product of the magnifications of the two lenses and is approximately

$$M \approx \frac{N\ell}{f_e f_o}, \qquad (33\text{–}10b)$$

where ℓ is the distance between the lenses, N is the near point of the eye, and f_o and f_e are the focal lengths of objective and eyepiece, respectively.]

[*Microscopes, telescopes, and other optical instruments are limited in the formation of sharp images by **lens aberrations**. These include **spherical aberration**, in which rays passing through the edge of a lens are not focused at the same point as those that pass near the center; and **chromatic aberration**, in which different colors are focused at different points. Compound lenses, consisting of several elements, can largely correct for aberrations.]

Questions

1. Where must the film be placed if a camera lens is to make a sharp image of an object far away?

2. A photographer moves closer to his subject and then refocuses. Does the camera lens move farther away from or closer to the sensor? Explain.

3. Can a diverging lens form a real image under any circumstances? Explain.

4. Use ray diagrams to show that a real image formed by a thin lens is always inverted, whereas a virtual image is always upright if the object is real.

5. Light rays are said to be "reversible." Is this consistent with the thin lens equation? Explain.

6. Can real images be projected on a screen? Can virtual images? Can either be photographed? Discuss carefully.

7. A thin converging lens is moved closer to a nearby object. Does the real image formed change (a) in position, (b) in size? If yes, describe how.

8. Compare the mirror equation with the thin lens equation. Discuss similarities and differences, especially the sign conventions for the quantities involved.

9. A lens is made of a material with an index of refraction $n = 1.30$. In air, it is a converging lens. Will it still be a converging lens if placed in water? Explain, using a ray diagram.

10. Explain how you could have a virtual object.

11. A dog with its tail in the air stands facing a converging lens. If the nose and the tail are each focused on a screen in turn, which will have the greater magnification?

12. A cat with its tail in the air stands facing a converging lens. Under what circumstances (if any) would the image of the nose be virtual and the image of the tail be real? Where would the image of the rest of the cat be?

13. Why, in Example 33–6, must the converging lens have a shorter focal length than the diverging lens if the latter's focal length is to be determined by combining them?

14. The thicker a double convex lens is in the center as compared to its edges, the shorter its focal length for a given lens diameter. Explain.

15. Does the focal length of a lens depend on the fluid in which it is immersed? What about the focal length of a spherical mirror? Explain.

16. An underwater lens consists of a carefully shaped thin-walled plastic container filled with air. What shape should it have in order to be (a) converging (b) diverging? Use ray diagrams to support your answer.

17. Consider two converging lenses separated by some distance. An object is placed so that the image from the first lens lies exactly at the focal point of the second lens. Will this combination produce an image? If so, where? If not, why not?

18. Will a nearsighted person who wears corrective lenses in her glasses be able to see clearly underwater when wearing those glasses? Use a diagram to show why or why not.

19. You can tell whether people are nearsighted or farsighted by looking at the width of their face through their glasses. If a person's face appears narrower through the glasses, (Fig. 33–45), is the person farsighted or nearsighted?

FIGURE 33–45
Question 19.

20. The human eye is much like a camera—yet, when a camera shutter is left open and the camera is moved, the image will be blurred. But when you move your head with your eyes open, you still see clearly. Explain.

21. In attempting to discern distant details, people will sometimes squint. Why does this help?

22. Is the image formed on the retina of the human eye upright or inverted? Discuss the implications of this for our perception of objects.

23. Reading glasses use converging lenses. A simple magnifier is also a converging lens. Are reading glasses therefore magnifiers? Discuss the similarities and differences between converging lenses as used for these two different purposes.

24. Why must a camera lens be moved farther from the film to focus on a closer object?

* 25. Spherical aberration in a thin lens is minimized if rays are bent equally by the two surfaces. If a planoconvex lens is used to form a real image of an object at infinity, which surface should face the object? Use ray diagrams to show why.

* 26. For both converging and diverging lenses, discuss how the focal length for red light differs from that for violet light.

Problems

33–1 and 33–2 Thin Lenses

1. (I) A sharp image is located 373 mm behind a 215-mm-focal-length converging lens. Find the object distance (a) using a ray diagram, (b) by calculation.

2. (I) Sunlight is observed to focus at a point 18.5 cm behind a lens. (a) What kind of lens is it? (b) What is its power in diopters?

3. (I) (a) What is the power of a 23.5-cm-focal-length lens? (b) What is the focal length of a -6.75-D lens? Are these lenses converging or diverging?

4. (II) A certain lens focuses an object 1.85 m away as an image 48.3 cm on the other side of the lens. What type of lens is it and what is its focal length? Is the image real or virtual?

5. (II) A 105-mm-focal-length lens is used to focus an image on the sensor of a camera. The maximum distance allowed between the lens and the sensor plane is 132 mm. (a) How far ahead of the sensor should the lens be if the object to be photographed is 10.0 m away? (b) 3.0 m away? (c) 1.0 m away? (d) What is the closest object this lens could photograph sharply?

6. (II) A stamp collector uses a converging lens with focal length 28 cm to view a stamp 18 cm in front of the lens. (a) Where is the image located? (b) What is the magnification?

7. (II) It is desired to magnify reading material by a factor of $2.5\times$ when a book is placed 9.0 cm behind a lens. (a) Draw a ray diagram and describe the type of image this would be. (b) What type of lens is needed? (c) What is the power of the lens in diopters?

8. (II) A -8.00-D lens is held 12.5 cm from an ant 1.00 mm high. Describe the position, type, and height of the image.

9. (II) An object is located 1.50 m from an 8.0-D lens. By how much does the image move if the object is moved (a) 0.90 m closer to the lens, and (b) 0.90 m farther from the lens?

10. (II) (a) How far from a 50.0-mm-focal-length lens must an object be placed if its image is to be magnified $2.50\times$ and be real? (b) What if the image is to be virtual and magnified $2.50\times$?

11. (II) How far from a converging lens with a focal length of 25 cm should an object be placed to produce a real image which is the same size as the object?

12. (II) (a) A 2.80-cm-high insect is 1.30 m from a 135-mm-focal-length lens. Where is the image, how high is it, and what type is it? (b) What if $f = -135$ mm?

13. (II) A bright object and a viewing screen are separated by a distance of 86.0 cm. At what location(s) between the object and the screen should a lens of focal length 16.0 cm be placed in order to produce a sharp image on the screen? [Hint: first draw a diagram.]

14. (II) How far apart are an object and an image formed by an 85-cm-focal-length converging lens if the image is $2.95\times$ larger than the object and is real?

15. (II) Show analytically that the image formed by a converging lens (a) is real and inverted if the object is beyond the focal point $(d_o > f)$, and (b) is virtual and upright if the object is within the focal point $(d_o < f)$. Next, describe the image if the object is itself an image (formed by another lens), and its position is on the opposite side of the lens from the incoming light, (c) for $-d_o > f$, and (d) for $0 < -d_o < f$.

16. (II) A converging lens has focal length f. When an object is placed a distance $d_o > f$ from this lens, a real image with magnification m is formed. (a) Show that $m = f/(f - d_o)$. (b) Sketch m vs. d_o over the range $f < d_o < \infty$ where $f = 0.45$ cm. (c) For what value of d_o will the real image have the same (lateral) size as the object? (d) To obtain a real image that is much larger than the object, in what general region should the object be placed relative to the lens?

17. (II) In a slide or movie projector, the film acts as the object whose image is projected on a screen (Fig. 33–46). If a 105-mm-focal-length lens is to project an image on a screen 6.50 m away, how far from the lens should the slide be? If the slide is 36 mm wide, how wide will the picture be on the screen?

FIGURE 33–46
Slide projector, Problem 17.

Slide   Lens   Screen

18. (III) A bright object is placed on one side of a converging lens of focal length f, and a white screen for viewing the image is on the opposite side. The distance $d_T = d_i + d_o$ between the object and the screen is kept fixed, but the lens can be moved. (a) Show that if $d_T > 4f$, there will be two positions where the lens can be placed and a sharp image will be produced on the screen. (b) If $d_T < 4f$, show that there will be no lens position where a sharp image is formed. (c) Determine a formula for the distance between the two lens positions in part (a), and the ratio of the image sizes.

19. (III) (a) Show that the lens equation can be written in the *Newtonian form*:

$$xx' = f^2,$$

where x is the distance of the object from the focal point on the front side of the lens, and x' is the distance of the image to the focal point on the other side of the lens. Calculate the location of an image if the object is placed 48.0 cm in front of a convex lens with a focal length of 38.0 cm using (b) the standard form of the thin lens formula, and (c) the Newtonian form, derived above.

33–3 Lens Combinations

20. (II) A diverging lens with $f = -33.5$ cm is placed 14.0 cm behind a converging lens with $f = 20.0$ cm. Where will an object at infinity be focused?

21. (II) Two 25.0-cm-focal-length converging lenses are placed 16.5 cm apart. An object is placed 35.0 cm in front of one lens. Where will the final image formed by the second lens be located? What is the total magnification?

22. (II) A 34.0-cm-focal-length converging lens is 24.0 cm behind a diverging lens. Parallel light strikes the diverging lens. After passing through the converging lens, the light is again parallel. What is the focal length of the diverging lens? [*Hint*: first draw a ray diagram.]

23. (II) The two converging lenses of Example 33–5 are now placed only 20.0 cm apart. The object is still 60.0 cm in front of the first lens as in Fig. 33–14. In this case, determine (a) the position of the final image, and (b) the overall magnification. (c) Sketch the ray diagram for this system.

24. (II) A diverging lens with a focal length of -14 cm is placed 12 cm to the right of a converging lens with a focal length of 18 cm. An object is placed 33 cm to the left of the converging lens. (a) Where will the final image be located? (b) Where will the image be if the diverging lens is 38 cm from the converging lens?

25. (II) Two lenses, one converging with focal length 20.0 cm and one diverging with focal length -10.0 cm, are placed 25.0 cm apart. An object is placed 60.0 cm in front of the converging lens. Determine (a) the position and (b) the magnification of the final image formed. (c) Sketch a ray diagram for this system.

26. (II) A diverging lens is placed next to a converging lens of focal length f_C, as in Fig. 33–15. If f_T represents the focal length of the combination, show that the focal length of the diverging lens, f_D, is given by

$$\frac{1}{f_D} = \frac{1}{f_T} - \frac{1}{f_C}.$$

27. (II) A lighted candle is placed 36 cm in front of a converging lens of focal length $f_1 = 13$ cm, which in turn is 56 cm in front of another converging lens of focal length $f_2 = 16$ cm (see Fig. 33–47). (a) Draw a ray diagram and estimate the location and the relative size of the final image. (b) Calculate the position and relative size of the final image.

FIGURE 33–47
Problem 27.

$f_1 = 13$ cm $f_2 = 16$ cm

$\longmapsto\!\!-36\text{ cm}\!-\!\!\longmapsto\!\!-56\text{ cm}\!-\!\!\longrightarrow$

*33–4 Lensmaker's Equation

*28. (I) A double concave lens has surface radii of 33.4 cm and 28.8 cm. What is the focal length if $n = 1.58$?

*29. (I) Both surfaces of a double convex lens have radii of 31.4 cm. If the focal length is 28.9 cm, what is the index of refraction of the lens material?

*30. (I) Show that if the lens of Example 33–7 is reversed, the focal length is unchanged.

*31. (I) A planoconvex lens (Fig. 33–2a) is to have a focal length of 18.7 cm. If made from fused quartz, what must be the radius of curvature of the convex surface?

*32. (II) An object is placed 90.0 cm from a glass lens ($n = 1.52$) with one concave surface of radius 22.0 cm and one convex surface of radius 18.5 cm. Where is the final image? What is the magnification?

*33. (II) A prescription for a corrective lens calls for $+3.50$ diopters. The lensmaker grinds the lens from a "blank" with $n = 1.56$ and convex front surface of radius of curvature of 30.0 cm. What should be the radius of curvature of the other surface?

33–5 Camera

34. (I) A properly exposed photograph is taken at $f/16$ and $\frac{1}{120}$ s. What lens opening is required if the shutter speed is $\frac{1}{1000}$ s?

35. (I) A television camera lens has a 17-cm focal length and a lens diameter of 6.0 cm. What is its f-number?

36. (II) A "pinhole" camera uses a tiny pinhole instead of a lens. Show, using ray diagrams, how reasonably sharp images can be formed using such a pinhole camera. In particular, consider two point objects 2.0 cm apart that are 1.0 m from a 1.0-mm-diameter pinhole. Show that on a piece of film 7.0 cm behind the pinhole the two objects produce two separate circles that do not overlap.

37. (II) Suppose that a correct exposure is $\frac{1}{250}$ s at $f/11$. Under the same conditions, what exposure time would be needed for a pinhole camera (Problem 36) if the pinhole diameter is 1.0 mm and the film is 7.0 cm from the hole?

38. (II) Human vision normally covers an angle of about 40° horizontally. A "normal" camera lens then is defined as follows: When focused on a distant horizontal object which subtends an angle of 40°, the lens produces an image that extends across the full horizontal extent of the camera's light-recording medium (film or electronic sensor). Determine the focal length f of the "normal" lens for the following types of cameras: (a) a 35-mm camera that records images on film 36 mm wide; (b) a digital camera that records images on a charge-coupled device (CCD) 1.00 cm wide.

39. (II) A nature photographer wishes to photograph a 38-m tall tree from a distance of 65 m. What focal-length lens should be used if the image is to fill the 24-mm height of the sensor?

33–6 Eye and Corrective Lenses

40. (I) A human eyeball is about 2.0 cm long and the pupil has a maximum diameter of about 8.0 mm. What is the "speed" of this lens?

41. (II) A person struggles to read by holding a book at arm's length, a distance of 55 cm away. What power of reading glasses should be prescribed for her, assuming they will be placed 2.0 cm from the eye and she wants to read at the "normal" near point of 25 cm?

42. (II) Reading glasses of what power are needed for a person whose near point is 105 cm, so that he can read a computer screen at 55 cm? Assume a lens–eye distance of 1.8 cm.

43. (II) If the nearsighted person in Example 33–13 wore contact lenses corrected for the far point ($=\infty$), what would be the near point? Would glasses be better in this case?

44. (II) An eye is corrected by a -4.50-D lens, 2.0 cm from the eye. (a) Is this eye near- or farsighted? (b) What is this eye's far point without glasses?

45. (II) A person's right eye can see objects clearly only if they are between 25 cm and 78 cm away. (a) What power of contact lens is required so that objects far away are sharp? (b) What will be the near point with the lens in place?

46. (II) A person has a far point of 14 cm. What power glasses would correct this vision if the glasses were placed 2.0 cm from the eye? What power contact lenses, placed on the eye, would the person need?

47. (II) One lens of a nearsighted person's eyeglasses has a focal length of -23.0 cm and the lens is 1.8 cm from the eye. If the person switches to contact lenses placed directly on the eye, what should be the focal length of the corresponding contact lens?

48. (II) What is the focal length of the eye lens system when viewing an object (a) at infinity, and (b) 38 cm from the eye? Assume that the lens–retina distance is 2.0 cm.

49. (II) A nearsighted person has near and far points of 10.6 and 20.0 cm respectively. If she puts on contact lenses with power $P = -4.00$ D, what are her new near and far points?

50. (II) The closely packed cones in the fovea of the eye have a diameter of about 2 μm. For the eye to discern two images on the fovea as distinct, assume that the images must be separated by at least one cone that is not excited. If these images are of two point-like objects at the eye's 25-cm near point, how far apart are these barely resolvable objects? Assume the diameter of the eye (cornea-to-fovea distance) is 2.0 cm.

33–7 Magnifying Glass

51. (I) What is the focal length of a magnifying glass of 3.8× magnification for a relaxed normal eye?

52. (I) What is the magnification of a lens used with a relaxed eye if its focal length is 13 cm?

53. (I) A magnifier is rated at 3.0× for a normal eye focusing on an image at the near point. (a) What is its focal length? (b) What is its focal length if the 3.0× refers to a relaxed eye?

54. (II) Sherlock Holmes is using an 8.80-cm-focal-length lens as his magnifying glass. To obtain maximum magnification, where must the object be placed (assume a normal eye), and what will be the magnification?

55. (II) A small insect is placed 5.85 cm from a $+6.00$-cm-focal-length lens. Calculate (a) the position of the image, and (b) the angular magnification.

56. (II) A 3.40-mm-wide bolt is viewed with a 9.60-cm-focal-length lens. A normal eye views the image at its near point. Calculate (a) the angular magnification, (b) the width of the image, and (c) the object distance from the lens.

57. (II) A magnifying glass with a focal length of 9.5 cm is used to read print placed at a distance of 8.3 cm. Calculate (a) the position of the image; (b) the angular magnification.

58. (II) A magnifying glass is rated at 3.0× for a normal eye that is relaxed. What would be the magnification for a relaxed eye whose near point is (a) 65 cm, and (b) 17 cm? Explain the differences.

59. (II) A converging lens of focal length $f = 12$ cm is being used by a writer as a magnifying glass to read some fine print on his book contract. Initially, the writer holds the lens above the fine print so that its image is at infinity. To get a better look, he then moves the lens so that the image is at his 25-cm near point. How far, and in what direction (toward or away from the fine print) did the writer move the lens? Assume the writer's eye is adjusted to remain always very near the magnifying glass.

33–8 Telescopes

60. (I) What is the magnification of an astronomical telescope whose objective lens has a focal length of 78 cm, and whose eyepiece has a focal length of 2.8 cm? What is the overall length of the telescope when adjusted for a relaxed eye?

61. (I) The overall magnification of an astronomical telescope is desired to be 35×. If an objective of 88 cm focal length is used, what must be the focal length of the eyepiece? What is the overall length of the telescope when adjusted for use by the relaxed eye?

62. (II) A 7.0× binocular has 3.0-cm-focal-length eyepieces. What is the focal length of the objective lenses?

63. (II) An astronomical telescope has an objective with focal length 75 cm and a $+35$ D eyepiece. What is the total magnification?

64. (II) An astronomical telescope has its two lenses spaced 78.0 cm apart. If the objective lens has a focal length of 75.5 cm, what is the magnification of this telescope? Assume a relaxed eye.

65. (II) A Galilean telescope adjusted for a relaxed eye is 33.8 cm long. If the objective lens has a focal length of 36.0 cm, what is the magnification?

66. (II) What is the magnifying power of an astronomical telescope using a reflecting mirror whose radius of curvature is 6.4 m and an eyepiece whose focal length is 2.8 cm?

67. (II) The Moon's image appears to be magnified 120× by a reflecting astronomical telescope with an eyepiece having a focal length of 3.1 cm. What are the focal length and radius of curvature of the main (objective) mirror?

68. (II) A 120× astronomical telescope is adjusted for a relaxed eye when the two lenses are 1.25 m apart. What is the focal length of each lens?

69. (II) An astronomical telescope longer than about 50 cm is not easy to hold by hand. Based on this fact, estimate the maximum angular magnification achievable for a telescope designed to be handheld. Assume its eyepiece lens, if used as a magnifying glass, provides a magnification of 5× for a relaxed eye with near point $N = 25$ cm.

70. (III) A reflecting telescope (Fig. 33–38b) has a radius of curvature of 3.00 m for its objective mirror and a radius of curvature of −1.50 m for its eyepiece mirror. If the distance between the two mirrors is 0.90 m, how far in front of the eyepiece should you place the electronic sensor to record the image of a star?

71. (III) A 7.5× pair of binoculars has an objective focal length of 26 cm. If the binoculars are focused on an object 4.0 m away (from the objective), what is the magnification? (The 7.5× refers to objects at infinity; Eq. 33–7 holds only for objects at infinity and not for nearby ones.)

*33–9 Microscopes

*72. (I) A microscope uses an eyepiece with a focal length of 1.50 cm. Using a normal eye with a final image at infinity, the barrel length is 17.5 cm and the focal length of the objective lens is 0.65 cm. What is the magnification of the microscope?

*73. (I) A 680× microscope uses a 0.40-cm-focal-length objective lens. If the barrel length is 17.5 cm, what is the focal length of the eyepiece? Assume a normal eye and that the final image is at infinity.

*74. (I) A 17-cm-long microscope has an eyepiece with a focal length of 2.5 cm and an objective with a focal length of 0.28 cm. What is the approximate magnification?

*75. (II) A microscope has a 13.0× eyepiece and a 58.0× objective lens 20.0 cm apart. Calculate (a) the total magnification, (b) the focal length of each lens, and (c) where the object must be for a normal relaxed eye to see it in focus.

*76. (II) Repeat Problem 75 assuming that the final image is located 25 cm from the eyepiece (near point of a normal eye).

*77. (II) A microscope has a 1.8-cm-focal-length eyepiece and a 0.80-cm objective. Assuming a relaxed normal eye, calculate (a) the position of the object if the distance between the lenses is 16.8 cm, and (b) the total magnification.

*78. (II) The eyepiece of a compound microscope has a focal length of 2.80 cm and the objective lens has $f = 0.740$ cm. If an object is placed 0.790 cm from the objective lens, calculate (a) the distance between the lenses when the microscope is adjusted for a relaxed eye, and (b) the total magnification.

*79. (II) An inexpensive instructional lab microscope allows the user to select its objective lens to have a focal length of 32 mm, 15 mm, or 3.9 mm. It also has two possible eyepieces with magnifications 5× and 10×. Each objective forms a real image 160 mm beyond its focal point. What are the largest and smallest overall magnifications obtainable with this instrument?

*80. (III) Given two 12-cm-focal-length lenses, you attempt to make a crude microscope using them. While holding these lenses a distance 55 cm apart, you position your microscope so that its objective lens is distance d_o from a small object. Assume your eye's near point $N = 25$ cm. (a) For your microscope to function properly, what should d_o be? (b) Assuming your eye is relaxed when using it, what magnification M does your microscope achieve? (c) Since the length of your microscope is not much greater than the focal lengths of its lenses, the approximation $M \approx N\ell/f_e f_o$ is not valid. If you apply this approximation to your microscope, what % error do you make in your microscope's true magnification?

*33–10 Lens Aberrations

*81. (II) A planoconvex lens (Fig. 33–2a) has one flat surface and the other has $R = 15.3$ cm. This lens is used to view a red and yellow object which is 66.0 cm away from the lens. The index of refraction of the glass is 1.5106 for red light and 1.5226 for yellow light. What are the locations of the red and yellow images formed by the lens?

*82. (II) An achromatic lens is made of two very thin lenses, placed in contact, that have focal lengths $f_1 = -28$ cm and $f_2 = +25$ cm. (a) Is the combination converging or diverging? (b) What is the net focal length?

General Problems

83. A 200-mm-focal-length lens can be adjusted so that it is 200.0 mm to 206.4 mm from the film. For what range of object distances can it be adjusted?

84. If a 135-mm telephoto lens is designed to cover object distances from 1.30 m to ∞, over what distance must the lens move relative to the plane of the sensor or film?

85. For a camera equipped with a 58-mm-focal-length lens, what is the object distance if the image height equals the object height? How far is the object from the image on the film?

86. Show that for objects very far away (assume infinity), the magnification of any camera lens is proportional to its focal length.

87. A small object is 25.0 cm from a diverging lens as shown in Fig. 33–48. A converging lens with a focal length of 12.0 cm is 30.0 cm to the right of the diverging lens. The two-lens system forms a real inverted image 17.0 cm to the right of the converging lens. What is the focal length of the diverging lens?

FIGURE 33–48   Problem 87.

88. A converging lens with focal length of 13.0 cm is placed in contact with a diverging lens with a focal length of −20.0 cm. What is the focal length of the combination, and is the combination converging or diverging?

89. An astronomical telescope has a magnification of 8.0×. If the two lenses are 28 cm apart, determine the focal length of each lens.

90. (a) Show that if two thin lenses of focal lengths f_1 and f_2 are placed in contact with each other, the focal length of the combination is given by $f_T = f_1 f_2 / (f_1 + f_2)$. (b) Show that the power P of the combination of two lenses is the sum of their separate powers, $P = P_1 + P_2$.

91. How large is the image of the Sun on film used in a camera with (a) a 28-mm-focal-length lens, (b) a 50-mm-focal-length lens, and (c) a 135-mm-focal-length lens? (d) If the 50-mm lens is considered normal for this camera, what relative magnification does each of the other two lenses provide? The Sun has diameter 1.4×10^6 km, and it is 1.5×10^8 km away.

92. Two converging lenses are placed 30.0 cm apart. The focal length of the lens on the right is 20.0 cm, and the focal length of the lens on the left is 15.0 cm. An object is placed to the left of the 15.0-cm-focal-length lens. A final image from both lenses is inverted and located halfway between the two lenses. How far to the left of the 15.0-cm-focal-length lens is the original object?

93. When an object is placed 60.0 cm from a certain converging lens, it forms a real image. When the object is moved to 40.0 cm from the lens, the image moves 10.0 cm farther from the lens. Find the focal length of this lens.

94. Figure 33–49 was taken from the NIST Laboratory (National Institute of Standards and Technology) in Boulder, CO, 2 km from the hiker in the photo. The Sun's image was 15 mm across on the film. Estimate the focal length of the camera lens (actually a telescope). The Sun has diameter 1.4×10^6 km, and it is 1.5×10^8 km away.

FIGURE 33–49 Problem 94.

95. A movie star catches a reporter shooting pictures of her at home. She claims the reporter was trespassing. To prove her point, she gives as evidence the film she seized. Her 1.75-m height is 8.25 mm high on the film, and the focal length of the camera lens was 220 mm. How far away from the subject was the reporter standing?

96. As early morning passed toward midday, and the sunlight got more intense, a photographer noted that, if she kept her shutter speed constant, she had to change the f-number from $f/5.6$ to $f/16$. By what factor had the sunlight intensity increased during that time?

97. A child has a near point of 15 cm. What is the maximum magnification the child can obtain using an 8.5-cm-focal-length magnifier? What magnification can a normal eye obtain with the same lens? Which person sees more detail?

98. A woman can see clearly with her right eye only when objects are between 45 cm and 155 cm away. Prescription bifocals should have what powers so that she can see distant objects clearly (upper part) and be able to read a book 25 cm away (lower part) with her right eye? Assume that the glasses will be 2.0 cm from the eye.

99. What is the magnifying power of a +4.0-D lens used as a magnifier? Assume a relaxed normal eye.

100. A physicist lost in the mountains tries to make a telescope using the lenses from his reading glasses. They have powers of +2.0 D and +4.5 D, respectively. (a) What maximum magnification telescope is possible? (b) Which lens should be used as the eyepiece?

101. A 50-year-old man uses +2.5-D lenses to read a newspaper 25 cm away. Ten years later, he must hold the paper 32 cm away to see clearly with the same lenses. What power lenses does he need now in order to hold the paper 25 cm away? (Distances are measured from the lens.)

102. An object is moving toward a converging lens of focal length f with constant speed v_o such that its distance d_o from the lens is always greater than f. (a) Determine the velocity v_i of the image as a function of d_o. (b) Which direction (toward or away from the lens) does the image move? (c) For what d_o does the image's speed equal the object's speed?

103. The objective lens and the eyepiece of a telescope are spaced 85 cm apart. If the eyepiece is +23 D, what is the total magnification of the telescope?

*104. Two converging lenses, one with $f = 4.0$ cm and the other with $f = 44$ cm, are made into a telescope. (a) What are the length and magnification? Which lens should be the eyepiece? (b) Assume these lenses are now combined to make a microscope; if the magnification needs to be 25×, how long would the microscope be?

105. Sam purchases +3.50-D eyeglasses which correct his faulty vision to put his near point at 25 cm. (Assume he wears the lenses 2.0 cm from his eyes.) (a) Calculate the focal length of Sam's glasses. (b) Calculate Sam's near point without glasses. (c) Pam, who has normal eyes with near point at 25 cm, puts on Sam's glasses. Calculate Pam's near point with Sam's glasses on.

106. The proper functioning of certain optical devices (e.g., optical fibers and spectrometers) requires that the input light be a collection of diverging rays within a cone of half-angle θ (Fig. 33–50). If the light initially exists as a collimated beam (i.e., parallel rays), show that a single lens of focal length f and diameter D can be used to create the required input light if $D/f = 2 \tan \theta$. If $\theta = 3.5°$ for a certain spectrometer, what focal length lens should be used if the lens diameter is 5.0 cm?

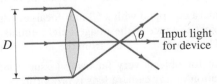

FIGURE 33–50 Problem 106.

107. In a science-fiction novel, an intelligent ocean-dwelling creature's eye functions underwater with a near point of 25 cm. This creature would like to create an underwater magnifier out of a thin plastic container filled with air. What shape should the air-filled plastic container have (i.e., determine radii of curvature of its surfaces) in order for it to be used by the creature as a 3.0× magnifier? Assume the eye is focused at its near point.

108. A telephoto lens system obtains a large magnification in a compact package. A simple such system can be constructed out of two lenses, one converging and one diverging, of focal lengths f_1 and $f_2 = -\frac{1}{2}f_1$, respectively, separated by a distance $\ell = \frac{3}{4}f_1$ as shown in Fig. 33–51. (a) For a distant object located at distance d_o from the first lens, show that the first lens forms an image with magnification $m_1 \approx -f_1/d_o$ located very close to its focal point. Go on to show that the total magnification for the two-lens system is $m \approx -2f_1/d_o$. (b) For an object located at infinity, show that the two-lens system forms an image that is a distance $\frac{5}{4}f_1$ behind the first lens. (c) A single 250-mm-focal-length lens would have to be mounted about 250 mm from a camera's film in order to produce an image of a distant object at d_o with magnification $-(250\,\text{mm})/d_o$. To produce an image of this object with the same magnification using the two-lens system, what value of f_1 should be used and how far in front of the film should the first lens be placed? How much smaller is the "focusing length" (i.e., first lens-to-final image distance) of this two-lens system in comparison with the 250-mm "focusing length" of the equivalent single lens?

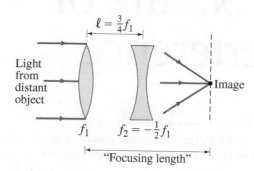

FIGURE 33–51 Problem 108.

*109. (III) In the "magnification" method, the focal length f of a converging lens is found by placing an object of known size at various locations in front of the lens and measuring the resulting real-image distances d_i and their associated magnifications m (minus sign indicates that image is inverted). The data taken in such an experiment are given here:

d_i (cm)	20	25	30	35	40
m	−0.43	−0.79	−1.14	−1.50	−1.89

(a) Show analytically that a graph of m vs. d_i should produce a straight line. What are the theoretically expected values for the slope and the y-intercept of this line? [*Hint*: d_o is not constant.] (b) Using the data above, graph m vs. d_i and show that a straight line does indeed result. Use the slope of this line to determine the focal length of the lens. Does the y-intercept of your plot have the expected value? (c) In performing such an experiment, one has the practical problem of locating the exact center of the lens since d_i must be measured from this point. Imagine, instead, that one measures the image distance d_i' from the back surface of the lens, which is a distance ℓ from the lens's center. Then, $d_i = d_i' + \ell$. Show that, when implementing the magnification method in this fashion, a plot of m vs. d_i' will still result in a straight line. How can f be determined from this straight line?

Answers to Exercises

A: Closer to it.

B: (b) and (d) are true.

C: $f = 10\,\text{cm}$ for both cases; $d_i = -10\,\text{cm}$ in (a) and 30 cm in (b).

D: −36 cm; diverging.

E: $P = -4.0\,\text{D}$.

F: 48 cm.

The beautiful colors from the surface of this soap bubble can be nicely explained by the wave theory of light. A soap bubble is a very thin spherical film filled with air. Light reflected from the outer and inner surfaces of this thin film of soapy water interferes constructively to produce the bright colors. Which color we see at any point depends on the thickness of the soapy water film at that point and also on the viewing angle. Near the top of the bubble, we see a small black area surrounded by a silver or white area. The bubble's thickness is smallest at that black spot, perhaps only about 30 nm thick, and is fully transparent (we see the black background).

We cover fundamental aspects of the wave nature of light, including two-slit interference and interference in thin films.

The Wave Nature of Light; Interference

CONTENTS

CHAPTER-OPENING QUESTION—Guess now!

When a thin layer of oil lies on top of water or wet pavement, you can often see swirls of color. We also see swirls of color on the soap bubble shown above. What causes these colors?

(a) Additives in the oil or soap reflect various colors.

(b) Chemicals in the oil or soap absorb various colors.

(c) Dispersion due to differences in index of refraction in the oil or soap.

(d) The interactions of the light with a thin boundary layer where the oil (or soap) and the water have mixed irregularly.

(e) Light waves reflected from the top and bottom surfaces of the thin oil or soap film can add up constructively for particular wavelengths.

That light carries energy is obvious to anyone who has focused the Sun's rays with a magnifying glass on a piece of paper and burned a hole in it. But how does light travel, and in what form is this energy carried? In our discussion of waves in Chapter 15, we noted that energy can be carried from place to place in basically two ways: by particles or by waves. In the first case, material objects or particles can carry energy, such as an avalanche of rocks or rushing water. In the second case, water waves and sound waves, for example, can carry energy over long distances even though the oscillating particles of the medium do not travel these distances. In view of this, what can we say about the nature of light: does light travel as a stream of particles away from its source, or does light travel in the form of waves that spread outward from the source?

Historically, this question has turned out to be a difficult one. For one thing, light does not reveal itself in any obvious way as being made up of tiny particles; nor do we see tiny light waves passing by as we do water waves. The evidence seemed to favor first one side and then the other until about 1830, when most physicists had accepted the wave theory. By the end of the nineteenth century, light was considered to be an *electromagnetic wave* (Chapter 31). In the early twentieth century, light was shown to have a particle nature as well, as we shall discuss in Chapter 37. We now speak of the wave–particle duality of light. The wave theory of light remains valid and has proved very successful. We now investigate the evidence for the wave theory and how it has been used to explain a wide range of phenomena.

34–1 Waves versus Particles; Huygens' Principle and Diffraction

The Dutch scientist Christian Huygens (1629–1695), a contemporary of Newton, proposed a wave theory of light that had much merit. Still useful today is a technique Huygens developed for predicting the future position of a wave front when an earlier position is known. By a wave front, we mean all the points along a two- or three-dimensional wave that form a wave crest—what we simply call a "wave" as seen on the ocean. Wave fronts are perpendicular to rays as we already discussed in Chapter 15 (Fig. 15–20). **Huygens' principle** can be stated as follows: *Every point on a wave front can be considered as a source of tiny wavelets that spread out in the forward direction at the speed of the wave itself. The new wave front is the envelope of all the wavelets—that is, the tangent to all of them.*

As a simple example of the use of Huygens' principle, consider the wave front AB in Fig. 34–1, which is traveling away from a source S. We assume the medium is *isotropic*—that is, the speed v of the waves is the same in all directions. To find the wave front a short time t after it is at AB, tiny circles are drawn with radius $r = vt$. The centers of these tiny circles are blue dots on the original wave front AB, and the circles represent Huygens' (imaginary) wavelets. The tangent to all these wavelets, the curved line CD, is the new position of the wave front.

Huygens' principle is particularly useful for analyzing what happens when waves impinge on an obstacle and the wave fronts are partially interrupted. Huygens' principle predicts that waves bend in behind an obstacle, as shown in Fig. 34–2. This is just what water waves do, as we saw in Chapter 15 (Figs. 15–31 and 15–32). The bending of waves behind obstacles into the "shadow region" is known as **diffraction**. Since diffraction occurs for waves, but not for particles, it can serve as one means for distinguishing the nature of light.

Note, as shown in Fig. 34–2, that diffraction is most prominent when the size of the opening is on the order of the wavelength of the wave. If the opening is much larger than the wavelength, diffraction goes unnoticed.

Does light exhibit diffraction? In the mid-seventeenth century, the Jesuit priest Francesco Grimaldi (1618–1663) had observed that when sunlight entered a darkened room through a tiny hole in a screen, the spot on the opposite wall was larger than would be expected from geometric rays. He also observed that the border of the image was not clear but was surrounded by colored fringes. Grimaldi attributed this to the diffraction of light.

The wave model of light nicely accounts for diffraction, and we discuss diffraction in detail in the next Chapter. But the ray model (Chapter 32) cannot account for diffraction, and it is important to be aware of such limitations to the ray model. Geometric optics using rays is successful in a wide range of situations only because normal openings and obstacles are much larger than the wavelength of the light, and so relatively little diffraction or bending occurs.

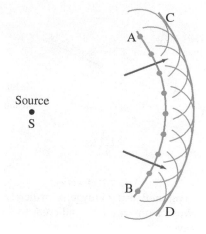

FIGURE 34–1 Huygens' principle, used to determine wave front CD when wave front AB is given.

FIGURE 34–2 Huygens' principle is consistent with diffraction (a) around the edge of an obstacle, (b) through a large hole, (c) through a small hole whose size is on the order of the wavelength of the wave.

(a)

(b)

(c)

34–2 Huygens' Principle and the Law of Refraction

FIGURE 34–3 Refraction explained, using Huygens' principle. Wave fronts are perpendicular to the rays.

The laws of reflection and refraction were well known in Newton's time. The law of reflection could not distinguish between the two theories we just discussed: waves versus particles. For when waves reflect from an obstacle, the angle of incidence equals the angle of reflection (Fig. 15–21). The same is true of particles—think of a tennis ball without spin striking a flat surface.

The law of refraction is another matter. Consider a ray of light entering a medium where it is bent toward the normal, as when traveling from air into water. As shown in Fig. 34–3, this bending can be constructed using Huygens' principle if we assume the speed of light is less in the second medium $(v_2 < v_1)$. In time t, point B on wave front AB (perpendicular to the incoming ray) travels a distance $v_1 t$ to reach point D. Point A on the wave front, traveling in the second medium, goes a distance $v_2 t$ to reach point C, and $v_2 t < v_1 t$. Huygens' principle is applied to points A and B to obtain the curved wavelets shown at C and D. The wave front is tangent to these two wavelets, so the new wave front is the line CD. Hence the rays, which are perpendicular to the wave fronts, bend toward the normal if $v_2 < v_1$, as drawn.

Newton favored a particle theory of light which predicted the opposite result, that the speed of light would be greater in the second medium $(v_2 > v_1)$. Thus the wave theory predicts that the speed of light in water, for example, is less than in air; and Newton's particle theory predicts the reverse. An experiment to actually measure the speed of light in water was performed in 1850 by the French physicist Jean Foucault, and it confirmed the wave-theory prediction. By then, however, the wave theory was already fully accepted, as we shall see in the next Section.

Snell's law of refraction follows directly from Huygens' principle, given that the speed of light v in any medium is related to the speed in a vacuum, c, and the index of refraction, n, by Eq. 32–4: that is, $v = c/n$. From the Huygens' construction of Fig. 34–3, angle ADC is equal to θ_2 and angle BAD is equal to θ_1. Then for the two triangles that have the common side AD, we have

$$\sin \theta_1 = \frac{v_1 t}{AD}, \qquad \sin \theta_2 = \frac{v_2 t}{AD}.$$

We divide these two equations and obtain

$$\frac{\sin \theta_1}{\sin \theta_2} = \frac{v_1}{v_2}.$$

Then, by Eq. 32–4 $v_1 = c/n_1$ and $v_2 = c/n_2$, so we have

$$n_1 \sin \theta_1 = n_2 \sin \theta_2,$$

which is Snell's law of refraction, Eq. 32–5. (The law of reflection can be derived from Huygens' principle in a similar way: see Problem 1 at the end of this Chapter.)

When a light wave travels from one medium to another, its frequency does not change, but its wavelength does. This can be seen from Fig. 34–3, where each of the blue lines representing a wave front corresponds to a crest (peak) of the wave. Then

$$\frac{\lambda_2}{\lambda_1} = \frac{v_2 t}{v_1 t} = \frac{v_2}{v_1} = \frac{n_1}{n_2},$$

where, in the last step, we used Eq. 32–4, $v = c/n$. If medium 1 is a vacuum (or air), so $n_1 = 1$, $v_1 = c$, and we call λ_1 simply λ, then the wavelength in another medium of index of refraction $n (= n_2)$ will be

$$\lambda_n = \frac{\lambda}{n}. \tag{34–1}$$

This result is consistent with the frequency f being unchanged no matter what medium the wave is traveling in, since $c = f\lambda$.

EXERCISE A A light beam in air with wavelength = 500 nm, frequency = 6.0×10^{14} Hz, and speed = 3.0×10^8 m/s goes into glass which has an index of refraction = 1.5. What are the wavelength, frequency, and speed of the light in the glass?

(a)

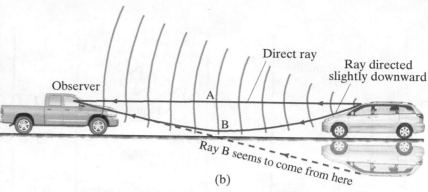

(b)

FIGURE 34–4 (a) A highway
mirage. (b) Drawing (greatly
exaggerated) showing wave fronts
and rays to explain highway mirages.
Note how sections of the wave fronts
near the ground move faster and so
are farther apart.

Wave fronts can be used to explain how mirages are produced by refraction of light. For example, on a hot day motorists sometimes see a mirage of water on the highway ahead of them, with distant vehicles seemingly reflected in it (Fig. 34–4a). On a hot day, there can be a layer of very hot air next to the roadway (made hot by the Sun beating on the road). Hot air is less dense than cooler air, so the index of refraction is slightly lower in the hot air. In Fig. 34–4b, we see a diagram of light coming from one point on a distant car (on the right) heading left toward the observer. Wave fronts and two rays (perpendicular to the wave fronts) are shown. Ray A heads directly at the observer and follows a straight-line path, and represents the normal view of the distant car. Ray B is a ray initially directed slightly downward, but it bends slightly as it moves through layers of air of different index of refraction. The wave fronts, shown in blue in Fig. 34–4b, move slightly faster in the layers of air nearer the ground. Thus ray B is bent as shown, and seems to the observer to be coming from below (dashed line) as if reflected off the road. Hence the mirage.

PHYSICS APPLIED
Highway mirages

34–3 Interference—Young's Double-Slit Experiment

In 1801, the Englishman Thomas Young (1773–1829) obtained convincing evidence for the wave nature of light and was even able to measure wavelengths for visible light. Figure 34–5a shows a schematic diagram of Young's famous double-slit experiment.

FIGURE 34–5 (a) Young's double-slit experiment. (b) If light consists of particles, we would expect to see two bright lines on the screen behind the slits. (c) In fact, many lines are observed. The slits and their separation need to be very thin.

(a) Viewing screen

(b) Viewing screen (particle theory prediction)

(c) Viewing screen (actual)

FIGURE 34–6 If light is a wave, light passing through one of two slits should interfere with light passing through the other slit.

To have light from a single source, Young used the Sun passing through a very narrow slit in a window covering. This beam of parallel rays falls on a screen containing two closely spaced slits, S_1 and S_2. (The slits and their separation are very narrow, not much larger than the wavelength of the light.) If light consists of tiny particles, we might expect to see two bright lines on a screen placed behind the slits as in (b). But instead a series of bright lines are seen, as in (c). Young was able to explain this result as a **wave-interference** phenomenon.

To understand why, we consider the simple situation of plane waves of light of a single wavelength—called **monochromatic**, meaning "one color"—falling on the two slits as shown in Fig. 34–6. Because of diffraction, the waves leaving the two small slits spread out as shown. This is equivalent to the interference pattern produced when two rocks are thrown into a lake (Fig. 15–23), or when sound from two loudspeakers interferes (Fig. 16–15). Recall Section 15–8 on wave interference.

FIGURE 34–7 How the wave theory explains the pattern of lines seen in the double-slit experiment. (a) At the center of the screen the waves from each slit travel the same distance and are in phase. (b) At this angle θ, the lower wave travels an extra distance of one whole wavelength, and the waves are in phase; note from the shaded triangle that the path difference equals $d \sin \theta$. (c) For this angle θ, the lower wave travels an extra distance equal to one-half wavelength, so the two waves arrive at the screen fully out of phase. (d) A more detailed diagram showing the geometry for parts (b) and (c).

FIGURE 34–8 Two traveling waves are shown undergoing (a) constructive interference, (b) destructive interference. (See also Section 15–8.)

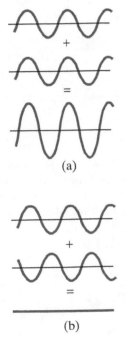

To see how an interference pattern is produced on the screen, we make use of Fig. 34–7. Waves of wavelength λ are shown entering the slits S_1 and S_2, which are a distance d apart. The waves spread out in all directions after passing through the slits (Fig. 34–6), but they are shown only for three different angles θ. In Fig. 34–7a, the waves reaching the center of the screen are shown ($\theta = 0°$). The waves from the two slits travel the same distance, so they are in phase: a crest of one wave arrives at the same time as a crest of the other wave. Hence the amplitudes of the two waves add to form a larger amplitude as shown in Fig. 34–8a. This is **constructive interference**, and there is a bright area at the center of the screen. Constructive interference also occurs when the paths of the two rays differ by one wavelength (or any whole number of wavelengths), as shown in Fig. 34–7b; also here there will be brightness on the screen. But if one ray travels an extra distance of one-half wavelength (or $\frac{3}{2}\lambda$, $\frac{5}{2}\lambda$, and so on), the two waves are exactly out of phase when they reach the screen: the crests of one wave arrive at the same time as the troughs of the other wave, and so they add to produce zero amplitude (Fig. 34–8b). This is **destructive interference**, and the screen is dark, Fig. 34–7c. Thus, there will be a series of bright and dark lines (or **fringes**) on the viewing screen.

To determine exactly where the bright lines fall, first note that Fig. 34–7 is somewhat exaggerated; in real situations, the distance d between the slits is very small compared to the distance ℓ to the screen. The rays from each slit for each case will therefore be essentially parallel, and θ is the angle they make with the horizontal as shown in Fig. 34–7d. From the shaded right triangles shown in Figs. 34–7b and c, we can see that the extra distance traveled by the lower ray is $d \sin \theta$ (seen more clearly in Fig. 34–7d). Constructive interference will occur, and a bright fringe will appear on the screen, when the *path difference*, $d \sin \theta$, equals a whole number of wavelengths:

$$d \sin \theta = m\lambda, \qquad m = 0, 1, 2, \cdots. \qquad \begin{bmatrix} \text{constructive} \\ \text{interference} \\ \text{(bright)} \end{bmatrix} \quad \textbf{(34–2a)}$$

The value of m is called the **order** of the interference fringe. The first order ($m = 1$), for example, is the first fringe on each side of the central fringe (which is at $\theta = 0$, $m = 0$). Destructive interference occurs when the path difference $d \sin \theta$ is $\frac{1}{2}\lambda$, $\frac{3}{2}\lambda$, and so on:

$$d \sin \theta = (m + \tfrac{1}{2})\lambda, \qquad m = 0, 1, 2, \cdots. \qquad \begin{bmatrix} \text{destructive} \\ \text{interference} \\ \text{(dark)} \end{bmatrix} \quad \textbf{(34–2b)}$$

The bright fringes are peaks or maxima of light intensity, the dark fringes are minima.

The intensity of the bright fringes is greatest for the central fringe $(m = 0)$ and decreases for higher orders, as shown in Fig. 34–9. How much the intensity decreases with increasing order depends on the width of the two slits.

Constructive interference

(a)

CONCEPTUAL EXAMPLE 34–1 | **Interference pattern lines.** (*a*) Will there be an infinite number of points on the viewing screen where constructive and destructive interference occur, or only a finite number of points? (*b*) Are neighboring points of constructive interference uniformly spaced, or is the spacing between neighboring points of constructive interference not uniform?

RESPONSE (*a*) When you look at Eqs. 34–2a and b you might be tempted to say, given the statement $m = 0, 1, 2, \cdots$ beside the equations, that there are an infinite number of points of constructive and destructive interference. However, recall that $\sin \theta$ cannot exceed 1. Thus, there is an upper limit to the values of m that can be used in these equations. For Eq. 34–2a, the maximum value of m is the integer closest in value but smaller than d/λ. So there are a *finite* number of points of constructive and destructive interference no matter how large the screen. (*b*) The spacing between neighboring points of constructive or destructive interference is not uniform: The spacing gets larger as θ gets larger, and you can verify this statement mathematically. For small values of θ the spacing is nearly uniform as you will see in Example 34–2.

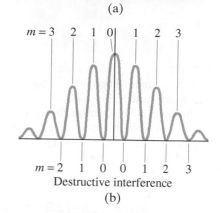

FIGURE 34–9 (a) Interference fringes produced by a double-slit experiment and detected by photographic film placed on the viewing screen. The arrow marks the central fringe. (b) Graph of the intensity of light in the interference pattern. Also shown are values of m for Eq. 34–2a (constructive interference) and Eq. 34–2b (destructive interference).

EXAMPLE 34–2 **Line spacing for double-slit interference.** A screen containing two slits 0.100 mm apart is 1.20 m from the viewing screen. Light of wavelength $\lambda = 500$ nm falls on the slits from a distant source. Approximately how far apart will adjacent bright interference fringes be on the screen?

APPROACH The angular position of bright (constructive interference) fringes is found using Eq. 34–2a. The distance between the first two fringes (say) can be found using right triangles as shown in Fig. 34–10.

SOLUTION Given $d = 0.100$ mm $= 1.00 \times 10^{-4}$ m, $\lambda = 500 \times 10^{-9}$ m, and $\ell = 1.20$ m, the first-order fringe $(m = 1)$ occurs at an angle θ given by

$$\sin \theta_1 = \frac{m\lambda}{d} = \frac{(1)(500 \times 10^{-9}\,\text{m})}{1.00 \times 10^{-4}\,\text{m}} = 5.00 \times 10^{-3}.$$

This is a very small angle, so we can take $\sin \theta \approx \theta$, with θ in radians. The first-order fringe will occur a distance x_1 above the center of the screen (see Fig. 34–10), given by $x_1/\ell = \tan \theta_1 \approx \theta_1$, so

$$x_1 \approx \ell\theta_1 = (1.20\,\text{m})(5.00 \times 10^{-3}) = 6.00\,\text{mm}.$$

The second-order fringe $(m = 2)$ will occur at

$$x_2 \approx \ell\theta_2 = \ell\frac{2\lambda}{d} = 12.0\,\text{mm}$$

above the center, and so on. Thus the lower order fringes are 6.00 mm apart.

NOTE The spacing between fringes is essentially uniform until the approximation $\sin \theta \approx \theta$ is no longer valid.

FIGURE 34–10 Examples 34–2 and 34–3. For small angles θ (give θ in radians), the interference fringes occur at distance $x = \theta\ell$ above the center fringe $(m = 0)$; θ_1 and x_1 are for the first-order fringe $(m = 1)$; θ_2 and x_2 are for $m = 2$.

CONCEPTUAL EXAMPLE 34–3 | **Changing the wavelength.** (*a*) What happens to the interference pattern shown in Fig. 34–10, Example 34–2, if the incident light (500 nm) is replaced by light of wavelength 700 nm? (*b*) What happens instead if the wavelength stays at 500 nm but the slits are moved farther apart?

RESPONSE (*a*) When λ increases in Eq. 34–2a but d stays the same, then the angle θ for bright fringes increases and the interference pattern spreads out. (*b*) Increasing the slit spacing d reduces θ for each order, so the lines are closer together.

White

|←2.0 mm→|

|←——3.5 mm——→|

FIGURE 34–11 First-order fringes are a full spectrum, like a rainbow. Also Example 34–4.

FIGURE 34–10 (Repeated.) For small angles θ (give θ in radians), the interference fringes occur at distance $x = \theta\ell$ above the center fringe ($m = 0$); θ_1 and x_1 are for the first-order fringe ($m = 1$), θ_2 and x_2 are for $m = 2$.

From Eqs. 34–2 we can see that, except for the zeroth-order fringe at the center, the position of the fringes depends on wavelength. Consequently, when white light falls on the two slits, as Young found in his experiments, the central fringe is white, but the first- (and higher-) order fringes contain a spectrum of colors like a rainbow; θ was found to be smallest for violet light and largest for red (Fig. 34–11). By measuring the position of these fringes, Young was the first to determine the wavelengths of visible light (using Eqs. 34–2). In doing so, he showed that what distinguishes different colors physically is their wavelength (or frequency), an idea put forward earlier by Grimaldi in 1665.

EXAMPLE 34–4 Wavelengths from double-slit interference. White light passes through two slits 0.50 mm apart, and an interference pattern is observed on a screen 2.5 m away. The first-order fringe resembles a rainbow with violet and red light at opposite ends. The violet light is about 2.0 mm and the red 3.5 mm from the center of the central white fringe (Fig. 34–11). Estimate the wavelengths for the violet and red light.

APPROACH We find the angles for violet and red light from the distances given and the diagram of Fig. 34–10. Then we use Eq. 34–2a to obtain the wavelengths. Because 3.5 mm is much less than 2.5 m, we can use the small-angle approximation.

SOLUTION We use Eq. 34–2a with $m = 1$ and $\sin\theta \approx \tan\theta \approx \theta$. Then for violet light, $x = 2.0$ mm, so (see also Fig. 34–10)

$$\lambda = \frac{d\sin\theta}{m} \approx \frac{d\theta}{m} \approx \frac{d}{m}\frac{x}{\ell} = \left(\frac{5.0 \times 10^{-4}\,\text{m}}{1}\right)\left(\frac{2.0 \times 10^{-3}\,\text{m}}{2.5\,\text{m}}\right) = 4.0 \times 10^{-7}\,\text{m},$$

or 400 nm. For red light, $x = 3.5$ mm, so

$$\lambda = \frac{d}{m}\frac{x}{\ell} = \left(\frac{5.0 \times 10^{-4}\,\text{m}}{1}\right)\left(\frac{3.5 \times 10^{-3}\,\text{m}}{2.5\,\text{m}}\right) = 7.0 \times 10^{-7}\,\text{m} = 700\,\text{nm}.$$

Coherence

The two slits in Fig. 34–7 act as if they were two sources of radiation. They are called **coherent sources** because the waves leaving them have the same wavelength and frequency, and bear the same phase relationship to each other at all times. This happens because the waves come from a single source to the left of the two slits in Fig. 34–7, splitting the original beam into two. An interference pattern is observed only when the sources are coherent. If two tiny lightbulbs replaced the two slits, an interference pattern would not be seen. The light emitted by one lightbulb would have a random phase with respect to the second bulb, and the screen would be more or less uniformly illuminated. Two such sources, whose output waves have phases that bear no fixed relationship to each other over time, are called **incoherent sources**.

*34–4 Intensity in the Double-Slit Interference Pattern

We saw in Section 34–3 that the interference pattern produced by the coherent light from two slits, S_1 and S_2 (Figs. 34–7 and 34–9), produces a series of bright and dark fringes. If the two monochromatic waves of wavelength λ are in phase at the slits, the maxima (brightest points) occur at angles θ given by (Eqs. 34–2)

$$d\sin\theta = m\lambda,$$

and the minima (darkest points) when

$$d\sin\theta = (m + \tfrac{1}{2})\lambda,$$

where m is an integer ($m = 0, 1, 2, \cdots$).

We now determine the intensity of the light at all points in the pattern, assuming that if either slit were covered, the light passing through the other would diffract sufficiently to illuminate a large portion of the screen uniformly. The intensity I of the light at any point is proportional to the square of its wave amplitude (Section 15–3). Treating light as an electromagnetic wave, I is proportional to the square of the electric field E (or to the magnetic field B, Section 31–8): $I \propto E^2$. The electric field $\vec{E}$ at any point P (see Fig. 34–12) will be the sum of the electric field vectors of the waves coming from each of the two slits, $\vec{E}_1$ and $\vec{E}_2$. Since $\vec{E}_1$ and $\vec{E}_2$ are essentially parallel (on a screen far away compared to the slit separation), the magnitude of the electric field at angle θ (that is, at point P) will be

$$E_\theta = E_1 + E_2.$$

FIGURE 34–12 Determining the intensity in a double-slit interference pattern. Not to scale: in fact $\ell \gg d$, and the two rays become essentially parallel.

Both E_1 and E_2 vary sinusoidally with frequency $f = c/\lambda$, but they differ in phase, depending on their different travel distances from the slits. The electric field at P can then be written for the light from each of the two slits, using $\omega = 2\pi f$, as

$$\begin{aligned} E_1 &= E_{10} \sin \omega t \\ E_2 &= E_{20} \sin(\omega t + \delta) \end{aligned} \tag{34–3}$$

where E_{10} and E_{20} are their respective amplitudes and δ is the phase difference. The value of δ depends on the angle θ, so let us now determine δ as a function of θ.

At the center of the screen (point 0), $\delta = 0$. If the difference in path length from P to S_1 and S_2 is $d \sin \theta = \lambda/2$, the two waves are exactly out of phase so $\delta = \pi$ (or 180°). If $d \sin \theta = \lambda$, the two waves differ in phase by $\delta = 2\pi$. In general, then, δ is related to θ by

$$\frac{\delta}{2\pi} = \frac{d \sin \theta}{\lambda}$$

or

$$\delta = \frac{2\pi}{\lambda} d \sin \theta. \tag{34–4}$$

To determine $E_\theta = E_1 + E_2$, we add the two scalars E_1 and E_2 which are sine functions differing by the phase δ. One way to determine the sum of E_1 and E_2 is to use a **phasor diagram**. (We used this technique before, in Chapter 30.) As shown in Fig. 34–13, we draw an arrow of length E_{10} to represent the amplitude of E_1 (Eq. 34–3); and the arrow of length E_{20}, which we draw to make a fixed angle δ with E_{10}, represents the amplitude of E_2. When the diagram rotates at angular frequency ω about the origin, the projections of E_{10} and E_{20} on the vertical axis represent E_1 and E_2 as a function of time (see Eq. 34–3). We let $E_{\theta 0}$ be the "vector" sum[†] of E_{10} and E_{20}; $E_{\theta 0}$ is the amplitude of the sum $E_\theta = E_1 + E_2$, and the projection of $E_{\theta 0}$ on the vertical axis is just E_θ. If the two slits provide equal illumination, so that $E_{10} = E_{20} = E_0$, then from *symmetry* in Fig. 34–13, the angle $\phi = \delta/2$, and we can write

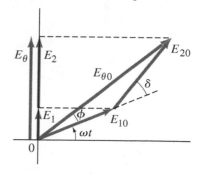

FIGURE 34–13 Phasor diagram for double-slit interference pattern.

$$E_\theta = E_{\theta 0} \sin \left(\omega t + \frac{\delta}{2} \right). \tag{34–5a}$$

From Fig. 34–13 we can also see that

$$E_{\theta 0} = 2 E_0 \cos \phi = 2 E_0 \cos \frac{\delta}{2}. \tag{34–5b}$$

Combining Eqs. 34–5a and b, we obtain

$$E_\theta = 2 E_0 \cos \frac{\delta}{2} \sin \left(\omega t + \frac{\delta}{2} \right), \tag{34–5c}$$

where δ is given by Eq. 34–4.

[†]We are not adding the actual electric field vectors; instead we are using the "phasor" technique to add the amplitudes, taking into account the phase difference of the two waves.

We are not really interested in E_θ as a function of time, since for visible light the frequency (10^{14} to 10^{15} Hz) is much too high to be noticeable. We are interested in the average intensity, which is proportional to the amplitude squared, $E_{\theta 0}^2$. We now drop the word "average," and we let I_θ ($I_\theta \propto E_\theta^2$) be the intensity at any point P at an angle θ to the horizontal. We let I_0 be the intensity at point O, the center of the screen, where $\theta = \delta = 0$, so $I_0 \propto (E_{10} + E_{20})^2 = (2E_0)^2$. Then the ratio I_θ / I_0 is equal to the ratio of the squares of the electric-field amplitudes at these two points, so

$$\frac{I_\theta}{I_0} = \frac{E_{\theta 0}^2}{(2E_0)^2} = \cos^2 \frac{\delta}{2}$$

where we used Eq. 34–5b. Thus the intensity I_θ at any point is related to the maximum intensity at the center of the screen by

$$I_\theta = I_0 \cos^2 \frac{\delta}{2}$$

$$= I_0 \cos^2 \left(\frac{\pi d \sin \theta}{\lambda} \right)$$

(34–6)

where δ was given by Eq. 34–4. This is the relation we sought.

From Eq. 34–6 we see that maxima occur where $\cos \delta/2 = \pm 1$, which corresponds to $\delta = 0, 2\pi, 4\pi, \cdots$. From Eq. 34–4, δ has these values when

$$d \sin \theta = m\lambda, \qquad m = 0, 1, 2, \cdots.$$

Minima occur where $\delta = \pi, 3\pi, 5\pi, \cdots$, which corresponds to

$$d \sin \theta = (m + \tfrac{1}{2})\lambda, \qquad m = 0, 1, 2, \cdots.$$

These are the same results we obtained in Section 34–3. But now we know not only the position of maxima and minima, but from Eq. 34–6 we can determine the intensity at all points.

In the usual situation where the distance ℓ to the screen from the slits is large compared to the slit separation d ($\ell \gg d$), if we consider only points P whose distance y from the center (point O) is small compared to ℓ ($y \ll \ell$)—see Fig. 34–12—then

$$\sin \theta = \frac{y}{\ell}.$$

From this it follows (see Eq. 34–4) that

$$\delta = \frac{2\pi}{\lambda} \frac{d}{\ell} y.$$

Equation 34–6 then becomes

$$I_\theta = I_0 \left[\cos \left(\frac{\pi d}{\lambda \ell} y \right) \right]^2. \qquad\qquad [y \ll \ell, \, d \ll \ell] \quad \text{(34–7)}$$

EXERCISE B What are the values for the intensity I_θ when (a) $y = 0$, (b) $y = \lambda\ell/4d$, and (c) $y = \lambda\ell/2d$?

The intensity I_θ as a function of the phase difference δ is plotted in Fig. 34–14. In the approximation of Eq. 34–7, the horizontal axis could as well be y, the position on the screen.

The intensity pattern expressed in Eqs. 34–6 and 34–7, and plotted in Fig. 34–14, shows a series of maxima of equal height, and is based on the assumption that each slit (alone) would illuminate the screen uniformly. This is never quite true, as we shall see when we discuss diffraction in the next Chapter. We will see that the center maximum is strongest and each succeeding maximum to each side is a little less strong.

EXAMPLE 34–5 **Antenna intensity.** Two radio antennas are located close to each other as shown in Fig. 34–15, separated by a distance d. The antennas radiate in phase with each other, emitting waves of intensity I_0 at wavelength λ. (*a*) Calculate the net intensity as a function of θ for points very far from the antennas. (*b*) For $d = \lambda$, determine I and find in which directions I is a maximum and a minimum. (*c*) Repeat part (*b*) when $d = \lambda/2$.

APPROACH This setup is similar to Young's double-slit experiment.

SOLUTION (*a*) Points of constructive and destructive interference are still given by Eqs. 34–2a and b, and the net intensity as a function of θ is given by Eq. 34–6. (*b*) We let $d = \lambda$ in Eq. 34–6, and find for the intensity,

$$I = I_0 \cos^2(\pi \sin \theta).$$

I is a maximum, equal to I_0, when $\sin \theta = 0$, 1, or -1, meaning $\theta = 0, 90°, 180°$, and $270°$. I is zero when $\sin \theta = \frac{1}{2}$ and $-\frac{1}{2}$, for which $\theta = 30°, 150°, 210°$, and $330°$. (*c*) For $d = \lambda/2$, I is maximized for $\theta = 0$ and $180°$, and minimized for $90°$ and $270°$.

FIGURE 34–15 Example 34–5. The two dots represent the antennas.

34–5 Interference in Thin Films

Interference of light gives rise to many everyday phenomena such as the bright colors reflected from soap bubbles and from thin oil or gasoline films on water, Fig. 34–16. In these and other cases, the colors are a result of constructive interference between light reflected from the two surfaces of the thin film.

FIGURE 34–16 Thin film interference patterns seen in (a) a soap bubble, (b) a thin film of soapy water, and (c) a thin layer of oil on wet pavement.

(a)

(b)

(c)

FIGURE 34–17 Light reflected from the upper and lower surfaces of a thin film of oil lying on water. This analysis assumes the light strikes the surface nearly perpendicularly, but is shown here at an angle so we can display each ray.

To see how this **thin-film interference** happens, consider a smooth surface of water on top of which is a thin uniform layer of another substance, say an oil whose index of refraction is less than that of water (we'll see why we assume this in a moment); see Fig. 34–17. Assume for the moment that the incident light is of a single wavelength. Part of the incident light is reflected at A on the top surface, and part of the light transmitted is reflected at B on the lower surface. The part reflected at the lower surface must travel the extra distance ABC. If this *path difference* ABC equals one or a whole number of wavelengths in the film (λ_n), the two waves will reach the eye in phase and interfere constructively. Hence the region AC on the surface film will appear bright. But if ABC equals $\frac{1}{2}\lambda_n, \frac{3}{2}\lambda_n$, and so on, the two waves will be exactly out of phase and destructive interference occurs: the area AC on the film will show no reflection—it will be dark (or better, transparent to the dark material below). The wavelength λ_n is *the wavelength in the film:* $\lambda_n = \lambda/n$, where n is the index of refraction in the film and λ is the wavelength in vacuum. See Eq. 34–1.

When white light falls on such a film, the path difference ABC will equal λ_n (or $m\lambda_n$, with m = an integer) for only one wavelength at a given viewing angle. The color corresponding to λ (λ in air) will be seen as very bright. For light viewed at a slightly different angle, the path difference ABC will be longer or shorter and a different color will undergo constructive interference. Thus, for an extended (nonpoint) source emitting white light, a series of bright colors will be seen next to one another. Variations in thickness of the film will also alter the path difference ABC and therefore affect the color of light that is most strongly reflected.

EXERCISE C Return to the Chapter-Opening Question, page 900, and answer it again now. Try to explain why you may have answered differently the first time.

When a curved glass surface is placed in contact with a flat glass surface, Fig. 34–18, a series of concentric rings is seen when illuminated from above by either white light (as shown) or by monochromatic light. These are called **Newton's rings**[†] and they are due to interference between waves reflected by the top and bottom surfaces of the very thin *air gap* between the two pieces of glass. Because this gap (which is equivalent to a thin film) increases in width from the central contact point out to the edges, the extra path length for the lower ray (equal to BCD) varies; where it equals $0, \frac{1}{2}\lambda, \lambda, \frac{3}{2}\lambda, 2\lambda$, and so on, it corresponds to constructive and destructive interference; and this gives rise to the series of bright colored circles seen in Fig. 34–18b. The color you see at a given radius corresponds to constructive interference; at that radius, other colors partially or fully destructively interfere. (If monochromatic light is used, the rings are alternately bright and dark.)

[†]Although Newton gave an elaborate description of them, they had been first observed and described by his contemporary, Robert Hooke.

FIGURE 34–18 Newton's rings. (a) Light rays reflected from upper and lower surfaces of the thin air gap can interfere. (b) Photograph of interference patterns using white light.

(a)

(b)

The point of contact of the two glass surfaces (A in Fig. 34–18a) is dark in Fig. 34–18b. Since the path difference is zero here, our previous analysis would suggest that the waves reflected from each surface are in phase and so this central area ought to be bright. But it is dark, which tells us something else is happening here: the two waves must be completely out of phase. This can happen if one of the waves, upon reflection, flips over—a crest becomes a trough—see Fig. 34–19. We say that the reflected wave has undergone a phase change of 180°, or of half a wave cycle. Indeed, this and other experiments reveal that, at normal incidence,

a beam of light reflected by a material with index of refraction greater than that of the material in which it is traveling, changes phase by 180° or $\frac{1}{2}$ cycle;

see Fig. 34–19. This phase change acts just like a path difference of $\frac{1}{2}\lambda$. If the index of refraction of the reflecting material is less than that of the material in which the light is traveling, no phase change occurs.[†]

Thus the wave reflected at the curved surface above the air gap in Fig. 34–18a undergoes no change in phase. But the wave reflected at the lower surface, where the beam in air strikes the glass, undergoes a $\frac{1}{2}$-cycle phase change, equivalent to a $\frac{1}{2}\lambda$ path difference. Thus the two waves reflected near the point of contact A of the two glass surfaces (where the air gap approaches zero thickness) will be a half cycle (or 180°) out of phase, and a dark spot occurs. Bright colored rings will occur when the path difference is $\frac{1}{2}\lambda$, $\frac{3}{2}\lambda$, and so on, because the phase change at one surface effectively adds a path difference of $\frac{1}{2}\lambda$ $\left(=\frac{1}{2}\text{ cycle}\right)$. (If monochromatic light is used, the bright Newton's rings will be separated by dark bands which occur when the path difference BCD in Fig. 34–18a is equal to an integral number of wavelengths.)

Returning for a moment to Fig. 34–17, the light reflecting at both interfaces, air–oil and oil–water, underwent a phase change of 180° equivalent to a path difference of $\frac{1}{2}\lambda$, since we assumed $n_{\text{water}} > n_{\text{oil}} > n_{\text{air}}$; since the phase changes were equal, they didn't affect our analysis.

EXAMPLE 34–6 **Thin film of air, wedge-shaped.** A very fine wire 7.35×10^{-3} mm in diameter is placed between two flat glass plates as in Fig. 34–20a. Light whose wavelength in air is 600 nm falls (and is viewed) perpendicular to the plates and a series of bright and dark bands is seen, Fig. 34–20b. How many light and dark bands will there be in this case? Will the area next to the wire be bright or dark?

APPROACH We need to consider two effects: (1) path differences for rays reflecting from the two close surfaces (thin wedge of air between the two glass plates), and (2) the $\frac{1}{2}$-cycle phase change at the lower surface (point E in Fig. 34–20a), where rays in air can enter glass. Because of the phase change at the lower surface, there will be a dark band (no reflection) when the path difference is 0, λ, 2λ, 3λ, and so on. Since the light rays are perpendicular to the plates, the extra path length equals $2t$, where t is the thickness of the air gap at any point.

SOLUTION Dark bands will occur where

$$2t = m\lambda, \qquad m = 0, 1, 2, \cdots.$$

Bright bands occur when $2t = \left(m + \frac{1}{2}\right)\lambda$, where m is an integer. At the position of the wire, $t = 7.35 \times 10^{-6}$ m. At this point there will be $2t/\lambda = (2)(7.35 \times 10^{-6}\text{ m})/(6.00 \times 10^{-7}\text{ m}) = 24.5$ wavelengths. This is a "half integer," so the area next to the wire will be bright. There will be a total of 25 dark lines along the plates, corresponding to path lengths of 0λ, 1λ, 2λ, 3λ, $\ldots$, 24λ, including the one at the point of contact A $(m = 0)$. Between them, there will be 24 bright lines plus the one at the end, or 25.

NOTE The bright and dark bands will be straight only if the glass plates are extremely flat. If they are not, the pattern is uneven, as in Fig. 34–20c. Thus we see a very precise way of testing a glass surface for flatness. Spherical lens surfaces can be tested for precision by placing the lens on a flat glass surface and observing Newton's rings (Fig. 34–18b) for perfect circularity.

[†]This result can be derived from Maxwell's equations. It corresponds to the reflection of a wave traveling along a cord when it reaches the end; as we saw in Fig. 15–18, if the end is tied down, the wave changes phase and the pulse flips over, but if the end is free, no phase change occurs.

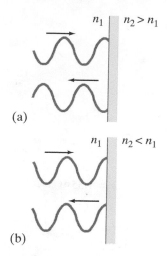

FIGURE 34–19 (a) Reflected ray changes phase by 180° or $\frac{1}{2}$ cycle if $n_2 > n_1$, but (b) does not if $n_2 < n_1$.

FIGURE 34–20 (a) Light rays reflected from the upper and lower surfaces of a thin wedge of air interfere to produce bright and dark bands. (b) Pattern observed when glass plates are optically flat; (c) pattern when plates are not so flat. See Example 34–6.

👤 PHYSICS APPLIED
Testing glass for flatness

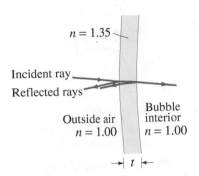

$n = 1.35$

Incident ray
Reflected rays

Outside air
$n = 1.00$

Bubble interior
$n = 1.00$

$\rightarrow| \; t \; |\leftarrow$

FIGURE 34–21 Example 34–7. The incident and reflected rays are assumed to be perpendicular to the bubble's surface. They are shown at a slight angle so we can distinguish them.

⚠ **C A U T I O N**

A formula is not enough: you must also check for phase changes at surfaces

FIGURE 34–16b (Repeated.)

If the wedge between the two glass plates of Example 34–6 is filled with some transparent substance other than air—say, water—the pattern shifts because the wavelength of the light changes. In a material where the index of refraction is n, the wavelength is $\lambda_n = \lambda/n$, where λ is the wavelength in vacuum (Eq. 34–1). For instance, if the thin wedge of Example 34–6 were filled with water, then $\lambda_n = 600 \text{ nm}/1.33 = 450 \text{ nm}$; instead of 25 dark lines, there would be 33.

When white light (rather than monochromatic light) is incident on the thin wedge of air in Figs. 34–18a or 34–20a, a colorful series of fringes is seen because constructive interference occurs for different wavelengths in the reflected light at different thicknesses along the wedge.

A soap bubble (Fig. 34–16a and Chapter-Opening Photo) is a thin spherical shell (or film) with air inside. The variations in thickness of a soap bubble film gives rise to bright colors reflected from the soap bubble. (There is air on both sides of the bubble film.) Similar variations in film thickness produce the bright colors seen reflecting from a thin layer of oil or gasoline on a puddle or lake (Fig. 34–16c). Which wavelengths appear brightest also depends on the viewing angle.

EXAMPLE 34–7 **Thickness of soap bubble skin.** A soap bubble appears green ($\lambda = 540 \text{ nm}$) at the point on its front surface nearest the viewer. What is the smallest thickness the soap bubble film could have? Assume $n = 1.35$.

APPROACH Assume the light is reflected perpendicularly from the point on a spherical surface nearest the viewer, Fig. 34–21. The light rays also reflect from the inner surface of the soap bubble film as shown. The path difference of these two reflected rays is $2t$, where t is the thickness of the soap film. Light reflected from the first (outer) surface undergoes a 180° phase change (index of refraction of soap is greater than that of air), whereas reflection at the second (inner) surface does not. To determine the thickness t for an interference maximum, we must use the wavelength of light in the soap ($n = 1.35$).

SOLUTION The 180° phase change at only one surface is equivalent to a $\frac{1}{2}\lambda$ path difference. Therefore, green light is bright when the minimum path difference equals $\frac{1}{2}\lambda_n$. Thus, $2t = \lambda/2n$, so

$$t = \frac{\lambda}{4n} = \frac{(540 \text{ nm})}{(4)(1.35)} = 100 \text{ nm}.$$

This is the smallest thickness; but the green color is more likely to be seen at the *next* thickness that gives constructive interference, $2t = 3\lambda/2n$, because other colors would be more fully cancelled by destructive interference. The more likely thickness is $3\lambda/4n = 300 \text{ nm}$, or even $5\lambda/4n = 500 \text{ nm}$. Note that green is seen in air, so $\lambda = 540 \text{ nm}$ (not λ/n).

*Colors in a Thin Soap Film

The thin film of soapy water shown in Fig. 34–16b (repeated here) has stood vertically for a long time so that gravity has pulled much of the soapy water toward the bottom. The top section is so thin (perhaps 30 nm thick) that light reflected from the front and back surfaces have almost no path difference. Thus the 180° phase change at the front surface assures that the two reflected waves are 180° out of phase for all wavelengths of visible light. The white light incident on this thin film does not reflect at the top part of the film. Thus the top **is** transparent, and we see the background which is black.

Below the black area at the top, there is a thin blue line, and then a white band. The film thickness is perhaps 75 to 100 nm, so the shortest wavelength (blue) light begins to partially interfere constructively; but just below, where the thickness is slightly greater (100 nm), the path length is reasonably close to $\lambda/2$ for much of the spectrum and we see white or silver. (Why? Recall that red starts at 600 nm in air; so most colors in the spectrum lie between 450 nm and 600 nm in air; but in water the wavelengths are $n = 1.33$ times smaller, 340 nm to 450 nm, so a 100 nm thickness is a 200 nm path length, not far from $\lambda/2$ for most colors.) Immediately below the white band we see a brown band (around 200 nm in thickness) where selected wavelengths (not all) are close to exactly λ and those colors destructively interfere, leaving only a few colors to partially interfere constructively, giving us murky brown.

Farther down, with increasing thickness t, a path length $2t = 510$ nm corresponds nicely to $\frac{3}{2}\lambda$ for blue, but not for other colors, so we see blue ($\frac{3}{2}\lambda$ path difference plus $\frac{1}{2}\lambda$ phase change = constructive interference). Other colors experience constructive interference (at $\frac{3}{2}\lambda$ and then at $\frac{5}{2}\lambda$) at still greater thicknesses, so we see a series of separated colors something like a rainbow.

In the soap bubble of our Chapter-Opening Photo (p. 900), similar things happen: at the top (where the film is thinnest) we see black and then silver-white, just as within the loop shown in Fig. 34–16b. And examine the oil film on wet pavement shown in Fig. 34–16c (repeated here); the oil film is thickest at the center and thins out toward the edges. Notice the whitish outer ring where most colors constructively interfere, which would suggest a thickness on the order of 100 nm as discussed above for the white band in the soap film. Beyond the outer white band of the oil film, Fig. 34–16c, there is still some oil, but the film is so thin that reflected light from upper and lower surfaces destructively interfere and you can see right through this very thin oil film.

FIGURE 34–16c (Repeated.)

Lens Coatings

An important application of thin-film interference is in the coating of glass to make it "nonreflecting," particularly for lenses. A glass surface reflects about 4% of the light incident upon it. Good-quality cameras, microscopes, and other optical devices may contain six to ten thin lenses. Reflection from all these surfaces can reduce the light level considerably, and multiple reflections produce a background haze that reduces the quality of the image. By reducing reflection, transmission is increased. A very thin coating on the lens surfaces can reduce reflections considerably. The thickness of the film is chosen so that light (at least for one wavelength) reflecting from the front and rear surfaces of the film destructively interferes. The amount of reflection at a boundary depends on the difference in index of refraction between the two materials. Ideally, the coating material should have an index of refraction which is the geometric mean ($= \sqrt{n_1 n_2}$) of those for air and glass, so that the amount of reflection at each surface is about equal. Then destructive interference can occur nearly completely for one particular wavelength depending on the thickness of the coating. Nearby wavelengths will at least partially destructively interfere, but a single coating cannot eliminate reflections for all wavelengths. Nonetheless, a single coating can reduce total reflection from 4% to 1% of the incident light. Often the coating is designed to eliminate the center of the reflected spectrum (around 550 nm). The extremes of the spectrum—red and violet—will not be reduced as much. Since a mixture of red and violet produces purple, the light seen reflected from such coated lenses is purple (Fig. 34–22). Lenses containing two or three separate coatings can more effectively reduce a wider range of reflecting wavelengths.

PHYSICS APPLIED
Lens coatings

FIGURE 34–22 A coated lens. Note color of light reflected from the front lens surface.

Interference

1. **Interference effects** depend on the simultaneous arrival of two or more waves at the same point in space.

2. **Constructive interference** occurs when the waves arrive in phase with each other: a crest of one wave arrives at the same time as a crest of the other wave. The amplitudes of the waves then add to form a larger amplitude. Constructive interference also occurs when the path difference is exactly one full wavelength or any integer multiple of a full wavelength: $1\lambda, 2\lambda, 3\lambda, \cdots$.

3. **Destructive interference** occurs when a crest of one wave arrives at the same time as a trough of the other wave. The amplitudes add, but they are of opposite sign, so the total amplitude is reduced to zero if the two amplitudes are equal. Destructive interference occurs whenever the phase difference is half a wave cycle, or the path difference is a half-integral number of wavelengths. Thus, the total amplitude will be zero if two identical waves arrive one-half wavelength out of phase, or $(m + \frac{1}{2})\lambda$ out of phase, where m is an integer.

4. For thin-film interference, an extra half-wavelength **phase shift** occurs when light **reflects** from an optically more dense medium (going from a material of lesser toward greater index of refraction).

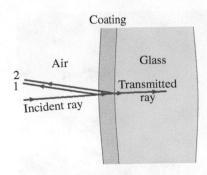

FIGURE 34–23 Example 34–8. Incident ray of light is partially reflected at the front surface of a lens coating (ray 1) and again partially reflected at the rear surface of the coating (ray 2), with most of the energy passing as the transmitted ray into the glass.

EXAMPLE 34–8 **Nonreflective coating.** What is the thickness of an optical coating of MgF$_2$ whose index of refraction is $n = 1.38$ and which is designed to eliminate reflected light at wavelengths (in air) around 550 nm when incident normally on glass for which $n = 1.50$?

APPROACH We explicitly follow the procedure outlined in the Problem Solving Strategy on page 913.

SOLUTION

1. **Interference effects.** Consider two rays reflected from the front and rear surfaces of the coating on the lens as shown in Fig. 34–23. The rays are drawn not quite perpendicular to the lens so we can see each of them. These two reflected rays will interfere with each other.

2. **Constructive interference.** We want to eliminate reflected light, so we do not consider constructive interference.

3. **Destructive interference.** To eliminate reflection, we want reflected rays 1 and 2 to be $\frac{1}{2}$ cycle out of phase with each other so that they destructively interfere. The phase difference is due to the path difference $2t$ traveled by ray 2, as well as any phase change in either ray due to reflection.

4. **Reflection phase shift.** Rays 1 and 2 *both* undergo a change of phase by $\frac{1}{2}$ cycle when they reflect from the coating's front and rear surfaces, respectively (at both surfaces the index of refraction increases). Thus there is no net change in phase due to the reflections. The net phase difference will be due to the extra path $2t$ taken by ray 2 in the coating, where $n = 1.38$. We want $2t$ to equal $\frac{1}{2}\lambda_n$ so that destructive interference occurs, where $\lambda_n = \lambda/n$ is the wavelength in the coating. With $2t = \lambda_n/2 = \lambda/2n$, then

$$t = \frac{\lambda_n}{4} = \frac{\lambda}{4n} = \frac{(550 \text{ nm})}{(4)(1.38)} = 99.6 \text{ nm}.$$

NOTE We could have set $2t = \left(m + \frac{1}{2}\right)\lambda_n$, where m is an integer. The smallest thickness ($m = 0$) is usually chosen because destructive interference will occur over the widest angle.

NOTE Complete destructive interference occurs only for the given wavelength of visible light. Longer and shorter wavelengths will have only partial cancellation.

*34–6 Michelson Interferometer

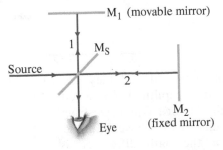

FIGURE 34–24 Michelson interferometer.

A useful instrument involving wave interference is the **Michelson interferometer** (Fig. 34–24),[†] invented by the American Albert A. Michelson (Section 31–7). Monochromatic light from a single point on an extended source is shown striking a half-silvered mirror M_S. This **beam splitter** mirror M_S has a thin layer of silver that reflects only half the light that hits it, so that half of the beam passes through to a fixed mirror M_2, where it is reflected back. The other half is reflected by M_S to a mirror M_1 that is movable (by a fine-thread screw), where it is also reflected back. Upon its return, part of beam 1 passes through M_S and reaches the eye; and part of beam 2, on its return, is reflected by M_S into the eye. If the two path lengths are identical, the two coherent beams entering the eye constructively interfere and brightness will be seen. If the movable mirror is moved a distance $\lambda/4$, one beam will travel an extra distance equal to $\lambda/2$ (because it travels back and forth over the distance $\lambda/4$). In this case, the two beams will destructively interfere and darkness will be seen. As M_1 is moved farther, brightness will recur (when the path difference is λ), then darkness, and so on.

Very precise length measurements can be made with an interferometer. The motion of mirror M_1 by only $\frac{1}{4}\lambda$ produces a clear difference between brightness and darkness. For $\lambda = 400$ nm, this means a precision of 100 nm or 10^{-4} mm! If mirror M_1 is tilted very slightly, the bright or dark spots are seen instead as a series of bright and dark lines or "fringes." By counting the number of fringes (or fractions thereof) that pass a reference line, extremely precise length measurements can be made.

[†]There are other types of interferometer, but Michelson's is the best known.

*34–7 Luminous Intensity

The *intensity* of light, as for any electromagnetic wave, is measured by the Poynting vector in W/m², and the total power output of a source can be measured in watts (the *radiant flux*). But for measuring the visual sensation we call brightness, we must consider *only* the visible spectrum as well as the eye's sensitivity to different wavelengths—the eye is most sensitive in the central, 550-nm (green), portion of the spectrum.

These factors are taken into account in the quantity **luminous flux**, F_ℓ, whose unit is the **lumen** (lm). One lumen is equivalent to $\frac{1}{683}$ watts of 555-nm light.

Since the luminous flux from a source may not be uniform over all directions, we define the **luminous intensity** I_ℓ as the luminous flux per unit solid angle[†] (steradian). Its unit is the **candela** (cd) where $1\,\text{cd} = 1\,\text{lm/sr}$, and it is one of the seven basic quantities in the SI. (See Section 1–4 and Table 1–5.)

The **illuminance**, E_ℓ, is the luminous flux incident on a surface per unit area of the surface: $E_\ell = F_\ell/A$. Its unit is the lumen per square meter (lm/m^2) and is a measure of the illumination falling on a surface.[‡]

EXAMPLE 34–9 **Lightbulb illuminance.** The brightness of a particular type of 100-W lightbulb is rated at 1700 lm. Determine (*a*) the luminous intensity and (*b*) the illuminance at a distance of 2.0 m.

APPROACH Assume the light output is uniform in all directions.

SOLUTION (*a*) A full sphere corresponds to 4π sr. Hence, $I_\ell = 1700\,\text{lm}/4\pi\,\text{sr} = 135\,\text{cd}$. It does not depend on distance. (*b*) At $d = 2.0\,\text{m}$ from the source, the luminous flux per unit area is

$$E_\ell = \frac{F_\ell}{4\pi d^2} = \frac{1700\,\text{lm}}{(4\pi)(2.0\,\text{m})^2} = 34\,\text{lm/m}^2.$$

The illuminance decreases as the square of the distance.

[†]A solid angle is a sort of two-dimensional angle and is measured in steradians. Think of a solid angle starting at a point and intercepting an area ΔA on a sphere of radius r surrounding that point. The solid angle has magnitude $\Delta A/r^2$ steradians. A solid angle including all of space intercepts the full surface area of the sphere, $4\pi r^2$, and so has magnitude $4\pi r^2/r^2 = 4\pi$ steradians. (Compare to a normal angle, for which a full circle subtends 2π radians.)

[‡]The British unit is the foot-candle, or lumen per square foot.

Summary

The wave theory of light is strongly supported by the observations that light exhibits **interference** and **diffraction**. Wave theory also explains the refraction of light and the fact that light travels more slowly in transparent solids and liquids than it does in air.

An aid to predicting wave behavior is **Huygens' principle**, which states that every point on a wave front can be considered as a source of tiny wavelets that spread out in the forward direction at the speed of the wave itself. The new wave front is the envelope (the common tangent) of all the wavelets.

The wavelength of light in a medium with index of refraction n is

$$\lambda_n = \frac{\lambda}{n}, \qquad (34–1)$$

where λ is the wavelength in vacuum; the frequency is not changed.

Young's double-slit experiment clearly demonstrated the interference of light. The observed bright spots of the interference pattern are explained as constructive interference between the beams coming through the two slits, where the beams differ in path length by an integral number of wavelengths. The dark areas in between are due to destructive interference when the path lengths differ by $\frac{1}{2}\lambda, \frac{3}{2}\lambda$, and so on. The angles θ at which **constructive interference** occurs are given by

$$\sin\theta = m\frac{\lambda}{d}, \qquad (34–2a)$$

where λ is the wavelength of the light, d is the separation of the slits, and m is an integer $(0, 1, 2, \cdots)$. **Destructive interference** occurs at angles θ given by

$$\sin\theta = \left(m + \tfrac{1}{2}\right)\frac{\lambda}{d}, \qquad (34–2b)$$

where m is an integer $(0, 1, 2, \cdots)$.

The light intensity I_θ at any point in a double-slit interference pattern can be calculated using a phasor diagram, which predicts that

$$I_\theta = I_0 \cos^2 \frac{\delta}{2} \tag{34–6}$$

where I_0 is the intensity at $\theta = 0$ and the phase angle δ is

$$\delta = \frac{2\pi d}{\lambda} \sin \theta. \tag{34–4}$$

Two sources of light are perfectly **coherent** if the waves leaving them are of the same single frequency and maintain the same phase relationship at all times. If the light waves from the two sources have a random phase with respect to each other over time (as for two incandescent lightbulbs) the two sources are **incoherent**.

Light reflected from the front and rear surfaces of a thin film of transparent material can interfere constructively or destructively, depending on the path difference. A phase change of 180° or $\frac{1}{2}\lambda$ occurs when the light reflects at a surface where the index of refraction increases. Such **thin-film interference** has many practical applications, such as lens coatings and using Newton's rings to check the uniformity of glass surfaces.

Questions

1. Does Huygens' principle apply to sound waves? To water waves?
2. What is the evidence that light is energy?
3. Why is light sometimes described as rays and sometimes as waves?
4. We can hear sounds around corners but we cannot see around corners; yet both sound and light are waves. Explain the difference.
5. Can the wavelength of light be determined from reflection or refraction measurements?
6. Two rays of light from the same source destructively interfere if their path lengths differ by how much?
7. Monochromatic red light is incident on a double slit and the interference pattern is viewed on a screen some distance away. Explain how the fringe pattern would change if the red light source is replaced by a blue light source.
8. If Young's double-slit experiment were submerged in water, how would the fringe pattern be changed?

9. Compare a double-slit experiment for sound waves to that for light waves. Discuss the similarities and differences.
10. Suppose white light falls on the two slits of Fig. 34–7, but one slit is covered by a red filter (700 nm) and the other by a blue filter (450 nm). Describe the pattern on the screen.
11. Why doesn't the light from the two headlights of a distant car produce an interference pattern?
12. Why are interference fringes noticeable only for a *thin* film like a soap bubble and not for a thick piece of glass, say?
13. Why are Newton's rings (Fig. 34–18) closer together farther from the center?
14. Some coated lenses appear greenish yellow when seen by reflected light. What wavelengths do you suppose the coating is designed to eliminate completely?
15. A drop of oil on a pond appears bright at its edges where its thickness is much less than the wavelengths of visible light. What can you say about the index of refraction of the oil compared to that of water?

Problems

34–2 Huygens' Principle

1. (II) Derive the law of reflection—namely, that the angle of incidence equals the angle of reflection from a flat surface—using Huygens' principle for waves.

34–3 Double-Slit Interference

2. (I) Monochromatic light falling on two slits 0.018 mm apart produces the fifth-order bright fringe at a 9.8° angle. What is the wavelength of the light used?
3. (I) The third-order bright fringe of 610 nm light is observed at an angle of 28° when the light falls on two narrow slits. How far apart are the slits?
4. (II) Monochromatic light falls on two very narrow slits 0.048 mm apart. Successive fringes on a screen 6.00 m away are 8.5 cm apart near the center of the pattern. Determine the wavelength and frequency of the light.
5. (II) If 720-nm and 660-nm light passes through two slits 0.68 mm apart, how far apart are the second-order fringes for these two wavelengths on a screen 1.0 m away?
6. (II) A red laser from the physics lab is marked as producing 632.8-nm light. When light from this laser falls on two closely spaced slits, an interference pattern formed on a wall several meters away has bright fringes spaced 5.00 mm apart near the center of the pattern. When the laser is replaced by a small laser pointer, the fringes are 5.14 mm apart. What is the wavelength of light produced by the pointer?

7. (II) Light of wavelength λ passes through a pair of slits separated by 0.17 mm, forming a double-slit interference pattern on a screen located a distance 35 cm away. Suppose that the image in Fig. 34–9a is an actual-size reproduction of this interference pattern. Use a ruler to measure a pertinent distance on this image; then utilize this measured value to determine λ (nm).
8. (II) Light of wavelength 680 nm falls on two slits and produces an interference pattern in which the third-order bright fringe is 38 mm from the central fringe on a screen 2.6 m away. What is the separation of the two slits?
9. (II) A parallel beam of light from a He–Ne laser, with a wavelength 633 nm, falls on two very narrow slits 0.068 mm apart. How far apart are the fringes in the center of the pattern on a screen 3.8 m away?
10. (II) A physics professor wants to perform a lecture demonstration of Young's double-slit experiment for her class using the 633-nm light from a He–Ne laser. Because the lecture hall is very large, the interference pattern will be projected on a wall that is 5.0 m from the slits. For easy viewing by all students in the class, the professor wants the distance between the $m = 0$ and $m = 1$ maxima to be 25 cm. What slit separation is required in order to produce the desired interference pattern?

11. (II) Suppose a thin piece of glass is placed in front of the lower slit in Fig. 34–7 so that the two waves enter the slits 180° out of phase (Fig. 34–25). Describe in detail the interference pattern on the screen.

FIGURE 34–25
Problem 11.

12. (II) In a double-slit experiment it is found that blue light of wavelength 480 nm gives a second-order maximum at a certain location on the screen. What wavelength of visible light would have a minimum at the same location?

13. (II) Two narrow slits separated by 1.0 mm are illuminated by 544 nm light. Find the distance between adjacent bright fringes on a screen 5.0 m from the slits.

14. (II) In a double-slit experiment, the third-order maximum for light of wavelength 500 nm is located 12 mm from the central bright spot on a screen 1.6 m from the slits. Light of wavelength 650 nm is then projected through the same slits. How far from the central bright spot will the second-order maximum of this light be located?

15. (II) Light of wavelength 470 nm in air falls on two slits 6.00×10^{-2} mm apart. The slits are immersed in water, as is a viewing screen 50.0 cm away. How far apart are the fringes on the screen?

16. (II) A very thin sheet of plastic $(n = 1.60)$ covers one slit of a double-slit apparatus illuminated by 680-nm light. The center point on the screen, instead of being a maximum, is dark. What is the (minimum) thickness of the plastic?

*34–4 Intensity in Two-Slit Interference

*17. (I) If one slit in Fig. 34–12 is covered, by what factor does the intensity at the center of the screen change?

*18. (II) Derive an expression similar to Eq. 34–2 which gives the angles for which the double-slit intensity is one-half its maximum value, $I_\theta = \frac{1}{2} I_0$.

*19. (II) Show that the angular full width at half maximum of the central peak in a double-slit interference pattern is given by $\Delta\theta = \lambda/2d$ if $\lambda \ll d$.

*20. (II) In a two-slit interference experiment, the path length to a certain point P on the screen differs for one slit in comparison with the other by 1.25λ. (a) What is the phase difference between the two waves arriving at point P? (b) Determine the intensity at P, expressed as a fraction of the maximum intensity I_0 on the screen.

*21. (III) Suppose that one slit of a double-slit apparatus is wider than the other so that the intensity of light passing through it is twice as great. Determine the intensity I as a function of position (θ) on the screen for coherent light.

*22. (III) (a) Consider three equally spaced and equal-intensity coherent sources of light (such as adding a third slit to the two slits of Fig. 34–12). Use the phasor method to obtain the intensity as a function of the phase difference δ (Eq. 34–4). (b) Determine the positions of maxima and minima.

34–5 Thin-Film Interference

23. (I) If a soap bubble is 120 nm thick, what wavelength is most strongly reflected at the center of the outer surface when illuminated normally by white light? Assume that $n = 1.32$.

24. (I) How far apart are the dark fringes in Example 34–6 if the glass plates are each 28.5 cm long?

25. (II) (a) What is the smallest thickness of a soap film $(n = 1.33)$ that would appear black if illuminated with 480-nm light? Assume there is air on both sides of the soap film. (b) What are two other possible thicknesses for the film to appear black? (c) If the thickness t was much less than λ, why would the film also appear black?

26. (II) A lens appears greenish yellow $(\lambda = 570$ nm is strongest) when white light reflects from it. What minimum thickness of coating $(n = 1.25)$ do you think is used on such a glass $(n = 1.52)$ lens, and why?

27. (II) A thin film of oil $(n_o = 1.50)$ with varying thickness floats on water $(n_w = 1.33)$. When it is illuminated from above by white light, the reflected colors are as shown in Fig. 34–26. In air, the wavelength of yellow light is 580 nm. (a) Why are there no reflected colors at point A? (b) What is the oil's thickness t at point B?

FIGURE 34–26
Problem 27.

28. (II) A thin oil slick $(n_o = 1.50)$ floats on water $(n_w = 1.33)$. When a beam of white light strikes this film at normal incidence from air, the only enhanced reflected colors are red (650 nm) and violet (390 nm). From this information, deduce the (minimum) thickness t of the oil slick.

29. (II) A total of 31 bright and 31 dark Newton's rings (not counting the dark spot at the center) are observed when 560-nm light falls normally on a planoconvex lens resting on a flat glass surface (Fig. 34–18). How much thicker is the center than the edges?

30. (II) A fine metal foil separates one end of two pieces of optically flat glass, as in Fig. 34–20. When light of wavelength 670 nm is incident normally, 28 dark lines are observed (with one at each end). How thick is the foil?

31. (II) How thick (minimum) should the air layer be between two flat glass surfaces if the glass is to appear bright when 450-nm light is incident normally? What if the glass is to appear dark?

32. (II) A uniform thin film of alcohol $(n = 1.36)$ lies on a flat glass plate $(n = 1.56)$. When monochromatic light, whose wavelength can be changed, is incident normally, the reflected light is a minimum for $\lambda = 512$ nm and a maximum for $\lambda = 635$ nm. What is the minimum thickness of the film?

33. (II) Show that the radius r of the mth dark Newton's ring, as viewed from directly above (Fig. 34–18), is given by $r = \sqrt{m\lambda R}$ where R is the radius of curvature of the curved glass surface and λ is the wavelength of light used. Assume that the thickness of the air gap is much less than R at all points and that $r \ll R$. [Hint: Use the binomial expansion.]

34. (II) Use the result of Problem 33 to show that the distance between adjacent dark Newton's rings is

$$\Delta r \approx \sqrt{\frac{\lambda R}{4m}}$$

for the mth ring, assuming $m \gg 1$.

35. (II) When a Newton's ring apparatus (Fig. 34–18) is immersed in a liquid, the diameter of the eighth dark ring decreases from 2.92 cm to 2.54 cm. What is the refractive index of the liquid? [Hint: see Problem 33.]

36. (II) A planoconvex lucite lens 3.4 cm in diameter is placed on a flat piece of glass as in Fig. 34–18. When 580-nm light is incident normally, 44 bright rings are observed, the last one right at the edge. What is the radius of curvature of the lens surface, and the focal length of the lens? [Hint: see Problem 33.]

37. (II) Let's explore why only "thin" layers exhibit thin-film interference. Assume a layer of water, sitting atop a flat glass surface, is illuminated from the air above by white light (all wavelengths from 400 nm to 700 nm). Further, assume that the water layer's thickness t is much greater than a micron ($= 1000$ nm); in particular, let $t = 200\,\mu$m. Take the index of refraction for water to be $n = 1.33$ for all visible wavelengths. (a) Show that a visible color will be reflected from the water layer if its wavelength is $\lambda = 2nt/m$, where m is an integer. (b) Show that the two extremes in wavelengths (400 nm and 700 nm) of the incident light are both reflected from the water layer and determine the m-value associated with each. (c) How many other visible wavelengths, besides $\lambda = 400$ nm and 700 nm, are reflected from the "thick" layer of water? (d) How does this explain why such a thick layer does not reflect colorfully, but is white or grey?

38. (III) A single optical coating reduces reflection to zero for $\lambda = 550$ nm. By what factor is the intensity reduced by the coating for $\lambda = 430$ nm and $\lambda = 670$ nm as compared to no coating? Assume normal incidence.

*39. (II) How far must the mirror M_1 in a Michelson interferometer be moved if 650 fringes of 589-nm light are to pass by a reference line?

*40. (II) What is the wavelength of the light entering an interferometer if 384 bright fringes are counted when the movable mirror moves 0.125 mm?

*41. (II) A micrometer is connected to the movable mirror of an interferometer. When the micrometer is tightened down on a thin metal foil, the net number of bright fringes that move, compared to the empty micrometer, is 272. What is the thickness of the foil? The wavelength of light used is 589 nm.

*42. (III) One of the beams of an interferometer (Fig. 34–27) passes through a small evacuated glass container 1.155 cm deep. When a gas is allowed to slowly fill the container, a total of 176 dark fringes are counted to move past a reference line. The light used has a wavelength of 632.8 nm. Calculate the index of refraction of the gas at its final density, assuming that the interferometer is in vacuum.

FIGURE 34–27 Problem 42.

*43. (III) The yellow sodium D lines have wavelengths of 589.0 and 589.6 nm. When they are used to illuminate a Michelson interferometer, it is noted that the interference fringes disappear and reappear periodically as the mirror M_1 is moved. Why does this happen? How far must the mirror move between one disappearance and the next?

*44. (II) The illuminance of direct sunlight on Earth is about 10^5 lm/m^2. Estimate the luminous flux and luminous intensity of the Sun.

*45. (II) The *luminous efficiency* of a lightbulb is the ratio of luminous flux to electric power input. (a) What is the luminous efficiency of a 100-W, 1700-lm bulb? (b) How many 40-W, 60-lm/W fluorescent lamps would be needed to provide an illuminance of 250 lm/m^2 on a factory floor of area 25 m × 30 m? Assume the lights are 10 m above the floor and that half their flux reaches the floor.

General Problems

46. Light of wavelength 5.0×10^{-7} m passes through two parallel slits and falls on a screen 4.0 m away. Adjacent bright bands of the interference pattern are 2.0 cm apart. (a) Find the distance between the slits. (b) The same two slits are next illuminated by light of a different wavelength, and the fifth-order minimum for this light occurs at the same point on the screen as the fourth-order minimum for the previous light. What is the wavelength of the second source of light?

47. Television and radio waves reflecting from mountains or airplanes can interfere with the direct signal from the station. (a) What kind of interference will occur when 75-MHz television signals arrive at a receiver directly from a distant station, and are reflected from a nearby airplane 122 m directly above the receiver? Assume $\frac{1}{2}\lambda$ change in phase of the signal upon reflection. (b) What kind of interference will occur if the plane is 22 m closer to the receiver?

48. A radio station operating at 88.5 MHz broadcasts from two identical antennas at the same elevation but separated by a 9.0-m horizontal distance d, Fig. 34–28. A maximum signal is found along the midline, perpendicular to d at its midpoint and extending horizontally in both directions. If the midline is taken as 0°, at what other angle(s) θ is a maximum signal detected? A minimum signal? Assume all measurements are made much farther than 9.0 m from the antenna towers.

FIGURE 34–28
Problem 48.

49. Light of wavelength 690 nm passes through two narrow slits 0.66 mm apart. The screen is 1.60 m away. A second source of unknown wavelength produces its second-order fringe 1.23 mm closer to the central maximum than the 690-nm light. What is the wavelength of the unknown light?

50. Monochromatic light of variable wavelength is incident normally on a thin sheet of plastic film in air. The reflected light is a maximum only for $\lambda = 491.4$ nm and $\lambda = 688.0$ nm in the visible spectrum. What is the thickness of the film $(n = 1.58)$? [*Hint*: Assume successive values of m.]

*51. Suppose the mirrors in a Michelson interferometer are perfectly aligned and the path lengths to mirrors M_1 and M_2 are identical. With these initial conditions, an observer sees a bright maximum at the center of the viewing area. Now one of the mirrors is moved a distance x. Determine a formula for the intensity at the center of the viewing area as a function of x, the distance the movable mirror is moved from the initial position.

52. A highly reflective mirror can be made for a particular wavelength at normal incidence by using two thin layers of transparent materials of indices of refraction n_1 and $n_2 (1 < n_1 < n_2)$ on the surface of the glass $(n > n_2)$. What should be the minimum thicknesses d_1 and d_2 in Fig. 34–29 in terms of the incident wavelength λ, to maximize reflection?

FIGURE 34–29
Problem 52.

53. Calculate the minimum thickness needed for an antireflective coating $(n = 1.38)$ applied to a glass lens in order to eliminate (*a*) blue (450 nm), or (*b*) red (720 nm) reflections for light at normal incidence.

54. Stealth aircraft are designed to not reflect radar, whose wavelength is typically 2 cm, by using an antireflecting coating. Ignoring any change in wavelength in the coating, estimate its thickness.

55. Light of wavelength λ strikes a screen containing two slits a distance d apart at an angle θ_i to the normal. Determine the angle θ_m at which the mth-order maximum occurs.

56. Consider two antennas radiating 6.0-MHz radio waves in phase with each other. They are located at points S_1 and S_2, separated by a distance $d = 175$ m, Fig. 34–30. Determine the points on the y axis where the signals from the two sources will be out of phase (crests of one meet troughs of the other).

FIGURE 34–30
Problem 56.

57. What is the minimum (non-zero) thickness for the air layer between two flat glass surfaces if the glass is to appear dark when 680-nm light is incident normally? What if the glass is to appear bright?

58. *Lloyd's mirror* provides one way of obtaining a double-slit interference pattern from a single source so the light is coherent. As shown in Fig. 34–31, the light that reflects from the plane mirror appears to come from the virtual image of the slit. Describe in detail the interference pattern on the screen.

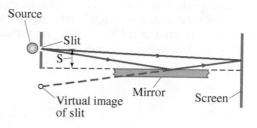

FIGURE 34–31   Problem 58.

59. Consider the antenna array of Example 34–5, Fig. 34–15. Let $d = \lambda/2$, and suppose that the two antennas are now 180° out of phase with each other. Find the directions for constructive and destructive interference, and compare with the case when the sources are in phase. (These results illustrate the basis for directional antennas.)

60. Suppose you viewed the light *transmitted* through a thin film layered on a flat piece of glass. Draw a diagram, similar to Fig. 34–17 or 34–23, and describe the conditions required for maxima and minima. Consider all possible values of index of refraction. Discuss the relative size of the minima compared to the maxima and to zero.

61. A thin film of soap $(n = 1.34)$ coats a piece of flat glass $(n = 1.52)$. How thick is the film if it reflects 643-nm red light most strongly when illuminated normally by white light?

62. Two identical sources S_1 and S_2, separated by distance d, coherently emit light of wavelength λ uniformly in all directions. Defining the x axis with its origin at S_1 as shown in Fig. 34–32, find the locations (expressed as multiples of λ) where the signals from the two sources are out of phase along this axis for $x > 0$, if $d = 3\lambda$.

FIGURE 34–32
Problem 62.

63. A two-slit interference set-up with slit separation $d = 0.10\ \text{mm}$ produces interference fringes at a particular set of angles θ_m (where $m = 0, 1, 2, \ldots$) for red light of frequency $f = 4.6 \times 10^{14}\ \text{Hz}$. If one wishes to construct an analogous two-slit interference set-up that produces interference fringes at the same set of angles θ_m for room-temperature sound of middle-C frequency $f_S = 262\ \text{Hz}$, what should the slit separation d_S be for this analogous set-up?

64. A radio telescope, whose two antennas are separated by 55 m, is designed to receive 3.0-MHz radio waves produced by astronomical objects. The received radio waves create 3.0-MHz electronic signals in the telescope's left and right antennas. These signals then travel by equal-length cables to a centrally located amplifier, where they are added together. The telescope can be "pointed" to a certain region of the sky by adding the instantaneous signal from the right antenna to a "time-delayed" signal received by the left antenna a time Δt ago. (This time delay of the left signal can be easily accomplished with the proper electronic circuit.) If a radio astronomer wishes to "view" radio signals arriving from an object oriented at a $12°$ angle to the vertical as in Fig. 34–33, what time delay Δt is necessary?

FIGURE 34–33
Problem 64.

65. In a compact disc (CD), digital information is stored as a sequence of raised surfaces called "pits" and recessed surfaces called "lands." Both pits and lands are highly reflective and are embedded in a thick plastic material with index of refraction $n = 1.55$ (Fig. 34–34). As a 780-nm wavelength (in air) laser scans across the pit–land sequence, the transition between a neighboring pit and land is sensed by monitoring the intensity of reflected laser light from the CD. At the moment when half the width of the laser beam is reflected from the pit and the other half from the land, we want the two reflected halves of the beam to be $180°$ out of phase with each other. What should be the (minimum) height difference t between a pit and land? [When this light enters a detector, cancellation of the two out-of-phase halves of the beam produces a minimum detector output.]

FIGURE 34–34
Problem 65.

*Numerical/Computer

*66. (II) A Michelson interferometer can be used to determine the index of refraction of a glass plate. A glass plate (thickness t) is placed on a platform that can rotate. The plate is placed in the light's path between the beam splitter and either the fixed or movable mirror, so that its thickness is in the direction of the laser beam. The platform is rotated to various angles, and the number of fringes shifted is counted. It can be shown that if N is the number of fringes shifted when the angle of rotation changes by θ, the index of refraction is $n = (2t - N\lambda)(1 - \cos\theta)/[2t(1 - \cos\theta) - N\lambda]$ where t is the thickness of the plate. The accompanying Table shows the data collected by a student in determining the index of refraction of a transparent plate by a Michelson interferometer.

N	25	50	75	100	125	150
θ (degree)	5.5	6.9	8.6	10.0	11.3	12.5

In the experiment $\lambda = 632.8\ \text{nm}$ and $t = 4.0\ \text{mm}$. Determine n for each θ and find the average n.

Answers to Exercises

A: 333 nm; $6.0 \times 10^{14}\ \text{Hz}$; $2.0 \times 10^8\ \text{m/s}$.

B: (a) I_0; (b) $0.50I_0$; (c) 0.

C: (e).

Parallel coherent light from a laser, which acts as nearly a point source, illuminates these shears. Instead of a clean shadow, there is a dramatic diffraction pattern, which is a strong confirmation of the wave theory of light. Diffraction patterns are washed out when typical extended sources of light are used, and hence are not seen, although a careful examination of shadows will reveal fuzziness. We will examine diffraction by a single slit, and how it affects the double-slit pattern. We also discuss diffraction gratings and diffraction of X-rays by crystals. We will see how diffraction affects the resolution of optical instruments, and that the ultimate resolution can never be greater than the wavelength of the radiation used. Finally we study the polarization of light.

Diffraction and Polarization

C H A P T E R 35

CHAPTER-OPENING QUESTION—Guess now!

Because of diffraction, a light microscope has a maximum useful magnification of about

(a) 50×;
(b) 100×;
(c) 500×;
(d) 2000×;
(e) 5000×;

and the smallest objects it can resolve have a size of about

(a) 10 nm;
(b) 100 nm;
(c) 500 nm;
(d) 2500 nm;
(e) 5500 nm.

Young's double-slit experiment put the wave theory of light on a firm footing. But full acceptance came only with studies on diffraction more than a decade later, in the 1810s and 1820s.

We have already discussed diffraction briefly with regard to water waves (Section 15–11) as well as for light (Section 34–1). We have seen that it refers to the spreading or bending of waves around edges. Now we look at diffraction in more detail, including its important practical effects of limiting the amount of detail, or *resolution*, that can be obtained with any optical instrument such as telescopes, cameras, and the eye.

CONTENTS

FIGURE 35–1 If light is a wave, a bright spot will appear at the center of the shadow of a solid disk illuminated by a point source of monochromatic light.

In 1819, Augustin Fresnel (1788–1827) presented to the French Academy a wave theory of light that predicted and explained interference and diffraction effects. Almost immediately Siméon Poisson (1781–1840) pointed out a counter-intuitive inference: according to Fresnel's wave theory, if light from a point source were to fall on a solid disk, part of the incident light would be diffracted around the edges and would constructively interfere at the center of the shadow (Fig. 35–1). That prediction seemed very unlikely. But when the experiment was actually carried out by François Arago, the bright spot was seen at the very center of the shadow (Fig. 35–2a). This was strong evidence for the wave theory.

Figure 35–2a is a photograph of the shadow cast by a coin using a coherent point source of light, a laser in this case. The bright spot is clearly present at the center. Note also the bright and dark fringes beyond the shadow. These resemble the interference fringes of a double slit. Indeed, they are due to interference of waves diffracted around the disk, and the whole is referred to as a **diffraction pattern**. A diffraction pattern exists around any sharp-edged object illuminated by a point source, as shown in Fig. 35–2b and c. We are not always aware of diffraction because most sources of light in everyday life are not points, so light from different parts of the source washes out the pattern.

FIGURE 35–2 Diffraction pattern of (a) a circular disk (a coin), (b) razorblade, (c) a single slit, each illuminated by a coherent point source of monochromatic light, such as a laser.

(a) (b) (c)

35–1 Diffraction by a Single Slit or Disk

To see how a diffraction pattern arises, we will analyze the important case of monochromatic light passing through a narrow slit. We will assume that parallel rays (plane waves) of light fall on the slit of width D, and pass through to a viewing screen very far away. If the viewing screen is not far away, lenses can be used to make the rays parallel.[†] As we know from studying water waves and from Huygens' principle, the waves passing through the slit spread out in all directions. We will now examine how the waves passing through different parts of the slit interfere with each other.

Parallel rays of monochromatic light pass through the narrow slit as shown in Fig. 35–3a. The slit width D is on the order of the wavelength λ of the light, but the slit's length (in and out of page) is large compared to λ. The light falls on a screen which is assumed to be very far away, so the rays heading for any point are very nearly parallel before they meet at the screen.

[†]Such a diffraction pattern, involving parallel rays, is called *Fraunhofer diffraction*. If the screen is close and no lenses are used, it is called *Fresnel diffraction*. The analysis in the latter case is rather involved, so we consider only the limiting case of Fraunhofer diffraction.

(a) $\theta = 0$
Bright

(b) $\sin \theta = \dfrac{\lambda}{D}$
Dark

(c) $\sin \theta = \dfrac{3\lambda}{2D}$
Bright

(d) $\sin \theta = \dfrac{2\lambda}{D}$
Dark

FIGURE 35–3 Analysis of diffraction pattern formed by light passing through a narrow slit of width D.

First we consider rays that pass straight through as in Fig. 35–3a. They are all in phase, so there will be a central bright spot on the screen (see Fig. 35–2c). In Fig. 35–3b, we consider rays moving at an angle θ such that the ray from the top of the slit travels exactly one wavelength farther than the ray from the bottom edge to reach the screen. The ray passing through the very center of the slit will travel one-half wavelength farther than the ray at the bottom of the slit. These two rays will be exactly out of phase with one another and so will destructively interfere when they overlap at the screen. Similarly, a ray slightly above the bottom one will cancel a ray that is the same distance above the central one. Indeed, each ray passing through the lower half of the slit will cancel with a corresponding ray passing through the upper half. Thus, all the rays destructively interfere in pairs, and so the light intensity will be zero on the viewing screen at this angle. The angle θ at which this takes place can be seen from Fig. 35–3b to occur when $\lambda = D \sin \theta$, so

$$ \sin \theta = \frac{\lambda}{D}. \qquad\qquad \text{[first minimum]} \quad \textbf{(35–1)} $$

The light intensity is a maximum at $\theta = 0°$ and decreases to a minimum (intensity = zero) at the angle θ given by Eq. 35–1.

Now consider a larger angle θ such that the top ray travels $\frac{3}{2}\lambda$ farther than the bottom ray, as in Fig. 35–3c. In this case, the rays from the bottom third of the slit will cancel in pairs with those in the middle third because they will be $\lambda/2$ out of phase. However, light from the top third of the slit will still reach the screen, so there will be a bright spot centered near $\sin \theta \approx 3\lambda/2D$, but it will not be nearly as bright as the central spot at $\theta = 0°$. For an even larger angle θ such that the top ray travels 2λ farther than the bottom ray, Fig. 35–3d, rays from the bottom quarter of the slit will cancel with those in the quarter just above it because the path lengths differ by $\lambda/2$. And the rays through the quarter of the slit just above center will cancel with those through the top quarter. At this angle there will again be a minimum of zero intensity in the diffraction pattern. A plot of the intensity as a function of angle is shown in Fig. 35–4. This corresponds well with the photo of Fig. 35–2c. Notice that minima (zero intensity) occur on both sides of center at

FIGURE 35–4 Intensity in the diffraction pattern of a single slit as a function of $\sin \theta$. Note that the central maximum is not only much higher than the maxima to each side, but it is also twice as wide ($2\lambda/D$ wide) as any of the others (only λ/D wide each).

$$ D \sin \theta = m\lambda, \qquad m = \pm 1, \pm 2, \pm 3, \cdots, \qquad \text{[minima]} \quad \textbf{(35–2)} $$

but *not* at $m = 0$ where there is the strongest maximum. Between the minima, smaller intensity maxima occur at approximately (not exactly) $m \approx \frac{3}{2}, \frac{5}{2}, \cdots$.

Note that the *minima* for a diffraction pattern, Eq. 35–2, satisfy a criterion that looks very similar to that for the *maxima* (bright fringes) for double-slit interference, Eq. 34–2a. Also note that D is a single slit width, whereas d in Eq. 34–2 is the distance between two slits.

⚠ **CAUTION**

Don't confuse Eqs. 34–2 for interference with Eq. 35–1 for diffraction: note the differences

FIGURE 35–5 Example 35–1.

EXAMPLE 35–1 **Single-slit diffraction maximum.** Light of wavelength 750 nm passes through a slit 1.0×10^{-3} mm wide. How wide is the central maximum (a) in degrees, and (b) in centimeters, on a screen 20 cm away?

APPROACH The width of the central maximum goes from the first minimum on one side to the first minimum on the other side. We use Eq. 35–1 to find the angular position of the first single-slit diffraction minimum.

SOLUTION (a) The first minimum occurs at

$$\sin \theta = \frac{\lambda}{D} = \frac{7.5 \times 10^{-7} \text{ m}}{1.0 \times 10^{-6} \text{ m}} = 0.75.$$

So $\theta = 49°$. This is the angle between the center and the first minimum, Fig. 35–5. The angle subtended by the whole central maximum, between the minima above and below the center, is twice this, or 98°.

(b) The width of the central maximum is $2x$, where $\tan \theta = x/20$ cm. So $2x = 2(20 \text{ cm})(\tan 49°) = 46$ cm.

NOTE A large width of the screen will be illuminated, but it will not normally be very bright since the amount of light that passes through such a small slit will be small and it is spread over a large area. Note also that we *cannot* use the small-angle approximation here ($\theta \approx \sin \theta \approx \tan \theta$) because θ is large.

EXERCISE A In Example 35–1, red light ($\lambda = 750$ nm) was used. If instead yellow light at 575 nm had been used, would the central maximum be wider or narrower?

FIGURE 35–6 Example 35–2.

Diffraction spreads. Light shines through a rectangular hole that is narrower in the vertical direction than the horizontal, Fig. 35–6. (a) Would you expect the diffraction pattern to be more spread out in the vertical direction or in the horizontal direction? (b) Should a rectangular loudspeaker horn at a stadium be high and narrow, or wide and flat?

RESPONSE (a) From Eq. 35–1 we can see that if we make the slit (width D) narrower, the pattern spreads out more. This is consistent with our study of waves in Chapter 15. The diffraction through the rectangular hole will be wider vertically, since the opening is smaller in that direction. (b) For a loudspeaker, the sound pattern desired is one spread out horizontally, so the horn should be tall and narrow (rotate Fig. 35–6 by 90°).

*35–2 Intensity in Single-Slit Diffraction Pattern

We have determined the positions of the minima in the diffraction pattern produced by light passing through a single slit, Eq. 35–2. We now discuss a method for predicting the amplitude and intensity at any point in the pattern using the phasor technique already discussed in Section 34–4.

Let us consider the slit divided into N very thin strips of width Δy as indicated in Fig. 35–7. Each strip sends light in all directions toward a screen on the right. Again we take the rays heading for any particular point on the distant screen to be parallel, all making an angle θ with the horizontal as shown. We choose the strip width Δy to be much smaller than the wavelength λ of the monochromatic light falling on the slit, so all the light from a given strip is in phase. The strips are of equal size, and if the whole slit is uniformly illuminated, we can take the electric field wave amplitudes ΔE_0 from each thin strip to be equal as long as θ is not too large. However, the separate amplitudes from the different strips will differ in phase. The phase difference in the light coming from adjacent strips will be (see Section 34–4, Eq. 34–4)

$$\Delta \beta = \frac{2\pi}{\lambda} \Delta y \sin \theta \tag{35–3}$$

since the difference in path length is $\Delta y \sin \theta$.

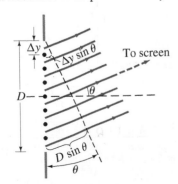

FIGURE 35–7 Slit of width D divided into N strips of width Δy.

The total amplitude on the screen at any angle θ will be the sum of the separate wave amplitudes due to each strip. These wavelets have the same amplitude ΔE_0 but differ in phase. To obtain the total amplitude, we can use a phasor diagram as we did in Section 34–4 (Fig. 34–13). The phasor diagrams for four different angles θ are shown in Fig. 35–8. At the center of the screen, $\theta = 0$, the waves from each strip are all in phase ($\Delta\beta = 0$, Eq. 35–3), so the arrows representing each ΔE_0 line up as shown in Fig. 35–8a. The total amplitude of the light arriving at the center of the screen is then $E_0 = N \Delta E_0$.

FIGURE 35–8 Phasor diagram for single-slit diffraction, giving the total amplitude E_θ at four different angles θ.

(a) At center, $\theta = 0$.

(b) Between center and first minimum.

(c) First minimum, $E_\theta = 0$ ($\beta = 2\pi = 360°$).

(d) Near secondary maximum.

At a small angle θ, for a point on the distant screen not far from the center, Fig. 35–8b shows how the wavelets of amplitude ΔE_0 add up to give E_θ, the total amplitude on the screen at this angle θ. Note that each wavelet differs in phase from the adjacent one by $\Delta\beta$. The phase difference between the wavelets from the top and bottom edges of the slit is

$$\beta = N \Delta\beta = \frac{2\pi}{\lambda} N \Delta y \sin\theta = \frac{2\pi}{\lambda} D \sin\theta \qquad (35\text{–}4)$$

where $D = N \Delta y$ is the total width of the slit. Although the "arc" in Fig. 35–8b has length $N \Delta E_0$, and so would equal E_0 (total amplitude at $\theta = 0$), the amplitude of the total wave E_θ at angle θ is the *vector* sum of each wavelet amplitude and so is equal to the length of the chord as shown. The chord is shorter than the arc, so $E_\theta < E_0$.

For greater θ, we eventually come to the case, illustrated in Fig. 35–8c, where the chain of arrows closes on itself. In this case the vector sum is zero, so $E_\theta = 0$ for this angle θ. This corresponds to the first minimum. Since $\beta = N \Delta\beta$ is 360° or 2π in this case, we have from Eq. 35–3,

$$2\pi = N \Delta\beta = N\left(\frac{2\pi}{\lambda} \Delta y \sin\theta\right)$$

or, since the slit width $D = N \Delta y$,

$$\sin\theta = \frac{\lambda}{D}.$$

Thus the first minimum $(E_\theta = 0)$ occurs where $\sin\theta = \lambda/D$, which is the same result we obtained in the previous Section, Eq. 35–1.

For even greater values of θ, the chain of arrows spirals beyond 360°. Figure 35–8d shows the case near the secondary maximum next to the first minimum. Here $\beta = N \Delta\beta \approx 360° + 180° = 540°$ or 3π. When greater angles θ are considered, new maxima and minima occur. But since the total length of the coil remains constant, equal to $N \Delta E_0 (= E_0)$, each succeeding maximum is smaller and smaller as the coil winds in on itself.

FIGURE 35–9 Determining amplitude E_θ as a function of θ for single-slit diffraction.

To obtain a quantitative expression for the amplitude (and intensity) for any point on the screen (that is, for any angle θ), we now consider the limit $N \to \infty$ so Δy becomes the infinitesimal width dy. In this case, the diagrams of Fig. 35–8 become smooth curves, one of which is shown in Fig. 35–9. For any angle θ, the wave amplitude on the screen is E_θ, equal to the chord in Fig. 35–9. The length of the arc is E_0, as before. If r is the radius of curvature of the arc, then

$$\frac{E_\theta}{2} = r \sin \frac{\beta}{2}.$$

Using radian measure for $\beta/2$, we also have

$$\frac{E_0}{2} = r \frac{\beta}{2}.$$

We combine these to obtain

$$E_\theta = E_0 \frac{\sin \beta/2}{\beta/2}. \tag{35–5}$$

The angle β is the phase difference between the waves from the top and bottom edges of the slit. The path difference for these two rays is $D \sin \theta$ (see Fig. 35–7 as well as Eq. 35–4), so

$$\beta = \frac{2\pi}{\lambda} D \sin \theta. \tag{35–6}$$

Intensity is proportional to the square of the wave amplitude, so the intensity I_θ at any angle θ is, from Eq. 35–5,

$$I_\theta = I_0 \left(\frac{\sin \beta/2}{\beta/2} \right)^2 \tag{35–7}$$

where I_0 ($\propto E_0^2$) is the intensity at $\theta = 0$ (the central maximum). We can combine Eqs. 35–7 and 35–6 (although it is often simpler to leave them as separate equations) to obtain

$$I_\theta = I_0 \left[\frac{\sin\left(\frac{\pi D \sin \theta}{\lambda} \right)}{\left(\frac{\pi D \sin \theta}{\lambda} \right)} \right]^2. \tag{35–8}$$

According to Eq. 35–8, minima ($I_\theta = 0$) occur where $\sin(\pi D \sin \theta/\lambda) = 0$, which means $\pi D \sin \theta/\lambda$ must be $\pi, 2\pi, 3\pi$, and so on, or

$$D \sin \theta = m\lambda, \qquad m = 1, 2, 3, \cdots \qquad \text{[minima]}$$

which is what we have obtained previously, Eq. 35–2. Notice that m cannot be zero: when $\beta/2 = \pi D \sin \theta/\lambda = 0$, the denominator as well as the numerator in Eqs. 35–7 or 35–8 vanishes. We can evaluate the intensity in this case by taking the limit as $\theta \to 0$ (or $\beta \to 0$); for very small angles, $\sin \beta/2 \approx \beta/2$, so $(\sin \beta/2)/(\beta/2) \to 1$ and $I_\theta = I_0$, the *maximum* at the center of the pattern.

The intensity I_θ as a function of θ, as given by Eq. 35–8, corresponds to the diagram of Fig. 35–4.

EXAMPLE 35–3 ESTIMATE | Intensity at secondary maxima. Estimate the intensities of the first two secondary maxima to either side of the central maximum.

APPROACH The secondary maxima occur close to halfway between the minima, at about

$$\frac{\beta}{2} = \frac{\pi D \sin \theta}{\lambda} \approx (m + \tfrac{1}{2})\pi. \qquad m = 1, 2, 3, \cdots$$

The actual maxima are not quite at these points—their positions can be determined by differentiating Eq. 35–7 (see Problem 14)—but we are only seeking an estimate.

SOLUTION Using these values for β in Eq. 35–7 or 35–8, with $\sin(m + \tfrac{1}{2})\pi = 1$, gives

$$I_\theta = \frac{I_0}{(m + \tfrac{1}{2})^2 \pi^2}. \qquad m = 1, 2, 3, \cdots$$

For $m = 1$ and 2, we get

$$I_\theta = \frac{I_0}{22.2} = 0.045 I_0 \qquad\qquad [m = 1]$$

$$I_\theta = \frac{I_0}{61.7} = 0.016 I_0. \qquad\qquad [m = 2]$$

The first maximum to the side of the central peak has only 1/22, or 4.5%, the intensity of the central peak, and succeeding ones are smaller still, just as we can see in Fig. 35–4 and the photo of Fig. 35–2c.

Diffraction by a circular opening produces a similar pattern (though circular rather than rectangular) and is of great practical importance, since lenses are essentially circular apertures through which light passes. We will discuss this in Section 35–4 and see how diffraction limits the resolution (or sharpness) of images.

*35–3 Diffraction in the Double-Slit Experiment

When we analyzed Young's double-slit experiment in Section 34–4, we assumed that the central portion of the screen was uniformly illuminated. This is equivalent to assuming the slits are infinitesimally narrow, so that the central diffraction peak is spread out over the whole screen. This can never be the case for real slits; diffraction reduces the intensity of the bright interference fringes to the side of center so they are not all of the same height as they were shown in Fig. 34–14. (They were shown more correctly in Fig. 34–9b.)

To calculate the intensity in a double-slit interference pattern, including diffraction, let us assume the slits have equal widths D and their centers are separated by a distance d. Since the distance to the screen is large compared to the slit separation d, the wave amplitude due to each slit is essentially the same at each point on the screen. Then the total wave amplitude at any angle θ will no longer be

$$E_{\theta 0} = 2E_0 \cos\frac{\delta}{2},$$

as was given by Eq. 34–5b. Rather, it must be modified, because of diffraction, by Eq. 35–5, so that

$$E_{\theta 0} = 2E_0 \left(\frac{\sin \beta/2}{\beta/2}\right) \cos\frac{\delta}{2}.$$

Thus the intensity will be given by

$$I_\theta = I_0 \left(\frac{\sin \beta/2}{\beta/2}\right)^2 \left(\cos\frac{\delta}{2}\right)^2 \qquad\qquad (35\text{–}9)$$

where $I_0 = 4E_0^2$, and from Eqs. 35–6 and 34–4 we have

$$\frac{\beta}{2} = \frac{\pi}{\lambda} D \sin\theta \qquad \text{and} \qquad \frac{\delta}{2} = \frac{\pi}{\lambda} d \sin\theta.$$

(a) Diffraction factor, $(\sin^2\beta/2)/(\beta/2)^2$ vs. θ

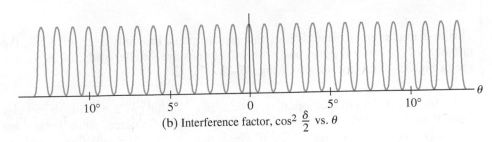

(b) Interference factor, $\cos^2\dfrac{\delta}{2}$ vs. θ

FIGURE 35–10
(a) Diffraction factor,
(b) interference factor, and
(c) the resultant intensity I_θ,
plotted as a function of θ
for $d = 6D = 60\lambda$.

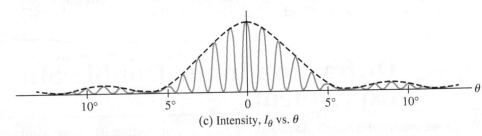

(c) Intensity, I_θ vs. θ

Equation 35–9 for the intensity in a double-slit pattern, as we just saw, is

$$I_\theta = I_0\left(\frac{\sin\beta/2}{\beta/2}\right)^2\left(\cos\frac{\delta}{2}\right)^2. \qquad (35\text{–}9)$$

The first term in parentheses is sometimes called the "diffraction factor" and the second one the "interference factor." These two factors are plotted in Fig. 35–10a and b for the case when $d = 6D$, and $D = 10\lambda$. (Figure 35–10b is essentially the same as Fig. 34–14.) Figure 35–10c shows the product of these two curves (times I_0) which is the actual intensity as a function of θ (or as a function of position on the screen for θ not too large) as given by Eq. 35–9. As indicated by the dashed lines in Fig. 35–10c, the diffraction factor acts as a sort of envelope that limits the interference peaks.

FIGURE 35–11 Photographs of a double-slit interference pattern using a laser beam showing effects of diffraction. In both cases $d = 0.50$ mm, whereas $D = 0.040$ mm in (a) and 0.080 mm in (b).

(a)

(b)

EXAMPLE 35–4 **Diffraction plus interference.** Show why the central diffraction peak in Fig. 35–10c contains 11 interference fringes.

APPROACH The first minimum in the diffraction pattern occurs where

$$\sin\theta = \frac{\lambda}{D}.$$

Since $d = 6D$,

$$d\sin\theta = 6D\left(\frac{\lambda}{D}\right) = 6\lambda.$$

SOLUTION From Eq. 34–2a, interference peaks (maxima) occur for $d\sin\theta = m\lambda$ where m can be $0, 1, \cdots$ or any integer. Thus the diffraction minimum ($d\sin\theta = 6\lambda$) coincides with $m = 6$ in the interference pattern, so the $m = 6$ peak won't appear. Hence the central diffraction peak encloses the central interference peak ($m = 0$) and five peaks ($m = 1$ to 5) on each side for a total of 11. Since the sixth order doesn't appear, it is said to be a "missing order."

Notice from Example 35–4 that the number of interference fringes in the central diffraction peak depends only on the ratio d/D. It does not depend on wavelength λ. The actual spacing (in angle, or in position on the screen) does depend on λ. For the case illustrated, $D = 10\lambda$, and so the first diffraction minimum occurs at $\sin\theta = \lambda/D = 0.10$ or about $6°$.

The decrease in intensity of the interference fringes away from the center, as graphed in Fig. 35–10, is shown in Fig. 35–11.

Interference vs. Diffraction

The patterns due to interference and diffraction arise from the same phenomenon—the superposition of coherent waves of different phase. The distinction between them is thus not so much physical as for convenience of description, as in this Section where we analyzed the two-slit pattern in terms of interference and diffraction separately. In general, we use the word "diffraction" when referring to an analysis by superposition of many infinitesimal and usually contiguous sources, such as when we subdivide a source into infinitesimal parts. We use the term "interference" when we superpose the wave from a finite (and usually small) number of coherent sources.

35–4 Limits of Resolution; Circular Apertures

The ability of a lens to produce distinct images of two point objects very close together is called the **resolution** of the lens. The closer the two images can be and still be seen as distinct (rather than overlapping blobs), the higher the resolution. The resolution of a camera lens, for example, is often specified as so many dots or lines per millimeter, as mentioned in Section 33–5.

Two principal factors limit the resolution of a lens. The first is lens aberrations. As we saw in Chapter 33, because of spherical and other aberrations, a point object is not a point on the image but a tiny blob. Careful design of compound lenses can reduce aberrations significantly, but they cannot be eliminated entirely. The second factor that limits resolution is *diffraction*, which cannot be corrected for because it is a natural result of the wave nature of light. We discuss it now.

In Section 35–1, we saw that because light travels as a wave, light from a point source passing through a slit is spread out into a diffraction pattern (Figs. 35–2 and 35–4). A lens, because it has edges, acts like a round slit. When a lens forms the image of a point object, the image is actually a tiny diffraction pattern. Thus *an image would be blurred even if aberrations were absent.*

In the analysis that follows, we assume that the lens is free of aberrations, so we can concentrate on diffraction effects and how much they limit the resolution of a lens. In Fig. 35–4 we saw that the diffraction pattern produced by light passing through a rectangular slit has a central maximum in which most of the light falls. This central peak falls to a minimum on either side of its center at an angle θ given by $\sin \theta = \lambda/D$ (this is Eq. 35–1), where D is the slit width and λ the wavelength of light used. θ is the angular half-width of the central maximum, and for small angles can be written

$$\theta \approx \sin \theta = \frac{\lambda}{D}.$$

There are also low-intensity fringes beyond.

For a lens, or any circular hole, the image of a point object will consist of a *circular* central peak (called the *diffraction spot* or *Airy disk*) surrounded by faint circular fringes, as shown in Fig. 35–12a. The central maximum has an angular half width given by

$$\theta = \frac{1.22\lambda}{D},$$

where D is the diameter of the circular opening. This is a theoretical result for a perfect circle or lens. For real lenses or circles, the factor is on the order of 1 to 2. This formula differs from that for a slit (Eq. 35–1) by the factor 1.22. This factor appears because the width of a circular hole is not uniform (like a rectangular slit) but varies from its diameter D to zero. A mathematical analysis shows that the "average" width is $D/1.22$. Hence we get the equation above rather than Eq. 35–1. The intensity of light in the diffraction pattern from a point source of light passing through a circular opening is shown in Fig. 35–13. The image for a non-point source is a superposition of such patterns. For most purposes we need consider only the central spot, since the concentric rings are so much dimmer.

If two point objects are very close, the diffraction patterns of their images will overlap as shown in Fig. 35–12b. As the objects are moved closer, a separation is

(a)

(b)

FIGURE 35–12 Photographs of images (greatly magnified) formed by a lens, showing the diffraction pattern of an image for: (a) a single point object; (b) two point objects whose images are barely resolved.

FIGURE 35–13 Intensity of light across the diffraction pattern of a circular hole.

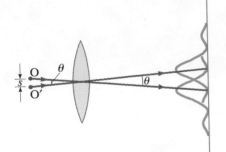

reached where you can't tell if there are two overlapping images or a single image. The separation at which this happens may be judged differently by different observers. However, a generally accepted criterion is that proposed by Lord Rayleigh (1842–1919). This **Rayleigh criterion** states that *two images are just resolvable when the center of the diffraction disk of one image is directly over the first minimum in the diffraction pattern of the other*. This is shown in Fig. 35–14. Since the first minimum is at an angle $\theta = 1.22\lambda/D$ from the central maximum, Fig. 35–14 shows that two objects can be considered *just resolvable* if they are separated by at least an angle θ given by

$$\theta = \frac{1.22\lambda}{D}. \qquad\qquad \text{[θ in radians]} \quad (35\text{–}10)$$

FIGURE 35–14 The *Rayleigh criterion*. Two images are just resolvable when the center of the diffraction peak of one is directly over the first minimum in the diffraction pattern of the other. The two point objects O and O′ subtend an angle θ at the lens; only one ray (it passes through the center of the lens) is drawn for each object, to indicate the center of the diffraction pattern of its image.

In this equation, D is the diameter of the lens, and applies also to a mirror diameter. This is the limit on resolution set by the wave nature of light due to diffraction. A smaller angle means better resolution: you can make out closer objects. We see from Eq. 35–10 that using a shorter wavelength λ can reduce θ and thus increase resolution.

EXERCISE B Green light (550 nm) passes through a 25-mm-diameter camera lens. What is the angular half-width of the resulting diffraction pattern? (*a*) 2.7×10^{-5} degrees, (*b*) 1.5×10^{-3} degrees, (*c*) $3.2°$, (*d*) $27°$, (*e*) 1.5×10^{3} degrees.

FIGURE 35–15 Hubble Space Telescope, with Earth in the background. The flat orange panels are solar cells that collect energy from the Sun.

EXAMPLE 35–5 Hubble Space Telescope. The Hubble Space Telescope (HST) is a reflecting telescope that was placed in orbit above the Earth's atmosphere, so its resolution would not be limited by turbulence in the atmosphere (Fig. 35–15). Its objective diameter is 2.4 m. For visible light, say $\lambda = 550$ nm, estimate the improvement in resolution the Hubble offers over Earth-bound telescopes, which are limited in resolution by movement of the Earth's atmosphere to about half an arc second. (Each degree is divided into 60 minutes each containing 60 seconds, so $1° = 3600$ arc seconds.)

APPROACH Angular resolution for the Hubble is given (in radians) by Eq. 35–10. The resolution for Earth telescopes is given, and we first convert it to radians so we can compare.

SOLUTION Earth-bound telescopes are limited to an angular resolution of

$$\theta = \tfrac{1}{2}\left(\frac{1}{3600}\right)^{\!\circ}\left(\frac{2\pi\,\text{rad}}{360°}\right) = 2.4 \times 10^{-6}\,\text{rad}.$$

The Hubble, on the other hand, is limited by diffraction (Eq. 35–10) which for $\lambda = 550$ nm is

$$\theta = \frac{1.22\lambda}{D} = \frac{1.22(550 \times 10^{-9}\,\text{m})}{2.4\,\text{m}} = 2.8 \times 10^{-7}\,\text{rad},$$

thus giving almost ten times better resolution $(2.4 \times 10^{-6}\,\text{rad}/2.8 \times 10^{-7}\,\text{rad} \approx 9\times)$.

EXAMPLE 35–6 ESTIMATE Eye resolution. You are in an airplane at an altitude of 10,000 m. If you look down at the ground, estimate the minimum separation s between objects that you could distinguish. Could you count cars in a parking lot? Consider only diffraction, and assume your pupil is about 3.0 mm in diameter and $\lambda = 550$ nm.

APPROACH We use the Rayleigh criterion, Eq. 35–10, to estimate θ. The separation s of objects is $s = \ell\theta$, where $\ell = 10^{4}$ m and θ is in radians.

SOLUTION In Eq. 35–10, we set $D = 3.0$ mm for the opening of the eye:

$$s = \ell\theta = \ell\frac{1.22\lambda}{D} = \frac{(10^{4}\,\text{m})(1.22)(550 \times 10^{-9}\,\text{m})}{3.0 \times 10^{-3}\,\text{m}} = 2.2\,\text{m}.$$

Yes, you could just resolve a car (roughly 2 m wide by 3 or 4 m long) and count them.

35–5 Resolution of Telescopes and Microscopes; the λ Limit

You might think that a microscope or telescope could be designed to produce any desired magnification, depending on the choice of focal lengths and quality of the lenses. But this is not possible, because of diffraction. An increase in magnification above a certain point merely results in magnification of the diffraction patterns. This can be highly misleading since we might think we are seeing details of an object when we are really seeing details of the diffraction pattern. To examine this problem, we apply the Rayleigh criterion: two objects (or two nearby points on one object) are just resolvable if they are separated by an angle θ (Fig. 35–14) given by Eq. 35–10:

$$\theta = \frac{1.22\lambda}{D}.$$

This formula is valid for either a microscope or a telescope, where D is the diameter of the objective lens or mirror. For a telescope, the resolution is specified by stating θ as given by this equation.[†]

EXAMPLE 35–7 **Telescope resolution (radio wave vs. visible light).** What is the theoretical minimum angular separation of two stars that can just be resolved by (a) the 200-inch telescope on Palomar Mountain (Fig. 33–38c); and (b) the Arecibo radiotelescope (Fig. 35–16), whose diameter is 300 m and whose radius of curvature is also 300 m. Assume $\lambda = 550$ nm for the visible-light telescope in part (a), and $\lambda = 4$ cm (the shortest wavelength at which the radiotelescope has been operated) in part (b).

APPROACH We apply the Rayleigh criterion (Eq. 35–10) for each telescope.

SOLUTION (a) Since $D = 200$ in. $= 5.1$ m, we have from Eq. 35–10 that

$$\theta = \frac{1.22\lambda}{D} = \frac{(1.22)(5.50 \times 10^{-7}\,\text{m})}{(5.1\,\text{m})} = 1.3 \times 10^{-7}\,\text{rad},$$

or 0.75×10^{-5} deg. (Note that this is equivalent to resolving two points less than 1 cm apart from a distance of 100 km!)
(b) For radio waves with $\lambda = 0.04$ m emitted by stars, the resolution is

$$\theta = \frac{(1.22)(0.04\,\text{m})}{(300\,\text{m})} = 1.6 \times 10^{-4}\,\text{rad}.$$

The resolution is less because the wavelength is so much larger, but the larger objective collects more radiation and thus detects fainter objects.

NOTE In both cases, we determined the limit set by diffraction. The resolution for a visible-light Earth-bound telescope is not this good because of aberrations and, more importantly, turbulence in the atmosphere. In fact, large-diameter objectives are not justified by increased resolution, but by their greater light-gathering ability—they allow more light in, so fainter objects can be seen. Radiotelescopes are not hindered by atmospheric turbulence, and the resolution found in (b) is a good estimate.

FIGURE 35–16 The 300-meter radiotelescope in Arecibo, Puerto Rico, uses radio waves (Fig. 31–12) instead of visible light.

[†]Earth-bound telescopes with large-diameter objectives are usually limited not by diffraction but by other effects such as turbulence in the atmosphere. The resolution of a high-quality microscope, on the other hand, normally *is* limited by diffraction; microscope objectives are complex compound lenses containing many elements of small diameter (since f is small), thus reducing aberrations.

For a microscope, it is more convenient to specify the actual distance, s, between two points that are just barely resolvable: see Fig. 35–14. Since objects are normally placed near the focal point of the microscope objective, the angle subtended by two objects is $\theta = s/f$, so $s = f\theta$. If we combine this with Eq. 35–10, we obtain the **resolving power (RP)** of a microscope

$$\text{RP} = s = f\theta = \frac{1.22\lambda f}{D}, \tag{35–11}$$

where f is the objective lens' focal length (not frequency). This distance s is called the resolving power of the lens because it is the minimum separation of two object points that can just be resolved—assuming the highest quality lens since this limit is imposed by the wave nature of light. A smaller RP means better resolution, better detail.

| **EXERCISE C** What is the resolving power of a microscope with a 5-mm-diameter objective which has $f = 9\,\text{mm}$? (a) 550 nm, (b) 750 nm, (c) 1200 nm, (d) 0.05 nm, (e) 0.005 nm.

Diffraction sets an ultimate limit on the detail that can be seen on any object. In Eq. 35–11 for resolving power of a microscope, the focal length of the lens cannot practically be made less than (approximately) the radius of the lens, and even that is very difficult (see the lensmaker's equation, Eq. 33–4). In this best case, Eq. 35–11 gives, with $f \approx D/2$.

$$\text{RP} \approx \frac{\lambda}{2}. \tag{35–12}$$

Thus we can say, to within a factor of 2 or so, that

it is not possible to resolve detail of objects smaller than the wavelength of the radiation being used.

λ limits resolution

This is an important and useful rule of thumb.

Compound lenses in microscopes are now designed so well that the actual limit on resolution is often set by diffraction—that is, by the wavelength of the light used. To obtain greater detail, one must use radiation of shorter wavelength. The use of UV radiation can increase the resolution by a factor of perhaps 2. Far more important, however, was the discovery in the early twentieth century that electrons have wave properties (Chapter 37) and that their wavelengths can be very small. The wave nature of electrons is utilized in the electron microscope (Section 37–8), which can magnify 100 to 1000 times more than a visible-light microscope because of the much shorter wavelengths. X-rays, too, have very short wavelengths and are often used to study objects in great detail (Section 35–10).

*35–6 Resolution of the Human Eye and Useful Magnification

The resolution of the human eye is limited by several factors, all of roughly the same order of magnitude. The resolution is best at the fovea, where the cone spacing is smallest, about $3\,\mu\text{m}$ ($= 3000\,\text{nm}$). The diameter of the pupil varies from about 0.1 cm to about 0.8 cm. So for $\lambda = 550\,\text{nm}$ (where the eye's sensitivity is greatest), the diffraction limit is about $\theta \approx 1.22\lambda/D \approx 8 \times 10^{-5}\,\text{rad}$ to $6 \times 10^{-4}\,\text{rad}$. The eye is about 2 cm long, giving a resolving power (Eq. 35–11) of $s \approx (2 \times 10^{-2}\,\text{m})(8 \times 10^{-5}\,\text{rad}) \approx 2\,\mu\text{m}$ at best, to about $10\,\mu\text{m}$ at worst (pupil small). Spherical and chromatic aberration also limit the resolution to about $10\,\mu\text{m}$. The net result is that the eye can just resolve objects whose angular separation is around

$$5 \times 10^{-4}\,\text{rad}. \qquad \begin{bmatrix} \text{best eye} \\ \text{resolution} \end{bmatrix}$$

This corresponds to objects separated by 1 cm at a distance of about 20 m.

The typical near point of a human eye is about 25 cm. At this distance, the eye can just resolve objects that are $(25\,\text{cm})(5 \times 10^{-4}\,\text{rad}) \approx 10^{-4}\,\text{m} = \frac{1}{10}\,\text{mm}$ apart. Since the best light microscopes can resolve objects no smaller than about 200 nm at best (Eq. 35–12 for violet light, $\lambda = 400\,\text{nm}$), the useful magnification

[= (resolution by naked eye)/(resolution by microscope)] is limited to about

$$\frac{10^{-4}\,\text{m}}{200 \times 10^{-9}\,\text{m}} \approx 500\times. \qquad \left[\begin{array}{l}\text{maximum useful} \\ \text{microscope magnification}\end{array}\right]$$

In practice, magnifications of about 1000× are often used to minimize eyestrain. Any greater magnification would simply make visible the diffraction pattern produced by the microscope objective lens.

Now you have the answers to the Chapter-Opening Question: (c), by the equation above, and (c) by the λ rule.

35–7 Diffraction Grating

A large number of equally spaced parallel slits is called a **diffraction grating**, although the term "interference grating" might be as appropriate. Gratings can be made by precision machining of very fine parallel lines on a glass plate. The untouched spaces between the lines serve as the slits. Photographic transparencies of an original grating serve as inexpensive gratings. Gratings containing 10,000 lines per centimeter are common, and are very useful for precise measurements of wavelengths. A diffraction grating containing slits is called a **transmission grating**. Another type of diffraction grating is the **reflection grating**, made by ruling fine lines on a metallic or glass surface from which light is reflected and analyzed. The analysis is basically the same as for a transmission grating, which we now discuss.

The analysis of a diffraction grating is much like that of Young's double-slit experiment. We assume parallel rays of light are incident on the grating as shown in Fig. 35–17. We also assume that the slits are narrow enough so that diffraction by each of them spreads light over a very wide angle on a distant screen beyond the grating, and interference can occur with light from all the other slits. Light rays that pass through each slit without deviation ($\theta = 0°$) interfere constructively to produce a bright line at the center of the screen. Constructive interference also occurs at an angle θ such that rays from adjacent slits travel an extra distance of $\Delta\ell = m\lambda$, where m is an integer. If d is the distance between slits, then we see from Fig. 35–17 that $\Delta\ell = d \sin\theta$, and

$$\sin\theta = \frac{m\lambda}{d}, \qquad m = 0, 1, 2, \cdots \qquad \left[\begin{array}{l}\text{diffraction grating,} \\ \text{principal maxima}\end{array}\right] \quad (35\text{–}13)$$

is the criterion to have a brightness maximum. This is the same equation as for the double-slit situation, and again m is called the order of the pattern.

There is an important difference between a double-slit and a multiple-slit pattern. The bright maxima are much *sharper* and *narrower* for a grating. Why? Suppose that the angle θ is increased just slightly beyond that required for a maximum. In the case of only two slits, the two waves will be only slightly out of phase, so nearly full constructive interference occurs. This means the maxima are wide (see Fig. 34–9). For a grating, the waves from two adjacent slits will also not be significantly out of phase. But waves from one slit and those from a second one a few hundred slits away may be exactly out of phase; all or nearly all the light can cancel in pairs in this way. For example, suppose the angle θ is very slightly different from its first-order maximum, so that the extra path length for a pair of adjacent slits is not exactly λ but rather 1.0010λ. The wave through one slit and another one 500 slits below will have a path difference of $1\lambda + (500)(0.0010\lambda) = 1.5000\lambda$, or $1\frac{1}{2}$ wavelengths, so the two will cancel. A pair of slits, one below each of these, will also cancel. That is, the light from slit 1 cancels with that from slit 501; light from slit 2 cancels with that from slit 502, and so on. Thus even for a tiny angle[†] corresponding to an extra path length of $\frac{1}{1000}\lambda$, there is much destructive interference, and so the maxima are very narrow. The more lines there are in a grating, the sharper will be the peaks (see Fig. 35–18). Because a grating produces much sharper lines than two slits alone can (and much brighter lines because there are many more slits), a grating is a far more precise device for measuring wavelengths.

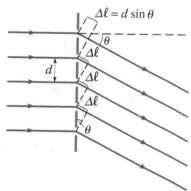

FIGURE 35–17 Diffraction grating.

⚠ **CAUTION**

Diffraction grating is analyzed using interference formulas, not diffraction formulas

FIGURE 35–18 Intensity as a function of viewing angle θ (or position on the screen) for (a) two slits, (b) six slits. For a diffraction grating, the number of slits is very large ($\approx 10^4$) and the peaks are narrower still.

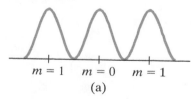

$m = 1 \qquad m = 0 \qquad m = 1$
(a)

$m = 1 \qquad m = 0 \qquad m = 1$
(b)

[†]Depending on the total number of slits, there may or may not be complete cancellation for such an angle, so there will be very tiny peaks between the main maxima (see Fig. 35–18b), but they are usually much too small to be seen.

Suppose the light striking a diffraction grating is not monochromatic, but consists of two or more distinct wavelengths. Then for all orders other than $m = 0$, each wavelength will produce a maximum at a different angle (Fig. 35–19a), just as for a double slit. If white light strikes a grating, the central $(m = 0)$ maximum will be a sharp white peak. But for all other orders, there will be a distinct spectrum of colors spread out over a certain angular width, Fig. 35–19b. Because a diffraction grating spreads out light into its component wavelengths, the resulting pattern is called a **spectrum**.

FIGURE 35–19 Spectra produced by a grating: (a) two wavelengths, 400 nm and 700 nm; (b) white light. The second order will normally be dimmer than the first order. (Higher orders are not shown.) If grating spacing is small enough, the second and higher orders will be missing.

EXAMPLE 35–8 Diffraction grating: lines. Determine the angular positions of the first- and second-order maxima for light of wavelength 400 nm and 700 nm incident on a grating containing 10,000 lines/cm.

APPROACH First we find the distance d between grating lines: if the grating has N lines in 1 m, then the distance between lines must be $d = 1/N$ meters. Then we use Eq. 35–13, $\sin \theta = m\lambda/d$, to find the angles for the two wavelengths for $m = 1$ and 2.

SOLUTION The grating contains 1.00×10^4 lines/cm $= 1.00 \times 10^6$ lines/m, which means the distance between lines is $d = (1/1.00 \times 10^6)\,\text{m} = 1.00 \times 10^{-6}\,\text{m} = 1.00\,\mu\text{m}$. In first order $(m = 1)$, the angles are

$$\sin \theta_{400} = \frac{m\lambda}{d} = \frac{(1)(4.00 \times 10^{-7}\,\text{m})}{1.00 \times 10^{-6}\,\text{m}} = 0.400$$

$$\sin \theta_{700} = \frac{(1)(7.00 \times 10^{-7}\,\text{m})}{1.00 \times 10^{-6}\,\text{m}} = 0.700$$

so $\theta_{400} = 23.6°$ and $\theta_{700} = 44.4°$. In second order,

$$\sin \theta_{400} = \frac{2\lambda}{d} = \frac{(2)(4.00 \times 10^{-7}\,\text{m})}{1.00 \times 10^{-6}\,\text{m}} = 0.800$$

$$\sin \theta_{700} = \frac{(2)(7.00 \times 10^{-7}\,\text{m})}{1.00 \times 10^{-6}\,\text{m}} = 1.40$$

so $\theta_{400} = 53.1°$. But the second order does not exist for $\lambda = 700\,\text{nm}$ because $\sin \theta$ cannot exceed 1. No higher orders will appear.

EXAMPLE 35–9 Spectra overlap. White light containing wavelengths from 400 nm to 750 nm strikes a grating containing 4000 lines/cm. Show that the blue at $\lambda = 450\,\text{nm}$ of the third-order spectrum overlaps the red at 700 nm of the second order.

APPROACH We use $\sin \theta = m\lambda/d$ to calculate the angular positions of the $m = 3$ blue maximum and the $m = 2$ red one.

SOLUTION The grating spacing is $d = (1/4000)$ cm $= 2.50 \times 10^{-6}$ m. The blue of the third order occurs at an angle θ given by

$$\sin \theta = \frac{m\lambda}{d} = \frac{(3)(4.50 \times 10^{-7} \text{ m})}{(2.50 \times 10^{-6} \text{ m})} = 0.540.$$

Red in second order occurs at

$$\sin \theta = \frac{(2)(7.00 \times 10^{-7} \text{ m})}{(2.50 \times 10^{-6} \text{ m})} = 0.560,$$

which is a greater angle; so the second order overlaps into the beginning of the third-order spectrum.

CONCEPTUAL EXAMPLE 35–10 | **Compact disk.** When you look at the surface of a music CD (Fig. 35–20), you see the colors of a rainbow. (a) Estimate the distance between the curved lines (they are read by a laser). (b) Estimate the distance between lines, noting that a CD contains at most 80 min of music, that it rotates at speeds from 200 to 500 rev/min, and that $\frac{2}{3}$ of its 6 cm radius contains the lines.

RESPONSE (a) The CD acts like a reflection diffraction grating. To satisfy Eq. 35–13, we might estimate the line spacing as one or a few (2 or 3) wavelengths ($\lambda \approx 550$ nm) or 0.5 to 1.5 μm. (b) Average rotation speed of 350 rev/min times 80 min gives 28,000 total rotations or 28,000 lines, which are spread over $(\frac{2}{3})(6 \text{ cm}) = 4$ cm. So we have a sort of reflection diffraction grating with about $(28{,}000 \text{ lines})/(4 \text{ cm}) = 7000$ lines/cm. The distance d between lines is roughly 1 cm/7000 lines $\approx 1.4 \times 10^{-6}$ m $= 1.4\ \mu$m. Our results in (a) and (b) agree.

FIGURE 35–20 A compact disk, Example 35–10.

35–8 The Spectrometer and Spectroscopy

A **spectrometer** or **spectroscope**, Fig. 35–21, is a device to measure wavelengths accurately using a diffraction grating (or a prism) to separate different wavelengths of light. Light from a source passes through a narrow slit S in the "collimator." The slit is at the focal point of the lens L, so parallel light falls on the grating. The movable telescope can bring the rays to a focus. Nothing will be seen in the viewing telescope unless it is positioned at an angle θ that corresponds to a diffraction peak (first order is usually used) of a wavelength emitted by the source. The angle θ can be measured to very high accuracy, so the wavelength of a line can be determined to high accuracy using Eq. 35–13:

$$\lambda = \frac{d}{m} \sin \theta,$$

where m is an integer representing the order, and d is the distance between grating lines. The line you see in a spectrometer corresponding to each wavelength is actually an image of the slit S. A narrower slit results in dimmer light but we can measure the angular positions more precisely. If the light contains a continuous range of wavelengths, then a continuous spectrum is seen in the spectroscope.

The spectrometer in Fig. 35–21 uses a transmission grating. Others may use a reflection grating, or sometimes a prism. A prism works because of dispersion (Section 32–6), bending light of different wavelengths into different angles. (A prism is not a linear device and must be calibrated.)

An important use of a spectrometer is for the identification of atoms or molecules. When a gas is heated or an electric current is passed through it, the gas emits a characteristic **line spectrum**. That is, only certain discrete wavelengths of light are emitted, and these are different for different elements and compounds.[†] Figure 35–22 shows the line spectra for a number of elements in the gas state. Line spectra occur only for gases at high temperatures and low pressure and density. The light from heated solids, such as a lightbulb filament, and even from a dense gaseous object such as the Sun, produces a **continuous spectrum** including a wide range of wavelengths.

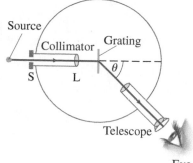

FIGURE 35–21 Spectrometer or spectroscope.

Source
Collimator Grating
S   L θ
Telescope
Eye

[†]Why atoms and molecules emit line spectra was a great mystery for many years and played a central role in the development of modern quantum theory, as we shall see in Chapter 37.

Atomic hydrogen

Mercury

Sodium

Solar absorption spectrum

FIGURE 35–22 Line spectra for the gases indicated, and the spectrum from the Sun showing absorption lines.

PHYSICS APPLIED
Chemical and biochemical analysis by spectroscopy

Figure 35–22 also shows the Sun's "continuous spectrum," which contains a number of *dark* lines (only the most prominent are shown), called **absorption lines**. Atoms and molecules can absorb light at the same wavelengths at which they emit light. The Sun's absorption lines are due to absorption by atoms and molecules in the cooler outer atmosphere of the Sun, as well as by atoms and molecules in the Earth's atmosphere. A careful analysis of all these thousands of lines reveals that at least two-thirds of all elements are present in the Sun's atmosphere. The presence of elements in the atmosphere of other planets, in interstellar space, and in stars, is also determined by spectroscopy.

Spectroscopy is useful for determining the presence of certain types of molecules in laboratory specimens where chemical analysis would be difficult. For example, biological DNA and different types of protein absorb light in particular regions of the spectrum (such as in the UV). The material to be examined, which is often in solution, is placed in a monochromatic light beam whose wavelength is selected by the placement angle of a diffraction grating or prism. The amount of absorption, as compared to a standard solution without the specimen, can reveal not only the presence of a particular type of molecule, but also its concentration.

Light emission and absorption also occur outside the visible part of the spectrum, such as in the UV and IR regions. Glass absorbs light in these regions, so reflection gratings and mirrors (in place of lenses) are used. Special types of film or sensors are used for detection.

EXAMPLE 35–11 **Hydrogen spectrum.** Light emitted by hot hydrogen gas is observed with a spectroscope using a diffraction grating having 1.00×10^4 lines/cm. The spectral lines nearest to the center $(0°)$ are a violet line at 24.2°, a blue line at 25.7°, a blue-green line at 29.1°, and a red line at 41.0° from the center. What are the wavelengths of these spectral lines of hydrogen?

APPROACH The wavelengths can be determined from the angles by using $\lambda = (d/m) \sin \theta$ where d is the spacing between slits, and m is the order of the spectrum (Eq. 35–13).

SOLUTION Since these are the closest lines to $\theta = 0°$, this is the first-order spectrum $(m = 1)$. The slit spacing is $d = 1/(1.00 \times 10^4 \, \text{cm}^{-1}) = 1.00 \times 10^{-6} \, \text{m}$. The wavelength of the violet line is

$$\lambda = \left(\frac{d}{m}\right) \sin \theta = \left(\frac{1.00 \times 10^{-6} \, \text{m}}{1}\right) \sin 24.2° = 4.10 \times 10^{-7} \, \text{m} = 410 \, \text{nm}.$$

The other wavelengths are:

blue: $\qquad \lambda = (1.00 \times 10^{-6} \, \text{m}) \sin 25.7° = 434 \, \text{nm},$

blue-green: $\quad \lambda = (1.00 \times 10^{-6} \, \text{m}) \sin 29.1° = 486 \, \text{nm},$

red: $\qquad \lambda = (1.00 \times 10^{-6} \, \text{m}) \sin 41.0° = 656 \, \text{nm}.$

NOTE In an unknown mixture of gases, these four spectral lines need to be seen to identify that the mixture contains hydrogen.

*35–9 Peak Widths and Resolving Power for a Diffraction Grating

We now look at the pattern of maxima produced by a multiple-slit grating using phasor diagrams. We can determine a formula for the width of each peak, and we will see why there are tiny maxima between the principal maxima, as indicated in Fig. 35–18b. First of all, it should be noted that the two-slit and six-slit patterns shown in Fig. 35–18 were drawn assuming very narrow slits so that diffraction does not limit the height of the peaks. For real diffraction gratings, this is not normally the case: the slit width D is often not much smaller than the slit separation d, and diffraction thus limits the intensity of the peaks so the central peak $(m = 0)$ is brighter than the side peaks. We won't worry about this effect on intensity except to note that if a diffraction minimum coincides with a particular order of the interference pattern, that order will not appear. (For example, if $d = 2D$, all the even orders, $m = 2, 4, \cdots$, will be missing. Can you see why? Hint: See Example 35–4.)

Figures 35–23 and 35–24 show phasor diagrams for a two-slit and a six-slit grating, respectively. Each short arrow represents the amplitude of a wave from a single slit, and their vector sum (as phasors) represents the total amplitude for a given viewing angle θ. Part (a) of each Figure shows the phasor diagram at $\theta = 0°$, at the center of the pattern, which is the central maximum $(m = 0)$. Part (b) of each Figure shows the condition for the adjacent minimum: where the arrows first close on themselves (add to zero) so the amplitude E_θ is zero. For two slits, this occurs when the two separate amplitudes are 180° out of phase. For six slits, it occurs when each amplitude makes a 60° angle with its neighbor. For two slits, the minimum occurs when the phase between slits is $\delta = 2\pi/2$ (in radians); for six slits it occurs when the phase δ is $2\pi/6$; and in the general case of N slits, the minimum occurs for a phase difference between adjacent slits of

$$\delta = \frac{2\pi}{N}. \tag{35–14}$$

What does this correspond to in θ? First note that δ is related to θ by (Eq. 34–4)

$$\frac{\delta}{2\pi} = \frac{d \sin \theta}{\lambda} \quad \text{or} \quad \delta = \frac{2\pi}{\lambda} d \sin \theta. \tag{35–15}$$

Let us call $\Delta\theta_0$ the angular position of the minimum next to the peak at $\theta = 0$. Then

$$\frac{\delta}{2\pi} = \frac{d \sin \Delta\theta_0}{\lambda}.$$

We insert Eq. 35–14 for δ and find

$$\sin \Delta\theta_0 = \frac{\lambda}{Nd}. \tag{35–16a}$$

Since $\Delta\theta_0$ is usually small (N is usually very large for a grating), $\sin \Delta\theta_0 \approx \Delta\theta_0$, so in the small angle limit we can write

$$\Delta\theta_0 = \frac{\lambda}{Nd}. \tag{35–16b}$$

It is clear from either of the last two relations that the larger N is, the narrower will be the central peak. (For $N = 2$, $\sin \Delta\theta_0 = \lambda/2d$, which is what we obtained earlier for the double slit, Eq. 34–2b with $m = 0$.)

Either of Eqs. 35–16 shows why the peaks become narrower for larger N. The origin of the small secondary maxima between the principal peaks (see Fig. 35–18b) can be deduced from the diagram of Fig. 35–25. This is just a continuation of Fig. 35–24b (where $\delta = 60°$); but now the phase δ has been increased to almost 90°, where E_θ is a relative maximum. Note that E_θ is much less than E_0 (Fig. 35–24a), so the intensity in this secondary maximum is much smaller than in a principal peak. As δ (and θ) is increased further, E_θ again decreases to zero (a "double circle"), then reaches another tiny maximum, and so on. Eventually the diagram unfolds again and when $\delta = 360°$, all the amplitudes again lie in a straight line (as in Fig. 35–24a) corresponding to the next principal maximum ($m = 1$ in Eq. 35–13).

(a) Central maximum: $\theta = 0$, $\delta = 0$

$E = 0$

$\delta = 180°$

(b) Minimum: $\delta = 180°$

FIGURE 35–23 Phasor diagram for two slits (a) at the central maximum, (b) at the nearest minimum.

FIGURE 35–24 Phasor diagram for six slits (a) at the central maximum, (b) at the nearest minimum.

E_0

(a) Central maximum: $\theta = 0$, $\delta = 0$

$\delta = 60°$

$\delta = 60°$

(b) Minimum: $\delta = 60°$, $E_\theta = 0$

FIGURE 35–25 Phasor diagram for the secondary peak.

E_θ

Equation 35–16b gives the half-width of the central $(m = 0)$ peak. To determine the half-width of higher order peaks, $\Delta\theta_m$ for order m, we differentiate Eq. 35–15 so as to relate the change $\Delta\delta$ in δ, to the change $\Delta\theta$ in the angle θ:

$$\Delta\delta \approx \frac{d\delta}{d\theta} \Delta\theta = \frac{2\pi d}{\lambda} \cos\theta \, \Delta\theta.$$

If $\Delta\theta_m$ represents the half-width of a peak of order m $(m = 1, 2, \cdots)$—that is, the angle between the peak maximum and the minimum to either side—then $\Delta\delta = 2\pi/N$ as given by Eq. 35–14. We insert this into the above relation and find

$$\Delta\theta_m = \frac{\lambda}{Nd \cos\theta_m}, \qquad (35\text{--}17)$$

where θ_m is the angular position of the mth peak as given by Eq. 35–13. This derivation is valid, of course, only for small $\Delta\delta \, (= 2\pi/N)$ which is indeed the case for real gratings since N is on the order of 10^4 or more.

An important property of any diffraction grating used in a spectrometer is its ability to resolve two very closely spaced wavelengths (wavelength difference $= \Delta\lambda$). The **resolving power** R of a grating is defined as

$$R = \frac{\lambda}{\Delta\lambda}. \qquad (35\text{--}18)$$

With a little work, using Eq. 35–17, we can show that $\Delta\lambda = \lambda/Nm$ where N is the total number of grating lines and m is the order. Then we have

$$R = \frac{\lambda}{\Delta\lambda} = Nm. \qquad (35\text{--}19)$$

The larger the value of R, the closer two wavelengths can be resolvable. If R is given, the minimum separation $\Delta\lambda$ between two wavelengths near λ, is (by Eq. 35–18)

$$\Delta\lambda = \frac{\lambda}{R}.$$

EXAMPLE 35–12 **Resolving two close lines.** Yellow sodium light, which consists of two wavelengths, $\lambda_1 = 589.00\,\text{nm}$ and $\lambda_2 = 589.59\,\text{nm}$, falls on a 7500-line/cm diffraction grating. Determine (a) the maximum order m that will be present for sodium light, (b) the width of grating necessary to resolve the two sodium lines.

APPROACH We first find $d = 1\,\text{cm}/7500 = 1.33 \times 10^{-6}\,\text{m}$, and then use Eq. 35–13 to find m. For (b) we use Eqs. 35–18 and 35–19.

SOLUTION (a) The maximum value of m at $\lambda = 589\,\text{nm}$, using Eq. 35–13 with $\sin\theta \le 1$, is

$$m = \frac{d}{\lambda}\sin\theta \le \frac{d}{\lambda} = \frac{1.33 \times 10^{-6}\,\text{m}}{5.89 \times 10^{-7}\,\text{m}} = 2.26,$$

so $m = 2$ is the maximum order present.

(b) The resolving power needed is

$$R = \frac{\lambda}{\Delta\lambda} = \frac{589\,\text{nm}}{0.59\,\text{nm}} = 1000.$$

From Eq. 35–19, the total number N of lines needed for the $m = 2$ order is $N = R/m = 1000/2 = 500$, so the grating need only be $500/7500\,\text{cm}^{-1} = 0.0667\,\text{cm}$ wide. A typical grating is a few centimeters wide, and so will easily resolve the two lines.

35–10 X-Rays and X-Ray Diffraction

In 1895, W. C. Roentgen (1845–1923) discovered that when electrons were accelerated by a high voltage in a vacuum tube and allowed to strike a glass or metal surface inside the tube, fluorescent minerals some distance away would glow, and photographic film would become exposed. Roentgen attributed these effects to a new type of radiation (different from cathode rays). They were given the name **X-rays** after the algebraic symbol x, meaning an unknown quantity. He soon found that X-rays penetrated through some materials better than through others, and within a few weeks he presented the first X-ray photograph (of his wife's hand). The production of X-rays today is usually done in a tube (Fig. 35–26) similar to Roentgen's, using voltages of typically 30 kV to 150 kV.

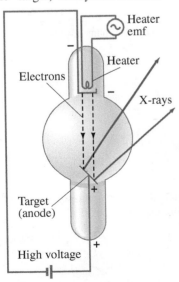

FIGURE 35–26 X-ray tube. Electrons emitted by a heated filament in a vacuum tube are accelerated by a high voltage. When they strike the surface of the anode, the "target," X-rays are emitted.

Investigations into the nature of X-rays indicated they were not charged particles (such as electrons) since they could not be deflected by electric or magnetic fields. It was suggested that they might be a form of invisible light. However, they showed no diffraction or interference effects using ordinary gratings. Indeed, if their wavelengths were much smaller than the typical grating spacing of 10^{-6} m $(= 10^3$ nm$)$, no effects would be expected. Around 1912, Max von Laue (1879–1960) suggested that if the atoms in a crystal were arranged in a regular array (see Fig. 17–2a), such a crystal might serve as a diffraction grating for very short wavelengths on the order of the spacing between atoms, estimated to be about 10^{-10} m $(= 10^{-1}$ nm$)$. Experiments soon showed that X-rays scattered from a crystal did indeed show the peaks and valleys of a diffraction pattern (Fig. 35–27). Thus it was shown, in a single blow, that X-rays have a wave nature and that atoms are arranged in a regular way in crystals. Today, X-rays are recognized as electromagnetic radiation with wavelengths in the range of about 10^{-2} nm to 10 nm, the range readily produced in an X-ray tube.

We saw in Section 35–5 that light of shorter wavelength provides greater resolution when we are examining an object microscopically. Since X-rays have much shorter wavelengths than visible light, they should in principle offer much greater resolution. However, there seems to be no effective material to use as lenses for the very short wavelengths of X-rays. Instead, the clever but complicated technique of **X-ray diffraction** (or **crystallography**) has proved very effective for examining the microscopic world of atoms and molecules. In a simple crystal such as NaCl, the atoms are arranged in an orderly cubical fashion, Fig. 35–28, with atoms spaced a distance d apart. Suppose that a beam of X-rays is incident on the crystal at an angle ϕ to the surface, and that the two rays shown are reflected from two subsequent planes of atoms as shown. The two rays will constructively interfere if the extra distance ray I travels is a whole number of wavelengths farther than the distance ray II travels. This extra distance is $2d \sin \phi$. Therefore, constructive interference will occur when

$$m\lambda = 2d \sin \phi, \qquad m = 1, 2, 3, \cdots, \qquad (35\text{–}20)$$

where m can be any integer. (Notice that ϕ is *not* the angle with respect to the normal to the surface.) This is called the **Bragg equation** after W. L. Bragg (1890–1971), who derived it and who, together with his father W. H. Bragg (1862–1942), developed the theory and technique of X-ray diffraction by crystals in 1912–1913. If the X-ray wavelength is known and the angle ϕ is measured, the distance d between atoms can be obtained. This is the basis for X-ray crystallography.

EXERCISE D When X-rays of wavelength 0.10×10^{-9} m are scattered from a sodium chloride crystal, a second-order diffraction peak is observed at 21°. What is the spacing between the planes of atoms for this scattering?

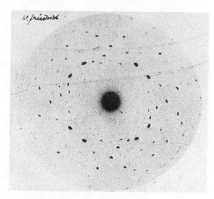

FIGURE 35–27 This X-ray diffraction pattern is one of the first observed by Max von Laue in 1912 when he aimed a beam of X-rays at a zinc sulfide crystal. The diffraction pattern was detected directly on a photographic plate.

FIGURE 35–28 X-ray diffraction by a crystal.

FIGURE 35–29 X-rays can be diffracted from many possible planes within a crystal.

Actual X-ray diffraction patterns are quite complicated. First of all, a crystal is a three-dimensional object, and X-rays can be diffracted from different planes at different angles within the crystal, as shown in Fig. 35–29. Although the analysis is complex, a great deal can be learned about any substance that can be put in crystalline form.

X-ray diffraction has also been very useful in determining the structure of biologically important molecules, such as the double helix structure of DNA, worked out by James Watson and Francis Crick in 1953. See Fig. 35–30, and for models of the double helix, Figs. 21–47a and 21–48. Around 1960, the first detailed structure of a protein molecule, myoglobin, was elucidated with the aid of X-ray diffraction. Soon the structure of an important constituent of blood, hemoglobin, was worked out, and since then the structures of a great many molecules have been determined with the help of X-rays.

FIGURE 35–30 X-ray diffraction photo of DNA molecules taken by Rosalind Franklin in the early 1950s. The cross of spots suggested that DNA is a helix.

FIGURE 35–31 Transverse waves on a rope polarized (a) in a vertical plane and (b) in a horizontal plane.

FIGURE 35–32 (a) Vertically polarized wave passes through a vertical slit, but (b) a horizontally polarized wave will not.

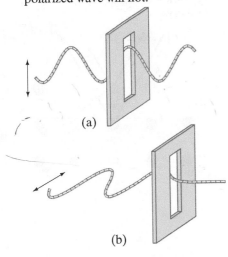

FIGURE 35–33 (below) (a) Oscillation of the electric field vectors in unpolarized light. The light is traveling into or out of the page. (b) Electric field in linear polarized light.

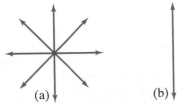

35–11 Polarization

An important and useful property of light is that it can be *polarized*. To see what this means, let us examine waves traveling on a rope. A rope can be set into oscillation in a vertical plane as in Fig. 35–31a, or in a horizontal plane as in Fig. 35–31b. In either case, the wave is said to be **linearly polarized** or **plane-polarized**—that is, the oscillations are in a plane.

If we now place an obstacle containing a vertical slit in the path of the wave, Fig. 35–32, a vertically polarized wave passes through the vertical slit, but a horizontally polarized wave will not. If a horizontal slit were used, the vertically polarized wave would be stopped. If both types of slit were used, both types of wave would be stopped by one slit or the other. Note that polarization can exist *only* for *transverse waves*, and not for longitudinal waves such as sound. The latter oscillate only along the direction of motion, and neither orientation of slit would stop them.

Light is not necessarily polarized. It can also be **unpolarized**, which means that the source has oscillations in many planes at once, as shown in Fig. 35–33. An ordinary incandescent lightbulb emits unpolarized light, as does the Sun.

Polaroids (Polarization by Absorption)

Plane-polarized light can be obtained from unpolarized light using certain crystals such as tourmaline. Or, more commonly, we use a **Polaroid sheet**. (Polaroid materials were invented in 1929 by Edwin Land.) A Polaroid sheet consists of long complex molecules arranged parallel to one another. Such a Polaroid acts like a series of parallel slits to allow one orientation of polarization to pass through nearly undiminished. This direction is called the *transmission axis* of the Polaroid. Polarization perpendicular to this direction is absorbed almost completely by the Polaroid.

Absorption by a Polaroid can be explained at the molecular level. An electric field $\vec{E}$ that oscillates parallel to the long molecules can set electrons into motion along the molecules, thus doing work on them and transferring energy. Hence, if $\vec{E}$ is parallel to the molecules, it gets absorbed. An electric field $\vec{E}$ perpendicular to the long molecules does not have this possibility of doing work and transferring its energy, and so passes through freely. When we speak of the *transmission axis* of a Polaroid, we mean the direction for which $\vec{E}$ is passed, so a Polaroid axis is *perpendicular* to the long molecules. If we want to think of there being slits between the parallel molecules in the sense of Fig. 35–32, then Fig. 35–32 would apply for the $\vec{B}$ field in the EM wave, not the $\vec{E}$ field.

If a beam of plane-polarized light strikes a Polaroid whose transmission axis is at an angle θ to the incident polarization direction, the beam will emerge plane-polarized parallel to the Polaroid transmission axis, and the amplitude of E will be reduced to $E \cos \theta$, Fig. 35–34. Thus, a Polaroid passes only that component of polarization (the electric field vector, $\vec{E}$) that is parallel to its transmission axis. Because the intensity of a light beam is proportional to the square of the amplitude (Sections 15–3 and 31–8), we see that the intensity of a plane-polarized beam transmitted by a polarizer is

$$I = I_0 \cos^2 \theta, \qquad \left[\begin{array}{l}\text{intensity of plane polarized} \\ \text{wave reduced by polarizer}\end{array}\right] \quad (35\text{–}21)$$

where I_0 is the incoming intensity and θ is the angle between the polarizer transmission axis and the plane of polarization of the incoming wave.

FIGURE 35–34 (right) Vertical Polaroid transmits only the vertical component of a wave (electric field) incident upon it.

Incident beam polarized at angle θ to the vertical; has amplitude E_0

A Polaroid can be used as a **polarizer** to produce plane-polarized light from unpolarized light, since only the component of light parallel to the axis is transmitted. A Polaroid can also be used as an **analyzer** to determine (1) if light is polarized and (2) the plane of polarization. A Polaroid acting as an analyzer will pass the same amount of light independent of the orientation of its axis if the light is unpolarized; try rotating one lens of a pair of Polaroid sunglasses while looking through it at a lightbulb. If the light is polarized, however, when you rotate the Polaroid the transmitted light will be a maximum when the plane of polarization is parallel to the Polaroid's axis, and a minimum when perpendicular to it. If you do this while looking at the sky, preferably at right angles to the Sun's direction, you will see that skylight is polarized. (Direct sunlight is unpolarized, but don't look directly at the Sun, even through a polarizer, for damage to the eye may occur.) If the light transmitted by an analyzer Polaroid falls to zero at one orientation, then the light is 100% plane-polarized. If it merely reaches a minimum, the light is *partially polarized*.

Unpolarized light consists of light with random directions of polarization. Each of these polarization directions can be resolved into components along two mutually perpendicular directions. On average, an unpolarized beam can be thought of as two plane-polarized beams of equal magnitude perpendicular to one another. When unpolarized light passes through a polarizer, one component is eliminated. So the intensity of the light passing through is reduced by half since half the light is eliminated: $I = \frac{1}{2} I_0$ (Fig. 35-35).

When two Polaroids are *crossed*—that is, their polarizing axes are perpendicular to one another—unpolarized light can be entirely stopped. As shown in Fig. 35-36, unpolarized light is made plane-polarized by the first Polaroid (the polarizer).

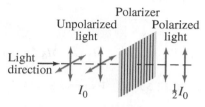

FIGURE 35-35 Unpolarized light has equal intensity vertical and horizontal components. After passing through a polarizer, one of these components is eliminated. The intensity of the light is reduced to half.

FIGURE 35-36 Crossed Polaroids completely eliminate light.

The second Polaroid, the analyzer, then eliminates this component since its transmission axis is perpendicular to the first. You can try this with Polaroid sunglasses (Fig. 35-37). Note that Polaroid sunglasses eliminate 50% of unpolarized light because of their polarizing property; they absorb even more because they are colored.

EXAMPLE 35-13 **Two Polaroids at 60°.** Unpolarized light passes through two Polaroids; the axis of one is vertical and that of the other is at 60° to the vertical. Describe the orientation and intensity of the transmitted light.

APPROACH Half of the unpolarized light is absorbed by the first Polaroid, and the remaining light emerges plane polarized. When that light passes through the second Polaroid, the intensity is further reduced according to Eq. 35-21, and the plane of polarization is then along the axis of the second Polaroid.

SOLUTION The first Polaroid eliminates half the light, so the intensity is reduced by half: $I_1 = \frac{1}{2} I_0$. The light reaching the second polarizer is vertically polarized and so is reduced in intensity (Eq. 35-21) to

$$I_2 = I_1 (\cos 60°)^2 = \frac{1}{4} I_1.$$

Thus, $I_2 = \frac{1}{8} I_0$. The transmitted light has an intensity one-eighth that of the original and is plane-polarized at a 60° angle to the vertical.

FIGURE 35-37 Crossed Polaroids. When the two polarized sunglass lenses overlap, with axes perpendicular, almost no light passes through.

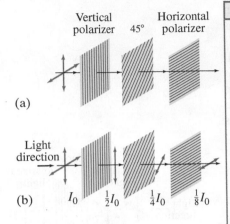

Vertical polarizer 45° Horizontal polarizer

(a)

Light direction

(b) I_0 $\frac{1}{2}I_0$ $\frac{1}{4}I_0$ $\frac{1}{8}I_0$

FIGURE 35–38 Example 35–14.

CONCEPTUAL EXAMPLE 35–14 | **Three Polaroids.** We saw in Fig. 35–36 that when unpolarized light falls on two crossed Polaroids (axes at 90°), no light passes through. What happens if a third Polaroid, with axis at 45° to each of the other two, is placed between them (Fig. 35–38a)?

RESPONSE We start just as in Example 35–13 and recall again that light emerging from each Polaroid is polarized parallel to that Polaroid's axis. Thus the angle in Eq. 35–21 is that between the transmission axes of each pair of Polaroids taken in turn. The first Polaroid changes the unpolarized light to plane-polarized and reduces the intensity from I_0 to $I_1 = \frac{1}{2}I_0$. The second polarizer further reduces the intensity by $(\cos 45°)^2$, Eq. 35–21:

$$I_2 = I_1(\cos 45°)^2 = \frac{1}{2}I_1 = \frac{1}{4}I_0.$$

The light leaving the second polarizer is plane polarized at 45° (Fig. 35–38b) relative to the third polarizer, so the third one reduces the intensity to

$$I_3 = I_2(\cos 45°)^2 = \frac{1}{2}I_2,$$

or $I_3 = \frac{1}{8}I_0$. Thus $\frac{1}{8}$ of the original intensity gets transmitted.

NOTE If we don't insert the 45° Polaroid, zero intensity results (Fig. 35–36).

EXERCISE E How much light would pass through if the 45° polarizer in Example 35–14 was placed not between the other two polarizers but (a) before the vertical (first) polarizer, or (b) after the horizontal polarizer?

FIGURE 35–39 Light reflected from a nonmetallic surface, such as the smooth surface of water in a lake, is partially polarized parallel to the surface.

Polarization by Reflection

Another means of producing polarized light from unpolarized light is by reflection. When light strikes a nonmetallic surface at any angle other than perpendicular, the reflected beam is polarized preferentially in the plane parallel to the surface, Fig. 35–39. In other words, the component with polarization in the plane perpendicular to the surface is preferentially transmitted or absorbed. You can check this by rotating Polaroid sunglasses while looking through them at a flat surface of a lake or road. Since most outdoor surfaces are horizontal, Polaroid sunglasses are made with their axes vertical to eliminate the more strongly reflected horizontal component, and thus reduce glare. People who go fishing wear Polaroids to eliminate reflected glare from the surface of a lake or stream and thus see beneath the water more clearly (Fig. 35–40).

FIGURE 35–40 Photographs of a river, (a) allowing all light into the camera lens, and (b) using a polarizer. The polarizer is adjusted to absorb most of the (polarized) light reflected from the water's surface, allowing the dimmer light from the bottom of the river, and any fish lying there, to be seen more readily.

(a)   (b)

The amount of polarization in the reflected beam depends on the angle, varying from no polarization at normal incidence to 100% polarization at an angle known as the **polarizing angle** θ_p.[†] This angle is related to the index of refraction of the two materials on either side of the boundary by the equation

$$\tan \theta_p = \frac{n_2}{n_1}, \tag{35-22a}$$

where n_1 is the index of refraction of the material in which the beam is traveling, and n_2 is that of the medium beyond the reflecting boundary. If the beam is traveling in air, $n_1 = 1$, and Eq. 35–22a becomes

$$\tan \theta_p = n. \tag{35-22b}$$

The polarizing angle θ_p is also called **Brewster's angle**, and Eqs. 35–22 *Brewster's law*, after the Scottish physicist David Brewster (1781–1868), who worked it out experimentally in 1812. Equations 35–22 can be derived from the electromagnetic wave theory of light. It is interesting that at Brewster's angle, the reflected ray and the transmitted (refracted) ray make a 90° angle to each other; that is, $\theta_p + \theta_r = 90°$, where θ_r is the refraction angle (Fig. 35–41). This can be seen by substituting Eq. 35–22a, $n_2 = n_1 \tan \theta_p = n_1 \sin \theta_p / \cos \theta_p$, into Snell's law, $n_1 \sin \theta_p = n_2 \sin \theta_r$, which gives $\cos \theta_p = \sin \theta_r$ which can only hold if $\theta_p = 90° - \theta_r$.

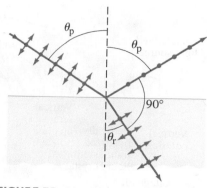

FIGURE 35–41 At θ_p the reflected light is plane-polarized parallel to the surface, and $\theta_p + \theta_r = 90°$, where θ_r is the refraction angle. (The large dots represent vibrations perpendicular to the page.)

EXAMPLE 35–15 **Polarizing angle.** (*a*) At what incident angle is sunlight reflected from a lake plane-polarized? (*b*) What is the refraction angle?

APPROACH The polarizing angle at the surface is Brewster's angle, Eq. 35–22b. We find the angle of refraction from Snell's law.

SOLUTION (*a*) We use Eq. 35–22b with $n = 1.33$, so $\tan \theta_p = 1.33$ giving $\theta_p = 53.1°$. (*b*) From Snell's law, $\sin \theta_r = \sin \theta_p / n = \sin 53.1°/1.33 = 0.601$ giving $\theta_r = 36.9°$.

NOTE $\theta_p + \theta_r = 53.1° + 36.9° = 90.0°$, as expected.

---

*35–12 Liquid Crystal Displays (LCD)

A wonderful use of polarization is in a **liquid crystal display** (LCD). LCDs are used as the display in hand-held calculators, digital wrist watches, cell phones, and in beautiful color flat-panel computer and television screens.

A liquid crystal display is made up of many tiny rectangles called **pixels**, or "picture elements." The picture you see depends on which pixels are dark or light and of what color, as suggested in Fig. 35–42 for a simple black and white picture.

Liquid crystals are organic materials that at room temperature exist in a phase that is neither fully solid nor fully liquid. They are sort of gooey, and their molecules display a randomness of position characteristic of liquids, as we discussed in Section 17–1 and Fig. 17–2. They also show some of the orderliness of a solid crystal (Fig. 17–2a), but only in one dimension. The liquid crystals we find useful are made up of relatively rigid rod-like molecules that interact weakly with each other and tend to align parallel to each other, as shown in Fig. 35–43.

FIGURE 35–42 Example of an image made up of many small squares or *pixels* (picture elements). This one has rather poor resolution.

FIGURE 35–43 Liquid crystal molecules tend to align in one dimension (parallel to each other) but have random positions (left-right, up-down).

[†]Only a fraction of the incident light is reflected at the surface of a transparent medium. Although this reflected light is 100% polarized (if $\theta = \theta_p$), the remainder of the light, which is transmitted into the new medium, is only partially polarized.

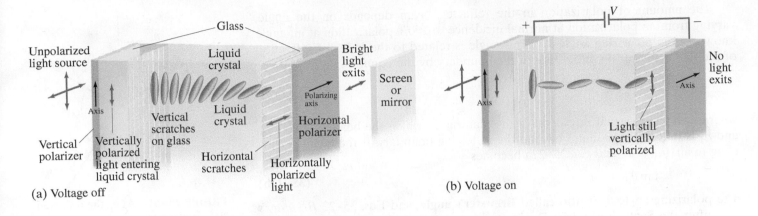

Glass

Unpolarized light source

Liquid crystal

Bright light exits

Screen or mirror

Axis

Vertical polarizer

Vertically polarized light entering liquid crystal

Vertical scratches on glass

Liquid crystal

Horizontal scratches

Polarizing axis

Horizontal polarizer

Horizontally polarized light

(a) Voltage off

Axis

Light still vertically polarized

No light exits

(b) Voltage on

FIGURE 35–44 (a) "Twisted" form of liquid crystal. Light polarization plane is rotated 90°, and so is transmitted by the horizontal polarizer. Only one line of molecules is shown. (b) Molecules disoriented by electric field. Plane of polarization is not changed, so light does not pass through the horizontal polarizer. (The transparent electrodes are not shown.)

FIGURE 35–45 Calculator LCD display. The black segments or pixels have a voltage applied to them. Note that the 8 uses all seven segments (pixels), whereas other numbers use fewer.

In a simple LCD, each pixel (picture element) contains a liquid crystal sandwiched between two glass plates whose inner surfaces have been brushed to form nanometer-wide parallel scratches. The rod-like liquid crystal molecules in contact with the scratches tend to line up along the scratches. The two plates typically have their scratches at 90° to each other, and the weak forces between the rod-like molecules tend to keep them nearly aligned with their nearest neighbors, resulting in the twisted pattern shown in Fig. 35–44a.

The outer surfaces of the glass plates each have a thin film polarizer, they too oriented at 90° to each other. Unpolarized light incident from the left becomes plane-polarized and the liquid crystal molecules keep this polarization aligned with their rod-like shape. That is, the plane of polarization of the light rotates with the molecules as the light passes through the liquid crystal. The light emerges with its plane of polarization rotated by 90°, and passes through the second polarizer readily (Fig. 35–44a). A tiny LCD pixel in this situation will appear bright.

Now suppose a voltage is applied to transparent electrodes on each glass plate of the pixel. The rod-like molecules are polar (or can acquire an internal separation of charge due to the applied electric field). The applied voltage tends to align the molecules and they no longer follow the twisted pattern shown in Fig. 35–44a, with the end molecules always lying in a plane parallel to the glass plates. Instead the applied electric field tends to align the molecules flat, left to right (perpendicular to the glass plates), and they don't affect the light polarization significantly. The entering plane-polarized light no longer has its plane of polarization rotated as it passes through, and no light can exit through the second (horizontal) polarizer (Fig. 35–44b). With the voltage on, the pixel appears dark.[†]

The simple display screens of watches and calculators use ambient light as the source (you can't see the display in the dark), and a mirror behind the LCD to reflect the light back. There are only a few pixels, corresponding to the elongated segments needed to form the numbers from 0 to 9 (and letters in some displays), as seen in Fig. 35–45. Any pixels to which a voltage is applied appear dark and form part of a number. With no voltage, pixels pass light through the polarizers to the mirror and back out, which forms a bright background to the dark numbers on the display.

Color television and computer LCDs are more sophisticated. A color pixel consists of three cells, or subpixels, each covered with a red, green, or blue filter. Varying brightnesses of these three primary colors can yield almost any natural color. A good-quality screen consists of a million or more pixels. Behind this array of pixels is a light source, often thin fluorescent tubes the diameter of a straw. The light passes through the pixels, or not, depending on the voltage applied to each subpixel, as in Fig. 35–44a and b.

[†]In some displays, the polarizers are parallel to each other (the scratches remain at 90° to maintain the twist). Then voltage off results in black (no light), and voltage on results in bright light.

*35–13 Scattering of Light by the Atmosphere

Sunsets are red, the sky is blue, and skylight is polarized (at least partially). These phenomena can be explained on the basis of the *scattering* of light by the molecules of the atmosphere. In Fig. 35–46 we see unpolarized light from the Sun impinging on a molecule of the Earth's atmosphere. The electric field of the EM wave sets the electric charges within the molecule into oscillation, and the molecule absorbs some of the incident radiation. But the molecule quickly reemits this light since the charges are oscillating. As discussed in Section 31–4, oscillating electric charges produce EM waves. The intensity is strongest along the direction perpendicular to the oscillation, and drops to zero along the line of oscillation (Section 31–4). In Fig. 35–46 the motion of the charges is resolved into two components. An observer at right angles to the direction of the sunlight, as shown, will see plane-polarized light because no light is emitted along the line of the other component of the oscillation. (When viewing along the line of an oscillation, you don't see that oscillation, and hence see no waves made by it.) At other viewing angles, both components will be present; one will be stronger, however, so the light appears partially polarized. Thus, the process of scattering explains the polarization of skylight.

Scattering of light by the Earth's atmosphere depends on wavelength λ. For particles much smaller than the wavelength of light (such as molecules of air), the particles will be less of an obstruction to long wavelengths than to short ones. The scattering decreases, in fact, as $1/\lambda^4$. Blue and violet light are thus scattered much more than red and orange, which is why the sky looks blue. At sunset, the Sun's rays pass through a maximum length of atmosphere. Much of the blue has been taken out by scattering. The light that reaches the surface of the Earth, and reflects off clouds and haze, is thus lacking in blue. That is why sunsets appear reddish.

The dependence of scattering on $1/\lambda^4$ is valid only if the scattering objects are much smaller than the wavelength of the light. This is valid for oxygen and nitrogen molecules whose diameters are about 0.2 nm. Clouds, however, contain water droplets or crystals that are much larger than λ. They scatter all frequencies of light nearly uniformly. Hence clouds appear white (or gray, if shadowed).

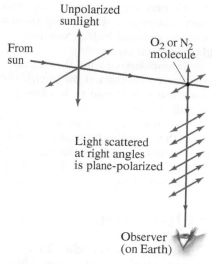

FIGURE 35–46 Unpolarized sunlight scattered by molecules of the air. An observer at right angles sees plane-polarized light, since the component of oscillation along the line of sight emits no light along that line.

PHYSICS APPLIED
Why the sky is blue
Why sunsets are red

PHYSICS APPLIED
Why clouds are white

Summary

Diffraction refers to the fact that light, like other waves, bends around objects it passes, and spreads out after passing through narrow slits. This bending gives rise to a **diffraction pattern** due to interference between rays of light that travel different distances.

Light passing through a very narrow slit of width D (on the order of the wavelength λ) will produce a pattern with a bright central maximum of half-width θ given by

$$\sin\theta = \frac{\lambda}{D}, \tag{35–1}$$

flanked by fainter lines to either side.

The minima in the diffraction pattern occur at

$$D\sin\theta = m\lambda \tag{35–2}$$

where $m = 1, 2, 3, \cdots$, but not $m = 0$ (for which the pattern has its strongest maximum).

The **intensity** at any point in the single-slit diffraction pattern can be calculated using **phasor** diagrams. The same technique can be used to determine the intensity of the pattern produced by two slits.

The pattern for two-slit interference can be described as a series of maxima due to interference of light from the two slits, modified by an "envelope" due to diffraction at each slit.

The wave nature of light limits the sharpness or **resolution** of images. Because of diffraction, it is not possible to *discern details smaller than the wavelength* of the radiation being used. The useful magnification of a light microscope is limited by diffraction to about 500×.

A **diffraction grating** consists of many parallel slits or lines, each separated from its neighbors by a distance d. The peaks of constructive interference occur at angles θ given by

$$\sin\theta = \frac{m\lambda}{d}, \tag{35–13}$$

where $m = 0, 1, 2, \cdots$. The peaks of constructive interference are much brighter and sharper for a diffraction grating than for a simple two-slit apparatus. [*Peak width is inversely proportional to the total number of lines in the grating.]

[*A diffraction grating (or a prism) is used in a **spectrometer** to separate different colors or to observe **line spectra**. For a given order m, θ depends on λ. Precise determination of wavelength can be done with a spectrometer by careful measurement of θ.]

*X-rays are a form of electromagnetic radiation of very short wavelength. They are produced when high-speed electrons, accelerated by high voltage in an evacuated tube, strike a glass or metal target.

In **unpolarized light**, the electric field vectors oscillate in all transverse directions. If the electric vector oscillates only in one plane, the light is said to be **plane-polarized**. Light can also be partially polarized.

When an unpolarized light beam passes through a **Polaroid** sheet, the emerging beam is plane-polarized. When a light beam is polarized and passes through a Polaroid, the intensity varies as the Polaroid is rotated. Thus a Polaroid can act as a **polarizer** or as an **analyzer**.

The intensity I of a plane-polarized light beam incident on a Polaroid is reduced by the factor

$$I = I_0 \cos^2 \theta \qquad (35\text{–}21)$$

where θ is the angle between the axis of the Polaroid and the initial plane of polarization.

Light can also be partially or fully **polarized by reflection**. If light traveling in air is reflected from a medium of index of refraction n, the reflected beam will be *completely* plane-polarized if the incident angle θ_p is given by

$$\tan \theta_p = n. \qquad (35\text{–}22b)$$

The fact that light can be polarized shows that it must be a transverse wave.

Questions

1. Radio waves and light are both electromagnetic waves. Why can a radio receive a signal behind a hill when we cannot see the transmitting antenna?

2. Hold one hand close to your eye and focus on a distant light source through a narrow slit between two fingers. (Adjust your fingers to obtain the best pattern.) Describe the pattern that you see.

3. Explain why diffraction patterns are more difficult to observe with an extended light source than for a point source. Compare also a monochromatic source to white light.

4. For diffraction by a single slit, what is the effect of increasing (a) the slit width, (b) the wavelength?

5. Describe the single-slit diffraction pattern produced when white light falls on a slit having a width of (a) 50 nm, (b) 50,000 nm.

6. What happens to the diffraction pattern of a single slit if the whole apparatus is immersed in (a) water, (b) a vacuum, instead of in air.

7. In the single-slit diffraction pattern, why does the first off-center maximum not occur at exactly $\sin \theta = \frac{3}{2}\lambda/D$?

8. Discuss the similarities, and differences, of double-slit interference and single-slit diffraction.

*9. Figure 35–10 shows a two-slit interference pattern for the case when d is larger than D. Can the reverse case occur, when d is less than D?

*10. When both diffraction and interference are taken into account in the double-slit experiment, discuss the effect of increasing (a) the wavelength, (b) the slit separation, (c) the slit width.

11. Does diffraction limit the resolution of images formed by (a) spherical mirrors, (b) plane mirrors?

12. Do diffraction effects occur for virtual as well as real images?

13. Give at least two advantages for the use of large reflecting mirrors in astronomical telescopes.

14. Atoms have diameters of about 10^{-8} cm. Can visible light be used to "see" an atom? Explain.

15. Which color of visible light would give the best resolution in a microscope? Explain.

16. Could a diffraction grating just as well be called an interference grating? Discuss.

17. Suppose light consisting of wavelengths between 400 nm and 700 nm is incident normally on a diffraction grating. For what orders (if any) would there be overlap in the observed spectrum? Does your answer depend on the slit spacing?

18. What is the difference in the interference patterns formed by two slits 10^{-4} cm apart as compared to a diffraction grating containing 10^4 lines/cm?

19. White light strikes (a) a diffraction grating and (b) a prism. A rainbow appears on a wall just below the direction of the horizontal incident beam in each case. What is the color of the top of the rainbow in each case? Explain.

20. Explain why there are tiny peaks between the main peaks produced by a diffraction grating illuminated with monochromatic light. Why are the peaks so tiny?

21. What does polarization tell us about the nature of light?

22. How can you tell if a pair of sunglasses is polarizing or not?

*23. What would be the color of the sky if the Earth had no atmosphere?

Problems

[Note: Assume light passing through slits is in phase, unless stated otherwise.]

35–1 Single-Slit Diffraction

1. (I) If 680-nm light falls on a slit 0.0365 mm wide, what is the angular width of the central diffraction peak?

2. (I) Monochromatic light falls on a slit that is 2.60×10^{-3} mm wide. If the angle between the first dark fringes on either side of the central maximum is 32.0° (dark fringe to dark fringe), what is the wavelength of the light used?

3. (II) Light of wavelength 580 nm falls on a slit that is 3.80×10^{-3} mm wide. Estimate how far the first brightest diffraction fringe is from the strong central maximum if the screen is 10.0 m away.

4. (II) Consider microwaves which are incident perpendicular to a metal plate which has a 1.6-cm slit in it. Discuss the angles at which there are diffraction minima for wavelengths of (a) 0.50 cm, (b) 1.0 cm, and (c) 3.0 cm.

5. (II) If parallel light falls on a single slit of width D at a 23.0° angle to the normal, describe the diffraction pattern.

6. (II) Monochromatic light of wavelength 633 nm falls on a slit. If the angle between the first bright fringes on either side of the central maximum is 35°, estimate the slit width.

7. (II) If a slit diffracts 580-nm light so that the diffraction maximum is 6.0 cm wide on a screen 2.20 m away, what will be the width of the diffraction maximum for light with a wavelength of 460 nm?

8. (II) (a) For a given wavelength λ, what is the minimum slit width for which there will be no diffraction minima? (b) What is the minimum slit width so that no visible light exhibits a diffraction minimum?

9. (II) When blue light of wavelength 440 nm falls on a single slit, the first dark bands on either side of center are separated by 55.0°. Determine the width of the slit.

10. (II) A single slit 1.0 mm wide is illuminated by 450-nm light. What is the width of the central maximum (in cm) in the diffraction pattern on a screen 5.0 m away?

11. (II) Coherent light from a laser diode is emitted through a rectangular area $3.0 \, \mu$m $\times 1.5 \, \mu$m (horizontal-by-vertical). If the laser light has a wavelength of 780 nm, determine the angle between the first diffraction minima (a) above and below the central maximum, (b) to the left and right of the central maximum.

*35–2 Intensity, Single-Slit Diffraction Pattern

*12. (II) If you double the width of a single slit, the intensity of the light passing through the slit is doubled. (a) Show, however, that the intensity at the center of the screen increases by a factor of 4. (b) Explain why this does not violate conservation of energy.

*13. (II) Light of wavelength 750 nm passes through a slit 1.0 μm wide and a single-slit diffraction pattern is formed vertically on a screen 25 cm away. Determine the light intensity I 15 cm above the central maximum, expressed as a fraction of the central maximum's intensity I_0.

*14. (III) (a) Explain why the secondary maxima in the single-slit diffraction pattern do not occur precisely at $\beta/2 = (m + \frac{1}{2})\pi$ where $m = 1, 2, 3, \cdots$. (b) By differentiating Eq. 35–7 with respect to β show that the secondary maxima occur when $\beta/2$ satisfies the relation $\tan(\beta/2) = \beta/2$. (c) Carefully and precisely plot the curves $y = \beta/2$ and $y = \tan \beta/2$. From their intersections, determine the values of β for the first and second secondary maxima. What is the percent difference from $\beta/2 = (m + \frac{1}{2})\pi$?

*35–3 Intensity, Double-Slit Diffraction

*15. (II) If a double-slit pattern contains exactly nine fringes in the central diffraction peak, what can you say about the slit width and separation? Assume the first diffraction minimum occurs at an interference minimum.

*16. (II) Design a double-slit apparatus so that the central diffraction peak contains precisely seventeen fringes. Assume the first diffraction minimum occurs at (a) an interference mimimum, (b) an interference maximum.

*17. (II) 605-nm light passes through a pair of slits and creates an interference pattern on a screen 2.0 m behind the slits. The slits are separated by 0.120 mm and each slit is 0.040 mm wide. How many constructive interference fringes are formed on the screen? [Many of these fringes will be of very low intensity.]

*18. (II) In a double-slit experiment, if the central diffraction peak contains 13 interference fringes, how many fringes are contained within each secondary diffraction peak (between $m = +1$ and $+2$ in Eq. 35–2). Assume the first diffraction minimum occurs at an interference minimum.

*19. (II) Two 0.010-mm-wide slits are 0.030 mm apart (center to center). Determine (a) the spacing between interference fringes for 580 nm light on a screen 1.0 m away and (b) the distance between the two diffraction minima on either side of the central maximum of the envelope.

*20. (II) Suppose $d = D$ in a double-slit apparatus, so that the two slits merge into one slit of width $2D$. Show that Eq. 35–9 reduces to the correct equation for single-slit diffraction.

*21. (II) In a double-slit experiment, let $d = 5.00 D = 40.0 \lambda$. Compare (as a ratio) the intensity of the third-order interference maximum with that of the zero-order maximum.

*22. (II) How many fringes are contained in the central diffraction peak for a double-slit pattern if (a) $d = 2.00D$, (b) $d = 12.0D$, (c) $d = 4.50D$, (d) $d = 7.20D$.

*23. (III) (a) Derive an expression for the intensity in the interference pattern for three equally spaced slits. Express in terms of $\delta = 2\pi d \sin \theta / \lambda$ where d is the distance between adjacent slits and assume the slit width $D \approx \lambda$. (b) Show that there is only one secondary maximum between principal peaks.

35–4 and 35–5 Resolution Limits

24. (I) What is the angular resolution limit (degrees) set by diffraction for the 100-inch (254-cm mirror diameter) Mt. Wilson telescope ($\lambda = 560$ nm)?

25. (II) Two stars 16 light-years away are barely resolved by a 66-cm (mirror diameter) telescope. How far apart are the stars? Assume $\lambda = 550$ nm and that the resolution is limited by diffraction.

26. (II) The nearest neighboring star to the Sun is about 4 light-years away. If a planet happened to be orbiting this star at an orbital radius equal to that of the Earth–Sun distance, what minimum diameter would an Earth-based telescope's aperture have to be in order to obtain an image that resolved this star–planet system? Assume the light emitted by the star and planet has a wavelength of 550 nm.

27. (II) If you shine a flashlight beam toward the Moon, estimate the diameter of the beam when it reaches the Moon. Assume that the beam leaves the flashlight through a 5.0-cm aperture, that its white light has an average wavelength of 550 nm, and that the beam spreads due to diffraction only.

28. (II) Suppose that you wish to construct a telescope that can resolve features 7.5 km across on the moon, 384,000 km away. You have a 2.0-m-focal-length objective lens whose diameter is 11.0 cm. What focal-length eyepiece is needed if your eye can resolve objects 0.10 mm apart at a distance of 25 cm? What is the resolution limit set by the size of the objective lens (that is, by diffraction)? Use $\lambda = 560$ nm.

29. (II) The normal lens on a 35-mm camera has a focal length of 50.0 mm. Its aperture diameter varies from a maximum of 25 mm ($f/2$) to a minimum of 3.0 mm ($f/16$). Determine the resolution limit set by diffraction for ($f/2$) and ($f/16$). Specify as the number of lines per millimeter resolved on the detector or film. Take $\lambda = 560$ nm.

35-7 and 35-8 Diffraction Grating, Spectroscopy

30. (I) At what angle will 480-nm light produce a second-order maximum when falling on a grating whose slits are 1.35×10^{-3} cm apart?

31. (I) A source produces first-order lines when incident normally on a 12,000-line/cm diffraction grating at angles 28.8°, 36.7°, 38.6°, and 47.9°. What are the wavelengths?

32. (I) A 3500-line/cm grating produces a third-order fringe at a 26.0° angle. What wavelength of light is being used?

33. (I) A grating has 6800 lines/cm. How many spectral orders can be seen (400 to 700 nm) when it is illuminated by white light?

34. (II) How many lines per centimeter does a grating have if the third order occurs at a 15.0° angle for 650-nm light?

35. (II) Red laser light from a He–Ne laser ($\lambda = 632.8$ nm) is used to calibrate a diffraction grating. If this light creates a second-order fringe at 53.2° after passing through the grating, and light of an unknown wavelength λ creates a first-order fringe at 20.6°, find λ.

36. (II) White light containing wavelengths from 410 nm to 750 nm falls on a grating with 7800 lines/cm. How wide is the first-order spectrum on a screen 2.80 m away?

37. (II) A diffraction grating has 6.0×10^5 lines/m. Find the angular spread in the second-order spectrum between red light of wavelength 7.0×10^{-7} m and blue light of wavelength 4.5×10^{-7} m.

38. (II) A tungsten–halogen bulb emits a continuous spectrum of ultraviolet, visible, and infrared light in the wavelength range 360 nm to 2000 nm. Assume that the light from a tungsten–halogen bulb is incident on a diffraction grating with slit spacing d and that the first-order brightness maximum for the wavelength of 1200 nm occurs at angle θ. What other wavelengths within the spectrum of incident light will produce a brightness maximum at this same angle θ? [Optical filters are used to deal with this bothersome effect when a continuous spectrum of light is measured by a spectrometer.]

39. (II) Show that the second- and third-order spectra of white light produced by a diffraction grating always overlap. What wavelengths overlap?

40. (II) Two first-order spectrum lines are measured by a 9650 line/cm spectroscope at angles, on each side of center, of $+26°38'$, $+41°02'$ and $-26°18'$, $-40°27'$. Calculate the wavelengths based on these data.

41. (II) Suppose the angles measured in Problem 40 were produced when the spectrometer (but not the source) was submerged in water. What then would be the wavelengths (in air)?

42. (II) The first-order line of 589-nm light falling on a diffraction grating is observed at a 16.5° angle. How far apart are the slits? At what angle will the third order be observed?

43. (II) White light passes through a 610-line/mm diffraction grating. First-order and second-order visible spectra ("rainbows") appear on the wall 32 cm away as shown in Fig. 35–47. Determine the widths ℓ_1 and ℓ_2 of the two "rainbows" (400 nm to 700 nm). In which order is the "rainbow" dispersed over a larger distance?

FIGURE 35–47
Problem 43.

44. (II) **Missing orders** occur for a diffraction grating when a diffraction minimum coincides with an interference maximum. Let D be the width of each slit and d the separation of slits. (a) Show that if $d = 2D$, all even orders ($m = 2, 4, 6, \cdots$) are missing. (b) Show there will be missing orders whenever

$$\frac{d}{D} = \frac{m_1}{m_2}$$

where m_1 and m_2 are integers. (c) Discusss the case $d = D$, the limit in which the space between slits becomes negligible.

45. (II) Monochromatic light falls on a transmission diffraction grating at an angle ϕ to the normal. (a) Show that Eq. 35–13 for diffraction maxima must be replaced by

$$d(\sin \phi + \sin \theta) = \pm m\lambda. \qquad m = 0, 1, 2, \cdots.$$

(b) Explain the $\pm$ sign. (c) Green light with a wavelength of 550 nm is incident at an angle of 15° to the normal on a diffraction grating with 5000 lines/cm. Find the angles at which the first-order maxima occur.

*35-9 Grating, Peak Widths, Resolving Power

*46. (II) A 6500-line/cm diffraction grating is 3.18 cm wide. If light with wavelengths near 624 nm falls on the grating, how close can two wavelengths be if they are to be resolved in any order? What order gives the best resolution?

*47. (II) A diffraction grating has 16,000 rulings in its 1.9 cm width. Determine (a) its resolving power in first and second orders, and (b) the minimum wavelength resolution ($\Delta\lambda$) it can yield for $\lambda = 410$ nm.

*48. (II) Let 580-nm light be incident normally on a diffraction grating for which $d = 3.00D = 1050$ nm. (a) How many orders (principal maxima) are present? (b) If the grating is 1.80 cm wide, what is the full angular width of each principal maximum?

35-10 X-Ray Diffraction

49. (II) X-rays of wavelength 0.138 nm fall on a crystal whose atoms, lying in planes, are spaced 0.285 nm apart. At what angle ϕ (relative to the surface, Fig. 35–28) must the X-rays be directed if the first diffraction maximum is to be observed?

50. (II) First-order Bragg diffraction is observed at 26.8° relative to the crystal surface, with spacing between atoms of 0.24 nm. (a) At what angle will second order be observed? (b) What is the wavelength of the X-rays?

51. (II) If X-ray diffraction peaks corresponding to the first three orders ($m = 1, 2,$ and 3) are measured, can both the X-ray wavelength λ and lattice spacing d be determined? Prove your answer.

35–11 Polarization

52. (I) Two polarizers are oriented at 65° to one another. Unpolarized light falls on them. What fraction of the light intensity is transmitted?

53. (I) Two Polaroids are aligned so that the light passing through them is a maximum. At what angle should one of them be placed so the intensity is subsequently reduced by half?

54. (I) What is Brewster's angle for an air–glass ($n = 1.58$) surface?

55. (I) What is Brewster's angle for a diamond submerged in water if the light is hitting the diamond ($n = 2.42$) while traveling in the water?

56. (II) The critical angle for total internal reflection at a boundary between two materials is 55°. What is Brewster's angle at this boundary? Give two answers, one for each material.

57. (II) At what angle should the axes of two Polaroids be placed so as to reduce the intensity of the incident unpolarized light to (a) $\frac{1}{3}$, (b) $\frac{1}{10}$?

58. (II) Two polarizers are oriented at 36.0° to one another. Light polarized at an 18.0° angle to each polarizer passes through both. What is the transmitted intensity (%)?

59. (II) What would Brewster's angle be for reflections off the surface of water for light coming from beneath the surface? Compare to the angle for total internal reflection, and to Brewster's angle from above the surface.

60. (II) Unpolarized light passes through six successive Polaroid sheets each of whose axis makes a 45° angle with the previous one. What is the intensity of the transmitted beam?

61. (II) Two polarizers A and B are aligned so that their transmission axes are vertical and horizontal, respectively. A third polarizer is placed between these two with its axis aligned at angle θ with respect to the vertical. Assuming vertically polarized light of intensity I_0 is incident upon polarizer A, find an expression for the light intensity I transmitted through this three-polarizer sequence. Calculate the derivative $dI/d\theta$; then use it to find the angle θ that maximizes I.

62. (III) The percent polarization P of a partially polarized beam of light is defined as

$$P = \frac{I_{max} - I_{min}}{I_{max} + I_{min}} \times 100$$

where I_{max} and I_{min} are the maximum and minimum intensities that are obtained when the light passes through a polarizer that is slowly rotated. Such light can be considered as the sum of two unequal plane-polarized beams of intensities I_{max} and I_{min} perpendicular to each other. Show that the light transmitted by a polarizer, whose axis makes an angle ϕ to the direction in which I_{max} is obtained, has intensity

$$\frac{1 + p \cos 2\phi}{1 + p} I_{max}$$

where $p = P/100$ is the "fractional polarization."

General Problems

63. When violet light of wavelength 415 nm falls on a single slit, it creates a central diffraction peak that is 8.20 cm wide on a screen that is 2.85 m away. How wide is the slit?

64. A series of polarizers are each placed at a 10° interval from the previous polarizer. Unpolarized light is incident on this series of polarizers. How many polarizers does the light have to go through before it is $\frac{1}{4}$ of its original intensity?

65. The wings of a certain beetle have a series of parallel lines across them. When normally incident 480-nm light is reflected from the wing, the wing appears bright when viewed at an angle of 56°. How far apart are the lines?

66. A teacher stands well back from an outside doorway 0.88 m wide, and blows a whistle of frequency 850 Hz. Ignoring reflections, estimate at what angle(s) it is *not* possible to hear the whistle clearly on the playground outside the doorway. Assume 340 m/s for the speed of sound.

67. Light is incident on a diffraction grating with 7600 lines/cm and the pattern is viewed on a screen located 2.5 m from the grating. The incident light beam consists of two wavelengths, $\lambda_1 = 4.4 \times 10^{-7}$ m and $\lambda_2 = 6.8 \times 10^{-7}$ m. Calculate the linear distance between the first-order bright fringes of these two wavelengths on the screen.

68. How many lines per centimeter must a grating have if there is to be no second-order spectrum for any visible wavelength?

69. When yellow sodium light, $\lambda = 589$ nm, falls on a diffraction grating, its first-order peak on a screen 66.0 cm away falls 3.32 cm from the central peak. Another source produces a line 3.71 cm from the central peak. What is its wavelength? How many lines/cm are on the grating?

70. Two of the lines of the atomic hydrogen spectrum have wavelengths of 656 nm and 410 nm. If these fall at normal incidence on a grating with 8100 lines/cm, what will be the angular separation of the two wavelengths in the first-order spectrum?

71. (a) How far away can a human eye distinguish two car headlights 2.0 m apart? Consider only diffraction effects and assume an eye diameter of 6.0 mm and a wavelength of 560 nm. (b) What is the minimum angular separation an eye could resolve when viewing two stars, considering only diffraction effects? In reality, it is about 1′ of arc. Why is it not equal to your answer in (b)?

72. A laser beam passes through a slit of width 1.0 cm and is pointed at the Moon, which is approximately 380,000 km from the Earth. Assume the laser emits waves of wavelength 633 nm (the red light of a He–Ne laser). Estimate the width of the beam when it reaches the Moon.

73. A He–Ne gas laser which produces monochromatic light of wavelength $\lambda = 6.328 \times 10^{-7}$ m is used to calibrate a reflection grating in a spectroscope. The first-order diffraction line is found at an angle of 21.5° to the incident beam. How many lines per meter are there on the grating?

74. The entrance to a boy's bedroom consists of two door-ways, each 1.0 m wide, which are separated by a distance of 3.0 m. The boy's mother yells at him through the two doors as shown in Fig. 35–48, telling him to clean up his room. Her voice has a frequency of 400 Hz. Later, when the mother discovers the room is still a mess, the boy says he never heard her telling him to clean his room. The velocity of sound is 340 m/s. (a) Find all of the angles θ (Fig. 35–48) at which no sound will be heard within the bedroom when the mother yells. Assume sound is completely absorbed when it strikes a bedroom wall. (b) If the boy was at the position shown when his mother yelled, does he have a good explanation for not having heard her? Explain.

FIGURE 35–48
Problem 74.

75. At what angle above the horizon is the Sun when light reflecting off a smooth lake is polarized most strongly?

76. Unpolarized light falls on two polarizer sheets whose axes are at right angles. (a) What fraction of the incident light intensity is transmitted? (b) What fraction is transmitted if a third polarizer is placed between the first two so that its axis makes a 66° angle with the axis of the first polarizer? (c) What if the third polarizer is in front of the other two?

77. At what angle should the axes of two Polaroids be placed so as to reduce the intensity of the incident unpolarized light by an additional factor (after the first Polaroid cuts it in half) of (a) 4, (b) 10, (c) 100?

78. Four polarizers are placed in succession with their axes vertical, at 30.0° to the vertical, at 60.0° to the vertical, and at 90.0° to the vertical. (a) Calculate what fraction of the incident unpolarized light is transmitted by the four polarizers. (b) Can the transmitted light be *decreased* by removing one of the polarizers? If so, which one? (c) Can the transmitted light intensity be extinguished by removing polarizers? If so, which one(s)?

79. Spy planes fly at extremely high altitudes (25 km) to avoid interception. Their cameras are reportedly able to discern features as small as 5 cm. What must be the minimum aperture of the camera lens to afford this resolution? (Use $\lambda = 580$ nm.)

80. Two polarizers are oriented at 48° to each other and plane-polarized light is incident on them. If only 25% of the light gets through both of them, what was the initial polarization direction of the incident light?

81. X-rays of wavelength 0.0973 nm are directed at an unknown crystal. The second diffraction maximum is recorded when the X-rays are directed at an angle of 23.4° relative to the crystal surface. What is the spacing between crystal planes?

82. X-rays of wavelength 0.10 nm fall on a microcrystalline powder sample. The sample is located 12 cm from the photographic film. The crystal structure of the sample has an atomic spacing of 0.22 nm. Calculate the radii of the diffraction rings corresponding to first- and second-order scattering. Note in Fig. 35–28 that the X-ray beam is deflected through an angle 2ϕ.

83. The Hubble Space Telescope with an objective diameter of 2.4 m, is viewing the Moon. Estimate the minimum distance between two objects on the Moon that the Hubble can distinguish. Consider diffraction of light with wavelength 550 nm. Assume the Hubble is near the Earth.

84. The Earth and Moon are separated by about 400×10^6 m. When Mars is 8×10^{10} m from Earth, could a person standing on Mars resolve the Earth and its Moon as two separate objects without a telescope? Assume a pupil diameter of 5 mm and $\lambda = 550$ nm.

85. A slit of width $D = 22$ μm is cut through a thin aluminum plate. Light with wavelength $\lambda = 650$ nm passes through this slit and forms a single-slit diffraction pattern on a screen a distance $\ell = 2.0$ m away. Defining x to be the distance between the first minima ($m = +1$ and $m = -1$) in this diffraction pattern, find the change Δx in this distance when the temperature T of the metal plate is changed by amount $\Delta T = 55$ C°. [*Hint*: Since $\lambda \ll D$, the first minima occur at a small angle.]

*Numerical/Computer

***86.** (II) A student shined a laser light onto a single slit of width 0.04000 mm. He placed a screen at a distance of 1.490 m from the slit to observe the diffraction pattern of the laser light. The accompanying Table shows the distances of the dark fringes from the center of the central bright fringe for different orders.

Order number, m:	1	2	3	4	5	6	7	8
Distance (m)	0.0225	0.0445	0.0655	0.0870	0.1105	0.1320	0.1540	0.1775

Determine the angle of diffraction, θ, and $\sin \theta$ for each order. Make a graph of $\sin \theta$ vs. order number, m, and find the wavelength, λ, of the laser from the best-fit straight line.

***87.** (III) Describe how to rotate the plane of polarization of a plane-polarized beam of light by 90° and produce only a 10% loss in intensity, using polarizers. Let N be the number of polarizers and θ be the (same) angle between successive polarizers.

88. (III) The "full-width at half-maximum" (FWHM) of the central peak for single-slit diffraction is defined as the angle $\Delta \theta$ between the two points on either side of center where the intensity is $\frac{1}{2} I_0$. (a) Determine $\Delta \theta$ in terms of (λ/D). Use graphs or a spreadsheet to solve $\sin \alpha = \alpha/\sqrt{2}$. (b) Determine $\Delta \theta$ (in degrees) for $D = \lambda$ and for $D = 100\lambda$.

Answers to Exercises

A: Narrower.

B: (b).

C: (c).

D: 0.28 nm.

E: Zero for both (a) and (b), because the two successive polarizers at 90° cancel all light. The 45° Polaroid must be inserted *between* the other two if any transmission is to occur.

An early science fantasy book (1940), called *Mr Tompkins in Wonderland* by physicist George Gamow, imagined a world in which the speed of light was only 10 m/s (20 mi/h). Mr Tompkins had studied relativity and when he began "speeding" on a bicycle, he "expected that he would be immediately shortened, and was very happy about it as his increasing figure had lately caused him some anxiety. To his great surprise, however, nothing happened to him or to his cycle. On the other hand, the picture around him completely changed. The streets grew shorter, the windows of the shops began to look like narrow slits, and the policeman on the corner became the thinnest man he had ever seen. 'By Jove!' exclaimed Mr Tompkins excitedly, 'I see the trick now. This is where the word *relativity* comes in.' "

Relativity does indeed predict that objects moving relative to us at high speed, close to the speed of light c, are shortened in length. We don't notice it as Mr Tompkins did, because $c = 3 \times 10^8$ m/s is incredibly fast. We will study length contraction, time dilation, simultaneity non-agreement, and how energy and mass are equivalent ($E = mc^2$).

The Special Theory of Relativity

CHAPTER 36

CHAPTER-OPENING QUESTION—Guess now!

A rocket is headed away from Earth at a speed of 0.80c. The rocket fires a missile at a speed of 0.70c (the missile is aimed away from Earth and leaves the rocket at 0.70c relative to the rocket). How fast is the missile moving relative to Earth?

(a) 1.50c;
(b) a little less than 1.50c;
(c) a little over c;
(d) a little under c;
(e) 0.75c.

Physics at the end of the nineteenth century looked back on a period of great progress. The theories developed over the preceding three centuries had been very successful in explaining a wide range of natural phenomena. Newtonian mechanics beautifully explained the motion of objects on Earth and in the heavens. Furthermore, it formed the basis for successful treatments of fluids, wave motion, and sound. Kinetic theory explained the behavior of gases and other materials. Maxwell's theory of electromagnetism not only brought together and explained electric and magnetic phenomena, but it predicted the existence of electromagnetic waves that would behave in every way just like light—so light came to be thought of as an electromagnetic wave. Indeed, it seemed that the natural world, as seen through the eyes of physicists, was very well explained. A few puzzles remained, but it was felt that these would soon be explained using already known principles.

CONTENTS

FIGURE 36–1 Albert Einstein (1879–1955), one of the great minds of the twentieth century, was the creator of the special and general theories of relativity.

It did not turn out so simply. Instead, these puzzles were to be solved only by the introduction, in the early part of the twentieth century, of two revolutionary new theories that changed our whole conception of nature: the *theory of relativity* and *quantum theory.*

Physics as it was known at the end of the nineteenth century (what we've covered up to now in this book) is referred to as **classical physics**. The new physics that grew out of the great revolution at the turn of the twentieth century is now called **modern physics**. In this Chapter, we present the special theory of relativity, which was first proposed by Albert Einstein (1879–1955; Fig. 36–1) in 1905. In Chapter 37, we introduce the equally momentous quantum theory.

36–1 Galilean–Newtonian Relativity

Einstein's special theory of relativity deals with how we observe events, particularly how objects and events are observed from different frames of reference. This subject had, of course, already been explored by Galileo and Newton.

The special theory of relativity deals with events that are observed and measured from so-called **inertial reference frames** (Sections 4–2 and 11–8), which are reference frames in which Newton's first law is valid: if an object experiences no net force, the object either remains at rest or continues in motion with constant speed in a straight line. It is usually easiest to analyze events when they are observed and measured by observers at rest in an inertial frame. The Earth, though not quite an inertial frame (it rotates), is close enough that for most purposes we can consider it an inertial frame. Rotating or otherwise accelerating frames of reference are noninertial frames,[†] and won't concern us in this Chapter (they are dealt with in Einstein's general theory of relativity).

A reference frame that moves with constant velocity with respect to an inertial frame is itself also an inertial frame, since Newton's laws hold in it as well. When we say that we observe or make measurements from a certain reference frame, it means that we are at rest in that reference frame.

Both Galileo and Newton were aware of what we now call the **relativity principle** applied to mechanics: that *the basic laws of physics are the same in all inertial reference frames.* You may have recognized its validity in everyday life. For example, objects move in the same way in a smoothly moving (constant-velocity) train or airplane as they do on Earth. (This assumes no vibrations or rocking which would make the reference frame noninertial.) When you walk, drink a cup of soup, play pool, or drop a pencil on the floor while traveling in a train, airplane, or ship moving at constant velocity, the objects move just as they do when you are at rest on Earth. Suppose you are in a car traveling rapidly at constant velocity. If you drop a coin from above your head inside the car, how will it fall? It falls straight downward with respect to the car, and hits the floor directly below the point of release, Fig. 36–2a.

FIGURE 36–2 A coin is dropped by a person in a moving car. The upper views show the moment of the coin's release, the lower views are a short time later. (a) In the reference frame of the car, the coin falls straight down (and the tree moves to the left). (b) In a reference frame fixed on the Earth, the coin has an initial velocity (= to car's) and follows a curved (parabolic) path.

[†]On a rotating platform (say a merry-go-round), for example, an object at rest starts moving outward even though no object exerts a force on it. This is therefore not an inertial frame. See Section 11–8.

(a)
Reference frame = car

(b)
Reference frame = Earth

This is just how objects fall on the Earth—straight down—and thus our experiment in the moving car is in accord with the relativity principle. (If you drop the coin out the car's window, this won't happen because the moving air drags the coin backward relative to the car.)

Note in this example, however, that to an observer on the Earth, the coin follows a curved path, Fig. 36–2b. The actual path followed by the coin is different as viewed from different frames of reference. This does not violate the relativity principle because this principle states that the *laws* of physics are the same in all inertial frames. The same law of gravity, and the same laws of motion, apply in both reference frames. The acceleration of the coin is the same in both reference frames. The difference in Figs. 36–2a and b is that in the Earth's frame of reference, the coin has an initial velocity (equal to that of the car). The laws of physics therefore predict it will follow a parabolic path like any projectile (Chapter 3). In the car's reference frame, there is no initial velocity, and the laws of physics predict that the coin will fall straight down. The laws are the same in both reference frames, although the specific paths are different.

Galilean–Newtonian relativity involves certain unprovable assumptions that make sense from everyday experience. It is assumed that the lengths of objects are the same in one reference frame as in another, and that time passes at the same rate in different reference frames. In classical mechanics, then, space and time intervals are considered to be **absolute**: their measurement does not change from one reference frame to another. The mass of an object, as well as all forces, are assumed to be unchanged by a change in inertial reference frame.

The position of an object, however, is different when specified in different reference frames, and so is velocity. For example, a person may walk inside a bus toward the front with a speed of 2 m/s. But if the bus moves 10 m/s with respect to the Earth, the person is then moving with a speed of 12 m/s with respect to the Earth. The acceleration of an object, however, is the same in any inertial reference frame according to classical mechanics. This is because the change in velocity, and the time interval, will be the same. For example, the person in the bus may accelerate from 0 to 2 m/s in 1.0 seconds, so $a = 2\,\text{m/s}^2$ in the reference frame of the bus. With respect to the Earth, the acceleration is $(12\,\text{m/s} - 10\,\text{m/s})/(1.0\,\text{s}) = 2\,\text{m/s}^2$, which is the same.

Since neither F, m, nor a changes from one inertial frame to another, then Newton's second law, $F = ma$, does not change. Thus Newton's second law satisfies the relativity principle. It is easily shown that the other laws of mechanics also satisfy the relativity principle.

That the laws of mechanics are the same in all inertial reference frames implies that no one inertial frame is special in any sense. We express this important conclusion by saying that **all inertial reference frames are equivalent** for the description of mechanical phenomena. No one inertial reference frame is any better than another. A reference frame fixed to a car or an aircraft traveling at constant velocity is as good as one fixed on the Earth. When you travel smoothly at constant velocity in a car or airplane, it is just as valid to say you are at rest and the Earth is moving as it is to say the reverse.[†] There is no experiment you can do to tell which frame is "really" at rest and which is moving. Thus, there is no way to single out one particular reference frame as being at absolute rest.

A complication arose, however, in the last half of the nineteenth century. Maxwell's comprehensive and successful theory of electromagnetism (Chapter 31) predicted that light is an electromagnetic wave. Maxwell's equations gave the velocity of light c as $3.00 \times 10^8\,\text{m/s}$; and this is just what is measured. The question then arose: in what reference frame does light have precisely the value predicted by Maxwell's theory? It was assumed that light would have a different speed in different frames of reference. For example, if observers were traveling on a rocket ship at a speed of $1.0 \times 10^8\,\text{m/s}$ away from a source of light, we might expect them to measure the speed of the light reaching them to be $(3.0 \times 10^8\,\text{m/s}) - (1.0 \times 10^8\,\text{m/s}) = 2.0 \times 10^8\,\text{m/s}$. But Maxwell's equations have no provision for relative velocity. They predicted the speed of light to be $c = 3.0 \times 10^8\,\text{m/s}$, which seemed to imply that there must be some preferred reference frame where c would have this value.

[†]We are ignoring the rotation and curvature of the Earth.

CAUTION

Laws are the same, but paths may be different in different reference frames

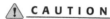

CAUTION

Position and velocity are different in different reference frames, but length is the same (classical)

We discussed in Chapters 15 and 16 that waves can travel on water and along ropes or strings, and sound waves travel in air and other materials. Nineteenth-century physicists viewed the material world in terms of the laws of mechanics, so it was natural for them to assume that light too must travel in some *medium*. They called this transparent medium the **ether** and assumed it permeated all space.[†] It was therefore assumed that the velocity of light given by Maxwell's equations must be with respect to the ether.

At first it appeared that Maxwell's equations did *not* satisfy the relativity principle. They were simplest in the frame where $c = 3.00 \times 10^8$ m/s; that is, in a reference frame at rest in the ether. In any other reference frame, extra terms would have to be added to take into account the relative velocity. Thus, although most of the laws of physics obeyed the relativity principle, the laws of electricity and magnetism apparently did not. Einstein's second postulate (Section 36–3) resolved this problem: Maxwell's equations do satisfy relativity.

Scientists soon set out to determine the speed of the Earth relative to this absolute frame, whatever it might be. A number of clever experiments were designed. The most direct were performed by A. A. Michelson and E. W. Morley in the 1880s. They measured the difference in the speed of light in different directions using Michelson's interferometer (Section 34–6). They expected to find a difference depending on the orientation of their apparatus with respect to the ether. For just as a boat has different speeds relative to the land when it moves upstream, downstream, or across the stream, so too light would be expected to have different speeds depending on the velocity of the ether past the Earth.

Strange as it may seem, they detected no difference at all. This was a great puzzle. A number of explanations were put forth over a period of years, but they led to contradictions or were otherwise not generally accepted. This **null result** was one of the great puzzles at the end of the nineteenth century.

Then in 1905, Albert Einstein proposed a radical new theory that reconciled these many problems in a simple way. But at the same time, as we shall see, it completely changed our ideas of space and time.

*36–2 The Michelson–Morley Experiment

The Michelson–Morley experiment was designed to measure the speed of the *ether*—the medium in which light was assumed to travel—with respect to the Earth. The experimenters thus hoped to find an absolute reference frame, one that could be considered to be at rest.

One of the possibilities nineteenth-century scientists considered was that the ether is fixed relative to the Sun, for even Newton had taken the Sun as the center of the universe. If this were the case (there was no guarantee, of course), the Earth's speed of about 3×10^4 m/s in its orbit around the Sun could produce a change of 1 part in 10^4 in the speed of light $(3.0 \times 10^8$ m/s$)$. Direct measurement of the speed of light to this precision was not possible. But A. A. Michelson, later with the help of E. W. Morley, was able to use his interferometer (Section 34–6) to measure the difference in the speed of light in different directions to this precision.

This famous experiment is based on the principle shown in Fig. 36–3. Part (a) is a diagram of the Michelson interferometer, and it is assumed that the "ether wind" is moving with speed v to the right. (Alternatively, the Earth is assumed to move to the left with respect to the ether at speed v.) The light from a source is split into two beams by a half-silvered mirror M_S. One beam travels to mirror M_1 and the other to mirror M_2. The beams are reflected by M_1 and M_2 and are joined again after passing through M_S. The now superposed beams interfere with each other and the resultant is viewed by the observer's eye as an interference pattern (discussed in Section 34–6).

Whether constructive or destructive interference occurs at the center of the interference pattern depends on the relative phases of the two beams after they have traveled their separate paths. Let us consider an analogy of a boat traveling up and

---

[†]The medium for light waves could not be air, since light travels from the Sun to Earth through nearly empty space. Therefore, another medium was postulated, the ether. The ether was not only transparent but, because of difficulty in detecting it, was assumed to have zero density.

(a)

(b)

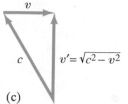

(c)

FIGURE 36–3 The Michelson–Morley experiment. (a) Michelson interferometer. (b) Boat analogy: boat 1 goes across the stream and back; boat 2 goes downstream and back upstream (boat has speed c relative to the water). (c) Calculation of the velocity of boat (or light beam) traveling perpendicular to the current (or ether wind).

down, and across, a river whose current moves with speed v, as shown in Fig. 36–3b. In still water, the boat can travel with speed c (not the speed of light in this case).

First we consider beam 2 in Fig. 36–3a, which travels parallel to the "ether wind." In its journey from M_S to M_2, the light would travel with speed $c + v$, according to classical physics, just as for a boat traveling downstream (see Fig. 36–3b) we add the speed of the river water to the boat's own speed (relative to the water) to get the boat's speed relative to the shore. Since the beam travels a distance ℓ_2, the time it takes to go from M_S to M_2 would be $t = \ell_2/(c + v)$. To make the return trip from M_2 to M_S, the light moves against the ether wind (like the boat going upstream), so its relative speed is expected to be $c - v$. The time for the return trip would be $\ell_2/(c - v)$. The total time for beam 2 to travel from M_S to M_2 and back to M_S is

$$t_2 = \frac{\ell_2}{c + v} + \frac{\ell_2}{c - v} = \frac{2\ell_2}{c\left(1 - v^2/c^2\right)}.$$

Now let us consider beam 1, which travels crosswise to the ether wind. Here the boat analogy (Fig. 36–3b) is especially helpful. The boat is to go from wharf A to wharf B directly across the stream. If it heads directly across, the stream's current will drag it downstream. To reach wharf B, the boat must head at an angle upstream. The precise angle depends on the magnitudes of c and v, but is of no interest to us in itself. Part (c) of Fig. 36–3 shows how to calculate the velocity v' of the boat relative to Earth as it crosses the stream. Since c, v, and v' form a right triangle, we have that $v' = \sqrt{c^2 - v^2}$. The boat has the same speed when it returns. If we now apply these principles to light beam 1 in Fig. 36–3a, we expect the beam to travel with speed $\sqrt{c^2 - v^2}$ in going from M_S to M_1 and back again. The total distance traveled is $2\ell_1$, so the time required for beam 1 to make the round trip would be $2\ell_1/\sqrt{c^2 - v^2}$, or

$$t_1 = \frac{2\ell_1}{c\sqrt{1 - v^2/c^2}}.$$

Notice that the denominator in this equation for t_1 involves a square root, whereas that for t_2 does not.

If $\ell_1 = \ell_2 = \ell$, we see that beam 2 will lag behind beam 1 by an amount

$$\Delta t = t_2 - t_1 = \frac{2\ell}{c}\left(\frac{1}{1 - v^2/c^2} - \frac{1}{\sqrt{1 - v^2/c^2}}\right).$$

If $v = 0$, then $\Delta t = 0$, and the two beams will return in phase since they were initially in phase. But if $v \neq 0$, then $\Delta t \neq 0$, and the two beams will return out of phase. If this change of phase from the condition $v = 0$ to that for $v \neq 0$ could be measured, then v could be determined. But the Earth cannot be stopped. Furthermore, we should not be too quick to assume that lengths are not affected by motion and therefore to assume $\ell_1 = \ell_2$.

Michelson and Morley realized that they could detect the difference in phase (assuming that $v \neq 0$) if they rotated their apparatus by 90°, for then the interference pattern between the two beams should change. In the rotated position, beam 1 would now move parallel to the ether and beam 2 perpendicular to it. Thus the roles could be reversed, and in the rotated position the times (designated by primes) would be

$$t_1' = \frac{2\ell_1}{c\left(1 - v^2/c^2\right)} \quad \text{and} \quad t_2' = \frac{2\ell_2}{c\sqrt{1 - v^2/c^2}}.$$

The time lag between the two beams in the nonrotated position (unprimed) would be

$$\Delta t = t_2 - t_1 = \frac{2\ell_2}{c\left(1 - v^2/c^2\right)} - \frac{2\ell_1}{c\sqrt{1 - v^2/c^2}}.$$

In the rotated position, the time difference would be

$$\Delta t' = t_2' - t_1' = \frac{2\ell_2}{c\sqrt{1 - v^2/c^2}} - \frac{2\ell_1}{c\left(1 - v^2/c^2\right)}.$$

When the rotation is made, the fringes of the interference pattern (Section 34–6) will shift an amount determined by the difference:

$$\Delta t - \Delta t' = \frac{2}{c}(\ell_1 + \ell_2)\left(\frac{1}{1 - v^2/c^2} - \frac{1}{\sqrt{1 - v^2/c^2}}\right).$$

This expression can be considerably simplified if we assume that $v/c \ll 1$. In this case we can use the binomial expansion (Appendix A), so

$$\frac{1}{1 - v^2/c^2} \approx 1 + \frac{v^2}{c^2} \quad \text{and} \quad \frac{1}{\sqrt{1 - v^2/c^2}} \approx 1 + \frac{1}{2}\frac{v^2}{c^2}.$$

Then

$$\Delta t - \Delta t' \approx \frac{2}{c}(\ell_1 + \ell_2)\left(1 + \frac{v^2}{c^2} - 1 - \frac{1}{2}\frac{v^2}{c^2}\right)$$

$$\approx (\ell_1 + \ell_2)\frac{v^2}{c^3}.$$

Now we assume $v = 3.0 \times 10^4\,\text{m/s}$, the speed of the Earth in its orbit around the Sun. In Michelson and Morley's experiments, the arms ℓ_1 and ℓ_2 were about 11 m long. The time difference would then be about

$$\frac{(22\,\text{m})(3.0 \times 10^4\,\text{m/s})^2}{(3.0 \times 10^8\,\text{m/s})^3} \approx 7.3 \times 10^{-16}\,\text{s}.$$

For visible light of wavelength $\lambda = 5.5 \times 10^{-7}\,\text{m}$, say, the frequency would be $f = c/\lambda = (3.0 \times 10^8\,\text{m/s})/(5.5 \times 10^{-7}\,\text{m}) = 5.5 \times 10^{14}\,\text{Hz}$, which means that wave crests pass by a point every $1/(5.5 \times 10^{14}\,\text{Hz}) = 1.8 \times 10^{-15}\,\text{s}$. Thus, with a time difference of $7.3 \times 10^{-16}\,\text{s}$, Michelson and Morley should have noted a movement in the interference pattern of $(7.3 \times 10^{-16}\,\text{s})/(1.8 \times 10^{-15}\,\text{s}) = 0.4$ fringe. They could easily have detected this, since their apparatus was capable of observing a fringe shift as small as 0.01 fringe.

But they found *no significant fringe shift whatever*! They set their apparatus at various orientations. They made observations day and night so that they would be at various orientations with respect to the Sun (due to the Earth's rotation).

They tried at different seasons of the year (the Earth at different locations due to its orbit around the Sun). Never did they observe a significant fringe shift.

This **null result** was one of the great puzzles of physics at the end of the nineteenth century. To explain it was a difficult challenge. One possibility to explain the null result was put forth independently by G. F. Fitzgerald and H. A. Lorentz (in the 1890s) in which they proposed that any length (including the arm of an interferometer) contracts by a factor $\sqrt{1 - v^2/c^2}$ in the direction of motion through the ether. According to Lorentz, this could be due to the ether affecting the forces between the molecules of a substance, which were assumed to be electrical in nature. This theory was eventually replaced by the far more comprehensive theory proposed by Albert Einstein in 1905—the special theory of relativity.

36–3 Postulates of the Special Theory of Relativity

The problems that existed at the start of the twentieth century with regard to electromagnetic theory and Newtonian mechanics were beautifully resolved by Einstein's introduction of the theory of relativity in 1905. Unaware of the Michelson–Morley null result, Einstein was motivated by certain questions regarding electromagnetic theory and light waves. For example, he asked himself: "What would I see if I rode a light beam?" The answer was that instead of a traveling electromagnetic wave, he would see alternating electric and magnetic fields at rest whose magnitude changed in space, but did not change in time. Such fields, he realized, had never been detected and indeed were not consistent with Maxwell's electromagnetic theory. He argued, therefore, that it was unreasonable to think that the speed of light relative to any observer could be reduced to zero, or in fact reduced at all. This idea became the second postulate of his theory of relativity.

In his famous 1905 paper, Einstein proposed doing away completely with the idea of the ether and the accompanying assumption of a preferred or absolute reference frame at rest. This proposal was embodied in two postulates. The first postulate was an extension of the Galilean–Newtonian relativity principle to include not only the laws of mechanics but also those of the rest of physics, including electricity and magnetism:

>*First postulate (the relativity principle):* **The laws of physics have the same form in all inertial reference frames.**

The first postulate can also be stated as: *There is no experiment you can do in an inertial reference frame to tell if you are at rest or moving uniformly at constant velocity.*

The second postulate is consistent with the first:

>*Second postulate (constancy of the speed of light):* **Light propagates through empty space with a definite speed c independent of the speed of the source or observer.**

These two postulates form the foundation of Einstein's **special theory of relativity**. It is called "special" to distinguish it from his later "general theory of relativity," which deals with noninertial (accelerating) reference frames (Chapter 44). The special theory, which is what we discuss here, deals only with inertial frames.

The second postulate may seem hard to accept, for it seems to violate common sense. First of all, we have to think of light traveling through empty space. Giving up the ether is not too hard, however, since it had never been detected. But the second postulate also tells us that the speed of light in vacuum is always the same, 3.00×10^8 m/s, no matter what the speed of the observer or the source. Thus, a person traveling toward or away from a source of light will measure the same speed for that light as someone at rest with respect to the source. This conflicts with our everyday experience: we would expect to have to add in the velocity of the observer. On the other hand, perhaps we can't expect our everyday experience to be helpful when dealing with the high velocity of light. Furthermore, the null result of the Michelson–Morley experiment is fully consistent with the second postulate.[†]

[†]The Michelson–Morley experiment can also be considered as evidence for the first postulate, since it was intended to measure the motion of the Earth relative to an absolute reference frame. Its failure to do so implies the absence of any such preferred frame.

Einstein's proposal has a certain beauty. By doing away with the idea of an absolute reference frame, it was possible to reconcile classical mechanics with Maxwell's electromagnetic theory. The speed of light predicted by Maxwell's equations *is* the speed of light in vacuum in *any* reference frame.

Einstein's theory required us to give up common sense notions of space and time, and in the following Sections we will examine some strange but interesting consequences of special relativity. Our arguments for the most part will be simple ones. We will use a technique that Einstein himself did: we will imagine very simple experimental situations in which little mathematics is needed. In this way, we can see many of the consequences of relativity theory without getting involved in detailed calculations. Einstein called these "thought" experiments.

36–4 Simultaneity

An important consequence of the theory of relativity is that we can no longer regard time as an absolute quantity. No one doubts that time flows onward and never turns back. But the time interval between two events, and even whether or not two events are simultaneous, depends on the observer's reference frame. By an **event**, which we use a lot here, we mean something that happens at a particular place and at a particular time.

Two events are said to occur simultaneously if they occur at exactly the same time. But how do we know if two events occur precisely at the same time? If they occur at the same point in space—such as two apples falling on your head at the same time—it is easy. But if the two events occur at widely separated places, it is more difficult to know whether the events are simultaneous since we have to take into account the time it takes for the light from them to reach us. Because light travels at finite speed, a person who sees two events must calculate back to find out when they actually occurred. For example, if two events are *observed* to occur at the same time, but one actually took place farther from the observer than the other, then the more distant one must have occurred earlier, and the two events were not simultaneous.

We now imagine a simple thought experiment. Assume an observer, called O, is located exactly halfway between points A and B where two events occur, Fig. 36–4. Suppose the two events are lightning that strikes the points A and B, as shown. For brief events like lightning, only short pulses of light (blue in Fig. 36–4) will travel outward from A and B and reach O. Observer O "sees" the events when the pulses of light reach point O. If the two pulses reach O at the same time, then the two events had to be simultaneous. This is because the two light pulses travel at the same speed (postulate 2), and since the distance OA equals OB, the time for the light to travel from A to O and B to O must be the same. Observer O can then definitely state that the two events occurred simultaneously. On the other hand, if O sees the light from one event before that from the other, then the former event occurred first.

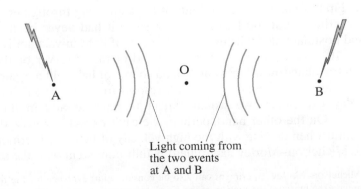

FIGURE 36–4 A moment after lightning strikes at points A and B, the pulses of light (shown as blue waves) are traveling toward the observer O, but O "sees" the lightning only when the light reaches O.

Light coming from the two events at A and B

The question we really want to examine is this: if two events are simultaneous to an observer in one reference frame, are they also simultaneous to another observer moving with respect to the first? Let us call the observers O_1 and O_2 and assume they are fixed in reference frames 1 and 2 that move with speed v relative to one another. These two reference frames can be thought of as two rockets or two trains (Fig. 36–5). O_2 says that O_1 is moving to the right with speed v, as in Fig. 36–5a; and O_1 says O_2 is moving to the left with speed v, as in Fig. 36–5b. Both viewpoints are legitimate according to the relativity principle. [There is no third point of view which will tell us which one is "really" moving.]

Now suppose that observers O_1 and O_2 observe and measure two lightning strikes. The lightning bolts mark both trains where they strike: at A_1 and B_1 on O_1's train, and at A_2 and B_2 on O_2's train, Fig. 36–6a. For simplicity, we assume that O_1 is exactly halfway between A_1 and B_1, and that O_2 is halfway between A_2 and B_2. Let us first put ourselves in O_2's reference frame, so we observe O_1 moving to the right with speed v. Let us also assume that the two events occur *simultaneously* in O_2's frame, and just at the instant when O_1 and O_2 are opposite each other, Fig. 36–6a. A short time later, Fig. 36–6b, the light from A_2 and B_2 reaches O_2 at the same time (we assumed this). Since O_2 knows (or measures) the distances O_2A_2 and O_2B_2 as equal, O_2 knows the two events are simultaneous in the O_2 reference frame.

FIGURE 36–5 Observers O_1 and O_2, on two different trains (two different reference frames), are moving with relative speed v. O_2 says that O_1 is moving to the right (a); O_1 says that O_2 is moving to the left (b). Both viewpoints are legitimate: it all depends on your reference frame.

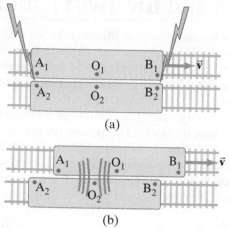

FIGURE 36–6 Thought experiment on simultaneity. In both (a) and (b) we are in the reference frame of observer O_2, who sees the reference frame of O_1 moving to the right. In (a), one lightning bolt strikes the two reference frames at A_1 and A_2, and a second lightning bolt strikes at B_1 and B_2. (b) A moment later, the light (shown in blue) from the two events reaches O_2 at the same time. So according to observer O_2, the two bolts of lightning struck simultaneously. But in O_1's reference frame, the light from B_1 has already reached O_1, whereas the light from A_1 has not yet reached O_1. So in O_1's reference frame, the event at B_1 must have preceded the event at A_1. Simultaneity in time is not absolute.

But what does observer O_1 observe and measure? From our (O_2) reference frame, we can predict what O_1 will observe. We see that O_1 moves to the right during the time the light is traveling to O_1 from A_1 and B_1. As shown in Fig. 36–6b, we can see from our O_2 reference frame that the light from B_1 has already passed O_1, whereas the light from A_1 has not yet reached O_1. That is, O_1 observes the light coming from B_1 before observing the light coming from A_1. Given (1) that light travels at the same speed c in any direction and in any reference frame, and (2) that the distance O_1A_1 equals O_1B_1, then observer O_1 can only conclude that the event at B_1 occurred before the event at A_1. The two events are *not* simultaneous for O_1, even though they are for O_2.

We thus find that two events which take place at different locations and are simultaneous to one observer, are actually not simultaneous to a second observer who moves relative to the first.

It may be tempting to ask: "Which observer is right, O_1 or O_2?" The answer, according to relativity, is that they are *both* right. There is no "best" reference frame we can choose to determine which observer is right. Both frames are equally good. We can only conclude that *simultaneity is not an absolute concept*, but is relative. We are not aware of this lack of agreement on simultaneity in everyday life because the effect is noticeable only when the relative speed of the two reference frames is very large (near c), or the distances involved are very large.

EXERCISE A Examine the experiment of Fig. 36–6 from O_1's reference frame. In this case, O_1 will be at rest and will see event B_1 occur before A_1. Will O_1 recognize that O_2, who is moving with speed v to the left, will see the two events as simultaneous? [*Hint*: Draw a diagram equivalent to Fig. 36–6.]

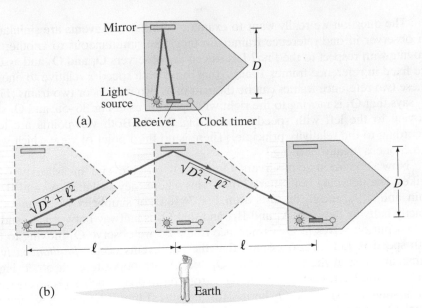

FIGURE 36–7 Time dilation can be shown by a thought experiment: the time it takes for light to travel across a spaceship and back is longer for the observer on Earth (b) than for the observer on the spaceship (a).

36–5 Time Dilation and the Twin Paradox

The fact that two events simultaneous to one observer may not be simultaneous to a second observer suggests that time itself is not absolute. Could it be that time passes differently in one reference frame than in another? This is, indeed, just what Einstein's theory of relativity predicts, as the following thought experiment shows.

Figure 36–7 shows a spaceship traveling past Earth at high speed. The point of view of an observer on the spaceship is shown in part (a), and that of an observer on Earth in part (b). Both observers have accurate clocks. The person on the spaceship (Fig. 36–7a) flashes a light and measures the time it takes the light to travel directly across the spaceship and return after reflecting from a mirror (the rays are drawn at a slight angle for clarity). In the reference frame of the spaceship, the light travels a distance $2D$ at speed c; so the time required to go across and back, which we call Δt_0, is

$$\Delta t_0 = 2D/c.$$

The observer on Earth, Fig. 36–7b, observes the same process. But to this observer, the spaceship is moving. So the light travels the diagonal path shown going across the spaceship, reflecting off the mirror, and returning to the sender. Although the light travels at the same speed to this observer (the second postulate), it travels a greater distance. Hence the time required, as measured by the observer on Earth, will be *greater* than that measured by the observer on the spaceship.

Let us determine the time interval Δt measured by the observer on Earth between sending and receiving the light. In time Δt, the spaceship travels a distance $2\ell = v\,\Delta t$ where v is the speed of the spaceship (Fig. 36–7b). The light travels a total distance on its diagonal path (Pythagorean theorem) of $2\sqrt{D^2 + \ell^2}$, where $\ell = v\,\Delta t/2$. Therefore

$$c = \frac{2\sqrt{D^2 + \ell^2}}{\Delta t} = \frac{2\sqrt{D^2 + v^2(\Delta t)^2/4}}{\Delta t}.$$

We square both sides,

$$c^2 = \frac{4D^2}{(\Delta t)^2} + v^2,$$

and solve for Δt, to find

$$\Delta t = \frac{2D}{c\sqrt{1 - v^2/c^2}}.$$

We combine this equation for Δt with the formula above, $\Delta t_0 = 2D/c$, and find

TIME DILATION

$$\Delta t = \frac{\Delta t_0}{\sqrt{1 - v^2/c^2}}. \qquad \textbf{(36–1a)}$$

Since $\sqrt{1 - v^2/c^2}$ is always less than 1, we see that $\Delta t > \Delta t_0$. That is, the time interval between the two events (the sending of the light, and its reception on the spaceship) is *greater* for the observer on Earth than for the observer on the spaceship. This is a general result of the theory of relativity, and is known as **time dilation**. Stated simply, the time dilation effect says that

> **clocks moving relative to an observer are measured to run more slowly (as compared to clocks at rest relative to that observer).**

However, we should not think that the clocks are somehow at fault. Time is actually measured to pass more slowly in any moving reference frame as compared to your own. This remarkable result is an inevitable outcome of the two postulates of the theory of relativity.

The factor $1/\sqrt{1 - v^2/c^2}$ occurs so often in relativity that we often give it the shorthand symbol γ (the Greek letter "gamma"), and write Eq. 36–1a as

$$\Delta t = \gamma \, \Delta t_0 \tag{36–1b}$$

where

$$\gamma = \frac{1}{\sqrt{1 - v^2/c^2}}. \tag{36–2}$$

Note that γ is never less than one, and has no units. At normal speeds, $\gamma = 1$ to a few decimal places; in general, $\gamma \geq 1$.

The concept of time dilation may be hard to accept, for it contradicts our experience. We can see from Eqs. 36–1 that the time dilation effect is indeed negligible unless v is reasonably close to c. If v is much less than c, then the term v^2/c^2 is much smaller than the 1 in the denominator of Eq. 36–1a, and then $\Delta t \approx \Delta t_0$ (see Example 36–2). The speeds we experience in everyday life are much smaller than c, so it is little wonder we don't ordinarily notice time dilation. Experiments have tested the time dilation effect, and have confirmed Einstein's predictions. In 1971, for example, extremely precise atomic clocks were flown around the Earth in jet planes. The speed of the planes $(10^3 \, \text{km/h})$ was much less than c, so the clocks had to be accurate to nanoseconds $(10^{-9} \, \text{s})$ in order to detect any time dilation. They were this accurate, and they confirmed Eqs. 36–1 to within experimental error. Time dilation had been confirmed decades earlier, however, by observations on "elementary particles" which have very small masses (typically 10^{-30} to $10^{-27} \, \text{kg}$) and so require little energy to be accelerated to speeds close to the speed of light, c. Many of these elementary particles are not stable and decay after a time into lighter particles. One example is the muon, whose mean lifetime is 2.2 μs when at rest. Careful experiments showed that when a muon is traveling at high speeds, its lifetime is measured to be longer than when it is at rest, just as predicted by the time dilation formula.

EXAMPLE 36–1 **Lifetime of a moving muon.** (a) What will be the mean lifetime of a muon as measured in the laboratory if it is traveling at $v = 0.60c = 1.80 \times 10^8 \, \text{m/s}$ with respect to the laboratory? Its mean lifetime at rest is $2.20 \, \mu\text{s} = 2.20 \times 10^{-6} \, \text{s}$. (b) How far does a muon travel in the laboratory, on average, before decaying?

APPROACH If an observer were to move along with the muon (the muon would be at rest to this observer), the muon would have a mean life of $2.20 \times 10^{-6} \, \text{s}$. To an observer in the lab, the muon lives longer because of time dilation. We find the mean lifetime using Eq. 36–1a and the average distance using $d = v \, \Delta t$.

SOLUTION (a) From Eq. 36–1a with $v = 0.60c$, we have

$$\Delta t = \frac{\Delta t_0}{\sqrt{1 - v^2/c^2}} = \frac{2.20 \times 10^{-6} \, \text{s}}{\sqrt{1 - 0.36c^2/c^2}} = \frac{2.20 \times 10^{-6} \, \text{s}}{\sqrt{0.64}} = 2.8 \times 10^{-6} \, \text{s}.$$

(b) Relativity predicts that a muon with speed $1.80 \times 10^8 \, \text{m/s}$ would travel an average distance $d = v \, \Delta t = (1.80 \times 10^8 \, \text{m/s})(2.8 \times 10^{-6} \, \text{s}) = 500 \, \text{m}$, and this is the distance that is measured experimentally in the laboratory.

NOTE At a speed of $1.8 \times 10^8 \, \text{m/s}$, classical physics would tell us that with a mean life of 2.2 μs, an average muon would travel $d = vt = (1.8 \times 10^8 \, \text{m/s})(2.2 \times 10^{-6} \, \text{s}) = 400 \, \text{m}$. This is shorter than the distance measured.

EXERCISE B What is the muon's mean lifetime (Example 36–1) if it is traveling at $v = 0.90c$? (a) 0.42 μs; (b) 2.3 μs; (c) 5.0 μs; (d) 5.3 μs; (e) 12.0 μs.

We need to clarify how to use Eqs. 36–1, and the meaning of Δt and Δt_0. The equation is true only when Δt_0 represents the time interval between the two events in a reference frame where the two events occur at *the same point in space* (as in Fig. 36–7a where the two events are the light flash being sent and being received). This time interval, Δt_0, is called the **proper time**. Then Δt in Eqs. 36–1 represents the time interval between the two events as measured in a reference frame moving with speed v with respect to the first. In Example 36–1 above, Δt_0 (and not Δt) was set equal to 2.2×10^{-6} s because it is only in the rest frame of the muon that the two events ("birth" and "decay") occur at the same point in space. The proper time Δt_0 is the shortest time between the events any observer can measure. In any other moving reference frame, the time Δt is greater.

⚠ CAUTION

Proper time Δt_0 is for 2 events at the same point in space.

EXAMPLE 36–2 **Time dilation at 100 km/h.** Let us check time dilation for everyday speeds. A car traveling 100 km/h covers a certain distance in 10.00 s according to the driver's watch. What does an observer at rest on Earth measure for the time interval?

APPROACH The car's speed relative to Earth is $100 \text{ km/h} = (1.00 \times 10^5 \text{ m})/(3600 \text{ s}) = 27.8 \text{ m/s}$. The driver is at rest in the reference frame of the car, so we set $\Delta t_0 = 10.00$ s in the time dilation formula.

SOLUTION We use Eq. 36–1a:

$$\Delta t = \frac{\Delta t_0}{\sqrt{1 - \dfrac{v^2}{c^2}}} = \frac{10.00 \text{ s}}{\sqrt{1 - \left(\dfrac{27.8 \text{ m/s}}{3.00 \times 10^8 \text{ m/s}}\right)^2}} = \frac{10.00 \text{ s}}{\sqrt{1 - (8.59 \times 10^{-15})}}.$$

If you put these numbers into a calculator, you will obtain $\Delta t = 10.00$ s, since the denominator differs from 1 by such a tiny amount. Indeed, the time measured by an observer on Earth would show no difference from that measured by the driver, even with the best instruments. A computer that could calculate to a large number of decimal places would reveal a difference between Δt and Δt_0. We can estimate the difference using the binomial expansion (Appendix A),

$$(1 \pm x)^n \approx 1 \pm nx. \qquad\qquad\qquad [\text{for } x \ll 1]$$

In our time dilation formula, we have the factor $\gamma = (1 - v^2/c^2)^{-\frac{1}{2}}$. Thus

$$\Delta t = \gamma \, \Delta t_0 = \Delta t_0\left(1 - \frac{v^2}{c^2}\right)^{-\frac{1}{2}} \approx \Delta t_0\left(1 + \frac{1}{2}\frac{v^2}{c^2}\right)$$

$$\approx 10.00 \text{ s}\left[1 + \frac{1}{2}\left(\frac{27.8 \text{ m/s}}{3.00 \times 10^8 \text{ m/s}}\right)^2\right] \approx 10.00 \text{ s} + 4 \times 10^{-14} \text{ s}.$$

So the difference between Δt and Δt_0 is predicted to be 4×10^{-14} s, an extremely small amount.

PROBLEM SOLVING

Use of the binomial expansion

EXERCISE C A certain atomic clock keeps perfect time on Earth. If the clock is taken on a spaceship traveling at a speed $v = 0.60c$, does this clock now run slow according to the people (*a*) on the spaceship, (*b*) on Earth?

EXAMPLE 36–3 **Reading a magazine on a spaceship.** A passenger on a high-speed spaceship traveling between Earth and Jupiter at a steady speed of $0.75c$ reads a magazine which takes 10.0 min according to her watch. (*a*) How long does this take as measured by Earth-based clocks? (*b*) How much farther is the spaceship from Earth at the end of reading the article than it was at the beginning?

APPROACH (*a*) The time interval in one reference frame is related to the time interval in the other by Eq. 36–1a or b. (*b*) At constant speed, distance is speed $\times$ time. Since there are two times (a Δt and a Δt_0) we will get two distances, one for each reference frame. [This surprising result is explored in the next Section (36–6).]

SOLUTION (a) The given 10.0-min time interval is the proper time—starting and finishing the magazine happen at the same place on the spaceship. Earth clocks measure

$$\Delta t = \frac{\Delta t_0}{\sqrt{1 - \frac{v^2}{c^2}}} = \frac{10.00 \text{ min}}{\sqrt{1 - (0.75)^2}} = 15.1 \text{ min.}$$

(b) In the Earth frame, the rocket travels a distance $D = v\,\Delta t = (0.75c)(15.1 \text{ min}) = (0.75)(3.0 \times 10^8 \text{ m/s})(15.1 \text{ min} \times 60 \text{ s/min}) = 2.04 \times 10^{11} \text{ m}$. In the spaceship's frame, the Earth is moving away from the spaceship at $0.75c$, but the time is only 10.0 min, so the distance is measured to be $D_0 = v\,\Delta t_0 = (2.25 \times 10^8 \text{ m/s})(600 \text{s}) = 1.35 \times 10^{11} \text{m}$.

Values for $\gamma = 1/\sqrt{1 - v^2/c^2}$ at a few speeds v are given in Table 36–1.

Space Travel?

Time dilation has aroused interesting speculation about space travel. According to classical (Newtonian) physics, to reach a star 100 light-years away would not be possible for ordinary mortals (1 light-year is the distance light can travel in 1 year = $3.0 \times 10^8 \text{ m/s} \times 3.16 \times 10^7 \text{ s} = 9.5 \times 10^{15} \text{ m}$). Even if a spaceship could travel at close to the speed of light, it would take over 100 years to reach such a star. But time dilation tells us that the time involved could be less. In a spaceship traveling at $v = 0.999c$, the time for such a trip would be only about $\Delta t_0 = \Delta t \sqrt{1 - v^2/c^2} = (100 \text{ yr})\sqrt{1 - (0.999)^2} = 4.5 \text{ yr}$. Thus time dilation allows such a trip, but the enormous practical problems of achieving such speeds may not be possible to overcome, certainly not in the near future.

In this example, 100 years would pass on Earth, whereas only 4.5 years would pass for the astronaut on the trip. Is it just the clocks that would slow down for the astronaut? No. All processes, including aging and other life processes, run more slowly for the astronaut according to the Earth observer. But to the astronaut, time would pass in a normal way. The astronaut would experience 4.5 years of normal sleeping, eating, reading, and so on. And people on Earth would experience 100 years of ordinary activity.

Twin Paradox

Not long after Einstein proposed the special theory of relativity, an apparent paradox was pointed out. According to this **twin paradox**, suppose one of a pair of 20-year-old twins takes off in a spaceship traveling at very high speed to a distant star and back again, while the other twin remains on Earth. According to the Earth twin, the astronaut twin will age less. Whereas 20 years might pass for the Earth twin, perhaps only 1 year (depending on the spacecraft's speed) would pass for the traveler. Thus, when the traveler returns, the earthbound twin could expect to be 40 years old whereas the traveling twin would be only 21.

This is the viewpoint of the twin on the Earth. But what about the traveling twin? If all inertial reference frames are equally good, won't the traveling twin make all the claims the Earth twin does, only in reverse? Can't the astronaut twin claim that since the Earth is moving away at high speed, time passes more slowly on Earth and the twin on Earth will age less? This is the opposite of what the Earth twin predicts. They cannot both be right, for after all the spacecraft returns to Earth and a direct comparison of ages and clocks can be made.

There is, however, no contradiction here. One of the viewpoints is indeed incorrect. The consequences of the special theory of relativity—in this case, time dilation—can be applied only by observers in an inertial reference frame. The Earth is such a frame (or nearly so), whereas the spacecraft is not. The spacecraft accelerates at the start and end of its trip and when it turns around at the far point of its journey. During the acceleration, the twin on the spacecraft is not in an inertial frame. In between, the astronaut twin may be in an inertial frame (and is justified in saying the Earth twin's clocks run slow), but it is not always the same frame. So she cannot use special relativity to predict their relative ages when she returns to Earth. The Earth twin stays in the same inertial frame, and we can thus trust her predictions based on special relativity. Thus, there is no paradox. The prediction of the Earth twin that the traveling twin ages less is the proper one.

TABLE 36–1 Values of γ

v	γ
0	1.000
0.01c	1.000
0.10c	1.005
0.50c	1.15
0.90c	2.3
0.99c	7.1

*Global Positioning System (GPS)

Airplanes, cars, boats, and hikers use **global positioning system (GPS)** receivers to tell them quite accurately where they are, at a given moment. The 24 global positioning system satellites send out precise time signals using atomic clocks. Your receiver compares the times received from at least four satellites, all of whose times are carefully synchronized to within 1 part in 10^{13}. By comparing the time differences with the known satellite positions and the fixed speed of light, the receiver can determine how far it is from each satellite and thus where it is on the Earth. It can do this to a typical accuracy of 15 m, if it has been constructed to make corrections such as the one below due to special relativity.

CONCEPTUAL EXAMPLE 36–4 | **A relativity correction to GPS.** GPS satellites move at about $4\,\text{km/s} = 4000\,\text{m/s}$. Show that a good GPS receiver needs to correct for time dilation if it is to produce results consistent with atomic clocks accurate to 1 part in 10^{13}.

RESPONSE Let us calculate the magnitude of the time dilation effect by inserting $v = 4000\,\text{m/s}$ into Eq. 36–1a:

$$\Delta t = \frac{1}{\sqrt{1 - \dfrac{v^2}{c^2}}} \Delta t_0$$

$$= \frac{1}{\sqrt{1 - \left(\dfrac{4 \times 10^3\,\text{m/s}}{3 \times 10^8\,\text{m/s}}\right)^2}} \Delta t_0$$

$$= \frac{1}{\sqrt{1 - 1.8 \times 10^{-10}}} \Delta t_0.$$

We use the binomial expansion: $(1 \pm x)^n \approx 1 \pm nx$ for $x \ll 1$ (see Appendix A) which here is $(1 - x)^{-\frac{1}{2}} \approx 1 + \frac{1}{2}x$. That is

$$\Delta t = \left(1 + \tfrac{1}{2}(1.8 \times 10^{-10})\right) \Delta t_0 = \left(1 + 9 \times 10^{-11}\right) \Delta t_0.$$

The time "error" divided by the time interval is

$$\frac{(\Delta t - \Delta t_0)}{\Delta t_0} = 1 + 9 \times 10^{-11} - 1 = 9 \times 10^{-11} \approx 1 \times 10^{-10}.$$

Time dilation, if not accounted for, would introduce an error of about 1 part in 10^{10}, which is 1000 times greater than the precision of the atomic clocks. Not correcting for time dilation means a receiver could give much poorer position accuracy.

NOTE GPS devices must make other corrections as well, including effects associated with general relativity.

36–6 Length Contraction

Time intervals are not the only things different in different reference frames. Space intervals—lengths and distances—are different as well, according to the special theory of relativity, and we illustrate this with a thought experiment.

Observers on Earth watch a spacecraft traveling at speed v from Earth to, say, Neptune, Fig. 36–8a. The distance between the planets, as measured by the Earth observers, is ℓ_0. The time required for the trip, measured from Earth, is

$$\Delta t = \frac{\ell_0}{v}. \qquad \text{[Earth observer]}$$

In Fig. 36–8b we see the point of view of observers on the spacecraft. In this frame of reference, the spaceship is at rest; Earth and Neptune move[†] with speed v. The time between departure of Earth and arrival of Neptune (observed from the spacecraft) is the "proper time," since the two events occur at the same point in space (i.e., on the spacecraft). Therefore the time interval is less for the spacecraft

---

[†] We assume v is much greater than the relative speed of Neptune and Earth, so the latter can be ignored.

Earth

(a) Earth at rest

Neptune

v

Earth

(b) Spacecraft at rest

v

Neptune

FIGURE 36–8 (a) A spaceship traveling at very high speed from Earth to the planet Neptune, as seen from Earth's frame of reference. (b) According to an observer on the spaceship, Earth and Neptune are moving at the very high speed v: Earth leaves the spaceship, and a time Δt_0 later Neptune arrives at the spaceship.

observers than for the Earth observers. That is, because of time dilation (Eq. 36–1a), the time for the trip as viewed by the spacecraft is

$$\Delta t_0 = \Delta t \sqrt{1 - v^2/c^2} = \Delta t/\gamma. \qquad \text{[spacecraft observer]}$$

Because the spacecraft observers measure the same speed but less time between these two events, they also measure the distance as less. If we let ℓ be the distance between the planets as viewed by the spacecraft observers, then $\ell = v\,\Delta t_0$, which we can rewrite as $\ell = v\,\Delta t_0 = v\,\Delta t\sqrt{1 - v^2/c^2} = \ell_0\sqrt{1 - v^2/c^2}$. Thus we have the important result that

$$\ell = \ell_0\sqrt{1 - v^2/c^2} \qquad \textbf{(36–3a)}$$

LENGTH CONTRACTION

or, using γ (Eq. 36–2),

$$\ell = \frac{\ell_0}{\gamma}. \qquad \textbf{(36–3b)}$$

This is a general result of the special theory of relativity and applies to lengths of objects as well as to distance between objects. The result can be stated most simply in words as:

> **the length of an object moving relative to an observer is measured to be shorter along its direction of motion than when it is at rest.**

This is called **length contraction**. The length ℓ_0 in Eqs. 36–3 is called the **proper length**. It is the length of the object (or distance between two points whose positions are measured at the same time) as determined by *observers at rest* with respect to the object. Equations 36–3 give the length ℓ that will be measured by observers when the object travels past them at speed v.

It is important to note that length contraction occurs *only along the direction of motion*. For example, the moving spaceship in Fig. 36–8a is shortened in length, but its height is the same as when it is at rest.

Length contraction, like time dilation, is not noticeable in everyday life because the factor $\sqrt{1 - v^2/c^2}$ in Eq. 36–3a differs from 1.00 significantly only when v is very large.

⚠️ **CAUTION**

Proper length is measured in reference frame where the two positions are at rest

EXAMPLE 36–5 Painting's contraction. A rectangular painting measures 1.00 m tall and 1.50 m wide. It is hung on the side wall of a spaceship which is moving past the Earth at a speed of 0.90c. See Fig. 36–9a. (*a*) What are the dimensions of the picture according to the captain of the spaceship? (*b*) What are the dimensions as seen by an observer on the Earth?

APPROACH We apply the length contraction formula, Eq. 36–3a, to the dimension parallel to the motion; v is the speed of the painting relative to the observer.

SOLUTION (*a*) The painting is at rest ($v = 0$) on the spaceship so it (as well as everything else in the spaceship) looks perfectly normal to everyone on the spaceship. The captain sees a 1.00-m by 1.50-m painting.

(*b*) Only the dimension in the direction of motion is shortened, so the height is unchanged at 1.00 m, Fig. 36–9b. The length, however, is contracted to

$$\ell = \ell_0\sqrt{1 - \frac{v^2}{c^2}}$$

$$= (1.50\,\text{m})\sqrt{1 - (0.90)^2} = 0.65\,\text{m}.$$

So the picture has dimensions 1.00 m × 0.65 m.

FIGURE 36–9 Example 36–5.

1.00 m

1.50 m

(a)

1.00 m

?

(b)

EXAMPLE 36–6 **A fantasy supertrain.** A very fast train with a proper length of 500 m is passing through a 200-m-long tunnel. Let us imagine the train's speed to be so great that the train fits completely within the tunnel as seen by an observer at rest on the Earth. That is, the engine is just about to emerge from one end of the tunnel at the time the last car disappears into the other end. What is the train's speed?

APPROACH Since the train just fits inside the tunnel, its length measured by the person on the ground is 200 m. The length contraction formula, Eq. 36–3a or b, can thus be used to solve for v.

SOLUTION Substituting $\ell = 200$ m and $\ell_0 = 500$ m into Eq. 36–3a gives

$$200 \text{ m} = 500 \text{ m} \sqrt{1 - \frac{v^2}{c^2}};$$

dividing both sides by 500 m and squaring, we get

$$(0.40)^2 = 1 - \frac{v^2}{c^2}$$

or

$$\frac{v}{c} = \sqrt{1 - (0.40)^2}$$

and

$$v = 0.92c.$$

NOTE No real train could go this fast. But it is fun to think about.

NOTE An observer on the *train* would *not* see the two ends of the train inside the tunnel at the same time. Recall that observers moving relative to each other do not agree about simultaneity.

EXERCISE D What is the length of the tunnel as measured by observers on the train in Example 36–6?

CONCEPTUAL EXAMPLE 36–7 **Resolving the train and tunnel length.** Observers at rest on the Earth see a very fast 200-m-long train pass through a 200-m-long tunnel (as in Example 36–6) so that the train momentarily disappears from view inside the tunnel. Observers on the train measure the train's length to be 500 m and the tunnel's length to be only 80 m (Exercise D, using Eq. 36–3a). Clearly a 500-m-long train cannot fit inside an 80-m-long tunnel. How is this apparent inconsistency explained?

RESPONSE Events simultaneous in one reference frame may not be simultaneous in another. Let the engine emerging from one end of the tunnel be "event A," and the last car disappearing into the other end of the tunnel "event B." To observers in the Earth frame, events A and B are simultaneous. To observers on the train, however, the events are not simultaneous. In the train's frame, event A occurs before event B. As the engine emerges from the tunnel, observers on the train observe the last car as still $500 \text{ m} - 80 \text{ m} = 420 \text{ m}$ from the entrance to the tunnel.

FIGURE 36–10 According to an accurate clock on a fast-moving train, a person (a) begins dinner at 7:00 and (b) finishes at 7:15. At the beginning of the meal, two observers on Earth set their watches to correspond with the clock on the train. These observers measure the eating time as 20 minutes.

(a)   (b)

36–7 Four-Dimensional Space–Time

Let us imagine a person is on a train moving at a very high speed, say $0.65c$, Fig. 36–10. This person begins a meal at 7:00 and finishes at 7:15, according to a clock on the train. The two events, beginning and ending the meal, take place at the same point on the train. So the proper time between these two events is 15 min. To observers on Earth, the meal will take longer—20 min according to Eqs. 36–1. Let us assume that the meal was served on a 20-cm-diameter plate. To observers on the Earth, the plate is only 15 cm wide (length contraction). Thus, to observers on the Earth, the meal looks smaller but lasts longer.

In a sense the two effects, time dilation and length contraction, balance each other. When viewed from the Earth, what an object seems to lose in size it gains in length of time it lasts. Space, or length, is exchanged for time.

Considerations like this led to the idea of **four-dimensional space–time**: space takes up three dimensions and time is a fourth dimension. Space and time are intimately connected. Just as when we squeeze a balloon we make one dimension larger and another smaller, so when we examine objects and events from different reference frames, a certain amount of space is exchanged for time, or vice versa.

Although the idea of four dimensions may seem strange, it refers to the idea that any object or event is specified by four quantities—three to describe where in space, and one to describe when in time. The really unusual aspect of four-dimensional space–time is that space and time can intermix: a little of one can be exchanged for a little of the other when the reference frame is changed.

It is difficult for most of us to understand the idea of four-dimensional space–time. Somehow we feel, just as physicists did before the advent of relativity, that space and time are completely separate entities. Yet we have found in our thought experiments that they are not completely separate. And think about Galileo and Newton. Before Galileo, the vertical direction, that in which objects fall, was considered to be distinctly different from the two horizontal dimensions. Galileo showed that the vertical dimension differs only in that it happens to be the direction in which gravity acts. Otherwise, all three dimensions are equivalent, a viewpoint we all accept today. Now we are asked to accept one more dimension, time, which we had previously thought of as being somehow different. This is not to say that there is no distinction between space and time. What relativity has shown is that space and time determinations are not independent of one another.

In Galilean–Newtonian relativity, the time interval between two events, Δt, and the distance between two events or points, Δx, are invariant quantities no matter what inertial reference frame they are viewed from. Neither of these quantities is invariant according to Einstein's relativity. But there is an invariant quantity in four-dimensional space–time, called the **space–time interval**, which is $(\Delta s)^2 = (c\,\Delta t)^2 - (\Delta x)^2$. We leave it as a Problem (97) to show that this quantity is indeed invariant under a Lorentz transformation (Section 36–8).

36–8 Galilean and Lorentz Transformations

We now examine in detail the mathematics of relating quantities in one inertial reference frame to the equivalent quantities in another. In particular, we will see how positions and velocities *transform* (that is, change) from one frame to the other.

We begin with the classical or Galilean viewpoint. Consider two inertial reference frames S and S' which are each characterized by a set of coordinate axes, Fig. 36–11. The axes x and y (z is not shown) refer to S and x' and y' to S'. The x' and x axes overlap one another, and we assume that frame S' moves to the right in the x direction at constant speed v with respect to S. For simplicity let us assume the origins 0 and 0' of the two reference frames are superimposed at time $t = 0$.

FIGURE 36–11 Inertial reference frame S' moves to the right at constant speed v with respect to frame S.

Now consider an event that occurs at some point P (Fig. 36–11) represented by the coordinates x', y', z' in reference frame S' at the time t'. What will be the coordinates of P in S? Since S and S' initially overlap precisely, after a time t', S' will have moved a distance vt'. Therefore, at time t', $x = x' + vt'$. The y and z coordinates, on the other hand, are not altered by motion along the x axis; thus $y = y'$ and $z = z'$. Finally, since time is assumed to be absolute in Galilean–Newtonian physics, clocks in the two frames will agree with each other; so $t = t'$. We summarize these in the following **Galilean transformation equations:**

$$x = x' + vt'$$
$$y = y'$$
$$z = z' \qquad \text{[Galilean]} \quad \textbf{(36–4)}$$
$$t = t'.$$

These equations give the coordinates of an event in the S frame when those in the S' frame are known. If those in the S frame are known, then the S' coordinates are obtained from

$$x' = x - vt, \qquad y' = y, \qquad z' = z, \qquad t' = t. \quad \text{[Galilean]}$$

These four equations are the "inverse" transformation and are very easily obtained from Eqs. 36–4. Notice that the effect is merely to exchange primed and unprimed quantities and replace v by $-v$. This makes sense because from the S' frame, S moves to the left (negative x direction) with speed v.

Now suppose the point P in Fig. 36–11 represents a particle that is moving. Let the components of its velocity vector in S' be u'_x, u'_y, u'_z. (We use u to distinguish it from the relative velocity of the two frames, v.) Now $u'_x = dx'/dt'$, $u'_y = dy'/dt'$ and $u'_z = dz'/dt'$. The velocity of P as seen from S will have components u_x, u_y, and u_z. We can show how these are related to the velocity components in S' by differentiating Eqs. 36–4. For u_x we get

$$u_x = \frac{dx}{dt} = \frac{d(x' + vt')}{dt'} = u'_x + v$$

since v is assumed constant. For the other components, $u'_y = u_y$ and $u'_z = u_z$, so we have

$$u_x = u'_x + v$$
$$u_y = u'_y$$
$$u_z = u'_z.$$

[Galilean] (36–5)

These are known as the **Galilean velocity transformation equations**. We see that the y and z components of velocity are unchanged, but the x components differ by v: $u_x = u'_x + v$. This is just what we have used before (see Chapter 3, Section 3–9) when dealing with relative velocity.

The Galilean transformations, Eqs. 36–4 and 36–5, are valid only when the velocities involved are much less than c. We can see, for example, that the first of Eqs. 36–5 will not work for the speed of light: light traveling in S′ with speed $u'_x = c$ would have speed $c + v$ in S, whereas the theory of relativity insists it must be c in S. Clearly, then, a new set of transformation equations is needed to deal with relativistic velocities.

We derive the required equation, looking again at Fig. 36–11. We will try the simple assumption that the transformation is linear and of the form

$$x = \gamma(x' + vt'), \qquad y = y', \qquad z = z'. \tag{i}$$

That is, we modify the first of Eqs. 36–4 by multiplying by a constant γ which is yet to be determined[†] ($\gamma = 1$ non-relativistically). But we assume the y and z equations are unchanged since there is no length contraction in these directions. We will not assume a form for t, but will derive it. The inverse equations must have the same form with v replaced by $-v$. (The principle of relativity demands it, since S′ moving to the right with respect to S is equivalent to S moving to the left with respect to S′.) Therefore

$$x' = \gamma(x - vt). \tag{ii}$$

Now if a light pulse leaves the common origin of S and S′ at time $t = t' = 0$, after a time t it will have traveled a distance $x = ct$ or $x' = ct'$ along the x axis. Therefore, from Eqs. (i) and (ii) above,

$$ct = \gamma(ct' + vt') = \gamma(c + v)t', \tag{iii}$$
$$ct' = \gamma(ct - vt) = \gamma(c - v)t. \tag{iv}$$

We substitute t' from Eq. (iv) into Eq. (iii) and find $ct = \gamma(c + v)\gamma(c - v)(t/c) = \gamma^2(c^2 - v^2)t/c$. We cancel out the t on each side and solve for γ to find

$$\gamma = \frac{1}{\sqrt{1 - v^2/c^2}}.$$

The constant γ here has the same value as the γ we used before, Eq. 36–2. Now that we have found γ, we need only find the relation between t and t'. To do so, we combine $x' = \gamma(x - vt)$ with $x = \gamma(x' + vt')$:

$$x' = \gamma(x - vt) = \gamma(\gamma[x' + vt'] - vt).$$

We solve for t and find $t = \gamma(t' + vx'/c^2)$. In summary,

$$x = \gamma(x' + vt')$$
$$y = y'$$
$$z = z'$$
$$t = \gamma\left(t' + \frac{vx'}{c^2}\right)$$

(36–6)

LORENTZ

TRANSFORMATIONS

These are called the **Lorentz transformation equations**. They were first proposed, in a slightly different form, by Lorentz in 1904 to explain the null result of the Michelson–Morley experiment and to make Maxwell's equations take the same form in all inertial reference frames. A year later Einstein derived them independently based on his theory of relativity. Notice that not only is the x equation modified as compared to the Galilean transformation, but so is the t equation; indeed, we see directly in this last equation how the space and time coordinates mix.

[†]γ here is not assumed to be given by Eq. 36–2.

Deriving Length Contraction

We now derive the length contraction formula, Eq. 36–3, from the Lorentz transformation equations. We consider two reference frames S and S' as in Fig. 36–11.

Let an object of length ℓ_0 be at rest on the x axis in S. The coordinates of its two end points are x_1 and x_2, so that $x_2 - x_1 = \ell_0$. At any instant in S', the end points will be at x_1' and x_2' as given by the Lorentz transformation equations. The length measured in S' is $\ell = x_2' - x_1'$. An observer in S' measures this length by measuring x_2' and x_1' at the same time (in the S' reference frame), so $t_2' = t_1'$. Then, from the first of Eqs. 36–6,

$$\ell_0 = x_2 - x_1 = \frac{1}{\sqrt{1 - v^2/c^2}}(x_2' + vt_2' - x_1' - vt_1').$$

Since $t_2' = t_1'$, we have

$$\ell_0 = \frac{1}{\sqrt{1 - v^2/c^2}}(x_2' - x_1') = \frac{\ell}{\sqrt{1 - v^2/c^2}},$$

or

$$\ell = \ell_0\sqrt{1 - v^2/c^2},$$

which is Eq. 36–3.

Deriving Time Dilation

We now derive the time-dilation formula, Eq. 36–1a, using the Lorentz transformation equations.

The time Δt_0 between two events that occur at the same place $(x_2' = x_1')$ in S' is measured to be $\Delta t_0 = t_2' - t_1'$. Since $x_2' = x_1'$, then from the last of Eqs. 36–6, the time Δt between the events as measured in S is

$$\Delta t = t_2 - t_1 = \frac{1}{\sqrt{1 - v^2/c^2}}\left(t_2' + \frac{vx_2'}{c^2} - t_1' - \frac{vx_1'}{c^2}\right)$$

$$= \frac{1}{\sqrt{1 - v^2/c^2}}(t_2' - t_1') = \frac{\Delta t_0}{\sqrt{1 - v^2/c^2}},$$

which is Eq. 36–1a. Note that we chose S' to be the frame in which the two events occur at the same place, so that $x_1' = x_2'$ and the terms containing x_1' and x_2' cancel out.

Relativistic Addition of Velocities

The relativistically correct velocity equations are readily obtained by differentiating Eqs. 36–6 with respect to time. For example (using $\gamma = 1/\sqrt{1 - v^2/c^2}$ and the chain rule for derivatives):

$$u_x = \frac{dx}{dt} = \frac{d}{dt}[\gamma(x' + vt')]$$

$$= \frac{d}{dt'}[\gamma(x' + vt')]\frac{dt'}{dt} = \gamma\left[\frac{dx'}{dt'} + v\right]\frac{dt'}{dt}.$$

But $dx'/dt' = u_x'$ and $dt'/dt = 1/(dt/dt') = 1/[\gamma(1 + vu_x'/c^2)]$ where we have differentiated the last of Eqs. 36–6 with respect to time. Therefore

$$u_x = \frac{[\gamma(u_x' + v)]}{[\gamma(1 + vu_x'/c^2)]} = \frac{u_x' + v}{1 + vu_x'/c^2}.$$

The others are obtained in the same way and we collect them here:

LORENTZ

VELOCITY

TRANSFORMATIONS

$$u_x = \frac{u_x' + v}{1 + vu_x'/c^2} \tag{36-7a}$$

$$u_y = \frac{u_y'\sqrt{1 - v^2/c^2}}{1 + vu_x'/c^2} \tag{36-7b}$$

$$u_z = \frac{u_z'\sqrt{1 - v^2/c^2}}{1 + vu_x'/c^2}. \tag{36-7c}$$

Note that even though the relative velocity $\vec{v}$ is in the x direction, if the object has y or z components of velocity, they too are affected by v and the x component of the object's velocity. This was not true for the Galilean transformation, Eqs. 36–5.

EXAMPLE 36-8 **Adding velocities.** Calculate the speed of rocket 2 in Fig. 36–12 with respect to Earth.

APPROACH Consider Earth as reference frame S, and rocket 1 as reference frame S'. Rocket 2 moves with speed $u' = 0.60c$ with respect to rocket 1. Rocket 1 has speed $v = 0.60c$ with respect to Earth. The velocities are along the same straight line which we take to be the x (and x') axis. We need use only the first of Eqs. 36–7.

SOLUTION The speed of rocket 2 with respect to Earth is

$$u = \frac{u' + v}{1 + \dfrac{vu'}{c^2}} = \frac{0.60c + 0.60c}{1 + \dfrac{(0.60c)(0.60c)}{c^2}} = \frac{1.20c}{1.36} = 0.88c.$$

NOTE The Galilean transformation would have given $u = 1.20c$.

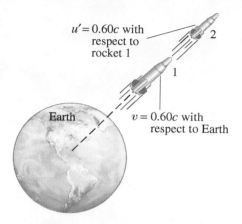

FIGURE 36–12 Rocket 1 moves away at speed $v = 0.60c$. Rocket 2 is fired from rocket 1 with speed $u' = 0.60c$. What is the speed of rocket 2 with respect to the Earth?

EXERCISE E Use Eqs. 36–7 to calculate the speed of rocket 2 in Fig. 36–12 relative to Earth if it was shot from rocket 1 at a speed $u' = 3000$ km/s $= 0.010c$. Assume rocket 1 had a speed $v = 6000$ km/s $= 0.020c$.

EXERCISE F Return to the Chapter-Opening Question, page 951, and answer it again now. Try to explain why you may have answered differently the first time.

Notice that Eqs. 36–7 reduce to the classical (Galilean) forms for velocities small compared to the speed of light, since $1 + vu'/c^2 \approx 1$ for v and $u' \ll c$. At the other extreme, let rocket 1 in Fig. 36–12 send out a beam of light, so that $u' = c$. Then Eq. 36–7a tells us the speed of light relative to Earth is

$$u = \frac{0.60c + c}{1 + \dfrac{(0.60c)(c)}{c^2}} = c,$$

which is consistent with the second postulate of relativity.

36-9 Relativistic Momentum

So far in this Chapter, we have seen that two basic mechanical quantities, length and time intervals, need modification because they are relative—their value depends on the reference frame from which they are measured. We might expect that other physical quantities might need some modification according to the theory of relativity, such as momentum, energy, and mass.

The analysis of collisions between two particles shows that if we want to preserve the law of conservation of momentum in relativity, we must redefine momentum as

$$p = \frac{mv}{\sqrt{1 - v^2/c^2}} = \gamma mv. \tag{36-8}$$

Here γ is shorthand for $1/\sqrt{1 - v^2/c^2}$ as before (Eq. 36–2). For speeds much less than the speed of light, Eq. 36–8 gives the classical momentum, $p = mv$.

Relativistic momentum has been tested many times on tiny elementary particles (such as muons), and it has been found to behave in accord with Eq. 36–8. We derive Eq. 36–8 in the optional subsection on the next page.

EXAMPLE 36–9 **Momentum of moving electron.** Compare the momentum of an electron when it has a speed of (a) 4.00×10^7 m/s in the CRT of a television set, and (b) $0.98c$ in an accelerator used for cancer therapy.

APPROACH We use Eq. 36–8 for the momentum of a moving electron.

SOLUTION (a) At $v = 4.00 \times 10^7$ m/s, the electron's momentum is

$$ p = \frac{mv}{\sqrt{1 - \dfrac{v^2}{c^2}}} = \frac{mv}{\sqrt{1 - \dfrac{(4.00 \times 10^7 \text{ m/s})^2}{(3.00 \times 10^8 \text{ m/s})^2}}} = 1.01mv. $$

The factor $\gamma = 1/\sqrt{1 - v^2/c^2} \approx 1.01$, so the momentum is only about 1% greater than the classical value. (If we put in the mass of an electron, $m = 9.11 \times 10^{-31}$ kg, the momentum is $p = 1.01mv = 3.68 \times 10^{-23}$ kg·m/s.)
(b) With $v = 0.98c$, the momentum is

$$ p = \frac{mv}{\sqrt{1 - \dfrac{v^2}{c^2}}} = \frac{mv}{\sqrt{1 - \dfrac{(0.98c)^2}{c^2}}} = \frac{mv}{\sqrt{1 - (0.98)^2}} = 5.0mv. $$

An electron traveling at 98% the speed of light has $\gamma = 5.0$ and a momentum 5.0 times its classical value.

Newton's second law, stated in its most general form, is

$$ \vec{F} = \frac{d\vec{p}}{dt} = \frac{d}{dt}(\gamma m \vec{v}) = \frac{d}{dt}\left(\frac{m\vec{v}}{\sqrt{1 - v^2/c^2}} \right) \tag{36–9} $$

and is valid relativistically.

*Derivation of Relativistic Momentum

Classically, momentum is a conserved quantity. We hope to find a formula for momentum that will also be valid relativistically. To do so, let us assume it has the general form given by $p = fmv$ where f is some function of v: $f(v)$. We consider a hypothetical collision between two objects—a thought experiment—and see what form $f(v)$ must take if momentum is to be conserved.

Our thought experiment involves the elastic collision of two identical balls, A and B. We consider two inertial reference frames, S and S′, moving along the x axis with a speed v with respect to each other, Fig. 36–13. That is, frame S′ moves to the right with velocity $\vec{v}$ as seen by observers on frame S; and frame S moves to the left with $-\vec{v}$ as seen by observers on S′. In reference frame S, ball A is thrown with speed u in the $+y$ direction. In reference frame S′, ball B is thrown with speed u in the negative $y′$ direction. The two balls are thrown at just the right time so that they collide. We assume that they rebound elastically and, from *symmetry*, that each moves with the same speed u back in the opposite direction in its thrower's reference frame. Figure 36–13a shows the collision as seen by an observer in reference frame S; and Fig. 36–13b shows the collision as seen from reference frame S′. In reference frame S, ball A has $v_x = 0$ both before and after the collision; it has $v_y = +u$ before the collision and $-u$ after the collision. In frame S′, ball A has x component of velocity $u'_x = -v$ both before and after the collision, and a $y′$ component (Eq. 36–7b with $u'_x = -v$) of magnitude

$$ u'_y = u \sqrt{1 - v^2/c^2}. $$

The same holds true for ball B, except in reverse. The velocity components are indicated in Fig. 36–13.

We now apply the law of conservation of momentum, which we hope remains valid in relativity, even if momentum has to be redefined. That is, we assume that the total momentum before the collision is equal to the total momentum after the

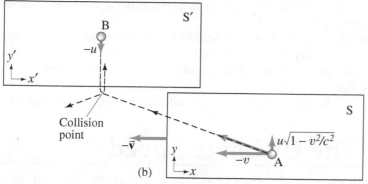

FIGURE 36–13 Deriving the momentum formula. Collision as seen by observers (a) in reference frame S, (b) in reference frame S'.

collision. We apply conservation of momentum to the y component of momentum in reference frame S (Fig. 36–13a). To make our task easier, let us assume $u \ll v$ so that the speed of ball B as seen in reference frame S is essentially v. Then B's y component of momentum in S before collision is $-f(v)mu\sqrt{1 - v^2/c^2}$ and after the collision is $+f(v)mu\sqrt{1 - v^2/c^2}$. Ball A in S has y component $f(u)mu$ before and $-f(u)mu$ after the collision. (We use $f(u)$ for A because its speed in S is only u.) Conservation of momentum in S for the y component is

$$(p_A + p_B)_{\text{before}} = (p_A + p_B)_{\text{after}}$$

$$f(u)mu - f(v)mu\sqrt{1 - v^2/c^2} = -f(u)mu + f(v)mu\sqrt{1 - v^2/c^2}.$$

We solve this for $f(v)$ and obtain

$$f(v) = \frac{f(u)}{\sqrt{1 - v^2/c^2}}.$$

To simplify this relation so we can solve for f, let us allow u to become very small so that it approaches zero (this corresponds to a glancing collision with one of the balls essentially at rest and the other moving with speed v). Then the momentum terms $f(u)mu$ are in the nonrelativistic realm and take on the classical form, simply mu, meaning that $f(u) = 1$. So the previous equation becomes

$$f(v) = \frac{1}{\sqrt{1 - v^2/c^2}}.$$

We see that $f(v)$ comes out to be the factor we used before and called γ, and here has been shown to be valid for ball A. Using Fig. 36–13b we can derive the same relation for ball B. Thus we can conclude that we need to define the relativistic momentum of a particle moving with velocity $\vec{v}$ as

$$\vec{p} = \frac{m\vec{v}}{\sqrt{1 - v^2/c^2}} = \gamma m\vec{v}.$$

With this definition the law of conservation of momentum will remain valid even in the relativistic realm. This relativistic momentum formula (Eq. 36–8) has been tested countless times on tiny elementary particles and been found valid.

*Relativistic Mass

The relativistic definition of momentum, Eq. 36–8, is sometimes interpreted as an increase in the mass of an object. In this interpretation, a particle can have a **relativistic mass**, m_{rel}, which increases with speed according to

$$m_{\text{rel}} = \frac{m}{\sqrt{1 - v^2/c^2}}.$$

In this "mass-increase" formula, m is referred to as the **rest mass** of the object. With this interpretation, *the mass of an object appears to increase as its speed increases*. But we must be careful in the use of relativistic mass. We cannot just plug it into formulas like $F = ma$ or $K = \frac{1}{2}mv^2$. For example, if we substitute it into $F = ma$, we obtain a formula that does not agree with experiment. If however, we write Newton's second law in its more general form, $\vec{F} = d\vec{p}/dt$, we do get a correct result (Eq. 36–9).

Also, be careful *not* to think a mass acquires more particles or more molecules as its speed becomes very large. It doesn't. In fact, many physicists believe an object has only one mass (its rest mass), and that it is only the momentum that increases with speed.

Whenever we talk about the mass of an object, we will always mean its rest mass (a fixed value).

36–10 The Ultimate Speed

A basic result of the special theory of relativity is that the speed of an object cannot equal or exceed the speed of light. That the speed of light is a natural speed limit in the universe can be seen from any of Eqs. 36–1, 36–2, 36–8, or the addition of velocities formula. It is perhaps easiest to see from Eq. 36–8. As an object is accelerated to greater and greater speeds, its momentum becomes larger and larger. Indeed, if v were to equal c, the denominator in this equation would be zero, and the momentum would be infinite. To accelerate an object up to $v = c$ would thus require infinite energy, and so is not possible.

36–11 $E = mc^2$; Mass and Energy

If momentum needs to be modified to fit with relativity as we just saw in Eq. 36–8, then we might expect energy too would need to be rethought. Indeed, Einstein not only developed a new formula for kinetic energy, but also found a new relation between mass and energy, and the startling idea that mass is a form of energy.

We start with the work-energy principle (Chapter 7), hoping it is still valid in relativity and will give verifiable results. That is, we assume the net work done on a particle is equal to its change in kinetic energy (K). Using this principle, Einstein showed that at high speeds the formula $K = \frac{1}{2}mv^2$ is not correct. Instead, as we show in the optional Subsection on page 978, the kinetic energy of a particle of mass m traveling at speed v is given by

$$K = \frac{mc^2}{\sqrt{1 - v^2/c^2}} - mc^2. \tag{36–10a}$$

In terms of $\gamma = 1/\sqrt{1 - v^2/c^2}$ we can rewrite Eq. 36–10a as

$$K = \gamma mc^2 - mc^2 = (\gamma - 1)mc^2. \tag{36–10b}$$

Equations 36–10 require some interpretation. The first term increases with the speed v of the particle. The second term, mc^2, is constant; it is called the **rest energy** of the particle, and represents a form of energy that a particle has even when at rest. Note that if a particle is at rest ($v = 0$) the first term in Eq. 36–10a becomes mc^2, so $K = 0$ as it should.

We can rearrange Eq. 36–10b to get

$$\gamma mc^2 = mc^2 + K.$$

We call γmc^2 the *total energy* E of the particle (assuming no potential energy), because it equals the rest energy plus the kinetic energy:

$$E = K + mc^2.$$ (36-11a)

The total energy can also be written, using Eqs. 36-10, as

$$E = \gamma mc^2 = \frac{mc^2}{\sqrt{1 - v^2/c^2}}.$$ (36-11b)

For a particle at rest in a given reference frame, K is zero in Eq. 36-11a, so the total energy is its rest energy:

$$E = mc^2.$$ (36-12)

MASS RELATED TO ENERGY

Here we have Einstein's famous formula, $E = mc^2$. This formula mathematically relates the concepts of energy and mass. But if this idea is to have any physical meaning, then mass ought to be convertible to other forms of energy and vice versa. Einstein suggested that this might be possible, and indeed changes of mass to other forms of energy, and vice versa, have been experimentally confirmed countless times in nuclear and elementary particle physics. For example, an electron and a positron (= a positive electron, Section 37-5) have often been observed to collide and disappear, producing pure electromagnetic radiation. The amount of electromagnetic energy produced is found to be exactly equal to that predicted by Einstein's formula, $E = mc^2$. The reverse process is also commonly observed in the laboratory: electromagnetic radiation under certain conditions can be converted into material particles such as electrons (see Section 37-5 on pair production). On a larger scale, the energy produced in nuclear power plants is a result of the loss in mass of the uranium fuel as it undergoes the process called fission. Even the radiant energy we receive from the Sun is an example of $E = mc^2$; the Sun's mass is continually decreasing as it radiates electromagnetic energy outward.

The relation $E = mc^2$ is now believed to apply to all processes, although the changes are often too small to measure. That is, when the energy of a system changes by an amount ΔE, the mass of the system changes by an amount Δm given by

$$\Delta E = (\Delta m)(c^2).$$

In a nuclear reaction where an energy E is required or released, the masses of the reactants and the products will be different by $\Delta m = \Delta E/c^2$.

EXAMPLE 36-10 Pion's kinetic energy. A π^0 meson ($m = 2.4 \times 10^{-28}\,\text{kg}$) travels at a speed $v = 0.80c = 2.4 \times 10^8\,\text{m/s}$. What is its kinetic energy? Compare to a classical calculation.

APPROACH We use Eq. 36-10 and compare to $\frac{1}{2}mv^2$.

SOLUTION We substitute values into Eq. 36-10a or b

$$K = (\gamma - 1)mc^2$$

where

$$\gamma = \frac{1}{\sqrt{1 - v^2/c^2}} = \frac{1}{\sqrt{1 - (0.80)^2}} = 1.67.$$

Then

$$K = (1.67 - 1)(2.4 \times 10^{-28}\,\text{kg})(3.0 \times 10^8\,\text{m/s})^2$$
$$= 1.4 \times 10^{-11}\,\text{J}.$$

PROBLEM SOLVING
Relativistic kinetic energy

Notice that the units of mc^2 are $\text{kg}\cdot\text{m}^2/\text{s}^2$, which is the joule.

NOTE If we were to do a classical calculation we would obtain $K = \frac{1}{2}mv^2 = \frac{1}{2}(2.4 \times 10^{-28}\,\text{kg})(2.4 \times 10^8\,\text{m/s})^2 = 6.9 \times 10^{-12}\,\text{J}$, about half as much, but this is not a correct result. Note that $\frac{1}{2}\gamma mv^2$ also does not work.

EXERCISE G A proton is traveling in an accelerator with a speed of $1.0 \times 10^8\,\text{m/s}$. By what factor does the proton's kinetic energy increase if its speed is doubled? (a) 1.3, (b) 2.0, (c) 4.0, (d) 5.6.

EXAMPLE 36-11 **Energy from nuclear decay.** The energy required or released in nuclear reactions and decays comes from a change in mass between the initial and final particles. In one type of radioactive decay, an atom of uranium ($m = 232.03714\,\text{u}$) decays to an atom of thorium ($m = 228.02873\,\text{u}$) plus an atom of helium ($m = 4.00260\,\text{u}$) where the masses given are in atomic mass units ($1\,\text{u} = 1.6605 \times 10^{-27}\,\text{kg}$). Calculate the energy released in this decay.

APPROACH The initial mass minus the total final mass gives the mass loss in atomic mass units (u); we convert that to kg, and multiply by c^2 to find the energy released, $\Delta E = \Delta m\, c^2$.

SOLUTION The initial mass is $232.03714\,\text{u}$, and after the decay the mass is $228.02873\,\text{u} + 4.00260\,\text{u} = 232.03133\,\text{u}$, so there is a decrease in mass of $0.00581\,\text{u}$. This mass, which equals $(0.00581\,\text{u})(1.66 \times 10^{-27}\,\text{kg}) = 9.64 \times 10^{-30}\,\text{kg}$, is changed into energy. By $\Delta E = \Delta m\, c^2$, we have

$$\Delta E = (9.64 \times 10^{-30}\,\text{kg})(3.0 \times 10^8\,\text{m/s})^2 = 8.68 \times 10^{-13}\,\text{J}.$$

Since $1\,\text{MeV} = 1.60 \times 10^{-13}\,\text{J}$ (Section 23–8), the energy released is $5.4\,\text{MeV}$.

In the tiny world of atoms and nuclei, it is common to quote energies in eV (electron volts) or multiples such as MeV ($10^6\,\text{eV}$). Momentum (see Eq. 36–8) can be quoted in units of eV/c (or MeV/c). And mass can be quoted (from $E = mc^2$) in units of eV/c^2 (or MeV/c^2). Note the use of c to keep the units correct. The rest masses of the electron and the proton are readily shown to be $0.511\,\text{MeV}/c^2$ and $938\,\text{MeV}/c^2$, respectively. See also the Table inside the front cover.

EXAMPLE 36-12 **A 1-TeV proton.** The Tevatron accelerator at Fermilab in Illinois can accelerate protons to a kinetic energy of $1.0\,\text{TeV}$ ($10^{12}\,\text{eV}$). What is the speed of such a proton?

APPROACH We solve the kinetic energy formula, Eq. 36–10a, for v.

SOLUTION The rest energy of a proton is $mc^2 = 938\,\text{MeV}$ or $9.38 \times 10^8\,\text{eV}$. Compared to the kinetic energy of $10^{12}\,\text{eV}$, the rest energy can be neglected, so we simplify Eq. 36–10a to

$$K \approx \frac{mc^2}{\sqrt{1 - v^2/c^2}}.$$

We solve this for v in the following steps:

$$\sqrt{1 - \frac{v^2}{c^2}} = \frac{mc^2}{K};$$

$$1 - \frac{v^2}{c^2} = \left(\frac{mc^2}{K}\right)^2;$$

$$\frac{v^2}{c^2} = 1 - \left(\frac{mc^2}{K}\right)^2 = 1 - \left(\frac{9.38 \times 10^8\,\text{eV}}{1.0 \times 10^{12}\,\text{eV}}\right)^2;$$

$$v = \sqrt{1 - (9.38 \times 10^{-4})^2}\, c = 0.99999956\, c.$$

So the proton is traveling at a speed very nearly equal to c.

At low speeds, $v \ll c$, the relativistic formula for kinetic energy reduces to the classical one, as we now show by using the binomial expansion, $(1 \pm x)^n = 1 \pm nx + n(n - 1)x^2/2! + \cdots$. With $n = -\tfrac{1}{2}$, we expand the square root in Eq. 36–10a

$$K = mc^2\left(\frac{1}{\sqrt{1 - v^2/c^2}} - 1\right)$$

so that

$$K \approx mc^2\left(1 + \frac{1}{2}\frac{v^2}{c^2} + \cdots - 1\right)$$

$$\approx \tfrac{1}{2}mv^2.$$

The dots in the first expression represent very small terms in the expansion which we neglect since we assumed that $v \ll c$. Thus at low speeds, the relativistic form for kinetic energy reduces to the classical form, $K = \frac{1}{2}mv^2$. This makes relativity a viable theory in that it can predict accurate results at low speed as well as at high. Indeed, the other equations of special relativity also reduce to their classical equivalents at ordinary speeds: length contraction, time dilation, and modifications to momentum as well as kinetic energy, all disappear for $v \ll c$ since $\sqrt{1 - v^2/c^2} \approx 1$.

A useful relation between the total energy E of a particle and its momentum p can also be derived. The momentum of a particle of mass m and speed v is given by Eq. 36–8

$$p = \gamma mv = \frac{mv}{\sqrt{1 - v^2/c^2}}.$$

The total energy is

$$E = K + mc^2$$

or

$$E = \gamma mc^2 = \frac{mc^2}{\sqrt{1 - v^2/c^2}}.$$

We square this equation (and we insert "$v^2 - v^2$" which is zero, but will help us):

$$E^2 = \frac{m^2c^2(v^2 - v^2 + c^2)}{1 - v^2/c^2}$$

$$= p^2c^2 + \frac{m^2c^4(1 - v^2/c^2)}{1 - v^2/c^2}$$

or

$$E^2 = p^2c^2 + m^2c^4. \tag{36–13}$$

Thus, the total energy can be written in terms of the momentum p, or in terms of the kinetic energy (Eqs. 36–11), where we have assumed there is no potential energy.

We can rewrite Eq. 36–13 as $E^2 - p^2c^2 = m^2c^4$. Since the mass m of a given particle is the same in any reference frame, we see that the quantity $E^2 - p^2c^2$ must also be the same in any reference frame. Thus, at any given moment the total energy E and momentum p of a particle will be different in different reference frames, but the quantity $E^2 - p^2c^2$ will have the same value in all inertial reference frames. We say that the quantity $E^2 - p^2c^2$ is **invariant** under a Lorentz transformation.

*When Do We Use Relativistic Formulas?

From a practical point of view, we do not have much opportunity in our daily lives to use the mathematics of relativity. For example, the γ factor, $\gamma = 1/\sqrt{1 - v^2/c^2}$, which appears in many relativistic formulas, has a value of 1.005 when $v = 0.10c$. Thus, for speeds even as high as $0.10c = 3.0 \times 10^7$ m/s, the factor $\sqrt{1 - v^2/c^2}$ in relativistic formulas gives a numerical correction of less than 1%. For speeds less than $0.10c$, or unless mass and energy are interchanged, we don't usually need to use the more complicated relativistic formulas, and can use the simpler classical formulas.

If you are given a particle's mass m and its kinetic energy K, you can do a quick calculation to determine if you need to use relativistic formulas or if classical ones are good enough. You simply compute the ratio K/mc^2 because (Eq. 36–10b)

$$\frac{K}{mc^2} = \gamma - 1 = \frac{1}{\sqrt{1 - v^2/c^2}} - 1.$$

If this ratio comes out to be less than, say, 0.01, then $\gamma \leq 1.01$ and relativistic equations will correct the classical ones by about 1%. If your expected precision is no better than 1%, classical formulas are good enough. But if your precision is 1 part in 1000 (0.1%) then you would want to use relativistic formulas. If your expected precision is only 10%, you need relativity if $(K/mc^2) \gtrsim 0.1$.

EXERCISE H For 1% accuracy, does an electron with $K = 100$ eV need to be treated relativistically? [*Hint:* The mass of an electron is 0.511 MeV.]

*Deriving Relativistic Energy

To find the mathematical relationship between mass and energy, we assume that the work-energy theorem is still valid in relativity for a particle, and we take the motion of the particle to be along the x axis. The work done to increase a particle's speed from zero to v is

$$W = \int_i^f F\,dx = \int_i^f \frac{dp}{dt}\,dx = \int_i^f \frac{dp}{dt}\,v\,dt = \int_i^f v\,dp$$

where i and f refer to the initial $(v = 0)$ and final $(v = v)$ states. Since $d(pv) = p\,dv + v\,dp$ we can write

$$v\,dp = d(pv) - p\,dv$$

so

$$W = \int_i^f d(pv) - \int_i^f p\,dv.$$

The first term on the right of the equal sign is

$$\int_i^f d(pv) = pv \Big|_i^f = (\gamma mv)v = \frac{mv^2}{\sqrt{1 - v^2/c^2}}.$$

The second term in our equation for W above is easily integrated since

$$\frac{d}{dv}\left(\sqrt{1 - v^2/c^2}\right) = -(v/c^2)/\sqrt{1 - v^2/c^2},$$

and so becomes

$$-\int_i^f p\,dv = -\int_0^v \frac{mv}{\sqrt{1 - v^2/c^2}}\,dv = mc^2\sqrt{1 - v^2/c^2}\,\Big|_0^v$$

$$= mc^2\sqrt{1 - v^2/c^2} - mc^2.$$

Finally, we have for W:

$$W = \frac{mv^2}{\sqrt{1 - v^2/c^2}} + mc^2\sqrt{1 - v^2/c^2} - mc^2.$$

We multiply the second term on the right by $\sqrt{1 - v^2/c^2}/\sqrt{1 - v^2/c^2} = 1$, and obtain

$$W = \frac{mc^2}{\sqrt{1 - v^2/c^2}} - mc^2.$$

By the work-energy theorem, the work done on the particle must equal its final kinetic energy K since the particle started from rest. Therefore

$$K = \frac{mc^2}{\sqrt{1 - v^2/c^2}} - mc^2$$

$$= \gamma mc^2 - mc^2 = (\gamma - 1)mc^2,$$

which are Eqs. 36–10.

*36–12 Doppler Shift for Light

In Section 16–7 we discussed how the frequency and wavelength of sound are altered if the source of the sound and the observer are moving toward or away from each other. When a source is moving toward us, the frequency is higher than when the source is at rest. If the source moves away from us, the frequency is lower. We obtained four different equations for the Doppler shift (Eqs. 16–9a and b, Eqs. 16–10a and b), depending on the direction of the relative motion and whether the source or the observer is moving. The Doppler effect occurs also for light; but the shifted frequency or wavelength is given by slightly different equations, and there are only two of them, because for light—according to special relativity—we can make no distinction between motion of the source and motion of the observer. (Recall that sound travels in a medium such as air, whereas light does not—there is no evidence for an ether.)

To derive the Doppler shift for light, let us consider a light source and an observer that move toward each other, and let their relative velocity be v as measured in the reference frame of either the source or the observer. Figure 36–14a shows a source at rest emitting light waves of frequency f_0 and wavelength $\lambda_0 = c/f_0$. Two wavecrests are shown, a distance λ_0 apart, the second crest just having been emitted. In Fig. 36–14b, the source is shown moving at speed v toward a stationary observer who will see the wavelength λ being somewhat less than λ_0. (This is much like Fig. 16–19 for sound.) Let Δt represent the time between crests as detected by the observer, whose reference frame is shown in Fig. 36–14b. From Fig. 36–14b we see that

$$\lambda = c\,\Delta t - v\,\Delta t,$$

where $c\,\Delta t$ is the distance crest 1 has moved in the time Δt after it was emitted, and $v\,\Delta t$ is the distance the source has moved in time Δt. So far our derivation has not differed from that for sound (Section 16–7). Now we invoke the theory of relativity. The time between emission of wavecrests has undergone time dilation:

$$\Delta t = \Delta t_0/\sqrt{1 - v^2/c^2}$$

where Δt_0 is the time between emissions of wavecrests in the reference frame where the source is at rest (the "proper" time). In the source's reference frame (Fig. 36–14a), we have

$$\Delta t_0 = \frac{1}{f_0} = \frac{\lambda_0}{c}$$

(Eqs. 5–2 and 31–14). Thus

$$\lambda = (c - v)\,\Delta t = (c - v)\frac{\Delta t_0}{\sqrt{1 - v^2/c^2}} = \frac{(c - v)}{\sqrt{c^2 - v^2}}\lambda_0$$

or

$$\lambda = \lambda_0\sqrt{\frac{c - v}{c + v}}. \qquad \begin{bmatrix} \text{source and observer} \\ \text{moving toward} \\ \text{each other} \end{bmatrix} \qquad \textbf{(36–14a)}$$

The frequency f is (recall $\lambda_0 = c/f_0$)

$$f = \frac{c}{\lambda} = f_0\sqrt{\frac{c + v}{c - v}}. \qquad \begin{bmatrix} \text{source and observer} \\ \text{moving toward} \\ \text{each other} \end{bmatrix} \qquad \textbf{(36–14b)}$$

Here f_0 is the frequency of the light as seen in the source's reference frame, and f is the frequency as measured by an observer moving toward the source or toward whom the source is moving. Equations 36–14 depend only on the relative velocity v. For relative motion *away* from each other we set $v < 0$ in Eqs. 36–14, and obtain

$$\lambda = \lambda_0\sqrt{\frac{c + v}{c - v}} \qquad \textbf{(36–15a)}$$

$$\begin{bmatrix} \text{source and observer} \\ \text{moving away from} \\ \text{each other} \end{bmatrix}$$

$$f = f_0\sqrt{\frac{c - v}{c + v}}. \qquad \textbf{(36–15b)}$$

From Eqs. 36–14 and 36–15 we see that light from a source moving toward us will have a higher frequency and shorter wavelength, whereas if a light source moves away from us, we will see a lower frequency and a longer wavelength. In the latter case, visible light will have its wavelength lengthened toward the red end of the visible spectrum (Fig. 32–26), an effect called a **redshift**. As we will see in the next Chapter, all atoms have their own distinctive signature in terms of the frequencies of the light they emit. In 1929 the American astronomer Edwin Hubble (1889–1953) found that radiation from atoms in many galaxies is redshifted. That is, the frequencies of light emitted are lower than those emitted by stationary atoms on Earth, suggesting that the galaxies are receding from us. This is the origin of the idea that the universe is expanding.

FIGURE 36–14 Doppler shift for light. (a) Source and observer at rest. (b) Source moving toward stationary observer.

EXAMPLE 36–13 **Speeding through a red light.** A driver claims that he did not go through a red light because the light was Doppler shifted and appeared green. Calculate the speed of a driver in order for a red light to appear green.

APPROACH We apply the Doppler shift equation for red light ($\lambda_0 \approx 650$ nm) and green light ($\lambda \approx 500$ nm).

SOLUTION Equation 36–14a holds for the source and the object moving toward each other:

$$\lambda = \lambda_0 \sqrt{\frac{c - v}{c + v}}.$$

We square this equation:

$$\frac{c - v}{c + v} = \left(\frac{\lambda}{\lambda_0}\right)^2$$

where $(\lambda/\lambda_0)^2 = (500 \text{ nm}/650 \text{ nm})^2 = 0.59$. We solve for v:

$$v = c \left[\frac{1 - (\lambda/\lambda_0)^2}{1 + (\lambda/\lambda_0)^2}\right] = 0.26c.$$

With this defense, the driver might not be guilty of running a red light, but he would clearly be guilty of speeding.

36–13 The Impact of Special Relativity

A great many experiments have been performed to test the predictions of the special theory of relativity. Within experimental error, no contradictions have been found. Scientists have therefore accepted relativity as an accurate description of nature.

At speeds much less than the speed of light, the relativistic formulas reduce to the old classical ones, as we have discussed. We would, of course, hope—or rather, insist—that this be true since Newtonian mechanics works so well for objects moving with speeds $v \ll c$. This insistence that a more general theory (such as relativity) give the same results as a more restricted theory (such as classical mechanics which works for $v \ll c$) is called the **correspondence principle**. The two theories must correspond where their realms of validity overlap. Relativity thus does not contradict classical mechanics. Rather, it is a more general theory, of which classical mechanics is now considered to be a limiting case.

The importance of relativity is not simply that it gives more accurate results, especially at very high speeds. Much more than that, it has changed the way we view the world. The concepts of space and time are now seen to be relative, and intertwined with one another, whereas before they were considered absolute and separate. Even our concepts of matter and energy have changed: either can be converted to the other. The impact of relativity extends far beyond physics. It has influenced the other sciences, and even the world of art and literature; it has, indeed, entered the general culture.

From a practical point of view, we do not have much opportunity in our daily lives to use the mathematics of relativity. For example, the γ factor $1/\sqrt{1 - v^2/c^2}$, which appears in relativistic formulas, has a value of only 1.005 even for a speed as high as $0.10c = 3.0 \times 10^7$ m/s, giving a correction of less than 1%. For speeds less than $0.10c$, or unless mass and energy are interchanged, we don't usually need to use the more complicated relativistic formulas, and can use the simpler classical formulas.

Summary

An **inertial reference frame** is one in which Newton's law of inertia holds. Inertial reference frames can move at constant velocity relative to one another; accelerating reference frames are **noninertial**.

The **special theory of relativity** is based on two principles: the **relativity principle**, which states that the laws of physics are the same in all inertial reference frames, and the principle of the **constancy of the speed of light**, which states that the speed of light in empty space has the same value in all inertial reference frames.

One consequence of relativity theory is that two events that are simultaneous in one reference frame may not be simultaneous in another. Other effects are **time dilation**: moving clocks are measured to run slow; and **length contraction**: the length of a moving object is measured to be shorter (in its direction of motion) than when it is at rest. Quantitatively,

$$\Delta t = \frac{\Delta t_0}{\sqrt{1 - v^2/c^2}} = \gamma \, \Delta t_0 \qquad \text{(36–1)}$$

$$\ell = \ell_0 \sqrt{1 - v^2/c^2} = \frac{\ell_0}{\gamma} \qquad \text{(36–3)}$$

where ℓ and Δt are the length and time interval of objects (or events) observed as they move by at the speed v; ℓ_0 and Δt_0 are the **proper length** and **proper time**—that is, the same quantities as measured in the rest frame of the objects or events. The quantity γ is shorthand for

$$\gamma = \frac{1}{\sqrt{1 - v^2/c^2}}. \qquad \text{(36–2)}$$

The theory of relativity has changed our notions of space and time, and of momentum, energy, and mass. Space and time are seen to be intimately connected, with time being the fourth dimension in addition to the three dimensions of space.

The **Lorentz transformations** relate the positions and times of events in one inertial reference frame to their positions and times in a second inertial reference frame.

$$
\begin{aligned}
x &= \gamma(x' + vt') \\
y &= y' \\
z &= z' \\
t &= \gamma\left(t' + \frac{vx'}{c^2}\right)
\end{aligned}
\qquad \text{(36–6)}
$$

where $\gamma = 1/\sqrt{1 - v^2/c^2}$.

Velocity addition also must be done in a special way. All these relativistic effects are significant only at high speeds, close to the speed of light, which itself is the ultimate speed in the universe.

The **momentum** of an object is given by

$$p = \gamma m v = \frac{mv}{\sqrt{1 - v^2/c^2}}. \qquad \text{(36–8)}$$

Mass and energy are interconvertible. The equation

$$E = mc^2 \qquad \text{(36–12)}$$

tells how much energy E is needed to create a mass m, or vice versa. Said another way, $E = mc^2$ is the amount of energy an object has because of its mass m. The law of conservation of energy must include mass as a form of energy.

The kinetic energy K of an object moving at speed v is given by

$$K = (\gamma - 1)mc^2 = \frac{mc^2}{\sqrt{1 - v^2/c^2}} - mc^2 \qquad \text{(36–10)}$$

where m is the mass of the object. The total energy E, if there is no potential energy, is

$$
\begin{aligned}
E &= K + mc^2 \\
&= \gamma mc^2.
\end{aligned}
\qquad \text{(36–11)}
$$

The momentum p of an object is related to its total energy E (assuming no potential energy) by

$$E^2 = p^2c^2 + m^2c^4. \qquad \text{(36–13)}$$

Questions

1. You are in a windowless car in an exceptionally smooth train moving at constant velocity. Is there any physical experiment you can do in the train car to determine whether you are moving? Explain.

2. You might have had the experience of being at a red light when, out of the corner of your eye, you see the car beside you creep forward. Instinctively you stomp on the brake pedal, thinking that you are rolling backward. What does this say about absolute and relative motion?

3. A worker stands on top of a moving railroad car, and throws a heavy ball straight up (from his point of view). Ignoring air resistance, will the ball land back in his hand or behind him?

4. Does the Earth really go around the Sun? Or is it also valid to say that the Sun goes around the Earth? Discuss in view of the relativity principle (that there is no best reference frame). Explain.

5. If you were on a spaceship traveling at $0.5c$ away from a star, at what speed would the starlight pass you?

6. The time dilation effect is sometimes expressed as "moving clocks run slowly." Actually, this effect has nothing to do with motion affecting the functioning of clocks. What then does it deal with?

7. Does time dilation mean that time actually passes more slowly in moving reference frames or that it only *seems* to pass more slowly?

8. A young-looking woman astronaut has just arrived home from a long trip. She rushes up to an old gray-haired man and in the ensuing conversation refers to him as her son. How might this be possible?

9. If you were traveling away from Earth at speed $0.5c$, would you notice a change in your heartbeat? Would your mass, height, or waistline change? What would observers on Earth using telescopes say about you?

10. Do time dilation and length contraction occur at ordinary speeds, say 90 km/h?

11. Suppose the speed of light were infinite. What would happen to the relativistic predictions of length contraction and time dilation?

12. Discuss how our everyday lives would be different if the speed of light were only 25 m/s.

13. Explain how the length contraction and time dilation formulas might be used to indicate that c is the limiting speed in the universe.

14. The drawing at the start of this Chapter shows the street as seen by Mr Tompkins, where the speed of light is $c = 20$ mi/h. What does Mr Tompkins look like to the people standing on the street (Fig. 36–15)? Explain.

FIGURE 36–15
Question 14.
Mr Tompkins as seen by people on the sidewalk. See also Chapter-Opening figure on page 951.

15. An electron is limited to travel at speeds less than c. Does this put an upper limit on the momentum of an electron? If so, what is this upper limit? If not, explain.

16. Can a particle of nonzero mass attain the speed of light?

17. Does the equation $E = mc^2$ conflict with the conservation of energy principle? Explain.

18. If mass is a form of energy, does this mean that a spring has more mass when compressed than when relaxed?

19. It is not correct to say that "matter can neither be created nor destroyed." What must we say instead?

20. Is our intuitive notion that velocities simply add, as in Section 3–9, completely wrong?

Problems

36–5 and 36–6 Time Dilation, Length Contraction

1. (I) A spaceship passes you at a speed of $0.850c$. You measure its length to be 38.2 m. How long would it be when at rest?

2. (I) A certain type of elementary particle travels at a speed of 2.70×10^8 m/s. At this speed, the average lifetime is measured to be 4.76×10^{-6} s. What is the particle's lifetime at rest?

3. (II) According to the special theory of relativity, the factor γ that determines the length contraction and the time dilation is given by $\gamma = 1/\sqrt{1 - v^2/c^2}$. Determine the numerical values of γ for an object moving at speed $v = 0.01c, 0.05c, 0.10c, 0.20c, 0.30c, 0.40c, 0.50c, 0.60c, 0.70c, 0.80c, 0.90c,$ and $0.99c$. Make a graph of γ versus v.

4. (II) If you were to travel to a star 135 light-years from Earth at a speed of 2.80×10^8 m/s, what would you measure this distance to be?

5. (II) What is the speed of a pion if its average lifetime is measured to be 4.40×10^{-8} s? At rest, its average lifetime is 2.60×10^{-8} s.

6. (II) In an Earth reference frame, a star is 56 light-years away. How fast would you have to travel so that to you the distance would be only 35 light-years?

7. (II) Suppose you decide to travel to a star 65 light-years away at a speed that tells you the distance is only 25 light-years. How many years would it take you to make the trip?

8. (II) At what speed v will the length of a 1.00-m stick look 10.0% shorter (90.0 cm)?

9. (II) Escape velocity from the Earth is 11.2 km/s. What would be the percent decrease in length of a 65.2-m-long spacecraft traveling at that speed as seen from Earth?

10. (II) A friend speeds by you in her spacecraft at a speed of $0.760c$. It is measured in your frame to be 4.80 m long and 1.35 m high. (a) What will be its length and height at rest? (b) How many seconds elapsed on your friend's watch when 20.0 s passed on yours? (c) How fast did you appear to be traveling according to your friend? (d) How many seconds elapsed on your watch when she saw 20.0 s pass on hers?

11. (II) At what speed do the relativistic formulas for (a) length and (b) time intervals differ from classical values by 1.00%? (This is a reasonable way to estimate when to do relativistic calculations rather than classical.)

12. (II) A certain star is 18.6 light-years away. How long would it take a spacecraft traveling $0.950c$ to reach that star from Earth, as measured by observers: (a) on Earth, (b) on the spacecraft? (c) What is the distance traveled according to observers on the spacecraft? (d) What will the spacecraft occupants compute their speed to be from the results of (b) and (c)?

13. (II) Suppose a news report stated that starship *Enterprise* had just returned from a 5-year voyage while traveling at $0.74c$. (a) If the report meant 5.0 years of *Earth time*, how much time elapsed on the ship? (b) If the report meant 5.0 years of *ship time*, how much time passed on Earth?

14. (II) An unstable particle produced in an accelerator experiment travels at constant velocity, covering 1.00 m in 3.40 ns in the lab frame before changing ("decaying") into other particles. In the rest frame of the particle, determine (a) how long it lived before decaying, (b) how far it moved before decaying.

15. (II) When it is stationary, the half-life of a certain subatomic particle is T_0. That is, if N of these particles are present at a certain time, then a time T_0 later only $N/2$ particles will be present, assuming the particles are at rest. A beam carrying N such particles per second is created at position $x = 0$ in a high-energy physics laboratory. This beam travels along the x axis at speed v in the laboratory reference frame and it is found that only $N/2$ particles per second travel in the beam at $x = 2cT_0$, where c is the speed of light. Find the speed v of the particles within the beam.

16. (II) In its own reference frame, a box has the shape of a cube 2.0 m on a side. This box is loaded onto the flat floor of a spaceship and the spaceship then flies past us with a horizontal speed of $0.80c$. What is the volume of the box as we observe it?

17. (II) When at rest, a spaceship has the form of an isosceles triangle whose two equal sides have length 2ℓ and whose base has length ℓ. If this ship flies past an observer with a relative velocity of $v = 0.95c$ directed along its base, what are the lengths of the ship's three sides according to the observer?

18. (II) How fast must a pion be moving on average to travel 25 m before it decays? The average lifetime, at rest, is 2.6×10^{-8} s.

36–8 Lorentz Transformations

19. (I) An observer on Earth sees an alien vessel approach at a speed of 0.60c. The *Enterprise* comes to the rescue (Fig. 36–16), overtaking the aliens while moving directly toward Earth at a speed of 0.90c relative to Earth. What is the relative speed of one vessel as seen by the other?

Enterprise

$v = 0.90c$

$v = 0.60c$

FIGURE 36–16 Problem 19.

20. (I) Suppose in Fig. 36–11 that the origins of S and S′ overlap at $t = t' = 0$ and that S′ moves at speed $v = 30$ m/s with respect to S. In S′, a person is resting at a point whose coordinates are $x' = 25$ m, $y' = 20$ m, and $z' = 0$. Calculate this person's coordinates in S (x, y, z) at (a) $t = 3.5$ s, (b) $t = 10.0$ s. Use the Galilean transformation.

21. (I) Repeat Problem 20 using the Lorentz transformation and a relative speed $v = 1.80 \times 10^8$ m/s, but choose the time t to be (a) 3.5 μs and (b) 10.0 μs.

22. (II) In Problem 21, suppose that the person moves with a velocity whose components are $u'_x = u'_y = 1.10 \times 10^8$ m/s, What will be her velocity with respect to S? (Give magnitude and direction.)

23. (II) Two spaceships leave Earth in opposite directions, each with a speed of 0.60c with respect to Earth. (a) What is the velocity of spaceship 1 relative to spaceship 2? (b) What is the velocity of spaceship 2 relative to spaceship 1?

24. (II) Reference frame S′ moves at speed $v = 0.92c$ in the $+x$ direction with respect to reference frame S. The origins of S and S′ overlap at $t = t' = 0$. An object is stationary in S′ at position $x' = 100$ m. What is the position of the object in S when the clock in S reads 1.00 μs according to the (a) Galilean and (b) Lorentz transformation equations?

25. (II) A spaceship leaves Earth traveling at 0.61c. A second spaceship leaves the first at a speed of 0.87c with respect to the first. Calculate the speed of the second ship with respect to Earth if it is fired (a) in the same direction the first spaceship is already moving, (b) directly backward toward Earth.

26. (II) Your spaceship, traveling at 0.90c, needs to launch a probe out the forward hatch so that its speed relative to the planet that you are approaching is 0.95c. With what speed must it leave your ship?

27. (II) A spaceship traveling at 0.76c away from Earth fires a module with a speed of 0.82c at right angles to its own direction of travel (as seen by the spaceship). What is the speed of the module, and its direction of travel (relative to the spaceship's direction), as seen by an observer on Earth?

28. (II) If a particle moves in the xy plane of system S (Fig. 36–11) with speed u in a direction that makes an angle θ with the x axis, show that it makes an angle θ' in S′ given by $\tan \theta' = (\sin \theta)\sqrt{1 - v^2/c^2}/(\cos \theta - v/u)$.

29. (II) A stick of length ℓ_0, at rest in reference frame S, makes an angle θ with the x axis. In reference frame S′, which moves to the right with velocity $\vec{v} = v\hat{i}$ with respect to S, determine (a) the length ℓ of the stick, and (b) the angle θ' it makes with the x' axis.

30. (III) In the old West, a marshal riding on a train traveling 35.0 m/s sees a duel between two men standing on the Earth 55.0 m apart parallel to the train. The marshal's instruments indicate that in his reference frame the two men fired simultaneously. (a) Which of the two men, the first one the train passes (A) or the second one (B) should be arrested for firing the first shot? That is, in the gunfighter's frame of reference, who fired first? (b) How much earlier did he fire? (c) Who was struck first?

31. (III) Two lightbulbs, A and B, are placed at rest on the x axis at positions $x_A = 0$ and $x_B = +\ell$. In this reference frame, the bulbs are turned on simultaneously. Use the Lorentz transformations to find an expression for the time interval between when the bulbs are turned on as measured by an observer moving at velocity v in the $+x$ direction. According to this observer, which bulb is turned on first?

32. (III) An observer in reference frame S notes that two events are separated in space by 220 m and in time by 0.80 μs. How fast must reference frame S′ be moving relative to S in order for an observer in S′ to detect the two events as occurring at the same location in space?

33. (III) A farm boy studying physics believes that he can fit a 12.0-m long pole into a 10.0-m long barn if he runs fast enough, carrying the pole. Can he do it? Explain in detail. How does this fit with the idea that when he is running the barn looks even shorter than 10.0 m?

36–9 Relativistic Momentum

34. (I) What is the momentum of a proton traveling at $v = 0.75c$?

35. (II) (a) A particle travels at $v = 0.10c$. By what percentage will a calculation of its momentum be wrong if you use the classical formula? (b) Repeat for $v = 0.60c$.

36. (II) A particle of mass m travels at a speed $v = 0.26c$. At what speed will its momentum be doubled?

37. (II) An unstable particle is at rest and suddenly decays into two fragments. No external forces act on the particle or its fragments. One of the fragments has a speed of 0.60c and a mass of 6.68×10^{-27} kg, while the other has a mass of 1.67×10^{-27} kg. What is the speed of the less massive fragment?

38. (II) What is the percent change in momentum of a proton that accelerates (a) from 0.45c to 0.80c, (b) from 0.80c to 0.98c?

36–11 Relativistic Energy

39. (I) Calculate the rest energy of an electron in joules and in MeV $(1 \text{ MeV} = 1.60 \times 10^{-13} \text{ J})$.

40. (I) When a uranium nucleus at rest breaks apart in the process known as fission in a nuclear reactor, the resulting fragments have a total kinetic energy of about 200 MeV. How much mass was lost in the process?

41. (I) The total annual energy consumption in the United States is about 8×10^{19} J. How much mass would have to be converted to energy to fuel this need?

42. (I) Calculate the mass of a proton in MeV/c^2.

43. (II) Suppose there was a process by which two photons, each with momentum 0.50 MeV/c, could collide and make a single particle. What is the maximum mass that the particle could possess?

44. (II) (a) How much work is required to accelerate a proton from rest up to a speed of 0.998c? (b) What would be the momentum of this proton?

45. (II) How much energy can be obtained from conversion of 1.0 gram of mass? How much mass could this energy raise to a height of 1.0 km above the Earth's surface?

46. (II) To accelerate a particle of mass m from rest to speed $0.90c$ requires work W_1. To accelerate the particle from speed $0.90c$ to $0.99c$, requires work W_2. Determine the ratio W_2/W_1.

47. (II) What is the speed of a particle when its kinetic energy equals its rest energy?

48. (II) What is the momentum of a 950-MeV proton (that is, its kinetic energy is 950 MeV)?

49. (II) Calculate the kinetic energy and momentum of a proton traveling 2.80×10^8 m/s.

50. (II) What is the speed of an electron whose kinetic energy is 1.25 MeV?

51. (II) What is the speed of a proton accelerated by a potential difference of 125 MV?

52. (II) Two identical particles of mass m approach each other at equal and opposite speeds, v. The collision is completely inelastic and results in a single particle at rest. What is the mass of the new particle? How much energy was lost in the collision? How much kinetic energy was lost in this collision?

53. (II) What is the speed of an electron just before it hits a television screen after being accelerated from rest by the 28,000 V of the picture tube?

54. (II) The kinetic energy of a particle is 45 MeV. If the momentum is 121 MeV/c, what is the particle's mass?

55. (II) Calculate the speed of a proton $(m = 1.67 \times 10^{-27} \text{ kg})$ whose kinetic energy is exactly half (a) its total energy, (b) its rest energy.

56. (II) Calculate the kinetic energy and momentum of a proton $(m = 1.67 \times 10^{-27} \text{ kg})$ traveling 8.15×10^7 m/s. By what percentages would your calculations have been in error if you had used classical formulas?

57. (II) Suppose a spacecraft of mass 17,000 kg is accelerated to $0.18c$. (a) How much kinetic energy would it have? (b) If you used the classical formula for kinetic energy, by what percentage would you be in error?

*58. (II) What magnetic field B is needed to keep 998-GeV protons revolving in a circle of radius 1.0 km (at, say, the Fermilab synchrotron)? Use the relativistic mass. The proton's rest mass is 0.938 GeV/c^2. (1 GeV = 10^9 eV.) [Hint: In relativity, $m_{rel} v^2/r = qvB$ is still valid in a magnetic field, where $m_{rel} = \gamma m$.]

59. (II) The americium nucleus, $^{241}_{95}$Am, decays to a neptunium nucleus, $^{237}_{93}$Np, by emitting an alpha particle of mass 4.00260 u and kinetic energy 5.5 MeV. Estimate the mass of the neptunium nucleus, ignoring its recoil, given that the americium mass is 241.05682 u.

60. (II) Make a graph of the kinetic energy versus momentum for (a) a particle of nonzero mass, and (b) a particle with zero mass.

61. (II) A negative muon traveling at 43% the speed of light collides head on with a positive muon traveling at 55% the speed of light. The two muons (each of mass 105.7 MeV/c^2) annihilate, and produce how much electromagnetic energy?

62. (II) Show that the kinetic energy K of a particle of mass m is related to its momentum p by the equation

$$p = \sqrt{K^2 + 2Kmc^2}/c.$$

63. (III) (a) In reference frame S, a particle has momentum $\vec{p} = p_x \hat{i}$ along the positive x axis. Show that in frame S′, which moves with speed v as in Fig. 36–11, the momentum has components

$$p'_x = \frac{p_x - vE/c^2}{\sqrt{1 - v^2/c^2}}$$

$$p'_y = p_y$$

$$p'_z = p_z$$

$$E' = \frac{E - p_x v}{\sqrt{1 - v^2/c^2}}.$$

(These transformation equations hold, actually, for any direction of $\vec{p}$, as long as the motion of S′ is along the x axis.) (b) Show that $p_x, p_y, p_z, E/c$ transform according to the Lorentz transformation in the same way as x, y, z, ct.

36–12 Doppler Shift for Light

64. (II) A certain galaxy has a Doppler shift given by $f_0 - f = 0.0987 f_0$. Estimate how fast it is moving away from us.

65. (II) A spaceship moving toward Earth at $0.70c$ transmits radio signals at 95.0 MHz. At what frequency should Earth receivers be tuned?

66. (II) Starting from Eq. 36–15a, show that the Doppler shift in wavelength is

$$\frac{\Delta \lambda}{\lambda} = \frac{v}{c}$$

if $v \ll c$.

67. (III) A radar "speed gun" emits microwaves of frequency $f_0 = 36.0$ GHz. When the gun is pointed at an object moving toward it at speed v, the object senses the microwaves at the Doppler-shifted frequency f. The moving object reflects these microwaves at this same frequency f. The stationary radar apparatus detects these reflected waves at a Doppler-shifted frequency f'. The gun combines its emitted wave at f_0 and its detected wave at f'. These waves interfere, creating a beat pattern whose beat frequency is $f_{beat} = f' - f_0$. (a) Show that

$$v \approx \frac{cf_{beat}}{2f_0},$$

if $f_{beat} \ll f_0$. If $f_{beat} = 6670$ Hz, what is v (km/h)? (b) If the object's speed is different by Δv, show that the difference in beat frequency Δf_{beat} is given by

$$\Delta f_{beat} = \frac{2f_0 \Delta v}{c}.$$

If the accuracy of the speed gun is to be 1 km/h, to what accuracy must the beat frequency be measured?

68. (III) A certain atom emits light of frequency f_0 when at rest. A monatomic gas composed of these atoms is at temperature T. Some of the gas atoms move toward and others away from an observer due to their random thermal motion. Using the rms speed of thermal motion, show that the fractional difference between the Doppler-shifted frequencies for atoms moving directly toward the observer and directly away from the observer is $\Delta f/f_0 \approx 2\sqrt{3kT/mc^2}$; assume $mc^2 \gg 3kT$. Evaluate $\Delta f/f_0$ for a gas of hydrogen atoms at 550 K. [This "Doppler-broadening" effect is commonly used to measure gas temperature, such as in astronomy.]

General Problems

69. An atomic clock is taken to the North Pole, while another stays at the Equator. How far will they be out of synchronization after 2.0 years has elapsed? [*Hint*: Use the binomial expansion, Appendix A.]

70. A spaceship in distress sends out two escape pods in opposite directions. One travels at a speed $v_1 = -0.60c$ in one direction, and the other travels at a speed $v_2 = +0.50c$ in the other direction, as observed from the spaceship. What speed does the first escape pod measure for the second escape pod?

71. An airplane travels 1300 km/h around the Earth in a circle of radius essentially equal to that of the Earth, returning to the same place. Using special relativity, estimate the difference in time to make the trip as seen by Earth and airplane observers. [*Hint*: Use the binomial expansion, Appendix A.]

72. The nearest star to Earth is Proxima Centauri, 4.3 light-years away. (*a*) At what constant velocity must a spacecraft travel from Earth if it is to reach the star in 4.6 years, as measured by travelers on the spacecraft? (*b*) How long does the trip take according to Earth observers?

73. A quasar emits familiar hydrogen lines whose wave-lengths are 7.0% longer than what we measure in the laboratory. (*a*) Using the Doppler formula for light, estimate the speed of this quasar. (*b*) What result would you obtain if you used the "classical" Doppler shift discussed in Chapter 16?

74. A healthy astronaut's heart rate is 60 beats/min. Flight doctors on Earth can monitor an astronaut's vital signs remotely while in flight. How fast would an astronaut have to be flying away from Earth in order for the doctor to measure her having a heart rate of 30 beats/min?

75. A spacecraft (reference frame S′) moves past Earth (reference frame S) at velocity $\vec{v}$, which points along the x and $x′$ axes. The spacecraft emits a light beam (speed c) along its $y′$ axis as shown in Fig. 36–17. (*a*) What angle θ does this light beam make with the x axis in the Earth's reference frame? (*b*) Use velocity transformations to show that the light moves with speed c also in the Earth's reference frame. (*c*) Compare these relativistic results to what you would have obtained classically (Galilean transformations).

FIGURE 36–17
Problem 75.

76. Rocket A passes Earth at a speed of $0.65c$. At the same time, rocket B passes Earth moving $0.85c$ relative to Earth in the same direction. How fast is B moving relative to A when it passes A?

77. (*a*) What is the speed v of an electron whose kinetic energy is 14,000 times its rest energy? You can state the answer as the difference $c - v$. Such speeds are reached in the Stanford Linear Accelerator, SLAC. (*b*) If the electrons travel in the lab through a tube 3.0 km long (as at SLAC), how long is this tube in the electrons' reference frame? [*Hint*: Use the binomial expansion.]

78. As a rough rule, anything traveling faster than about $0.1c$ is called *relativistic*—that is, special relativity is a significant effect. Determine the speed of an electron in a hydrogen atom (radius 0.53×10^{-10} m) and state whether or not it is relativistic. (Treat the electron as though it were in a circular orbit around the proton.)

79. What minimum amount of electromagnetic energy is needed to produce an electron and a positron together? A positron is a particle with the same mass as an electron, but has the opposite charge. (Note that electric charge is conserved in this process. See Section 37–5.)

80. How many grams of matter would have to be totally destroyed to run a 75-W lightbulb for 1.0 year?

81. If E is the total energy of a particle with zero potential energy, show that $dE/dp = v$, where p and v are the momentum and velocity of the particle, respectively.

82. A free neutron can decay into a proton, an electron, and a neutrino. Assume the neutrino's mass is zero; the other masses can be found in the Table inside the front cover. Determine the total kinetic energy shared among the three particles when a neutron decays at rest.

83. The Sun radiates energy at a rate of about 4×10^{26} W. (*a*) At what rate is the Sun's mass decreasing? (*b*) How long does it take for the Sun to lose a mass equal to that of Earth? (*c*) Estimate how long the Sun could last if it radiated constantly at this rate.

84. An unknown particle is measured to have a negative charge and a speed of 2.24×10^8 m/s. Its momentum is determined to be 3.07×10^{-22} kg·m/s. Identify the particle by finding its mass.

85. How much energy would be required to break a helium nucleus into its constituents, two protons and two neutrons? The rest masses of a proton (including an electron), a neutron, and neutral helium are, respectively, 1.00783 u, 1.00867 u, and 4.00260 u. (This energy difference is called the *total binding energy* of the $_2^4$He nucleus.)

86. Show analytically that a particle with momentum p and energy E has a speed given by

$$v = \frac{pc^2}{E} = \frac{pc}{\sqrt{m^2c^2 + p^2}}.$$

87. Two protons, each having a speed of $0.985c$ in the laboratory, are moving toward each other. Determine (*a*) the momentum of each proton in the laboratory, (*b*) the total momentum of the two protons in the laboratory, and (*c*) the momentum of one proton as seen by the other proton.

88. When two moles of hydrogen molecules (H_2) and one mole of oxygen molecules (O_2) react to form two moles of water (H_2O), the energy released is 484 kJ. How much does the mass decrease in this reaction? What % of the total original mass of the system does this mass change represent?

89. The fictional starship *Enterprise* obtains its power by combining matter and antimatter, achieving complete conversion of mass into energy. If the mass of the *Enterprise* is approximately 6×10^9 kg, how much mass must be converted into kinetic energy to accelerate it from rest to one-tenth the speed of light?

90. A spaceship and its occupants have a total mass of 180,000 kg. The occupants would like to travel to a star that is 35 light-years away at a speed of 0.70c. To accelerate, the engine of the spaceship changes mass directly to energy. How much mass will be converted to energy to accelerate the spaceship to this speed? Assume the acceleration is rapid, so the speed for the entire trip can be taken to be 0.70c, and ignore decrease in total mass for the calculation. How long will the trip take according to the astronauts on board?

91. In a nuclear reaction two identical particles are created, traveling in opposite directions. If the speed of each particle is 0.85c, relative to the laboratory frame of reference, what is one particle's speed relative to the other particle?

92. A 32,000-kg spaceship is to travel to the vicinity of a star 6.6 light-years from Earth. Passengers on the ship want the (one-way) trip to take no more than 1.0 year. How much work must be done on the spaceship to bring it to the speed necessary for this trip?

93. Suppose a 14,500-kg spaceship left Earth at a speed of 0.98c. What is the spaceship's kinetic energy? Compare with the total U.S. annual energy consumption (about 10^{20} J).

94. A pi meson of mass m_π decays at rest into a muon (mass m_μ) and a neutrino of negligible or zero mass. Show that the kinetic energy of the muon is $K_\mu = (m_\pi - m_\mu)^2 c^2 / (2m_\pi)$.

95. Astronomers measure the distance to a particular star to be 6.0 light-years (1 ly = distance light travels in 1 year). A spaceship travels from Earth to the vicinity of this star at steady speed, arriving in 2.50 years as measured by clocks on the spaceship. (a) How long does the trip take as measured by clocks in Earth's reference frame (assumed inertial)? (b) What distance does the spaceship travel as measured in its own reference frame?

96. A 1.88-kg mass oscillates on the end of a spring whose spring stiffness constant is $k = 84.2$ N/m. If this system is in a spaceship moving past Earth at 0.900c, what is its period of oscillation according to (a) observers on the ship, and (b) observers on Earth?

97. Show that the space–time interval, $(c\,\Delta t)^2 - (\Delta x)^2$, is invariant, meaning that all observers in all inertial reference frames calculate the same number for this quantity for any pair of events.

98. A slab of glass with index of refraction n moves to the right with speed v. A flash of light is emitted at point A (Fig. 36–18) and passes through the glass arriving at point B a distance ℓ away. The glass has thickness d in the reference frame where it is at rest, and the speed of light in the glass is c/n. How long does it take the light to go from point A to point B according to an observer at rest with respect to points A and B? Check your answer for the cases $v = c$, $v = 0$, and $n = 1$.

FIGURE 36–18
Problem 98.

*Numerical/Computer

* **99.** (II) For a 1.0-kg mass, make a plot of the kinetic energy as a function of speed for speeds from 0 to 0.9c, using both the classical formula $\left(K = \frac{1}{2}mv^2\right)$ and the correct relativistic formula $\left(K = (\gamma - 1)mc^2\right)$.

* **100.** (III) A particle of mass m is projected horizontally at a relativistic speed v_0 in the $+x$ direction. There is a constant downward force F acting on the particle. Using the definition of relativistic momentum $\vec{p} = \gamma m\vec{v}$ and Newton's second law $\vec{F} = d\vec{p}/dt$, (a) show that the x and y components of the velocity of the particle at time t are given by

$$v_x(t) = p_0 c / (m^2 c^2 + p_0^2 + F^2 t^2)^{\frac{1}{2}}$$

$$v_y(t) = -Fct / (m^2 c^2 + p_0^2 + F^2 t^2)^{\frac{1}{2}}$$

where p_0 is the initial momentum of the particle. (b) Assume the particle is an electron $(m = 9.11 \times 10^{-31}$ kg), with $v_0 = 0.50c$ and $F = 1.00 \times 10^{-15}$ N. Calculate the values of v_x and v_y of the electron as a function of time t from $t = 0$ to $t = 5.00\ \mu$s in intervals of 0.05 μs. Graph the values to show how the velocity components change with time during this interval. (c) Is the path parabolic, as it would be in classical mechanics (Sections 3–7 and 3–8)? Explain.

Answers to Exercises

A: Yes.

B: (c).

C: (a) No; (b) yes.

D: 80 m.

E: 0.030c, same as classical, to an accuracy of better than 0.1%.

F: (d).

G: (d).

H: No.

Electron microscopes produce images using electrons which have wave properties just as light does. Since the wavelength of electrons can be much smaller than that of visible light, much greater resolution and magnification can be obtained. A scanning electron microscope (SEM) can produce images with a three-dimensional quality, as for these *Giardia* cells inside a human small intestine. Magnification here is about 2000×. *Giardia* is on the minds of backpackers because it has become too common in untreated water, even in the high mountains, and causes an unpleasant intestinal infection not easy to get rid of.

Early Quantum Theory and Models of the Atom

CHAPTER 37

CHAPTER-OPENING QUESTION—Guess now!

It has been found experimentally that

- **(a)** light behaves as a wave.
- **(b)** light behaves as a particle.
- **(c)** electrons behave as particles.
- **(d)** electrons behave as waves.
- **(e)** all of the above are true.
- **(f)** none of the above are true.

The second aspect of the revolution that shook the world of physics in the early part of the twentieth century was the quantum theory (the other was Einstein's theory of relativity). Unlike the special theory of relativity, the revolution of quantum theory required almost three decades to unfold, and many scientists contributed to its development. It began in 1900 with Planck's quantum hypothesis, and culminated in the mid-1920s with the theory of quantum mechanics of Schrödinger and Heisenberg which has been so effective in explaining the structure of matter.

37–1 Planck's Quantum Hypothesis; Blackbody Radiation

Blackbody Radiation

One of the observations that was unexplained at the end of the nineteenth century was the spectrum of light emitted by hot objects. We saw in Section 19–10 that all objects emit radiation whose total intensity is proportional to the fourth power of the Kelvin (absolute) temperature (T^4). At normal temperatures $(\approx 300\,\text{K})$, we are not aware of this electromagnetic radiation because of its low intensity.

CONTENTS

FIGURE 37–1 Measured spectra of wavelengths and frequencies emitted by a blackbody at three different temperatures.

At higher temperatures, there is sufficient infrared radiation that we can feel heat if we are close to the object. At still higher temperatures (on the order of 1000 K), objects actually glow, such as a red-hot electric stove burner or the heating element in a toaster. At temperatures above 2000 K, objects glow with a yellow or whitish color, such as white-hot iron and the filament of a lightbulb. The light emitted is of a continuous range of wavelengths or frequencies, and the *spectrum* is a plot of intensity vs. wavelength or frequency. As the temperature increases, the electromagnetic radiation emitted by objects not only increases in total intensity but reaches a peak at higher and higher frequencies.

The spectrum of light emitted by a hot dense object is shown in Fig. 37–1 for an idealized **blackbody**. A blackbody is a body that would absorb all the radiation falling on it (and so would appear black under reflection when illuminated by other sources). The radiation such an idealized blackbody would emit when hot and luminous, called **blackbody radiation** (though not necessarily black in color), approximates that from many real objects. The 6000-K curve in Fig. 37–1, corresponding to the temperature of the surface of the Sun, peaks in the visible part of the spectrum. For lower temperatures, the total radiation drops considerably and the peak occurs at longer wavelengths (or lower frequencies). (This is why objects glow with a red color at around 1000 K.) It is found experimentally that the wavelength at the peak of the spectrum, λ_P, is related to the Kelvin temperature T by

$$\lambda_P T = 2.90 \times 10^{-3}\,\text{m} \cdot \text{K}. \tag{37–1}$$

This is known as **Wien's law**.

EXAMPLE 37–1 **The Sun's surface temperature.** Estimate the temperature of the surface of our Sun, given that the Sun emits light whose peak intensity occurs in the visible spectrum at around 500 nm.

APPROACH We assume the Sun acts as a blackbody, and use $\lambda_P = 500\,\text{nm}$ in Wien's law (Eq. 37–1).

SOLUTION Wien's law gives

$$T = \frac{2.90 \times 10^{-3}\,\text{m} \cdot \text{K}}{\lambda_P} = \frac{2.90 \times 10^{-3}\,\text{m} \cdot \text{K}}{500 \times 10^{-9}\,\text{m}} \approx 6000\,\text{K}.$$

EXAMPLE 37–2 **Star color.** Suppose a star has a surface temperature of 32,500 K. What color would this star appear?

APPROACH We assume the star emits radiation as a blackbody, and solve for λ_P in Wien's law, Eq. 37–1.

SOLUTION From Wien's law we have

$$\lambda_P = \frac{2.90 \times 10^{-3}\,\text{m} \cdot \text{K}}{T} = \frac{2.90 \times 10^{-3}\,\text{m} \cdot \text{K}}{3.25 \times 10^4\,\text{K}} = 89.2\,\text{nm}.$$

The peak is in the UV range of the spectrum, and will be way to the left in Fig. 37–1. In the visible region, the curve will be descending, so the shortest visible wavelengths will be strongest. Hence the star will appear bluish (or blue-white).

NOTE This example helps us to understand why stars have different colors (reddish for the coolest stars, orangish, yellow, white, bluish for "hotter" stars.)

Planck's Quantum Hypothesis

A major problem facing scientists in the 1890s was to explain blackbody radiation. Maxwell's electromagnetic theory had predicted that oscillating electric charges produce electromagnetic waves, and the radiation emitted by a hot object could be due to the oscillations of electric charges in the molecules of the material. Although this would explain where the radiation came from, it did not correctly predict the observed spectrum of emitted light. Two important theoretical curves based on classical ideas were those proposed by W. Wien (in 1896) and by Lord Rayleigh (in 1900). The latter was modified later by J. Jeans and since then has been known as the Rayleigh–Jeans theory. As experimental data came in, it became clear that neither Wien's nor the Rayleigh–Jeans formulations were in accord with experiment (see Fig. 37–2).

FIGURE 37–2 Comparison of the Wien and the Rayleigh–Jeans theories to that of Planck, which closely follows experiment. The dashed lines show lack of agreement of older theories.

In the year 1900 Max Planck (1858–1947) proposed an empirical formula that nicely fit the data (now often called *Planck's radiation formula*):

$$I(\lambda, T) = \frac{2\pi hc^2 \lambda^{-5}}{e^{hc/\lambda kT} - 1}.$$

$I(\lambda, T)$ is the radiation intensity as a function of wavelength λ at the temperature T; k is Boltzman's constant, c is the speed of light, and h is a new constant, now called **Planck's constant**. The value of h was estimated by Planck by fitting his formula for the blackbody radiation curve to experiment. The value accepted today is

$$h = 6.626 \times 10^{-34} \, \text{J·s}.$$

To provide a theoretical basis for his formula, Planck made a new and radical assumption: that the energy of the oscillations of atoms within molecules cannot have just any value; instead each has energy which is a multiple of a minimum value related to the frequency of oscillation by

$$E = hf.$$

Planck's assumption suggests that the energy of any molecular vibration could be only a whole number multiple of the minimum energy hf:

$$E = nhf, \qquad n = 1, 2, 3, \cdots, \tag{37–2}$$

where n is called a **quantum number** ("quantum" means "discrete amount" as opposed to "continuous"). This idea is often called **Planck's quantum hypothesis**, although little attention was brought to this point at the time. In fact, it appears that Planck considered it more as a mathematical device to get the "right answer" rather than as an important discovery in its own right. Planck himself continued to seek a classical explanation for the introduction of h. The recognition that this was an important and radical innovation did not come until later, after about 1905 when others, particularly Einstein, entered the field.

The quantum hypothesis, Eq. 37–2, states that the energy of an oscillator can be $E = hf$, or $2hf$, or $3hf$, and so on, but there cannot be vibrations with energies between these values. That is, energy would not be a continuous quantity as had been believed for centuries; rather it is **quantized**—it exists only in discrete amounts. The smallest amount of energy possible (hf) is called the **quantum of energy**. Recall from Chapter 14 that the energy of an oscillation is proportional to the amplitude squared. Another way of expressing the quantum hypothesis is that not just any amplitude of vibration is possible. The possible values for the amplitude are related to the frequency f.

A simple analogy may help. Compare a ramp, on which a box can be placed at any height, to a flight of stairs on which the box can have only certain discrete amounts of potential energy, as shown in Fig. 37–3.

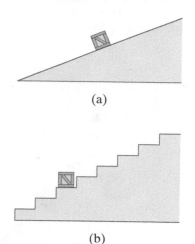

(a)

(b)

FIGURE 37–3 Ramp versus stair analogy. (a) On a ramp, a box can have continuous values of potential energy. (b) But on stairs, the box can have only discrete (quantized) values of energy.

37–2 Photon Theory of Light and the Photoelectric Effect

In 1905, the same year that he introduced the special theory of relativity, Einstein made a bold extension of the quantum idea by proposing a new theory of light. Planck's work had suggested that the vibrational energy of molecules in a radiating object is quantized with energy $E = nhf$, where n is an integer and f is the frequency of molecular vibration. Einstein argued that when light is emitted by a molecular oscillator, the molecule's vibrational energy of nhf must decrease by an amount hf (or by $2hf$, etc.) to another integer times hf, such as $(n - 1)hf$. Then to conserve energy, the light ought to be emitted in packets, or *quanta*, each with an energy

$$E = hf, \tag{37–3}$$

where f is here the frequency of the emitted light.

Again h is Planck's constant. Since all light ultimately comes from a radiating source, this suggests that perhaps *light is transmitted as tiny particles*, or **photons**, as they are now called, as well as via waves predicted by Maxwell's electromagnetic theory. The photon theory of light was a radical departure from classical ideas. Einstein proposed a test of the quantum theory of light: quantitative measurements on the photoelectric effect.

Light source

Light

C — P

Photocell

(A)

V

+ | −

FIGURE 37–4 The photoelectric effect.

When light shines on a metal surface, electrons are found to be emitted from the surface. This effect is called the **photoelectric effect** and it occurs in many materials, but is most easily observed with metals. It can be observed using the apparatus shown in Fig. 37–4. A metal plate P and a smaller electrode C are placed inside an evacuated glass tube, called a **photocell**. The two electrodes are connected to an ammeter and a source of emf, as shown. When the photocell is in the dark, the ammeter reads zero. But when light of sufficiently high frequency illuminates the plate, the ammeter indicates a current flowing in the circuit. We explain completion of the circuit by imagining that electrons, ejected from the plate by the impinging radiation, flow across the tube from the plate to the "collector" C as indicated in Fig. 37–4.

That electrons should be emitted when light shines on a metal is consistent with the electromagnetic (EM) wave theory of light: the electric field of an EM wave could exert a force on electrons in the metal and eject some of them. Einstein pointed out, however, that the wave theory and the photon theory of light give very different predictions on the details of the photoelectric effect. For example, one thing that can be measured with the apparatus of Fig. 37–4 is the maximum kinetic energy (K_{max}) of the emitted electrons. This can be done by using a variable voltage source and reversing the terminals so that electrode C is negative and P is positive. The electrons emitted from P will be repelled by the negative electrode, but if this reverse voltage is small enough, the fastest electrons will still reach C and there will be a current in the circuit. If the reversed voltage is increased, a point is reached where the current reaches zero—no electrons have sufficient kinetic energy to reach C. This is called the *stopping potential*, or *stopping voltage*, V_0, and from its measurement, K_{max} can be determined using conservation of energy (loss of kinetic energy = gain in potential energy):

$$K_{max} = eV_0.$$

Now let us examine the details of the photoelectric effect from the point of view of the wave theory versus Einstein's particle theory.

First the wave theory, assuming monochromatic light. The two important properties of a light wave are its intensity and its frequency (or wavelength). When these two quantities are varied, the wave theory makes the following predictions:

Wave

theory

predictions

1. If the light intensity is increased, the number of electrons ejected and their maximum kinetic energy should be increased because the higher intensity means a greater electric field amplitude, and the greater electric field should eject electrons with higher speed.

2. The frequency of the light should not affect the kinetic energy of the ejected electrons. Only the intensity should affect K_{max}.

The photon theory makes completely different predictions. First we note that in a monochromatic beam, all photons have the same energy ($= hf$). Increasing the intensity of the light beam means increasing the number of photons in the beam, but does not affect the energy of each photon as long as the frequency is not changed. According to Einstein's theory, an electron is ejected from the metal by a collision with a single photon. In the process, all the photon energy is transferred to the electron and the photon ceases to exist. Since electrons are held in the metal by attractive forces, some minimum energy W_0 is required just to get an electron out through the surface. W_0 is called the **work function**, and is a few electron volts ($1\,eV = 1.6 \times 10^{-19}\,J$) for most metals. If the frequency f of the incoming light is so low that hf is less than W_0, then the photons will not have enough energy to eject any electrons at all. If $hf > W_0$, then electrons will be ejected and energy will be conserved in the process. That is, the input energy (of the photon), hf, will equal the outgoing kinetic energy K of the electron plus the energy required to get it out of the metal, W:

$$hf = K + W. \qquad (37\text{–}4a)$$

The least tightly held electrons will be emitted with the most kinetic energy (K_{max}), in which case W in this equation becomes the work function W_0, and K becomes K_{max}:

$$hf = K_{max} + W_0. \qquad \text{[least bound electrons]} \quad \textbf{(37-4b)}$$

Many electrons will require more energy than the bare minimum (W_0) to get out of the metal, and thus the kinetic energy of such electrons will be less than the maximum.

From these considerations, the photon theory makes the following predictions:

1. An increase in intensity of the light beam means more photons are incident, so more electrons will be ejected; but since the energy of each photon is not changed, the maximum kinetic energy of electrons is not changed by an increase in intensity.

2. If the frequency of the light is increased, the maximum kinetic energy of the electrons increases linearly, according to Eq. 37-4b. That is,

$$K_{max} = hf - W_0.$$

This relationship is plotted in Fig. 37-5.

3. If the frequency f is less than the "cutoff" frequency f_0, where $hf_0 = W_0$, no electrons will be ejected, no matter how great the intensity of the light.

These predictions of the photon theory are clearly very different from the predictions of the wave theory. In 1913-1914, careful experiments were carried out by R. A. Millikan. The results were fully in agreement with Einstein's photon theory.

One other aspect of the photoelectric effect also confirmed the photon theory. If extremely low light intensity is used, the wave theory predicts a time delay before electron emission so that an electron can absorb enough energy to exceed the work function. The photon theory predicts no such delay—it only takes one photon (if its frequency is high enough) to eject an electron—and experiments showed no delay. This too confirmed Einstein's photon theory.

Photon

theory

predictions

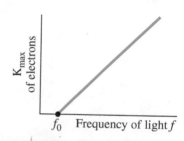

FIGURE 37-5 Photoelectric effect: the maximum kinetic energy of ejected electrons increases linearly with the frequency of incident light. No electrons are emitted if $f < f_0$.

EXAMPLE 37-3 **Photon energy.** Calculate the energy of a photon of blue light, $\lambda = 450\,\text{nm}$ in air (or vacuum).

APPROACH The photon has energy $E = hf$ (Eq. 37-3) where $f = c/\lambda$.

SOLUTION Since $f = c/\lambda$, we have

$$E = hf = \frac{hc}{\lambda} = \frac{(6.63 \times 10^{-34}\,\text{J}\cdot\text{s})(3.0 \times 10^8\,\text{m/s})}{(4.5 \times 10^{-7}\,\text{m})} = 4.4 \times 10^{-19}\,\text{J},$$

or $(4.4 \times 10^{-19}\,\text{J})/(1.60 \times 10^{-19}\,\text{J/eV}) = 2.8\,\text{eV}$. (See definition of eV in Section 23-8, $1\,\text{eV} = 1.60 \times 10^{-19}\,\text{J}$.)

EXAMPLE 37-4 **ESTIMATE** **Photons from a lightbulb.** Estimate how many visible light photons a 100-W lightbulb emits per second. Assume the bulb has a typical efficiency of about 3% (that is, 97% of the energy goes to heat).

APPROACH Let's assume an average wavelength in the middle of the visible spectrum, $\lambda \approx 500\,\text{nm}$. The energy of each photon is $E = hf = hc/\lambda$. Only 3% of the 100-W power is emitted as light, or $3\,\text{W} = 3\,\text{J/s}$. The number of photons emitted per second equals the light output of $3\,\text{J/s}$ divided by the energy of each photon.

SOLUTION The energy emitted in one second $(= 3\,\text{J})$ is $E = Nhf$ where N is the number of photons emitted per second and $f = c/\lambda$. Hence

$$N = \frac{E}{hf} = \frac{E\lambda}{hc} = \frac{(3\,\text{J})(500 \times 10^{-9}\,\text{m})}{(6.63 \times 10^{-34}\,\text{J}\cdot\text{s})(3.0 \times 10^8\,\text{m/s})} \approx 8 \times 10^{18}$$

per second, or almost 10^{19} photons emitted per second, an enormous number.

EXERCISE A Compare a light beam that contains infrared light of a single wavelength, 1000 nm, with a beam of monochromatic UV at 100 nm, both of the same intensity. Are there more 100-nm photons or more 1000-nm photons?

Photoelectron speed and energy. What is the kinetic energy and the speed of an electron ejected from a sodium surface whose work function is $W_0 = 2.28 \, \text{eV}$ when illuminated by light of wavelength (a) 410 nm, (b) 550 nm?

APPROACH We first find the energy of the photons $(E = hf = hc/\lambda)$. If the energy is greater than W_0, then electrons will be ejected with varying amounts of kinetic energy, with a maximum of $K_{max} = hf - W_0$.

SOLUTION (a) For $\lambda = 410 \, \text{nm}$,

$$ hf = \frac{hc}{\lambda} = 4.85 \times 10^{-19} \, \text{J} \quad \text{or} \quad 3.03 \, \text{eV}. $$

The maximum kinetic energy an electron can have is given by Eq. 37–4b, $K_{max} = 3.03 \, \text{eV} - 2.28 \, \text{eV} = 0.75 \, \text{eV}$, or $(0.75 \, \text{eV})(1.60 \times 10^{-19} \, \text{J/eV}) = 1.2 \times 10^{-19} \, \text{J}$. Since $K = \frac{1}{2}mv^2$ where $m = 9.11 \times 10^{-31} \, \text{kg}$,

$$ v_{max} = \sqrt{\frac{2K}{m}} = 5.1 \times 10^5 \, \text{m/s}. $$

Most ejected electrons will have less kinetic energy and less speed than these maximum values.

(b) For $\lambda = 550 \, \text{nm}$, $hf = hc/\lambda = 3.61 \times 10^{-19} \, \text{J} = 2.26 \, \text{eV}$. Since this photon energy is less than the work function, no electrons are ejected.

NOTE In (a) we used the nonrelativistic equation for kinetic energy. If v had turned out to be more than about $0.1c$, our calculation would have been inaccurate by at least a percent or so, and we would probably prefer to redo it using the relativistic form (Eq. 36–10).

EXERCISE B Determine the lowest frequency and the longest wavelength needed to emit electrons from sodium.

It is easy to show that the energy of a photon in electron volts, when given the wavelength λ in nm, is

$$ E \, (\text{eV}) = \frac{1.240 \times 10^3 \, \text{eV} \cdot \text{nm}}{\lambda \, (\text{nm})}. \qquad \text{[photon energy in eV]} $$

Applications of the Photoelectric Effect

The photoelectric effect, besides playing an important historical role in confirming the photon theory of light, also has many practical applications. Burglar alarms and automatic door openers often make use of the photocell circuit of Fig. 37–4. When a person interrupts the beam of light, the sudden drop in current in the circuit activates a switch—often a solenoid—which operates a bell or opens the door. UV or IR light is sometimes used in burglar alarms because of its invisibility. Many smoke detectors use the photoelectric effect to detect tiny amounts of smoke that interrupt the flow of light and so alter the electric current. Photographic light meters use this circuit as well. Photocells are used in many other devices, such as absorption spectrophotometers, to measure light intensity. One type of film sound track is a variably shaded narrow section at the side of the film. Light passing through the film is thus "modulated," and the output electrical signal of the photocell detector follows the frequencies on the sound track. See Fig. 37–6. For many applications today, the vacuum-tube photocell of Fig. 37–4 has been replaced by a semiconductor device known as a **photodiode** (Section 40–9). In these semiconductors, the absorption of a photon liberates a bound electron, which changes the conductivity of the material, so the current through a photodiode is altered.

FIGURE 37–6 Optical sound track on movie film. In the projector, light from a small source (different from that for the picture) passes through the sound track on the moving film. The light and dark areas on the sound track vary the intensity of the transmitted light which reaches the photocell, whose output current is then a replica of the original sound. This output is amplified and sent to the loudspeakers. High-quality projectors can show movies containing several parallel sound tracks to go to different speakers around the theater.

37–3 Energy, Mass, and Momentum of a Photon

We have just seen (Eq. 37–3) that the total energy of a single photon is given by $E = hf$. Because a photon always travels at the speed of light, it is truly a relativistic particle. Thus we must use relativistic formulas for dealing with its energy and momentum. The momentum of any particle of mass m is given by $p = mv/\sqrt{1 - v^2/c^2}$. Since $v = c$ for a photon, the denominator is zero. To avoid having an infinite momentum, we conclude that the photon's mass must be zero: $m = 0$. This makes sense too because a photon can never be at rest (it always moves at the speed of light). A photon's kinetic energy is its total energy:

$$K = E = hf. \qquad \text{[photon]}$$

The momentum of a photon can be obtained from the relativistic formula (Eq. 36–13) $E^2 = p^2c^2 + m^2c^4$ where we set $m = 0$, so $E^2 = p^2c^2$ or

$$p = \frac{E}{c}. \qquad \text{[photon]}$$

⚠ CAUTION

Momentum of photon is not mv

Since $E = hf$ for a photon, its momentum is related to its wavelength by

$$p = \frac{E}{c} = \frac{hf}{c} = \frac{h}{\lambda}. \qquad \textbf{(37–5)}$$

EXAMPLE 37–6 **ESTIMATE** **Photon momentum and force.** Suppose the 10^{19} photons emitted per second from the 100-W lightbulb in Example 37–4 were all focused onto a piece of black paper and absorbed. (a) Calculate the momentum of one photon and (b) estimate the force all these photons could exert on the paper.

APPROACH Each photon's momentum is obtained from Eq. 37–5, $p = h/\lambda$. Next, each absorbed photon's momentum changes from $p = h/\lambda$ to zero. We use Newton's second law, $F = \Delta p/\Delta t$, to get the force. Let $\lambda = 500\,\text{nm}$.

SOLUTION (a) Each photon has a momentum

$$p = \frac{h}{\lambda} = \frac{6.63 \times 10^{-34}\,\text{J}\cdot\text{s}}{500 \times 10^{-9}\,\text{m}} = 1.3 \times 10^{-27}\,\text{kg}\cdot\text{m/s}.$$

(b) Using Newton's second law for $N = 10^{19}$ photons (Example 37–4) whose momentum changes from h/λ to 0, we obtain

$$F = \frac{\Delta p}{\Delta t} = \frac{Nh/\lambda - 0}{1\,\text{s}} = N\frac{h}{\lambda} \approx \left(10^{19}\,\text{s}^{-1}\right)\left(10^{-27}\,\text{kg}\cdot\text{m/s}\right) \approx 10^{-8}\,\text{N}.$$

This is a tiny force, but we can see that a very strong light source could exert a measurable force, and near the Sun or a star the force due to photons in electromagnetic radiation could be considerable. See Section 31–9.

EXAMPLE 37–7 **Photosynthesis.** In *photosynthesis*, pigments such as chlorophyll in plants capture the energy of sunlight to change CO_2 to useful carbohydrate. About nine photons are needed to transform one molecule of CO_2 to carbohydrate and O_2. Assuming light of wavelength $\lambda = 670\,\text{nm}$ (chlorophyll absorbs most strongly in the range 650 nm to 700 nm), how efficient is the photosynthetic process? The reverse chemical reaction releases an energy of 4.9 eV/molecule of CO_2.

APPROACH The efficiency is the minimum energy required (4.9 eV) divided by the actual energy absorbed, nine times the energy (hf) of one photon.

SOLUTION The energy of nine photons, each of energy $hf = hc/\lambda$ is $(9)(6.63 \times 10^{-34}\,\text{J}\cdot\text{s})(3.0 \times 10^8\,\text{m/s})/(6.7 \times 10^{-7}\,\text{m}) = 2.7 \times 10^{-18}\,\text{J}$ or 17 eV. Thus the process is $(4.9\,\text{eV}/17\,\text{eV}) = 29\%$ efficient.

BEFORE COLLISION   AFTER COLLISION

FIGURE 37–7 The Compton effect. A single photon of wavelength λ strikes an electron in some material, knocking it out of its atom. The scattered photon has less energy (some energy is given to the electron) and hence has a longer wavelength λ′.

FIGURE 37–8 Plots of intensity of radiation scattered from a target such as graphite (carbon), for three different angles. The values for λ′ match Eq. 37–6. For (a) $\phi = 0°$, $\lambda' = \lambda_0$. In (b) and (c) a peak is found not only at λ′ due to photons scattered from free electrons (or very nearly free), but also a peak at almost precisely λ_0. The latter is due to scattering from electrons very tightly bound to their atoms so the mass in Eq. 37–6 becomes very large (mass of the atom) and Δλ becomes very small.

37–4 Compton Effect

Besides the photoelectric effect, a number of other experiments were carried out in the early twentieth century which also supported the photon theory. One of these was the **Compton effect** (1923) named after its discoverer, A. H. Compton (1892–1962). Compton scattered short-wavelength light (actually X-rays) from various materials. He found that the scattered light had a slightly longer wavelength than did the incident light, and therefore a slightly lower frequency indicating a loss of energy. He explained this result on the basis of the photon theory as incident photons colliding with electrons of the material, Fig. 37–7. Using Eq. 37–5 for momentum of a photon, Compton applied the laws of conservation of momentum and energy to the collision of Fig. 37–7 and derived the following equation for the wavelength of the scattered photons:

$$\lambda' = \lambda + \frac{h}{m_e c}(1 - \cos\phi), \tag{37-6a}$$

where m_e is the mass of the electron. For $\phi = 0$, the wavelength is unchanged (there is no collision for this case of the photon passing straight through). At any other angle, λ′ is longer than λ. The difference in wavelength,

$$\Delta\lambda = \lambda' - \lambda = \frac{h}{m_e c}(1 - \cos\phi), \tag{37-6b}$$

is called the **Compton shift**. The quantity $h/m_e c$, which has the dimensions of length, is called the **Compton wavelength** λ_C of a free electron,

$$\lambda_C = \frac{h}{m_e c} = 2.43 \times 10^{-3}\,\text{nm} = 2.43\,\text{pm}. \qquad \text{[electron]}$$

Equations 37–6 predict that λ′ depends on the angle ϕ at which the photons are detected. Compton's measurements of 1923 were consistent with this formula, confirming the value of λ_C and the dependence of λ′ on ϕ. See Fig. 37–8. The wave theory of light predicts no wavelength shift: an incoming electromagnetic wave of frequency f should set electrons into oscillation at the same frequency f, and such oscillating electrons should reemit EM waves of this same frequency f (Chapter 31), and would not change with the angle ϕ. Hence the Compton effect adds to the firm experimental foundation for the photon theory of light.

EXERCISE C When a photon scatters off an electron by the Compton effect, which of the following increase: its energy, frequency, or wavelength?

EXAMPLE 37–8 X-ray scattering. X-rays of wavelength 0.140 nm are scattered from a very thin slice of carbon. What will be the wavelengths of X-rays scattered at (a) 0°, (b) 90°, (c) 180°?

APPROACH This is an example of the Compton effect, and we use Eq. 37–6a to find the wavelengths.

SOLUTION (a) For $\phi = 0°$, $\cos\phi = 1$ and $1 - \cos\phi = 0$. Then Eq. 37–6 gives $\lambda' = \lambda = 0.140$ nm. This makes sense since for $\phi = 0°$, there really isn't any collision as the photon goes straight through without interacting.

(b) For $\phi = 90°$, $\cos\phi = 0$, and $1 - \cos\phi = 1$. So

$$\lambda' = \lambda + \frac{h}{m_e c} = 0.140\,\text{nm} + \frac{6.63 \times 10^{-34}\,\text{J}\cdot\text{s}}{(9.11 \times 10^{-31}\,\text{kg})(3.00 \times 10^8\,\text{m/s})}$$

$$= 0.140\,\text{nm} + 2.4 \times 10^{-12}\,\text{m} = 0.142\,\text{nm};$$

that is, the wavelength is longer by one Compton wavelength (= 0.0024 nm for an electron).

(c) For $\phi = 180°$, which means the photon is scattered backward, returning in the direction from which it came (a direct "head-on" collision), $\cos\phi = -1$, and $1 - \cos\phi = 2$. So

$$\lambda' = \lambda + 2\frac{h}{m_e c} = 0.140\,\text{nm} + 2(0.0024\,\text{nm}) = 0.145\,\text{nm}.$$

NOTE The maximum shift in wavelength occurs for backward scattering, and it is twice the Compton wavelength.

The Compton effect has been used to diagnose bone disease such as osteoporosis. Gamma rays, which are photons of even shorter wavelength than X-rays, coming from a radioactive source are scattered off bone material. The total intensity of the scattered radiation is proportional to the density of electrons, which is in turn proportional to the bone density. Changes in the density of bone can indicate the onset of osteoporosis.

*Derivation of Compton Shift

If the incoming photon in Fig. 37–7 has wavelength λ, then its total energy and momentum are

$$E = hf = \frac{hc}{\lambda} \quad \text{and} \quad p = \frac{h}{\lambda}.$$

After the collision of Fig. 37–7, the photon scattered at the angle ϕ has a wavelength which we call λ'. Its energy and momentum are

$$E' = \frac{hc}{\lambda'} \quad \text{and} \quad p' = \frac{h}{\lambda'}.$$

The electron, assumed at rest before the collision but free to move when struck, is scattered at an angle θ as shown in Fig. 37–8. The electron's kinetic energy is (see Eq. 36–10):

$$K_e = \left(\frac{1}{\sqrt{1 - v^2/c^2}} - 1\right)m_e c^2$$

where m_e is the mass of the electron and v is its speed. The electron's momentum is

$$p_e = \frac{1}{\sqrt{1 - v^2/c^2}}m_e v.$$

We apply conservation of energy to the collision (see Fig. 37–7):

$$\text{incoming photon} \longrightarrow \text{scattered photon} + \text{electron}$$

$$\frac{hc}{\lambda} = \frac{hc}{\lambda'} + \left(\frac{1}{\sqrt{1 - v^2/c^2}} - 1\right)m_e c^2.$$

We apply conservation of momentum to the x and y components of momentum:

$$\frac{h}{\lambda} = \frac{h}{\lambda'}\cos\phi + \frac{m_e v \cos\theta}{\sqrt{1 - v^2/c^2}}$$

$$0 = \frac{h}{\lambda'}\sin\phi - \frac{m_e v \sin\theta}{\sqrt{1 - v^2/c^2}}.$$

We can combine these three equations to eliminate v and θ, and we obtain, as Compton did, an equation for the wavelength of the scattered photon in terms of its scattering angle ϕ:

$$\lambda' = \lambda + \frac{h}{m_e c}(1 - \cos\phi),$$

which is Eq. 37–6a.

37–5 Photon Interactions; Pair Production

When a photon passes through matter, it interacts with the atoms and electrons. There are four important types of interactions that a photon can undergo:

1. The *photoelectric effect*: A photon may knock an electron out of an atom and in the process the photon disappears.

2. The photon may knock an atomic electron to a higher energy state in the atom if its energy is not sufficient to knock the electron out altogether. In this process the photon also disappears, and all its energy is given to the atom. Such an atom is then said to be in an *excited state*, and we shall discuss it more later.

3. The photon can be scattered from an electron (or a nucleus) and in the process lose some energy; this is the *Compton effect* (Fig. 37–7). But notice that the photon is not slowed down. It still travels with speed c, but its frequency will be lower because it has lost some energy.

4. *Pair production*: A photon can actually create matter, such as the production of an electron and a positron, Fig. 37–9. (A positron has the same mass as an electron, but the opposite charge, $+e$.)

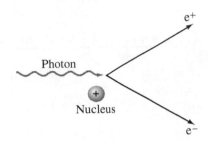

FIGURE 37–9 Pair production: a photon disappears and produces an electron and a positron.

In process 4, **pair production**, the photon disappears in the process of creating the electron–positron pair. This is an example of mass being created from pure energy, and it occurs in accord with Einstein's equation $E = mc^2$. Notice that a photon cannot create an electron alone since electric charge would not then be conserved. The inverse of pair production also occurs: if an electron collides with a positron, the two **annihilate** each other and their energy, including their mass, appears as electromagnetic energy of photons. Because of this process, positrons usually do not last long in nature.

EXAMPLE 37–9 **Pair production.** (a) What is the minimum energy of a photon that can produce an electron–positron pair? (b) What is this photon's wavelength?

APPROACH The minimum photon energy E equals the rest energy (mc^2) of the two particles created, via Einstein's famous equation $E = m_0 c^2$ (Eq. 36–12). There is no energy left over, so the particles produced will have zero kinetic energy. The wavelength is $\lambda = c/f$ where $E = hf$ for the original photon.

SOLUTION (a) Because $E = mc^2$, and the mass created is equal to two electron masses, the photon must have energy

$$E = 2(9.11 \times 10^{-31}\,\text{kg})(3.0 \times 10^8\,\text{m/s})^2 = 1.64 \times 10^{-13}\,\text{J} = 1.02\,\text{MeV}$$

$(1\,\text{MeV} = 10^6\,\text{eV} = 1.60 \times 10^{-13}\,\text{J})$. A photon with less energy cannot undergo pair production.

(b) Since $E = hf = hc/\lambda$, the wavelength of a 1.02-MeV photon is

$$\lambda = \frac{hc}{E} = \frac{(6.63 \times 10^{-34}\,\text{J}\cdot\text{s})(3.0 \times 10^8\,\text{m/s})}{(1.64 \times 10^{-13}\,\text{J})} = 1.2 \times 10^{-12}\,\text{m},$$

which is 0.0012 nm. Such photons are in the gamma-ray (or very short X-ray) region of the electromagnetic spectrum (Fig. 31–12).

NOTE Photons of higher energy (shorter wavelength) can also create an electron–positron pair, with the excess energy becoming kinetic energy of the particles.

Pair production cannot occur in empty space, for momentum could not be conserved. In Example 37–9, for instance, energy is conserved, but only enough energy was provided to create the electron–positron pair at rest, and thus with zero momentum, which could not equal the initial momentum of the photon. Indeed, it can be shown that at any energy, an additional massive object, such as an atomic nucleus, must take part in the interaction to carry off some of the momentum.

37–6 Wave–Particle Duality; the Principle of Complementarity

The photoelectric effect, the Compton effect, and other experiments have placed the particle theory of light on a firm experimental basis. But what about the classic experiments of Young and others (Chapters 34 and 35) on interference and diffraction which showed that the wave theory of light also rests on a firm experimental basis?

We seem to be in a dilemma. Some experiments indicate that light behaves like a wave; others indicate that it behaves like a stream of particles. These two theories seem to be incompatible, but both have been shown to have validity. Physicists finally came to the conclusion that this duality of light must be accepted as a fact of life. It is referred to as the **wave–particle duality**. Apparently, light is a more complex phenomenon than just a simple wave or a simple beam of particles.

To clarify the situation, the great Danish physicist Niels Bohr (1885–1962, Fig. 37–10) proposed his famous **principle of complementarity**. It states that to understand an experiment, sometimes we find an explanation using wave theory and sometimes using particle theory. Yet we must be aware of both the wave and particle aspects of light if we are to have a full understanding of light. Therefore these two aspects of light complement one another.

It is not easy to "visualize" this duality. We cannot readily picture a combination of wave and particle. Instead, we must recognize that the two aspects of light are different "faces" that light shows to experimenters.

Part of the difficulty stems from how we think. Visual pictures (or models) in our minds are based on what we see in the everyday world. We apply the concepts of waves and particles to light because in the macroscopic world we see that energy is transferred from place to place by these two methods. We cannot see directly whether light is a wave or particle, so we do indirect experiments. To explain the experiments, we apply the models of waves or of particles to the nature of light. But these are abstractions of the human mind. When we try to conceive of what light really "is," we insist on a visual picture. Yet there is no reason why light should conform to these models (or visual images) taken from the macroscopic world. The "true" nature of light—if that means anything—is not possible to visualize. The best we can do is recognize that our knowledge is limited to the indirect experiments, and that in terms of everyday language and images, light reveals both wave and particle properties.

It is worth noting that Einstein's equation $E = hf$ itself links the particle and wave properties of a light beam. In this equation, E refers to the energy of a particle; and on the other side of the equation, we have the frequency f of the corresponding wave.

FIGURE 37–10 Niels Bohr (right), walking with Enrico Fermi along the Appian Way outside Rome. This photo shows one important way physics is done.

⚠ **CAUTION**

*Not correct to say light is a wave and/or a particle. Light can **act** like a wave or like a particle.*

37–7 Wave Nature of Matter

In 1923, Louis de Broglie (1892–1987) extended the idea of the wave–particle duality. He appreciated the *symmetry* in nature, and argued that if light sometimes behaves like a wave and sometimes like a particle, then perhaps those things in nature thought to be particles—such as electrons and other material objects—might also have wave properties. De Broglie proposed that the wavelength of a material particle would be related to its momentum in the same way as for a photon, Eq. 37–5, $p = h/\lambda$. That is, for a particle having linear momentum $p = mv$, the wavelength λ is given by

$$\lambda = \frac{h}{p}, \tag{37–7}$$

and is valid classically ($p = mv$ for $v \ll c$) and relativistically ($p = \gamma mv = mv/\sqrt{1 - v^2/c^2}$). This is sometimes called the **de Broglie wavelength** of a particle.

EXAMPLE 37–10 **Wavelength of a ball.** Calculate the de Broglie wavelength of a 0.20-kg ball moving with a speed of 15 m/s.

APPROACH We use Eq. 37–7.

SOLUTION $\lambda = \dfrac{h}{p} = \dfrac{h}{mv} = \dfrac{(6.6 \times 10^{-34}\,\text{J·s})}{(0.20\,\text{kg})(15\,\text{m/s})} = 2.2 \times 10^{-34}\,\text{m}.$

Ordinary size objects, such as the ball of Example 37–10, have unimaginably small wavelengths. Even if the speed is extremely small, say 10^{-4} m/s, the wavelength would be about 10^{-29} m. Indeed, the wavelength of any ordinary object is much too small to be measured and detected. The problem is that the properties of waves, such as interference and diffraction, are significant only when the size of objects or slits is not much larger than the wavelength. And there are no known objects or slits to diffract waves only 10^{-30} m long, so the wave properties of ordinary objects go undetected.

But tiny elementary particles, such as electrons, are another matter. Since the mass m appears in the denominator of Eq. 37–7, a very small mass should have a much larger wavelength.

EXAMPLE 37–11 **Wavelength of an electron.** Determine the wavelength of an electron that has been accelerated through a potential difference of 100 V.

APPROACH If the kinetic energy is much less than the rest energy, we can use the classical formula, $K = \frac{1}{2}mv^2$ (see Section 36–11). For an electron, $mc^2 = 0.511$ MeV. We then apply conservation of energy: the kinetic energy acquired by the electron equals its loss in potential energy. After solving for v, we use Eq. 37–7 to find the de Broglie wavelength.

SOLUTION Gain in kinetic energy equals loss in potential energy: $\Delta U = eV - 0$. Thus $K = eV$, so $K = 100$ eV. The ratio $K/mc^2 = 100\,\text{eV}/(0.511 \times 10^6\,\text{eV}) \approx 10^{-4}$, so relativity is not needed. Thus

$$\frac{1}{2}mv^2 = eV$$

and

$$v = \sqrt{\frac{2eV}{m}} = \sqrt{\frac{(2)(1.6 \times 10^{-19}\,\text{C})(100\,\text{V})}{(9.1 \times 10^{-31}\,\text{kg})}} = 5.9 \times 10^6\,\text{m/s}.$$

Then

$$\lambda = \frac{h}{mv} = \frac{(6.63 \times 10^{-34}\,\text{J·s})}{(9.1 \times 10^{-31}\,\text{kg})(5.9 \times 10^6\,\text{m/s})} = 1.2 \times 10^{-10}\,\text{m},$$

or 0.12 nm.

FIGURE 37–11 Diffraction pattern of electrons scattered from aluminum foil, as recorded on film.

EXERCISE D As a particle travels faster, does its de Broglie wavelength decrease, increase, or remain the same?

From Example 37–11, we see that electrons can have wavelengths on the order of 10^{-10} m, and even smaller. Although small, this wavelength can be detected: the spacing of atoms in a crystal is on the order of 10^{-10} m and the orderly array of atoms in a crystal could be used as a type of diffraction grating, as was done earlier for X-rays (see Section 35–10). C. J. Davisson and L. H. Germer performed the crucial experiment; they scattered electrons from the surface of a metal crystal and, in early 1927, observed that the electrons were scattered into a pattern of regular peaks. When they interpreted these peaks as a diffraction pattern, the wavelength of the diffracted electron wave was found to be just that predicted by de Broglie, Eq. 37–7. In the same year, G. P. Thomson (son of J. J. Thomson) used a different experimental arrangement and also detected diffraction of electrons. (See Fig. 37–11. Compare it to X-ray diffraction, Section 35–10.) Later experiments showed that protons, neutrons, and other particles also have wave properties.

Thus the wave–particle duality applies to material objects as well as to light. The principle of complementarity applies to matter as well. That is, we must be aware of both the particle and wave aspects in order to have an understanding of matter, including electrons. But again we must recognize that a visual picture of a "wave–particle" is not possible.

EXAMPLE 37–12 **Electron diffraction.** The wave nature of electrons is manifested in experiments where an electron beam interacts with the atoms on the surface of a solid. By studying the angular distribution of the diffracted electrons, one can indirectly measure the geometrical arrangement of atoms. Assume that the electrons strike perpendicular to the surface of a solid (see Fig. 37–12), and that their energy is low, $K = 100\,\text{eV}$, so that they interact only with the surface layer of atoms. If the smallest angle at which a diffraction maximum occurs is at 24°, what is the separation d between the atoms on the surface?

SOLUTION Treating the electrons as waves, we need to determine the condition where the difference in path traveled by the wave diffracted from adjacent atoms is an integer multiple of the de Broglie wavelength, so that constructive interference occurs. The path length difference is $d \sin\theta$; so for the smallest value of θ we must have

$$d \sin\theta = \lambda.$$

However, λ is related to the (non-relativistic) kinetic energy K by

$$K = \frac{p^2}{2m_e} = \frac{h^2}{2m_e \lambda^2}.$$

Thus

$$\lambda = \frac{h}{\sqrt{2m_e K}} = \frac{(6.63 \times 10^{-34}\,\text{J·s})}{\sqrt{2(9.11 \times 10^{-31}\,\text{kg})(100\,\text{eV})(1.6 \times 10^{-19}\,\text{J/eV})}} = 0.123\,\text{nm}.$$

The surface inter-atomic spacing is

$$d = \frac{\lambda}{\sin\theta} = \frac{0.123\,\text{nm}}{\sin 24°} = 0.30\,\text{nm}.$$

EXERCISE E Return to the Chapter-Opening Question, page 987, and answer it again now. Try to explain why you may have answered differently the first time.

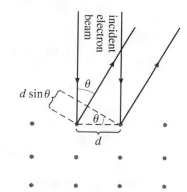

PHYSICS APPLIED
Electron diffraction

FIGURE 37–12 Example 37–12. The red dots represent atoms in an orderly array in a solid.

What Is an Electron?

We might ask ourselves: "What is an electron?" The early experiments of J. J. Thomson (Section 27–7) indicated a glow in a tube, and that glow moved when a magnetic field was applied. The results of these and other experiments were best interpreted as being caused by tiny negatively charged particles which we now call electrons. No one, however, has actually seen an electron directly. The drawings we sometimes make of electrons as tiny spheres with a negative charge on them are merely convenient pictures (now recognized to be inaccurate). Again we must rely on experimental results, some of which are best interpreted using the particle model and others using the wave model. These models are mere pictures that we use to extrapolate from the macroscopic world to the tiny microscopic world of the atom. And there is no reason to expect that these models somehow reflect the reality of an electron. We thus use a wave or a particle model (whichever works best in a situation) so that we can talk about what is happening. But we should not be led to believe that an electron *is* a wave or a particle. Instead we could say that an electron is the set of its properties that we can measure. Bertrand Russell said it well when he wrote that an electron is "a logical construction."

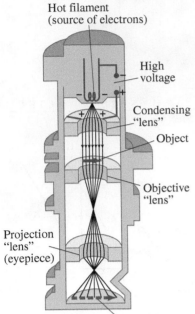

Hot filament
(source of electrons)

High
voltage

Condensing
"lens"

Object

Objective
"lens"

Projection
"lens"
(eyepiece)

Image (on screen, film,
or semiconductor detector)

FIGURE 37–13 Transmission electron microscope. The magnetic field coils are designed to be "magnetic lenses," which bend the electron paths and bring them to a focus, as shown.

FIGURE 37–14 Scanning electron microscope. Scanning coils move an electron beam back and forth across the specimen. Secondary electrons produced when the beam strikes the specimen are collected and modulate the intensity of the beam in the CRT to produce a picture.

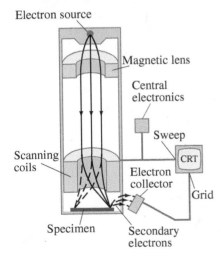

Electron source

Magnetic lens

Central electronics

Sweep

Scanning coils

CRT

Electron collector

Grid

Specimen

Secondary electrons

*37–8 Electron Microscopes

The idea that electrons have wave properties led to the development of the **electron microscope**, which can produce images of much greater magnification than does a light microscope. Figures 37–13 and 37–14 are diagrams of two types, developed around the middle of the twentieth century: the **transmission electron microscope**, which produces a two-dimensional image, and the **scanning electron microscope** (SEM), which produces images with a three-dimensional quality. In both types, the objective and eyepiece lenses are actually magnetic fields that exert forces on the electrons to bring them to a focus. The fields are produced by carefully designed current-carrying coils of wire. Photographs using each type are shown in Fig. 37–15.

As discussed in Section 35–5, the maximum resolution of details on an object is about the size of the wavelength of the radiation used to view it. Electrons accelerated by voltages on the order of 10^5 V have wavelengths of about 0.004 nm. The maximum resolution obtainable would be on this order, but in practice, aberrations in the magnetic lenses limit the resolution in transmission electron microscopes to at best about 0.1 to 0.5 nm. This is still 10^3 times better than that attainable with a visible-light microscope, and corresponds to a useful magnification of about a million. Such magnifications are difficult to attain, and more common magnifications are 10^4 to 10^5. The maximum resolution attainable with a scanning electron microscope is somewhat less, typically 5 to 10 nm although new high-resolution SEMs approach 1 nm.

We discuss other sophisticated electron microscopes in the next Chapter, Section 38–10.

FIGURE 37–15 Electron micrographs (in false color) of viruses attacking a cell of the bacterium *Escherichia coli*: (a) transmission electron micrograph ($\approx 50,000\times$); (b) scanning electron micrograph ($\approx 35,000\times$).

(a)   (b)

37–9 Early Models of the Atom

The idea that matter is made up of atoms was accepted by most scientists by 1900. With the discovery of the electron in the 1890s, scientists began to think of the atom itself as having a structure with electrons as part of that structure. We now introduce our modern approach to the atom and the quantum theory with which it is intertwined.[†]

[†]Some readers may say: "Tell us the facts as we know them today, and don't bother us with the historical background and its outmoded theories." Such an approach would ignore the creative aspect of science and thus give a false impression of how science develops. Moreover, it is not really possible to understand today's view of the atom without insight into the concepts that led to it.

A typical model of the atom in the 1890s visualized the atom as a homogeneous sphere of positive charge inside of which there were tiny negatively charged electrons, a little like plums in a pudding, Fig. 37–16.

Around 1911, Ernest Rutherford (1871–1937) and his colleagues performed experiments whose results contradicted the plum-pudding model of the atom. In these experiments a beam of positively charged alpha (α) particles was directed at a thin sheet of metal foil such as gold, Fig. 37–17a. (These newly discovered α particles were emitted by certain radioactive materials and were soon shown to be doubly ionized helium atoms—that is, having a charge of $+2e$.) It was expected from the plum-pudding model that the alpha particles would not be deflected significantly because electrons are so much lighter than alpha particles, and the alpha particles should not have encountered any massive concentration of positive charge to strongly repel them. The experimental results completely contradicted these predictions. It was found that most of the alpha particles passed through the foil unaffected, as if the foil were mostly empty space. And of those deflected, a few were deflected at very large angles—some even backward, nearly in the direction from which they had come. This could happen, Rutherford reasoned, only if the positively charged alpha particles were being repelled by a massive positive charge concentrated in a very small region of space (see Fig. 37–17b).

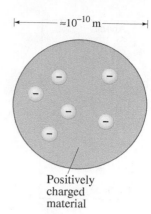

FIGURE 37–16 Plum-pudding model of the atom.

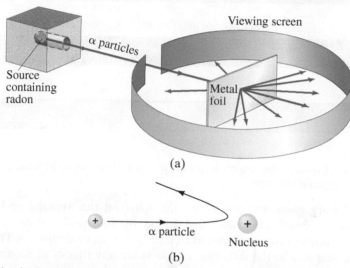

(a)

(b)

FIGURE 37–17 (a) Experimental setup for Rutherford's experiment: α particles emitted by radon are deflected by a thin metallic foil and a few rebound backward; (b) backward rebound of α particles explained as the repulsion from a heavy positively charged nucleus.

He hypothesized that the atom must consist of a tiny but massive positively charged nucleus, containing over 99.9% of the mass of the atom, surrounded by electrons some distance away. The electrons would be moving in orbits about the nucleus—much as the planets move around the Sun—because if they were at rest, they would fall into the nucleus due to electrical attraction, Fig. 37–18. Rutherford's experiments suggested that the nucleus must have a radius of about 10^{-15} to 10^{-14} m. From kinetic theory, and especially Einstein's analysis of Brownian motion (see Section 17–1), the radius of atoms was estimated to be about 10^{-10} m. Thus the electrons would seem to be at a distance from the nucleus of about 10,000 to 100,000 times the radius of the nucleus itself. (If the nucleus were the size of a baseball, the atom would have the diameter of a big city several kilometers across.) So an atom would be mostly empty space.

Rutherford's "planetary" model of the atom (also called the "nuclear model of the atom") was a major step toward how we view the atom today. It was not, however, a complete model and presented some major problems, as we shall see.

FIGURE 37–18 Rutherford's model of the atom, in which electrons orbit a tiny positive nucleus (not to scale). The atom is visualized as mostly empty space.

37–10 Atomic Spectra: Key to the Structure of the Atom

Earlier in this Chapter we saw that heated solids (as well as liquids and dense gases) emit light with a continuous spectrum of wavelengths. This radiation is assumed to be due to oscillations of atoms and molecules, which are largely governed by the interaction of each atom or molecule with its neighbors.

FIGURE 37–19 Gas-discharge tube: (a) diagram; (b) photo of an actual discharge tube for hydrogen.

FIGURE 37–21 Balmer series of lines for hydrogen.

Rarefied gases can also be excited to emit light. This is done by intense heating, or more commonly by applying a high voltage to a "discharge tube" containing the gas at low pressure, Fig. 37–19. The radiation from excited gases had been observed early in the nineteenth century, and it was found that the spectrum was not continuous, but *discrete*. Since excited gases emit light of only certain wavelengths, when this light is analyzed through the slit of a spectroscope or spectrometer, a **line spectrum** is seen rather than a continuous spectrum. The line spectra in the visible region emitted by a number of elements are shown below in Fig. 37–20, and in Chapter 35, Fig. 35–22. The **emission spectrum** is characteristic of the material and can serve as a type of "fingerprint" for identification of the gas.

We also saw (Chapter 35) that if a continuous spectrum passes through a rarefied gas, dark lines are observed in the emerging spectrum, at wavelengths corresponding to lines normally emitted by the gas. This is called an **absorption spectrum** (Fig. 37–20c), and it became clear that gases can absorb light at the same frequencies at which they emit. Using film sensitive to ultraviolet and to infrared light, it was found that gases emit and absorb discrete frequencies in these regions as well as in the visible.

FIGURE 37–20 Emission spectra of the gases (a) atomic hydrogen, (b) helium, and (c) the *solar absorption* spectrum.

In low-density gases, the atoms are far apart on the average and hence the light emitted or absorbed is assumed to be by *individual atoms* rather than through interactions between atoms, as in a solid, liquid, or dense gas. Thus the line spectra serve as a key to the structure of the atom: any theory of atomic structure must be able to explain why atoms emit light only of discrete wavelengths, and it should be able to predict what these wavelengths are.

Hydrogen is the simplest atom—it has only one electron. It also has the simplest spectrum. The spectrum of most atoms shows little apparent regularity. But the spacing between lines in the hydrogen spectrum decreases in a regular way, Fig. 37–21. Indeed, in 1885, J. J. Balmer (1825–1898) showed that the four lines in the visible portion of the hydrogen spectrum (with measured wavelengths 656 nm, 486 nm, 434 nm, and 410 nm) have wavelengths that fit the formula

$$\frac{1}{\lambda} = R\left(\frac{1}{2^2} - \frac{1}{n^2}\right), \qquad n = 3, 4, \cdots. \qquad \textbf{(37–8)}$$

Here n takes on the values 3, 4, 5, 6 for the four visible lines, and R, called the **Rydberg constant**, has the value $R = 1.0974 \times 10^7 \, \text{m}^{-1}$. Later it was found that this **Balmer series** of lines extended into the UV region, ending at $\lambda = 365$ nm, as shown in Fig. 37–21. Balmer's formula, Eq. 37–8, also worked for these lines with higher integer values of n. The lines near 365 nm became too close together to distinguish, but the limit of the series at 365 nm corresponds to $n = \infty$ (so $1/n^2 = 0$ in Eq. 37–8).

Later experiments on hydrogen showed that there were similar series of lines in the UV and IR regions, and each series had a pattern just like the Balmer series, but at different wavelengths, Fig. 37–22. Each of these series was found to fit a formula with the same form as Eq. 37–8 but with the $1/2^2$ replaced by $1/1^2, 1/3^2, 1/4^2$, and so on. For example, the so-called **Lyman series** contains lines with wavelengths from 91 nm to 122 nm (in the UV region) and fits the formula

$$\frac{1}{\lambda} = R\left(\frac{1}{1^2} - \frac{1}{n^2}\right), \qquad n = 2, 3, \cdots.$$

The wavelengths of the **Paschen series** (in the IR region) fit

$$\frac{1}{\lambda} = R\left(\frac{1}{3^2} - \frac{1}{n^2}\right), \qquad n = 4, 5, \cdots.$$

The Rutherford model was unable to explain why atoms emit line spectra. It had other difficulties as well. According to the Rutherford model, electrons orbit the nucleus, and since their paths are curved the electrons are accelerating. Hence they should give off light like any other accelerating electric charge (Chapter 31), with a frequency equal to its orbital frequency. Since light carries off energy and energy is conserved, the electron's own energy must decrease to compensate. Hence electrons would be expected to spiral into the nucleus. As they spiraled inward, their frequency would increase in a short time and so too would the frequency of the light emitted. Thus the two main difficulties with the Rutherford model are these: (1) it predicts that light of a continuous range of frequencies will be emitted, whereas experiment shows line spectra; (2) it predicts that atoms are unstable—electrons would quickly spiral into the nucleus—but we know that atoms in general are stable, because there is stable matter all around us.

Clearly Rutherford's model was not sufficient. Some sort of modification was needed, and Niels Bohr provided it in a model that included the quantum hypothesis. Although the Bohr model has been superceded, it did provide a crucial stepping stone to our present understanding. And some aspects of the Bohr model are still useful today, so we examine it in detail in the next Section.

37–11 The Bohr Model

Bohr had studied in Rutherford's laboratory for several months in 1912 and was convinced that Rutherford's planetary model of the atom had validity. But in order to make it work, he felt that the newly developing quantum theory would somehow have to be incorporated in it. The work of Planck and Einstein had shown that in heated solids, the energy of oscillating electric charges must change discontinuously—from one discrete energy state to another, with the emission of a quantum of light. Perhaps, Bohr argued, the electrons in an atom also cannot lose energy continuously, but must do so in quantum "jumps." In working out his model during the next year, Bohr postulated that electrons move about the nucleus in circular orbits, but that only certain orbits are allowed. He further postulated that an electron in each orbit would have a definite energy and would move in the orbit *without radiating energy* (even though this violated classical ideas since accelerating electric charges are supposed to emit EM waves; see Chapter 31). He thus called the possible orbits **stationary states**. Light is emitted, he hypothesized, only when an electron jumps from a higher (upper) stationary state to another of lower energy, Fig. 37–23. When such a transition occurs, a single photon of light is emitted whose energy, by energy conservation, is given by

$$hf = E_U - E_L, \tag{37–9}$$

where E_U refers to the energy of the upper state and E_L the energy of the lower state.

FIGURE 37–23 An atom emits a photon (energy $= hf$) when its energy changes from E_U to a lower energy E_L.

In 1912–13, Bohr set out to determine what energies these orbits would have in the simplest atom, hydrogen; the spectrum of light emitted could then be predicted from Eq. 37–9. In the Balmer formula he had the key he was looking for. Bohr quickly found that his theory would be in accord with the Balmer formula if he assumed that the electron's angular momentum L is quantized and equal to an integer n times $h/2\pi$. As we saw in Chapter 11 angular momentum is given by $L = I\omega$, where I is the moment of inertia and ω is the angular velocity. For a single particle of mass m moving in a circle of radius r with speed v, $I = mr^2$ and $\omega = v/r$; hence, $L = I\omega = (mr^2)(v/r) = mvr$. Bohr's **quantum condition** is

$$L = mvr_n = n\frac{h}{2\pi}, \qquad n = 1, 2, 3, \cdots, \qquad \textbf{(37–10)}$$

where n is an integer and r_n is the radius of the nth possible orbit. The allowed orbits are numbered $1, 2, 3, \cdots$, according to the value of n, which is called the **principal quantum number** of the orbit.

Equation 37–10 did not have a firm theoretical foundation. Bohr had searched for some "quantum condition," and such tries as $E = hf$ (where E represents the energy of the electron in an orbit) did not give results in accord with experiment. Bohr's reason for using Eq. 37–10 was simply that it worked; and we now look at how. In particular, let us determine what the Bohr theory predicts for the measurable wavelengths of emitted light.

An electron in a circular orbit of radius r_n (Fig. 37–24) would have a centripetal acceleration v^2/r_n produced by the electrical force of attraction between the negative electron and the positive nucleus. This force is given by Coulomb's law,

$$F = \frac{1}{4\pi\epsilon_0}\frac{(Ze)(e)}{r_n^2}.$$

The charge on the nucleus is $+Ze$, where Z is the number of positive charges[†] (i.e., protons). For the hydrogen atom, $Z = +1$.

In Newton's second law, $F = ma$, we substitute Coulomb's law for F, and $a = v^2/r_n$ for a particular allowed orbit of radius r_n, and obtain

$$F = ma$$
$$\frac{1}{4\pi\epsilon_0}\frac{Ze^2}{r_n^2} = \frac{mv^2}{r_n}.$$

We solve this for r_n, and then substitute for v from Eq. 37–10 (which says $v = nh/2\pi mr_n$):

$$r_n = \frac{Ze^2}{4\pi\epsilon_0 mv^2} = \frac{Ze^2 4\pi^2 mr_n^2}{4\pi\epsilon_0 n^2 h^2}.$$

We solve for r_n (it appears on both sides, so we cancel one of them) and find

$$r_n = \frac{n^2 h^2 \epsilon_0}{\pi m Z e^2} = \frac{n^2}{Z} r_1 \qquad \textbf{(37–11)}$$

where

$$r_1 = \frac{h^2 \epsilon_0}{\pi m e^2}.$$

Equation 37–11 gives the radii of all possible orbits. The smallest orbit is for $n = 1$, and for hydrogen $(Z = 1)$ has the value

$$r_1 = \frac{(1)^2 (6.626 \times 10^{-34}\,\text{J}\cdot\text{s})^2 (8.85 \times 10^{-12}\,\text{C}^2/\text{N}\cdot\text{m}^2)}{(3.14)(9.11 \times 10^{-31}\,\text{kg})(1.602 \times 10^{-19}\,\text{C})^2}$$

FIGURE 37–24 Electric force (Coulomb's law) keeps the negative electron in orbit around the positively charged nucleus.

$$F = \frac{1}{4\pi\epsilon_0}\frac{(Ze)(e)}{r^2}$$

[†]We include Z in our derivation so that we can treat other single-electron ("hydrogenlike") atoms such as the ions He^+ $(Z = 2)$ and Li^{2+} $(Z = 3)$. Helium in the neutral state has two electrons: if one electron is missing, the remaining He^+ ion consists of one electron revolving around a nucleus of charge $+2e$. Similarly, doubly ionized lithium, Li^{2+}, also has a single electron, and in this case $Z = 3$.

or
$$r_1 = 0.529 \times 10^{-10}\,\text{m}. \qquad \qquad \textbf{(37–12)}$$

The radius of the smallest orbit in hydrogen, r_1, is sometimes called the **Bohr radius**. From Eq. 37–11, we see that the radii of the larger orbits[†] increase as n^2, so

$$r_2 = 4r_1 = 2.12 \times 10^{-10}\,\text{m},$$
$$r_3 = 9r_1 = 4.76 \times 10^{-10}\,\text{m},$$
$$\vdots$$
$$r_n = n^2 r_1.$$

The first four orbits are shown in Fig. 37–25. Notice that, according to Bohr's model, an electron can exist only in the orbits given by Eq. 37–11. There are no allowable orbits in between.

For an atom with $Z \neq 1$, we can write the orbital radii, r_n, using Eq. 37–11:

$$r_n = \frac{n^2}{Z}(0.529 \times 10^{-10}\,\text{m}), \qquad n = 1, 2, 3, \cdots. \qquad \textbf{(37–13)}$$

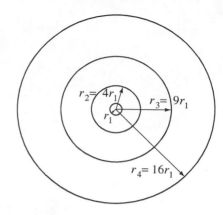

FIGURE 37–25 The four smallest orbits in the Bohr model of hydrogen; $r_1 = 0.529 \times 10^{-10}\,\text{m}$.

In each of its possible orbits, the electron would have a definite energy, as the following calculation shows. The total energy equals the sum of the kinetic and potential energies. The potential energy of the electron is given by $U = qV = -eV$, where V is the potential due to a point charge $+Ze$ as given by Eq. 23–5: $V = (1/4\pi\epsilon_0)(Q/r) = (1/4\pi\epsilon_0)(Ze/r)$. So

$$U = -eV = -\frac{1}{4\pi\epsilon_0}\frac{Ze^2}{r}.$$

The total energy E_n for an electron in the nth orbit of radius r_n is the sum of the kinetic and potential energies:

$$E_n = \tfrac{1}{2}mv^2 - \frac{1}{4\pi\epsilon_0}\frac{Ze^2}{r_n}.$$

When we substitute v from Eq. 37–10 and r_n from Eq. 37–11 into this equation, we obtain

$$E_n = -\left(\frac{Z^2 e^4 m}{8\epsilon_0^2 h^2}\right)\left(\frac{1}{n^2}\right), \qquad n = 1, 2, 3, \cdots. \qquad \textbf{(37–14a)}$$

If we evaluate the constant term in Eq. 37–14a and convert it to electron volts, as is customary in atomic physics, we obtain

$$E_n = -(13.6\,\text{eV})\frac{Z^2}{n^2}, \qquad n = 1, 2, 3, \cdots. \qquad \textbf{(37–14b)}$$

The lowest energy level $(n = 1)$ for hydrogen $(Z = 1)$ is

$$E_1 = -13.6\,\text{eV}.$$

Since n^2 appears in the denominator of Eq. 37–14b, the energies of the larger orbits in hydrogen $(Z = 1)$ are given by

$$E_n = \frac{-13.6\,\text{eV}}{n^2}.$$

For example,

$$E_2 = \frac{-13.6\,\text{eV}}{4} = -3.40\,\text{eV},$$

$$E_3 = \frac{-13.6\,\text{eV}}{9} = -1.51\,\text{eV}.$$

We see that not only are the orbit radii quantized, but from Eqs. 37–14 so is the energy. The quantum number n that labels the orbit radii also labels the energy levels. The lowest **energy level** or **energy state** has energy E_1, and is called the **ground state**. The higher states, E_2, E_3, and so on, are called **excited states**. The fixed energy levels are also called **stationary states**.

[†]Be careful not to believe that these well-defined orbits actually exist. Today electrons are better thought of as forming "clouds," as discussed in Chapter 39.

Notice that although the energy for the larger orbits has a smaller numerical value, all the energies are less than zero. Thus, $-3.4\,\text{eV}$ is a higher energy than $-13.6\,\text{eV}$. Hence the orbit closest to the nucleus (r_1) has the lowest energy. The reason the energies have negative values has to do with the way we defined the zero for potential energy (U). For two point charges, $U = (1/4\pi\epsilon_0)(q_1 q_2/r)$ corresponds to zero potential energy when the two charges are infinitely far apart. Thus, an electron that can just barely be free from the atom by reaching $r = \infty$ (or, at least, far from the nucleus) with zero kinetic energy will have $E = 0$, corresponding to $n = \infty$ in Eqs. 37–14. If an electron is free and has kinetic energy, then $E > 0$. To remove an electron that is part of an atom requires an energy input (otherwise atoms would not be stable). Since $E \geq 0$ for a free electron, then an electron bound to an atom needs to have $E < 0$. That is, energy must be added to bring its energy up, from a negative value, to at least zero in order to free it.

The minimum energy required to remove an electron from an atom initially in the ground state is called the **binding energy** or **ionization energy**. The ionization energy for hydrogen has been measured to be $13.6\,\text{eV}$, and this corresponds precisely to removing an electron from the lowest state, $E_1 = -13.6\,\text{eV}$, up to $E = 0$ where it can be free.

Spectra Lines Explained

It is useful to show the various possible energy values as horizontal lines on an energy-level diagram. This is shown for hydrogen in Fig. 37–26.[†] The electron in a hydrogen atom can be in any one of these levels according to Bohr's theory. But it could never be in between, say at $-9.0\,\text{eV}$. At room temperature, nearly all H atoms will be in the ground state $(n = 1)$. At higher temperatures, or during an electric discharge when there are many collisions between free electrons and atoms, many atoms can be in excited states $(n > 1)$. Once in an excited state, an atom's electron can jump down to a lower state, and give off a photon in the process. This is, according to the Bohr model, the origin of the emission spectra of excited gases.

[†]Note that above $E = 0$, an electron is free and can have any energy (E is not quantized). Thus there is a continuum of energy states above $E = 0$, as indicated in the energy-level diagram of Fig. 37–26.

FIGURE 37–26 Energy-level diagram for the hydrogen atom, showing the transitions for the spectral lines of the Lyman, Balmer, and Paschen series (Fig. 37–22). Each vertical arrow represents an atomic transition that gives rise to the photons of one spectral line (a single wavelength or frequency).

The vertical arrows in Fig. 37–26 represent the transitions or jumps that correspond to the various observed spectral lines. For example, an electron jumping from the level $n = 3$ to $n = 2$ would give rise to the 656-nm line in the Balmer series, and the jump from $n = 4$ to $n = 2$ would give rise to the 486-nm line (see Fig. 37–21). We can predict wavelengths of the spectral lines emitted by combining Eq. 37–9 with Eq. 37–14a. Since $hf = hc/\lambda$, we have from Eq. 37–9

$$\frac{1}{\lambda} = \frac{hf}{hc} = \frac{1}{hc}(E_n - E_{n'}),$$

where n refers to the upper state and n' to the lower state. Then using Eq. 37–14a,

$$\frac{1}{\lambda} = \frac{Z^2 e^4 m}{8\epsilon_0^2 h^3 c}\left(\frac{1}{(n')^2} - \frac{1}{(n)^2}\right). \tag{37–15}$$

This theoretical formula has the same form as the experimental Balmer formula, Eq. 37–8, with $n' = 2$. Thus we see that the Balmer series of lines corresponds to transitions or "jumps" that bring the electron down to the second energy level. Similarly, $n' = 1$ corresponds to the Lyman series and $n' = 3$ to the Paschen series (see Fig. 37–26).

When the constant in Eq. 37–15 is evaluated with $Z = 1$, it is found to have the measured value of the Rydberg constant, $R = 1.0974 \times 10^7 \, \text{m}^{-1}$ in Eq. 37–8, in accord with experiment (see Problem 58).

The great success of Bohr's model is that it gives an explanation for why atoms emit line spectra, and accurately predicts the wavelengths of emitted light for hydrogen. The Bohr model also explains absorption spectra: photons of just the right wavelength can knock an electron from one energy level to a higher one. To conserve energy, only photons that have just the right energy will be absorbed. This explains why a continuous spectrum of light entering a gas will emerge with dark (absorption) lines at frequencies that correspond to emission lines (Fig. 37–20c).

The Bohr theory also ensures the stability of atoms. It establishes stability by decree: the ground state is the lowest state for an electron and there is no lower energy level to which it can go and emit more energy. Finally, as we saw above, the Bohr theory accurately predicts the ionization energy of 13.6 eV for hydrogen. However, the Bohr model was not so successful for other atoms, and has been superseded as we shall discuss in the next Chapter. We discuss the Bohr model because it *was* an important start, and because we still use the concept of stationary states, the ground state, and transitions between states. Also, the terminology used in the Bohr model is still used by chemists and spectroscopists.

EXAMPLE 37–13 **Wavelength of a Lyman line.** Use Fig. 37–26 to determine the wavelength of the first Lyman line, the transition from $n = 2$ to $n = 1$. In what region of the electromagnetic spectrum does this lie?

APPROACH We use Eq. 37–9, $hf = E_U - E_L$, with the energies obtained from Fig. 37–26 to find the energy and the wavelength of the transition. The region of the electromagnetic spectrum is found using the EM spectrum in Fig. 31–12.
SOLUTION In this case, $hf = E_2 - E_1 = \{-3.4\,\text{eV} - (-13.6\,\text{eV})\} = 10.2\,\text{eV}$ $= (10.2\,\text{eV})(1.60 \times 10^{-19}\,\text{J/eV}) = 1.63 \times 10^{-18}\,\text{J}$. Since $\lambda = c/f$, we have

$$\lambda = \frac{c}{f} = \frac{hc}{E_2 - E_1} = \frac{(6.63 \times 10^{-34}\,\text{J·s})(3.00 \times 10^8\,\text{m/s})}{1.63 \times 10^{-18}\,\text{J}} = 1.22 \times 10^{-7}\,\text{m},$$

or 122 nm, which is in the UV region of the EM spectrum, Fig. 31–12. See also Fig. 37–22.

NOTE An alternate approach would be to use Eq. 37–15 to find λ, and it gives the same result.

EXAMPLE 37–14 **Wavelength of a Balmer line.** Determine the wavelength of light emitted when a hydrogen atom makes a transition from the $n = 6$ to the $n = 2$ energy level according to the Bohr model.

APPROACH We can use Eq. 37–15 or its equivalent, Eq. 37–8, with $R = 1.097 \times 10^7 \, \text{m}^{-1}$.

SOLUTION We find

$$\frac{1}{\lambda} = (1.097 \times 10^7 \, \text{m}^{-1})\left(\frac{1}{4} - \frac{1}{36}\right) = 2.44 \times 10^6 \, \text{m}^{-1}.$$

So $\lambda = 1/(2.44 \times 10^6 \, \text{m}^{-1}) = 4.10 \times 10^{-7} \, \text{m}$ or 410 nm. This is the fourth line in the Balmer series, Fig. 37–21, and is violet in color.

EXERCISE F The energy of the photon emitted when a hydrogen atom goes from the $n = 6$ state to the $n = 3$ state is (a) 0.378 eV; (b) 0.503 eV; (c) 1.13 eV; (d) 3.06 eV; (e) 13.6 eV.

EXAMPLE 37–15 **Absorption wavelength.** Use Fig. 37–26 to determine the maximum wavelength that hydrogen in its ground state can absorb. What would be the next smaller wavelength that would work?

APPROACH Maximum wavelength corresponds to minimum energy, and this would be the jump from the ground state up to the first excited state (Fig. 37–26). The next smaller wavelength occurs for the jump from the ground state to the second excited state. In each case, the energy difference can be used to find the wavelength.

SOLUTION The energy needed to jump from the ground state to the first excited state is $13.6 \, \text{eV} - 3.4 \, \text{eV} = 10.2 \, \text{eV}$; the required wavelength, as we saw in Example 37–13, is 122 nm. The energy to jump from the ground state to the second excited state is $13.6 \, \text{eV} - 1.5 \, \text{eV} = 12.1 \, \text{eV}$, which corresponds to a wavelength

$$\lambda = \frac{c}{f} = \frac{hc}{hf} = \frac{hc}{E_3 - E_1}$$

$$= \frac{(6.63 \times 10^{-34} \, \text{J} \cdot \text{s})(3.00 \times 10^8 \, \text{m/s})}{(12.1 \, \text{eV})(1.60 \times 10^{-19} \, \text{J/eV})} = 103 \, \text{nm}.$$

EXAMPLE 37–16 **He⁺ ionization energy.** (a) Use the Bohr model to determine the ionization energy of the He⁺ ion, which has a single electron. (b) Also calculate the maximum wavelength a photon can have to cause ionization.

APPROACH We want to determine the minimum energy required to lift the electron from its ground state and to barely reach the free state at $E = 0$. The ground state energy of He⁺ is given by Eq. 37–14b with $n = 1$ and $Z = 2$.

SOLUTION (a) Since all the symbols in Eq. 37–14b are the same as for the calculation for hydrogen, except that Z is 2 instead of 1, we see that E_1 will be $Z^2 = 2^2 = 4$ times the E_1 for hydrogen:

$$E_1 = 4(-13.6 \, \text{eV}) = -54.4 \, \text{eV}.$$

Thus, to ionize the He⁺ ion should require 54.4 eV, and this value agrees with experiment.

(b) The maximum wavelength photon that can cause ionization will have energy $hf = 54.4 \, \text{eV}$ and wavelength

$$\lambda = \frac{c}{f} = \frac{hc}{hf} = \frac{(6.63 \times 10^{-34} \, \text{J} \cdot \text{s})(3.00 \times 10^8 \, \text{m/s})}{(54.4 \, \text{eV})(1.60 \times 10^{-19} \, \text{J/eV})} = 22.8 \, \text{nm}.$$

NOTE If the atom absorbed a photon of greater energy (wavelength shorter than 22.8 nm), the atom could still be ionized and the freed electron would have kinetic energy of its own. If $\lambda > 22.8$ nm, the photon has too little energy to cause ionization.

In this last Example, we saw that E_1 for the He⁺ ion is four times more negative than that for hydrogen. Indeed, the energy-level diagram for He⁺ looks just like that for hydrogen, Fig. 37–26, except that the numerical values for each energy level are four times larger. Note, however, that we are talking here about the He⁺ *ion*. Normal (neutral) helium has two electrons and its energy level diagram is entirely different.

CONCEPTUAL EXAMPLE 37–17 | **Hydrogen at 20°C.** Estimate the average kinetic energy of whole hydrogen atoms (not just the electrons) at room temperature, and use the result to explain why nearly all H atoms are in the ground state at room temperature, and hence emit no light.

RESPONSE According to kinetic theory (Chapter 18), the average kinetic energy of atoms or molecules in a gas is given by Eq. 18–4:

$$\bar{K} = \tfrac{3}{2}kT,$$

where $k = 1.38 \times 10^{-23}$ J/K is Boltzmann's constant, and T is the kelvin (absolute) temperature. Room temperature is about $T = 300$ K, so

$$\bar{K} = \tfrac{3}{2}(1.38 \times 10^{-23}\,\text{J/K})(300\,\text{K}) = 6.2 \times 10^{-21}\,\text{J},$$

or, in electron volts:

$$\bar{K} = \frac{6.2 \times 10^{-21}\,\text{J}}{1.6 \times 10^{-19}\,\text{J/cV}} = 0.04\,\text{eV}.$$

The average kinetic energy of an atom as a whole is thus very small compared to the energy between the ground state and the next higher energy state (13.6 eV − 3.4 eV = 10.2 eV). Any atoms in excited states quickly fall to the ground state and emit light. Once in the ground state, collisions with other atoms can transfer energy of only 0.04 eV on the average. A small fraction of atoms can have much more energy (see Section 18–2 on the distribution of molecular speeds), but even a kinetic energy that is 10 times the average is not nearly enough to excite atoms into states above the ground state. Thus, at room temperature, nearly all atoms are in the ground state. Atoms can be excited to upper states by very high temperatures, or by passing a current of high energy electrons through the gas, as in a discharge tube (Fig. 37–19).

Correspondence Principle

We should note that Bohr made some radical assumptions that were at variance with classical ideas. He assumed that electrons in fixed orbits do not radiate light even though they are accelerating (moving in a circle), and he assumed that angular momentum is quantized. Furthermore, he was not able to say how an electron moved when it made a transition from one energy level to another. On the other hand, there is no real reason to expect that in the tiny world of the atom electrons would behave as ordinary-sized objects do. Nonetheless, he felt that where quantum theory overlaps with the macroscopic world, it should predict classical results. This is the **correspondence principle**, already mentioned in regard to relativity (Section 36–13). This principle does work for Bohr's theory of the hydrogen atom. The orbit sizes and energies are quite different for $n = 1$ and $n = 2$, say. But orbits with $n = 100,000,000$ and $100,000,001$ would be very close in radius and energy (see Fig. 37–26). Indeed, jumps between such large orbits (which would approach macroscopic sizes), would be imperceptible. Such orbits would thus appear to be continuously spaced, which is what we expect in the everyday world.

Finally, it must be emphasized that the well-defined orbits of the Bohr model do not actually exist. The Bohr model is only a model, not reality. The idea of electron orbits was rejected a few years later, and today electrons are thought of (Chapter 39) as forming "probability clouds."

37–12 de Broglie's Hypothesis Applied to Atoms

Bohr's theory was largely of an *ad hoc* nature. Assumptions were made so that theory would agree with experiment. But Bohr could give no reason why the orbits were quantized, nor why there should be a stable ground state. Finally, ten years later, a reason was proposed by Louis de Broglie. We saw in Section 37–7 that in 1923, de Broglie proposed that material particles, such as electrons, have a wave nature; and that this hypothesis was confirmed by experiment several years later.

FIGURE 37–27 An ordinary standing wave compared to a circular standing wave.

FIGURE 37–28 When a wave does not close (and hence interferes destructively with itself), it rapidly dies out.

FIGURE 37–29 Standing circular waves for two, three, and five wavelengths on the circumference; n, the number of wavelengths, is also the quantum number.

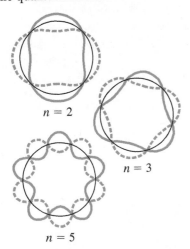

$n = 2$

$n = 3$

$n = 5$

One of de Broglie's original arguments in favor of the wave nature of electrons was that it provided an explanation for Bohr's theory of the hydrogen atom. According to de Broglie, a particle of mass m moving with a nonrelativistic speed v would have a wavelength (Eq. 37–7) of

$$\lambda = \frac{h}{mv}.$$

Each electron orbit in an atom, he proposed, is actually a standing wave. As we saw in Chapter 15, when a violin or guitar string is plucked, a vast number of wavelengths are excited. But only certain ones—those that have nodes at the ends—are sustained. These are the *resonant* modes of the string. Waves with other wavelengths interfere with themselves upon reflection and their amplitudes quickly drop to zero. With electrons moving in circles, according to Bohr's theory, de Broglie argued that the electron wave was a *circular* standing wave that closes on itself, Fig. 37–27. If the wavelength of a wave does not close on itself, as in Fig. 37–28, destructive interference takes place as the wave travels around the loop, and the wave quickly dies out. Thus, the only waves that persist are those for which the circumference of the circular orbit contains a whole number of wavelengths, Fig. 37–29. The circumference of a Bohr orbit of radius r_n is $2\pi r_n$, so to have constructive interference, we need

$$2\pi r_n = n\lambda, \qquad n = 1, 2, 3, \cdots.$$

When we substitute $\lambda = h/mv$, we get $2\pi r_n = nh/mv$, or

$$mvr_n = \frac{nh}{2\pi}.$$

This is just the *quantum condition* proposed by Bohr on an *ad hoc* basis, Eq. 37–10. It is from this equation that the discrete orbits and energy levels were derived. Thus we have a first explanation for the quantized orbits and energy states in the Bohr model: they are due to the wave nature of the electron, and only resonant "standing" waves can persist.[†] This implies that the *wave–particle duality* is at the root of atomic structure.

In viewing the circular electron waves of Fig. 37–29, the electron is not to be thought of as following the oscillating wave pattern. In the Bohr model of hydrogen, the electron moves in a circle. The circular wave, on the other hand, represents the *amplitude* of the electron "matter wave," and in Fig. 37–29 the wave amplitude is shown superimposed on the circular path of the particle orbit for convenience.

Bohr's theory worked well for hydrogen and for one-electron ions. But it did not prove successful for multi-electron atoms. Bohr's theory could not predict line spectra even for the next simplest atom, helium. It could not explain why some emission lines are brighter than others, nor why some lines are split into two or more closely spaced lines ("fine structure"). A new theory was needed and was indeed developed in the 1920s. This new and radical theory is called *quantum mechanics*. It finally solved the problem of atomic structure, but it gives us a very different view of the atom: the idea of electrons in well-defined orbits was replaced with the idea of electron "clouds." This new theory of quantum mechanics has given us a wholly different view of the basic mechanisms underlying physical processes.

[†]We note, however, that Eq. 37–10 is no longer considered valid, as discussed in Chapter 39.

Summary

Quantum theory has its origins in **Planck's quantum hypothesis** that molecular oscillations are **quantized**: their energy E can only be integer (n) multiples of hf, where h is Planck's constant and f is the natural frequency of oscillation:

$$E = nhf. \qquad (37\text{–}2)$$

This hypothesis explained the spectrum of radiation emitted by a **blackbody** at high temperature.

Einstein proposed that for some experiments, light could be pictured as being emitted and absorbed as **quanta** (particles), which we now call **photons**, each with energy

$$E = hf \qquad (37\text{–}3)$$

and momentum

$$p = \frac{E}{c} = \frac{hf}{c} = \frac{h}{\lambda}. \qquad (37\text{–}5)$$

He proposed the photoelectric effect as a test for the photon theory of light. In the **photoelectric effect**, the photon theory says that each incident photon can strike an electron in a material and eject it if the photon has sufficient energy. The maximum energy of ejected electrons is then linearly related to the frequency of the incident light.

The photon theory is also supported by the **Compton effect** and the observation of electron–positron **pair production**.

The **wave–particle duality** refers to the idea that light and matter (such as electrons) have both wave and particle properties. The wavelength of an object is given by

$$\lambda = \frac{h}{p}, \tag{37–7}$$

where p is the momentum of the object ($p = mv$ for a particle of mass m and speed v).

The **principle of complementarity** states that we must be aware of both the particle and wave properties of light and of matter for a complete understanding of them.

Early models of the atom include the plum-pudding model, and Rutherford's planetary (or nuclear) model of an atom which consists of a tiny but massive positively charged nucleus surrounded (at a relatively great distance) by electrons.

To explain the **line spectra** emitted by atoms, as well as the stability of atoms, **Bohr's theory** postulated that: (1) electrons bound in an atom can only occupy orbits for which the angular momentum is quantized, which results in discrete values for the radius and energy; (2) an electron in such a **stationary state** emits no radiation; (3) if an electron jumps to a lower state, it emits a photon whose energy equals the difference in energy between the two states; (4) the angular momentum L of atomic electrons is quantized by the rule

$$L = \frac{nh}{2\pi}, \tag{37–10}$$

where n is an integer called the **quantum number**. The $n = 1$ state is the **ground state**, which in hydrogen has an energy $E_1 = -13.6 \, \text{eV}$. Higher values of n correspond to **excited states**, and their energies are

$$E_n = -(13.6 \, \text{eV}) \frac{Z^2}{n^2}. \tag{37–14b}$$

Atoms are excited to these higher states by collisions with other atoms or electrons, or by absorption of a photon of just the right frequency.

De Broglie's hypothesis that electrons (and other matter) have a wavelength $\lambda = h/mv$ gave an explanation for Bohr's quantized orbits by bringing in the wave–particle duality: the orbits correspond to circular standing waves in which the circumference of the orbit equals a whole number of wavelengths.

Questions

1. What can be said about the relative temperatures of whitish-yellow, reddish, and bluish stars? Explain.

2. If energy is radiated by all objects, why can we not see most of them in the dark?

3. Does a lightbulb at a temperature of 2500 K produce as white a light as the Sun at 6000 K? Explain.

4. Darkrooms for developing black-and-white film were sometimes lit by a red bulb. Why red? Would such a bulb work in a darkroom for developing color photographs?

5. If the threshold wavelength in the photoelectric effect increases when the emitting metal is changed to a different metal, what can you say about the work functions of the two metals?

6. Explain why the existence of a cutoff frequency in the photoelectric effect more strongly favors a particle theory rather than a wave theory of light.

7. UV light causes sunburn, whereas visible light does not. Suggest a reason.

8. The work functions for sodium and cesium are 2.28 eV and 2.14 eV, respectively. For incident photons of a given frequency, which metal will give a higher maximum kinetic energy for the electrons?

9. (a) Does a beam of infrared photons always have less energy than a beam of ultraviolet photons? Explain. (b) Does a single photon of infrared light always have less energy than a single photon of ultraviolet light?

10. Light of 450-nm wavelength strikes a metal surface, and a stream of electrons emerges from the metal. If light of the same intensity but of wavelength 400 nm strikes the surface, are more electrons emitted? Does the energy of the emitted electrons change? Explain.

11. Explain how the photoelectric circuit of Fig. 37–4 could be used in (a) a burglar alarm, (b) a smoke detector, (c) a photographic light meter.

12. If an X-ray photon is scattered by an electron, does the photon's wavelength change? If so, does it increase or decrease?

13. In both the photoelectric effect and in the Compton effect, a photon collides with an electron causing the electron to fly off. What then, is the difference between the two processes?

14. Consider a point source of light. How would the intensity of light vary with distance from the source according to (a) wave theory, (b) particle (photon) theory? Would this help to distinguish the two theories?

15. If an electron and a proton travel at the same speed, which has the shorter de Broglie wavelength? Explain.

16. Why do we say that light has wave properties? Why do we say that light has particle properties?

17. Why do we say that electrons have wave properties? Why do we say that electrons have particle properties?

18. What are the differences between a photon and an electron? Be specific: make a list.

19. In Rutherford's planetary model of the atom, what keeps the electrons from flying off into space?

20. How can you tell if there is oxygen near the surface of the Sun?

21. When a wide spectrum of light passes through hydrogen gas at room temperature, absorption lines are observed that correspond only to the Lyman series. Why don't we observe the other series?

22. Explain how the closely spaced energy levels for hydrogen near the top of Fig. 37–26 correspond to the closely spaced spectral lines at the top of Fig. 37–21.

23. Is it possible for the de Broglie wavelength of a "particle" to be greater than the dimensions of the particle? To be smaller? Is there any direct connection?

24. In a helium atom, which contains two electrons, do you think that on average the electrons are closer to the nucleus or farther away than in a hydrogen atom? Why?

25. How can the spectrum of hydrogen contain so many lines when hydrogen contains only one electron?

26. The Lyman series is brighter than the Balmer series because this series of transitions ends up in the most common state for hydrogen, the ground state. Why then was the Balmer series discovered first?

27. Use conservation of momentum to explain why photons emitted by hydrogen atoms have slightly less energy than that predicted by Eq. 37–9.

28. Suppose we obtain an emission spectrum for hydrogen at very high temperature (when some of the atoms are in excited states), and an absorption spectrum at room temperature, when all atoms are in the ground state. Will the two spectra contain identical lines?

Problems

37–1 Planck's Quantum Hypothesis

1. (I) Estimate the peak wavelength for radiation from (a) ice at 273 K, (b) a floodlamp at 3500 K, (c) helium at 4.2 K, (d) for the universe at $T = 2.725$ K, assuming blackbody emission. In what region of the EM spectrum is each?

2. (I) How hot is metal being welded if it radiates most strongly at 460 nm?

3. (I) An HCl molecule vibrates with a natural frequency of 8.1×10^{13} Hz. What is the difference in energy (in joules and electron volts) between successive values of the oscillation energy?

4. (II) Estimate the peak wavelength of light issuing from the pupil of the human eye (which approximates a blackbody) assuming normal body temperature.

5. (III) Planck's radiation law is given by:

$$I(\lambda, T) = \frac{2\pi hc^2\lambda^{-5}}{e^{hc/\lambda kT} - 1}$$

where $I(\lambda, T)$ is the rate energy is radiated per unit surface area per unit wavelength interval at wavelength λ and Kelvin temperature T. (a) Show that Wien's displacement law follows from this relationship. (b) Determine the value of h from the experimental value of $\lambda_\mathrm{P} T$ given in the text. [You may want to use graphing techniques.] (c) Derive the T^4 dependence of the rate at which energy is radiated (as in the Stefan-Boltzmann law, Eq. 19–17), by integrating Planck's formula over all wavelengths; that is, show that

$$\int I(\lambda, T) \, d\lambda \propto T^4.$$

37–2 and 37–3 Photons and the Photoelectric Effect

6. (I) What is the energy of photons (in joules) emitted by a 104.1-MHz FM radio station?

7. (I) What is the energy range (in joules and eV) of photons in the visible spectrum, of wavelength 410 nm to 750 nm?

8. (I) A typical gamma ray emitted from a nucleus during radioactive decay may have an energy of 380 keV. What is its wavelength? Would we expect significant diffraction of this type of light when it passes through an everyday opening, such as a door?

9. (I) About 0.1 eV is required to break a "hydrogen bond" in a protein molecule. Calculate the minimum frequency and maximum wavelength of a photon that can accomplish this.

10. (I) Calculate the momentum of a photon of yellow light of wavelength 6.20×10^{-7} m.

11. (I) What minimum frequency of light is needed to eject electrons from a metal whose work function is 4.8×10^{-19} J?

12. (I) What is the longest wavelength of light that will emit electrons from a metal whose work function is 3.70 eV?

13. (II) What wavelength photon would have the same energy as a 145-gram baseball moving 30.0 m/s?

14. (II) The human eye can respond to as little as 10^{-18} J of light energy. For a wavelength at the peak of visual sensitivity, 550 nm, how many photons lead to an observable flash?

15. (II) The work functions for sodium, cesium, copper, and iron are 2.3, 2.1, 4.7, and 4.5 eV, respectively. Which of these metals will not emit electrons when visible light shines on it?

16. (II) In a photoelectric-effect experiment it is observed that no current flows unless the wavelength is less than 520 nm. (a) What is the work function of this material? (b) What is the stopping voltage required if light of wavelength 470 nm is used?

17. (II) What is the maximum kinetic energy of electrons ejected from barium $(W_0 = 2.48 \text{ eV})$ when illuminated by white light, $\lambda = 410$ to 750 nm?

18. (II) Barium has a work function of 2.48 eV. What is the maximum kinetic energy of electrons if the metal is illuminated by UV light of wavelength 365 nm? What is their speed?

19. (II) When UV light of wavelength 285 nm falls on a metal surface, the maximum kinetic energy of emitted electrons is 1.70 eV. What is the work function of the metal?

20. (II) The threshold wavelength for emission of electrons from a given surface is 320 nm. What will be the maximum kinetic energy of ejected electrons when the wavelength is changed to (a) 280 nm, (b) 360 nm?

21. (II) When 230-nm light falls on a metal, the current through a photoelectric circuit (Fig. 37–4) is brought to zero at a stopping voltage of 1.84 V. What is the work function of the metal?

22. (II) A certain type of film is sensitive only to light whose wavelength is less than 630 nm. What is the energy (eV and kcal/mol) needed for the chemical reaction to occur which causes the film to change?

23. (II) The range of visible light wavelengths extends from about 410 nm to 750 nm. (a) Estimate the minimum energy (eV) necessary to initiate the chemical process on the retina that is responsible for vision. (b) Speculate as to why, at the other end of the visible range, there is a threshold photon energy beyond which the eye registers no sensation of sight. Determine this threshold photon energy (eV).

24. (II) In a photoelectric experiment using a clean sodium surface, the maximum energy of the emitted electrons was measured for a number of different incident frequencies, with the following results.

Frequency $(\times 10^{14}$ Hz)	Energy (eV)
11.8	2.60
10.6	2.11
9.9	1.81
9.1	1.47
8.2	1.10
6.9	0.57

Plot the graph of these results and find: (a) Planck's constant; (b) the cutoff frequency of sodium; (c) the work function.

25. (II) A **photomultiplier tube** (a very sensitive light sensor), is based on the photoelectric effect: incident photons strike a metal surface and the resulting ejected electrons are collected. By counting the number of collected electrons, the number of incident photons (i.e., the incident light intensity) can be determined. (a) If a photomultiplier tube is to respond properly for incident wavelengths throughout the visible range (410 nm to 750 nm), what is the maximum value for the work function W_0 (eV) of its metal surface? (b) If W_0 for its metal surface is above a certain threshold value, the photomultiplier will only function for incident ultraviolet wavelengths and be unresponsive to visible light. Determine this threshold value (eV).

26. (III) A group of atoms is confined to a very small (point-like) volume in a laser-based **atom trap**. The incident laser light causes each atom to emit 1.0×10^6 photons of wavelength 780 nm every second. A sensor of area 1.0 cm^2 measures the light intensity emanating from the trap to be 1.6 nW when placed 25 cm away from the trapped atoms. Assuming each atom emits photons with equal probability in all directions, determine the number of trapped atoms.

27. (III) Assume light of wavelength λ is incident on a metal surface, whose work function is known precisely (i.e., its uncertainty is better than 0.1% and can be ignored). Show that if the stopping voltage can be determined to an accuracy of ΔV_0, the fractional uncertainty (magnitude) in wavelength is

$$\frac{\Delta \lambda}{\lambda} = \frac{\lambda e}{hc} \Delta V_0 .$$

Determine this fractional uncertainty if $\Delta V_0 = 0.01$ V and $\lambda = 550$ nm.

37–4 Compton Effect

28. (I) A high-frequency photon is scattered off of an electron and experiences a change of wavelength of 1.5×10^{-4} nm. At what angle must a detector be placed to detect the scattered photon (relative to the direction of the incoming photon)?

29. (II) Determine the Compton wavelength for (a) an electron, (b) a proton. (c) Show that if a photon has wavelength equal to the Compton wavelength of a particle, the photon's energy is equal to the rest energy of the particle.

30. (II) X-rays of wavelength $\lambda = 0.120$ nm are scattered from carbon. What is the expected Compton wavelength shift for photons detected at angles (relative to the incident beam) of exactly (a) 60°, (b) 90°, (c) 180°?

31. (II) In the Compton effect, determine the ratio $(\Delta\lambda/\lambda)$ of the maximum change $\Delta\lambda$ in a photon's wavelength to the photon's initial wavelength λ, if the photon is (a) a visible-light photon with $\lambda = 550$ nm, (b) an X-ray photon with $\lambda = 0.10$ nm.

32. (II) A 1.0-MeV gamma-ray photon undergoes a sequence of Compton-scattering events. If the photon is scattered at an angle of 0.50° in each event, estimate the number of events required to convert the photon into a visible-light photon with wavelength 555 nm. You can use an expansion for small θ; see Appendix A. [Gamma rays created near the center of the Sun are transformed to visible wavelengths as they travel to the Sun's surface through a sequence of small-angle Compton scattering events.]

33. (III) In the Compton effect, a 0.160-nm photon strikes a free electron in a head-on collision and knocks it into the forward direction. The rebounding photon recoils directly backward. Use conservation of (relativistic) energy and momentum to determine (a) the kinetic energy of the electron, and (b) the wavelength of the recoiling photon. Use Eq. 37–5, but not Eq. 37–6.

34. (III) In the Compton effect (see Fig. 37–7), use the relativistic equations for conservation of energy and of linear momentum to show that the Compton shift in wavelength is given by Eq. 37–6.

37–5 Pair Production

35. (I) How much total kinetic energy will an electron–positron pair have if produced by a 2.67-MeV photon?

36. (II) What is the longest wavelength photon that could produce a proton–antiproton pair? (Each has a mass of 1.67×10^{-27} kg.)

37. (II) What is the minimum photon energy needed to produce a $\mu^+ - \mu^-$ pair? The mass of each μ (muon) is 207 times the mass of an electron. What is the wavelength of such a photon?

38. (II) An electron and a positron, each moving at 2.0×10^5 m/s, collide head on, disappear, and produce two photons moving in opposite directions, each with the same energy and momentum. Determine the energy and momentum of each photon.

39. (II) A gamma-ray photon produces an electron and a positron, each with a kinetic energy of 375 keV. Determine the energy and wavelength of the photon.

37–7 Wave Nature of Matter

40. (I) Calculate the wavelength of a 0.23-kg ball traveling at 0.10 m/s.

41. (I) What is the wavelength of a neutron $(m = 1.67 \times 10^{-27}$ kg) traveling at 8.5×10^4 m/s?

42. (I) Through how many volts of potential difference must an electron be accelerated to achieve a wavelength of 0.21 nm?

43. (II) What is the theoretical limit of resolution for an electron microscope whose electrons are accelerated through 85 kV? (Relativistic formulas should be used.)

44. (II) The speed of an electron in a particle accelerator is $0.98c$. Find its de Broglie wavelength. (Use relativistic momentum.)

45. (II) Calculate the ratio of the kinetic energy of an electron to that of a proton if their wavelengths are equal. Assume that the speeds are nonrelativistic.

46. (II) Neutrons can be used in diffraction experiments to probe the lattice structure of crystalline solids. Since the neutron's wavelength needs to be on the order of the spacing between atoms in the lattice, about 0.3 nm, what should the speed of the neutrons be?

47. (II) An electron has a de Broglie wavelength $\lambda = 6.0 \times 10^{-10}$ m. (a) What is its momentum? (b) What is its speed? (c) What voltage was needed to accelerate it to this speed?

48. (II) What is the wavelength of an electron of energy (a) 20 eV, (b) 200 eV, (c) 2.0 keV?

49. (II) Show that if an electron and a proton have the same nonrelativistic kinetic energy, the proton has the shorter wavelength.

50. (II) Calculate the de Broglie wavelength of an electron in a TV picture tube if it is accelerated by 33,000 V. Is it relativistic? How does its wavelength compare to the size of the "neck" of the tube, typically 5 cm? Do we have to worry about diffraction problems blurring our picture on the screen?

51. (II) After passing through two slits separated by a distance of $3.0\,\mu m$, a beam of electrons creates an interference pattern with its second-order maximum at an angle of 55°. Find the speed of the electrons in this beam.

*37–8 Electron Microscope

*52. (II) What voltage is needed to produce electron wavelengths of 0.28 nm? (Assume that the electrons are nonrelativistic.)

*53. (II) Electrons are accelerated by 3450 V in an electron microscope. Estimate the maximum possible resolution of the microscope.

37–10 and 37–11 Bohr Model

54. (I) For the three hydrogen transitions indicated below, with n being the initial state and n' being the final state, is the transition an absorption or an emission? Which is higher, the initial state energy or the final state energy of the atom? Finally, which of these transitions involves the largest energy photon? (a) $n = 1$, $n' = 3$; (b) $n = 6$, $n' = 2$; (c) $n = 4$, $n' = 5$.

55. (I) How much energy is needed to ionize a hydrogen atom in the $n = 3$ state?

56. (I) (a) Determine the wavelength of the second Balmer line ($n = 4$ to $n = 2$ transition) using Fig. 37–26. Determine likewise (b) the wavelength of the third Lyman line and (c) the wavelength of the first Balmer line.

57. (I) Calculate the ionization energy of doubly ionized lithium, Li^{2+}, which has $Z = 3$.

58. (I) Evaluate the Rydberg constant R using the Bohr model (compare Eqs. 37–8 and 37–15) and show that its value is $R = 1.0974 \times 10^7\,m^{-1}$.

59. (II) What is the longest wavelength light capable of ionizing a hydrogen atom in the ground state?

60. (II) In the Sun, an ionized helium (He^+) atom makes a transition from the $n = 5$ state to the $n = 2$ state, emitting a photon. Can that photon be absorbed by hydrogen atoms present in the Sun? If so, between what energy states will the hydrogen atom transition occur?

61. (II) What wavelength photon would be required to ionize a hydrogen atom in the ground state and give the ejected electron a kinetic energy of 20.0 eV?

62. (II) For what maximum kinetic energy is a collision between an electron and a hydrogen atom in its ground state definitely elastic?

63. (II) Construct the energy-level diagram for the He^+ ion (like Fig. 37–26).

64. (II) Construct the energy-level diagram (like Fig. 37–26) for doubly ionized lithium, Li^{2+}.

65. (II) Determine the electrostatic potential energy and the kinetic energy of an electron in the ground state of the hydrogen atom.

66. (II) An excited hydrogen atom could, in principle, have a diameter of 0.10 mm. What would be the value of n for a Bohr orbit of this size? What would its energy be?

67. (II) Is the use of nonrelativistic formulas justified in the Bohr atom? To check, calculate the electron's velocity, v, in terms of c, for the ground state of hydrogen, and then calculate $\sqrt{1 - v^2/c^2}$.

68. (II) A hydrogen atom has an angular momentum of $5.273 \times 10^{-34}\,kg\cdot m^2/s$. According to the Bohr model, what is the energy (eV) associated with this state?

69. (II) Assume hydrogen atoms in a gas are initially in their ground state. If free electrons with kinetic energy 12.75 eV collide with these atoms, what photon wavelengths will be emitted by the gas?

70. (II) Suppose an electron was bound to a proton, as in the hydrogen atom, but by the gravitational force rather than by the electric force. What would be the radius, and energy, of the first Bohr orbit?

71. (II) *Correspondence principle*: Show that for large values of n, the difference in radius Δr between two adjacent orbits (with quantum numbers n and $n - 1$) is given by

$$\Delta r = r_n - r_{n-1} \approx \frac{2r_n}{n},$$

so $\Delta r/r_n \to 0$ as $n \to \infty$ in accordance with the correspondence principle. [Note that we can check the correspondence principle by either considering large values of n $(n \to \infty)$ or by letting $h \to 0$. Are these equivalent?]

General Problems

72. If a 75-W lightbulb emits 3.0% of the input energy as visible light (average wavelength 550 nm) uniformly in all directions, estimate how many photons per second of visible light will strike the pupil (4.0 mm diameter) of the eye of an observer 250 m away.

73. At low temperatures, nearly all the atoms in hydrogen gas will be in the ground state. What minimum frequency photon is needed if the photoelectric effect is to be observed?

74. A beam of 125-eV electrons is scattered from a crystal, as in X-ray diffraction, and a first-order peak is observed at $\theta = 38°$. What is the spacing between planes in the diffracting crystal? (See Section 35–10.)

75. A microwave oven produces electromagnetic radiation at $\lambda = 12.2$ cm and produces a power of 860 W. Calculate the number of microwave photons produced by the microwave oven each second.

76. Sunlight reaching the Earth has an intensity of about 1350 W/m^2. Estimate how many photons per square meter per second this represents. Take the average wavelength to be 550 nm.

77. A beam of red laser light $(\lambda = 633 \text{ nm})$ hits a black wall and is fully absorbed. If this light exerts a total force $F = 6.5 \text{ nN}$ on the wall, how many photons per second are hitting the wall?

78. The Big Bang theory states that the beginning of the universe was accompanied by a huge burst of photons. Those photons are still present today and make up the so-called cosmic microwave background radiation. The universe radiates like a blackbody with a temperature of about 2.7 K. Calculate the peak wavelength of this radiation.

79. An electron and a positron collide head on, annihilate, and create two 0.755-MeV photons traveling in opposite directions. What were the initial kinetic energies of electron and positron?

80. By what potential difference must (a) a proton $(m = 1.67 \times 10^{-27} \text{ kg})$, and (b) an electron $(m = 9.11 \times 10^{-31} \text{ kg})$, be accelerated to have a wavelength $\lambda = 6.0 \times 10^{-12} \text{ m}$?

81. In some of Rutherford's experiments (Fig. 37–17) the α particles $(\text{mass} = 6.64 \times 10^{-27} \text{ kg})$ had a kinetic energy of 4.8 MeV. How close could they get to the center of a silver nucleus $(\text{charge} = +47e)$? Ignore the recoil motion of the nucleus.

82. Show that the magnitude of the electrostatic potential energy of an electron in any Bohr orbit of a hydrogen atom is twice the magnitude of its kinetic energy in that orbit.

83. Calculate the ratio of the gravitational force to the electric force for the electron in a hydrogen atom. Can the gravitational force be safely ignored?

84. Electrons accelerated by a potential difference of 12.3 V pass through a gas of hydrogen atoms at room temperature. What wavelengths of light will be emitted?

85. In a particular photoelectric experiment, a stopping potential of 2.70 V is measured when ultraviolet light of wavelength 380 nm is incident on the metal. If blue light of wavelength 440 nm is used, what is the new stopping potential?

86. In an X-ray tube (see Fig. 35–26 and discussion in Section 35–10), the high voltage between filament and target is V. After being accelerated through this voltage, an electron strikes the target where it is decelerated (by positively charged nuclei) and in the process one or more X-ray photons are emitted. (a) Show that the photon of shortest wavelength will have

$$\lambda_0 = \frac{hc}{eV}.$$

(b) What is the shortest wavelength of X-ray emitted when accelerated electrons strike the face of a 33-kV television picture tube?

87. The intensity of the Sun's light in the vicinity of Earth is about 1350 W/m^2. Imagine a spacecraft with a mirrored square sail of dimension 1.0 km. Estimate how much thrust (in newtons) this craft will experience due to collisions with the Sun's photons. [Hint: Assume the photons bounce perpendicularly off the sail with no change in the magnitude of their momentum.]

88. Photons of energy 9.0 eV are incident on a metal. It is found that current flows from the metal until a stopping potential of 4.0 V is applied. If the wavelength of the incident photons is doubled, what is the maximum kinetic energy of the ejected electrons? What would happen if the wavelength of the incident photons was tripled?

89. Light of wavelength 360 nm strikes a metal whose work function is 2.4 eV. What is the shortest de Broglie wavelength for the electrons that are produced as photoelectrons?

90. Visible light incident on a diffraction grating with slit spacing of 0.012 mm has the first maximum at an angle of 3.5° from the central peak. If electrons could be diffracted by the same grating, what electron velocity would produce the same diffraction pattern as the visible light?

91. (a) Suppose an unknown element has an absorption spectrum with lines corresponding to 2.5, 4.7, and 5.1 eV above its ground state, and an ionization energy of 11.5 eV. Draw an energy level diagram for this element. (b) If a 5.1-eV photon is absorbed by an atom of this substance, in which state was the atom before absorbing the photon? What will be the energies of the photons that can subsequently be emitted by this atom?

92. Light of wavelength 424 nm falls on a metal which has a work function of 2.28 eV. (a) How much voltage should be applied to bring the current to zero? (b) What is the maximum speed of the emitted electrons? (c) What is the de Broglie wavelength of these electrons?

93. (a) Apply Bohr's assumptions to the Earth–Moon system to calculate the allowed energies and radii of motion. (b) Given the known distance between Earth and the Moon, is the quantization of the energy and radius apparent?

94. Show that the wavelength of a particle of mass m with kinetic energy K is given by the relativistic formula $\lambda = hc/\sqrt{K^2 + 2mc^2K}$.

95. A small flashlight is rated at 3.0 W. As the light leaves the flashlight in one direction, a reaction force is exerted on the flashlight in the opposite direction. Estimate the size of this reaction force.

96. At the atomic-scale, the electron volt and nanometer are well-suited units for energy and distance, respectively. (a) Show that the energy E in eV of a photon, whose wavelength λ is in nm, is given by

$$E = \frac{1240 \text{ eV} \cdot \text{nm}}{\lambda \text{ (nm)}}.$$

(b) How much energy (eV) does a 650-nm photon have?

*97. Three fundamental constants of nature—the gravitational constant G, Planck's constant h, and the speed of light c—have the dimensions of $[L^3/MT^2]$, $[ML^2/T]$, and $[L/T]$, respectively. (a) Find the mathematical combination of these fundamental constants that has the dimension of time. This combination is called the "Planck time" t_P and is thought to be the earliest time, after the creation of the universe, at which the currently known laws of physics can be applied. (b) Determine the numerical value of t_P. (c) Find the mathematical combination of these fundamental constants that has the dimension of length. This combination is called the "Planck length" λ_P and is thought to be the smallest length over which the currently known laws of physics can be applied. (d) Determine the numerical value of λ_P.

98. Imagine a free particle of mass m bouncing back and forth between two perfectly reflecting walls, separated by distance ℓ. Imagine that the two oppositely directed matter waves associated with this particle interfere to create a standing wave with a node at each of the walls. Show that the ground state (first harmonic) and first excited state (second harmonic) have (non-relativistic) kinetic energies $h^2/8m\ell^2$ and $h^2/2m\ell^2$, respectively.

99. (a) A rubidium atom $(m = 85\,\text{u})$ is at rest with one electron in an excited energy level. When the electron jumps to the ground state, the atom emits a photon of wavelength $\lambda = 780\,\text{nm}$. Determine the resulting (nonrelativistic) recoil speed v of the atom. (b) The recoil speed sets the lower limit on the temperature to which an ideal gas of rubidium atoms can be cooled in a laser-based **atom trap**. Using the kinetic theory of gases (Chapter 18), estimate this "lowest achievable" temperature.

100. A rubidium atom (atomic mass 85) is initially at room temperature and has a velocity $v = 290\,\text{m/s}$ due to its thermal motion. Consider the absorption of photons by this atom from a laser beam of wavelength $\lambda = 780\,\text{nm}$. Assume the rubidium atom's initial velocity v is directed into the laser beam (the photons are moving right and the atom is moving left) and that the atom absorbs a new photon every 25 ns. How long will it take for this process to completely stop ("cool") the rubidium atom? [*Note*: a more detailed analysis predicts that the atom can be slowed to about 1 cm/s by this light absorption process, but it cannot be completely stopped.]

*Numerical/Computer

*101. (III) (a) Graph Planck's radiation formula (top of page 989) as a function of wavelength from $\lambda = 20\,\text{nm}$ to $2000\,\text{nm}$ in 20 nm steps for two lightbulb filaments, one at 2700 K and the other at 3300 K. Plot both curves on the same set of axes. (b) Approximately how much more intense is the visible light from the hotter bulb? Use numerical integration.

*102. (III) Estimate what % of emitted sunlight energy is in the visible range. Use Planck's radiation formula (top of page 989) and numerical integration.

*103. (III) Potassium has one of the lowest work functions of all metals and so is useful in photoelectric devices using visible light. Light from a source is incident on a potassium surface. Data for the stopping voltage V_0 as a function of wavelength λ is shown below. (a) Explain why a graph of V_0 vs. $1/\lambda$ is expected to yield a straight line. What are the theoretical expectations for the slope and the y-intercept of this line? (b) Using the data below, graph V_0 vs. $1/\lambda$ and show that a straight-line plot does indeed result. (c) Determine the slope a and y-intercept b of this line. Using your values for a and b, determine (d) potassium's work function (eV) and (e) Planck's constant h (J·s).

λ (μm)	0.400	0.430	0.460	0.490	0.520
V_0 (V)	0.803	0.578	0.402	0.229	0.083

Answers to Exercises

A: More 1000-nm photons (lower frequency).

B: 5.50×10^{14} Hz, 545 nm.

C: Only λ.

D: Decrease.

E: (e).

F: (c).

Participants in the 1927 Solvay Conference. Albert Einstein, seated at front center, had difficulty accepting that nature could behave according to the rules of quantum mechanics. We present a brief summary of quantum mechanics in this Chapter starting with the wave function and the uncertainty principle. We examine the Schrödinger equation and its solutions for some simple cases: free particles, the square well, and tunneling through a barrier.

C H A P T E R

38

Quantum Mechanics

CHAPTER-OPENING QUESTION—Guess now!

The uncertainty principle states that

(a) no measurement can be perfect because it is technologically impossible to make perfect measuring instruments.

(b) it is impossible to measure exactly where a particle is, unless it is at rest.

(c) it is impossible to simultaneously know both the position and the momentum of a particle with complete certainty.

(d) a particle cannot actually have a completely certain value of momentum.

Bohr's model of the atom gave us a first (though rough) picture of what an atom is like. It proposed explanations for why there is emission and absorption of light by atoms at only certain wavelengths. The wavelengths of the line spectra and the ionization energy for hydrogen (and one-electron ions) are in excellent agreement with experiment. But the Bohr theory had important limitations. It was not able to predict line spectra for more complex atoms—not even for the neutral helium atom, which has only two electrons. Nor could it explain why emission lines, when viewed with great precision, consist of two or more very closely spaced lines (referred to as *fine structure*). The Bohr model also did not explain why some spectral lines were brighter than others. And it could not explain the bonding of atoms in molecules or in solids and liquids.

From a theoretical point of view, too, the Bohr theory was not satisfactory: it was a strange mixture of classical and quantum ideas. Moreover, the wave–particle duality was not really resolved.

CONTENTS

FIGURE 38–1 Erwin Schrödinger with Lise Meitner (see Chapter 42).

FIGURE 38–2 Werner Heisenberg (center) on Lake Como with Enrico Fermi (left) and Wolfgang Pauli (right).

We mention these limitations of the Bohr theory not to disparage it—for it was a landmark in the history of science. Rather, we mention them to show why, in the early 1920s, it became increasingly evident that a new, more comprehensive theory was needed. It was not long in coming. Less than two years after de Broglie gave us his matter–wave hypothesis, Erwin Schrödinger (1887–1961; Fig. 38–1) and Werner Heisenberg (1901–1976; Fig. 38–2) independently developed a new comprehensive theory.

38–1 Quantum Mechanics—A New Theory

The new theory, called **quantum mechanics**, has been extremely successful. It unifies the wave–particle duality into a single consistent theory and has successfully dealt with the spectra emitted by complex atoms, even the fine details. It explains the relative brightness of spectral lines and how atoms form molecules. It is also a much more general theory that covers all quantum phenomena from blackbody radiation to atoms and molecules. It has explained a wide range of natural phenomena and from its predictions many new practical devices have become possible. Indeed, it has been so successful that it is accepted today by nearly all physicists as the fundamental theory underlying physical processes.

Quantum mechanics deals mainly with the microscopic world of atoms and light. But this new theory, when it is applied to macroscopic phenomena, must be able to produce the old classical laws. This, the **correspondence principle** (already mentioned in Section 37–11), is satisfied fully by quantum mechanics.

This doesn't mean we should throw away classical theories such as Newton's laws. In the everyday world, the latter are far easier to apply and they give sufficiently accurate descriptions. But when we deal with high speeds, close to the speed of light, we must use the theory of relativity; and when we deal with the tiny world of the atom, we use quantum mechanics.

Although we won't go into the detailed mathematics of quantum mechanics, we will discuss the main ideas and how they involve the wave and particle properties of matter to explain atomic structure and other applications.

38–2 The Wave Function and Its Interpretation; the Double-Slit Experiment

The important properties of any wave are its wavelength, frequency, and amplitude. For an electromagnetic wave, the frequency (or wavelength) determines whether the light is in the visible spectrum or not, and if so, what color it is. We also have seen (Eq. 37–3) that the frequency is a measure of the energy of the corresponding photons ($E = hf$). The amplitude or displacement of an electromagnetic wave at any point is the strength of the electric (or magnetic) field at that point, and is related to the intensity of the wave (the brightness of the light).

For material particles such as electrons, quantum mechanics relates the wavelength to momentum according to de Broglie's formula, $\lambda = h/p$, Eq. 37–7. But what corresponds to the *amplitude* or *displacement* of a matter wave? The amplitude of an electromagnetic wave is represented by the electric and magnetic fields, E and B. In quantum mechanics, this role is played by the **wave function**, which is given the symbol Ψ (the Greek capital letter psi, pronounced "sigh"). Thus Ψ represents the wave displacement, as a function of time and position, of a new kind of field which we might call a "matter" field or a matter wave.

To understand how to interpret the wave function Ψ, we make an analogy with light using the wave–particle duality.

We saw in Chapter 15 that the intensity I of any wave is proportional to the square of the amplitude. This holds true for light waves as well, as we saw in Chapter 31. That is,

$$I \propto E^2,$$

where E is the electric field strength. From the *particle* point of view, the intensity of a light beam (of given frequency) is proportional to the number of photons, N, that pass through a given area per unit time. The more photons there are, the greater the intensity. Thus

$$I \propto E^2 \propto N.$$

This proportion can be turned around so that we have

$$N \propto E^2.$$

That is, the number of photons (striking a page of this book, say) is proportional to the square of the electric field strength.

If the light beam is very weak, only a few photons will be involved. Indeed, it is possible to "build up" a photograph in a camera using very weak light so the effect of individual photons can be seen.

If we are dealing with only one photon, the relationship above $(N \propto E^2)$ can be interpreted in a slightly different way. At any point the square of the electric field strength, E^2, is a measure of the *probability* that a photon will be at that location. At points where E^2 is large, there is a high probability the photon will be there; where E^2 is small, the probability is low.

We can interpret matter waves in the same way, as was first suggested by Max Born (1882–1970) in 1927. The wave function Ψ may vary in magnitude from point to point in space and time. If Ψ describes a collection of many electrons, then $|\Psi|^2$ at any point will be proportional to the number of electrons expected to be found at that point.[†] When dealing with small numbers of electrons we can't make very exact predictions, so $|\Psi|^2$ takes on the character of a probability. If Ψ, which depends on time and position, represents a single electron (say, in an atom), then $|\Psi|^2$ is interpreted as follows: $|\Psi|^2$ *at a certain point in space and time represents the probability of finding the electron at the given position and time.* Thus $|\Psi|^2$ is often referred to as the **probability density** or **probability distribution**.

Double-Slit Interference Experiment for Electrons

To understand this better, we take as a thought experiment the familiar double-slit experiment, and consider it both for light and for electrons.

Consider two slits whose size and separation are on the order of the wavelength of whatever we direct at them, either light or electrons, Fig. 38–3. We know very well what would happen in this case for light, since this is just Young's double-slit experiment (Section 34–3): an interference pattern would be seen on the screen behind. If light were replaced by electrons with wavelength comparable to the slit size, they too would produce an interference pattern (recall Fig. 37–11). In the case of light, the pattern would be visible to the eye or could be recorded on film. For electrons, a fluorescent screen could be used (it glows where an electron strikes).

[†]The wave function Ψ is generally a complex quantity (that is, it involves $i = \sqrt{-1}$) and hence is not directly observable. On the other hand, $|\Psi|^2$, the absolute value of Ψ squared, is always a real quantity and it is to $|\Psi|^2$ that we can give a physical interpretation.

FIGURE 38–3 Parallel beam, of light or electrons, falls on two slits whose sizes are comparable to the wavelength. An interference pattern is observed.

Light or electrons

Intensity on screen

FIGURE 38–4 Young's double-slit experiment done with electrons—note that the pattern is not evident with only a few electrons (top photo), but with more and more electrons (second and third photos), the familiar double-slit interference pattern (Chapter 34) is seen.

If we reduced the flow of electrons (or photons) so they passed through the slits one at a time, we would see a flash each time one struck the screen. At first, the flashes would seem random. Indeed, there is no way to predict just where any one electron would hit the screen. If we let the experiment run for a long time, and kept track of where each electron hit the screen, we would soon see a pattern emerging—the interference pattern predicted by the wave theory; see Fig. 38–4. Thus, although we could not predict where a given electron would strike the screen, we could predict probabilities. (The same can be said for photons.) The probability, as mentioned before, is proportional to $|\Psi|^2$. Where $|\Psi|^2$ is zero, we would get a minimum in the interference pattern. And where $|\Psi|^2$ is a maximum, we would get a peak in the interference pattern.

The interference pattern would thus occur even when electrons (or photons) passed through the slits one at a time. So the interference pattern could not arise from the interaction of one electron with another. It is as if an electron passed through both slits at the same time, interfering with itself. This is possible because an electron is not precisely a particle. It is as much a wave as it is a particle, and a wave could travel through both slits at once. But what would happen if we covered one of the slits so we knew that the electron passed through the other slit, and a little later we covered the second slit so the electron had to have passed through the first slit? The result would be that no interference pattern would be seen. We would see, instead, two bright areas (or diffraction patterns) on the screen behind the slits. This confirms our idea that if both slits are open, the screen shows an interference pattern as if each electron passed through both slits, like a wave. Yet each electron would make a tiny spot on the screen as if it were a particle.

The main point of this discussion is this: if we treat electrons (and other particles) as if they were waves, then Ψ represents the wave amplitude. If we treat them as particles, then we must treat them on a *probabilistic* basis. The square of the wave function, $|\Psi|^2$, gives the probability of finding a given electron at a given point. We cannot predict—or even follow—the path of a single electron precisely through space and time.

38–3 The Heisenberg Uncertainty Principle

Whenever a measurement is made, some uncertainty is always involved. For example, you cannot make an absolutely exact measurement of the length of a table. Even with a measuring stick that has markings 1 mm apart, there will be an inaccuracy of perhaps $\frac{1}{2}$ mm or so. More precise instruments will produce more precise measurements. But there is always some uncertainty involved in a measurement, no matter how good the measuring device. We expect that by using more precise instruments, the uncertainty in a measurement can be made indefinitely small.

But according to quantum mechanics, there is actually a limit to the precision of certain measurements. This limit is not a restriction on how well instruments can be made; rather, it is inherent in nature. It is the result of two factors: the wave–particle duality, and the unavoidable interaction between the thing observed and the observing instrument. Let us look at this in more detail.

To make a measurement on an object without disturbing it, at least a little, is not possible. Consider trying to locate a Ping-Pong ball in a completely dark room. You grope about trying to find its position; and just when you touch it with your finger, you bump it and it bounces away. Whenever we measure the position of an object, whether it is a ball or an electron, we always touch it with something else that gives us the information about its position. To locate a lost Ping-Pong ball in a dark room, you could probe about with your hand or a stick; or you could shine a light and detect the light reflecting off the ball. When you search with your hand or a stick, you find the ball's position when you touch it, but at the same time you unavoidably bump it and give it some momentum.

Thus you won't know its *future* position. The same would be true if you observe the Ping-Pong ball using light. In order to "see" the ball, at least one photon must scatter from it, and the reflected photon must enter your eye or some other detector. When a photon strikes an ordinary-sized object, it does not appreciably alter the motion or position of the object. But when a photon strikes a very tiny object like an electron, it can transfer momentum to the object and thus greatly change the object's motion and position in an unpredictable way. The mere act of measuring the position of an object at one time makes our knowledge of its future position imprecise.

Now let us see where the wave–particle duality comes in. Imagine a thought experiment in which we are trying to measure the position of an object, say an electron, with photons, Fig. 38–5. (The arguments would be similar if we were using, instead, an electron microscope.) As we saw in Chapter 35, objects can be seen to a precision at best of about the wavelength of the radiation used due to diffraction. If we want a precise position measurement, we must use a short wavelength. But a short wavelength corresponds to high frequency and large momentum ($p = h/\lambda$); and the more momentum the photons have, the more momentum they can give the object when they strike it. If we use photons of longer wavelength, and correspondingly smaller momentum, the object's motion when struck by the photons will not be affected as much. But the longer wavelength means lower resolution, so the object's position will be less accurately known. Thus the act of observing produces an uncertainty in both the *position* and the *momentum* of the electron. This is the essence of the *uncertainty principle* first enunciated by Heisenberg in 1927.

Quantitatively, we can make an approximate calculation of the magnitude of this effect. If we use light of wavelength λ, the position can be measured at best to a precision of about λ. That is, the uncertainty in the position measurement, Δx, is approximately

$$\Delta x \approx \lambda.$$

Suppose that the object can be detected by a single photon. The photon has a momentum $p_x = h/\lambda$ (Eq. 37–5). When the photon strikes our object, it will give some or all of this momentum to the object, Fig. 38–5. Therefore, the final x momentum of our object will be uncertain in the amount

$$\Delta p_x \approx \frac{h}{\lambda}$$

since we can't tell beforehand how much momentum will be transferred. The product of these uncertainties is

$$(\Delta x)(\Delta p_x) \approx h.$$

The uncertainties could be worse than this, depending on the apparatus and the number of photons needed for detection. A more careful mathematical calculation shows the product of the uncertainties as, at best, about

$$(\Delta x)(\Delta p_x) \gtrsim \frac{h}{2\pi} \qquad \qquad \textbf{(38–1)}$$

UNCERTAINTY PRINCIPLE
(Δx and Δp)

where Δp_x is the uncertainty of the momentum in the x direction.[†] This is a mathematical statement of the **Heisenberg uncertainty principle**, or, as it is sometimes called, the **indeterminancy principle**. It tells us that we cannot measure both the position *and* momentum of an object precisely at the same time. The more accurately we try to measure the position so that Δx is small, the greater will be the uncertainty in momentum, Δp_x. If we try to measure the momentum very accurately, then the uncertainty in the position becomes large.

[†]Note, however, that quantum mechanics does allow simultaneous precise measurements of p_x and y: that is, $(\Delta y)(\Delta p_x) \gtrsim 0$.

FIGURE 38–5 Thought experiment for observing an electron with a powerful light microscope. At least one photon must scatter from the electron (transferring some momentum to it) and enter the microscope.

The uncertainty principle does not forbid individual precise measurements, however. For example, in principle we could measure the position of an object exactly. But then its momentum would be completely unknown. Thus, although we might know the position of the object exactly at one instant, we could have no idea at all where it would be a moment later. The uncertainties expressed here are inherent in nature, and reflect the best precision theoretically attainable even with the best instruments.

| **EXERCISE A** Return to the Chapter-Opening Question on p. 1017, and answer it again now.

Another useful form of the uncertainty principle relates energy and time, and we examine this as follows. The object to be detected has an uncertainty in position $\Delta x \approx \lambda$. The photon that detects it travels with speed c, and it takes a time $\Delta t \approx \Delta x/c \approx \lambda/c$ to pass through the distance of uncertainty. Hence, the measured time when our object is at a given position is uncertain by about

$$\Delta t \approx \frac{\lambda}{c}.$$

Since the photon can transfer some or all of its energy ($= hf = hc/\lambda$) to our object, the uncertainty in energy of our object as a result is

$$\Delta E \approx \frac{hc}{\lambda}.$$

The product of these two uncertainties is

$$(\Delta E)(\Delta t) \approx h.$$

A more careful calculation gives

$$(\Delta E)(\Delta t) \gtrsim \frac{h}{2\pi}. \tag{38–2}$$

This form of the uncertainty principle tells us that the energy of an object can be uncertain (or can be interpreted as briefly nonconserved) by an amount ΔE for a time $\Delta t \approx h/(2\pi \, \Delta E)$.

The quantity $(h/2\pi)$ appears so often in quantum mechanics that for convenience it is given the symbol $\hbar$ ("h-bar"). That is,

$$\hbar = \frac{h}{2\pi} = \frac{6.626 \times 10^{-34} \, \text{J} \cdot \text{s}}{2\pi} = 1.055 \times 10^{-34} \, \text{J} \cdot \text{s}.$$

By using this notation, Eqs. 38–1 and 38–2 for the uncertainty principle can be written

$$(\Delta x)(\Delta p_x) \gtrsim \hbar \quad \text{and} \quad (\Delta E)(\Delta t) \gtrsim \hbar.$$

We have been discussing the position and velocity of an electron as if it were a particle. But it isn't simply a particle. Indeed, we have the uncertainty principle because an electron—and matter in general—has wave as well as particle properties. What the uncertainty principle really tells us is that if we insist on thinking of the electron as a particle, then there are certain limitations on this simplified view—namely, that the position and velocity cannot both be known precisely at the same time; and even that the electron does not *have* a precise position and momentum at the same time (because it is not simply a particle). Similarly, the energy can be uncertain in the amount ΔE for a time $\Delta t \approx \hbar/\Delta E$.

Because Planck's constant, h, is so small, the uncertainties expressed in the uncertainty principle are usually negligible on the macroscopic level. But at the level of atomic sizes, the uncertainties are significant. Because we consider ordinary objects to be made up of atoms containing nuclei and electrons, the uncertainty principle is relevant to our understanding of all of nature. The uncertainty principle expresses, perhaps most clearly, the probabilistic nature of quantum mechanics. It thus is often used as a basis for philosophic discussion.

EXAMPLE 38–1 **Position uncertainty of an electron.** An electron moves in a straight line with a constant speed $v = 1.10 \times 10^6$ m/s which has been measured to a precision of 0.10%. What is the maximum precision with which its position could be simultaneously measured?

APPROACH The momentum is $p = mv$, and the uncertainty in p is $\Delta p = 0.0010p$. The uncertainty principle (Eq. 38–1) gives us the lowest Δx using the equals sign.

SOLUTION The momentum of the electron is

$$p = mv = (9.11 \times 10^{-31} \text{ kg})(1.10 \times 10^6 \text{ m/s}) = 1.00 \times 10^{-24} \text{ kg} \cdot \text{m/s}.$$

The uncertainty in the momentum is 0.10% of this, or $\Delta p = 1.0 \times 10^{-27}$ kg·m/s. From the uncertainty principle, the best simultaneous position measurement will have an uncertainty of

$$\Delta x \approx \frac{\hbar}{\Delta p} = \frac{1.055 \times 10^{-34} \text{ J} \cdot \text{s}}{1.0 \times 10^{-27} \text{ kg} \cdot \text{m/s}} = 1.1 \times 10^{-7} \text{ m},$$

or 110 nm.

NOTE This is about 1000 times the diameter of an atom.

EXAMPLE 38–2 **Position uncertainty of a baseball.** What is the uncertainty in position, imposed by the uncertainty principle, on a 150-g baseball thrown at (93 ± 2) mi/h $= (42 \pm 1)$ m/s?

APPROACH The uncertainty in the speed is $\Delta v = 1$ m/s. We multiply Δv by m to get Δp and then use the uncertainty principle, solving for Δx.

SOLUTION The uncertainty in the momentum is

$$\Delta p = m \, \Delta v = (0.150 \text{ kg})(1 \text{ m/s}) = 0.15 \text{ kg} \cdot \text{m/s}.$$

Hence the uncertainty in a position measurement could be as small as

$$\Delta x = \frac{\hbar}{\Delta p} = \frac{1.055 \times 10^{-34} \text{ J} \cdot \text{s}}{0.15 \text{ kg} \cdot \text{m/s}} = 7 \times 10^{-34} \text{ m}.$$

NOTE This distance is far smaller than any we could imagine observing or measuring. It is trillions of trillions of times smaller than an atom. Indeed, the uncertainty principle sets no relevant limit on measurement for macroscopic objects.

EXAMPLE 38–3 **ESTIMATE** **J/ψ lifetime calculated.** The J/ψ meson, discovered in 1974, was measured to have an average mass of 3100 MeV/c^2 (note the use of energy units since $E = mc^2$) and an intrinsic width of 63 keV/c^2. By this we mean that the masses of different J/ψ mesons were actually measured to be slightly different from one another. This mass "width" is related to the very short lifetime of the J/ψ before it decays into other particles. From the uncertainty principle, if the particle exists for only a time Δt, its mass (or rest energy) will be uncertain by $\Delta E \approx \hbar/\Delta t$. Estimate the J/ψ lifetime.

APPROACH We use the energy–time version of the uncertainty principle, Eq. 38–2.

SOLUTION The uncertainty of 63 keV/c^2 in the J/ψ's mass is an uncertainty in its rest energy, which in joules is

$$\Delta E = (63 \times 10^3 \text{ eV})(1.60 \times 10^{-19} \text{ J/eV}) = 1.01 \times 10^{-14} \text{ J}.$$

Then we expect its lifetime τ ($= \Delta t$ using Eq. 38–2) to be

$$\tau \approx \frac{\hbar}{\Delta E} = \frac{1.06 \times 10^{-34} \text{ J} \cdot \text{s}}{1.01 \times 10^{-14} \text{ J}} \approx 1 \times 10^{-20} \text{ s}.$$

Lifetimes this short are difficult to measure directly, and the assignment of very short lifetimes depends on this use of the uncertainty principle. (See Chapter 43.)

The uncertainty principle applies also for angular variables:

$$(\Delta L_z)(\Delta \phi) \gtrsim \hbar$$

where L is the component of angular momentum along a given axis (z) and ϕ is the angular position in a plane perpendicular to that axis.

38–4 Philosophic Implications; Probability Versus Determinism

The classical Newtonian view of the world is a deterministic one (see Section 6–5). One of its basic ideas is that once the position and velocity of an object are known at a particular time, its future position can be predicted if the forces on it are known. For example, if a stone is thrown a number of times with the same initial velocity and angle, and the forces on it remain the same, the path of the projectile will always be the same. If the forces are known (gravity and air resistance, if any), the stone's path can be precisely predicted. This mechanistic view implies that the future unfolding of the universe, assumed to be made up of particulate objects, is completely determined.

This classical deterministic view of the physical world has been radically altered by quantum mechanics. As we saw in the analysis of the double-slit experiment (Section 38–2), electrons all prepared in the same way will not all end up in the same place. According to quantum mechanics, certain probabilities exist that an electron will arrive at different points. This is very different from the classical view, in which the path of a particle is precisely predictable from the initial position and velocity and the forces exerted on it. According to quantum mechanics, the position and velocity of an object cannot even be known accurately at the same time. This is expressed in the uncertainty principle, and arises because basic entities, such as electrons, are not considered simply as particles: they have wave properties as well. Quantum mechanics allows us to calculate only the probability[†] that, say, an electron (when thought of as a particle) will be observed at various places. Quantum mechanics says there is some inherent unpredictability in nature.

Since matter is considered to be made up of atoms, even ordinary-sized objects are expected to be governed by probability, rather than by strict determinism. For example, quantum mechanics predicts a finite (but negligibly small) probability that when you throw a stone, its path will suddenly curve upward instead of following the downward-curved parabola of normal projectile motion. Quantum mechanics predicts with extremely high probability that ordinary objects will behave just as the classical laws of physics predict. But these predictions are considered probabilities, not certainties. The reason that macroscopic objects behave in accordance with classical laws with such high probability is due to the large number of molecules involved: when large numbers of objects are present in a statistical situation, deviations from the average (or most probable) approach zero. It is the average configuration of vast numbers of molecules that follows the so-called fixed laws of classical physics with such high probability, and gives rise to an apparent "determinism." Deviations from classical laws are observed when small numbers of molecules are dealt with. We can say, then, that although there are no precise deterministic laws in quantum mechanics, there are statistical laws based on probability.

It is important to note that there is a difference between the probability imposed by quantum mechanics and that used in the nineteenth century to understand thermodynamics and the behavior of gases in terms of molecules (Chapters 18 and 20). In thermodynamics, probability is used because there are far too many particles to keep track of. But the molecules are still assumed to move and interact in a deterministic way following Newton's laws. Probability in quantum mechanics is quite different; it is seen as *inherent* in nature, and not as a limitation on our abilities to calculate or to measure.

The view presented here is the generally accepted one and is called the **Copenhagen interpretation** of quantum mechanics in honor of Niels Bohr's home, since it was largely developed there through discussions between Bohr and other prominent physicists.

Because electrons are not simply particles, they cannot be thought of as following particular paths in space and time. This suggests that a description of matter in space and time may not be completely correct. This deep and far-reaching

---

[†]Note that these probabilities can be calculated precisely, just like exact predictions of probabilities at rolling dice or playing cards, but they are unlike predictions of probabilities at sporting events or for natural or man-made disasters, which are only estimates.

conclusion has been a lively topic of discussion among philosophers. Perhaps the most important and influential philosopher of quantum mechanics was Bohr. He argued that a space–time description of actual atoms and electrons is not possible. Yet a description of experiments on atoms or electrons must be given in terms of space and time and other concepts familiar to ordinary experience, such as waves and particles. We must not let our *descriptions* of experiments lead us into believing that atoms or electrons themselves actually move in space and time as classical particles.

38–5 The Schrödinger Equation in One Dimension—Time-Independent Form

In order to describe physical systems quantitatively using quantum mechanics, we must have a means of determining the wave function Ψ mathematically. The basic equation (in the nonrelativistic realm) for determining Ψ is the *Schrödinger equation*. We cannot, however, derive the Schrödinger equation from some higher principles, just as Newton's second law, for example, cannot be derived. The relation $\vec{F} = m\vec{a}$ was *invented* by Newton to describe how the motion of an object is related to the net applied force. As we saw early in this book, Newton's second law works exceptionally well. In the realm of classical physics it is the starting point for analytically solving a wide range of problems, and the solutions it yields are fully consistent with experiment. The validity of any fundamental equation resides in its agreement with experiment. The Schrödinger equation forms part of a new theory, and it too had to be *invented*—and then checked against experiment, a test that it passed splendidly.

The Schrödinger equation can be written in two forms: the time-dependent version and the time-independent version. We will mainly be interested in steady-state situations—that is, when there is no time dependence—and so we mainly deal with the time-independent version. (We briefly discuss the time-dependent version in the optional Section 38–6.) The time-independent version involves a wave function with only spatial dependence which we represent by lowercase psi, $\psi(x)$, for the simple one-dimensional case we deal with here. In three dimensions, we write $\psi(x, y, z)$ or $\psi(r, \theta, \phi)$.

In classical mechanics, we solved problems using two approaches: via Newton's laws with the concept of force, and by using the energy concept with the conservation laws. The Schrödinger equation is based on the energy approach. Even though the Schrödinger equation cannot be derived, we can suggest what form it might take by using conservation of energy and considering a very simple case: that of a free particle on which no forces act, so that its potential energy U is constant. We assume that our particle moves along the x axis, and since no force acts on it, its momentum remains constant and its wavelength ($\lambda = h/p$) is fixed. To describe a wave for a free particle such as an electron, we expect that its wave function will satisfy a differential equation that is akin to (but not identical to) the classical wave equation. Let us see what we can infer about this equation. Consider a simple traveling wave of a single wavelength λ whose wave displacement, as we saw in Chapter 15 for mechanical waves and in Chapter 31 for electromagnetic waves, is given by $A \sin(kx - \omega t)$, or more generally as a superposition of sine and cosine: $A \sin(kx - \omega t) + B \cos(kx - \omega t)$. We are only interested in the spatial dependence, so we consider the wave at a specific moment, say $t = 0$. Thus we write as the wave function for our free particle

$$\psi(x) = A \sin kx + B \cos kx, \qquad \textbf{(38–3a)}$$

where A and B are constants[†] and $k = 2\pi/\lambda$ (Eq. 15–11). For a particle of mass m and velocity v, the de Broglie wavelength is $\lambda = h/p$, where $p = mv$ is the particle's momentum. Hence

$$k = \frac{2\pi}{\lambda} = \frac{2\pi p}{h} = \frac{p}{\hbar}. \qquad \textbf{(38–3b)}$$

[†]In quantum mechanics, constants can be complex (i.e., with a real and/or imaginary part).

One requirement for our wave equation, then, is that it have the wave function $\psi(x)$ as given by Eq. 38–3 as a solution for a free particle. A second requirement is that it be consistent with the conservation of energy, which we can express as

$$\frac{p^2}{2m} + U = E,$$

where E is the total energy, U is the potential energy, and (since we are considering the nonrelativistic realm) the kinetic energy K of our particle of mass m is $K = \frac{1}{2}mv^2 = p^2/2m$. Since $p = \hbar k$ (Eq. 38–3b), we can write the conservation of energy condition as

$$\frac{\hbar^2 k^2}{2m} + U = E. \tag{38–4}$$

Thus we are seeking a differential equation that satisfies conservation of energy (Eq. 38–4) when $\psi(x)$ is its solution. Now, note that if we take two derivatives of our expression for $\psi(x)$, Eq. 38–3a, we get a factor $-k^2$ multiplied by $\psi(x)$:

$$\frac{d\psi(x)}{dx} = \frac{d}{dx}(A \sin kx + B \cos kx) = k(A \cos kx - B \sin kx)$$

$$\frac{d^2\psi(x)}{dx^2} = k\frac{d}{dx}(A \cos kx - B \sin kx) = -k^2(A \sin kx + B \cos kx) = -k^2\psi(x).$$

Can this last term be related to the k^2 term in Eq. 38–4? Indeed, if we multiply this last relation by $-\hbar^2/2m$, we obtain

$$-\frac{\hbar^2}{2m}\frac{d^2\psi(x)}{dx^2} = \frac{\hbar^2 k^2}{2m}\psi(x).$$

The right side is just the first term on the left in Eq. 38–4 multiplied by $\psi(x)$. If we multiply Eq. 38–4 through by $\psi(x)$, and make this substitution, we obtain

$$-\frac{\hbar^2}{2m}\frac{d^2\psi(x)}{dx^2} + U(x)\psi(x) = E\psi(x). \tag{38–5}$$

SCHRÖDINGER EQUATION
(time-independent form)

This is, in fact, the one-dimensional **time-independent Schrödinger equation**, where for generality we have written $U = U(x)$. It is the basis for solving problems in nonrelativistic quantum mechanics. For a particle moving in three dimensions there would be additional derivatives with respect to y and z (see Chapter 39).

Note that we have by no means derived the Schrödinger equation. Although we have made a good argument in its favor, other arguments could also be made which might or might not lead to the same equation. The Schrödinger equation as written (Eq. 38–5) is useful and valid only because it has given results in accord with experiment for a wide range of situations.

There are some requirements we impose on any wave function that is a solution of the Schrödinger equation in order that it be physically meaningful. First, we insist that it be a continuous function; after all, if $|\psi|^2$ represents the probability of finding a particle at a certain point, we expect the probability to be continuous from point to point and not to take discontinuous jumps. Second, we want the wave function to be *normalized*. By this we mean that for a single particle, the probability of finding the particle at one point or another (i.e., the probabilities summed over all space) must be exactly 1 (or 100%). For a single particle, $|\psi|^2$ represents the probability of finding the particle in unit volume. Then

$$|\psi|^2 \, dV \tag{38–6a}$$

is the probability of finding the particle within a volume dV, where ψ is the value of the wave function in this infinitesimal volume dV. For the one-dimensional case, $dV = dx$, so the probability of finding a particle within dx of position x is

$$|\psi(x)|^2 \, dx. \tag{38–6b}$$

Then the sum of the probabilities over all space—that is, the probability of finding the particle somewhere—becomes

$$\int_{\text{all space}} |\psi|^2 \, dV = \int |\psi|^2 \, dx = 1. \qquad \text{(38–6c)}$$

This is called the **normalization condition**, and the integral is taken over whatever region of space in which the particle has a chance of being found, which is often all of space, from $x = -\infty$ to $x = \infty$.

*38–6 Time-Dependent Schrödinger Equation

The more general form of the Schrödinger equation, including time dependence, for a particle of mass m moving in one dimension, is

$$-\frac{\hbar^2}{2m} \frac{\partial^2 \Psi(x,t)}{\partial x^2} + U(x)\Psi(x,t) = i\hbar \frac{\partial \Psi(x,t)}{\partial t}. \qquad \text{(38–7)}$$

This is the **time-dependent Schrödinger equation**; here $U(x)$ is the potential energy of the particle as a function of position, and i is the imaginary number $i = \sqrt{-1}$. For a particle moving in three dimensions, there would be additional derivatives with respect to y and z, just as for the classical wave equation discussed in Section 15–5. Indeed, it is worth noting the similarity between the Schrödinger wave equation for zero potential energy $(U = 0)$ and the classical wave equation: $\partial^2 D/\partial t^2 = v^2 \partial^2 D/\partial x^2$, where D is the wave displacement (equivalent of the wave function). In both equations there is the second derivative with respect to x; but in the Schrödinger equation there is only the first derivative with respect to time, whereas the classical wave equation has the second derivative for time.

As we pointed out in the preceding Section, we cannot derive the time-dependent Schrödinger equation. But we can show how the time-independent Schrödinger equation (Eq. 38–5) is obtained from it. For many problems in quantum mechanics, it is possible to write the wave function as a product of separate functions of space and time:

$$\Psi(x,t) = \psi(x)f(t).$$

Substituting this into the time-dependent Schrödinger equation (Eq. 38–7), we get:

$$-\frac{\hbar^2}{2m} f(t) \frac{d^2\psi(x)}{dx^2} + U(x)\psi(x)f(t) = i\hbar\psi(x) \frac{df(t)}{dt}.$$

We divide both sides of this equation by $\psi(x)f(t)$ and obtain an equation that involves only x on one side and only t on the other:

$$-\frac{\hbar^2}{2m} \frac{1}{\psi(x)} \frac{d^2\psi(x)}{dx^2} + U(x) = i\hbar \frac{1}{f(t)} \frac{df(t)}{dt}.$$

This **separation of variables** is very convenient. Since the left side is a function only of x, and the right side is a function only of t, the equality can be valid for all values of x and all values of t only if each side is equal to a constant (the same constant), which we call C:

$$-\frac{\hbar^2}{2m} \frac{1}{\psi(x)} \frac{d^2\psi(x)}{dx^2} + U(x) = C \qquad \text{(38–8a)}$$

$$i\hbar \frac{1}{f(t)} \frac{df(t)}{dt} = C. \qquad \text{(38–8b)}$$

We multiply the first of these (Eq. 38–8a) through by $\psi(x)$ and obtain

$$-\frac{\hbar^2}{2m} \frac{d^2\psi(x)}{dx^2} + U(x)\psi(x) = C\psi(x). \qquad \text{(38–8c)}$$

This we recognize immediately as the time-independent Schrödinger equation, Eq. 38–5, where the constant C equals the total energy E. Thus we have obtained the time-independent form of Schrödinger's equation from the time-dependent form.

Equation 38–8b is easy to solve. Putting $C = E$, we rewrite Eq. 38–8b as

$$\frac{df(t)}{dt} = -i\frac{E}{\hbar}f(t)$$

(note that since $i^2 = -1$, $i = -1/i$), and then as

$$\frac{df(t)}{f(t)} = -i\frac{E}{\hbar}dt.$$

We integrate both sides to obtain

$$\ln f(t) = -i\frac{E}{\hbar}t$$

or

$$f(t) = e^{-i\left(\frac{E}{\hbar}\right)t}.$$

Thus the total wave function is

$$\Psi(x,t) = \psi(x)e^{-i\left(\frac{E}{\hbar}\right)t}, \tag{38–9}$$

where $\psi(x)$ satisfies Eq. 38–5. It is, in fact, the solution of the time-independent Schrödinger equation (Eq. 38–5) that is the major task of nonrelativistic quantum mechanics. Nonetheless, we should note that in general the wave function $\Psi(x,t)$ is a complex function since it involves $i = \sqrt{-1}$. It has both a real and an imaginary part.[†] Since $\Psi(x,t)$ is not purely real, it cannot itself be physically measurable. Rather it is only $|\Psi|^2$, which *is* real, that can be measured physically.

Note also that

$$|f(t)| = \left|e^{-i\left(\frac{E}{\hbar}\right)t}\right| = 1,$$

so $|f(t)|^2 = 1$. Hence the probability density in space does not depend on time:

$$|\Psi(x,t)|^2 = |\psi(x)|^2.$$

We thus will be interested only in the time-independent Schrödinger equation, Eq. 38–5, which we will now examine for a number of simple situations.

38–7 Free Particles; Plane Waves and Wave Packets

A **free particle** is one that is not subject to any force, and we can therefore take its potential energy to be zero. (Although we dealt with the free particle in Section 38–5 in arguing for Schrödinger's equation, here we treat it directly using Schrödinger's equation as the basis.) Schrödinger's equation (Eq. 38–5) with $U(x) = 0$ becomes

$$-\frac{\hbar^2}{2m}\frac{d^2\psi(x)}{dx^2} = E\psi(x),$$

which can be written

$$\frac{d^2\psi}{dx^2} + \frac{2mE}{\hbar^2}\psi = 0.$$

This is a familiar equation that we encountered in Chapter 14 (Eq. 14–3) in connection with the simple harmonic oscillator. The solution to this equation, but with appropriate variable changes[‡] for our case here, is

$$\psi = A\sin kx + B\cos kx, \qquad \text{[free particle]} \tag{38–10}$$

where

$$k = \sqrt{\frac{2mE}{\hbar^2}}. \tag{38–11a}$$

Since $U = 0$, the total energy E of the particle is $E = \frac{1}{2}mv^2 = p^2/2m$ (where p is the momentum); thus

$$k = \frac{p}{\hbar} = \frac{h}{\lambda\hbar} = \frac{2\pi}{\lambda}. \tag{38–11b}$$

[†]Recall that $e^{-i\theta} = \cos\theta - i\sin\theta$.
[‡]In Eq. 14–3, t becomes x and ω becomes $k = \sqrt{2mE/\hbar^2}$. (Don't confuse this k with the spring constant k of Chapter 14.) We could also write our solution (Eq. 38–10) as $\psi = A\cos(kx + \phi)$ where ϕ is a phase constant.

So a free particle of momentum p and energy E can be represented by a plane wave that varies sinusoidally. If we are not interested in the phase, we can choose $B = 0$ in Eq. 38–10, and we show this sine wave in Fig. 38–6a.

EXAMPLE 38–4 **Free electron.** An electron with energy $E = 6.3 \, \text{eV}$ is in free space (where $U = 0$). Find (a) the wavelength λ and (b) the wave function ψ for the electron, assuming $B = 0$.

APPROACH The wavelength $\lambda = 2\pi/k$ (Eq. 38–11b) where the wave number k is given by Eq. 38–11a. The wave function is given by $\psi = A \sin kx$.

SOLUTION

(a) $\lambda = \dfrac{2\pi}{k} = \dfrac{2\pi\hbar}{\sqrt{2mE}}$

$= \dfrac{2\pi(1.055 \times 10^{-34} \, \text{J} \cdot \text{s})}{\sqrt{2(9.11 \times 10^{-31} \, \text{kg})(6.3 \, \text{eV})(1.60 \times 10^{-19} \, \text{J/eV})}}$

$= 4.9 \times 10^{-10} \, \text{m} = 0.49 \, \text{nm}.$

(b) $k = \dfrac{2\pi}{\lambda}$

$= 1.28 \times 10^{10} \, \text{m}^{-1},$

so

$\psi = A \sin kx = A \sin\left[(1.28 \times 10^{10} \, \text{m}^{-1})(x)\right].$

(a)

(b)

FIGURE 38–6 (a) A plane wave describing a free particle. (b) A wave packet of "width" Δx.

Note in Fig. 38–6a that the sine wave will extend indefinitely[†] in the $+x$ and $-x$ directions. Thus, since $|\psi|^2$ represents the probability of finding the particle, the particle could be anywhere between $x = -\infty$ and $x = \infty$. This is fully consistent with the uncertainty principle (Section 38–3): the momentum of the particle was given and hence is known precisely ($p = \hbar k$), so the particle's position must be totally unpredictable. Mathematically, if $\Delta p = 0$, $\Delta x \gtrsim \hbar/\Delta p = \infty$.

To describe a particle whose position is well localized—that is, it is known to be within a small region of space—we can use the concept of a **wave packet**. Figure 38–6b shows an example of a wave packet whose width is about Δx as shown, meaning that the particle is most likely to be found within this region of space. A well-localized particle moving through space can thus be represented by a moving wave packet.

A wave packet can be represented mathematically as the sum of many plane waves (sine waves) of slightly different wavelengths. That this will work can be seen by looking carefully at Fig. 16–17. There we combined only two nearby frequencies (to explain why there are "beats") and found that the sum of two sine waves looked like a series of wave packets. If we add additional waves with other nearby frequencies, we can eliminate all but one of the packets and arrive at Fig. 38–6b. Thus a wave packet consists of waves of a *range* of wavelengths; hence it does not have a definite momentum $p \, (= h/\lambda)$, but rather, a range of momenta. This is consistent with the uncertainty principle: we have made Δx small, so the momentum cannot be precise; that is, Δp cannot be zero. Instead, our particle can be said to have a range of momenta, Δp, or to have an uncertainty in its momentum, Δp. It is not hard to show, even for this simple situation (see Problem 20), that $\Delta p \approx h/\Delta x$, in accordance with the uncertainty principle.

[†]Such an infinite wave makes problems for normalization since $\int_{-\infty}^{\infty} |\psi|^2 \, dx = A^2 \int_{-\infty}^{\infty} \sin^2 kx \, dx$ is infinite for any nonzero value for A. For practical purposes we can usually normalize the waves ($A \neq 0$) by assuming that the particle is in a large but finite region of space. The region can be chosen large enough so that momentum is still rather precisely fixed.

38–8 Particle in an Infinitely Deep Square Well Potential (a Rigid Box)

FIGURE 38–7 A plot of potential energy U vs. x for an infinitely deep square well potential.

The Schrödinger equation can be solved analytically only for a few possible forms of the potential energy U. We consider some simple cases here which at first may not seem realistic, but have simple solutions that can be used as approximations to understand a variety of phenomena.

In our first case, we assume that a particle of mass m is confined to a one-dimensional box of width ℓ whose walls are perfectly rigid. (This can serve as an approximation for an electron in a metal, for example.) The particle is trapped in this box and collisions with the walls are perfectly elastic. The potential energy for this situation, which is commonly known as an **infinitely deep square well potential** or **rigid box**, is shown in Fig. 38–7. We can write the potential energy $U(x)$ as

$$U(x) = 0 \qquad 0 < x < \ell$$
$$U(x) = \infty \qquad x \le 0 \quad \text{and} \quad x \ge \ell.$$

For the region $0 < x < \ell$, where $U(x) = 0$, we already know the solution of the Schrödinger equation from our discussion in Section 38–7: it is just Eq. 38–10,

$$\psi(x) = A \sin kx + B \cos kx,$$

where (from Eq. 38–11a)

$$k = \sqrt{\frac{2mE}{\hbar^2}}.$$

(We could also use $\psi(x) = A \sin(kx + \phi)$ where ϕ is a phase constant.) Outside the well $U(x) = \infty$, so $\psi(x)$ must be zero. (If it weren't, the product $U\psi$ in the Schrödinger equation wouldn't be finite; besides, if $U = \infty$, we can't expect a particle of finite total energy to be in such a region.) So we are concerned only with the wave function within the well, and we must determine the constants A and B as well as any restrictions on the value of k (and hence on the energy E).

We have insisted that the wave function must be continuous. Hence, if $\psi = 0$ outside the well, it must be zero at $x = 0$ and at $x = \ell$:

$$\psi(0) = 0 \quad \text{and} \quad \psi(\ell) = 0.$$

These are the **boundary conditions** for this problem. At $x = 0$, $\sin kx = 0$ but $\cos kx = 1$, so at this point Eq. 38–10 yields

$$0 = \psi(0) = A \sin 0 + B \cos 0 = 0 + B.$$

Thus B must be zero. Our solution is reduced to

$$\psi(x) = A \sin kx.$$

Now we apply the other boundary condition, $\psi = 0$ at $x = \ell$:

$$0 = \psi(\ell) = A \sin k\ell.$$

We don't want $A = 0$ or we won't have a particle at all ($|\psi|^2 = 0$ everywhere). Therefore, we set

$$\sin k\ell = 0.$$

The sine is zero for angles of $0, \pi, 2\pi, 3\pi, \cdots$ radians, which means that $k\ell = 0, \pi, 2\pi, 3\pi, \cdots$. In other words,

$$k\ell = n\pi, \qquad n = 1, 2, 3, \cdots, \tag{38–12}$$

where n is an integer. We eliminate the case $n = 0$ since that would make $\psi = 0$ everywhere. Thus k, and hence E, cannot have just any value; rather, k is limited to values

$$k = \frac{n\pi}{\ell}.$$

Putting this expression in Eq. 38–11a (and substituting $h/2\pi$ for $\hbar$), we find that E

can have only the values

$$E = n^2 \frac{h^2}{8m\ell^2}, \qquad n = 1, 2, 3, \cdots. \qquad (38\text{–}13)$$

A particle trapped in a rigid box thus can only have certain *quantized energies*. The lowest energy (the ground state) has $n = 1$ and is given by

$$E_1 = \frac{h^2}{8m\ell^2}. \qquad \text{[ground state]}$$

The next highest energy $(n = 2)$ is

$$E_2 = 4E_1,$$

and for higher energies (see Fig. 38–8),

$$E_3 = 9E_1$$
$$\vdots$$
$$E_n = n^2 E_1.$$

The integer n is called the **quantum number** of the state.

That the lowest energy, E_1, is not zero means that the particle in the box can never be at rest. This is contrary to classical ideas, according to which a particle can have $E = 0$. E_1 is called the **zero-point energy**. One outcome of this result is that even at a temperature of absolute zero $(0\,\text{K})$, quantum mechanics predicts that particles in a box would not be at rest but would have a zero-point energy.

We also note that both the energy E_1 and momentum $p_1 = \hbar k = \hbar\pi/\ell$ (Eq. 38–11b) in the ground state are related inversely to the width of the box. The smaller the width ℓ, the larger the momentum (and energy). This can be considered a direct result of the uncertainty principle (see Problem 25).

The wave function $\psi = A \sin kx$ for each of the quantum states is (since $k = n\pi/\ell$)

$$\psi_n = A \sin\left(\frac{n\pi}{\ell} x\right). \qquad (38\text{–}14)$$

We can determine the constant A by imposing the normalization condition (Eq. 38–6c):

$$1 = \int_{-\infty}^{\infty} \psi^2 \, dx = \int_0^{\ell} A^2 \sin^2\left(\frac{n\pi}{\ell} x\right) dx, \qquad (38\text{–}15)$$

where the integral needs to be done only over the range $0 < x < \ell$ because outside these limits $\psi = 0$. The integral (see Example 38–6) is equal to $A^2\ell/2$, so we have

$$A = \sqrt{\frac{2}{\ell}} \qquad \text{and} \qquad \psi_n = \sqrt{\frac{2}{\ell}} \sin\left(\frac{n\pi}{\ell} x\right).$$

The amplitude A is the same for all the quantum numbers. Figure 38–9 shows the wave functions (Eq. 38–14) for $n = 1, 2, 3,$ and 10. They look just like standing waves on a string—see Fig. 15–26. This is not surprising since the wave function solutions, Eq. 38–14, are the same as for the standing waves on a string, and the condition $k\ell = n\pi$ is the same in the two cases (page 414).

Figure 38–10 shows the probability distribution, $|\psi|^2$, for the same states $(n = 1, 2, 3, 10)$ for which ψ is shown in Fig. 38–9. We see immediately that the particle is more likely to be found in some places than in others. For example, in the ground state $(n = 1)$, the electron is much more likely to be found near the center of the box than near the walls. This is clearly at variance with classical ideas, which predict a uniform probability density—the particle would be as likely to be found at one point in the box as at any other. The quantum-mechanical probability densities for higher states are even more complicated, with areas of low probability not only near the walls but also at regular intervals in between.

FIGURE 38–8 Possible energy levels for a particle in a box with perfectly rigid walls (infinite square well potential).

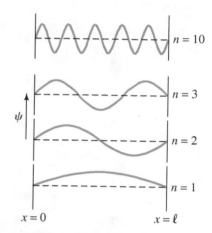

FIGURE 38–9 Wave functions corresponding to the quantum number n being 1, 2, 3, and 10 for a particle confined to a rigid box.

FIGURE 38–10 The probability distribution for a particle in a rigid box for the states with $n = 1, 2, 3,$ and 10.

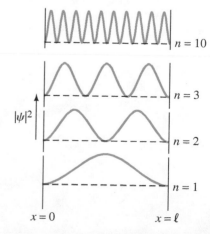

EXAMPLE 38–5 **Electron in an infinite potential well.** (*a*) Calculate the three lowest energy levels for an electron trapped in an infinitely deep square well potential of width $\ell = 1.00 \times 10^{-10}$ m (about the diameter of a hydrogen atom in its ground state). (*b*) If a photon were emitted when the electron jumps from the $n = 2$ state to the $n = 1$ state, what would its wavelength be?

APPROACH The energy levels are given by Eq. 38–13. In (*b*), $hf = hc/\lambda = E_2 - E_1$.

SOLUTION (*a*) The ground state $(n = 1)$ has energy

$$E_1 = \frac{h^2}{8m\ell^2} = \frac{(6.63 \times 10^{-34}\,\text{J·s})^2}{8(9.11 \times 10^{-31}\,\text{kg})(1.00 \times 10^{-10}\,\text{m})^2} = 6.03 \times 10^{-18}\,\text{J}.$$

In electron volts this is

$$E_1 = \frac{6.03 \times 10^{-18}\,\text{J}}{1.60 \times 10^{-19}\,\text{J/eV}} = 37.7\,\text{eV}.$$

Then

$$E_2 = (2)^2 E_1 = 151\,\text{eV}$$
$$E_3 = (3)^2 E_1 = 339\,\text{eV}.$$

(*b*) The energy difference is $E_2 - E_1 = 151\,\text{eV} - 38\,\text{eV} = 113\,\text{eV}$ or 1.81×10^{-17} J, and this would equal the energy of the emitted photon (energy conservation). Its wavelength would be

$$\lambda = \frac{c}{f} = \frac{hc}{E} = \frac{(6.63 \times 10^{-34}\,\text{J·s})(3.00 \times 10^8\,\text{m/s})}{1.81 \times 10^{-17}\,\text{J}} = 1.10 \times 10^{-8}\,\text{m}$$

or 11.0 nm, which is in the ultraviolet region of the spectrum.

EXERCISE B The wavelength of a photon emitted in an $n = 3$ to $n = 1$ transition is (*a*) 0.062 nm, (*b*) 620 nm, (*c*) 301 nm, (*d*) 3.2×10^{-15} m, (*e*) 4.1 nm.

EXAMPLE 38–6 **Calculating a normalization constant.** Show that the normalization constant A for all wave functions describing a particle in an infinite potential well of width ℓ has a value of $A = \sqrt{2/\ell}$.

APPROACH The wave functions for various n are

$$\psi = A \sin \frac{n\pi x}{\ell}.$$

To normalize ψ, we must have (Eq. 38–15)

$$1 = \int_0^\ell |\psi|^2\, dx = \int_0^\ell A^2 \sin^2 \frac{n\pi x}{\ell}\, dx.$$

SOLUTION We need integrate only from 0 to ℓ since $\psi = 0$ for all other values of x. To evaluate this integral we let $\theta = n\pi x/\ell$ and use the trigonometric identity $\sin^2 \theta = \frac{1}{2}(1 - \cos 2\theta)$. Then, with $dx = \ell\, d\theta/n\pi$, we have

$$1 = A^2 \int_0^{n\pi} \sin^2 \theta \left(\frac{\ell}{n\pi}\right) d\theta = \frac{A^2 \ell}{2n\pi} \int_0^{n\pi} (1 - \cos 2\theta)\, d\theta$$

$$= \frac{A^2 \ell}{2n\pi} \left(\theta - \tfrac{1}{2}\sin 2\theta\right)\Big|_0^{n\pi}$$

$$= \frac{A^2 \ell}{2}.$$

Thus $A^2 = 2/\ell$ and

$$A = \sqrt{\frac{2}{\ell}}.$$

EXAMPLE 38–7 **ESTIMATE** **Probability near center of rigid box.** An electron is in an infinitely deep square well potential of width $\ell = 1.00 \times 10^{-10}$ m. If the electron is in the ground state, what is the probability of finding it in a region of width $\Delta x = 1.0 \times 10^{-12}$ m at the center of the well (at $x = 0.50 \times 10^{-10}$ m)?

APPROACH The probability of finding a particle in a small region of width dx is $|\psi|^2 \, dx$ (Eq. 38–6b). Using A from Example 38–6, the wave function for the ground state is

$$\psi(x) = \sqrt{\frac{2}{\ell}} \sin \frac{\pi x}{\ell}.$$

SOLUTION The $n = 1$ curve in Fig. 38–9 shows that ψ is roughly constant near the center of the well. So we can avoid doing an integral over dx and just set $dx \approx \Delta x$ and find

$$|\psi|^2 \, \Delta x \;=\; \frac{2}{\ell} \sin^2 \left[\frac{\pi x}{\ell} \right] \Delta x$$

$$= \frac{2}{(1.00 \times 10^{-10}\,\text{m})} \sin^2 \left[\frac{\pi (0.50 \times 10^{-10}\,\text{m})}{(1.00 \times 10^{-10}\,\text{m})} \right] (1.0 \times 10^{-12}\,\text{m}) \;=\; 0.02.$$

The probability of finding the electron in this region at the center of the well is thus 2%.

NOTE Since $\Delta x = 1.0 \times 10^{-12}$ m is 1% of the well width of 1.00×10^{-10} m, our result of 2% probability is not what would be expected classically. Classically, the electron would be equally likely to be anywhere in the box, and we would expect the probability to be 1% instead of 2%.

EXAMPLE 38–8 **Probability of e^- in $\frac{1}{4}$ of box.** Determine the probability of finding an electron in the left quarter of a rigid box—i.e., between one wall at $x = 0$ and position $x = \ell/4$. Assume the electron is in the ground state.

APPROACH We cannot make the assumption we did in Example 38–7 that $|\psi|^2 \approx$ constant and Δx is small. Here we need to integrate $|\psi|^2 \, dx$ from $x = 0$ to $x = \ell/4$, which is equal to the area under the curve shown colored in Fig. 38–11.

SOLUTION The wave function in the ground state is $\psi_1 = \sqrt{2/\ell} \, \sin(\pi x/\ell)$. To find the probability of the electron in the left quarter of the box, we integrate just as in Example 38–6 but with different limits on the integral (and now we know that $A = \sqrt{2/\ell}$). That is, we set $\theta = \pi x/\ell$ (then $x = \ell/4$ corresponds to $\theta = \pi/4$) and use the identity $\sin^2 \theta = \frac{1}{2}(1 - \cos 2\theta)$. Thus, with $dx = (\ell/\pi)d\theta$,

$$\int_0^{\ell/4} |\psi|^2 \, dx = \frac{2}{\ell} \int_0^{\ell/4} \sin^2 \left(\frac{\pi}{\ell} x \right) dx$$

$$= \frac{1}{\ell} \int_0^{\pi/4} (1 - \cos 2\theta) \left(\frac{\ell}{\pi} \right) d\theta$$

$$= \frac{1}{\pi} \left(\theta - \frac{1}{2} \sin 2\theta \right) \Bigg|_0^{\pi/4}$$

$$= \frac{1}{4} - \frac{1}{2\pi} = 0.091.$$

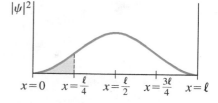

FIGURE 38–11 Ground-state probability distribution $|\psi|^2$ for an electron in a rigid box. Same as $n = 1$ graph of Fig. 38–10; but here we show the area under the curve from $x = 0$ to $x = \ell/4$ which represents the probability of finding the electron in that region.

NOTE The electron spends only 9.1% of its time in the left quarter of the box. Classically it would spend 25%.

EXERCISE C What is the probability of finding the electron between $x = \ell/4$ and $x = \ell/2$? (Do you need to integrate?) (a) 9.1%; (b) 18.2%; (c) 25%; (d) 33%; (e) 40.9%.

EXAMPLE 38–9 **Most likely and average positions.** Two interesting quantities are the most likely position of a particle and the average position of the particle. Consider an electron in a rigid box of width 1.00×10^{-10} m in the first excited state $n = 2$. (a) What is its most likely position? (b) What is its average position?

APPROACH To find (a) the most likely position (or positions), we find the maximum value(s) of the probability distribution $|\psi|^2$ by taking its derivative and setting it equal to zero. For (b), the average position, we integrate $\overline{x} = \int_0^\ell x |\psi|^2 \, dx$.

SOLUTION (a) The wave function for $n = 2$ is $\psi(x) = \sqrt{\dfrac{2}{\ell}} \sin\left(\dfrac{2\pi}{\ell} x\right)$, so $|\psi(x)|^2 = \dfrac{2}{\ell} \sin^2\left(\dfrac{2\pi}{\ell} x\right)$. To find maxima and minima, we set $d|\psi|^2/dx = 0$:

$$\frac{d}{dx} |\psi|^2 = \frac{2}{\ell} (2) \frac{2\pi}{\ell} \sin\left(\frac{2\pi}{\ell} x\right) \cos\left(\frac{2\pi}{\ell} x\right).$$

This quantity is zero when either the sine is zero ($2\pi x/\ell = 0, \pi, 2\pi, \cdots$), or the cosine is zero ($2\pi x/\ell = \pi/2, 3\pi/2, \cdots$). The maxima and minima occur at $x = 0$, $\ell/2, \ell$, and $x = \ell/4, 3\ell/4$. The latter ($\ell/4, 3\ell/4$) are the maxima—see the $n = 2$ curve of Fig. 38–10; the others are minima. [To confirm, you can take the second derivative, $d^2|\psi|^2/dx^2$, which is >0 for minima and <0 for maxima.]

(b) The average position is (again we use $\sin^2 \theta = \frac{1}{2}(1 - \cos 2\theta)$):

$$\overline{x} = \int_0^\ell x |\psi|^2 \, dx = \int_0^\ell \frac{2}{\ell} x \sin^2\left(\frac{2\pi}{\ell} x\right) dx = \frac{1}{\ell} \int_0^\ell x \left[1 - \cos\left(\frac{4\pi}{\ell} x\right)\right] dx,$$

which gives (integrating by parts, Appendix B: $u = x$, $dv = \cos(4\pi x/\ell) \, dx$):

$$\overline{x} = \frac{1}{\ell} \left[\frac{x^2}{2} - \frac{x\ell}{4\pi} \sin\left(\frac{4\pi}{\ell} x\right) - \frac{\ell^2}{16\pi^2} \cos\left(\frac{4\pi}{\ell} x\right)\right]_0^\ell = \frac{\ell}{2}.$$

Since the curves for $|\psi|^2$ are symmetric about the center of the box, we expect this answer. But note that for $n = 2$, the probability of finding the particle at the point $x = \ell/2$ is actually zero (Fig. 38–10).

EXAMPLE 38–10 **ESTIMATE** **Confined bacterium.** A tiny bacterium with a mass of about 10^{-14} kg is confined between two rigid walls 0.1 mm apart. (a) Estimate its minimum speed. (b) If, instead, its speed is about 1 mm in 100 s, estimate the quantum number of its state.

APPROACH We assume $U = 0$ inside the potential well, so $E = \frac{1}{2} mv^2$. In (a) the minimum speed occurs in the ground state, $n = 1$, so $v = \sqrt{2E/m}$ where E is the ground-state energy. In (b) we solve Eq. 38–13 for n.

SOLUTION (a) With $n = 1$, Eq. 38–13 gives $E = h^2/8m\ell^2$ so

$$v = \sqrt{\frac{2E}{m}} = \sqrt{\frac{h^2}{4m^2\ell^2}} = \frac{h}{2m\ell} = \frac{6.6 \times 10^{-34} \text{ J} \cdot \text{s}}{2(10^{-14} \text{ kg})(10^{-4} \text{ m})} \approx 3 \times 10^{-16} \text{ m/s}.$$

This is a speed so small that we could not measure it and the object would seem at rest, consistent with classical physics.

(b) Given $v = 10^{-3} \text{ m}/100 \text{ s} = 10^{-5} \text{ m/s}$, the kinetic energy of the bacterium is

$$E = \tfrac{1}{2} mv^2 = \tfrac{1}{2}(10^{-14} \text{ kg})(10^{-5} \text{ m/s})^2 = 0.5 \times 10^{-24} \text{ J}.$$

From Eq. 38–13, the quantum number of this state is

$$n = \sqrt{E\left(\frac{8m\ell^2}{h^2}\right)} = \sqrt{\frac{(0.5 \times 10^{-24} \text{ J})(8)(10^{-14} \text{ kg})(10^{-4} \text{ m})^2}{(6.6 \times 10^{-34} \text{ J} \cdot \text{s})^2}} \approx 3 \times 10^{10}.$$

NOTE This number is so large that we could never distinguish between adjacent energy states (between $n = 3 \times 10^{10}$ and $3 \times 10^{10} + 1$). The energy states would appear to form a continuum. Thus, even though the energies involved here are small ($\ll 1$ eV), we are still dealing with a macroscopic object (though visible only under a microscope) and the quantum result is not distinguishable from a classical one. This is in accordance with the correspondence principle.

38–9 Finite Potential Well

Let us now look at a particle in a box whose walls are not perfectly rigid. That is, the potential energy outside the box or well is not infinite, but rises to some level U_0, as shown in Fig. 38–12. This is called a **finite potential well**. It can serve as an approximation for, say, a neutron in a nucleus. There are some significant new features that arise for the finite well as compared to the infinite well. We divide the well into three regions as shown in Fig. 38–12. In region II, inside the well, the Schrödinger equation is the same as before $(U = 0)$, although the boundary conditions will be different. So we write the solution for region II as

$$\psi_{II} = A \sin kx + B \cos kx \quad (0 < x < \ell)$$

but we don't immediately set $B = 0$ or assume that k is given by Eq. 38–12.

In regions I and III, the Schrödinger equation, now with $U(x) = U_0$, is

$$-\frac{\hbar^2}{2m}\frac{d^2\psi}{dx^2} + U_0\psi = E\psi.$$

We rewrite this as

$$\frac{d^2\psi}{dx^2} - \left[\frac{2m(U_0 - E)}{\hbar^2}\right]\psi = 0.$$

Let us assume that E is less than U_0, so the particle is "trapped" in the well (at least classically). There might be only one such **bound state**, or several, or even none, as we shall discuss later. We define the constant G by

$$G^2 = \frac{2m(U_0 - E)}{\hbar^2} \tag{38–16}$$

and rewrite the Schrödinger equation as

$$\frac{d^2\psi}{dx^2} - G^2\psi = 0.$$

This equation has the general solution

$$\psi_{I, III} = Ce^{Gx} + De^{-Gx},$$

which can be confirmed by direct substitution, since

$$\frac{d^2}{dx^2}\left(e^{\pm Gx}\right) = G^2 e^{\pm Gx}.$$

In region I, x is always negative, so D must be zero (otherwise, $\psi \to \infty$ as $x \to -\infty$, giving an unacceptable result). Similarly in region III, where x is always positive, C must be zero. Hence

$$\psi_I = Ce^{Gx} \quad (x < 0)$$

$$\psi_{III} = De^{-Gx} \quad (x > \ell).$$

In regions I and III, the wave function decreases exponentially with distance from the well. The mathematical forms of the wave function inside and outside the well are different, but we insist that the wave function be continuous even at the two walls. We also insist that the slope of ψ, which is its first derivative, be continuous at the walls. Hence we have the boundary conditions:

$$\psi_I = \psi_{II} \quad \text{and} \quad \frac{d\psi_I}{dx} = \frac{d\psi_{II}}{dx} \quad \text{at } x = 0$$

$$\psi_{II} = \psi_{III} \quad \text{and} \quad \frac{d\psi_{II}}{dx} = \frac{d\psi_{III}}{dx} \quad \text{at } x = \ell.$$

At the left-hand wall $(x = 0)$ these boundary conditions become

$$Ce^0 = A \sin 0 + B \cos 0 \quad \text{or} \quad C = B$$

and

$$GCe^0 = kA \cos 0 - kB \sin 0 \quad \text{or} \quad GC = kA.$$

These are two of the relations that link the constants A, B, C, D and the energy E.

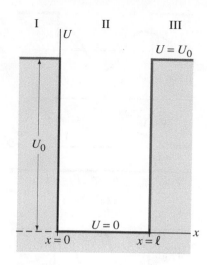

FIGURE 38–12 Potential energy U vs. x for a finite one-dimensional square well.

(a)

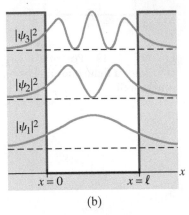

(b)

FIGURE 38–13 The wave functions (a), and probability distributions (b), for the three lowest possible states of a particle in a finite potential well. Each of the ψ and $|\psi|^2$ curves has been superposed on its energy level (dashed lines) for convenience.

FIGURE 38–14 The wave function of a particle of energy E traveling over a potential well whose depth U_0 is less than E (measured in the well).

We get two more relations from the boundary conditions at $x = \ell$, and a fifth relation from normalizing the wave functions over all space, $\int_{-\infty}^{\infty} |\psi|^2 \, dx = 1$. These five relations allow us to solve for the five unknowns, including the energy E. We will not go through the detailed mathematics, but we will discuss some of the results.

Figure 38–13a shows the wave function ψ for the three lowest possible states, and Fig. 38–13b shows the probability distributions $|\psi|^2$. We see that the wave functions are smooth at the walls of the well. Within the well ψ has the form of a sinusoidal wave; for the ground state, there is less than a half wavelength. Compare this to the infinite well (Fig. 38–9), where the ground-state wave function is exactly a half wavelength: $\lambda = 2\ell$. For our finite well, $\lambda > 2\ell$. Thus for a finite well the momentum of a particle $(p = h/\lambda)$, and hence its ground-state energy, will be less than for an infinite well of the same width ℓ.

Outside the finite well we see that the wave function drops off exponentially on either side of the walls. That ψ is not zero beyond the walls means that the particle can sometimes be found outside the well. This completely contradicts classical ideas. Outside the well, the potential energy of the particle is greater than its total energy: $U_0 > E$. This violates conservation of energy. But we clearly see in Fig. 38–13b that the particle can spend some time outside the well, where $U_0 > E$ (although the penetration into this classically forbidden region is generally not far since $|\psi|^2$ decreases exponentially with distance from either wall). The penetration of a particle into a classically forbidden region is a very important result of quantum mechanics. But how can it be? How can we accept this nonconservation of energy? We can look to the uncertainty principle, in the form

$$\Delta E \, \Delta t \gtrsim \hbar.$$

It tells us that the energy can be uncertain, and can even be nonconserved, by an amount ΔE for very short times $\Delta t \sim \hbar/\Delta E$.

Now let us consider the situation when the total energy E of the particle is greater than U_0. In this case the particle is a free particle and everywhere its wave function is sinusoidal, Fig. 38–14. Its wavelength is different outside the well than inside, as shown. Since $K = \frac{1}{2}mv^2 = p^2/2m$, the wavelength in region II $(U = 0)$ is

$$\lambda = \frac{h}{p} = \frac{h}{\sqrt{2mE}} \qquad 0 < x < \ell,$$

whereas in regions I and III, where $p^2/2m = K = E - U_0$, the wavelength is longer and is given by

$$\lambda = \frac{h}{p} = \frac{h}{\sqrt{2m(E - U_0)}} \qquad x < 0 \quad \text{and} \quad x > \ell.$$

For $E > U_0$, any energy E is possible. But for $E < U_0$, as we saw above, the energy is quantized and only certain states are possible.

EXERCISE D An electron with energy $E = 6.0 \, \text{eV}$ is near a potential well of depth $U_0 = 4.5 \, \text{eV}$ and width $\ell = 10.0 \, \text{nm}$. What is the wavelength of the electron when it is inside the well? (a) $0.50 \, \text{nm}$; (b) $0.58 \, \text{nm}$; (c) $1.0 \, \text{nm}$; (d) $10 \, \text{nm}$; (e) $20 \, \text{nm}$.

[Another very interesting but more complicated well is the **simple harmonic oscillator** which has $U(x) = \frac{1}{2}Cx^2$ as we discussed in Chapter 14. Some quantum mechanical results, such as a zero-point energy of $\frac{1}{2}\hbar\omega$ (E cannot be zero), are treated briefly in Problem 52.]

38–10 Tunneling through a Barrier

We saw in Section 38–9 that, according to quantum mechanics, a particle such as an electron can penetrate a barrier into a region forbidden by classical mechanics. There are a number of important applications of this phenomenon, particularly as applied to penetration of a thin barrier.

We consider a particle of mass m and energy E traveling to the right along the x axis in free space where the potential energy $U = 0$ so the energy is all kinetic energy ($E = K$). The particle encounters a narrow potential barrier whose height U_0 (in energy units) is greater than E, and whose thickness is ℓ (distance units); see Fig. 38–15a. Since $E < U_0$, we would expect from classical physics that the particle could not penetrate the barrier but would simply be reflected and would return in the opposite direction. Indeed, this is what happens for macroscopic objects. But quantum mechanics predicts a nonzero probability for finding the particle on the other side of the barrier. We can see how this can happen in part (b) of Fig. 38–15, which shows the wave function. The approaching particle has a sinusoidal wave function. Within the barrier the solution to the Schrödinger equation is a decaying exponential just as for the finite well of Section 38–9. However, before the exponential dies away to zero, the barrier ends (at $x = \ell$), and for $x > \ell$ there is again a sinusoidal wave function, since $U = 0$ and $E = K > 0$. But it is a sine wave of greatly reduced amplitude. Nonetheless, because $|\psi|^2$ is nonzero beyond the barrier, we see that there is a nonzero probability that the particle penetrates the barrier. This process is called **tunneling** through the barrier, or **barrier penetration**. Although we cannot observe the particle within the barrier (it would violate conservation of energy), we can detect it after it has penetrated the barrier.

Quantitatively, we can describe the tunneling probability with a *transmission coefficient*, T, and a *reflection coefficient*, R. Suppose, for example, that $T = 0.03$ and $R = 0.97$; then if 100 particles struck the barrier, on the average 3 would tunnel through and 97 would be reflected. Note that $T + R = 1$, since an incident particle must either reflect or tunnel through. The transmission coefficient can be determined by writing the wave function for each of the three regions, just as we did for the finite well, and then applying the boundary conditions that ψ and $d\psi/dx$ must be continuous at the edges of the barrier ($x = 0$ and $x = \ell$). The calculation shows (see Problem 44) that if T is small ($\ll 1$), then

$$T \approx e^{-2G\ell}, \tag{38–17a}$$

where

$$G = \sqrt{\frac{2m(U_0 - E)}{\hbar^2}}. \tag{38–17b}$$

(This is the same G as in Section 38–9, Eq. 38–16.) We note that increasing the height of the barrier, U_0, or increasing its thickness, ℓ, will drastically reduce T. Indeed, for macroscopic situations, T is extremely small, in accord with classical physics, which predicts no tunneling (again the correspondence principle).

EXAMPLE 38–11 **Barrier penetration.** A 50-eV electron approaches a square barrier 70 eV high and (*a*) 1.0 nm thick, (*b*) 0.10 nm thick. What is the probability that the electron will tunnel through?

APPROACH We convert eV to joules and use Eqs. 38–17.

SOLUTION (*a*) Inside the barrier $U_0 - E = (70\,\text{eV} - 50\,\text{eV})(1.6 \times 10^{-19}\,\text{J/eV}) = 3.2 \times 10^{-18}\,\text{J}$. Then, using Eqs. 38–17, we have

$$2G\ell = 2\sqrt{\frac{2(9.11 \times 10^{-31}\,\text{kg})(3.2 \times 10^{-18}\,\text{J})}{(1.055 \times 10^{-34}\,\text{J·s})^2}}(1.0 \times 10^{-9}\,\text{m}) = 46$$

and

$$T = e^{-2G\ell} = e^{-46} \approx 1 \times 10^{-20},$$

which is extremely small.

(*b*) For $\ell = 0.10\,\text{nm}$, $2G\ell = 4.6$ and

$$T = e^{-4.6} = 0.010.$$

Thus the electron has a 1% chance of penetrating a 0.1-nm-thick barrier, but only 1 chance in 10^{20} to penetrate a 1-nm barrier. By reducing the barrier thickness by a factor of 10, the probability of tunneling through increases 10^{18} times! Clearly the transmission coefficient is extremely sensitive to the values of ℓ, $U_0 - E$, and m.

FIGURE 38–15 (a) A potential barrier of height U_0 and thickness ℓ. (b) The wave function for a particle of energy $E (< U_0)$ that approaches from the left. The curve for ψ is superposed, for convenience, on the energy level line (dashed).

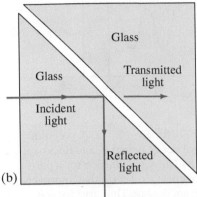

FIGURE 38–16 (a) Light traveling in glass strikes the interface with air at an angle greater than the critical angle, and is totally internally reflected. (b) A small amount of light tunnels through a narrow air gap between two pieces of glass.

FIGURE 38–17 Potential energy seen by an alpha particle (charge q) in presence of nucleus (charge Q), showing the wave function for tunneling out.

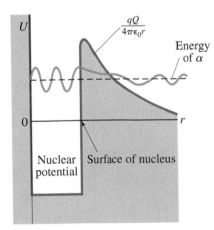

Tunneling of Light Wave

Tunneling is a result of the wave properties of material particles, and also occurs for classical waves. For example, we saw in Section 32–7 that, when light traveling in glass strikes a glass–air boundary at an angle greater than the critical angle, the light is 100% totally reflected. We studied this phenomenon of total internal reflection from the point of view of ray optics, and we show it here in Fig. 38–16a. The wave theory, however, predicts that waves actually penetrate the air for a few wavelengths—almost as if they "needed" to pass the interface to find out there is air beyond and hence need to be totally reflected. Indeed, if a second piece of glass is brought near the first as shown in Fig. 38–16b, a transmitted wave that has tunneled through the air gap can be experimentally observed. You can actually observe this for yourself by looking down into a glass of water at an angle such that light entering your eye has been totally internally reflected from the (outer) glass surface (it will look silvery). If you press a moistened fingertip against the glass, you can see the whorls of the ridges on your fingerprints, because at the ridges you have interfered with the total internal reflection at the outer surface of the glass. So you see light that has penetrated the gap and reflected off the ridges on your finger.

Applications of Tunneling

Tunneling thus occurs even for classical waves. What is new in quantum mechanics is that material particles have wave properties and hence can tunnel. Tunneling has provided the basis for a number of useful devices, as well as helped to explain a number of important phenomena, some of which we mention briefly now.

Some atomic nuclei undergo **radioactive decay** by the emission of an alpha (α) particle, which consists of two protons and two neutrons. Inside a radioactive nucleus, we can imagine that the protons and neutrons are moving about, and sometimes two of each come together and form this stable entity, the alpha particle. We will study alpha decay in more detail in Chapter 41, but for now we note that the potential energy diagram for the alpha particle inside this type of nucleus looks something like Fig. 38–17. The square well represents the attractive nuclear force that holds the nucleus together. To this is added the $1/r$ Coulomb potential energy of repulsion between the positive alpha particle and the remaining positively charged nucleus. The barrier that results is called the **Coulomb barrier**. The wave function for the tunneling particle shown must have energy greater than zero (or the barrier would be infinitely wide and tunneling could not occur), but less than the height of the barrier. If the alpha particle had energy higher than the barrier, it would always be free and the original nucleus wouldn't exist. Thus the barrier keeps the nucleus together, but occasionally a nucleus of this type can decay by the tunneling of an alpha particle. The probability of an α particle escaping, and hence the "lifetime" of a nucleus, depends on the height and width of the barrier, and can take on a very wide range of values for only a limited change in barrier width as we saw in Example 38–11. Lifetimes of α-decaying radioactive nuclei range from less than $1\,\mu\text{s}$ to 10^{10} yr.

A so-called **tunnel diode** is an electronic device made of two types of semiconductor carrying opposite-sign charge carriers, separated by a very thin neutral region. Current can tunnel through this thin barrier and can be controlled by the voltage applied to it, which affects the height of the barrier.

The **scanning tunneling electron microscope** (STM), developed in the 1980s, makes use of tunneling through a vacuum. A tiny probe, whose tip may be only one (or a few) atoms wide, is moved across the specimen to be examined in a series of linear passes, like those made by the electron beam in a TV tube or CRT. The tip, as it scans, remains very close to the surface of the specimen, about 1 nm above it, Fig. 38–18. A small voltage applied between the probe and the surface causes electrons to tunnel through the vacuum between them. This tunneling current is very sensitive to the gap width (see Example 38–11), so that a feedback mechanism can be used to raise and lower the probe to maintain a constant electron tunneling current. The probe's vertical motion, following the surface of the specimen, is then plotted as a function of position, scan after scan, producing a three-dimensional image of the surface. Surface features as fine as the size of an atom can be resolved: a resolution better than 0.1 nm laterally and 10^{-2} to 10^{-3} nm vertically. This kind of resolution was not available previously and has given a great impetus to the study of the surface structure of materials. The "topographic" image of a surface actually represents the distribution of electron charge (electron wave probability distributions) on the surface.

The new **atomic force microscope** (AFM) is in many ways similar to an STM, but can be used on a wider range of sample materials. Instead of detecting an electric current, the AFM measures the force between a cantilevered tip and the sample, a force which depends strongly on the tip–sample separation at each point. The tip is moved as for the STM.

FIGURE 38–18 The probe tip of a scanning tunneling microscope, as it is moved horizontally, automatically moves up and down to maintain a constant tunneling current, thus producing an image of the surface.

Summary

In 1925, Schrödinger and Heisenberg separately worked out a new theory, **quantum mechanics**, which is now considered to be the fundamental theory at the atomic level. It is a statistical theory rather than a deterministic one.

An important aspect of quantum mechanics is the **Heisenberg uncertainty principle**. It results from the wave–particle duality and the unavoidable interaction between the observed object and the observer.

One form of the uncertainty principle states that the position x and momentum p_x of an object cannot both be measured precisely at the same time. The products of the uncertainties, $(\Delta x)(\Delta p_x)$, can be no less than $\hbar \ (= h/2\pi)$:

$$(\Delta x)(\Delta p_x) \gtrsim \hbar. \tag{38–1}$$

Another form states that the energy can be uncertain, or nonconserved, by an amount ΔE for a time Δt where

$$(\Delta E)(\Delta t) \gtrsim \hbar. \tag{38–2}$$

A particle such as an electron is represented by a **wave function** ψ. The square of the wave function, $|\psi|^2$, at any point in space represents the **probability** of finding the particle at that point. The wave function must be **normalized**, meaning that $\int |\psi|^2 \, dV$ over all space must equal 1, since the particle must be found at one place or another.

In nonrelativistic quantum mechanics, ψ satisfies the **Schrödinger equation**:

$$-\frac{\hbar^2}{2m}\frac{d^2\psi}{dx^2} + U\psi = E\psi, \tag{38–5}$$

here in its one-dimensional time-independent form, where U is the potential energy as a function of position and E is the total energy of the particle.

A **free particle** subject to no forces has a sinusoidal wave function $\psi = A \sin kx + B \cos kx$ with $k = p/\hbar$ and p is the particle's momentum. Such a wave of fixed momentum is spread out indefinitely in space as a plane wave.

A **wave packet**, localized in space, is a superposition of sinusoidal waves with a range of momenta.

For a particle confined to an **infinitely deep square well potential**, or **rigid box**, the Schrödinger equation gives the wave functions as

$$\psi = A \sin k\ell,$$

where ℓ is the width of the box, $A = \sqrt{2/\ell}$, and $k = n\pi/\ell$ with n an integer, as solutions inside the well. The energy is quantized,

$$E = \frac{\hbar^2 k^2}{2m} = \frac{n^2 h^2}{8m\ell^2}. \tag{38–13}$$

In a **finite potential well**, the wave function extends into the classically forbidden region where the total energy is less than the potential energy. That this is possible is consistent with the uncertainty principle. The solutions to the Schrödinger equation in these areas are decaying exponentials.

Because quantum-mechanical particles can penetrate such classically forbidden areas, they can **tunnel** through thin barriers even though the potential energy in the barrier is greater than the total energy of the particle.

Questions

1. Compare a matter wave ψ to (a) a wave on a string, (b) an EM wave. Discuss similarities and differences.
2. Explain why Bohr's theory of the atom is not compatible with quantum mechanics, particularly the uncertainty principle.
3. Explain why it is that the more massive an object is, the easier it becomes to predict its future position.
4. In view of the uncertainty principle, why does a baseball seem to have a well-defined position and speed, whereas an electron does not?

5. Would it ever be possible to balance a very sharp needle precisely on its point? Explain.

6. When you check the pressure in a tire, doesn't some air inevitably escape? Is it possible to avoid this escape of air altogether? What is the relation to the uncertainty principle?

7. It has been said that the ground-state energy in the hydrogen atom can be precisely known but that the excited states have some uncertainty in their values (an "energy width"). Is this consistent with the uncertainty principle in its energy form? Explain.

8. If Planck's constant were much larger than it is, how would this affect our everyday life?

9. In what ways is Newtonian mechanics contradicted by quantum mechanics?

10. If you knew the position of an object precisely, with no uncertainty, how well would you know its momentum?

11. A cold thermometer is placed in a hot bowl of soup. Will the temperature reading of the thermometer be the same as the temperature of the hot soup before the measurement was made? Explain.

12. Does the uncertainty principle set a limit to how well you can make any single measurement of position?

13. Discuss the connection between the zero-point energy for a particle in a rigid box and the uncertainty principle.

14. The wave function for a particle in a rigid box is zero at points within the box (except for $n = 1$). Does this mean that the probability of finding the particle at these points is zero? Does it mean that the particle cannot pass by these points? Explain.

15. What does the probability density look like for a particle in an infinite potential well for large values of n, say $n = 100$ or $n = 1000$? As n becomes very large, do your predictions approach classical predictions in accord with the correspondence principle?

16. For a particle in an infinite potential well the separation between energy states increases as n increases (see Eq. 38–13). But doesn't the correspondence principle require closer spacing between states as n increases so as to approach a classical (nonquantized) situation? Explain.

17. A particle is trapped in an infinite potential well. Describe what happens to the particle's ground-state energy and wave function as the potential walls become finite and get lower and lower until they finally reach zero ($U = 0$ everywhere).

18. A hydrogen atom and a helium atom, each with 4 eV of kinetic energy, approach a thin barrier 6 MeV high. Which has the greater probability of tunneling through?

Problems

38–2 Wave Function, Double-Slit

1. (II) The neutrons in a parallel beam, each having kinetic energy 0.030 eV, are directed through two slits 0.60 mm apart. How far apart will the interference peaks be on a screen 1.0 m away? [*Hint*: First find the wavelength of the neutron.]

2. (II) Pellets of mass 3.0 g are fired in parallel paths with speeds of 150 m/s through a hole 3.0 mm in diameter. How far from the hole must you be to detect a 1.0-cm-diameter spread in the beam of pellets?

38–3 Uncertainty Principle

3. (I) A proton is traveling with a speed of $(7.560 \pm 0.012) \times 10^5$ m/s. With what maximum precision can its position be ascertained?

4. (I) An electron remains in an excited state of an atom for typically 10^{-8} s. What is the minimum uncertainty in the energy of the state (in eV)?

5. (I) If an electron's position can be measured to a precision of 2.6×10^{-8} m, how precisely can its speed be known?

6. (I) The lifetime of a typical excited state in an atom is about 10 ns. Suppose an atom falls from one such excited state and emits a photon of wavelength about 500 nm. Find the fractional energy uncertainty $\Delta E/E$ and wavelength uncertainty $\Delta \lambda/\lambda$ of this photon.

7. (I) A radioactive element undergoes an alpha decay with a lifetime of $12\,\mu s$. If alpha particles are emitted with 5.5-keV kinetic energy, find the uncertainty $\Delta E/E$ in the particle energy.

8. (II) A 12-g bullet leaves a rifle horizontally at a speed of 180 m/s. (a) What is the wavelength of this bullet? (b) If the position of the bullet is known to a precision of 0.65 cm (radius of the barrel), what is the minimum uncertainty in its vertical momentum?

9. (II) An electron and a 140-g baseball are each traveling 95 m/s measured to a precision of 0.085%. Calculate and compare the uncertainty in position of each.

10. (II) What is the uncertainty in the mass of a muon ($m = 105.7$ MeV/c^2), specified in eV/c^2, given its lifetime of $2.20\,\mu s$?

11. (II) A free neutron ($m = 1.67 \times 10^{-27}$ kg) has a mean life of 900 s. What is the uncertainty in its mass (in kg)?

12. (II) Use the uncertainty principle to show that if an electron were present in the nucleus ($r \approx 10^{-15}$ m), its kinetic energy (use relativity) would be hundreds of MeV. (Since such electron energies are not observed, we conclude that electrons are not present in the nucleus.) [*Hint*: Assume a particle can have energy as large as its uncertainty.]

13. (II) An electron in the $n = 2$ state of hydrogen remains there on average about 10^{-8} s before jumping to the $n = 1$ state. (a) Estimate the uncertainty in the energy of the $n = 2$ state. (b) What fraction of the transition energy is this? (c) What is the wavelength, and width (in nm), of this line in the spectrum of hydrogen?

14. (II) How accurately can the position of a 3.50-keV electron be measured assuming its energy is known to 1.00%?

15. (III) In a double-slit experiment on electrons (or photons), suppose that we use indicators to determine which slit each electron went through (Section 38–2). These indicators must tell us the y coordinate to within $d/2$, where d is the distance between slits. Use the uncertainty principle to show that the interference pattern will be destroyed. [*Note*: First show that the angle θ between maxima and minima of the interference pattern is given by $\frac{1}{2}\lambda/d$, Fig. 38–19.]

FIGURE 38–19 Problem 15.

*38–6 Time-Dependent Schrödinger Equation

*16. (II) Show that the superposition principle holds for the time-dependent Schrödinger equation. That is, show that if $\Psi_1(x, t)$ and $\Psi_2(x, t)$ are solutions, then $A\Psi_1(x, t) + B\Psi_2(x, t)$ is also a solution where A and B are arbitrary constants.

*17. (III) (a) Show that $\Psi(x, t) = Ae^{i(kx-\omega t)}$ is a solution to the time-dependent Schrödinger equation for a free particle $[U(x) = U_0 = \text{constant}]$ but that $\Psi(x, t) = A\cos(kx - \omega t)$ and $\Psi(x, t) = A\sin(kx - \omega t)$ are not. (b) Show that the valid solution of part (a) satisfies conservation of energy if the de Broglie relations hold; $\lambda = h/p$, $\omega = E/\hbar$. That is, show that direct substitution into Eq. 38–7 gives

$$\hbar\omega = \frac{\hbar^2 k^2}{2m} + U_0.$$

38–7 Free Particles; Plane Waves; Wave Packets

18. (I) A free electron has a wave function $\psi(x) = A\sin(2.0 \times 10^{10} x)$, where x is given in meters. Determine the electron's (a) wavelength, (b) momentum, (c) speed, and (d) kinetic energy.

19. (I) Write the wave function for (a) a free electron and (b) a free proton, each having a constant velocity $v = 3.0 \times 10^5$ m/s.

20. (III) Show that the uncertainty principle holds for a "wave packet" that is formed by two waves of similar wavelength λ_1 and λ_2. To do so, follow the argument leading up to Eq. 16–8, but use as the two waves $\psi_1 = A\sin k_1 x$ and $\psi_2 = A\sin k_2 x$. Then show that the width of each "wave packet" is $\Delta x = 2\pi/(k_1 - k_2) = 2\pi/\Delta k$ (from $t = 0.05$ s to $t = 0.15$ s in Fig. 16–17). Finally, show that $\Delta x \Delta p = h$ for this simple situation.

38–8 Infinite Square Well

21. (II) What is the minimum speed of an electron trapped in a 0.20-nm-wide infinitely deep square well?

22. (II) Show that for a particle in a perfectly rigid box, the wavelength of the wave function for any state is the de Broglie wavelength.

23. (II) An electron trapped in an infinitely deep square well has a ground-state energy $E = 9.0$ eV. (a) What is the longest wavelength photon that an excited state of this system can emit? (b) What is the width of the well?

24. (II) An $n = 4$ to $n = 1$ transition for an electron trapped in a rigid box produces a 340-nm photon. What is the width of the box?

25. (II) For a particle in a box with rigid walls, determine whether our results for the ground state are consistent with the uncertainty principle by calculating the product $\Delta p \Delta x$. Take $\Delta x \approx \ell$, since the particle is somewhere within the box. For Δp, note that although p is known $(= \hbar k)$, the direction of $\vec{p}$ is not known, so the x component could vary from $-p$ to $+p$; hence take $\Delta p \approx 2p$.

26. (II) The longest-wavelength line in the spectrum emitted by an electron trapped in an infinitely deep square well is 610 nm. What is the width of the well?

27. (II) Determine the lowest four energy levels and wave functions for an electron trapped in an infinitely deep potential well of width 2.0 nm.

28. (II) Write a formula for the positions of (a) the maxima and (b) the minima in $|\psi|^2$ for a particle in the nth state in an infinite square well.

29. (II) Consider an atomic nucleus to be a rigid box of width 2.0×10^{-14} m. What would be the ground-state energy for (a) an electron, (b) a neutron, and (c) a proton in this nucleus?

30. (II) A proton in a nucleus can be roughly modeled as a particle in a box of nuclear dimensions. Calculate the energy released when a proton confined in a nucleus of width 1.0×10^{-14} m makes a transition from the first excited state to the ground state.

31. (II) Consider a single oxygen molecule confined in a one-dimensional rigid box of width 4.0 mm. (a) Treating this as a particle in a rigid box, determine the ground-state energy. (b) If the molecule has an energy equal to the one-dimensional average thermal energy $\frac{1}{2}kT$ at $T = 300$ K, what is the quantum number n? (c) What is the energy difference between the nth state and the next higher state?

32. (II) An electron is trapped in a 1.00-nm-wide rigid box. Determine the probability of finding the electron within 0.15 nm of the center of the box (on either side of center) for (a) $n = 1$, (b) $n = 5$, and (c) $n = 20$. (d) Compare to the classical prediction.

33. (III) If an infinitely deep well of width ℓ is redefined to be located from $x = -\frac{1}{2}\ell$ to $x = \frac{1}{2}\ell$ (as opposed to $x = 0$ to $x = \ell$), speculate how this will change the wave function for a particle in this well. Investigate your speculation(s) by determining the wave functions and energy levels for this newly defined well. [*Hint*: Try $\psi = A\sin(kx + \phi)$.]

38–9 Finite Potential Well

34. (II) An electron with 180 eV of kinetic energy in free space passes over a finite potential well 56 eV deep that stretches from $x = 0$ to $x = 0.50$ nm. What is the electron's wavelength (a) in free space, (b) when over the well? (c) Draw a diagram showing the potential energy and total energy as a function of x, and on the diagram sketch a possible wave function.

35. (II) Sketch the wave functions and the probability distributions for the $n = 4$ and $n = 5$ states for a particle trapped in a finite square well.

36. (II) Suppose that a particle of mass m is trapped in a finite potential well that has a rigid wall at $x = 0$ ($U = \infty$ for $x < 0$) and a finite wall of height $U = U_0$ at $x = \ell$, Fig. 38–20. (a) Sketch the wave functions for the lowest three states. (b) What is the form of the wave function in the ground state in the three regions $x < 0$, $0 < x < \ell$, $x > \ell$?

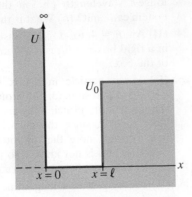

FIGURE 38–20
Problem 36.

37. (II) An electron is trapped in a 0.16-nm-wide finite square well of height $U_0 = 2.0\,\text{keV}$. Estimate at what distance outside the walls of the well the ground state wave function drops to 1.0% of its value at the walls.

38–10 Tunneling

38. (II) A potential barrier has a height $U_0 = 14\,\text{eV}$ and thickness $\ell = 0.85\,\text{nm}$. If the transmission coefficient for an incident electron is 0.00050, what is the electron's energy?

39. (II) An electron approaches a potential barrier 18 eV high and 0.55 nm wide. If the electron has a 1.0% probability of tunneling through the barrier, what is the electron's energy?

40. (II) A proton and a helium nucleus approach a 25-MeV potential energy barrier. If each has a kinetic energy of 5.0 MeV, what is the probability of each to tunnel through the barrier, assuming it is rectangular and 3.6 fm thick?

41. (II) An electron with an energy of 8.0 eV is incident on a potential barrier which is 9.2 eV high and 0.25 nm wide. (a) What is the probability that the electron will pass through the barrier? (b) What is the probability that the electron will be reflected?

42. (II) A 1.0-mA current of 1.6-MeV protons strikes a 2.6-MeV-high potential barrier 2.8×10^{-13} m thick. Estimate the transmitted current.

43. (II) For part (b) of Example 38–11, what effect will there be on the transmission coefficient if (a) the barrier height is raised 2.0%, (b) the barrier thickness is increased by 2.0%?

44. (II) Show that the transmission coefficient is given roughly by Eqs. 38–17 for a high or thick barrier, by calculating $|\psi(x = \ell)|^2/|\psi(0)|^2$. [Hint: Assume that ψ is a decaying exponential inside the barrier.]

45. (III) A uranium-238 nucleus ($Q = +92e$) lasts about 4.5×10^9 years before it decays by emission of an alpha particle ($q = +2e$, $M = 4M_{\text{proton}}$). (a) Assuming that the α particle is a point, and the nucleus is roughly 8 fm in radius, estimate the height of the Coulomb barrier (the peak in Fig. 38–17). (b) The alpha particle, when free, has kinetic energy $\approx 4\,\text{MeV}$. Estimate the width of the barrier. (c) Assuming that the square well has $U = 0$ inside (and $U = 0$ far from the nucleus), calculate the speed of the alpha particle and how often it hits the barrier inside, and from this (and Eqs. 38–17) estimate the uranium lifetime. [Hint: Replace the $1/r$ Coulomb barrier with an "averaged" rectangular barrier (as in Fig. 38–15) of width equal to $\frac{1}{3}$ that calculated in (b).]

General Problems

46. The Z^0 boson, discovered in 1985, is the mediator of the weak nuclear force, and it typically decays very quickly. Its average rest energy is 91.19 GeV, but its short lifetime shows up as an intrinsic width of 2.5 GeV. What is the lifetime of this particle?

47. Estimate the lowest possible energy of a neutron contained in a typical nucleus of radius 1.2×10^{-15} m. [Hint: A particle can have an energy at least as large as its uncertainty.]

48. A neutron is trapped in an infinitely deep potential well 2.5 fm in width. Determine (a) the four lowest possible energy states and (b) their wave functions. (c) What is the wavelength and energy of a photon emitted when the neutron makes a transition between the two lowest states? In what region of the EM spectrum does this photon lie? [Note: This is a rough model of an atomic nucleus.]

49. Protons are accelerated from rest across 650 V. They are then directed at two slits 0.80 mm apart. How far apart will the interference peaks be on a screen 18 m away?

50. An electron and a proton, each initially at rest, are accelerated across the same voltage. Assuming that the uncertainty in their position is given by their de Broglie wavelength, find the ratio of the uncertainty in their momentum.

51. Use the uncertainty principle to estimate the position uncertainty for the electron in the ground state of the hydrogen atom. [Hint: Determine the momentum using the Bohr model of Section 37–11 and assume the momentum can be anywhere between this value and zero.] How does this compare to the Bohr radius?

52. **Simple Harmonic Oscillator.** Suppose that a particle of mass m is trapped not in a square well, but in one whose potential energy is that of a simple harmonic oscillator: $U(x) = \frac{1}{2}Cx^2$. That is, if the particle is displaced from $x = 0$, a restoring force $F = -Cx$ acts on it, where C is constant. (a) Sketch this potential energy. (b) Show that $\psi = Ae^{-Bx^2}$ is a solution to the Schrödinger equation and that the energy of this state is $E = \frac{1}{2}\hbar\omega$, where $\omega = \sqrt{C/m}$ (as classically, Eq. 14–5) and $B = m\omega/2\hbar$. [Note: This is the ground state, and this energy $\frac{1}{2}\hbar\omega$ is the zero-point energy for a harmonic oscillator. The energies of higher states are $E_n = (n + \frac{1}{2})\hbar\omega$, where n is an integer.]

53. Estimate the kinetic energy and speed of an alpha particle ($q = +2e$, $M = 4M_{\text{proton}}$) trapped in a nucleus 1.5×10^{-14} m wide. Assume an infinitely deep square well potential.

54. A small ball of mass 3.0×10^{-6} kg is dropped on a table from a height of 2.0 m. After each bounce the ball rises to 65% of its height before the bounce because of its inelastic collision with the table. Estimate how many bounces occur before the uncertainty principle plays a role in the problem. [*Hint*: Determine when the uncertainty in the ball's speed is comparable to its speed of impact on the table.]

55. By how much does the tunneling current through the tip of an STM change if the tip rises 0.020 nm from some initial height above a sodium surface with a work function $W_0 = 2.28$ eV? [*Hint*: Let the work function (see Section 37–2) equal the energy needed to raise the electron to the top of the barrier.]

56. Show that the function $\psi(x) = Ae^{ikx}$, where A is a constant and k is given by Eq. 38–11, is a solution of the time-independent Schrödinger equation for the case $U = 0$.

57. Show that the average value of the square of the position x of a particle in state n inside an infinite well of width ℓ is $\overline{x^2} = \int x^2 |\psi_n|^2 \, dx = \ell^2 [\frac{1}{3} - \frac{1}{2}(n\pi)^{-2}]$. Calculate the values of $\overline{x^2}$ for $n = 1$ to 20 and make a graph of $\overline{x^2}$ versus n. [*Hint*: You may want to consult a detailed Table of integrals.]

58. Consider a particle that can exist anywhere in space with a wave function given by $\psi(x) = b^{-\frac{3}{2}} |x/b|^{\frac{1}{2}} e^{-(x/b)^2/2}$, where $b = 1.0$ nm. (*a*) Check that the wave function is normalized. (*b*) What is the most probable position for the particle in the region $x > 0$? (*c*) What is the probability of finding the particle between $x = 0$ nm and $x = 0.50$ nm?

59. A 7.0-gram pencil, 18 cm long, is balanced on its point. Classically, this is a configuration of (unstable) equilibrium, so the pencil could remain there forever if it were perfectly placed. A quantum mechanical analysis shows that the pencil must fall. (*a*) Why is this the case? (*b*) Estimate (within a factor of 2) how long it will take the pencil to hit the table if it is initially positioned as well as possible? [*Hint*: Use the uncertainty principle in its angular form to obtain an expression for the initial angle $\phi_0 \approx \Delta\phi$.]

*Numerical/Computer

*60. (III) An electron is trapped in the ground state of an infinite potential well of width $\ell = 0.10$ nm. The probability that the electron will be found in the central 1% of the well was estimated in Example 38–7 by $|\psi|^2 \Delta x$. Use numerical methods to determine how large Δx could be to cause less than a 10% error in such an estimate.

*61. (III) Consider a particle of mass m and energy E traveling to the right where it encounters a narrow potential barrier of height U_0 and width ℓ as shown in Fig. 38–21. It can be shown that:
(i) for $E < U_0$, the transmission probability is

$$T = \left[1 + \frac{(e^{G\ell} - e^{-G\ell})^2}{16(E/U_0)(1 - E/U_0)} \right]^{-1}$$

where

$$G = \sqrt{\frac{2m(U_0 - E)}{\hbar^2}}$$

and the reflection probability is $R = 1 - T$;
(ii) for $E > U_0$, the transmission probability is

$$T = \left[1 + \frac{\sin^2(G'\ell)}{4(E/U_0)(E/U_0 - 1)} \right]^{-1}$$

where

$$G' = \sqrt{\frac{2m(E - U_0)}{\hbar^2}}$$

and $R = 1 - T$. Consider that the particle is an electron and it is incident on a rectangular barrier of height $U_0 = 10$ eV and width $\ell = 1.0 \times 10^{-10}$ m. (*a*) Calculate T and R for the electron from $E/U_0 = 0$ to 10, in steps of 0.1. Make a single graph showing the two curves of T and R as a function of E/U_0. (*b*) From the graph determine the energies (E/U_0) at which the electron will have transmission probabilities of 10%, 20%, 50%, and 80%.

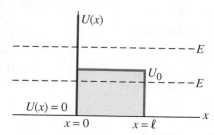

FIGURE 38–21 Problem 61.

Answers to Exercises

A: (*c*).

B: (*e*).

C: (*e*).

D: (*a*).

A neon tube is a thin glass tube, moldable into various shapes, filled with neon (or other) gas that glows with a particular color when a current at high voltage passes through it. Gas atoms, excited to upper energy levels, jump down to lower energy levels and emit light (photons) whose wavelengths (color) are characteristic of the type of gas.

In this Chapter we study what quantum mechanics tells us about atoms, their wave functions and energy levels, including the effect of the exclusion principle. We also discuss interesting applications such as lasers and holography.

Quantum Mechanics of Atoms

CHAPTER-OPENING QUESTIONS—Guess now!

1. Thousands of hydrogen atoms are all in their ground state. Which statement below is true?
   - (a) All of the atoms have the electron in a circular orbit at the Bohr radius.
   - (b) All of the atoms have the electron in the same orbit, but it's not the same orbit for the ground state in the Bohr model.
   - (c) The electron is not in an actual orbit, but the distance between the nucleus and the electron is the same in all of the atoms.
   - (d) If the distance from the nucleus to the electron could be measured, it would be found at different locations in different atoms. The most probable distance would be the Bohr radius.

2. The state of an electron in an atom can be specified by a set of quantum numbers. Which of the following statements are valid?
   - (a) No two electrons in the universe can be identical to each other.
   - (b) All electrons in the universe are identical.
   - (c) No two electrons in an atom can occupy the same quantum state.
   - (d) There cannot be more than one electron in a given electron orbit.
   - (e) Electrons must be excluded from the nucleus because only positive charges are allowed in the nucleus to give rise to stable electronic orbits according to Bohr's model.

At the beginning of Chapter 38 we discussed the limitations of the Bohr theory of atomic structure and why a new theory was needed. Although the Bohr theory had great success in predicting the wavelengths of light emitted and absorbed by the hydrogen atom, it could not do so for more complex atoms. Nor did it explain *fine structure*, the splitting of emission lines into two or more closely spaced lines. And, as a theory, it was an uneasy mixture of classical and quantum ideas.

Quantum mechanics came to the rescue in 1925 and 1926, and in this Chapter we examine the quantum-mechanical theory of atomic structure, which is far more complete than the old Bohr theory.

39–1 Quantum-Mechanical View of Atoms

Although the Bohr model has been discarded as an accurate description of nature, nonetheless, quantum mechanics reaffirms certain aspects of the older theory, such as that electrons in an atom exist only in discrete states of definite energy, and that a photon of light is emitted (or absorbed) when an electron makes a transition from one state to another. But quantum mechanics is a much deeper theory, and has provided us with a very different view of the atom. According to quantum mechanics, electrons do not exist in well-defined circular orbits as in the Bohr theory. Rather, the electron (because of its wave nature) can be thought of as spread out in space as if it were a "**cloud.**" The size and shape of the electron cloud can be calculated for a given state of an atom. For the ground state in the hydrogen atom, the solution of the Schrödinger equation, as we will discuss in more detail in Section 39–3, gives

$$\psi(r) = \frac{1}{\sqrt{\pi r_0^3}} e^{-\frac{r}{r_0}}.$$

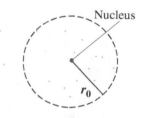

Here $\psi(r)$ is the wave function as a function of position, and it depends only on the radial distance r from the center, and not on angular position θ or ϕ. (The constant r_0 happens to be equal to the first Bohr radius.) Thus the electron cloud, whose density is $|\psi|^2$, for the ground state of hydrogen is spherically symmetric as shown in Fig. 39–1. The extent of the electron cloud at its higher densities roughly indicates the "size" of an atom, but just as a cloud may not have a distinct border, atoms do not have a precise boundary or a well-defined size. Not all electron clouds have a spherical shape, as we shall see later in this Chapter. But note that $\psi(r)$, while becoming extremely small for large r (see the equation above), does not equal zero in any finite region. So quantum mechanics suggests that an atom is not mostly empty space. (Indeed, since $\psi \to 0$ only for $r \to \infty$, we might question the idea that there is any truly empty space in the universe.)

FIGURE 39–1 Electron cloud or "probability distribution" $|\psi|^2$ for the ground state of the hydrogen atom, as seen from afar. The circle represents the Bohr radius r_0. The dots represent a hypothetical detection of an electron at that point: dots closer together represent more probable presence of an electron (denser cloud).

The electron cloud can be interpreted from either the particle or the wave viewpoint. Remember that by a particle we mean something that is localized in space—it has a definite position at any given instant. By contrast, a wave is spread out in space. The electron cloud, spread out in space as in Fig. 39–1, is a result of the wave nature of electrons. Electron clouds can also be interpreted as **probability distributions** (or **probability density**) for a particle. As we saw in Section 38–3, we cannot predict the path an electron will follow. After one measurement of its position we cannot predict exactly where it will be at a later time. We can only calculate the probability that it will be found at different points. If you were to make 500 different measurements of the position of an electron, considering it as a particle, the majority of the results would show the electron at points where the probability is high (darker area in Fig. 39–1). Only occasionally would the electron be found where the probability is low.

39–2 Hydrogen Atom: Schrödinger Equation and Quantum Numbers

The hydrogen atom is the simplest of all atoms, consisting of a single electron of charge $-e$ moving around a central nucleus (a single proton) of charge $+e$. It is with hydrogen that a study of atomic structure must begin.

FIGURE 39–2 Potential energy $U(r)$ for the hydrogen atom. The radial distance r of the electron from the nucleus is given in terms of the Bohr radius r_0.

The Schrödinger equation (see Eq. 38–5) includes a term containing the potential energy. For the hydrogen (H) atom, the potential energy is due to the Coulomb force between electron and proton:

$$U = -\frac{1}{4\pi\epsilon_0}\frac{e^2}{r}$$

where r is the radial distance from the proton (situated at $r = 0$) to the electron. See Fig. 39–2. The (time-independent) Schrödinger equation, which must now be written in three dimensions, is then

$$-\frac{\hbar^2}{2m}\left(\frac{\partial^2\psi}{\partial x^2} + \frac{\partial^2\psi}{\partial y^2} + \frac{\partial^2\psi}{\partial z^2}\right) - \frac{1}{4\pi\epsilon_0}\frac{e^2}{r}\psi = E\psi, \qquad \text{(39–1)}$$

where $\partial^2\psi/\partial x^2$, $\partial^2\psi/\partial y^2$, and $\partial^2\psi/\partial z^2$ are partial derivatives with respect to x, y, and z. To solve the Schrödinger equation for the H atom, it is usual to write it in terms of spherical coordinates (r, θ, ϕ). We will not, however, actually go through the process of solving it. Instead, we look at the properties of the solutions, and (in the next Section) at the wave functions themselves.

Recall from Chapter 38 that the solutions of the Schrödinger equation in one dimension for the infinite square well were characterized by a single quantum number, which we called n, which arises from applying the boundary conditions. In the three-dimensional problem of the H atom, the solutions of the Schrödinger equation are characterized by three quantum numbers corresponding to boundary conditions applied in the three dimensions. However, four different quantum numbers are actually needed to specify each state in the H atom, the fourth coming from a relativistic treatment. We now discuss each of these quantum numbers. Much of our analysis here will also apply to more complex atoms, which we discuss starting in Section 39–4.

Quantum mechanics predicts the same energy levels (Fig. 37–26) for the H atom as does the Bohr theory. That is,

$$E_n = -\frac{13.6\ \text{eV}}{n^2} \qquad n = 1, 2, 3, \cdots, \qquad \text{(39–2)}$$

where n is an integer. In the simple Bohr theory, there was only one quantum number, n. In quantum mechanics, four different quantum numbers are needed to specify each state in the atom:

(1) The *quantum number*, n, from the Bohr theory is found also in quantum mechanics and is called the **principal quantum number**. It can have any integer value from 1 to ∞. The total energy of a state in the hydrogen atom depends on n, as we saw above.

(2) The **orbital quantum number**, ℓ, is related to the magnitude of the angular momentum of the electron; ℓ can take on integer values from 0 to $(n - 1)$. For the ground state $(n = 1)$, ℓ can only be zero.[†] For $n = 3$, ℓ can be 0, 1, or 2. The actual magnitude of the angular momentum L is related to the quantum number ℓ by

$$L = \sqrt{\ell(\ell + 1)}\,\hbar. \qquad \text{(39–3)}$$

The value of ℓ has almost no effect on the total energy in the hydrogen atom; only n does to any appreciable extent (but see *fine structure* below). In atoms with two or more electrons, the energy does depend on ℓ as well as n, as we shall see.

(3) The **magnetic quantum number**, m_ℓ, is related to the *direction* of the electron's angular momentum, and it can take on integer values ranging from $-\ell$ to $+\ell$. For example, if $\ell = 2$, then m_ℓ can be $-2, -1, 0, +1$, or $+2$. Since angular momentum is a vector, it is not surprising that both its magnitude and its direction would be quantized. For $\ell = 2$, the five different directions allowed can be represented by the diagram of Fig. 39–3.

FIGURE 39–3 Quantization of angular momentum direction for $\ell = 2$. (Magnitude of $\vec{L}$ is $\sqrt{6}\,\hbar$).

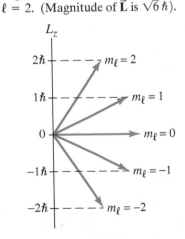

[†]This replaces Bohr theory, which had $\ell = 1$ for the ground state (Eq. 37–10).

This limitation on the direction of $\vec{\mathbf{L}}$ is often called **space quantization**. In quantum mechanics, the direction of the angular momentum is usually specified by giving its component along the z axis (this choice is arbitrary). Then L_z is related to m_ℓ by the equation

$$L_z = m_\ell \hbar. \tag{39-4}$$

The values of L_x and L_y are not definite, however. The name for m_ℓ derives not from theory (which relates it to L_z), but from experiment. It was found that when a gas-discharge tube was placed in a magnetic field, the spectral lines were split into several very closely spaced lines. This splitting, known as the **Zeeman effect**, implies that the energy levels must be split (Fig. 39–4), and thus that the energy of a state depends not only on n but also on m_ℓ when a magnetic field is applied—hence the name "magnetic quantum number."

(4) Finally, there is the **spin quantum number**, m_s, which for an electron can have only two values, $m_s = +\frac{1}{2}$ and $m_s = -\frac{1}{2}$. The existence of this quantum number did not come out of Schrödinger's original theory, as did n, ℓ, and m_ℓ. Instead, a subsequent modification by P. A. M. Dirac (1902–1984) explained its presence as a relativistic effect. The first hint that m_s was needed, however, came from experiment. A careful study of the spectral lines of hydrogen showed that each actually consisted of two (or more) very closely spaced lines even in the absence of an external magnetic field. It was at first hypothesized that this tiny splitting of energy levels, called **fine structure**, was due to angular momentum associated with a spinning of the electron. That is, the electron might spin on its axis as well as orbit the nucleus, just as the Earth spins on its axis as it orbits the Sun. The interaction between the tiny current of the spinning electron could then interact with the magnetic field due to the orbiting charge and cause the small observed splitting of energy levels. (The energy thus depends slightly on m_ℓ and m_s. Fine structure is said to be due to a **spin-orbit interaction**.) Today we consider the picture of a spinning electron as not legitimate. We cannot even view an electron as a localized object, much less a spinning one. What is important is that the electron can have two different states due to some intrinsic property that behaves like an angular momentum, and we still call this property "spin." The electron is said to have a spin quantum number $s = \frac{1}{2}$, which produces a spin angular momentum

$$S = \sqrt{s(s + 1)}\,\hbar = \frac{\sqrt{3}}{2}\hbar.$$

The z component is

$$S_z = m_s \hbar$$

where the two possible values of m_s $\left(+\frac{1}{2} \text{ and } -\frac{1}{2}\right)$ are often said to be "spin up" and "spin down," referring to the two possible directions of the spin angular momentum. See Fig. 39–5. A state with spin down $\left(m_s = -\frac{1}{2}\right)$ has slightly lower energy than a state with spin up. (Note that we include m_s, but not s, in our list of quantum numbers since s is the same for all electrons.)

The possible values of the four quantum numbers for an electron in the hydrogen atom are summarized in Table 39–1.

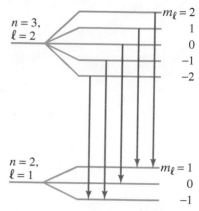

FIGURE 39–4 When a magnetic field is applied, an $n = 3$, $\ell = 2$ energy level is split into five separate levels (shown exaggerated—not to scale) corresponding to the five values of m_ℓ (2, 1, 0, −1, −2). An $n = 2$, $\ell = 1$ level is split into three levels $(m_\ell = 1, 0, -1)$. Transitions can occur between levels (not all transitions are shown), with photons of several slightly different frequencies being given off (the Zeeman effect).

FIGURE 39–5 The spin angular momentum S can take on only two directions, $m_s = +\frac{1}{2}$ or $-\frac{1}{2}$, called "spin up" and "spin down."

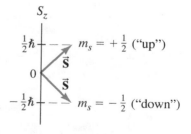

TABLE 39–1 Quantum Numbers for an Electron

Name	Symbol	Possible Values
Principal	n	$1, 2, 3, \cdots, \infty$.
Orbital	ℓ	For a given n: ℓ can be $0, 1, 2, \cdots, n - 1$.
Magnetic	m_ℓ	For given n and ℓ: m_ℓ can be $\ell, \ell - 1, \cdots, 0, \cdots, -\ell$.
Spin	m_s	For each set of n, ℓ, and m_ℓ: m_s can be $+\frac{1}{2}$ or $-\frac{1}{2}$.

CONCEPTUAL EXAMPLE 39–1 **Possible states for $n = 3$.** How many different states are possible for an electron whose principal quantum number is $n = 3$?

RESPONSE For $n = 3$, ℓ can have the values $\ell = 2, 1, 0$. For $\ell = 2$, m_ℓ can be 2, 1, 0, −1, −2, which is five different possibilities. For each of these, m_s can be either up or down ($+\frac{1}{2}$ or $-\frac{1}{2}$); so for $\ell = 2$, there are $2 \times 5 = 10$ states. For $\ell = 1$, m_ℓ can be 1, 0, −1, and since m_s can be $+\frac{1}{2}$ or $-\frac{1}{2}$ for each of these, we have 6 more possible states. Finally, for $\ell = 0$, m_ℓ can only be 0, and there are only 2 states corresponding to $m_s = +\frac{1}{2}$ and $-\frac{1}{2}$. The total number of states is $10 + 6 + 2 = 18$, as detailed in the following Table:

n	ℓ	m_ℓ	m_s	n	ℓ	m_ℓ	m_s
3	2	2	$\frac{1}{2}$	3	1	1	$\frac{1}{2}$
3	2	2	$-\frac{1}{2}$	3	1	1	$-\frac{1}{2}$
3	2	1	$\frac{1}{2}$	3	1	0	$\frac{1}{2}$
3	2	1	$-\frac{1}{2}$	3	1	0	$-\frac{1}{2}$
3	2	0	$\frac{1}{2}$	3	1	−1	$\frac{1}{2}$
3	2	0	$-\frac{1}{2}$	3	1	−1	$-\frac{1}{2}$
3	2	−1	$\frac{1}{2}$	3	0	0	$\frac{1}{2}$
3	2	−1	$-\frac{1}{2}$	3	0	0	$-\frac{1}{2}$
3	2	−2	$\frac{1}{2}$				
3	2	−2	$-\frac{1}{2}$				

EXERCISE A An electron has $n = 4$, $\ell = 2$. Which of the following values of m_ℓ are possible: 4, 3, 2, 1, 0, −1, −2, −3, −4?

EXAMPLE 39–2 **E and L for $n = 3$.** Determine (a) the energy and (b) the orbital angular momentum for an electron in each of the hydrogen atom states of Example 39–1.

APPROACH The energy of a state depends only on n, except for the very small corrections mentioned above, which we will ignore. Energy is calculated as in the Bohr theory, $E_n = -13.6\,\text{eV}/n^2$. For angular momentum we use Eq. 39–3.

SOLUTION (a) Since $n = 3$ for all these states, they all have the same energy,

$$E_3 = -\frac{13.6\,\text{eV}}{(3)^2} = -1.51\,\text{eV}.$$

(b) For $\ell = 0$, Eq. 39–3 gives

$$L = \sqrt{\ell(\ell + 1)}\,\hbar = 0.$$

For $\ell = 1$,

$$L = \sqrt{1(1 + 1)}\,\hbar = \sqrt{2}\,\hbar = 1.49 \times 10^{-34}\,\text{J·s}.$$

For $\ell = 2$, $L = \sqrt{2(2 + 1)}\,\hbar = \sqrt{6}\,\hbar$.

NOTE Atomic angular momenta are generally given as a multiple of $\hbar$ ($\sqrt{2}\,\hbar$ or $\sqrt{6}\,\hbar$ in this case), rather than in SI units.

EXERCISE B What is the magnitude of the orbital angular momentum for orbital quantum number $\ell = 3$? (a) $3\hbar$; (b) $3.5\hbar$; (c) $4\hbar$; (d) $12\hbar$.

Selection Rules: Allowed and Forbidden Transitions

Another prediction of quantum mechanics is that when a photon is emitted or absorbed, transitions can occur only between states with values of ℓ that differ by exactly one unit:

$$\Delta\ell = \pm 1.$$

According to this **selection rule**, an electron in an $\ell = 2$ state can jump only to a state with $\ell = 1$ or $\ell = 3$. It cannot jump to a state with $\ell = 2$ or $\ell = 0$.

A transition such as $\ell = 2$ to $\ell = 0$ is called a **forbidden transition**. Actually, such a transition is not absolutely forbidden and can occur, but only with very low probability compared to **allowed transitions**—those that satisfy the selection rule $\Delta\ell = \pm 1$. Since the orbital angular momentum of an H atom must change by one unit when it emits a photon, conservation of angular momentum tells us that the photon must carry off angular momentum. Indeed, experimental evidence of many sorts shows that the photon can be assigned a spin angular momentum of $1\hbar$.

39–3 Hydrogen Atom Wave Functions

The solution of the Schrödinger equation for the ground state of hydrogen (the state with lowest energy) has an energy $E_1 = -13.6\,\text{eV}$, as we have seen. The wave function for the ground state depends only on r and so is spherically symmetric. As already mentioned in Section 39–1, its form is

$$\psi_{100} = \frac{1}{\sqrt{\pi r_0^3}}\, e^{-\frac{r}{r_0}} \tag{39–5a}$$

where $r_0 = h^2\epsilon_0/\pi m e^2 = 0.0529\,\text{nm}$ is the Bohr radius (Section 37–11). The subscript 100 on ψ represents the quantum numbers n, ℓ, m_ℓ:

$$\psi_{n\ell m_\ell}.$$

For the ground state, $n = 1, \ell = 0, m_\ell = 0,$ and there is only one wave function that serves for both $m_s = +\frac{1}{2}$ and $m_s = -\frac{1}{2}$ (the value of m_s does not affect the spatial dependence of the wave function for any state, since spin is an *internal* or *intrinsic* property of the electron). The probability density for the ground state is

$$|\psi_{100}|^2 = \frac{1}{\pi r_0^3}\, e^{-\frac{2r}{r_0}} \tag{39–5b}$$

which falls off exponentially with r. Note that ψ_{100}, like all other wave functions we discuss, has been normalized:

$$\int_{\text{all space}} |\psi_{100}|^2\, dV = 1.$$

The quantity $|\psi|^2\, dV$ gives the probability of finding the electron in a volume dV about a given point. It is often more useful to specify the **radial probability distribution**, P_r, which is defined so that $P_r\, dr$ is the probability of finding the electron at a radial distance between r and $r + dr$ from the nucleus. That is, $P_r\, dr$ specifies the probability of finding the electron within a thin shell of thickness dr of inner radius r and outer radius $r + dr$, regardless of direction (see Fig. 39–6). The volume of this shell is the product of its surface area, $4\pi r^2$, and its thickness, dr:

$$dV = 4\pi r^2\, dr.$$

Hence

$$|\psi|^2\, dV = |\psi|^2 4\pi r^2\, dr$$

and the radial probability distribution is

$$P_r = 4\pi r^2 |\psi|^2. \tag{39–6}$$

For the ground state of hydrogen, P_r becomes

$$P_r = 4\frac{r^2}{r_0^3}\, e^{-\frac{2r}{r_0}} \tag{39–7}$$

and is plotted in Fig. 39–7. The peak of the curve is the "most probable" value of r and occurs for $r = r_0$, the Bohr radius, which we show in the following Example.

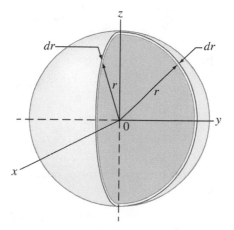

FIGURE 39–6 A spherical shell of thickness dr, inner radius r, and outer radius $r + dr$. Its volume is $dV = 4\pi r^2\, dr$.

FIGURE 39–7 The radial probability distribution P_r for the ground state of hydrogen, $n = 1$, $\ell = 0$. The peak occurs at $r = r_0$, the Bohr radius.

FIGURE 39–7 (Repeated.) The radial probability distribution P_r for the ground state of hydrogen, $n = 1$, $\ell = 0$. The peak occurs at $r = r_0$, the Bohr radius.

EXAMPLE 39–3 **Most probable electron radius in hydrogen.** Determine the most probable distance r from the nucleus at which to find the electron in the ground state of hydrogen.

APPROACH The peak of the curve in Fig. 39–7 corresponds to the most probable value of r. At this point the curve has zero slope, so we take the derivative of Eq. 39–7, set it equal to zero, and solve for r.

SOLUTION We find

$$\frac{d}{dr}\left(4\frac{r^2}{r_0^3}e^{-\frac{2r}{r_0}}\right) = 0$$

$$\left(8\frac{r}{r_0^3} - \frac{8r^2}{r_0^4}\right)e^{-\frac{2r}{r_0}} = 0.$$

Since $e^{-\frac{2r}{r_0}}$ goes to zero only at $r = \infty$, it is the term in parentheses that must be zero:

$$8\frac{r}{r_0^3} - 8\frac{r^2}{r_0^4} = 0.$$

Therefore,

$$\frac{r}{r_0^3} = \frac{r^2}{r_0^4}$$

or

$$r = r_0.$$

The most probable radial distance of the electron from the nucleus according to quantum mechanics is at the Bohr radius, an interesting coincidence.

EXERCISE C Return to the first Chapter-Opening Question, page 1044, and answer it again now. Try to explain why you may have answered differently the first time.

EXAMPLE 39–4 **Calculating probability.** Determine the probability of finding the electron in the ground state of hydrogen within two Bohr radii of the nucleus.

APPROACH We need to integrate P_r from $r = 0$ out to $r = 2r_0$.

SOLUTION We want to find

$$P = \int_{r=0}^{2r_0} |\psi|^2 \, dV = \int_0^{2r_0} 4\frac{r^2}{r_0^3}e^{-\frac{2r}{r_0}} \, dr.$$

We first make the substitution

$$x = 2\frac{r}{r_0}$$

and then integrate by parts ($\int u \, dv = uv - \int v \, du$) letting $u = x^2$ and $dv = e^{-x} \, dx$ (and note that $dx = 2 \, dr/r_0$, and the upper limit is $x = 2(2r_0)/r_0 = 4$):

$$P = \frac{1}{2}\int_{x=0}^{4} x^2 e^{-x} \, dx = \frac{1}{2}\left[-x^2 e^{-x} + \int 2x e^{-x} \, dx\right]\Bigg|_0^4.$$

The second term we also integrate by parts with $u = 2x$ and $dv = e^{-x} \, dx$:

$$P = \frac{1}{2}\left[-x^2 e^{-x} - 2x e^{-x} + 2\int e^{-x} \, dx\right]\Bigg|_0^4$$

$$= \left(-\frac{1}{2}x^2 - x - 1\right)e^{-x}\Bigg|_0^4.$$

We evaluate this at $x = 0$ and at $x = 4$:

$$P = (-8 - 4 - 1)e^{-4} + e^0 = 0.76$$

or 76%. Thus the electron would be found 76% of the time within 2 Bohr radii of the nucleus and 24% of the time farther away.

NOTE This result depends on our wave function being properly normalized, which it is, as is readily shown by letting $r \to \infty$ and integrating over all space: $\int_0^{\infty} |\psi|^2 \, dV = 1$; that is, let the upper limit in the equation above be ∞.

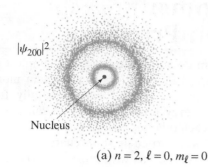

$|\psi_{200}|^2$

Nucleus

(a) $n = 2, \ell = 0, m_\ell = 0$

P_r (nm^{-1})

$n = 2, \ell = 0$

$5r_0$ $10r_0$ r

(b)

FIGURE 39–8 (a) Electron cloud, or probability distribution, for $n = 2$, $\ell = 0$ state in hydrogen. (b) The radial probability distribution P_r for the $n = 2$, $\ell = 0$ state in hydrogen.

The first excited state in hydrogen has $n = 2$. For $\ell = 0$, the solution of the Schrödinger equation (Eq. 39–1) is a wave function that is again spherically symmetric:

$$\psi_{200} = \frac{1}{\sqrt{32\pi r_0^3}}\left(2 - \frac{r}{r_0}\right)e^{-\frac{r}{2r_0}}. \qquad \textbf{(39–8)}$$

Figure 39–8a shows the probability distribution $|\psi_{200}|^2$ and Fig. 39–8b shows[†] a plot of the radial probability distribution

$$P_r = 4\pi r^2|\psi|^2 = \frac{1}{8}\frac{r^2}{r_0^3}\left(2 - \frac{r}{r_0}\right)^2 e^{-\frac{r}{r_0}}.$$

There are two peaks in this curve; the second, at $r \approx 5r_0$, is higher and corresponds to the most probable value for r in the $n = 2$, $\ell = 0$ state. We see that the electron tends to be somewhat farther from the nucleus in the $n = 2$, $\ell = 0$ state than in the $n = 1$, $\ell = 0$ state. (Compare to the Bohr model that gave $r_2 = 4r_0$.)

For the state with $n = 2$, $\ell = 1$, there are three possible wave functions, corresponding to $m_\ell = +1$, 0, or −1:

$$\psi_{210} = \frac{z}{\sqrt{32\pi r_0^5}}\, e^{-\frac{r}{2r_0}}$$

$$\psi_{211} = \frac{x + iy}{\sqrt{64\pi r_0^5}}\, e^{-\frac{r}{2r_0}} \qquad \textbf{(39–9)}$$

$$\psi_{21-1} = \frac{x - iy}{\sqrt{64\pi r_0^5}}\, e^{-\frac{r}{2r_0}}$$

where i is the imaginary number $i = \sqrt{-1}$. These wave functions are *not* spherically symmetric. The probability distributions, $|\psi|^2$, are shown in Fig. 39–9a, where we can see their directional orientation.

You may wonder how such non-spherically symmetric wave functions arise when the potential energy in the Schrödinger equation has spherical symmetry. Indeed, how could an electron select one of these states? In the absence of any external influence, such as a magnetic field in a particular direction, all three of these states are equally likely, and they all have the same energy. Thus an electron can be considered to spend one-third of its time in each of these states. The net effect, then, is the sum of these three wave functions squared:

$$|\psi_{210}|^2 + |\psi_{211}|^2 + |\psi_{21-1}|^2,$$

which is spherically symmetric, since $x^2 + y^2 + z^2 = r^2$. The radial probability distribution for this sum is shown in Fig. 39–9b.

Although the spatial distributions of the electron can be calculated for the various states, it is difficult to measure them experimentally. Indeed, most of the experimental information about atoms has come from a careful examination of the emission spectra under various conditions.

[†]Just as for a particle in a deep square well potential (see Figs. 38–9 and 38–10), the higher the energy, the more nodes there are in ψ and $|\psi|^2$ also for the H atom.

FIGURE 39–9 (a) The probability distribution for the three states with $n = 2$, $\ell = 1$. (b) Radial probability distribution for the sum of the three states with $n = 2$, $\ell = 1$, and $m_\ell = +1$, 0, or −1.

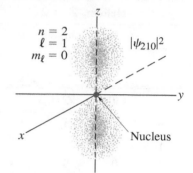

$n = 2$
$\ell = 1$
$m_\ell = 0$

$|\psi_{210}|^2$

Nucleus

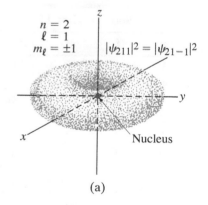

$n = 2$
$\ell = 1$
$m_\ell = \pm 1$

$|\psi_{211}|^2 = |\psi_{21-1}|^2$

Nucleus

(a)

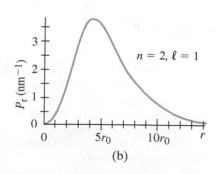

P_r (nm^{-1})

$n = 2, \ell = 1$

$5r_0$ $10r_0$ r

(b)

39–4 Complex Atoms; the Exclusion Principle

We have discussed the hydrogen atom in detail because it is the simplest to deal with. Now we briefly discuss more complex atoms, those that contain more than one electron. Their energy levels can be determined experimentally from an analysis of their emission spectra. The energy levels are *not* the same as in the H atom, since the electrons interact with each other as well as with the nucleus. Each electron in a complex atom still occupies a particular state characterized by the same quantum numbers n, ℓ, m_ℓ, and m_s. For atoms with more than one electron, the energy levels depend on both n and ℓ.

The number of electrons in a neutral atom is called its **atomic number**, Z; Z is also the number of positive charges (protons) in the nucleus, and determines what kind of atom it is. That is, Z determines the fundamental properties that distinguish one type of atom from another.

Quantum mechanics in the years after 1925 proved successful also in dealing with complex atoms. The mathematics becomes very difficult, however, since in multi-electron atoms, each electron is not only attracted to the nucleus but is also repelled by the other electrons.

To understand the possible arrangements of electrons in an atom, a new principle was needed. It was introduced by Wolfgang Pauli (1900–1958; Fig. 38–2) and is called the **Pauli exclusion principle**. It states:

No two electrons in an atom can occupy the same quantum state.

Thus, no two electrons in an atom can have exactly the same set of the quantum numbers n, ℓ, m_ℓ, and m_s. The Pauli exclusion principle forms the basis not only for understanding complex atoms, but also for understanding molecules and bonding, and other phenomena as well.

Let us now look at the structure of some of the simpler atoms when they are in the ground state. After hydrogen, the next simplest atom is *helium* with two electrons. Both electrons can have $n = 1$, since one can have spin up $\left(m_s = +\frac{1}{2}\right)$ and the other spin down $\left(m_s = -\frac{1}{2}\right)$, thus satisfying the exclusion principle. Since $n = 1$, then ℓ and m_ℓ must be zero (Table 39–1, p. 1047). Thus the two electrons have the quantum numbers indicated in Table 39–2.

Lithium has three electrons, two of which can have $n = 1$. But the third cannot have $n = 1$ without violating the exclusion principle. Hence the third electron must have $n = 2$. It happens that the $n = 2$, $\ell = 0$ level has a lower energy than $n = 2$, $\ell = 1$. So the electrons in the ground state have the quantum numbers indicated in Table 39–2. The quantum numbers of the third electron could also be, say, $(n, \ell, m_\ell, m_s) = \left(3, 1, -1, \frac{1}{2}\right)$. But the atom in this case would be in an excited state since it would have greater energy. It would not be long before it jumped to the ground state with the emission of a photon. At room temperature, unless extra energy is supplied (as in a discharge tube), the vast majority of atoms are in the ground state.

We can continue in this way to describe the quantum numbers of each electron in the ground state of larger and larger atoms. The quantum numbers for sodium, with its eleven electrons, are shown in Table 39–2.

Figure 39–10 shows a simple energy level diagram where occupied states are shown as up or down arrows ($m_s = +\frac{1}{2}$ or $-\frac{1}{2}$), and possible empty states are shown as a small circle.

TABLE 39–2 Ground-State Quantum Numbers

Helium, $Z = 2$

n	ℓ	m_ℓ	m_s
1	0	0	$\frac{1}{2}$
1	0	0	$-\frac{1}{2}$

Lithium, $Z = 3$

n	ℓ	m_ℓ	m_s
1	0	0	$\frac{1}{2}$
1	0	0	$-\frac{1}{2}$
2	0	0	$\frac{1}{2}$

Sodium, $Z = 11$

n	ℓ	m_ℓ	m_s
1	0	0	$\frac{1}{2}$
1	0	0	$-\frac{1}{2}$
2	0	0	$\frac{1}{2}$
2	0	0	$-\frac{1}{2}$
2	1	1	$\frac{1}{2}$
2	1	1	$-\frac{1}{2}$
2	1	0	$\frac{1}{2}$
2	1	0	$-\frac{1}{2}$
2	1	-1	$\frac{1}{2}$
2	1	-1	$-\frac{1}{2}$
3	0	0	$\frac{1}{2}$

FIGURE 39–10 Energy level diagram (not to scale) showing occupied states (arrows) and unoccupied states (o) for the ground states of He, Li, and Na. Note that we have shown the $n = 2$, $\ell = 1$ level of Li even though it is empty.

Helium (He, $Z = 2$)
Lithium (Li, $Z = 3$)
Sodium (Na, $Z = 11$)

The ground-state configuration for all atoms is given in the Periodic Table, which is displayed inside the back cover of this book, and discussed in the next Section.

| **EXERCISE D** Construct a Table of the ground-state quantum numbers for beryllium, $Z = 4$ (like those in Table 39–2).

The exclusion principle applies to identical particles whose spin quantum number is a half-integer ($\frac{1}{2}$, $\frac{3}{2}$, and so on), including electrons, protons, and neutrons; such particles are called **fermions**, after Enrico Fermi who derived a statistical theory describing them. A basic assumption is that all electrons are **identical**, indistinguishable one from another. Similarly, all protons are identical, all neutrons are identical, and so on. The exclusion principle does not apply to particles with integer spin (0, 1, 2, and so on), such as the photon and π meson, all of which are referred to as **bosons** (after Satyendranath Bose, who derived a statistical theory for them).

| **EXERCISE E** Return to the second Chapter-Opening Question, page 1044, and answer it again now. Try to explain why you may have answered differently the first time.

39–5 Periodic Table of Elements

More than a century ago, Dmitri Mendeleev (1834–1907) arranged the (then) known elements into what we now call the **Periodic Table** of the elements. The atoms were arranged according to increasing mass, but also so that elements with similar chemical properties would fall in the same column. Today's version is shown inside the back cover of this book. Each square contains the atomic number Z, the symbol for the element, and the atomic mass (in atomic mass units). Finally, the lower left corner shows the configuration of the ground state of the atom. This requires some explanation. Electrons with the same value of n are referred to as being in the same **shell**. Electrons with $n = 1$ are in one shell (the K shell), those with $n = 2$ are in a second shell (the L shell), those with $n = 3$ are in the third (M) shell, and so on. Electrons with the same values of n and ℓ are referred to as being in the same **subshell**. Letters are often used to specify the value of ℓ as shown in Table 39–3. That is, $\ell = 0$ is the s subshell; $\ell = 1$ is the p subshell; $\ell = 2$ is the d subshell; beginning with $\ell = 3$, the letters follow the alphabet, f, g, h, i, and so on. (The first letters s, p, d, and f were originally abbreviations of "sharp," "principal," "diffuse," and "fundamental," experimental terms referring to the spectra.)

The Pauli exclusion principle limits the number of electrons possible in each shell and subshell. For any value of ℓ, there are $2\ell + 1$ possible m_ℓ values (m_ℓ can be any integer from 1 to ℓ, from -1 to $-\ell$, or zero), and two possible m_s values. There can be, therefore, at most $2(2\ell + 1)$ electrons in any ℓ subshell. For example, for $\ell = 2$, five m_ℓ values are possible (2, 1, 0, −1, −2), and for each of these, m_s can be $+\frac{1}{2}$ or $-\frac{1}{2}$ for a total of $2(5) = 10$ states. Table 39–3 lists the maximum number of electrons that can occupy each subshell.

Since the energy levels depend almost entirely on the values of n and ℓ, it is customary to specify the electron configuration simply by giving the n value and the appropriate letter for ℓ, with the number of electrons in each subshell given as a superscript. The ground-state configuration of sodium, for example, is written as $1s^2 2s^2 2p^6 3s^1$. This is simplified in the Periodic Table by specifying the configuration only of the outermost electrons and any other nonfilled subshells (see Table 39–4 here, and the Periodic Table inside the back cover).

TABLE 39–3 Value of ℓ

Value of ℓ	Letter Symbol	Maximum Number of Electrons in Subshell
0	s	2
1	p	6
2	d	10
3	f	14
4	g	18
5	h	22
⋮	⋮	⋮

TABLE 39–4 Electron Configuration of Some Elements

Z (Number of Electrons)	Element[†]	Ground State Configuration (outer electrons)
1	H	$1s^1$
2	He	$1s^2$
3	Li	$2s^1$
4	Be	$2s^2$
5	B	$2s^2 2p^1$
6	C	$2s^2 2p^2$
7	N	$2s^2 2p^3$
8	O	$2s^2 2p^4$
9	F	$2s^2 2p^5$
10	Ne	$2s^2 2p^6$
11	Na	$3s^1$
12	Mg	$3s^2$
13	Al	$3s^2 3p^1$
14	Si	$3s^2 3p^2$
15	P	$3s^2 3p^3$
16	S	$3s^2 3p^4$
17	Cl	$3s^2 3p^5$
18	Ar	$3s^2 3p^6$
19	K	$4s^1$
20	Ca	$4s^2$
21	Sc	$3d^1 4s^2$
22	Ti	$3d^2 4s^2$
23	V	$3d^3 4s^2$
24	Cr	$3d^5 4s^1$
25	Mn	$3d^5 4s^2$
26	Fe	$3d^6 4s^2$

[†] Names of elements can be found in Appendix F.

Electron configurations. Which of the following electron configurations are possible, and which are not: (*a*) $1s^2 2s^2 2p^6 3s^3$; (*b*) $1s^2 2s^2 2p^6 3s^2 3p^5 4s^2$; (*c*) $1s^2 2s^2 2p^6 2d^1$?

RESPONSE (*a*) This is not allowed, because too many electrons (three) are shown in the *s* subshell of the M ($n = 3$) shell. The *s* subshell has $m_\ell = 0$, with two slots only, for "spin up" and "spin down" electrons. (*b*) This is allowed, but it is an excited state. One of the electrons from the 3*p* subshell has jumped up to the 4*s* subshell. Since there are 19 electrons, the element is potassium. (*c*) This is not allowed, because there is no *d* ($\ell = 2$) subshell in the $n = 2$ shell (Table 39–1). The outermost electron will have to be (at least) in the $n = 3$ shell.

| **EXERCISE F** Write the complete ground-state configuration for gallium, with its 31 electrons.

The grouping of atoms in the Periodic Table is according to increasing atomic number, *Z*. There is also a strong regularity according to chemical properties. Although this is treated in chemistry textbooks, we discuss it here briefly because it is a result of quantum mechanics. See the Periodic Table inside the back cover.

All the **noble gases** (in column VIII of the Periodic Table) have completely filled shells or subshells. That is, their outermost subshell is completely full, and the electron distribution is spherically symmetric. With such full spherical symmetry, other electrons are not attracted nor are electrons readily lost (ionization energy is high). This is why the noble gases are chemically inert (more on this when we discuss molecules and bonding in Chapter 40). Column VII contains the **halogens**, which lack one electron from a filled shell. Because of the shapes of the orbits (see Section 40–1), an additional electron can be accepted from another atom, and hence these elements are quite reactive. They have a valence of -1, meaning that when an extra electron is acquired, the resulting ion has a net charge of $-1e$. Column I of the Periodic Table contains the **alkali metals**, all of which have a single outer *s* electron. This electron spends most of its time outside the inner closed shells and subshells which shield it from most of the nuclear charge. Indeed, it is relatively far from the nucleus and is attracted to it by a net charge of only about $+1e$, because of the shielding effect of the other electrons. Hence this outer electron is easily removed and can spend much of its time around another atom, forming a molecule. This is why the alkali metals are chemically active and have a valence of $+1$. The other columns of the Periodic Table can be treated similarly.

The presence of the **transition elements** in the center of the Table, as well as the lanthanides (rare earths) and actinides below, is a result of incomplete inner shells. For the lowest *Z* elements, the subshells are filled in a simple order: first 1*s*, then 2*s*, followed by 2*p*, 3*s*, and 3*p*. You might expect that 3*d* ($n = 3, \ell = 2$) would be filled next, but it isn't. Instead, the 4*s* level actually has a slightly lower energy than the 3*d* (due to electrons interacting with each other), so it fills first (K and Ca). Only then does the 3*d* shell start to fill up, beginning with Sc, as can be seen in Table 39–4. (The 4*s* and 3*d* levels are close, so some elements have only one 4*s* electron, such as Cr.) Most of the chemical properties of these transition elements are governed by the relatively loosely held 4*s* electrons, and hence they usually have valences of $+1$ or $+2$. A similar effect is responsible for the *lanthanides* and *actinides*, which are shown at the bottom of the Periodic Table for convenience. All have very similar chemical properties, which are determined by their two outer 6*s* or 7*s* electrons, whereas the different numbers of electrons in the unfilled inner shells have little effect.

⚠ CAUTION

Subshells are not always filled in "order"

39–6 X-Ray Spectra and Atomic Number

The line spectra of atoms in the visible, UV, and IR regions of the EM spectrum are mainly due to transitions between states of the outer electrons. Much of the charge of the nucleus is shielded from these electrons by the negative charge on the inner electrons. But the innermost electrons in the $n = 1$ shell "see" the full charge of the nucleus. Since the energy of a level is proportional to Z^2 (see Eq. 37–14), for an atom with $Z = 50$, we would expect wavelengths about $50^2 = 2500$ times shorter than those found in the Lyman series of hydrogen (around 100 nm), or 10^{-2} to 10^{-1} nm. Such short wavelengths lie in the X-ray region of the spectrum.

X-rays are produced when electrons accelerated by a high voltage strike the metal target inside the X-ray tube (Section 35–10). If we look at the spectrum of wavelengths emitted by an X-ray tube, we see that the spectrum consists of two parts: a continuous spectrum with a cutoff at some λ_0 which depends only on the voltage across the tube, and a series of peaks superimposed. A typical example is shown in Fig. 39–11. The smooth curve and the cutoff wavelength λ_0 move to the left as the voltage across the tube increases. The sharp lines or peaks (labeled K_α and K_β in Fig. 39–11), however, remain at the same wavelength when the voltage is changed, although they are located at different wavelengths when different target materials are used. This observation suggests that the peaks are characteristic of the target material used. Indeed, we can explain the peaks by imagining that the electrons accelerated by the high voltage of the tube can reach sufficient energies that when they collide with the atoms of the target, they can knock out one of the very tightly held inner electrons. Then we explain these **characteristic X-rays** (the peaks in Fig. 39–11) as photons emitted when an electron in an upper state drops down to fill the vacated lower state. The K lines result from transitions *into* the K shell $(n = 1)$. The K_α line consists of photons emitted in a transition that originates from the $n = 2$ (L) shell and drops to the $n = 1$ (K) shell, whereas the K_β line reflects a transition from the $n = 3$ (M) shell down to the K shell. An L line, on the other hand, is due to a transition into the L shell, and so on.

Measurement of the characteristic X-ray spectra has allowed a determination of the inner energy levels of atoms. It has also allowed the determination of Z values for many atoms, since (as we have seen) the wavelength of the shortest characteristic X-rays emitted will be inversely proportional to Z^2. Actually, for an electron jumping from, say, the $n = 2$ to the $n = 1$ level (K_α line), the wavelength is inversely proportional to $(Z - 1)^2$ because the nucleus is shielded by the one electron that still remains in the 1s level. In 1914, H. G. J. Moseley (1887–1915) found that a plot of $\sqrt{1/\lambda}$ vs. Z produced a straight line, Fig. 39–12 where λ is the wavelength of the K_α line. The Z values of a number of elements were determined by fitting them to such a **Moseley plot**. The work of Moseley put the concept of atomic number on a firm experimental basis.

FIGURE 39–11 Spectrum of X-rays emitted from a molybdenum target in an X-ray tube operated at 50 kV.

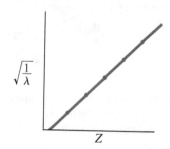

FIGURE 39–12 Plot of $\sqrt{1/\lambda}$ vs. Z for K_α X-ray lines.

EXAMPLE 39–6 X-ray wavelength. Estimate the wavelength for an $n = 2$ to $n = 1$ transition in molybdenum $(Z = 42)$. What is the energy of such a photon?

APPROACH We use the Bohr formula, Eq. 37–15 for $1/\lambda$, with Z^2 replaced by $(Z - 1)^2 = (41)^2$.

SOLUTION Equation 37–15 gives

$$\frac{1}{\lambda} = \left(\frac{e^4 m}{8\epsilon_0^2 h^3 c}\right)(Z - 1)^2 \left(\frac{1}{n'^2} - \frac{1}{n^2}\right)$$

where $n = 2$ and $n' = 1$. We substitute in values:

$$\frac{1}{\lambda} = (1.097 \times 10^7 \text{ m}^{-1})(41)^2 \left(\frac{1}{1} - \frac{1}{4}\right) = 1.38 \times 10^{10} \text{ m}^{-1}.$$

So

$$\lambda = \frac{1}{1.38 \times 10^{10} \text{ m}^{-1}} = 0.072 \text{ nm}.$$

This is close to the measured value (Fig. 39–11) of 0.071 nm. Each of these photons would have energy (in eV) of:

$$E = hf = \frac{hc}{\lambda} = \frac{(6.63 \times 10^{-34} \text{ J} \cdot \text{s})(3.00 \times 10^8 \text{ m/s})}{(7.2 \times 10^{-11} \text{ m})(1.60 \times 10^{-19} \text{ J/eV})} = 17 \text{ keV}.$$

The denominator includes the conversion factor from joules to eV.

FIGURE 39-11 (Repeated.) Spectrum of X-rays emitted from a molybdenum target in an X-ray tube operated at 50 kV.

FIGURE 39-13 Bremsstrahlung photon produced by an electron decelerated by interaction with a target atom.

APPROACH The highest intensity X-rays are generally for the K_α line (see Fig. 39–11) which occurs when high-energy external electrons knock out K shell electrons (the innermost orbit, $n = 1$) and their place is taken by electrons from the L shell $(n = 2)$. We use the Bohr model, and assume the electrons "see" a nuclear charge of $Z - 1$ (screened by one electron).

SOLUTION The hydrogen transition $n = 2$ to $n = 1$ would yield about 10.2 eV (see Fig. 37–26 or Example 37–13). Energy E is proportional to Z^2 (Eq. 37–14), or rather $(Z - 1)^2$ because the nucleus is shielded by the one electron in a $1s$ state (see above), so we can use ratios:

$$\frac{(Z - 1)^2}{1^2} = \frac{66.3 \times 10^3 \text{ eV}}{10.2 \text{ eV}} = 6.50 \times 10^3,$$

so $Z - 1 = \sqrt{6500} = 81$, and $Z = 82$, which makes it lead.

Now we briefly analyze the continuous part of an X-ray spectrum (Fig. 39–11) based on the photon theory of light. When electrons strike the target, they collide with atoms of the material and give up most of their energy as heat (about 99%, so X-ray tubes must be cooled). Electrons can also give up energy by emitting a photon: an electron decelerated by interaction with atoms of the target (Fig. 39–13) emits radiation because of its deceleration (Chapter 31), and in this case it is called **bremsstrahlung** (German for "braking radiation"). Because energy is conserved, the energy of the emitted photon, hf, must equal the loss of kinetic energy of the electron, $\Delta K = K - K'$, so

$$hf = \Delta K.$$

An electron may lose all or a part of its energy in such a collision. The continuous X-ray spectrum (Fig. 39–11) is explained as being due to such bremsstrahlung collisions in which varying amounts of energy are lost by the electrons. The shortest-wavelength X-ray (the highest frequency) must be due to an electron that gives up *all* its kinetic energy to produce one photon in a single collision. Since the initial kinetic energy of an electron is equal to the energy given it by the accelerating voltage, V, then $K = eV$. In a single collision in which the electron is brought to rest $(K' = 0)$, then $\Delta K = eV$ and

$$hf_0 = eV.$$

We set $f_0 = c/\lambda_0$ where λ_0 is the cutoff wavelength (Fig. 39–11) and find

$$\lambda_0 = \frac{hc}{eV}. \tag{39–10}$$

This prediction for λ_0 corresponds precisely with that observed experimentally. This result is further evidence that X-rays are a form of electromagnetic radiation (light)[†] and that the photon theory of light is valid.

APPROACH The electrons striking the target will have a kinetic energy of 50 keV. The shortest-wavelength photons are due to collisions in which all of the electron's kinetic energy is given to the photon so $K = eV = hf_0$.

SOLUTION From Eq. 39–10,

$$\lambda_0 = \frac{hc}{eV} = \frac{(6.63 \times 10^{-34} \text{ J·s})(3.0 \times 10^8 \text{ m/s})}{(1.6 \times 10^{-19} \text{ C})(5.0 \times 10^4 \text{ V})} = 2.5 \times 10^{-11} \text{ m},$$

or 0.025 nm.

NOTE This result agrees well with experiment, Fig. 39–11.

[†]If X-rays were not photons but rather neutral particles with mass m, Eq. 39–10 would not hold.

*39-7 Magnetic Dipole Moment; Total Angular Momentum

*Magnetic Dipole Moment and the Bohr Magneton

An electron orbiting the nucleus of an atom can be considered as a current loop, classically, and thus might be expected to have a **magnetic dipole moment** as discussed in Chapter 27. Indeed, in Example 27–12 we did a classical calculation of the magnetic dipole moment of the electron in the ground state of hydrogen based, essentially, on the Bohr model, and found it to give

$$\mu = IA = \tfrac{1}{2}evr.$$

Here v is the orbital velocity of the electron, and for a particle moving in a circle of radius r, its angular momentum is

$$L = mvr.$$

So we can write

$$\mu = \frac{1}{2}\frac{e}{m}L.$$

The direction of the angular momentum $\vec{\mathbf{L}}$ is perpendicular to the plane of the current loop. So is the direction of the magnetic dipole moment vector $\vec{\boldsymbol{\mu}}$, although in the opposite direction since the electron's charge is negative. Hence we can write the vector equation

$$\vec{\boldsymbol{\mu}} = -\frac{1}{2}\frac{e}{m}\vec{\mathbf{L}}. \tag{39–11}$$

This rough semiclassical derivation was based on the Bohr theory. The same result (Eq. 39–11) is obtained using quantum mechanics. Since $\vec{\mathbf{L}}$ is quantized in quantum mechanics, the magnetic dipole moment, too, must be quantized. The magnitude of the dipole moment is given by (see Eq. 39–3)

$$\mu = \frac{e\hbar}{2m}\sqrt{\ell(\ell+1)}.$$

When a magnetic dipole moment is in a magnetic field $\vec{\mathbf{B}}$, it experiences a torque as we saw in Section 27–5, and the potential energy U of such a system depends on $\vec{\mathbf{B}}$ and the orientation of $\vec{\boldsymbol{\mu}}$ relative to $\vec{\mathbf{B}}$ (Eq. 27–12):

$$U = -\vec{\boldsymbol{\mu}} \cdot \vec{\mathbf{B}}.$$

If the magnetic field $\vec{\mathbf{B}}$ is in the z direction, then

$$U = -\mu_z B_z$$

and from Eq. 39–4 $\left(L_z = m_\ell \hbar\right)$ and Eq. 39–11, we have

$$\mu_z = -\frac{e\hbar}{2m}m_\ell.$$

(Be careful here not to confuse the electron mass m with the magnetic quantum number, m_ℓ.) It is useful to define the quantity

$$\mu_B = \frac{e\hbar}{2m} \tag{39–12}$$

which is called the **Bohr magneton** and has the value $\mu_B = 9.27 \times 10^{-24}\,\text{J/T}$ (joule/tesla). Then we can write

$$\mu_z = -\mu_B m_\ell, \tag{39–13}$$

where m_ℓ has integer values from 0 to $\pm\ell$ (see Table 39–1). An atom placed in a magnetic field would have its energy split into levels that differ by $\Delta U = \mu_B B$; this is the *Zeeman effect*, and was shown in Fig. 39–4.

*Stern-Gerlach Experiment and the *g*-Factor for Electron Spin

The first evidence for the splitting of atomic energy levels, known as *space quantization* (Section 39–2), came in 1922 in a famous experiment known as the **Stern-Gerlach experiment**. Silver atoms (and later others) were heated in an oven from which they escaped as shown in Fig. 39–14. The atoms were made to pass through a

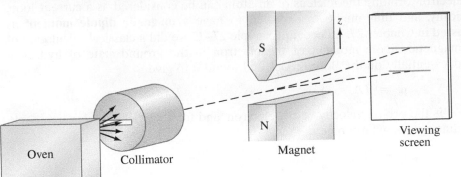

FIGURE 39–14 The Stern-Gerlach experiment, which is done inside a vacuum chamber.

collimator, which eliminated all but a narrow beam. The beam then passed into a *nonhomogeneous* magnetic field. The field was deliberately made nonhomogeneous so that it would exert a force on atomic magnetic moments: remember that the potential energy (in this case $-\vec{\mu} \cdot \vec{B}$) must change in space if there is to be a force ($F_x = -dU/dx$, etc., Section 8–2). If $\vec{B}$ has a gradient along the z axis, as in Fig. 39–14, then the force is along z:

$$F_z = -\frac{dU}{dz} = \mu_z \frac{dB_z}{dz}.$$

Thus the silver atoms would be deflected up or down depending on the value of μ for each atom. Classically, we would expect to see a continuous distribution on the viewing screen, since we would expect the atoms to have randomly oriented magnetic moments. But Stern and Gerlach saw instead two distinct lines for silver (and for other atoms sometimes more than two lines). These observations were the first evidence for space quantization, though not fully explained until a few years later. If the lines were due to orbital angular momentum, there should have been an odd number of them, corresponding to the possible values of m_ℓ (since $\mu_z = -\mu_B m_\ell$). For $\ell = 0$, there is only one possibility, $m_\ell = 0$. For $\ell = 1, m_\ell$ can be $1, 0$, or -1, and we would expect three lines, and so on. Why there are only two lines was eventually explained by the concept of electron spin. With a spin of $\frac{1}{2}$, the electron spin can have only two orientations in space, as we saw in Fig. 39–5. Hence a magnetic dipole moment associated with spin would have only two positions. Thus, the two states for silver seen in the Stern-Gerlach experiment must be due to the spin of its one valence electron. Silver atoms must thus have zero orbital angular momentum but a total spin of $\frac{1}{2}$ due to this one valence electron. (Of silver's 47 electrons, the spins of the first 46 cancel.) For the H atom in its ground state, again only two lines were seen on the screen of Fig. 39–14: due to the spin $\frac{1}{2}$ of its electron since the orbital angular momentum is zero.

The Stern-Gerlach deflection is proportional to the magnetic dipole moment, μ_z, and for a spin $\frac{1}{2}$ particle we expect $\mu_z = -\mu_B m_s = -\left(\frac{1}{2}\right)(e\hbar/2m)$ as for the case of orbital angular momentum, Eq. 39–13. Instead, μ_z for spin was found to be about twice as large:

$$\mu_z = -g\mu_B m_s, \qquad \text{[electron spin]} \quad \textbf{(39–14)}$$

where g, called the **g-factor** or **gyromagnetic ratio**, has been measured to be slightly larger than 2: $g = 2.0023 \cdots$ for a free electron. This unexpected factor of (about) 2 clearly indicates that spin cannot be viewed as a classical angular momentum. It is a purely quantum-mechanical effect. Equation 39–14 is the same as Eq. 39–13 for orbital angular momentum with m_s replacing m_ℓ. But for the orbital case, $g = 1$.

*Total Angular Momentum $\vec{J}$

An atom can have both orbital and spin angular momenta. For example, in the $2p$ state of hydrogen $\ell = 1$ and $s = \frac{1}{2}$. In the $4d$ state, $\ell = 2$ and $s = \frac{1}{2}$. The **total angular momentum** is the vector sum of the orbital angular momentum $\vec{L}$ and the spin $\vec{S}$:

$$\vec{J} = \vec{L} + \vec{S}.$$

According to quantum mechanics, the magnitude of the total angular momentum $\vec{J}$ is quantized:

$$J = \sqrt{j(j + 1)}\,\hbar. \tag{39–15}$$

For the single electron in the H atom, quantum mechanics gives the result that j can be

$$j = \ell + s = \ell + \frac{1}{2}$$

or

$$j = \ell - s = \ell - \frac{1}{2}$$

but never less than zero, just as for ℓ and s. For the $1s$ state, $\ell = 0$ and $j = \frac{1}{2}$ is the only possibility. For p states, say the $2p$ state, $\ell = 1$ and j can be either $\frac{3}{2}$ or $\frac{1}{2}$. The z component for j is quantized in the usual way:

$$m_j = j, j - 1, \cdots, -j.$$

For a $2p$ state with $j = \frac{1}{2}$, m_j can be $\frac{1}{2}$ or $-\frac{1}{2}$; for $j = \frac{3}{2}$, m_j can be $\frac{3}{2}, \frac{1}{2}, -\frac{1}{2}, -\frac{3}{2}$, for a total of four states. Note that the state of a single electron can be specified by giving n, ℓ, m_ℓ, m_s, or by giving n, j, ℓ, m_j (only one of these descriptions at a time).

| **EXERCISE G** What are the possibilities for j in the $3d$ state of hydrogen? $(a)\ \frac{3}{2}, \frac{1}{2}$; $(b)\ \frac{5}{2}, \frac{3}{2}, \frac{1}{2}$; $(c)\ \frac{7}{2}, \frac{5}{2}, \frac{3}{2}, \frac{1}{2}$; $(d)\ \frac{5}{2}, \frac{3}{2}$; $(e)\ \frac{7}{2}, \frac{5}{2}$.

The interaction of magnetic fields with atoms, as in the Zeeman effect and the Stern-Gerlach experiment, involves the *total* angular momentum. Thus the Stern-Gerlach experiment on H atoms in the ground state shows two lines (for $m_j = +\frac{1}{2}$ and $-\frac{1}{2}$), but for the first excited state it shows four lines corresponding to the four possible m_j values $(\frac{3}{2}, \frac{1}{2}, -\frac{1}{2}, -\frac{3}{2})$.

*Spectroscopic Notation

We can specify the state of an atom, including the total angular momentum quantum number j, using the following **spectroscopic notation**. For a single electron state we can write

$$nL_j,$$

where the value of L (the orbital quantum number) is specified using the same letters as in Table 39–3, but in upper case:

$$L = 0 \quad 1 \quad 2 \quad 3 \quad 4 \quad \cdots$$
$$\text{letter} = S \quad P \quad D \quad F \quad G \quad \cdots.$$

So the $2P_{3/2}$ state has $n = 2$, $\ell = 1$, $j = \frac{3}{2}$, whereas $1S_{1/2}$ specifies the ground state in hydrogen.

A magnetic effect also produces the *fine structure* splitting mentioned in Section 39–2, but it occurs in the absence of any external field. Instead, it is due to a magnetic field produced by the atom itself. We can see how it occurs by putting ourselves in the reference frame of the electron, in which case we see the nucleus revolving about us as a moving charge or electric current that produces a magnetic field, B_n. The electron has an intrinsic magnetic dipole moment μ_s (Eq. 39–14) and hence its energy will be altered by an amount (Eq. 27–12)

$$\Delta U = -\vec{\mu}_s \cdot \vec{B}_n.$$

Since μ_s takes on quantized values according to the values of m_s, the energy of a single electron state will split into two closely spaced energy levels (for $m_s = +\frac{1}{2}$ and $-\frac{1}{2}$). This tiny splitting of energy levels produces a tiny splitting in spectral lines. For example, in the H atom, the 2P → 1S transition is split into two lines corresponding to $2P_{1/2} \to 1S_{1/2}$ and $2P_{3/2} \to 1S_{1/2}$. The difference in energy between these two is only about 5×10^{-5} eV, which is very small compared to the 2P → 1S transition energy of 13.6 eV $- 3.4$ eV $= 10.2$ eV.

The magnetic field $\vec{B}_n$ produced by the orbital motion is proportional to the orbital angular momentum $\vec{L}$, and since $\vec{\mu}_s$ is proportional to the spin $\vec{S}$, then $\Delta U = -\vec{\mu}_s \cdot \vec{B}_n$ can be written

$$\Delta U \propto \vec{L} \cdot \vec{S}.$$

This interaction, which produces the fine structure, is thus called the **spin-orbit interaction**. Its magnitude is related to a dimensionless constant known as the **fine structure constant**,

$$\alpha = \frac{e^2}{2\epsilon_0 hc} \approx \frac{1}{137},$$

which also appears elsewhere in atomic physics.

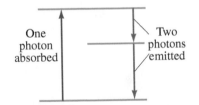

One photon absorbed / Two photons emitted

FIGURE 39–15 Fluorescence.

FIGURE 39–16 When UV light (a range of wavelengths) illuminates these various "fluorescent" rocks, they fluoresce in the visible region of the spectrum.

39–8 Fluorescence and Phosphorescence

When an atom is excited from one energy state to a higher one by the absorption of a photon, it may return to the lower level in a series of two (or more) jumps if there is an energy level in between (Fig. 39–15). The photons emitted will consequently have lower energy and frequency than the absorbed photon. When the absorbed photon is in the UV and the emitted photons are in the visible region of the spectrum, this phenomenon is called **fluorescence** (Fig. 39–16).

The wavelength for which fluorescence will occur depends on the energy levels of the particular atoms. Because the frequencies are different for different substances, and because many substances fluoresce readily, fluorescence is a powerful tool for identification of compounds. It is also used for assaying—determining how much of a substance is present—and for following substances along a natural pathway as in plants and animals. For detection of a given compound, the stimulating light must be monochromatic, and solvents or other materials present must not fluoresce in the same region of the spectrum. Sometimes the observation of fluorescent light being emitted is sufficient to detect a compound. In other cases, spectrometers are used to measure the wavelengths and intensities of the emitted light.

Fluorescent lightbulbs work in a two-step process. The applied voltage accelerates electrons that strike atoms of the gas in the tube and cause them to be excited. When the excited atoms jump down to their normal levels, they emit UV photons which strike a fluorescent coating on the inside of the tube. The light we see is a result of this material fluorescing in response to the UV light striking it.

Materials such as those used for luminous watch dials are said to be **phosphorescent**. When an atom is raised to a normal excited state, it drops back down within about 10^{-8} s. In phosphorescent substances, atoms can be excited by photon absorption to energy levels, called **metastable**, which are states that last much longer because to jump down is a "forbidden" transition as discussed in Section 39–2. Metastable states can last even a few seconds or longer. In a collection of such atoms, many of the atoms will descend to the lower state fairly soon, but many will remain in the excited state for over an hour. Hence light will be emitted even after long periods. When you put your luminous watch dial close to a bright lamp, many atoms are excited to metastable states, and you can see the glow for a long time afterward.

39–9 Lasers

A **laser** is a device that can produce a very narrow intense beam of monochromatic coherent light. (By *coherent*, we mean that across any cross section of the beam, all parts have the same phase.) The emitted beam is a nearly perfect plane wave. An ordinary light source, on the other hand, emits light in all directions (so the intensity decreases rapidly with distance), and the emitted light is incoherent (the different parts of a beam are not in phase with each other). The excited atoms that emit the light in an ordinary lightbulb act independently, so each photon emitted can be considered as a short wave train that lasts about 10^{-8} s. Different wave trains bear no phase relation to one another. Just the opposite is true of lasers.

The action of a laser is based on quantum theory. We have seen that a photon can be absorbed by an atom if (and only if) the photon energy hf corresponds to the energy difference between an occupied energy level of the atom and an available excited state, Fig. 39–17a. If the atom is already in the excited state, it may of course jump down spontaneously (i.e., no apparent stimulus) to the lower state with the emission of a photon. However, if a photon with this same energy strikes the excited atom, it can stimulate the atom to make the transition sooner to the lower state, Fig. 39–17b. This phenomenon is called **stimulated emission**: not only do we still have the original photon, but also a second one of the same frequency as a result of the atom's transition. These two photons are exactly *in phase*, and they are moving in the same direction. This is how coherent light is produced in a laser. Hence the name "laser," which is an acronym for **L**ight **A**mplification by **S**timulated **E**mission of **R**adiation.

The natural population in energy states of atoms in thermal equilibrium at any temperature T (in K) is given by the **Boltzmann distribution** (or **Boltzmann factor**):

$$N_n = Ce^{-\frac{E_n}{kT}}, \tag{39–16a}$$

where N_n is the number of atoms in the state with energy E_n. For two states n and n', the ratio of the number of atoms in the two states is

$$\frac{N_n}{N_{n'}} = e^{-\left(\frac{E_n - E_{n'}}{kT}\right)}. \tag{39–16b}$$

Thus most atoms are in the ground state unless the temperature is very high. In the two-level system of Fig. 39–17, most atoms are normally in the lower state, so the majority of incident photons will be absorbed. In order to obtain the coherent light from stimulated emission, two conditions must be satisfied. First, atoms must be excited to the higher state, so that an **inverted population** is produced, one in which more atoms are in the upper state than in the lower one (Fig. 39–18). Then *emission* of photons will dominate over absorption. Hence the system will not be in thermal equilibrium. And second, the higher state must be a **metastable state**— a state in which the electrons remain longer than usual[†] so that the transition to the lower state occurs by stimulated emission rather than spontaneously. (How inverted populations are created will be discussed shortly.)

[†] An atom excited to such a state can jump to a lower state only by a so-called forbidden transition (discussed in Section 39–2), which is why the lifetime is longer than normal.

FIGURE 39–17 (a) Absorption of a photon. (b) Stimulated emission. E_u and E_ℓ refer to "upper" and "lower" energy states.

FIGURE 39–18 Two energy levels for a collection of atoms. Each dot represents the energy state of one atom. (a) A normal situation; (b) an inverted population.

FIGURE 39–19 Laser diagram, showing excited atoms stimulated to emit light.

Figure 39–19 is a schematic diagram of a laser: the "lasing" material is placed in a long narrow tube at the ends of which are two mirrors, one of which is partially transparent (transmitting perhaps 1 or 2%). Some of the excited atoms drop down fairly soon after being excited. One of these is the blue atom shown on the far left in Fig. 39–19. If the emitted photon strikes another atom in the excited state, it stimulates this atom to emit a photon of the *same* frequency, moving in the *same* direction, and *in phase* with it. These two photons then move on to strike other atoms causing more stimulated emission. As the process continues, the number of photons multiplies. When the photons strike the end mirrors, most are reflected back, and as they move in the opposite direction, they continue to stimulate more atoms to emit photons. As the photons move back and forth between the mirrors, a small percentage passes through the partially transparent mirror at one end. These photons make up the narrow coherent external laser beam.

Inside the tube, some spontaneously emitted photons will be emitted at an angle to the axis, and these will merely go out the side of the tube and not affect the narrowness of the main beam. In a well-designed laser, the spreading of the beam is limited only by diffraction, so the angular spread is $\approx \lambda/D$ (see Eq. 35–1 or 35–10), where D is the diameter of the end mirror. The diffraction spreading can be incredibly small. The light energy, instead of spreading out in space as it does for an ordinary light source, can be a pencil-thin beam.

Creating an Inverted Population

The excitation of the atoms in a laser can be done in several ways to produce the necessary inverted population. In a **ruby laser**, the lasing material is a ruby rod consisting of Al_2O_3 with a small percentage of aluminum (Al) atoms replaced by chromium (Cr) atoms. The Cr atoms are the ones involved in lasing. In a process called **optical pumping**, the atoms are excited by strong flashes of light of wavelength 550 nm, which corresponds to a photon energy of 2.2 eV. As shown in Fig. 39–20, the atoms are excited from state E_0 to state E_2. The atoms quickly decay either back to E_0 or to the intermediate state E_1, which is metastable with a lifetime of about 3×10^{-3} s (compared to 10^{-8} s for ordinary levels). With strong pumping action, more atoms can be found in the E_1 state than are in the E_0 state. Thus we have the inverted population needed for lasing. As soon as a few atoms in the E_1 state jump down to E_0, they emit photons that produce stimulated emission of the other atoms, and the lasing action begins. A ruby laser thus emits a beam whose photons have energy 1.8 eV and a wavelength of 694.3 nm (or "ruby-red" light).

In a helium–neon (He–Ne) laser, the lasing material is a gas, a mixture of about 85% He and 15% Ne. The atoms are excited by applying a high voltage to the tube so that an electric discharge takes place within the gas. In the process, some of the He atoms are raised to the metastable state E_1 shown in Fig. 39–21, which corresponds to a jump of 20.61 eV, almost exactly equal to an excited state in neon, 20.66 eV. The He atoms do not quickly return to the ground state by spontaneous emission, but instead often give their excess energy to a Ne atom when they collide—see Fig. 39–21. In such a collision, the He drops to the ground state and the Ne atom is excited to the state E_3' (the prime refers to neon states). The slight difference in energy (0.05 eV) is supplied by the kinetic energy of the moving atoms. In this manner, the E_3' state in Ne—which is metastable—becomes more populated than the E_2' level. This inverted population between E_3' and E_2' is what is needed for lasing.

FIGURE 39–20 Energy levels of chromium in a ruby crystal. Photons of energy 2.2 eV "pump" atoms from E_0 to E_2, which then decay to metastable state E_1. Lasing action occurs by stimulated emission of photons in transition from E_1 to E_0.

FIGURE 39–21 Energy levels for He and Ne. He is excited in the electric discharge to the E_1 state. This energy is transferred to the E_3' level of the Ne by collision. E_3' is metastable and decays to E_2' by stimulated emission.

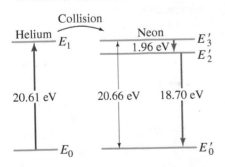

Very common now are **semiconductor diode lasers**, also called **pn junction lasers**, which utilize an inverted population of electrons between the conduction band of the n side of the diode and the lower-energy valence band of the p side (Sections 40–7 to 40–9). When an electron jumps down, a photon can be emitted, which in turn can stimulate another electron to make the transition and emit another photon, in phase. The needed mirrors (as in Fig. 39–19) are made by the polished ends of the pn crystal. Semiconductor lasers are used in CD and DVD players (see below), and in many other applications.

Other types of laser include: *chemical lasers*, in which the energy input comes from the chemical reaction of highly reactive gases; *dye lasers*, whose frequency is tunable; CO_2 *gas lasers*, capable of high-power output in the infrared; and *rare-earth solid-state lasers* such as the high-power Nd:YAG laser.

The excitation of the atoms in a laser can be done continuously or in pulses. In a **pulsed laser**, the atoms are excited by periodic inputs of energy. In a **continuous laser**, the energy input is continuous: as atoms are stimulated to jump down to the lower level, they are soon excited back up to the upper level so the output is a continuous laser beam.

No laser is a source of energy. Energy must be put in, and the laser converts a part of it into an intense narrow beam output.

*Applications

The unique feature of light from a laser, that it is a coherent narrow beam, has found many applications. In everyday life, lasers are used as bar-code readers (at store checkout stands) and in compact disc (CD) and digital video disc (DVD) players. The laser beam reflects off the stripes and spaces of a bar code, and off the tiny pits of a CD or DVD as shown in Fig. 39–22a. The recorded information on a CD or DVD is a series of pits and spaces representing 0s and 1s (or "off" and "on") of a binary code that is decoded electronically before being sent to the audio or video system. The laser of a CD player starts reading at the inside of the disc which rotates at about 500 rpm at the start. As the disc rotates, the laser follows the spiral track (Fig. 39–22b), and as it moves outward the disc must slow down because each successive circumference ($C = 2\pi r$) is slightly longer as r increases; at the outer edge, the disc is rotating about 200 rpm. A 1-hour CD has a track roughly 5 km long; the track width is about 1600 nm ($= 1.6\ \mu$m) and the distance between pits is about 800 nm. DVDs contain much more information. Standard DVDs use a thinner track ($0.7\ \mu$m) and shorter pit length (400 nm). New high-definition DVDs use a "blue" laser with a short wavelength (405 nm) and narrower beam, allowing a narrower track ($0.3\ \mu$m) that can store much more data for high definition. DVDs can also have two layers, one below the other. When the laser focuses on the second layer, the light passes through the semitransparent surface layer. The second layer may start reading at the outer edge instead of inside. DVDs can also have a single or double layer on *both* surfaces of the disc.

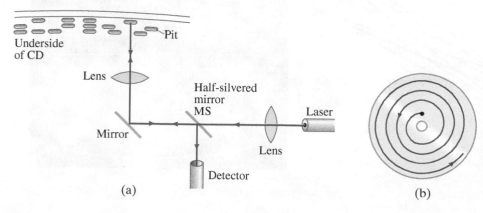

(a)

(b)

FIGURE 39–22 (a) Reading a CD (or DVD). The fine beam of a laser, focused even more finely with lenses, is directed at the undersurface of a rotating compact disc. The beam is reflected back from the areas between pits but reflects much less from pits. The reflected light is detected as shown, reflected by a half-reflecting mirror MS. The strong and weak reflections correspond to the 0s and 1s of the binary code representing the audio or video signal. (b) A laser follows the CD track which starts near the center and spirals outward.

FIGURE 39–23 Laser being used in eye surgery.

Lasers are a useful surgical tool. The narrow intense beam can be used to destroy tissue in a localized area, or to break up gallstones and kidney stones. Because of the heat produced, a laser beam can be used to "weld" broken tissue, such as a detached retina, Fig. 39–23, or to mold the cornea of the eye (by vaporizing tiny bits of material) to correct myopia and other eye defects (LASIK surgery). The laser beam can be carried by an optical fiber (Section 32–7) to the surgical point, sometimes as an additional fiber-optic path on an endoscope (again Section 32–7). An example is the removal of plaque clogging human arteries. Tiny organelles within a living cell have been destroyed using lasers by researchers studying how the absence of that organelle affects the behavior of the cell. Laser beams are used to destroy cancerous and precancerous cells; and the heat seals off capillaries and lymph vessels, thus "cauterizing" the wound to prevent spread of the disease.

The intense heat produced in a small area by a laser beam is used for welding and machining metals and for drilling tiny holes in hard materials. Because a laser beam is coherent, monochromatic, narrow, and essentially parallel, lenses can be used to focus the light into even smaller areas. The precise straightness of a laser beam is also useful to surveyors for lining up equipment accurately, especially in inaccessible places.

*39–10 Holography

One of the most interesting applications of laser light is the production of three-dimensional images called **holograms** (see Fig. 39–24). In an ordinary photograph, the film simply records the intensity of light reaching it at each point. When the photograph or transparency is viewed, light reflecting from it or passing through it gives us a two-dimensional picture. In holography, the images are formed by interference, without lenses. When a laser hologram is made on film, a broadened laser beam is split into two parts by a half-silvered mirror, Fig. 39–24a. One part goes directly to the film; the rest passes to the object to be photographed, from which it is reflected to the film. Light from every point on the object reaches each point on the film, and the interference of the two beams allows the film to record both the intensity and relative phase of the light at each point. It is crucial that the incident light be coherent—that is, in phase at all points—which is why a laser is used. After the film is developed, it is placed again in a laser beam and a three-dimensional image of the object is created. You can walk around such an image and see it from different sides as if it were the original object (Fig. 39–24b). Yet, if you try to touch it with your hand, there will be nothing material there.

FIGURE 39–24 (a) Making a hologram. Light reflected from various points on the object interferes (at the film) with light from the direct beam. (b) A boy is looking at a hologram of two women talking on telephones. Holograms do not photograph well—they must be seen directly.

(a)

(b)

The details of how the image is formed are quite complicated. But we can get the basic idea by considering one single point on the object. In Fig. 39–25a the rays OA and OB have reflected from one point on our object. The rays CA and DB come directly from the source and interfere with OA and OB at points A and B on the film. A set of interference fringes is produced as shown in Fig. 39–25b. The spacing between the fringes changes from top to bottom as shown. Why this happens is explained in Fig. 39–26. Thus the hologram of a single point object would have the fringe pattern shown in Fig. 39–25b. The film in this case looks like a diffraction grating with variable spacing. Hence, when coherent laser light is passed back through the developed film to reconstruct the image, the diffracted rays in the first order maxima occur at slightly different angles because the spacing changes. (Remember Eq. 35–13, $\sin \theta = \lambda/d$: where the spacing d is greater, the angle θ is less.) Hence, the rays diffracted upward (in first order) seem to diverge from a single point, Fig. 39–27. This is a virtual image of the original object, which can be seen with the eye. Rays diffracted in first order *downward* converge to make a real image, which can be seen and also photographed. (Note that the straight-through undiffracted rays are of no interest.) Of course real objects consist of many points, so a hologram will be a complex interference pattern which, when laser light is incident on it, will reproduce an image of the object. Each image point will be at the correct (three-dimensional) position with respect to other points, so the image accurately represents the original object. And it can be viewed from different angles as if viewing the original object. Holograms can be made in which a viewer can walk entirely around the image (360°) and see all sides of it.

FIGURE 39–25 (a) Light from point O on the object interferes with light of the direct beam (rays CA and DB). (b) Interference fringes produced.

FIGURE 39–26 Each of the rays shown leaving point O is one wavelength shorter than the one above it. If the top ray is in phase with the direct beam (not shown), which has the same phase at all points on the screen, each of the rays shown produces a constructive interference fringe. From this diagram it can be seen that the fringe spacing increases toward the bottom.

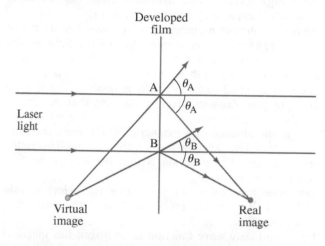

FIGURE 39–27 Reconstructing the image of one point on the object. Laser beam strikes the developed film, which is like a diffraction grating of variable spacing. Rays corresponding to the first diffraction maxima are shown emerging. The angle $\theta_A > \theta_B$ because the spacing at B is greater than at A ($\sin \theta = \lambda/d$). Hence real and virtual images of the point are reproduced as shown.

Volume or **white-light holograms** do not require a laser to see the image, but can be viewed with ordinary white light (preferably a nearly point source, such as the Sun or a clear bulb with a small bright filament). Such holograms must be made, however, with a laser. They are made not on thin film, but on a *thick* emulsion. The interference pattern in the film emulsion can be thought of as an array of bands or ribbons where constructive interference occurred. This array, and the reconstruction of the image, can be compared to Bragg scattering of X-rays from the atoms in a crystal (see Section 35–10). White light can reconstruct the image because the Bragg condition ($m\lambda = 2d \sin \theta$) selects out the appropriate single wavelength. If the hologram is originally produced by lasers emitting the three additive primary colors (red, green, and blue), the three-dimensional image can be seen in full color when viewed with white light.

Summary

In the quantum-mechanical view of the atom, the electrons do not have well-defined orbits, but instead exist as a "cloud." Electron clouds can be interpreted as an electron wave spread out in space, or as a **probability distribution** for electrons considered as particles.

For the simplest atom, hydrogen, the Schrödinger equation contains the potential energy

$$U = -\frac{1}{4\pi\epsilon_0}\frac{e^2}{r}.$$

The solutions give the same values of energy as the old Bohr theory.

According to quantum mechanics, the state of an electron in an atom is specified by four **quantum numbers:** n, ℓ, m_ℓ, and m_s:

1. n, the **principal quantum number**, can take on any integer value $(1, 2, 3, \cdots)$ and corresponds to the quantum number of the old Bohr theory;

2. ℓ, the **orbital quantum number**, can take on integer values from 0 up to $n - 1$;

3. m_ℓ, the **magnetic quantum number**, can take on integer values from $-\ell$ to $+\ell$;

4. m_s, the **spin quantum number**, can be $+\frac{1}{2}$ or $-\frac{1}{2}$.

The energy levels in the hydrogen atom depend on n, whereas in other atoms they depend on n and ℓ.

The orbital angular momentum of an atom has magnitude $L = \sqrt{\ell(\ell + 1)}\,\hbar$ and z component $L_z = m_\ell\hbar$. Spin angular momentum has magnitude $S = \sqrt{s(s + 1)}\,\hbar$ and z component $S_z = m_s\hbar$ where $s = \frac{1}{2}$ and $m_s = \pm\frac{1}{2}$.

When an external magnetic field is applied, the spectral lines are split (the **Zeeman effect**), indicating that the energy depends also on m_ℓ in this case.

Even in the absence of a magnetic field, precise measurements of spectral lines show a tiny splitting of the lines called **fine structure**, whose explanation is that the energy depends very slightly on m_ℓ and m_s.

Transitions between states that obey the **selection rule** $\Delta\ell = \pm 1$ are far more probable than other so-called **forbidden** transitions.

The ground-state wave function in hydrogen has spherical symmetry, as do other $\ell = 0$ states. States with $\ell > 0$ have some directionality in space.

The **probability density** (or probability distribution), $|\psi|^2$, and the **radial probability density**, $P_r = 4\pi r^2|\psi|^2$, are both useful to illustrate the spatial extent of the electron cloud.

The arrangement of electrons in multi-electron atoms is governed by the **Pauli exclusion principle**, which states that no two electrons can occupy the same quantum state—that is, they cannot have the same set of quantum numbers n, ℓ, m_ℓ, and m_s.

As a result, electrons in multi-electron atoms are grouped into **shells** (according to the value of n) and **subshells** (according to ℓ).

Electron configurations are specified using the numerical values of n, and using letters for ℓ: s, p, d, f, etc., for $\ell = 0, 1, 2, 3$, and so on, plus a superscript for the number of electrons in that subshell. Thus, the ground state of hydrogen is $1s^1$, whereas that for oxygen is $1s^22s^22p^4$.

In the **Periodic Table**, the elements are arranged in horizontal rows according to increasing atomic number (number of electrons in the neutral atom). The shell structure gives rise to a periodicity in the properties of the elements, so that each vertical column can contain elements with similar chemical properties.

X-rays, which are a form of electromagnetic radiation of very short wavelength, are produced when high-speed electrons strike a target. The spectrum of X-rays so produced consists of two parts, a continuous spectrum produced when the electrons are decelerated by atoms of the target, and peaks representing photons emitted by atoms of the target after being excited by collision with the high-speed electrons. Measurement of these peaks allows determination of inner energy levels of atoms and determination of atomic number Z.

[*An atom has a **magnetic dipole moment** $\vec{\mu}$ related to its orbital angular momentum $\vec{L}$, which produces a potential energy when in a magnetic field, $U = -\vec{\mu}\cdot\vec{B}$. Electron spin also yields a magnetic moment, but the energy in a magnetic field is a factor $g = 2.0023 \cdots$ times larger than expected, as determined in Stern-Gerlach experiments.]

[*Atoms have a total angular momentum $\vec{J} = \vec{L} + \vec{S}$ which is quantized as for L and S, namely $J = \sqrt{j(j + 1)}\,\hbar$ where j is a half-integer equal to $\ell \pm \frac{1}{2}$ in hydrogen.]

Fluorescence occurs when absorbed UV photons are followed by emission of visible light, due to the special arrangement of energy levels of atoms of the material. **Phosphorescent** materials have **metastable** states (long-lived) that emit light seconds or minutes after absorption of light.

Lasers produce a narrow beam of monochromatic coherent light (light waves *in phase*). [*Holograms** are images with a 3-dimensional quality, formed by interference of laser light.]

Questions

1. Discuss the differences between Bohr's view of the atom and the quantum-mechanical view.

2. The probability density $|\psi|^2$ is a maximum at the center of the H atom $(r = 0)$ for the ground state, whereas the radial probability density $P_r = 4\pi r^2|\psi|^2$ is zero at this point. Explain why.

3. Which model of the hydrogen atom, the Bohr model or the quantum-mechanical model, predicts that the electron spends more time near the nucleus?

4. The size of atoms varies by only a factor of three or so, from largest to smallest, yet the number of electrons varies from one to over 100. Why?

5. Excited hydrogen and excited helium atoms both radiate light as they jump down to the $n = 1, \ell = 0, m_\ell = 0$ state. Yet the two elements have very different emission spectra. Why?

6. In Fig. 39–4, why do the upper and lower levels have different energy splittings in a magnetic field?

7. Why do three quantum numbers come out of the Schrödinger theory (rather than, say, two or four)?

8. The 589-nm yellow line in sodium is actually two very closely spaced lines. This splitting is due to an "internal" Zeeman effect. Can you explain this? [*Hint*: Put yourself in the reference frame of the electron.]

9. Which of the following electron configurations are not allowed: (a) $1s^2 2s^2 2p^4 3s^2 4p^2$; (b) $1s^2 2s^2 2p^8 3s^1$; (c) $1s^2 2s^2 2p^6 3s^2 3p^5 4s^2 4d^5 4f^1$? If not allowed, explain why.

10. Give the complete electron configuration for a uranium atom (careful scrutiny across the Periodic Table on the inside back cover will provide useful hints).

11. In what column of the Periodic Table would you expect to find the atom with each of the following configurations? (a) $1s^2 2s^2 2p^6 3s^2$; (b) $1s^2 2s^2 2p^6 3s^2 3p^6$; (c) $1s^2 2s^2 2p^6 3s^2 3p^6 4s^1$; (d) $1s^2 2s^2 2p^5$.

12. On what factors does the periodicity of the Periodic Table depend? Consider the exclusion principle, quantization of angular momentum, spin, and any others you can think of.

13. How would the Periodic Table look if there were no electron spin but otherwise quantum mechanics were valid? Consider the first 20 elements or so.

14. The ionization energy for neon ($Z = 10$) is 21.6 eV and that for sodium ($Z = 11$) is 5.1 eV. Explain the large difference.

15. Why do chlorine and iodine exhibit similar properties?

16. Explain why potassium and sodium exhibit similar properties.

17. Why are the chemical properties of the rare earths so similar?

18. Why do we not expect perfect agreement between measured values of characteristic X-ray line wavelengths and those calculated using Bohr theory, as in Example 39–6?

19. Why does the Bohr theory, which does not work at all well for normal transitions involving the outer electrons for He and more complex atoms, nevertheless predict reasonably well the atomic X-ray spectra for transitions deep inside the atom?

20. Why does the cutoff wavelength in Fig. 39–11 imply a photon nature for light?

21. How would you figure out which lines in an X-ray spectrum correspond to K_α, K_β, L, etc., transitions?

22. Why do the characteristic X-ray spectra vary in a systematic way with Z, whereas the visible spectra (Fig. 35–22) do not?

23. Why do we expect electron transitions deep within an atom to produce shorter wavelengths than transitions by outer electrons?

*24. Why is the direction of the magnetic dipole moment of an electron opposite to that of its orbital angular momentum?

*25. Why is a nonhomogeneous field used in the Stern-Gerlach experiment?

26. Compare spontaneous emission to stimulated emission.

27. Does the intensity of light from a laser fall off as the inverse square of the distance?

28. How does laser light differ from ordinary light? How is it the same?

29. Explain how a 0.0005-W laser beam, photographed at a distance, can seem much stronger than a 1000-W street lamp at the same distance.

Problems

39–2 Hydrogen Atom Quantum Numbers

1. (I) For $n = 7$, what values can ℓ have?

2. (I) For $n = 6$, $\ell = 3$, what are the possible values of m_ℓ and m_s?

3. (I) How many different states are possible for an electron whose principal quantum number is $n = 5$? Write down the quantum numbers for each state.

4. (I) If a hydrogen atom has $m_\ell = -4$, what are the possible values of n, ℓ, and m_s?

5. (I) A hydrogen atom has $\ell = 5$. What are the possible values for n, m_ℓ, and m_s?

6. (I) Calculate the magnitude of the angular momentum of an electron in the $n = 5$, $\ell = 3$ state of hydrogen.

7. (II) A hydrogen atom is in the 7g state. Determine (a) the principal quantum number, (b) the energy of the state, (c) the orbital angular momentum and its quantum number ℓ, and (d) the possible values for the magnetic quantum number.

8. (II) (a) Show that the number of different states possible for a given value of ℓ is equal to $2(2\ell + 1)$. (b) What is this number for $\ell = 0, 1, 2, 3, 4, 5,$ and 6?

9. (II) Show that the number of different electron states possible for a given value of n is $2n^2$. (See Problem 8.)

10. (II) An excited H atom is in a 5d state. (a) Name all the states to which the atom is "allowed" to jump with the emission of a photon. (b) How many different wavelengths are there (ignoring fine structure)?

11. (II) The magnitude of the orbital angular momentum in an excited state of hydrogen is 6.84×10^{-34} J·s and the z component is 2.11×10^{-34} J·s. What are all the possible values of n, ℓ, and m_ℓ for this state?

39–3 Hydrogen Atom Wave Functions

12. (I) Show that the ground-state wave function, Eq. 39–5, is normalized. [Hint: See Example 39–4.]

13. (II) For the ground state of hydrogen, what is the value of (a) ψ, (b) $|\psi|^2$, and (c) P_r, at $r = 1.5 r_0$?

14. (II) For the $n = 2$, $\ell = 0$ state of hydrogen, what is the value of (a) ψ, (b) $|\psi|^2$, and (c) P_r, at $r = 4 r_0$?

15. (II) By what factor is it more likely to find the electron in the ground state of hydrogen at the Bohr radius (r_0) than at twice the Bohr radius ($2r_0$)?

16. (II) (a) Show that the probability of finding the electron in the ground state of hydrogen at less than one Bohr radius from the nucleus is 32%. (b) What is the probability of finding a 1s electron between $r = r_0$ and $r = 2r_0$?

17. (II) Determine the radius r of a sphere centered on the nucleus within which the probability of finding the electron for the ground state of hydrogen is (a) 50%, (b) 90%, (c) 99%.

18. (II) (a) Estimate the probability of finding an electron, in the ground state of hydrogen, within the nucleus assuming it to be a sphere of radius $r = 1.1$ fm. (b) Repeat the estimate assuming the electron is replaced with a muon, which is very similar to an electron (Chapter 43) except that its mass is 207 times greater.

19. (II) Show that the mean value of r for an electron in the ground state of hydrogen is $\bar{r} = \frac{3}{2}r_0$, by calculating

$$\bar{r} = \int_{\text{all space}} r|\psi_{100}|^2 \, dV = \int_0^\infty r|\psi_{100}|^2 4\pi r^2 \, dr.$$

20. (II) Show that ψ_{200} as given by Eq. 39–8 is normalized.

21. (II) Determine the average radial probability distribution P_r for the $n = 2, \ell = 1$ state in hydrogen by calculating

$$P_r = 4\pi r^2 \left[\frac{1}{3}|\psi_{210}|^2 + \frac{1}{3}|\psi_{211}|^2 + \frac{1}{3}|\psi_{21-1}|^2\right].$$

22. (II) Use the result of Problem 21 to show that the most probable distance r from the nucleus for an electron in the $2p$ state of hydrogen is $r = 4r_0$, which is just the second Bohr radius (Eq. 37–11, Fig. 37–25).

23. (II) For the ground state of hydrogen, what is the probability of finding the electron within a spherical shell of inner radius $0.99r_0$ and outer radius $1.01r_0$?

24. (III) For the $n = 2, \ell = 0$ state of hydrogen, what is the probability of finding the electron within a spherical shell of inner radius $4.00\,r_0$ and outer radius $5.00\,r_0$? [Hint: You might integrate by parts.]

25. (III) Show that ψ_{100} (Eq. 39–5a) satisfies the Schrödinger equation (Eq. 39–1) with the Coulomb potential, for energy $E = -me^4/8\epsilon_0^2 h^2$.

26. (III) Show that the probability of finding the electron within 1 Bohr radius of the nucleus in the hydrogen atom is (a) 3.4% for the $n = 2, \ell = 0$ state, and (b) 0.37% for the $n = 2, \ell = 1$ state. (See Problem 21.)

27. (III) The wave function for the $n = 3, \ell = 0$ state in hydrogen is

$$\psi_{300} = \frac{1}{\sqrt{27\pi r_0^3}}\left(1 - \frac{2r}{3r_0} + \frac{2r^2}{27r_0^2}\right)e^{-\frac{r}{3r_0}}.$$

(a) Determine the radial probability distribution P_r for this state, and (b) draw the curve for it on a graph. (c) Determine the most probable distance from the nucleus for an electron in this state.

39–4 and 39–5 Complex Atoms

28. (I) List the quantum numbers for each electron in the ground state of oxygen ($Z = 8$).

29. (I) List the quantum numbers for each electron in the ground state of (a) carbon ($Z = 6$), (b) aluminum ($Z = 13$).

30. (I) How many electrons can be in the $n = 6, \ell = 4$ subshell?

31. (II) An electron has $m_\ell = 2$ and is in its lowest possible energy state. What are the values of n and ℓ for this electron?

32. (II) If the principal quantum number n were limited to the range from 1 to 6, how many elements would we find in nature?

33. (II) What is the full electron configuration for (a) nickel (Ni), (b) silver (Ag), (c) uranium (U)? [Hint: See the Periodic Table inside the back cover.]

34. (II) Estimate the binding energy of the third electron in lithium using Bohr theory. [Hint: This electron has $n = 2$ and "sees" a net charge of approximately $+1e$.] The measured value is 5.36 eV.

35. (II) Using the Bohr formula for the radius of an electron orbit, estimate the average distance from the nucleus for an electron in the innermost ($n = 1$) orbit in uranium ($Z = 92$). Approximately how much energy would be required to remove this innermost electron?

36. (II) Let us apply the exclusion principle to an infinitely high square well (Section 38–8). Let there be five electrons confined to this rigid box whose width is ℓ. Find the lowest energy state of this system, by placing the electrons in the lowest available levels, consistent with the Pauli exclusion principle.

37. (II) Show that the total angular momentum is zero for a filled subshell.

39–6 X-rays

38. (I) If the shortest-wavelength bremsstrahlung X-rays emitted from an X-ray tube have $\lambda = 0.027$ nm, what is the voltage across the tube?

39. (I) What are the shortest-wavelength X-rays emitted by electrons striking the face of a 32.5-kV TV picture tube? What are the longest wavelengths?

40. (I) Show that the cutoff wavelength λ_0 in an X-ray spectrum is given by

$$\lambda_0 = \frac{1240}{V}\,\text{nm},$$

where V is the X-ray tube voltage in volts.

41. (II) Estimate the wavelength for an $n = 2$ to $n = 1$ transition in iron ($Z = 26$).

42. (II) Use the result of Example 39–6 to estimate the X-ray wavelength emitted when a cobalt atom ($Z = 27$) makes a transition from $n = 2$ to $n = 1$.

43. (II) A mixture of iron and an unknown material are bombarded with electrons. The wavelength of the K_α lines are 194 pm for iron and 229 pm for the unknown. What is the unknown material?

44. (II) Use Bohr theory to estimate the wavelength for an $n = 3$ to $n = 1$ transition in molybdenum ($Z = 42$). The measured value is 0.063 nm. Why do we not expect perfect agreement?

45. (II) Use conservation of energy and momentum to show that a moving electron cannot give off an X-ray photon unless there is a third object present, such as an atom or nucleus.

*39–7 Magnetic Dipole Moment; $\vec{J}$

*46. (I) Verify that the Bohr magneton has the value $\mu_B = 9.27 \times 10^{-24}$ J/T (see Eq. 39–12).

*47. (I) If the quantum state of an electron is specified by (n, ℓ, m_ℓ, m_s), estimate the energy difference between the states $\left(1, 0, 0, -\frac{1}{2}\right)$ and $\left(1, 0, 0, +\frac{1}{2}\right)$ of an electron in the $1s$ state of helium in an external magnetic field of 2.5 T.

*48. (II) Silver atoms (spin $= \frac{1}{2}$) are placed in a 1.0-T magnetic field which splits the ground state into two close levels. (a) What is the difference in energy between these two levels, and (b) what wavelength photon could cause a transition from the lower level to the upper one? (c) How would your answer differ if the atoms were hydrogen?

*49. (II) In a Stern-Gerlach experiment, Ag atoms exit the oven with an average speed of 780 m/s and pass through a magnetic field gradient $dB/dz = 1.8 \times 10^3$ T/m for a distance of 5.0 cm. (a) What is the separation of the two beams as they emerge from the magnet? (b) What would the separation be if the g-factor were 1 for electron spin?

*50. (II) For an electron in a $5g$ state, what are all the possible values of j, m_j, J, and J_z?

*51. (II) What are the possible values of j for an electron in (a) the $4p$, (b) the $4f$, and (c) the $3d$ state of hydrogen? (d) What is J in each case?

*52. (II) (a) Write down the quantum numbers for each electron in the gallium atom. (b) Which subshells are filled? (c) The last electron is in the $4p$ state; what are the possible values of the total angular momentum quantum number, j, for this electron? (d) Explain why the angular momentum of this last electron also represents the total angular momentum for the entire atom (ignoring any angular momentum of the nucleus). (e) How could you use a Stern-Gerlach experiment to determine which value of j the atom has?

*53. (III) The difference between the $2P_{3/2}$ and $2P_{1/2}$ energy levels in hydrogen is about 5×10^{-5} eV, due to the spin-orbit interaction. (a) Taking the electron's (orbital) magnetic moment to be 1 Bohr magneton, estimate the internal magnetic field due to the electron's orbital motion. (b) Estimate the internal magnetic field using a simple model of the nucleus revolving in a circle about the electron.

39–9 Lasers

54. (II) A laser used to weld detached retinas puts out 23-ms-long pulses of 640-nm light which average 0.63-W output during a pulse. How much energy can be deposited per pulse and how many photons does each pulse contain?

55. (II) Estimate the angular spread of a laser beam due to diffraction if the beam emerges through a 3.6-mm-diameter mirror. Assume that $\lambda = 694$ nm. What would be the diameter of this beam if it struck (a) a satellite 380 km above the Earth, (b) the Moon? [Hint: See Chapter 35.]

56. (II) A low-power laser used in a physics lab might have a power of 0.50 mW and a beam diameter of 3.0 mm. Calculate (a) the average light intensity of the laser beam, and (b) compare it to the intensity of a lightbulb emitting 15 W of light viewed from a distance of 2.0 m.

57. (II) Calculate the wavelength of a He–Ne laser.

58. (II) Suppose that the energy level system in Fig. 39–20 is not being pumped and is in thermal equilibrium. Determine the fraction of atoms in levels E_2 and E_1 relative to E_0 at $T = 300$ K.

59. (II) To what temperature would the system in Fig. 39–20 have to be raised (see Problem 58) so that in thermal equilibrium the level E_2 would have half as many atoms as E_0? (Note that pumping mechanisms do not maintain thermal equilibrium.)

60. (II) Show that a population inversion for two levels (as in a pumped laser) corresponds to a negative Kelvin temperature in the Boltzmann distribution. Explain why such a situation does not contradict the idea that negative Kelvin temperatures cannot be reached in the normal sense of temperature.

General Problems

61. The ionization (binding) energy of the outermost electron in boron is 8.26 eV. (a) Use the Bohr model to estimate the "effective charge," Z_{eff}, seen by this electron. (b) Estimate the average orbital radius.

62. How many electrons can there be in an "h" subshell?

63. What is the full electron configuration in the ground state for elements with Z equal to (a) 25, (b) 34, (c) 39? [Hint: See the Periodic Table inside the back cover.]

64. What are the largest and smallest possible values for the angular momentum L of an electron in the $n = 6$ shell?

65. Estimate (a) the quantum number ℓ for the orbital angular momentum of the Earth about the Sun, and (b) the number of possible orientations for the plane of Earth's orbit.

66. Use the Bohr theory (especially Eq. 37–15) to show that the Moseley plot (Fig. 39–12) can be written

$$\sqrt{\frac{1}{\lambda}} = a(Z - b),$$

where $b \approx 1$, and evaluate a.

67. Determine the most probable distance from the nucleus of an electron in the $n = 2, \ell = 0$ state of hydrogen.

68. Show that the diffractive spread of a laser beam, $\approx \lambda/D$ as described in Section 39–9, is precisely what you might expect from the uncertainty principle. [Hint: Since the beam's width is constrained by the dimension of the aperture D, the component of the light's momentum perpendicular to the laser axis is uncertain.]

69. In the so-called **vector model** of the atom, space quantization of angular momentum (Fig. 39–3) is illustrated as shown in Fig. 39–28. The angular momentum vector of magnitude $L = \sqrt{\ell(\ell + 1)}\,\hbar$ is thought of as precessing around the z axis (like a spinning top or gyroscope) in such a way that the z component of angular momentum, $L_z = m_\ell \hbar$, also stays constant. Calculate the possible values for the angle θ between $\vec{L}$ and the z axis (a) for $\ell = 1$, (b) $\ell = 2$, and (c) $\ell = 3$. (d) Determine the minimum value of θ for $\ell = 100$ and $\ell = 10^6$. Is this consistent with the correspondence principle?

FIGURE 39–28 The vector model for orbital angular momentum. The orbital angular momentum vector $\vec{L}$ is imagined to precess about the z axis; L and L_z remain constant, but L_x and L_y continually change. Problems 69 and 70.

70. The vector model (Problem 69) gives some insight into the uncertainty principle for angular momentum, which is

$$\Delta L_z \Delta\phi \geq \hbar$$

for the z component. Here ϕ is the angular position measured in the plane perpendicular to the z axis. Once m_ℓ for an atom is known, L_z is known precisely, so $\Delta L_z = 0$. (a) What does this tell us about ϕ? (b) What can you say about L_x and L_y, which are not quantized (only L and L_z are)? (c) Show that although L_x and L_y are not quantized, nonetheless $(L_x^2 + L_y^2)^{1/2} = [\ell(\ell + 1) - m_\ell^2]^{1/2}\,\hbar$ is.

71. (a) Show that the mean value for $1/r$ of an electron in the ground state of hydrogen equals $1/r_0$, and from this conclude that the mean value of the potential energy is

$$\bar{U} = -\frac{1}{4\pi\epsilon_0}\frac{e^2}{r_0}.$$

(b) Using $E = \bar{U} + \bar{K}$, find a relationship between the average kinetic energy and the average potential energy in the ground state. [Hint: For (a), see Problem 19 or Example 38–9.]

72. The angular momentum in the hydrogen atom is given both by the Bohr model and by quantum mechanics. Compare the results for $n = 2$.

73. For each of the following atomic transitions, state whether the transition is *allowed* or *forbidden*, and why: (a) $4p \rightarrow 3p$; (b) $3p \rightarrow 1s$; (c) $4d \rightarrow 3d$; (d) $4d \rightarrow 3s$; (e) $4s \rightarrow 2p$.

74. It is possible for atoms to be excited into states with very high values of the principal quantum number. Electrons in these so-called *Rydberg states* have very small ionization energies and huge orbital radii. This makes them particularly sensitive to external perturbation, as would be the case if the atom were in an electric field. Consider the $n = 45$ state of the hydrogen atom. Determine the binding energy, the radius of the orbit, and the effective cross-sectional area of this Rydberg state.

75. Suppose that the spectrum of an unknown element shows a series of lines with one out of every four matching a line from the Lyman series of hydrogen. Assuming that the unknown element is an ion with Z protons and one electron, determine Z and the element in question.

*76. Suppose that the splitting of energy levels shown in Fig. 39–4 was produced by a 1.6-T magnetic field. (a) What is the separation in energy between adjacent m_ℓ levels for the same ℓ? (b) How many different wavelengths will there be for $3d$ to $2p$ transitions, if m_ℓ can change only by ± 1 or 0? (c) What is the wavelength for each of these transitions?

77. *Populations in the H atom.* Use the Boltzmann factor (Eq. 39–16) to estimate the fraction of H atoms in the $n = 2$ and $n = 3$ levels (relative to the ground state) for thermal equilibrium at (a) $T = 300\,\text{K}$ and (b) $T = 6000\,\text{K}$. [Note: Since there are eight states with $n = 2$ and only two with $n = 1$, multiply your result for $n = 2$ by $\frac{8}{2} = 4$; do similarly for $n = 3$.] (c) Given 1.0 g of hydrogen, estimate the number of atoms in each state at $T = 6000\,\text{K}$. (d) Estimate the number of $n = 3$ to $n = 1$ and $n = 2$ to $n = 1$ photons that will be emitted per second at $T = 6000\,\text{K}$. Assume that the lifetime of each excited state is $10^{-8}\,\text{s}$. [Hint: To evaluate a large exponent, you can use base-10 logarithms, Appendix A.]

Answers to Exercises

A: 2, 1, 0, −1, −2.

B: (b).

C: (d).

D: Add one line to Li in Table 39–2: 2, 0, 0, $-\frac{1}{2}$.

E: (b), (c).

F: $1s^2 2s^2 2p^6 3s^2 3p^6 3d^{10} 4s^2 4p^1$.

G: (d).

This computer processor chip contains over 800 million transistors, plus diodes and other semiconductor electronic elements, all in a space smaller than a penny.

Before discussing semiconductors and their applications, we study the quantum theory description of bonding between atoms to form molecules, and how it explains molecular behavior. We then examine how atoms and molecules form solids, with emphasis on metals as well as on semiconductors and their use in electronics.

Molecules and Solids

CHAPTER-OPENING QUESTION—Guess now!
As a metal is heated, how does the rms speed (v_{rms}) of the electrons change? Assume a temperature change of about 30C° near room temperature.

(a) v_{rms} increases linearly with temperature.
(b) v_{rms} decreases linearly with temperature.
(c) v_{rms} increases exponentially with temperature.
(d) v_{rms} decreases exponentially with temperature.
(e) v_{rms} changes very little as the temperature is increased.

S ince its development in the 1920s, quantum mechanics has had a profound influence on our lives, both intellectually and technologically. Even the way we view the world has changed, as we have seen in the last few Chapters. Now we discuss how quantum mechanics has given us an understanding of the structure of molecules and matter in bulk, as well as a number of important applications including semiconductor devices.

CONTENTS

40–1 Bonding in Molecules

One of the great successes of quantum mechanics was to give scientists, at last, an understanding of the nature of chemical bonds. Since it is based in physics, and because this understanding is so important in many fields, we discuss it here.

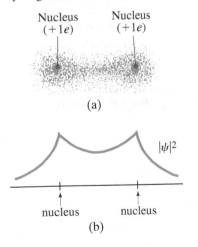

Nucleus
(+1e)

Nucleus
(+1e)

(a)

$|\psi|^2$

nucleus   nucleus

(b)

FIGURE 40–1 Electron probability distribution (electron cloud) for two H atoms when the spins are the same $(S = 1)$: (a) electron cloud; (b) projection of $|\psi|^2$ along the line through the centers of the two atoms.

FIGURE 40–2 Electron probability distribution for two H atoms when the spins are opposite $(S = 0)$: (a) electron cloud; (b) projection of $|\psi|^2$ along the line through the centers of the atoms. In this case a bond is formed because the positive nuclei are attracted to the concentration of negative charge between them. This is a hydrogen molecule, H_2.

Nucleus
(+1e)

Nucleus
(+1e)

(a)

$|\psi|^2$

nucleus   nucleus

(b)

By a molecule, we mean a group of two or more atoms that are strongly held together so as to function as a single unit. When atoms make such an attachment, we say that a chemical **bond** has been formed. There are two main types of strong chemical bond: covalent and ionic. Many bonds are actually intermediate between these two types.

Covalent Bonds

To understand how *covalent bonds* are formed, we take the simplest case, the bond that holds two hydrogen atoms together to form the hydrogen molecule, H_2. The mechanism is basically the same for other covalent bonds. As two H atoms approach each other, the electron clouds begin to overlap, and the electrons from each atom can "orbit" both nuclei. (This is sometimes called "sharing" electrons.) If both electrons are in the ground state $(n = 1)$ of their respective atoms, there are two possibilities: their spins can be parallel (both up or both down), in which case the total spin is $S = \frac{1}{2} + \frac{1}{2} = 1$; or their spins can be opposite $(m_s = +\frac{1}{2}$ for one, $m_s = -\frac{1}{2}$ for the other), so that the total spin $S = 0$. We shall now see that a bond is formed only for the $S = 0$ state, when the spins are opposite.

First we consider the $S = 1$ state, for which the spins are the same. The two electrons cannot both be in the lowest energy state and be attached to the same atom, for then they would have identical quantum numbers in violation of the exclusion principle. The exclusion principle tells us that, because no two electrons can occupy the same quantum state, if two electrons have the same quantum numbers, they must be different in some other way—namely, by being in different places in space (for example, attached to different atoms). Thus, for $S = 1$, when the two atoms approach each other, the electrons will stay away from each other as shown by the probability distribution of Fig. 40–1. The electrons spend very little time between the two nuclei, so the positively charged nuclei repel each other and no bond is formed.

For the $S = 0$ state, on the other hand, the spins are opposite and the two electrons are consequently in different quantum states (m_s is different, $+\frac{1}{2}$ for one, $-\frac{1}{2}$ for the other). Hence the two electrons can come close together, and the probability distribution looks like Fig. 40–2: the electrons can spend much of their time between the two nuclei. The two positively charged nuclei are attracted to the negatively charged electron cloud between them, and this is the attraction that holds the two hydrogen atoms together to form a hydrogen molecule. This is a **covalent bond**.

The probability distributions of Figs. 40–1 and 40–2 can perhaps be better understood on the basis of waves. What the exclusion principle requires is that when the spins are the same, there is destructive interference of the electron wave functions in the region between the two atoms. But when the spins are opposite, constructive interference occurs in the region between the two atoms, resulting in a large amount of negative charge there. Thus a covalent bond can be said to be the result of constructive interference of the electron wave functions in the space between the two atoms, and of the electrostatic attraction of the two positive nuclei for the negative charge concentration between them.

Why a bond is formed can also be understood from the energy point of view. When the two H atoms approach close to one another, if the spins of their electrons are opposite, the electrons can occupy the same space, as discussed above. This means that each electron can now move about in the space of two atoms instead of in the volume of only one. Because each electron now occupies more space, it is less well localized. From the uncertainty principle with Δx larger, we see that Δp and the minimum momentum can be less. With less momentum, each electron has less energy when the two atoms combine than when they are separate. That is, the molecule has less energy than the two separate atoms, and so is more stable. An energy input is required to break the H_2 molecule into two separate H atoms, so the H_2 molecule is a stable entity.

This is what we mean by a *bond*. The energy required to break a bond is called the **bond energy**, the **binding energy**, or the **dissociation energy**. For the hydrogen molecule, H_2, the bond energy is 4.5 eV.

Ionic Bonds

An *ionic bond* is, in a sense, a special case of the covalent bond. Instead of the electrons being shared equally, they are shared unequally. For example, in sodium chloride (NaCl), the outer electron of the sodium spends nearly all its time around the chlorine (Fig. 40–3). The chlorine atom acquires a net negative charge as a result of the extra electron, whereas the sodium atom is left with a net positive charge. The electrostatic attraction between these two charged atoms holds them together. The resulting bond is called an **ionic bond** because it is created by the attraction between the two ions (Na^+ and Cl^-). But to understand the ionic bond, we must understand why the extra electron from the sodium spends so much of its time around the chlorine. After all, the chlorine atom is neutral; why should it attract another electron?

The answer lies in the probability distributions of the two neutral atoms. Sodium contains 11 electrons, 10 of which are in spherically symmetric closed shells (Fig. 40–4). The last electron spends most of its time beyond these closed shells. Because the closed shells have a total charge of $-10e$ and the nucleus has charge $+11e$, the outermost electron in sodium "feels" a net attraction due to $+1e$. It is not held very strongly. On the other hand, 12 of chlorine's 17 electrons form closed shells, or subshells (corresponding to $1s^2 2s^2 2p^6 3s^2$). These 12 electrons form a spherically symmetric shield around the nucleus. The other five electrons are in $3p$ states whose probability distributions are not spherically symmetric and have a form similar to those for the $2p$ states in hydrogen shown in Fig. 39–9. Four of these $3p$ electrons can have "doughnut-shaped" distributions symmetric about the z axis, as shown in Fig. 40–5. The fifth can have a "barbell-shaped" distribution (as for $m_\ell = 0$ in Fig. 39–9), which in Fig. 40–5 is shown only in dashed outline because it is half empty. That is, the exclusion principle allows one more electron to be in this state (it will have spin opposite to that of the electron already there). If an extra electron—say from a Na atom—happens to be in the vicinity, it can be in this state, perhaps at point x in Fig. 40–5. It could experience an attraction due to as much as $+5e$ because the $+17e$ of the nucleus is partly shielded at this point by the 12 inner electrons. Thus, the outer electron of a sodium atom will be more strongly attracted by the $+5e$ of the chlorine atom than by the $+1e$ of its own atom. This, combined with the strong attraction between the two ions when the extra electron stays with the Cl^-, produces the charge distribution of Fig. 40–3, and hence the ionic bond.

FIGURE 40–3 Probability distribution $|\psi|^2$ for the outermost electron of Na in NaCl.

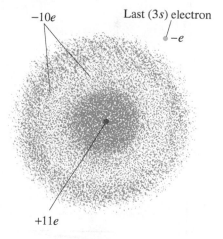

FIGURE 40–4 In a neutral sodium atom, the 10 inner electrons shield the nucleus, so the single outer electron is attracted by a net charge of $+1e$.

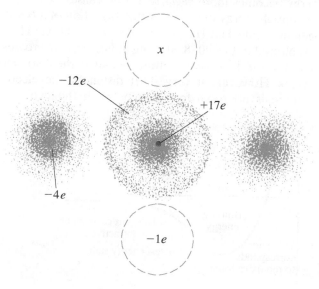

FIGURE 40–5 Neutral chlorine atom. The $+17e$ of the nucleus is shielded by the 12 electrons in the inner shells and subshells. Four of the five $3p$ electrons are shown in doughnut-shaped clouds (seen in cross section at left and right), and the fifth is in the dashed-line cloud concentrated about the z axis (vertical). An extra electron at x will be attracted by a net charge that can be as much as $+5e$.

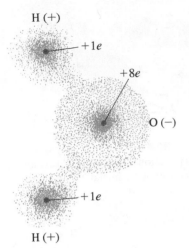

H (+)

+1e

+8e

O (−)

+1e

H (+)

FIGURE 40–6 The water molecule H_2O is polar.

FIGURE 40–7 Potential energy U as a function of separation r for two point charges of (a) like sign and (b) opposite sign.

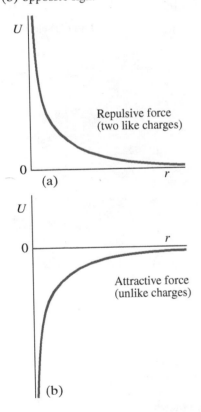

Partial Ionic Character of Covalent Bonds

A pure covalent bond in which the electrons are shared equally occurs mainly in symmetrical molecules such as H_2, O_2, and Cl_2. When the atoms involved are different from each other, it is usual to find that the shared electrons are more likely to be in the vicinity of one atom than the other. The extreme case is an ionic bond; in intermediate cases the covalent bond is said to have a *partial ionic character*. The molecules themselves are **polar**—that is, one part (or parts) of the molecule has a net positive charge and other parts a net negative charge. An example is the water molecule, H_2O (Fig. 40–6). The shared electrons are more likely to be found around the oxygen atom than around the two hydrogens. The reason is similar to that discussed above in connection with ionic bonds. Oxygen has eight electrons $(1s^2 2s^2 2p^4)$, of which four form a spherically symmetric core and the other four could have, for example, a doughnut-shaped distribution. The barbell-shaped distribution on the z axis (like that shown dashed in Fig. 40–5) could be empty, so electrons from hydrogen atoms can be attracted by a net charge of $+4e$. They are also attracted by the H nuclei, so they partly orbit the H atoms as well as the O atom. The net effect is that there is a net positive charge on each H atom (less than $+1e$), because the electrons spend only part of their time there. And, there is a net negative charge on the O atom.

40–2 Potential-Energy Diagrams for Molecules

It is useful to analyze the interaction between two objects—say, between two atoms or molecules—with the use of a potential-energy diagram, which is a plot of the potential energy versus the separation distance.

For the simple case of two point charges, q_1 and q_2, the potential energy U is given by (see Chapter 23)

$$U = \frac{1}{4\pi\epsilon_0} \frac{q_1 q_2}{r},$$

where r is the distance between the charges, and the constant $(1/4\pi\epsilon_0)$ is equal to $9.0 \times 10^9 \, \text{N} \cdot \text{m}^2/\text{C}^2$. If the two charges have the same sign, the potential energy U is positive for all values of r, and a graph of U versus r in this case is shown in Fig. 40–7a. The force is repulsive (the charges have the *same* sign) and the curve rises as r decreases; this makes sense since work is done to bring the charges together, thereby increasing their potential energy. If, on the other hand, the two charges are of the *opposite* sign, the potential energy is negative because the product $q_1 q_2$ is negative. The force is attractive in this case, and the graph of U ($\propto -1/r$) versus r looks like Fig. 40–7b. The potential energy becomes more *negative* as r decreases.

Now let us look at the potential-energy diagram for the formation of a covalent bond, such as for the hydrogen molecule, H_2. The potential energy U of one H atom in the presence of the other is plotted in Fig. 40–8. Starting at large r, U decreases as the atoms approach, because the electrons concentrate between the two nuclei (Fig. 40–2), so attraction occurs. However, at very short distances, the electrons would be "squeezed out"—there is no room for them between the two nuclei.

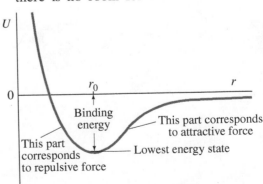

FIGURE 40–8 (right) Potential-energy diagram for H_2 molecule; r is the separation of the two H atoms. The binding energy (the energy difference between $U = 0$ and the lowest energy state near the bottom of the well) is 4.5 eV, and $r_0 = 0.074$ nm.

Without the electrons between them, each nucleus would feel a repulsive force due to the other, so the curve rises as r decreases further. There is an optimum separation of the atoms, r_0 in Fig. 40–8, at which the energy is lowest. This is the point of greatest stability for the hydrogen molecule, and r_0 is the average separation of atoms in the H_2 molecule. The depth of this "well" is the *binding energy*,[†] as shown. This is how much energy must be put into the system to separate the two atoms to infinity, where $U = 0$. For the H_2 molecule, the binding energy is about 4.5 eV and $r_0 = 0.074$ nm.

In molecules made of larger atoms, say, oxygen or nitrogen, repulsion also occurs at short distances, because the closed inner electron shells begin to overlap and the exclusion principle forbids their coming too close. The repulsive part of the curve rises even more steeply than $1/r$. A reasonable approximation to the potential energy, at least in the vicinity of r_0, is

$$U = -\frac{A}{r^m} + \frac{B}{r^n}, \tag{40-1}$$

where A and B are constants associated with the attractive and repulsive parts of the potential energy and the exponents m and n are small integers. For ionic and some covalent bonds, the attractive term can often be written with $m = 1$ (Coulomb potential).

For many bonds, the potential-energy curve has the shape shown in Fig. 40–9. There is still an optimum distance r_0 at which the molecule is stable. But when the atoms approach from a large distance, the force is initially repulsive rather than attractive. The atoms thus do not interact spontaneously. Instead, some additional energy must be injected into the system to get it over the "hump" (or barrier) in the potential-energy diagram. This required energy is called the **activation energy**.

The curve of Fig. 40–9 is much more common than that of Fig. 40–8. The activation energy often reflects a need to break other bonds, before the one under discussion can be made. For example, to make water from O_2 and H_2, the H_2 and O_2 molecules must first be broken into H and O atoms by an input of energy; this is what the activation energy represents. Then the H and O atoms can combine to form H_2O with the release of a great deal more energy than was put in initially. The initial activation energy can be provided by applying an electric spark to a mixture of H_2 and O_2, breaking a few of these molecules into H and O atoms. The resulting explosive release of energy when these atoms combine to form H_2O quickly provides the activation energy needed for further reactions, so additional H_2 and O_2 molecules are broken up and recombined to form H_2O.

The potential-energy diagrams for ionic bonds can have similar shapes. In NaCl, for example, the Na^+ and Cl^- ions attract each other at distances a bit larger than some r_0, but at shorter distances the overlapping of inner electron shells gives rise to repulsion. The two atoms thus are most stable at some intermediate separation, r_0, and for many bonds there is an activation energy.

[†]The binding energy corresponds not quite to the bottom of the potential energy curve, but to the lowest quantum energy state, slightly above the bottom, as shown in Fig. 40–8.

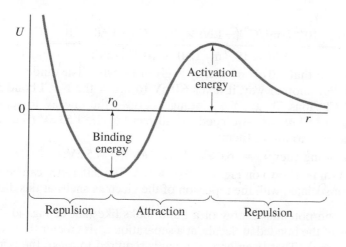

FIGURE 40–9 Potential-energy diagram for a bond requiring an activation energy.

EXAMPLE 40–1 **ESTIMATE** **Sodium chloride bond.** A potential-energy diagram for the NaCl ionic bond is shown in Fig. 40–10, where we have set $U = 0$ for free Na and Cl neutral atoms (which are represented on the right in Fig. 40–10). Measurements show that 5.14 eV are required to remove an electron from a neutral Na atom to produce the Na$^+$ ion; and 3.61 eV of energy is released when an electron is "grabbed" by a Cl atom to form the Cl$^-$ ion. Thus, forming Na$^+$ and Cl$^-$ ions from neutral Na and Cl atoms requires 5.14 eV − 3.61 eV = 1.53 eV of energy, a form of activation energy. This is shown as the "bump" in Fig. 40–10. But note that the potential-energy diagram from here out to the right is not really a function of distance—it is drawn dashed to remind us that it only represents the energy difference between the ions and the neutral atoms (for which we have chosen $U = 0$). (a) Calculate the separation distance, r_1, at which the potential of the Na$^+$ and Cl$^-$ ions drops to zero (measured value is $r_1 = 0.94$ nm). (b) Estimate the binding energy of the NaCl bond, which occurs at a separation $r_0 = 0.24$ nm. Ignore the repulsion of the overlapping electron shells that occurs at this distance (and causes the rise of the potential-energy curve for $r < r_0$, Fig. 40–10).

FIGURE 40–10 Example 40–1. Potential-energy diagram for the NaCl bond. Beyond about $r = 1.2$ nm, the diagram is schematic only, and represents the energy difference between ions and neutral atoms. $U = 0$ is chosen for the two separated atoms Na and Cl (not for the ions). [For the two ions, Na$^+$ and Cl$^-$, the zero of potential energy at $r = \infty$ corresponds to $U \approx 1.53$ eV on this diagram.]

SOLUTION (a) The potential energy of two point charges is given by Coulomb's law:

$$U' = \frac{1}{4\pi\epsilon_0} \frac{q_1 q_2}{r},$$

where we distinguish U' from the U in Fig. 40–10. This formula works for our two ions if we set $U' = 0$ at $r = \infty$, which in the plot of Fig. 40–10 corresponds to $U = +1.53$ eV (Fig. 40–10 is drawn for $U = 0$ for the free *atoms*). The point r_1 in Fig. 40–10 corresponds to $U' = -1.53$ eV relative to the two free ions. We solve the U' equation above for r, setting $q_1 = +e$ and $q_2 = -e$:

$$r_1 = \frac{1}{4\pi\epsilon_0} \frac{q_1 q_2}{U'} = \frac{(9.0 \times 10^9 \, \text{N} \cdot \text{m}^2/\text{C}^2)(-1.60 \times 10^{-19} \, \text{C})(+1.60 \times 10^{-19} \, \text{C})}{(-1.53 \, \text{eV})(1.60 \times 10^{-19} \, \text{J/eV})}$$

$$= 0.94 \, \text{nm},$$

which is just the measured value.

(b) At $r_0 = 0.24$ nm, the potential energy of the two ions (relative to $r = \infty$ for the two ions) is

$$U' = \frac{1}{4\pi\epsilon_0} \frac{q_1 q_2}{r}$$

$$= \frac{(9.0 \times 10^9 \, \text{N} \cdot \text{m}^2/\text{C}^2)(-1.60 \times 10^{-19} \, \text{C})(+1.60 \times 10^{-19} \, \text{C})}{(0.24 \times 10^{-9} \, \text{m})(1.60 \times 10^{-19} \, \text{J/eV})} = -6.0 \, \text{eV}.$$

Thus, we estimate that 6.0 eV of energy is given up when Na$^+$ and Cl$^-$ ions form a NaCl bond. Put another way, it takes 6.0 eV to break the NaCl bond and form the Na$^+$ and Cl$^-$ ions. To get the binding energy—the energy to separate the NaCl into Na and Cl *atoms*—we need to subtract out the 1.53 eV (the "bump" in Fig. 40–10) needed to ionize them:

$$\text{binding energy} = 6.0 \, \text{eV} - 1.53 \, \text{eV} = 4.5 \, \text{eV}.$$

The measured value (shown on Fig. 40–10) is 4.2 eV. The difference can be attributed to the energy associated with the repulsion of the electron shells at this distance.

Sometimes the potential energy of a bond looks like that of Fig. 40–11. In this case, the energy of the bonded molecule, at a separation r_0, is greater than when there is no bond ($r = \infty$). That is, an energy *input* is required to make the bond (hence the binding energy is negative), and there is energy release when the bond is broken.

Such a bond is stable only because there is the barrier of the activation energy. This type of bond is important in living cells, for it is in such bonds that energy can be stored efficiently in certain molecules, particularly ATP (adenosine triphosphate). The bond that connects the last phosphate group (designated Ⓟ in Fig. 40–11) to the rest of the molecule (ADP, meaning adenosine diphosphate, since it contains only two phosphates) has potential energy of the shape shown in Fig. 40–11. Energy is stored in this bond. When the bond is broken (ATP → ADP + Ⓟ), energy is released and this energy can be used to make other chemical reactions "go."

In living cells, many chemical reactions have activation energies that are often on the order of several eV. Such energy barriers are not easy to overcome in the cell. This is where enzymes come in. They act as *catalysts*, which means they act to lower the activation energy so that reactions can occur that otherwise would not. Enzymes act via the electrostatic force to distort the bonding electron clouds, so that the initial bonds are easily broken.

FIGURE 40–11 Potential-energy diagram for the formation of ATP from ADP and phosphate (Ⓟ).

| **EXAMPLE 40–2** | **Bond length.** Suppose a diatomic molecule has a potential |

energy given by $U = -(1/4\pi\epsilon_0)(e^2/r) + B/r^6$ where $B = 1.0 \times 10^{-78}$ J·m^6 and r is the distance between the centers of the two atoms. Determine the expected equilibrium separation of the two atoms (bond length of the molecule).

APPROACH The force between the two atoms is given by $F = -dU/dr$ (analogous to Eq. 8–7). The classical equilibrium separation is found by setting $F = 0$.
SOLUTION
$$F = -dU/dr = (1/4\pi\epsilon_0)(-e^2/r^2) - B(-6/r^7) = -(1/4\pi\epsilon_0)(e^2/r^2) + 6B/r^7 = 0.$$
Then
$$r^5 = 6B(4\pi\epsilon_0)/e^2 = 2.6 \times 10^{-50}\,\text{m}^5.$$
So $r = 1.2 \times 10^{-10}$ m $= 0.12$ nm.

NOTE This can be shown to be a stable equilibrium point by checking the sign of d^2U/dr^2, or by evaluating F at positions slightly larger and smaller than the equilibrium position.

40–3 Weak (van der Waals) Bonds

Once a bond between two atoms or ions is made, energy must normally be supplied to break the bond and separate the atoms. As mentioned in Section 40–1, this energy is called the *bond energy* or *binding energy*. The binding energy for covalent and ionic bonds is typically 2 to 5 eV. These bonds, which hold atoms together to *form* molecules, are often called **strong bonds** to distinguish them from so-called "weak bonds." The term **weak bond**, as we use it here, refers to attachments *between* molecules due to simple electrostatic attraction—such as *between* polar molecules (and not *within* a polar molecule, which is a strong bond). The strength of the attachment is much less than for the strong bonds. Binding energies are typically in the range 0.04 to 0.3 eV—hence their name "weak bonds."

Weak bonds are generally the result of attraction between dipoles (Sections 21–11, 23–6). For example, Fig. 40–12 shows two molecules, which have permanent dipole moments, attracting one another. Besides such **dipole–dipole bonds**, there can also be **dipole–induced dipole bonds**, in which a polar molecule with a permanent dipole moment can induce a dipole moment in an otherwise electrically balanced (nonpolar) molecule, just as a single charge can induce a separation of charge in a nearby object (see Fig. 21–7). There can even be an attraction between two nonpolar molecules, because their electrons are moving about: at any instant there may be a transient separation of charge, creating a brief dipole moment and weak attraction. All these weak bonds are referred to as **van der Waals bonds**, and the forces involved **van der Waals forces**. The potential energy has the general shape shown in Fig. 40–8, with the attractive van der Waals potential energy varying as $1/r^6$.

When one of the atoms in a dipole–dipole bond is hydrogen, as in Fig. 40–12, it is called a **hydrogen bond**. A hydrogen bond is generally the strongest of the weak bonds, because the hydrogen atom is the smallest atom and can be approached more closely. Hydrogen bonds also have a partial "covalent" character: that is, electrons between the two dipoles may be shared to a small extent, making a stronger, more lasting bond.

FIGURE 40–12 The $C^+ - O^-$ and $H^+ - N^-$ dipoles attract each other. (These dipoles may be part of, for example, the nucleotide bases cytosine and guanine in DNA molecules. See Fig. 40–13.) The + and − charges typically have magnitudes of a fraction of e.

FIGURE 40–13 (a) Section of a DNA double helix. The red dots represent hydrogen bonds between the two strands. (b) "Close-up" view: cytosine (C) and guanine (G) molecules on separate strands of a DNA double helix are held together by the hydrogen bonds (red dots) involving an H^+ on one molecule attracted to an N^- or $C^+ \!\!-\!\! O^-$ of a molecule on the adjacent chain. See also Section 21–12 and Figs. 21–47 and 21–48.

(a)

(b)

Weak bonds are important in liquids and solids when strong bonds are absent (see Section 40–5). They are also very important for understanding the activities of cells, such as the double helix shape of DNA (Fig. 40–13), and DNA replication. The average kinetic energy of molecules in a living cell at normal temperatures ($T \approx 300\,\text{K}$) is around $\frac{3}{2}kT \approx 0.04\,\text{eV}$, about the magnitude of weak bonds. This means that a weak bond can readily be broken just by a molecular collision. Hence weak bonds are not very permanent—they are, instead, brief attachments. This helps them play particular roles in the cell. On the other hand, strong bonds—those that hold molecules together—are almost never broken simply by molecular collision. Thus they are relatively permanent. They can be broken by chemical action (the making of even stronger bonds), and this usually happens in the cell with the aid of an enzyme, which is a protein molecule.

EXAMPLE 40–3 **Nucleotide energy.** Calculate the potential energy between a C═O dipole of the nucleotide base cytosine and the nearby H—N dipole of guanine, assuming that the two dipoles are lined up as shown in Fig. 40–12. Dipole moment ($= q\ell$) measurements (see Table 23–2 and Fig. 40–12) give

$$q_H = -q_N = \frac{3.0 \times 10^{-30}\,\text{C}\cdot\text{m}}{0.10 \times 10^{-9}\,\text{m}} = 3.0 \times 10^{-20}\,\text{C} = 0.19e,$$

and

$$q_C = -q_O = \frac{8.0 \times 10^{-30}\,\text{C}\cdot\text{m}}{0.12 \times 10^{-9}\,\text{m}} = 6.7 \times 10^{-20}\,\text{C} = 0.42e.$$

APPROACH We want to find the potential energy of the two charges in one dipole due to the two charges in the other, since this will be equal to the work needed to pull the two dipoles infinitely far apart. The potential energy U of a charge q_1 in the presence of a charge q_2 is $U = (1/4\pi\epsilon_0)(q_1 q_2/r_{12})$ where $1/4\pi\epsilon_0 = 9.0 \times 10^9\,\text{N}\cdot\text{m}^2/\text{C}^2$ and r_{12} is the distance between the two charges.

SOLUTION The potential energy U consists of four terms:

$$U = U_{CH} + U_{CN} + U_{OH} + U_{ON},$$

where U_{CH} means the potential energy of C in the presence of H, and similarly for the other terms. We do not have terms corresponding to C and O, or N and H, because the two dipoles are assumed to be stable entities. Then, using the distances shown in Fig. 40–12, we get:

$$U = \frac{1}{4\pi\epsilon_0}\left[\frac{q_C q_H}{r_{CH}} + \frac{q_C q_N}{r_{CN}} + \frac{q_O q_H}{r_{OH}} + \frac{q_O q_N}{r_{ON}}\right]$$

$$= (9.0 \times 10^9\,\text{N}\cdot\text{m}^2/\text{C}^2)(6.7)(3.0)\left(\frac{1}{0.31} - \frac{1}{0.41} - \frac{1}{0.19} + \frac{1}{0.29}\right)\frac{(10^{-20}\,\text{C})^2}{(10^{-9}\,\text{m})}$$

$$= -1.86 \times 10^{-20}\,\text{J} = -0.12\,\text{eV}.$$

The potential energy is negative, meaning 0.12 eV of work (or energy input) is required to separate the dipoles. That is, the binding energy of this "weak" or hydrogen bond is 0.12 eV. This is only an estimate, of course, since other charges in the vicinity would have an influence too.

FIGURE 40–14 Protein synthesis.
See text for details.

*Protein Synthesis

Weak bonds, especially hydrogen bonds, are crucial to the process of protein synthesis. Proteins serve as structural parts of the cell and as enzymes to catalyze chemical reactions needed for the growth and survival of the organism. A protein molecule consists of one or more chains of small molecules known as *amino acids*. There are 20 different amino acids, and a single protein chain may contain hundreds of them in a specific order. The standard model for how amino acids are connected together in the correct order to form a protein molecule is shown schematically in Fig. 40–14.

It begins at the DNA double helix: each gene on a chromosome contains the information for producing one protein. The ordering of the four bases, A, C, G, and T, provides the "code," the **genetic code**, for the order of amino acids in the protein. First, the DNA double helix unwinds and a new molecule called *messenger*-RNA (m-RNA) is synthesized using one strand of the DNA as a "template." m-RNA is a chain molecule containing four different bases, like those of DNA (Section 21–12) except that thymine (T) is replaced by the similar uracil molecule (U). Near the top left in Fig. 40–14, a C has just been added to the growing m-RNA chain in much the same way that DNA replicates; and an A, attracted and held close to the T on the DNA chain by the electrostatic force, will soon be attached to the C by an enzyme. The order of the bases, and thus the genetic information, is preserved in the m-RNA because the shapes of the molecules only allow the "proper" one to get close enough so the electrostatic force can act to form weak bonds.

Next, the m-RNA is buffeted about in the cell (kinetic theory) until it gets close to a tiny organelle known as a *ribosome*, to which it can attach by electrostatic attraction (on the right in Fig. 40–14), because their shapes allow the charged parts to get close enough to form weak bonds. Also held by the electrostatic force to the ribosome are one or two *transfer*-RNA (t-RNA) molecules. These t-RNA molecules "translate" the genetic code of nucleotide bases into amino acids in the following way. There is a different t-RNA molecule for each amino acid and each combination of three bases. On one end of a t-RNA molecule is an amino acid. On the other end of the t-RNA molecule is the appropriate "anticodon," a set of three nucleotide bases that "code" for that amino acid. If all three bases of an anticodon match the three bases of the "codon" on the m-RNA (in the sense of G to C and A to U), the anticodon is attracted electrostatically to the m-RNA codon and that t-RNA molecule is held there briefly. The ribosome has two particular attachment sites which hold two t-RNA molecules while enzymes link their two amino acids together to lengthen the amino acid chain (yellow in Fig. 40–14). As each amino acid is connected by an enzyme (four are already connected in Fig. 40–14, top right, and a fifth is about to be connected), the old t-RNA molecule is removed—perhaps by a random collision with some molecule in the cellular fluid. A new one soon becomes attracted as the ribosome moves along the m-RNA.

This process of protein synthesis is often presented as if it occurred in clockwork fashion—as if each molecule knew its role and went to its assigned place. But this is not the case. The forces of attraction between the electric charges of the molecules are rather weak and become significant only when the molecules can come close together and several weak bonds can be made. Indeed, if the shapes are not just right, there is almost no electrostatic attraction, which is why there are few mistakes. The fact that weak bonds are weak is very important. If they were strong, collisions with other molecules would not allow a t-RNA molecule to be released from the ribosome, or the m-RNA to be released from the DNA. If they were not temporary encounters, metabolism would grind to a halt.

As each amino acid is added to the next, the protein molecule grows in length until it is complete. Even as it is being made, this chain is being buffeted about in the cellular sea—we might think of a wiggling worm. But a protein molecule has electrically charged polar groups along its length. And as it takes on various shapes, the electric forces of attraction between different parts of the molecule will eventually lead to a particular configuration that is quite stable. Each type of protein has its own special shape, depending on the location of charged atoms. In the last analysis, the final shape depends on the order of the amino acids.

40–4 Molecular Spectra

When atoms combine to form molecules, the probability distributions of the outer electrons overlap and this interaction alters the energy levels. Nonetheless, molecules can undergo transitions between electron energy levels just as atoms do. For example, the H_2 molecule can absorb a photon of just the right frequency to excite one of its ground-state electrons to an excited state. The excited electron can then return to the ground state, emitting a photon. The energy of photons emitted by molecules can be of the same order of magnitude as for atoms, typically 1 to 10 eV, or less.

Additional energy levels become possible for molecules (but not for atoms) because the molecule as a whole can rotate, and the atoms of the molecule can vibrate relative to each other. The energy levels for both rotational and vibrational levels are quantized, and are generally spaced much more closely (10^{-3} to 10^{-1} eV) than the electronic levels. Each atomic energy level thus becomes a set of closely spaced levels corresponding to the vibrational and rotational motions, Fig. 40–15. Transitions from one level to another appear as many very closely spaced lines. In fact, the lines are not always distinguishable, and these spectra are called **band spectra**. Each type of molecule has its own characteristic spectrum, which can be used for identification and for determination of structure. We now look in more detail at rotational and vibrational states in molecules.

Rotational Energy Levels in Molecules

We consider only diatomic molecules, although the analysis can be extended to polyatomic molecules. When a diatomic molecule rotates about its center of mass as shown in Fig. 40–16, its kinetic energy of rotation (see Section 10–8) is

$$E_{\text{rot}} = \frac{1}{2} I\omega^2 = \frac{(I\omega)^2}{2I},$$

where $I\omega$ is the angular momentum (Section 11–1). Quantum mechanics predicts quantization of angular momentum just as in atoms (see Eq. 39–3):

$$I\omega = \sqrt{\ell(\ell + 1)}\,\hbar, \qquad \ell = 0, 1, 2, \cdots,$$

where ℓ is an integer called the **rotational angular momentum quantum number**. Thus the rotational energy is quantized:

$$E_{\text{rot}} = \frac{(I\omega)^2}{2I} = \ell(\ell + 1)\frac{\hbar^2}{2I}. \qquad \ell = 0, 1, 2, \cdots. \qquad \textbf{(40–2)}$$

Transitions between rotational energy levels are subject to the **selection rule** (as in Section 39–2):

$$\Delta\ell = \pm 1.$$

The energy of a photon emitted or absorbed for a transition between rotational

3p

2s

Isolated atom   Atom in a molecule

(a)   (b)

FIGURE 40–15 (a) The individual energy levels of an isolated atom become (b) bands of closely spaced levels in molecules, as well as in solids and liquids.

FIGURE 40–16 Diatomic molecule rotating about a vertical axis.

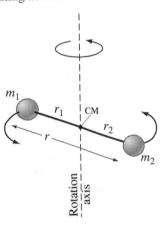

states with angular momentum quantum number ℓ and $\ell - 1$ will be

$$\Delta E_{\text{rot}} = E_\ell - E_{\ell-1} = \frac{\hbar^2}{2I}\ell(\ell+1) - \frac{\hbar^2}{2I}(\ell-1)(\ell)$$

$$= \frac{\hbar^2}{I}\ell. \qquad \begin{bmatrix} \ell \text{ is for upper} \\ \text{energy state} \end{bmatrix} \quad \text{(40–3)}$$

We see that the transition energy increases directly with ℓ. Figure 40–17 shows some of the allowed rotational energy levels and transitions. Measured absorption lines fall in the microwave or far-infrared regions of the spectrum, and their frequencies are generally $2, 3, 4, \cdots$ times higher than the lowest one, as predicted by Eq. 40–3.

EXERCISE A Determine the three lowest rotational energy states (in eV) for a nitrogen molecule which has a moment of inertia $I = 1.39 \times 10^{-46} \, \text{kg} \cdot \text{m}^2$.

The moment of inertia of the molecule in Fig. 40–16 rotating about its center of mass (Section 10–5) is

$$I = m_1 r_1^2 + m_2 r_2^2,$$

where r_1 and r_2 are the distances of each atom from their common center of mass. We can show (in Example 40–4 below) that I can be written

$$I = \frac{m_1 m_2}{m_1 + m_2} r^2 = \mu r^2, \qquad \text{(40–4)}$$

where $r = r_1 + r_2$ is the distance between the two atoms of the molecule and $\mu = m_1 m_2 / (m_1 + m_2)$ is called the **reduced mass**. If $m_1 = m_2$, then $\mu = \frac{1}{2}m_1 = \frac{1}{2}m_2$.

EXAMPLE 40–4 **Reduced mass.** Show that the moment of inertia of a diatomic molecule rotating about its center of mass can be written

$$I = \mu r^2,$$

where

$$\mu = \frac{m_1 m_2}{m_1 + m_2}$$

is the reduced mass, Eq. 40–4, and r is the distance between the atoms.

SOLUTION The moment of inertia of a single particle of mass m a distance r from the rotation axis is $I = mr^2$ (Eq. 10–11 or 10–13). For our diatomic molecule (Fig. 40–16)

$$I = m_1 r_1^2 + m_2 r_2^2.$$

Now $r = r_1 + r_2$ and $m_1 r_1 = m_2 r_2$ because the axis of rotation passes through the center of mass. Hence

$$r_1 = r - r_2 = r - \frac{m_1}{m_2}r_1.$$

Solving for r_1 gives

$$r_1 = \frac{r}{1 + \dfrac{m_1}{m_2}} = \frac{m_2 r}{m_1 + m_2}.$$

Similarly,

$$r_2 = \frac{m_1 r}{m_1 + m_2}.$$

Then (see first equation of this Solution)

$$I = m_1\left(\frac{m_2 r}{m_1 + m_2}\right)^2 + m_2\left(\frac{m_1 r}{m_1 + m_2}\right)^2 = \frac{m_1 m_2(m_1 + m_2)r^2}{(m_1 + m_2)^2}$$

$$= \frac{m_1 m_2}{m_1 + m_2}r^2 = \mu r^2,$$

where

$$\mu = \frac{m_1 m_2}{m_1 + m_2},$$

which is what we wished to show.

FIGURE 40–17 Rotational energy levels and allowed transitions (emission and absorption) for a diatomic molecule. Upward-pointing arrows represent absorption of a photon, and downward arrows represent emission of a photon.

EXAMPLE 40–5 **Rotational transition.** A rotational transition $\ell = 1$ to $\ell = 0$ for the molecule CO has a measured absorption wavelength $\lambda_1 = 2.60\,\text{mm}$ (microwave region). Use this to calculate (a) the moment of inertia of the CO molecule, and (b) the CO bond length, r. (c) Calculate the wavelengths of the next three rotational transitions, and the energies of the photon emitted for each of these four transitions.

APPROACH The absorption wavelength is used to find the energy of the absorbed photon. The moment of inertia I is found from Eq. 40–3, and the bond length r from Eq. 40–4.

SOLUTION (a) The photon energy, $E = hf = hc/\lambda$, equals the rotational energy level difference, ΔE_{rot}. From Eq. 40–3, we can write

$$\frac{\hbar^2}{I}\ell = \Delta E = hf = \frac{hc}{\lambda_1}.$$

With $\ell = 1$ (the upper state) in this case, we solve for I:

$$I = \frac{\hbar^2 \ell}{hc}\lambda_1 = \frac{h\lambda_1}{4\pi^2 c} = \frac{(6.63 \times 10^{-34}\,\text{J}\cdot\text{s})(2.60 \times 10^{-3}\,\text{m})}{4\pi^2(3.00 \times 10^8\,\text{m/s})}$$

$$= 1.46 \times 10^{-46}\,\text{kg}\cdot\text{m}^2.$$

(b) The masses of C and O are 12.0 u and 16.0 u, respectively, where $1\,\text{u} = 1.66 \times 10^{-27}\,\text{kg}$. Thus the reduced mass is

$$\mu = \frac{m_1 m_2}{m_1 + m_2} = \frac{(12.0)(16.0)}{28.0}(1.66 \times 10^{-27}\,\text{kg}) = 1.14 \times 10^{-26}\,\text{kg}$$

or 6.86 u. Then, from Eq. 40–4, the bond length is

$$r = \sqrt{\frac{I}{\mu}} = \sqrt{\frac{1.46 \times 10^{-46}\,\text{kg}\cdot\text{m}^2}{1.14 \times 10^{-26}\,\text{kg}}} = 1.13 \times 10^{-10}\,\text{m} = 0.113\,\text{nm}.$$

(c) From Eq. 40–3, $\Delta E \propto \ell$. Hence $\lambda = c/f = hc/\Delta E$ is proportional to $1/\ell$. Thus, for $\ell = 2$ to $\ell = 1$ transitions, $\lambda_2 = \frac{1}{2}\lambda_1 = 1.30\,\text{mm}$. For $\ell = 3$ to $\ell = 2$, $\lambda_3 = \frac{1}{3}\lambda_1 = 0.87\,\text{mm}$. And for $\ell = 4$ to $\ell = 3$, $\lambda_4 = 0.65\,\text{mm}$. All are close to measured values. The energies of the photons, $hf = hc/\lambda$, are respectively $4.8 \times 10^{-4}\,\text{eV}$, $9.5 \times 10^{-4}\,\text{eV}$, $1.4 \times 10^{-3}\,\text{eV}$, and $1.9 \times 10^{-3}\,\text{eV}$.

Vibrational Energy Levels in Molecules

The potential energy of the two atoms in a typical diatomic molecule has the shape shown in Fig. 40–8 or 40–9, and Fig. 40–18 again shows the potential energy for the H_2 molecule. We note that the potential energy, at least in the vicinity of the equilibrium separation r_0, closely resembles the potential energy of a simple harmonic oscillator, $U = \frac{1}{2}kx^2$, which is shown superposed in dashed lines. Thus, for small displacements from r_0, each atom experiences a

FIGURE 40–18 Potential energy for the H_2 molecule and for a simple harmonic oscillator ($U_{\text{SHO}} = \frac{1}{2}kx^2$, with $|x| = |r - r_0|$). The 0.50-eV energy height marked is for use in Example 40–6 to estimate k. [Note that $U_{\text{SHO}} = 0$ is not the same as $U = 0$ for the molecule.]

restoring force approximately proportional to the displacement, and the molecule vibrates as a simple harmonic oscillator (SHO). The classical frequency of vibration is

$$f = \frac{1}{2\pi}\sqrt{\frac{k}{\mu}}, \tag{40–5}$$

where k is the "stiffness constant" (as for a spring, Chapter 14) and instead of the mass m we must again use the reduced mass $\mu = m_1 m_2/(m_1 + m_2)$. (This is shown in Problem 19.) The Schrödinger equation for the SHO potential energy yields solutions for energy that are quantized according to

$$E_{vib} = \left(v + \tfrac{1}{2}\right)hf \qquad v = 0, 1, 2, \cdots, \qquad \text{(40–6)}$$

where f is given by Eq. 40–5 and v is an integer called the **vibrational quantum number**. The lowest energy state $(v = 0)$ is not zero (as for rotation) but has $E = \tfrac{1}{2}hf$. This is called the **zero-point energy.**[†] Higher states have energy $\tfrac{3}{2}hf$, $\tfrac{5}{2}hf$, and so on, as shown in Fig. 40–19. Transitions are subject to the **selection rule**

$$\Delta v = \pm 1,$$

so allowed transitions occur only between adjacent states and all give off photons of energy

$$\Delta E_{vib} = hf. \qquad \text{(40–7)}$$

This is very close to experimental values for small v; but for higher energies, the potential-energy curve (Fig. 40–18) begins to deviate from a perfect SHO curve, which affects the wavelengths and frequencies of the transitions. Typical transition energies are on the order of 10^{-1} eV, about 10 to 100 times larger than for rotational transitions, with wavelengths in the infrared region of the spectrum $(\approx 10^{-5}\,\text{m})$.[‡]

FIGURE 40–19 Allowed vibrational energies of a diatomic molecule, where f is the fundamental frequency of vibration, given by Eq. 40–5. The energy levels are equally spaced. Transitions are allowed only between adjacent levels $(\Delta v = \pm 1)$.

EXAMPLE 40–6 ESTIMATE Wavelength for H_2. (a) Use the curve of Fig. 40–18 to estimate the value of the stiffness constant k for the H_2 molecule, and then (b) estimate the fundamental wavelength for vibrational transitions.

APPROACH To find k, we arbitrarily choose an energy height of 0.50 eV which is indicated in Fig. 40–18. By measuring directly on the graph, we find that this energy corresponds to a vibration on either side of $r_0 = 0.074$ nm of about $x = \pm 0.017$ nm.

SOLUTION (a) For SHO, $U_{SHO} = \tfrac{1}{2}kx^2$ and $U_{SHO} = 0$ at $x = 0$ $(r = r_0)$; then

$$k = \frac{2U_{SHO}}{x^2} \approx \frac{2(0.50\,\text{eV})(1.6 \times 10^{-19}\,\text{J/eV})}{(1.7 \times 10^{-11}\,\text{m})^2} \approx 550\,\text{N/m}.$$

NOTE This value of k would also be reasonable for a macroscopic spring.

(b) The reduced mass is $\mu = m_1 m_2/(m_1 + m_2) = m_1/2 = \tfrac{1}{2}(1.0\,\text{u})(1.66 \times 10^{-27}\,\text{kg}) = 0.83 \times 10^{-27}$ kg. Hence, using Eq. 40–5,

$$\lambda = \frac{c}{f} = 2\pi c\sqrt{\frac{\mu}{k}} = 2\pi(3.0 \times 10^8\,\text{m/s})\sqrt{\frac{0.83 \times 10^{-27}\,\text{kg}}{550\,\text{N/m}}} = 2300\,\text{nm},$$

which is in the infrared region of the spectrum.

Experimentally, we do the inverse process: The wavelengths of vibrational transitions for a given molecule are measured, and from this the stiffness constant k can be calculated. The values of k calculated in this way are a measure of the strength of the molecular bond.

EXAMPLE 40–7 Vibrational energy levels in hydrogen. Hydrogen molecule vibrations emit infrared radiation of wavelength around 2300 nm. (a) What is the separation in energy between adjacent vibrational levels? (b) What is the lowest vibrational energy state?

APPROACH The energy separation between adjacent vibrational levels is $\Delta E_{vib} = hf = hc/\lambda$. The lowest energy (Eq. 40–6) has $v = 0$.

SOLUTION (a)

$$\Delta E_{vib} = hf = \frac{hc}{\lambda} = \frac{(6.63 \times 10^{-34}\,\text{J}\cdot\text{s})(3.00 \times 10^8\,\text{m/s})}{(2300 \times 10^{-9}\,\text{m})(1.60 \times 10^{-19}\,\text{J/eV})} = 0.54\,\text{eV},$$

where the denominator includes the conversion factor from joules to eV.

(b) The lowest vibrational energy has $v = 0$ in Eq. 40–6:

$$E_{vib} = \left(v + \tfrac{1}{2}\right)hf = \tfrac{1}{2}hf = 0.27\,\text{eV}.$$

[†]Recall this phenomenon for a square well, Fig. 38–8.

[‡]Forbidden transitions with $\Delta v = 2$ are emitted somewhat more weakly, but their observation can be important in some cases, such as in astronomy.

FIGURE 40-20 Combined electronic, vibrational, and rotational energy levels. Transitions marked with an × are not allowed by selection rules.

Rotational plus Vibrational Levels

When energy is imparted to a molecule, both the rotational and vibrational modes can be excited. Because rotational energies are an order of magnitude or so smaller than vibrational energies, which in turn are smaller than the electronic energy levels, we can represent the grouping of levels as shown in Fig. 40–20. Transitions between energy levels, with emission of a photon, are subject to the **selection rules**:

$$\Delta \nu = \pm 1 \qquad \text{and} \qquad \Delta \ell = \pm 1.$$

Some allowed and forbidden (marked ×) transitions are indicated in Fig. 40–20. Not all transitions and levels are shown, and the separation between vibrational levels, and (even more) between rotational levels, has been exaggerated. But we can clearly see the origin of the very closely spaced lines that give rise to the band spectra, as mentioned with reference to Fig. 40–15 earlier in this Section.

The spectra are quite complicated, so we consider briefly only transitions within the same electronic level, such as those at the top of Fig. 40–20. A transition from a state with quantum numbers ν and ℓ, to one with quantum numbers $\nu + 1$ and $\ell \pm 1$ (see the selection rules above), will absorb[†] a photon of energy:

$$\Delta E = \Delta E_{\text{vib}} + \Delta E_{\text{rot}}$$

$$= hf + (\ell + 1)\frac{\hbar^2}{I} \quad \begin{bmatrix} \ell \to \ell + 1 \\ (\Delta \ell = +1) \end{bmatrix}, \quad \ell = 0, 1, 2, \cdots \quad \textbf{(40–8a)}$$

$$= hf - \ell \frac{\hbar^2}{I} \quad \begin{bmatrix} \ell \to \ell - 1 \\ (\Delta \ell = -1) \end{bmatrix}, \quad \ell = 1, 2, 3, \cdots, \quad \textbf{(40–8b)}$$

where we have used Eqs. 40–3 and 40–7. Note that for $\ell \to \ell - 1$ transitions, ℓ cannot be zero because there is then no state with $\ell = -1$. Equations 40–8 predict an absorption spectrum like that shown schematically in Fig. 40–21, with transitions $\ell \to \ell - 1$ on the left and $\ell \to \ell + 1$ on the right. Figure 40–22 shows the molecular absorption spectrum of HCl, which follows this pattern very well.

[†]Eqs. 40–8 are for absorption; for emission of a photon, the transition would be $\nu \to \nu - 1$, $\ell \to \ell \pm 1$.

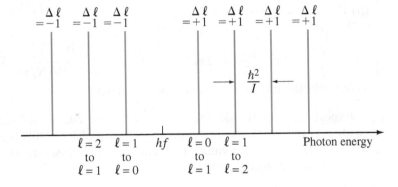

FIGURE 40–21 Expected spectrum for transitions between combined rotational and vibrational states.

FIGURE 40–22 Absorption spectrum for HCl molecules. Lines on the left correspond to transitions where $\ell \to \ell - 1$; those on the right are for $\ell \to \ell + 1$. Each line has a double peak because chlorine has two isotopes of different mass and different moment of inertia.

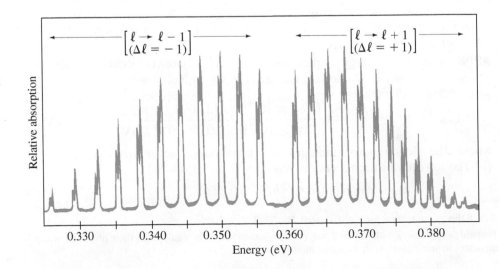

(Each line in the spectrum of Fig. 40–22 is split into two because Cl consists of two isotopes of different mass; hence there are two kinds of HCl molecule with slightly different moments of inertia I.)

EXAMPLE 40–8 **ESTIMATE** **The HCl molecule.** Estimate the moment of inertia of the HCl molecule using the absorption spectrum shown in Fig. 40–22. For the purposes of a rough estimate you can ignore the difference between the two isotopes.

APPROACH The locations of the peaks in Fig. 40–22 should correspond to Eqs. 40–8. We don't know what value of ℓ each peak corresponds to in Fig. 40–22, but we can estimate the energy difference between peaks to be about $\Delta E' = 0.0025 \text{ eV}$.

SOLUTION From Eqs. 40–8, the energy difference between two peaks is given by

$$\Delta E' = \Delta E_{\ell+1} - \Delta E_\ell = \frac{\hbar^2}{I}.$$

Then

$$I = \frac{\hbar^2}{\Delta E'} = \frac{(6.626 \times 10^{-34} \text{ J·s}/2\pi)^2}{(0.0025 \text{ eV})(1.6 \times 10^{-19} \text{ J/eV})} = 2.8 \times 10^{-47} \text{ kg·m}^2.$$

NOTE To get an idea of what this number means, we write $I = \mu r^2$ (Eq. 40–4), where μ is the reduced mass (Example 40–4); then we calculate μ:

$$\mu = \frac{m_1 m_2}{m_1 + m_2} = \frac{(1.0\,\text{u})(35\,\text{u})}{36\,\text{u}}(1.66 \times 10^{-27} \text{ kg/u}) = 1.6 \times 10^{-27} \text{ kg};$$

the bond length is given by (Eq. 40–4)

$$r = \left(\frac{I}{\mu}\right)^{\frac{1}{2}} = \left(\frac{2.8 \times 10^{-47} \text{ kg·m}^2}{1.6 \times 10^{-27} \text{ kg}}\right)^{\frac{1}{2}} = 1.3 \times 10^{-10} \text{ m},$$

which is the expected order of magnitude for a bond length.

40–5 Bonding in Solids

Quantum mechanics has been a great tool for understanding the structure of solids. This active field of research today is called **solid-state physics**, or **condensed-matter physics** so as to include liquids as well. The rest of this Chapter is devoted to this subject, and we begin with a brief look at the structure of solids and the bonds that hold them together.

Although some solid materials are *amorphous* in structure, in that the atoms and molecules show no long-range order, we will be interested here in the large class of *crystalline* substances whose atoms, ions, or molecules are generally believed to form an orderly array known as a **lattice**. Figure 40–23 shows three of the possible arrangements of atoms in a crystal: simple cubic, face-centered cubic, and body-centered cubic. The NaCl crystal is face-centered cubic (see Fig. 40–24), with one Na$^+$ ion or one Cl$^-$ ion at each lattice point (i.e., considering Na and Cl separately).

The molecules of a solid are held together in a number of ways. The most common are by *covalent* bonding (such as between the carbon atoms of the diamond crystal) or *ionic* bonding (as in a NaCl crystal). Often the bonds are partially covalent and partially ionic. Our discussion of these bonds earlier in this Chapter for molecules applies equally well here to solids.

Let us look for a moment at the NaCl crystal of Fig. 40–24. Each Na$^+$ ion feels an attractive Coulomb potential due to each of the six "nearest neighbor" Cl$^-$ ions surrounding it. Note that one Na$^+$ does not "belong" exclusively to one Cl$^-$, so we must not think of ionic solids as consisting of individual molecules. Each Na$^+$ also feels a repulsive Coulomb potential due to other Na$^+$ ions, although this is weaker since the other Na$^+$ ions are farther away. Thus we expect a net attractive potential

$$U = -\alpha \frac{1}{4\pi\epsilon_0} \frac{e^2}{r}.$$

The factor α is called the *Madelung constant*. If each Na$^+$ were surrounded by only the six Cl$^-$ ions, α would be 6, but the influence of all the other ions reduces it to a value $\alpha = 1.75$ for the NaCl crystal. The potential must also include a term representing the repulsive force when the wave functions of the inner shells and subshells overlap, and this has the form $U = B/r^m$, where m is a small integer.

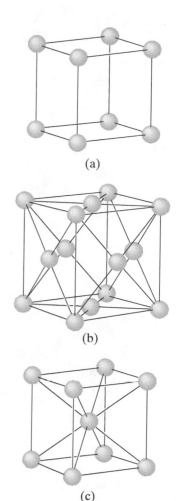

(a)

(b)

(c)

FIGURE 40–23 Arrangement of atoms in (a) a simple cubic crystal, (b) face-centered cubic crystal (note the atom at the center of each face), and (c) body-centered cubic crystal. Each shows the relationship of the bonds. Each of these "cells" is repeated in three dimensions to the edges of the macroscopic crystal.

FIGURE 40–24 Diagram of an NaCl crystal, showing the "packing" of atoms.

The sum of these two terms suggests a potential energy

$$U = -\frac{\alpha}{4\pi\epsilon_0}\frac{e^2}{r} + \frac{B}{r^m},$$

(40–9)

which has the same form as Eq. 40–1 for molecules (Section 40–2). It can be shown (Problem 25) that, at the equilibrium distance r_0,

$$U = U_0 = -\frac{\alpha}{4\pi\epsilon_0}\frac{e^2}{r_0}\left(1 - \frac{1}{m}\right).$$

This U_0 is known as the *ionic cohesive energy*; it is a sort of "binding energy"—the energy (per ion) needed to take the solid apart into separated ions, one by one.

A different type of bond occurs in metals. Metal atoms have relatively loosely held outer electrons. Present-day **metallic bond** theories propose that in a metallic solid, these outer electrons roam rather freely among all the metal atoms which, without their outer electrons, act like positive ions. The electrostatic attraction between the metal ions and this negative electron "gas" is what is believed, at least in part, to hold the solid together. The binding energy of metal bonds are typically 1 to 3 eV, somewhat weaker than ionic or covalent bonds (5 to 10 eV in solids). The "free electrons," according to this theory, are responsible for the high electrical and thermal conductivity of metals (see Sections 40–6 and 40–7). This theory also nicely accounts for the shininess of smooth metal surfaces: the electrons are free and can vibrate at any frequency, so when light of a range of frequencies falls on a metal, the electrons can vibrate in response and re-emit light of those same frequencies. Hence the reflected light will consist largely of the same frequencies as the incident light. Compare this to nonmetallic materials that have a distinct color—the atomic electrons exist only in certain energy states, and when white light falls on them, the atoms absorb at certain frequencies, and reflect other frequencies which make up the color we see.

Here is a brief summary of important strong bonds:

- ionic: an electron is stolen from one atom by another;
- covalent: electrons are shared by atoms within a single molecule;
- metallic: electrons are shared by all atoms in the metal.

The atoms or molecules of some materials, such as the noble gases, can form only *weak bonds* with each other. As we saw in Section 40–3, weak bonds have very low binding energies and would not be expected to hold atoms together as a liquid or solid at room temperature. The noble gases condense only at very low temperatures, where the atomic kinetic energy is small and the weak attraction can then hold the atoms together.

40–6 Free-Electron Theory of Metals; Fermi Energy

Let us look more closely at the free-electron theory of metals mentioned in the preceding Section. Let us imagine the electrons trapped within the metal as being in a potential well: inside the metal, the potential energy is zero, but at the edges of the metal there are high potential walls. Since very few electrons leave the metal at room temperature, we can imagine the walls as being infinitely high (as in Section 38–8). At higher temperatures, electrons do leave the metal (we know that thermionic emission occurs, Section 23–9), so we must recognize that the well is of finite depth. In this simple model, the electrons are trapped within the metal, but are free to move about inside the well whose size is macroscopic—the size of the piece of metal. The energy will be quantized, but the spacing between energy levels will be very tiny (see Eq. 38–13) because the width of the potential well ℓ is very large. Indeed, for a cube 1 cm on a side, the number of states with energy between, say, 5.0 and 5.5 eV, is on the order of 10^{22} (see Example 40–9).

To deal with such vast numbers of states, which are so closely spaced as to seem continuous, we need to use statistical methods. We define a quantity known as the **density of states**, $g(E)$, whose meaning is similar to the Maxwell distribution, Eq. 18–6 (see Section 18–2). That is, the quantity $g(E)\,dE$ represents the number of states per unit volume that have energy between E and $E + dE$. A careful calculation (see Problem 41), which must treat the potential well as three dimensional, shows that

$$g(E) = \frac{8\sqrt{2}\,\pi m^{3/2}}{h^3} E^{1/2} \qquad (40\text{–}10)$$

where m is the mass of the electron. This function is plotted in Fig. 40–25.

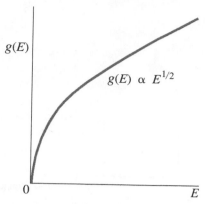

FIGURE 40–25 Density of states $g(E)$ as a function of energy E (Eq. 40–10).

EXAMPLE 40–9 **ESTIMATE** **Electron states in copper.** Estimate the number of states in the range 5.0 to 5.5 eV available to electrons in a 1.0-cm cube of copper metal.

APPROACH Since $g(E)$ is the number of states per unit volume per unit energy interval, the number N of states is approximately (it is approximate because ΔE is not small)

$$N \approx g(E)V\,\Delta E,$$

where the volume $V = 1.0\,\text{cm}^3 = 1.0 \times 10^{-6}\,\text{m}^3$ and $\Delta E = 0.50\,\text{eV}$.

SOLUTION We evaluate $g(E)$ at 5.25 eV, and find (Eq. 40–10):

$$N \approx g(E)V\,\Delta E = \frac{8\sqrt{2}\,\pi(9.1 \times 10^{-31}\,\text{kg})^{\frac{3}{2}}}{(6.63 \times 10^{-34}\,\text{J}\cdot\text{s})^3}\sqrt{(5.25\,\text{eV})(1.6 \times 10^{-19}\,\text{J/eV})}$$
$$\times\,(1.0 \times 10^{-6}\,\text{m}^3)(0.50\,\text{eV})(1.6 \times 10^{-19}\,\text{J/eV})$$
$$\approx 8 \times 10^{21}$$

states in 1.0 cm³. Note that the type of metal did not enter the calculation.

Equation 40–10 gives us the density of states. Now we must ask: How are the states available to an electron gas actually populated? Let us first consider the situation at absolute zero, $T = 0\,\text{K}$. For a classical ideal gas, all the particles would be in the lowest state, with zero kinetic energy $(= \frac{3}{2}kT = 0)$. But the situation is vastly different for an electron gas because electrons obey the exclusion principle. Electrons do not obey classical statistics but rather a quantum statistics called **Fermi–Dirac statistics**[†] that takes into account the exclusion principle. All particles that have spin $\frac{1}{2}$ (or other half-integral spin: $\frac{3}{2}$, $\frac{5}{2}$, etc.), such as electrons, protons, and neutrons, obey Fermi–Dirac statistics and are referred to as **fermions**.[‡] The electron gas in a metal is often called a **Fermi gas**. According to the exclusion principle, no two electrons in the metal can have the same set of quantum numbers. Therefore, in each of the states of our potential well, there can be at most two electrons: one with spin up $(m_s = +\frac{1}{2})$ and one with spin down $(m_s = -\frac{1}{2})$. (This factor of 2 has already been included in Eq. 40–10.) Thus, at $T = 0\,\text{K}$, the possible energy levels will be filled, two electrons each, up to a maximum level called the **Fermi level**. This is shown in Fig. 40–26, where the vertical axis is labeled $n_0(E)$ for "density of occupied states." The energy of the state at the Fermi level is called the **Fermi energy**, E_F. To determine E_F, we integrate Eq. 40–10 from $E = 0$ to $E = E_F$ (all states up to E_F are filled at $T = 0\,\text{K}$):

$$\frac{N}{V} = \int_0^{E_F} g(E)\,dE, \qquad (40\text{–}11)$$

where N/V is the number of conduction electrons per unit volume in the metal.

FIGURE 40–26 At $T = 0\,\text{K}$, all states up to energy E_F, called the Fermi energy, are filled.

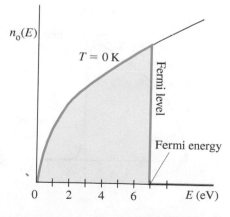

[†]Developed independently by Enrico Fermi (Figs. 41–8, 38–2, 37–10) in early 1926 and by P. A. M. Dirac a few months later.

[‡]Particles with integer spin (0, 1, 2, etc.), such as the photon, obey *Bose–Einstein* statistics and are called *bosons*, as mentioned in Section 39–4.

Then, solving for E_F, the result (see Example 40–10 below) is

$$E_F = \frac{h^2}{8m}\left(\frac{3}{\pi}\frac{N}{V}\right)^{\frac{2}{3}}. \tag{40–12}$$

The average energy in this distribution (see Problem 35) is

$$\overline{E} = \tfrac{3}{5}E_F. \tag{40–13}$$

For copper, $E_F = 7.0\,\text{eV}$ (see Example 40–10) and $\overline{E} = 4.2\,\text{eV}$. This is very much greater than the energy of thermal motion at room temperature $(\tfrac{3}{2}kT \approx 0.04\,\text{eV})$. Clearly, all motion does not stop at absolute zero.

Thus, at $T = 0$, all states with energy below E_F are occupied, and all states above E_F are empty. What happens for $T > 0$? We expect that some (at least) of the electrons will increase in energy due to thermal motion. Classically, the distribution of occupied states would be given by the Boltzmann factor, $e^{-E/kT}$ (see Eqs. 39–16). But for our electron gas, a quantum-mechanical system obeying the exclusion principle, the probability of a given state of energy E being occupied is given by the **Fermi–Dirac probability function** (or **Fermi factor**):

$$f(E) = \frac{1}{e^{(E-E_F)/kT} + 1}, \tag{40–14}$$

where E_F is the Fermi energy. This function is plotted in Fig. 40–27 for two temperatures, $T = 0\,\text{K}$ and $T = 1200\,\text{K}$ (just below the melting point of copper). At $T = 0$ (or as T approaches zero) the factor $e^{(E-E_F)/kT}$ in Eq. 40–14 is zero if $E < E_F$ and is ∞ if $E > E_F$. Thus

$$f(E) = \begin{cases} 1 & E < E_F \\ 0 & E > E_F \end{cases} \quad \text{at} \quad T = 0.$$

This is what is plotted in black in Fig. 40–27 and is consistent with Fig. 40–26: all states up to the Fermi level are occupied [probability $f(E) = 1$] and all states above are unoccupied. For $T = 1200\,\text{K}$, the Fermi factor changes only a little, as shown in Fig. 40–27 as the blue curve. Note that at any temperature T, when $E = E_F$, then Eq. 40–14 gives $f(E) = 0.50$, meaning the state at $E = E_F$ has a 50% chance of being occupied. To see how $f(E)$ affects the actual distribution of electrons in energy states, we must weight the density of possible states, $g(E)$, by the probability that those states will be occupied, $f(E)$. The product of these two functions then gives the **density of occupied states**,

$$n_o(E) = g(E)f(E) = \frac{8\sqrt{2}\,\pi m^{3/2}}{h^3}\frac{E^{1/2}}{e^{(E-E_F)/kT} + 1}. \tag{40–15}$$

Then $n_o(E)\,dE$ represents the number of electrons per unit volume with energy between E and $E + dE$ in thermal equilibrium at temperature T. This is plotted in Fig. 40–28 for $T = 1200\,\text{K}$, a temperature at which a metal is so hot it would glow. We see immediately that the distribution differs very little from that at $T = 0$. We see also that the changes that do occur are concentrated about the Fermi level. A few electrons from slightly below the Fermi level move to energy states slightly above it. The average energy of the electrons increases only very slightly when the temperature is increased from $T = 0\,\text{K}$ to $T = 1200\,\text{K}$. This is very different from the behavior of an ideal gas, for which kinetic energy increases directly with T. Nonetheless, this behavior is readily understood as follows. Energy of thermal motion at $T = 1200\,\text{K}$ is about $\tfrac{3}{2}kT \approx 0.1\,\text{eV}$. The Fermi level, on the other hand, is on the order of several eV: for copper it is $E_F \approx 7.0\,\text{eV}$. An electron at $T = 1200\,\text{K}$ may have 7 eV of energy, but it can acquire at most only a few times 0.1 eV of energy by a (thermal) collision with the lattice. Only electrons very near the Fermi level would find vacant states close enough to make such a transition. Essentially none of the electrons could increase in energy by, say, 3 eV, so electrons farther down in the electron gas are unaffected. Only electrons near the top of the energy distribution can be thermally excited to higher states. And their new energy is on the average only slightly higher than their old energy.

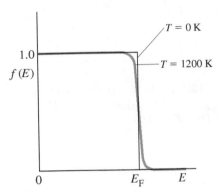

FIGURE 40–27 The Fermi–Dirac probability function for two temperatures, $T = 0\,\text{K}$ (black line) and $T = 1200\,\text{K}$ (blue curve). For $f(E) = 1$, a state with energy E is certainly occupied. For $f(E) = 0.5$, which occurs at $E = E_F$, the state with E_F has a 50% chance of being occupied.

FIGURE 40–28 The density of occupied states for the electron gas in copper. The width kT shown above the graph represents thermal energy at $T = 1200\,\text{K}$.

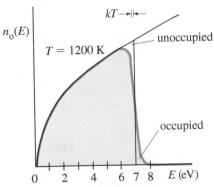

EXERCISE B Return to the Chapter-Opening Question, page 1071, and answer it again now. Try to explain why you may have answered differently the first time.

EXAMPLE 40–10 **The Fermi level.** For the metal copper, determine (a) the Fermi energy, (b) the average energy of electrons, and (c) the speed of electrons at the Fermi level (this is called the *Fermi speed*).

APPROACH We first derive Eq. 40–12 by combining Eqs. 40–10 and 40–11:

$$\frac{N}{V} = \frac{8\sqrt{2}\,\pi m^{3/2}}{h^3} \int_0^{E_F} E^{1/2}\, dE = \frac{8\sqrt{2}\,\pi m^{3/2}}{h^3}\frac{2}{3}E_F^{3/2}.$$

Solving for E_F, we obtain

$$E_F = \frac{h^2}{8m}\left(\frac{3}{\pi}\frac{N}{V}\right)^{\frac{2}{3}}$$

[note: $(2\sqrt{2})^{\frac{2}{3}} = (2^{\frac{3}{2}})^{\frac{2}{3}} = 2$], and this is Eq. 40–12. We calculated N/V, the number of conduction electrons per unit volume in copper, in Example 25–14 to be $N/V = 8.4 \times 10^{28}\,\text{m}^{-3}$.

SOLUTION (a) The Fermi energy for copper is thus

$$E_F = \frac{(6.63 \times 10^{-34}\,\text{J·s})^2}{8(9.1 \times 10^{-31}\,\text{kg})}\left[\frac{3(8.4 \times 10^{28}\,\text{m}^{-3})}{\pi}\right]^{\frac{2}{3}}\frac{1}{1.6 \times 10^{-19}\,\text{J/eV}} = 7.0\,\text{eV}.$$

(b) From Eq. 40–13,

$$\overline{E} = \tfrac{3}{5}E_F = 4.2\,\text{eV}.$$

(c) In our model, we have taken $U = 0$ inside the metal (assuming a 3-D infinite potential well, Section 38–8, Eq. 40–10, and Problem 41). Then E is only kinetic energy $= \frac{1}{2}mv^2$. Therefore, at the Fermi level, the Fermi speed is

$$v_F = \sqrt{\frac{2E_F}{m}} = \sqrt{\frac{2(7.0\,\text{eV})(1.6 \times 10^{-19}\,\text{J/eV})}{9.1 \times 10^{-31}\,\text{kg}}} = 1.6 \times 10^6\,\text{m/s},$$

a very high speed. The temperature of a classical gas would have to be extremely high to produce an average particle speed this large.

EXAMPLE 40–11 **Incorrect classical calculation.** Let us see what result we get if the electrons are treated as a classical ideal gas. That is, estimate the average kinetic energy of electrons at room temperature using the kinetic theory of gases, Chapter 18.

APPROACH The average kinetic energy of particles in an ideal gas was given in Chapter 18, Eq. 18–4, as

$$\overline{K} = \tfrac{3}{2}kT,$$

where k is Boltzmann's constant and $T \approx 300\,\text{K}$.

SOLUTION The ideal gas model gives

$$\overline{K} = \tfrac{3}{2}(1.38 \times 10^{-23}\,\text{J/K})(300\,\text{K})\left(\frac{1}{1.6 \times 10^{-19}\,\text{J/eV}}\right) = 0.039\,\text{eV}.$$

This result is far from correct. It is off by a factor of 100: Example 40–10 gave 4.2 eV. The ideal gas model does not work for electrons which obey the exclusion principle. Indeed, we see here how important and powerful the exclusion principle is.

EXERCISE C Determine the Fermi energy for gold (density = 19,300 kg/m³). (a) 5.5 eV, (b) 6.2 eV, (c) 7.2 eV, (d) 8.1 eV, (e) 8.4 eV.

FIGURE 40–29 Potential energy for an electron in a metal crystal, with deep potential wells in the vicinity of each ion in the crystal lattice.

The simple model of an electron gas presented here provides good explanations for the electrical and thermal properties of conductors. But it does not explain why some materials are good conductors and others are good insulators. To provide an explanation, our model of electrons inside a metal moving in a uniform potential well needs to be refined to include the effect of the lattice. Figure 40–29 shows a "periodic" potential that takes into account the attraction of electrons for each atomic ion in the lattice. Here we have taken $U = 0$ for an electron free of the metal; so within the metal, electron energies are less than zero (just as for molecules, or for the H atom in which the ground state has $E = -13.6\,\text{eV}$). The quantity eW_0 represents the minimum energy to remove an electron from the metal, where W_0 is the *work function* (see Section 37–2). The crucial outcome of putting a periodic potential (more easily approximated with narrow square wells) into the Schrödinger equation is that the allowed energy states are divided into *bands*, with energy gaps in between. Only electrons in the highest band, close to the Fermi level, are able to move about freely within the metal crystal. In the next Section we will see physically why there are bands and how they explain the properties of conductors, insulators, and semiconductors.

40–7 Band Theory of Solids

We saw in Section 40–1 that when two hydrogen atoms approach each other, the wave functions overlap, and the two 1s states (one for each atom) divide into two states of different energy. (As we saw, only one of these states, $S = 0$, has low enough energy to give a bound H_2 molecule.) Figure 40–30a shows this situation for 1s and 2s states for two atoms: as the two atoms get closer (toward the left in Fig. 40–30a), the 1s and 2s states split into two levels. If six atoms come together, as in Fig. 40–30b, each of the states splits into six levels. If a large number of atoms come together to form a solid, then each of the original atomic levels becomes a **band** as shown in Fig. 40–30c. The energy levels are so close together in each band that they seem essentially continuous. This is why the spectrum of heated solids (Section 37–1) appears continuous. (See also Fig. 40–15 and its discussion at the start of Section 40–4.)

FIGURE 40–30 The splitting of 1s and 2s atomic energy levels as (a) two atoms approach each other (the atomic separation decreases toward the left on the graph), (b) the same for six atoms, and (c) for many atoms when they come together to form a solid.

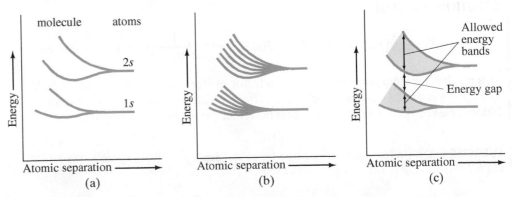

The crucial aspect of a good **conductor** is that the highest energy band containing electrons is only partially filled. Consider sodium metal, for example, whose energy bands are shown in Fig. 40–31. The 1s, 2s, and 2p bands are full (just as in a sodium atom) and don't concern us. The 3s band, however, is only half full. To see why, recall that the exclusion principle stipulates that in an atom, only two electrons can be in the 3s state, one with spin up and one with spin down. These two states have slightly different energy. For a solid consisting of N atoms, the 3s band will contain 2N possible energy states. A sodium atom has a single 3s electron, so in a sample of sodium metal containing N atoms, there are N electrons in the 3s band, and N unoccupied states. When a potential difference is applied across the metal, electrons can respond by accelerating and increasing their energy, since there are plenty of unoccupied states of slightly higher energy available. Hence, a current flows readily and sodium is a good conductor. The characteristic of all good conductors is that the highest energy band is only partially filled, or two bands overlap so that unoccupied states are available. An example of the latter is magnesium, which has two 3s electrons, so its 3s band is filled. But the unfilled 3p band overlaps the 3s band in energy, so there are lots of available states for the electrons to move into. Thus magnesium, too, is a good conductor.

In a material that is a good **insulator**, on the other hand, the highest band containing electrons, called the **valence band**, is completely filled. The next highest energy band, called the **conduction band**, is separated from the valence band by a "forbidden" **energy gap** (or **band gap**), E_g, of typically 5 to 10 eV. So at room temperature (300 K), where thermal energies (that is, average kinetic energy—see Chapter 18) are on the order of $\frac{3}{2}kT \approx 0.04$ eV, almost no electrons can acquire the 5 eV needed to reach the conduction band. When a potential difference is applied across the material, no available states are accessible to the electrons, and no current flows. Hence, the material is a good insulator.

Figure 40–32 compares the relevant energy bands (a) for conductors, (b) for insulators, and also (c) for the important class of materials known as **semiconductors**. The bands for a pure (or **intrinsic**) semiconductor, such as silicon or germanium, are like those for an insulator, except that the unfilled conduction band is separated from the filled valence band by a much smaller energy gap, E_g, typically on the order of 1 eV. At room temperature, a few electrons can acquire enough thermal energy to reach the conduction band, and so a very small current may flow when a voltage is applied. At higher temperatures, more electrons have enough energy to jump the gap. Often this effect can more than offset the effects of more frequent collisions due to increased disorder at higher temperature, so the resistivity of semiconductors can *decrease* with increasing temperature (see Table 25–1). But this is not the whole story of semiconductor conduction. When a potential difference is applied to a semiconductor, the few electrons in the conduction band move toward the positive electrode. Electrons in the valence band try to do the same thing, and a few can because there are a small number of unoccupied states which were left empty by the electrons reaching the conduction band. Such unfilled electron states are called **holes**. Each electron in the valence band that fills a hole in this way as it moves toward the positive electrode leaves behind its own hole, so the holes migrate toward the negative electrode. As the electrons tend to accumulate at one side of the material, the holes tend to accumulate on the opposite side. We will look at this phenomenon in more detail in the next Section.

FIGURE 40–31 Energy bands for sodium (Na).

$3s$

$2p$

$2s$

$1s$

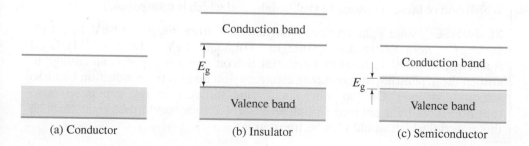

(a) Conductor

Conduction band

E_g

Valence band

(b) Insulator

Conduction band

E_g

Valence band

(c) Semiconductor

FIGURE 40–32 Energy bands for (a) a conductor, (b) an insulator, which has a large energy gap E_g, and (c) a semiconductor, which has a small energy gap E_g. Shading represents occupied states. Pale shading in (c) represents electrons that can pass from the top of the valence band to the bottom of the conduction band due to thermal agitation at room temperature (exaggerated).

EXAMPLE 40–12 **Calculating the energy gap.** It is found that the conductivity of a certain semiconductor increases when light of wavelength 345 nm or shorter strikes it, suggesting that electrons are being promoted from the valence band to the conduction band. What is the energy gap, E_g, for this semiconductor?

APPROACH The longest wavelength (lowest energy) photon to cause an increase in conductivity has $\lambda = 345$ nm, and its energy ($= hf$) equals the energy gap.

SOLUTION The gap energy equals the energy of a $\lambda = 345$-nm photon:

$$E_g = hf = \frac{hc}{\lambda} = \frac{(6.63 \times 10^{-34}\,\text{J}\cdot\text{s})(3.00 \times 10^8\,\text{m/s})}{(345 \times 10^{-9}\,\text{m})(1.60 \times 10^{-19}\,\text{J/eV})} = 3.6\,\text{eV}.$$

EXAMPLE 40–13 **ESTIMATE** **Free electrons in semiconductors and insulators.** Use the Fermi–Dirac probability function, Eq. 40–14, to estimate the order of magnitude of the numbers of free electrons in the conduction band of a solid containing 10^{21} atoms, assuming the solid is at room temperature ($T = 300$ K) and is (a) a semiconductor with $E_g \approx 1.1$ eV, (b) an insulator with $E_g \approx 5$ eV. Compare to a conductor.

APPROACH At $T = 0$, all states above the Fermi energy E_F are empty, and all those below are full. So for semiconductors and insulators we can take E_F to be about midway between the valence and conduction bands, Fig. 40–33, and it does not change significantly as we go to room temperature. We can thus use Eq. 40–14 to find the fraction of electrons in the conduction band at room temperature for the two cases.

SOLUTION (a) For the semiconductor, the gap $E_g \approx 1.1$ eV, so $E - E_F \approx 0.55$ eV for the lowest states in the conduction band. Since at room temperature we have $kT \approx 0.026$ eV, then $(E - E_F)/kT \approx 0.55\,\text{eV}/0.026\,\text{eV} \approx 21$ and

$$f(E) = \frac{1}{e^{(E-E_F)/kT} + 1} \approx \frac{1}{e^{21}} \approx 10^{-9}.$$

Thus about 1 atom in 10^9 can contribute an electron to the conductivity.
(b) For the insulator with $E - E_F \approx 5.0\,\text{eV} - \frac{1}{2}(5.0\,\text{eV}) = 2.5\,\text{eV}$, we get

$$f(E) \approx \frac{1}{e^{2.5/0.026} + 1} \approx \frac{1}{e^{96}} \approx 10^{-42}.$$

Thus in an ordinary sample containing 10^{21} atoms, there would be no free electrons in an insulator $(10^{21} \times 10^{-42} = 10^{-21})$, about 10^{12} $(10^{21} \times 10^{-9})$ free electrons in a semiconductor, and about 10^{21} free electrons in a good conductor.

Conduction band

E_g - - - - - - - - - - - - - - - E_F

Valence band

FIGURE 40–33 Example 40–13: The Fermi energy is midway between the valence band and the conduction band.

CONCEPTUAL EXAMPLE 40–14 **Which is transparent?** The energy gap for silicon is 1.14 eV at room temperature, whereas that of zinc sulfide (ZnS) is 3.6 eV. Which one of these is opaque to visible light, and which is transparent?

RESPONSE Visible light photons span energies from roughly 1.8 eV to 3.1 eV ($E = hf = hc/\lambda$ where $\lambda = 400$ nm to 700 nm and 1 eV $= 1.6 \times 10^{-19}$ J). Light is absorbed by the electrons in a material. Silicon's energy gap is small enough to absorb these photons, thus bumping electrons well up into the conduction band, so silicon is opaque. On the other hand, zinc sulfide's energy gap is so large that no visible light photons would be absorbed; they would pass right through the material which would thus be transparent.

40–8 Semiconductors and Doping

Nearly all electronic devices today use semiconductors. The most common are silicon (Si) and germanium (Ge). An atom of silicon or germanium has four outer electrons that act to hold the atoms in the regular lattice structure of the crystal, shown schematically in Fig. 40–34a. Germanium and silicon acquire properties useful for electronics when a tiny amount of impurity is introduced into the crystal structure (perhaps 1 part in 10^6 or 10^7). This is called **doping** the semiconductor. Two kinds of doped semiconductor can be made, depending on the type of impurity used. If the impurity is an element whose atoms have five outer electrons, such as arsenic, we have the situation shown in Fig. 40–34b, with the arsenic atoms holding positions in the crystal lattice where normally silicon atoms would be. Only four of arsenic's electrons fit into the bonding structure. The fifth does not fit in and can move relatively freely, somewhat like the electrons in a conductor. Because of this small number of extra electrons, a doped semiconductor becomes slightly conducting.

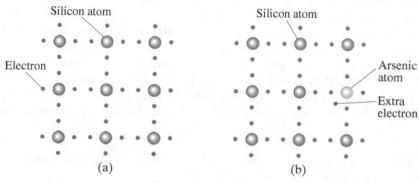

(a)　　　　　　(b)

FIGURE 40–34 Two-dimensional representation of a silicon crystal. (a) Four (outer) electrons surround each silicon atom. (b) Silicon crystal doped with a small percentage of arsenic atoms: the extra electron doesn't fit into the crystal lattice and so is free to move about. This is an *n*-type semiconductor.

The density of conduction electrons in an intrinsic (undoped) semiconductor at room temperature is very low, usually less than 1 per 10^9 atoms. With an impurity concentration of 1 in 10^6 or 10^7 when doped, the conductivity will be much higher and it can be controlled with great precision. An arsenic-doped silicon crystal is called an **n-type semiconductor** because *negative* charges (electrons) carry the electric current.

In a **p-type semiconductor**, a small percentage of semiconductor atoms are replaced by atoms with three outer electrons—such as gallium. As shown in Fig. 40–35a, there is a "hole" in the lattice structure near a gallium atom since it has only three outer electrons. Electrons from nearby silicon atoms can jump into this hole and fill it. But this leaves a hole where that electron had previously been, Fig. 40–35b. The vast majority of atoms are silicon, so holes are almost always next to a silicon atom. Since silicon atoms require four outer electrons to be neutral, this means that there is a net positive charge at the hole. Whenever an electron moves to fill a hole, the positive hole is then at the previous position of that electron. Another electron can then fill this hole, and the hole thus moves to a new location; and so on. This type of semiconductor is called *p-type* because it is the positive holes that seem to carry the electric current. Note, however, that both *p-type* and *n-type* semiconductors have *no net charge* on them.

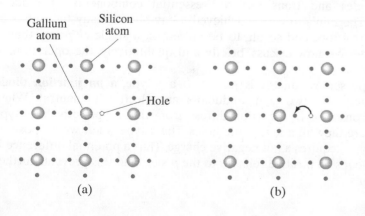

(a)　　　　　　(b)

FIGURE 40–35 A *p*-type semiconductor, gallium-doped silicon. (a) Gallium has only three outer electrons, so there is an empty spot, or *hole* in the structure. (b) Electrons from silicon atoms can jump into the hole and fill it. As a result, the hole moves to a new location (to the right in this Figure), to where the electron used to be.

FIGURE 40–36 Impurity energy levels in doped semiconductors.

According to the band theory (Section 40–7), in a doped semiconductor the impurity provides additional energy states between the bands as shown in Fig. 40–36. In an *n*-type semiconductor, the impurity energy level lies just below the conduction band, Fig. 40–36a. Electrons in this energy level need only about 0.05 eV in Si (even less in Ge) to reach the conduction band; this is on the order of the thermal energy, $\frac{3}{2}kT$ ($= 0.04$ eV at 300 K), so transitions occur readily at room temperature. This energy level can thus supply electrons to the conduction band, so it is called a **donor** level. In *p*-type semiconductors, the impurity energy level is just above the valence band (Fig. 40–36b). It is called an **acceptor** level because electrons from the valence band can easily jump into it. Positive holes are left behind in the valence band, and as other electrons move into these holes, the holes move as discussed earlier.

EXERCISE D Which of the following impurity atoms would produce a *p*-type semiconductor? (*a*) Ge; (*b*) Ne; (*c*) Al; (*d*) As; (*e*) none of the above.

(a)

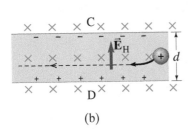

(b)

FIGURE 27–32 (Repeated.) The Hall effect. (a) Negative charges moving to the right as the current. (b) The same current, but as positive charges moving to the left.

| CONCEPTUAL EXAMPLE 40–15 | **Determining charge of conductors.** How can we determine if a *p*-type semiconductor has a current that is really due to the motion of holes? Or, is this just a convenient model?

RESPONSE Recall from Section 27–8 that the Hall effect can be used to distinguish the sign of the charges involved in a current. When placed in a magnetic field, the current in a particular direction can result in a voltage perpendicular to that current due to the magnetic force on the moving charges (Fig. 27–32, repeated here). The direction of this *Hall voltage* depends on the sign of the charges carrying the current. In this way, it has been demonstrated that it really is moving holes that are responsible for the current in a *p*-type semiconductor.

40–9 Semiconductor Diodes

Semiconductor diodes and transistors are essential components of modern electronic devices. The miniaturization achieved today allows many thousands of diodes, transistors, resistors, and so on, to be placed on a single *chip* less than a millimeter on a side. We now discuss, briefly and qualitatively, the operation of diodes and transistors.

When an *n*-type semiconductor is joined to a *p*-type, a ***pn* junction diode** is formed. Separately, the two semiconductors are electrically neutral. When joined, a few electrons near the junction diffuse from the *n*-type into the *p*-type semiconductor, where they fill a few of the holes. The *n*-type is left with a positive charge, and the *p*-type acquires a net negative charge. Thus a potential difference is established, with the *n* side positive relative to the *p* side, and this prevents further diffusion of electrons.

If a battery is connected to a diode with the positive terminal to the p side and the negative terminal to the n side as in Fig. 40–37a, the externally applied voltage opposes the internal potential difference and the diode is said to be **forward biased**. If the voltage is great enough (about 0.3 V for Ge, 0.6 V for Si at room temperature), a current will flow. The positive holes in the p-type semiconductor are repelled by the positive terminal of the battery, and the electrons in the n-type are repelled by the negative terminal of the battery. The holes and electrons meet at the junction, and the electrons cross over and fill the holes. A current is flowing. Meanwhile, the positive terminal of the battery is continually pulling electrons off the p end, forming new holes, and electrons are being supplied by the negative terminal at the n end. Consequently, a large current flows through the diode.

When the diode is **reverse biased**, as in Fig. 40–37b, the holes in the p end are attracted to the battery's negative terminal and the electrons in the n end are attracted to the positive terminal. The current carriers do not meet near the junction and, ideally, no current flows.

A graph of current versus voltage for a typical diode is shown in Fig. 40–38. As can be seen, a real diode does allow a small amount of reverse current to flow. For most practical purposes, it is negligible. (At room temperature, the reverse current is a few μA in Ge and a few pA in Si; but it increases rapidly with temperature, and may render a diode ineffective above 200°C.)

FIGURE 40–37 Schematic diagram showing how a semiconductor diode operates. Current flows when the voltage is connected in forward bias, as in (a), but not when connected in reverse bias, as in (b).

FIGURE 40–38 Current through a silicon pn diode as a function of applied voltage.

EXAMPLE 40–16 **A diode.** The diode whose current–voltage characteristics are shown in Fig. 40–38 is connected in series with a 4.0-V battery in forward bias and a resistor. If a current of 15 mA is to pass through the diode, what resistance must the resistor have?

APPROACH We use Fig. 40–38, where we see that the voltage drop across the diode is about 0.7 V when the current is 15 mA. Then we use simple circuit analysis and Ohm's law (Chapters 25 and 26).

SOLUTION The voltage drop across the resistor is $4.0\,\text{V} - 0.7\,\text{V} = 3.3\,\text{V}$, so $R = V/I = (3.3\,\text{V})/(1.5 \times 10^{-2}\,\text{A}) = 220\,\Omega$.

The symbol for a diode is

$$\longrightarrow\!\!\!\!\blacktriangleright\!\!|\!\longrightarrow$$

[diode]

where the arrow represents the direction conventional ($+$) current flows readily.

If the voltage across a diode connected in reverse bias is increased greatly, a point is reached where breakdown occurs. The electric field across the junction becomes so large that ionization of atoms results. The electrons thus pulled off their atoms contribute to a larger and larger current as breakdown continues. The voltage remains constant over a wide range of currents. This is shown on the far left in Fig. 40–38. This property of diodes can be used to accurately regulate a voltage supply. A diode designed for this purpose is called a **zener diode**. When placed across the output of an unregulated power supply, a zener diode can maintain the voltage at its own breakdown voltage as long as the supply voltage is always above this point. Zener diodes can be obtained corresponding to voltages of a few volts to hundreds of volts.

FIGURE 40–39 (a) A simple (half-wave) rectifier circuit using a semiconductor diode. (b) AC source input voltage, and output voltage across R, as functions of time.

FIGURE 40–40 (a) Full-wave rectifier circuit (including a transformer so the magnitude of the voltage can be changed). (b) Output voltage in the absence of capacitor C. (c) Output voltage with the capacitor in the circuit.

FIGURE 40–41 LED traffic light.

Since a _pn_ junction diode allows current to flow only in one direction (as long as the voltage is not too high), it can serve as a **rectifier**—to change ac into dc. A simple rectifier circuit is shown in Fig. 40–39a. The ac source applies a voltage across the diode alternately positive and negative. Only during half of each cycle will a current pass through the diode; only then is there a current through the resistor R. Hence, a graph of the voltage V_{ab} across R as a function of time looks like the output voltage shown in Fig. 40–39b. This **half-wave rectification** is not exactly dc, but it is unidirectional. More useful is a **full-wave rectifier** circuit, which uses two diodes (or sometimes four) as shown in Fig. 40–40a. At any given instant, either one diode or the other will conduct current to the right. Therefore, the output across the load resistor R will be as shown in Fig. 40–40b. Actually this is the voltage if the capacitor C were not in the circuit. The capacitor tends to store charge and, if the time constant RC is sufficiently long, helps to smooth out the current as shown in Fig. 40–40c. (The variation in output shown in Fig. 40–40c is called **ripple voltage**.)

Rectifier circuits are important because most line voltage in buildings is ac, and most electronic devices require a dc voltage for their operation. Hence, diodes are found in nearly all electronic devices including radio and TV sets, calculators, and computers.

(a)

(b) Without capacitor

(c) With capacitor

Another useful device is a **light-emitting diode** (LED), invented in the 1960s. When a _pn_ junction is forward biased, a current begins to flow. Electrons cross from the _n_ region into the _p_ region and combine with holes, and a photon can be emitted with an energy approximately equal to the band gap, E_g (see Figs. 40–32c and 40–36). Often the energy, and hence the wavelength, is in the red region of the visible spectrum, producing the familiar LED displays on electronic devices, car instrument panels, digital clocks, and so on. Infrared (i.e., nonvisible) LEDs are used in remote controls for TVs, DVDs, and stereos. New types of LEDs emit other colors, and LED "bulbs" are beginning to replace other types of lighting in applications such as flashlights, traffic signals, car brake lights, and outdoor signs, billboards, and theater displays. LED bulbs, sometimes called **solid-state** lighting, are costly, but they offer advantages: they are long-lived, efficient, and rugged. LED traffic lights, for example (Fig. 40–41), last 5 to 10 times longer than traditional incandescent bulbs, and use only 20% of the energy for the same light output. As car brake lights, they light up a fraction of a second sooner, allowing a driver an extra 5 or 6 meters (15–20 ft) more stopping distance at highway speeds.

Solar cells and **photodiodes** (Section 37–2) are _pn_ junctions used in the reverse way. Photons are absorbed, creating electron–hole pairs if the photon energy is greater than the band gap energy, E_g. The created electrons and holes produce a current that, when connected to an external circuit, becomes a source of emf and power. _Particle detectors_ (Section 41–11) operate similarly.

A diode is called a **nonlinear device** because the current is not proportional to the voltage. That is, a graph of current versus voltage (Fig. 40–38) is not a straight line, as it is for a resistor (which ideally _is_ linear). Transistors are also _nonlinear_ devices.

40–10 Transistors and Integrated Circuits (Chips)

A simple **junction transistor** consists of a crystal of one type of doped semiconductor sandwiched between two crystals of the opposite type. Both *npn* and *pnp* transistors are made, and they are shown schematically in Fig. 40–42a. The three semiconductors are given the names *collector*, *base*, and *emitter*. The symbols for *npn* and *pnp* transistors are shown in Fig. 40–42b. The arrow is always placed on the emitter and indicates the direction of (conventional) current flow in normal operation.

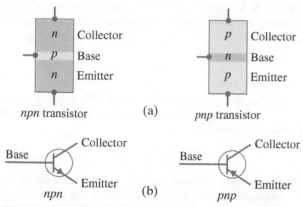

FIGURE 40–42 (a) Schematic diagram of *npn* and *pnp* transistors. (b) Symbols for *npn* and *pnp* transistors.

FIGURE 40–43 An *npn* transistor used as an amplifier. I_B is the current produced by $\mathcal{E}_B$ (in the absence of a signal), i_B is the ac signal current (= change in I_B).

The operation of a transistor can be analyzed qualitatively—very briefly—as follows. Consider an *npn* transistor connected as shown in Fig. 40–43. A voltage V_{CE} is maintained between the collector and emitter by the battery $\mathcal{E}_C$. The voltage applied to the base is called the *base bias voltage*, V_{BE}. If V_{BE} is positive, conduction electrons in the emitter are attracted into the base. Since the base region is very thin (less than 1 μm—much less if on a chip), most of these electrons flow right across into the collector, which is maintained at a positive voltage. A large current, I_C, flows between collector and emitter and a much smaller current, I_B, through the base. In the steady state, I_B and I_C can be considered dc. A small variation in the base voltage due to an input signal causes a large change in the collector current and therefore a large change in the voltage drop across the output resistor R_C. Hence a transistor can *amplify* a small signal into a larger one.

Typically a small ac signal (call it i_B) is to be amplified, and when added to the base bias voltage and current causes the voltage and current at the collector to vary at the same rate but magnified. Thus, what is important for amplification is the *change* in collector current for a given input *change* in base current. We label these ac signal currents (= changes in I_C and I_B) as i_C and i_B. The **current gain** is defined as the ratio

$$\beta_I = \frac{\text{output (collector) ac current}}{\text{input (base) ac current}} = \frac{i_C}{i_B}.$$

β_I is typically on the order of 10 to 100. Similarly, the **voltage gain** is

$$\beta_V = \frac{\text{output (collector) ac voltage}}{\text{input (base) ac voltage}}.$$

Transistors are the basic elements in modern electronic **amplifiers** of all sorts.

A *pnp* transistor operates like an *npn*, except that holes move instead of electrons. The collector voltage is negative, and so is the base voltage in normal operation.

In **digital circuits**, including computers, where "off" and "on" (or zero and one) make up the binary code, transistors act like a **gate** or switch. That is, they let current pass ("on") or they block it ("off").

Transistors were a great advance in miniaturization of electronic circuits. Although individual transistors are very small compared to the once-used vacuum tubes, they are huge compared to **integrated circuits** or **chips** (see photo at start of this Chapter). Tiny amounts of impurities can be placed at particular locations within a single silicon crystal. These can be arranged to form diodes, transistors, and resistors (undoped semiconductors). Capacitors and inductors can also be formed, although they are often connected separately. A tiny chip, a few millimeters on a side, may contain millions of transistors and other circuit elements. Integrated circuits are the heart of computers, televisions, calculators, cameras, and the electronic instruments that control aircraft, space vehicles, and automobiles. The "miniaturization" produced by integrated circuits not only allows extremely complicated circuits to be placed in a small space, but also has allowed a great increase in the speed of operation of, say, computers, because the distances the electronic signals travel are so tiny.

Summary

Quantum mechanics explains the bonding together of atoms to form **molecules**. In a **covalent bond**, the electron clouds of two or more atoms overlap because of constructive interference between the electron waves. The positive nuclei are attracted to this concentration of negative charge between them, forming the bond.

An **ionic bond** is an extreme case of a covalent bond in which one or more electrons from one atom spend much more time around the other atom than around their own. The atoms then act as oppositely charged ions that attract each other, forming the bond.

These **strong bonds** hold molecules together, and also hold atoms and molecules together in solids. Also important are **weak bonds** (or **van der Waals bonds**), which are generally dipole attractions between molecules.

When atoms combine to form molecules, the energy levels of the outer electrons are altered because they now interact with each other. Additional energy levels also become possible because the atoms can vibrate with respect to each other, and the molecule as a whole can rotate. The energy levels for both vibrational and rotational motion are quantized, and are very close together (typically, 10^{-1} eV to 10^{-3} eV apart). Each atomic energy level thus becomes a set of closely spaced levels corresponding to the vibrational and rotational motions. Transitions from one level to another appear as many very closely spaced lines. The resulting spectra are called **band spectra**.

The quantized rotational energy levels are given by

$$E_{rot} = \ell(\ell + 1)\frac{\hbar^2}{2I}, \qquad \ell = 0, 1, 2, \cdots, \quad \textbf{(40–2)}$$

where I is the moment of inertia of the molecule.

The energy levels for vibrational motion are given by

$$E_{vib} = \left(\nu + \tfrac{1}{2}\right)hf, \qquad \nu = 0, 1, 2, \cdots, \quad \textbf{(40–6)}$$

where f is the classical natural frequency of vibration for the molecule. Transitions between energy levels are subject to the selection rules $\Delta\ell = \pm 1$ and $\Delta\nu = \pm 1$.

Some **solids** are bound together by covalent and ionic bonds, just as molecules are. In metals, the electrostatic force between free electrons and positive ions helps form the **metallic bond**.

In the free-electron theory of metals, electrons occupy the possible energy states according to the exclusion principle. At $T = 0$ K, all possible states are filled up to a maximum energy level called the **Fermi energy**, E_F, the magnitude of which is typically a few eV. All states above E_F are vacant at $T = 0$ K.

At normal temperatures (300 K) the distribution of occupied states is only slightly altered and is given by the **Fermi–Dirac probability function**

$$f(E) = \frac{1}{e^{(E - E_F)/kT} + 1}. \quad \textbf{(40–14)}$$

In a crystalline solid, the possible energy states for electrons are arranged in **bands**. Within each band the levels are very close together, but between the bands there may be forbidden **energy gaps**. Good conductors are characterized by the highest occupied band (the **conduction band**) being only partially full, so there are many accessible states available to electrons to move about and accelerate when a voltage is applied. In a good insulator, the highest occupied energy band (the **valence band**) is completely full, and there is a large energy gap (5 to 10 eV) to the next highest band, the *conduction band*. At room temperature, molecular kinetic energy (thermal energy) available due to collisions is only about 0.04 eV, so almost no electrons can jump from the valence to the conduction band. In a **semiconductor**, the gap between valence and conduction bands is much smaller, on the order of 1 eV, so a few electrons can make the transition from the essentially full valence band to the nearly empty conduction band.

In a **doped** semiconductor, a small percentage of impurity atoms with five or three valence electrons replace a few of the normal silicon atoms with their four valence electrons. A five-electron impurity produces an **n-type** semiconductor with negative electrons as carriers of current. A three-electron impurity produces a **p-type** semiconductor in which positive **holes** carry the current. The energy level of impurity atoms lies slightly below the conduction band in an *n*-type semiconductor, and acts as a **donor** from which electrons readily pass into the conduction band. The energy level of impurity atoms in a *p*-type semiconductor lies slightly above the valence band and acts as an **acceptor** level, since electrons from the valence band easily reach it, leaving holes behind to act as charge carriers.

A semiconductor **diode** consists of a *pn* **junction** and allows current to flow in one direction only; it can be used as a **rectifier** to change ac to dc. Common **transistors** consist of three semiconductor sections, either as *pnp* or *npn*. Transistors can amplify electrical signals and in computers serve as switches or **gates** for the 1s and 0s. An integrated circuit consists of a tiny semiconductor crystal or **chip** on which many transistors, diodes, resistors, and other circuit elements have been constructed using careful placement of impurities.

Questions

1. What type of bond would you expect for (a) the N_2 molecule, (b) the HCl molecule, (c) Fe atoms in a solid?

2. Describe how the molecule $CaCl_2$ could be formed.

3. Does the H_2 molecule have a permanent dipole moment? Does O_2? Does H_2O? Explain.

4. Although the molecule H_3 is not stable, the ion H_3^+ is. Explain, using the Pauli exclusion principle.

5. The energy of a molecule can be divided into four categories. What are they?

6. Would you expect the molecule H_2^+ to be stable? If so, where would the single electron spend most of its time?

7. Explain why the carbon atom $(Z = 6)$ usually forms four bonds with hydrogen-like atoms.

8. Explain on the basis of energy bands why the sodium chloride crystal is a good insulator. [*Hint*: Consider the shells of Na^+ and Cl^- ions.]

9. If conduction electrons are free to roam about in a metal, why don't they leave the metal entirely?

10. Explain why the resistivity of metals increases with increasing temperature whereas the resistivity of semiconductors may decrease with increasing temperature.

11. Figure 40–44 shows a "bridge-type" full-wave rectifier. Explain how the current is rectified and how current flows during each half cycle.

FIGURE 40–44
Question 11.

12. Discuss the differences between an ideal gas and a Fermi electron gas.

13. Compare the resistance of a *pn* junction diode connected in forward bias to its resistance when connected in reverse bias.

14. Which aspects of Fig. 40–28 are peculiar to copper, and which are valid in general for other metals?

15. Explain how a transistor can be used as a switch.

16. What is the main difference between *n*-type and *p*-type semiconductors?

17. Draw a circuit diagram showing how a *pnp* transistor can operate as an amplifier.

18. In a transistor, the base–emitter junction and the base–collector junction are essentially diodes. Are these junctions reverse-biased or forward-biased in the application shown in Fig. 40–43?

19. A transistor can amplify an electronic signal, meaning it can increase the power of an input signal. Where does it get the energy to increase the power?

20. A silicon semiconductor is doped with phosphorus. Will these atoms be donors or acceptors? What type of semiconductor will this be?

21. Do diodes and transistors obey Ohm's law? Explain.

22. Can a diode be used to amplify a signal? Explain.

23. If $\mathscr{E}_C$ were reversed in Fig. 40–43, how would the amplification be altered?

Problems

40–1 to 40–3 Molecular Bonds

1. (I) Estimate the binding energy of a KCl molecule by calculating the electrostatic potential energy when the K^+ and Cl^- ions are at their stable separation of 0.28 nm. Assume each has a charge of magnitude $1.0e$.

2. (II) The measured binding energy of KCl is 4.43 eV. From the result of Problem 1, estimate the contribution to the binding energy of the repelling electron clouds at the equilibrium distance $r_0 = 0.28$ nm.

3. (II) Estimate the binding energy of the H_2 molecule, assuming the two H nuclei are 0.074 nm apart and the two electrons spend 33% of their time midway between them.

4. (II) The equilibrium distance r_0 between two atoms in a molecule is called the **bond length**. Using the bond lengths of homogeneous molecules (like H_2, O_2, and N_2), one can estimate the bond length of heterogeneous molecules (like CO, CN, and NO). This is done by summing half of each bond length of the homogenous molecules to estimate that of the heterogeneous molecule. Given the following bond lengths: H_2 (= 74 pm), N_2 (= 145 pm), O_2 (= 121 pm), C_2 (= 154 pm), estimate the bond lengths for: HN, CN, and NO.

5. (II) Estimate the energy associated with the repulsion of the electron shells of a lithium fluoride (LiF) molecule. The ionization energy of lithium is 5.39 eV, and it takes 3.41 eV to remove the extra electron from an F^- ion. The bond length is 0.156 nm, and the binding energy of LiF is 5.95 eV.

6. (II) Binding energies are often measured experimentally in kcal per mole, and then the binding energy in eV per molecule is calculated from that result. What is the conversion factor in going from kcal per mole to eV per molecule? What is the binding energy of KCl (= 4.43 eV) in kcal per mole?

7. (III) (a) Apply reasoning similar to that in the text for the $S = 0$ and $S = 1$ states in the formation of the H_2 molecule to show why the molecule He_2 is *not* formed. (b) Explain why the He_2^+ molecular ion *could* form. (Experiment shows it has a binding energy of 3.1 eV at $r_0 = 0.11$ nm.)

40–4 Molecular Spectra

8. (I) Show that the quantity $\hbar^2/I$ has units of energy.

9. (I) What is the reduced mass of the molecules (a) KCl; (b) O_2; (c) HCl?

10. (II) (a) Calculate the "characteristic rotational energy," $\hbar^2/2I$, for the O_2 molecule whose bond length is 0.121 nm. (b) What are the energy and wavelength of photons emitted in an $\ell = 2$ to $\ell = 1$ transition?

11. (II) The "characteristic rotational energy," $\hbar^2/2I$, for N_2 is 2.48×10^{-4} eV. Calculate the N_2 bond length.

12. (II) Estimate the longest wavelength emitted by a lithium hydride (LiH) molecule for a change in its rotational state if its equilibrium separation is 0.16 nm.

13. (II) The equilibrium separation of H atoms in the H_2 molecule is 0.074 nm (Fig. 40–8). Calculate the energies and wavelengths of photons for the rotational transitions (a) $\ell = 1$ to $\ell = 0$, (b) $\ell = 2$ to $\ell = 1$, and (c) $\ell = 3$ to $\ell = 2$.

14. (II) Explain why there is no transition for $\Delta E = hf$ in Fig. 40–21 (and Fig. 40–22). See Eqs. 40–8.

15. (II) The fundamental vibration frequency for the CO molecule is 6.42×10^{13} Hz. Determine (a) the reduced mass, and (b) the effective value of the "stiffness" constant k. Compare to k for the H_2 molecule.

16. (II) Li and Br form a molecule for which the lowest vibrational frequency is 1.7×10^{13} Hz. What is the effective stiffness constant k?

17. (II) Calculate the bond length for the NaCl molecule given that three successive wavelengths for rotational transitions are 23.1 mm, 11.6 mm, and 7.71 mm.

18. (II) (a) Use the curve of Fig. 40–18 to estimate the stiffness constant k for the H_2 molecule. (Recall that $U = \frac{1}{2}kx^2$.) (b) Then estimate the fundamental wavelength for vibrational transitions using the classical formula (Chapter 14), but use only $\frac{1}{2}$ the mass of an H atom (because both H atoms move).

19. (III) Imagine the two atoms of a diatomic molecule as if they were connected by a spring, Fig. 40–45. Show that the classical frequency of vibration is given by Eq. 40–5. [Hint: Let x_1 and x_2 be the displacements of each mass from initial equilibrium positions; then $m_1 \, d^2x_1/dt^2 = -kx$, and $m_2 \, d^2x_2/dt^2 = -kx$, where $x = x_1 + x_2$. Find another relationship between x_1 and x_2, assuming that the center of mass of the system stays at rest, and then show that $\mu \, d^2x/dt^2 = -kx$.]

FIGURE 40–45
Problem 19.

40–5 Bonding in Solids

20. (I) Estimate the ionic cohesive energy for NaCl taking $\alpha = 1.75$, $m = 8$, and $r_0 = 0.28$ nm.

21. (II) Common salt, NaCl, has a density of 2.165 g/cm^3. The molecular weight of NaCl is 58.44. Estimate the distance between nearest neighbor Na and Cl ions. [Hint: Each ion can be considered to have one "cube" or "cell" of side s (our unknown) extending out from it.]

22. (II) Repeat the previous Problem for KCl whose density is 1.99 g/cm^3.

23. (II) The spacing between "nearest neighbor" Na and Cl ions in a NaCl crystal is 0.24 nm. What is the spacing between two nearest neighbor Na ions?

24. (III) For a long one-dimensional chain of alternating positive and negative ions, show that the Madelung constant would be $\alpha = 2 \ln 2$. [Hint: Use a series expansion for $\ln(1 + x)$.]

25. (III) (a) Starting from Eq. 40–9, show that the ionic cohesive energy is given by $U_0 = -(\alpha e^2/4\pi\epsilon_0 r_0)(1 - 1/m)$. Determine U_0 for (b) NaI ($r_0 = 0.33$ nm) and (c) MgO ($r_0 = 0.21$ nm). Assume $m = 10$. (d) If you used $m = 8$ instead, how far off would your answers be? Assume $\alpha = 1.75$.

40–6 Free-Electron Theory of Metals

26. (II) Estimate the number of possible electron states in a 1.00-cm^3 cube of silver between $0.985E_F$ and E_F $(= 5.48$ eV$)$.

27. (II) Estimate the number of states between 7.00 eV and 7.05 eV that are available to electrons in a 1.0-cm^3 cube of copper.

28. (II) What, roughly, is the ratio of the density of molecules in an ideal gas at 285 K and 1 atm (say O_2) to the density of free electrons (assume one per atom) in a metal (copper) also at 285 K?

29. (II) Calculate the energy which has 85.0% occupancy probability for copper at (a) $T = 295$ K; (b) $T = 750$ K.

30. (II) Calculate the energy which has 15.0% occupancy probability for copper at (a) $T = 295$ K; (b) $T = 950$ K.

31. (II) What is the occupancy probability for a conduction electron in copper at $T = 295$ K for an energy $E = 1.015E_F$?

32. (II) The atoms in zinc metal $(\rho = 7.1 \times 10^3$ kg/m$^3)$ each have two free electrons. Calculate (a) the density of conduction electrons, (b) their Fermi energy, and (c) their Fermi speed.

33. (II) Calculate the Fermi energy and Fermi speed for sodium, which has a density of 0.97×10^3 kg/m^3 and has one conduction electron per atom.

34. (II) Given that the Fermi energy of aluminum is 11.63 eV, (a) calculate the density of free electrons using Eq. 40–12, and (b) estimate the valence of aluminum using this model and the known density $(2.70 \times 10^3$ kg/m$^3)$ and atomic mass (27.0) of aluminum.

35. (II) Show that the average energy of conduction electrons in a metal at $T = 0$ K is $\overline{E} = \frac{3}{5}E_F$ (Eq. 40–13) by calculating

$$\overline{E} = \frac{\int E \, n_o(E) \, dE}{\int n_o(E) \, dE}.$$

36. (II) The neutrons in a neutron star (Chapter 44) can be treated as a Fermi gas with neutrons in place of the electrons in our model of an electron gas. Determine the Fermi energy for a neutron star of radius 12 km and mass 2.5 times that of our Sun. Assume that the star is made entirely of neutrons and is of uniform density.

37. (II) For a one-dimensional potential well of width ℓ, start with Eq. 38–13 and show that the number of states per unit energy interval for an electron gas is given by

$$g_\ell(E) = \sqrt{\frac{8m\ell^2}{h^2E}}.$$

Remember that there can be two electrons (spin up and spin down) for each value of n. [Hint: Write the quantum number n in terms of E. Then $g_\ell(E) = 2 \, dn/dE$ where dn is the number of energy levels between E and $E + dE$.]

38. (II) Show that the probability for the state at the Fermi energy being occupied is exactly $\frac{1}{2}$, independent of temperature.

39. (II) A very simple model of a "one-dimensional" metal consists of N electrons confined to a rigid box of width ℓ. We neglect the Coulomb interaction between the electrons. (a) Calculate the Fermi energy for this one-dimensional metal (E_F = the energy of the most energetic electron at $T = 0\,\text{K}$), taking into account the Pauli exclusion principle. You can assume for simplicity that N is even. (b) What is the smallest amount of energy, ΔE, that this 1-D metal can absorb? (c) Find the limit of $\Delta E / E_F$ for large N. What does this result say about how well metals can conduct?

40. (II) (a) For copper at room temperature ($T = 293\,\text{K}$), calculate the Fermi factor, Eq. 40–14, for an electron with energy 0.12 eV above the Fermi energy. This represents the probability that this state is occupied. Is this reasonable? (b) What is the probability that a state 0.12 eV below the Fermi energy is occupied? (c) What is the probability that the state in part (b) is unoccupied?

41. (III) Proceed as follows to derive the density of states, $g(E)$, the number of states per unit volume per unit energy interval, Eq. 40–10. Let the metal be a cube of side ℓ. Extend the discussion of Section 38–8 for an infinite well to three dimensions, giving energy levels

$$ E = \frac{h^2}{8m\ell^2}\left(n_1^2 + n_2^2 + n_3^2\right). $$

(Explain the meaning of n_1, n_2, n_3.) Each set of values for the quantum numbers n_1, n_2, n_3 corresponds to one state. Imagine a space where n_1, n_2, n_3 are the axes, and each state is represented by a point on a cubic lattice in this space, each separated by 1 unit along an axis. Consider the octant $n_1 > 0$, $n_2 > 0$, $n_3 > 0$. Show that the number of states N within a radius $R = \left(n_1^2 + n_2^2 + n_3^2\right)^{\frac{1}{2}}$ is $2\left(\frac{1}{8}\right)\left(\frac{4}{3}\pi R^3\right)$. Then, to get Eq. 40–10, set $g(E) = (1/V)(dN/dE)$, where $V = \ell^3$ is the volume of the metal.

40–7 Band Theory of Solids

42. (I) A semiconductor is struck by light of slowly increasing frequency and begins to conduct when the wavelength of the light is 580 nm; estimate the size of the energy gap E_g.

43. (I) Calculate the longest-wavelength photon that can cause an electron in silicon ($E_g = 1.14\,\text{eV}$) to jump from the valence band to the conduction band.

44. (II) The energy gap between valence and conduction bands in germanium is 0.72 eV. What range of wavelengths can a photon have to excite an electron from the top of the valence band into the conduction band?

45. (II) We saw that there are $2N$ possible electron states in the $3s$ band of Na, where N is the total number of atoms. How many possible electron states are there in the (a) $2s$ band, (b) $2p$ band, and (c) $3p$ band? (d) State a general formula for the total number of possible states in any given electron band.

46. (II) The energy gap E_g in germanium is 0.72 eV. When used as a photon detector, roughly how many electrons can be made to jump from the valence to the conduction band by the passage of a 730-keV photon that loses all its energy in this fashion?

40–8 Semiconductors and Doping

47. (II) Suppose that a silicon semiconductor is doped with phosphorus so that one silicon atom in 1.2×10^6 is replaced by a phosphorus atom. Assuming that the "extra" electron in every phosphorus atom is donated to the conduction band, by what factor is the density of conduction electrons increased? The density of silicon is $2330\,\text{kg/m}^3$, and the density of conduction electrons in pure silicon is about $10^{16}\,\text{m}^{-3}$ at room temperature.

40–9 Diodes

48. (I) At what wavelength will an LED radiate if made from a material with an energy gap $E_g = 1.6\,\text{eV}$?

49. (I) If an LED emits light of wavelength $\lambda = 680\,\text{nm}$, what is the energy gap (in eV) between valence and conduction bands?

50. (II) A silicon diode, whose current–voltage characteristics are given in Fig. 40–38, is connected in series with a battery and an 860-Ω resistor. What battery voltage is needed to produce a 12-mA current?

51. (II) Suppose that the diode of Fig. 40–38 is connected in series to a 150-Ω resistor and a 2.0-V battery. What current flows in the circuit? [Hint: Draw a line on Fig. 40–38 representing the current in the resistor as a function of the voltage across the diode; the intersection of this line with the characteristic curve will give the answer.]

52. (II) Sketch the resistance as a function of current, for $V > 0$, for the diode shown in Fig. 40–38.

53. (II) An ac voltage of 120 V rms is to be rectified. Estimate very roughly the average current in the output resistor R (35 kΩ) for (a) a half-wave rectifier (Fig. 40–39), and (b) a full-wave rectifier (Fig. 40–40) without capacitor.

54. (II) A semiconductor diode laser emits 1.3-μm light. Assuming that the light comes from electrons and holes recombining, what is the band gap in this laser material?

55. (II) A silicon diode passes significant current only if the forward-bias voltage exceeds about 0.6 V. Make a rough estimate of the average current in the output resistor R of (a) a half-wave rectifier (Fig. 40–39), and (b) a full-wave rectifier (Fig. 40–40) without a capacitor. Assume that $R = 120\,\Omega$ in each case and that the ac voltage is 9.0 V rms in each case.

56. (III) A 120-V rms 60-Hz voltage is to be rectified with a full-wave rectifier as in Fig. 40–40, where $R = 28\,\text{k}\Omega$, and $C = 35\,\mu\text{F}$. (a) Make a rough estimate of the average current. (b) What happens if $C = 0.10\,\mu\text{F}$? [Hint: See Section 26–5.]

40–10 Transistors

57. (II) If the current gain of the transistor amplifier in Fig. 40–43 is $\beta = i_C/i_B = 95$, what value must R_C have if a 1.0-μA ac base current is to produce an ac output voltage of 0.35 V?

58. (II) Suppose that the current gain of the transistor in Fig. 40–43 is $\beta = i_C/i_B = 85$. If $R_C = 4.3\,\text{k}\Omega$, calculate the ac output voltage for an ac input current of 2.0 μA.

59. (II) An amplifier has a voltage gain of 65 and a 25-kΩ load (output) resistance. What is the peak output current through the load resistor if the input voltage is an ac signal with a peak of 0.080 V?

60. (II) A transistor, whose current gain $\beta = i_C/i_B = 75$, is connected as in Fig. 40–43 with $R_B = 3.8\,k\Omega$ and $R_C = 7.8\,k\Omega$. Calculate (a) the voltage gain, and (b) the power amplification.

61. (II) From Fig. 40–43, write an equation for the relationship between the base current (I_B), the collector current (I_C), and the emitter current $(I_E,$ not labeled in Fig. 40–43). Assume $i_B = i_C = 0$.

General Problems

62. Use the uncertainty principle to estimate the binding energy of the H_2 molecule by calculating the difference in kinetic energy of the electrons between when they are in separate atoms and when they are in the molecule. Take Δx for the electrons in the separated atoms to be the radius of the first Bohr orbit, 0.053 nm, and for the molecule take Δx to be the separation of the nuclei, 0.074 nm. [*Hint:* Let $\Delta p \approx \Delta p_x$.]

63. The average translational kinetic energy of an atom or molecule is about $\overline{K} = \frac{3}{2}kT$ (see Chapter 18), where $k = 1.38 \times 10^{-23}\,J/K$ is Boltzmann's constant. At what temperature T will $\overline{K}$ be on the order of the bond energy (and hence the bond easily broken by thermal motion) for (a) a covalent bond (say H_2) of binding energy 4.0 eV, and (b) a "weak" hydrogen bond of binding energy 0.12 eV?

64. In the ionic salt KF, the separation distance between ions is about 0.27 nm. (a) Estimate the electrostatic potential energy between the ions assuming them to be point charges (magnitude $1e$). (b) When F "grabs" an electron, it releases 3.41 eV of energy, whereas 4.34 eV is required to ionize K. Find the binding energy of KF relative to free K and F atoms, neglecting the energy of repulsion.

65. A diatomic molecule is found to have an activation energy of 1.4 eV. When the molecule is disassociated, 1.6 eV of energy is released. Draw a potential energy curve for this molecule.

66. One possible form for the potential energy (U) of a diatomic molecule (Fig. 40–8) is called the *Morse Potential*:

$$U = U_0\left[1 - e^{-a(r-r_0)}\right]^2.$$

(a) Show that r_0 represents the equilibrium distance and U_0 the dissociation energy. (b) Graph U from $r = 0$ to $r = 4r_0$, assuming $a = 18\,nm^{-1}$, $U_0 = 4.6$ eV, and $r_0 = 0.13$ nm.

67. The fundamental vibration frequency for the HCl molecule is 8.66×10^{13} Hz. Determine (a) the reduced mass, and (b) the effective value of the stiffness constant k. Compare to k for the H_2 molecule.

68. For H_2, estimate how many rotational states there are between vibrational states.

69. Explain, using the Boltzmann factor (Eq. 39–16), why the heights of the peaks in Fig. 40–22 are different from one another. Explain also why the lines are not equally spaced. [*Hint:* Does the moment of inertia necessarily remain constant?]

70. The rotational absorption spectrum of a molecule displays peaks about 8.4×10^{11} Hz apart. Determine the moment of inertia of this molecule.

71. A TV remote control emits IR light. If the detector on the TV set is *not* to react to visible light, could it make use of silicon as a "window" with its energy gap $E_g = 1.14$ eV? What is the shortest-wavelength light that can strike silicon without causing electrons to jump from the valence band to the conduction band?

72. Do we need to consider quantum effects for everyday rotating objects? Estimate the differences between rotational energy levels for a spinning baton compared to the energy of the baton. Assume the baton consists of a uniform 32-cm-long bar with a mass of 260 g and two small end masses, each of mass 380 g, and that it rotates at 1.6 rev/s about the bar's center.

73. Consider a monatomic solid with a weakly bound cubic lattice, with each atom connected to six neighbors, each bond having a binding energy of 3.9×10^{-3} eV. When this solid melts, its latent heat of fusion goes directly into breaking the bonds between the atoms. Estimate the latent heat of fusion for this solid, in J/mol. [*Hint:* Show that in a simple cubic lattice (Fig. 40–46), there are *three* times as many bonds as there are atoms, when the number of atoms is large.]

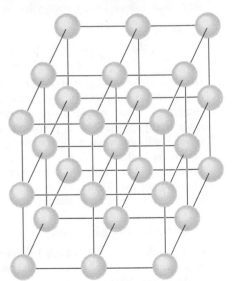

FIGURE 40–46
Problem 73.

74. The energy gap between valence and conduction bands in zinc sulfide is 3.6 eV. What range of wavelengths can a photon have to excite an electron from the top of the valence band into the conduction band?

75. When EM radiation is incident on diamond, it is found that light with wavelengths shorter than 226 nm will cause the diamond to conduct. What is the energy gap between the valence band and the conduction band for diamond?

76. The **Fermi temperature** T_F is defined as that temperature at which the thermal energy kT (without the $\frac{3}{2}$) is equal to the Fermi energy: $kT_F = E_F$. (a) Determine the Fermi temperature for copper. (b) Show that for $T \gg T_F$, the Fermi factor (Eq. 40–14) approaches the Boltzmann factor. (Note: This last result is not very useful for understanding conductors. Why?)

77. Estimate the number of states from 4.0 eV to 6.2 eV available to electrons in a 10-cm cube of iron.

78. The band gap of silicon is 1.14 eV. (a) For what range of wavelengths will silicon be transparent? (See Example 40–14.) In what region of the electromagnetic spectrum does this transparent range begin? (b) If window glass is transparent for all visible wavelengths, what is the minimum possible band gap value for glass (assume $\lambda = 450$ nm to 750 nm)? [Hint: If the photon has less energy than the band gap, the photon will pass through the solid without being absorbed.]

79. For a certain semiconductor, the longest wavelength radiation that can be absorbed is 1.92 mm. What is the energy gap in this semiconductor?

80. Assume conduction electrons in a semiconductor behave as an ideal gas. (This is not true for conduction electrons in a metal.) (a) Taking mass $m = 9 \times 10^{-31}$ kg and temperature $T = 300$ K, determine the de Broglie wavelength of a semiconductor's conduction electrons. (b) Given that the spacing between atoms in a semiconductor's atomic lattice is on the order of 0.3 nm, would you expect room-temperature conduction electrons to travel in straight lines or diffract when traveling through this lattice? Explain.

81. Most of the Sun's radiation has wavelengths shorter than 1100 nm. For a solar cell to absorb all this, what energy gap ought the material have?

82. Green and blue LEDs became available many years after red LEDs were first developed. Approximately what energy gaps would you expect to find in green (525 nm) and in blue (465 nm) LEDs?

83. For an arsenic donor atom in a doped silicon semiconductor, assume that the "extra" electron moves in a Bohr orbit about the arsenic ion. For this electron in the ground state, take into account the dielectric constant $K = 12$ of the Si lattice (which represents the weakening of the Coulomb force due to all the other atoms or ions in the lattice), and estimate (a) the binding energy, and (b) the orbit radius for this extra electron. [Hint: Substitute $\epsilon = K\epsilon_0$ in Coulomb's law; see Section 24–5.]

84. A strip of silicon 1.8 cm wide and 1.0 mm thick is immersed in a magnetic field of strength 1.3 T perpendicular to the strip (Fig. 40–47). When a current of 0.28 mA is run through the strip, there is a resulting Hall effect voltage of 18 mV across the strip (Section 27–8). How many electrons per silicon atom are in the conduction band? The density of silicon is 2330 kg/m³.

FIGURE 40–47   Problem 84.

85. A zener diode voltage regulator is shown in Fig. 40–48. Suppose that $R = 2.80$ kΩ and that the diode breaks down at a reverse voltage of 130 V. (The current increases rapidly at this point, as shown on the far left of Fig. 40–38 at a voltage of -12 V on that diagram.) The diode is rated at a maximum current of 120 mA. (a) If $R_{load} = 18.0$ kΩ, over what range of supply voltages will the circuit maintain the output voltage at 130 V? (b) If the supply voltage is 245 V, over what range of load resistance will the voltage be regulated?

FIGURE 40–48
Problem 85.

86. A full-wave rectifier (Fig. 40–40) uses two diodes to rectify a 95-V rms 60 Hz ac voltage. If $R = 7.8$ kΩ and $C = 36$ μF, what will be the approximate percent variation in the output voltage? The variation in output voltage (Fig. 40–40c) is called ripple voltage. [Hint: See Section 26–5 and assume the discharge of the capacitor is approximately linear.]

Numerical/Computer

*87. (II) Write a program that will determine the Fermi–Dirac probability function (Eq. 40–14). Make separate plots of this function versus E/E_F for copper at (a) $T = 500$ K; (b) $T = 1000$ K; (c) $T = 5000$ K; and (d) $T = 10,000$ K. For copper, $E_F = 7.0$ eV. Interpret each plot accordingly.

*88. (III) A simple picture of an H_2 molecule sharing two electrons is shown in Fig. 40–49. We assume the electrons are symmetrically located between the two protons, which are separated by $r_0 = 0.074$ nm. (a) When the electrons are separated by a distance d, write the total potential energy U in terms of d and r_0. (b) Make a graph of U in eV as a function of d in nm, and state where U has a minimum on your graph, and for what range of d values U is negative. (c) Determine analytically the value of d that gives minimum U (greatest stability).

FIGURE 40–49   Problem 88.

*89. (III) Estimate the current produced per cm² of area in a flat silicon semiconductor placed perpendicular to sunlight. Assume the sunlight has an intensity of 1000 W/m² and that only photons that have more energy than the band gap can create an electron–hole pair in the semiconductor. Assume the Sun is a blackbody emitter at 6000 K, and find the fraction of photons that have energy above the band gap (1.14 eV). See Section 37–1 and integrate the Planck formula numerically.

Answers to Exercises

A: $0, 5.00 \times 10^{-4}$ eV, 1.50×10^{-3} eV.

B: (e).

C: (a).

D: (c).

This archeologist has unearthed the remains of a sea-turtle within an ancient man-made stone circle. Carbon dating of the remains can tell her when humans inhabited the site.

In this Chapter we begin our discussion of nuclear physics. We study the properties of nuclei, the various forms of radioactivity, and how radioactive decay can be used in a variety of fields to determine the age of old objects, from bones and trees to rocks and other mineral substances, and obtain information on the history of the Earth.

C H A P T E R

41

Nuclear Physics and Radioactivity

CHAPTER-OPENING QUESTION—Guess now!

If half of an 80-μg sample of $^{60}_{27}$Co decays in 5.3 years, how much $^{60}_{27}$Co is left in 15.9 years?

(a) 10 μg.

(b) 20 μg.

(c) 30 μg.

(d) 40 μg.

(e) 0 μg.

In the early part of the twentieth century, Rutherford's experiments led to the idea that at the center of an atom there is a tiny but massive nucleus. At the same time that quantum theory was being developed and scientists were attempting to understand the structure of the atom and its electrons, investigations into the nucleus itself had also begun. In this Chapter and the next, we take a brief look at *nuclear physics*.

41–1 Structure and Properties of the Nucleus

An important question for physicists was whether the nucleus had a structure, and what that structure might be. We now understand the nucleus to be a complicated entity that is not fully understood even today. By the early 1930s, a model of the nucleus had been developed that is still useful. According to this model, a nucleus is considered to be an aggregate of two types of particles: protons and neutrons. (These "particles" also have wave properties, but for ease of visualization and language, we often refer to them simply as "particles.") A **proton** is the nucleus of the simplest atom, hydrogen. It has a positive charge ($= +e = +1.60 \times 10^{-19}$ C, the same magnitude as for the electron) and a mass

$$m_p = 1.67262 \times 10^{-27} \text{ kg}.$$

The **neutron**, whose existence was ascertained in 1932 by the English physicist James Chadwick (1891–1974), is electrically neutral ($q = 0$), as its name implies. Its mass is very slightly larger than that of the proton:

$$m_n = 1.67493 \times 10^{-27} \text{ kg}.$$

These two constituents of a nucleus, neutrons and protons, are referred to collectively as **nucleons**.

Although the hydrogen nucleus consists of a single proton alone, the nuclei of all other elements consist of both neutrons and protons. The different nuclei are often referred to as **nuclides**. The number of protons in a nucleus (or nuclide) is called the **atomic number** and is designated by the symbol Z. The total number of nucleons, neutrons plus protons, is designated by the symbol A and is called the **atomic mass number**, or sometimes simply **mass number**. This name is used since the mass of a nucleus is very closely A times the mass of one nucleon. A nuclide with 7 protons and 8 neutrons thus has $Z = 7$ and $A = 15$. The **neutron number** N is $N = A - Z$.

To specify a given nuclide, we need give only A and Z. A special symbol is commonly used which takes the form

$$^A_Z X,$$

where X is the chemical symbol for the element (see Appendix F, and the Periodic Table inside the back cover), A is the atomic mass number, and Z is the atomic number. For example, $^{15}_7 N$ means a nitrogen nucleus containing 7 protons and 8 neutrons for a total of 15 nucleons. In a neutral atom, the number of electrons orbiting the nucleus is equal to the atomic number Z (since the charge on an electron has the same magnitude but opposite sign to that of a proton). The main properties of an atom, and how it interacts with other atoms, are largely determined by the number of electrons in the neutral atom. Hence Z determines what kind of atom it is: carbon, oxygen, gold, or whatever. It is redundant to specify both the symbol of a nucleus and its atomic number Z as described above. If the nucleus is nitrogen, for example, we know immediately that $Z = 7$. The subscript Z is thus sometimes dropped and $^{15}_7 N$ is then written simply ^{15}N; in words we say "nitrogen fifteen."

For a particular type of atom (say, carbon), nuclei are found to contain different numbers of neutrons, although they all have the same number of protons. For example, carbon nuclei always have 6 protons, but they may have 5, 6, 7, 8, 9, or 10 neutrons. Nuclei that contain the same number of protons but different numbers of neutrons are called **isotopes**. Thus, $^{11}_6 C$, $^{12}_6 C$, $^{13}_6 C$, $^{14}_6 C$, $^{15}_6 C$, and $^{16}_6 C$ are all isotopes of carbon. The isotopes of a given element are not all equally common. For example, 98.9% of naturally occurring carbon (on Earth) is the isotope $^{12}_6 C$, and about 1.1% is $^{13}_6 C$. These percentages are referred to as the **natural abundances**.[†] Even hydrogen has isotopes: 99.99% of natural hydrogen is $^1_1 H$, a simple proton, as the nucleus; there are also $^2_1 H$, called **deuterium**, and $^3_1 H$, **tritium**, which besides the proton contain 1 or 2 neutrons.

[†]The mass value for each element as given in the Periodic Table (inside back cover) is an average weighted according to the natural abundances of its isotopes.

Many isotopes that do not occur naturally can be produced in the laboratory by means of nuclear reactions (more on this later). Indeed, all elements beyond uranium ($Z > 92$) do not occur naturally on Earth and are only produced artificially (that is, in the laboratory), as are many nuclides with $Z \leq 92$.

The approximate size of nuclei was determined originally by Rutherford from the scattering of charged particles by thin metal foils (Fig. 37–17). We cannot speak about a definite size for nuclei because of the wave–particle duality: their spatial extent must remain somewhat fuzzy. Nonetheless a rough "size" can be measured by scattering high-speed electrons off nuclei. It is found that nuclei have a roughly spherical shape with a radius that increases with A according to the approximate formula

$$r \approx (1.2 \times 10^{-15} \text{ m})(A^{\frac{1}{3}}). \qquad (41-1)$$

Since the volume of a sphere is $V = \frac{4}{3}\pi r^3$, we see that the volume of a nucleus is approximately proportional to the number of nucleons, $V \propto A$. This is what we would expect if nucleons were like impenetrable billiard balls: if you double the number of balls, you double the total volume. Hence, all nuclei have nearly the same density, and it is enormous (see Example 41–1).

The metric abbreviation for 10^{-15} m is the fermi (after Enrico Fermi) or the femtometer, fm (Table 1–4 or inside the front cover). Thus 1.2×10^{-15} m = 1.2 fm or 1.2 fermis.

Because nuclear radii vary as $A^{\frac{1}{3}}$, the largest nuclei, such as uranium with $A = 238$, have a radius only about $\sqrt[3]{238} \approx 6$ times that of the smallest, hydrogen ($A = 1$).

EXAMPLE 41–1 **ESTIMATE** **Nuclear and atomic densities.** Compare the density of nuclear matter to the density of normal solids.

APPROACH The density of normal liquids and solids is on the order of 10^3 to 10^4 kg/m^3 (see Table 13–1), and because the atoms are close packed, atoms have about this density too. We therefore compare the density (mass per volume) of a nucleus to that of its atom as a whole.

SOLUTION The mass of a proton is greater than the mass of an electron by a factor

$$\frac{1.7 \times 10^{-27} \text{ kg}}{9.1 \times 10^{-31} \text{ kg}} \approx 2 \times 10^3.$$

Thus, over 99.9% of the mass of an atom is in the nucleus, and for our estimate we can say the mass of the atom equals the mass of the nucleus, $m_{\text{nucl}}/m_{\text{atom}} = 1$. Atoms have a radius of about 10^{-10} m (Chapter 37) and nuclei on the order of 10^{-15} m (Eq. 41–1). Thus the ratio of nuclear density to atomic density is about

$$\frac{\rho_{\text{nucl}}}{\rho_{\text{atom}}} = \frac{(m_{\text{nucl}}/V_{\text{nucl}})}{(m_{\text{atom}}/V_{\text{atom}})} = \left(\frac{m_{\text{nucl}}}{m_{\text{atom}}}\right)\frac{\frac{4}{3}\pi r_{\text{atom}}^3}{\frac{4}{3}\pi r_{\text{nucl}}^3} \approx (1)\frac{(10^{-10})^3}{(10^{-15})^3} = 10^{15}.$$

The nucleus is 10^{15} times more dense than ordinary matter.

The masses of nuclei can be determined from the radius of curvature of fast-moving nuclei (as ions) in a known magnetic field using a mass spectrometer, as discussed in Section 27–9. Indeed the existence of different isotopes of the same element (different number of neutrons) was discovered using this device. Nuclear masses can be specified in **unified atomic mass units** (u). On this scale, a neutral $^{12}_{6}$C atom is given the precise value 12.000000 u. A neutron then has a measured mass of 1.008665 u, a proton 1.007276 u, and a neutral hydrogen atom $^{1}_{1}$H (proton plus electron) 1.007825 u. The masses of many nuclides are given in Appendix F. It should be noted that the masses in this Table, as is customary, are for the *neutral atom* (including electrons), and not for a bare nucleus.

⚠ **CAUTION**

Masses are for neutral atom (nucleus plus electrons)

Masses are often specified using the electron-volt energy unit. This can be done because mass and energy are related, and the precise relationship is given by Einstein's equation $E = mc^2$ (Chapter 36). Since the mass of a proton is 1.67262×10^{-27} kg, or 1.007276 u, then

$$1.0000 \text{ u} = (1.0000 \text{ u})\left(\frac{1.67262 \times 10^{-27} \text{ kg}}{1.007276 \text{ u}}\right) = 1.66054 \times 10^{-27} \text{ kg};$$

this is equivalent to an energy (see Table inside front cover) in MeV ($= 10^6$ eV) of

$$E = mc^2 = \frac{(1.66054 \times 10^{-27} \text{ kg})(2.9979 \times 10^8 \text{ m/s})^2}{(1.6022 \times 10^{-19} \text{ J/eV})} = 931.5 \text{ MeV}.$$

Thus

$$1 \text{ u} = 1.6605 \times 10^{-27} \text{ kg} = 931.5 \text{ MeV}/c^2.$$

The masses of some of the basic particles are given in Table 41–1.

TABLE 41–1 Masses in Kilograms, Unified Atomic Mass Units, and MeV/c^2

Object	Mass		
	kg	u	MeV/c^2
Electron	9.1094×10^{-31}	0.00054858	0.51100
Proton	1.67262×10^{-27}	1.007276	938.27
$^1_1$H atom	1.67353×10^{-27}	1.007825	938.78
Neutron	1.67493×10^{-27}	1.008665	939.57

Just as an electron has intrinsic spin and orbital angular momentum quantum numbers, so too do nuclei and their constituents, the proton and neutron. Both the proton and the neutron are spin-$\frac{1}{2}$ particles, just like the electron. A nucleus, made up of protons and neutrons, has a **nuclear spin** quantum number I that is the vector sum of the spins of all its nucleons (plus any orbital angular momentum), and can be either integer or half integer, depending on whether it is made up of an even or an odd number of nucleons. [Orbital angular momentum is integer and doesn't affect half integer or whole for I.] The **total nuclear angular momentum** of a nucleus is given, as might be expected (see Section 39–2 and Eq. 39–15), by $\sqrt{I(I + 1)}\,\hbar$.

Nuclear magnetic moments are measured in terms of the **nuclear magneton**

$$\mu_N = \frac{e\hbar}{2m_p}, \tag{41–2}$$

which is defined by analogy with the Bohr magneton for electrons ($\mu_B = e\hbar/2m_e$, Section 39–7). Since μ_N contains the proton mass, m_p, instead of the electron mass, it is about 2000 times smaller. The electron spin magnetic moment is about 2 Bohr magnetons. The proton's magnetic moment μ_p has been measured to be

$$\mu_p = 2.7928\,\mu_N.$$

There is no satisfactory explanation for this large factor. The neutron has a magnetic moment

$$\mu_n = -1.9135\,\mu_N,$$

which suggests that, although the neutron carries no net charge, it may have internal structure (quarks, as we discuss later). The minus sign for μ_n indicates that its magnetic moment is opposite to its spin.

Important applications based on nuclear spin are nuclear magnetic resonance (NMR) and magnetic resonance imaging (MRI). They are discussed in the next Chapter (Section 42–10).

41-2 Binding Energy and Nuclear Forces

Binding Energies

The total mass of a stable nucleus is always less than the sum of the masses of its separate protons and neutrons, as the following Example shows.

PROBLEM SOLVING

Keep track of electron masses

EXAMPLE 41–2 $^4_2$**He mass compared to its constituents.** Compare the mass of a $^4_2$He atom to the total mass of its constituent particles.

APPROACH The $^4_2$He nucleus contains 2 protons and 2 neutrons. Tables normally give the masses of neutral atoms—that is, nucleus plus its Z electrons—since this is how masses are measured. We must therefore be sure to balance out the electrons when we compare masses. Thus we use the mass of $^1_1$H rather than that of a proton alone. We look up the mass of the $^4_2$He atom in Appendix F (it includes the mass of 2 electrons), as well as the mass for the 2 neutrons and 2 hydrogen atoms (= 2 protons + 2 electrons).

SOLUTION The mass of a neutral $^4_2$He atom, from Appendix F, is 4.002603 u. The mass of two neutrons and two H atoms (2 protons including the 2 electrons) is

$$2m_n = 2(1.008665\,u) = 2.017330\,u$$
$$2m(^1_1H) = 2(1.007825\,u) = \underline{2.015650\,u}$$
$$sum = 4.032980\,u.$$

Thus the mass of $^4_2$He is measured to be less than the masses of its constituents by an amount 4.032980 u − 4.002603 u = 0.030377 u.

Where has this lost mass of 0.030377 u disappeared to? It must be $E = mc^2$.

If the four nucleons suddenly came together to form a $^4_2$He nucleus, the mass "loss" would appear as energy of another kind (such as γ radiation, or kinetic energy). The mass (or energy) difference in the case of $^4_2$He, given in energy units, is (0.030377 u)(931.5 MeV/u) = 28.30 MeV. This difference is referred to as the **total binding energy** of the nucleus. The total binding energy represents the amount of energy that must be put *into* a nucleus in order to break it apart into its constituents. If the mass of, say, a $^4_2$He nucleus were exactly equal to the mass of two neutrons plus two protons, the nucleus could fall apart without any input of energy. To be stable, the mass of a nucleus *must* be less than that of its constituent nucleons, so that energy input *is* needed to break it apart. Note that the binding energy is not something a nucleus has—it is energy it "lacks" relative to the total mass of its separate constituents.

We saw in Chapter 37 that the binding energy of the one electron in the hydrogen atom is 13.6 eV; so the mass of a $^1_1$H atom is less than that of a single proton plus a single electron by 13.6 eV/c^2. Compared to the total mass of the hydrogen atom (939 MeV/c^2), this is incredibly small, 1 part in 10^8. The binding energies of nuclei are on the order of MeV, so the eV binding energies of electrons can be ignored. Note that nuclear binding energies, compared to nuclear masses, are on the order of (28 MeV/4000 MeV) $\approx 1 \times 10^{-2}$, where we used helium's binding energy (see above) and mass $\approx 4 \times 940$ MeV ≈ 4000 MeV.

EXERCISE A Determine how much less the mass of the $^7_3$Li nucleus is compared to that of its constituents.

The **binding energy per nucleon** is defined as the total binding energy of a nucleus divided by A, the total number of nucleons. We calculated above that the binding energy of $^4_2$He is 28.3 MeV, so its binding energy per nucleon is 28.3 MeV/4 = 7.1 MeV. Figure 41–1 shows the binding energy per nucleon as a function of A for stable nuclei. The curve rises as A increases and reaches a plateau at about 8.7 MeV per nucleon above $A \approx 40$. Beyond $A \approx 80$, the curve decreases slowly, indicating that larger nuclei are held together a little less tightly than those in the middle of the Periodic Table. We will see later that these characteristics allow the release of nuclear energy in the processes of fission and fusion.

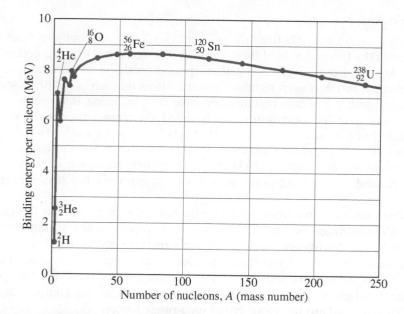

FIGURE 41–1 Binding energy per nucleon for the more stable nuclides as a function of mass number A.

EXAMPLE 41–3 **Binding energy for iron.** Calculate the total binding energy and the binding energy per nucleon for $^{56}_{26}Fe$, the most common stable isotope of iron.

APPROACH We subtract the mass of an $^{56}_{26}Fe$ atom from the total mass of 26 hydrogen atoms and 30 neutrons, all found in Appendix F. Then we convert mass units to energy units; finally we divide by $A = 56$, the total number of nucleons.

SOLUTION $^{56}_{26}Fe$ has 26 protons and 30 neutrons whose separate masses are

$$26m(^1_1H) = (26)(1.007825\,u) = 26.20345\,u \text{ (includes 26 electrons)}$$
$$30m_n = (30)(1.008665\,u) = \underline{30.25995\,u}$$
$$\text{sum} = 56.46340\,u.$$
$$\text{Subtract mass of } ^{56}_{26}Fe\colon = \underline{-55.93494\,u} \text{ (Appendix F)}$$
$$\Delta m = 0.52846\,u.$$

The total binding energy is thus

$$(0.52846\,u)(931.5\,MeV/u) = 492.26\,MeV$$

and the binding energy per nucleon is

$$\frac{492.26\,MeV}{56 \text{ nucleons}} = 8.79\,MeV.$$

NOTE The binding energy per nucleon graph (Fig. 41–1) peaks about here, for iron, so the iron nucleus (and its neighbors) is the most stable of nuclei.

| **EXERCISE B** Determine the binding energy per nucleon for $^{16}_8O$.

EXAMPLE 41–4 **Binding energy of last neutron.** What is the binding energy of the last neutron in $^{13}_6C$?

APPROACH If $^{13}_6C$ lost one neutron, it would be $^{12}_6C$. We subtract the mass of $^{13}_6C$ from the masses of $^{12}_6C$ and a free neutron.

SOLUTION Obtaining the masses from Appendix F, we have

$$\text{Mass } ^{12}_6C = 12.000000\,u$$
$$\text{Mass } ^1_0n = \underline{1.008665\,u}$$
$$\text{Total} = 13.008665\,u.$$
$$\text{Subtract mass of } ^{13}_6C\colon \underline{-13.003355\,u}$$
$$\Delta m = 0.005310\,u$$

which in energy is $(931.5\,MeV/u)(0.005310\,u) = 4.95\,MeV$. That is, it would require 4.95 MeV input of energy to remove one neutron from $^{13}_6C$.

Nuclear Forces

We can analyze nuclei not only from the point of view of energy, but also from the point of view of the forces that hold them together. We would not expect a collection of protons and neutrons to come together spontaneously, since protons are all positively charged and thus exert repulsive electric forces on each other. Since stable nuclei *do* stay together, it is clear that another force must be acting. Because this new force is stronger than the electric force, it is called the **strong nuclear force**. The strong nuclear force is an attractive force that acts between all nucleons—protons and neutrons alike. Thus protons attract each other via the strong nuclear force at the same time they repel each other via the electric force. Neutrons, since they are electrically neutral, only attract other neutrons or protons via the strong nuclear force.

The strong nuclear force turns out to be far more complicated than the gravitational and electromagnetic forces. One important aspect of the strong nuclear force is that it is a **short-range** force: it acts only over a very short distance. It is very strong between two nucleons if they are less than about 10^{-15} m apart, but it is essentially zero if they are separated by a distance greater than this. Compare this to electric and gravitational forces, which decrease as $1/r^2$ but continue acting over any distances and are therefore called **long-range** forces.

The strong nuclear force has some strange features. For example, if a nuclide contains too many or too few neutrons relative to the number of protons, the binding of the nucleons is reduced; nuclides that are too unbalanced in this regard are unstable. As shown in Fig. 41–2, stable nuclei tend to have the same number of protons as neutrons $(N = Z)$ up to about $A = 30$. Beyond this, stable nuclei contain more neutrons than protons. This makes sense since, as Z increases, the electrical repulsion increases, so a greater number of neutrons—which exert only the attractive strong nuclear force—are required to maintain stability. For very large Z, no number of neutrons can overcome the greatly increased electric repulsion. Indeed, there are no completely stable nuclides above $Z = 82$.

What we mean by a *stable nucleus* is one that stays together indefinitely. What then is an *unstable nucleus*? It is one that comes apart; and this results in radioactive decay. Before we discuss the important subject of radioactivity (next Section), we note that there is a second type of nuclear force that is much weaker than the strong nuclear force. It is called the **weak nuclear force**, and we are aware of its existence only because it shows itself in certain types of radioactive decay. These two nuclear forces, the strong and the weak, together with the gravitational and electromagnetic forces, comprise the four basic types of force in nature.

FIGURE 41–2 Number of neutrons versus number of protons for stable nuclides, which are represented by dots. The straight line represents $N = Z$.

41–3 Radioactivity

Nuclear physics had its beginnings in 1896. In that year, Henri Becquerel (1852–1908) made an important discovery: in his studies of phosphorescence, he found that a certain mineral (which happened to contain uranium) would darken a photographic plate even when the plate was wrapped to exclude light. It was clear that the mineral emitted some new kind of radiation that, unlike X-rays, occurred without any external stimulus. This new phenomenon eventually came to be called **radioactivity**.

Soon after Becquerel's discovery, Marie Curie (1867–1934) and her husband, Pierre Curie (1859–1906), isolated two previously unknown elements that were very highly radioactive (Fig. 41–3). These were named polonium and radium. Other radioactive elements were soon discovered as well. The radioactivity was found in every case to be unaffected by the strongest physical and chemical treatments, including strong heating or cooling or the action of strong chemical reagents. It was suspected that the source of radioactivity must be deep within the atom, emanating from the nucleus. It became apparent that radioactivity is the result of the **disintegration** or **decay** of an unstable nucleus. Certain isotopes are not stable, and they decay with the emission of some type of radiation or "rays."

FIGURE 41–3 Marie and Pierre Curie in their laboratory (about 1906) where radium was discovered.

Many unstable isotopes occur in nature, and such radioactivity is called "natural radioactivity." Other unstable isotopes can be produced in the laboratory by nuclear reactions (Section 42–1); these are said to be produced "artificially" and to have "artificial radioactivity." Radioactive isotopes are sometimes referred to as **radioisotopes** or **radionuclides**.

Rutherford and others began studying the nature of the rays emitted in radioactivity about 1898. They classified the rays into three distinct types according to their penetrating power. One type of radiation could barely penetrate a piece of paper. The second type could pass through as much as 3 mm of aluminum. The third was extremely penetrating: it could pass through several centimeters of lead and still be detected on the other side. They named these three types of radiation alpha (α), beta (β), and gamma (γ), respectively, after the first three letters of the Greek alphabet.

Each type of ray was found to have a different charge and hence is bent differently in a magnetic field, Fig. 41–4; α rays are positively charged, β rays are negatively charged, and γ rays are neutral. It was soon found that all three types of radiation consisted of familiar kinds of particles. Gamma rays are very high-energy photons whose energy is even higher than that of X-rays. Beta rays are electrons, identical to those that orbit the nucleus, but they are created within the nucleus itself. Alpha rays (or α particles) are simply the nuclei of helium atoms, $_2^4$He; that is, an α ray consists of two protons and two neutrons bound together.

We now discuss each of these three types of radioactivity, or decay, in more detail.

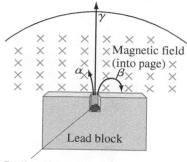

FIGURE 41–4 Alpha and beta rays are bent in opposite directions by a magnetic field, whereas gamma rays are not bent at all.

41–4 Alpha Decay

Experiments show that when nuclei decay, the number of nucleons (= mass number A) is conserved, as well as electric charge (= Ze). When a nucleus emits an α particle ($_2^4$He), the remaining nucleus will be different from the original: it has lost two protons and two neutrons. Radium 226 ($_{88}^{226}$Ra), for example, is an α emitter. It decays to a nucleus with $Z = 88 - 2 = 86$ and $A = 226 - 4 = 222$. The nucleus with $Z = 86$ is radon (Rn)—see Appendix F or the Periodic Table. Thus the radium decays to radon with the emission of an α particle. This is written

$$_{88}^{226}\text{Ra} \rightarrow \,_{86}^{222}\text{Rn} + \,_2^4\text{He}.$$

See Fig. 41–5.

When α decay occurs, a different element is formed. The **daughter** nucleus ($_{86}^{222}$Rn in this case) is different from the **parent** nucleus ($_{88}^{226}$Ra in this case). This changing of one element into another is called **transmutation**.

Alpha decay can be written in general as

$$_Z^A\text{N} \rightarrow \,_{Z-2}^{A-4}\text{N}' + \,_2^4\text{He} \qquad\qquad [\alpha \text{ decay}]$$

where N is the parent, N' the daughter, and Z and A are the atomic number and atomic mass number, respectively, of the parent.

EXERCISE C $_{66}^{154}$Dy decays by α emission to what element? (a) Pb, (b) Gd, (c) Sm, (d) Er, (e) Yb.

Alpha decay occurs because the strong nuclear force is unable to hold very large nuclei together. The nuclear force is a short-range force: it acts only between neighboring nucleons. But the electric force acts all the way across a large nucleus. For very large nuclei, the large Z means the repulsive electric force becomes so large (Coulomb's law) that the strong nuclear force is unable to hold the nucleus together.

FIGURE 41–5 Radioactive decay of radium to radon with emission of an alpha particle.

We can express the instability of the parent nucleus in terms of energy (or mass): the mass of the parent nucleus is greater than the mass of the daughter nucleus plus the mass of the α particle. The mass difference appears as kinetic energy, which is carried away by the α particle and the recoiling daughter nucleus. The total energy released is called the **disintegration energy**, Q, or the **Q-value** of the decay. From conservation of energy,

$$M_P c^2 = M_D c^2 + m_\alpha c^2 + Q,$$

where Q equals the kinetic energy of the daughter and α particle, and M_P, M_D, and m_α are the masses of the parent, daughter, and α particle, respectively. Thus

$$Q = M_P c^2 - (M_D + m_\alpha)c^2. \qquad (41\text{--}3)$$

If the parent had *less* mass than the daughter plus the α particle (so $Q < 0$), the decay could not occur spontaneously, for the conservation of energy law would be violated.

EXAMPLE 41–5 **Uranium decay energy release.** Calculate the disintegration energy when $^{232}_{92}\text{U}$ (mass $= 232.037156$ u) decays to $^{228}_{90}\text{Th}$ (228.028741 u) with the emission of an α particle. (As always, masses given are for neutral atoms.)

APPROACH We use conservation of energy as expressed in Eq. 41–3. $^{232}_{92}\text{U}$ is the parent, $^{228}_{90}\text{Th}$ is the daughter.

SOLUTION Since the mass of the $^{4}_{2}\text{He}$ is 4.002603 u (Appendix F), the total mass in the final state is

$$228.028741 \text{ u} + 4.002603 \text{ u} = 232.031344 \text{ u}.$$

The mass lost when the $^{232}_{92}\text{U}$ decays is

$$232.037156 \text{ u} - 232.031344 \text{ u} = 0.005812 \text{ u}.$$

Since $1 \text{ u} = 931.5 \text{ MeV}$, the energy Q released is

$$Q = (0.005812 \text{ u})(931.5 \text{ MeV/u}) = 5.4 \text{ MeV}$$

and this energy appears as kinetic energy of the α particle and the daughter nucleus.

EXAMPLE 41–6 **Kinetic energy of the α in $^{232}_{92}\text{U}$ decay.** For the $^{232}_{92}\text{U}$ decay of Example 41–5, how much of the 5.4-MeV disintegration energy will be carried off by the α particle?

APPROACH In any reaction, momentum must be conserved as well as energy.

SOLUTION Before disintegration, the nucleus can be assumed to be at rest, so the total momentum was zero. After disintegration, the total vector momentum must still be zero so the magnitude of the α particle's momentum must equal the magnitude of the daughter's momentum (Fig. 41–6):

$$m_\alpha v_\alpha = m_D v_D.$$

Thus $v_\alpha = m_D v_D / m_\alpha$ and the α's kinetic energy is

$$K_\alpha = \tfrac{1}{2} m_\alpha v_\alpha^2 = \tfrac{1}{2} m_\alpha \left(\frac{m_D v_D}{m_\alpha} \right)^2 = \tfrac{1}{2} m_D v_D^2 \left(\frac{m_D}{m_\alpha} \right) = \left(\frac{m_D}{m_\alpha} \right) K_D$$

$$= \left(\frac{228.028741 \text{ u}}{4.002603 \text{ u}} \right) K_D = 57 K_D.$$

The total disintegration energy is $Q = K_\alpha + K_D = 57 K_D + K_D = 58 K_D$. Hence

$$K_\alpha = \frac{57}{58} Q = 5.3 \text{ MeV}.$$

The lighter α particle carries off (57/58) or 98% of the total kinetic energy.

FIGURE 41–6 Momentum conservation in Example 41–6.

α-Decay Theory—Tunneling

If the mass of the daughter nucleus plus the mass of the α particle is less than the mass of the parent nucleus (so the parent is energetically allowed to decay), why are there any parent nuclei at all? That is, why haven't radioactive nuclei all decayed long ago, right after they were formed (in supernovae)? We can understand decay using a model of a nucleus that has an alpha particle trapped inside it. The potential energy "seen" by the α particle would have a shape something like that shown in Fig. 41–7. The potential energy well (approximately square) between $r = 0$ and $r = R_0$ represents the short-range attractive nuclear force.

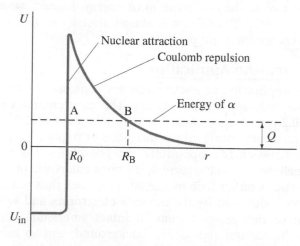

FIGURE 41–7 Potential energy for alpha particle and (daughter) nucleus, showing the Coulomb barrier through which the α particle must tunnel to escape. The Q-value of the reaction is also shown. This plot assumes spherical symmetry, so the central well has diameter $2R_0$.

Beyond the nuclear radius, R_0, the Coulomb repulsion dominates (since the nuclear force drops to zero) and we see the characteristic $1/r$ dependence of the Coulomb potential. The α particle, trapped within the nucleus, can be thought of as moving back and forth between the potential walls. Since the potential energy just beyond $r = R_0$ is greater than the energy of the α particle (dashed line), the α particle could not escape the nucleus if it were governed by classical physics. But according to quantum mechanics, there is a nonzero probability that the α particle can **tunnel** through the Coulomb barrier, from point A to point B in Fig. 41–7, as we discussed in Section 38–10. The height and width of the barrier affect the rate at which nuclei decay (Section 41–8). Because of this barrier, the lifetimes of α-unstable nuclei can be quite long, from a fraction of a microsecond to over 10^{10} years. Note in Fig. 41–7 that the Q-value represents the total kinetic energy when the α particle is far from the nucleus.

A simple way to look at tunneling is via the uncertainty principle which tells us that energy conservation can be violated by an amount ΔE for a length of time Δt given by

$$(\Delta E)(\Delta t) \approx \frac{h}{2\pi}.$$

Thus quantum mechanics allows conservation of energy to be violated for brief periods that may be long enough for an α particle to "tunnel" through the barrier. ΔE would represent the energy difference between the average barrier height and the particle's energy, and Δt the time to pass through the barrier. The higher and wider the barrier, the less time the α particle has to escape and the less likely it is to do so. It is therefore the height and width of this barrier that controls the rate of decay and half-life of an isotope.

Why α Particles?

Why, you may wonder, do nuclei emit this combination of four nucleons called an α particle? Why not just four separate nucleons, or even one? The answer is that the α particle is very strongly bound, so that its mass is significantly less than that of four separate nucleons. As we saw in Example 41–2, two protons and two neutrons separately have a total mass of about 4.032980 u (electrons included). For the decay of $^{232}_{92}\text{U}$ discussed in Example 41–5, the total mass of the daughter $^{228}_{90}\text{Th}$ plus four separate nucleons is $228.028741 + 4.032980 = 232.061721$ u, which is greater than the mass of the $^{232}_{92}\text{U}$ parent (232.037156). Such a decay could not occur because it would violate the conservation of energy. Indeed, we have never seen $^{232}_{92}\text{U} \rightarrow {}^{228}_{90}\text{Th} + 2n + 2p$. Similarly, it is almost always true that the emission of a single nucleon is energetically not possible.

Smoke Detectors—An Application

One widespread application of nuclear physics is present in nearly every home in the form of an ordinary **smoke detector**. The most common type of detector contains about 0.2 mg of the radioactive americium isotope, $^{241}_{95}\text{Am}$, in the form of AmO_2. The radiation continually ionizes the nitrogen and oxygen molecules in the air space between two oppositely charged plates. The resulting conductivity allows a small steady electric current. If smoke enters, the radiation is absorbed by the smoke particles rather than by the air molecules, thus reducing the current. The current drop is detected by the device's electronics and sets off the alarm. The radiation dose that escapes from an intact americium smoke detector is much less than the natural radioactive background, and so can be considered relatively harmless. There is no question that smoke detectors save lives and reduce property damage.

41–5 Beta Decay

β^- Decay

Transmutation of elements also occurs when a nucleus decays by β decay—that is, with the emission of an electron or β^- particle. The nucleus $^{14}_6\text{C}$, for example, emits an electron when it decays:

$$^{14}_6\text{C} \rightarrow {}^{14}_7\text{N} + e^- + \text{neutrino},$$

where e^- is the symbol for the electron. The particle known as the neutrino, whose charge $q = 0$ and whose mass is very small or zero, was not initially detected and was only later hypothesized to exist, as we shall discuss later in this Section. No nucleons are lost when an electron is emitted, and the total number of nucleons, A, is the same in the daughter nucleus as in the parent. But because an electron has been emitted from the nucleus itself, the charge on the daughter nucleus is $+1e$ greater than that on the parent. The parent nucleus in the decay written above had $Z = +6$, so from charge conservation the nucleus remaining behind must have a charge of $+7e$. So the daughter nucleus has $Z = 7$, which is nitrogen.

It must be carefully noted that the electron emitted in β decay is *not* an orbital electron. Instead, the electron is created *within the nucleus itself*. What happens is that one of the neutrons changes to a proton and in the process (to conserve charge) emits an electron. Indeed, free neutrons actually do decay in this fashion:

$$n \rightarrow p + e^- + \text{neutrino}.$$

To remind us of their origin in the nucleus, the electrons emitted in β decay are often referred to as "β particles." They are, nonetheless, indistinguishable from orbital electrons.

EXAMPLE 41–7 **Energy release in $^{14}_{6}C$ decay.** How much energy is released when $^{14}_{6}C$ decays to $^{14}_{7}N$ by β emission?

APPROACH We find the mass difference before and after decay, Δm. The energy released is $E = (\Delta m)c^2$. The masses given in Appendix F are those of the neutral atom, and we have to keep track of the electrons involved. Assume the parent nucleus has six orbiting electrons so it is neutral; its mass is 14.003242 u. The daughter in this decay, $^{14}_{7}N$, is not neutral since it has the same six orbital electrons circling it but the nucleus has a charge of $+7e$. However, the mass of this daughter with its six electrons, plus the mass of the emitted electron (which makes a total of seven electrons), is just the mass of a neutral nitrogen atom.

SOLUTION The total mass in the final state is

$$\text{(mass of } ^{14}_{7}N \text{ nucleus } + \text{ 6 electrons)} + \text{(mass of 1 electron)},$$

and this is equal to

$$\text{mass of neutral } ^{14}_{7}N \text{ (includes 7 electrons)},$$

which from Appendix F is a mass of 14.003074 u. So the mass difference is 14.003242 u − 14.003074 u = 0.000168 u, which is equivalent to an energy change $\Delta m\, c^2 = (0.000168\,\text{u})(931.5\,\text{MeV/u}) = 0.156\,\text{MeV}$ or $156\,\text{keV}$.

NOTE The neutrino doesn't contribute to either the mass or charge balance since it has $q = 0$ and $m \approx 0$.

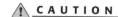

⚠ **CAUTION**

Be careful with atomic and electron masses in β decay

According to Example 41–7, we would expect the emitted electron to have a kinetic energy of 156 keV. (The daughter nucleus, because its mass is very much larger than that of the electron, recoils with very low velocity and hence gets very little of the kinetic energy—see Example 41–6.) Indeed, very careful measurements indicate that a few emitted β particles do have kinetic energy close to this calculated value. But the vast majority of emitted electrons have somewhat less energy. In fact, the energy of the emitted electron can be anywhere from zero up to the maximum value as calculated above. This range of electron kinetic energy was found for any β decay. It was as if the law of conservation of energy was being violated, and indeed Bohr actually considered this possibility. Careful experiments indicated that linear momentum and angular momentum also did not seem to be conserved. Physicists were troubled at the prospect of giving up these laws, which had worked so well in all previous situations.

In 1930, Wolfgang Pauli proposed an alternate solution: perhaps a new particle that was very difficult to detect was emitted during β decay in addition to the electron. This hypothesized particle could be carrying off the energy, momentum, and angular momentum required to maintain the conservation laws. This new particle was named the **neutrino**—meaning "little neutral one"—by the great Italian physicist Enrico Fermi (1901–1954; Fig. 41–8), who in 1934 worked out a detailed theory of β decay. (It was Fermi who, in this theory, postulated the existence of the fourth force in nature which we call the *weak nuclear force*.) The neutrino has zero charge, spin of $\frac{1}{2}\hbar$, and was long thought to have zero mass, although today we are quite sure that it has a very tiny mass ($< 0.14\,\text{eV}/c^2$). If its mass were zero, it would be much like a photon in that it is neutral and would travel at the speed of light. But the neutrino is very difficult to detect. In 1956, complex experiments produced further evidence for the existence of the neutrino; but by then, most physicists had already accepted its existence.

The symbol for the neutrino is the Greek letter nu (ν). The correct way of writing the decay of $^{14}_{6}C$ is then

$$^{14}_{6}C \rightarrow\ ^{14}_{7}N + e^- + \bar{\nu}.$$

The bar ($^-$) over the neutrino symbol is to indicate that it is an "antineutrino." (Why this is called an antineutrino rather than simply a neutrino need not concern us now; it is discussed in Chapter 43.)

FIGURE 41–8 Enrico Fermi, as portrayed on a US postage stamp. Fermi contributed significantly to both theoretical and experimental physics, a feat almost unique in modern times.

FIGURE 41–2 (Repeated.)
Number of neutrons versus number of protons for stable nuclides, which are represented by dots. The straight line represents $N = Z$.

β^+ Decay

Many isotopes decay by electron emission. They are always isotopes that have too many neutrons compared to the number of protons. That is, they are isotopes that lie above the stable isotopes plotted in Fig. 41–2. But what about unstable isotopes that have too few neutrons compared to their number of protons—those that fall below the stable isotopes of Fig. 41–2? These, it turns out, decay by emitting a **positron** instead of an electron. A positron (sometimes called an e^+ or β^+ particle) has the same mass as the electron, but it has a positive charge of $+1e$. Because it is so like an electron, except for its charge, the positron is called the **antiparticle**[†] to the electron. An example of a β^+ decay is that of $^{19}_{10}\text{Ne}$:

$$^{19}_{10}\text{Ne} \rightarrow ^{19}_{9}\text{F} + e^+ + \nu,$$

where e^+ stands for a positron. Note that the ν emitted here is a neutrino, whereas that emitted in β^- decay is called an antineutrino. Thus an antielectron (= positron) is emitted with a neutrino, whereas an antineutrino is emitted with an electron; this gives a certain balance as discussed in Chapter 43.

We can write β^- and β^+ decay, in general, as follows:

$$^{A}_{Z}\text{N} \rightarrow ^{A}_{Z+1}\text{N}' + e^- + \bar{\nu} \qquad [\beta^- \text{ decay}]$$
$$^{A}_{Z}\text{N} \rightarrow ^{A}_{Z-1}\text{N}' + e^+ + \nu, \qquad [\beta^+ \text{ decay}]$$

where N is the parent nucleus and N′ is the daughter.

Electron Capture

Besides β^- and β^+ emission, there is a third related process. This is **electron capture** (abbreviated EC in Appendix F) and occurs when a nucleus absorbs one of its orbiting electrons. An example is $^{7}_{4}\text{Be}$, which as a result becomes $^{7}_{3}\text{Li}$. The process is written

$$^{7}_{4}\text{Be} + e^- \rightarrow ^{7}_{3}\text{Li} + \nu,$$

or, in general,

$$^{A}_{Z}\text{N} + e^- \rightarrow ^{A}_{Z-1}\text{N}' + \nu. \qquad [\text{electron capture}]$$

Usually it is an electron in the innermost (K) shell that is captured, in which case the process is called **K-capture**. The electron disappears in the process, and a proton in the nucleus becomes a neutron; a neutrino is emitted as a result. This process is inferred experimentally by detection of emitted X-rays (due to other electrons jumping down to fill the empty state) of just the proper energy.

In β decay, it is the weak nuclear force that plays the crucial role. The neutrino is unique in that it interacts with matter only via the weak force, which is why it is so hard to detect.

41–6 Gamma Decay

Gamma rays are photons having very high energy. They have their origin in the decay of a nucleus, much like emission of photons by excited atoms. Like an atom, a nucleus itself can be in an excited state. When it jumps down to a lower energy state, or to the ground state, it emits a photon which we call a γ ray. The possible energy levels of a nucleus are much farther apart than those of an atom: on the order of keV or MeV, as compared to a few eV for electrons in an atom. Hence, the emitted photons have energies that can range from a few keV to several MeV. For a given decay, the γ ray always has the same energy. Since a γ ray carries no charge, there is no change in the element as a result of a γ decay.

How does a nucleus get into an excited state? It may occur because of a violent collision with another particle. More commonly, the nucleus remaining after a previous radioactive decay may be in an excited state. A typical example is shown in the energy-level diagram of Fig. 41–9. $^{12}_{5}\text{B}$ can decay by β decay directly

FIGURE 41–9 Energy-level diagram showing how $^{12}_{5}\text{B}$ can decay to the ground state of $^{12}_{6}\text{C}$ by β decay (total energy released = 13.4 MeV), or can instead β decay to an excited state of $^{12}_{6}\text{C}$ (indicated by *), which subsequently decays to its ground state by emitting a 4.4-MeV γ ray.

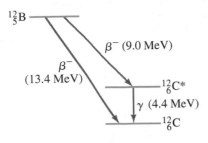

[†]Discussed in Chapter 43. Briefly, an antiparticle has the same mass as its corresponding particle, but opposite charge. A particle and its antiparticle can quickly annihilate each other, releasing energy (γ rays).

to the ground state of $^{12}_{6}\text{C}$; or it can go by β decay to an excited state of $^{12}_{6}\text{C}$, which then decays by emission of a 4.4-MeV γ ray to the ground state.

We can write γ decay as

$$^{A}_{Z}\text{N}^* \rightarrow {}^{A}_{Z}\text{N} + \gamma, \qquad \text{[}\gamma\text{ decay]}$$

where the asterisk means "excited state" of that nucleus.

What, you may wonder, is the difference between a γ ray and an X-ray? They both are electromagnetic radiation (photons) and, though γ rays usually have higher energy than X-rays, their range of energies overlap to some extent. The difference is not intrinsic. We use the term X-ray if the photon is produced by an electron–atom interaction, and γ ray if the photon is produced in a nuclear process.

Isomers; Internal Conversion

In some cases, a nucleus may remain in an excited state for some time before it emits a γ ray. The nucleus is then said to be in a **metastable state** and is called an **isomer**.

An excited nucleus can sometimes return to the ground state by another process known as **internal conversion** with no γ ray emitted. In this process, the excited nucleus interacts with one of the orbital electrons and ejects this electron from the atom with the same kinetic energy (minus the binding energy of the electron) that an emitted γ ray would have had.

41–7 Conservation of Nucleon Number and Other Conservation Laws

In all three types of radioactive decay, the classical conservation laws hold. Energy, linear momentum, angular momentum, and electric charge are all conserved. These quantities are the same before the decay as after. But a new conservation law is also revealed, the **law of conservation of nucleon number**. According to this law, the total number of nucleons (A) remains constant in any process, although one type can change into the other type (protons into neutrons or vice versa). This law holds in all three types of decay. Table 41–2 gives a summary of α, β, and γ decay. [In Chapter 43 we will generalize this and call it conservation of baryon number.]

TABLE 41–2 The Three Types of Radioactive Decay
α *decay:*
$\qquad {}^{A}_{Z}\text{N} \rightarrow {}^{A-4}_{Z-2}\text{N}' + {}^{4}_{2}\text{He}$
β *decay:*
$\qquad {}^{A}_{Z}\text{N} \rightarrow {}^{A}_{Z+1}\text{N}' + e^- + \bar{\nu}$
$\qquad {}^{A}_{Z}\text{N} \rightarrow {}^{A}_{Z-1}\text{N}' + e^+ + \nu$
$\qquad {}^{A}_{Z}\text{N} + e^- \rightarrow {}^{A}_{Z-1}\text{N}' + \nu \text{ [EC]}^\dagger$
γ *decay:*
$\qquad {}^{A}_{Z}\text{N}^* \rightarrow {}^{A}_{Z}\text{N} + \gamma$

† Electron capture.
* Indicates the excited state of a nucleus.

41–8 Half-Life and Rate of Decay

A macroscopic sample of any radioactive isotope consists of a vast number of radioactive nuclei. These nuclei do not all decay at one time. Rather, they decay one by one over a period of time. This is a random process: we can not predict exactly when a given nucleus will decay. But we can determine, on a probabilistic basis, approximately how many nuclei in a sample will decay over a given time period, by assuming that each nucleus has the same probability of decaying in each second that it exists.

The number of decays ΔN that occur in a very short time interval Δt is then proportional to Δt and to the total number N of radioactive nuclei present:

$$\Delta N = -\lambda N \, \Delta t \qquad \textbf{(41–4a)}$$

where the minus sign means N is decreasing. We rewrite this to get the rate of decay:

$$\frac{\Delta N}{\Delta t} = -\lambda N. \qquad \textbf{(41–4b)}$$

In these equations, λ is a constant of proportionality called the **decay constant**, which is different for different isotopes. The greater λ is, the greater the rate of decay and the more "radioactive" that isotope is said to be. The number of decays that occur in the short time interval Δt is designated ΔN because each decay that

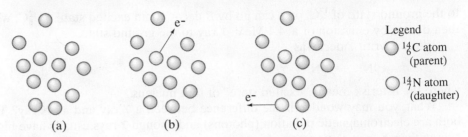

FIGURE 41–10 Radioactive nuclei decay one by one. Hence, the number of parent nuclei in a sample is continually decreasing. When a $^{14}_{6}$C nucleus emits an electron, the nucleus becomes a $^{14}_{7}$N nucleus.

Legend
$^{14}_{6}$C atom (parent)
$^{14}_{7}$N atom (daughter)

(a)　　(b)　　(c)

occurs corresponds to a decrease by one in the number N of nuclei present. That is, radioactive decay is a "one-shot" process, Fig. 41–10. Once a particular parent nucleus decays into its daughter, it cannot do it again.

If we take the limit $\Delta t \to 0$ in Eq. 41–4, ΔN will be small compared to N, and we can write the equation in infinitesimal form as

$$dN = -\lambda N\, dt. \tag{41–5}$$

We can determine N as a function of t by rearranging this equation to

$$\frac{dN}{N} = -\lambda\, dt$$

and then integrating from $t = 0$ to $t = t$:

$$\int_{N_0}^{N} \frac{dN}{N} = -\int_{0}^{t} \lambda\, dt,$$

where N_0 is the number of parent nuclei present at $t = 0$ and N is the number remaining at time t. The integration gives

$$\ln \frac{N}{N_0} = -\lambda t$$

or

$$N = N_0\, e^{-\lambda t}. \tag{41–6}$$

Equation 41–6 is called the **radioactive decay law**. It tells us that the number of radioactive nuclei in a given sample decreases exponentially in time. This is shown in Fig. 41–11a for the case of $^{14}_{6}$C whose decay constant is $\lambda = 3.83 \times 10^{-12}\,\text{s}^{-1}$.

The rate of decay in a pure sample, or number of decays per second, is

$$\left| \frac{dN}{dt} \right|,$$

also called the **activity** of the sample. We use absolute value signs to make activity a positive number (dN/dt is negative because the number of parent nuclei N is decreasing). The symbol R is also used for activity, $R = |dN/dt|$.

FIGURE 41–11 (a) The number N of parent nuclei in a given sample of $^{14}_{6}$C decreases exponentially. We set $N_0 = 1.00 \times 10^{22}$ here, as we do in the text shortly. (b) The number of decays per second also decreases exponentially. The half-life (Eq. 41–8) of $^{14}_{6}$C is about 5730 yr, which means that the number of parent nuclei, N, and the rate of decay, $|dN/dt|$, decrease by half every 5730 yr.

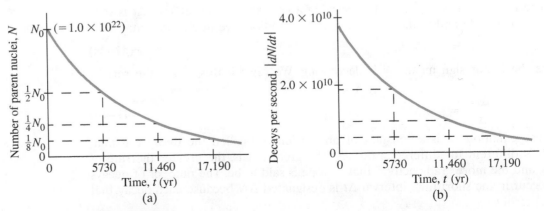

From Eqs. 41–5 and 41–6,

$$\left|\frac{dN}{dt}\right| = \lambda N = \lambda N_0 e^{-\lambda t}. \tag{41–7a}$$

At $t = 0$, the activity is

$$\left|\frac{dN}{dt}\right|_0 = \lambda N_0. \tag{41–7b}$$

Hence, at any other time t the activity is

$$\left|\frac{dN}{dt}\right| = \left|\frac{dN}{dt}\right|_0 e^{-\lambda t}, \tag{41–7c}$$

so the activity decreases exponentially in time at the same rate as for N (Fig. 41–11b). Equation 41–7c is sometimes referred to as the **radioactive decay law** (so is Eq. 41–6), and can be written using R to represent activity, $R = |dN/dt|$, as

$$R = R_0 e^{-\lambda t}. \tag{41–7d}$$

The rate of decay of any isotope is often specified by giving its half-life rather than the decay constant λ. The **half-life** of an isotope is defined as the time it takes for half the original amount of isotope in a given sample to decay. For example, the half-life of $^{14}_{6}C$ is about 5730 years. If at some time a piece of petrified wood contains, say, 1.00×10^{22} $^{14}_{6}C$ nuclei, then 5730 yr later it will contain only 0.50×10^{22} nuclei. After another 5730 yr it will contain 0.25×10^{22} nuclei, and so on. This is characteristic of the exponential function, and is shown in Fig. 41–11a. Since the rate of decay $|dN/dt|$ is proportional to N, it too decreases by a factor of 2 every half-life, Fig. 41–11b.

EXERCISE D The half-life of $^{22}_{11}Na$ is 2.6 years. How much will be left of a 1.0-μg sample of $^{22}_{11}Na$ after 5.2 yr? (a) None. (b) $\frac{1}{8}\mu$g. (c) $\frac{1}{4}\mu$g. (d) $\frac{1}{2}\mu$g. (e) 0.693 μg.

EXERCISE E Return to the Chapter-Opening Question, page 1104, and answer it again now. Try to explain why you may have answered differently the first time.

The half-lives of known radioactive isotopes vary from as short as 10^{-22} s to about 10^{28} s (about 10^{21} yr). The half-lives of many isotopes are given in Appendix F. It should be clear that the half-life (which we designate $T_{\frac{1}{2}}$) bears an inverse relationship to the decay constant. The longer the half-life of an isotope, the more slowly it decays, and hence λ is smaller. The precise relation is obtained from Eq. 41–6 by setting $N = N_0/2$ at $t = T_{\frac{1}{2}}$:

$$\frac{N_0}{2} = N_0 e^{-\lambda T_{\frac{1}{2}}} \qquad \text{or} \qquad e^{\lambda T_{\frac{1}{2}}} = 2.$$

We take natural logs of both sides ("ln" and "e" are inverse operations, meaning $\ln(e^x) = x$) and find

$$\ln(e^{\lambda T_{\frac{1}{2}}}) = \ln 2, \qquad \text{so} \qquad \lambda T_{\frac{1}{2}} = \ln 2$$

and

$$T_{\frac{1}{2}} = \frac{\ln 2}{\lambda} = \frac{0.693}{\lambda}. \tag{41–8}$$

We can then write Eq. 41–6 as

$$N = N_0 e^{-0.693 t/T_{\frac{1}{2}}}.$$

Sometimes the **mean life** τ of an isotope is quoted, which is defined as $\tau = 1/\lambda$ (see also Problem 80), so then Eq. 41–6 can be written

$$N = N_0 e^{-t/\tau}$$

just as for RC and LR circuits (Chapters 26 and 30, where τ is called the time constant). Since

$$\tau = \frac{1}{\lambda} = \frac{T_{\frac{1}{2}}}{0.693} \tag{41–9a}$$

the mean life and half-life differ by a factor 0.693; confusing them can cause serious error. The *radioactive decay law*, Eq. 41–7d, can be written simply as

$$R = R_0 e^{-t/\tau}. \tag{41–9b}$$

EXAMPLE 41–8 **Sample activity.** The isotope $^{14}_{6}C$ has a half-life of 5730 yr. If a sample contains 1.00×10^{22} carbon-14 nuclei, what is the activity of the sample?

APPROACH We first use the half-life to find the decay constant (Eq. 41–8), and use that to find the activity, Eq. 41–7b or 41–5. The number of seconds in a year is $(60 \text{ s/min})(60 \text{ min/h})(24 \text{ h/d})(365\frac{1}{4} \text{ d/yr}) = 3.156 \times 10^7 \text{ s}$.

SOLUTION The decay constant λ from Eq. 41–8 is

$$\lambda = \frac{0.693}{T_{\frac{1}{2}}} = \frac{0.693}{(5730 \text{ yr})(3.156 \times 10^7 \text{ s/yr})} = 3.83 \times 10^{-12} \text{ s}^{-1}.$$

From Eq. 41–7b, the activity or rate of decay is

$$\left|\frac{dN}{dt}\right|_0 = \lambda N_0 = (3.83 \times 10^{-12} \text{ s}^{-1})(1.00 \times 10^{22}) = 3.83 \times 10^{10} \text{ decays/s}.$$

Notice that the graph of Fig. 41–11b starts at this value, corresponding to the original value of $N_0 = 1.0 \times 10^{22}$ nuclei in Fig. 41–11a.

NOTE The unit "decays/s" is often written simply as s^{-1} since "decays" is not a unit but refers only to the number. This simple unit of activity is called the becquerel: $1 \text{ Bq} = 1 \text{ decay/s}$, as discussed in Chapter 42.

| **EXERCISE F** Determine the decay constant for radium $(T_{\frac{1}{2}} = 1600 \text{ yr})$.

CONCEPTUAL EXAMPLE 41–9 **Safety: Activity versus half-life.** One might think that a short half-life material is safer than a long half-life material because it will not last as long. Is that true?

RESPONSE No. A shorter half-life means the activity is higher and thus more "radioactive" and can cause more biological damage. On the other hand, a longer half-life for the same sample size N means a lower activity but we have to worry about it for longer and find safe storage until it reaches a safe (low) level of activity.

EXAMPLE 41–10 **A sample of radioactive $^{13}_{7}N$.** A laboratory has 1.49 μg of pure $^{13}_{7}N$, which has a half-life of 10.0 min (600 s). (a) How many nuclei are present initially? (b) What is the activity initially? (c) What is the activity after 1.00 h? (d) After approximately how long will the activity drop to less than one per second $(= 1 \text{ s}^{-1})$?

APPROACH We use the definition of the mole and Avogadro's number (Sections 17–7 and 17–9) to find the number of nuclei. For (b) we get λ from the given half-life and use Eq. 41–7b for the activity. For (c) and (d) we use Eq. 41–7c, and/or make a Table of the times.

SOLUTION (a) The atomic mass is 13.0, so 13.0 g will contain 6.02×10^{23} nuclei (Avogadro's number). We have only 1.49×10^{-6} g, so the number of nuclei N_0 that we have initially is given by the ratio

$$\frac{N_0}{6.02 \times 10^{23}} = \frac{1.49 \times 10^{-6} \text{ g}}{13.0 \text{ g}}.$$

Solving, we find $N_0 = 6.90 \times 10^{16}$ nuclei.

(b) From Eq. 41–8,

$$\lambda = 0.693/T_{\frac{1}{2}} = (0.693)/(600 \text{ s}) = 1.155 \times 10^{-3} \text{ s}^{-1}.$$

Then, at $t = 0$ (Eq. 41–7b),

$$\left|\frac{dN}{dt}\right|_0 = \lambda N_0 = (1.155 \times 10^{-3} \text{ s}^{-1})(6.90 \times 10^{16}) = 7.97 \times 10^{13} \text{ decays/s}.$$

(c) After $1.00 \text{ h} = 3600 \text{ s}$, the magnitude of the activity will be (Eq. 41–7c)

$$\left|\frac{dN}{dt}\right| = \left|\frac{dN}{dt}\right|_0 e^{-\lambda t} = (7.97 \times 10^{13} \text{ s}^{-1})e^{-(1.155\times10^{-3} \text{ s}^{-1})(3600 \text{ s})} = 1.25 \times 10^{12} \text{ s}^{-1}.$$

(d) We want to determine the time t when $|dN/dt| = 1.00 \text{ s}^{-1}$. From Eq. 41–7c, we have

$$e^{-\lambda t} = \frac{|dN/dt|}{|dN/dt|_0} = \frac{1.00 \text{ s}^{-1}}{7.97 \times 10^{13} \text{ s}^{-1}} = 1.25 \times 10^{-14}.$$

We take the natural log (ln) of both sides $(\ln e^{-\lambda t} = -\lambda t)$ and divide by λ to find

$$t = -\frac{\ln(1.25 \times 10^{-14})}{\lambda} = 2.77 \times 10^4 \, \text{s} = 7.70 \, \text{h}.$$

Easy Alternate Solution to (c) 1.00 h = 60.0 minutes is 6 half-lives, so the activity will decrease to $\left(\frac{1}{2}\right)\left(\frac{1}{2}\right)\left(\frac{1}{2}\right)\left(\frac{1}{2}\right)\left(\frac{1}{2}\right)\left(\frac{1}{2}\right) = \left(\frac{1}{2}\right)^6 = \frac{1}{64}$ of its original value, or $(7.97 \times 10^{13})/(64) = 1.25 \times 10^{12}$ per second.

EXERCISE G Technicium $^{98}_{43}$Tc has a half-life of 4.2×10^6 yr. Strontium $^{90}_{38}$Sr has a half-life of 28.79 yr. Which statements are true?
(*a*) The decay constant of Sr is greater than the decay constant of Tc.
(*b*) The activity of 100 g of Sr is less than the activity of 100 g of Tc.
(*c*) The long half-life of Tc means that it decays by alpha decay.
(*d*) A Tc atom has a higher probability of decaying in 1 yr than a Sr atom.
(*e*) 28.79 g of Sr has the same activity as 4.2×10^6 g of Tc.

41–9 Decay Series

It is often the case that one radioactive isotope decays to another isotope that is also radioactive. Sometimes this daughter decays to yet a third isotope which also is radioactive. Such successive decays are said to form a **decay series**. An important example is illustrated in Fig. 41–12. As can be seen, $^{238}_{92}$U decays by α emission to $^{234}_{90}$Th, which in turn decays by β decay to $^{234}_{91}$Pa. The series continues as shown, with several possible branches near the bottom, ending at the stable lead isotope, $^{206}_{82}$Pb. The two last decays can be

$$^{206}_{81}\text{Tl} \rightarrow \, ^{206}_{82}\text{Pb} + e^- + \bar{\nu}, \qquad (T_{\frac{1}{2}} = 4.2 \, \text{min})$$

or

$$^{210}_{84}\text{Po} \rightarrow \, ^{206}_{82}\text{Pb} + \alpha. \qquad (T_{\frac{1}{2}} = 138 \, \text{days})$$

Other radioactive series also exist.

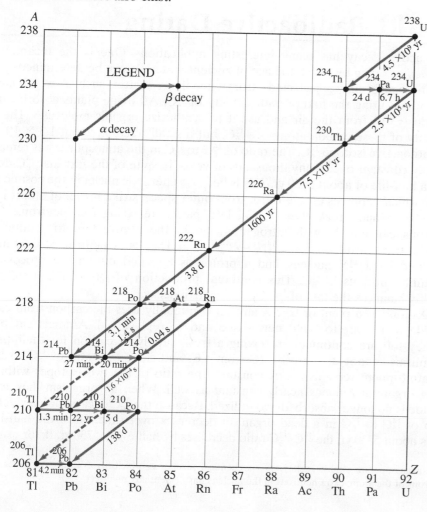

FIGURE 41–12 Decay series beginning with $^{238}_{92}$U. Nuclei in the series are specified by a dot representing A and Z values. Half-lives are given in seconds (s), minutes (min), hours (h), days (d), or years (yr). Note that a horizontal arrow represents β decay (A does not change), whereas a diagonal line represents α decay (A changes by 4, Z changes by 2). For the four nuclides shown that can decay by both α and β decay, the more prominent decay (in these four cases, > 99.9%) is shown as a solid arrow and the less common decay (< 0.1%) as a dashed arrow.

Because of such decay series, certain radioactive elements are found in nature that otherwise would not be. When the solar system (including Earth) was formed about 5 billion years ago, it is believed that nearly all nuclides were present, having been formed (by fusion and neutron capture, Sections 42–4 and 44–2) in a nearby supernova explosion (Section 44–2). Many isotopes with short half-lives decayed quickly and no longer are detected in nature today. But long-lived isotopes, such as $^{238}_{92}U$ with a half-life of 4.5×10^9 yr, still do exist in nature today. Indeed, about half of the original $^{238}_{92}U$ still remains. We might expect, however, that radium $\left(^{226}_{88}Ra\right)$, with a half-life of 1600 yr, would long since have disappeared from the Earth. Indeed, the original $^{226}_{88}Ra$ nuclei must by now have all decayed. However, because $^{238}_{92}U$ decays (in several steps) to $^{226}_{88}Ra$, the supply of $^{226}_{88}Ra$ is continually replenished, which is why it is still found on Earth today. The same can be said for many other radioactive nuclides.

CONCEPTUAL EXAMPLE 41–11 **Decay chain.** In the decay chain of Fig. 41–12, if we start looking below $^{234}_{92}U$, we see four successive nuclides with half-lives of 250,000 yr, 75,000 yr, 1600 yr, and a little under 4 days. Each decay in the chain has an alpha particle of a characteristic energy, and so we can monitor the radioactive decay rate of each nuclide. Given a sample that was pure $^{234}_{92}U$ a million years ago, which alpha decay would you expect to have the highest activity in the sample?

RESPONSE The first instinct is to say that the process with the shortest half-life would show the highest activity. Surprisingly, perhaps, the activities of the four nuclides in this sample are all the same. The reason is that in each case the decay of the parent acts as a bottleneck to the decay of the daughter. Compared to the 1600-yr half-life of $^{226}_{88}Ra$, for example, its daughter $^{222}_{86}Rn$ decays almost immediately, but it cannot decay until it is made. (This is like an automobile assembly line: if worker A takes 20 minutes to do a task and then worker B takes only 1 minute to do the next task, worker B still does only one car every 20 minutes.)

41–10 Radioactive Dating

Radioactive decay has many interesting applications. One is the technique of *radioactive dating* by which the age of ancient materials can be determined.

The age of any object made from once-living matter, such as wood, can be determined using the natural radioactivity of $^{14}_6C$. All living plants absorb carbon dioxide (CO_2) from the air and use it to synthesize organic molecules. The vast majority of these carbon atoms are $^{12}_6C$, but a small fraction, about 1.3×10^{-12}, is the radioactive isotope $^{14}_6C$. The ratio of $^{14}_6C$ to $^{12}_6C$ in the atmosphere has remained roughly constant over many thousands of years, in spite of the fact that $^{14}_6C$ decays with a half-life of about 5730 yr. This is because energetic nuclei in the cosmic radiation, which impinges on the Earth from outer space, strike nuclei of atoms in the atmosphere and break those nuclei into pieces, releasing free neutrons. Those neutrons can collide with nitrogen nuclei in the atmosphere to produce the nuclear transformation $n + {}^{14}_7N \rightarrow {}^{14}_6C + p$. That is, a neutron strikes and is absorbed by a $^{14}_7N$ nucleus, and a proton is knocked out in the process. The remaining nucleus is $^{14}_6C$. This continual production of $^{14}_6C$ in the atmosphere roughly balances the loss of $^{14}_6C$ by radioactive decay.

As long as a plant or tree is alive, it continually uses the carbon from carbon dioxide in the air to build new tissue and to replace old. Animals eat plants, so they too are continually receiving a fresh supply of carbon for their tissues. Organisms cannot distinguish[†] $^{14}_6C$ from $^{12}_6C$, and since the ratio of $^{14}_6C$ to $^{12}_6C$ in the atmosphere remains nearly constant, the ratio of the two isotopes within the living organism remains nearly constant as well. When an organism dies, carbon dioxide is no longer absorbed and utilized. Because the $^{14}_6C$ decays radioactively, the ratio of $^{14}_6C$ to $^{12}_6C$ in a dead organism decreases over time. Since the half-life of $^{14}_6C$ is about 5730 yr, the $^{14}_6C/^{12}_6C$ ratio decreases by half every 5730 yr. If, for example,

---

[†]Organisms operate almost exclusively via chemical reactions—which involve only the outer orbital electrons of the atom; extra neutrons in the nucleus have essentially no effect.

the $^{14}_{6}C/^{12}_{6}C$ ratio of an ancient wooden tool is half of what it is in living trees, then the object must have been made from a tree that was felled about 5730 years ago.

Actually, corrections must be made for the fact that the $^{14}_{6}C/^{12}_{6}C$ ratio in the atmosphere has not remained precisely constant over time. The determination of what this ratio has been over the centuries has required techniques such as comparing the expected ratio to the actual ratio for objects whose age is known, such as very old trees whose annual rings can be counted reasonably accurately.

EXAMPLE 41–12 **An ancient animal.** The mass of carbon in an animal bone fragment found in an archeological site is 200 g. If the bone registers an activity of 16 decays/s, what is its age?

PHYSICS APPLIED
Archeological dating

APPROACH First we determine how many $^{14}_{6}C$ atoms there were in our 200-g sample when the animal was alive, given the known fraction of $^{14}_{6}C$, 1.3×10^{-12}. Then we use Eq. 41–7b to find the activity back then, and Eq. 41–7c to find out how long ago that was by solving for the time t.

SOLUTION The 200 g of carbon is nearly all $^{12}_{6}C$; 12.0 g of $^{12}_{6}C$ contains 6.02×10^{23} atoms, so 200 g contains

$$\left(\frac{6.02 \times 10^{23} \text{ atoms/mol}}{12 \text{ g/mol}} \right)(200 \text{ g}) = 1.00 \times 10^{25} \text{ atoms.}$$

When the animal was alive, the ratio of $^{14}_{6}C$ to $^{12}_{6}C$ in the bone was 1.3×10^{-12}. The number of $^{14}_{6}C$ nuclei at that time was

$$N_0 = (1.00 \times 10^{25} \text{ atoms})(1.3 \times 10^{-12}) = 1.3 \times 10^{13} \text{ atoms.}$$

From Eq. 41–7b, with $\lambda = 3.83 \times 10^{-12} \text{ s}^{-1}$ for $^{14}_{6}C$ (Example 41–8), the magnitude of the activity when the animal was still alive ($t = 0$) was

$$\left| \frac{dN}{dt} \right|_0 = \lambda N_0 = (3.83 \times 10^{-12} \text{ s}^{-1})(1.3 \times 10^{13}) = 50 \text{ s}^{-1}.$$

From Eq. 41–7c,

$$\left| \frac{dN}{dt} \right| = \left| \frac{dN}{dt} \right|_0 e^{-\lambda t},$$

where $|dN/dt|$ is given as 16 s^{-1}. Then

$$e^{\lambda t} = \frac{|dN/dt|_0}{|dN/dt|} = \frac{50 \text{ s}^{-1}}{16 \text{ s}^{-1}}.$$

We take the natural log (ln) of both sides (and divide by λ) to get

$$t = \frac{1}{\lambda} \ln \left[\frac{|dN/dt|_0}{|dN/dt|} \right] = \frac{1}{3.83 \times 10^{-12} \text{ s}^{-1}} \ln \left[\frac{50 \text{ s}^{-1}}{16 \text{ s}^{-1}} \right]$$

$$= 2.98 \times 10^{11} \text{ s} = 9400 \text{ yr,}$$

which is the time elapsed since the death of the animal.

Geological Time Scale Dating

Carbon dating is useful only for determining the age of objects less than about 60,000 years old. The amount of $^{14}_{6}C$ remaining in objects older than that is usually too small to measure accurately, although new techniques are allowing detection of even smaller amounts of $^{14}_{6}C$, pushing the time frame further back. On the other hand, radioactive isotopes with longer half-lives can be used in certain circumstances to obtain the age of older objects. For example, the decay of $^{238}_{92}U$, because of its long half-life of 4.5×10^9 years, is useful in determining the ages of rocks on a geologic time scale. When molten material on Earth long ago solidified into rock as the temperature dropped, different compounds solidified according to the melting points, and thus different compounds separated to some extent. Uranium

PHYSICS APPLIED
Geological dating

present in a material became fixed in position and the daughter nuclei that result from the decay of uranium were also fixed in that position. Thus, by measuring the amount of $^{238}_{92}$U remaining in the material relative to the amount of daughter nuclei, the time when the rock solidified can be determined.

Radioactive dating methods using $^{238}_{92}$U and other isotopes have shown the age of the oldest Earth rocks to be about 4×10^9 yr. The age of rocks in which the oldest fossilized organisms are embedded indicates that life appeared more than $3\frac{1}{2}$ billion years ago. The earliest fossilized remains of mammals are found in rocks 200 million years old, and humanlike creatures seem to have appeared about 2 million years ago. Radioactive dating has been indispensable for the reconstruction of Earth's history.

PHYSICS APPLIED
Oldest Earth rocks and earliest life

FIGURE 41–13 Diagram of a Geiger counter.

41–11 Detection of Radiation

Individual particles such as electrons, protons, α particles, neutrons, and γ rays are not detected directly by our senses. Consequently, a variety of instruments have been developed to detect them.

Counters

One of the most common is the **Geiger counter**. As shown in Fig. 41–13, it consists of a cylindrical metal tube filled with a certain type of gas. A long wire runs down the center and is kept at a high positive voltage ($\approx 10^3$ V) with respect to the outer cylinder. The voltage is just slightly less than that required to ionize the gas atoms. When a charged particle enters through the thin "window" at one end of the tube, it ionizes a few atoms of the gas. The freed electrons are attracted toward the positive wire, and as they are accelerated they strike and ionize additional atoms. An "avalanche" of electrons is quickly produced, and when it reaches the wire anode, it produces a voltage pulse. The pulse, after being amplified, can be sent to an electronic counter, which counts how many particles have been detected. Or the pulses can be sent to a loudspeaker and each detection of a particle is heard as a "click." Only a fraction of the radiation emitted by a sample is detected by any detector.

A **scintillation counter** makes use of a solid, liquid, or gas known as a **scintillator** or **phosphor**. The atoms of a scintillator are easily excited when struck by an incoming particle and emit visible light when they return to their ground states. Typical scintillators are crystals of NaI and certain plastics. One face of a solid scintillator is cemented to a photomultiplier tube, and the whole is wrapped with opaque material to keep it light-tight (in the dark) or is placed within a light-tight container. The **photomultiplier** (PM) **tube** converts the energy of the scintillator-emitted photon(s) into an electric signal. A PM tube is a vacuum tube containing several electrodes (typically 8 to 14), called *dynodes*, which are maintained at successively higher voltages as shown in Fig. 41–14. At its top surface is a photoelectric surface, called the *photocathode*, whose work function (Section 37–2) is low enough that an electron is easily released when struck by a photon from the scintillator. Such an electron is accelerated toward the positive voltage of the first dynode. When it strikes the first dynode, the electron has acquired sufficient kinetic energy so that it can eject two to five more electrons. These, in turn, are accelerated toward the higher voltage second dynode, and a multiplication process begins. The number of electrons striking the last dynode may be 10^6 or more. Thus the passage of a particle through the scintillator results in an electric signal at the output of the PM tube that can be sent to an electronic counter just as for a Geiger tube. Solid scintillators are much more dense than the gas of a Geiger counter, and so are much more efficient detectors—especially for γ rays, which interact less with matter than do α or β particles. Scintillators that can measure the total energy deposited are much used today and are called **calorimeters**.

FIGURE 41–14 Scintillation counter with a photomultiplier tube.

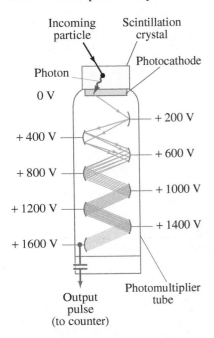

In tracer work (Section 42–8), **liquid scintillators** are often used. Radioactive samples taken at different times or from different parts of an organism are placed directly in small bottles containing the liquid scintillator. This is particularly convenient for detection of β rays from ^3_1H and $^{14}_6C$, which have very low energies and have difficulty passing through the outer covering of a crystal scintillator or Geiger tube. A PM tube is still used to produce the electric signal from the liquid scintillator.

A **semiconductor detector** consists of a reverse-biased pn junction diode (Sections 40–8 and 40–9). A particle passing through the junction can excite electrons into the conduction band, leaving holes in the valence band. The freed charges produce a short electrical pulse that can be counted just as for Geiger and scintillation counters.

Hospital workers and others who work around radiation may carry *film badges* which detect the accumulation of radiation exposure. The film inside is periodically replaced and developed, the darkness being related to total exposure (see Section 42–6).

Visualization

The devices discussed so far are used for counting the number of particles (or decays of a radioactive isotope). There are also devices that allow the track of charged particles to be *seen*. Very important are semiconductor detectors. **Silicon wafer semiconductors** have their surface etched into separate tiny pixels, each providing particle position information. They are much used in elementary particle physics (Chapter 43) to track the positions of particles produced and to determine their point of origin and/or their momentum (with the help of a magnetic field). The pixel arrangement can be CCD or CMOS (Section 33–5), the latter able to incorporate electronics inside, allowing fast readout.

One of the oldest tracking devices is the **photographic emulsion**, which can be small and portable, used now particularly for cosmic-ray studies from balloons. A charged particle passing through an emulsion ionizes the atoms along its path. These points undergo a chemical change, and when the emulsion is developed (like film) the particle's path is revealed.

In a **cloud chamber**, used in the early days of nuclear physics, a gas is cooled to a temperature slightly below its usual condensation point ("supercooled"), and gas molecules condense on any ionized molecules present. Tiny droplets form around ions produced when a charged particle passes through (Fig. 41–15). Light scattering from these droplets reveals the track of the particle.

The **bubble chamber**, invented in 1952 by D. A. Glaser (1926–   ), makes use of a superheated liquid kept close to its normal boiling point. Bubbles characteristic of boiling form around ions produced by the passage of a charged particle, revealing paths of particles that recently passed through. Because a bubble chamber uses a liquid, often liquid hydrogen, many more interactions can occur than in a cloud chamber. A magnetic field is usually applied across the chamber so the momentum of the moving particles can be determined from the radius of curvature of their paths.

A **wire drift chamber** consists of a set of closely spaced fine wires immersed in a gas (Fig. 41–16). Many wires are grounded, and the others between are kept at very high voltage. A charged particle passing through produces ions in the gas. Freed electrons drift toward the nearest high voltage wire, creating an "avalanche" of many more ions, and producing an electric pulse or signal at that wire. The positions of the particles are determined electronically by the position of the wire and by the time it takes the pulses to reach "readout" electronics at the ends of the wires. The paths of the particles are reconstructed electronically by computers which can "draw" a picture of the tracks, as shown in the photo at the start of Chapter 43. An external magnetic field curves the paths, allowing the momentum of the particles to be measured.

In many detectors, the energy of the particles can be measured by the strength of the electronic signal; such detectors are referred to as **calorimeters**, as already mentioned.

FIGURE 41–15 In a cloud chamber or bubble chamber, droplets or bubbles are formed around ions produced by the passage of a charged particle.

FIGURE 41–16 Wire-drift chamber inside the Collider Detector at Fermilab (CDF). The photo at the start of Chapter 43 (page 1164) was done with this detector.

Summary

Nuclear physics is the study of atomic nuclei. Nuclei contain **protons** and **neutrons**, which are collectively known as **nucleons**. The total number of nucleons, A, is the nucleus's **atomic mass number**. The number of protons, Z, is the **atomic number**. The number of neutrons equals $A - Z$. **Isotopes** are nuclei with the same Z, but with different numbers of neutrons. For an element X, an isotope of given Z and A is represented by

$$\_Z^A X.$$

The nuclear radius is approximately proportional to $A^{\frac{1}{3}}$, indicating that all nuclei have about the same density. Nuclear masses are specified in **unified atomic mass units** (u), where the mass of $^{12}_6C$ (including its 6 electrons) is defined as exactly 12.000000 u. In terms of the energy equivalent (because $E = mc^2$),

$$1\,u = 931.5\,\text{MeV}/c^2 = 1.66 \times 10^{-27}\,\text{kg}.$$

The mass of a stable nucleus is less than the sum of the masses of its constituent nucleons. The difference in mass (times c^2) is the **total binding energy**. It represents the energy needed to break the nucleus into its constituent nucleons. The **binding energy per nucleon** averages about 8 MeV per nucleon, and is lowest for low mass and high mass nuclei.

Unstable nuclei undergo **radioactive decay**; they change into other nuclei with the emission of an α, β, or γ particle. An α particle is a $^4_2$He nucleus; a β particle is an electron or positron; and a γ ray is a high-energy photon. In β decay, a **neutrino** is also emitted. The transformation of the **parent** into the **daughter** nucleus is called **transmutation** of the elements. Radioactive decay occurs spontaneously only when the mass of the products is less than the mass of the parent nucleus. The loss in mass appears as kinetic energy of the products.

Alpha decay occurs via the purely quantum mechanical process of **tunneling** through a barrier.

Nuclei are held together by the **strong nuclear force**. The **weak nuclear force** makes itself apparent in β decay. These two forces, plus the gravitational and electromagnetic forces, are the four known types of force.

Electric charge, linear and angular momentum, mass–energy, and **nucleon number** are **conserved** in all decays.

Radioactive decay is a statistical process. For a given type of radioactive nucleus, the number of nuclei that decay (ΔN) in a time Δt is proportional to the number N of parent nuclei present:

$$\Delta N = -\lambda N\,\Delta t; \qquad \textbf{(41–4a)}$$

the minus sign means N *decreases* in time.

The proportionality constant λ is called the **decay constant** and is characteristic of the given nucleus. The number N of nuclei remaining after a time t decreases exponentially

$$N = N_0 e^{-\lambda t}, \qquad \textbf{(41–6)}$$

as does the **activity**, $R = |dN/dt|$:

$$\left|\frac{dN}{dt}\right| = \left|\frac{dN}{dt}\right|_0 e^{-\lambda t}. \qquad \textbf{(41–7c)}$$

The **half-life**, $T_{\frac{1}{2}}$, is the time required for half the nuclei of a radioactive sample to decay. It is related to the decay constant by

$$T_{\frac{1}{2}} = \frac{0.693}{\lambda}. \qquad \textbf{(41–8)}$$

Radioactive decay can be used to determine the age of certain objects, such as once-living biological material ($^{14}_6$C) or geological formations ($^{238}_{92}$U).

Particle **detectors** include **Geiger counters**, **scintillators** with attached **photomultiplier tubes**, and **semiconductor detectors**. Detectors that can image particle tracks include **semiconductors**, photographic **emulsions**, **bubble chambers**, and **wire drift chambers**.

Questions

1. What do different isotopes of a given element have in common? How are they different?

2. What are the elements represented by the X in the following: (a) $^{232}_{92}$X; (b) $^{18}_7$X; (c) $^1_1$X; (d) $^{82}_{38}$X; (e) $^{247}_{97}$X?

3. How many protons and how many neutrons do each of the isotopes in Question 2 have?

4. Identify the element that has 88 nucleons and 50 neutrons.

5. Why are the atomic masses of many elements (see the Periodic Table) not close to whole numbers?

6. How do we know there is such a thing as the strong nuclear force?

7. What are the similarities and the differences between the strong nuclear force and the electric force?

8. What is the experimental evidence in favor of radioactivity being a nuclear process?

9. The isotope $^{64}_{29}$Cu is unusual in that it can decay by γ, β^-, and β^+ emission. What is the resulting nuclide for each case?

10. A $^{238}_{92}$U nucleus decays via α decay to a nucleus containing how many neutrons?

11. Describe, in as many ways as you can, the difference between α, β, and γ rays.

12. What element is formed by the radioactive decay of (a) $^{24}_{11}$Na (β^-); (b) $^{22}_{11}$Na (β^+); (c) $^{210}_{84}$Po (α)?

13. What element is formed by the decay of (a) $^{32}_{15}$P (β^-); (b) $^{35}_{16}$S (β^-); (c) $^{211}_{83}$Bi (α)?

14. Fill in the missing particle or nucleus:
    (a) $^{45}_{20}$Ca $\rightarrow$? $+ e^- + \bar{\nu}$
    (b) $^{58}_{29}$Cu* $\rightarrow$? $+ \gamma$
    (c) $^{46}_{24}$Cr $\rightarrow$ $^{46}_{23}$V $+$?
    (d) $^{234}_{94}$Pu $\rightarrow$? $+ \alpha$
    (e) $^{239}_{93}$Np $\rightarrow$ $^{239}_{94}$Pu $+$?

15. Immediately after a $^{238}_{92}$U nucleus decays to $^{234}_{90}$Th $+ {}^4_2$He, the daughter thorium nucleus may still have 92 electrons circling it. Since thorium normally holds only 90 electrons, what do you suppose happens to the two extra ones?

16. When a nucleus undergoes either β^- or β^+ decay, what happens to the energy levels of the atomic electrons? What is likely to happen to these electrons following the decay?

17. The alpha particles from a given alpha-emitting nuclide are generally monoenergetic; that is, they all have the same kinetic energy. But the beta particles from a beta-emitting nuclide have a spectrum of energies. Explain the difference between these two cases.

18. Do isotopes that undergo electron capture generally lie above or below the stable nuclides in Fig. 41–2?

19. Can hydrogen or deuterium emit an α particle? Explain.

20. Why are many artificially produced radioactive isotopes rare in nature?

21. An isotope has a half-life of one month. After two months, will a given sample of this isotope have completely decayed? If not, how much remains?

22. Why are none of the elements with $Z > 92$ stable?

23. A proton strikes a $^6_3$Li nucleus. As a result, an α particle and another particle are released. What is the other particle?

24. Can $^{14}_6$C dating be used to measure the age of stone walls and tablets of ancient civilizations? Explain.

25. In both internal conversion and β decay, an electron is emitted. How could you determine which decay process occurred?

26. Describe how the potential energy curve for an α particle in an α-emitting nucleus differs from that for a stable nucleus.

27. Explain the absence of β^+ emitters in the radioactive decay series of Fig. 41–12.

28. As $^{222}_{86}$Rn decays into $^{206}_{82}$Pb, how many alpha and beta particles are emitted? Does it matter which path in the decay series is chosen? Why or why not?

Problems

41–1 Nuclear Properties

1. (I) A pi meson has a mass of 139 MeV/c^2. What is this in atomic mass units?

2. (I) What is the approximate radius of an alpha particle ($^4_2$He)?

3. (I) By what % is the radius of $^{238}_{92}$U greater than the radius of $^{232}_{92}$U?

4. (II) (a) What is the approximate radius of a $^{112}_{48}$Cd nucleus? (b) Approximately what is the value of A for a nucleus whose radius is 3.7×10^{-15} m?

5. (II) What is the mass of a bare α particle (without electrons) in MeV/c^2?

6. (II) Suppose two alpha particles were held together so they were just touching. Estimate the electrostatic repulsive force each would exert on the other. What would be the acceleration of an alpha particle subjected to this force?

7. (II) (a) Show that the density of nuclear matter is essentially the same for all nuclei. (b) What would be the radius of the Earth if it had its actual mass but had the density of nuclei? (c) What would be the radius of a $^{238}_{92}$U nucleus if it had the density of the Earth?

8. (II) What stable nucleus has approximately half the radius of a uranium nucleus? [Hint: Find A and use Appendix F to get Z.]

9. (II) If an alpha particle were released from rest near the surface of a $^{257}_{100}$Fm nucleus, what would its kinetic energy be when far away?

10. (II) (a) What is the fraction of the hydrogen atom's mass that is in the nucleus? (b) What is the fraction of the hydrogen atom's volume that is occupied by the nucleus?

11. (II) Approximately how many nucleons are there in a 1.0-kg object? Does it matter what the object is made of? Why or why not?

12. (II) How much kinetic energy must an α particle have to just "touch" the surface of a $^{238}_{92}$U nucleus?

41–2 Binding Energy

13. (I) Estimate the total binding energy for $^{63}_{29}$Cu, using Fig. 41–1.

14. (II) Use Appendix F to calculate the binding energy of $^2_1$H (deuterium).

15. (II) Determine the binding energy of the last neutron in a $^{32}_{15}$P nucleus.

16. (II) Calculate the total binding energy, and the binding energy per nucleon, for (a) $^7_3$Li, (b) $^{197}_{79}$Au. Use Appendix F.

17. (II) Compare the average binding energy of a nucleon in $^{23}_{11}$Na to that in $^{24}_{11}$Na.

18. (III) How much energy is required to remove (a) a proton, (b) a neutron, from $^{15}_7$N? Explain the difference in your answers.

19. (III) (a) Show that the nucleus $^8_4$Be (mass = 8.005305 u) is unstable and will decay into two α particles. (b) Is $^{12}_6$C stable against decay into three α particles? Show why or why not.

41–3 to 41–7 Radioactive Decay

20. (I) How much energy is released when tritium, $^3_1$H, decays by β^- emission?

21. (I) What is the maximum kinetic energy of an electron emitted in the β decay of a free neutron?

22. (I) Show that the decay $^{11}_6$C $\rightarrow$ $^{10}_5$B + p is not possible because energy would not be conserved.

23. (I) The $^7_3$Li nucleus has an excited state 0.48 MeV above the ground state. What wavelength gamma photon is emitted when the nucleus decays from the excited state to the ground state?

24. (II) Give the result of a calculation that shows whether or not the following decays are possible:
    (a) $^{233}_{92}$U $\rightarrow$ $^{232}_{92}$U + n;
    (b) $^{14}_7$N $\rightarrow$ $^{13}_7$N + n;
    (c) $^{40}_{19}$K $\rightarrow$ $^{39}_{19}$K + n.

25. (II) $^{24}_{11}$Na is radioactive. (a) Is it a β^- or β^+ emitter? (b) Write down the decay reaction, and estimate the maximum kinetic energy of the emitted β.

26. (II) When $^{23}_{10}$Ne (mass = 22.9945 u) decays to $^{23}_{11}$Na (mass = 22.9898 u), what is the maximum kinetic energy of the emitted electron? What is its minimum energy? What is the energy of the neutrino in each case? Ignore recoil of the daughter nucleus.

27. (II) A $^{238}_{92}$U nucleus emits an α particle with kinetic energy = 4.20 MeV. (a) What is the daughter nucleus, and (b) what is the approximate atomic mass (in u) of the daughter atom? Ignore recoil of the daughter nucleus.

28. (II) What is the maximum kinetic energy of the emitted β particle during the decay of $^{60}_{27}$Co?

29. (II) A nucleus of mass 256 u, initially at rest, emits an α particle with a kinetic energy of 5.0 MeV. What is the kinetic energy of the recoiling daughter nucleus?

30. (II) The isotope $^{218}_{84}$Po can decay by either α or β^- emission. What is the energy release in each case? The mass of $^{218}_{84}$Po is 218.008965 u.

31. (II) The nuclide $^{32}_{15}$P decays by emitting an electron whose maximum kinetic energy can be 1.71 MeV. (a) What is the daughter nucleus? (b) Calculate the daughter's atomic mass (in u).

32. (II) A photon with a wavelength of 1.00×10^{-13} m is ejected from an atom. Calculate its energy and explain why it is a γ ray from the nucleus or a photon from the atom.

33. (II) How much energy is released in electron capture by beryllium: $^7_4$Be + e$^- \rightarrow ^7_3$Li + ν?

34. (II) How much recoil energy does a $^{40}_{19}$K nucleus get when it emits a 1.46-MeV gamma ray?

35. (II) Determine the maximum kinetic energy of β^+ particles released when $^{11}_6$C decays to $^{11}_5$B. What is the maximum energy the neutrino can have? What is the minimum energy of each?

36. (III) The α particle emitted when $^{238}_{92}$U decays has 4.20 MeV of kinetic energy. Calculate the recoil kinetic energy of the daughter nucleus and the Q-value of the decay.

37. (III) What is the energy of the α particle emitted in the decay $^{210}_{84}$Po $\rightarrow$ $^{206}_{82}$Pb + α? Take into account the recoil of the daughter nucleus.

38. (III) Show that when a nucleus decays by β^+ decay, the total energy released is equal to

$$(M_P - M_D - 2m_e)c^2,$$

where M_P and M_D are the masses of the parent and daughter atoms (neutral), and m_e is the mass of an electron or positron.

41–8 to 41–10 Half-Life, Decay Rates, Decay Series, Dating

39. (I) (a) What is the decay constant of $^{238}_{92}$U whose half-life is 4.5×10^9 yr? (b) The decay constant of a given nucleus is 3.2×10^{-5} s^{-1}. What is its half-life?

40. (I) A radioactive material produces 1280 decays per minute at one time, and 3.6 h later produces 320 decays per minute. What is its half-life?

41. (I) What fraction of a sample of $^{68}_{32}$Ge, whose half-life is about 9 months, will remain after 2.0 yr?

42. (I) What is the activity of a sample of $^{14}_6$C that contains 8.1×10^{20} nuclei?

43. (I) What fraction of a sample is left after exactly 6 half-lives?

44. (II) A sample of $^{60}_{27}$Co and a sample of $^{131}_{53}$I both have N_0 atoms at $t = 0$. How long will it take until both have the same activity? (Use Appendix F for half-life data.)

45. (II) How many nuclei of $^{238}_{92}$U remain in a rock if the activity registers 340 decays per second?

46. (II) In a series of decays, the nuclide $^{235}_{92}$U becomes $^{207}_{82}$Pb. How many α and β^- particles are emitted in this series?

47. (II) The iodine isotope $^{131}_{53}$I is used in hospitals for diagnosis of thyroid function. If 782 μg are ingested by a patient, determine the activity (a) immediately, (b) 1.00 h later when the thyroid is being tested, and (c) 4.0 months later. Use Appendix F.

48. (II) $^{124}_{55}$Cs has a half-life of 30.8 s. (a) If we have 7.8 μg initially, how many Cs nuclei are present? (b) How many are present 2.6 min later? (c) What is the activity at this time? (d) After how much time will the activity drop to less than about 1 per second?

49. (II) Calculate the mass of a sample of pure $^{40}_{19}$K with an initial decay rate of 2.0×10^5 s^{-1}. The half-life of $^{40}_{19}$K is 1.265×10^9 yr.

50. (II) Calculate the activity of a pure 8.7-μg sample of $^{32}_{15}$P $(T_{\frac{1}{2}} = 1.23 \times 10^6$ s).

51. (II) The activity of a sample of $^{35}_{16}$S $(T_{\frac{1}{2}} = 87.32$ days) is 3.65×10^4 decays per second. What is the mass of the sample?

52. (II) A sample of $^{233}_{92}$U $(T_{\frac{1}{2}} = 1.59 \times 10^5$ yr) contains 5.50×10^{18} nuclei. (a) What is the decay constant? (b) Approximately how many disintegrations will occur per minute?

53. (II) The activity of a sample drops by a factor of 4.0 in 8.6 minutes. What is its half-life?

54. (II) A 385-g sample of pure carbon contains 1.3 parts in 10^{12} (atoms) of $^{14}_6$C. How many disintegrations occur per second?

55. (II) A sample of $^{238}_{92}$U is decaying at a rate of 3.70×10^2 decays/s. What is the mass of the sample?

56. (II) **Rubidium–strontium dating.** The rubidium isotope $^{87}_{37}$Rb, a β emitter with a half-life of 4.75×10^{10} yr, is used to determine the age of rocks and fossils. Rocks containing fossils of ancient animals contain a ratio of $^{87}_{38}$Sr to $^{87}_{37}$Rb of 0.0260. Assuming that there was no $^{87}_{38}$Sr present when the rocks were formed, estimate the age of these fossils.

57. (II) The activity of a radioactive source decreases by 2.5% in 31.0 hours. What is the half-life of this source?

58. (II) $^7_4$Be decays with a half-life of about 53 d. It is produced in the upper atmosphere, and filters down onto the Earth's surface. If a plant leaf is detected to have 350 decays/s of $^7_4$Be, (a) how long do we have to wait for the decay rate to drop to 15 per second? (b) Estimate the initial mass of $^7_4$Be on the leaf.

59. (II) Two of the naturally occurring radioactive decay sequences start with $^{232}_{90}$Th and with $^{235}_{92}$U. The first five decays of these two sequences are:

$$\alpha, \beta, \beta, \alpha, \alpha$$

and

$$\alpha, \beta, \alpha, \beta, \alpha.$$

Determine the resulting intermediate daughter nuclei in each case.

60. (II) An ancient wooden club is found that contains 85 g of carbon and has an activity of 7.0 decays per second. Determine its age assuming that in living trees the ratio of ^{14}C/^{12}C atoms is about 1.3×10^{-12}.

61. (III) At $t = 0$, a pure sample of radioactive nuclei contains N_0 nuclei whose decay constant is λ. Determine a formula for the number of daughter nuclei, N_D, as a function of time; assume the daughter is stable and that $N_D = 0$ at $t = 0$.

General Problems

62. Which radioactive isotope of lead is being produced if the measured activity of a sample drops to 1.050% of its original activity in 4.00 h?

63. An old wooden tool is found to contain only 6.0% of the $^{14}_{6}C$ that an equal mass of fresh wood would. How old is the tool?

64. A neutron star consists of neutrons at approximately nuclear density. Estimate, for a 10-km-diameter neutron star, (a) its mass number, (b) its mass (kg), and (c) the acceleration of gravity at its surface.

65. **Tritium dating**. The $^{3}_{1}H$ isotope of hydrogen, which is called *tritium* (because it contains three nucleons), has a half-life of 12.3 yr. It can be used to measure the age of objects up to about 100 yr. It is produced in the upper atmosphere by cosmic rays and brought to Earth by rain. As an application, determine approximately the age of a bottle of wine whose $^{3}_{1}H$ radiation is about $\frac{1}{10}$ that present in new wine.

66. Some elementary particle theories (Section 43–11) suggest that the proton may be unstable, with a half-life $\geq 10^{33}$ yr. How long would you expect to wait for one proton in your body to decay (approximate your body as all water)?

67. Show, using the decays given in Section 41–5, that the neutrino has either spin $\frac{1}{2}$ or $\frac{3}{2}$.

68. The original experiments which established that an atom has a heavy, positive nucleus were done by shooting alpha particles through gold foil. The alpha particles used had a kinetic energy of 7.7 MeV. What is the closest they could get to a gold nucleus? How does this compare with the size of the nucleus?

69. How long must you wait (in half-lives) for a radioactive sample to drop to 1.00% of its original activity?

70. If the potassium isotope $^{40}_{19}K$ gives 45 decays/s in a liter of milk, estimate how much $^{40}_{19}K$ and regular $^{39}_{19}K$ are in a liter of milk. Use Appendix F.

71. (a) In α decay of, say, a $^{226}_{88}Ra$ nucleus, show that the nucleus carries away a fraction $1/(1 + \frac{1}{4}A_D)$ of the total energy available, where A_D is the mass number of the daughter nucleus. [*Hint*: Use conservation of momentum as well as conservation of energy.] (b) Approximately what percentage of the energy available is thus carried off by the α particle when $^{226}_{88}Ra$ decays?

72. Strontium-90 is produced as a nuclear fission product of uranium in both reactors and atomic bombs. Look at its location in the Periodic Table to see what other elements it might be similar to chemically, and tell why you think it might be dangerous to ingest. It has too many neutrons, and it decays with a half-life of about 29 yr. How long will we have to wait for the amount of $^{90}_{38}Sr$ on the Earth's surface to reach 1% of its current level, assuming no new material is scattered about? Write down the decay reaction, including the daughter nucleus. The daughter is radioactive: write down its decay.

73. Using the uncertainty principle and the radius of a nucleus, estimate the minimum possible kinetic energy of a nucleon in, say, iron. Ignore relativistic corrections. [*Hint*: A particle can have a momentum at least as large as its momentum uncertainty.]

74. (a) Calculate the kinetic energy of the α particle emitted when $^{236}_{92}U$ decays. (b) Use Eq. 41–1 to estimate the radius of an α particle and a $^{232}_{90}Th$ nucleus. Use this to estimate (c) the maximum height of the Coulomb barrier, and (d) its width AB in Fig. 41–7.

75. The nuclide $^{191}_{76}Os$ decays with β^- energy of 0.14 MeV accompanied by γ rays of energy 0.042 MeV and 0.129 MeV. (a) What is the daughter nucleus? (b) Draw an energy-level diagram showing the ground states of the parent and daughter and excited states of the daughter. (c) To which of the daughter states does β^- decay of $^{191}_{76}Os$ occur?

76. Determine the activities of (a) 1.0 g of $^{131}_{53}I$ ($T_{\frac{1}{2}} = 8.02$ days) and (b) 1.0 g of $^{238}_{92}U$ ($T_{\frac{1}{2}} = 4.47 \times 10^9$ yr).

77. Use Fig. 41–1 to estimate the total binding energy for copper and then estimate the energy, in joules, needed to break a 3.0-g copper penny into its constituent nucleons.

78. Instead of giving atomic masses for nuclides as in Appendix F, some Tables give the **mass excess**, Δ, defined as $\Delta = M - A$, where A is the atomic mass number and M is the mass in u. Determine the mass excess, in u and in MeV/c^2, for: (a) $^{4}_{2}He$; (b) $^{12}_{6}C$; (c) $^{86}_{38}Sr$; (d) $^{235}_{92}U$. (e) From a glance at Appendix F, can you make a generalization about the sign of Δ as a function of Z or A?

79. When water is placed near an intense neutron source, the neutrons can be slowed down by collisions with the water molecules and eventually captured by a hydrogen nucleus to form the stable isotope called deuterium, $^{2}_{1}H$, giving off a gamma ray. What is the energy of the gamma ray?

80. (a) Show that the **mean life** of a radioactive nuclide, defined as

$$\tau = \frac{\int_0^\infty t\, N(t)\, dt}{\int_0^\infty N(t)\, dt},$$

is $\tau = 1/\lambda$. (b) What fraction of the original number of nuclei remains after one mean life?

81. (a) A 72-gram sample of natural carbon contains the usual fraction of $^{14}_{6}C$. Estimate how long it will take before there is only one $^{14}_{6}C$ nucleus left. (b) How does the answer in (a) change if the sample is 270 grams? What does this tell you about the limits of carbon dating?

82. If the mass of the proton were just a little closer to the mass of the neutron, the following reaction would be possible even at low collision energies:

$$e^- + p \rightarrow n + \nu.$$

(a) Why would this situation be catastrophic? (b) By what percentage would the proton's mass have to be increased to make this reaction possible?

83. What is the ratio of the kinetic energies for an alpha particle and a beta particle if both make tracks with the same radius of curvature in a magnetic field, oriented perpendicular to the paths of the particles?

84. A 1.00-g sample of natural samarium emits α particles at a rate of $120 \, \text{s}^{-1}$ due to the presence of $^{147}_{62}\text{Sm}$. The natural abundance of $^{147}_{62}\text{Sm}$ is 15%. Calculate the half-life for this decay process.

85. Almost all of naturally occurring uranium is $^{238}_{92}\text{U}$ with a half-life of $4.468 \times 10^9 \, \text{yr}$. Most of the rest of natural uranium is $^{235}_{92}\text{U}$ with a half-life of $7.04 \times 10^8 \, \text{yr}$. Today a sample contains 0.720% $^{235}_{92}\text{U}$. (a) What was this percentage 1.0 billion years ago? (b) What percentage of $^{235}_{92}\text{U}$ will remain 100 million years from now?

86. A typical banana contains 400 mg of potassium, of which a small fraction is the radioactive isotope $^{40}_{19}\text{K}$ (see Appendix F). Estimate the activity of an average banana due to $^{40}_{19}\text{K}$.

87. Some radioactive isotopes have half-lives that are larger than the age of the universe (like gadolinium or samarium). The only way to determine these half-lives is to monitor the decay rate of a sample that contains these isotopes. For example, suppose we find an asteroid that currently contains about 15,000 kg of $^{152}_{64}\text{Gd}$ (gadolinium) and we detect an activity of 1 decay/s. What is the half-life of gadolinium (in years)?

88. Decay series, such as that shown in Fig. 41–12, can be classified into four families, depending on whether the mass numbers have the form $4n$, $4n + 1$, $4n + 2$, or $4n + 3$, where n is an integer. Justify this statement and show that for a nuclide in any family, all its daughters will be in the same family.

*Numerical/Computer

*89. (I) A laboratory has a 1.80-μg sample of radioactive $^{13}_{7}\text{N}$ whose decay constant $\lambda = 1.16 \times 10^{-3} \, \text{s}^{-1}$. Calculate the initial number of nuclei, N_0, present in the sample. Use the radioactive decay law, $N = N_0 e^{-\lambda t}$, to determine the number of nuclei N present at time t for $t = 0$ to 30 minutes (1800 s) in steps of 0.5 min (30 s). Make a graph of N versus t and from the graph determine the half-life of the sample.

*90. (II) Construct a spreadsheet (or other numerical tool) that will reproduce Fig. 41–1, the graph of binding energy per nucleon (in MeV) vs. the mass number A. Using Appendix F, calculate the binding energy per nucleon for the most stable isotope of each possible mass number $A \geq 2$. [The first few values will be for $^{2}_{1}\text{H}$, $^{3}_{2}\text{He}$ (it is more stable than $^{3}_{1}\text{H}$), $^{4}_{2}\text{He}$, $^{6}_{3}\text{Li}$, and $^{7}_{3}\text{Li}$ (since it is more stable than $^{7}_{4}\text{Be}$).] To reduce the amount of data, for $A \geq 20$ plot only points for even values of A, and plot to a maximum of $A = 142$.

Answers to Exercises

A: 0.042130 u.

B: 7.98 MeV/nucleon.

C: (b).

D: (c).

E: (a).

F: $1.37 \times 10^{-11} \, \text{s}^{-1}$.

G: (a).

Diagram of ITER (International Thermonuclear Experimental Reactor), which will hopefully begin operation around 2016. Inside its cavity, over 12 m in diameter, a plasma of electrons and light nuclei will be heated to high temperatures that rival the Sun. Confining a plasma by magnetic fields has proved difficult, and intense research is needed if the fusion of smaller nuclei is to fulfill its promise as a source of abundant and relatively clean power.

This Chapter covers the basic physics topics of nuclear reactions, nuclear fission, nuclear fusion, and how we obtain nuclear energy. We also examine the health aspects of radiation dosimetry, therapy, and imaging by CAT, PET, SPET, and MRI.

42

Nuclear Energy; Effects and Uses of Radiation

CHAPTER-OPENING QUESTIONS—Guess now!

1. The Sun is powered by
   (a) nuclear alpha decay.
   (b) nuclear beta decay.
   (c) nuclear gamma decay.
   (d) nuclear fission.
   (e) nuclear fusion.

2. Which radiation induces the most biological damage for a given amount of energy deposited in tissue?
   (a) Alpha particles.
   (b) Gamma radiation.
   (c) Beta radiation.
   (d) They all do the same damage for the same deposited energy.
   (e) It depends on the type of tissue.

We continue our study of nuclear physics in this Chapter. We begin with a discussion of nuclear reactions, and then we examine the important large energy-releasing processes of fission and fusion. This Chapter also deals with the effects of nuclear radiation passing through matter, particularly biological matter, and how radiation is used medically for therapy, diagnosis, and imaging techniques.

CONTENTS

1131

42–1 Nuclear Reactions and the Transmutation of Elements

When a nucleus undergoes α or β decay, the daughter nucleus is a different element from the parent. The transformation of one element into another, called **transmutation**, also occurs by means of nuclear reactions. A **nuclear reaction** is said to occur when a given nucleus is struck by another nucleus, or by a simpler particle such as a γ ray or neutron, and an interaction takes place. Ernest Rutherford was the first to report seeing a nuclear reaction. In 1919 he observed that some of the α particles passing through nitrogen gas were absorbed and protons emitted. He concluded that nitrogen nuclei had been transformed into oxygen nuclei via the reaction

$$^4_2\text{He} + ^{14}_7\text{N} \rightarrow ^{17}_8\text{O} + ^1_1\text{H},$$

where ^4_2He is an α particle, and ^1_1H is a proton.

Since then, a great many nuclear reactions have been observed. Indeed, many of the radioactive isotopes used in the laboratory are made by means of nuclear reactions. Nuclear reactions can be made to occur in the laboratory, but they also occur regularly in nature. In Chapter 41 we saw an example: $^{14}_6\text{C}$ is continually being made in the atmosphere via the reaction $\text{n} + ^{14}_7\text{N} \rightarrow ^{14}_6\text{C} + \text{p}$.

Nuclear reactions are sometimes written in a shortened form: for example, the reaction

$$\text{n} + ^{14}_7\text{N} \rightarrow ^{14}_6\text{C} + \text{p}$$

can be written

$$^{14}_7\text{N} \,(\text{n}, \text{p})\, ^{14}_6\text{C}.$$

The symbols outside the parentheses on the left and right represent the initial and final nuclei, respectively. The symbols inside the parentheses represent the bombarding particle (first) and the emitted small particle (second).

In any nuclear reaction, both electric charge and nucleon number are conserved. These conservation laws are often useful, as the following Example shows.

CONCEPTUAL EXAMPLE 42–1 **Deuterium reaction.** A neutron is observed to strike an $^{16}_8\text{O}$ nucleus, and a deuteron is given off. (A **deuteron**, or **deuterium**, is the isotope of hydrogen containing one proton and one neutron, ^2_1H; it is sometimes given the symbol d or D.) What is the nucleus that results?

RESPONSE We have the reaction $\text{n} + ^{16}_8\text{O} \rightarrow ? + ^2_1\text{H}$. The total number of nucleons initially is $1 + 16 = 17$, and the total charge is $0 + 8 = 8$. The same totals apply after the reaction. Hence the product nucleus must have $Z = 7$ and $A = 15$. From the Periodic Table, we find that it is nitrogen that has $Z = 7$, so the nucleus produced is $^{15}_7\text{N}$.

| **EXERCISE A** Determine the resulting nucleus in the reaction $\text{n} + ^{137}_{56}\text{Ba} \rightarrow ? + \gamma$.

Energy and momentum are also conserved in nuclear reactions, and can be used to determine whether or not a given reaction can occur. For example, if the total mass of the final products is less than the total mass of the initial particles, this decrease in mass (recall $\Delta E = \Delta m\, c^2$) is converted to kinetic energy (K) of the outgoing particles. But if the total mass of the products is greater than the total mass of the initial reactants, the reaction requires energy. The reaction will then not occur unless the bombarding particle has sufficient kinetic energy. Consider a nuclear reaction of the general form

$$a + X \rightarrow Y + b, \tag{42–1}$$

where a is a projectile particle (or small nucleus) that strikes nucleus X, producing nucleus Y and particle b (typically, p, n, α, γ). We define the **reaction energy**, or **Q-value**, in terms of the masses involved, as

$$Q = (M_a + M_X - M_b - M_Y)c^2. \qquad \text{(42–2a)}$$

For a γ ray, $M = 0$.

Because energy is conserved, Q has to be equal to the change in kinetic energy (final minus initial):

$$Q = K_b + K_Y - K_a - K_X. \qquad \text{(42–2b)}$$

If X is a target nucleus at rest (or nearly so) struck by incoming particle a, then $K_X = 0$. For $Q > 0$, the reaction is said to be *exothermic* or *exoergic*; energy is released in the reaction, so the total kinetic energy is greater after the reaction than before. If Q is negative ($Q < 0$), the reaction is said to be *endothermic* or *endoergic*: the final total kinetic energy is less than the initial kinetic energy, and an energy input is required to make the reaction happen. The energy input comes from the kinetic energy of the initial colliding particles (a and X).

EXAMPLE 42–2 **A slow-neutron reaction.** The nuclear reaction

$$n + {}^{10}_{5}B \rightarrow {}^{7}_{3}Li + {}^{4}_{2}He$$

is observed to occur even when very slow-moving neutrons (mass $M_n = 1.0087\ u$) strike a boron atom at rest. For a particular reaction in which $K_n \approx 0$, the outgoing helium ($M_{He} = 4.0026\ u$) is observed to have a speed of $9.30 \times 10^6\ m/s$. Determine (*a*) the kinetic energy of the lithium ($M_{Li} = 7.0160\ u$), and (*b*) the Q-value of the reaction.

APPROACH Since the neutron and boron are both essentially at rest, the total momentum before the reaction is zero; momentum is conserved and so must be zero afterward as well. Thus,

$$M_{Li} v_{Li} = M_{He} v_{He}.$$

We solve this for v_{Li} and substitute it into the equation for kinetic energy. In (*b*) we use Eq. 42–2b.

SOLUTION (*a*) We can use classical kinetic energy with little error, rather than relativistic formulas, because $v_{He} = 9.30 \times 10^6\ m/s$ is not close to the speed of light c, and v_{Li} will be even less since $M_{Li} > M_{He}$. Thus we can write:

$$K_{Li} = \frac{1}{2} M_{Li} v_{Li}^2 = \frac{1}{2} M_{Li} \left(\frac{M_{He} v_{He}}{M_{Li}} \right)^2$$

$$= \frac{M_{He}^2 v_{He}^2}{2 M_{Li}}.$$

We put in numbers, changing the mass in u to kg and recall that $1.60 \times 10^{-13}\ J = 1\ MeV$:

$$K_{Li} = \frac{(4.0026\ u)^2 (1.66 \times 10^{-27}\ kg/u)^2 (9.30 \times 10^6\ m/s)^2}{2(7.0160\ u)(1.66 \times 10^{-27}\ kg/u)}$$

$$= 1.64 \times 10^{-13}\ J = 1.02\ MeV.$$

(*b*) We are given the data $K_a = K_X = 0$ in Eq. 42–2b, so $Q = K_{Li} + K_{He}$, where

$$K_{He} = \tfrac{1}{2} M_{He} v_{He}^2$$

$$= \tfrac{1}{2}(4.0026\ u)(1.66 \times 10^{-27}\ kg/u)(9.30 \times 10^6\ m/s)^2$$

$$= 2.87 \times 10^{-13}\ J = 1.80\ MeV.$$

Hence, $Q = 1.02\ MeV + 1.80\ MeV = 2.82\ MeV.$

Will the reaction "go"? Can the reaction

$$p + {}^{13}_{6}C \rightarrow {}^{13}_{7}N + n$$

occur when ${}^{13}_{6}C$ is bombarded by 2.0-MeV protons?

APPROACH The reaction will "go" if the reaction is exothermic ($Q > 0$) and even if $Q < 0$ if the input momentum and kinetic energy are sufficient. First we calculate Q from the difference between final and initial masses using Eq. 42–2a, and looking up the masses in Appendix F.

SOLUTION The total masses before and after the reaction are:

Before		After	
$M({}^{13}_{6}C) =$	13.003355	$M({}^{13}_{7}N) =$	13.005739
$M({}^{1}_{1}H) =$	1.007825	$M(n) =$	1.008665
	14.011180		14.014404

(We must use the mass of the ${}^{1}_{1}H$ atom rather than that of the bare proton because the masses of ${}^{13}_{6}C$ and ${}^{13}_{7}N$ include the electrons, and we must include an equal number of electron masses on each side of the equation since none are created or destroyed.) The products have an excess mass of

$$(14.014404 - 14.011180)\,u = 0.003224\,u \times 931.5\,\text{MeV}/u = 3.00\,\text{MeV}.$$

Thus $Q = -3.00\,\text{MeV}$, and the reaction is endothermic. This reaction requires energy, and the 2.0-MeV protons do not have enough to make it go.

NOTE The incoming proton in this Example would have to have somewhat more than 3.00 MeV of kinetic energy to make this reaction go; 3.00 MeV would be enough to conserve energy, but a proton of this energy would produce the ${}^{13}_{7}N$ and n with no kinetic energy and hence no momentum. Since an incident 3.0-MeV proton has momentum, conservation of momentum would be violated. A calculation using conservation of energy *and* of momentum, as we did in Examples 41–6 and 42–2, shows that the minimum proton energy, called the **threshold energy**, is 3.23 MeV in this case (= Problem 16).

(a) Neutron captured by ${}^{238}_{92}U$.

(b) ${}^{239}_{92}U$ decays by β decay to neptunium-239.

(c) ${}^{239}_{93}Np$ itself decays by β decay to produce plutonium-239.

FIGURE 42–1 Neptunium and plutonium are produced in this series of reactions, after bombardment of ${}^{238}_{92}U$ by neutrons.

Neutron Physics

The artificial transmutation of elements took a great leap forward in the 1930s when Enrico Fermi realized that neutrons would be the most effective projectiles for causing nuclear reactions and in particular for producing new elements. Because neutrons have no net electric charge, they are not repelled by positively charged nuclei as are protons or alpha particles. Hence the probability of a neutron reaching the nucleus and causing a reaction is much greater than for charged projectiles,[†] particularly at low energies. Between 1934 and 1936, Fermi and his co-workers in Rome produced many previously unknown isotopes by bombarding different elements with neutrons. Fermi realized that if the heaviest known element, uranium, is bombarded with neutrons, it might be possible to produce new elements with atomic numbers greater than that of uranium. After several years of hard work, it was suspected that two new elements had been produced, neptunium ($Z = 93$) and plutonium ($Z = 94$). The full confirmation that such "transuranic" elements could be produced came several years later at the University of California, Berkeley. The reactions are shown in Fig. 42–1.

It was soon shown that what Fermi had actually observed when he bombarded uranium was an even stranger process—one that was destined to play an extraordinary role in the world at large. We discuss it in Section 42–3.

[†]That is, positively charged particles. Electrons rarely cause nuclear reactions because they do not interact via the strong nuclear force.

42–2 Cross Section

Some reactions have a higher probability of occurring than others. The reaction probability is specified by a quantity called the **cross section**. Although the size of a nucleus, like that of an atom, is not a clearly defined quantity since the edges are not distinct like those of a tennis ball or baseball, we can nonetheless define a *cross section* for nuclei undergoing collisions by using an analogy. Suppose that projectile particles strike a stationary target of total area A and thickness ℓ, as shown in Fig. 42–2. Assume also that the target is made up of identical objects (such as marbles or nuclei), each of which has a cross-sectional area σ, and we assume the incoming projectiles are small by comparison. We assume that the target objects are fairly far apart and the thickness ℓ is so small that we don't have to worry about overlapping. This is often a reasonable assumption because nuclei have diameters on the order of 10^{-14} m but are at least 10^{-10} m (atomic size) apart even in solids. If there are n nuclei per unit volume, the total cross-sectional area of all these tiny targets is

$$A' = nA\ell\sigma$$

since $nA\ell = (n)(\text{volume})$ is the total number of targets and σ is the cross-sectional area of each. If $A' \ll A$, most of the incident projectile particles will pass through the target without colliding. If R_0 is the rate at which the projectile particles strike the target (number/second), the rate at which collisions occur, R, is

$$R = R_0 \frac{A'}{A} = R_0 \frac{nA\ell\sigma}{A}$$

so

$$R = R_0 n\ell\sigma.$$

Thus, by measuring the collision rate, R, we can determine σ:

$$\sigma = \frac{R}{R_0 n\ell}. \tag{42–3}$$

If nuclei were simple billiard balls, and R the number of particles that are deflected per second, σ would represent the real cross-sectional area of each ball. But nuclei are complicated objects that cannot be considered to have distinct boundaries. Furthermore, collisions can be either elastic or inelastic, and reactions can occur in which the nature of the particles can change. By measuring R for each possible process, we can determine an **effective cross section**, σ, for each process. None of these cross sections is necessarily related to a geometric cross-sectional area. Rather, σ is an "effective" target area. It is a *measure of the probability of a collision or of a particular reaction occurring* per target nucleus, independent of the dimensions of the entire target. The concept of cross section is useful because σ depends only on the properties of the interacting particles, whereas R depends on the thickness and area of the physical (macroscopic) target, on the number of particles in the incident beam, and so on.

When a given pair of particles interact, we define their **elastic cross section** σ_{el} using Eq. 42–3, where R for a given experimental setup is the rate of elastic collisions (or **elastic scattering**), by which we mean collisions for which the final particles are the same as the initial particles (a = b, X = Y in Eq. 42–1) and $Q = 0$. Similarly, the inelastic cross section, σ_{inel}, is related to the rate of inelastic collisions, or **inelastic scattering**, which involves the same final and initial particles but $Q \neq 0$, usually because excited states are involved. For each reaction in which the final particles are different than the initial particles, there is a particular cross section. For protons (p) incident on $^{13}_{6}\text{C}$, for example, we could have various reactions, such as $\text{p} + ^{13}_{6}\text{C} \rightarrow ^{13}_{7}\text{N} + \text{n}$ or $\text{p} + ^{13}_{6}\text{C} \rightarrow ^{10}_{5}\text{B} + ^{4}_{2}\text{He}$, and so on. The sum of all the separate reaction cross sections (for a given pair of initial particles) is called the **total reaction cross section**, σ_{R}. The **total cross section**, σ_{T}, is

$$\sigma_{\text{T}} = \sigma_{\text{el}} + \sigma_{\text{inel}} + \sigma_{\text{R}}$$

and is a measure of all possible interactions or collisions starting with given initial particles. Said another way, σ_{T} is a measure of how many of the incident particles interact in some way and hence are eliminated from the incident beam.

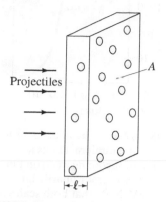

FIGURE 42–2 Projectile particles strike a target of area A and thickness ℓ made up of n nuclei per unit volume.

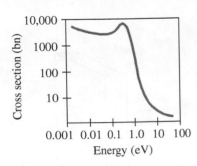

FIGURE 42–3 The neutron cross section for cadmium-114 as a function of incoming neutron kinetic energy. It is extraordinarily large for $K \lesssim 1\,\text{eV}$. Note that both scales are logarithmic.

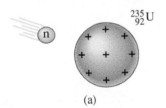

FIGURE 42–4 Fission of a $^{235}_{92}\text{U}$ nucleus after capture of a neutron, according to the liquid-drop model.

$^{235}_{92}\text{U}$

(a)

(b) $^{236}_{92}\text{U}$ (excited)

(c)

X_1 X_2

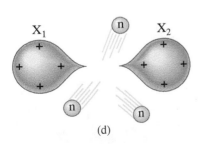

(d)

We can also define **differential cross sections**, which represent the probability of the deflected (or emitted) particles leaving at particular angles.

It is said that when one of the first nuclear cross sections was measured, a physicist, surprised that it was as large as it was ($\approx 10^{-28}\,\text{m}^2$), remarked, "it's as big as a barn." Ever since then nuclear cross sections have been measured in "barns," where $1\text{ barn (bn)} = 10^{-28}\,\text{m}^2$.

The value of σ for a given reaction depends on, among other things, the incident kinetic energy. Typical nuclear cross sections are on the order of barns, but they can vary from millibarns to kilobarns or more. Figure 42–3 shows the cross section for neutron capture in cadmium ($n + {}^{114}_{48}\text{Cd} \rightarrow {}^{115}_{48}\text{Cd} + \gamma$) as a function of neutron kinetic energy. Neutron cross sections for most materials are greater at low energies, as in Fig. 42–3. To produce nuclear reactions at a high rate it is therefore desirable that the bombarding neutrons have low energy. Neutrons that have been slowed down and have reached equilibrium with matter at room temperature ($\tfrac{3}{2}kT \approx 0.04\,\text{eV}$ at $T = 300\,\text{K}$) are called **thermal neutrons**.

EXAMPLE 42–4 **Using cross section.** The reaction

$$p + {}^{56}_{26}\text{Fe} \rightarrow {}^{56}_{27}\text{Co} + n$$

has a cross section of 0.65 bn for a particular incident proton energy. Suppose the iron target has an area of $1.5\,\text{cm}^2$, and is $2.0\,\mu\text{m}$ thick. The density of iron is $7.8 \times 10^3\,\text{kg/m}^3$. If the protons are incident at a rate of 2.0×10^{13} particles/s, calculate the rate at which neutrons are produced.

APPROACH We use Eq. 42–3 in the form: $R = R_0\, n\ell\sigma$.

SOLUTION We are given $R_0 = 2.0 \times 10^{13}$ particles/s, $\ell = 2.0 \times 10^{-6}\,\text{m}$, and $\sigma = 0.65\,\text{bn}$. Recalling from Chapter 17 that one mole (mass = 56 g for iron) contains 6.02×10^{23} atoms, then the number of iron atoms per unit volume is

$$n = (6.02 \times 10^{23}\,\text{atoms/mole})\frac{(7.8 \times 10^3\,\text{kg/m}^3)}{(56 \times 10^{-3}\,\text{kg/mole})} = 8.4 \times 10^{28}\,\text{atoms/m}^3.$$

Then we find that the rate at which neutrons are produced is

$$
\begin{aligned}
R &= R_0\, n\ell\sigma \\
&= (2.0 \times 10^{13}\,\text{particles/s})(8.4 \times 10^{28}\,\text{atoms/m}^3)(2.0 \times 10^{-6}\,\text{m})(0.65 \times 10^{-28}\,\text{m}^2) \\
&= 2.2 \times 10^8\,\text{particles/s}.
\end{aligned}
$$

42–3 Nuclear Fission; Nuclear Reactors

In 1938, the German scientists Otto Hahn and Fritz Strassmann made an amazing discovery. Following up on Fermi's work, they found that uranium bombarded by neutrons sometimes produced smaller nuclei that were roughly half the size of the original uranium nucleus. Lise Meitner and Otto Frisch quickly realized what had happened: the uranium nucleus, after absorbing a neutron, actually had split into two roughly equal pieces. This was startling, for until then the known nuclear reactions involved knocking out only a tiny fragment (for example, n, p, or α) from a nucleus.

Nuclear Fission and Chain Reactions

This new phenomenon was named **nuclear fission** because of its resemblance to biological fission (cell division). It occurs much more readily for $^{235}_{92}\text{U}$ than for the more common $^{238}_{92}\text{U}$. The process can be visualized by imagining the uranium nucleus to be like a liquid drop. According to this **liquid-drop model**, the neutron absorbed by the $^{235}_{92}\text{U}$ nucleus gives the nucleus extra internal energy (like heating a drop of water). This intermediate state, or **compound nucleus**, is $^{236}_{92}\text{U}$ (because of the absorbed neutron). The extra energy of this nucleus—it is in an excited state—appears as increased motion of the individual nucleons, which causes the nucleus to take on abnormal elongated shapes, Fig. 42–4. When the nucleus elongates (in this model) into the shape shown in Fig. 42–4c, the attraction of the two ends via the short-range nuclear force is greatly weakened by the increased separation distance, and the electric repulsive force becomes dominant, and the nucleus splits in two (Fig. 42–4d). The two resulting nuclei, X_1 and X_2, are called **fission fragments**, and in the process a number of neutrons (typically two or three) are also given off. The reaction can be written

$$n + {}^{235}_{92}U \rightarrow {}^{236}_{92}U \rightarrow X_1 + X_2 + \text{neutrons.} \qquad (42-4)$$

The compound nucleus, ${}^{236}_{92}U$, exists for less than 10^{-12} s, so the process occurs very quickly. The two fission fragments, X_1 and X_2, more often split the original uranium mass as about 40%–60% rather than precisely half and half. A typical fission reaction is

$$n + {}^{235}_{92}U \rightarrow {}^{141}_{56}Ba + {}^{92}_{36}Kr + 3n, \qquad (42-5)$$

although many others also occur.

CONCEPTUAL EXAMPLE 42–5 **Counting nucleons.** Identify the element X in the fission reaction $n + {}^{235}_{92}U \rightarrow {}^{A}_{Z}X + {}^{93}_{38}Sr + 2n$.

RESPONSE The number of nucleons is conserved (Section 41–7). The uranium nucleus with 235 nucleons plus the incoming neutron make $235 + 1 = 236$ nucleons. So there must be 236 nucleons after the reaction. The Sr has 93 nucleons, and the two neutrons make 95 nucleons, so X has $A = 236 - 95 = 141$. Electric charge is also conserved: before the reaction, the total charge is $92e$. After the reaction the total charge is $(Z + 38)e$ and must equal $92e$. Thus $Z = 92 - 38 = 54$. The element with $Z = 54$ is xenon (see Appendix F or the Periodic Table inside the back cover), so the isotope is ${}^{141}_{54}Xe$.

Figure 42–5 shows the distribution of ${}^{235}_{92}U$ fission fragments according to mass. Only rarely (about 1 in 10^4) does a fission result in equal mass fragments (arrow in Fig. 42–5).

A tremendous amount of energy is released in a fission reaction because the mass of ${}^{235}_{92}U$ is considerably greater than the total mass of the fission fragments plus released neutrons. This can be seen from the binding-energy-per-nucleon curve of Fig. 41–1; the binding energy per nucleon for uranium is about 7.6 MeV/nucleon, but for fission fragments that have intermediate mass (in the center portion of the graph, $A \approx 100$), the average binding energy per nucleon is about 8.5 MeV/nucleon. Since the fission fragments are more tightly bound, the sum of their masses is less than the mass of the uranium. The difference in mass, or energy, between the original uranium nucleus and the fission fragments is about $8.5 - 7.6 = 0.9$ MeV per nucleon. Since there are 236 nucleons involved in each fission, the total energy released per fission is

$$(0.9 \text{ MeV/nucleon})(236 \text{ nucleons}) \approx 200 \text{ MeV.} \qquad (42-6)$$

This is an enormous amount of energy for one single nuclear event. At a practical level, the energy from one fission is tiny. But if many such fissions could occur in a short time, an enormous amount of energy at the macroscopic level would be available. A number of physicists, including Fermi, recognized that the neutrons released in each fission (Eqs. 42–4 and 42–5) could be used to create a **chain reaction**. That is, one neutron initially causes one fission of a uranium nucleus; the two or three neutrons released can go on to cause additional fissions, so the process multiplies as shown schematically in Fig. 42–6.

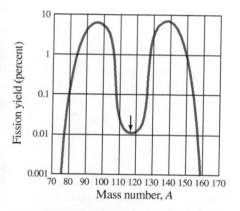

FIGURE 42–5 Mass distribution of fission fragments from ${}^{235}_{92}U + n$. The small arrow indicates equal mass fragments ($\frac{1}{2} \times (236 - 2) = 117$, assuming 2 neutrons are liberated). Note that the vertical scale is logarithmic.

Neutron

Fission fragment nuclei

${}^{235}_{92}U$ nucleus

FIGURE 42–6 Chain reaction.

FIGURE 42–7 This is the only photograph of the first nuclear reactor, built by Fermi under the grandstand of Stagg Field at the University of Chicago. It is shown here under construction as a layer of graphite (used as moderator) was being placed over a layer of natural uranium. On December 2, 1942, Fermi slowly withdrew the cadmium control rods and the reactor went critical. This first self-sustaining chain reaction was announced to Washington, via telephone, by Arthur Compton who witnessed the event and reported: "The Italian navigator has just landed in the new world."

If a **self-sustaining chain reaction** was actually possible in practice, the enormous energy available in fission could be released on a larger scale. Fermi and his co-workers (at the University of Chicago) showed it was possible by constructing the first **nuclear reactor** in 1942 (Fig. 42–7).

Nuclear Reactors

Several problems have to be overcome to make any nuclear reactor function. First, the probability that a $^{235}_{92}U$ nucleus will absorb a neutron is large only for slow neutrons, but the neutrons emitted during a fission (which are needed to sustain a chain reaction) are moving very fast. A substance known as a **moderator** must be used to slow down the neutrons. The most effective moderator will consist of atoms whose mass is as close as possible to that of the neutrons. (To see why this is true, recall from Chapter 9 that a billiard ball striking an equal mass ball at rest can itself be stopped in one collision; but a billiard ball striking a heavy object bounces off with nearly unchanged speed.) The best moderator would thus contain ^1_1H atoms. Unfortunately, ^1_1H tends to absorb neutrons. But the isotope of hydrogen called *deuterium*, ^2_1H, does not absorb many neutrons and is thus an almost ideal moderator. Either ^1_1H or ^2_1H can be used in the form of water. In the latter case, it is **heavy water**, in which the hydrogen atoms have been replaced by deuterium. Another common moderator is *graphite*, which consists of $^{12}_6C$ atoms.

FIGURE 42–8 If the amount of uranium exceeds the critical mass, as in (b), a sustained chain reaction is possible. If the mass is less than critical, as in (a), too many neutrons escape before additional fissions occur, and the chain reaction is not sustained.

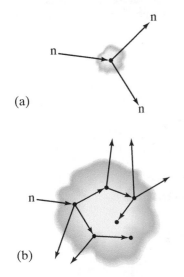

A second problem is that the neutrons produced in one fission may be absorbed and produce other nuclear reactions with other nuclei in the reactor, rather than produce further fissions. In a "light-water" reactor, the ^1_1H nuclei absorb neutrons, as does $^{238}_{92}U$ to form $^{239}_{92}U$ in the reaction $n + {}^{238}_{92}U \rightarrow {}^{239}_{92}U + \gamma$. Naturally occurring uranium[†] contains 99.3% $^{238}_{92}U$ and only 0.7% fissionable $^{235}_{92}U$. To increase the probability of fission of $^{235}_{92}U$ nuclei, natural uranium can be **enriched** to increase the percentage of $^{235}_{92}U$ by using processes such as diffusion or centrifugation. Enrichment is not usually necessary for reactors using heavy water as moderator since heavy water doesn't absorb neutrons.

The third problem is that some neutrons will escape through the surface of the reactor core before they can cause further fissions (Fig. 42–8). Thus the mass of fuel must be sufficiently large for a self-sustaining chain reaction to take place. The minimum mass of uranium needed is called the **critical mass**. The value of the critical mass depends on the moderator, the fuel ($^{239}_{94}Pu$ may be used instead of $^{235}_{92}U$), and how much the fuel is enriched, if at all. Typical values are on the order of a few kilograms (that is, neither grams nor thousands of kilograms).

To have a self-sustaining chain reaction, on average at least one neutron produced in each fission must go on to produce another fission. The average number of neutrons per fission that do go on to produce further fissions is called the **multiplication factor**, f. For a self-sustaining chain reaction, we must have $f \geq 1$.

[†]$^{238}_{92}U$ will fission, but only with fast neutrons ($^{238}_{92}U$ is more stable than $^{235}_{92}U$). The probability of absorbing a fast neutron and producing a fission is too low to produce a self-sustaining chain reaction.

If $f < 1$, the reactor is "subcritical." If $f > 1$, it is "supercritical" (and could become dangerously explosive). Reactors are equipped with movable **control rods** (good neutron absorbers like cadmium or boron), whose function is to absorb neutrons and maintain the reactor at just barely "critical," $f = 1$. The release of neutrons and subsequent fissions occur so quickly that manipulation of the control rods to maintain $f = 1$ would not be possible if it weren't for the small percentage ($\approx 1\%$) of so-called **delayed neutrons**. They come from the decay of neutron-rich fission fragments (or their daughters) having lifetimes on the order of seconds—sufficient to allow enough reaction time to operate the control rods and maintain $f = 1$.

Nuclear reactors have been built for use in research and to produce electric power. Fission produces many neutrons and a "research reactor" is basically an intense source of neutrons. These neutrons can be used as projectiles in nuclear reactions to produce nuclides not found in nature, including isotopes used as tracers and for therapy. A "power reactor" is used to produce electric power. The energy released in the fission process appears as heat, which is used to boil water and produce steam to drive a turbine connected to an electric generator (Fig. 42–9). The **core** of a nuclear reactor consists of the fuel and a moderator (water in most U.S. commercial reactors). The fuel is usually uranium enriched so that it contains 2 to 4 percent $^{235}_{92}$U. Water at high pressure or other liquid (such as liquid sodium) is allowed to flow through the core. The thermal energy it absorbs is used to produce steam in the heat exchanger, so the fissionable fuel acts as the heat input for a heat engine (Chapter 20).

FIGURE 42–9 A nuclear reactor. The heat generated by the fission process in the fuel rods is carried off by hot water or liquid sodium and is used to boil water to steam in the heat exchanger. The steam drives a turbine to generate electricity and is then cooled in the condenser.

FIGURE 42–10 Devastation around Chernobyl in Russia, after the nuclear power plant meltdown in 1986.

There are problems associated with nuclear power plants. Besides the usual thermal pollution associated with any heat engine (Section 20–11), there is the serious problem of disposal of the radioactive fission fragments produced in the reactor, plus radioactive nuclides produced by neutrons interacting with the structural parts of the reactor. Fission fragments, like their uranium or plutonium parents, have about 50% more neutrons than protons. Nuclei with atomic number in the typical range for fission fragments ($Z \approx 30$ to 60) are stable only if they have more nearly equal numbers of protons and neutrons (see Fig. 41–2). Hence the highly neutron-rich fission fragments are very unstable and decay radioactively. The accidental release of highly radioactive fission fragments into the atmosphere poses a serious threat to human health (Section 42–5), as does possible leakage of the radioactive wastes when they are disposed of. The accidents at Three Mile Island, Pennsylvania (1979), and at Chernobyl, Russia (1986), have illustrated some of the dangers and have shown that nuclear plants must be constructed, maintained, and operated with great care and precision (Fig. 42–10).

Finally, the lifetime of nuclear power plants is limited to 30-some years, due to buildup of radioactivity and the fact that the structural materials themselves are weakened by the intense conditions inside. "Decommissioning" of a power plant could take a number of forms, but the cost of any method of decommissioning a large plant is very great.

So-called **breeder reactors** were proposed as a solution to the problem of limited supplies of fissionable uranium, $^{235}_{92}\text{U}$. A breeder reactor is one in which some of the neutrons produced in the fission of $^{235}_{92}\text{U}$ are absorbed by $^{238}_{92}\text{U}$, and $^{239}_{94}\text{Pu}$ is produced via the set of reactions shown in Fig. 42–1. $^{239}_{94}\text{Pu}$ is fissionable with slow neutrons, so after separation it can be used as a fuel in a nuclear reactor. Thus a breeder reactor "breeds" new fuel ($^{239}_{94}\text{Pu}$) from otherwise useless $^{238}_{92}\text{U}$. Since natural uranium is 99.3% $^{238}_{92}\text{U}$, this means that the supply of fissionable fuel could be increased by more than a factor of 100. But breeder reactors have the same problems as other reactors, plus other serious problems. Not only is plutonium considered to be a serious health hazard in itself (radioactive with a half-life of 24,000 years), but plutonium produced in a reactor can readily be used in a bomb, increasing the danger of nuclear proliferation and theft of fuel by terrorists to produce a bomb.

Nuclear power presents risks. Other large-scale energy-conversion methods, such as conventional oil and coal-burning steam plants, also present health and environmental hazards; some of them were discussed in Section 20–11, and include air pollution, oil spills, and the release of CO_2 gas which can trap heat as in a greenhouse to raise the Earth's temperature. The solution to the world's needs for energy is not only technological, but also economic and political. A major factor surely is to "conserve"—to minimize our use of energy. "Reduce, reuse, recycle."

EXAMPLE 42–6 **Uranium fuel amount.** Estimate the minimum amount of $^{235}_{92}\text{U}$ that needs to undergo fission in order to run a 1000-MW power reactor per year of continuous operation. Assume an efficiency (Chapter 20) of about 33%.

APPROACH At 33% efficiency, we need $3 \times 1000\,\text{MW} = 3000 \times 10^6\,\text{J/s}$ input. Each fission releases about 200 MeV (Eq. 42–6), so we divide the energy for a year by 200 MeV to get the number of fissions needed per year. Then we multiply by the mass of one uranium atom.

SOLUTION For 1000 MW output, the total power generation needs to be 3000 MW, of which 2000 MW is dumped as "waste" heat. Thus the total energy release in 1 yr $(3 \times 10^7\,\text{s})$ from fission needs to be about

$$(3 \times 10^9\,\text{J/s})(3 \times 10^7\,\text{s}) \approx 10^{17}\,\text{J}.$$

If each fission releases 200 MeV of energy, the number of fissions required for a year is

$$\frac{(10^{17}\,\text{J})}{(2 \times 10^8\,\text{eV/fission})(1.6 \times 10^{-19}\,\text{J/eV})} \approx 3 \times 10^{27}\,\text{fissions}.$$

The mass of a single uranium atom is about $(235\,\text{u})(1.66 \times 10^{-27}\,\text{kg/u}) \approx 4 \times 10^{-25}\,\text{kg}$, so the total uranium mass needed is

$$(4 \times 10^{-25}\,\text{kg/fission})(3 \times 10^{27}\,\text{fissions}) \approx 1000\,\text{kg},$$

or about a ton of $^{235}_{92}\text{U}$.

NOTE Since $^{235}_{92}\text{U}$ makes up only 0.7% of natural uranium, the yearly requirement for uranium is on the order of a hundred tons. This is orders of magnitude less than coal, both in mass and volume. Coal releases $2.8 \times 10^7\,\text{J/kg}$, whereas $^{235}_{92}\text{U}$ can release $10^{17}\,\text{J}/10^3\,\text{kg} = 10^{14}\,\text{J/kg}$. For natural uranium, the figure is 100 times less, $10^{12}\,\text{J/kg}$.

EXERCISE B A nuclear-powered submarine needs 6000-kW input power. How many $^{235}_{92}$U fissions is this per second?

Atom Bomb

The first use of fission, however, was not to produce electric power. Instead, it was first used as a fission bomb (called the "atomic bomb"). In early 1940, with Europe already at war, Germany's leader, Adolf Hitler, banned the sale of uranium from the Czech mines he had recently taken over. Research into the fission process suddenly was enshrouded in secrecy. Physicists in the United States were alarmed. A group of them approached Einstein—a man whose name was a household word—to send a letter to President Franklin Roosevelt about the possibilities of using nuclear fission for a bomb far more powerful than any previously known, and inform him that Germany might already have begun development of such a bomb. Roosevelt responded by authorizing the program known as the Manhattan Project, to see if a bomb could be built. Work began in earnest after Fermi's demonstration in 1942 that a sustained chain reaction was possible. A new secret laboratory was developed on an isolated mesa in New Mexico known as Los Alamos. Under the direction of J. Robert Oppenheimer (1904–1967; Fig. 42–11), it became the home of famous scientists from all over Europe and the United States.

To build a bomb that was subcritical during transport but that could be made supercritical (to produce a chain reaction) at just the right moment, two pieces of uranium were used, each less than the critical mass but together greater than the critical mass. The two masses, kept separate until the moment of detonation, were then forced together quickly by a kind of gun, and a chain reaction of explosive proportions occurred. An alternate bomb detonated conventional explosives (TNT) surrounding a plutonium sphere to compress it by implosion to double its density, making it more than critical and causing a nuclear explosion. The first fission bomb was tested in the New Mexico desert in July 1945. It was successful. In early August, a fission bomb using uranium was dropped on Hiroshima and a second, using plutonium, was dropped on Nagasaki (Fig. 42–12), both in Japan. World War II ended shortly thereafter.

Besides its great destructive power, a fission bomb produces many highly radioactive fission fragments, as does a nuclear reactor. When a fission bomb explodes, these radioactive isotopes are released into the atmosphere and are known as **radioactive fallout**.

Testing of nuclear bombs in the atmosphere after World War II was a cause of concern, for the movement of air masses spread the fallout all over the globe. Radioactive fallout eventually settles to the Earth, particularly in rainfall, and is absorbed by plants and grasses and enters the food chain. This is a far more serious problem than the same radioactivity on the exterior of our bodies, since α and β particles are largely absorbed by clothing and the outer (dead) layer of skin. But inside our bodies via food, the isotopes are in direct contact with living cells. One particularly dangerous radioactive isotope is $^{90}_{38}$Sr, which is chemically much like calcium and becomes concentrated in bone, where it causes bone cancer and destruction of bone marrow. The 1963 treaty signed by over 100 nations that bans nuclear weapons testing in the atmosphere was motivated because of the hazards of fallout.

FIGURE 42–11 J. Robert Oppenheimer, on the left, with General Leslie Groves, who was the administrative head of Los Alamos during World War II. The photograph was taken at the Trinity site in the New Mexico desert, where the first atomic bomb was exploded.

FIGURE 42–12 Photo taken a month after the bomb was dropped on Nagasaki. The shacks were constructed afterwards from debris in the ruins.

42–4 Nuclear Fusion

The mass of every stable nucleus is less than the sum of the masses of its constituent protons and neutrons. For example, the mass of the helium isotope $^4_2$He is less than the mass of two protons plus the mass of two neutrons, as we saw in Example 41–2. Thus, if two protons and two neutrons were to come together to form a helium nucleus, there would be a loss of mass. This mass loss is manifested in the release of a large amount of energy.

FIGURE 42–13 Average binding energy per nucleon as a function of mass number A for stable nuclei. Same as Fig. 41–1.

Nuclear Fusion; Stars

The process of building up nuclei by bringing together individual protons and neutrons, or building larger nuclei by combining small nuclei, is called **nuclear fusion**. A glance at Fig. 42–13 (same as Fig. 41–1) shows why small nuclei can combine to form larger ones with the release of energy: it is because the binding energy per nucleon is smaller for light nuclei than it is for those of increasing mass (up to about $A \approx 60$). It is believed that many of the elements in the universe were originally formed through the process of fusion (see Chapter 44), and that fusion is today continually taking place within the stars, including our Sun, producing the prodigious amounts of radiant energy they emit.

EXAMPLE 42–7 **Fusion energy release.** One of the simplest fusion reactions involves the production of deuterium, ^2_1H, from a neutron and a proton: $^1_1\text{H} + \text{n} \rightarrow {}^2_1\text{H} + \gamma$. How much energy is released in this reaction?

APPROACH The energy released equals the difference in mass (times c^2) between the initial and final masses.

SOLUTION From Appendix F, the initial mass is

$$1.007825\,\text{u} + 1.008665\,\text{u} = 2.016490\,\text{u},$$

and after the reaction the mass is that of the ^2_1H, namely 2.014082 u (the γ is massless). The mass difference is

$$2.016490\,\text{u} - 2.014082\,\text{u} = 0.002408\,\text{u},$$

so the energy released is

$$(\Delta m)c^2 = (0.002408\,\text{u})(931.5\,\text{MeV/u}) = 2.24\,\text{MeV},$$

and it is carried off by the ^2_1H nucleus and the γ ray.

The energy output of our Sun is believed to be due principally to the following sequence of fusion reactions:

$$^1_1\text{H} + {}^1_1\text{H} \rightarrow {}^2_1\text{H} + e^+ + \nu \qquad (0.44\,\text{MeV}) \qquad \textbf{(42–7a)}$$

$$^1_1\text{H} + {}^2_1\text{H} \rightarrow {}^3_2\text{He} + \gamma \qquad (5.48\,\text{MeV}) \qquad \textbf{(42–7b)}$$

$$^3_2\text{He} + {}^3_2\text{He} \rightarrow {}^4_2\text{He} + {}^1_1\text{H} + {}^1_1\text{H} \qquad (12.86\,\text{MeV}) \qquad \textbf{(42–7c)}$$

where the energy released (Q-value) for each reaction is given in parentheses. The net effect of this sequence, which is called the **proton–proton cycle**, is for four protons to combine to form one $^4_2$He nucleus plus two positrons, two neutrinos, and two gamma rays:

$$4\,^1_1\text{H} \rightarrow\ ^4_2\text{He} + 2e^+ + 2\nu + 2\gamma. \qquad (42\text{–}8)$$

Note that it takes two of each of the first two reactions (Eqs. 42–7a and b) to produce the two $^3_2$He for the third reaction. So the total energy release for the net reaction, Eq. 42–8, is $(2 \times 0.44\,\text{MeV} + 2 \times 5.48\,\text{MeV} + 12.86\,\text{MeV}) = 24.7\,\text{MeV}$. In addition, each of the two e^+ (Eq. 42–7a) quickly annihilates with an electron to produce $2m_e c^2 = 1.02\,\text{MeV}$; so the total energy released is $(24.7\,\text{MeV} + 2 \times 1.02\,\text{MeV}) = 26.7\,\text{MeV}$. The first reaction, the formation of deuterium from two protons (Eq. 42–7a), has a very low probability, and the infrequency of that reaction serves to limit the rate at which the Sun produces energy.

EXERCISE C Return to the first Chapter-Opening Question, page 1131, and answer it again now. Try to explain why you may have answered it differently the first time.

EXERCISE D If the Sun is generating a constant amount of energy via fusion, the mass of the Sun must be (a) increasing, (b) decreasing, (c) constant, (d) irregular.

EXAMPLE 42–8 **ESTIMATE** **Estimating fusion energy.** Estimate the energy released if the following reaction occurred:

$$^2_1\text{H} + ^2_1\text{H} \rightarrow\ ^4_2\text{He}.$$

APPROACH We use Fig. 42–13 for a quick estimate.

SOLUTION We see in Fig. 42–13 that each $^2_1$H has a binding energy of about $1\frac{1}{4}\,\text{MeV/nucleon}$, which for 2 nuclei of mass 2 is $4 \times (1\frac{1}{4}) \approx 5\,\text{MeV}$. The $^4_2$He has a binding energy per nucleon of about $7\,\text{MeV}$ for a total of $4 \times 7\,\text{MeV} = 28\,\text{MeV}$. Hence the energy release is about $28\,\text{MeV} - 5\,\text{MeV} = 23\,\text{MeV}$.

In stars hotter than the Sun, it is more likely that the energy output comes principally from the **carbon** (or **CNO**) **cycle**, which comprises the following sequence of reactions:

$$^{12}_{6}\text{C} + ^1_1\text{H} \rightarrow\ ^{13}_{7}\text{N} + \gamma$$
$$^{13}_{7}\text{N} \rightarrow\ ^{13}_{6}\text{C} + e^+ + \nu$$
$$^{13}_{6}\text{C} + ^1_1\text{II} \rightarrow\ ^{14}_{7}\text{N} + \gamma$$
$$^{14}_{7}\text{N} + ^1_1\text{H} \rightarrow\ ^{15}_{8}\text{O} + \gamma$$
$$^{15}_{8}\text{O} \rightarrow\ ^{15}_{7}\text{N} + e^+ + \nu$$
$$^{15}_{7}\text{N} + ^1_1\text{H} \rightarrow\ ^{12}_{6}\text{C} + ^4_2\text{He}.$$

It is easy to see (see Problem 47) that no carbon is consumed in this cycle (see first and last equations) and that the net effect is the same as the proton–proton cycle, Eq. 42–8 (plus one extra γ). The theory of the proton–proton cycle and of the carbon cycle as the source of energy for the Sun and stars was first worked out by Hans Bethe (1906–2005) in 1939.

CONCEPTUAL EXAMPLE 42–9 **Stellar fusion.** What is the heaviest element likely to be produced in fusion processes in stars?

RESPONSE Fusion is possible if the final products have more binding energy (less mass) than the reactants, for then there is a net release of energy. Since the binding energy curve in Fig. 42–13 (or Fig. 41–1) peaks near $A \approx 56$ to 58 which corresponds to iron or nickel, it would not be energetically favorable to produce elements heavier than that. Nevertheless, in the center of massive stars or in supernova explosions, there is enough initial kinetic energy available to drive endothermic reactions that produce heavier elements, as well.

Possible Fusion Reactors

The possibility of utilizing the energy released in fusion to make a power reactor is very attractive. The fusion reactions most likely to succeed in a reactor involve the isotopes of hydrogen, ^2_1H (deuterium) and ^3_1H (tritium), and are as follows, with the energy released given in parentheses:

$$^2_1H + {}^2_1H \rightarrow {}^3_1H + {}^1_1H \qquad\qquad (4.00\ \text{MeV}) \qquad \textbf{(42–9a)}$$

$$^2_1H + {}^2_1H \rightarrow {}^3_2He + n \qquad\qquad (3.23\ \text{MeV}) \qquad \textbf{(42–9b)}$$

$$^2_1H + {}^3_1H \rightarrow {}^4_2He + n. \qquad\qquad (17.57\ \text{MeV}) \qquad \textbf{(42–9c)}$$

Comparing these energy yields with that for the fission of $^{235}_{92}U$, we can see that the energy released in fusion reactions can be greater for a given mass of fuel than in fission. Furthermore, as fuel, a fusion reactor could use deuterium, which is very plentiful in the water of the oceans (the natural abundance of ^2_1H is 0.0115% on average, or about 1 g of deuterium per 80 L of water). The simple proton–proton reaction of Eq. 42–7a, which could use a much more plentiful source of fuel, ^1_1H, has such a small probability of occurring that it cannot be considered a possibility on Earth.

Although a useful fusion reactor has not yet been achieved, considerable progress has been made in overcoming the inherent difficulties. The problems are associated with the fact that all nuclei have a positive charge and repel each other. However, if they can be brought close enough together so that the short-range attractive strong nuclear force can come into play, it can pull the nuclei together and fusion will occur. For the nuclei to get close enough together, they must have large kinetic energy to overcome the electric repulsion. High kinetic energies are easily attainable with particle accelerators (Chapter 43), but the number of particles involved is too small. To produce realistic amounts of energy, we must deal with matter in bulk, for which high kinetic energy means higher temperatures. Indeed, very high temperatures are required for fusion to occur, and fusion devices are often referred to as **thermonuclear devices**. The interiors of the Sun and other stars are very hot, many millions of degrees, so the nuclei are moving fast enough for fusion to take place, and the energy released keeps the temperature high so that further fusion reactions can occur. The Sun and the stars represent huge self-sustaining thermonuclear reactors that stay together because of their great gravitational mass; but on Earth, containment of the fast-moving nuclei at the high temperatures and densities required has proven difficult.

It was realized after World War II that the temperature produced within a fission (or "atomic") bomb was close to 10^8 K. This suggested that a fission bomb could be used to ignite a fusion bomb (popularly known as a thermonuclear or hydrogen bomb) to release the vast energy of fusion. The uncontrollable release of fusion energy in an H-bomb (in 1952) was relatively easy to obtain. But to realize usable energy from fusion at a slow and controlled rate has turned out to be a serious challenge.

EXAMPLE 42–10 **ESTIMATE** **Temperature needed for d–t fusion.** Estimate the temperature required for deuterium–tritium fusion (d–t) to occur.

APPROACH We assume the nuclei approach head-on, each with kinetic energy K, and that the nuclear force comes into play when the distance between their centers equals the sum of their nuclear radii. The electrostatic potential energy (Chapter 23) of the two particles at this distance equals the minimum total kinetic energy of the two particles when far apart. The average kinetic energy is related to Kelvin temperature by Eq. 18–4.

SOLUTION The radii of the two nuclei ($A_d = 2$ and $A_t = 3$) are given by Eq. 41–1: $r_d \approx 1.5$ fm, $r_t \approx 1.7$ fm, so $r_d + r_t = 3.2 \times 10^{-15}$ m. We equate the kinetic energy of the two initial particles to the potential energy when at this distance:

$$2K \approx \frac{1}{4\pi\epsilon_0}\frac{e^2}{(r_d + r_t)}$$

$$\approx \left(9.0 \times 10^9\ \frac{\text{N·m}^2}{\text{C}^2}\right)\frac{(1.6 \times 10^{-19}\ \text{C})^2}{(3.2 \times 10^{-15}\ \text{m})(1.6 \times 10^{-19}\ \text{J/eV})} \approx 0.45\ \text{MeV}.$$

Thus, $K \approx 0.22$ MeV, and if we ask that the average kinetic energy be this high, then from Eq. 18–4, $\frac{3}{2}kT = \bar{K}$, we have a temperature of

$$T = \frac{2\bar{K}}{3k} = \frac{2(0.22\,\text{MeV})(1.6 \times 10^{-13}\,\text{J/MeV})}{3(1.38 \times 10^{-23}\,\text{J/K})} \approx 2 \times 10^9\,\text{K}.$$

NOTE More careful calculations show that the temperature required for fusion is actually about an order of magnitude less than this rough estimate, partly because it is not necessary that the *average* kinetic energy be 0.22 MeV—a small percentage with this much energy (particles in the high-energy tail of the Maxwell distribution, Fig. 18–3) would be sufficient. Reasonable estimates for a usable fusion reactor are in the range $T \gtrsim 1$ to $4 \times 10^8\,\text{K}$.

It is not only a high temperature that is required for a fusion reactor. There must also be a high density of nuclei to ensure a sufficiently high collision rate. A real difficulty with controlled fusion is to contain nuclei long enough and at a high enough density for sufficient reactions to occur that a usable amount of energy is obtained. At the temperatures needed for fusion, the atoms are ionized, and the resulting collection of nuclei and electrons is referred to as a **plasma**. Ordinary materials vaporize at a few thousand degrees at most, and hence cannot be used to contain a high-temperature plasma. Two major containment techniques are *magnetic confinement* and *inertial confinement*.

In **magnetic confinement**, magnetic fields are used to try to contain the hot plasma. A simple approach is the "magnetic bottle" shown in Fig. 42–14. The paths of the charged particles in the plasma are bent by the magnetic field; where magnetic field lines are close together, the force on the particles reflects them back toward the center. Unfortunately, magnetic bottles develop "leaks" and the charged particles slip out before sufficient fusion takes place. The most promising design today is the **tokamak**, first developed in Russia. A tokamak (Fig. 42–15) is toroid-shaped and involves complicated magnetic fields: current-carrying conductors produce a magnetic field directed along the axis of the toroid ("toroidal" field); an additional field is produced by currents within the plasma itself ("poloidal" field). The combination produces a helical field as shown in Fig. 42–15, confining the plasma, at least briefly, so it doesn't touch the vacuum chamber's metal walls.

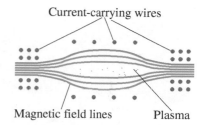

FIGURE 42–14 "Magnetic bottle" used to confine a plasma.

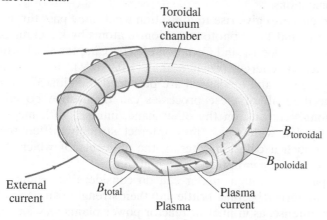

FIGURE 42–15 Tokamak configuration, showing the total $\vec{B}$ field due to external current plus current in the plasma itself.

In 1957, J. D. Lawson showed that the product of ion density n and confinement time τ must exceed a minimum value of approximately

$$n\tau \gtrsim 3 \times 10^{20}\,\text{s/m}^3.$$

This **Lawson criterion** must be reached to produce **ignition**, meaning fusion that continues after all external heating is turned off. Practically, it is expected to be achieved with $n \approx 1$ to $3 \times 10^{20}\,\text{m}^{-3}$ and $\tau \approx 1$–$3\,\text{s}$. To reach **break-even**, the point at which the energy output due to fusion is equal to the energy input to heat the plasma, requires an $n\tau$ about an order of magnitude less. The break-even point was very closely approached in the 1990s at the Tokamak Fusion Test Reactor (TFTR) at Princeton, and the very high temperature needed for ignition $(4 \times 10^8\,\text{K})$ was exceeded—although not both of these at the same time.

Tokamak fusion research continues throughout the world, from the Princeton Plasma Physics Laboratory (PPPL) in the U.S. to the KSTAR tokamak in South Korea. This research will help us in developing the huge multinational test device (European Union, India, Japan, South Korea, Russia, China, and the U.S.), called ITER (International Thermonuclear Experimental Reactor). It is hoped that ITER will be finished and running by 2016, in southeast France, with an expected power output of about 500 MW, 10 times the input energy. ITER (see Chapter-Opening Photograph on page 1131) is planned to be the final research step before building a commercial reactor.

The second method for containing the fuel for fusion is **inertial confinement**: a small pellet or capsule of deuterium and tritium is struck simultaneously from several directions by very intense laser beams. The intense influx of energy heats and ionizes the pellet into a plasma, compressing it and heating it to temperatures at which fusion can occur. The confinement time is on the order of 10^{-11} to 10^{-9} s, during which time the ions do not move appreciably because of their own inertia, and fusion can take place.

42–5 Passage of Radiation Through Matter; Radiation Damage

When we speak of *radiation*, we include α, β, γ, and X-rays, as well as protons, neutrons, and other particles such as pions (see Chapter 43). Because charged particles can ionize the atoms or molecules of any material they pass through, they are referred to as **ionizing radiation**. And because radiation produces ionization, it can cause considerable damage to materials, particularly to biological tissue.

Charged particles, such as α and β rays and protons, cause ionization because of electric forces. That is, when they pass through a material, they can attract or repel electrons strongly enough to remove them from the atoms of the material. Since the α and β rays emitted by radioactive substances have energies on the order of 1 MeV (10^4 to 10^7 eV), whereas ionization of atoms and molecules requires on the order of 10 eV, it is clear that a single α or β particle can cause thousands of ionizations.

Neutral particles also give rise to ionization when they pass through materials. For example, X-ray and γ-ray photons can ionize atoms by knocking out electrons by means of the photoelectric and Compton effects (Chapter 37). Furthermore, if a γ ray has sufficient energy (greater than 1.02 MeV), it can undergo pair production: an electron and a positron are produced (Section 37–5). The charged particles produced in all of these processes can themselves go on to produce further ionization. Neutrons, on the other hand, interact with matter mainly by collisions with nuclei, with which they interact strongly. Often the nucleus is broken apart by such a collision, altering the molecule of which it was a part. The fragments produced can in turn cause ionization.

Radiation passing through matter can do considerable damage. Metals and other structural materials become brittle and their strength can be weakened if the radiation is very intense, as in nuclear reactor power plants and for space vehicles that must pass through areas of intense cosmic radiation.

*Biological Damage

PHYSICS APPLIED
Biological radiation damage

The radiation damage produced in biological organisms is due primarily to ionization produced in cells. Several related processes can occur. Ions or radicals are produced that are highly reactive and take part in chemical reactions that interfere with the normal operation of the cell. All forms of radiation can ionize atoms by knocking out electrons. If these are bonding electrons, the molecule may break apart, or its structure may be altered so it does not perform its normal function or may perform a harmful function. In the case of proteins, the loss of one molecule is not serious if there are other copies of it in the cell and additional copies can be made from the gene that codes for it. However, large doses of radiation may damage so many molecules that new copies cannot be made quickly enough, and the cell dies. Damage to the DNA is more serious, since a cell may have only one copy. Each alteration in the DNA can affect a gene and alter the molecule it codes for (Section 40–3), so that needed proteins or other materials may not be made at all. Again the cell may die. The death of a single cell is not normally a problem, since the body can replace it with a new one. (There are exceptions, such as neurons, which are mostly not replaceable, so their loss is serious.) But if many cells die, the organism may not be able to recover. On the other hand, a cell may survive but be defective. It may go on dividing and produce many more defective cells, to the detriment of the whole organism. Thus radiation can cause cancer—the rapid uncontrolled production of cells.

The possible damage done by the medical use of X-rays and other radiation must be balanced against the medical benefits and prolongation of life as a result of their use.

42–6 Measurement of Radiation— Dosimetry

Although the passage of ionizing radiation through the human body can cause considerable damage, radiation can also be used to treat certain diseases, particularly cancer, often by using very narrow beams directed at a cancerous tumor in order to destroy it (Section 42–7). It is therefore important to be able to quantify the amount, or **dose**, of radiation. This is the subject of **dosimetry**.

The strength of a source can be specified at a given time by stating the **source activity**: how many nuclear decays (or disintegrations) occur per second. The traditional unit is the **curie** (Ci), defined as

$$1 \, \text{Ci} = 3.70 \times 10^{10} \, \text{decays per second.}$$

(This number comes from the original definition as the activity of exactly one gram of radium.) Although the curie is still in common use, the SI unit for source activity is the **becquerel** (Bq), defined as

$$1 \, \text{Bq} = 1 \, \text{decay/s.}$$

Commercial suppliers of **radionuclides** (radioactive nuclides) specify the activity at a given time. Since the activity decreases over time, more so for short-lived isotopes, it is important to take this into account.

The magnitude of the source activity $|dN/dt|$ is related to the number of radioactive nuclei present, N, and to the half-life, $T_{\frac{1}{2}}$, by (see Section 41–8):

$$\left| \frac{dN}{dt} \right| = \lambda N = \frac{0.693}{T_{\frac{1}{2}}} N.$$

EXAMPLE 42–11 **Radioactivity taken up by cells.** In a certain experiment, 0.016 μCi of $^{32}_{15}$P is injected into a medium containing a culture of bacteria. After 1.0 h the cells are washed and a 70% efficient detector (counts 70% of emitted β rays) records 720 counts per minute from the cells. What percentage of the original $^{32}_{15}$P was taken up by the cells?

APPROACH The half-life of $^{32}_{15}$P is about 14 days (Appendix F), so we can ignore any loss of activity over 1 hour. From the given activity, we find how many β rays are emitted. We can compare 70% of this to the $(720/\text{min})/(60 \, \text{s/min}) = 12$ per second detected.

SOLUTION The total number of decays per second originally was $(0.016 \times 10^{-6})(3.7 \times 10^{10}) = 590$. The counter could be expected to count 70% of this, or 410 per second. Since it counted $720/60 = 12$ per second, then $12/410 = 0.029$ or 2.9% was incorporated into the cells.

Another type of measurement is the exposure or **absorbed dose**—that is, the effect the radiation has on the absorbing material. The earliest unit of dosage was the **roentgen** (R), defined in terms of the amount of ionization produced by the radiation ($1 R = 1.6 \times 10^{12}$ ion pairs per gram of dry air at standard conditions). Today, 1 R is defined as the amount of X or γ radiation that deposits 0.878×10^{-2} J of energy per kilogram of air. The roentgen was largely superseded by another unit of absorbed dose applicable to any type of radiation, the **rad**: *1 rad is that amount of radiation which deposits energy per unit mass of 1.00×10^{-2} J/kg in any absorbing material.* (This is quite close to the roentgen for X- and γ rays.) The proper SI unit for absorbed dose is the **gray** (Gy):

$$1 \, \text{Gy} = 1 \, \text{J/kg} = 100 \, \text{rad}. \tag{42–10}$$

The absorbed dose depends not only on the strength of a given radiation beam (number of particles per second) and the energy per particle, but also on the type of material that is absorbing the radiation. Bone, for example, absorbs more of the radiation normally used than does flesh, so the same beam passing through a human body deposits a greater dose (in rads or grays) in bone than in flesh.

The gray and the rad are physical units of dose—the energy deposited per unit mass of material. They are, however, not the most meaningful units for measuring the biological damage produced by radiation because equal doses of different types of radiation cause differing amounts of damage. For example, 1 rad of α radiation does 10 to 20 times the amount of damage as 1 rad of β or γ rays. This difference arises largely because α rays (and other heavy particles such as protons and neutrons) move much more slowly than β and γ rays of equal energy due to their greater mass. Hence, ionizing collisions occur closer together, so more irreparable damage can be done. The **relative biological effectiveness** (RBE) or **quality factor** (QF) of a given type of radiation is defined as the number of rads of X or γ radiation that produces the same biological damage as 1 rad of the given radiation. Table 42–1 gives the QF for several types of radiation. The numbers are approximate since they depend somewhat on the energy of the particles and on the type of damage that is used as the criterion.

The **effective dose** can be given as the product of the dose in rads and the QF, and this unit is known as the **rem** (which stands for *rad equivalent man*):

$$\text{effective dose (in rem)} = \text{dose (in rad)} \times \text{QF}. \tag{42–11a}$$

This unit is being replaced by the SI unit for "effective dose," the **sievert** (Sv):

$$\text{effective dose (Sv)} = \text{dose (Gy)} \times \text{QF}. \tag{42–11b}$$

By these definitions, 1 rem (or 1 Sv) of any type of radiation does approximately the same amount of biological damage. For example, 50 rem of fast neutrons does the same damage as 50 rem of γ rays. But note that 50 rem of fast neutrons is only 5 rads, whereas 50 rem of γ rays is 50 rads.

EXERCISE E Return to the second Chapter-Opening Question, page 1131, and answer it again now. Try to explain why you many have answered it differently the first time.

Human Exposure to Radiation

PHYSICS APPLIED
Radon

We are constantly exposed to low-level radiation from natural sources: cosmic rays, natural radioactivity in rocks and soil, and naturally occurring radioactive isotopes in our food, such as $^{40}_{19}$K. **Radon**, $^{222}_{86}$Rn, is of considerable concern today. It is the product of radium decay and is an intermediate in the decay series from uranium (see Fig. 41–12). Most intermediates remain in the rocks where formed, but radon is a gas that can escape from rock (and from building material like concrete) to enter the air we breathe, and attack the interior of the lung.

PHYSICS APPLIED
Human radiation exposure

The **natural radioactive background** averages about 0.30 rem (300 mrem) per year per person in the U.S., although there are large variations. From medical X-rays and scans, the average person receives about 50 to 60 mrem per year, giving an average total dose of about 360 mrem (3.6 mSv) per person. Government regulators suggest an upper limit of allowed radiation for an individual in the

TABLE 42–1 Quality Factor (QF) of Different Kinds of Radiation

Type	QF
X- and γ rays	1
β (electrons)	≈ 1
Fast protons	1
Slow neutrons	≈ 3
Fast neutrons	Up to 10
α particles and heavy ions	Up to 20

general populace at about 100 mrem (1 mSv) per year in addition to natural background. It is believed that even low doses of radiation increase the chances of cancer or genetic defects; there is no safe level or threshold of radiation exposure.

The upper limit for people who work around radiation—in hospitals, in power plants, in research—has been set higher, a maximum of 5 rem (50 mSv) whole-body dose in any one year, and significantly less averaged over more years (below 2 rem/yr averaged over 5 years). To monitor exposure, those people who work around radiation generally carry some type of dosimeter, one common type being a **radiation film badge** which is a piece of film wrapped in light-tight material. The passage of ionizing radiation through the film changes it so that the film is darkened upon development, and thus indicates the received dose. Newer types include the *thermoluminescent dosimeter* (TLD). Dosimeters and badges do not protect the worker, but high levels detected suggest reassignment or modified work practices to reduce radiation exposure to acceptable levels.

Large doses of radiation can cause unpleasant symptoms such as nausea, fatigue, and loss of body hair. Such effects are sometimes referred to as **radiation sickness**. Large doses can be fatal, although the time span of the dose is important. A short dose of 1000 rem (10 Sv) is nearly always fatal. A 400-rem (4-Sv) dose in a short period of time is fatal in 50% of the cases. However, the body possesses remarkable repair processes, so that a 400-rem dose spread over several weeks is usually not fatal. It will, nonetheless, cause considerable damage to the body.

The effects of low doses over a long time are difficult to determine and are not well known as yet.

⊕ **PHYSICS APPLIED**
Radiation worker exposure
Film badge

⊕ **PHYSICS APPLIED**
Radiation sickness

EXAMPLE 42–12 **Whole-body dose.** What whole-body dose is received by a 70-kg laboratory worker exposed to a 40-mCi $^{60}_{27}$Co source, assuming the person's body has cross-sectional area 1.5 m² and is normally about 4.0 m from the source for 4.0 h per day? $^{60}_{27}$Co emits γ rays of energy 1.33 MeV and 1.17 MeV in quick succession. Approximately 50% of the γ rays interact in the body and deposit all their energy. (The rest pass through.)

APPROACH Of the given energy emitted, only a fraction passes through the worker, equal to *her* area divided by the total area over a full sphere of radius 4.0 m (Fig. 42–16).

SOLUTION The total γ-ray energy per decay is $(1.33 + 1.17)$ MeV = 2.50 MeV, so the total energy emitted by the source per second is

$$(0.040 \text{ Ci})(3.7 \times 10^{10} \text{ decays/Ci} \cdot \text{s})(2.50 \text{ MeV}) = 3.7 \times 10^9 \text{ MeV/s}.$$

The proportion of this energy intercepted by the body is its 1.5-m² area divided by the area of a sphere of radius 4.0 m (Fig. 42–16):

$$\frac{1.5 \text{ m}^2}{4\pi r^2} = \frac{1.5 \text{ m}^2}{4\pi (4.0 \text{ m})^2} = 7.5 \times 10^{-3}.$$

So the rate energy is deposited in the body (remembering that only 50% of the γ rays interact in the body) is

$$E = (\tfrac{1}{2})(7.5 \times 10^{-3})(3.7 \times 10^9 \text{ MeV/s})(1.6 \times 10^{-13} \text{ J/MeV}) = 2.2 \times 10^{-6} \text{ J/s}.$$

Since 1 Gy = 1 J/kg, the whole-body dose rate for this 70-kg person is $(2.2 \times 10^{-6} \text{ J/s})/(70 \text{ kg}) = 3.1 \times 10^{-8} \text{ Gy/s}$. In 4.0 h, this amounts to a dose of

$$(4.0 \text{ h})(3600 \text{ s/h})(3.1 \times 10^{-8} \text{ Gy/s}) = 4.5 \times 10^{-4} \text{ Gy}.$$

Since QF $\approx$ 1 for gammas, the effective dose is 450 μSv (Eqs. 42–11b and 42–10) or:

$$(100 \text{ rad/Gy})(4.5 \times 10^{-4} \text{ Gy})(1 \text{ rem/rad}) = 45 \text{ mrem} = 0.45 \text{ mSv}.$$

NOTE This 45-mrem effective dose is almost 50% of the normal allowed dose for a whole year (100 mrem/yr), or 1% of the maximum one-year allowance for radiation workers. This worker should not receive such a large dose every day and should seek ways to reduce it (shield the source, vary the work, work farther from the source, work less time this close to source, etc.).

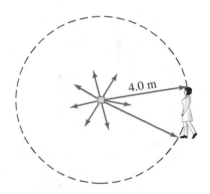

FIGURE 42–16 Radiation spreads out in all directions. A person 4.0 m away intercepts only a fraction: her cross-sectional area divided by the area of a sphere of radius 4.0 m. Example 42–12.

EXAMPLE 42–13 **Radon exposure.** In the U.S., yearly deaths from radon exposure (the second leading cause of lung cancer) are estimated to exceed the yearly deaths from drunk driving. The Environmental Protection Agency recommends taking action to reduce the radon concentration in living areas if it exceeds 4 pCi/L of air. In some areas 50% of houses exceed this level from naturally occurring radon in the soil. Estimate the mass of radon that emits 4.0 pCi of $^{222}_{86}$Rn radiation.

APPROACH We can use the definition of the curie to determine how many decays per second correspond to 4 pCi, then Eq. 41–7b to determine how many nuclei of radon it takes to have this activity $|dN/dt|$.

SOLUTION We saw at the start of Section 42–6 that 1 Ci = 3.70×10^{10} decays/s. Thus

$$\left|\frac{dN}{dt}\right| = 4.0\,\text{pCi}$$
$$= (4.0 \times 10^{-12}\,\text{Ci})(3.70 \times 10^{10}\,\text{decays/s/Ci})$$
$$= 0.148\,\text{s}^{-1}.$$

From Eqs. 41–7a and 41–8

$$\left|\frac{dN}{dt}\right| = \lambda N = \frac{0.693}{T_{\frac{1}{2}}}N.$$

Appendix F tells us $T_{\frac{1}{2}}$ = 3.8232 days, so

$$N = \left|\frac{dN}{dt}\right|\frac{T_{\frac{1}{2}}}{0.693}$$
$$= (0.148\,\text{s}^{-1})\frac{(3.8232\,\text{days})(8.64 \times 10^4\,\text{s/day})}{0.693}$$
$$= 7.05 \times 10^4\,\text{atoms of radon-222}.$$

The molar mass (222 u) and Avogadro's number are used to find the mass:

$$m = \frac{(7.05 \times 10^4\,\text{atoms})(222\,\text{g/mol})}{6.02 \times 10^{23}\,\text{atoms/mol}} = 2.6 \times 10^{-17}\,\text{g}$$

or 26 attograms in 1 L of air. This 2.6×10^{-17} g/L = 2.6×10^{-14} g/m^3 of radon is about 150 atoms decaying per second in every meter of air at the limit of 4 pCi/L.

NOTE Each radon atom emits 4 α particles and 4 β particles before the decay sequence reaches a stable element, each one capable of causing many harmful ionizations.

*42–7 Radiation Therapy

The medical application of radioactivity and radiation to human beings involves two basic aspects: (1) **radiation therapy**—the treatment of disease (mainly cancer)—which we discuss in this Section; and (2) the *diagnosis* of disease, which we discuss in the following Sections of this Chapter.

Radiation can cause cancer. It can also be used to treat it. Rapidly growing cancer cells are especially susceptible to destruction by radiation. Nonetheless, large doses are needed to kill the cancer cells, and some of the surrounding normal cells are inevitably killed as well. It is for this reason that cancer patients receiving radiation therapy often suffer side effects characteristic of radiation sickness. To minimize the destruction of normal cells, a narrow beam of γ or X-rays is often used when a cancerous tumor is well localized. The beam is directed at the tumor, and the source (or body) is rotated so that the beam passes through various parts of the body to keep the dose at any one place as low as possible—except at the tumor and its immediate surroundings, where the beam passes at all times (Fig. 42–17). The radiation may be from a radioactive source such as $^{60}_{27}$Co, or it may be from an X-ray machine that produces photons in the range 200 keV to 5 MeV. Protons, neutrons, electrons, and pions, which are produced in particle accelerators (Section 43–1), are also being used in cancer therapy.

Protons used to kill tumors have a special property that makes them particularly useful. As shown in Fig. 42–18, when protons enter tissue, most of their energy is deposited at the end of their path. The protons' initial kinetic energy can be chosen so that most of the energy is deposited at the depth of the tumor itself, to destroy it. The incoming protons deposit only a small amount of energy in the tissue in front of the tumor, and none at all behind the tumor, thus having less negative effect on healthy tissue than X- or γ rays. Because tumors have physical size, even several centimeters in diameter, a range of proton energies is often used. Heavier ions, such as α particles or carbon ions, are similarly useful. This **proton therapy** technique is more than a half century old, but the necessity of having a large accelerator has meant that few hospitals have used the technique until now. Many such "proton centers" are now being built.

FIGURE 42–17 Radiation source rotates so that the beam always passes through the diseased tissue, but minimizes the dose in the rest of the body.

Proton therapy

FIGURE 42–18 Energy deposited in tissue as a function of depth for 170-MeV protons (red curve) and 190-MeV protons (green). The peak of each curve is often called the Bragg peak.

Another form of treatment is to insert a tiny radioactive source directly inside a tumor, which will eventually kill the majority of the cells. A similar technique is used to treat cancer of the thyroid with the radioactive isotope $^{131}_{53}$I. The thyroid gland concentrates iodine present in the bloodstream, particularly in any area where abnormal growth is taking place. Its intense radioactivity can destroy the defective cells.

Another application of radiation is for sterilizing bandages, surgical equipment, and even packaged foods, since bacteria and viruses can be killed or deactivated by large doses of radiation.

*42–8 Tracers in Research and Medicine

Radioactive isotopes are commonly used in biological and medical research as **tracers**. A given compound is artificially synthesized using a radioactive isotope such as $^{14}_{6}$C or $^{3}_{1}$H. Such "tagged" molecules can then be traced as they move through an organism or as they undergo chemical reactions. The presence of these tagged molecules (or parts of them, if they undergo chemical change) can be detected by a Geiger or scintillation counter, which detects emitted radiation (see Section 41–11). How food molecules are digested, and to what parts of the body they are diverted, can be traced in this way.

Tracers in medicine and biology

(a)

(b)

FIGURE 42–19 (a) Autoradiograph of a leaf exposed for 30 s to $^{14}CO_2$. The photosynthetic (green) tissue has become radioactive; the nonphotosynthetic tissue of the veins is free of $^{14}_6C$ and therefore does not blacken the X-ray sheet. This technique is useful in following patterns of nutrient transport in plants. (b) Autoradiograph of chromosomal DNA. The dashed arrays of film grains show the Y-shaped growing point of replicating DNA.

Radioactive tracers have been used to determine how amino acids and other essential compounds are synthesized by organisms. The permeability of cell walls to various molecules and ions can be determined using radioactive isotopes: the tagged molecule or ion is injected into the extracellular fluid, and the radioactivity present inside and outside the cells is measured as a function of time.

In a technique known as **autoradiography**, the position of the radioactive isotopes is detected on film. For example, the distribution of carbohydrates produced in the leaves of plants from absorbed CO_2 can be observed by keeping the plant in an atmosphere where the carbon atom in the CO_2 is $^{14}_6C$. After a time, a leaf is placed firmly on a photographic plate and the emitted radiation darkens the film most strongly where the isotope is most strongly concentrated (Fig. 42–19a). Autoradiography using labeled nucleotides (components of DNA) has revealed much about the details of DNA replication (Fig. 42–19b).

For medical diagnosis, the radionuclide commonly used today is $^{99m}_{43}Tc$, a long-lived excited state of technetium-99 (the "m" in the symbol stands for "metastable" state). It is formed when $^{99}_{42}Mo$ decays. The great usefulness of $^{99m}_{43}Tc$ derives from its convenient half-life of 6 h (short, but not too short) and the fact that it can combine with a large variety of compounds. The compound to be labeled with the radionuclide is so chosen because it concentrates in the organ or region of the anatomy to be studied. Detectors outside the body then record, or image, the distribution of the radioactively labeled compound. The detection could be done by a single detector (Fig. 42–20a) which is moved across the body, measuring the intensity of radioactivity at a large number of points. The image represents the relative intensity of radioactivity at each point. The relative radioactivity is a diagnostic tool. For example, high or low radioactivity may represent overactivity or underactivity of an organ or part of an organ, or in another case may represent a lesion or tumor. More complex **gamma cameras** make use of many detectors which simultaneously record the radioactivity at many points. The measured intensities can be displayed on a TV or computer monitor. The image is sometimes called a scintigram (after scintillator), Fig. 42–20b. Gamma cameras are relatively inexpensive, but their resolution is limited—by non-perfect collimation[†]; but they allow "dynamic" studies: images that change in time, like a movie.

[†] To "collimate" means to "make parallel," usually by blocking non-parallel rays with a narrow tube inside lead, as in Fig. 42–20a.

(a)   (b)

Photomultiplier tube

Scintillator crystal

Lead collimator

Collimating hole

Patient

FIGURE 42–20 (a) Collimated gamma-ray detector for scanning (moving) over a patient. The collimator selects γ rays that come in a (nearly) straight line from the patient. Without the collimator, γ rays from all parts of the body could strike the scintillator, producing a poor image. Detectors today usually have many collimator tubes and are called *gamma cameras*. (b) Gamma camera image (scintigram) of a leg with a fatigue fracture detecting γs from $^{99m}_{43}Tc$. The image is gray scale, but is colored here for visibility.

Imaging by Tomography: CAT Scans and Emission Tomography

*Normal X-ray Image

For a conventional medical or dental X-ray photograph, the X-rays emerging from the tube (Section 35–10) pass through the body and are detected on photographic film or a fluorescent screen, Fig. 42–21. The rays travel in very nearly straight lines through the body with minimal deviation since at X-ray wavelengths there is little diffraction or refraction. There is absorption (and scattering), however; and the difference in absorption by different structures in the body is what gives rise to the image produced by the transmitted rays. The less the absorption, the greater the transmission and the darker the film. The image is, in a sense, a "shadow" of what the rays have passed through. The X-ray image is *not* produced by focusing rays with lenses as for the instruments discussed in Chapter 33.

PHYSICS APPLIED
Normal X-ray image is a sort of shadow (no lenses involved)

X-ray source

FIGURE 42–21 Conventional X-ray imaging, which is essentially shadowing.

*Tomography Images (CT)

In conventional X-ray images, the entire thickness of the body is projected onto the film; structures overlap and in many cases are difficult to distinguish. In the 1970s, a revolutionary new X-ray technique was developed called **computed tomography** (CT), which produces an image of a *slice* through the body. (The word **tomography** comes from the Greek: *tomos* = slice, *graph* = picture.) Structures and lesions previously impossible to visualize can now be seen with remarkable clarity. The principle behind CT is shown in Fig. 42–22: a thin collimated beam of X-rays (to "collimate" means to "make parallel") passes through the body to a detector that measures the transmitted intensity. Measurements are made at a large number of points as the source and detector are moved past the body together. The apparatus is then rotated slightly about the body axis and again scanned; this is repeated at (perhaps) 1° intervals for 180°. The intensity of the transmitted beam for the many points of each scan, and for each angle, are sent to a computer that reconstructs the image of the slice. Note that the imaged slice is perpendicular to the long axis of the body. For this reason, CT is sometimes called **computerized axial tomography** (CAT), although the abbreviation CAT, as in CAT scan, can also be read as **computer-assisted tomography**.

The use of a single detector as in Fig. 42–22 would require a few minutes for the many scans needed to form a complete image. Much faster scanners use

PHYSICS APPLIED
Computed tomography images

Video monitor

Computer

Collimator

Detector

Collimator

X-ray source

FIGURE 42–22 Tomographic imaging: the X-ray source and detector move together across the body, the transmitted intensity being measured at a large number of points. Then the source–detector assembly is rotated slightly (say, 1°) and another scan is made. This process is repeated for perhaps 180°. The computer reconstructs the image of the slice and it is presented on a TV or computer monitor.

(a)   (b)

FIGURE 42–23 (a) Fan-beam scanner. Rays transmitted through the entire body are measured simultaneously at each angle. The source and detector rotate to take measurements at different angles. In another type of fan-beam scanner, there are detectors around the entire 360° of the circle which remain fixed as the source moves. (b) In still another type, a beam of electrons from a source is directed by magnetic fields at tungsten targets surrounding the patient.

a fan beam, Fig. 42–23a, in which beams passing through the entire cross section of the body are detected simultaneously by many detectors. The source and detectors are then rotated about the patient, and an image requires only a few seconds. Even faster, and therefore useful for heart scans, are fixed source machines wherein an electron beam is directed (by magnetic fields) to tungsten targets surrounding the patient, creating the X-rays. See Fig. 42–23b.

*Image Formation

But how is the image formed? We can think of the slice to be imaged as being divided into many tiny picture elements (or **pixels**), which could be squares. (See Fig. 35–42.) For CT, the width of each pixel is chosen according to the width of the detectors and/or the width of the X-ray beams, and this determines the resolution of the image, which might be 1 mm. An X-ray detector measures the intensity of the transmitted beam. When we subtract this value from the intensity of the beam at the source, we obtain the total absorption (called a "projection") along that beam line. Complicated mathematical techniques are used to analyze all the absorption projections for the huge number of beam scans measured (see the next Subsection), obtaining the absorption at each pixel and assigning each a "grayness value" according to how much radiation was absorbed. The image is made up of tiny spots (pixels) of varying shades of gray. Often the amount of absorption is color-coded. The colors in the resulting **false-color** image have nothing to do, however, with the actual color of the object. The real medical images are monochromatic (various shades of gray). Only *visible* light has color; X-rays and γ rays don't.

Figure 42–24 illustrates what actual CT images look like. It is generally agreed that CT scanning has revolutionized some areas of medicine by providing much less invasive, and/or more accurate, diagnosis.

Computed tomography can also be applied to ultrasound imaging (Section 16–9) and to emissions from radioisotopes and nuclear magnetic resonance, which we discuss in Section 42–10.

*Tomographic Image Reconstruction

How can the "grayness" of each pixel be determined even though all we can measure is the total absorption along each beam line in the slice? It can be done only by using the many beam scans made at a great many different angles. Suppose the image is to be an array of 100×100 elements for a total of 10^4 pixels. If we have 100 detectors and measure the absorption projections at 100 different angles, then we get 10^4 pieces of information. From this information, an image can be reconstructed, but not precisely. If more angles are measured, the reconstruction of the image can be done more accurately.

FIGURE 42–24 Two CT images, with different resolutions, each showing a cross section of a brain. Photo (a) is of low resolution. Photo (b), of higher resolution, shows a brain tumor, and uses false color to highlight it.

(a)

(b)

To suggest how mathematical reconstruction is done, we consider a very simple case using the "iterative" technique ("to iterate" is from the Latin "to repeat"). Suppose our sample slice is divided into the simple 2 × 2 pixels as shown in Fig. 42–25. The number inside each pixel represents the amount of absorption by the material in that area (say, in tenths of a percent): that is, 4 represents twice as much absorption as 2. But we cannot directly measure these values—they are the unknowns we want to solve for. All we can measure are the projections—the total absorption along each beam line—and these are shown in the diagram as the sum of the absorptions for the pixels along each line at four different angles. These projections (given at the tip of each arrow) are what we can measure, and we now want to work back from them to see how close we can get to the true absorption value for each pixel. We start our analysis with each pixel being assigned a zero value, Fig. 42–26a. In the iterative technique, we use the projections to estimate the absorption value in each square, and repeat for each angle. The angle 1 projections are 7 and 13. We divide each of these equally between their two squares: each square in the left column gets $3\frac{1}{2}$ (half of 7), and each square in the right column gets $6\frac{1}{2}$ (half of 13); see Fig. 42–26b. Next we use the projections at angle 2. We

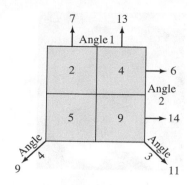

FIGURE 42–25 A simple 2 × 2 image showing true absorption values and measured projections.

FIGURE 42–26 Reconstructing the image using projections in an iterative procedure.

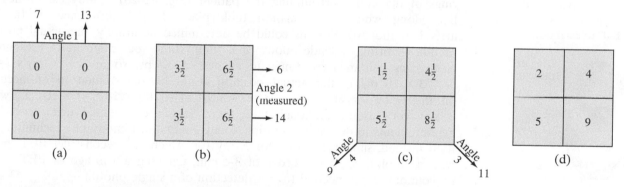

calculate the difference between the measured projections at angle 2 (6 and 14) and the projections based on the previous estimate (top row: $3\frac{1}{2} + 6\frac{1}{2} = 10$; same for bottom row). Then we distribute this difference equally to the squares in that row. For the top row, we have

$$3\frac{1}{2} + \frac{6 - 10}{2} = 1\frac{1}{2} \quad \text{and} \quad 6\frac{1}{2} + \frac{6 - 10}{2} = 4\frac{1}{2};$$

and for the bottom row,

$$3\frac{1}{2} + \frac{14 - 10}{2} = 5\frac{1}{2} \quad \text{and} \quad 6\frac{1}{2} + \frac{14 - 10}{2} = 8\frac{1}{2}.$$

These values are inserted as shown in Fig. 42–26c. Next, the projection at angle 3 gives

$$\text{(upper left)} \quad 1\frac{1}{2} + \frac{11 - 10}{2} = 2 \quad \text{and} \quad \text{(lower right)} \quad 8\frac{1}{2} + \frac{11 - 10}{2} = 9;$$

and that for angle 4 gives

$$\text{(lower left)} \quad 5\frac{1}{2} + \frac{9 - 10}{2} = 5 \quad \text{and} \quad \text{(upper right)} \quad 4\frac{1}{2} + \frac{9 - 10}{2} = 4.$$

The result, shown in Fig. 42–26d, corresponds exactly to the true values. (In real situations, the true values are not known, which is why these computer techniques are required.) To obtain these numbers exactly, we used six pieces of information (two each at angles 1 and 2, one each at angles 3 and 4). For the much larger number of pixels used for actual images, exact values are generally not attained. Many iterations may be needed, and the calculation is considered sufficiently precise when the difference between calculated and measured projections is sufficiently small. The above example illustrates the "convergence" of the process: the first iteration (b to c in Fig. 42–26) changed the values by 2, the last iteration (c to d) by only $\frac{1}{2}$.

FIGURE 42-27 SPECT scan of brain (false color) with Mesulam's syndrome, labeled with $^{99m}_{43}$Tc.

Ⓧ **PHYSICS APPLIED**

Emission tomography (SPECT, PET)

FIGURE 42-28 Positron emission tomography (PET) system showing a ring of detectors to detect the two annihilation γ rays $(e^+ + e^- \rightarrow 2\gamma)$ emitted at 180° to each other.

Ring of detectors

*Emission Tomography

It is possible to image the emissions of a radioactive tracer (see Section 42–8) in a single plane or slice through a body using computed tomography techniques. A basic gamma detector (Fig. 42–20a) can be moved around the patient to measure the radioactive intensity from the tracer at many points and angles; the data are processed in much the same way as for X-ray CT scans. This technique is referred to as **single photon emission tomography** (SPET), or SPECT (single photon emission computed tomography); see Fig. 42–27.

Another important technique is **positron emission tomography** (PET), which makes use of positron emitters such as $^{11}_{6}$C, $^{13}_{7}$N, $^{15}_{8}$O, and $^{18}_{9}$F. These isotopes are incorporated into molecules that, when inhaled or injected, accumulate in the organ or region of the body to be studied. When such a nuclide undergoes β^+ decay, the emitted positron travels at most a few millimeters before it collides with a normal electron. In this collision, the positron and electron are annihilated, producing two γ rays $(e^+ + e^- \rightarrow 2\gamma)$. The two γ rays fly off in opposite directions $(180° \pm 0.25°)$ since they must have almost exactly equal and opposite momenta to conserve momentum (the momenta of the initial e^+ and e^- are essentially zero compared to the momenta of the γ rays). Because the photons travel along the same line in opposite directions, their detection in coincidence by rings of detectors surrounding the patient (Fig. 42–28) readily establishes the line along which the emission took place. If the difference in time of arrival of the two photons could be determined accurately, the actual position of the emitting nuclide along that line could be calculated. Present-day electronics can measure times to at best ± 300 ps, so at the γ ray's speed $(c = 3 \times 10^8 \text{ m/s})$, the actual position could be determined to an accuracy on the order of about $d = vt \approx (3 \times 10^8 \text{ m/s})(300 \times 10^{-12} \text{ s}) \approx 10 \text{ cm}$, which is not very useful. Although there may be future potential for time-of-flight measurements to determine position, today computed tomography techniques are used instead, similar to those for X-ray CT, which can reconstruct PET images with a resolution on the order of 3–5 mm. One big advantage of PET is that no collimators are needed (as for detection of a single photon—see Fig. 42–20a). Thus, fewer photons are "wasted" and lower doses can be administered to the patient with PET.

Both PET and SPET systems can give images related to biochemistry, metabolism, and function. This is to be compared to X-ray CT scans, whose images reflect shape and structure—that is, the anatomy of the imaged region.

*42–10 Nuclear Magnetic Resonance (NMR); Magnetic Resonance Imaging (MRI)

Nuclear magnetic resonance (NMR) is a phenomenon which soon after its discovery in 1946 became a powerful research tool in a variety of fields from physics to chemistry and biochemistry. It is also an important medical imaging technique. We first briefly discuss the phenomenon, and then look at its applications.

*Nuclear Magnetic Resonance (NMR)

We saw in Chapter 39 that the energy levels in atoms are split when they are placed in a magnetic field B (the Zeeman effect) according to the angular momentum or spin of the state. The splitting is proportional to B and to the magnetic moment, μ. Nuclei too have magnetic moments (Section 41–1), and we examine only the simplest, the hydrogen ($^1_1$H) nucleus which consists of a single proton. Its spin angular momentum (and its magnetic moment), like that of the electron, can take on only two values when placed in a magnetic field: spin up (parallel to the field) and spin down (antiparallel to the field) as suggested in Fig. 42–29.

FIGURE 42-29 Schematic picture of a proton in a magnetic field $\vec{B}$ (pointing upward) with the two possible states of proton spin, up and down.

$\vec{B}$

Up   Down

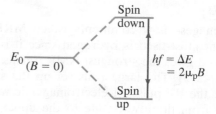

FIGURE 42–30 Energy E_0 in the absence of a magnetic field splits into two levels in the presence of a magnetic field.

When a magnetic field is present, an energy state splits into two levels as shown in Fig. 42–30 with the spin-up state (parallel to field) having the lower energy. The spin-down state acquires an additional energy $\mu_p B_T$ and the spin-up state has its energy changed by $-\mu_p B_T$ (Eq. 27–12 and Section 39–7), where B_T is the total magnetic field at the nucleus. The difference in energy between the two states (Fig. 42–30) is thus

$$\Delta E = 2\mu_p B_T,$$

where μ_p is the magnetic moment of the proton.

In a standard nuclear magnetic resonance (NMR) setup, the sample to be examined is placed in a static magnetic field. A radiofrequency (RF) pulse of electromagnetic radiation (that is, photons) is applied to the sample. If the frequency, f, of this pulse corresponds precisely to the energy difference between the two energy levels (Fig. 42–30), so that

$$hf = \Delta E = 2\mu_p B_T, \tag{42–12}$$

then the photons of the RF beam will be absorbed, exciting many of the nuclei from the lower state to the upper state. This is a resonance phenomenon since there is significant absorption only if f is very near $f = 2\mu_p B_T/h$. Hence the name "nuclear magnetic resonance." For free $_1^1$H nuclei, the frequency is 42.58 MHz for a field $B_T = 1.0$ T (Example 42–14). If the H atoms are bound in a molecule, the total magnetic field B_T at the H nuclei will be the sum of the external applied field (B_{ext}) plus the local magnetic field (B_{loc}) due to electrons and nuclei of neighboring atoms. Since f is proportional to B_T, the value of f for a given external field will be slightly different for bound H atoms than for free atoms:

$$hf = 2\mu_p(B_{ext} + B_{loc}).$$

This change in frequency, which can be measured, is called the "chemical shift." A great deal has been learned about the structure of molecules and bonds using this NMR technique.

EXAMPLE 42–14 **NMR for free protons.** Calculate the resonant frequency for free protons in a 1.000-T magnetic field.

APPROACH We use Eq. 42–12, where the magnetic moment of the proton (Section 41–1) is

$$\mu_p = 2.7928\mu_N = 2.7928\left(\frac{e\hbar}{2m_p}\right) = 2.7928\left(\frac{eh}{4\pi m_p}\right).$$

SOLUTION We solve for f in Eq. 42–12 and find

$$f = \frac{\Delta E}{h} = \frac{2\mu_p B}{h}$$

$$= (2.7928)\left(\frac{eB}{2\pi m_p}\right) = 2.7928\left[\frac{(1.6022 \times 10^{-19}\,\text{C})(1.000\,\text{T})}{2\pi(1.6726 \times 10^{-27}\,\text{kg})}\right]$$

$$= 42.58\,\text{MHz}.$$

* Magnetic Resonance Imaging (MRI)

For producing medically useful NMR images—now commonly called MRI, or **magnetic resonance imaging**—the element most used is hydrogen since it is the commonest element in the human body and gives the strongest NMR signals. The experimental apparatus is shown in Fig. 42–31. The large coils set up the static magnetic field, and the RF coils produce the RF pulse of electromagnetic waves (photons) that cause the nuclei to jump from the lower state to the upper one (Fig. 42–30). These same coils (or another coil) can detect the absorption of energy or the emitted radiation (also of frequency $f = \Delta E/h$) when the nuclei jump back down to the lower state.

Magnetic field coils

RF coils

(a) (b)

FIGURE 42–31 Typical MRI imaging setup: (a) diagram; (b) photograph.

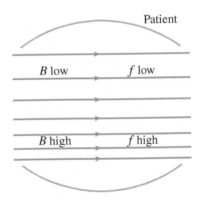

Patient

B low f low

B high f high

FIGURE 42–32 A static field that is stronger at the bottom than at the top. The frequency of absorbed or emitted radiation is proportional to B in NMR.

FIGURE 42–33 False-color NMR image (MRI) of a vertical section through the head showing structures in the normal brain.

The formation of a two-dimensional or three-dimensional image can be done using techniques similar to those for computed tomography (Section 42–9). The simplest thing to measure for creating an image is the intensity of absorbed and/or reemitted radiation from many different points of the body, and this would be a measure of the density of H atoms at each point. But how do we determine from what part of the body a given photon comes? One technique is to give the static magnetic field a gradient; that is, instead of applying a uniform magnetic field, B_T, the field is made to vary with position across the width of the sample (or patient). Since the frequency absorbed by the H nuclei is proportional to B_T (Eq. 42–12), only one plane within the body will have the proper value of B_T to absorb photons of a particular frequency f. By varying f, absorption by different planes can be measured. Alternately, if the field gradient is applied *after* the RF pulse, the frequency of the emitted photons will be a measure of where they were emitted. See Fig. 42–32. If a magnetic field gradient in one direction is applied during excitation (absorption of photons) and photons of a single frequency are transmitted, only H nuclei in one thin slice will be excited. By applying a gradient during reemission in a direction perpendicular to the first, the frequency f of the reemitted radiation will represent depth in that slice. Other ways of varying the magnetic field throughout the volume of the body can be used in order to correlate NMR frequency with position.

A reconstructed image based on the density of H atoms (that is, the intensity of absorbed or emitted radiation) is not very interesting. More useful are images based on the rate at which the nuclei decay back to the ground state, and such images can produce resolution of 1 mm or better. This NMR technique (sometimes called **spin-echo**) produces images of great diagnostic value, both in the delineation of structure (anatomy) and in the study of metabolic processes. An NMR image is shown in Fig. 42–33, color enhanced—no medical imaging uses visible light, so the colors shown here are added. The original images, those looked at by your doctor, are various shades of gray, representing intensity (or counts).

NMR imaging is considered to be noninvasive. We can calculate the energy of the photons involved: as determined in Example 42–14, in a 1.0-T magnetic field, $f = 42.58$ MHz for $^1_1$H. This corresponds to an energy of $hf = (6.6 \times 10^{-34}\,\text{J}\cdot\text{s})(43 \times 10^6\,\text{Hz}) \approx 3 \times 10^{-26}$ J or about 10^{-7} eV. Since molecular bonds are on the order of 1 eV, it is clear that the RF photons can cause little cellular disruption. This should be compared to X- or γ rays whose energies are 10^4 to 10^6 eV and thus can cause significant damage. The static magnetic fields, though often large (~ 0.1 to 1 T), are believed to be harmless (except for people wearing heart pacemakers).

Table 42–2 lists the major techniques we have discussed for imaging the interior of the human body, along with the optimum resolution attainable today. Resolution is just one factor that must be considered, as the different imaging techniques provide different types of information, useful for different types of diagnosis.

TABLE 42–2 Medical Imaging Techniques

Technique	Resolution
Conventional X-ray	$\frac{1}{2}$ mm
CT scan, X-ray	$\frac{1}{2}$ mm
Nuclear medicine (tracers)	1 cm
SPET (single photon emission)	1 cm
PET (positron emission)	3–5 mm
NMR (MRI)	$\frac{1}{2}$–1 mm
Ultrasound (Section 16–9)	2 mm

Summary

A **nuclear reaction** occurs when two nuclei collide and two or more other nuclei (or particles) are produced. In this process, as in radioactivity, **transmutation** (change) of elements occurs.

The **reaction energy** or **Q-value** of a reaction $a + X \rightarrow Y + b$ is

$$Q = (M_a + M_X - M_b - M_Y)c^2 \qquad \textbf{(42–2a)}$$

$$= K_b + K_Y - K_a - K_X. \qquad \textbf{(42–2b)}$$

The effective **cross section** σ for a reaction is a measure of the reaction probability per target nucleus.

In **fission**, a heavy nucleus such as uranium splits into two intermediate-sized nuclei after being struck by a neutron. $^{235}_{92}$U is fissionable by slow neutrons, whereas some fissionable nuclei require fast neutrons. Much energy is released in fission (≈ 200 MeV per fission) because the binding energy per nucleon is lower for heavy nuclei than it is for intermediate-sized nuclei, so the mass of a heavy nucleus is greater than the total mass of its fission products. The fission process releases neutrons, so that a **chain reaction** is possible. The **critical mass** is the minimum mass of fuel needed to sustain a chain reaction. In a **nuclear reactor** or nuclear bomb, a **moderator** is used to slow down the released neutrons.

The **fusion** process, in which small nuclei combine to form larger ones, also releases energy. The energy from our Sun originates in the fusion reactions known as the **proton–proton cycle** in which four protons fuse to form a $^4_2$He nucleus producing 25 MeV of energy. A useful fusion reactor for power generation has not yet proved possible because of the difficulty in containing the fuel (e.g., deuterium) long enough at the extremely high temperature required ($\approx 10^8$ K). Nonetheless, great progress has been made in confining the collection of charged ions known as a **plasma**. The two main methods are **magnetic confinement**, using a magnetic field in a device such as the toroidal-shaped **tokamak**, and **inertial confinement** in which intense laser beams compress a fuel pellet of deuterium and tritium.

Radiation can cause damage to materials, including biological tissue. Quantifying amounts of radiation is the subject of **dosimetry**. The **curie** (Ci) and the **becquerel** (Bq) are units that measure the **source activity** or rate of decay of a sample: $1\,\text{Ci} = 3.70 \times 10^{10}$ decays per second, whereas $1\,\text{Bq} = 1$ decay/s. The **absorbed dose**, often specified in **rads**, measures the amount of energy deposited per unit mass of absorbing material: 1 rad is the amount of radiation that deposits energy at the rate of 10^{-2} J/kg of material. The SI unit of absorbed dose is the **gray**: $1\,\text{Gy} = 1\,\text{J/kg} = 100\,\text{rad}$. The **effective dose** is often specified by the **rem** $= \text{rad} \times \text{QF}$, where QF is the "quality factor" of a given type of radiation; 1 rem of any type of radiation does approximately the same amount of biological damage. The average dose received per person per year in the United States is about 360 mrem. The SI unit for effective dose is the **sievert**: $1\,\text{Sv} = 10^2\,\text{rem}$.

[*Nuclear radiation is used in medicine for cancer therapy, and for imaging of biological structure and processes. **Tomographic imaging** of the human body, which can provide 3-dimensional detail, includes several types: CT scans, PET, SPET (= SPECT), and MRI; the latter makes use of **nuclear magnetic resonance** (NMR).]

Questions

(NOTE: Masses are found in Appendix F.)

1. Fill in the missing particles or nuclei:

   (a) $n + {}^{137}_{56}$Ba $\rightarrow$? $+ \gamma$;

   (b) $n + {}^{137}_{56}$Ba $\rightarrow {}^{137}_{55}$Cs $+$?;

   (c) $d + {}^2_1$H $\rightarrow {}^4_2$He $+$?;

   (d) $\alpha + {}^{197}_{79}$Au $\rightarrow$? $+ d$

   where d stands for deuterium.

2. The isotope $^{32}_{15}$P is produced by the reaction: $n + ? \rightarrow {}^{32}_{15}\text{P} + p$. What must be the target nucleus?

3. When $^{22}_{11}$Na is bombarded by deuterons ($^2_1$H), an α particle is emitted. What is the resulting nuclide?

4. Why are neutrons such good projectiles for producing nuclear reactions?

5. A proton strikes a $^{20}_{10}$Ne nucleus, and an α particle is observed to emerge. What is the residual nucleus? Write down the reaction equation.

6. Are fission fragments β^+ or β^- emitters? Explain.

7. The energy from nuclear fission appears in the form of thermal energy—but the thermal energy of what?

8. $^{238}_{92}U$ releases an average of 2.5 neutrons per fission compared to 2.9 for $^{239}_{94}Pu$. Which of these two nuclei do you think would have the smaller critical mass? Explain.

9. If $^{235}_{92}U$ released only 1.5 neutrons per fission on the average, would a chain reaction be possible? If so, how would the chain reaction be different than if 3 neutrons were released per fission?

10. Why can't uranium be enriched by chemical means?

11. How can a neutron, with practically no kinetic energy, excite a nucleus to the extent shown in Fig. 42–4?

12. Why would a porous block of uranium be more likely to explode if kept under water rather than in air?

13. A reactor that uses highly enriched uranium can use ordinary water (instead of heavy water) as a moderator and still have a self-sustaining chain reaction. Explain.

14. Why must the fission process release neutrons if it is to be useful?

15. Why are neutrons released in a fission reaction?

16. What is the reason for the "secondary system" in a nuclear reactor, Fig. 42–9? That is, why is the water heated by the fuel in a nuclear reactor not used directly to drive the turbines?

17. What is the basic difference between fission and fusion?

18. Discuss the relative merits and disadvantages, including pollution and safety, of power generation by fossil fuels, nuclear fission, and nuclear fusion.

19. A higher temperature is required for deuterium–deuterium ignition than for deuterium–tritium. Explain.

20. Light energy emitted by the Sun and stars comes from the fusion process. What conditions in the interior of stars make this possible?

21. How do stars, and our Sun, maintain confinement of the plasma for fusion?

22. Why is the recommended maximum radiation dose higher for women beyond the child-bearing age than for younger women?

23. People who work around metals that emit alpha particles are trained that there is little danger from proximity or touching the material, but they must take extreme precautions against ingesting it. Why? (Eating and drinking while working are forbidden.)

24. What is the difference between absorbed dose and effective dose? What are the SI units for each?

25. Radiation is sometimes used to sterilize medical supplies and even food. Explain how it works.

*26. How might radioactive tracers be used to find a leak in a pipe?

Problems

(NOTE: Masses are found in Appendix F.)

42–1 Nuclear Reactions, Transmutation

1. (I) Natural aluminum is all $^{27}_{13}Al$. If it absorbs a neutron, what does it become? Does it decay by β^+ or β^-? What will be the product nucleus?

2. (I) Determine whether the reaction $^2_1H + ^2_1H \rightarrow ^3_2He + n$ requires a threshold energy.

3. (I) Is the reaction $n + ^{238}_{92}U \rightarrow ^{239}_{92}U + \gamma$ possible with slow neutrons? Explain.

4. (II) Does the reaction $p + ^7_3Li \rightarrow ^4_2He + \alpha$ require energy, or does it release energy? How much energy?

5. (II) Calculate the energy released (or energy input required) for the reaction $\alpha + ^9_4Be \rightarrow ^{12}_6C + n$.

6. (II) (a) Can the reaction $n + ^{24}_{12}Mg \rightarrow ^{23}_{11}Na + d$ occur if the bombarding particles have 16.00 MeV of kinetic energy? (d stands for deuterium, ^2_1H.) (b) If so, how much energy is released? If not, what kinetic energy is needed?

7. (II) (a) Can the reaction $p + ^7_3Li \rightarrow ^4_2He + \alpha$ occur if the incident proton has kinetic energy = 3500 keV? (b) If so, what is the total kinetic energy of the products? If not, what kinetic energy is needed?

8. (II) In the reaction $\alpha + ^{14}_7N \rightarrow ^{17}_8O + p$, the incident α particles have 9.68 MeV of kinetic energy. The mass of $^{17}_8O$ is 16.999132 u. (a) Can this reaction occur? (b) If so, what is the total kinetic energy of the products? If not, what kinetic energy is needed?

9. (II) Calculate the Q-value for the "capture" reaction $\alpha + ^{16}_8O \rightarrow ^{20}_{10}Ne + \gamma$.

10. (II) Calculate the total kinetic energy of the products of the reaction $d + ^{13}_6C \rightarrow ^{14}_7N + n$ if the incoming deuteron has kinetic energy $K = 44.4$ MeV.

11. (II) Radioactive $^{14}_6C$ is produced in the atmosphere when a neutron is absorbed by $^{14}_7N$. Write the reaction and find its Q-value.

12. (II) An example of a **stripping** nuclear reaction is $d + ^6_3Li \rightarrow X + p$. (a) What is X, the resulting nucleus? (b) Why is it called a "stripping" reaction? (c) What is the Q-value of this reaction? Is the reaction endothermic or exothermic?

13. (II) An example of a **pick-up** nuclear reaction is $^3_2He + ^{12}_6C \rightarrow X + \alpha$. (a) Why is it called a "pick-up" reaction? (b) What is the resulting nucleus? (c) What is the Q-value of this reaction? Is the reaction endothermic or exothermic?

14. (II) (a) Complete the following nuclear reaction, $p + ? \rightarrow ^{32}_{16}S + \gamma$. (b) What is the Q-value?

15. (II) The reaction $p + ^{18}_8O \rightarrow ^{18}_9F + n$ requires an input of energy equal to 2.438 MeV. What is the mass of $^{18}_9F$?

16. (III) Use conservation of energy and momentum to show that a bombarding proton must have an energy of 3.23 MeV in order to make the reaction $^{13}_6C(p, n)^{13}_7N$ occur. (See Example 42–3.)

17. (III) How much kinetic energy (if any) would the proton require for the reaction $^{14}_6C(p, n)^{14}_7N$ to proceed?

42–2 Cross Section

18. (I) The cross section for the reaction $n + ^{10}_5B \rightarrow ^7_3Li + ^4_2He$ is about 40 bn for an incident neutron of low energy (kinetic energy ≈ 0). The boron is contained in a gas with $n = 1.7 \times 10^{21}$ nuclei/m^3 and the target has thickness $\ell = 12.0$ cm. What fraction of incident neutrons will be scattered?

19. (I) What is the effective cross section for the collision of two hard spheres of radius R_1 and R_2?

20. (II) When the target is thick, the rate at which projectile particles collide with nuclei in the rear of the target is less than in the front of the target, since some scattering (i.e., collisions) takes place in the front layers. Let R_0 be the rate at which incident particles strike the front of the target, and R_x be the rate at a distance x into the target ($R_x = R_0$ at $x = 0$). Then show that the rate at which particles are scattered (and therefore lost from the incident beam) in a thickness dx is $-dR_x = R_x n\sigma\, dx$, where the minus sign means that R_x is decreasing and n is the number of nuclei per unit volume. Then show that $R_x = R_0 e^{-n\sigma x}$, where σ is the total cross section. If the thickness of the target is ℓ, what does $R_x = R_0 e^{-n\sigma\ell}$ represent?

21. (II) A 1.0-cm-thick lead target reduces a beam of gamma rays to 25% of its original intensity. What thickness of lead will allow only one γ in 10^6 to penetrate (see Problem 20)?

22. (II) Use Fig. 42–3 to estimate what thickness of $^{114}_{48}$Cd $(\rho = 8650\ \text{kg/m}^3)$ will cause a 2.0% reaction rate $(R/R_0 = 0.020)$ for (a) 0.10-eV neutrons (b) 5.0-eV neutrons.

42–3 Nuclear Fission

23. (I) What is the energy released in the fission reaction of Eq. 42–5? (The masses of $^{141}_{56}$Ba and $^{92}_{36}$Kr are 140.914411 u and 91.926156 u, respectively.)

24. (I) Calculate the energy released in the fission reaction $\text{n} + ^{235}_{92}\text{U} \rightarrow ^{88}_{38}\text{Sr} + ^{136}_{54}\text{Xe} + 12\text{n}$. Use Appendix F, and assume the initial kinetic energy of the neutron is very small.

25. (I) How many fissions take place per second in a 200-MW reactor? Assume 200 MeV is released per fission.

26. (I) The energy produced by a fission reactor is about 200 MeV per fission. What fraction of the mass of a $^{235}_{92}$U nucleus is this?

27. (II) Suppose that the average electric power consumption, day and night, in a typical house is 880 W. What initial mass of $^{235}_{92}$U would have to undergo fission to supply the electrical needs of such a house for a year? (Assume 200 MeV is released per fission, as well as 100% efficiency.)

28. (II) Consider the fission reaction

$$^{235}_{92}\text{U} + \text{n} \rightarrow ^{133}_{51}\text{Sb} + ^{98}_{41}\text{Nb} + ?\text{n}.$$

(a) How many neutrons are produced in this reaction? (b) Calculate the energy release. The atomic masses for Sb and Nb isotopes are 132.915250 u and 97.910328 u, respectively.

29. (II) How much mass of $^{238}_{92}$U is required to produce the same amount of energy as burning 1.0 kg of coal (about 3×10^7 J)?

30. (II) What initial mass of $^{235}_{92}$U is required to operate a 950-MW reactor for 1 yr? Assume 38% efficiency.

31. (II) If a 1.0-MeV neutron emitted in a fission reaction loses one-half of its kinetic energy in each collision with moderator nuclei, how many collisions must it make to reach thermal energy $(\frac{3}{2}kT = 0.040\ \text{eV})$?

32. (II) Assuming a fission of $^{236}_{92}$U into two roughly equal fragments, estimate the electric potential energy just as the fragments separate from each other. Assume that the fragments are spherical (see Eq. 41–1) and compare your calculation to the nuclear fission energy released, about 200 MeV.

33. (II) Estimate the ratio of the height of the Coulomb barrier for α decay to that for fission of $^{236}_{92}$U. (Both are described by a potential energy diagram of the shape shown in Fig. 41–7.)

34. (II) Suppose that the neutron multiplication factor is 1.0004. If the average time between successive fissions in a chain of reactions is 1.0 ms, by what factor will the reaction rate increase in 1.0 s?

42–4 Nuclear Fusion

35. (I) What is the average kinetic energy of protons at the center of a star where the temperature is 2×10^7 K? [Hint: See Eq. 18–4.]

36. (II) Show that the energy released in the fusion reaction $^2_1\text{H} + ^3_1\text{H} \rightarrow ^4_2\text{He} + \text{n}$ is 17.57 MeV.

37. (II) Show that the energy released when two deuterium nuclei fuse to form ^3_2He with the release of a neutron is 3.23 MeV.

38. (II) Verify the Q-value stated for each of the reactions of Eqs. 42–7. [Hint: Be careful with electrons.]

39. (II) (a) Calculate the energy release per gram of fuel for the reactions of Eqs. 42–9a, b, and c. (b) Calculate the energy release per gram of uranium $^{235}_{92}$U in fission, and give its ratio to each reaction in (a).

40. (II) How much energy is released when $^{238}_{92}$U absorbs a slow neutron (kinetic energy ≈ 0) and becomes $^{239}_{92}$U?

41. (II) If a typical house requires 850 W of electric power on average, what minimum amount of deuterium fuel would have to be used in a year to supply these electrical needs? Assume the reaction of Eq. 42–9b.

42. (II) If $^6_3$Li is struck by a slow neutron, it can form $^4_2$He and another isotope. (a) What is the second isotope? (This is a method of generating this isotope.) (b) How much energy is released in the process?

43. (II) Suppose a fusion reactor ran on "d–d" reactions, Eqs. 42–9a and b in equal amounts. Estimate how much natural water, for fuel, would be needed per hour to run a 1250-MW reactor, assuming 33% efficiency.

44. (II) Show that the energies carried off by the $^4_2$He nucleus and the neutron for the reaction of Eq. 42–9c are about 3.5 MeV and 14 MeV, respectively. Are these fixed values, independent of the plasma temperature?

45. (II) How much energy (J) is contained in 1.00 kg of water if its natural deuterium is used in the fusion reaction of Eq. 42–9a? Compare to the energy obtained from the burning of 1.0 kg of gasoline, about 5×10^7 J.

46. (III) (a) Give the ratio of the energy needed for the first reaction of the carbon cycle to the energy needed for a deuterium–tritium reaction (Example 42–10). (b) If a deuterium–tritium reaction requires $T \approx 3 \times 10^8$ K, estimate the temperature needed for the first carbon-cycle reaction.

47. (III) The energy output of massive stars is believed to be due to the carbon cycle (see text). (a) Show that no carbon is consumed in this cycle and that the net effect is the same as for the proton–proton cycle. (b) What is the total energy release? (c) Determine the energy output for each reaction and decay. (d) Why might the carbon cycle require a higher temperature $(\approx 2 \times 10^7\ \text{K})$ than the proton–proton cycle $(\approx 1.5 \times 10^7\ \text{K})$?

42–6 Dosimetry

48. (I) 250 rads of α-particle radiation is equivalent to how many rads of X-rays in terms of biological damage?

49. (I) A dose of 4.0 Sv of γ rays in a short period would be lethal to about half the people subjected to it. How many grays is this?

50. (I) How much energy is deposited in the body of a 65-kg adult exposed to a 3.0-Gy dose?

51. (I) How many rads of slow neutrons will do as much biological damage as 65 rads of fast neutrons?

52. (II) A cancer patient is undergoing radiation therapy in which protons with an energy of 1.2 MeV are incident on a 0.25-kg tumor. (a) If the patient receives an effective dose of 1.0 rem, what is the absorbed dose? (b) How many protons are absorbed by the tumor? Assume QF ≈ 1.

53. (II) A 0.035-μCi sample of $^{32}_{15}$P is injected into an animal for tracer studies. If a Geiger counter intercepts 25% of the emitted β particles, what will be the counting rate, assumed 85% efficient?

54. (II) About 35 eV is required to produce one ion pair in air. Show that this is consistent with the two definitions of the roentgen given in the text.

55. (II) A 1.6-mCi source of $^{32}_{15}$P (in NaHPO$_4$), a β emitter, is implanted in a tumor where it is to administer 36 Gy. The half-life of $^{32}_{15}$P is 14.3 days, and 1.0 mCi delivers about 10 mGy/min. Approximately how long should the source remain implanted?

56. (II) What is the mass of a 2.00-μCi $^{14}_{6}$C source?

57. (II) Huge amounts of radioactive $^{131}_{53}$I were released in the accident at Chernobyl in 1986. Chemically, iodine goes to the human thyroid. (Doctors can use it for diagnosis and treatment of thyroid problems.) In a normal thyroid, $^{131}_{53}$I absorption can cause damage to the thyroid. (a) Write down the reaction for the decay of $^{131}_{53}$I. (b) Its half-life is 8.0 d; how long would it take for ingested $^{131}_{53}$I to become 7.0% of the initial value? (c) Absorbing 1 mCi of $^{131}_{53}$I can be harmful; what mass of iodine is this?

58. (II) Assume a liter of milk typically has an activity of 2000 pCi due to $^{40}_{19}$K. If a person drinks two glasses (0.5 L) per day, estimate the total effective dose (in Sv and in rem) received in a year. As a crude model, assume the milk stays in the stomach 12 hr and is then released. Assume also that very roughly 10% of the 1.5 MeV released per decay is absorbed by the body. Compare your result to the normal allowed dose of 100 mrem per year. Make your estimate for (a) a 60-kg adult, and (b) a 6-kg baby.

59. (II) $^{57}_{27}$Co emits 122-keV γ rays. If a 58-kg person swallowed 1.55 μCi of $^{57}_{27}$Co, what would be the dose rate (Gy/day) averaged over the whole body? Assume that 50% of the γ-ray energy is deposited in the body. [Hint: Determine the rate of energy deposited in the body and use the definition of the gray.]

60. (II) Ionizing radiation can be used on meat products to reduce the levels of microbial pathogens. Refrigerated meat is limited to 4.5 kGy. If 1.2-MeV electrons irradiate 5 kg of beef, how many electrons would it take to reach the allowable limit?

61. (II) Radon gas, $^{222}_{86}$Rn, is considered a serious health hazard (see discussion in text). It decays by α-emission. (a) What is the daughter nucleus? (b) Is the daughter nucleus stable or radioactive? If the latter, how does it decay, and what is its half-life? (See Fig. 41–12.) (c) Is the daughter nucleus also a noble gas, or is it chemically reactive? (d) Suppose 1.6 ng of $^{222}_{86}$Rn seeps into a basement. What will be its activity? If the basement is then sealed, what will be the activity 1 month later?

*42–9 Imaging by Tomography

*62. (II) (a) Suppose for a conventional X-ray image that the X-ray beam consists of parallel rays. What would be the magnification of the image? (b) Suppose, instead, that the X-rays come from a point source (as in Fig. 42–21) that is 15 cm in front of a human body which is 25 cm thick, and the film is pressed against the person's back. Determine and discuss the range of magnifications that result.

*42–10 NMR

*63. (I) Calculate the wavelength of photons needed to produce NMR transitions in free protons in a 1.000-T field. In what region of the spectrum is this wavelength?

*64. (II) Carbon-13 has a magnetic moment $\mu = 0.7023\mu_N$ (see Eq. 41–2). What magnetic field would be necessary if $^{13}_{6}$C were to be detected in a proton NMR spectrometer operating at 42.58 MHz? (This large field necessitates that a $^{13}_{6}$C spectrometer operate at a lower frequency.)

General Problems

65. J. Chadwick discovered the neutron by bombarding $^{9}_{4}$Be with the popular projectile of the day, alpha particles. (a) If one of the reaction products was the then unknown neutron, what was the other product? (b) What is the Q-value of this reaction?

66. Fusion temperatures are often given in keV. Determine the conversion factor from kelvins to keV using, as is common in this field, $\overline{K} = kT$ without the factor $\frac{3}{2}$.

67. One means of enriching uranium is by diffusion of the gas UF$_6$. Calculate the ratio of the speeds of molecules of this gas containing $^{235}_{92}$U and $^{238}_{92}$U, on which this process depends.

68. (a) What mass of $^{235}_{92}$U was actually fissioned in the first atomic bomb, whose energy was the equivalent of about 20 kilotons of TNT (1 kiloton of TNT releases 5×10^{12} J)? (b) What was the actual mass transformed to energy?

69. The average yearly background radiation in a certain town consists of 29 mrad of X-rays and γ rays plus 3.6 mrad of particles having a QF of 10. How many rem will a person receive per year on the average?

70. Deuterium makes up 0.0115% of natural hydrogen on average. Make a rough estimate of the total deuterium in the Earth's oceans and estimate the total energy released if all of it were used in fusion reactors.

71. A shielded γ-ray source yields a dose rate of 0.052 rad/h at a distance of 1.0 m for an average-sized person. If workers are allowed a maximum dose of 5.0 rem in 1 year, how close to the source may they operate, assuming a 35-h work week? Assume that the intensity of radiation falls off as the square of the distance. (It actually falls off more rapidly than $1/r^2$ because of absorption in the air, so your answer will give a better-than-permissible value.)

72. Radon gas, $^{222}_{86}$Rn, is formed by α decay. (a) Write the decay equation. (b) Ignoring the kinetic energy of the daughter nucleus (it's so massive), estimate the kinetic energy of the α particle produced. (c) Estimate the momentum of the alpha and of the daughter nucleus. (d) Estimate the kinetic energy of the daughter, and show that your approximation in (b) was valid.

73. Consider a system of nuclear power plants that produce 2400 MW. (a) What total mass of $^{235}_{92}$U fuel would be required to operate these plants for 1 yr, assuming that 200 MeV is released per fission? (b) Typically 6% of the $^{235}_{92}$U nuclei that fission produce $^{90}_{38}$Sr, a β^- emitter with a half-life of 29 yr. What is the total radioactivity of the $^{90}_{38}$Sr, in curies, produced in 1 yr? (Neglect the fact that some of it decays during the 1-yr period.)

74. In the net reaction, Eq. 42–8, for the proton–proton cycle in the Sun, the neutrinos escape from the Sun with energy of about 0.5 MeV. The remaining energy, 26.2 MeV, is available within the Sun. Use this value to calculate the "heat of combustion" per kilogram of hydrogen fuel and compare it to the heat of combustion of coal, about 3×10^7 J/kg.

75. Energy reaches Earth from the Sun at a rate of about 1300 W/m^2. Calculate (a) the total power output of the Sun, and (b) the number of protons consumed per second in the reaction of Eq. 42–8, assuming that this is the source of all the Sun's energy. (c) Assuming that the Sun's mass of 2.0×10^{30} kg was originally all protons and that all could be involved in nuclear reactions in the Sun's core, how long would you expect the Sun to "glow" at its present rate? See Problem 74.

76. Estimate how many solar neutrinos pass through a 180-m^2 ceiling of a room, at latitude 38°, for an hour around midnight on midsummer night. [*Hint*: See Problems 74 and 75.]

77. Estimate how much total energy would be released via fission if 2.0 kg of uranium were enriched to 5% of the isotope $^{235}_{92}$U.

78. Some stars, in a later stage of evolution, may begin to fuse two $^{12}_6$C nuclei into one $^{24}_{12}$Mg nucleus. (a) How much energy would be released in such a reaction? (b) What kinetic energy must two carbon nuclei each have when far apart, if they can then approach each other to within 6.0 fm, center-to-center? (c) Approximately what temperature would this require?

79. An average adult body contains about 0.10 μCi of $^{40}_{19}$K, which comes from food. (a) How many decays occur per second? (b) The potassium decay produces beta particles with energies of around 1.4 MeV. Estimate the dose per year in sieverts for a 55-kg adult. Is this a significant fraction of the 3.6-mSv/yr background rate?

80. When the nuclear reactor accident occurred at Chernobyl in 1986, 2.0×10^7 Ci were released into the atmosphere. Assuming that this radiation was distributed uniformly over the surface of the Earth, what was the activity per square meter? (The actual activity was not uniform; even within Europe wet areas received more radioactivity from rainfall.)

81. A star with a large helium abundance can burn helium in the reaction $^4_2$He + $^4_2$He + $^4_2$He $\rightarrow$ $^{12}_6$C. What is the Q-value for this reaction?

82. A 1.2-μCi $^{137}_{55}$Cs source is used for 1.6 hours by a 65-kg worker. Radioactive $^{137}_{55}$Cs decays by β^- decay with a half-life of 30 yr. The average energy of the emitted betas is about 190 keV per decay. The β decay is quickly followed by a γ with an energy of 660 keV. Assuming the person absorbs *all* emitted energy, what effective dose (in rem) is received?

83. A large amount of $^{90}_{38}$Sr was released during the Chernobyl nuclear reactor accident in 1986. The $^{90}_{38}$Sr enters the body through the food chain. How long will it take for 85% of the $^{90}_{38}$Sr released during the accident to decay? See Appendix F.

84. Three radioactive sources have the same activity, 35 mCi. Source A emits 1.0-MeV γ rays, source B emits 2.0-MeV γ rays, and source C emits 2.0-MeV alphas. What is the relative danger of these sources?

85. A 60-kg patient is to be given a medical test involving the ingestion of $^{99m}_{43}$Tc (Section 42–8) which decays by emitting a 140-keV gamma. The half-life for this decay is 6 hours. Assuming that about half the gamma photons exit the body without interacting with anything, what must be the initial activity of the Tc sample if the whole-body dose cannot exceed 50 mrem? Make the rough approximation that biological elimination of Tc can be ignored.

86. Centuries ago, paint generally contained a different amount of cobalt ($^{59}_{27}$Co) than paint today. A certain "old" painting is suspected of being a new forgery, and an examiner has decided to use **neutron activation analysis** to test this hypothesis. After placing the painting in a neutron flux of 5.0×10^{12} neutrons/cm^2/s for 5.0 minutes, an activity of 55 decays/s of $^{60}_{27}$Co ($T_{\frac{1}{2}} = 5.27$ yr) is observed. Assuming $^{59}_{27}$Co has a cross section of 19 bn, how much cobalt (in grams) does the paint contain?

87. Show, using the laws of conservation of energy and momentum, that for a nuclear reaction requiring energy, the minimum kinetic energy of the bombarding particle (the **threshold energy**) is equal to $[-Qm_{pr}/(m_{pr} - m_b)]$, where $-Q$ is the energy required (difference in total mass between products and reactants), m_b is the mass of the bombarding particle, and m_{pr} is the total mass of the products. Assume the target nucleus is at rest before an interaction takes place, and that all speeds are nonrelativistic.

88. The early scattering experiments performed around 1910 in Ernest Rutherford's laboratory in England produced the first evidence that an atom consists of a heavy nucleus surrounded by electrons. In one of these experiments, α particles struck a gold-foil target 4.0×10^{-5} cm thick in which there were 5.9×10^{28} gold atoms per cubic meter. Although most α particles either passed straight through the foil or were scattered at small angles, approximately 1.6×10^{-3} percent were scattered at angles greater than 90°—that is, in the backward direction. (a) Calculate the cross section, in barns, for backward scattering. (b) Rutherford concluded that such backward scattering could occur only if an atom consisted of a very tiny, massive, and positively charged nucleus with electrons orbiting some distance away. Assuming that backward scattering occurs for nearly direct collisions (i.e., $\sigma \approx$ area of nucleus), estimate the diameter of a gold nucleus.

Answers to Exercises

A: $^{138}_{56}$Ba.

B: 2×10^{17}.

C: (e).

D: (b).

E: (a).

This computer-generated reconstruction of a proton–antiproton collision at Fermilab (Fig. 43–3) occurred at a combined energy of nearly 2 TeV. It is one of the events that provided evidence for the top quark (1995). The wire drift chamber (Section 41–11) is in a magnetic field, and the radius of curvature of the charged particle tracks is a measure of each particle's momentum (Section 27–4).

The white dots represent the signals seen on the electric wires of the drift chamber. The colored lines are the particle paths.

The top quark (t) has too brief a lifetime $(\approx 10^{-23}\,\text{s})$ to be detected itself, so we look for its possible decay products. Analysis indicates the following interaction and subsequent decays:

$$p + \bar{p} \longrightarrow t + \bar{t}$$
$$\hookrightarrow W^- + \bar{b}$$
$$\hookrightarrow \text{jet}$$
$$\rightarrow \mu^- + \bar{\nu}_\mu$$
$$\hookrightarrow W^+ + b$$
$$\hookrightarrow \text{jet}$$
$$\hookrightarrow u + \bar{d}$$
$$\hookrightarrow \text{jet}$$
$$\rightarrow \text{jet}$$

The tracks in the photo include jets (groups of particles moving in roughly the same direction), and a muon (μ^-) whose track is the pink one enclosed by a yellow rectangle to make it stand out. After reading this Chapter, try to name each symbol above and comment on whether all conservation laws hold.

C H A P T E R
43

Elementary Particles

CONTENTS

CHAPTER-OPENING QUESTIONS—Guess now!

1. Electrons are still considered fundamental particles (in the group called leptons). But protons and neutrons are no longer considered fundamental; they have substructure and are made up of

   (a) pions.
   (b) leptons.
   (c) quarks.
   (d) bosons.
   (e) photons.

2. Thus the elementary particles as we see them today are

   (a) atoms and electrons.
   (b) protons, neutrons, and electrons.
   (c) protons, neutrons, electrons, and photons.
   (d) quarks, leptons, and gauge bosons.
   (e) hadrons, leptons, and gauge bosons.

I n the final two Chapters of this book we discuss two of the most exciting areas of contemporary physics: elementary particles in this Chapter, and cosmology and astrophysics in Chapter 44. These are subjects at the forefront of knowledge—elementary particles treats the smallest objects in the universe; cosmology treats the largest (and oldest) aspects of the universe.

In this penultimate Chapter we discuss *elementary particle* physics, which represents the human endeavor to understand the basic building blocks of all matter, and the fundamental forces that govern their interactions. By the mid-1930s, it was recognized that all atoms can be considered to be made up of neutrons, protons, and electrons. The basic constituents of the universe were no longer considered to be atoms but rather the proton, neutron, and electron. Besides these three "elementary particles," several others were also known: the positron (a positive electron), the neutrino, and the γ particle (or photon), for a total of six elementary particles.

By the 1950s and 1960s many new types of particles similar to the neutron and proton were discovered, as well as many "midsized" particles called *mesons* whose masses were mostly less than nucleon masses but more than the electron mass. (Other mesons, found later, have masses greater than nucleons.) Physicists felt that all of these particles could not be fundamental, and must be made up of even smaller constituents (later confirmed by experiment), which were given the name *quarks*.

Today, the basic constituents of matter are considered to be **quarks** (they make up protons and neutrons as well as mesons) and **leptons** (a class that includes electrons, positrons, and neutrinos). In addition, there are the "carriers of force" including **gluons**, the photon, and other "gauge bosons." The theory that describes our present view is called the **Standard Model**. How we came to our present understanding of elementary particles is the subject of this Chapter.

One of the exciting recent developments of the last few years is an emerging synthesis between the study of elementary particles and astrophysics (Chapter 44). In fact, recent observations in astrophysics have led to the conclusion that the greater part of the mass–energy content of the universe is not ordinary matter but two mysterious and invisible forms known as "dark matter" and "dark energy" which cannot be explained by the Standard Model in its present form.

Indeed, we are now aware that the Standard Model is not sufficient. There are problems and important questions still unanswered, and we will mention some of them in this Chapter and how we hope to answer them.

43–1 High-Energy Particles and Accelerators

In the years after World War II, it was found that if the incoming particle in a nuclear reaction has sufficient energy, new types of particles can be produced. The earliest experiments used **cosmic rays**—particles that impinge on the Earth from space. In the laboratory, various types of particle accelerators have been constructed to accelerate protons or electrons to high energies, although heavy ions can also be accelerated. These **high-energy accelerators** have been used to probe more deeply into matter, to produce and study new particles, and to give us information about the basic forces and constituents of nature. Because the projectile particles are at high energy, this field is sometimes called **high-energy physics**.

Wavelength and Resolution

Particles accelerated to high energy can probe the interior of nuclei and nucleons or other particles they strike. An important factor is that faster-moving projectiles can reveal more detail. The wavelength of projectile particles is given by de Broglie's wavelength formula (Eq. 37–7),

$$\lambda = \frac{h}{p}, \tag{43-1}$$

showing that the greater the momentum p of the bombarding particle, the shorter its wavelength. As discussed in Chapter 35 on diffraction, resolution of details in images is limited by the wavelength: the shorter the wavelength, the finer the detail that can be obtained. This is one reason why particle accelerators of higher and higher energy have been built in recent years: to probe ever deeper into the structure of matter, to smaller and smaller size.

EXAMPLE 43–1 **High resolution with electrons.** What is the wavelength, and hence the expected resolution, for 1.3-GeV electrons?

APPROACH Because 1.3 GeV is much larger than the electron mass, we must be dealing with relativistic speeds. The momentum of the electrons is found from Eq. 36–13, and the wavelength is $\lambda = h/p$.

SOLUTION Each electron has $K = 1.3\,\text{GeV} = 1300\,\text{MeV}$, which is about 2500 times the rest energy of the electron $(mc^2 = 0.51\,\text{MeV})$. Thus we can ignore the term $(mc^2)^2$ in Eq. 36–13, $E^2 = p^2c^2 + m^2c^4$, and we solve for p:

$$p = \sqrt{\frac{E^2 - m^2c^4}{c^2}} \approx \sqrt{\frac{E^2}{c^2}} = \frac{E}{c}.$$

Therefore the de Broglie wavelength is

$$\lambda = \frac{h}{p} = \frac{hc}{E},$$

where $E = 1.3\,\text{GeV}$. Hence

$$\lambda = \frac{(6.63 \times 10^{-34}\,\text{J·s})(3.0 \times 10^8\,\text{m/s})}{(1.3 \times 10^9\,\text{eV})(1.6 \times 10^{-19}\,\text{J/eV})} = 0.96 \times 10^{-15}\,\text{m},$$

or 0.96 fm. This resolution of about 1 fm is on the order of the size of nuclei (see Eq. 41–1).

NOTE The maximum possible resolution of this beam of electrons is far greater than for a light beam in a light microscope $(\lambda \approx 500\,\text{nm})$.

| **EXERCISE A** What is the wavelength of a proton with $K = 1.00\,\text{TeV}$?

Another major reason for building high-energy accelerators is that new particles of greater mass can be produced at higher energies, transforming the kinetic energy of the colliding particles into massive particles by $E = mc^2$, as we will discuss shortly. Now we look at particle accelerators.

FIGURE 43–1 Ernest O. Lawrence, around 1930, holding the first cyclotron (we see the vacuum chamber enclosing it).

FIGURE 43–2 Diagram of a cyclotron. The magnetic field, applied by a large electromagnet, points into the page. The protons start at A, the ion source. The red electric field lines shown are for the alternating electric field in the gap at a certain moment.

Cyclotron

The cyclotron was developed in 1930 by E. O. Lawrence (1901–1958; Fig. 43–1) at the University of California, Berkeley. It uses a magnetic field to maintain charged ions—usually protons—in nearly circular paths. Although particle physicists no longer use simple cyclotrons, they are used in medicine for treating cancer, and their operating principles are useful for understanding modern accelerators. The protons move in a vacuum inside two D-shaped cavities, as shown in Fig. 43–2. Each time they pass into the gap between the "dees," a voltage accelerates them (the electric force), increasing their speed and increasing the radius of curvature of their path in the magnetic field. After many revolutions, the protons acquire high kinetic energy and reach the outer edge of the cyclotron where they strike a target. The protons speed up only when they are in the gap *between* the dees, and the voltage must be alternating. When protons are moving to the right across the gap in Fig. 43–2, the right dee must be electrically negative and the left one positive. A half-cycle later, the protons are moving to the left, so the left dee must be negative in order to accelerate them.

The frequency, f, of the applied voltage must be equal to that of the circulating protons. When ions of charge q are circulating *within* the hollow dees, the net force F on each is due to the magnetic field B, so $F = qvB$, where v is the speed of the ion at a given moment (Eq. 27–5). The magnetic force is perpendicular to both $\vec{v}$ and $\vec{B}$ and causes the ions to move in circles; the acceleration within the dees is thus centripetal and equals v^2/r, where r is the radius of the ion's path at a given moment.

We use Newton's second law, $F = ma$, and find that

$$F = ma$$

$$qvB = \frac{mv^2}{r}$$

when the protons are within the dees (not the gap), so

$$v = \frac{qBr}{m}.$$

The time required for a complete revolution is the period T and is equal to

$$T = \frac{\text{distance}}{\text{speed}} = \frac{2\pi r}{qBr/m} = \frac{2\pi m}{qB}.$$

Hence the frequency of revolution f is

$$f = \frac{1}{T} = \frac{qB}{2\pi m}. \tag{43–2}$$

This is known as the **cyclotron frequency**.

EXAMPLE 43–2 **Cyclotron.** A small cyclotron of maximum radius $R = 0.25$ m accelerates protons in a 1.7-T magnetic field. Calculate (a) the frequency needed for the applied alternating voltage, and (b) the kinetic energy of protons when they leave the cyclotron.

APPROACH The frequency of the protons revolving within the dees (Eq. 43–2) must equal the frequency of the voltage applied across the gap if the protons are going to increase in speed.

SOLUTION (a) From Eq. 43–2,

$$f = \frac{qB}{2\pi m}$$

$$= \frac{(1.6 \times 10^{-19}\,\text{C})(1.7\,\text{T})}{(6.28)(1.67 \times 10^{-27}\,\text{kg})} = 2.6 \times 10^7\,\text{Hz} = 26\,\text{MHz},$$

which is in the radio-wave region of the EM spectrum (Fig. 31–12).
(b) The protons leave the cyclotron at $r = R = 0.25$ m. From $qvB = mv^2/r$ (see above), we have $v = qBr/m$, so their kinetic energy is

$$K = \frac{1}{2}mv^2 = \frac{1}{2}m\frac{q^2 B^2 R^2}{m^2} = \frac{q^2 B^2 R^2}{2m}$$

$$= \frac{(1.6 \times 10^{-19}\,\text{C})^2(1.7\,\text{T})^2(0.25\,\text{m})^2}{(2)(1.67 \times 10^{-27}\,\text{kg})} = 1.4 \times 10^{-12}\,\text{J} = 8.7\,\text{MeV}.$$

The kinetic energy is much less than the rest energy of the proton (938 MeV), so relativity is not needed.

NOTE The magnitude of the voltage applied to the dees does not appear in the formula for K, and so does not affect the final energy. But the higher this voltage, the fewer the revolutions required to bring the protons to full energy.

An important aspect of the cyclotron is that the frequency of the applied voltage, as given by Eq. 43–2, does not depend on the radius r of the particle's path. Thus the frequency does not have to be changed as the protons or ions start from the source and are accelerated to paths of larger and larger radii. But this is only true at nonrelativistic energies. At higher speeds, the momentum (Eq. 36–8) is $p = mv/\sqrt{1 - v^2/c^2}$, so m in Eq. 43–2 has to be replaced by γm and the cyclotron frequency f (Eq. 43–2) depends on speed v. To keep the particles in sync, machines called **synchrocyclotrons** reduce their frequency in time to correspond with Eq. 43–2 as m increases, as a packet of charged particles increases in speed at larger orbits.

(a)   (b)

FIGURE 43–3 (a) Aerial view of Fermilab, near Chicago in Illinois; the main accelerator is a circular ring 1.0 km in radius. (b) The interior of the tunnel of the main accelerator at Fermilab, showing (red) the ring of superconducting magnets for the 1-TeV Tevatron.

Synchrotron

Another way to accelerate relativistic particles is to increase the magnetic field B in time so as to keep f (Eq. 43–2) constant as the particles speed up. Such devices are called **synchrotrons**; the particles move in a circle of fixed radius, which can be very large. At the European Center for Nuclear Research (CERN) in Geneva, Switzerland, the new Large Hadron Collider (LHC) is 4.3 km in radius and accelerates protons to 7 TeV. The *Tevatron* accelerator at Fermilab (the Fermi National Accelerator Laboratory) at Batavia, Illinois, has a radius of 1.0 km.[†] The Tevatron uses superconducting magnets to accelerate protons to about 1000 GeV = 1 TeV (hence its name); 1 TeV = 10^{12} eV. These large synchrotrons use a narrow ring of magnets (see Fig. 43–3) with each magnet placed at the same radius from the center of the circle. The magnets are interrupted by gaps where high voltage accelerates the particles. Another way to describe the acceleration is to say the particles "surf" on a traveling electromagnetic wave within radiofrequency (RF) cavities. (The particles are first given considerable energy in a smaller accelerator, "the injector," before being injected into the large ring of the large synchrotron.)

One problem of any accelerator is that accelerating electric charges radiate electromagnetic energy (see Chapter 31). Since ions or electrons are accelerated in an accelerator, we can expect considerable energy to be lost by radiation. The effect increases with energy and is especially important in circular machines where centripetal acceleration is present, such as synchrotrons, and hence is called **synchrotron radiation**. Synchrotron radiation can be useful, however. Intense beams of photons (γ rays) are sometimes needed, and they are usually obtained from an electron synchrotron.

| **EXERCISE B** By what factor is the diameter of the Fermilab Tevatron (Fig. 43–3) greater than Lawrence's original cyclotron (estimate from Fig. 43–1)?

[†]Robert Wilson, who helped design the Tevatron, and founded the field of proton therapy (Section 42–7), expressed his views on accelerators and national security in this exchange with Senator John Pastore during testimony before a Congressional Committee in 1969:

> Pastore: "Is there anything connected with the hopes of this accelerator [the Tevatron] that in any way involves the security of the country?"
>
> Robert Wilson: "No sir, I don't believe so."
>
> Pastore: "Nothing at all?"
>
> Wilson: "Nothing at all. . . ."
>
> Pastore: "It has no value in that respect?"
>
> Wilson: "It has only to do with the respect with which we regard one another, the dignity of men, our love of culture. . . . It has to do with are we good painters, good sculptors, great poets? I mean all the things we really venerate in our country and are patriotic about . . . it has nothing to do directly with defending our country except to make it worth defending."

Linear Accelerators

In a **linear accelerator** (linac), electrons or ions are accelerated along a straight-line path, Fig. 43–4, passing through a series of tubular conductors. Voltage applied to the tubes is alternating so that when electrons (say) reach a gap, the tube in front of them is positive and the one they just left is negative. At low speeds, the particles cover less distance in the same amount of time, so the tubes are shorter at first. Electrons, with their small mass, get close to the speed of light quickly, $v \approx c$, and the tubes are nearly equal in length. Linear accelerators are particularly important for accelerating electrons to avoid loss of energy due to synchrotron radiation. The largest electron linear accelerator has been at Stanford University (Stanford Linear Accelerator Center, or SLAC), about 3 km (2 mi) long, accelerating electrons to 50 GeV. It is now being decommissioned. Linacs accelerating protons are used as injectors into circular machines to provide initial kinetic energy. Many hospitals have 10-MeV electron linacs that strike a metal foil to produce γ ray photons to irradiate tumors.

FIGURE 43–4 Diagram of a simple linear accelerator.

Colliding Beams

High-energy physics experiments were once done by aiming a beam of particles from an accelerator at a stationary target. But to obtain the maximum possible collision energy from a given accelerator, two beams of particles are now accelerated to very high energy and are steered so that they collide head-on. One way to accomplish such **colliding beams** with a single accelerator is through the use of **storage rings**, in which oppositely circulating beams can be repeatedly brought into collision with one another at particular points. For example, in the experiments that provided strong evidence for the top quark (Chapter-Opening Photo and Section 43–9), the Fermilab Tevatron accelerated protons and antiprotons each to 900 GeV, so that the combined energy of head-on collisions was 1.8 TeV.

The largest collider is the brand new Large Hadron Collider (LHC) at CERN, with a circumference of 26.7 km (Fig. 43–5). The two colliding beams each carry 7-TeV protons for a total interaction energy of 14 TeV.

FIGURE 43–5 The large circle represents the position of the tunnel, about 100 m below the ground at CERN (near Geneva) on the French-Swiss border, which houses the LHC. The smaller circle shows the position of the Super Proton Synchrotron that will be used for accelerating protons prior to injection into the LHC.

FIGURE 43–6 ATLAS, one of
several large complex detectors at
the LHC, is shown here as it was
being built. It is hoped the LHC will
provide evidence for the Higgs
boson (to help understand the
Standard Model), and perhaps to
find supersymmetric particles which
are candidates for the unknown dark
matter that makes up a large part of
the mass–energy of the universe. We
will touch on these topics later in
this Chapter.

Figure 43–6 shows part of one of the detectors (ATLAS) as it was being constructed at the LHC. The detectors within ATLAS include silicon semiconductor detectors with huge numbers of pixels used to track particle paths, to find their point of interaction, and to measure their radius of curvature in a magnetic field and thus determine their momentum (Section 27–4). Their energy is determined in "calorimeters" utilizing plastic, liquid, or dense metal compound crystal scintillators (Section 41–11).

In the planning stage is the International Linear Collider (ILC) which would have colliding beams of e^- and e^+ at around 0.3 to 1 TeV, with semiconductor detectors using CMOS (Section 33–5) with embedded transistors to allow fast readout.

EXAMPLE 43–3 **Protons at relativistic speeds.** Determine the energy required to accelerate a proton in a high-energy accelerator (a) from rest to $v = 0.900c$, and (b) from $v = 0.900c$ to $v = 0.999c$. (c) What is the kinetic energy achieved by the proton in each case?

APPROACH We use the work-energy principle, which is still valid relativistically as mentioned in Section 36–11: $W = \Delta K$.

SOLUTION The kinetic energy of a proton of mass m is given by Eq. 36–10,

$$K = (\gamma - 1)mc^2,$$

where the relativistic factor γ is

$$\gamma = \frac{1}{\sqrt{1 - v^2/c^2}}.$$

The work-energy theorem becomes

$$W = \Delta K = (\Delta\gamma)mc^2$$

since m and c are constant.

(a) For $v = 0, \gamma = 1$; and for $v = 0.900c$

$$\gamma = \frac{1}{\sqrt{1 - (0.900)^2}} = 2.29.$$

For a proton, $mc^2 = 938\ \text{MeV}$, so the work (or energy) needed to accelerate it from rest to $v = 0.900c$ is

$$W = \Delta K = (\Delta\gamma)mc^2$$
$$= (2.29 - 1.00)(938\ \text{MeV}) = 1.21\ \text{GeV}.$$

(b) For $v = 0.999c$,

$$\gamma = \frac{1}{\sqrt{1 - (0.999)^2}} = 22.4.$$

So the work needed to accelerate a proton from $0.900c$ to $0.999c$ is

$$W = \Delta K = (\Delta\gamma)mc^2$$
$$= (22.4 - 2.29)(938\ \text{MeV}) = 18.9\ \text{GeV},$$

which is 15 times as much.

(c) The kinetic energy reached by the proton in (a) is just equal to the work done on it, $K = 1.21\ \text{GeV}$. The final kinetic energy of the proton in (b), moving at $v = 0.999c$, is

$$K = (\gamma - 1)mc^2 = (21.4)(938\ \text{MeV}) = 20.1\ \text{GeV},$$

which makes sense since, starting from rest, we did work $W = 1.21\ \text{GeV} + 18.9\ \text{GeV} = 20.1\ \text{GeV}$ on it.

EXAMPLE 43–4 **Speed of a 1.0-TeV proton.** What is the speed of a 1.0-TeV proton produced at Fermilab?

APPROACH The kinetic energy $K = 1.0\,\text{TeV} = 1.0 \times 10^{12}\,\text{eV}$ is much greater than the mass of the proton, $0.938 \times 10^9\,\text{eV}$, so relativistic calculations must be used. In particular, we use Eq. 36–10:

$$K = (\gamma - 1)mc^2 = \frac{mc^2}{\sqrt{1 - v^2/c^2}} - mc^2.$$

SOLUTION Compared to $K = 1.0 \times 10^{12}\,\text{eV}$, the rest energy $(\approx 10^{-3}\,\text{TeV})$ can be neglected, so we write

$$K = \frac{mc^2}{\sqrt{1 - v^2/c^2}}.$$

Then

$$1 - \frac{v^2}{c^2} = \left(\frac{mc^2}{K}\right)^2$$

or

$$\frac{v}{c} = \sqrt{1 - \left(\frac{mc^2}{K}\right)^2} = \sqrt{1 - \left(\frac{938 \times 10^6\,\text{eV}}{1.0 \times 10^{12}\,\text{eV}}\right)^2}$$

$$v = 0.9999996\,c.$$

The proton is traveling at a speed extremely close to c, the speed of light.

43–2 Beginnings of Elementary Particle Physics—Particle Exchange

The accepted model for elementary particles today views *quarks* and *leptons* as the basic constituents of ordinary matter. To understand our present-day view of elementary particles, it is necessary to understand the ideas leading up to its formulation.

Elementary particle physics might be said to have begun in 1935 when the Japanese physicist Hidcki Yukawa (1907–1981) predicted the existence of a new particle that would in some way mediate the strong nuclear force. To understand Yukawa's idea, we first consider the electromagnetic force. When we first discussed electricity, we saw that the electric force acts over a distance, without contact. To better perceive how a force can act over a distance, we used the idea of a **field**. The force that one charged particle exerts on a second can be said to be due to the electric field set up by the first. Similarly, the magnetic field can be said to carry the magnetic force. Later (Chapter 31), we saw that electromagnetic (EM) fields can travel through space as waves. Finally, in Chapter 37, we saw that electromagnetic radiation (light) can be considered as either a wave or as a collection of particles called *photons*. Because of this wave–particle duality, it is possible to imagine that the electromagnetic force between charged particles is due to

(1) the EM field set up by one charged particle and felt by the other, or
(2) an exchange of photons (γ particles) between them.

It is (2) that we want to concentrate on here, and a crude analogy for how an exchange of particles could give rise to a force is suggested in Fig. 43–7. In part (a), two children start throwing heavy pillows at each other; each throw and each catch results in the child being pushed backward by the impulse. This is the equivalent of a repulsive force. On the other hand, if the two children exchange pillows by grabbing them out of the other person's hand, they will be pulled toward each other, as when an attractive force acts.

FIGURE 43–7 Forces equivalent to particle exchange. (a) Repulsive force (children on roller skates throwing pillows at each other). (b) Attractive force (children grabbing pillows from each other's hands).

(a) Repulsive force (children throwing pillows)

(b) Attractive force (children grabbing pillows from each other's hands)

FIGURE 43–8 Feynman diagram showing a photon acting as the carrier of the electromagnetic force between two electrons. This is sort of an *x* vs. *t* graph, with *t* increasing upward. Starting at the bottom, two electrons approach each other (the distance between them decreases in time). As they get close, momentum and energy get transferred from one to the other, carried by a photon (or, perhaps, by more than one), and the two electrons bounce apart.

FIGURE 43–9 Early model showing meson exchange when a proton and neutron interact via the strong nuclear force. (Today, as we shall see shortly, we view the strong force as carried by gluons between quarks.)

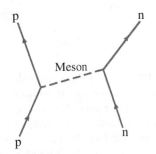

For the electromagnetic force, it is photons that are exchanged between two charged particles that give rise to the force between them. A simple diagram describing this photon exchange is shown in Fig. 43–8. Such a diagram, called a **Feynman diagram** after its inventor, the American physicist Richard Feynman (1918–1988), is based on the theory of **quantum electrodynamics** (QED).

Figure 43–8 represents the simplest case in QED, in which a single photon is exchanged. One of the charged particles emits the photon and recoils somewhat as a result; and the second particle absorbs the photon. In any collision or *interaction*, energy and momentum are transferred from one charged particle to the other, carried by the photon. The photon is absorbed by the second particle after it is emitted by the first and is not observable. Hence it is referred to as a **virtual** photon, in contrast to one that is free and can be detected by instruments. The photon is said to **mediate**, or **carry**, the electromagnetic force.

By analogy with photon exchange that mediates the electromagnetic force, Yukawa argued that there ought to be a particle that mediates the strong nuclear force—the force that holds nucleons together in the nucleus. Yukawa called this predicted particle a **meson** (meaning "medium mass"). Figure 43–9 is a Feynman diagram showing the original model of meson exchange: a meson carrying the strong force between a neutron and a proton.

A rough estimate of the mass of the meson can be made as follows. Suppose the proton on the left in Fig. 43–9 is at rest. For it to emit a meson would require energy (to make the meson's mass) which, coming from nowhere, would violate conservation of energy. But the uncertainty principle allows nonconservation of energy by an amount ΔE if it occurs only for a time Δt given by $(\Delta E)(\Delta t) \approx h/2\pi$. We set ΔE equal to the energy needed to create the mass m of the meson: $\Delta E = mc^2$. Conservation of energy is violated only as long as the meson exists, which is the time Δt required for the meson to pass from one nucleon to the other, where it is absorbed and disappears. If we assume the meson travels at relativistic speed, close to the speed of light c, then Δt need be at most about $\Delta t = d/c$, where d is the maximum distance that can separate the interacting nucleons. Thus we can write

$$\Delta E\, \Delta t \approx \frac{h}{2\pi}$$

$$mc^2 \left(\frac{d}{c}\right) \approx \frac{h}{2\pi}$$

or

$$mc^2 \approx \frac{hc}{2\pi d}. \tag{43–3}$$

The range of the strong nuclear force (the maximum distance away it can be felt) is small—not much more than the size of a nucleon or small nucleus (see Eq. 41–1)—so let us take $d \approx 1.5 \times 10^{-15}$ m. Then from Eq. 43–3,

$$mc^2 \approx \frac{hc}{2\pi d} = \frac{(6.6 \times 10^{-34}\,\text{J·s})(3.0 \times 10^8\,\text{m/s})}{(6.28)(1.5 \times 10^{-15}\,\text{m})} \approx 2.1 \times 10^{-11}\,\text{J} = 130\,\text{MeV}.$$

The mass of the predicted meson, roughly $130\,\text{MeV}/c^2$, is about 250 times the electron mass of $0.51\,\text{MeV}/c^2$.

EXERCISE C What effect does an increase in the mass of the virtual exchange particle have on the range of the force it mediates? (*a*) Decreases it; (*b*) increases it; (*c*) has no appreciable effect; (*d*) decreases the range for charged particles and increases the range for neutral particles.

Note that since the electromagnetic force has infinite range, Eq. 43–3 with $d = \infty$ tells us that the exchanged particle for the electromagnetic force, the photon, will have zero mass, which it does.

The particle predicted by Yukawa was discovered in cosmic rays by C. F. Powell and G. Occhialini in 1947, and is called the "π" or pi meson, or simply the **pion**. It comes in three charge states: $+e$, $-e$, or 0, where $e = 1.6 \times 10^{-19}\,$C. The π^+ and π^- have mass of 139.6 MeV/c^2 and the π^0 a mass of 135.0 MeV/c^2, all close to Yukawa's prediction. All three interact strongly with matter. Reactions observed in the laboratory, using a particle accelerator, include

$$p + p \rightarrow p + p + \pi^0,$$
$$p + p \rightarrow p + n + \pi^+. \qquad (43\text{–}4)$$

The incident proton from the accelerator must have sufficient energy to produce the additional mass of the free pion.

Yukawa's theory of pion exchange as carrier of the strong force has been superseded by *quantum chromodynamics* in which protons, neutrons, and other strongly interacting particles are made up of basic entities called *quarks*, and the basic carriers of the strong force are *gluons*, as we shall discuss shortly. But the basic idea of the earlier theory, that forces can be understood as the exchange of particles, remains valid.

There are four known types of force—or interactions—in nature. The electromagnetic force is carried by the photon, the strong force by gluons. What about the other two: the weak force and gravity? These too are believed to be mediated by particles. The particles that transmit the weak force are referred to as the W^+, W^-, and Z^0, and were detected in 1983 (Fig. 43–10). The quantum (or carrier) of the gravitational force is called the **graviton**, and if it exists it has not yet been observed.

FIGURE 43–10 (a) Computer reconstruction of a Z-particle decay into an electron and a positron ($Z^0 \rightarrow e^+ + e^-$) whose tracks are shown in white, which took place in the UA1 detector at CERN. (b) Photo of the UA1 detector at CERN as it was being built.

(a)

(b)

A comparison of the four forces is given in Table 43–1, where they are listed according to their (approximate) relative strengths. Notice that although gravity may be the most obvious force in daily life (because of the huge mass of the Earth), on a nuclear scale it is by far the weakest of the four forces, and its effect at the particle level can nearly always be ignored.

TABLE 43–1 The Four Forces in Nature

Type	Relative Strength (approx., for 2 protons in nucleus)	Field Particle
Strong	1	Gluons
Electromagnetic	10^{-2}	Photon
Weak	10^{-6}	$W^{\pm}$ and Z^0
Gravitational	10^{-38}	Graviton (?)

43–3 Particles and Antiparticles

The positron, as we discussed in Sections 37–5 (pair production) and 41–5 (β^+ decay), is basically a positive electron. That is, many of its properties are the same as for the electron, such as mass, but it has the opposite electric charge $(+e)$. Other quantum numbers that we will discuss shortly are also reversed. The positron is said to be the **antiparticle** to the electron.

The original idea for antiparticles came from a relativistic wave equation developed in 1928 by the Englishman P. A. M. Dirac (1902–1984). Recall that the non-relativistic Schrödinger equation took conservation of energy as a starting point. The Dirac equation too was based in part on conservation of energy. In Chapter 36, we saw that the total energy E of a particle with mass m and momentum p and zero potential energy is given by Eq. 36–13, $E^2 = p^2c^2 + m^2c^4$. Thus

$$E = \pm\sqrt{p^2c^2 + m^2c^4}.$$

Dirac applied his new equation and found that it included solutions with both $+$ and $-$ signs. He could not ignore the solution with the negative sign, which we might have thought unphysical. If those negative energy states are real, then we would expect normal free electrons to drop down into those states, emitting photons—never experimentally seen. To deal with this difficulty, Dirac postulated that all those negative energy states are *normally occupied*. That is, what we thought was the **vacuum** is instead a vast **sea of electrons** in negative energy states (Fig. 43–11a). These electrons are not normally observable. But if a photon strikes one of these negative energy electrons, that electron can be knocked up to a normal $(E > mc^2)$ energy state as shown in Fig. 43–11b. (Note in Fig. 43–11 that there are no energy states between $E = -mc^2$ and $E = +mc^2$ because p^2 cannot be negative in the equation $E = \pm\sqrt{p^2c^2 + m^2c^4}$.) The photon that knocks an e^- from the negative sea up to a normal state (Fig. 43–11b) must have an energy greater than $2mc^2$. What is left behind is a hole (as in semiconductors, Sections 40–7 and 40–8) with positive charge. We call that "hole" a **positron**, and it can move around as a free particle with positive energy. Thus Fig. 43–11b represents (Section 37–5) **pair production**: $\gamma \rightarrow e^- e^+$.

The positron was first detected as a curved path in a cloud chamber in a magnetic field by Carl Anderson in 1932. It was predicted that other particles also would have antiparticles. It was decades before another type was found. Finally, in 1955 the antiparticle to the proton, the **antiproton** ($\bar{p}$), which carries a negative charge (Fig. 43–12), was discovered at the University of California, Berkeley,

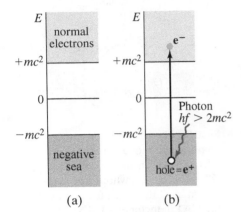

FIGURE 43–11 (a) Possible energy states for an electron. Note the vast sea of fully occupied electron states at $E < -mc^2$. (b) An electron in the negative sea is hit by a photon $(E > 2mc^2)$ and knocks it up to a normal positive energy state. The positive "hole" left behind acts like a positive electron—it is a positron.

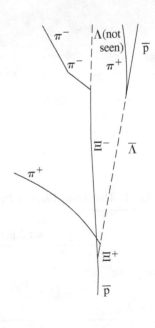

FIGURE 43–12 Liquid-hydrogen bubble-chamber photograph of an antiproton ($\bar{p}$) colliding with a proton at rest, producing a Xi–anti-Xi pair ($\bar{p} + p \rightarrow \Xi^- + \overline{\Xi}{}^+$) that subsequently decay into other particles. The drawing indicates the assignment of particles to each track, which is based on how or if that particle decays, and on mass values estimated from measurement of momentum (curvature of track in magnetic field) and energy (thickness of track, for example). Neutral particle paths are shown by dashed lines since neutral particles produce no bubbles and hence no tracks.

by Emilio Segrè (1905–1989, Fig. 43–13) and Owen Chamberlain (1920–2006). A bar, such as over the p, is used in general to indicate the antiparticle ($\bar{p}$). Soon after, the antineutron ($\bar{n}$) was found. All particles have antiparticles. But a few, like the photon and the π^0, do not have distinct antiparticles—we say that they are their own antiparticles.

Antiparticles are produced in nuclear reactions when there is sufficient energy available to produce the required mass, and they do not live very long in the presence of matter. For example, a positron is stable when by itself; but if it encounters an electron, the two annihilate each other. The energy of their vanished mass, plus any kinetic energy they possessed, is converted into the energy of γ rays or of other particles. Annihilation also occurs for all other particle–antiparticle pairs.

The vast sea of electrons with negative energy in Fig. 43–11 is the vacuum (or **vacuum state**). According to quantum mechanics, the vacuum is not empty, but contains electrons and other particles as well. The uncertainty principle allows a particle to jump briefly up to a normal energy, thus creating a **particle–antiparticle** pair. It is possible that they could be the source of the recently discovered *dark energy* that fills the universe (Chapter 44). We still have a lot to learn.

Antimatter is a term referring to material that would be made up of "antiatoms" in which antiprotons and antineutrons would form the nucleus around which positrons (antielectrons) would move. The term is also used for antiparticles in general. If there were pockets of antimatter in the universe, a huge explosion would occur if it should encounter normal matter. It is believed that antimatter was prevalent in the very early universe (Section 44–7).

FIGURE 43–13 Emilio Segrè: he worked with Fermi in the 1930s, later discovered the first "man-made" element, technetium, and other elements, and then the antiproton. The inscription below the photo is from a book by Segrè given to this book's author.

43–4 Particle Interactions and Conservation Laws

One of the important uses of high-energy accelerators is to study the interactions of elementary particles with each other. As a means of ordering this subnuclear world, the conservation laws are indispensable. The laws of conservation of energy, of momentum, of angular momentum, and of electric charge are found to hold precisely in all particle interactions.

A study of particle interactions has revealed a number of new conservation laws which (just like the old ones) are ordering principles: they help to explain why some reactions occur and others do not. For example, the following reaction has never been observed:

$$p + n \nrightarrow p + p + \bar{p}$$

even though charge, energy, and so on, are conserved ($\nrightarrow$ means the reaction does not occur). To understand why such a reaction does not occur, physicists hypothesized a new conservation law, the conservation of **baryon number**. (Baryon number is a generalization of nucleon number, which we saw earlier is conserved in nuclear reactions and decays.) All nucleons are defined to have baryon number $B = +1$, and all antinucleons (antiprotons, antineutrons) have $B = -1$. All other types of particles, such as photons, mesons, and electrons and other leptons, have $B = 0$. The reaction shown at the start of this paragraph does not conserve baryon number since the left side has $B = (+1) + (+1) = +2$, and the right has $B = (+1) + (+1) + (-1) = +1$. On the other hand, the following reaction does conserve B and *does* occur if the incoming proton has sufficient energy:

$$p + p \rightarrow p + p + \bar{p} + p,$$
$$B = +1 + 1 = +1 + 1 - 1 + 1.$$

As indicated, $B = +2$ on both sides of this equation. From these and other reactions, the **conservation of baryon number** has been established as a basic principle of physics.

Also useful are conservation laws for the three **lepton numbers**, associated with weak interactions including decays. In ordinary β decay, an electron or positron is emitted along with a neutrino or antineutrino. In another type of decay, a particle known as a "μ" or mu meson, or **muon**, can be emitted instead of an electron. The muon (discovered in 1937) seems to be much like an electron, except its mass is 207 times larger ($106 \, \text{MeV}/c^2$). The neutrino (ν_e) that accompanies an emitted electron is found to be different from the neutrino (ν_μ) that accompanies an emitted muon.

⚠ **C A U T I O N**

The different types of neutrinos are not identical

Each of these neutrinos has an antiparticle: $\bar{\nu}_e$ and $\bar{\nu}_\mu$. In ordinary β decay we have, for example,

$$n \rightarrow p + e^- + \bar{\nu}_e$$

but not $n \not\rightarrow p + e^- + \bar{\nu}_\mu$. To explain why these do not occur, the concept of **electron lepton number**, L_e, was invented. If the electron (e^-) and the electron neutrino (ν_e) are assigned $L_e = +1$, and e^+ and $\bar{\nu}_e$ are assigned $L_e = -1$, whereas all other particles have $L_e = 0$, then all observed decays conserve L_e. For example, in $n \rightarrow p + e^- + \bar{\nu}_e$, initially $L_e = 0$, and afterward $L_e = 0 + (+1) + (-1) = 0$. Decays that do not conserve L_e, even though they would obey the other conservation laws, are not observed to occur.

In a decay involving muons, such as

$$\pi^+ \rightarrow \mu^+ + \nu_\mu,$$

a second quantum number, **muon lepton number** (L_μ), is conserved. The μ^- and ν_μ are assigned $L_\mu = +1$, and their antiparticles μ^+ and $\bar{\nu}_\mu$ have $L_\mu = -1$, whereas all other particles have $L_\mu = 0$. L_μ too is conserved in interactions and decays. Similar assignments can be made for the **tau lepton number**, L_τ, associated with the τ lepton (discovered in 1976 with mass more than 3000 times the electron mass) and its neutrino, ν_τ.

Keep in mind that antiparticles have not only opposite electric charge from their particles, but also opposite B, L_e, L_μ, and L_τ. For example, a neutron has $B = +1$, an antineutron has $B = -1$ (and all the L's are zero).

CONCEPTUAL EXAMPLE 43–5 **Lepton number in muon decay.** Which of the following decay schemes is possible for muon decay: (a) $\mu^- \rightarrow e^- + \bar{\nu}_e$; (b) $\mu^- \rightarrow e^- + \bar{\nu}_e + \nu_\mu$; (c) $\mu^- \rightarrow e^- + \nu_e$? All of these particles have $L_\tau = 0$.

RESPONSE A μ^- has $L_\mu = +1$ and $L_e = 0$. This is the initial state for all decays given, and the final state must also have $L_\mu = +1$, $L_e = 0$. In (a), the final state has $L_\mu = 0 + 0 = 0$, and $L_e = +1 - 1 = 0$; L_μ would not be conserved and indeed this decay is not observed to occur. The final state of (b) has $L_\mu = 0 + 0 + 1 = +1$ and $L_e = +1 - 1 + 0 = 0$, so both L_μ and L_e are conserved. This is in fact the most common decay mode of the μ^-. Lastly, (c) does not occur because L_e ($= +2$ in the final state) is not conserved, nor is L_μ.

EXAMPLE 43–6 **Energy and momentum are conserved.** In addition to the "number" conservation laws which help explain the decay schemes of particles, we can also apply the laws of conservation of energy and momentum. The decay of a Σ^+ particle at rest with a mass of $1189 \text{ MeV}/c^2$ (Table 43–2 in Section 43–6) commonly yields a proton (mass $= 938 \text{ MeV}/c^2$) and a neutral pion, π^0 (mass $= 135 \text{ MeV}/c^2$):

$$\Sigma^+ \rightarrow p + \pi^0.$$

What are the kinetic energies of the decay products, assuming the Σ^+ parent particle was at rest?

APPROACH We find the energy release from the change in mass $(E = mc^2)$ as we did for nuclear processes (Eq. 41–3 or 42–2a), and apply conservation of energy and momentum.

SOLUTION The energy released, or Q-value, is the change in mass times c^2:

$$Q = [m_{\Sigma^+} - (m_p + m_{\pi^0})]c^2 = [1189 - (938 + 135)] \text{ MeV} = 116 \text{ MeV}.$$

This energy Q becomes the kinetic energy of the resulting decay particles, p and π^0:

$$Q = K_p + K_{\pi^0}$$

with each particle's kinetic energy related to its momentum by (Eqs. 36–11 and 13):

$$K_p = E_p - m_p c^2 = \sqrt{(p_p c)^2 + (m_p c^2)^2} - m_p c^2,$$

and similarly for the pion. From momentum conservation, the proton and pion have the same magnitude of momentum since the original Σ^+ was at rest: $p_p = p_{\pi^0} = p$. Then, $Q = K_p + K_{\pi^0}$ gives $116 \text{ MeV} = [\sqrt{(pc)^2 + (938 \text{ MeV})^2} - 938 \text{ MeV}] + [\sqrt{(pc)^2 + (135 \text{ MeV})^2} - 135 \text{ MeV}]$. We solve this for pc, which gives $pc = 189 \text{ MeV}$. Substituting into the expression above for the kinetic energy, first for the proton, then for the pion, we obtain $K_p = 19 \text{ MeV}$ and $K_{\pi^0} = 97 \text{ MeV}$.

43–5 Neutrinos—Recent Results

We first met neutrinos with regard to β^- decay in Section 41–5. The study of neutrinos is a "hot" subject today. Experiments are being carried out in deep underground laboratories, sometimes in deep mine shafts. The thick layer of earth above is meant to filter out all other "background" particles, leaving mainly the very weakly interacting neutrinos to arrive at the detectors.

Some very important results have come to the fore in recent years. First there was the **solar neutrino problem**. The energy output of the Sun is believed to be due to the nuclear fusion reactions discussed in Chapter 42, Eqs. 42–7 and 42–8. The neutrinos emitted in these reactions are all ν_e (accompanied by e^+). But the rate at which ν_e arrive at Earth is measured to be much less than expected based on the power output of the Sun. It was then proposed that perhaps, on the long trip between Sun and Earth, ν_e might turn into ν_μ or ν_τ. Subsequent experiments confirmed this hypothesis. Thus the three neutrinos, ν_e, ν_μ, ν_τ, can change into one another in certain circumstances, a phenomenon called **neutrino flavor oscillation** (each of the three neutrino types being called, whimsically, a different "flavor"). This result suggests that the lepton numbers $L_e, L_\mu,$ and L_τ are not perfectly conserved. But the sum, $L_e + L_\mu + L_\tau$, is believed to be always conserved.

The second exceptional result has long been speculated on: are neutrinos massless as originally thought, or do they have a nonzero mass? Rough upper limits on the masses have been made. Today astrophysical experiments show that the sum of all three neutrino masses is less than about $0.14 \, \text{eV}/c^2$. But can the masses be zero? Not if there are the flavor oscillations discussed above. It seems likely that at least one neutrino type has a mass of at least $0.04 \, \text{eV}/c^2$.

As a result of neutrino oscillations, the three types of neutrino may not be exactly what we thought they were (e, μ, τ). If not, the three basic neutrinos, called 1, 2, and 3, are linear combinations of $\nu_e, \nu_\mu,$ and ν_τ.

Another outstanding question is whether or not neutrinos are in the category called **Majorana particles**,[†] meaning they would be their own antiparticles. If so, a lot of other questions (and answers) would appear.

*Neutrino Mass Estimate from a Supernova

The supernova of 1987 offered an opportunity to estimate electron neutrino mass. If neutrinos do have mass, then $v < c$ and neutrinos of different energy would take different times to travel the 170,000 light-years from the supernova to Earth. To get an idea of how such a measurement could be done, suppose two neutrinos from "SN1987a" were emitted at the same time and detected on Earth (via the reaction $\bar{\nu}_e + p \rightarrow n + e^+$) 10 seconds apart, with measured kinetic energies of about 20 MeV and 10 MeV. Since we expect the neutrino mass to be surely less than 100 eV (from other laboratory measurements), and since our neutrinos have kinetic energy of 20 MeV and 10 MeV, we can make the approximation $m_\nu c^2 \ll E$, so that E (the total energy) is essentially equal to the kinetic energy. We use Eq. 36–11, which tells us

$$E = \frac{m_\nu c^2}{\sqrt{1 - v^2/c^2}}.$$

We solve this for v, the velocity of a neutrino with energy E:

$$v = c\left(1 - \frac{m_\nu^2 c^4}{E^2}\right)^{\frac{1}{2}} = c\left(1 - \frac{m_\nu^2 c^4}{2E^2} + \cdots\right),$$

where we have used the binomial expansion $(1 - x)^{\frac{1}{2}} = 1 - \frac{1}{2}x + \cdots$, and we ignore higher-order terms since $m_\nu^2 c^4 \ll E^2$. The time t for a neutrino to travel a distance $d \, (= 170,000 \, \text{ly})$ is

$$t = \frac{d}{v} = \frac{d}{c\left(1 - \frac{m_\nu^2 c^4}{2E^2}\right)} \approx \frac{d}{c}\left(1 + \frac{m_\nu^2 c^4}{2E^2}\right),$$

where again we used the binomial expansion $[(1 - x)^{-1} = 1 + x + \cdots]$.

[†]The brilliant young physicist Ettore Majorana (1906–1938) disappeared from a ship under mysterious circumstances in 1938 at the age of 31.

The difference in arrival times for our two neutrinos of energies $E_1 = 20\,\text{MeV}$ and $E_2 = 10\,\text{MeV}$ is

$$t_2 - t_1 = \frac{d}{c}\,\frac{m_\nu^2 c^4}{2}\left(\frac{1}{E_2^2} - \frac{1}{E_1^2}\right).$$

We solve this for $m_\nu c^2$ and set $t_2 - t_1 = 10\,\text{s}$:

$$m_\nu c^2 = \left[\frac{2c(t_2 - t_1)}{d}\,\frac{E_1^2 E_2^2}{E_1^2 - E_2^2}\right]^{\frac{1}{2}}$$

$$= \left[\frac{2(3.0 \times 10^8\,\text{m/s})(10\,\text{s})}{(1.7 \times 10^5\,\text{ly})(1.0 \times 10^{16}\,\text{m/ly})}\,\frac{(400\,\text{MeV}^2)(100\,\text{MeV}^2)}{(400\,\text{MeV}^2 - 100\,\text{MeV}^2)}\right]^{\frac{1}{2}}$$

$$= 22 \times 10^{-6}\,\text{MeV} = 22\,\text{eV}.$$

We thus estimate the mass of the neutrino to be $22\,\text{eV}/c^2$, but there would of course be experimental uncertainties, not to mention the unwarranted assumption that the two neutrinos were emitted at the same time.

Theoretical models of supernova explosions suggest that the neutrinos are emitted in a burst that lasts from a second or two up to perhaps 10 s. If we assume the neutrinos are not emitted simultaneously but rather at any time over a 10-s interval, what then could we say about the neutrino mass based on the data given above? The 10-s difference in their arrival times could be due to a 10-s difference in their emission time. In this case our data would be consistent with zero mass, and it puts an approximate *upper limit* on the neutrino mass of $22\,\text{eV}/c^2$.

The actual detection of these neutrinos was brilliant—it was a rare event that allowed us to detect something other than EM radiation from beyond the solar system, and was an exceptional confirmation of theory. In the experiments, the most sensitive detector consisted of several thousand tons of water in an underground chamber. It detected 11 events in 12 seconds, probably via the reaction $\bar{\nu}_e + \text{p} \rightarrow \text{n} + \text{e}^+$. There was not a clear correlation between energy and time of arrival. Nonetheless, a careful analysis of that experiment set a rough upper limit on the electron anti-neutrino mass of about $4\,\text{eV}/c^2$. The more recent results mentioned above are much more definitive—they provide evidence that mass is much smaller, and that it is *not zero*.

43–6 Particle Classification

In the decades following the discovery of the π meson in the late 1940s, hundreds of other subnuclear particles were discovered. One way of arranging the particles in categories is according to their interactions, since not all particles interact by means of all four of the forces known in nature (though all interact via gravity). Table 43–2 (next page) lists some of the more common particles classified in this way along with many of their properties. At the top of Table 43–2 are the so-called "fundamental" particles which we believe have no internal structure. Below them are some of the "composite" particles which are made up of quarks, according to the Standard Model.

The fundamental particles include the **gauge bosons** (so-named after the theory that describes them, "gauge theory"), which include the gluons, the photon, and the W and Z particles; these are the particles that mediate the strong, electromagnetic, and weak interactions, respectively. Also fundamental are the **leptons**, which are particles that do not interact via the strong force but do interact via the weak nuclear force. Leptons that carry electric charge also interact via the electromagnetic force. The leptons include the electron, the muon, and the tau, and three types of neutrino: the electron neutrino (ν_e), the muon neutrino (ν_μ), and the tau neutrino (ν_τ). Each has an antiparticle.

TABLE 43–2 Particles (selected)[†]

Category	Forces involved	Particle name	Symbol	Anti-particle	Spin	Mass (MeV/c^2)	B	L_e	L_μ	L_τ	S	Mean life (s)	Principal Decay Modes
Fundamental													
Gauge bosons (force carriers)	str	Gluons	g	Self	1	0	0	0	0	0	0	Stable	
	em	Photon	γ	Self	1	0	0	0	0	0	0	Stable	
	w, em	W	W^+	W^-	1	80.40×10^3	0	0	0	0	0	$\approx 10^{-24}$	$e\nu_e$, $\mu\nu_\mu$, $\tau\nu_\tau$, hadrons
	w	Z	Z^0	Self	1	91.19×10^3	0	0	0	0	0	$\approx 10^{-24}$	e^+e^-, $\mu^+\mu^-$, $\tau^+\tau^-$, hadrons
Leptons	w, em[‡]	Electron	e^-	e^+	$\frac{1}{2}$	0.511	0	+1	0	0	0	Stable	
		Neutrino (e)	ν_e	$\bar{\nu}_e$	$\frac{1}{2}$	0 (<0.14 eV)[‡]	0	+1	0	0	0	Stable	
		Muon	μ^-	μ^+	$\frac{1}{2}$	105.7	0	0	+1	0	0	2.20×10^{-6}	$e^-\bar{\nu}_e\nu_\mu$
		Neutrino (μ)	ν_μ	$\bar{\nu}_\mu$	$\frac{1}{2}$	0 (<0.14 eV)[‡]	0	0	+1	0	0	Stable	
		Tau	τ^-	τ^+	$\frac{1}{2}$	1777	0	0	0	+1	0	2.91×10^{-13}	$\mu^-\bar{\nu}_\mu\nu_\tau$, $e^-\bar{\nu}_e\nu_\tau$, hadrons $+\nu_\tau$
		Neutrino (τ)	ν_τ	$\bar{\nu}_\tau$	$\frac{1}{2}$	0 (<0.14 eV)[‡]	0	0	0	+1	0	Stable	
Hadrons (composite), selected													
Mesons (quark–antiquark)	str, em, w	Pion	π^+	π^-	0	139.6	0	0	0	0	0	2.60×10^{-8}	$\mu^+\nu_\mu$
			π^0	Self	0	135.0	0	0	0	0	0	0.84×10^{-16}	2γ
		Kaon	K^+	K^-	0	493.7	0	0	0	0	+1	1.24×10^{-8}	$\mu^+\nu_\mu$, $\pi^+\pi^0$
			K_S^0	$\bar{K}_S^0$	0	497.7	0	0	0	0	+1	0.89×10^{-10}	$\pi^+\pi^-$, $2\pi^0$
			K_L^0	$\bar{K}_L^0$	0	497.7	0	0	0	0	+1	5.17×10^{-8}	$\pi^\pm e^\mp \overset{(-)}{\nu}_e$, $\pi^\pm \mu^\mp \overset{(-)}{\nu}_\mu$, 3π
		Eta	η^0	Self	0	547.5	0	0	0	0	0	$\approx 10^{-18}$	2γ, $3\pi^0$, $\pi^+\pi^-\pi^0$
		Rho	ρ^0	Self	1	775	0	0	0	0	0	$\approx 10^{-23}$	$\pi^+\pi^-$, $2\pi^0$
			ρ^+	ρ^-	1	775	0	0	0	0	0	$\approx 10^{-23}$	$\pi^+\pi^0$
		and others											
Baryons (3 quarks)	str, em, w	Proton	p	$\bar{p}$	$\frac{1}{2}$	938.3	+1	0	0	0	0	Stable	
		Neutron	n	$\bar{n}$	$\frac{1}{2}$	939.6	+1	0	0	0	0	886	$pe^-\bar{\nu}_e$
		Lambda	Λ^0	$\bar{\Lambda}^0$	$\frac{1}{2}$	1115.7	+1	0	0	0	-1	2.63×10^{-10}	$p\pi^-$, $n\pi^0$
		Sigma	Σ^+	$\bar{\Sigma}^-$	$\frac{1}{2}$	1189.4	+1	0	0	0	-1	0.80×10^{-10}	$p\pi^0$, $n\pi^+$
			Σ^0	$\bar{\Sigma}^0$	$\frac{1}{2}$	1192.6	+1	0	0	0	-1	7.4×10^{-20}	$\Lambda^0\gamma$
			Σ^-	$\bar{\Sigma}^+$	$\frac{1}{2}$	1197.4	+1	0	0	0	-1	1.48×10^{-10}	$n\pi^-$
		Xi	Ξ^0	$\bar{\Xi}^0$	$\frac{1}{2}$	1314.8	+1	0	0	0	-2	2.90×10^{-10}	$\Lambda^0\pi^0$
			Ξ^-	$\bar{\Xi}^+$	$\frac{1}{2}$	1321.3	+1	0	0	0	-2	1.64×10^{-10}	$\Lambda^0\pi^-$
		Omega	Ω^-	Ω^+	$\frac{3}{2}$	1672.5	+1	0	0	0	-3	0.82×10^{-10}	$\Xi^0\pi^-$, $\Lambda^0 K^-$, $\Xi^-\pi^0$
		and others											

[†]See also Table 43–4 for particles with charm and bottomness. S in this Table stands for "strangeness" (see Section 43–8). More detail online at: pdg.lbl.gov.
[‡]Neutrinos partake only in the weak interaction. Experimental upper limits on neutrino masses are given in parentheses, as obtained mainly from the WMAP survey (Chapter 44). Detection of neutrino oscillations suggests that at least one type of neutrino has a nonzero mass greater than 0.04 eV.

The second category of particle in Table 43–2 is the **hadrons**, which are composite particles as we will discuss shortly. Hadrons are those particles that interact via the strong nuclear force. Hence they are said to be **strongly interacting particles**. They also interact via the other forces, but the strong force predominates at short distances. The hadrons include the proton, neutron, pion, and a large number of other particles. They are divided into two subgroups: **baryons**, which are those particles that have baryon number +1 (or −1 in the case of their antiparticles) and, as we shall see, are each made up of three quarks; and **mesons**, which have baryon number = 0, and are made up of a quark and an antiquark.

Only a few of the hundreds of hadrons (a veritable "zoo") are included in Table 43–2. Notice that the baryons Λ, Σ, Ξ, and Ω all decay to lighter-mass baryons, and eventually to a proton or neutron. All these processes conserve baryon number. Since there is no particle lighter than the proton with $B = +1$, if baryon number is strictly conserved, the proton itself cannot decay and is stable. (But see Section 43–11.) Note that Table 43–2 gives the *mean life* (τ) of each particle (as is done in particle physics), not the half-life ($T_{\frac{1}{2}}$). Recall that they differ by a factor 0.693: $\tau = T_{\frac{1}{2}}/\ln 2 = T_{\frac{1}{2}}/0.693$, Eq. 41–9. The term **lifetime** in particle physics means the mean life τ (= mean lifetime).

The baryon and lepton numbers (B, L_e, L_μ, L_τ), as well as strangeness S (Section 43–8), as given in Table 43–2 are for particles; their antiparticles have opposite sign for these numbers.

Baryon decay. Show that the decay modes of the Σ^+ baryon given in Table 43–2 do not violate the conservation laws we have studied up to now: energy, charge, baryon number, lepton numbers.

APPROACH Table 43–2 shows two possible decay modes, (a) $\Sigma^+ \rightarrow p + \pi^0$, (b) $\Sigma^+ \rightarrow n + \pi^+$. We check each for energy conservation, charge conservation, and conservation of baryon number. All the particles have lepton numbers equal to zero.

SOLUTION (a) Energy: for $\Sigma^+ \rightarrow p + \pi^0$ the change in mass-energy is

$$\Delta M = m_\Sigma c^2 - m_p c^2 - m_{\pi^0} c^2$$
$$= 1189.4 \, \text{MeV}/c^2 - 938.3 \, \text{MeV}/c^2 - 135.0 \, \text{MeV}/c^2 = +116.1 \, \text{MeV}/c^2,$$

so energy can be conserved with the resulting particles having kinetic energy.
Charge: $+e = +e + 0$, so charge is conserved.
Baryon number: $+1 = +1 + 0$, so baryon number is conserved.
(b) Energy: for $\Sigma^+ \rightarrow n + \pi^+$, the mass-energy change is

$$\Delta M = m_\Sigma c^2 - m_n c^2 - m_{\pi^+} c^2$$
$$= 1189.4 \, \text{MeV}/c^2 - 939.6 \, \text{MeV}/c^2 - 139.6 \, \text{MeV}/c^2 = 110.2 \, \text{MeV}/c^2.$$

This reaction releases 110.2 MeV of energy as kinetic energy of the products.
Charge: $+e = 0 + e$, so charge is conserved.
Baryon number: $+1 = +1 + 0$, so baryon number is conserved.

43–7 Particle Stability and Resonances

Many particles listed in Table 43–2 are unstable. The lifetime of an unstable particle depends on which force is most active in causing the decay. When a stronger force influences a decay, that decay occurs more quickly. Decays caused by the weak force typically have lifetimes of 10^{-13} s or longer (W and Z are exceptions). Decays via the electromagnetic force have much shorter lifetimes, typically about 10^{-16} to 10^{-19} s, and normally involve a γ (photon). The unstable particles listed in Table 43–2 decay either via the weak or the electromagnetic interaction.

Many particles have been found that decay via the strong interaction, with very short lifetimes, typically about 10^{-23} s. Their lifetimes are so short they do not travel far enough to be detected before decaying. The existence of such short-lived particles is inferred from their decay products. Consider the first such particle discovered (by Fermi), using a beam of π^+ particles with varying amounts of energy directed through a hydrogen target (protons). The number of interactions (π^+ scattered) plotted versus the pion's kinetic energy is shown in Fig. 43–14.

FIGURE 43–14 Number of π^+ particles scattered by a proton target as a function of the incident π^+ kinetic energy. The resonance shape represents the formation of a short-lived particle, the Δ, which has a charge in this case of $+2e$ (Δ^{++}).

The large number of interactions around 200 MeV led Fermi to conclude that the π^+ and proton combined momentarily to form a short-lived particle before coming apart again, or at least that they resonated together for a short time. Indeed, the large peak in Fig. 43–14 resembles a resonance curve (see Figs. 14–23, 14–26, and 30–22), and this new "particle"—now called the Δ—is referred to as a **resonance**. Hundreds of other resonances have been found, and are regarded as excited states of lighter mass particles such as the nucleon.

The **width** of a resonance—in Fig. 43–14 the full width of the Δ peak at half the peak height is on the order of 100 MeV—is an interesting application of the uncertainty principle. If a particle lives only 10^{-23} s, then its mass (i.e., its rest energy) will be uncertain by an amount

$$\Delta E \approx h/(2\pi \, \Delta t)$$

$$\approx (6.6 \times 10^{-34}\,\text{J·s})/(6)(10^{-23}\,\text{s}) \approx 10^{-11}\,\text{J} \approx 100\,\text{MeV},$$

which is what is observed. Actually, the lifetimes of $\approx 10^{-23}$ s for such resonances are inferred by the reverse process: from the measured width being ≈ 100 MeV.

43–8 Strange Particles? Charm? Towards a New Model

In the early 1950s, the newly found particles K, Λ, and Σ were found to behave rather strangely in two ways. First, they were always produced in pairs. For example, the reaction

$$\pi^- + \text{p} \rightarrow \text{K}^0 + \Lambda^0$$

occurred with high probability, but the similar reaction $\pi^- + \text{p} \nrightarrow \text{K}^0 + \text{n}$, was never observed to occur even though it did not violate any known conservation law. The second feature of these **strange particles**, as they came to be called, was that they were produced via the strong interaction (that is, at a high interaction rate), but did not decay at a fast rate characteristic of the strong interaction (even though they decayed into strongly interacting particles).

To explain these observations, a new quantum number, **strangeness**, and a new conservation law, **conservation of strangeness**, were introduced. By assigning the strangeness numbers (S) indicated in Table 43–2, the production of strange particles in pairs was explained. Antiparticles were assigned opposite strangeness from their particles. For example, in the reaction $\pi^- + \text{p} \rightarrow \text{K}^0 + \Lambda^0$, the initial state has strangeness $S = 0 + 0 = 0$, and the final state has $S = +1 - 1 = 0$, so strangeness is conserved. But for $\pi^- + \text{p} \nrightarrow \text{K}^0 + \text{n}$, the initial state has $S = 0$ and the final state has $S = +1 + 0 = +1$, so strangeness would not be conserved; and this reaction is not observed.

To explain the decay of strange particles, it is assumed that strangeness is conserved in the strong interaction but is *not conserved in the weak interaction*. Thus, strange particles were forbidden by strangeness conservation to decay to nonstrange particles of lower mass via the strong interaction, but could decay by means of the weak interaction at the observed longer lifetimes of 10^{-10} to 10^{-8} s.

The conservation of strangeness was the first example of a *partially conserved* quantity. In this case, the quantity strangeness is conserved by strong interactions but not by weak.

⚠ CAUTION

Partially conserved quantities

| CONCEPTUAL EXAMPLE 43–8 | **Guess the missing particle.** Using the conservation laws for particle interactions, determine the possibilities for the missing particle in the reaction

$$\pi^- + p \rightarrow K^0 + ?$$

in addition to $K^0 + \Lambda^0$ mentioned above.

RESPONSE We write equations for the conserved numbers in this reaction, with B, L_e, S, and Q as unknowns whose determination will reveal what the possible particle might be:

Baryon number: $\quad 0 + 1 = 0 + B$
Lepton number: $\quad 0 + 0 = 0 + L_e$
Charge: $\quad\quad\quad -1 + 1 = 0 + Q$
Strangeness: $\quad\ 0 + 0 = 1 + S$.

The unknown product particle would have to have these characteristics:

$$B = +1 \quad L_e = 0 \quad Q = 0 \quad S = -1.$$

In addition to Λ^0, a neutral sigma particle, Σ^0, is also consistent with these numbers.

In the next Section we will discuss another partially conserved quantity which was given the name **charm**. The discovery in 1974 of a particle with charm helped solidify a new theory involving quarks, which we now discuss.

43–9 Quarks

All particles, except the gauge bosons (Section 43–6), are either leptons or hadrons. One difference between these two groups is that the hadrons interact via the strong interaction, whereas the leptons do not.

There is another major difference. The six leptons $(e^-, \mu^-, \tau^-, \nu_e, \nu_\mu, \nu_\tau)$ are considered to be truly fundamental particles because they do not show any internal structure, and have no measurable size. (Attempts to determine the size of leptons have put an upper limit of about 10^{-18} m.) On the other hand, there are hundreds of hadrons, and experiments indicate they do have an internal structure.

In 1963, M. Gell-Mann and G. Zweig proposed that none of the hadrons, not even the proton and neutron, are truly fundamental, but instead are made up of combinations of three more fundamental pointlike entities called (somewhat whimsically) **quarks**.[†] Today, the quark theory is well-accepted, and quarks are considered truly fundamental particles, like leptons. The three quarks originally proposed were labeled u, d, s, and have the names **up**, **down**, and **strange**. The theory today has six quarks, just as there are six leptons—based on a presumed symmetry in nature. The other three quarks are called **charmed**, **bottom**, and **top**. The names apply also to new properties of each (quantum numbers c, b, t) that distinguish the new quarks from the old quarks (see Table 43–3), and which (like strangeness) are conserved in strong, but not weak, interactions.

[†]Gell-Mann chose the word from a phrase in James Joyce's *Finnegans Wake*.

TABLE 43–3 Properties of Quarks (Antiquarks have opposite sign Q, B, S, c, t, b)

				Quarks				
Name	Symbol	Mass (MeV/c^2)	Charge Q	Baryon Number B	Strangeness S	Charm c	Bottomness b	Topness t
Up	u	2	$+\frac{2}{3}e$	$\frac{1}{3}$	0	0	0	0
Down	d	5	$-\frac{1}{3}e$	$\frac{1}{3}$	0	0	0	0
Strange	s	95	$-\frac{1}{3}e$	$\frac{1}{3}$	-1	0	0	0
Charmed	c	1250	$+\frac{2}{3}e$	$\frac{1}{3}$	0	$+1$	0	0
Bottom	b	4200	$-\frac{1}{3}e$	$\frac{1}{3}$	0	0	-1	0
Top	t	173,000	$+\frac{2}{3}e$	$\frac{1}{3}$	0	0	0	$+1$

Category	Particle	Anti-particle	Spin	Mass (MeV/c^2)	Baryon Number B	Strangeness S	Charm c	Bottomness b	Mean life (s)	Principal Decay Modes
Mesons	D^+	D^-	0	1869.4	0	0	+1	0	10.6×10^{-13}	K + others, e + others
	D^0	$\overline{D}^0$	0	1864.5	0	0	+1	0	4.1×10^{-13}	K + others, μ or e + others
	D_S^+	D_S^-	0	1968	0	+1	+1	0	5.0×10^{-13}	K + others
	J/ψ (3097)	Self	1	3096.9	0	0	0	0	$\approx 10^{-20}$	Hadrons, e^+e^-, $\mu^+\mu^-$
	Υ (9460)	Self	1	9460	0	0	0	0	$\approx 10^{-20}$	Hadrons, $\mu^+\mu^-$, e^+e^-, $\tau^+\tau^-$
	B^-	B^+	0	5279	0	0	0	-1	1.6×10^{-12}	D^0 + others
	B^0	$\overline{B}^0$	0	5279	0	0	0	-1	1.5×10^{-12}	D^0 + others
Baryons	Λ_c^+	Λ_c^-	$\frac{1}{2}$	2286	+1	0	+1	0	2.0×10^{-13}	Hadrons (e.g., Λ + others)
	Σ_c^{++}	Σ_c^{--}	$\frac{1}{2}$	2454	+1	0	+1	0	$\approx 10^{-21}$	$\Lambda_c^+\pi^+$
	Σ_c^+	Σ_c^-	$\frac{1}{2}$	2453	+1	0	+1	0	$\approx 10^{-21}$	$\Lambda_c^+\pi^0$
	Σ_c^0	$\overline{\Sigma}_c^0$	$\frac{1}{2}$	2454	+1	0	+1	0	$\approx 10^{-21}$	$\Lambda_c^+\pi^-$
	Λ_b^0	$\overline{\Lambda}_b^0$	$\frac{1}{2}$	5620	+1	0	0	-1	1.2×10^{-12}	$J/\psi\Lambda^0$, $pD^0\pi^-$, $\Lambda_c^+\pi^+\pi^-\pi^-$

All quarks have spin $\frac{1}{2}$ and an electric charge of either $+\frac{2}{3}e$ or $-\frac{1}{3}e$ (that is, a fraction of the previously thought smallest charge e). Antiquarks have opposite sign of electric charge Q, baryon number B, strangeness S, charm c, bottomness b, and topness t. Other properties of quarks are shown in Table 43–3.

All hadrons are considered to be made up of combinations of quarks (plus the gluons that hold them together), and their properties are described by looking at their quark content. Mesons consist of a quark–antiquark pair. For example, a π^+ meson is a $u\overline{d}$ combination: note that for the $u\overline{d}$ pair (Table 43–3), $Q = \frac{2}{3}e + \frac{1}{3}e = +1e$, $B = \frac{1}{3} - \frac{1}{3} = 0$, $S = 0 + 0 = 0$, as they must for a π^+; and a $K^+ = u\overline{s}$, with $Q = +1$, $B = 0$, $S = +1$.

Baryons, on the other hand, consist of three quarks. For example, a neutron is $n = ddu$, whereas an antiproton is $\overline{p} = \overline{u}\,\overline{u}\,\overline{d}$. See Fig. 43–15. Strange particles all contain an s or $\overline{s}$ quark, whereas charmed particles contain a c or $\overline{c}$ quark. A few of these hadrons are listed in Table 43–4.

After the quark theory was proposed, physicists began looking for these fractionally charged particles, but direct detection has not been successful. Current models suggest that quarks may be so tightly bound together that they may not ever exist singly in the free state. But observations of very high energy electrons scattered off protons suggest that protons are indeed made up of constituents.

Today, the truly **fundamental particles** are considered to be the six quarks, the six leptons, and the gauge bosons that carry the fundamental forces. See Table 43–5, where the quarks and leptons are arranged in three "families" or "generations." Ordinary matter—atoms made of protons, neutrons, and electrons—is contained in the "first generation." The others are thought to have existed in the very early universe, but are seen by us today only at powerful accelerators or in cosmic rays. All of the hundreds of hadrons can be accounted for by combinations of the six quarks and six antiquarks.

EXERCISE D Return to the Chapter-Opening Questions, page 1164, and answer them again now. Try to explain why you may have answered differently the first time.

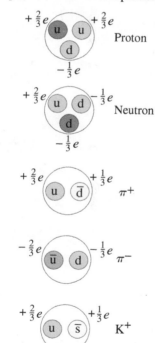

FIGURE 43–15 Quark compositions for several particles.

TABLE 43–5 The Fundamental Particles† as Seen Today

Gauge bosons	Force		First generation	Second generation	Third generation
Gluons	Strong	Quarks	u, d	s, c	b, t
$W^\pm$, Z_0	Weak	Leptons	e, ν_e	μ, ν_μ	τ, ν_τ
γ (photon)	EM				

†The quarks and leptons are arranged into three generations each.

Quark combinations. Find the baryon number, charge, and strangeness for the following quark combinations, and identify the hadron particle that is made up of these quark combinations: (a) udd, (b) uū, (c) uss, (d) sdd, and (e) bū.

RESPONSE We use Table 43–3 to get the properties of the quarks, then Table 43–2 or 43–4 to find the particle that has these properties.

(a) udd has

$$Q = +\tfrac{2}{3}e - \tfrac{1}{3}e - \tfrac{1}{3}e = 0,$$
$$B = \tfrac{1}{3} + \tfrac{1}{3} + \tfrac{1}{3} = 1,$$
$$S = 0 + 0 + 0 = 0,$$

as well as $c = 0$, bottomness $= 0$, topness $= 0$. The only baryon $(B = +1)$ that has $Q = 0$, $S = 0$, etc., is the neutron (Table 43–2).

(b) uū has $Q = \tfrac{2}{3}e - \tfrac{2}{3}e = 0$, $B = \tfrac{1}{3} - \tfrac{1}{3} = 0$, and all other quantum numbers $= 0$. Sounds like a π^0 (dd̄ also gives a π^0).

(c) uss has $Q = 0$, $B = +1$, $S = -2$, others $= 0$. This is a Ξ^0.

(d) sdd has $Q = -1$, $B = +1$, $S = -1$, so must be a Σ^-.

(e) bū has $Q = -1$, $B = 0$, $S = 0$, $c = 0$, bottomness $= -1$, topness $= 0$. This must be a B^- meson (Table 43–4).

| **EXERCISE E** What is the quark composition of a K^- meson?

43–10 The "Standard Model": Quantum Chromodynamics (QCD) and Electroweak Theory

Not long after the quark theory was proposed, it was suggested that quarks have another property (or quality) called **color**, or "color charge" (analogous to electric charge). The distinction between the six types of quark (u, d, s, c, b, t) was referred to as **flavor**. According to theory, each of the flavors of quark can have three colors, usually designated red, green, and blue. (These are the three primary colors which, when added together in appropriate amounts, as on a TV screen, produce white.) Note that the names "color" and "flavor" have nothing to do with our senses, but are purely whimsical—as are other names, such as charm, in this new field. (We did, however, "color" the quarks in Fig. 43–15.) The antiquarks are colored antired, antigreen, and antiblue. Baryons are made up of three quarks, one of each color. Mesons consist of a quark–antiquark pair of a particular color and its anticolor. Both baryons and mesons are thus colorless or white.

Originally, the idea of quark color was proposed to preserve the Pauli exclusion principle (Section 39–4). Not all particles obey the exclusion principle. Those that do, such as electrons, protons, and neutrons, are called **fermions**. Those that don't are called **bosons**. These two categories are distinguished also in their spin (Section 39–2): bosons have integer spin (0, 1, 2, etc.) whereas fermions have half-integer spin, usually $\tfrac{1}{2}$ as for electrons and nucleons, but other fermions have spin $\tfrac{3}{2}, \tfrac{5}{2}$, etc. Matter is made up mainly of fermions, but the carriers of the forces (γ, W, Z, and gluons) are all bosons. Quarks are fermions (they have spin $\tfrac{1}{2}$) and therefore should obey the exclusion principle. Yet for three particular baryons (uuu, ddd, and sss), all three quarks would have the same quantum numbers, and at least two quarks have their spin in the same direction (since there are only two choices, spin up $\left[m_s = +\tfrac{1}{2}\right]$ or spin down $\left[m_s = -\tfrac{1}{2}\right]$). This would seem to violate the exclusion principle; but if quarks have an additional quantum number (color), which is different for each quark, it would serve to distinguish them and allow the exclusion principle to hold. Although quark color, and the resulting threefold increase in the number of quarks, was originally an *ad hoc* idea, it also served to bring the theory into better agreement with experiment, such as predicting the correct lifetime of the π^0 meson, and the measured rate of hadron production in observed e^+e^- collisions at accelerators. The idea of color soon became a central feature of the theory as determining the force binding quarks together in a hadron.

(a)

(b)

(c)

FIGURE 43–16 (a) The force between two quarks holding them together as part of a proton, for example, is carried by a gluon, which in this case involves a change in color. (b) Strong interaction $n + p \rightarrow n + p$ with the exchange of a charged π meson (+ or −, depending on whether it is considered moving to the left or to the right). (c) Quark representation of the same interaction $n + p \rightarrow n + p$. The blue coiled lines between quarks represent gluon exchanges holding the hadrons together. (The exchanged meson may be regarded as $\bar{u}d$ emitted by the n and absorbed by the p, or as $u\bar{d}$ emitted by p and absorbed by n, because a u (or d) quark going to the left in the diagram is equivalent to a $\bar{u}$ (or $\bar{d}$) going to the right.)

Each quark is assumed to carry a *color charge*, analogous to electric charge, and the strong force between quarks is referred to as the **color force**. This theory of the strong force is called **quantum chromodynamics** (*chroma* = color in Greek), or **QCD**, to indicate that the force acts between color charges (and not between, say, electric charges). The strong force between two hadrons is considered to be a force between the quarks that make them up, as suggested in Fig. 43–16. The particles that transmit the color force (analogous to photons for the EM force) are called **gluons** (a play on "glue"). They are included in Tables 43–2 and 43–5. There are eight gluons, according to the theory, all massless and all have color charge.[†]

You might ask what would happen if we try to see a single quark with color by reaching deep inside a hadron and extracting a single quark. Quarks are so tightly bound to other quarks that extracting one would require a tremendous amount of energy, so much that it would be sufficient to create more quarks $(E = mc^2)$. Indeed, such experiments are done at modern particle colliders and all we get is more hadrons (quark–antiquark pairs, or triplets, which we observe as mesons or baryons), never an isolated quark. This property of quarks, that they are always bound in groups that are colorless, is called **confinement**.

The color force has the interesting property that, as two quarks approach each other very closely (equivalently, have high energy), the force between them becomes small. This aspect is referred to as **asymptotic freedom**.

The weak force, as we have seen, is thought to be mediated by the W^+, W^-, and Z^0 particles. It acts between the "weak charges" that each particle has. Each elementary particle can thus have electric charge, weak charge, color charge, and gravitational mass, although one or more of these could be zero. For example, all leptons have color charge of zero, so they do not interact via the strong force.

FIGURE 43–17 Quark representation of the Feynman diagram for β decay of a neutron into a proton.

CONCEPTUAL EXAMPLE 43–10 **Beta decay.** Draw a Feynman diagram, showing what happens in beta decay using quarks.

RESPONSE Beta decay is a result of the weak interaction, and the mediator is either a $W^\pm$ or Z^0 particle. What happens, in part, is that a neutron (udd quarks) decays into a proton (uud). Apparently a d quark (charge $-\frac{1}{3}e$) has turned into a u quark (charge $+\frac{2}{3}e$). Charge conservation means that a negatively charged particle, namely a W^-, was emitted by the d quark. Since an electron and an anti-neutrino appear in the final state, they must have come from the decay of the virtual W^-, as shown in Fig. 43–17.

[†]Compare to the EM interaction, where the photon has no electric charge. Because gluons have color charge, they could attract each other and form composite particles (photons cannot). Such "glueballs" are being searched for.

To summarize, the Standard Model says that the truly fundamental particles (Table 43–5) are the leptons, the quarks, and the gauge bosons (photon, W and Z, and the gluons). The photon, leptons, W^+, W^-, and Z^0 have all been observed in experiments. But so far only combinations of quarks (baryons and mesons) have been observed, and it seems likely that free quarks and gluons are unobservable.

One important aspect of theoretical work is the attempt to find a **unified** basis for the different forces in nature. This was a long-held hope of Einstein, which he was never able to fulfill. A so-called **gauge theory** that unifies the weak and electromagnetic interactions was put forward in the 1960s by S. Weinberg, S. Glashow, and A. Salam. In this **electroweak theory**, the weak and electromagnetic forces are seen as two different manifestations of a single, more fundamental, *electroweak* interaction. The electroweak theory has had many successes, including the prediction of the $W^\pm$ particles as carriers of the weak force, with masses of $80.38 \pm 0.02 \,\mathrm{GeV}/c^2$ in excellent agreement with the measured values of $80.403 \pm 0.029 \,\mathrm{GeV}/c^2$ (and similar accuracy for the Z^0).

The combination of electroweak theory plus QCD for the strong interaction is often referred to today as the **Standard Model**.

EXAMPLE 43–11 ESTIMATE Range of weak force. The weak nuclear force is of very short range, meaning it acts over only a very short distance. Estimate its range using the masses (Table 43–2) of the $W^\pm$ and Z: $m \approx 80$ or $90 \,\mathrm{GeV}/c^2 \approx 10^2 \,\mathrm{GeV}/c^2$.

APPROACH We assume the $W^\pm$ or Z^0 exchange particles can exist for a time Δt given by the uncertainty principle, $\Delta t \approx \hbar/\Delta E$, where $\Delta E \approx mc^2$ is the energy needed to create the virtual particle $(W^\pm, Z)$ that carries the weak force.

SOLUTION Let Δx be the distance the virtual W or Z can move before it must be reabsorbed within the time $\Delta t \approx \hbar/\Delta E$. To find an upper limit on Δx, and hence the maximum range of the weak force, we let the W or Z travel close to the speed of light, so $\Delta x \lesssim c\,\Delta t$. Recalling that $1 \,\mathrm{GeV} = 1.6 \times 10^{-10} \,\mathrm{J}$, then

$$\Delta x \lesssim c\,\Delta t \approx \frac{c\hbar}{\Delta E} \approx \frac{(3 \times 10^8 \,\mathrm{m/s})(10^{-34} \,\mathrm{J \cdot s})}{(10^2 \,\mathrm{GeV})(1.6 \times 10^{-10} \,\mathrm{J/GeV})} \approx 10^{-18} \,\mathrm{m}.$$

This is indeed a very small range.

NOTE Compare this to the range of the electromagnetic force whose range is infinite ($1/r^2$ never becomes zero for any finite r), which makes sense because the mass of its virtual exchange particle, the photon, is zero (in the denominator of the above equation).

We did a similar calculation for the strong force in Section 43–2, and estimated the mass of the π meson as exchange particle between nucleons, based on the apparent range of $10^{-15} \,\mathrm{m}$ (size of nuclei). This is only one aspect of the strong force. In our deeper view, namely the color force between quarks within a nucleon, the gluons have zero mass, which implies (see the formula above in Example 43–11) infinite range. We might have expected a range of about $10^{-15} \,\mathrm{m}$; but according to the Standard Model, the color force is weak at very close distances and increases greatly with distance (causing quark confinement). Thus its range could be infinite.

Theoreticians have wondered why the W and Z have large masses rather than being massless like the photon. Electroweak theory suggests an explanation by means of an hypothesized **Higgs field** and its particle, the **Higgs boson**, which interact with the W and Z to "slow them down." In being forced to go slower than the speed of light, they would have to have mass ($m = 0$ only if $v = c$). Indeed, the Higgs is thought to permeate the vacuum ("empty space") and to perhaps confer mass on all particles with mass by slowing them down. The search for the Higgs boson is a priority for experimental particle physicists at CERN's Large Hadron Collider (Section 43–1). So far, searches suggest the Higgs mass is greater than $115 \,\mathrm{GeV}/c^2$. Yet it is expected to have a mass no larger than $1 \,\mathrm{TeV}/c^2$. We are narrowing in on it.

43–11 Grand Unified Theories

The Standard Model, for all its success, cannot explain some important issues—such as why the charge on the electron has *exactly* the same magnitude as the charge on the proton. This is crucial, because if the charge magnitudes were even a little different, atoms would not be neutral and the resulting large electric forces would surely have made life impossible. Indeed, the Standard Model is now considered to be a low-energy approximation to a more complete theory.

With the success of unified electroweak theory, theorists are trying to incorporate it and QCD for the strong (color) force into a so-called **grand unified theory** (GUT).

One type of such a grand unified theory of the electromagnetic, weak, and strong forces has been worked out in which there is only one class of particle—leptons and quarks belong to the same family and are able to change freely from one type to the other—and the three forces are different aspects of a single underlying force. The unity is predicted to occur, however, only on a scale of less than about 10^{-31} m, corresponding to a typical particle energy of about 10^{16} GeV. If two elementary particles (leptons or quarks) approach each other to within this **unification scale**, the apparently fundamental distinction between them would not exist at this level, and a quark could readily change to a lepton, or vice versa. Baryon and lepton numbers would not be conserved. The weak, electromagnetic, and strong (color) force would blend to a force of a single strength.

What happens between the unification distance of 10^{-31} m and more normal (larger) distances is referred to as **symmetry breaking**. As an analogy, consider an atom in a crystal. Deep within the atom, there is much symmetry—in the innermost regions the electron cloud is spherically symmetric (Chapter 39). Farther out, this symmetry breaks down—the electron clouds are distributed preferentially along the lines (bonds) joining the atoms in the crystal. In a similar way, at 10^{-31} m the force between elementary particles is theorized to be a single force—it is symmetrical and does not single out one type of "charge" over another. But at larger distances, that symmetry is broken and we see three distinct forces. (In the "Standard Model" of electroweak interactions, Section 43–10, the symmetry breaking between the electromagnetic and the weak interactions occurs at about 10^{-18} m.)

CONCEPTUAL EXAMPLE 43–12 **Symmetry.** The table in Fig. 43–18 has four identical place settings. Four people sit down to eat. Describe the symmetry of this table and what happens to it when someone starts the meal.

RESPONSE The table has several kinds of symmetry. It is symmetric to rotations of 90°: that is, the table will look the same if everyone moved one chair to the left or to the right. It is also north–south symmetric and east–west symmetric, so that swaps across the table don't affect the way the table looks. It also doesn't matter whether any person picks up the fork to the left of the plate or the fork to the right. But once that first person picks up either fork, the choice is set for all the rest at the table as well. The symmetry has been *broken*. The underlying symmetry is still there—the blue glasses could still be chosen either way—but some choice must get made and at that moment the symmetry of the diners is broken.

Another example of symmetry breaking is a pencil standing on its point before falling. Standing, it looks the same from any horizontal direction. From above, it is a tiny circle. But when it falls to the table, it points in one particular direction—the symmetry is broken.

Proton Decay

Since unification is thought to occur at such tiny distances and huge energies, the theory is difficult to test experimentally. But it is not completely impossible. One testable prediction is the idea that the proton might decay (via, for example, $p \rightarrow \pi^0 + e^+$) and violate conservation of baryon number. This could happen if two quarks approached to within 10^{-31} m of each other. But it is very unlikely at normal temperature and energy, so the decay of a proton can only be an unlikely process.

FIGURE 43–18 Symmetry around a table. Example 43–12.

In the simplest form of GUT, the theoretical estimate of the proton mean life for the decay mode $p \to \pi^0 + e^+$ is about 10^{31} yr, and this is now within the realm of testability.[†] Proton decays have still not been seen, and experiments put the lower limit on the proton mean life for the above mode to be about 10^{33} yr, somewhat greater than this prediction. This may seem a disappointment, but on the other hand, it presents a challenge. Indeed more complex GUTs are not affected by this result.

EXAMPLE 43–13 **ESTIMATE** | **Proton decay.** An experiment uses 3300 tons of water waiting to see a proton decay of the type $p \to \pi^0 + e^+$. If the experiment is run for 4 years without detecting a decay, estimate the lower limit on the proton mean life.

APPROACH As with radioactive decay, the number of decays is proportional to the number of parent species (N), the time interval (Δt), and the decay constant (λ) which is related to the mean life τ by (see Eqs. 41–4 and 41–9a):

$$\Delta N = -\lambda N \, \Delta t = -\frac{N \, \Delta t}{\tau}.$$

SOLUTION Dealing only with magnitudes, we solve for τ:

$$\tau = \frac{N \, \Delta t}{\Delta N}.$$

Thus for $\Delta N < 1$ over the four-year trial,

$$\tau > N \, (4 \, \text{yr}),$$

where N is the number of protons in 3300 tons of water. To determine N, we note that each molecule of H_2O contains $2 + 8 = 10$ protons. So one mole of water $(18 \, \text{g}, \ 6 \times 10^{23} \text{ molecules})$ contains $10 \times 6 \times 10^{23}$ protons in 18 g of water, or about 3×10^{26} protons per kilogram. One ton is 10^3 kg, so the chamber contains $(3.3 \times 10^6 \, \text{kg})(3 \times 10^{26} \text{ protons/kg}) \approx 1 \times 10^{33}$ protons. Then our very rough estimate for a lower limit on the proton mean life is $\tau > (10^{33})(4 \, \text{yr}) \approx 4 \times 10^{33}$ yr.

GUT and Cosmology

An interesting prediction of unified theories relates to cosmology (Chapter 44). It is thought that during the first 10^{-35} s after the theorized Big Bang that created the universe, the temperature was so extremely high that particles had energies corresponding to the unification scale. Baryon number would not have been conserved then, perhaps allowing an imbalance that might account for the observed predominance of matter ($B > 0$) over antimatter ($B < 0$) in the universe. The fact that we are surrounded by matter, with no significant antimatter in sight, is considered a problem in search of an explanation (not given by the Standard Model). See also Chapter 44. We call this the **matter–antimatter problem**. To understand it may require still undiscovered phenomena—perhaps related to quarks or neutrinos, or the Higgs boson or supersymmetry (next Section).

This last example is interesting, for it illustrates a deep connection between investigations at either end of the size scale: theories about the tiniest objects (elementary particles) have a strong bearing on the understanding of the universe on a large scale. We will look at this more in the next Chapter.

Figure 43–19 is a rough diagram indicating how the four fundamental forces in nature "condensed out" (a symmetry was broken) as time went on after the Big Bang (Chapter 44), and as the mean temperature of the universe and the typical particle energy decreased.

FIGURE 43–19 Time and energy plot of the four fundamental forces, unified at the Planck time, and how each condensed out. The symbol t_{abu} = time after the birth of the universe. Note that the typical particle energy (and average temperature of the universe) decreases to the right, as time after the Big Bang increases. We discuss the Big Bang in the next Chapter.

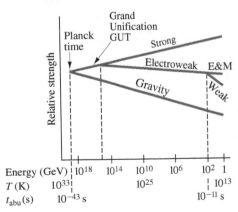

[†]This is much larger than the age of the universe ($\approx 14 \times 10^9$ yr). But we don't have to wait 10^{31} yr to see. Instead we can wait for one decay among 10^{31} protons over a year (see Eqs. 41–4 and 41–9a, $\Delta N = \lambda N \, \Delta t = N \, \Delta t / \tau$).

43–12 Strings and Supersymmetry

We have seen that the Standard Model is unable to address important experimental issues, and that theoreticians are attacking the problem as experimenters search for new data, new particles, new concepts.

Even more ambitious than grand unified theories are attempts to also incorporate gravity, and thus unify all four forces in nature into a single theory. (Such theories are sometimes referred to misleadingly as **theories of everything**.) There are consistent theories that attempt to unify all four forces called **string theories**, in which each fundamental particle (Table 43–5) is imagined not as a point but as a one-dimensional string, perhaps 10^{-35} m long, which vibrates in a particular standing wave pattern. (You might say each particle is a different note on a tiny stretched string.) More sophisticated theories propose the fundamental entities as being multidimensional **branes** (after 2-D membranes).

A related idea that also goes way beyond the Standard Model is **supersymmetry**, which applied to strings is known as **superstring theory**. Supersymmetry, developed by Bruno Zumino (1923–) and Julius Wess (1934–2007), predicts that interactions exist that would change fermions into bosons and vice versa, and that each known fermion would have a supersymmetric boson partner of the same mass. Thus, for each quark (a fermion), there would be a **squark** (a *boson*) or "supersymmetric" quark. For every lepton there would be a **slepton**. Likewise, for every known boson (photons and gluons, for example), there would be a supersymmetric fermion (**photinos** and **gluinos**). Supersymmetry predicts also that a *graviton*, which transmits the gravity force, has a partner, the **gravitino**. Supersymmetric particles are sometimes called "SUSYs" for short, and are a candidate for the "dark matter" of the universe (discussed in Chapter 44). But why hasn't this "missing part" of the universe ever been detected? The best guess is that supersymmetric particles might be heavier than their conventional counterparts, perhaps too heavy to have been produced in today's accelerators. A search for supersymmetric particles is already in the works for CERN's new Large Hadron Collider.

Versions of supersymmetry predict other interesting properties, such as that space has 11 dimensions, but 7 of them are "coiled up" so we normally only notice the 4-D of space–time. We would like to know if and how many extra dimensions there are, and how and why they are hidden. We hope to have some answers from the new LHC and the future ILC (Section 43–1).

The world of elementary particles is opening new vistas. What happens in the future is bound to be exciting.

Summary

Particle accelerators are used to accelerate charged particles, such as electrons and protons, to very high energy. High-energy particles have short wavelength and so can be used to probe the structure of matter in great detail (very small distances). High kinetic energy also allows the creation of new particles through collisions (via $E = mc^2$).

Cyclotrons and **synchrotrons** use a magnetic field to keep the particles in a circular path and accelerate them at intervals by high voltage. **Linear accelerators** accelerate particles along a line. **Colliding beams** allow higher interaction energy.

An **antiparticle** has the same mass as a particle but opposite charge. Certain other properties may also be opposite: for example, the antiproton has **baryon number** (nucleon number) opposite ($B = -1$) to that for the proton ($B = +1$).

In all nuclear and particle reactions, the following conservation laws hold: momentum, angular momentum, mass–energy, electric charge, baryon number, and **lepton numbers**.

Certain particles have a property called **strangeness**, which is conserved by the strong force but not by the weak force. The properties **charm, bottomness**, and **topness** also are conserved by the strong force but not by the weak force.

Just as the electromagnetic force can be said to be due to an exchange of photons, the strong nuclear force is carried by massless **gluons**. The W and Z particles carry the weak force. These fundamental force carriers (photon, W and Z, gluons) are called **gauge bosons**.

Other particles can be classified as either *leptons* or *hadrons*. **Leptons** participate only in gravity, the weak, and the electromagnetic interactions. **Hadrons**, which today are considered to be made up of **quarks**, participate in all four interactions, including the strong interaction. The hadrons can be classified as **mesons**, with baryon number zero, and **baryons**, with nonzero baryon number.

All particles, except for the photon, electron, neutrinos, and proton, decay with measurable mean lives varying from 10^{-25} s to 10^3 s. The mean life depends on which force is predominant. Weak decays usually have mean lives greater than about 10^{-13} s. Electromagnetic decays typically have mean lives on the order of 10^{-16} to 10^{-19} s. The shortest lived particles, called **resonances**, decay via the strong interaction and live typically for only about 10^{-23} s.

Today's Standard Model of elementary particles considers **quarks** as the basic building blocks of the hadrons. The six quark "flavors" are called **up, down, strange, charmed, bottom,** and **top**. It is expected that there are the same number of quarks as leptons (six of each), and that quarks and leptons are the truly fundamental particles along with the gauge bosons (γ, W, Z, gluons). Quarks are said to have **color**, and, according to **quantum chromodynamics** (QCD), the strong color force acts between their color charges and is transmitted by **gluons**. **Electroweak theory** views the weak and electromagnetic forces as two aspects of a single underlying interaction. QCD plus the electroweak theory are referred to as the **Standard Model**.

Grand unified theories of forces suggest that at very short distance (10^{-31} m) and very high energy, the weak, electromagnetic, and strong forces appear as a single force, and the fundamental difference between quarks and leptons disappears.

According to **string theory**, the fundamental particles may be tiny strings, 10^{-35} m long, distinguished by their standing wave pattern. **Supersymmetry** hypothesizes that each fermion (or boson) has a corresponding boson (or fermion) partner.

Questions

1. Give a reaction between two nucleons, similar to Eq. 43–4, that could produce a π^-.

2. If a proton is moving at very high speed, so that its kinetic energy is much greater than its rest energy (mc^2), can it then decay via p $\rightarrow$ n + π^+?

3. What would an "antiatom," made up of the antiparticles to the constituents of normal atoms, consist of? What might happen if *antimatter*, made of such antiatoms, came in contact with our normal world of matter?

4. What particle in a decay signals the electromagnetic interaction?

5. (a) Does the presence of a neutrino among the decay products of a particle necessarily mean that the decay occurs via the weak interaction? (b) Do all decays via the weak interaction produce a neutrino? Explain.

6. Why is it that a neutron decays via the weak interaction even though the neutron and one of its decay products (proton) are strongly interacting?

7. Which of the four interactions (strong, electromagnetic, weak, gravitational) does an electron take part in? A neutrino? A proton?

8. Check that charge and baryon number are conserved in each of the decays in Table 43–2.

9. Which of the particle decays listed in Table 43–2 occur via the electromagnetic interaction?

10. Which of the particle decays listed in Table 43–2 occur by the weak interaction?

11. The Δ baryon has spin $\frac{3}{2}$, baryon number 1, and charge $Q = +2, +1, 0,$ or -1. Why is there no charge state $Q = -2$?

12. Which of the particle decays in Table 43–4 occur via the electromagnetic interaction?

13. Which of the particle decays in Table 43–4 occur by the weak interaction?

14. Quarks have spin $\frac{1}{2}$. How do you account for the fact that baryons have spin $\frac{1}{2}$ or $\frac{3}{2}$, and mesons have spin 0 or 1?

15. Suppose there were a kind of "neutrinolet" that was massless, had no color charge or electrical charge, and did not feel the weak force. Could you say that this particle even exists?

16. Is it possible for a particle to be both (a) a lepton and a baryon? (b) a baryon and a hadron? (c) a meson and a quark? (d) a hadron and a lepton? Explain.

17. Using the ideas of quantum chromodynamics, would it be possible to find particles made up of two quarks and no antiquarks? What about two quarks and two antiquarks?

18. Why can neutrons decay when they are free, but not when they are inside a stable nucleus?

19. Is the reaction e$^-$ + p $\rightarrow$ n + $\bar{\nu}_e$ possible? Explain.

20. Occasionally, the Λ will decay by the following reaction: $\Lambda^0 \rightarrow$ p$^+$ + e$^-$ + $\bar{\nu}_e$. Which of the four forces in nature is responsible for this decay? How do you know?

Problems

43–1 Particles and Accelerators

1. (I) What is the total energy of a proton whose kinetic energy is 4.65 GeV?

2. (I) Calculate the wavelength of 28-GeV electrons.

3. (I) What strength of magnetic field is used in a cyclotron in which protons make 3.1×10^7 revolutions per second?

4. (I) What is the time for one complete revolution for a very high-energy proton in the 1.0-km-radius Fermilab accelerator?

5. (I) If α particles are accelerated by the cyclotron of Example 43–2, what must be the frequency of the voltage applied to the dees?

6. (II) (a) If the cyclotron of Example 43–2 accelerated α particles, what maximum energy could they attain? What would their speed be? (b) Repeat for deuterons ($^2_1$H). (c) In each case, what frequency of voltage is required?

7. (II) Which is better for resolving details of the nucleus: 25-MeV alpha particles or 25-MeV protons? Compare each of their wavelengths with the size of a nucleon in a nucleus.

8. (II) What magnetic field intensity is needed at the 1.0-km-radius Fermilab synchrotron for 1.0-TeV protons?

9. (II) What magnetic field is required for the 7.0-TeV protons in the 4.25-km-radius Large Hadron Collider (LHC)?

10. (II) A cyclotron with a radius of 1.0 m is to accelerate deuterons ($^2_1$H) to an energy of 12 MeV. (a) What is the required magnetic field? (b) What frequency is needed for the voltage between the dees? (c) If the potential difference between the dees averages 22 kV, how many revolutions will the particles make before exiting? (d) How much time does it take for one deuteron to go from start to exit? (e) Estimate how far it travels during this time.

11. (II) What is the wavelength (= minimum resolvable size) of 7.0-TeV protons?

12. (II) The 1.0-km radius Fermilab Tevatron takes about 20 seconds to bring the energies of the stored protons from 150 GeV to 1.0 TeV. The acceleration is done once per turn. Estimate the energy given to the protons on each turn. (You can assume that the speed of the protons is essentially c the whole time.)

13. (II) Show that the energy of a particle (charge e) in a synchrotron, in the relativistic limit ($v \approx c$), is given by E (in eV) = Brc, where B is the magnetic field and r is the radius of the orbit (SI units).

14. (I) About how much energy is released when a Λ^0 decays to n + π^0? (See Table 43–2.)

15. (I) How much energy is released in the decay
$$\pi^+ \rightarrow \mu^+ + \nu_\mu?$$
See Table 43–2.

16. (I) Estimate the range of the strong force if the mediating particle were the kaon in place of a pion.

17. (I) How much energy is required to produce a neutron–antineutron pair?

18. (II) Determine the energy released when Σ^0 decays to Λ^0 and then to a proton.

19. (II) Two protons are heading toward each other with equal speeds. What minimum kinetic energy must each have if a π^0 meson is to be created in the process? (See Table 43–2.)

20. (II) What minimum kinetic energy must two neutrons each have if they are traveling at the same speed toward each other, collide, and produce a K^+K^- pair in addition to themselves? (See Table 43–2.)

21. (II) For the decay $K^0 \rightarrow \pi^- + e^+ + \nu_e$, determine the maximum kinetic energy of (a) the positron, and (b) the π^-. Assume the K^0 is at rest.

22. (II) What are the wavelengths of the two photons produced when a proton and antiproton at rest annihilate?

23. (II) The Λ^0 cannot decay by the following reactions. What conservation laws are violated in each of the reactions?
   (a) $\Lambda^0 \not\rightarrow n + \pi^-$
   (b) $\Lambda^0 \not\rightarrow p + K^-$
   (c) $\Lambda^0 \not\rightarrow \pi^+ + \pi^-$

24. (II) For the decay $\Lambda^0 \rightarrow p + \pi^-$, calculate (a) the Q-value (energy released), and (b) the kinetic energy of the p and π^-, assuming the Λ^0 decays from rest. (Use relativistic formulas.)

25. (II) (a) Show, by conserving momentum and energy, that it is impossible for an isolated electron to radiate only a single photon. (b) With this result in mind, how can you defend the photon exchange diagram in Fig. 43–8?

26. (II) What would be the wavelengths of the two photons produced when an electron and a positron, each with 420 keV of kinetic energy, annihilate in a head-on collision?

27. (II) In the rare decay $\pi^+ \rightarrow e^+ + \nu_e$, what is the kinetic energy of the positron? Assume the π^+ decays from rest.

28. (II) Which of the following reactions and decays are possible? For those forbidden, explain what laws are violated.
   (a) $\pi^- + p \rightarrow n + \eta^0$
   (b) $\pi^+ + p \rightarrow n + \pi^0$
   (c) $\pi^+ + p \rightarrow p + e^+$
   (d) $p \rightarrow e^+ + \nu_e$
   (e) $\mu^+ \rightarrow e^+ + \bar{\nu}_\mu$
   (f) $p \rightarrow n + e^+ + \nu_e$

29. (II) Calculate the kinetic energy of each of the two products in the decay $\Xi^- \rightarrow \Lambda^0 + \pi^-$. Assume the Ξ^- decays from rest.

30. (II) Antiprotons can be produced when a proton with sufficient energy hits a stationary proton. Even if there is enough energy, which of the following reactions will not happen?
$$p + p \rightarrow p + \bar{p}$$
$$p + p \rightarrow p + p + \bar{p}$$
$$p + p \rightarrow p + p + p + \bar{p}$$
$$p + p \rightarrow p + e^+ + e^+ + \bar{p}$$

31. (III) Calculate the maximum kinetic energy of the electron when a muon decays from rest via $\mu^- \rightarrow e^- + \bar{\nu}_e + \nu_\mu$. [Hint: In what direction do the two neutrinos move relative to the electron in order to give the electron the maximum kinetic energy? Both energy and momentum are conserved; use relativistic formulas.]

32. (III) Could a π^+ meson be produced if a 110-MeV proton struck a proton at rest? What minimum kinetic energy must the incoming proton have?

33. (I) The mean life of the Σ^0 particle is 7×10^{-20} s. What is the uncertainty in its rest energy? Express your answer in MeV.

34. (I) The measured width of the ψ (3686) meson is about 300 keV. Estimate its mean life.

35. (I) The measured width of the J/ψ meson is 88 keV. Estimate its mean life.

36. (I) The B$^-$ meson is a b$\bar{u}$ quark combination. (a) Show that this is consistent for all quantum numbers. (b) What are the quark combinations for B$^+$, B^0, $\bar{B}^0$?

37. (I) What is the energy width (or uncertainty) of (a) η^0, and (b) ρ^+? See Table 43–2.

38. (II) Which of the following decays are possible? For those that are forbidden, explain which laws are violated.
   (a) $\Xi^0 \rightarrow \Sigma^+ + \pi^-$
   (b) $\Omega^- \rightarrow \Sigma^0 + \pi^- + \nu$
   (c) $\Sigma^0 \rightarrow \Lambda^0 + \gamma + \gamma$

39. (II) What quark combinations produce (a) a Ξ^0 baryon and (b) a Ξ^- baryon?

40. (II) What are the quark combinations that can form (a) a neutron, (b) an antineutron, (c) a Λ^0, (d) a $\bar{\Sigma}^0$?

41. (II) What particles do the following quark combinations produce: (a) uud, (b) $\bar{u}\bar{u}\bar{s}$, (c) $\bar{u}s$, (d) d$\bar{u}$, (e) $\bar{c}s$?

42. (II) What is the quark combination needed to produce a D^0 meson ($Q = B = S = 0$, $c = +1$)?

43. (II) The D$_S^+$ meson has $S = c = +1$, $B = 0$. What quark combination would produce it?

44. (II) Draw a possible Feynman diagram using quarks (as in Fig. 43–16c) for the reaction $\pi^- + p \rightarrow \pi^0 + n$.

45. (II) Draw a Feynman diagram for the reaction $n + \nu_\mu \rightarrow p + \mu^-$.

General Problems

46. The mean lifetimes listed in Table 43–2 are in terms of *proper time*, measured in a reference frame where the particle is at rest. If a tau lepton is created with a kinetic energy of 950 MeV, how long would its track be as measured in the lab, on average, ignoring any collisions?

47. Assume there are 5.0×10^{13} protons at 1.0 TeV stored in the 1.0-km-radius ring of the Tevatron. (a) How much current (amperes) is carried by this beam? (b) How fast would a 1500-kg car have to move to carry the same kinetic energy as this beam?

48. (a) How much energy is released when an electron and a positron annihilate each other? (b) How much energy is released when a proton and an antiproton annihilate each other? (All particles have $K \approx 0$.)

49. Protons are injected into the 1.0-km-radius Fermilab Tevatron with an energy of 150 GeV. If they are accelerated by 2.5 MV each revolution, how far do they travel and approximately how long does it take for them to reach 1.0 TeV?

50. Which of the following reactions are possible, and by what interaction could they occur? For those forbidden, explain why.

(a) $\pi^- + p \rightarrow K^0 + p + \pi^0$
(b) $K^- + p \rightarrow \Lambda^0 + \pi^0$
(c) $K^+ + n \rightarrow \Sigma^+ + \pi^0 + \gamma$
(d) $K^+ \rightarrow \pi^0 + \pi^0 + \pi^+$
(e) $\pi^+ \rightarrow e^+ + \nu_e$

51. Which of the following reactions are possible, and by what interaction could they occur? For those forbidden, explain why.

(a) $\pi^- + p \rightarrow K^+ + \Sigma^-$
(b) $\pi^+ + p \rightarrow K^+ + \Sigma^+$
(c) $\pi^- + p \rightarrow \Lambda^0 + K^0 + \pi^0$
(d) $\pi^+ + p \rightarrow \Sigma^0 + \pi^0$
(e) $\pi^- + p \rightarrow p + e^- + \bar{\nu}_e$

52. One decay mode for a π^+ is $\pi^+ \rightarrow \mu^+ + \nu_\mu$. What would be the equivalent decay for a π^-? Check conservation laws.

53. Symmetry breaking occurs in the electroweak theory at about 10^{-18} m. Show that this corresponds to an energy that is on the order of the mass of the $W^\pm$.

54. Calculate the Q-value for each of the reactions, Eq. 43–4, for producing a pion.

55. How many fundamental fermions are there in a water molecule?

56. The mass of a π^0 can be measured by observing the reaction $\pi^- + p \rightarrow \pi^0 + n$ at very low incident π^- kinetic energy (assume it is zero). The neutron is observed to be emitted with a kinetic energy of 0.60 MeV. Use conservation of energy and momentum to determine the π^0 mass.

57. (a) Show that the so-called unification distance of 10^{-31} m in grand unified theory is equivalent to an energy of about 10^{16} GeV. Use the uncertainty principle, and also de Broglie's wavelength formula, and explain how they apply. (b) Calculate the temperature corresponding to 10^{16} GeV.

58. Calculate the Q-value for the reaction $\pi^- + p \rightarrow \Lambda^0 + K^0$, when negative pions strike stationary protons. Estimate the minimum pion kinetic energy needed to produce this reaction. [Hint: Assume Λ^0 and K^0 move off with the same velocity.]

59. A proton and an antiproton annihilate each other at rest and produce two pions, π^- and π^+. What is the kinetic energy of each pion?

60. For the reaction $p + p \rightarrow 3p + \bar{p}$, where one of the initial protons is at rest, use relativistic formulas to show that the threshold energy is $6m_p c^2$, equal to three times the magnitude of the Q-value of the reaction, where m_p is the proton mass. [Hint: Assume all final particles have the same velocity.]

61. What is the total energy of a proton whose kinetic energy is 15 GeV? What is its wavelength?

62. At about what kinetic energy (in eV) can the rest energy of a proton be ignored when calculating its wavelength, if the wavelength is to be within 1.0% of its true value? What are the corresponding wavelength and speed of the proton?

63. Use the quark model to describe the reaction
$$\bar{p} + n \rightarrow \pi^- + \pi^0.$$

64. Identify the missing particle in the following reactions.

(a) $p + p \rightarrow p + n + \pi^+ + ?$
(b) $p + ? \rightarrow n + \mu^+$

65. What fraction of the speed of light c is the speed of a 7.0-TeV proton?

66. A particle at rest, with a rest energy of mc^2, decays into two fragments with rest energies of $m_1 c^2$ and $m_2 c^2$. Show that the kinetic energy of fragment 1 is

$$K_1 = \frac{1}{2mc^2} \left[(mc^2 - m_1 c^2)^2 - (m_2 c^2)^2 \right].$$

*Numerical/Computer

*67. (II) In a particle physics experiment to determine the mean lifetime of muons, the muons enter a scintillator and decay. Students have sampled the individual lifetimes of muons decaying within a time interval between 1 μs and 10 μs after being stopped in the scintillator. It is assumed that the muons obey the radioactive decay law $R = R_0 e^{-t/\tau}$ where R_0 is the unknown activity at $t = 0$ and R is the activity (counts/μs) at time t. Here is their data:

Time (μs)	1.5	2.5	3.5	4.5	5.5	6.5
$R(t)$	55	35	23	18	12	5

Make a graph of $\ln (R/R_0)$ versus time t (μs), and from the best fit of the graph to a straight line find the mean life τ. The accepted value of the mean life of the muon is $\tau = 2.19703 \ \mu$s $\pm \ 0.00004 \ \mu$s. What is the percentage error of their result from the accepted value?

Answers to Exercises

A: 1.24×10^{-18} m = 1.24 am.

B: $\approx 2 \times 10^3$ m/0.1 m $\approx 10^4$.

C: (a).

D: (c); (d).

E: s$\bar{u}$.

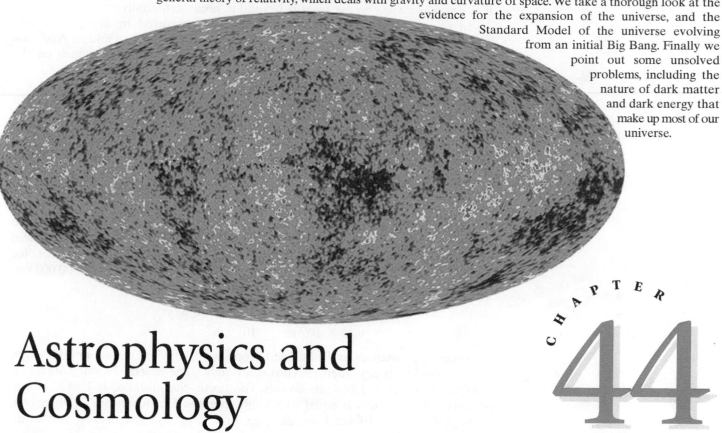

This map of the entire sky (WMAP) is color-coded to represent slight temperature variations in the almost perfectly uniform 2.7-kelvin microwave background radiation that reaches us from all directions in the sky. This latest version (2006) is providing detailed information on the origins of our universe and its structures. The tiny temperature variations, red slightly hotter, blue slightly cooler (on the order of 1 part in 10^4) are "quantum fluctuations" that are the seeds on which galaxies and clusters of galaxies eventually grew.

To discuss the nature of the universe as we understand it today, we examine the latest theories on how stars and galaxies form and evolve, including the role of nucleosynthesis. We briefly discuss Einstein's general theory of relativity, which deals with gravity and curvature of space. We take a thorough look at the evidence for the expansion of the universe, and the Standard Model of the universe evolving from an initial Big Bang. Finally we point out some unsolved problems, including the nature of dark matter and dark energy that make up most of our universe.

Astrophysics and Cosmology

CHAPTER-OPENING QUESTION—Guess now!

Until recently, astronomers expected the expansion rate of the universe would be decreasing. Why?

(a) Friction.
(b) The second law of thermodynamics.
(c) Gravity.
(d) The electromagnetic force.

I n the previous Chapter, we studied the tiniest objects in the universe—the elementary particles. Now we leap to the grandest objects in the universe— stars, galaxies, and clusters of galaxies. These two extreme realms, elementary particles and the cosmos, are among the most intriguing and exciting subjects in science. And, surprisingly, these two extreme realms are related in a fundamental way, as already hinted in Chapter 43.

Use of the techniques and ideas of physics to study the heavens is often referred to as **astrophysics**. Central to our present theoretical understanding of the universe (or cosmos) is Einstein's *general theory of relativity* which represents our most complete understanding of gravitation. Many other aspects of physics are involved, from electromagnetism and thermodynamics to atomic and nuclear physics as well as elementary particles. General Relativity serves also as the foundation for modern **cosmology**, which is the study of the universe as a whole. Cosmology deals especially with the search for a theoretical framework to understand the observed universe, its origin, and its future.

CONTENTS

The questions posed by cosmology are profound and difficult; the possible answers stretch the imagination. They are questions like "Has the universe always existed, or did it have a beginning in time?" Either alternative is difficult to imagine: time going back indefinitely into the past, or an actual moment when the universe began (but, then, what was there before?). And what about the size of the universe? Is it infinite in size? It is hard to imagine infinity. Or is it finite in size? This is also hard to imagine, for if the universe is finite, it does not make sense to ask what is beyond it, because the universe is all there is.

In the last few years, so much progress has occurred in astrophysics and cosmology that many scientists are calling recent work a "Golden Age" for cosmology. Our survey will be qualitative, but we will nonetheless touch on the major ideas. We begin with a look at what can be seen beyond the Earth.

44–1 Stars and Galaxies

According to the ancients, the stars, except for the few that seemed to move relative to the others (the planets), were fixed on a sphere beyond the last planet. The universe was neatly self-contained, and we on Earth were at or near its center. But in the centuries following Galileo's first telescopic observations of the night sky in 1610, our view of the universe has changed dramatically. We no longer place ourselves at the center, and we view the universe as vastly larger. The distances involved are so great that we specify them in terms of the time it takes light to travel the given distance: for example, 1 light-second $= (3.0 \times 10^8 \, \text{m/s})(1.0 \, \text{s}) = 3.0 \times 10^8 \, \text{m} = 300{,}000 \, \text{km}$; 1 light-minute $= 18 \times 10^6 \, \text{km}$; and 1 **light-year** (ly) is

$$1 \, \text{ly} = (2.998 \times 10^8 \, \text{m/s})(3.156 \times 10^7 \, \text{s/yr})$$
$$= 9.46 \times 10^{15} \, \text{m} \approx 10^{13} \, \text{km}.$$

For specifying distances to the Sun and Moon, we usually use meters or kilometers, but we could specify them in terms of light. The Earth–Moon distance is 384,000 km, which is 1.28 light-seconds. The Earth–Sun distance is $1.50 \times 10^{11} \, \text{m}$, or 150,000,000 km; this is equal to 8.3 light-minutes. Far out in our solar system, Pluto is about $6 \times 10^9 \, \text{km}$ from the Sun, or $6 \times 10^{-4} \, \text{ly}$. The nearest star to us, other than the Sun, is Proxima Centauri, about 4.3 ly away.

On a clear moonless night, thousands of stars of varying degrees of brightness can be seen, as well as the long cloudy stripe known as the Milky Way (Fig. 44–1). Galileo first observed, with his telescope, that the Milky Way is comprised of countless individual stars. A century and a half later (about 1750), Thomas Wright suggested that the Milky Way was a flat disk of stars extending to great distances in a plane, which we call the **Galaxy** (Greek for "milky way").

FIGURE 44–1 Sections of the Milky Way. In (a), the thin line is the trail of an artificial Earth satellite in this long time exposure. The dark diagonal area is due to dust absorption of visible light, blocking the view. In (b) the view is toward the center of the Galaxy (taken in summer from Arizona).

(a)   (b)

Our Galaxy has a diameter of almost 100,000 light-years and a thickness of roughly 2000 ly. It has a bulging central "nucleus" and spiral arms (Fig. 44–2). Our Sun, which is a star like many others, is located about halfway from the galactic center to the edge, some 26,000 ly from the center. Our Galaxy contains roughly 100 billion (10^{11}) stars. The Sun orbits the galactic center approximately once every 250 million years, so its speed is about 200 km/s relative to the center of the Galaxy. The total mass of all the stars in our Galaxy is estimated to be about 3×10^{41} kg, which is ordinary matter. In addition, there is strong evidence that our Galaxy is surrounded by an invisible "halo" of "dark matter," which we discuss in Section 44–9.

FIGURE 44–2 Our Galaxy, as it would appear from the outside: (a) "edge view," in the plane of the disk; (b) "top view," looking down on the disk. (If only we could see it like this—from the outside!) (c) Infrared photograph of the inner reaches of the Milky Way, showing the central bulge and disk of our Galaxy. This very wide angle photo taken from the COBE satellite (Section 44–6) extends over 180° of sky, and to be viewed properly it should be wrapped in a semicircle with your eyes at the center. The white dots are nearby stars.

(b)

(a)

(c)

EXAMPLE 44–1 **ESTIMATE** **Our Galaxy's mass.** Estimate the total mass of our Galaxy using the orbital data above for the Sun about the center of the Galaxy. Assume that most of the mass of the Galaxy is concentrated near the center of the Galaxy.

APPROACH We assume that the Sun (including our solar system) has total mass m and moves in a circular orbit about the center of the Galaxy (total mass M), and that the mass M can be considered as being located at the center of the Galaxy. We then apply Newton's second law, $F = ma$, with a being the centripetal acceleration, $a = v^2/r$, and F being the universal law of gravitation (Chapter 6).

SOLUTION Our Sun and solar system orbit the center of the Galaxy, according to the best measurements as mentioned above, with a speed of about $v = 200$ km/s at a distance from the Galaxy center of about $r = 26,000$ ly. We use Newton's second law:

$$F = ma$$

$$G\frac{Mm}{r^2} = m\frac{v^2}{r}$$

where M is the mass of the Galaxy and m is the mass of our Sun and solar system. Solving this, we find

$$M = \frac{rv^2}{G} \approx \frac{(26,000\,\text{ly})(10^{16}\,\text{m/ly})(2 \times 10^5\,\text{m/s})^2}{6.67 \times 10^{-11}\,\text{N}\cdot\text{m}^2/\text{kg}^2} \approx 2 \times 10^{41}\,\text{kg}.$$

NOTE In terms of *numbers* of stars, if they are like our Sun $(m = 2.0 \times 10^{30}\,\text{kg})$, there would be about $(2 \times 10^{41}\,\text{kg})/(2 \times 10^{30}\,\text{kg}) \approx 10^{11}$ or on the order of 100 billion stars.

FIGURE 44–3 This globular star cluster is located in the constellation Hercules.

FIGURE 44–4 This gaseous nebula, found in the constellation Carina, is about 9000 light-years from us.

In addition to stars both within and outside the Milky Way, we can see by telescope many faint cloudy patches in the sky which were all referred to once as "nebulae" (Latin for "clouds"). A few of these, such as those in the constellations Andromeda and Orion, can actually be discerned with the naked eye on a clear night. Some are **star clusters** (Fig. 44–3), groups of stars that are so numerous they appear to be a cloud. Others are glowing clouds of gas or dust (Fig. 44–4), and it is for these that we now mainly reserve the word **nebula**. Most fascinating are those that belong to a third category: they often have fairly regular elliptical shapes and seem to be a great distance beyond our Galaxy. Immanuel Kant (about 1755) seems to have been the first to suggest that these latter might be circular disks, but appear elliptical because we see them at an angle, and are faint because they are so distant. At first it was not universally accepted that these objects were **extragalactic**—that is, outside our Galaxy. The very large telescopes constructed in the twentieth century revealed that individual stars could be resolved within these extragalactic objects and that many contain spiral arms. Edwin Hubble (1889–1953) did much of this observational work in the 1920s using the 2.5-m (100-inch) telescope[†] on Mt. Wilson near Los Angeles, California, then the world's largest. Hubble demonstrated that these objects were indeed extragalactic because of their great distances. The distance to our nearest large galaxy,[‡] Andromeda, is over 2 million light-years, a distance 20 times greater than the diameter of our Galaxy. It seemed logical that these nebulae must be **galaxies** similar to ours. (Note that it is usual to capitalize the word "galaxy" only when it refers to our own.) Today it is thought there are roughly 10^{11} galaxies in the observable universe—that is, roughly as many galaxies as there are stars in a galaxy. See Fig. 44–5.

Many galaxies tend to be grouped in **galaxy clusters** held together by their mutual gravitational attraction. There may be anywhere from a few to many thousands of galaxies in each cluster. Furthermore, clusters themselves seem to be

[†]2.5 m (= 100 inches) refers to the diameter of the curved objective mirror. The bigger the mirror, the more light it collects (greater intensity) and the less diffraction there is (better resolution), so more and fainter stars can be seen. See Chapters 33 and 35. Until recently, photographic films or plates were used to take long time exposures. Now large solid-state CCD or CMOS sensors (Section 33–5) are available containing hundreds of millions of pixels (compared to 10 million pixels in a good-quality digital camera).

[‡]The *Magellanic clouds* are much closer than Andromeda, but are small and are usually considered small satellite galaxies of our own Galaxy.

FIGURE 44–5 Photographs of galaxies. (a) Spiral galaxy in the constellation Hydra. (b) Two galaxies: the larger and more dramatic one is known as the Whirlpool galaxy. (c) An infrared image (given "false" colors) of the same galaxies as in (b), here showing the arms of the spiral as having more substance than in the visible light photo (b); the different colors correspond to different light intensities. Visible light is scattered and absorbed by interstellar dust much more than infrared is, so infrared gives us a clearer image.

(a)　　　　　(b)　　　　　(c)

organized into even larger aggregates: clusters of clusters of galaxies, or **superclusters**. The farthest detectable galaxies are more than 10^{10} ly distant. See Table 44–1.

TABLE 44–1 Astronomical Distances

Object	Approx. Distance from Earth (ly)
Moon	4×10^{-8}
Sun	1.6×10^{-5}
Size of solar system (distance to Pluto)	6×10^{-4}
Nearest star (Proxima Centauri)	4.3
Center of our Galaxy	2.6×10^4
Nearest large galaxy	2.4×10^6
Farthest galaxies	10^{10}

CONCEPTUAL EXAMPLE 44–2 **Looking back in time.** Astronomers often think of their telescopes as time machines, looking back toward the origin of the universe. How far back do they look?

RESPONSE The distance in light-years measures how long in years the light has been traveling to reach us, so Table 44–1 tells us also how far back in time we are looking. For example, if we saw Proxima Centauri explode into a supernova today, then the event would have really occurred 4.3 years ago. The most distant galaxies emitted the light we see now roughly 10^{10} years ago. What we see was how they were then, 10^{10} yr ago, or about 10^9 years after the universe was born in the Big Bang.

EXERCISE A Suppose we could place a huge mirror 1 light-year away from us. What would we see in this mirror if it is facing us on Earth? When did it take place? (This might be called a "time machine.")

Besides the usual stars, clusters of stars, galaxies, and clusters and superclusters of galaxies, the universe contains many other interesting objects. Among these are stars known as *red giants*, *white dwarfs*, *neutron stars*, exploding stars called *novae* and *supernovae*, and *black holes* whose gravity is so strong even light can not escape them. In addition, there is electromagnetic radiation that reaches the Earth but does not emanate from the bright pointlike objects we call stars: particularly important is the microwave background radiation that arrives nearly uniformly from all directions in the universe. We will discuss all these phenomena.

Finally, there are *active galactic nuclei* (AGN), which are very luminous pointlike sources of light in the centers of distant galaxies. The most dramatic examples of AGN are *quasars* ("quasistellar objects" or QSOs), which are so luminous that the surrounding starlight of the galaxy is drowned out. Their luminosity is thought to come from matter falling into a giant black hole at a galaxy's center.

44–2 Stellar Evolution: Nucleosynthesis, and the Birth and Death of Stars

The stars appear unchanging. Night after night the night sky reveals no significant variations. Indeed, on a human time scale, the vast majority of stars change very little (except for novae, supernovae, and certain variable stars). Although stars *seem* fixed in relation to each other, many move sufficiently for the motion to be detected. Speeds of stars relative to neighboring stars can be hundreds of km/s, but at their great distance from us, this motion is detectable only by careful measurement. Furthermore, there is a great range of brightness among stars. The differences in brightness are due both to differences in the rate at which stars emit energy and to their different distances from us.

Luminosity and Brightness of Stars

A useful parameter for a star or galaxy is its **intrinsic luminosity**, L (or simply **luminosity**), by which we mean the total power radiated in watts. Also important is the **apparent brightness**, b, defined as the power crossing unit area at the Earth perpendicular to the path of the light. Given that energy is conserved, and ignoring any absorption in space, the total emitted power L when it reaches a distance d from the star will be spread over a sphere of surface area $4\pi d^2$. If d is the distance from the star to the Earth, then L must be equal to $4\pi d^2$ times b (power per unit area at Earth). That is,

$$b = \frac{L}{4\pi d^2}. \qquad (44-1)$$

Apparent brightness. Suppose a particular star has intrinsic luminosity equal to that of our Sun, but is 10 ly away from Earth. By what factor will it appear dimmer than the Sun?

APPROACH The luminosity L is the same for both stars, so the apparent brightness depends only on their relative distances. We use the inverse square law as stated in Eq. 44–1 to determine the relative brightness.

SOLUTION Using the inverse square law, the star appears dimmer by a factor

$$\frac{b_{\text{star}}}{b_{\text{Sun}}} = \frac{d_{\text{Sun}}^2}{d_{\text{star}}^2} = \frac{(1.5 \times 10^8 \text{ km})^2}{(10 \text{ ly})^2 (10^{13} \text{ km/ly})^2} \approx 2 \times 10^{-12}.$$

Careful study of nearby stars has shown that the luminosity for most stars depends on the mass: *the more massive the star, the greater its luminosity*[†]. Indeed, we might expect that more massive stars would have higher core temperature and pressure to counterbalance the greater gravitational attraction, and thus be more luminous. Another important parameter of a star is its surface temperature, which can be determined from the spectrum of electromagnetic frequencies it emits (stars are "good" blackbodies—see Section 37–1). As we saw in Chapter 37, as the temperature of a body increases, the spectrum shifts from predominantly lower frequencies (and longer wavelengths, such as red) to higher frequencies (and shorter wavelengths such as blue). Quantitatively, the relation is given by Wien's law (Eq. 37–1): the peak wavelength λ_P in the spectrum of light emitted by a blackbody (we often approximate stars as blackbodies) is inversely proportional to its Kelvin temperature T; that is, $\lambda_P T = 2.90 \times 10^{-3} \text{ m} \cdot \text{K}$. The surface temperatures of stars typically range from about 3000 K (reddish) to about 50,000 K (UV).

Determining star temperature and star size. Suppose that the distances from Earth to two nearby stars can be reasonably estimated, and that their measured apparent brightnesses suggest the two stars have about the same luminosity, L. The spectrum of one of the stars peaks at about 700 nm (so it is reddish). The spectrum of the other peaks at about 350 nm (bluish). Use Wien's law (Eq. 37–1) and the Stefan-Boltzmann equation (Section 19–10) to determine (a) the surface temperature of each star, and (b) how much larger one star is than the other.

APPROACH We determine the surface temperature T for each star using Wien's law and each star's peak wavelength. Then, using the Stefan-Boltzmann equation (power output or luminosity $\propto AT^4$ where $A =$ surface area of emitter), we can find the surface area ratio and relative sizes of the two stars.

SOLUTION (a) Wien's law (Eq. 37–1) states that $\lambda_P T = 2.90 \times 10^{-3} \text{ m} \cdot \text{K}$. So the temperature of the reddish star is

$$T_{\text{r}} = \frac{2.90 \times 10^{-3} \text{ m} \cdot \text{K}}{700 \times 10^{-9} \text{ m}} = 4140 \text{ K}.$$

The temperature of the bluish star will be double this since its peak wavelength is half (350 nm vs. 700 nm):

$$T_{\text{b}} = 8280 \text{ K}.$$

(b) The Stefan-Boltzmann equation, Eq. 19–17, states that the power radiated *per unit area* of surface from a blackbody is proportional to the fourth power of the Kelvin temperature, T^4. The temperature of the bluish star is double that of the reddish star, so the bluish one must radiate $(2^4) = 16$ times as much energy per unit area. But we are given that they have the same luminosity (the same total power output); so the surface area of the blue star must be $\frac{1}{16}$ that of the red one. The surface area of a sphere is $4\pi r^2$, so the radius of the reddish star is $\sqrt{16} = 4$ times larger than the radius of the bluish star (or $4^3 = 64$ times the volume).

[†]Applies to "main-sequence" stars (see next page). The mass of a star can be determined by observing its gravitational effects. Many stars are part of a cluster, the simplest being a binary star in which two stars orbit around each other, allowing their masses to be determined using rotational mechanics.

FIGURE 44–6 Hertzsprung–Russell (H–R) diagram is a logarithmic graph of luminosity vs. surface temperature T of stars (note that T increases to the left).

H–R Diagram

An important astronomical discovery, made around 1900, was that for most stars, the color is related to the intrinsic luminosity and therefore to the mass. A useful way to present this relationship is by the so-called Hertzsprung–Russell (H–R) diagram. On the H–R diagram, the horizontal axis shows the surface temperature T whereas the vertical axis is the luminosity L; each star is represented by a point on the diagram, Fig. 44–6. Most stars fall along the diagonal band termed the **main sequence**. Starting at the lower right we find the coolest stars, reddish in color; they are the least luminous and therefore of low mass. Farther up toward the left we find hotter and more luminous stars that are whitish, like our Sun. Still farther up we find even more massive and more luminous stars, bluish in color. Stars that fall on this diagonal band are called *main-sequence stars*. There are also stars that fall outside the main sequence. Above and to the right we find extremely large stars, with high luminosities but with low (reddish) color temperature: these are called **red giants**. At the lower left, there are a few stars of low luminosity but with high temperature: these are the **white dwarfs**.

EXAMPLE 44–5 ESTIMATE **Distance to a star using the H–R diagram and color.** Suppose that detailed study of a certain star suggests that it most likely fits on the main sequence of an H–R diagram. Its measured apparent brightness is $b = 1.0 \times 10^{-12}$ W/m², and the peak wavelength of its spectrum is $\lambda_P \approx 600$ nm. Estimate its distance from us.

APPROACH We find the temperature using Wien's law, Eq. 37–1. The luminosity is estimated for a main sequence star on the H–R diagram of Fig. 44–6, and then the distance is found using the relation between brightness and luminosity, Eq. 44–1.

SOLUTION The star's temperature, from Wien's law (Eq. 37–1), is

$$T \approx \frac{2.90 \times 10^{-3} \, \text{m} \cdot \text{K}}{600 \times 10^{-9} \, \text{m}} \approx 4800 \, \text{K}.$$

A star on the main sequence of an H–R diagram at this temperature has intrinsic luminosity of about $L \approx 1 \times 10^{26}$ W, read off of Fig. 44–6. Then, from Eq. 44–1,

$$d = \sqrt{\frac{L}{4\pi b}} \approx \sqrt{\frac{1 \times 10^{26} \, \text{W}}{4(3.14)(1.0 \times 10^{-12} \, \text{W/m}^2)}} \approx 3 \times 10^{18} \, \text{m}.$$

Its distance from us in light-years is

$$d = \frac{3 \times 10^{18} \, \text{m}}{10^{16} \, \text{m/ly}} \approx 300 \, \text{ly}.$$

EXERCISE B Estimate the distance to a 6000-K main-sequence star with an apparent brightness of 2.0×10^{-12} W/m².

Stellar Evolution; Nucleosynthesis

Why are there different types of stars, such as red giants and white dwarfs, as well as main-sequence stars? Were they all born this way, in the beginning? Or might each different type represent a different age in the life cycle of a star? Astronomers and astrophysicists today believe the latter is the case. Note, however, that we cannot actually follow any but the tiniest part of the life cycle of any given star since they live for ages vastly greater than ours, on the order of millions or billions of years. Nonetheless, let us follow the process of **stellar evolution** from the birth to the death of a star, as astrophysicists have theoretically reconstructed it today.

Stars are born, it is believed, when gaseous clouds (mostly hydrogen) contract due to the pull of gravity. A huge gas cloud might fragment into numerous contracting masses, each mass centered in an area where the density was only slightly greater than that at nearby points. Once such "globules" formed, gravity would cause each to contract in toward its center of mass. As the particles of such a *protostar* accelerate inward, their kinetic energy increases. When the kinetic energy is sufficiently high, the Coulomb repulsion between the positive charges is not strong enough to keep the hydrogen nuclei apart, and nuclear fusion can take place.

In a star like our Sun, the fusion of hydrogen (sometimes referred to as "burning")[†] occurs via the *proton–proton cycle* (Section 42–4, Eqs. 42–7), in which four protons fuse to form a $^4_2$He nucleus with the release of γ rays, positrons, and neutrinos: $4\,^1_1\text{H} \rightarrow\ ^4_2\text{He} + 2\,e^+ + 2\nu_e + 2\gamma$. These reactions require a temperature of about 10^7 K, corresponding to an average kinetic energy ($\approx kT$) of about 1 keV (Eq. 18–4). In more massive stars, the carbon cycle produces the same net effect: four $^1_1$H produce a $^4_2$He—see Section 42–4. The fusion reactions take place primarily in the core of a star, where T may be on the order of 10^7 to 10^8 K. (The surface temperature is much lower—on the order of a few thousand kelvins.) The tremendous release of energy in these fusion reactions produces an outward pressure sufficient to halt the inward gravitational contraction. Our protostar, now really a young *star*, stabilizes on the main sequence. Exactly where the star falls along the main sequence depends on its mass. The more massive the star, the farther up (and to the left) it falls on the H–R diagram of Fig. 44–6. Our Sun required perhaps 30 million years to reach the main sequence, and is expected to remain there about 10 billion years (10^{10} yr). Although most stars are billions of years old, evidence is strong that stars are actually being born at this moment. More massive stars have shorter lives, because they are hotter and the Coulomb repulsion is more easily overcome, so they use up their fuel faster. If our Sun remains on the main sequence for 10^{10} years, a star ten times more massive may reside there for only 10^7 years.

As hydrogen fuses to form helium, the helium that is formed is denser and tends to accumulate in the central core where it was formed. As the core of helium grows, hydrogen continues to fuse in a shell around it: see Fig. 44–7. When much of the hydrogen within the core has been consumed, the production of energy decreases at the center and is no longer sufficient to prevent the huge gravitational forces from once again causing the core to contract and heat up. The hydrogen in the shell around the core then fuses even more fiercely because of this rise in temperature, allowing the outer envelope of the star to expand and to cool. The surface temperature, thus reduced, produces a spectrum of light that peaks at longer wavelength (reddish).

FIGURE 44–7 A shell of "burning" hydrogen (fusing to become helium) surrounds the core where the newly formed helium gravitates.

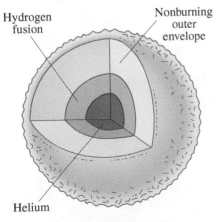

Hydrogen fusion

Nonburning outer envelope

Helium

[†]The word "burn" is put in quotation marks because these high-temperature fusion reactions occur via a *nuclear* process, and must not be confused with ordinary burning (of, say, paper, wood, or coal) in air, which is a *chemical* reaction, occurring at the *atomic* level (and at a much lower temperature).

By this time the star has left the main sequence. It has become redder, and as it has grown in size, it has become more luminous. So it will have moved to the right and upward on the H–R diagram, as shown in Fig. 44–8. As it moves upward, it enters the **red giant** stage. Thus, theory explains the origin of red giants as a natural step in a star's evolution. Our Sun, for example, has been on the main sequence for about $4\frac{1}{2}$ billion years. It will probably remain there another 4 or 5 billion years. When our Sun leaves the main sequence, it is expected to grow in diameter (as it becomes a red giant) by a factor of 100 or more, possibly swallowing up inner planets such as Mercury.

If the star is like our Sun, or larger, further fusion can occur. As the star's outer envelope expands, its core continues to shrink and heat up. When the temperature reaches about 10^8 K, even helium nuclei, in spite of their greater charge and hence greater electrical repulsion, can come close enough to each other to undergo fusion. The reactions are

$$\begin{aligned} {}^{4}_{2}\text{He} + {}^{4}_{2}\text{He} &\rightarrow {}^{8}_{4}\text{Be} \\ {}^{4}_{2}\text{He} + {}^{8}_{4}\text{Be} &\rightarrow {}^{12}_{6}\text{C} \end{aligned}$$
(44–2)

with the emission of two γ rays. These two reactions must occur in quick succession (because ${}^{8}_{4}\text{Be}$ is very unstable), and the net effect is

$$3\,{}^{4}_{2}\text{He} \rightarrow {}^{12}_{6}\text{C}. \qquad (Q = 7.3\,\text{MeV})$$

This fusion of helium causes a change in the star which moves rapidly to the "horizontal branch" on the H–R diagram (Fig. 44–8). Further fusion reactions are possible, with ${}^{4}_{2}\text{He}$ fusing with ${}^{12}_{6}\text{C}$ to form ${}^{16}_{8}\text{O}$. In more massive stars, higher Z elements like ${}^{20}_{10}\text{Ne}$ or ${}^{24}_{12}\text{Mg}$ can be made. This process of creating heavier nuclei from lighter ones (or by absorption of neutrons which tends to occur at higher Z) is called **nucleosynthesis**.

The final fate of a star depends on its mass. Stars can lose mass as parts of their outer envelope move off into space. Stars born with a mass less than about 8 (or perhaps 10) solar masses eventually end up with a residual mass less than about 1.4 solar masses, which is known as the **Chandrasekhar limit**. For them, no further fusion energy can be obtained. The core of such a "low mass" star (original mass $\lesssim$ 8–10 solar masses) contracts under gravity; the outer envelope expands again and the star becomes an even larger red giant. Eventually the outer layers escape into space, the core shrinks, the star cools, and typically follows the dashed route shown in Fig. 44–8, descending downward, becoming a **white dwarf**. A white dwarf with a residual mass equal to that of the Sun would be about the size of the Earth. A white dwarf contracts to the point at which the electron clouds start to overlap, but no further because, by the Pauli exclusion principle, no two electrons can be in the same quantum state. At this point the star is supported against further collapse by this **electron degeneracy** pressure. A white dwarf continues to lose internal energy by radiation, decreasing in temperature and becoming dimmer until it glows no more. It has then become a cold dark chunk of extremely dense material.

Stars whose residual mass is greater than the Chandrasekhar limit of 1.4 solar masses (original mass greater than about 8 or 10 solar masses) are thought to follow a quite different scenario. A star with this great a mass can contract under gravity and heat up even further. In the range $T = (2.5\text{–}5) \times 10^9$ K, nuclei as heavy as ${}^{56}_{26}\text{Fe}$ and ${}^{56}_{28}\text{Ni}$ can be made. But here the formation of heavy nuclei from lighter ones, by fusion, ends. As we saw in Fig. 41–1, the average binding energy per nucleon begins to decrease for A greater than about 60. Further fusions would *require* energy, rather than release it.

Elements heavier than Ni are thought to form mainly by neutron capture, particularly in exploding stars called *supernovae* (singular is **supernova**). Large numbers of free neutrons, resulting from nuclear reactions, are present inside these highly evolved stars and they can readily combine with, say, a ${}^{56}_{26}\text{Fe}$ nucleus to form (if three are captured) ${}^{59}_{26}\text{Fe}$, which decays to ${}^{59}_{27}\text{Co}$. The ${}^{59}_{27}\text{Co}$ can capture neutrons, also becoming neutron rich and decaying by β^- to the next higher Z element, and so on to the highest Z elements.

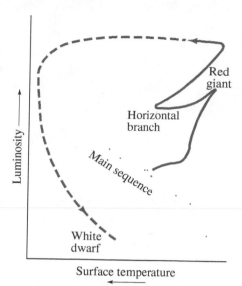

FIGURE 44–8 Evolutionary "track" of a star like our Sun represented on an H–R diagram.

Yet at these extremely high temperatures, well above 10^9 K, the kinetic energy of the nuclei is so high that fusion of elements heavier than iron is still possible even though the reactions require energy input. But the high-energy collisions can also cause the breaking apart of iron and nickel nuclei into He nuclei, and eventually into protons and neutrons:

$$^{56}_{26}\text{Fe} \rightarrow 13\,^{4}_{2}\text{He} + 4\text{n}$$
$$^{4}_{2}\text{He} \rightarrow 2\text{p} + 2\text{n}.$$

These are energy-requiring (endothermic) reactions, but at such extremely high temperature and pressure there is plenty of energy available, enough even to force electrons and protons together to form neutrons in **inverse β decay**:

$$\text{e}^- + \text{p} \rightarrow \text{n} + \nu.$$

As a result of these reactions, the pressure in the core drops precipitously. As the core collapses under the huge gravitational forces, the tremendous mass becomes essentially an enormous nucleus made up almost exclusively of neutrons. The size of the star is no longer limited by the exclusion principle applied to electrons, but rather by **neutron degeneracy** pressure, and the star contracts rapidly to form an enormously dense **neutron star**. The core of a neutron star contracts to the point at which all neutrons are as close together as they are in an atomic nucleus. That is, the density of a neutron star is on the order of 10^{14} times greater than normal solids and liquids on Earth. A cupful of such dense matter would weigh billions of tons. A neutron star that has a mass 1.5 times that of our Sun would have a diameter of only about 20 km. (Compare this to a white dwarf with 1 solar mass whose diameter would be $\approx 10^4$ km, as already mentioned.)

The contraction of the core of a massive star would mean a great reduction in gravitational potential energy. Somehow this energy would have to be released. Indeed, it was suggested in the 1930s that the final core collapse to a neutron star may be accompanied by a catastrophic explosion (a *supernova*—see previous page) whose tremendous energy could form virtually all elements of the Periodic Table and blow away the entire outer envelope of the star (Fig. 44–9), spreading its contents into interstellar space. The presence of heavy elements on Earth and in our solar system suggests that our solar system formed from the debris of such a supernova explosion.

FIGURE 44–9 The star indicated by the arrow in (a) exploded in 1987 as a supernova (SN1987a), as shown in (b). The bright spot in (b) does not represent the physical size. Part (c) is a photo taken a few years later, showing shock waves moving outward from where SN1987a was (blow-up in corner). Part (c) is magnified relative to (a) and (b).

(a)

(b)

(c)

If the final mass of a neutron star is less than about two or three solar masses, its subsequent evolution is thought to resemble that of a white dwarf. If the mass is greater than this, the star collapses under gravity, overcoming even the neutron exclusion principle. Gravity would then be so strong that even light emitted from the star could not escape—it would be pulled back in by the force of gravity. Since no radiation could escape from such a star, we could not see it—it would be black. An object may pass by it and be deflected by its gravitational field, but if it came too close it would be swallowed up, never to escape. This is a **black hole**.

Novae and Supernovae

Novae (singular is *nova*, meaning "new" in Latin) are faint stars that have suddenly increased in brightness by as much as a factor of 10^4 and last for a month or two before fading. Novae are thought to be faint white dwarfs that have pulled mass from a nearby companion (they make up a *binary* system), as illustrated in Fig. 44–10. The captured mass of hydrogen suddenly fuses into helium at a high rate for a few weeks. Many novae (maybe all) are *recurrent*—they repeat their bright glow years later.

Supernovae are also brief explosive events, but release millions of times more energy than novae, up to 10^{10} times more luminous than our Sun. The peak of brightness may exceed that of the entire galaxy in which they are located, but lasts only a few days or weeks. They slowly fade over a few months. Many supernovae form by core collapse to a neutron star as described above. See Fig. 44–9.

Type Ia supernovae are different. They all seem to have very nearly the same luminosity. They are believed to be binary stars, one of which is a white dwarf that pulls mass from its companion, much like for a nova, Fig. 44–10. The mass is higher, and as mass is captured and the total mass reaches the Chandrasekhar limit of 1.4 solar masses, it explodes as a supernova by undergoing a "thermonuclear runaway"—an uncontrolled chain of nuclear reactions. What is left is a neutron star or (if the mass is great enough) a black hole.

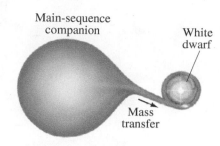

FIGURE 44–10 Hypothetical model for novae and type Ia supernovae, showing how a white dwarf could pull mass from its normal companion.

44–3 Distance Measurements

We have talked about the vast distances of objects in the universe. But how do we measure these distances? One basic technique employs simple geometry to measure the **parallax** of a star. By parallax we mean the apparent motion of a star, against the background of much more distant stars, due to the Earth's motion about the Sun. As shown in Fig. 44–11, the sighting angle of a star relative to the plane of Earth's orbit (angle θ) can be determined at different times of the year. Since we know the distance d from Earth to Sun, we can reconstruct the right triangles shown in Fig. 44–11 and can determine[†] the distance D to the star.

[†]This is essentially the way the heights of mountains are determined, by "triangulation." See Example 1–7.

(a)

(b)

FIGURE 44–11 (a) Simple example of determining the distance D to a relatively nearby star using parallax. Horizontal distances are greatly exaggerated: in reality ϕ is a very small angle. (b) Diagram of the sky showing the apparent position of the "nearby" star relative to more distant stars, at two different times (January and July). The viewing angle in January puts the star more to the right relative to distant stars, whereas in July it is more to the left (dashed circle shows January location).

EXAMPLE 44–6 **ESTIMATE** **Distance to a star using parallax.** Estimate the distance D to a star if the angle θ in Fig. 44–11 is measured to be 89.99994°.

APPROACH From trigonometry, $\tan\phi = d/D$ in Fig. 44–11. The Sun–Earth distance is $d = 1.5 \times 10^8$ km.

SOLUTION The angle $\phi = 90° - 89.99994° = 0.00006°$, or about 1.0×10^{-6} radians. We can use $\tan\phi \approx \phi$ since ϕ is very small. We solve for D in $\tan\phi = d/D$. The distance D to the star is

$$D = \frac{d}{\tan\phi} \approx \frac{d}{\phi} = \frac{1.5 \times 10^8 \text{ km}}{1.0 \times 10^{-6} \text{ rad}} = 1.5 \times 10^{14} \text{ km},$$

or about 15 ly.

Distances to stars are often specified in terms of parallax angle (ϕ in Fig. 44–11a) given in seconds of arc: 1 second (1″) is $\frac{1}{60}$ of one minute (1′) of arc, which is $\frac{1}{60}$ of a degree, so $1'' = \frac{1}{3600}$ of a degree. The distance is then specified in **parsecs** (pc) (meaning *par*allax angle in *sec*onds of arc): $D = 1/\phi$ with ϕ in seconds of arc. In Example 44–6, $\phi = (6 \times 10^{-5})°(3600) = 0.22''$ of arc, so we would say the star is at a distance of $1/0.22'' = 4.5$ pc. One parsec is given by (recall $D = d/\phi$, and we set the Sun–Earth distance (Fig. 44–11a) as $d = 1.496 \times 10^{11}$ m):

$$1 \text{ pc} = \frac{d}{1''} = \frac{1.496 \times 10^{11} \text{ m}}{(1'')\left(\frac{1'}{60''}\right)\left(\frac{1°}{60'}\right)\left(\frac{2\pi \text{ rad}}{360°}\right)} = 3.086 \times 10^{16} \text{ m}$$

$$1 \text{ pc} = (3.086 \times 10^{16} \text{ m})\left(\frac{1 \text{ ly}}{9.46 \times 10^{15} \text{ m}}\right) = 3.26 \text{ ly}.$$

Parallax can be used to determine the distance to stars as far away as about 100 light-years (≈ 30 parsecs) from Earth, and from an orbiting spacecraft perhaps 5 to 10 times farther. Beyond that distance, parallax angles are too small to measure. For greater distances, more subtle techniques must be employed. We might compare the apparent brightnesses of two stars, or two galaxies, and use the inverse square law (apparent brightness drops off as the square of the distance) to roughly estimate their relative distances. We can't expect this technique to be very precise because we don't expect any two stars, or two galaxies, to have the same intrinsic luminosity. When comparing galaxies, a perhaps better estimate assumes the brightest stars in all galaxies (or the brightest galaxies in galaxy clusters) are similar and have about the same intrinsic luminosity. Consequently, their *apparent brightness* would be a measure of how far away they were.

Another technique makes use of the H–R diagram. Measurement of a star's surface temperature (from its spectrum) places it at a certain point (within 20%) on the H–R diagram, assuming it is a main-sequence star, and then its luminosity can be estimated off the vertical axis (Fig. 44–6). Its apparent brightness and Eq. 44–1 give its approximate distance; see Example 44–5.

A better estimate comes from comparing *variable stars*, especially *Cepheid variables* whose luminosity varies over time with a period that is found to be related to their average luminosity. Thus, from their period and apparent brightness we get their distance.

The largest distances are estimated by comparing the apparent brightnesses of type Ia supernovae (SNIa). Type Ia supernovae all have a similar origin (as described on the previous page, Fig. 44–10), and their brief explosive burst of light is expected to be of nearly the same luminosity. They are thus sometimes referred to as "standard candles."

Another important technique for estimating the distance of very distant stars is from the "redshift" in the line spectra of elements and compounds. The redshift is related to the expansion of the universe, as we shall discuss in Section 44–5. It is useful for objects farther than 10^7 to 10^8 ly away.

As we look farther and farther away, the measurement techniques are less and less reliable, so there is more and more uncertainty in the measurements of large distances.

44–4 General Relativity: Gravity and the Curvature of Space

We have seen that the force of gravity plays an important role in the processes that occur in stars. Gravity too is important for the evolution of the universe as a whole. The reasons gravity plays a dominant role in the universe, and not one of the other of the four forces in nature, are (1) it is long-range and (2) it is always attractive. The strong and weak nuclear forces act over very short distances only, on the order of the size of a nucleus; hence they do not act over astronomical distances (they do act between nuclei and nucleons in stars to produce nuclear reactions). The electromagnetic force, like gravity, acts over great distances. But it can be either attractive or repulsive. And since the universe does not seem to contain large areas of net electric charge, a large net force does not occur. But gravity acts as an attractive force between *all* masses, and there are large accumulations in the universe of only the one "sign" of mass (not + and − as with electric charge). The force of gravity as Newton described it in his law of universal gravitation was modified by Einstein. In his general theory of relativity, Einstein developed a theory of gravity that now forms the basis of cosmological dynamics.

In the *special theory of relativity* (Chapter 36), Einstein concluded that there is no way for an observer to determine whether a given frame of reference is at rest or is moving at constant velocity in a straight line. Thus the laws of physics must be the same in different inertial reference frames. But what about the more general case of motion where reference frames can be *accelerating*?

Einstein tackled the problem of accelerating reference frames in his **general theory of relativity** and in it also developed a theory of gravity. The mathematics of General Relativity is complex, so our discussion will be mainly qualitative.

We begin with Einstein's **principle of equivalence**, which states that

no experiment can be performed that could distinguish between a uniform gravitational field and an equivalent uniform acceleration.

If observers sensed that they were accelerating (as in a vehicle speeding around a sharp curve), they could not prove by any experiment that in fact they weren't simply experiencing the pull of a gravitational field. Conversely, we might think we are being pulled by gravity when in fact we are undergoing an acceleration having nothing to do with gravity.

As a thought experiment, consider a person in a freely falling elevator near the Earth's surface. If our observer held out a book and let go of it, what would happen? Gravity would pull it downward toward the Earth, but at the same rate ($g = 9.8\,\text{m/s}^2$) at which the person and elevator were falling. So the book would hover right next to the person's hand (Fig. 44–12). The effect is exactly the same as if this reference frame was at rest and *no* forces were acting. On the other hand, if the elevator was out in space where the gravitational field is essentially zero, the released book would float, just as it does in Fig. 44–12. Next, if the elevator (out in space) is accelerating upward at an acceleration of $9.8\,\text{m/s}^2$, the book as seen by our observer would fall to the floor with an acceleration of $9.8\,\text{m/s}^2$, just as if it were falling due to gravity at the surface of the Earth. According to the principle of equivalence, the observer could not determine whether the book fell because the elevator was accelerating upward, or because a gravitational field was acting downward and the elevator was at rest. The two descriptions are equivalent.

The principle of equivalence is related to the concept that there are two types of mass. Newton's second law, $F = ma$, uses **inertial mass**. We might say that inertial mass represents "resistance" to any type of force. The second type of mass is **gravitational mass**. When one object attracts another by the gravitational force (Newton's law of universal gravitation, $F = Gm_1m_2/r^2$, Chapter 6), the strength of the force is proportional to the product of the *gravitational masses* of the two objects.

FIGURE 44–12 In an elevator falling freely under gravity, (a) a person releases a book; (b) the released book hovers next to the owner's hand; (b) is a few moments after (a).

(a)

(b)

This is much like Coulomb's law for the electric force between two objects which is proportional to the product of their electric charges. The electric charge on an object is not related to its inertial mass; so why should we expect that an object's gravitational mass (call it gravitational charge if you like) be related to its inertial mass? All along we have assumed they were the same. Why? Because no experiment—not even of high precision—has been able to discern any measurable difference between inertial mass and gravitational mass. (For example, in the absence of air resistance, all objects fall at the same acceleration, g, on Earth.) This is another way to state the equivalence principle: *gravitational mass is equivalent to inertial mass.*

FIGURE 44–13 (a) Light beam goes straight across an elevator which is not accelerating. (b) The light beam bends (exaggerated) in an accelerating elevator whose speed increases in the upward direction. Both views are as seen by an outside observer in an inertial reference frame.

(a)   (b)

FIGURE 44–14 (a) Three stars in the sky observed from Earth. (b) If the light from one of these stars passes very near the Sun, whose gravity bends the rays, the star will appear higher than it actually is (follow the ray backwards).

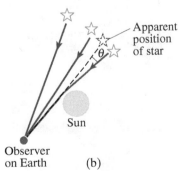

The principle of equivalence can be used to show that light ought to be deflected due to the gravitational force of a massive object. Consider another thought experiment, in which an elevator is in free space where virtually no gravity acts. If a light beam is emitted by a flashlight attached to the side of the elevator, the beam travels straight across the elevator and makes a spot on the opposite side if the elevator is at rest or moving at constant velocity (Fig. 44–13a). If instead the elevator is accelerating upward, as in Fig. 44–13b, the light beam still travels straight across in a reference frame at rest. In the upwardly accelerating elevator, however, the beam is observed to curve downward. Why? Because during the time the light travels from one side of the elevator to the other, the elevator is moving upward at a vertical speed that is increasing relative to the light. Next we note that according to the equivalence principle, an upwardly accelerating reference frame is equivalent to a downward gravitational field. Hence, we can picture the curved light path in Fig. 44–13b as being due to the effect of a gravitational field. Thus, from the principle of equivalence, we expect gravity to exert a force on a beam of light and to bend it out of a straight-line path!

That light is affected by gravity is an important prediction of Einstein's general theory of relativity. And it can be tested. The amount a light beam would be deflected from a straight-line path must be small even when passing a massive object. (For example, light near the Earth's surface after traveling 1 km is predicted to drop only about 10^{-10} m, which is equal to the diameter of a small atom and not detectable.) The most massive object near us is the Sun, and it was calculated that light from a distant star would be deflected by 1.75″ of arc (tiny but detectable) as it passed by the edge of the Sun (Fig. 44–14). However, such a measurement could be made only during a total eclipse of the Sun, so that the Sun's tremendous brightness would not obscure the starlight passing near its edge. An opportune eclipse occurred in 1919, and scientists journeyed to the South Atlantic to observe it.

(a)   (b)

FIGURE 44–15 (a) Hubble Space Telescope photograph of the so-called "Einstein cross", thought to represent "gravitational lensing": the central spot is a relatively nearby galaxy, whereas the four other spots are thought to be images of a single quasar *behind* the galaxy. (b) Diagram showing how the galaxy could bend the light coming from the quasar behind it to produce the four images. See also Fig. 44–14. [If the shape of the nearby galaxy and distant quasar were perfect spheres, we would expect the "image" of the distant quasar to be a circular ring or halo instead of the four separate images seen here. Such a ring is called an "Einstein ring."]

Their photos of stars around the Sun revealed shifts in accordance with Einstein's prediction. Another example is gravitational lensing, as shown in Fig. 44–15.

Fermat showed that optical phenomena, including reflection, refraction, and effects of lenses, can be derived from a simple principle: that light traveling between two points follows the shortest path in space. Thus if gravity curves the path of light, then gravity must be able to curve space itself. That is, *space itself can be curved*, and it is gravitational mass that causes the curvature. Indeed, the curvature of space—or rather, of four-dimensional space-time—is a basic aspect of Einstein's General Relativity (GR).

What is meant by **curved space**? To understand, recall that our normal method of viewing the world is via Euclidean plane geometry. In Euclidean geometry, there are many axioms and theorems we take for granted, such as that the sum of the angles of any triangle is 180°. Non-Euclidean geometries, which involve curved space, have also been imagined by mathematicians. It is hard enough to imagine three-dimensional curved space, much less curved four-dimensional space-time. So let us try to understand the idea of curved space by using two-dimensional surfaces.

Consider, for example, the two-dimensional surface of a sphere. It is clearly curved, Fig. 44–16, at least to us who view it from the outside—from our three-dimensional world. But how would hypothetical two-dimensional creatures determine whether their two-dimensional space was flat (a plane) or curved? One way would be to measure the sum of the angles of a triangle. If the surface is a plane, the sum of the angles is 180°, as we learn in plane geometry. But if the space is curved, and a sufficiently large triangle is constructed, the sum of the angles will *not* be 180°. To construct a triangle on a curved surface, say the sphere of Fig. 44–16, we must use the equivalent of a straight line: that is, the shortest distance between two points, which is called a **geodesic**. On a sphere, a geodesic is an arc of a great circle (an arc in a plane passing through the center of the sphere) such as the Earth's equator and the Earth's longitude lines. Consider, for example, the large triangle of Fig. 44–16: its sides are two longitude lines passing from the north pole to the equator, and the third side is a section of the equator as shown. The two longitude lines make 90° angles with the equator (look at a world globe to see this more clearly). They make an angle with each other at the north pole, which could be, say, 90° as shown; the sum of these angles is 90° + 90° + 90° = 270°. This is clearly *not* a Euclidean space. Note, however, that if the triangle is small in comparison to the radius of the sphere, the angles will add up to nearly 180°, and the triangle (and space) will seem flat.

FIGURE 44–16 On a two-dimensional curved surface, the sum of the angles of a triangle may not be 180°.

FIGURE 44–17 On a spherical surface (a two-dimensional world) a circle of circumference *C* is drawn (red) about point O as the center. The radius of the circle (not the sphere) is the distance *r* along the surface. (Note that in our three-dimensional view, we can tell that $C = 2\pi a$. Since $r > a$, then $C < 2\pi r$.)

FIGURE 44–18 Example of a two-dimensional surface with negative curvature.

Another way to test the curvature of space is to measure the radius *r* and circumference *C* of a large circle. On a plane surface, $C = 2\pi r$. But on a two-dimensional spherical surface, *C* is *less* than $2\pi r$, as can be seen in Fig. 44–17. The proportionality between *C* and *r* is *less* than 2π. Such a surface is said to have *positive curvature*. On the saddlelike surface of Fig. 44–18, the circumference of a circle is greater than $2\pi r$, and the sum of the angles of a triangle is less than 180°. Such a surface is said to have a *negative curvature*.

Curvature of the Universe

What about our universe? On a large scale (not just near a large mass), what is the overall curvature of the universe? Does it have positive curvature, negative curvature, or is it flat (zero curvature)? We perceive our world as Euclidean (flat), but we can not exclude the possibility that space could have a curvature so slight that we don't normally notice it. This is a crucial question in cosmology, and it can be answered only by precise experimentation.

If the universe had a positive curvature, the universe would be *closed*, or *finite* in volume. This would *not* mean that the stars and galaxies extended out to a certain boundary, beyond which there is empty space. There is no boundary or edge in such a universe. The universe is all there is. If a particle were to move in a straight line in a particular direction, it would eventually return to the starting point—perhaps eons of time later.

On the other hand, if the curvature of space was zero or negative, the universe would be *open*. It could just go on forever. An open universe could be *infinite*; but according to recent research, even that may not necessarily be so.

Today the evidence is very strong that the universe on a large scale is very close to being flat. Indeed, it is so close to being flat that we can't tell if it might have very slightly positive or very slightly negative curvature.

Black Holes

FIGURE 44–19 Rubber-sheet analogy for space-time curved by matter.

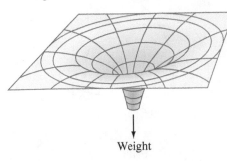

Weight

According to Einstein's theory, space-time is curved near massive objects. We might think of space as being like a thin rubber sheet: if a heavy weight is hung from it, it curves as shown in Fig. 44–19. The weight corresponds to a huge mass that causes space (space itself!) to curve. Thus, in Einstein's theory[†] we do not speak of the "force" of gravity acting on objects. Instead we say that objects and light rays move as they do because space-time is curved. An object starting at rest or moving slowly near the great mass of Fig. 44–19 would follow a geodesic (the equivalent of a straight line in plane geometry) toward that great mass.

[†]Alexander Pope (1688–1744) wrote an epitaph for Newton:
  "Nature, and Nature's laws lay hid in night:
  God said, *Let Newton be!* and all was light."
Sir John Squire (1884–1958), perhaps uncomfortable with Einstein's profound thoughts, added:
  "It did not last: the Devil howling 'Ho!
  Let Einstein be!' restored the status quo."

The extreme curvature of space-time shown in Fig. 44–19 could be produced by a **black hole**. A black hole, as we mentioned in Section 44–2, is so dense that even light cannot escape from it. To become a black hole, an object of mass M must undergo **gravitational collapse**, contracting by gravitational self-attraction to within a radius called the **Schwarzschild radius**:

$$R = \frac{2GM}{c^2},$$

where G is the gravitational constant and c the speed of light. If an object collapses to within this radius, it is predicted by general relativity to rapidly $(\approx 10^{-5}\,\text{s})$ collapse to a point at $r = 0$, forming an infinitely dense singularity. This prediction is uncertain, however, because in this realm we need to combine quantum mechanics with gravity, a unification of theories not yet achieved (Section 43–12).

| **EXERCISE C** What is the Schwarzschild radius for an object with 2 solar masses?

The Schwarzschild radius also represents the event horizon of a black hole. By **event horizon** we mean the surface beyond which no emitted signals can ever reach us, and thus inform us of events that happen beyond that surface. As a star collapses toward a black hole, the light it emits is pulled harder and harder by gravity, but we can still see it. Once the matter passes within the event horizon, the emitted light cannot escape but is pulled back in by gravity.

All we can know about a black hole is its mass, its angular momentum (there could be rotating black holes), and its electric charge. No other information, no details of its structure or the kind of matter it was formed of, can be known because no information can escape.

How might we observe black holes? We cannot see them because no light can escape from them. They would be black objects against a black sky. But they do exert a gravitational force on nearby objects. The black hole believed to be at the center of our Galaxy ($M \approx 2 \times 10^6\,M_{\text{Sun}}$) was discovered by examining the motion of matter in its vicinity. Another technique is to examine stars which appear to move as if they were one member of a *binary system* (two stars rotating about their common center of mass), but without a visible companion. If the unseen star is a black hole, it might be expected to pull off gaseous material from its visible companion (as in Fig. 44–10). As this matter approached the black hole, it would be highly accelerated and should emit X-rays of a characteristic type before plunging inside the event horizon. Such X-rays, plus a sufficiently high mass estimate from the rotational motion, can provide evidence for a black hole. One of the many candidates for a black hole is in the binary-star system Cygnus X-1. It is widely believed that the center of most galaxies is occupied by a black hole with a mass 10^6 to 10^9 times the mass of a typical star like our Sun.

| **EXERCISE D** A black hole has radius R. Its mass is proportional to (a) R, (b) R^2, (c) R^3. Justify your answer.

44–5 The Expanding Universe: Redshift and Hubble's Law

We discussed in Section 44–2 how individual stars evolve from their birth to their death as white dwarfs, neutron stars, and black holes. But what about the universe as a whole: is it static, or does it change? One of the most important scientific discoveries of the twentieth century was that distant galaxies are racing away from us, and that the farther they are from us, the faster they are moving away. How astronomers arrived at this astonishing idea, and what it means for the past history of the universe as well as its future, will occupy us for the remainder of the book.

Low redshift galaxy spectrum
z = 0.004

(a)

Higher redshift galaxy spectrum
z = 0.104

(b)

FIGURE 44–20 Atoms and molecules emit and absorb light of particular frequencies depending on the spacing of their energy levels, as we saw in Chapters 37 to 40. (a) The spectrum of light received from a relatively slow-moving galaxy. (b) Spectrum of a galaxy moving away from us at a much higher speed. Note how the peaks (or lines) in the spectrum have moved to longer wavelengths. The redshift is $z = (\lambda_{obs} - \lambda_{rest})/\lambda_{rest}$.

That the universe is expanding was first put forth by Edwin Hubble in 1929. This idea was based on distance measurements of galaxies (Section 44–3), and determination of their velocities by the Doppler shift of spectral lines in the light received from them (Fig. 44–20). In Chapter 16 we saw how the frequency of sound is higher and the wavelength shorter if the source and observer move toward each other. If the source moves away from the observer, the frequency is lower and the wavelength longer. The **Doppler effect** occurs also for light, and we saw in Section 36–12 (Eq. 36–15) that according to special relativity, the Doppler shift is given by

$$\lambda_{obs} = \lambda_{rest} \sqrt{\frac{1 + v/c}{1 - v/c}}, \quad \left[\begin{array}{l}\text{source and observer moving} \\ \text{away from each other}\end{array}\right] \quad \textbf{(44–3)}$$

where λ_{rest} is the emitted wavelength as seen in a reference frame at rest with respect to the source, and λ_{obs} is the wavelength observed in a frame moving with velocity v away from the source along the line of sight. (For relative motion *toward* each other, $v < 0$ in this formula.) When a distant source emits light of a particular wavelength, and the source is moving away from us, the wavelength appears longer to us: the color of the light (if it is visible) is shifted toward the red end of the visible spectrum, an effect known as a **redshift**. (If the source moves toward us, the color shifts toward the blue or shorter wavelength.)

In the spectra of stars in other galaxies, lines are observed that correspond to lines in the known spectra of particular atoms (see Section 37–10 and Figs. 35–22 and 37–20). What Hubble found was that the lines seen in the spectra from distant galaxies were generally *redshifted*, and that the amount of shift seemed to be approximately proportional to the distance of the galaxy from us. That is, the velocity v of a galaxy moving away from us is proportional to its distance d from us:

HUBBLE'S LAW

$$v = Hd. \quad \textbf{(44–4)}$$

This is **Hubble's law**, one of the most fundamental astronomical ideas. The constant H is called the **Hubble parameter**.

The value of H until recently was uncertain by over 20%, and thought to be between 50 and 80 km/s/Mpc. But recent measurements now put its value more precisely at

$$H = 71 \text{ km/s/Mpc}$$

(that is, 71 km/s per megaparsec of distance). The current uncertainty is about 5%, or ± 4 km/s/Mpc. If we use light-years for distance, then $H = 22$ km/s per million light-years of distance:

$$H = 22 \text{ km/s/Mly}$$

with an estimated uncertainty of ± 1 km/s/Mly.

Redshift Origins

Galaxies very near us seem to be moving randomly relative to us: some move towards us (blueshifted), others away from us (redshifted); their speeds are on the order of $0.001c$. But for more distant galaxies, the velocity of recession is much greater than the velocity of local random motion, and so is dominant and Hubble's law (Eq. 44–4) holds very well. More distant galaxies have higher recession velocity and a larger redshift, and we call their redshift a **cosmological redshift**. We interpret this redshift today as due to the *expansion of space* itself. We can think of the originally emitted wavelength λ_{rest} as being stretched out (becoming longer) along with the expanding space around it, as suggested in Fig. 44–21. Although Hubble thought of the redshift as a Doppler shift, now we understand it in this sense of expanding space.

Contrast the cosmological redshift, due to the expansion of space itself, with an ordinary *Doppler redshift* which is due to the relative motion of emitter and observer in a space that can be considered fixed over the time interval of observation.

There is a third way to produce a redshift, which we mention for completeness: a **gravitational redshift**. Light leaving a massive star is gaining in gravitational potential energy (just like a stone thrown upward from Earth). So the kinetic energy of each photon, hf, must be getting smaller (to conserve energy). A smaller frequency f means a larger (longer) wavelength λ $(= c/f)$, which is a redshift.

The amount of a redshift is specified by the **redshift parameter**, z, defined as

$$z = \frac{\lambda_{obs} - \lambda_{rest}}{\lambda_{rest}} = \frac{\Delta\lambda}{\lambda_{rest}}, \tag{44–5a}$$

where λ_{rest} is a wavelength as seen by an observer at rest relative to the source, and λ_{obs} is the wavelength measured by a moving observer. Equation 44–5a can also be written as

$$z = \frac{\lambda_{obs}}{\lambda_{rest}} - 1 \tag{44–5b}$$

and

$$z + 1 = \frac{\lambda_{obs}}{\lambda_{rest}}. \tag{44–5c}$$

For low speeds not close to the speed of light ($v \lesssim 0.1c$), the Doppler formula (Eq. 44–3) can be used to show (Problem 29) that z is proportional to the speed of the source toward or away from us:

$$z = \frac{\lambda_{obs} - \lambda_{rest}}{\lambda_{rest}} \approx \frac{v}{c}. \qquad [v \ll c] \tag{44–6}$$

But redshifts are not always small, in which case the approximation of Eq. 44–6 is not valid. Modern telescopes regularly observe galaxies with $z \approx 5$ (Fig. 44–22); for large z galaxies, not even Eq. 44–3 applies because the redshift is due to the expansion of space (cosmological redshift), not the Doppler effect.

Scale Factor

The expansion of space can be described as a simple scaling of the typical distance between two points or objects in the universe. If two distant galaxies are a distance d_0 apart at some initial time, then a time t later they will be separated by a greater distance $d(t)$. The **scale factor** is the same as for light, expressed in Eq. 44–5a. That is,

$$\frac{d(t) - d_0}{d_0} = \frac{\Delta\lambda}{\lambda} = z$$

or

$$\frac{d(t)}{d_0} = 1 + z.$$

Thus, for example, if a galaxy has $z = 3$, then the scale factor is now $(1 + 3) = 4$ times larger than when the light was emitted from that galaxy. That is, the average distance between galaxies has become 4 times larger. Thus the factor by which the wavelength has increased since it was emitted tells us by what factor the universe (or the typical distance between objects) has increased.

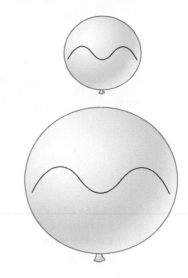

FIGURE 44–21 Simplified model of a 2-dimensional universe, imagined as a balloon. As you blow up the balloon (= expanding universe), the wavelength of a wave on its surface gets longer (redshifted).

FIGURE 44–22 Hubble Ultra Deep Field photograph showing what may be among the most distant galaxies from us (small red dots, highlighted by squares), with $z \approx 5$ or 6, existing when the universe was only about 800 million years old. The two distant galaxies in this photo are shown enlarged below.

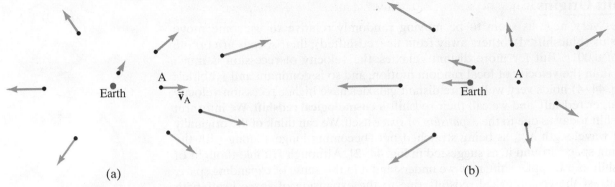

FIGURE 44–23 Expansion of the universe looks the same from any point in the universe. If you are on Earth as shown in part (a) or you are instead at point A (which is at rest in the reference frame shown in (b)), all other galaxies appear to be racing away from you.

Expansion, and the Cosmological Principle

What does it mean that distant galaxies are all moving away from us, and with ever greater speed the farther they are from us? It seems to suggest some kind of explosive expansion that started at some very distant time in the past. And at first sight we seem to be in the middle of it all. But we aren't. The expansion appears the same from any other point in the universe. To understand why, see Fig. 44–23. In Fig. 44–23a we have the view from Earth (or from our Galaxy). The velocities of surrounding galaxies are indicated by arrows, pointing away from us, and the arrows are longer for galaxies more distant from us. Now, what if we were on the galaxy labeled A in Fig. 44–23a? From Earth, galaxy A appears to be moving to the right at a velocity, call it $\vec{v}_A$, represented by the arrow pointing to the right. If we were *on* galaxy A, Earth would appear to be moving to the left at velocity $-\vec{v}_A$. To determine the velocities of other galaxies relative to A, we vectorially add the velocity vector, $-\vec{v}_A$, to all the velocity arrows shown in Fig. 44–23a. This yields Fig. 44–23b, where we see clearly that the universe is expanding away from galaxy A as well; and the velocities of galaxies receding from A are proportional to their current distance from A. The universe looks pretty much the same from different points.

Thus the expansion of the universe can be stated as follows: all galaxies are racing away from *each other* at an average rate of about 22 km/s per million light-years of distance between them. The ramifications of this idea are profound, and we discuss them in a moment.

A basic assumption in cosmology has been that on a large scale, the universe would look the same to observers at different places at the same time. In other words, the universe is both *isotropic* (looks the same in all directions) and *homogeneous* (would look the same if we were located elsewhere, say in another galaxy). This assumption is called the **cosmological principle**. On a local scale, say in our solar system or within our Galaxy, it clearly does not apply (the sky looks different in different directions). But it has long been thought to be valid if we look on a large enough scale, so that the average population density of galaxies and clusters of galaxies ought to be the same in different areas of the sky. This seems to be valid on distances greater than about 200 Mpc (700 Mly). The expansion of the universe (Fig. 44–23) is consistent with the cosmological principle; and the near uniformity of the cosmic microwave background radiation (discussed in Section 44–6) supports it. Another way to state the cosmological principle is that *our place in the universe is not special.*

The expansion of the universe, as described by Hubble's law, strongly suggests that galaxies must have been closer together in the past than they are now. This is, in fact, the basis of the *Big Bang* theory of the origin of the universe, which pictures the universe as a relentless expansion starting from a very hot and compressed beginning. We discuss the Big Bang in detail shortly, but first let us see what can be said about the age of the universe.

One way to estimate the age of the universe uses the Hubble parameter. With $H \approx 22$ km/s per 10^6 light-years, the time required for the galaxies to arrive at their present separations would be approximately (starting with $v = d/t$ and using Hubble's law, Eq. 44–4),

$$t = \frac{d}{v} = \frac{d}{Hd} = \frac{1}{H} \approx \frac{(10^6 \, \text{ly})(0.95 \times 10^{13} \, \text{km/ly})}{(22 \, \text{km/s})(3.16 \times 10^7 \, \text{s/yr})} \approx 14 \times 10^9 \, \text{yr},$$

or 14 billion years. The age of the universe calculated in this way is called the *characteristic expansion time* or "Hubble age." It is a very rough estimate and assumes the rate of expansion of the universe was constant (which today we are quite sure is not true). Today's best measurements give the age of the universe as 13.7×10^9 yr, in remarkable agreement with the rough Hubble age estimate.

*Steady-State Model

Before discussing the Big Bang in detail, we mention one alternative to the Big Bang—the **steady-state model**—which assumed that the universe is infinitely old and on average looks the same now as it always has. (This assumed uniformity in time as well as space was called the *perfect cosmological principle*.) According to the steady-state model, no large-scale changes have taken place in the universe as a whole, particularly no Big Bang. To maintain this view in the face of the recession of galaxies away from each other, matter must be created continuously to maintain the assumption of uniformity. The rate of mass creation required is very small—about one nucleon per cubic meter every 10^9 years.

The steady-state model provided the Big Bang model with healthy competition in the mid-twentieth century. But the discovery of the cosmic microwave background radiation (next Section), as well as other observations of the universe, has made the Big Bang model universally accepted.

44–6 The Big Bang and the Cosmic Microwave Background

The expansion of the universe suggests that typical objects in the universe were once much closer together than they are now. This is the basis for the idea that the universe began about 14 billion years ago as an expansion from a state of very high density and temperature known affectionately as the **Big Bang**.

The birth of the universe was not an explosion, because an explosion blows pieces out into the surrounding space. Instead, the Big Bang was the start of an expansion of space itself. The observable universe was very small at the start and has been expanding ever since. The initial tiny universe of extremely dense matter is not to be thought of as a concentrated mass in the midst of a much larger space around it. The initial tiny but dense universe was the entire universe. There wouldn't have been anything else. When we say that the universe was once smaller than it is now, we mean that the average separation between objects (such as galaxies) was less. It is thought the universe was infinite in extent then, and it still is (only bigger). The observable universe, however, is finite.

A major piece of evidence supporting the Big Bang is the **cosmic microwave background** radiation (or CMB) whose discovery came about as follows.

In 1964, Arno Penzias and Robert Wilson pointed their radiotelescope (a large antenna device for detecting radio waves) into the night sky (Fig. 44–24). With it they detected widespread emission, and became convinced that it was coming from outside our Galaxy. They made precise measurements at a wavelength $\lambda = 7.35$ cm, in the microwave region of the electromagnetic spectrum (Fig. 31–12). The intensity of this radiation was found initially not to vary by day or night or time of year, nor to depend on direction. It came from all directions in the universe with equal intensity, to a precision of better than 1%. It could only be concluded that this radiation came from the universe as a whole.

FIGURE 44–24 Arno Penzias (left) and Robert Wilson, and behind them their "horn antenna."

Wavelength (cm)

Blackbody spectrum
(T = 2.725 K)

Penzias and
Wilson

Intensity

Frequency (GHz)

FIGURE 44–25 Spectrum of cosmic microwave background radiation, showing blackbody curve and experimental measurements including at the frequency detected by Penzias and Wilson. (Thanks to G. F. Smoot and D. Scott. The vertical bars represent the most recent experimental uncertainty in a measurement.)

FIGURE 44–26 COBE scientists John Mather (left, chief scientist and responsible for measuring the blackbody form of the spectrum) and George Smoot (chief investigator for anisotropy experiment) shown here during celebrations for their Dec. 2006 Nobel Prize, given for their discovery of the spectrum and anisotropy of the CMB using the COBE instrument.

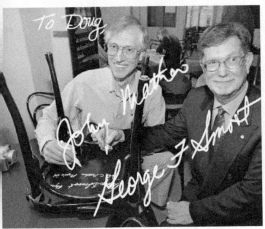

They measured this cosmic microwave background radiation at λ = 7.35 cm, and its intensity corresponds to blackbody radiation (see Section 37–1) at a temperature of about 3 K. When radiation at other wavelengths was measured by the COBE satellite (COsmic Background Explorer), the intensities were found to fall on a nearly perfect blackbody curve as shown in Fig. 44–25, corresponding to a temperature of 2.725 K ($\pm$ 0.002 K).

The remarkable uniformity of the cosmic microwave background radiation was in accordance with the cosmological principle. But theorists felt that there needed to be some small inhomogeneities, or "anisotropies," in the CMB that would have provided "seeds" around which galaxy formation could have started. Small areas of slightly higher density, which could have contracted under gravity to form stars and galaxies, were indeed found. These tiny inhomogeneities in density and temperature were detected first by the COBE satellite experiment in 1992, led by John Mather and George Smoot (Fig. 44–26).

This discovery of the **anisotropy** of the CMB ranks with the discovery of the CMB itself in the history of cosmology. It was the culmination of decades of research by pioneers such as Paul Richards and David Wilkinson. Subsequent experiments with greater detail culminated in 2003 with the WMAP (Wilkinson Microwave Anisotropy Probe) results. See Fig. 44–27 which presents the latest (2006) results.

The CMB provides strong evidence in support of the Big Bang, and gives us information about conditions in the very early universe. In fact, in the late 1940s, George Gamow and his collaborators calculated that a Big Bang origin of the universe should have generated just such a microwave background radiation.

To understand why, let us look at what a Big Bang might have been like. (Today we usually use the term "Big Bang" to refer to the *process*, starting from the birth of the universe through the subsequent expansion.) The temperature must have been extremely high at the start, so high that there could not have been any atoms in the very early stages of the universe. Instead, the universe

FIGURE 44–27 Measurements of the cosmic microwave background radiation over the entire sky, color-coded to represent differences in temperature from the average 2.725 K: the color scale ranges from +200 μK (red) to −200 μK (dark blue), representing slightly hotter and colder spots (associated with variations in density). Results are from the WMAP satellite in 2006: the angular resolution is 0.2°. The white lines are added to show the measured polarization direction of the earliest light, which gives further clues to the early universe.

would have consisted solely of radiation (photons) and a plasma of charged electrons and other elementary particles. The universe would have been opaque—the photons in a sense "trapped," traveling very short distances before being scattered again, primarily by electrons. Indeed, the details of the microwave background radiation is strong evidence that matter and radiation were once in equilibrium at a very high temperature. As the universe expanded, the energy spread out over an increasingly larger volume and the temperature dropped. Only when the temperature had fallen to about 3000 K, some 380,000 years later, could nuclei and electrons combine together as atoms. With the disappearance of free electrons, as they combined with nuclei to form atoms, the radiation would have been freed—**decoupled** from matter, we say. The universe became *transparent* because photons were now free to travel nearly unimpeded straight through the universe.

It is this radiation, from 380,000 years after the birth of the universe, that we now see as the CMB. As the universe expanded, so too the wavelengths of the radiation lengthened, thus redshifting to longer wavelengths that correspond to lower temperature (recall Wien's law, $\lambda_P T = $ constant, Section 37–1), until they would have reached the 2.7-K background radiation we observe today.

Looking Back toward the Big Bang—Lookback Time

Figure 44–28 shows our Earth point of view, looking out in all directions back toward the Big Bang and the brief (380,000-year-long) period when radiation was trapped in the early plasma (yellow band). The time it takes light to reach us from an event is called its **lookback time**. The "close-up" insert in Fig. 44–28 shows a photon scattering repeatedly inside that early plasma and then exiting the plasma in a straight line. No matter what direction we look, our view of the very early universe is blocked by this wall of plasma. It is like trying to look into a very thick fog or into the surface of the Sun—we can see only as far as its surface, called the **surface of last scattering**, but not into it. Wavelengths from there are redshifted by $z \approx 1100$. Time $\Delta t'$ in Fig. 44–28 is the lookback time (not real time that goes forward).

Recall that when we view an object far away, we are seeing it as it was then, when the light was emitted, not as it would appear today.

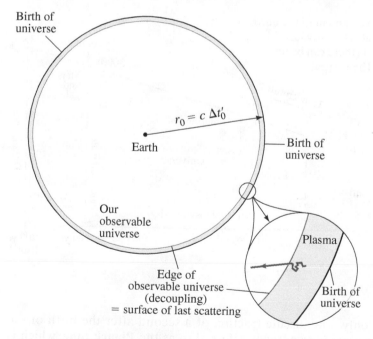

FIGURE 44–28 When we look out from the Earth, we look back in time. Any other observer in the universe would see more or less the same thing. The farther an object is from us, the longer ago the light we see had to have left it. We cannot see quite as far as the Big Bang; we can see only as far as the "surface of last scattering," which radiated the CMB. The insert on the lower right shows the earliest 380,000 years of the universe when it was opaque: a photon is shown scattering many times and then (at decoupling, 380,000 yr after the birth of the universe) becoming free to travel in a straight line. If this photon wasn't heading our way when "liberated," many others were. Galaxies are not shown, but would be concentrated close to Earth in this diagram because they were created relatively recently. *Note:* This diagram is not a normal map. Maps show a section of the world as might be seen all *at a given time*. This diagram shows space (like a map), but each point is *not* at the same time. The light coming from a point a distance r from Earth took a time $\Delta t' = r/c$ to reach Earth, and thus shows an event that took place long ago, a time $\Delta t' = r/c$ in the past, which we call its "lookback time." The universe began $\Delta t_0' = 13.7$ Gyr ago.

The Observable Universe

Figure 44–28 is a bit dangerous: it is not a picture of the universe at a given instant, but is intended to suggest how we look out in all directions from our observation point (the Earth, or near it). Be careful not to think that the birth of the universe took place in a circle or a sphere surrounding us as if Fig. 44–28 were a photo taken at a given moment. What Fig. 44–28 does show is what we can see, the *observable universe*. Better yet, it shows the *most* we could see.

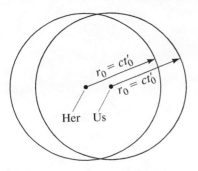

FIGURE 44–29 Two observers, on widely separated galaxies, have different horizons, different observable universes.

We would undoubtedly be arrogant to think that we could see the entire universe. Indeed, theories assume that we cannot see everything, that the **entire universe** is greater than the **observable universe**, which is a sphere of radius $r_0 = ct_0$ centered on the observer, with t_0 being the age of the universe. We can never see further back than the time it takes light to reach us.

Consider, for example, an observer in another galaxy, very far from us, located to the left of our observation point in Fig. 44–28. That observer would not yet have seen light coming from the far right of the large circle in Fig. 44–28 that we see—it will take some time for that light to reach her. But she will have already, some time ago, seen the light coming from the left that we are seeing now. In fact, her observable universe, superimposed on ours, is suggested by Fig. 44–29.

The edge of our observable universe is called the **horizon**. We could, in principle, see as far as the horizon, but not beyond it. An observer in another galaxy, far from us, will have a different horizon.

44–7 The Standard Cosmological Model: Early History of the Universe

In the last decade or two, a convincing theory of the origin and evolution of the universe has been developed, now called the **Standard Cosmological Model**, or (sometimes) the *concordance model*. Part of this theory is based on recent theoretical and experimental advances in elementary particle physics, and part from observations of the universe including COBE and WMAP. Indeed, cosmology and elementary particle physics have cross-fertilized to a surprising extent.

Let us go back to the earliest of times—as close as possible to the Big Bang—and follow a Standard Model scenario of events as the universe expanded and cooled after the Big Bang. Initially we talk of extremely small time intervals as well as extremely high temperatures, far beyond anything in the universe today. Figure 44–30 is a compressed graphical representation of the events, and it may be helpful to consult it as we go along.

FIGURE 44–30 Compressed graphical representation of the development of the universe after the Big Bang, according to modern cosmology. [The time scale is mostly logarithmic (each factor of 10 in time gets equal treatment), except at the start (there can be no $t = 0$ on a log scale), and just after $t = 10^{-35}$ s (to save space). The vertical height is a rough indication of the size of the universe, mainly to suggest expansion of the universe.]

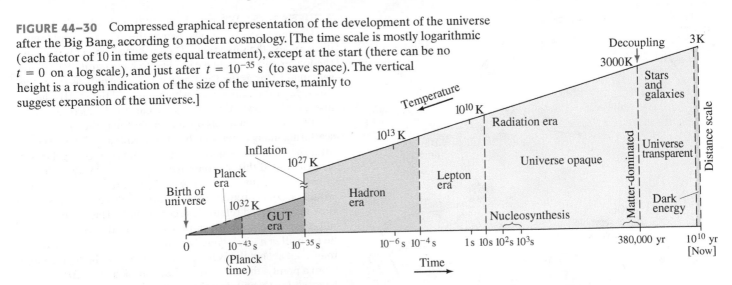

The History

We begin at a time only a minuscule fraction of a second after the birth of the universe, 10^{-43} s. This time is sometimes referred to as the **Planck time**, which is a value determined by the fundamental constants. It is related to the *Planck length* λ_P which we obtained in Chapter 1 (Example 1–10) by dimensional analysis: $\lambda_P = \sqrt{Gh/c^3} \approx 4 \times 10^{-35}$ m. The Planck time is the time it takes light to travel the Planck length: $t_P = \lambda_P/c \approx (4 \times 10^{-35} \text{ m})/(3 \times 10^8 \text{ m/s}) \approx 10^{-43}$ s. This is an unimaginably short time, and predictions can be only speculative. Earlier, we can say nothing because we do not have a theory of quantum gravity which would be needed for the incredibly high densities and temperatures during this "Planck era." It is thought that, perhaps as early as 10^{-43} s, the four forces in nature were unified—there was only one force (Chapter 43, Fig. 43–19). The temperature would have been about 10^{32} K, corresponding to randomly moving particles with an average kinetic energy K of 10^{19} GeV (see Eq. 18–4):

$$K \approx kT \approx \frac{(1.4 \times 10^{-23} \text{ J/K})(10^{32} \text{ K})}{1.6 \times 10^{-19} \text{ J/eV}} \approx 10^{28} \text{ eV} = 10^{19} \text{ GeV}.$$

(Note that the factor $\frac{3}{2}$ in Eq. 18–4 is usually ignored in such order of magnitude calculations.) At $t = 10^{-43}$ s, a kind of "phase transition" is believed to have occurred during which the gravitational force, in effect, "condensed out" as a separate force. This, and subsequent phase transitions, are analogous to the phase transitions water undergoes as it cools from a gas, condenses into a liquid, and with further cooling freezes into ice.† The *symmetry* of the four forces was broken, but the strong, weak, and electromagnetic forces were still unified, and the universe entered the **grand unified era** (GUT—see Chapter 43). There was no distinction between quarks and leptons; baryon and lepton numbers were not conserved. Very shortly thereafter, as the universe expanded considerably and the temperature had dropped to about 10^{27} K, there was another phase transition and the strong force condensed out at about 10^{-35} s after the Big Bang. Now the universe was filled with a "soup" of leptons and quarks. The quarks were initially free, but soon began to "condense" into more normal particles: nucleons and the other hadrons and their antiparticles. With this **confinement of quarks**, the universe entered the **hadron era**.

About this time, when the universe was only 10^{-35} s old, a strange thing may have happened, according to theorists. A brilliant idea, proposed around 1980, suggests that the universe underwent an incredible exponential expansion, increasing in size by a factor of 10^{40} or maybe much more, in a tiny fraction of a second, perhaps 10^{-35} s. The usefulness of this **inflationary scenario** is that it solved major problems with earlier Big Bang models, such as explaining why the universe is flat, as well as the thermal equilibrium to provide the nearly uniform CMB, as discussed below.

After the very brief inflationary period, the universe would have settled back into its more regular expansion. The universe was now a "soup" of leptons and hadrons. We can think of this "soup" as a plasma of particles and antiparticles, as well as photons—all in roughly equal numbers—colliding with one another frequently and exchanging energy.

By the time the universe was only about a microsecond (10^{-6} s) old, it had cooled to about 10^{13} K, corresponding to an average kinetic energy of 1 GeV, and the vast majority of hadrons disappeared. To see why, let us focus on the most familiar hadrons: nucleons and their antiparticles. When the average kinetic energy of particles was somewhat higher than 1 GeV, protons, neutrons, and their antiparticles were continually being created out of the energies of collisions involving photons and other particles, such as

$$\text{photons} \rightarrow \text{p} + \bar{\text{p}}$$
$$\rightarrow \text{n} + \bar{\text{n}}.$$

But just as quickly, particles and antiparticles would annihilate: for example

$$\text{p} + \bar{\text{p}} \rightarrow \text{photons or leptons.}$$

So the processes of creation and annihilation of nucleons were in equilibrium. The numbers of nucleons and antinucleons were high—roughly as many as there were electrons, positrons, or photons. But as the universe expanded and cooled, and the average kinetic energy of particles dropped below about 1 GeV, which is the minimum energy needed in a typical collision to create nucleons and antinucleons (about 940 MeV each), the process of nucleon creation could not continue. The process of annihilation could continue, however, with antinucleons annihilating nucleons, until there were almost no nucleons left. But not quite zero. Somehow we need to explain our present world of matter (nucleons and electrons) with very little antimatter in sight.

† It may be interesting to note that our story of origins here bears some resemblance to ancient accounts that mention the "void," "formless wasteland" (or "darkness over the deep"), "abyss," "divide the waters" (possibly a phase transition?), not to mention the sudden appearance of light.

To explain our world of matter, we might suppose that earlier in the universe, perhaps around 10^{-35} s after the Big Bang, a slight excess of quarks over antiquarks was formed.[†] This would have resulted in a slight excess of nucleons over antinucleons. And it is these "leftover" nucleons that we are made of today. The excess of nucleons over antinucleons was probably about one part in 10^9. During the hadron era, there should have been about as many nucleons as photons. After it ended, the "leftover" nucleons thus numbered only about one nucleon per 10^9 photons, and this ratio has persisted to this day. Protons, neutrons, and all other heavier particles were thus tremendously reduced in number by about 10^{-6} s after the Big Bang. The lightest hadrons, the pions, soon disappeared, about 10^{-4} s after the Big Bang; because they are the lightest mass hadrons (140 MeV), they were the last hadrons to be able to be created as the temperature (and average kinetic energy) dropped. Lighter particles, including electrons and neutrinos, were the dominant form of matter, and the universe entered the **lepton era**.

By the time the first full second had passed (clearly the most eventful second in history!), the universe had cooled to about 10 billion degrees, 10^{10} K. The average kinetic energy was about 1 MeV. This was still sufficient energy to create electrons and positrons and balance their annihilation reactions, since their masses correspond to about 0.5 MeV. So there were about as many e^+ and e^- as there were photons. But within a few more seconds, the temperature had dropped sufficiently so that e^+ and e^- could no longer be formed. Annihilation $(e^+ + e^- \rightarrow$ photons) continued. And, like nucleons before them, electrons and positrons all but disappeared from the universe—except for a slight excess of electrons over positrons (later to join with nuclei to form atoms). Thus, about $t = 10$ s after the Big Bang, the universe entered the **radiation era** (Fig. 44–30). Its major constituents were photons and neutrinos. But the neutrinos, partaking only in the weak force, rarely interacted. So the universe, until then experiencing significant amounts of energy in matter and in radiation, now became **radiation-dominated**: much more energy was contained in radiation than in matter, a situation that would last more than 50,000 years.

FIGURE 44–30 (Repeated.) Compressed graphical representation of the development of the universe after the Big Bang, according to modern cosmology.

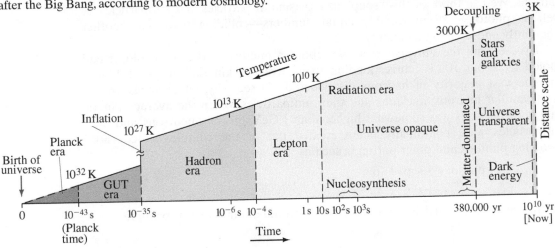

Meanwhile, during the next few minutes, crucial events were taking place. Beginning about 2 or 3 minutes after the Big Bang, nuclear fusion began to occur. The temperature had dropped to about 10^9 K, corresponding to an average kinetic energy $\bar{K} \approx 100$ keV, where nucleons could strike each other and be able to fuse (Section 42–4), but now cool enough so newly formed nuclei would not be immediately broken apart by subsequent collisions. Deuterium, helium, and very tiny amounts of lithium nuclei were made. But the universe was cooling too quickly, and larger nuclei were not made. After only a few minutes, probably not even a quarter of an hour after the Big Bang, the temperature dropped far enough that nucleosynthesis stopped, not to start again for millions of years (in stars).

[†]Why this could have happened is a question for which we are seeking an answer today.

Thus, after the first quarter hour or so of the universe, matter consisted mainly of bare nuclei of hydrogen (about 75%) and helium (about 25%)[†] and electrons. But radiation (photons) continued to dominate.

Our story is almost complete. The next important event is thought to have occurred 380,000 years later. The universe had expanded to about $\frac{1}{1000}$ of its present scale, and the temperature had cooled to about 3000 K. The average kinetic energy of nuclei, electrons, and photons was less than an electron volt. Since ionization energies of atoms are on the order of eV, then as the temperature dropped below this point, electrons could orbit the bare nuclei and remain there (without being ejected by collisions), thus forming atoms. This period is often called the **recombination** epoch (a misnomer since electrons had never before been combined with nuclei to form atoms). With the disappearance of free electrons and the birth of atoms, the photons—which had been continually scattering from the free electrons—now became free to spread throughout the universe. As mentioned in the previous Section, we say that the photons became **decoupled** from matter. Thus *decoupling* occurred at *recombination*. The total energy contained in radiation had been decreasing (lengthening in wavelength as the universe expanded); and at about $t = 56,000\,\text{yr}$ (even before decoupling) the total energy contained in matter became dominant over radiation. The universe was said to have become **matter-dominated** (marked on Fig. 44–30). As the universe continued to expand, the electromagnetic radiation cooled further, to 2.7 K today, forming the cosmic microwave background radiation we detect from everywhere in the universe.

After the birth of atoms, then stars and galaxies could begin to form: by self-gravitation around mass concentrations (inhomogeneities). Stars began to form about 200 million years after the Big Bang, galaxies after almost 10^9 years. The universe continued to evolve until today, some 14 billion years after it started.

* * *

This scenario, like other scientific models, cannot be said to be "proven." Yet this model is remarkably effective in explaining the evolution of the universe we live in, and makes predictions which can be tested against the next generation of observations.

A major event, and something only discovered very recently, is that when the universe was more than half as old as it is now (about 5 Gyr ago), its expansion began to accelerate. This was a big surprise because it was assumed the expansion of the universe would slow down due to gravitational attraction of all objects towards each other. Another major recent discovery is that ordinary matter makes up very little of the total mass–energy of the universe ($\approx 5\%$). Instead, as we discuss in Section 44–9, the major contributors to the energy density of the universe are *dark matter* and *dark energy*. On the right in Fig. 44–30 is a narrow vertical strip that represents the most recent 5 billion years of the universe, during which *dark energy* seems to have dominated.

44–8 Inflation: Explaining Flatness, Uniformity, and Structure

The idea that the universe underwent a period of exponential inflation early in its life, expanding by a factor of 10^{40} or more (previous Section), was first put forth by Alan Guth in 1981. Many more sophisticated models have since been proposed. The energy required for this wild expansion may have been released when the electroweak force separated from the strong force (end of GUT era, Fig. 43–19). So far, the evidence for inflation is indirect; yet it is a feature of most viable cosmological models because it is able to provide natural explanations for several remarkable features of our universe.

[†]This Standard Model prediction of a 25% primordial production of helium agrees with what we observe today—the universe *does* contain about 25% He—and it is strong evidence in support of the Standard Big Bang Model. Furthermore, the theory says that 25% He abundance is fully consistent with there being three neutrino types, which is the number we observe. And it sets an upper limit of four to the maximum number of possible neutrino types. This is a striking example of the exciting interface between particle physics and cosmology.

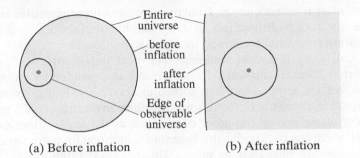

FIGURE 44–31 (a) Simple 2-D model of the entire universe; the observable universe is suggested by the small circle centered on us (blue dot). (b) Edge of universe is essentially flat after the 10^{40}–fold expansion during inflation.

(a) Before inflation   (b) After inflation

Flatness

First of all, our best measurements suggest that the universe is flat, that it has zero curvature. As scientists, we would like some reason for this remarkable result. To see how inflation explains flatness, let us consider a simple 2-dimensional model of the universe (as we did earlier in Figs. 44–16 and 44–21). A circle in this 2-dimensional universe (= surface of a sphere, Fig. 44–31a) represents the *observable* universe as seen by an observer at the circle's center. A possible hypothesis is that inflation occurred over a time interval that very roughly doubled the age of the universe, from let us say, $t = 1 \times 10^{-35}$ s to $t = 2 \times 10^{-35}$ s. The size of the observable universe ($r = ct$) would have increased by a factor of two during inflation, while the radius of curvature of the entire universe increased by an enormous factor of 10^{40} or more. Thus the edge of our 2-D sphere representing the entire universe would have seemed flat to a high degree of precision, Fig. 44–31b. Even if the time of inflation was a factor of 10 or 100 (instead of 2), the expansion factor of 10^{40} or more would have blotted out any possibility of observing anything but a flat universe.

CMB Uniformity

Inflation also explains why the CMB is so uniform. Without inflation, the tiny universe at 10^{-35} s was too large for all parts of it to have been in contact so as to reach the same temperature (information cannot travel faster than c). Imagine a universe about 1 cm in diameter at $t = 10^{-36}$ s, as per original Big Bang theory. In that 10^{-36} s, light could have traveled $d = ct = (3 \times 10^8 \text{ m/s})(10^{-36} \text{ s}) = 10^{-27}$ m, way too small for opposite sides of a 1-cm-wide universe to have been in communication. But if the universe had been 10^{40} times smaller ($= 10^{-42}$ m), as proposed by the inflation model, there could have been contact and thermal equilibrium to produce the observed nearly uniform CMB. Inflation, by making the early universe very small, assures that all parts could have been in thermal equilibrium; and after inflation the universe could be large enough to give us today's observable universe.

Galaxy Seeds, Fluctuations, Magnetic Monopoles

Inflation also gives us a clue as to how the present structure of the universe (galaxies and clusters of galaxies) came about. We saw earlier that, according to the uncertainty principle, energy may not be conserved by an amount ΔE for a time $\Delta t \approx \hbar/\Delta E$. Forces, whether electromagnetic or other types, can undergo such tiny **quantum fluctuations** according to quantum theory, but they are so tiny they are not detectable unless magnified in some way. That is what inflation might have done: it could have magnified those fluctuations perhaps 10^{40} times in size, which would give us the density irregularities seen in the cosmic microwave background (WMAP, Fig. 44–27). That would be very nice, because the density variations we see in the CMB are what we believe were the seeds that later coalesced under gravity into galaxies and galaxy clusters, including their substructures (stars and planets), and our models fit the data extremely well.

Sometimes it is said that the quantum fluctuations occurred in the **vacuum state** or vacuum energy. This could be possible because the vacuum is no longer considered to be empty, as we discussed in Section 43–3 relative to positrons and a negative energy sea of electrons. Indeed, the vacuum is thought to be filled with fields and particles occupying all the possible negative energy states. Also, the virtual exchange particles that carry the forces, as discussed in Chapter 43, could leave their brief virtual states and actually become real as a result of the 10^{40} magnification of space (according to inflation) and the very short time over which it occurred ($\Delta t = \hbar/\Delta E$).

Inflation helps us too with the puzzle of why **magnetic monopoles** have never been observed, yet isolated magnetic poles may well have been copiously produced at the start. After inflation, they would have been so far apart that we have never stumbled on one.

Some theorists have proposed that inflation may not have occurred in the entire universe. Perhaps only some regions of that tiny early universe became unstable (maybe it was a quantum fluctuation) and inflated into cosmic "bubbles." If so, we would be living in one of the bubbles. The universe outside the bubble would be hopelessly **unobservable** to us.

Inflation may solve outstanding problems, but it needs to be confirmed and we may need new physics just to understand how inflation occurred.

44–9 Dark Matter and Dark Energy

According to the Standard Big Bang Model, the universe is evolving and changing. Individual stars are being created, evolving, and then dying to become white dwarfs, neutron stars, black holes. At the same time, the universe as a whole is expanding. One important question is whether the universe will continue to expand forever. Until the late 1990s, the universe was thought to be dominated by matter which interacts by gravity, and this question was connected to the curvature of space-time (Section 44–4). If the universe had *negative* curvature, the expansion of the universe would never stop, although the rate of expansion would decrease due to the gravitational attraction of its parts. Such a universe would be *open* and infinite. If the universe is *flat* (no curvature), it would still be open and infinite but its expansion would slowly approach a zero rate. Finally, if the universe had *positive* curvature, it would be *closed* and finite; the effect of gravity would be strong enough that the expansion would eventually stop and the universe would begin to contract, collapsing back onto itself in a **big crunch**.

| **EXERCISE E** Return to the Chapter-Opening Question, page 1193, and answer it again. Try to explain why you may have answered differently the first time.

Critical Density

According to the above scenario (which does not include inflation or the recently discovered acceleration of the universe), the fate of the universe would depend on the average mass–energy density in the universe. For an average mass density greater than a critical value known as the **critical density**, estimated to be about

$$\rho_c \approx 10^{-26} \, \text{kg/m}^3$$

(i.e., a few nucleons/m^3 on average throughout the universe), gravity would prevent expansion from continuing forever. Eventually (if $\rho > \rho_c$) gravity would pull the universe back into a big crunch and space-time would have a positive curvature. If instead the actual density was equal to the critical density, $\rho = \rho_c$, the universe would be flat and open. If the actual density was less than the critical density, $\rho < \rho_c$, the universe would have negative curvature. See Fig. 44–32. Today we believe the universe is very close to flat. But recent evidence suggests the universe is expanding at an *accelerating* rate, as discussed below.

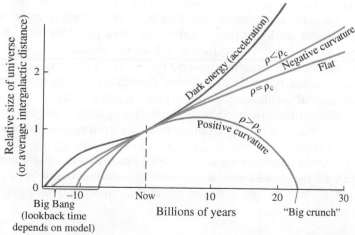

FIGURE 44–32 Three future possibilities for the universe, depending on the density ρ of ordinary matter, plus a fourth possibility that includes dark energy. Note that all curves have been chosen to have the same slope ($= H$, the Hubble parameter) right now. Looking back in time, the Big Bang occurs where each curve touches the horizontal (time) axis.

EXAMPLE 44–7 **ESTIMATE** **Critical density of the universe.** Use energy conservation and escape velocity (Section 8–7) to estimate the critical density of the universe.

APPROACH At the critical density, ρ_c, any given galaxy of mass m will just be able to "escape" away from our Galaxy. As we saw in Section 8–7, escape can just occur if the total energy E of the galaxy satisfies

$$E = K + U = \tfrac{1}{2}mv^2 - G\frac{mM}{R} = 0.$$

Here R is the distance of that galaxy m from us. We approximate the total mass M that pulls inward on m as the total mass within a sphere of radius R around us (Appendix D). If we assume the density of galaxies is roughly constant, then $M = \tfrac{4}{3}\pi\rho_c R^3$.

SOLUTION Substituting this M into the equation above, and setting $v = HR$ (Hubble's law, Eq. 44–4), we obtain

$$\frac{GM}{R} = \tfrac{1}{2}v^2$$

or

$$\frac{G(\tfrac{4}{3}\pi\rho_c R^3)}{R} = \tfrac{1}{2}(HR)^2.$$

We solve for ρ_c:

$$\rho_c = \frac{3H^2}{8\pi G} \approx \frac{3[(22\,\text{km/s/Mly})(1\,\text{Mly}/10^{19}\,\text{km})]^2}{8(3.14)(6.67\times10^{-11}\,\text{N}\cdot\text{m}^2/\text{kg}^2)} \approx 10^{-26}\,\text{kg/m}^3.$$

Dark Matter

WMAP and other experiments have convinced scientists that the universe is flat and $\rho = \rho_c$. But this ρ cannot be only normal baryonic matter (atoms are 99.9% baryons—protons and neutrons—by weight). These recent experiments put the amount of normal baryonic matter in the universe at only about 5% of the critical density. What is the other 95%? There is strong evidence for a significant amount of nonluminous matter in the universe referred to as **dark matter**, which acts normally under gravity, but does not absorb or radiate light. For example, observations of the rotation of galaxies suggest that they rotate as if they had considerably more mass than we can see. Recall from Chapter 6, Eq. 6–5, that for a satellite of mass m revolving around Earth (mass M)

$$m\frac{v^2}{r} = G\frac{mM}{r^2}$$

and hence $v = \sqrt{GM/r}$. If we apply this equation to stars in a galaxy, we see that their speed depends on galactic mass. Observations show that stars farther from the galactic center revolve much faster than expected if there is only the pull of visible matter, suggesting a great deal of invisible matter. Similarly, observations of the motion of galaxies within clusters also suggest that they have considerably more mass than can be seen. Without dark matter, galaxies and stars probably would not have formed and would not exist; it would seem to hold the universe together. But what might this nonluminous matter in the universe be? We don't know yet. But we hope to find out soon. It cannot be made of ordinary (baryonic) matter, so it must consist of some other sort of elementary particle, perhaps created at a very early time. Perhaps it is a supersymmetric particle (Section 43–12), maybe the lightest one. We are anxiously awaiting details both from particle accelerators and the cosmos.

Dark matter makes up about 20% of the mass–energy of the universe, according to the latest observations and models. Thus the total mass–energy is 20% dark matter plus 5% baryons for a total of about 25%, which does not bring ρ up to ρ_c. What is the other 75%? We are not sure about that either, but we have given it a name: "dark energy."

Dark Energy—Cosmic Acceleration

In 1998, just before the turn of the millennium, cosmologists received a huge surprise. Gravity was assumed to be the predominant force on a large scale in the universe, and it was thought that the expansion of the universe ought to be slowing down in time because gravity acts as an attractive force between objects. But measurements of type Ia supernovae (SNIa, our best standard candles—see Section 44–3) unexpectedly showed that very distant (high z) SNIa's were dimmer than expected. That is, given their great distance d as determined from their low brightness, their speed v as determined from the measured z was less than expected according to Hubble's law. This result suggests that nearer galaxies are moving away from us relatively faster than those very distant ones, meaning the expansion of the universe in more recent epochs has sped up. This **acceleration** in the expansion of the universe (in place of the expected deceleration due to gravitational attraction between masses) seems to have begun roughly 5 billion years ago (5 Gyr, which would be 8 to 9 Gyr after the Big Bang).

What could be causing the universe to accelerate in its expansion, against the attractive force of gravity? Does our understanding of gravity need to be revised? We don't know the answers to these questions. Many scientists say dark energy is the biggest mystery facing physical science today. There are several speculations. But somehow it seems to have a long-range *repulsive* effect on space, like a negative gravity, causing objects to speed away from each other ever faster. Whatever it is, it has been given the name **dark energy**.

One idea is a sort of quantum field given the name **quintessence**. Another possibility suggests an energy latent in space itself (**vacuum energy**) and relates to an aspect of General Relativity known as the **cosmological constant** (symbol Λ). When Einstein developed his equations, he found that they offered no solutions for a static universe. In those days (1917) it was thought the universe was static—unchanging and everlasting. Einstein added an arbitrary constant to his equations to provide solutions for a static universe. A decade later, when Hubble showed us an expanding universe, Einstein discarded his cosmological constant as no longer needed ($\Lambda = 0$). But today, measurements are consistent with dark energy being due to a nonzero cosmological constant, although further measurements are needed to see subtle differences among theories.

There is increasing evidence that the effects of some form of dark energy are very real. Observations of the CMB, supernovae, and large-scale structure (Section 44–10) agree well with theories and computer models when they input dark energy as providing 75% of the mass–energy in the universe, and when the total mass–energy density equals the critical density ρ_c.

Today's best estimate of how the mass–energy in the universe is distributed is approximately (Fig. 44–33):

75% dark energy

25% matter, subject to the known gravitational force.

    Of this 25%, about

20% is dark matter

    5% is baryons (what atoms are made of); of this 5% only $\frac{1}{10}$ is readily visible matter—stars and galaxies (that is, 0.5% of the total); the other $\frac{9}{10}$ of ordinary matter, which is not visible, is mainly gaseous plasma.

It is remarkable that only 0.5% of all the mass–energy in the universe is visible as stars and galaxies.

The idea that the universe is dominated by completely unknown forms of energy seems bizarre. Nonetheless, the ability of our present model to precisely explain observations of the CMB anisotropy, cosmic expansion, and large-scale structure (next Section) presents a compelling case.

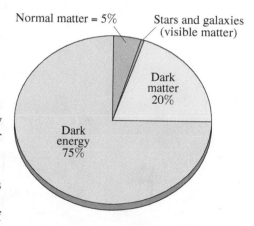

FIGURE 44–33 Portions of total mass–energy in the universe.

Normal matter = 5%

Stars and galaxies (visible matter)

Dark matter 20%

Dark energy 75%

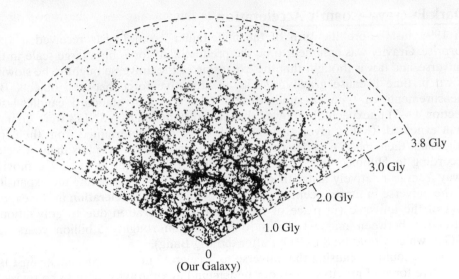

FIGURE 44–34 Distribution of some 50,000 galaxies in a 2.5° slice through almost half of the sky above the equator, as measured by the Sloan Digital Sky Survey (SDSS). Each dot represents a galaxy. The distance from us is obtained from the redshift and Hubble's law, and is given in units of 10^9 light-years (Gly). At greater distances, fewer galaxies are bright enough to be detected, thus resulting in an apparent thinning out of galaxies. The point 0 represents us, our observation point. Note the "walls" and "voids" of galaxies.

3.8 Gly
3.0 Gly
2.0 Gly
1.0 Gly
0
(Our Galaxy)

44–10 Large-Scale Structure of the Universe

The beautiful WMAP pictures of the sky (Fig. 44–27 and Chapter-Opening Photo) show small but significant inhomogeneities in the temperature of the CMB. These anisotropies reflect compressions and expansions in the primordial plasma just before decoupling, from which stars, galaxies, and clusters of galaxies formed. Analysis of the irregularities in the CMB using mammoth computer simulations predict a large-scale distribution of galaxies very similar to what is seen today (Fig. 44–34). These simulations are very successful if they contain dark energy and dark matter; and the dark matter needs to be *cold* (slow speed—think of Eq. 18–4, $\frac{1}{2}m\overline{v^2} = \frac{3}{2}kT$ where T is temperature), rather than "hot" dark matter such as neutrinos which move at or very near the speed of light. Indeed, the modern **cosmological model** is called the Λ**CDM** model, where lambda (Λ) stands for the cosmological constant, and CDM is **cold dark matter**.

Cosmologists have gained substantial confidence in this cosmological model from such a precise fit between observations and theory. They can also extract very precise values for cosmological parameters which previously were only known with low accuracy. The CMB is such an important cosmological observable that every effort is being made to extract all of the information it contains. A new generation of ground, balloon, and satellite experiments will observe the CMB with greater resolution and sensitivity. They may detect interaction of **gravity waves** (produced in the inflationary epoch) with the CMB and thereby provide direct evidence for cosmic inflation, and also provide information about elementary particle physics at energies far beyond the reach of man-made accelerators.

44–11 Finally . . .

When we look up into the night sky, we see stars; and with the best telescopes, we see galaxies and the exotic objects we discussed earlier, including rare supernovae. But even with our best instruments we do not see the processes going on inside stars and supernovae that we hypothesized (and believe). We are dependent on brilliant theorists who come up with viable theories and verifiable models. We depend on complicated computer models whose parameters are varied until the outputs compare favorably with our observations and analyses of WMAP and other experiments. And we now have a surprisingly precise idea about some aspects of our universe: it is flat, it is about 14 billion years old, it contains only 5% "normal" baryonic matter (for atoms), and so on.

The questions raised by cosmology are difficult and profound, and may seem removed from everyday "reality." We can always say, "the Sun is shining, it's going to burn on for an unimaginably long time, all is well." Nonetheless, the questions of cosmology are deep ones that fascinate the human intellect. One aspect that is especially intriguing is this: calculations on the formation and evolution of the universe have been performed that deliberately varied the values—just slightly—of certain fundamental physical constants. The result? A universe in which life as we know it could not exist. [For example, if the difference in mass between proton and neutron were zero, or small (less than the mass of the electron, $0.511 \text{ MeV}/c^2$), there would be no atoms: electrons would be captured by protons never to be freed again.] Such results have contributed to a philosophical idea called the **Anthropic principle**, which says that if the universe were even a little different than it is, we could not be here. We physicists are trying to find out if there are some undiscovered fundamental laws that determined those conditions that allowed us to exist. A poet might say that the universe is exquisitely tuned, almost as if to accommodate us.

Summary

The night sky contains myriads of stars including those in the Milky Way, which is a "side view" of our **Galaxy** looking along the plane of the disk. Our Galaxy includes over 10^{11} stars. Beyond our Galaxy are billions of other galaxies.

Astronomical distances are measured in **light-years** ($1 \text{ ly} \approx 10^{13} \text{ km}$). The nearest star is about 4 ly away and the nearest large galaxy is 2 million ly away. Our Galactic disk has a diameter of about 100,000 ly. Distances are often specified in **parsecs**, where 1 parsec = 3.26 ly.

Stars are believed to begin life as collapsing masses of gas (protostars), largely hydrogen. As they contract, they heat up (potential energy is transformed to kinetic energy). When the temperature reaches about 10 million degrees, nuclear fusion begins and forms heavier elements (**nucleosynthesis**), mainly helium at first. The energy released during these reactions heats the gas so its outward pressure balances the inward gravitational force, and the young star stabilizes as a **main-sequence** star. The tremendous luminosity of stars comes from the energy released during these thermonuclear reactions. After billions of years, as helium is collected in the core and hydrogen is used up, the core contracts and heats further. The envelope expands and cools, and the star becomes a **red giant** (larger diameter, redder color).

The next stage of stellar evolution depends on the mass of the star, which may have lost much of its original mass as its outer envelope escaped into space. Stars of residual mass less than about 1.4 solar masses cool further and become **white dwarfs**, eventually fading and going out altogether. Heavier stars contract further due to their greater gravity: the density approaches nuclear density, the huge pressure forces electrons to combine with protons to form neutrons, and the star becomes essentially a huge nucleus of neutrons. This is a **neutron star**, and the energy released from its final core collapse is believed to produce **supernova** explosions. If the star is very massive, it may contract even further and form a **black hole**, which is so dense that no matter or light can escape from it.

In the **general theory of relativity**, the **equivalence principle** states that an observer cannot distinguish acceleration from a gravitational field. Said another way, gravitational and inertial masses are the same. The theory predicts gravitational bending of light rays to a degree consistent with experiment. Gravity is treated as a curvature in space and time, the curvature being greater near massive objects. The universe as a whole may be curved. With sufficient mass, the curvature of the universe would be positive, and the universe is *closed* and *finite*; otherwise, it would be *open* and *infinite*. Today we believe the universe is **flat**.

Distant galaxies display a **redshift** in their spectral lines, originally interpreted as a Doppler shift. The universe seems to be **expanding**, its galaxies racing away from each other at speeds (v) proportional to the distance (d) between them:

$$v = Hd, \tag{44-4}$$

which is known as **Hubble's law** (H is the **Hubble parameter**). This expansion of the universe suggests an explosive origin, the **Big Bang**, which occurred about 13.7 billion years ago. It is not like an ordinary explosion, but rather an expansion of space itself.

The **cosmological principle** assumes that the universe, on a large scale, is homogeneous and isotropic.

Important evidence for the Big Bang model of the universe was the discovery of the **cosmic microwave background** radiation (CMB), which conforms to a blackbody radiation curve at a temperature of 2.725 K.

The **Standard Model** of the Big Bang provides a possible scenario as to how the universe developed as it expanded and cooled after the Big Bang. Starting at 10^{-43} seconds after the Big Bang, according to this model, there were a series of **phase transitions** during which previously unified forces of nature "condensed out" one by one. The **inflationary scenario** assumes that during one of these phase transitions, the universe underwent a brief but rapid exponential expansion. Until about 10^{-35} s, there was no distinction between quarks and leptons. Shortly thereafter, quarks were **confined** into hadrons (the **hadron era**). About 10^{-4} s after the Big Bang, the majority of hadrons disappeared, having combined with anti-hadrons, producing photons, leptons, and energy, leaving mainly photons and leptons to freely move, thus introducing the **lepton era**. By the time the universe was about 10 s old, the electrons too had mostly disappeared, having combined with their antiparticles; the universe was **radiation-dominated**. A couple of minutes later, nucleosynthesis began, but lasted only a few minutes. It then took almost four hundred thousand years before the universe was cool enough for electrons to combine with nuclei to form atoms (**recombination**). Photons, up to then continually being scattered off of free electrons, could now move freely—they were **decoupled** from matter and the universe became transparent. The background radiation had expanded and cooled so much that its total energy became less than the energy in matter, and **matter dominated** increasingly over radiation. Then stars and galaxies formed, producing a universe not much different than it is today—some 14 billion years later.

Recent observations indicate that the universe is flat, that it contains an as-yet unknown type of **dark matter**, and that it is dominated by a mysterious **dark energy** which exerts a sort of negative gravity causing the expansion of the universe to accelerate. The total contributions of baryonic (normal) matter, dark matter, and dark energy sum up to the **critical density**.

Questions

1. The Milky Way was once thought to be "murky" or "milky" but is now considered to be made up of point sources. Explain.

2. A star is in equilibrium when it radiates at its surface all the energy generated in its core. What happens when it begins to generate more energy than it radiates? Less energy? Explain.

3. Describe a red giant star. List some of its properties.

4. Select a point on the H–R diagram. Mark several directions away from this point. Now describe the changes that would take place in a star moving in each of these directions.

5. Does the H–R diagram reveal anything about the core of a star?

6. Why do some stars end up as white dwarfs, and others as neutron stars or black holes?

7. Can we tell, by looking at the population on the H–R diagram, that hotter main-sequence stars have shorter lives? Explain.

8. If you were measuring star parallaxes from the Moon instead of Earth, what corrections would you have to make? What changes would occur if you were measuring parallaxes from Mars?

9. *Cepheid variable* stars change in luminosity with a typical period of several days. The period has been found to have a definite relationship with the intrinsic luminosity of the star. How could these stars be used to measure the distance to galaxies?

10. What is a geodesic? What is its role in General Relativity?

11. If it were discovered that the redshift of spectral lines of galaxies was due to something other than expansion, how might our view of the universe change? Would there be conflicting evidence? Discuss.

12. All galaxies appear to be moving away from us. Are we therefore at the center of the universe? Explain.

13. If you were located in a galaxy near the boundary of our observable universe, would galaxies in the direction of the Milky Way appear to be approaching you or receding from you? Explain.

14. Compare an explosion on Earth to the Big Bang. Consider such questions as: Would the debris spread at a higher speed for more distant particles, as in the Big Bang? Would the debris come to rest? What type of universe would this correspond to, open or closed?

15. If nothing, not even light, escapes from a black hole, then how can we tell if one is there?

16. What mass will give a Schwarzschild radius equal to that of the hydrogen atom in its ground state?

17. The Earth's age is often given as about 4 billion years. Find that time on Fig. 44–30. People have lived on Earth on the order of a million years. Where is that on Fig. 44–30?

18. Explain what the 2.7-K cosmic microwave background radiation is. Where does it come from? Why is its temperature now so low?

19. Why were atoms, as opposed to bare nuclei, unable to exist until hundreds of thousands of years after the Big Bang?

20. (a) Why are type Ia supernovae so useful for determining the distances of galaxies? (b) How are their distances actually measured?

21. Explain why the CMB radiation should not be that of a perfect blackbody. (The deviations from a blackbody spectrum are slightly less than one part in 10^4.)

22. Under what circumstances would the universe eventually collapse in on itself?

23. When stable nuclei first formed, about 3 minutes after the Big Bang, there were about 7 times more protons than neutrons. Explain how this leads to a ratio of the mass of hydrogen to the mass of helium of 3 : 1. This is about the actual ratio observed in the universe.

24. (a) Why did astronomers expect that the expansion rate of the universe would be decreasing (decelerating) with time? (b) How, in principle, could astronomers hope to determine whether the universe used to expand faster than it does now?

Problems

44–1 to 44–3 Stars, Galaxies, Stellar Evolution, Distances

1. (I) The parallax angle of a star is 0.00029°. How far away is the star?

2. (I) A star exhibits a parallax of 0.27 seconds of arc. How far away is it?

3. (I) What is the parallax angle for a star that is 65 ly away? How many parsecs is this?

4. (I) A star is 56 pc away. What is its parallax angle? State (a) in seconds of arc, and (b) in degrees.

5. (I) If one star is twice as far away from us as a second star, will the parallax angle of the farther star be greater or less than that of the nearer star? By what factor?

6. (II) A star is 85 pc away. How long does it take for its light to reach us?

7. (II) What is the relative brightness of the Sun as seen from Jupiter, as compared to its brightness from Earth? (Jupiter is 5.2 times farther from the Sun than the Earth is.)

8. (II) We saw earlier (Chapter 19) that the rate energy reaches the Earth from the Sun (the "solar constant") is about $1.3 \times 10^3 \text{ W/m}^2$. What is (a) the apparent brightness b of the Sun, and (b) the intrinsic luminosity L of the Sun?

9. (II) When our Sun becomes a red giant, what will be its average density if it expands out to the orbit of Mercury (6×10^{10} m, from the Sun)?

10. (II) Estimate the angular width that our Galaxy would subtend if observed from the nearest galaxy to us (Table 44–1). Compare to the angular width of the Moon from Earth.

11. (II) Calculate the Q-values for the He burning reactions of Eq. 44–2. (The mass of the very unstable $^8_4$Be is 8.005305 u.)

12. (II) When our Sun becomes a white dwarf, it is expected to be about the size of the Moon. What angular width would it subtend from the present distance to Earth?

13. (II) Calculate the density of a white dwarf whose mass is equal to the Sun's and whose radius is equal to the Earth's. How many times larger than Earth's density is this?

14. (II) A neutron star whose mass is 1.5 solar masses has a radius of about 11 km. Calculate its average density and compare to that for a white dwarf (Problem 13) and to that of nuclear matter.

15. (III) Stars located in a certain cluster are assumed to be about the same distance from us. Two such stars have spectra that peak at $\lambda_1 = 470$ nm and $\lambda_2 = 720$ nm, and the ratio of their apparent brightness is $b_1/b_2 = 0.091$. Estimate their relative sizes (give ratio of their diameters) using Wien's law and the Stefan-Boltzmann equation, Eq. 19–17.

16. (III) Suppose two stars of the same apparent brightness b are also believed to be the same size. The spectrum of one star peaks at 750 nm whereas that of the other peaks at 450 nm. Use Wien's law and the Stefan-Boltzmann equation (Eq. 19–17) to estimate their relative distances from us.

44–4 General Relativity, Gravity and Curved Space

17. (I) Show that the Schwarzschild radius for a star with mass equal to that of Earth is 8.9 mm.

18. (II) What is the Schwarzschild radius for a typical galaxy (like ours)?

19. (II) What is the maximum sum-of-the-angles for a triangle on a sphere?

20. (II) Calculate the escape velocity, using Newtonian mechanics, from an object that has collapsed to its Schwarzschild radius.

21. (II) What is the apparent deflection of a light beam in an elevator (Fig. 44–13) which is 2.4 m wide if the elevator is accelerating downward at 9.8 m/s^2?

44–5 Redshift, Hubble's Law

22. (I) The redshift of a galaxy indicates a velocity of 1850 km/s. How far away is it?

23. (I) If a galaxy is traveling away from us at 1.5% of the speed of light, roughly how far away is it?

24. (II) A galaxy is moving away from Earth. The "blue" hydrogen line at 434 nm emitted from the galaxy is measured on Earth to be 455 nm. (a) How fast is the galaxy moving? (b) How far is it from Earth?

25. (II) Estimate the wavelength shift for the 656-nm line in the Balmer series of hydrogen emitted from a galaxy whose distance from us is (a) 7.0×10^6 ly, (b) 7.0×10^7 ly.

26. (II) If an absorption line of calcium is normally found at a wavelength of 393.4 nm in a laboratory gas, and you measure it to be at 423.4 nm in the spectrum of a galaxy, what is the approximate distance to the galaxy?

27. (II) What is the speed of a galaxy with $z = 0.060$?

28. (II) What would be the redshift parameter z for a galaxy traveling away from us at $v = 0.075\,c$?

29. (II) Starting from Eq. 44–3, show that the Doppler shift in wavelength is $\Delta\lambda/\lambda_{\text{rest}} \approx v/c$ (Eq. 44–6) for $v \ll c$. [Hint: Use the binomial expansion.]

30. (II) Radiotelescopes are designed to observe 21-cm waves emitted by atomic hydrogen gas. A signal from a distant radio-emitting galaxy is found to have a wavelength that is 0.10 cm longer than the normal 21-cm wavelength. Estimate the distance to this galaxy.

44–6 to 44–8 The Big Bang, CMB, Universe Expansion

31. (I) Calculate the wavelength at the peak of the blackbody radiation distribution at 2.7 K using Wien's law.

32. (II) Calculate the peak wavelength of the CMB at 1.0 s after the birth of the universe. In what part of the EM spectrum is this radiation?

33. (II) The critical density for closure of the universe is $\rho_c \approx 10^{-26}$ kg/m^3. State ρ_c in terms of the average number of nucleons per cubic meter.

34. (II) The scale factor of the universe (average distance between galaxies) at any given time is believed to have been inversely proportional to the absolute temperature. Estimate the size of the universe, compared to today, at (a) $t = 10^6$ yr, (b) $t = 1$ s, (c) $t = 10^{-6}$ s, and (d) $t = 10^{-35}$ s.

35. (II) At approximately what time had the universe cooled below the threshold temperature for producing (a) kaons ($M \approx 500$ MeV/c^2), (b) Υ ($M \approx 9500$ MeV/c^2), and (c) muons ($M \approx 100$ MeV/c^2)?

44–9 Dark Matter, Dark Energy

36. (II) Only about 5% of the energy in the universe is composed of baryonic matter. (a) Estimate the average density of baryonic matter in the observable universe with a radius of 14 billion light-years that contains 10^{11} galaxies, each with about 10^{11} stars like our Sun. (b) Estimate the density of dark matter in the universe.

General Problems

37. The evolution of stars, as discussed in Section 44–2, can lead to a white dwarf, a neutron star, or even a black hole, depending on the mass. (a) Referring to Sections 44–2 and 44–4, give the radius of (i) a white dwarf of 1 solar mass, (ii) a neutron star of 1.5 solar masses, and (iii) a black hole of 3 solar masses. (b) Express these three radii as ratios $(r_i : r_{ii} : r_{iii})$.

38. Use conservation of angular momentum to estimate the angular velocity of a neutron star which has collapsed to a diameter of 16 km, from a star whose radius was equal to that of our Sun $(7 \times 10^8$ m). Assume its mass is 1.5 times that of the Sun, and that it rotated (like our Sun) about once a month.

39. By what factor does the rotational kinetic energy change when the star in Problem 38 collapses to a neutron star?

40. Assume that the nearest stars to us have an intrinsic luminosity about the same as the Sun's. Their apparent brightness, however, is about 10^{11} times fainter than the Sun. From this, estimate the distance to the nearest stars. (Newton did this calculation, although he made a numerical error of a factor of 100.)

41. Suppose that three main-sequence stars could undergo the three changes represented by the three arrows, A, B, and C, in the H–R diagram of Fig. 44–35. For each case, describe the changes in temperature, intrinsic luminosity, and size.

FIGURE 44–35 Problem 41.

42. A certain pulsar, believed to be a neutron star of mass 1.5 times that of the Sun, with diameter 16 km, is observed to have a rotation speed of 1.0 rev/s. If it loses rotational kinetic energy at the rate of 1 part in 10^9 per day, which is all transformed into radiation, what is the power output of the star?

43. The nearest large galaxy to our Galaxy is about 2×10^6 ly away. If both galaxies have a mass of 3×10^{41} kg, with what gravitational force does each galaxy attract the other?

44. Estimate what neutrino mass (in eV/c^2) would provide the critical density to close the universe. Assume the neutrino density is, like photons, about 10^9 times that of nucleons, and that nucleons make up only (a) 2% of the mass needed, or (b) 5% of the mass needed.

45. Two stars, whose spectra peak at 660 nm and 480 nm, respectively, both lie on the main sequence. Use Wien's law, the Stefan-Boltzmann equation, and the H–R diagram (Fig. 44–6) to estimate the ratio of their diameters.

46. (a) In order to measure distances with parallax at 100 parsecs, what minimum angular resolution (in degrees) is needed? (b) What diameter mirror or lens would be needed?

47. What is the temperature that corresponds to 1.96-TeV collisions at the Fermilab collider? To what era in cosmological history does this correspond? [Hint: See Fig. 44–30.]

48. Astronomers have measured the rotation of gas around a possible supermassive black hole of about 2 billion solar masses at the center of a galaxy. If the radius from the galactic center to the gas clouds is 68 light-years, estimate the value of z.

49. In the later stages of stellar evolution, a star (if massive enough) will begin fusing carbon nuclei to form, for example, magnesium:

$$^{12}_{6}C + ^{12}_{6}C \rightarrow ^{24}_{12}Mg + \gamma.$$

(a) How much energy is released in this reaction (see Appendix F)? (b) How much kinetic energy must each carbon nucleus have (assume equal) in a head-on collision if they are just to "touch" (use Eq. 41–1) so that the strong force can come into play? (c) What temperature does this kinetic energy correspond to?

50. Consider the reaction

$$^{16}_{8}O + ^{16}_{8}O \rightarrow ^{28}_{14}Si + ^{4}_{2}He,$$

and answer the same questions as in Problem 49.

51. Calculate the Schwarzschild radius using a semi-classical (Newtonian) gravitational theory, by calculating the minimum radius R for a sphere of mass M such that a photon can escape from the surface. (General Relativity gives $R = 2GM/c^2$.)

52. How large would the Sun be if its density equaled the critical density of the universe, $\rho_c \approx 10^{-26}$ kg/m³? Express your answer in light-years and compare with the Earth–Sun distance and the diameter of our Galaxy.

53. The Large Hadron Collider in Geneva, Switzerland, can collide two beams of protons at an energy of 14 TeV. Estimate the time after the Big Bang probed by this energy.

54. (a) Use special relativity and Newton's law of gravitation to show that a photon of mass $m = E/c^2$ just grazing the Sun will be deflected by an angle $\Delta\theta$ given by

$$\Delta\theta = \frac{2GM}{c^2 R}$$

where G is the gravitational constant, R and M are the radius and mass of the Sun, and c is the speed of light. (b) Put in values and show $\Delta\theta = 0.87''$. (General Relativity predicts an angle twice as large, $1.74''$.)

55. Astronomers use an **apparent magnitude** (m) scale to describe apparent brightness. It uses a logarithmic scale, where a higher number corresponds to a less bright star. (For example, the Sun has magnitude -27, whereas most stars have positive magnitudes.) On this scale, a change in apparent magnitude by $+5$ corresponds to a decrease in apparent brightness by a factor of 100. If Venus has an apparent magnitude of -4.4, whereas Sirius has an apparent magnitude of -1.4, which is brighter? What is the ratio of the apparent brightness of these two objects?

56. Estimate the radius of a white dwarf whose mass is equal to that of the Sun by the following method, assuming there are N nucleons and $\frac{1}{2}N$ electrons (why $\frac{1}{2}$?): (a) Use Fermi-Dirac statistics (Section 40–6) to show that the total energy of all the electrons is

$$E_e = \frac{3}{5}\left(\frac{1}{2}N\right)\frac{h^2}{8m_e}\left(\frac{3}{\pi}\frac{N}{2V}\right)^{\frac{2}{3}}.$$

[Hint: See Eqs. 40–12 and 40–13; we assume electrons fill energy levels from 0 up to the Fermi energy.] (b) The nucleons contribute to the total energy mainly via the gravitational force (note that the Fermi energy for nucleons is negligible compared to that for electrons—why?). Use a gravitational form of Gauss's law to show that the total gravitational potential energy of a uniform sphere of radius R is

$$-\frac{3}{5}\frac{GM^2}{R},$$

by considering the potential energy of a spherical shell of radius r due only to the mass inside it (why?) and integrate from $r = 0$ to $r = R$. (See also Appendix D.) (c) Write the total energy as a sum of these two terms, and set $dE/dR = 0$ to find the equilibrium radius, and evaluate it for a mass equal to the Sun's $(2.0 \times 10^{30}$ kg).

57. Determine the radius of a neutron star using the same argument as in Problem 56 but for N neutrons only. Show that the radius of a neutron star, of 1.5 solar masses, is about 11 km.

58. Use *dimensional analysis* with the fundamental constants c, G, and $\hbar$ to estimate the value of the so-called *Planck time*. It is thought that physics as we know it can say nothing about the universe before this time.

Answers to Exercises

A: Ourselves, 2 years ago.

B: 600 ly (estimating L from Fig. 44–6 as $L \approx 8 \times 10^{26}$ W; note that on a log scale, 6000 K is closer to 7000 K than it is to 5000 K).

C: 6 km.

D: (a); not the usual R^3, but R: see formula for the Schwarzschild radius.

E: (c).

Mathematical Formulas

A–1 Quadratic Formula

If
$$ax^2 + bx + c = 0$$

then
$$x = \frac{-b \pm \sqrt{b^2 - 4ac}}{2a}$$

A–2 Binomial Expansion

$$(1 \pm x)^n = 1 \pm nx + \frac{n(n-1)}{2!}x^2 \pm \frac{n(n-1)(n-2)}{3!}x^3 + \cdots$$

$$(x + y)^n = x^n\left(1 + \frac{y}{x}\right)^n = x^n\left(1 + n\frac{y}{x} + \frac{n(n-1)}{2!}\frac{y^2}{x^2} + \cdots\right)$$

A–3 Other Expansions

$$e^x = 1 + x + \frac{x^2}{2!} + \frac{x^3}{3!} + \cdots$$

$$\ln(1 + x) = x - \frac{x^2}{2} + \frac{x^3}{3} - \frac{x^4}{4} + \cdots$$

$$\sin \theta = \theta - \frac{\theta^3}{3!} + \frac{\theta^5}{5!} - \cdots$$

$$\cos \theta = 1 - \frac{\theta^2}{2!} + \frac{\theta^4}{4!} - \cdots$$

$$\tan \theta = \theta + \frac{\theta^3}{3} + \frac{2}{15}\theta^5 + \cdots \qquad |\theta| < \frac{\pi}{2}$$

In general:
$$f(x) = f(0) + \left(\frac{df}{dx}\right)_0 x + \left(\frac{d^2f}{dx^2}\right)_0 \frac{x^2}{2!} + \cdots$$

A–4 Exponents

$$(a^n)(a^m) = a^{n+m}$$
$$(a^n)(b^n) = (ab)^n$$
$$(a^n)^m = a^{nm}$$

$$\frac{1}{a^n} = a^{-n}$$
$$a^n a^{-n} = a^0 = 1$$
$$a^{\frac{1}{2}} = \sqrt{a}$$

A–5 Areas and Volumes

Object	Surface area	Volume
Circle, radius r	πr^2	—
Sphere, radius r	$4\pi r^2$	$\frac{4}{3}\pi r^3$
Right circular cylinder, radius r, height h	$2\pi r^2 + 2\pi r h$	$\pi r^2 h$
Right circular cone, radius r, height h	$\pi r^2 + \pi r\sqrt{r^2 + h^2}$	$\frac{1}{3}\pi r^2 h$

A–6 Plane Geometry

1. *Equal angles:*

FIGURE A–1 If line a_1 is parallel to line a_2, then $\theta_1 = \theta_2$.

2. *Equal angles:*

FIGURE A–2 If $a_1 \perp a_2$ and $b_1 \perp b_2$, then $\theta_1 = \theta_2$.

3. The sum of the angles in any plane triangle is 180°.

4. *Pythagorean theorem:*

FIGURE A–3

In any right triangle (one angle = 90°) of sides a, b, and c:

$$a^2 + b^2 = c^2$$

where c is the length of the hypotenuse (opposite the 90° angle).

5. *Similar triangles:* Two triangles are said to be similar if all three of their angles are equal (in Fig. A–4, $\theta_1 = \phi_1$, $\theta_2 = \phi_2$, and $\theta_3 = \phi_3$). Similar triangles can have different sizes and different orientations.

(*a*) Two triangles are similar if any two of their angles are equal. (This follows because the third angles must also be equal since the sum of the angles of a triangle is 180°.)

(*b*) The ratios of corresponding sides of two similar triangles are equal (Fig. A–4):

$$\frac{a_1}{b_1} = \frac{a_2}{b_2} = \frac{a_3}{b_3}.$$

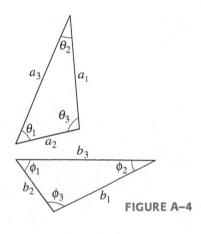

FIGURE A–4

6. *Congruent triangles:* Two triangles are congruent if one can be placed precisely on top of the other. That is, they are similar triangles and they have the same size. Two triangles are congruent if any of the following holds:

(*a*) The three corresponding sides are equal.

(*b*) Two sides and the enclosed angle are equal ("side-angle-side").

(*c*) Two angles and the enclosed side are equal ("angle-side-angle").

A–7 Logarithms

Logarithms are defined in the following way:

$$\text{if} \quad y = A^x, \quad \text{then} \quad x = \log_A y.$$

That is, the logarithm of a number y to the base A is that number which, as the exponent of A, gives back the number y. For **common logarithms**, the base is 10, so

$$\text{if} \quad y = 10^x, \quad \text{then} \quad x = \log y.$$

The subscript 10 on $\log_{10}$ is usually omitted when dealing with common logs. Another important base is the exponential base $e = 2.718\ldots$, a natural number. Such logarithms are called **natural logarithms** and are written ln. Thus,

$$\text{if} \quad y = e^x, \quad \text{then} \quad x = \ln y.$$

For any number y, the two types of logarithm are related by

$$\ln y = 2.3026 \log y.$$

Some simple rules for logarithms are as follows:

$$\log(ab) = \log a + \log b, \tag{i}$$

which is true because if $a = 10^n$ and $b = 10^m$, then $ab = 10^{n+m}$. From the definition of logarithm, $\log a = n$, $\log b = m$, and $\log(ab) = n + m$; hence, $\log(ab) = n + m = \log a + \log b$. In a similar way, we can show that

$$\log\left(\frac{a}{b}\right) = \log a - \log b \qquad \textbf{(ii)}$$

and

$$\log a^n = n \log a. \qquad \textbf{(iii)}$$

These three rules apply to any kind of logarithm.

If you do not have a calculator that calculates logs, you can easily use a **log table**, such as the small one shown here (Table A–1): the number N whose log we want is given to two digits. The first digit is in the vertical column to the left, the second digit is in the horizontal row across the top. For example, Table A–1 tells us that $\log 1.0 = 0.000$, $\log 1.1 = 0.041$, and $\log 4.1 = 0.613$. Table A–1 does not include the decimal point. The Table gives logs for numbers between 1.0 and 9.9. For larger or smaller numbers, we use rule (i) above, $\log(ab) = \log a + \log b$. For example, $\log(380) = \log(3.8 \times 10^2) = \log(3.8) + \log(10^2)$. From the Table, $\log 3.8 = 0.580$; and from rule (iii) above $\log(10^2) = 2 \log(10) = 2$, since $\log(10) = 1$. [This follows from the definition of the logarithm: if $10 = 10^1$, then $1 = \log(10)$.] Thus,

$$\begin{aligned}
\log(380) &= \log(3.8) + \log(10^2) \\
&= 0.580 + 2 \\
&= 2.580.
\end{aligned}$$

Similarly,

$$\begin{aligned}
\log(0.081) &= \log(8.1) + \log(10^{-2}) \\
&= 0.908 - 2 = -1.092.
\end{aligned}$$

The reverse process of finding the number N whose log is, say, 2.670, is called "taking the **antilogarithm**." To do so, we separate our number 2.670 into two parts, making the separation at the decimal point:

$$\begin{aligned}
\log N &= 2.670 = 2 + 0.670 \\
&= \log 10^2 + 0.670.
\end{aligned}$$

We now look at Table A–1 to see what number has its log equal to 0.670; none does, so we must **interpolate**: we see that $\log 4.6 = 0.663$ and $\log 4.7 = 0.672$. So the number we want is between 4.6 and 4.7, and closer to the latter by $\frac{7}{9}$. Approximately we can say that $\log 4.68 = 0.670$. Thus

$$\begin{aligned}
\log N &= 2 + 0.670 \\
&= \log(10^2) + \log(4.68) = \log(4.68 \times 10^2),
\end{aligned}$$

so $N = 4.68 \times 10^2 = 468$.

If the given logarithm is negative, say, -2.180, we proceed as follows:

$$\begin{aligned}
\log N &= -2.180 = -3 + 0.820 \\
&= \log 10^{-3} + \log 6.6 = \log 6.6 \times 10^{-3},
\end{aligned}$$

so $N = 6.6 \times 10^{-3}$. Notice that we added to our given logarithm the next largest integer (3 in this case) so that we have an integer, plus a decimal number between 0 and 1.0 whose antilogarithm can be looked up in the Table.

TABLE A–1 Short Table of Common Logarithms

N	0.0	0.1	0.2	0.3	0.4	0.5	0.6	0.7	0.8	0.9
1	000	041	079	114	146	176	204	230	255	279
2	301	322	342	362	380	398	415	431	447	462
3	477	491	505	519	531	544	556	568	580	591
4	602	613	623	633	643	653	663	672	681	690
5	699	708	716	724	732	740	748	756	763	771
6	778	785	792	799	806	813	820	826	833	839
7	845	851	857	863	869	875	881	886	892	898
8	903	908	914	919	924	929	935	940	944	949
9	954	959	964	968	973	978	982	987	991	996

A–8 Vectors

Vector addition is covered in Sections 3–2 to 3–5.
Vector multiplication is covered in Sections 3–3, 7–2, and 11–2.

A–9 Trigonometric Functions and Identities

The trigonometric functions are defined as follows (see Fig. A–5, o = side opposite, a = side adjacent, h = hypotenuse. Values are given in Table A–2):

$$\sin \theta = \frac{o}{h} \qquad\qquad \csc \theta = \frac{1}{\sin \theta} = \frac{h}{o}$$

$$\cos \theta = \frac{a}{h} \qquad\qquad \sec \theta = \frac{1}{\cos \theta} = \frac{h}{a}$$

$$\tan \theta = \frac{o}{a} = \frac{\sin \theta}{\cos \theta} \qquad \cot \theta = \frac{1}{\tan \theta} = \frac{a}{o}$$

and recall that

$$a^2 + o^2 = h^2 \qquad\qquad \text{[Pythagorean theorem]}.$$

Figure A–6 shows the signs (+ or −) that cosine, sine, and tangent take on for angles θ in the four quadrants (0° to 360°). Note that angles are measured counterclockwise from the x axis as shown; negative angles are measured from *below* the x axis, clockwise: for example, −30° = +330°, and so on.

The following are some useful identities among the trigonometric functions:

$$\sin^2 \theta + \cos^2 \theta = 1$$

$$\sec^2 \theta - \tan^2 \theta = 1, \quad \csc^2 \theta - \cot^2 \theta = 1$$

$$\sin 2\theta = 2 \sin \theta \cos \theta$$

$$\cos 2\theta = \cos^2 \theta - \sin^2 \theta = 2 \cos^2 \theta - 1 = 1 - 2 \sin^2 \theta$$

$$\tan 2\theta = \frac{2 \tan \theta}{1 - \tan^2 \theta}$$

$$\sin(A \pm B) = \sin A \cos B \pm \cos A \sin B$$

$$\cos(A \pm B) = \cos A \cos B \mp \sin A \sin B$$

$$\tan(A \pm B) = \frac{\tan A \pm \tan B}{1 \mp \tan A \tan B}$$

$$\sin(180° - \theta) = \sin \theta$$

$$\cos(180° - \theta) = -\cos \theta$$

$$\sin(90° - \theta) = \cos \theta$$

$$\cos(90° - \theta) = \sin \theta$$

$$\sin(-\theta) = -\sin \theta$$

$$\cos(-\theta) = \cos \theta$$

$$\tan(-\theta) = -\tan \theta$$

$$\sin\tfrac{1}{2}\theta = \sqrt{\frac{1 - \cos \theta}{2}}, \quad \cos\tfrac{1}{2}\theta = \sqrt{\frac{1 + \cos \theta}{2}}, \quad \tan\tfrac{1}{2}\theta = \sqrt{\frac{1 - \cos \theta}{1 + \cos \theta}}$$

$$\sin A \pm \sin B = 2 \sin\left(\frac{A \pm B}{2}\right) \cos\left(\frac{A \mp B}{2}\right).$$

For any triangle (see Fig. A–7):

$$\frac{\sin \alpha}{a} = \frac{\sin \beta}{b} = \frac{\sin \gamma}{c} \qquad\qquad \text{[Law of sines]}$$

$$c^2 = a^2 + b^2 - 2ab \cos \gamma. \qquad\qquad \text{[Law of cosines]}$$

Values of sine, cosine, tangent are given in Table A–2.

FIGURE A–5

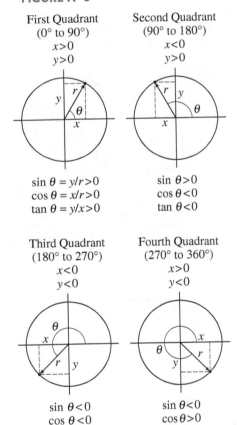

FIGURE A–6

First Quadrant
(0° to 90°)
$x>0$
$y>0$

$\sin \theta = y/r>0$
$\cos \theta = x/r>0$
$\tan \theta = y/x>0$

Second Quadrant
(90° to 180°)
$x<0$
$y>0$

$\sin \theta>0$
$\cos \theta<0$
$\tan \theta<0$

Third Quadrant
(180° to 270°)
$x<0$
$y<0$

$\sin \theta<0$
$\cos \theta<0$
$\tan \theta>0$

Fourth Quadrant
(270° to 360°)
$x>0$
$y<0$

$\sin \theta<0$
$\cos \theta>0$
$\tan \theta<0$

FIGURE A–7

Angle in Degrees	Angle in Radians	Sine	Cosine	Tangent	Angle in Degrees	Angle in Radians	Sine	Cosine	Tangent
0°	0.000	0.000	1.000	0.000					
1°	0.017	0.017	1.000	0.017	46°	0.803	0.719	0.695	1.036
2°	0.035	0.035	0.999	0.035	47°	0.820	0.731	0.682	1.072
3°	0.052	0.052	0.999	0.052	48°	0.838	0.743	0.669	1.111
4°	0.070	0.070	0.998	0.070	49°	0.855	0.755	0.656	1.150
5°	0.087	0.087	0.996	0.087	50°	0.873	0.766	0.643	1.192
6°	0.105	0.105	0.995	0.105	51°	0.890	0.777	0.629	1.235
7°	0.122	0.122	0.993	0.123	52°	0.908	0.788	0.616	1.280
8°	0.140	0.139	0.990	0.141	53°	0.925	0.799	0.602	1.327
9°	0.157	0.156	0.988	0.158	54°	0.942	0.809	0.588	1.376
10°	0.175	0.174	0.985	0.176	55°	0.960	0.819	0.574	1.428
11°	0.192	0.191	0.982	0.194	56°	0.977	0.829	0.559	1.483
12°	0.209	0.208	0.978	0.213	57°	0.995	0.839	0.545	1.540
13°	0.227	0.225	0.974	0.231	58°	1.012	0.848	0.530	1.600
14°	0.244	0.242	0.970	0.249	59°	1.030	0.857	0.515	1.664
15°	0.262	0.259	0.966	0.268	60°	1.047	0.866	0.500	1.732
16°	0.279	0.276	0.961	0.287	61°	1.065	0.875	0.485	1.804
17°	0.297	0.292	0.956	0.306	62°	1.082	0.883	0.469	1.881
18°	0.314	0.309	0.951	0.325	63°	1.100	0.891	0.454	1.963
19°	0.332	0.326	0.946	0.344	64°	1.117	0.899	0.438	2.050
20°	0.349	0.342	0.940	0.364	65°	1.134	0.906	0.423	2.145
21°	0.367	0.358	0.934	0.384	66°	1.152	0.914	0.407	2.246
22°	0.384	0.375	0.927	0.404	67°	1.169	0.921	0.391	2.356
23°	0.401	0.391	0.921	0.424	68°	1.187	0.927	0.375	2.475
24°	0.419	0.407	0.914	0.445	69°	1.204	0.934	0.358	2.605
25°	0.436	0.423	0.906	0.466	70°	1.222	0.940	0.342	2.747
26°	0.454	0.438	0.899	0.488	71°	1.239	0.946	0.326	2.904
27°	0.471	0.454	0.891	0.510	72°	1.257	0.951	0.309	3.078
28°	0.489	0.469	0.883	0.532	73°	1.274	0.956	0.292	3.271
29°	0.506	0.485	0.875	0.554	74°	1.292	0.961	0.276	3.487
30°	0.524	0.500	0.866	0.577	75°	1.309	0.966	0.259	3.732
31°	0.541	0.515	0.857	0.601	76°	1.326	0.970	0.242	4.011
32°	0.559	0.530	0.848	0.625	77°	1.344	0.974	0.225	4.331
33°	0.576	0.545	0.839	0.649	78°	1.361	0.978	0.208	4.705
34°	0.593	0.559	0.829	0.675	79°	1.379	0.982	0.191	5.145
35°	0.611	0.574	0.819	0.700	80°	1.396	0.985	0.174	5.671
36°	0.628	0.588	0.809	0.727	81°	1.414	0.988	0.156	6.314
37°	0.646	0.602	0.799	0.754	82°	1.431	0.990	0.139	7.115
38°	0.663	0.616	0.788	0.781	83°	1.449	0.993	0.122	8.144
39°	0.681	0.629	0.777	0.810	84°	1.466	0.995	0.105	9.514
40°	0.698	0.643	0.766	0.839	85°	1.484	0.996	0.087	11.43
41°	0.716	0.656	0.755	0.869	86°	1.501	0.998	0.070	14.301
42°	0.733	0.669	0.743	0.900	87°	1.518	0.999	0.052	19.081
43°	0.750	0.682	0.731	0.933	88°	1.536	0.999	0.035	28.636
44°	0.768	0.695	0.719	0.966	89°	1.553	1.000	0.017	57.290
45°	0.785	0.707	0.707	1.000	90°	1.571	1.000	0.000	∞

APPENDIX

B Derivatives and Integrals

B–1 Derivatives: General Rules

(See also Section 2–3.)

$$\frac{dx}{dx} = 1$$

$$\frac{d}{dx}[af(x)] = a\frac{df}{dx} \quad [a = \text{constant}]$$

$$\frac{d}{dx}[f(x) + g(x)] = \frac{df}{dx} + \frac{dg}{dx}$$

$$\frac{d}{dx}[f(x)g(x)] = \frac{df}{dx}g + f\frac{dg}{dx}$$

$$\frac{d}{dx}[f(y)] = \frac{df}{dy}\frac{dy}{dx} \quad [\text{chain rule}]$$

$$\frac{dx}{dy} = \frac{1}{\left(\dfrac{dy}{dx}\right)} \quad \text{if } \frac{dy}{dx} \neq 0.$$

B–2 Derivatives: Particular Functions

$$\frac{da}{dx} = 0 \quad [a = \text{constant}]$$

$$\frac{d}{dx}x^n = nx^{n-1}$$

$$\frac{d}{dx}\sin ax = a\cos ax$$

$$\frac{d}{dx}\cos ax = -a\sin ax$$

$$\frac{d}{dx}\tan ax = a\sec^2 ax$$

$$\frac{d}{dx}\ln ax = \frac{1}{x}$$

$$\frac{d}{dx}e^{ax} = ae^{ax}$$

B–3 Indefinite Integrals: General Rules

(See also Section 7–3.)

$$\int dx = x$$

$$\int a f(x)\, dx = a\int f(x)\, dx \quad [a = \text{constant}]$$

$$\int [f(x) + g(x)]\, dx = \int f(x)\, dx + \int g(x)\, dx$$

$$\int u\, dv = uv - \int v\, du \quad [\text{integration by parts: see also B–6}]$$

B–4 Indefinite Integrals: Particular Functions

(An arbitrary constant can be added to the right side of each equation.)

$$\int a\,dx = ax \qquad [a = \text{constant}]$$

$$\int x^m\,dx = \frac{1}{m+1}x^{m+1} \qquad [m \neq -1]$$

$$\int \sin ax\,dx = -\frac{1}{a}\cos ax$$

$$\int \cos ax\,dx = \frac{1}{a}\sin ax$$

$$\int \tan ax\,dx = \frac{1}{a}\ln|\sec ax|$$

$$\int \frac{1}{x}\,dx = \ln x$$

$$\int e^{ax}\,dx = \frac{1}{a}e^{ax}$$

$$\int \frac{dx}{\sqrt{x^2 \pm a^2}} = \ln(x + \sqrt{x^2 \pm a^2})$$

$$\int \frac{dx}{\sqrt{a^2 - x^2}} = \sin^{-1}\left(\frac{x}{a}\right) = -\cos^{-1}\left(\frac{x}{a}\right) \qquad [\text{if } x^2 \leq a^2]$$

$$\int \frac{dx}{(x^2 \pm a^2)^{\frac{3}{2}}} = \frac{\pm x}{a^2\sqrt{x^2 \pm a^2}}$$

$$\int \frac{x\,dx}{(x^2 \pm a^2)^{\frac{3}{2}}} = \frac{-1}{\sqrt{x^2 \pm a^2}}$$

$$\int \sin^2 ax\,dx = \frac{x}{2} - \frac{\sin 2ax}{4a}$$

$$\int xe^{-ax}\,dx = -\frac{e^{-ax}}{a^2}(ax + 1)$$

$$\int x^2 e^{-ax}\,dx = -\frac{e^{-ax}}{a^3}(a^2x^2 + 2ax + 2)$$

$$\int \frac{dx}{x^2 + a^2} = \frac{1}{a}\tan^{-1}\frac{x}{a}$$

$$\int \frac{dx}{x^2 - a^2} = \frac{1}{2a}\ln\left(\frac{x-a}{x+a}\right) \qquad [x^2 > a^2]$$

$$= -\frac{1}{2a}\ln\left(\frac{a+x}{a-x}\right) \qquad [x^2 < a^2]$$

B–5 A Few Definite Integrals

$$\int_0^\infty x^n e^{-ax}\,dx = \frac{n!}{a^{n+1}}$$

$$\int_0^\infty e^{-ax^2}\,dx = \sqrt{\frac{\pi}{4a}}$$

$$\int_0^\infty xe^{-ax^2}\,dx = \frac{1}{2a}$$

$$\int_0^\infty x^2 e^{-ax^2}\,dx = \sqrt{\frac{\pi}{16a^3}}$$

$$\int_0^\infty x^3 e^{-ax^2}\,dx = \frac{1}{2a^2}$$

$$\int_0^\infty x^{2n} e^{-ax^2}\,dx = \frac{1\cdot 3\cdot 5\cdots(2n-1)}{2^{n+1}a^n}\sqrt{\frac{\pi}{a}}$$

B–6 Integration by Parts

Sometimes a difficult integral can be simplified by carefully choosing the functions u and v in the identity:

$$\int u\,dv = uv - \int v\,du. \qquad [\text{Integration by parts}]$$

This identity follows from the property of derivatives

$$\frac{d}{dx}(uv) = u\frac{dv}{dx} + v\frac{du}{dx}$$

or as differentials: $d(uv) = u\,dv + v\,du$.

For example $\int xe^{-x}\,dx$ can be integrated by choosing $u = x$ and $dv = e^{-x}\,dx$ in the "integration by parts" equation above:

$$\int xe^{-x}\,dx = (x)(-e^{-x}) + \int e^{-x}\,dx$$

$$= -xe^{-x} - e^{-x} = -(x+1)e^{-x}.$$

More on Dimensional Analysis

An important use of dimensional analysis (Section 1–7) is to obtain the *form* of an equation: how one quantity depends on others. To take a concrete example, let us try to find an expression for the period T of a simple pendulum. First, we try to figure out what T could depend on, and make a list of these variables. It might depend on its length ℓ, on the mass m of the bob, on the angle of swing θ, and on the acceleration due to gravity, g. It might also depend on air resistance (we would use the viscosity of air), the gravitational pull of the Moon, and so on; but everyday experience suggests that the Earth's gravity is the major force involved, so we ignore the other possible forces. So let us assume that T is a function of ℓ, m, θ, and g, and that each of these factors is present to some power:

$$T = C\ell^w m^x \theta^y g^z.$$

C is a dimensionless constant, and w, x, y, and z are exponents we want to solve for. We now write down the dimensional equation (Section 1–7) for this relationship:

$$[T] = [L]^w [M]^x [L/T^2]^z.$$

Because θ has no dimensions (a radian is a length divided by a length—see Eq. 10–1a), it does not appear. We simplify and obtain

$$[T] = [L]^{w+z} [M]^x [T]^{-2z}$$

To have dimensional consistency, we must have

$$1 = -2z$$
$$0 = w + z$$
$$0 = x.$$

We solve these equations and find that $z = -\frac{1}{2}$, $w = \frac{1}{2}$, and $x = 0$. Thus our desired equation must be

$$T = C\sqrt{\ell/g}\, f(\theta), \tag{C–1}$$

where $f(\theta)$ is some function of θ that we cannot determine using this technique. Nor can we determine in this way the dimensionless constant C. (To obtain C and f, we would have to do an analysis such as that in Chapter 14 using Newton's laws, which reveals that $C = 2\pi$ and $f \approx 1$ for small θ). But look what we *have* found, using only dimensional consistency. We obtained the form of the expression that relates the period of a simple pendulum to the major variables of the situation, ℓ and g (see Eq. 14–12c), and saw that it does not depend on the mass m.

How did we do it? And how useful is this technique? Basically, we had to use our intuition as to which variables were important and which were not. This is not always easy, and often requires a lot of insight. As to usefulness, the final result in our example could have been obtained from Newton's laws, as in Chapter 14. But in many physical situations, such a derivation from other laws cannot be done. In those situations, dimensional analysis can be a powerful tool.

In the end, any expression derived by the use of dimensional analysis (or by any other means, for that matter) must be checked against experiment. For example, in our derivation of Eq. C–1, we can compare the periods of two pendulums of different lengths, ℓ_1 and ℓ_2, whose amplitudes (θ) are the same. For, using Eq. C–1, we would have

$$\frac{T_1}{T_2} = \frac{C\sqrt{\ell_1/g}\, f(\theta)}{C\sqrt{\ell_2/g}\, f(\theta)} = \sqrt{\frac{\ell_1}{\ell_2}}.$$

Because C and $f(\theta)$ are the same for both pendula, they cancel out, so we can experimentally determine if the ratio of the periods varies as the ratio of the square roots of the lengths. This comparison to experiment checks our derivation, at least in part; C and $f(\theta)$ could be determined by further experiments.

D Gravitational Force due to a Spherical Mass Distribution

In Chapter 6 we stated that the gravitational force exerted by or on a uniform sphere acts as if all the mass of the sphere were concentrated at its center, if the other object (exerting or feeling the force) is outside the sphere. In other words, the gravitational force that a uniform sphere exerts on a particle outside it is

$$F = G\frac{mM}{r^2},$$ [m outside sphere of mass M]

where m is the mass of the particle, M the mass of the sphere, and r the distance of m from the center of the sphere. Now we will derive this result. We will use the concepts of infinitesimally small quantities and integration.

First we consider a very thin, uniform spherical shell (like a thin-walled basketball) of mass M whose thickness t is small compared to its radius R (Fig. D–1). The force on a particle of mass m at a distance r from the center of the shell can be calculated as the vector sum of the forces due to all the particles of the shell. We imagine the shell divided up into thin (infinitesimal) circular strips so that all points on a strip are equidistant from our particle m. One of these circular strips, labeled AB, is shown in Fig. D–1. It is $R\,d\theta$ wide, t thick, and has a radius $R\sin\theta$. The force on our particle m due to a tiny piece of the strip at point A is represented by the vector $\vec{F}_A$ shown. The force due to a tiny piece of the strip at point B, which is diametrically opposite A, is the force $\vec{F}_B$. We take the two pieces at A and B to be of equal mass, so $F_A = F_B$. The horizontal components of $\vec{F}_A$ and $\vec{F}_B$ are each equal to

$$F_A \cos\phi$$

and point toward the center of the shell. The vertical components of $\vec{F}_A$ and $\vec{F}_B$ are of equal magnitude and point in opposite directions, and so cancel. Since for every point on the strip there is a corresponding point diametrically opposite (as with A and B), we see that the net force due to the entire strip points toward the center of the shell. Its magnitude will be

$$dF = G\frac{m\,dM}{\ell^2}\cos\phi,$$

where dM is the mass of the entire circular strip and ℓ is the distance from all points on the strip to m, as shown. We write dM in terms of the density ρ; by density we mean the mass per unit volume (Section 13–2). Hence, $dM = \rho\,dV$, where dV is the volume of the strip and equals $(2\pi R\sin\theta)(t)(R\,d\theta)$. Then the force dF due to the circular strip shown is

$$dF = G\frac{m\rho 2\pi R^2 t \sin\theta\,d\theta}{\ell^2}\cos\phi. \qquad\qquad \textbf{(D–1)}$$

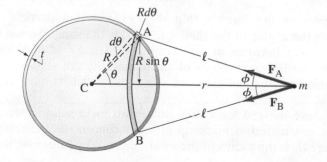

FIGURE D–1 Calculating the gravitational force on a particle of mass m due to a uniform spherical shell of radius R and mass M.

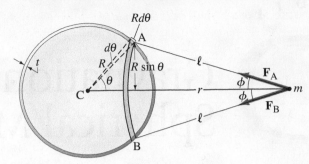

FIGURE D–1 (repeated) Calculating the gravitational force on a particle of mass m due to a uniform spherical shell of radius R and mass M.

To get the total force F that the entire shell exerts on the particle m, we must integrate over all the circular strips: that is, we integrate

$$dF = G \frac{m\rho 2\pi R^2 t \sin\theta \, d\theta}{\ell^2} \cos\phi \qquad \textbf{(D–1)}$$

from $\theta = 0°$ to $\theta = 180°$. But our expression for dF contains ℓ and ϕ, which are functions of θ. From Fig. D–1 we can see that

$$\ell \cos\phi = r - R\cos\theta.$$

Furthermore, we can write the law of cosines for triangle CmA:

$$\cos\theta = \frac{r^2 + R^2 - \ell^2}{2rR}. \qquad \textbf{(D–2)}$$

With these two expressions we can reduce our three variables (ℓ, θ, ϕ) to only one, which we take to be ℓ. We do two things with Eq. D–2: (1) We put it into the equation for $\ell \cos\phi$ above:

$$\cos\phi = \frac{1}{\ell}(r - R\cos\theta) = \frac{r^2 + \ell^2 - R^2}{2r\ell}.$$

and (2) we take the differential of both sides of Eq. D–2 (because $\sin\theta \, d\theta$ appears in the expression for dF, Eq. D–1), considering r and R to be constants when summing over the strips:

$$-\sin\theta \, d\theta = -\frac{2\ell \, d\ell}{2rR} \quad \text{or} \quad \sin\theta \, d\theta = \frac{\ell \, d\ell}{rR}.$$

We insert these into Eq. D–1 for dF and find

$$dF = Gm\rho\pi t \frac{R}{r^2}\left(1 + \frac{r^2 - R^2}{\ell^2}\right) d\ell.$$

Now we integrate to get the net force on our thin shell of radius R. To integrate over all the strips ($\theta = 0°$ to $180°$), we must go from $\ell = r - R$ to $\ell = r + R$ (see Fig. D–1). Thus,

$$F = Gm\rho\pi t \frac{R}{r^2}\left[\ell - \frac{r^2 - R^2}{\ell}\right]_{\ell = r - R}^{\ell = r + R}$$

$$= Gm\rho\pi t \frac{R}{r^2}(4R).$$

The volume V of the spherical shell is its area $(4\pi R^2)$ times the thickness t. Hence the mass $M = \rho V = \rho 4\pi R^2 t$, and finally

$$F = G\frac{mM}{r^2}. \qquad \left[\begin{array}{l}\text{particle of mass } m \text{ outside a}\\ \text{thin uniform spherical shell of mass } M\end{array}\right]$$

This result gives us the force a thin shell exerts on a particle of mass m a distance r from the center of the shell, and *outside* the shell. We see that the force is the same as that between m and a particle of mass M at the center of the shell. In other words, for purposes of calculating the gravitational force exerted on or by a uniform spherical shell, we can consider all its mass concentrated at its center.

What we have derived for a shell holds also for a solid sphere, since a solid sphere can be considered as made up of many concentric shells, from $R = 0$ to $R = R_0$, where R_0 is the radius of the solid sphere. Why? Because if each shell has mass dM, we write for each shell, $dF = Gm\,dM/r^2$, where r is the distance from the center C to mass m and is the same for all shells. Then the total force equals the sum or integral over dM, which gives the total mass M. Thus the result

$$F = G\frac{mM}{r^2} \qquad \left[\begin{array}{c}\text{particle of mass } m \text{ outside} \\ \text{solid sphere of mass } M\end{array}\right] \quad \textbf{(D–3)}$$

is valid for a solid sphere of mass M even if the density varies with distance from the center. (It is not valid if the density varies within each shell—that is, depends not only on R.) Thus the gravitational force exerted on or by spherical objects, including nearly spherical objects like the Earth, Sun, and Moon, can be considered to act as if the objects were point particles.

This result, Eq. D–3, is true only if the mass m is outside the sphere. Let us next consider a point mass m that is located inside the spherical shell of Fig. D–1. Here, r would be less than R, and the integration over ℓ would be from $\ell = R - r$ to $\ell = R + r$, so

$$\left[\ell - \frac{r^2 - R^2}{\ell}\right]_{R-r}^{R+r} = 0.$$

Thus the force on any mass inside the shell would be zero. This result has particular importance for the electrostatic force, which is also an inverse square law. For the gravitational situation, we see that at points within a solid sphere, say 1000 km below the Earth's surface, only the mass up to that radius contributes to the net force. The outer shells beyond the point in question contribute zero net gravitational effect.

The results we have obtained here can also be reached using the gravitational analog of Gauss's law for electrostatics (Chapter 22).

Differential Form of Maxwell's Equations

Maxwell's equations can be written in another form that is often more convenient than Eqs. 31–5. This material is usually covered in more advanced courses, and is included here simply for completeness.

We quote here two theorems, without proof, that are derived in vector analysis textbooks. The first is called **Gauss's theorem** or the **divergence theorem**. It relates the integral over a surface of any vector function $\vec{\mathbf{F}}$ to a volume integral over the volume enclosed by the surface:

$$\oint_{\text{Area } A} \vec{\mathbf{F}} \cdot d\vec{\mathbf{A}} = \int_{\text{Volume } V} \vec{\boldsymbol{\nabla}} \cdot \vec{\mathbf{F}} \, dV.$$

The operator $\vec{\boldsymbol{\nabla}}$ is the **del operator**, defined in Cartesian coordinates as

$$\vec{\boldsymbol{\nabla}} = \hat{\mathbf{i}} \frac{\partial}{\partial x} + \hat{\mathbf{j}} \frac{\partial}{\partial y} + \hat{\mathbf{k}} \frac{\partial}{\partial z}.$$

The quantity

$$\vec{\boldsymbol{\nabla}} \cdot \vec{\mathbf{F}} = \frac{\partial F_x}{\partial x} + \frac{\partial F_y}{\partial y} + \frac{\partial F_z}{\partial z}$$

is called the **divergence** of $\vec{\mathbf{F}}$. The second theorem is **Stokes's theorem**, and relates a line integral around a closed path to a surface integral over any surface enclosed by that path:

$$\oint_{\text{Line}} \vec{\mathbf{F}} \cdot d\vec{\boldsymbol{\ell}} = \int_{\text{Area } A} \vec{\boldsymbol{\nabla}} \times \vec{\mathbf{F}} \cdot d\vec{\mathbf{A}}.$$

The quantity $\vec{\boldsymbol{\nabla}} \times \vec{\mathbf{F}}$ is called the **curl** of $\vec{\mathbf{F}}$. (See Section 11–2 on the vector product.)

We now use these two theorems to obtain the differential form of Maxwell's equations in free space. We apply Gauss's theorem to Eq. 31–5a (Gauss's law):

$$\oint_A \vec{\mathbf{E}} \cdot d\vec{\mathbf{A}} = \int \vec{\boldsymbol{\nabla}} \cdot \vec{\mathbf{E}} \, dV = \frac{Q}{\epsilon_0}.$$

Now the charge Q can be written as a volume integral over the charge density ρ: $Q = \int \rho \, dV$. Then

$$\int \vec{\boldsymbol{\nabla}} \cdot \vec{\mathbf{E}} \, dV = \frac{1}{\epsilon_0} \int \rho \, dV.$$

Both sides contain volume integrals over the same volume, and for this to be true over *any* volume, whatever its size or shape, the integrands must be equal:

$$\vec{\boldsymbol{\nabla}} \cdot \vec{\mathbf{E}} = \frac{\rho}{\epsilon_0}. \tag{E–1}$$

This is the differential form of Gauss's law. The second of Maxwell's equations, $\oint \vec{\mathbf{B}} \cdot d\vec{\mathbf{A}} = 0$, is treated in the same way, and we obtain

$$\vec{\boldsymbol{\nabla}} \cdot \vec{\mathbf{B}} = 0. \tag{E–2}$$

Next, we apply Stokes's theorem to the third of Maxwell's equations,

$$\oint \vec{\mathbf{E}} \cdot d\vec{\boldsymbol{\ell}} = \int \vec{\boldsymbol{\nabla}} \times \vec{\mathbf{E}} \cdot d\vec{\mathbf{A}} = -\frac{d\Phi_B}{dt}.$$

Since the magnetic flux $\Phi_B = \int \vec{\mathbf{B}} \cdot d\vec{\mathbf{A}}$, we have

$$\int \vec{\boldsymbol{\nabla}} \times \vec{\mathbf{E}} \cdot d\vec{\mathbf{A}} = -\frac{\partial}{\partial t} \int \vec{\mathbf{B}} \cdot d\vec{\mathbf{A}}$$

where we use the partial derivative, $\partial \vec{\mathbf{B}}/\partial t$, since B may also depend on position. These are surface integrals over the same area, and to be true over any area, even a very small one, we must have

$$\vec{\boldsymbol{\nabla}} \times \vec{\mathbf{E}} = -\frac{\partial \vec{\mathbf{B}}}{\partial t}. \qquad\qquad \textbf{(E–3)}$$

This is the third of Maxwell's equations in differential form. Finally, to the last of Maxwell's equations,

$$\oint \vec{\mathbf{B}} \cdot d\vec{\boldsymbol{\ell}} = \mu_0 I + \mu_0 \epsilon_0 \frac{d\Phi_E}{dt},$$

we apply Stokes's theorem and write $\Phi_E = \int \vec{\mathbf{E}} \cdot d\vec{\mathbf{A}}$:

$$\int \vec{\boldsymbol{\nabla}} \times \vec{\mathbf{B}} \cdot d\vec{\mathbf{A}} = \mu_0 I + \mu_0 \epsilon_0 \frac{\partial}{\partial t} \int \vec{\mathbf{E}} \cdot d\vec{\mathbf{A}}.$$

The conduction current I can be written in terms of the current density $\vec{\mathbf{j}}$, using Eq. 25–12:

$$I = \int \vec{\mathbf{j}} \cdot d\vec{\mathbf{A}}.$$

Then Maxwell's fourth equation becomes:

$$\int \vec{\boldsymbol{\nabla}} \times \vec{\mathbf{B}} \cdot d\vec{\mathbf{A}} = \mu_0 \int \vec{\mathbf{j}} \cdot d\vec{\mathbf{A}} + \mu_0 \epsilon_0 \frac{\partial}{\partial t} \int \vec{\mathbf{E}} \cdot d\vec{\mathbf{A}}.$$

For this to be true over any area A, whatever its size or shape, the integrands on each side of the equation must be equal:

$$\vec{\boldsymbol{\nabla}} \times \vec{\mathbf{B}} = \mu_0 \vec{\mathbf{j}} + \mu_0 \epsilon_0 \frac{\partial \vec{\mathbf{E}}}{\partial t}. \qquad\qquad \textbf{(E–4)}$$

Equations E–1, 2, 3, and 4 are Maxwell's equations in differential form for free space. They are summarized in Table E–1.

TABLE E–1 Maxwell's Equations in Free Space[†]

Integral form	Differential form
$\oint \vec{\mathbf{E}} \cdot d\vec{\mathbf{A}} = \dfrac{Q}{\epsilon_0}$	$\vec{\boldsymbol{\nabla}} \cdot \vec{\mathbf{E}} = \dfrac{\rho}{\epsilon_0}$
$\oint \vec{\mathbf{B}} \cdot d\vec{\mathbf{A}} = 0$	$\vec{\boldsymbol{\nabla}} \cdot \vec{\mathbf{B}} = 0$
$\oint \vec{\mathbf{E}} \cdot d\vec{\boldsymbol{\ell}} = -\dfrac{d\Phi_B}{dt}$	$\vec{\boldsymbol{\nabla}} \times \vec{\mathbf{E}} = -\dfrac{\partial \vec{\mathbf{B}}}{\partial t}$
$\oint \vec{\mathbf{B}} \cdot d\vec{\boldsymbol{\ell}} = \mu_0 I + \mu_0 \epsilon_0 \dfrac{d\Phi_E}{dt}$	$\vec{\boldsymbol{\nabla}} \times \vec{\mathbf{B}} = \mu_0 \vec{\mathbf{j}} + \mu_0 \epsilon_0 \dfrac{\partial \vec{\mathbf{E}}}{\partial t}$

[†] $\vec{\boldsymbol{\nabla}}$ stands for the *del operator* $\vec{\boldsymbol{\nabla}} = \hat{\mathbf{i}} \frac{\partial}{\partial x} + \hat{\mathbf{j}} \frac{\partial}{\partial y} + \hat{\mathbf{k}} \frac{\partial}{\partial z}$ in Cartesian coordinates.

F Selected Isotopes

(1) Atomic Number Z	(2) Element	(3) Symbol	(4) Mass Number A	(5) Atomic Mass[†]	(6) % Abundance (or Radioactive Decay[‡] Mode)	(7) Half-life (if radioactive)
0	(Neutron)	n	1	1.008665	β^-	10.23 min
1	Hydrogen	H	1	1.007825	99.9885%	
	Deuterium	d or D	2	2.014082	0.0115%	
	Tritium	t or T	3	3.016049	β^-	12.312 yr
2	Helium	He	3	3.016029	0.000137%	
			4	4.002603	99.999863%	
3	Lithium	Li	6	6.015123	7.59%	
			7	7.016005	92.41%	
4	Beryllium	Be	7	7.016930	EC, γ	53.22 days
			9	9.012182	100%	
5	Boron	B	10	10.012937	19.9%	
			11	11.009305	80.1%	
6	Carbon	C	11	11.011434	β^+, EC	20.370 min
			12	12.000000	98.93%	
			13	13.003355	1.07%	
			14	14.003242	β^-	5730 yr
7	Nitrogen	N	13	13.005739	β^+, EC	9.9670 min
			14	14.003074	99.632%	
			15	15.000109	0.368%	
8	Oxygen	O	15	15.003066	β^+, EC	122.5 min
			16	15.994915	99.757%	
			18	17.999161	0.205%	
9	Fluorine	F	19	18.998403	100%	
10	Neon	Ne	20	19.992440	90.48%	
			22	21.991385	9.25%	
11	Sodium	Na	22	21.994436	β^+, EC, γ	2.6027 yr
			23	22.989769	100%	
			24	23.990963	β^-, γ	14.9574 h
12	Magnesium	Mg	24	23.985042	78.99%	
13	Aluminum	Al	27	26.981539	100%	
14	Silicon	Si	28	27.976927	92.2297%	
			31	30.975363	β^-, γ	157.3 min
15	Phosphorus	P	31	30.973762	100%	
			32	31.973907	β^-	14.284 days

[†] The masses given in column (5) are those for the neutral atom, including the Z electrons.

[‡] Chapter 41; EC = electron capture.

(1) Atomic Number Z	(2) Element	(3) Symbol	(4) Mass Number A	(5) Atomic Mass	(6) % Abundance (or Radioactive Decay Mode)	(7) Half-life (if radioactive)
16	Sulfur	S	32	31.972071	94.9%	
			35	34.969032	β^-	87.32 days
17	Chlorine	Cl	35	34.968853	75.78%	
			37	36.965903	24.22%	
18	Argon	Ar	40	39.962383	99.600%	
19	Potassium	K	39	38.963707	93.258%	
			40	39.963998	0.0117%	
					β^-, EC, γ, β^+	1.265×10^9 yr
20	Calcium	Ca	40	39.962591	96.94%	
21	Scandium	Sc	45	44.955912	100%	
22	Titanium	Ti	48	47.947946	73.72%	
23	Vanadium	V	51	50.943960	99.750%	
24	Chromium	Cr	52	51.940508	83.789%	
25	Manganese	Mn	55	54.938045	100%	
26	Iron	Fe	56	55.934938	91.75%	
27	Cobalt	Co	59	58.933195	100%	
			60	59.933817	β^-, γ	5.2710 yr
28	Nickel	Ni	58	57.935343	68.077%	
			60	59.930786	26.223%	
29	Copper	Cu	63	62.929598	69.17%	
			65	64.927790	30.83%	
30	Zinc	Zn	64	63.929142	48.6%	
			66	65.926033	27.9%	
31	Gallium	Ga	69	68.925574	60.108%	
32	Germanium	Ge	72	71.922076	27.5%	
			74	73.921178	36.3%	
33	Arsenic	As	75	74.921596	100%	
34	Selenium	Se	80	79.916521	49.6%	
35	Bromine	Br	79	78.918337	50.69%	
36	Krypton	Kr	84	83.911507	57.00%	
37	Rubidium	Rb	85	84.911790	72.17%	
38	Strontium	Sr	86	85.909260	9.86%	
			88	87.905612	82.58%	
			90	89.907738	β^-	28.80 yr
39	Yttrium	Y	89	88.905848	100%	
40	Zirconium	Zr	90	89.904704	51.4%	
41	Niobium	Nb	93	92.906378	100%	
42	Molybdenum	Mo	98	97.905408	24.1%	
43	Technetium	Tc	98	97.907216	β^-, γ	4.2×10^6 yr
44	Ruthenium	Ru	102	101.904349	31.55%	
45	Rhodium	Rh	103	102.905504	100%	
46	Palladium	Pd	106	105.903486	27.33%	
47	Silver	Ag	107	106.905097	51.839%	
			109	108.904752	48.161%	
48	Cadmium	Cd	114	113.903359	28.7%	
49	Indium	In	115	114.903878	95.71%; β^-	4.41×10^{14} yr
50	Tin	Sn	120	119.902195	32.58%	
51	Antimony	Sb	121	120.903816	57.21%	

(1) Atomic Number Z	(2) Element	(3) Symbol	(4) Mass Number A	(5) Atomic Mass	(6) % Abundance (or Radioactive Decay Mode)	(7) Half-life (if radioactive)
52	Tellurium	Te	130	129.906224	34.1%; $\beta^-\beta^-$	$>9.7 \times 10^{22}$ yr
53	Iodine	I	127	126.904473	100%	
			131	130.906125	β^-, γ	8.0233 days
54	Xenon	Xe	132	131.904154	26.89%	
			136	135.907219	8.87%; $\beta^-\beta^-$	$>8.5 \times 10^{21}$ yr
55	Cesium	Cs	133	132.905452	100%	
56	Barium	Ba	137	136.905827	11.232%	
			138	137.905247	71.70%	
57	Lanthanum	La	139	138.906353	99.910%	
58	Cerium	Ce	140	139.905439	88.45%	
59	Praseodymium	Pr	141	140.907653	100%	
60	Neodymium	Nd	142	141.907723	27.2%	
61	Promethium	Pm	145	144.912749	EC, α	17.7 yr
62	Samarium	Sm	152	151.919732	26.75%	
63	Europium	Eu	153	152.921230	52.19%	
64	Gadolinium	Gd	158	157.924104	24.84%	
65	Terbium	Tb	159	158.925347	100%	
66	Dysprosium	Dy	164	163.929175	28.2%	
67	Holmium	Ho	165	164.930322	100%	
68	Erbium	Er	166	165.930293	33.6%	
69	Thulium	Tm	169	168.934213	100%	
70	Ytterbium	Yb	174	173.938862	31.8%	
71	Lutetium	Lu	175	174.940772	97.41%	
72	Hafnium	Hf	180	179.946550	35.08%	
73	Tantalum	Ta	181	180.947996	99.988%	
74	Tungsten (wolfram)	W	184	183.950931	30.64%; α	$>8.9 \times 10^{21}$ yr
75	Rhenium	Re	187	186.955753	62.60%; β^-	4.35×10^{10} yr
76	Osmium	Os	191	190.960930	β^-, γ	15.4 days
			192	191.961481	40.78%	
77	Iridium	Ir	191	190.960594	37.3%	
			193	192.962926	62.7%	
78	Platinum	Pt	195	194.964791	33.832%	
79	Gold	Au	197	196.966569	100%	
80	Mercury	Hg	199	198.968280	16.87%	
			202	201.970643	29.9%	
81	Thallium	Tl	205	204.974428	70.476%	
82	Lead	Pb	206	205.974465	24.1%	
			207	206.975897	22.1%	
			208	207.976652	52.4%	
			210	209.984188	β^-, γ, α	22.23 yr
			211	210.988737	β^-, γ	36.1 min
			212	211.991898	β^-, γ	10.64 h
			214	213.999805	β^-, γ	26.8 min
83	Bismuth	Bi	209	208.980399	100%	
			211	210.987269	α, γ, β^-	2.14 min
84	Polonium	Po	210	209.982874	α, γ, EC	138.376 days
			214	213.995201	α, γ	162.3 μs
85	Astatine	At	218	218.008694	α, β^-	1.4 s

(1) Atomic Number Z	(2) Element	(3) Symbol	(4) Mass Number A	(5) Atomic Mass	(6) % Abundance (or Radioactive Decay Mode)	(7) Half-life (if radioactive)
86	Radon	Rn	222	222.017578	α, γ	3.8232 days
87	Francium	Fr	223	223.019736	β^-, γ, α	22.00 min
88	Radium	Ra	226	226.025410	α, γ	1600 yr
89	Actinium	Ac	227	227.027752	β^-, γ, α	21.772 yr
90	Thorium	Th	228	228.028741	α, γ	698.60 days
			232	232.038055	100%; α, γ	1.405×10^{10} yr
91	Protactinium	Pa	231	231.035884	α, γ	3.276×10^4 yr
92	Uranium	U	232	232.037156	α, γ	68.9 yr
			233	233.039635	α, γ	1.592×10^5 yr
			235	235.043930	0.720%; α, γ	7.04×10^8 yr
			236	236.045568	α, γ	2.342×10^7 yr
			238	238.050788	99.274%; α, γ	4.468×10^9 yr
			239	239.054293	β^-, γ	23.46 min
93	Neptunium	Np	237	237.048173	α, γ	2.144×10^6 yr
			239	239.052939	β^-, γ	2.356 days
94	Plutonium	Pu	239	239.052163	α, γ	24,100 yr
			244	244.064204	α	8.00×10^7 yr
95	Americium	Am	243	243.061381	α, γ	7370 yr
96	Curium	Cm	247	247.070354	α, γ	1.56×10^7 yr
97	Berkelium	Bk	247	247.070307	α, γ	1380 yr
98	Californium	Cf	251	251.079587	α, γ	898 yr
99	Einsteinium	Es	252	252.082980	α, EC, γ	471.7 days
100	Fermium	Fm	257	257.095105	α, γ	100.5 days
101	Mendelevium	Md	258	258.098431	α, γ	51.5 days
102	Nobelium	No	259	259.10103	α, EC	58 min
103	Lawrencium	Lr	262	262.10963	α, EC, fission	≈ 4 h
104	Rutherfordium	Rf	263	263.11255	fission	10 min
105	Dubnium	Db	262	262.11408	α, fission, EC	35 s
106	Seaborgium	Sg	266	266.12210	α, fission	≈ 21 s
107	Bohrium	Bh	264	264.12460	α	≈ 0.44 s
108	Hassium	Hs	269	269.13406	α	≈ 10 s
109	Meitnerium	Mt	268	268.13870	α	21 ms
110	Darmstadtium	Ds	271	271.14606	α	≈ 70 ms
111	Roentgenium	Rg	272	272.15360	α	3.8 ms
112		Uub	277	277.16394	α	≈ 0.7 ms

Preliminary evidence (unconfirmed) has been reported for elements 113, 114, 115, 116 and 118.

Answers to Odd-Numbered Problems

CHAPTER 14

1. 0.72 m.

3. 1.5 Hz.

5. 350 N/m.

7. 0.13 m/s, 0.12 m/s², 1.2%.

9. (a) 0.16 N/m;
(b) 2.8 Hz.

11. $\dfrac{\sqrt{3k/M}}{2\pi}$.

13. (a) 2.5 m, 3.5 m;
(b) 0.25 Hz, 0.50 Hz;
(c) 4.0 s, 2.0 s;
(d) $x_A = (2.5\,\text{m})\,\sin(\tfrac{1}{2}\pi t)$,
$x_B = (3.5\,\text{m})\,\cos(\pi t)$.

15. (a) $y(t) =$
$(0.280\,\text{m})\,\sin[(34.3\,\text{rad/s})t]$;
(b) $t_{\text{longest}} =$
$4.59 \times 10^{-2}\,\text{s} + n(0.183\,\text{s})$,
$n = 0, 1, 2, \cdots$;
$t_{\text{shortest}} =$
$1.38 \times 10^{-1}\,\text{s} + n(0.183\,\text{s})$,
$n = 0, 1, 2, \cdots$.

17. (a) 1.6 s, $\frac{5}{8}$ Hz;
(b) 3.3 m, -7.5 m/s;
(c) -13 m/s, 29 m/s².

19. 0.75 s.

21. 3.1 s, 6.3 s, 9.4 s.

23. 88.8 N/m, 17.8 m.

27. (a) 0.650 m;
(b) 1.18 Hz;
(c) 13.3 J;
(d) 11.2 J, 2.1 J.

29.

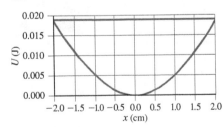

(a) 0.011 J;
(b) 0.008 J;
(c) 0.5 m/s.

31. 10.2 m/s.

33. $A_{\text{high energy}} = \sqrt{5}\,A_{\text{low energy}}$.

35. (a) 430 N/m;
(b) 3.7 kg.

37. 309.8 m/s.

39. (a) 0.410 s, 2.44 Hz;
(b) 0.148 m;
(c) 34.6 m/s²;
(d) $x = (0.148\,\text{m})\,\sin(4.87\pi t)$;
(e) 2.00 J;
(f) 1.68 J.

41. 2.2 s.

43. (a) $-5.4°$;
(b) $8.4°$;
(c) $-13°$.

45. $\frac{1}{3}$.

47. $\sqrt{2g\ell(1 - \cos\theta)}$.

49. 0.41 g.

51. (a) $\theta = \theta_0 \cos(\omega t + \phi)$, $\omega = \sqrt{\dfrac{K}{I}}$.

53. 2.9 s.

55. 1.08 s.

57. Decreased by a factor of 6.

59. (a) $(-1.21 \times 10^{-3})\%$;
(b) 32.3 periods.

63. (a) $0°$;
(b) 0, $\pm A$;
(c) $\frac{1}{2}\pi$ or $90°$.

65. 3.1 m/s.

67. 23.7.

69. (a) 170 s;
(b) 1.3×10^{-5} W;
(c) 1.0×10^{-3} Hz on either side.

71. 0.11 m.

73. (a) $1.22\,f$;
(b) $0.71\,f$.

75. (a) 0.41 s;
(b) 9 mm.

77. 0.9922 m, 1.6 mm, 0.164 m.

79. $x = \pm\dfrac{\sqrt{3}A}{2} \approx \pm 0.866A$.

81. $\rho_{\text{water}}\, g\,(\text{area}_{\text{bottom side}})$.

83. (a) 130 N/m;
(b) 0.096 m.

85. (a) $x = \pm\dfrac{\sqrt{3}x_0}{2} \approx \pm 0.866x_0$;
(b) $x = \pm\frac{1}{2}x_0$.

87. 84.5 min.

89. 1.25 Hz.

91. ~ 3000 N/m.

93. (a) $k = \dfrac{4\pi^2}{\text{slope}}$, y-intercept $= 0$;

(b) slope $= 0.13\,\text{s}^2/\text{kg}$,
y-intercept $= 0.14\,\text{s}^2$

(c) $k = \dfrac{4\pi^2}{\text{slope}} = 310$ N/m,

y-intercept $= \dfrac{4\pi^2 m_0}{k}$,

$m_0 = 1.1$ kg;
(d) portion of spring's mass that is effectively oscillating.

CHAPTER 15

1. 2.7 m/s.

3. (a) 1400 m/s;
(b) 4100 m/s;
(c) 5100 m/s.

5. 0.62 m.

7. 4.3 N.

9. (a) 78 m/s;
(b) 8300 N.

11. (a)

(b) -4 cm/s.

13. 18 m.

15. $A_{\text{more energy}}/A_{\text{less energy}} = \sqrt{3}$.

19. (a) 0.38 W;
(b) 0.25 cm.

21. (b) 420 W.

23. $D = A\sin\left[2\pi\left(\dfrac{x}{\lambda} + \dfrac{t}{T}\right) + \phi\right]$.

25. (a) 41 m/s;
(b) 6.4×10^4 m/s²;
(c) 35 m/s, 3.2×10^4 m/s².

27. (b) $D =$
$(0.45\,\text{m})\cos[2.6(x - 2.0t) + 1.2]$;
(d) $D =$
$(0.45\,\text{m})\cos[2.6(x + 2.0t) + 1.2]$.

29. $D = (0.020\,\text{cm}) \times$
$\sin[(9.54\,\text{m}^{-1})x - (3290\,\text{rad/s})t + \tfrac{3}{2}\pi]$

31. Yes, it is a solution.

35. Yes, it is a solution.

37. (a) 0.84 m;
(b) 0.26 N;
(c) 0.59 m.

39. (a) $t = \dfrac{2}{v}\sqrt{D^2 + \left(\dfrac{x}{2}\right)^2}$;

(b) slope $= \dfrac{1}{v^2}$,

y-intercept $= \dfrac{4}{v^2}D^2$.

41. (a)

(b)

(c) all kinetic energy.

43. 662 Hz.

45. $T_n = \dfrac{(1.5\,\text{s})}{n}$, $n = 1, 2, 3, \cdots$,

$f_n = n(0.67\,\text{Hz})$, $n = 1, 2, 3, \cdots$.

47. $f_{0.50}/f_{1.00} = \sqrt{2}$.

49. 80 Hz.

53. 11.

55. (a) $D_2 = 4.2\sin(0.84x + 47t + 2.1)$;
(b) $8.4\sin(0.84x + 2.1)\cos(47t)$.

57. 315 Hz.

59. (a)

(b)

61. $n = 4, n = 8$, and $n = 12$.

63. $x = \pm\left(n + \tfrac{1}{2}\right)\dfrac{\pi}{2}$ m, $n = 0, 1, 2, \cdots$.

65. 5.2 km/s.

67. $(3.0 \times 10^1)°$.

69. 44°.

71. (a) 0.042 m;
(b) 0.55 radians.

73. The speed is greater in the less dense rod, by a factor of $\sqrt{2.5} = 1.6$.

75. (a) 0.05 m;
(b) 2.25.

77. 0.69 m.

79. (a) $t = 0$ s;

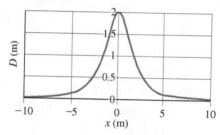

(b) $D = \dfrac{4.0\,\text{m}^3}{(x - 2.4t)^2 + 2.0\,\text{m}^2}$
(c) $t = 1.0$ s, moving right;

(d) $D = \dfrac{4.0\,\text{m}^3}{(x + 2.4t)^2 + 2.0\,\text{m}^2}$,
$t = 1.0$ s, moving left.

81. (a) G: 784 Hz, 1180 Hz, B: 988 Hz, 1480 Hz;
(b) 1.59;
(c) 1.26;
(d) 0.630.

83. 6.3 m from the end where the first pulse originated.

85. $\lambda = \dfrac{4\ell}{2n - 1}$, $n = 1, 2, 3, \cdots$.

87. $D(x, t) =$
$(3.5\,\text{cm})\cos(0.10\pi x - 1.5\pi t)$, with x in cm and t in s.

89. 12 min.

93. speed $= 0.50$ m/s; direction of motion $= +x$, period $= 2\pi$ s, wavelength $= \pi$ m.

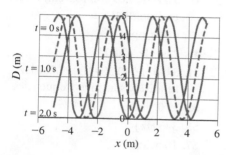

CHAPTER 16

1. 340 m.

3. (a) 1.7 cm to 17 m;
(b) 2.3×10^{-5} m.

5. (a) 0.17 m;
(b) 11 m;
(c) 0.5%.

7. 41 m.

9. (a) 8%;
(b) 4%.

11. (a) 4.4×10^{-5} Pa;
(b) 4.4×10^{-3} Pa.

13. (a) 5.3 m;
(b) 675 Hz;
(c) 3600 m/s;
(d) 1.0×10^{-13} m.

15. 63 dB.

17. (a) 10^9;
(b) 10^{12}.

19. 2.9×10^{-9} J.

21. 124 dB.

23. (a) 9.4×10^{-6} W;
(b) 8.0×10^6 people.

25. (a) 122 dB, 115 dB;
(b) no.

27. 7 dB.

29. (a) The higher frequency wave, 2.6;
   (b) 6.8.

31. (a) 3.2×10^{-5} m;
   (b) 3.0×10^1 Pa.

33. 1.24 m.

35. (a) 69.2 Hz, 207 Hz, 346 Hz, 484 Hz;
   (b) 138 Hz, 277 Hz, 415 Hz, 553 Hz.

37. 8.6 mm to 8.6 m.

39. (a) 0.18 m;
   (b) 1.1 m;
   (c) 440 Hz, 0.78 m.

41. −3.0%.

43. (a) 1.31 m;
   (b) 3, 4, 5, 6.

45. 3.65 cm, 7.09 cm, 10.3 cm, 13.4 cm, 16.3 cm, 19.0 cm.

47. 4.3 m, open.

49. 21.4 Hz, 42.8 Hz.

51. 3430 Hz, 10,300 Hz, 17,200 Hz, relatively sensitive frequencies.

53. ± 0.50 Hz.

55. 346 Hz.

57. 10 beats/s.

59. (a) 221.5 Hz or 218.5 Hz;
   (b) 1.4% increase, 1.3% decrease.

61. (a) 1470 Hz;
   (b) 1230 Hz.

63. (a) 2430 Hz, 2420 Hz, difference of 10 Hz;
   (b) 4310 Hz, 3370 Hz, difference of 940 Hz;
   (c) 34,300 Hz, 4450 Hz, difference of 29,900 Hz;

(d) $f'_{\text{source moving}} \approx f'_{\text{observer moving}}$
$$= f\left(1 + \frac{v_{\text{object}}}{v_{\text{sound}}}\right).$$

65. (a) 1420 Hz, 1170 Hz;
   (b) 1520 Hz, 1080 Hz;
   (c) 1330 Hz, 1240 Hz.

67. 3 Hz.

69. (a) Every 1.3 s;
   (b) every 15 s.

71. 8.9 cm/s.

73. (a) 93;
   (b) 0.62°.

77. 19 km.

79. (a) 57 Hz, 69 Hz, 86 Hz, 110 Hz, 170 Hz.

81. 90 dB.

83. 11 W.

85. 51 dB.

87. 1.07.

89. (a) 280 m/s, 57 N;
   (b) 0.19 m;
   (c) 880 Hz, 1320 Hz.

91. 3 Hz.

93. 141 Hz, 422 Hz, 703 Hz, 984 Hz.

95. 22 m/s.

97. (a) No beats;
   (b) 20 Hz;
   (c) no beats.

99. 55.2 kHz.

101. 11.5 m.

103. 2.3 Hz.

105. 17 km/h.

107. (a) 3400 Hz;
   (b) 1.50 m;
   (c) 0.10 m.

109. (a)

(b)

CHAPTER 31

1. $110 \, \text{kV/m·s}$.

3. $1.2 \times 10^{15} \, \text{V/m·s}$.

7. (b) With R in meters, for $R \le R_0$,
$B_0 = (6.3 \times 10^{-11} \, \text{T/m})R$;

for $R > R_0$, $B_0 = \dfrac{5.7 \times 10^{-14} \, \text{T·m}}{R}$.

(c)

9. $3.75 \, \text{V/m}$.

11. (a) $-\hat{\mathbf{k}}$;

(b) $\dfrac{E_0}{c}, -\hat{\mathbf{j}}$.

13. $2.00 \times 10^{10} \, \text{Hz}$.

15. $5.00 \times 10^2 \, \text{s} = 8.33 \, \text{min}$.

17. (a) $3.00 \times 10^5 \, \text{m}$;

(b) $34.1 \, \text{cm}$;

(c) no.

19. (a) $261 \, \text{s}$;

(b) $1260 \, \text{s}$.

21. $3.4 \, \text{krad/s}$.

23. $2.77 \times 10^7 \, \text{s}$.

25. $4.8 \, \text{W/m}^2$, $42 \, \text{V/m}$.

27. $4.50 \, \mu\text{J}$.

29. $3.80 \times 10^{26} \, \text{W}$.

31. (a) $5 \, \text{cm}^2$, yes;

(b) $20 \, \text{m}^2$, yes;

(c) $100 \, \text{m}^2$, no.

33. (a) $2 \times 10^8 \, \text{ly}$;

(b) 2000 times larger.

35. $8 \times 10^6 \, \text{m/s}^2$.

37. $27 \, \text{m}^2$.

39. $16 \, \text{cm}$.

41. $3.5 \, \text{nH}$ to $5.3 \, \text{nH}$.

43. $6.25 \times 10^{-4} \, \text{V/m}$;

$1.04 \times 10^{-9} \, \text{W/m}^2$.

45. $3 \, \text{m}$.

47. $1.35 \, \text{s}$.

49. $34 \, \text{V/m}$, $0.11 \, \mu\text{T}$.

51. Down, $2.2 \, \mu\text{T}$, $650 \, \text{V/m}$.

53. (a) $0.18 \, \text{nJ}$;

(b) $8.7 \, \mu\text{V/m}$, $2.9 \times 10^{-14} \, \text{T}$.

57. $4 \times 10^{10} \, \text{W}$.

59. 5 nodes, $6.1 \, \text{cm}$.

61. (a) $+x$;

(b) $\beta = \alpha c$;

(c) $\dfrac{E_0}{c} e^{-(\alpha x - \beta t)^2}$.

63. (d) Both $\vec{\mathbf{E}}$ and $\vec{\mathbf{B}}$ rotate counterclockwise.

CHAPTER 32

1.

3. $7°$.

7.

9. $37.6 \, \text{cm}$.

11. $1.0 \, \text{m}$.

13. $2.1 \, \text{cm}$ behind front surface of ball; virtual, upright.

15. Concave, $5.3 \, \text{cm}$.

17. $-6.0 \, \text{m}$.

19. Convex, $-32.0 \, \text{cm}$.

21.

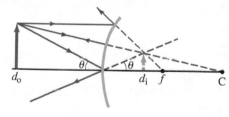

23. -3.9 m.

25. (a) Convex;

    (b) 20 cm behind mirror;

    (c) -91 cm;

    (d) -1.8 m.

27. (b)

    (c) 0.90 m;

    (d) just beyond focal point.

31. Because the image is inverted.

33. (a) 2.21×10^8 m/s;

    (b) 1.99×10^8 m/s;

    (c) 1.97×10^8 m/s.

35. 8.33 min.

37. 3 m.

39. $35°$.

41. $38.6°$.

43. 2.6 cm.

45. 4.4 m.

47. 3.2 mm.

49. $38.9°$.

53. $0.22°$.

55. $0.80°$.

57. $33.3°$, diamond.

59. 82.1 cm.

61. $n \geq 1.5$.

63. (a) 2.3 μs;

    (b) 17 ns.

65. $n \geq 1.72$.

67. 17.3 cm.

71. 0.25 m, 0.50 m.

73. (a) 3.0 m, 4.4 m, 7.4 m;

    (b) toward, away, toward.

75. 3.80 m.

77. 31 cm for real image, 15 cm for virtual image.

83. $\dfrac{d}{n-1}$.

85. The light would totally internally reflect only if $\theta_i \leq 32.5°$.

---

87. $A = 1.5005$, $B = 5740$ nm^2.

CHAPTER 33

1. (a)

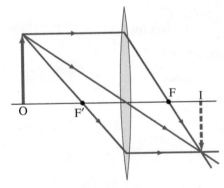

    (b) 508 mm.

3. (a) 4.26 D, converging;

    (b) -14.8 cm, diverging.

5. (a) 106 mm;

    (b) 109 mm;

    (c) 117 mm;

    (d) an object 0.513 m away.

7. (a) Virtual, upright, magnified;

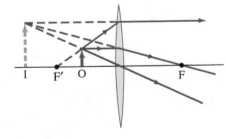

    (b) converging;

    (c) 6.7 D.

9. (a) 0.02 m;

    (b) 0.004 m.

11. 50 cm.

---

13. 21.3 cm, 64.7 cm.

15. (c) Real, upright; (d) real, upright.

17. 0.107 m, 2.2 m.

19. (b) 182 cm; (c) 182 cm.

21. 18.5 cm beyond second lens, $-0.651\times$.

23. (a) 7.14 cm beyond second lens;

    (b) $-0.357\times$; (c)

25. (a) 0.10 m to right of diverging lens; (b) $-1.0\times$;

    (c)

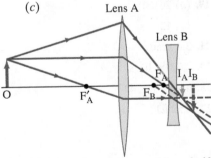

27. (a) 30 cm beyond second lens, half the size of object;

    (b) 29 cm beyond second lens, 0.46 times the size of object.

29. 1.54.

31. 8.6 cm.

33. 34 cm.

35. $f/2.8$.

37. $\frac{1}{6}$ s.

39. 41 mm.

41. $+2.5$ D.

43. 41 cm, yes.

45. (a) −1.3 D;
  (b) 37 cm.
47. −24.8 cm.
49. 18.4 cm, 1.00 m.
51. 6.6 cm.
53. (a) 13 cm;
  (b) 8.3 cm.
55. (a) −234 cm;
  (b) 4.17×.
57. (a) −66 cm;
  (b) 3.0×.
59. 4 cm, toward.
61. 2.5 cm, 91 cm.
63. −26×.
65. 16×.
67. 3.7 m, 7.4 m.
69. −9×.
71. 8.0×.
73. 1.6 cm.
75. (a) 754×;
  (b) 1.92 cm, 0.307 cm;
  (c) 0.312 cm.
77. (a) 0.85 cm;
  (b) 250×.
79. 410×, 25×.
81. 79.4 cm, 75.5 cm.
83. $6.450 \text{ m} \leq d_0 \leq \infty$.
85. 116 mm, 232 mm.
87. −19.0 cm.
89. 3.1 cm, 25 cm.
91. (a) 0.26 mm;
  (b) 0.47 mm;
  (c) 1.3 mm;
  (d) 0.56×, 2.7×.
93. 20.0 cm.
95. 47 m.
97. 2.8×, 3.9×, person with normal eye.
99. 1.0×.
101. +3.4 D.
103. −19×.
105. (a) 28.6 cm;
  (b) 120 cm;
  (c) 15 cm.
107. −6.2 cm.
109. (a) $-1/f$, 1;
  (b) 14 cm, yes,
    y-intercept = 1.03;

  (c) $f = -1/\text{slope}$.

CHAPTER 34

3. 3.9 µm.
5. 0.2 mm.
7. 660 nm.
9. 3.5 cm.
11. Inverted, starts with central dark line, and every place there was bright fringe before is now dark fringe and vice versa.
13. 2.7 mm.
15. 2.94 mm.
17. $\frac{1}{4}$.
21. $I_0 \left[\dfrac{3 + 2\sqrt{2} \cos\left(\dfrac{2\pi d \sin\theta}{\lambda}\right)}{3 + 2\sqrt{2}} \right]$.
23. 634 nm.
25. (a) 180 nm;
  (b) 361 nm, 541 nm.
27. (b) 290 nm.
29. 8.68 µm.
31. 113 nm, 225 nm.
35. 1.32.
37. (c) 571 nm.
39. 0.191 mm.
41. 80.1 µm.
43. 0.3 mm.
45. (a) 17 lm/W;
  (b) 160 lamps.
47. (a) Constructive;
  (b) destructive.
49. 440 nm.
51. $I_0 \cos^2\left(\dfrac{2\pi x}{\lambda}\right)$.
53. (a) 81.5 nm;
  (b) 0.130 µm.
55. $\theta = \sin^{-1}\left(\sin\theta_i \pm \dfrac{m\lambda}{d}\right)$.
57. 340 nm, 170 nm.
59. Constructive: 90°, 270°; destructive: 0°, 180°; exactly switched.
61. 240 nm.
63. 0.20 km.
65. 126 nm.

CHAPTER 35

1. 37.3 mrad = 2.13°.
3. 2.35 m.
5. Entire pattern is shifted, with central maximum at 23° to the normal.
7. 4.8 cm.
9. 953 nm.
11. (a) 63°;
  (b) 30°.

13. 0.15.
15. $d = 5D$.
17. 265 fringes.
19. (a) 1.9 cm;
  (b) 12 cm.
21. 0.255.
23. (a) $I_\theta = I_0 \left(\dfrac{1 + 2\cos\delta}{3} \right)^2$.
25. 1.5×10^{11} m.
27. 1.0×10^4 m.
29. 730 lines/mm, 88 lines/mm.
31. 0.40 µm, 0.50 µm, 0.52 µm, 0.62 µm.
33. Two full orders, plus part of a third order.
35. 556 nm.
37. 24°.
39. $\lambda_2 > 600$ nm overlap with $\lambda_3 < 467$ nm.
41. $\lambda_1 = 614$ nm, $\lambda_2 = 899$ nm.
43. 7 cm, 35 cm, second order.
45. (c) −32°, 0.9°.
47. (a) 16,000 and 32,000;
  (b) 26 pm, 13 pm.
49. 14.0°.
51. No.
53. 45°.
55. 61.2°.
57. (a) 35.3°;
  (b) 63.4°.
59. 36.9°, smaller than both angles.
61. $I = \dfrac{I_0}{4} \sin^2(2\theta)$, 45°.
63. 28.8 µm.
65. 580 nm.
67. 0.6 m.
69. 658 nm, 853 lines/cm.
71. (a) 18 km;
  (b) 23″, atmospheric distortions make it worse.
73. 5.79×10^5 lines/m.
75. 36.9°.
77. (a) 60°;
  (b) 71.6°;
  (c) 84.3°.
79. 0.4 m.
81. 0.245 nm.
83. 110 m.
85. −0.17 mm.
87. Use 24 polarizers, each rotated 3.75° from previous axis.

CHAPTER 36

1. 72.5 m.

3. 1.00, 1.00, 1.01, 1.02, 1.05, 1.09, 1.15, 1.25, 1.40, 1.67, 2.29, 7.09.

5. 2.42×10^8 m/s.

7. 27 yr.

9. $(6.97 \times 10^{-8})\%$.

11. (a) 0.141c;
    (b) 0.140c.

13. (a) 3.4 yr;
    (b) 7.4 yr.

15. 0.894c.

17. Base: 0.30ℓ, sides: 1.94ℓ.

19. 0.65c.

21. (a) (820 m, 20 m, 0);
    (b) (2280 m, 20 m, 0).

23. (a) 0.88c;
    (b) −0.88c.

25. (a) 0.97c;
    (b) 0.55c.

27. 0.93c at 35°.

29. (a) $\ell_0\sqrt{1 - \dfrac{v^2}{c^2}\cos^2\theta}$;

    (b) $\tan^{-1}\left[\dfrac{\tan\theta}{\sqrt{1 - \dfrac{v^2}{c^2}}}\right]$.

31. $t'_B - t'_A = -\dfrac{v\ell}{c^2\sqrt{1 - \dfrac{v^2}{c^2}}}$,

    B is turned on first.

33. Not possible in boy's frame of reference.

35. (a) −0.5%;
    (b) −20%.

37. 0.95c.

39. 8.20×10^{-14} J, 0.511 MeV.

41. 900 kg.

43. $1.00\ \text{MeV}/c^2$, or 1.78×10^{-30} kg.

45. 9.0×10^{13} J, 9.2×10^9 kg.

47. 0.866c.

49. 1670 MeV, 2440 MeV/c.

51. 0.470c.

53. 0.32c.

55. 0.866c, 0.745c.

57. (a) 2.5×10^{19} J;
    (b) −2.4%.

59. 237.04832 u.

61. 240 MeV.

65. 230 MHz.

67. (a) 1.00×10^2 km/h;
    (b) 67 Hz.

69. 75 μs.

71. 8.0×10^{-8} s.

73. (a) 0.067c;
    (b) 0.070c.

75. (a) $\tan^{-1}\sqrt{\dfrac{c^2}{v^2} - 1}$;

    (c) $\tan^{-1}\dfrac{c}{v}$, $u = \sqrt{c^2 + v^2}$.

77. (a) 0.77 m/s;
    (b) 0.21 m.

79. 1.022 MeV.

83. (a) 4×10^9 kg/s;
    (b) 4×10^7 yr;
    (c) 1×10^{13} yr.

85. 28.32 MeV.

87. (a) 2.86×10^{-18} kg·m/s;
    (b) 0;
    (c) 3.31×10^{-17} kg·m/s.

89. 3×10^7 kg.

91. 0.987c.

93. 5.3×10^{21} J, 53 times as great.

95. (a) 6.5 yr;
    (b) 2.3 ly.

99.

CHAPTER 37

1. (a) 10.6 μm, far infrared;
   (b) 829 nm, infrared;
   (c) 0.69 mm, microwave;
   (d) 1.06 mm, microwave.

3. 5.4×10^{-20} J, 0.34 eV.

5. (b) 6.62×10^{-34} J·s.

7. 2.7×10^{-19} J $< E < 4.9 \times 10^{-19}$ J, 1.7 eV $< E <$ 3.0 eV.

9. 2×10^{13} Hz, 1×10^{-5} m.

11. 7.2×10^{14} Hz.

13. 3.05×10^{-27} m.

15. Copper and iron.

17. 0.55 eV.

19. 2.66 eV.

21. 3.56 eV.

23. (a) 1.66 eV;
    (b) 3.03 eV.

25. (a) 1.66 eV;
    (b) 3.03 eV.

27. 0.004, or 0.4%.

29. (a) 2.43 pm;
    (b) 1.32 fm.

31. (a) 8.8×10^{-6};
    (b) 0.049.

33. (a) 229 eV;
    (b) 0.165 nm.

35. 1.65 MeV.

37. 212 MeV, 5.86 fm.

39. 1.772 MeV, 702 fm.

41. 4.7 pm.

43. 4.0 pm.

45. 1840.

47. (a) 1.1×10^{-24} kg·m/s;
    (b) 1.2×10^6 m/s;
    (c) 4.2 V.

51. 590 m/s.

53. 20.9 pm.

55. 1.51 eV

57. 122 eV.

59. 91.4 nm.

61. 37.0 nm.

63.

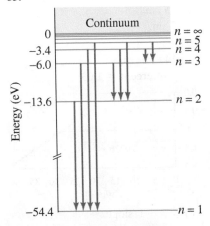

65. -27.2 eV, 13.6 eV.

67. Yes: $v = 7 \times 10^{-3} c$;
$1/\gamma = 0.99997$.

69. 97.23 nm, 102.6 nm, 121.5 nm,
486.2 nm, 656.3 nm, 1875 nm.

71. Yes.

73. 3.28×10^{15} Hz.

75. 5.3×10^{26} photons/s.

77. 6.2×10^{18} photons/s.

79. 0.244 MeV for both.

81. 28 fm.

83. 4.4×10^{-40}, yes.

85. 2.25 V.

87. 9.0 N.

89. 1.2 nm.

91. *(a)*

(b) Ground state, 0.4 eV, 2.2 eV,
2.5 eV, 2.6 eV, 4.7 eV, 5.1 eV.

93. *(a)* $E_n = -\dfrac{2.84 \times 10^{165}\,\text{J}}{n^2}$,
$r_n = n^2(5.17 \times 10^{-129}\,\text{m})$;

(b) no, because $n \approx 10^{68}$ so $\Delta n = 1$
is negligible compared to n.

95. 1.0×10^{-8} N.

97. *(a)* $\sqrt{\dfrac{Gh}{c^5}}$; *(b)* 1.34×10^{-43} s;

(c) $\sqrt{\dfrac{Gh}{c^3}}$; *(d)* 4.05×10^{-35} m.

99. *(a)* 6.0×10^{-3} m/s;

(b) 1.2×10^{-7} K.

101. *(a)*

(b) 4.8 times more intense.

103. *(a)* $\dfrac{hc}{e}$, $-\dfrac{W_0}{e}$;

(b)

(c) 1.2×10^{-6} V·m, -2.31 V;

(d) 2.31 eV;

(e) 6.63×10^{-34} J·s.

CHAPTER 38

1. 2.8×10^{-7} m.

3. 5.3×10^{-11} m.

5. 4500 m/s.

7. 1.0×10^{-14}.

9. $\Delta x_{\text{electron}} \geq 1.4 \times 10^{-3}$ m,
$\Delta x_{\text{baseball}} \geq 9.3 \times 10^{-33}$ m,
$\dfrac{\Delta x_{\text{electron}}}{\Delta x_{\text{baseball}}} = 1.5 \times 10^{29}$.

11. 1.3×10^{-54} kg.

13. *(a)* 10^{-7} eV;

(b) $1/10^8$;

(c) 100 nm, 10^{-6} nm.

19. *(a)* $A \sin[(2.6 \times 10^9\,\text{m}^{-1})x]$
$+ B \cos[(2.6 \times 10^9\,\text{m}^{-1})x]$;

(b) $A \sin[(4.7 \times 10^{12}\,\text{m}^{-1})x]$
$+ B \cos[(4.7 \times 10^{12}\,\text{m}^{-1})x]$.

21. 1.8×10^6 m/s.

23. *(a)* 46 nm;

(b) 0.20 nm.

25. $\Delta p\,\Delta x \approx h$, which is consistent with
the uncertainty principle.

27. $n = 1$: 0.094 eV,
$(1.0\,\text{nm}^{-1/2}) \sin[(1.6\,\text{nm}^{-1})x]$;
$n = 2$: 0.38 eV,
$(1.0\,\text{nm}^{-1/2}) \sin[(3.1\,\text{nm}^{-1})x]$;
$n = 3$: 0.85 eV,
$(1.0\,\text{nm}^{-1/2}) \sin[(4.7\,\text{nm}^{-1})x]$;
$n = 4$: 1.5 eV,
$(1.0\,\text{nm}^{-1/2}) \sin[(6.3\,\text{nm}^{-1})x]$.

29. *(a)* 940 MeV;

(b) 0.51 MeV;

(c) 0.51 MeV.

31. *(a)* 4.0×10^{-19} eV;

(b) 2×10^8;

(c) 1.4×10^{-10} eV.

33. n odd:
$\psi = [(-1)^{(n-1)/2}]\sqrt{\dfrac{2}{\ell}} \cos\left(\dfrac{n\pi x}{\ell}\right)$,
$E_n = \dfrac{n^2 h^2}{8m\ell^2}$;

n even:
$\psi = [(-1)^{n/2}]\sqrt{\dfrac{2}{\ell}} \sin\left(\dfrac{n\pi x}{\ell}\right)$,
$E_n = \dfrac{n^2 h^2}{8m\ell^2}$.

35.

37. 0.020 nm.

39. 17 eV.

41. *(a)* 6.1%;

(b) 93.9%.

43. *(a)* 12% decrease;

(b) 6.2% decrease.

45. *(a)* 32 MeV;

(b) 57 fm;

(c) 1.4×10^7 m/s, 8.6×10^{20} Hz,
7×10^9 yr.

47. 14 MeV.

49. 25 nm.

51. $\Delta x = r_1$ (the Bohr radius).

53. 0.23 MeV, 3.3×10^6 m/s.

55. 27% decrease.

57.

59. *(a)* $\Delta \phi > 0$ so $\phi \neq 0$ exactly;

(b) 4 s.

61. (*a*)

(*b*) 10%: $E/U_0 = 0.146$;
20%: $E/U_0 = 0.294$;
50%: $E/U_0 = 0.787$;
80%: $E/U_0 = 1.56$.

CHAPTER 39

1. 0, 1, 2, 3, 4, 5, 6.
3. 18 states, $(3, 0, 0, -\frac{1}{2})$, $(3, 0, 0, +\frac{1}{2})$,
$(3, 1, -1, -\frac{1}{2})$, $(3, 1, -1, +\frac{1}{2})$,
$(3, 1, 0, -\frac{1}{2})$, $(3, 1, 0, +\frac{1}{2})$,
$(3, 1, 1, -\frac{1}{2})$, $(3, 1, 1, +\frac{1}{2})$,
$(3, 2, -2, -\frac{1}{2})$, $(3, 2, -2, +\frac{1}{2})$,
$(3, 2, -1, -\frac{1}{2})$, $(3, 2, -1, +\frac{1}{2})$,
$(3, 2, 0, -\frac{1}{2})$, $(3, 2, 0, +\frac{1}{2})$,
$(3, 2, 1, -\frac{1}{2})$, $(3, 2, 1, +\frac{1}{2})$,
$(3, 2, 2, -\frac{1}{2})$, $(3, 2, 2, +\frac{1}{2})$.
5. $n \geq 6$; $m_\ell = -5, -4, -3, -2, -1$,
$0, 1, 2, 3, 4, 5$; $m_s = -\frac{1}{2}, +\frac{1}{2}$.
7. (*a*) 7;
(*b*) -0.278 eV;
(*c*) 4.72×10^{-34} J·s, 4;
(*d*) $-4, -3, -2, -1, 0, 1, 2, 3, 4$.
11. $n \geq 7$, $\ell = 6$, $m_\ell = 2$.
13. (*a*) $\dfrac{1}{\sqrt{\pi r_0^3}} e^{-1.5}$;
(*b*) $\dfrac{1}{\pi r_0^3} e^{-3}$;
(*c*) $\dfrac{4}{r_0} e^{-3}$.
15. 1.85.
17. (*a*) $1.3r_0$;
(*b*) $2.7r_0$;
(*c*) $4.2r_0$.
21. $\dfrac{r^4}{24r_0^5} e^{-r/r_0}$.
23. 1.1%.
27. (*a*) $\dfrac{4r^2}{27r_0^3}\left(1 - \dfrac{2r}{3r_0} + \dfrac{2r^2}{27r_0^2}\right) e^{-2r/3r_0}$;
(*b*)

(*c*) $13.1r_0$.

29. (*a*) $(1, 0, 0, -\frac{1}{2})$, $(1, 0, 0, +\frac{1}{2})$,
$(2, 0, 0, -\frac{1}{2})$, $(2, 0, 0, +\frac{1}{2})$,
$(2, 1, -1, -\frac{1}{2})$, $(2, 1, -1, +\frac{1}{2})$;
(*b*) $(1, 0, 0, -\frac{1}{2})$, $(1, 0, 0, +\frac{1}{2})$,
$(2, 0, 0, -\frac{1}{2})$, $(2, 0, 0, +\frac{1}{2})$,
$(2, 1, -1, -\frac{1}{2})$, $(2, 1, -1, +\frac{1}{2})$,
$(2, 1, 0, -\frac{1}{2})$, $(2, 1, 0, +\frac{1}{2})$,
$(2, 1, 1, -\frac{1}{2})$, $(2, 1, 1, +\frac{1}{2})$,
$(3, 0, 0, -\frac{1}{2})$, $(3, 0, 0, +\frac{1}{2})$,
$(3, 1, -1, -\frac{1}{2})$.
31. $n = 3$, $\ell = 2$.
33. (*a*) $1s^2 2s^2 2p^6 3s^2 3p^6 3d^8 4s^2$;
(*b*) $1s^2 2s^2 2p^6 3s^2 3p^6 3d^{10} 4s^2 4p^6 4d^{10} 5s^1$;
(*c*) $1s^2 2s^2 2p^6 3s^2 3p^6 3d^{10} 4s^2 4p^6 4d^{10}$-$4f^{14} 5s^2 5p^6 5d^{10} 6s^2 6p^6 5f^3 6d^1 7s^2$.
35. 5.75×10^{-13} m, 115 keV.
39. 0.0383 nm, 1 nm.
41. 0.194 nm.
43. Chromium.
47. 2.9×10^{-4} eV.
49. (*a*) 0.38 mm; (*b*) 0.19 mm.
51. (*a*) $\frac{1}{2}, \frac{3}{2}$; (*b*) $\frac{5}{2}, \frac{7}{2}$; (*c*) $\frac{3}{2}, \frac{5}{2}$;
(*d*) $4p$: $\frac{\sqrt{3}}{2}\hbar, \frac{\sqrt{15}}{2}\hbar$; $4f$: $\frac{\sqrt{35}}{2}\hbar, \frac{\sqrt{63}}{2}\hbar$;
$3d$: $\frac{\sqrt{15}}{2}\hbar, \frac{\sqrt{35}}{2}\hbar$.
53. (*a*) 0.4 T;
(*b*) 0.5 T.
55. 4.7×10^{-4} rad; (*a*) 180 m;
(*b*) 1.8×10^5 m.
57. 634 nm.
59. 3.7×10^4 K.
61. (*a*) 1.56;
(*b*) 1.36×10^{-10} m.
63. (*a*) $1s^2 2s^2 2p^6 3s^2 3p^6 3d^5 4s^2$;
(*b*) $1s^2 2s^2 2p^6 3s^2 3p^6 3d^{10} 4s^2 4p^4$;
(*c*) $1s^2 2s^2 2p^6 3s^2 3p^6 3d^{10} 4s^2 4p^6 4d^{15} 5s^2$.
65. (*a*) 2.5×10^{74};
(*b*) 5.1×10^{74}.
67. $5.24r_0$.
69. (*a*) 45°, 90°, 135°;
(*b*) 35.3°, 65.9°, 90°, 114.1°, 144.7°;
(*c*) 30°, 54.7°, 73.2°, 90°, 106.8°,
125.3°, 150°;
(*d*) 5.71°, 0.0573°, yes.
71. (*b*) $\overline{K} = -\frac{1}{2}\overline{U}$.
73. (*a*) Forbidden; (*b*) allowed;
(*c*) forbidden; (*d*) forbidden;
(*e*) allowed.
75. 4, beryllium.
77. (*a*) 3×10^{-171}, 1×10^{-202};
(*b*) 1×10^{-8}, 6×10^{-10};
(*c*) 7×10^{15}, 4×10^{14};
(*d*) 4×10^{22} photons/s,
7×10^{23} photons/s.

CHAPTER 40

1. 5.1 eV.
3. 4.7 eV.
5. 1.28 eV.
9. (*a*) 18.59 u;
(*b*) 8.00 u;
(*c*) 0.9801 u.
11. 1.10×10^{-10} m.
13. (*a*) 1.5×10^{-2} eV, 0.082 mm;
(*b*) 3.0×10^{-2} eV, 0.041 mm;
(*c*) 4.6×10^{-2} eV, 0.027 mm.
15. (*a*) 6.86 u;
(*b*) 1850 N/m, $k_{CO}/k_{H_2} = 3.4$.
17. 2.36×10^{-10} m.
19. $m_1 x_1 = m_2 x_2$.
21. 0.2826 nm.
23. 0.34 nm.
25. (*b*) -6.9 eV;
(*c*) -11 eV;
(*d*) -2.8%.
27. 9.0×10^{20}.
29. (*a*) 6.96 eV;
(*b*) 6.89 eV.
31. 1.6%.
33. 3.2 eV, 1.1×10^6 m/s.
39. (*a*) $\dfrac{h^2 N^2}{32m\ell^2}$;
(*b*) $\dfrac{h^2 (N + 1)}{8m\ell^2}$;
(*c*) $\dfrac{4}{N}$.
43. 1.09 μm.
45. (*a*) $2N$;
(*b*) $6N$;
(*c*) $6N$;
(*d*) $2N(2\ell + 1)$.
47. 4×10^6.
49. 1.8 eV.
51. 8.6 mA.
53. (*a*) 1.7 mA; (*b*) 3.4 mA.
55. (*a*) 35 mA; (*b*) 70 mA.
57. 3700 Ω.
59. 0.21 mA.
61. $I_B + I_C = I_E$.
63. (*a*) 3.1×10^4 K;
(*b*) 930 K.
65.

67. (a) 0.9801 u;

(b) 482 N/m, $k_{HCl}/k_{H_2} = 0.88$.

71. Yes, 1.09 μm.

73. 1100 J/mol.

75. 5.50 eV.

77. 3×10^{25}.

79. 6.47×10^{-4} eV.

81. 1.1 eV.

83. (a) 0.094 eV; (b) 0.63 nm.

85. (a) 150 V $\leq V \leq$ 486 V;

(b) 3.16 k$\Omega \leq R_{load} < \infty$.

87. (a)

(b)

(c)

(d)

89. 32 mA.

CHAPTER 41

1. 0.149 u.

3. 0.85%.

5. 3727 MeV/c^2.

7. (b) 180 m; (c) 2.58×10^{-10} m.

9. 30 MeV.

11. 6×10^{26} nucleons, no, mass of all nucleons is approximately the same.

13. 550 MeV.

15. 7.94 MeV.

17. $^{23}_{11}$Na: 8.113 MeV/nucleon; $^{24}_{11}$Na: 8.063 MeV/nucleon.

19. (b) Yes, binding energy is positive.

21. 0.782 MeV.

23. 2.6×10^{-12} m.

25. (a) β^-;

(b) $^{24}_{11}$Na $\rightarrow$ $^{24}_{12}$Mg + β^- + $\bar{\nu}$, 5.52 MeV.

27. (a) $^{234}_{90}$Th; (b) 234.04368 u.

29. 0.079 MeV.

31. (a) $^{32}_{16}$S;

(b) 31.972071 u.

33. 0.862 MeV.

35. 0.9612 MeV, 0.9612 MeV, 0, 0.

37. 5.31 MeV.

39. (a) 1.5×10^{-10} yr^{-1};

(b) 6.0 h.

41. 0.16.

43. 0.015625.

45. 6.9×10^{19} nuclei.

47. (a) 3.60×10^{12} decays/s;

(b) 3.58×10^{12} decays/s;

(c) 9.72×10^7 decays/s.

49. 0.76 g.

51. 2.30×10^{-11} g.

53. 4.3 min.

55. 2.98×10^{-2} g.

57. 35.4 d.

59. $^{228}_{88}$Ra, $^{228}_{89}$Ac, $^{228}_{90}$Th, $^{224}_{88}$Ra, $^{220}_{86}$Rn; $^{231}_{90}$Th, $^{231}_{91}$Pa, $^{227}_{89}$Ac, $^{227}_{90}$Th, $^{223}_{88}$Ra.

61. $N_D = N_0(1 - e^{-\lambda t})$.

63. 2.3×10^4 yr.

65. 41 yr.

69. $6.64T_{1/2}$.

71. (b) 98.2%.

73. 1 MeV.

75. (a) $^{191}_{77}$Ir;

(b)

(c) The higher excited state.

77. 550 MeV, 2.5×10^{12} J.

79. 2.243 MeV.

81. (a) 2.4×10^5 yr;

(b) no significant change, maximum age is on the order of 10^5 yr.

83. 5.48×10^{-4}.

85. (a) 1.63%;

(b) 0.663%.

87. 1.3×10^{21} yr.

89. 8.33×10^{16} nuclei,

600 s.

CHAPTER 42

1. $^{28}_{13}$Al, β^-, $^{28}_{14}$Si.

3. Yes, because $Q = 4.807$ MeV.

5. 5.701 MeV released.

7. (a) Yes;

(b) 20.8 MeV.

9. 4.730 MeV.

11. n + $^{14}_7$N $\rightarrow$ $^{14}_6$C + p, 0.626 MeV.

13. (a) The He has picked up a neutron from the C;

(b) $^{11}_6$C;

(c) 1.856 MeV, exothermic.

15. 18.000938 u.

17. 0.671 MeV.

19. $\pi(R_1 + R_2)^2$.

21. 10 cm.

23. 173.3 MeV.

25. 6×10^{18} fissions/s.

27. 0.34 g.

29. 5×10^{-5} kg.

31. 25 collisions.

33. 0.11.

35. 3000 eV.

39. (a) 5.98×10^{23} MeV/g, 4.83×10^{23} MeV/g, 2.10×10^{24} MeV/g;

(b) 5.13×10^{23} MeV/g; Eq. 42–9a gives about 17% more energy per gram, 42–9b gives about 6% less, and 42–9c gives about 4× more.

41. 0.35 g.

43. 6100 kg/h.

45. 2.46×10^9 J, 50 times more than gasoline.

47. (b) 26.73 MeV;

(c) 1.943 MeV, 2.218 MeV, 7.551 MeV, 7.296 MeV, 2.752 MeV, 4.966 MeV;

(d) larger Coulomb repulsion to overcome.

49. 4.0 Gy.

51. 220 rad.

53. 280 counts/s.

55. 1.6 days.

57. (a) $^{131}_{53}\text{I} \rightarrow {}^{131}_{54}\text{Xe} + \beta^- + \bar{\nu}$;

    (b) 31 d;

    (c) 8×10^{-12} kg.

59. 8.3×10^{-7} Gy/d.

61. (a) $^{218}_{84}\text{Po}$;

    (b) radioactive, alpha and beta decay, 3.1 min;

    (c) chemically reactive;

    (d) 9.1×10^6 Bq, 4.0×10^4 Bq.

63. 7.041 m, radio wave.

65. (a) $^{12}_{6}\text{C}$;

    (b) 5.701 MeV.

67. $1.0043 : 1$.

69. 6.5×10^{-2} rem/yr.

71. 4.4 m.

73. (a) 920 kg;

    (b) 3×10^6 Ci.

75. (a) 3.7×10^{26} W;

    (b) 3.5×10^{38} protons/s;

    (c) 1.1×10^{11} yr.

77. 8×10^{12} J.

79. (a) 3700 decays/s;

    (b) 4.8×10^{-4} Sv/yr, yes (13% of the background rate).

81. 7.274 MeV.

83. 79 yr.

85. 2 mCi.

CHAPTER 43

1. 5.59 GeV.

3. 2.0 T.

5. 13 MHz.

7. Alpha particles,
$\lambda_\alpha \approx d_{\text{nucleon}}$, $\lambda_p \approx 2d_{\text{nucleon}}$.

9. 5.5 T.

11. 1.8×10^{-19} m.

15. 33.9 MeV.

17. 1879.2 MeV.

19. 67.5 MeV.

21. (a) 178.5 MeV;

    (b) 128.6 MeV.

23. (a) Charge, strangeness;

    (b) energy;

    (c) baryon number, strangeness, spin.

25. (b) The photon exists for such a short time that the uncertainty principle allows energy to not be conserved during the exchange.

27. 69.3 MeV.

29. $K_{\Lambda^0} = 8.6$ MeV, $K_{\pi^-} = 57.4$ MeV.

31. 52.3 MeV.

33. 9 keV.

35. 7.5×10^{-21} s.

37. (a) 700 eV;

    (b) 70 MeV.

39. (a) uss;

    (b) dss.

41. (a) Proton;

    (b) $\overline{\Sigma^-}$;

    (c) K^-;

    (d) π^-;

    (e) D_S^-.

43. $c\bar{s}$.

45.

47. (a) 0.38 A;

    (b) 1.0×10^2 m/s.

49. 2.1×10^9 m, 7.1 s.

51. (a) Possible, strong interaction;

    (b) possible, strong interaction;

    (c) possible, strong interaction;

    (d) not possible, charge is not conserved;

    (e) possible, weak interaction.

55. 64.

57. (b) 10^{29} K.

59. 798.7 MeV, 798.7 MeV.

61. 16 GeV, 7.8×10^{-17} m.

63. Some possibilities:

or [see Example 43–9b]

65. $v/c = 1 - (9.0 \times 10^9)$.

67.

2.3 μs, 3.1%.

CHAPTER 44

1. 3.1 ly.

3. $0.050''$, 20 pc.

5. Less than, a factor of 2.

7. 0.037.

9. 2×10^{-3} kg/m³.

11. -0.092 MeV, 7.366 MeV.

13. 1.83×10^9 kg/m³, 3.33×10^5 times.

15. $D_1/D_2 = 0.13$.

19. 540°.

21. 1.3×10^{-16} m.

23. 200 Mly.

25. (a) 656 nm;

    (b) 659 nm.

27. $0.0589\,c$.

31. 1.1×10^{-3} m.

33. 6 nucleons/m³.

35. (a) 10^{-5} s;

    (b) 10^{-7} s;

    (c) 10^{-4} s.

37. (a) 6380 km, 20 km, 8.85 km;

    (b) $700 : 2 : 1$.

39. 8×10^9.

41. A: Temperature increases, luminosity stays the same, and size decreases;

    B: Temperature stays the same, and luminosity and size decrease;

    C: Temperature decreases, and luminosity and size increase.

43. 2×10^{28} N.

45. $d_{480}/d_{660} = 1.7$.

47. 2×10^{16} K, hadron era.

49. (a) 13.93 MeV;

    (b) 4.7 MeV;

    (c) 5.5×10^{10} K.

51. $R_{\text{min}} = GM/c^2$.

53. $\approx 10^{-15}$ s.

55. Venus, $b_{\text{Venus}}/b_{\text{Sirius}} = 16$.

57. $\dfrac{h^2}{4m_n^{8/3}\,GM^{1/3}} \left(\dfrac{9}{4\pi^2} \right)^{2/3}$.

Index

Note: The abbreviation *defn* means the page cited gives the definition of the term; *fn* means the reference is in a footnote; *pr* means it is found in a Problem or Question; *ff* means "also the following pages."

A (atomic mass number), 1105
Aberration:
    chromatic, 889 *fn*, 892, 932
    of lenses, 891–92, 929, 931
    spherical, 843, 857, 891, 892, 932
Absolute pressure, 345
Absolute space, 953, 957
Absolute temperature scale, 457, 464, 469–70
Absolute time, 953
Absolute zero, 464, 549
Absorbed dose, 1148
Absorption lines, 936, 1002, 1081, 1084–85
Absorption spectra, 936, 1002, 1084
Absorption wavelength, 1008
Abundances, natural, 1105
Ac circuits, 664–65, 677 *fn*, 790–803
Ac generator, 766–67
Ac motor, 720
Accelerating reference frames, 85, 88, 155–56, 300–2
Acceleration, 24–42, 60–62
    angular, 251–56, 258–63
    average, 24–26
    centripetal, 120 *ff*
    constant, 28–29, 62
    constant angular, 255
    Coriolis, 301–2
    cosmic, 1223
    in *g*'s, 37
    due to gravity, 34–39, 87 *fn*, 92, 143–45
    instantaneous, 27–28, 60–61
    of the Moon, 121, 140
    motion at constant, 28–39, 62–71
    radial, 120 *ff*, 128
    related to force, 86–88
    tangential, 128–29, 251–52
    uniform, 28–39, 62–71
    variable, 39–43
Accelerators, particle, 1165–71
Accelerometer, 100
Acceptor level, 1094
Accommodation of eye, 883
Accuracy, 3–5
    precision vs., 5
Achromatic doublet, 892
Achromatic lens, 892
Actinides, 1054
Action at a distance, 154, 568
Action potential, 670
Action–reaction (Newton's third law), 89–91
Activation energy, 481, 1075, 1077
Active galactic nuclei (AGN), 1197

Active solar heating, 550
Activity, 1118
    and half-life, 1120
    source, 1147
Addition of vectors, 52–58
Addition of velocities:
    classical, 71–74
    relativistic, 970–71
Adhesion, 360
Adiabatic lapse rate, 525 *pr*
Adiabatic processes, 508, 514–15
ADP, 1076–77
AFM, 1039
AGN, 1197
Air bags, 31
Air cleaner, electrostatic, 645 *pr*
Air columns, vibrations of, 434–36
Air conditioners, 537–38
Air parcel, 525 *pr*
Air pollution, 551
Air resistance, 34–35, 129–30
Airplane wing, 356–57
Airy disk, 929
Alkali metals, 1054
Allowed transitions, 1048–49, 1080–81, 1083, 1084
Alpha decay, 1111–14, 1117
    and tunneling, 1038, 1113
Alpha particle (or ray), 1038, 1111–14
Alternating current (ac), 664–65, 677 *fn*, 796–803
Alternators, 768
AM radio, 830
Amino acids, 1079
Ammeter, 695–97, 721
    digital, 695, 697
Amorphous solids, 1085
Ampère, André, 654, 737
Ampere (A) (unit), 654, 736
    operational definition of, 736
Ampère's law, 737–43, 813–17
Amplifiers, 1097
Amplitude, 371, 397, 404
    intensity related to, 430
    pressure, 427
    of vibration, 371
    of wave, 371, 397, 402, 404, 426, 430, 1019
Amplitude modulation (AM), 830
Analog information, 775
Analog meters, 695–97, 721
Analyzer (of polarized light), 941
Anderson, Carl, 1174
Andromeda, 1196
Aneroid barometer, 347
Aneroid gauge, 347
Angle, 7 *fn*, 249
    attack, 356
    Brewster's, 943, 949 *pr*
    critical, 854
    of dip, 709
    of incidence, 410, 415, 838, 850
    phase, 373, 405, 800

polarizing, 943–44
radian measure of, 249
of reflection, 410, 838
of refraction, 415, 850
solid, 7 *fn*, 915 *fn*
Angstrom (Å) (unit), 17 *pr*, 852 *fn*
Angular acceleration, 251–56, 258–63
    constant, 255
Angular displacement, 250, 381
Angular frequency, 373
Angular magnification, 886
Angular momentum, 285–89, 291–300, 1003
    in atoms, 1004, 1046–49, 1057–60
    conservation, law of, 285–89, 297–98, 1117
    directional nature of, 288–89, 291 *ff*
    nuclear, 1107
    of a particle, 291–92
    quantized in atoms, 1046–47
    quantized in molecules, 1080–81
    relation between torque and, 292–97
    total, 1059
    and uncertainty principle, 1023
    vector, 288, 291
Angular position, 249, 1023
Angular quantities, 249 *ff*
    vector nature, 254
Angular velocity, 250–55
    of precession, 299–300
Anisotropy of CMB, 1214, 1220
Annihilation (e^-e^+, particle–antiparticle), 996, 1175, 1217
Anode, 620
Antenna, 812, 817, 824, 831, 909
Anthropic principle, 1225
Anticodon, 1079
Antilogarithm, A-3
Antimatter, 1175, 1188, 1190 *pr* (*see also* Antiparticle)
Antineutrino, 1115–16, 1179
Antineutron, 1175
Antinodes, 412, 433, 434, 435
Antiparticle, 1116, 1174–76, 1179 (*see also* Antimatter)
Antiproton, 1164, 1174–75
Antiquark, 1179, 1183
Apparent brightness, 1197–98
Apparent magnitude, 1228 *pr*
Apparent weight, 148–49, 350
Apparent weightlessness, 148–49
Approximations, 9–12
Arago, F., 922
Arches, 327–28
Archimedes, 349–50
Archimedes' principle, 348–52
    and geology, 351
Area, 9, A-1, inside back cover
    under a curve or graph, 169–71
Arecibo, 931
Aristotle, 2, 84
Armature, 720, 766
Arteriosclerosis, 359

Photo Credits

Useful Geometry Formulas—Areas, Volumes

Circumference of circle $C = \pi d = 2\pi r$

Area of circle $A = \pi r^2 = \dfrac{\pi d^2}{4}$

Area of rectangle $A = \ell w$

Area of parallelogram $A = bh$

Area of triangle $A = \frac{1}{2} hb$

Right triangle (Pythagoras) $c^2 = a^2 + b^2$

Sphere: surface area $A = 4\pi r^2$
    volume $V = \frac{4}{3}\pi r^3$

Rectangular solid: volume $V = \ell wh$

Cylinder (right):
    surface area $A = 2\pi r\ell + 2\pi r^2$
    volume $V = \pi r^2 \ell$

Right circular cone:
    surface area $A = \pi r^2 + \pi r \sqrt{r^2 + h^2}$
    volume $V = \frac{1}{3}\pi r^2 h$

Quadratic Formula

Equation with unknown x, in the form

$ax^2 + bx + c = 0,$

has solutions

$$x = \frac{-b \pm \sqrt{b^2 - 4ac}}{2a}.$$

Exponents

$(a^n)(a^m) = a^{n+m}$ [Example: $(a^3)(a^2) = a^5$]

$(a^n)(b^n) = (ab)^n$ [Example: $(a^3)(b^3) = (ab)^3$]

$(a^n)^m = a^{nm}$ $\begin{bmatrix} \text{Example: } (a^3)^2 = a^6 \\ \text{Example: } (a^{\frac{1}{4}})^4 = a \end{bmatrix}$

$a^{-1} = \dfrac{1}{a}$ $a^{-n} = \dfrac{1}{a^n}$ $a^0 = 1$

$a^{\frac{1}{2}} = \sqrt{a}$ $a^{\frac{1}{4}} = \sqrt{\sqrt{a}}$

$(a^n)(a^{-m}) = \dfrac{a^n}{a^m} = a^{n-m}$ [Ex.: $(a^5)(a^{-2}) = a^3$]

$\dfrac{a^n}{b^n} = \left(\dfrac{a}{b}\right)^n$

Logarithms [Appendix A–7; Table A–1]

If $y = 10^x$,   then $x = \log_{10} y = \log y$.

If $y = e^x$,   then $x = \log_e y = \ln y$.

$\log(ab) = \log a + \log b$

$\log\left(\dfrac{a}{b}\right) = \log a - \log b$

$\log a^n = n \log a$

Some Derivatives and Integrals[†]

$\dfrac{d}{dx} x^n = n x^{n-1}$ $\displaystyle\int \sin ax \, dx = -\dfrac{1}{a}\cos ax$

$\dfrac{d}{dx} \sin ax = a \cos ax$ $\displaystyle\int \cos ax \, dx = \dfrac{1}{a}\sin ax$

$\dfrac{d}{dx} \cos ax = -a \sin ax$ $\displaystyle\int \dfrac{1}{x} dx = \ln x$

$\displaystyle\int x^m \, dx = \dfrac{1}{m+1} x^{m+1}$ $\displaystyle\int e^{ax} \, dx = \dfrac{1}{a} e^{ax}$

[†] See Appendix B for more.

Binomial Expansion

$(1 \pm x)^n = 1 \pm nx + \dfrac{n(n-1)}{2\cdot1} x^2 \pm \dfrac{n(n-1)(n-2)}{3\cdot2\cdot1} x^3 + \cdots$ [for $x^2 < 1$]

$\approx 1 \pm nx$ [for $x \ll 1$]

Trigonometric Formulas [Appendix A–9]

$\sin\theta = \dfrac{\text{opp}}{\text{hyp}}$

$\cos\theta = \dfrac{\text{adj}}{\text{hyp}}$

$\tan\theta = \dfrac{\text{opp}}{\text{adj}}$

$\text{adj}^2 + \text{opp}^2 = \text{hyp}^2$ (Pythagorean theorem)

$\tan\theta = \dfrac{\sin\theta}{\cos\theta}$

$\sin^2\theta + \cos^2\theta = 1$

$\sin 2\theta = 2\sin\theta\cos\theta$

$\cos 2\theta = (\cos^2\theta - \sin^2\theta) = (1 - 2\sin^2\theta) = (2\cos^2\theta - 1)$

$\sin(180° - \theta) = \sin\theta$ $\cos(180° - \theta) = -\cos\theta$

$\sin(90° - \theta) = \cos\theta$

$\cos(90° - \theta) = \sin\theta$

$\sin\frac{1}{2}\theta = \sqrt{(1 - \cos\theta)/2}$ $\cos\frac{1}{2}\theta = \sqrt{(1 + \cos\theta)/2}$

$\sin\theta \approx \theta$ [for small $\theta \lesssim 0.2$ rad]

$\cos\theta \approx 1 - \dfrac{\theta^2}{2}$ [for small $\theta \lesssim 0.2$ rad]

$\sin(A \pm B) = \sin A \cos B \pm \cos A \sin B$

$\cos(A \pm B) = \cos A \cos B \mp \sin A \sin B$

For any triangle:

$c^2 = a^2 + b^2 - 2ab\cos\gamma$ (law of cosines)

$\dfrac{\sin\alpha}{a} = \dfrac{\sin\beta}{b} = \dfrac{\sin\gamma}{c}$ (law of sines)